WOMEN'S AMERICA

WOMEN'S AMERICA

Refocusing the Past

FOURTH EDITION

EDITED BY

LINDA K. KERBER
University of Iowa

JANE SHERRON DE HART
University of California, Santa Barbara

New York   Oxford
OXFORD UNIVERSITY PRESS
1995

Oxford University Press

Oxford   New York
Athens   Auckland   Bangkok   Bombay
Calcutta   Cape Town   Dar es Salaam   Delhi
Florence   Hong Kong   Istanbul   Karachi
Kuala Lumpur   Madras   Madrid   Melbourne
Mexico City   Nairobi   Paris   Singapore
Taipei   Tokyo   Toronto

and associated companies in
Berlin   Ibadan

Published by Oxford University Press, Inc.,
198 Madison Avenue, New York, New York 10016-4314

Oxford is a registered trademark of Oxford University Press

Library of Congress Cataloging-in-Publication Data
Women's America : refocusing the past /
edited by Linda K. Kerber, Jane Sherron De Hart.—4th ed.
p.   cm.   Includes bibliographical references and index.
ISBN 0-19-509146-9—ISBN 0-19-509147-7 (paper)
1. Women—United States—History—Sources.
2. Women—Employment—United States—History—Sources.
3. Women in politics—United States—History—Sources.
4. Women—Health and hygiene—United States—History—Sources.
5. Feminism–United States—History—Sources.
I. Kerber, Linda K.   II. De Hart, Jane Sherron.
HQ1426.W663   1995   305.4'0973—dc20   94-18219

5 7 9 8 6 4

Printed in the United States of America
on acid-free paper

To our nieces

Carol Anne Coulter and Jane De Hart Coulter,
Meredith Harper Epstein, Lauren Elizabeth Epstein,
Elyse Marin Kerber, and Erica Beth Kerber

Acknowledgments

Women's America goes to press nearly a year before the first copies are in readers' hands. In the two years between the appearance of the third edition and our completion of this revision, the field of women's history has grown faster than ever, in complex directions. With new and sophisticated work on the historical experience of Hispanic and Asian-American women, it is more extensive than it has been. With new work on the relationships among ethnic and racial groups of women, and on the ways in which gender itself has been socially constructed—by public policy, by educational choices, even by the meaning assigned to sports—women's historians are posing more sophisticated and complex questions than they have before. And by insisting that what is learned about women's experience has important implications for what we think we understand about men, about gender, about citizenship and nationality, and about the meaning of political, social, and cultural history, women's historians have engaged the central questions of the historical narrative. A new generation of historians has been entering this work in ever-increasing numbers, historians who entered graduate school in the 1980s intending to focus on the historical construction of gender, and their first books represent fresh and innovative interpretations. And an older generation of historians, writing their second and third books, are bringing to their work an impressive maturity of vision and of scholarship.

Perhaps the most rewarding aspect of working in women's history remains the extraordinary collegiality and support displayed by those working in the field. Spanning generational and geographical boundaries, they form a network bonded by a common commitment to the recovery of women's historical experience. The generosity with which they share insights and expertise is a measure of that commitment. We are grateful once again to be the beneficiaries.

In preparing this fourth edition, we are especially indebted to Nell Irwin Painter of Princeton University, who took time from her own work on a biography of Sojourner Truth to write the essay that appears here. Leslie Schwalm of the University of Iowa suggested the Reconstruction documents. Martha Chamallas of the University of Pittsburgh School of Law and Susan Klepp of Rider College offered good counsel. We feel very lucky to have encountered Peg Roberts, who provided the photograph and accompanying caption for a group of her fellow WASPs.

As research assistants, Daniel Gomes of the University of California, Santa Barbara, and Doris Malkmus, Kim Nielsen, Catherine Rymph, Eric Fure-Slocum, and Leslie Taylor of the University of Iowa tackled assignments—some intellectually challenging, some tedious—with intelligence, ingenuity, and care. We are, as always, grateful to Nancy Lane of Oxford University Press, whose editorial experience and friendship continue to make our collaborative efforts rewarding.

Iowa City, Iowa   L. K. K.
Santa Barbara, Calif.   J. S. DeH.
May 1994

Contents

Essential Documents

WOMEN'S AMERICA

Introduction
Jane Sherron De Hart and Linda K. Kerber
Gender and the New Women's History

One of the most effective ways in which dominant groups maintain their power is by depriving the people they dominate of the knowledge of their own history. The Martiniquian psychiatrist Frantz Fanon, a leader of the Algerian resistance against the French in the 1950s, understood this well. In *The Wretched of the Earth*, his classic attack on colonialism, Fanon observed that "colonialism is not satisfied merely with holding a people in its grip . . . [but] by a kind of perverted logic, it turns to the past of an oppressed people, and distorts, disfigures and destroys it." Lacking an appreciation of their own historical experience and the dignity, even glory, of the actions of their own people, the colonized are encouraged to think that they have no alternative to oppressive conditions. "The effect consciously sought . . . [is] to drive into the natives' heads the idea that if the settlers were to leave, they would at once fall back into barbarism, degradation and bestiality."[1]

Throughout history, certain women have understood this. When, in 1404, Christine de Pizan undertook to write the earliest modern chronicle of the lives of great women of the past, she explained to her readers that she hoped to bring them "out of the ignorance which so blinds your own intellect." Although they knew "for a certainty" from their own experience that women were capable of virtue and fortitude, they were vulnerable to "philosophers" who defined women as trivial. Pizan described her contemporaries as "valiant women" who, denied a knowledge of their own history, had been "abandoned . . . exposed like a field without a surrounding hedge, without finding a champion to afford them an adequate defense. . . . Where is there a city so strong which could not be taken immediately if no resistance were forthcoming . . . ?" To provide women with their history was to build "a city wall, strongly constructed and well founded."[2]

WOMEN'S HISTORY AS A FIELD OF RESEARCH

A fictional woman in Jane Austen's novel *Northanger Abbey* (1818) complains that she reads history only a little, "as a duty, but it tells me little that does not either vex or weary me. The quarrels of popes and kings, with wars or pestilences, in every page; the men all so good for nothing, and hardly any women at all."[3] As recently as ten years ago, students in high school and college history classes could examine the index of their American history survey texts and reach the same conclusion.

In mid-nineteenth-century America, women activists self-consciously created a historical archive. Fearing that women would be denied knowledge of their own history, knowing that the actions of women were little regarded by historians, and predicting that pioneering activists on behalf of women's rights would die before their experiences had been recorded, Elizabeth Cady Stanton and Susan B. Anthony energetically collected evidence of the women's movement of their own time. The rich collection of documents that they published—six large volumes, entitled *History of Woman Suffrage*—was intended to be "an arsenal of facts" for the next generation of activists and historians.[4] But most historians ignored it. Ralph Henry Gabriel's *The Course of American Democratic Thought*, the standard text widely used throughout the 1940s and 1950s in college history courses, failed to cite a single work by a woman, not even the massive *History of Woman Suffrage*. "[I]f women were doing any thinking . . . ," the historian Mary Beard acidly observed in 1946, "it is difficult to find out from this treatise what it was."[5] In 1933 she herself edited a documentary collection, *America Through Women's Eyes,* in which she argued that an accurate understanding of the past required that women's experience be analyzed with as much care as historians normally devote to the experience of men. Our perspective and our goals in this book are similar to hers. We offer essays that we not only enjoy reading and rereading but that represent some of the best work done during the past three decades in which women's history emerged as a research field.

Surveying those decades, the historian Gerda Lerner suggested that the writing of women's history can be arranged in four stages of development, each stage more complex and sophisticated than the last, but all useful and necessary.[6] The first stage she called "compensatory history," in which the historian wanders, like Diogenes with a lantern, seeking to identify women and their activities. In the decade of the 1970s, some historians began to search for women whose work and experiences deserved to be more widely known. The accomplishments of these women ranged from feats of exploration and endurance to scientific discoveries, artistic achievements, and humanitarian reforms. They included such pioneers as Amelia Earhart, the pilot whose solo flight across the Atlantic in 1933 dramatically demonstrated women's courage and daring; Alice Hamilton, the social reformer and physician whose innovative work in the 1920s on lead poisoning and other toxins made her a world authority on industrial disease and a strong critic of American industry; Maria Goeppert-Mayer, the brilliant theoretical physicist whose research on the structure of the atom and its nucleus won her the Nobel Prize; and Zora Neale Hurston, the novelist and folklorist who mastered African-American folk idiom and depicted independent black women. One result of this search has been the publication of *Notable American Women*, four volumes of fascinating biographies of 1,800 remarkable individuals.[7]

"The next level of conceptualizing women's history," Lerner suggested, has been "contribution history." In this stage, historians describe women's contribution to topics, issues, and themes that have already been determined to be important. The main actors in the historical narrative remain men; women are subordinate, "helping" or "contributing" to the work of male activists. If the tone of "compensatory history" is delighted discovery of previously unknown women, the tone of contributory history can often be reproachful: how is it that men did not acknowledge women's help? Still, the work of contributory history can be very important in connecting women to major movements in the past: the women of Hull House "contribute" to Progressive reforms, the women in cotton factories in Lowell, Massachusetts, are an important part of the story of the industrialization of America. Pioneering historians in the late 1920s and 1930s, among them Julia Cherry Spruill, Mary Beard, and Caroline Ware, wrote important books that firmly established women's participation in and contribution to significant developments in American history: frontier settlement, abolition, urbanization and industralization, populism and progressivism.

It could be said that a third stage of women's history—which developed as a vigorous field of study and research in the 1970s and 1980s—is to move past a recounting of women's "contributions" and to seek to test familiar generalizations and to rewrite the historical narrative. Things we thought we "knew" about American history turn out to be more complex than we had suspected. For example, most textbooks suggest that the frontier meant opportunity for Americans, "a gate of escape from the bondage of the past." But it was men who more readily found on the frontier compensation for their hard work; many women found only drudgery. (In fact, women were more likely to find economic opportunity in cities than on the frontier.) Other generalizations turn out to be equally suspect. We have often assumed that American slaves were provided with at least adequate diets, but the generalization holds better for male slaves than for pregnant women and nursing mothers; for them, the slaves' diet meant semistarvation. The new women's history challenges us to re-examine the social relations of the sexes, to *reconstruct* many historical generalizations, and to *reconfigure* the historical narrative.

Finally, women's history challenges us to understand that gender itself is a social construction. Historians increasingly ask questions about how people construct meaning for their historical experience, and how difference between the sexes operates to shape the construction of meaning. Women's history also suggests a more complex understanding of traditional categories of historical interpretation. Conventional periodization has used presidential administrations or wars as major guideposts in organizing our description of the past: the Revolutionary Era, the Age of Jackson, the Civil War, the Eisenhower Years. Conventional interpretations have tended to emphasize the accomplishments of men, whether they be presidents, generals, farmers, or ranch hands. But all men had women for contemporaries, and women experienced the same great social phenomena that men did.

This book is divided into three major chronological sections. Because dates that mark major turning points in traditional historical accounts do not automatically coincide with those dates that mark significant changes in the lives of American women, women's history challenges us to re-examine conventional periodization. Our sections are generally congruent with familiar periodization; they also reflect changing realities in women's experience. The dividing date between traditional and industrial America is 1820, by which time forces were in motion that would erode the domestic economy of an agrarian society, slowly transforming women's lives in the process. The long period of industrialization that followed 1820 may conveniently be broken at 1880, by which time large-scale industries in which women were employed were firmly established. By this time, too, women's rights leaders had come to recognize that suffrage would not be granted by the courts on the basis of a fresh interpretation of the Constitution, and they demanded a specific constitutional amendment. The second major period ends at 1920, when the necessary ingredients for emancipation were present. Gerda Lerner has identified these as "urbanization; industrialization with technology permitting society to remove food preparation and care of the sick from the home; the mechanization of heating and laundry; spread of health and medical care sufficient to lower infant mortality and protect maternal health; birth control; . . . and availability of education on all levels to all children."[8] These conditions existed in varying measure by 1920, which was also the year of the passage of the Equal Suffrage Amendment, the first year in which women attended large state universities in numbers comparable to men, and the first year in which more women were working in factories and white-collar jobs than in domestic service.

THE SHARED HISTORICAL EXPERIENCE OF WOMEN AND MEN

However historical experience is periodized, women shared in that experience. The history of industrialization is a history that involves female workers quite as much as it does male. Like their male counterparts, most women workers relied on their wages for their own support and that of their families. In the first factory labor force—the mill hands of Samuel Slater's first textile factory in Pawtucket, Rhode Island, in 1790—women and children actually outnumbered men. Extensively employed in manufacturing by the nineteenth century, they worked in a wide variety of trades as bookbinders, printers, shoemakers, seamstresses, laundresses, glass painters, button makers. In the twentieth century they worked in shipyards, airplane factories, and automobile plants turning out the military equipment essential to allied victory in two world wars.

Women were at the forefront of working-class protest. Women weavers in Pawtucket, Rhode Island, who walked off work in 1824 were among the first American workers to strike against low wages and long hours; a significant number of strikes by women workers followed in the 1830s.[9] Women at the textile mills in Lowell, Massachusetts, in the 1840s were the first industrial workers in the nation to demand state regulation of the length of the workday. In the twentieth century, large-scale strikes organized by men in mines and railroads had their counterparts in large-scale strikes organized by women in textile mills and garment factories.[10]

Similarly, enslaved workers—primarily Africans but also, in the early centuries, Indians—were as likely to be women as men. Enslaved women workers were to be found in the fields, toiling alongside men, in the same jobs.

THE DIFFERENT HISTORICAL EXPERIENCE OF WOMEN AND MEN

The historical experience of the two sexes, for all its similarities, was in many important ways profoundly different. Difference itself is a comparative term. As legal scholar Martha Minow writes, "I am no more different from you than you are from me. A short person is different only in relation to a tall one." While making distinctions helps people cope with complexity, descriptions of difference usually carry with them unstated assumptions of value and hierarchy. As Minow puts it, "Women are compared to the unstated norm of men, 'minority' races to white, handicapped persons to the able-bodied, and 'minority' religions to 'majorities.'"[11] Difference, therefore, is not a neutral term.

Differences among women are also multiple. Differences of culture, nationality, and historical memory are exacerbated by distinctions of race, class, ethnicity, and sexual preference. Because women are apt to live with men—husbands, fathers, sons—who share their racial, class, and ethnic identities, commonalities with women who don't share that identity are often obscured. Because each of these differences carries with it implications of hierarchy, further distancing can develop. Affluent women may feel superior to poor women; white women may feel hostile to black women; Asian-American women may feel that they have little in common with Hispanic women.

Hispanic women, who are often identified as a single ethnic group, are in fact people of many nationalities: Puerto Ricans, Cubans, Mexicans, Brazilians—to name a few. Moreover, most are of Central American Indian descent and share the gene pool of North American Indians. They learned to speak Spanish—hence the name "Hispanic"—only because their original land was conquered by Spain. "Hispanic" women differ from each other not only with respect to ethnicity but also class. Affluent women who are part of the Miami Cuban community may feel that they have little in common with migrant agricultural workers from Mexico. By the same token, Asian-American women who came from such countries as China, Japan, the Philippines, Korea, Thailand, or Vietnam are separated by diverse heritages, various languages, and disparate economic resources. So are white women who are separated by multiple ethnic backgrounds, religious affiliations, and class positions.

Differences in sexual preference further divide women, stigmatizing lesbians and obscuring the commonalities they share with heterosexual women. Even those heterosexual women who reject negative stereotypes of homosexuals may view their lesbian counterparts with ambivalence. Women who are able to tolerate same-sex relationships as long as they remain discreetly hidden are often uncomfortable with open displays of homosexual preference and distance themselves from the women involved. Lesbians who have struggled for self-validation and a life-style that allows them to express same-sex love, affection, and sexuality feel no less alienated from women whose discomfort is a measure of their identification with a system that has stigmatized and oppressed other women.

That the factors which women share with men and which separate them from other women have been so powerful and persistent should not blind us to fundamental divergence in the historical experience of women and men. Gender differences in life cycles and family experiences have been a central factor in that divergence. Employment patterns of white women in a large New England textile factory make this clear. As young single women at the turn of the century, women went into the mill to supplement family income, often allowing brothers to improve their job prospects by staying in school; as wives, they withdrew when children were born and returned as mothers of small children when the perilous state of family finances required them to do so. As mothers of grown children, they returned to stay. Thus family responsibilities were a crucial factor not only in determining at what stage in their life cycle women were gainfully employed but also in explaining why their employment patterns differed from those of male workers.

Once in the work force, the jobs to which women were assigned, the wages they were paid, the opportunities for unionization they encountered, and the relationship they forged with governmental regulators all reinforced fundamental differences between the sexes. Even when they entered the factory together, with comparable skills, men and women were assigned by management to different tasks at markedly different pay scales. Despite the low wages, which should have made them ripe recruits for unionization, most unions were loath to organize women workers. In part because women lacked the leverage that unions afforded skilled male workers, federal and state governments reluctantly agreed to regulate women's hours, wages, and working conditions long before they regulated men's.

Most people, male and female, particularly if they were white and middle class, understood difference to mean advantage. They assumed that women were spared heavy physical labor and fierce competitive pressures. Excused from primary responsibility for family support, wives and daughters could spend most of their adult lives at home rather than in the work force, devoting their time to such congenial tasks as caring for children, doing charitable deeds, and socializing with friends. Those who were employed outside the home were thought to work for "pin money," which they could use to indulge their whims as consumers.

Recent research makes clear that most of these "advantages" were class-specific and illusory. Exhausting labor performed in hazardous conditions characterized many women's jobs. Responsibility for supporting other family members was not limited to men, especially among the working class. Unmarried women often returned their wages to their parents, who relied on daughters' wages for essentials. Most adult women— whether they were single, widows, or wives—worked to feed and shelter themselves, their children, other members of their families. Their expenditure of money was rarely capricious; in fact they accepted low wages in nonunionized jobs because they were so likely to be in desperate need.

The notion that the home protected working-class housewives from the competitive pressures of the marketplace and all housewives from real work was also an illusion. The home has always been less a haven than a workplace. It was the site of housework— heavy physical labor and unremitting toil—work that was no less strenuous for all the denial that it was work at all since it was performed for love of family rather than wages. Even the middle-class housewife who enjoyed the conveniences of nineteenth-century town life and possibly a servant to help with the laundry and cooking struggled with an exhausting array of tasks that included washing, starching, ironing, sorting, and putting away laundry; scrubbing, sweeping, and dusting floors, walls, windows, furniture, and accessories; growing, pickling, preserving, and baking food; sewing, mending, and knitting clothes, towels, pillowcases, quilts, curtains, carpets, and rugs; birthing, nursing, tending, instructing, and disciplining children. According to one harried antebellum housewife, every day was "hurry, hurry, hurry, and drive, drive, drive."[12] For rural women the workload was even heavier. There were farm-related chores to perform and raw materials such as soap and cloth to produce in addition to core household tasks. Through much of the nineteenth century rural black women were enslaved; after the

Civil War most lived in sharecropping families in which the level of subsistence was scarcely higher and the physical work load almost as heavy, although the psychological conditions were generally better. Reflecting on the workload of her mother's generation, a nineteenth-century daughter spoke for millions when she lamented that her mother had been robbed of "her health, her strength, and her life."[13] In some respects, little has changed. In the 1980s, a farm woman in northern Iowa told an interviewer, "I plant the garden, I feed the chickens, I sell the eggs, I put up a year's worth of vegetables. I don't have *time* to work!"[14]

Although twentieth-century technology has lightened the onerous physical burden, the equation of homemaking with leisure remains an illusion carefully nurtured by the advertising industry. From the introduction of the electrical washing machine in the 1920s—"an entire new day will be added to your week"—to the dishwashers, ranges, and microwave ovens of the 1990s that will do the work "whether you are at home or not," promises of relief from drudgery through the purchase of new products have been accompanied by new expectations that entailed more work.[15] Laundry—and there was more of it—had to be done more frequently; cooking demanded more creativity; clothing necessitated hours spent shopping; child care involved properly sterilized bottles, regular feeding schedules, greater attention to toilet training, nutrition, hygiene, and properly supervised play. If the nature of housework had changed, the time spent doing it did not. In 1960, nonemployed urban women were spending 55 hours per week in housework—three hours more than rural homemakers in the 1920s. Fully employed women in the 1980s each week pack an additional 25 hours of work—housework—into evenings and weekends, leading one expert to conclude that their work days are probably longer than were their grandmothers'.[16]

If women seldom found the home that tranquil center of repose depicted in popular literature, they had equal difficulty finding in it the much celebrated "haven" from the competitive pressures of a "heartless world." We have long understood that severe downturns in the market have enormous economic and psychic impact on family life. During the Great Depression of the 1930s, for example, many homemakers were thrust into the work force, joining the long lines of men desperate for work. Refusing to sit by passively when their families lacked basic necessities, others opened their homes to boarders and applied their sewing skills to piecework—measures that wives of laborers had long used to supplement family income even in periods of prosperity. Resorting to the home production that had engaged their grandmothers, middle- and working-class women alike raised and canned vegetables and patched, mended, and recycled clothes in order to keep cash outlays at a minimum.

What historians have only begun to appreciate is the extent to which in more prosperous times such enterprise and frugality benefited not only the household economy but the national economy as well. By helping out husbands in shops, buying in bulk, taking in boarders, doing piecework, taking in wash, peddling goods on the street, scavenging for food and fuel, wives in laboring-class households throughout the nineteenth and early twentieth century managed to transform a husband's wages below subsistence level into subsistence wages. Because of such efforts, businesses employing those husbands were able to stay afloat in an undercapitalized and volatile economy. Among the emerging middle class where a husband's income was sufficient for maintenance, it was the value of the wife's labor that frequently provided the kind of savings and investments that buffered the family against market vicissitudes and fueled economic growth in an industrializing nation. In sum, even in the nineteenth century, the boundaries between home and market, domestic sphere and public sphere, were far more permeable than once assumed.

GENDER AS A SOCIAL CONSTRUCTION

The adverse economic implications for women associated with the old perception that housework was not real work suggest that in this instance, as in many others, difference has meant disadvantage. Women's historians have not only documented this disadvantage, but have sought to explain it. The factors involved in this explanation are very complex and still imperfectly understood. The explanation traditionally offered has been a variant of biological essentialism. As Supreme Court Justice David Brewer put it in 1908, "The two sexes differ in the structure of the body, in the functions to be performed by each, in the amount of physical strength, in the capacity for long continuing labor . . . , [in] the self reliance which enables one to assert full rights, and in the capacity to maintain the struggle for subsistence." Woman's "physical structure and a proper discharge of her maternal functions" place her at a disadvantage in that struggle, he continued, and justify legislation to protect her.[17]

Justice Brewer's statement reveals a common confusion of sex and gender. To the extent that his view of difference is based on anatomical and hormonal features that differentiate males and females biologically, he is talking about *sexual* difference. When, however, he speaks of "the self-reliance that enables . . . [men] to assert full rights," "the capacity [of men] to maintain the struggle for subsistence," and the "proper discharge of [woman's] maternal functions," he is referring to *gender* difference. The assumption that men are self-reliant and that women are not, that men struggle for subsistence and women do not, that women nurture their children and men cannot, reflects the ways in which Justice Brewer and most of his generation understood the implications of being male or female.

In antebellum America, for example, white southern males, whether members of the low-country planter class or the backcountry working class, identified masculinity with a concept of personal honor, in defense of which duels were fought and fists flew. In the cities of the North, many young working-class males shared their southern counterparts' obsession with physical prowess and bellicosity. So synonymous were masculinity and toughness for those New Yorkers known as "Bowery boys" that when the Bowery boy was represented on stage, he was immediately recognizable by his swaggering gait and aggressive persona. Although the black abolitionist Frederick Douglass would not have been comfortable with the flamboyant aggressiveness and virility flaunted by the Bowery boys as a badge of working-class masculinity, the identification of force and power with manhood was a concept he well understood. In *Narrative of the Life of Frederick Douglass* (1845), Douglass's autobiographical account of his life as a slave and his escape to freedom, the author prefaced a description of his brutal fight with the vicious slave breaker Covey with a single sentence: "You have seen how a man was made a slave; you shall see how a slave was made a man."

Not all social groups defined masculinity in this fashion, even in antebellum America. Although aggressiveness, self-reliance, and competitiveness were cultivated in most boys because these traits were needed in the work world of adult males, families whose values were shaped by evangelical Protestantism emphasized that manliness also involved self-restraint, moral self-discipline, and sobriety. These qualities became even more important in the new urban bourgeois culture of the late nineteenth century. A bureaucratized corporate capitalism would require of the middle class a model of masculinity different from the rougher, more "macho" ideal characteristic of the frontier. A "real" man, while projecting a virile and, if necessary, tough demeanor, also needed to be a "team player"—an attribute cultivated in boyhood games and team sports. Indeed, competitive sports, virility, and masculinity have become so intertwined in the twentieth century . . . that "the boy or man who dislikes competitive sports or virile postures has little choice but to affect 'manly' interests and behavior and to hope these affectations will not be exposed."[18] To behave otherwise was to risk being called a "sissy" or a "queer." Such labels reflected popular assumptions that "real" men were sportsmen and that nonathletes, whether heterosexual or not, were males who wished to have sexual relations only with males, were effeminate, and/or wished to be women. In other words, sex refers to biological differences that are unchanging; gender involves the *meaning* that a particular society and culture attach to sexual difference. Because that meaning varies over time and among cultures, gender differences are both socially constructed and subject to change. Definitions of what is masculine and feminine are learned as each society instructs its members from infancy through adulthood as to what behavior and personality attributes are appropriate for males and females of that generation.

Sexuality is also socially constructed. Anatomical and hormonal characteristics set certain boundaries within which we operate. Within those boundaries socially constructed scripts provide cues as to how we respond sexually—what or who arouses our desire. How sexual preference is first determined or chosen—and when—is a matter experts do not fully understand. But here, too, culture plays a part. It is helpful, writes historian Carroll Smith-Rosenberg, to "view sexual and emotional impulses as part of a continuum or spectrum. . . . At one end of the continuum lies committed heterosexuality, at the other uncompromising homosexuality; between, a wide latitude of emotions and sexual feelings."[19] Where we place ourselves on that continuum and whether we move within it is affected by cultural norms as well as a strong biological component.

Sexuality has its own history. Conceptions of sexuality, attitudes as to how sexual feelings should be expressed, with whom, and where, have been continually reshaped by the changing nature of the economy and politics. In the seventeenth century, for example, women were believed to be more lustful and carnal than men. Female sexuality was seen as a source of power and corruption to be feared and controlled. By the nineteenth century, when sexual restraints had to be internalized, sexuality was redefined. Women—at least white, native-born, middle- and upper-class women—were viewed as having weaker sexual desires than men. Sensuality was attached to poor or "darker" women—who, by definition, "invited" male advances.

As we begin to uncover the history of sexuality, we can better understand what part sexuality played in women's subordination. We can also see how women tried to devise ways to enhance sexual control and expression. In the nineteenth century, for example, some married women used the concept of women as passionless to reduce the frequency of sexual intercourse so as to reduce the likelihood of pregnancy and enhance sexual pleasure. Women who wished to express themselves sexually as well as emotionally in single-sex relationships constructed life-styles that opened up new realms of freedom. Indeed, we are just beginning to understand the ways in which these private relationships sustained the public activism of women such as Jane Addams or Lillian Wald.

GENDER AND ITS IMPLICATIONS

Understanding the difference between sex and gender provides a key to understanding the differences in men's and women's historical experience. In the workplace, for example, women and men were assigned jobs that reflected the employers' beliefs about the kind of work each sex should do. In a society whose understanding of gender included the conviction that women's primary obligations were familial and their basic talents domestic, female wage earners were persistently channeled into jobs that corresponded with the kind of work done in the domestic sphere or with characteristics long associated with women.

In the preindustrial domestic economy, women did both heavy physical labor—hauling water, slaughtering chickens—and skilled tasks—spinning, weaving, nursing. When women sought new avenues through which to gain economic independence they followed these chores into the marketplace. As slaves and as "hired help" they toiled on other people's farms; as "mill girls" they tended dangerous spinning machinery for twelve hours a day; as packinghouse workers they labored amid stench and slime. Upwardly mobile women laid claim to the teaching and nursing professions by emphasizing that the personality characteristics and skills required for such work were precisely those believed to be unique to the female sex. Thus nursing, considered in pre–Civil War years an occupation no respectable woman would enter, was eventually touted as a profession eminently suited to women. Providence, after all, had endowed the fairer sex with that "compassion which penetrate[s] the heart, that instinct which divines and anticipates the wants of the sick, and the patience which pliantly bends to all their caprices."[20] As the economy grew more complex, middle-class women infiltrated the ranks of librarians and secretaries. These occupations had been primarily male, but, like teaching and nursing, were redefined so as to emphasize the nurturing, service-oriented qualities ascribed to women—with a corresponding decrease in pay. Newer industries provided new job titles but old work categories. Receptionists and social workers were hired by employers still convinced that the tasks required in these jobs were consistent with the personality characteristics and skills traditionally associated with women. New white-collar jobs were also segregated by race, even in the North where segregation was not officially practiced. White women were overwhelmingly hired as stewardesses on national airlines until after the civil rights legislation of the 1960s. Because gender rather than individual talent or capability has been the primary consideration, the result of this kind of stereotyping has been to segregate women into certain kinds of work, whether in the professions or in industry. Of the 299 occupations listed by the Bureau of Labor Statistics in 1990, only 56 are thoroughly integrated by sex. Males overwhelmingly dominate 164 occupations. Seventy-nine occupations are predominantly female, and it is into these that over 80 percent of women workers cluster, working as waitresses, salespersons, secretaries, nurses, and teachers.[21]

Once a form of work has been identified with women, it has invariably become associated with low pay and minimal prestige. "Theoretically, the market treats men and women neutrally, judging only the characteristics of their labor," writes the historian Alice Kessler-Harris. "In the world of economists, the wage is rooted in the play of supply and demand." In practice, she continues, "the wage is neither neutral nor natural, but reveals a set of social constructs . . . that convey messages about the nature of the world, and about . . . men and women and . . . the relations between them." Low pay was appropriate for people assumed to be marginal workers, whose place was in the home where purity and virtue could be protected and family duties fulfilled. In this way the home subsidized the factory.[22]

Gender was embedded not only in economic relations but in legal relations as well. In the legal tradition English colonists brought to America, the husband was understood to be the head of the family and to represent it in its dealings with the world. Upon marriage, the woman lost her separate civil identity; it was assumed that she had voluntarily forsworn the claim to make choices at odds with those of her husband. In a powerful legal fiction, man and wife were understood to be one person; the married woman was the *feme covert*, "covered" with her husband's legal identity for virtually all purposes except crime.[23] All personal property she brought to the marriage became her husband's; he could sell her jewelry, gamble away her money. He could not sell her real estate unless she consented, but he could decide how it was to be used: whether land was to be farmed, rented out, planted in corn or vegetables, whether trees on it were to be cultivated or cut down. Since married women did not own property they could not make legal contracts affecting it; they could not buy and sell without their husband's consent. A married woman could not decide whether their children were to be kept at home or apprenticed or, if apprenticed, who their masters would be. She could not sign a contract independently; not until she was a widow could she leave a will. So powerful was the fiction that husband and wife are one person that marital rape was inconceivable. Indeed, marital rape was not outlawed anywhere in the world until 1978, when New York State passed a statute prohibiting forced sexual intercourse whether by a stranger, an acquaintance, or a spouse. As of 1990, only nine states have followed New York's lead. In most states, for husbands to force sex upon unwilling, even resisting wives is a crime only under certain circumstances. In four states it is not a crime at all.[24]

Gender also defined political relationships. In Anglo-American tradition the right to participate in political activities—voting, office-holding, jury duty—was conditioned on the holding of property. Since married women could not direct the use of their property, it seemed to follow that they could be neither jurors, nor voters, nor officeholders. That politics was considered a male domain, that women were not political beings, is an understanding as old as Western civilization. Aristotle, whose classic work provided the basic terms by which westerners have understood politics, said that men alone realized themselves as citizens. It is no accident that the civic *virtue* he extolled derives from the same root as the word *virile.* Women, Aristotle maintained, realized themselves only within the confines of the household. Their relationship to the world of politics, like their legal status, was derivative—through fathers, husbands, and sons.

This derivative relationship forced women to carve out a political role that rested upon their ability to influence those who held political power. A time-honored tradition, this use of influence was employed in the interests of a wide range of important social issues and philanthropic causes in the years before 1920. Women found that the wielding of influence benefited their communities and enlarged their political skills. The uses of influence continued to be exploited by American women even after they got the vote. As primary adviser to Al Smith, governor of New York and presidential candidate in the 1920s, Belle Moskowitz had enormous impact both on the policies of his administration and on the politics of the Democratic party. But she was uncomfortable claiming power for herself and never ran for political office. Mary McLeod Bethune, a prominent African-American educator, was equally adept in the uses of influence. As president of the National Association of Colored Women and the National Council of Negro Women, Bethune met Eleanor Roosevelt. The first lady, admiring the effectiveness with which this forceful, articulate black woman championed the needs of her people, used her own influence to secure for Bethune appointments to a number of positions, notably in the National Youth Administration. From her position within the administration, Bethune in turn organized the Federal Council on Negro Affairs, a group of black leaders who worked effectively to focus the attention of the media as well as the administration on the desperate problems facing blacks in the Depression.

The gendering of politics forced women to clothe their political claims in domestic language. Deflecting male hostility to their entry into the political arena, they argued that women should have the vote in order to elect city officials who would see to it that rotting garbage was removed from homes, decaying meat taken out of markets, and polluted water purified; otherwise, the best efforts of mothers to assure their children clean homes and wholesome food were to no avail. Women in the nuclear disarmament movement also used gendered language, naming their organization "Mothers Strike for Peace."

THE DIFFICULTIES OF UNDERSTANDING GENDER AS A SYSTEM

Economics, law, politics—each, as we have seen, was permeated by assumptions, practices, and expectations that were deeply gendered. So widely shared were these assumptions, practices, and expectations and so much a part of the ordinary, everyday experience that they acquired an aura of naturalness, rightness, even inevitability. Common sense dictated that "this is simply the way things are." But "common sense," as anthropologist Clifford Geertz has shrewdly observed, "is not what the mind cleared of cant spontaneously apprehends; it is what the mind filled with presuppositions . . . concludes."[25] The consequence of comprehending the world in this way—whether in the nineteenth century or in our own time—is that it obscures the workings of a system in which economic, political, and cultural forces interact and reinforce each other in ways that benefit one group and disadvantage the other. Unable to recognize the system, failing to understand that what shapes and defines our lives has been constructed piece by interlocking piece over time by other human beings, we constantly reproduce the world we know believing we have no other choice. As a result the inequities persist, becoming more difficult to challenge because they, too, seem as natural and inevitable as the system that has produced them.

To develop a way of looking that allows one to "see" economic and social relationships, which are presumed to be neutral and natural, as socially constructed arrangements which in fact benefit one group at the expense of others is always a difficult task. That task is made even more difficult by the fact that language itself has embedded within it the values, norms, and assumptions of the dominant group. Consequently it reflects and re-creates reality as it is perceived by that group. Using language that is not one's own to expose unequal relationships or to create an alternative to those relationships challenges the ingenuity and analytical abilities of even the most clearheaded and imaginative thinkers.

Analytical skills, however, are not inborn. They are developed slowly and painfully within an educational process that values and encourages those skills as contrasted, for example, with simple memorization or rote learning. Throughout history, women have been explicitly excluded from the intellectual community. Prior to the seventeenth century when most people were illiterate, elite families in which sons learned to read and write rarely provided such opportunities for their daughters. A major literacy gap existed until well into the nineteenth century throughout the world and, in many underdeveloped countries, persists today. At the time of the American Revolution, when it has been estimated that 70 percent of the men in Northern cities could read, only 35 percent of their female counterparts could do so. Slaves were denied by law access to instruction in reading and writing lest they learn about alternatives to slavery. Not until the second half of the nineteenth century were white women admitted to major state universities. Between 1870 and 1890 a few elite colleges were founded that were designed to provide upper middle-class young women an education equivalent to that which their brothers were receiving at Harvard, Yale, and Princeton universities. These new women's colleges reluctantly admitted a few black students. It was left to black women with meager resources in a rigidly segregated society—notably Mary McLeod Bethune and Charlotte Hawkins Brown—to develop their own institutions. Because public schools served black children so badly, these private institutions often began not as colleges, but as elementary or secondary schools and later grew into larger and higher-level colleges. Only in recent generations have women in substantial numbers been able to acquire not only a basic education, but the rigorous training that would facilitate their ability to analyze and question the social and cultural arrangements within which they lived.

Another consequence of women's educational deprivation was their ignorance of history and, therefore, their lack of an intimate acquaintance with other historical actors—male or female—who had faced challenges that in some way resembled their own. Lacking a history of their own, they had few models—heroes to emulate or strategies to adopt. The lack of a history in which women were actors made it particularly difficult for even educated women to envision a world other than one in which men—their experiences and needs—were the norm. Marginality in the past thus confirmed and reinforced marginality in the present.

Understanding economic and social relationships that benefit one sex at the expense of another, developing language with which to critique those hierarchical relationships and articulate an alternative vision, and forging the group solidarity necessary to realize that vision, have been the tasks of feminism. The term *feminism* came into use in the United States around 1910 at a time when women were engaged in the fight for suffrage as well as a host of other reforms. As historian Nancy Cott has pointed out, feminism included suffrage and other measures to promote women's welfare that had emerged out of the nineteenth-century women's movement.[26] However, feminism encompassed a wider range of fundamental changes, amounting to a revolution in the relation of the sexes. "As an *ism* (an ideology)," Cott notes, "feminism presupposed a set of principles not necessarily belonging to every woman—nor limited to women."[27] In other words, not all women would oppose a sex hierarchy that privileged men as a group nor would they feel compelled to struggle for sexual equality. Some men would, joining feminist women in their efforts to dismantle a system that conferred on one sex the power to define the other. While this system has been partially dismantled—the goal of suffrage was realized in law in 1920[28]—the wider revolution remains to be accomplished.

RETHINKING THE SOCIAL CONSTRUCTION OF GENDER

Embracing the goals of their feminist predecessors and enriched by current scholarship on gender, contemporary feminists seek to reconstruct social relations between the sexes. To do so, they believe, requires change in both public life and private behavior. This double agenda has a long history.

In 1848, when American feminists drafted their first manifesto, Elizabeth Cady Stanton demanded change in both law and custom. She called for legal change in the form of property rights for married women and voting rights for all women. Recognizing the ways in which women's self-esteem and autonomy were undermined, she also urged women to work for wide-ranging cultural change, such as equal standards of sexual behavior and equal roles in churches.

When twentieth-century feminists began to understand gender as a social construction, they too realized that the feminist revolution had to be waged in personal life as well as public life; in home as well as in workplace; in the most intimate relationships as well as the most remote. "It must be womanly as well as manly to earn your own living, to stand on your own feet," observed the feminist Crystal Eastman shortly after the national suffrage amendment was passed in 1920. "And it must be manly as well as womanly to know how to cook and sew and clean and take care of yourself in the ordinary exigencies of life. . . . [T]he second part of this revolution will be more passionately resisted than the first. Men will not give up their privilege of helplessness without a struggle. The average man has a carefully cultivated ignorance about household matters . . . a sort of cheerful inefficiency."[29] But it was fifty years before Eastman's insights became an agenda for action.

Feminists of the 1970s captured national attention with bitter criticisms of parents who gave nurses' kits to their daughters and doctors' bags to their sons and of guidance counselors who urged mathematically talented girls to become bookkeepers and boys to become engineers. Feminists condemned stereotypes that fit children to conventional roles in their adult life and encouraged the publication of books and toys designed to demonstrate to both boys and girls that they need not shape their aspirations to gendered stereotypes. (The popular TV show, record, and book, *Free to Be You and Me*, encapsulated these themes.) Feminists also urged a new set of private decisions in the family, so that both sexes would share more equitably the burdens and pleasures associated with earning a living, maintaining a household, and rearing a family. But gender stereotypes turned out to be more resilient than many had anticipated; socialization is a lifetime process.

Feminists themselves had to wrestle with a culture that maintained a hierarchy of values, reserving strength, competence, independence, and rationality for men and nurture, supportiveness, and empathy for women. Questioning both the hierarchy and the dualisms embedded in this gendering of values, feminists argued that these should be viewed as shared human qualities that are not sex-specific.

Sexual hierarchy was not the only cultural hierarchy that posed problems. There were also hierarchies of race and class. White feminists in the 1970s were criticized for promoting a vision of feminism that ignored black women and assumed that all women who were impatient with contemporary culture were white and middle-class. The upwardly mobile vision was a contested vision; the priorities of women of different classes and races did not necessarily converge. Many black women supported many elements of the agenda of middle-class white feminists of the 1970s—equal pay for equal work, access to jobs—but they disagreed on priorities. They were skeptical of those who placed the needs of middle-class women ahead of the needs of working women. Middle-class white women, the employers of domestic workers, were markedly more enthusiastic about the elimination of quotas for female students in law and medical schools than they were about the establishment of minimum wage and social security protection for domestic workers. The first generation of white radical feminists fought vigorously for the repeal of all abortion laws and for safe access to birth control; for black feminists the need for access to abortion was only one of a wide range of medical services for which many black women struggled.

Differences in sexual preference also posed problems for this generation of feminists. Challenges to traditional gender arrangements have always inspired charges of sexual deviance from those seeking to discredit the movement and trivialize grievances; the 1960s were no exception. Concerned about the movement's image, many feminists, rejecting the charge, attempted to push lesbians out of sight. They insisted that equality, not sexual preference, was the issue. Lesbian feminists disagreed, arguing that autonomy in sexual matters involved more than access to reproductive control. In time, tensions eased as many heterosexual feminists accepted the legitimacy of lesbian involvement and the validity of their contention that straight/gay divisions also constituted a form of cultural hierarchy that reinforced male supremacy.

THE COMPLEXITY OF CREATING EQUALITY

Recognizing the magnitude of cultural and personal change required if each woman was to realize her full human potential, feminists of the 1970s simultaneously challenged the institutions and the laws that denied women equal treatment. They launched a barrage of test cases in state and federal courts challenging practices of unequal responsibility for jury service, unequal benefits for dependents, unequal age requirements for drinking and marriage. In 1971, in an Idaho case testing who was to be the administrator of a will, feminists persuaded the Supreme Court for the first time in American history to treat discrimination on the basis of sex as a denial of equal protection under the law.[30] But the Supreme Court was reluctant to build on this precedent in subsequent cases. The Court's refusal to apply as strict a standard to sex discrimination as to racial discrimination prompted feminists to try to insert a ban on sex discrimination in the Constitution. The Equal Rights Amendment, passed overwhelmingly by Congress in 1972, failed to garner the last three states necessary for the three-quarter majority required for ratification. A contributing factor in its failure was basic disagreement on whether equality under law requires equality of military obligation.

Lobbying vigorously with both Congress and the executive branch, feminists won guarantees of equal pay for equal work, equal employment opportunities, equal access to credit and to education.[31] Building on the tactics and achievements of the civil rights movement, feminists secured major gains in the 1960s and 1970s. In the process, however, they discovered that guarantees of equality in a system structured with men's needs as the norm does not always produce a gender-neutral result. In many professions, for example, there is enormous pressure to demonstrate mastery of one's field in the early stages of a career, precisely when the physical hazards of childbearing are relatively minimal. Although the standard appears to be gender-neutral, it presents young women with excruciating choices that do not confront their male peers.

Nowhere was the challenge of achieving gender-neutrality in the workplace greater than on the matter of pregnancy. Aware of the long history of discrimination against pregnant employees, feminists successfully attacked regulations that prevented women from making their own decisions about whether and how long to work when pregnant. But initial legislative "solutions" raised new complexities challenging the assumption that equality always requires identical treatment. If employers could no longer fire pregnant women, they could still exclude from the company's disability program those temporarily unable to work during some portion of their pregnancy or at childbirth. Pregnancy, according to the Supreme Court, was not temporary disability but a "voluntary physical condition."[32] Outraged at the Court's ruling, feminists and their allies demanded congressional action that would require pregnancy and childbirth be treated like any other physical event that befalls workers. Responding in 1978 with model legislation mandating *equal* treatment in the workplace, Congress required employers to give physically disabled pregnant workers the same benefits given to other disabled workers. The problem, however, was not yet resolved.

If employers denied disability leave to all employees as a matter of company policy, federal legislation mandating equal treatment for both sexes with respect to pregnancy disability would, in effect, penalize female employees unable to work because of pregnancy-related illness. Equality, in this instance, seemed to require *special* treatment. Lawmakers in California and a few other states agreed and required employers to provide pregnant workers disability coverage even if no other illnesses were covered. Employers complained that this constituted "preferential treatment" for women. Some feminists, aware of the ways in which legislation designating women as a special class of employees because of their reproductive capacity had penalized female workers in the past, questioned whether such legislation was in the best interests of women. Would it reinforce sexist stereotypes of men as "natural" breadwinners and women as "natural" childbearers and rearers, making employers reluctant to hire married women of childbearing age and further marginalizing women as workers? Wouldn't it be better strategy to concentrate on extending disability benefits to workers of both sexes? Other feminists were untroubled. Pregnancy is unique to women, they argued, and calls for "special treatment" in recognition of that uniqueness. Such legislation, they insisted, acknowledges reality at a time when growing numbers of women become pregnant within one year of their employment.

Writing for the majority in a 1987 decision upholding a controversial California law on pregnancy disability benefits, Justice Thurgood Marshall went to the heart of the equality/difference dilemma. He noted that "while federal law mandates the same treatment of pregnant and non-pregnant employees, it would be violating the spirit of the law to read it as barring preferential treatment of pregnancy." The California law, he reasoned, "promotes equal employment opportunities because it allows women as well as men to have families without losing their jobs."[33]

The difficulty of determining what is fair treatment for pregnant women dramatically illustrates the complexities involved in reconciling equality and sexual difference. Part of the difficulty has to do with the meaning of equality. Is equality to be thought of, as it has been throughout American history, as equality of opportunity? Or is equality to be defined as equality of results? In either case, do the methods used to achieve equality demand the same treatment or different treatment? The stakes in this debate are high, as the debate over pregnancy in the workplace illustrates, because childbearing impacts so directly on women's struggle for economic independence.

Childbearing is only one aspect of sexual difference that complicates efforts to achieve equality between the sexes. Closely related are other issues surrounding reproduction. In the first half of the twentieth century, access to birth control was the contested issue. Feminists argued that the right to choose if and when to bear children was the foundation on which authentic equality between men and women must rest. The debate was intense and emotionally charged because reproductive issues involve sexuality, ethical and religious values, medical technology, constitutional rights to privacy, as well as matters of economic dependence, physical vulnerability, and state power. In the second half of the twentieth century, particularly in the wake of the Supreme Court's decision in *Roe* v. *Wade* (1973), these issues were fought out over policies governing access to abortion. Issues of race, class, and gender intersected. For many white middle-class feminists, preserving abortion rights was a top priority. Advocates of birth control, they saw abortion as a measure of last resort. Without that option, women's efforts to plan their lives, to set priorities, and to make choices were severely constrained, and constrained in ways that men's were not. For poor women and women of color who had been the subject of involuntary sterilization and who lacked access to a wide range of medical services, abortion was only one among many essential needs, and not necessarily the most pressing one. For many other women, abortion was not an essential need at all. Believing that the fetus is a human being from the moment of conception and that motherhood is women's key reason for being, they denied any connection between equality and access to abortion. They rejected the feminist contention that denying women access to abortion is a way in which men use the power of the state to reinforce their own power over women. Whether the state should permit and/or fund abortions for teen-age victims of incest is the most dramatic of the issues in conflict.

Incest is only one aspect of the larger problem of sexual violence that feminists contend is the ultimate expression of male dominance. Sexual violence, they insist, is violence, not sex, and it is a public, not a private, matter. Rape crisis centers, battered women's shelters, and "Take Back the Night" marches are expressions of their insistence that government respond to male violence against women. Feminists also attack directly the notion that female victims of violence are in some measure to blame by virtue of provocative dress and behavior or prior sexual experience. In the late 1970s they convinced policymakers that sexual harassment was a form of economic discrimination and that those who maintained workplaces were legally obliged to take action to prevent it.

Feminists also exposed the link between sexual violence and pornography. Many of them argued that material that objectifies women and equates violence against them with sexual pleasure is an invasion of their civil liberties. This interpretation represents a radical reformulation of traditional civil liberties arguments and a willingness on the part of some feminists to entertain reconsideration of the boundaries of protected speech. The controversial nature of pornography and the complex issues of civil rights and civil liberties raised by efforts to deal with it once again exemplifies the challenges involved in creating a society in which men and women are equal.

THE ANGUISH OF FUNDAMENTAL CHANGE

Reconciling equality and difference, equity and justice, involves feminists in a task as consequential as any in human history. Relationships assumed to be the result of choice, even of love, were now exposed as hierarchical relationships involving power and control. Such exposures are always traumatic. "All the decent drapery of life is . . . rudely torn off," complained the British legislator Edmund Burke when revolutionaries in France challenged the divine right of kings two hundred years ago. "When ancient opinions and rules of life are taken away, the loss cannot possibly be estimated. From that moment we have no compass to govern us; nor can we know distinctly to what port we steer."[34]

Even those in the vanguard of change can appreciate its difficulty; old habits are hard to break even for those determined to break them. For those who are not the initiators, challenges to long-standing beliefs and behaviors, whether issued now or in the past, can be, at best, unwelcome and, at worst, profoundly threatening. Feminism is no exception. Demands for equality in terms of power, resources, and prestige are usually seen as redistributive. Giving one party its share of the pie may result in a smaller share for the others. Even individuals who believe in equality in the abstract may find themselves loath to share power and privileges in practice, especially when their own lives are affected intimately. Moreover, new governmental policies designed to provide women equal protection in the law, equity in the workplace, and parity in politics were only part of what feminists were about. Cultural values as well as social institutions were under scrutiny. Even the definition of family was being tampered with as the 1980 White House Conference on Families made clear. Family had always meant that members were related by blood, marriage, or adoption. The term was now being applied to two mothers with children or an unmarried heterosexual couple who were childless; "anybody living under the same roof that provides support for each other *regardless* of blood, marriage, or adoption" seemed to qualify. To recognize these arrangements as multiple family forms, which many feminists did, was to legitimate people who, from the viewpoint of traditionalists, were living "illegitimate lifestyles."[35]

From this perspective it is hardly surprising that gender changes that feminists saw as expanding options for women and men alike, were seen by traditionalists as rejecting cherished beliefs and practices—"neuterizing society."[36] Women who believe they have lived useful and admirable lives by the old rules often regard feminists' attacks on traditional gender roles as an attack on a way of life they have mastered—and hence an attack on them personally. They fear that "a woman who has been a good wife and homemaker for decades" will be "turned out to pasture with impunity" by "a new, militant breed of women's liberationist" prepared to sacrifice justice for equality.[37] At issue are not just economic security and personal identity of individuals but the larger social order. Convinced that biological differences between the sexes dictate "natural" roles, traditionalists see the maintenance of these roles as socially and morally necessary—a source of stability in a world of flux. Thus feminist insistence that women should be able to seek fulfillment in the public world of work and power as well as in the private world of home and family is viewed by traditionalists as an egocentric demand that places personal gratification above familial duty. "Feminists praise self-centeredness and call it liberation," observed activist Connie Marshner.[38] By the same token, the demand that women themselves be the ultimate judge of whether and when to bear children is seen by some not as a legitimate desire to ensure a good life for those children who are born but as an escape from maternal obligations that threatens the future of the family and ultimately, therefore, society itself.

To suggest that some women find feminism an essential part of their identity and that other women define themselves and their lives in terms of traditionalism is not to suggest that the ideological history of women is bipolar. It embraces many variants. Nor do we suggest that there is little on which the two groups agree. Traditionalist women may be as suspicious of male-controlled institutions as feminists. Traditionalists may also be as vocal and publicly active on behalf of their goals. Feminists may be just as dedicated to family as traditionalists. Both groups identify with "sisterhood" and see "women's issues" as special ones, although they do not consistently agree on what they are or how they should be addressed. Partisans of these issues may unite or divide along class, occupational, or political lines. But no matter where they fall on the ideological spectrum, *all* women are a part of women's history.

"Woman has always been acting and thinking . . . at the center of life," wrote Mary Beard a half century ago;[39] but the significance of women's activities has, until recent years, often been discounted and rarely been understood. The scholarship of the past decades has spotlighted much that has lain in the shadows of history unnoticed and unappreciated. As we have examined that scholarship, we find ourselves less impressed by gender-based constraints—which were very real—than by the vigor and subtlety with which women have defined the terms of their existence. These creative experiences show how the private lives of historical persons can help us understand the rich complexities of change. To study women's history, then, is to take part in a bold enterprise that can eventually lead us to a new history, one that, by taking into account both sexes, should tell us more about each other and, therefore, our collective selves.

NOTES

1. Frantz Fanon, *The Wretched of the Earth*, translated by Constance Farrington (New York, 1963), p. 170.
2. Christine de Pizan, *The Book of the City of Ladies*, translated by Earl Jeffrey Prichards (New York, 1982), pp. 6–8, 10–11.

3. Jane Austen, *Northanger Abbey and Persuasion*, ed. John Davie, (London, 1971), pp. 97–99.

4. Elizabeth Cady Stanton, Susan B. Anthony and Matilda Joslyn Gage, *History of Woman Suffrage*, vol. I. (New York, 1881), pp. 7–8.

5. Mary R. Beard, *Woman as Force in History: A Study in Traditions and Realities* (New York, 1946), pp. 59–60.

6. "Placing Women in History: Definitions and Challenges," *Feminist Studies* III (1975):5–14; reprinted in Gerda Lerner, *The Majority Finds Its Past: Placing Women in History* (New York, 1979), pp. 145–59.

7. Edward T. James, Janet Wilson James, and Paul Boyer, eds. *Notable American Women, 1607–1950: A Biographical Dictionary*, 3 vols. (Cambridge, Mass., 1971); and Barbara Sicherman and Carol Hurd Green, eds., *Notable American Women: The Modern Period* (Cambridge, Mass., 1980).

8. Lerner, *The Majority Finds Its Past*, pp. 49–50.

9. Alice Kessler-Harris, *Out to Work: A History of Wage-Earning Women in the United States* (New York, 1982), p. 40.

10. For detailed essays on the wave of garment workers' strikes of the early twentieth century, see Joan M. Jensen and Sue Davidson, eds., *A Needle, A Bobbin, A Strike: Women Needleworkers in America* (Philadelphia, 1984), pp. 81–182.

11. Martha Minow, "The Supreme Court—1986 Term. Foreword: Justice Engendered," *Harvard Law Review* 101 (1987):13. Minow points out that "'Minority' itself is a relative term. . . . Only in relation to white Westerners are [people of color] minorities."

12. Quoted from Harriet Beecher Stowe in Jeanne Boydston, *Home and Work: Housework, Wages, and the Ideology of Labor in the Early Republic* (New York, 1991), chap. 4.

13. George S. Merriam, ed., *Reminiscences and Letters of Caroline C. Briggs* (New York, 1897), pp. 21–23. Quoted in Boydston, *Home and Work*, chap. 4.

14. See Deborah Fink, *Open Country, Iowa: Rural Women, Tradition and Change* (Albany, N.Y., 1986), pp. 62–65.

15. Quoted in Susan Strasser, *Never Done: A History of American Housework* (New York, 1982), pp. 268, 278.

16. Joann Vanek, "Time Spent in Housework," *Scientific American* 231 (1974):116–20.

17. *Mueller* v. *Oregon*, 208 U.S. 412.

18. Mark C. Carnes and Clyde Griffin, eds., *Meanings for Manhood: Constructions of Masculinity in Victorian America* (Chicago, 1990), p. 203.

19. Carroll Smith-Rosenberg, "The Female World of Love and Ritual: Relations between Women in Nineteenth Century America," *Signs: Journal of Women in Culture and Society* 1 (1975):29–30.

20. *Raleigh* (N.C.) *News and Observer*, November 24, 1904.

21. For purposes of these calculations, predominantly female occupations were defined as those hiring 70% or more women; predominantly male occupations were defined as those hiring 30% or less women. The calculations were made by Jennifer Lettieri on the basis of materials supplied by the U.S. Department of Labor, Bureau of Labor Statistics. See especially *Employment and Earnings* (Washington, D.C., January 1989), pp. 183–88.

22. Alice Kessler-Harris, *A Woman's Wages* (Lexington, Ky., 1990).

23. If, however, she committed a crime under his direction or surveillance, it was understood that he was the culprit. In most elements of criminal law, however, even married women were understood to have independent moral and ethical responsibilities; women could be charged with murder or treason.

24. New York Penal Law, Sec. # 130.00 1978. *McKinney's Consolidated Laws of New York Annotated* (St. Paul, 1987). For a basic review of the laws, see Herma Hill Kay, ed., *Sex-Based Discrimination* (St. Paul, 1988), pp. 239–62.

25. Clifford Geertz, *Local Knowledge: Further Essays in Interpretive Anthropology* (New York, 1983), p. 84.

26. Nancy F. Cott, *The Grounding of Modern Feminism* (New Haven, Conn., 1987), pp. 13–16.

27. Ibid., p. 3.

28. But in a segregated South, poll taxes and other devices barred black women (as well as men) from voting; not until the civil rights revolution of the 1950s and 1960s did the suffrage slowly and irregularly become available.

29. "Now We Can Begin," in Blanche Weisen Cook, ed., *Crystal Eastman on Women and Revolution* (New York, 1978), pp. 54–55. Originally published in *The Liberator* (December 1920).

30. *Reed* v. *Reed* 404 U.S. 71 (1971).

31. Equal Pay Act of 1963; Equal Credit Opportunity Act of 1974; Title VII of the Civil Rights Act of 1964; Title IX of the Educational Amendments Act of 1974.

32. *Geduldig* v. *Aiello* 417 U.S. 484 (1974); and *General Electric* v. *Martha Gilbert* 97 S. Ct. 401 (1976).

33. *California Federal Savings and Loan Association* v. *Guerra* 479 U.S. 272 (1987). "Promoting equal employment opportunities" requires new child care policies. Giving men and women equal access to a workplace that lacks provisions for child care is not gender neutral in its results when over 50% of these women have children under six. Working mothers, whatever the ages of their children and whatever their income level, currently spend 25 hours per week on domestic work compared with only 11 hours spent by their male partners. With less time and energy available for the kind of job-related activities and training programs that would improve their economic position, many are penalized with respect to both pay and promotion. Others who accept low-paying jobs for which they are overqualified because the hours or location allow them to more easily integrate

wage work and family responsibilities find themselves similarly immobilized. For women who are single parents and heads of household, the penalties are especially severe.

34. Edmund Burke, *Reflections on the Revolution in France* (London, 1910), pp. 74–75.

35. Paul Weyrich, "Debate with Michael Lerner," speech presented at the Family Forum II conference, Washington, D.C., July 28, 1982. Quoted in Rebecca Klatch, *Women of the New Right* (Philadelphia, 1987), pp. 125–26.

36. Phyllis Schlafly, *The Power of the Positive Woman* (New Rochelle, N.Y., 1977), p. 25.

37. Ibid., p. 81.

38. Connaught Marshner, *The New Traditional Woman* (Washington, D.C., 1982), pp. 1, 3–4, 12. See also Klatch, *Women of the New Right,* p. 129.

39. Mary R. Beard, ed., *America Through Women's Eyes* (New York, 1933), pp. 4–5.

The wyfe of an Herowan of Secotan.

This portrait of a Carolina Algonquin woman at her home settlement Secoton was drawn in the summer of 1585 by John White, the official artist of the Roanoke Expedition. His drawings are important representations of Algonquin life before extensive European contact. The woman, who looks skeptically at the viewer, is the wife of a leading male chief or counselor. Her body is decorated with gray, brown, and blue tattoos on the face, neck, arms, and legs. Women's tattoos simulated elaborate necklaces and other ornamentation; men used body paint for ceremonial purposes. (Courtesy of The British Museum. See Also Paul Hulton, America 1585: The Complete Drawings of John White [Chapel Hill: University of North Carolina Press and British Museum Publications, 1984], pp. 66–67)

I

Traditional America
1600–1820

Most American histories treat the colonial period as a time when government and order were imposed upon a wilderness. The important subjects tend to be Indian wars, international trade, the establishment of legislatures, and rivalries between British colonies and those of other nations. The first woman mentioned is usually Pocahontas, the innocent Indian princess who allegedly saved the life of the hero of Jamestown, Captain John Smith. The second woman who appears is often Anne Hutchinson, who was banished from Massachusetts Bay Colony for heresy. Both met premature and unpleasant deaths. Unaccustomed to the climate of England, where she had been taken to be shown to Queen Anne, Pocahontas died of pneumonia. Hutchinson was massacred by Indians during a raid on her lonely dwelling in what is now Westchester County, New York. The reader who concludes from these examples that women were not very important in colonial America, and that the few women whom we remember are likely to have been troublesome and to have come to a bad end, may be pardoned.

But if we pose Mary Beard's question and ask, What did colonial America look like, seen through women's eyes? the picture changes. More constructive than troublesome, women were among the founders of virtually every colony. Indeed, a settlement counted itself as having passed the stage of a temporary camp only after it had attracted a reasonable complement of women. A sex ratio approaching 100 (that is, 100 women to every 100 men) was taken to be evidence that the settlement was here to stay. Once founded, communities were maintained in large part by women's labor. The productivity of housekeepers is not easily measured, but over fifty years ago Julia Cherry Spruill established the complexity of the tasks performed in frontier households.[1]

It may be that America seemed to women less radical a change from the Old World than it did to men. The terrors of the ocean crossing and of the wilderness were, of course, shared by all. In the farming communities Europeans established along the eastern seaboard daily tasks proceeded in the manner of England, whether the agricultural laborer were farmer or farmer's wife. The rituals of childbirth were transmitted intact from Old World to New, although it may well have been that the rate of survival of mother and infant was better in the American countryside, where the dangers of infection were far fewer than in the towns and cities of Europe. By contrast, the innovations that made the colonies most distinctive from the Old World—especially governmental institutions like town meetings and provincial legislatures—were settings from which women were barred.

One institution in which women were welcome was the church, but despite repeated quotation of St. Paul's rule that "in Christ there is neither man or woman," believers of every faith were very conscious of gender distinctions. Hutchinson's heresy was compounded by the fact that it was formulated by a woman. Many of the questions in her trial were grounded in the objection that she had stepped out of her proper place. For women, Puritans had special expectations and understood there to be special punishments. When dissenting women like Mary Dyer were delivered of malformed infants, John Winthrop saw no reason to be surprised at the divine punishment. Witchcraft, too, was a religious heresy; it, too, was gender specific, a woman's crime. Although witchcraft accusations normally arose in places where the entire community was troubled, the accusers were usually teen-aged girls, and the "witches" usually women.

English colonists brought with them a system of property rights that assumed that a married woman's civil identity fused with her husband's. The principle of "unity of person" created what historian Marylynn Salmon has called "a special kind of legal partnership," in which married women's legal activities were extensively restricted. "Covered" by her husband's civil identity, the married woman could not execute a contract without his signature (although a husband could manage the family's property without asking her consent). Without his agreement, she could not buy, sell, or trade; she could not apprentice her children or execute a valid will (until she was a widow.)[2]

In English colonies, some women nevertheless managed to control their property after marriage through prenuptial agreements or marriage settlements. When the United States purchased the Louisiana Territory, it acquired vast expanses of land that had been ruled by Spanish and French law, systems not marked by coverture, in which the property husbands and wives brought to their marriage became "community property." Although husbands were "head and master" of their households and had wide discretion in their use of family property, married women could keep separate property in their own names and pass it on to whomever they chose as heirs. These practices were not erased when the land passed to the United States; Louisiana, Texas, New Mexico, Arizona, Idaho, Nevada, California, and Washington remained community property states, offering significant legal advantages to married women deep into the twentieth century.

In English colonies, the right to participate in the political system—to vote and to hold office—was conditioned on holding property. It therefore seemed logical to colonists that political rights be granted only to men. Since girls could not grow up to be legislators or ministers or lawyers, little care was taken to provide them with any but the most elementary forms of schooling. "How many female minds, rich with native genius and noble sentiment, have been lost to the world, and all their mental treasures buried in oblivion?" mourned one writer.[3]

Like it or not, women were part of the community. What they chose to do or not to do set constraints on men's options. The Revolutionary army, lacking an effective quartermaster corps, was dependent on women for nursing, cooking, and cleaning. The army, in turn, could not march as quickly as Washington would have liked because provision had to be made for the "woemin of the army." The task of the recruiting officer was eased when men could rely on their female relatives to keep family farms and mills in operation, fend off squatters, and protect family property by their heavy labor, often at grave physical risk. We have no simple calculus for measuring the extent to which women's services made it possible for men to act in certain ways during the Revolution, but it is clear that women's work provided the civilian context in which the war was carried on.

When the war was over and the political structure of the new nation was being reshaped in federal and state constitutions, little attention was given to the political role women might directly play. Yet women did have distinctive political interests. For example, if women had had the vote in 1789, they might well have used it to establish pensions for widows of veterans and to claim independent property rights for married women. Women's distinctive needs tended to be discounted as trivial. It was left to women of succeeding generations to accomplish for themselves what the Revolution had not.

NOTES

1. Julia Cherry Spruill, *Women's Life and Work in the Southern Colonies* (Chapel Hill, 1938).

2. Marylynn Salmon, *Women and the Law of Property in Early America* (Chapel Hill, 1986), pp. 14–15; on Louisiana, see Elizabeth Bowles Warbasse, *The Changing Legal Rights of Married Women 1800–1861* (New York, 1987, 1960), pp. 48–56.

3. Clio [pseud.], "Thoughts on Female Education," *Royal American Magazine,* Jan. 1774, pp. 9–10.

SARA EVANS
The First American Women

The first American women were Indian women. The religious, economic, and political roles that they played within their own societies prior to the arrival of Europeans suggest that Europeans and Indians held dramatically different ideas about what women and men should be and should do. The difficulty that Europeans had in understanding the alternative gender realities to which they were exposed tells us how strong is the impulse to view established gender definitions in one's own culture as natural rather than socially constructed.

Note the importance Evans attaches to Indian women's religious functions. How did the sexual division of labor within Indian tribes she describes affect women's economic importance in a subsistence economy? To what extent did the Iroquois provide the authors of American constitutions with a democratic model?

According to the Iroquois, the creation of the earth began when a woman came from heaven and fluttered above the sea, unable to find a resting place for her feet. The fish and animals of the sea, having compassion on her, debated in council about which of them should help her. The tortoise offered his back, which became the land, and the woman made her home there. A spirit noticed her loneliness and with her begot three children to provide her company. The quarrels of her two sons can still be heard in the thunder. But her daughter became the mother of the great nations of the Iroquois.[1]

Women appear frequently at the cosmic center of native American myths and legends, tales that are undoubtedly very ancient. The history of women on the North American continent began 20,000 years ago with the migration of people from the Asian continent across the land bridge that now is the Bering Strait. These early ancestors of contemporary native Americans gradually created a great diversity of cultures as they adapted to varied environmental circumstances and conditions over time. The archaeological record indicates that 2,000 years ago some North American cultures lived nomadically, hunting and gathering plants and animals. Others settled in villages and subsisted on domesticated plants as well as wild resources. Still others built complex, hierarchically organized societies centered in relatively large cities or towns. In these latter groups, archaeological remains reveal widespread trade relations and religious systems uniting people over vast areas of the continent. When the first Europeans reached North America in the fifteenth and sixteenth centuries, there were some 2,000 native American languages in use, a cultural diversity that made Europe look homogeneous.[2]

GATHERERS AND NURTURERS, TRADERS AND SHAMANS

Among the peoples of North America whose tribes lived in the woods, along the rivers, and on the edges of the plains, women were essential to group survival. In a subsistence economy, daily life revolved around finding food for the next meal or, at the most, the next season. Women's work as gatherers and processors of food and as nurturers of small children was not only visible to the whole community, but it also shaped ritual life and processes of community decision making.

Women's activities were sharply divided from those of men in most Indian societies. Women gathered seeds, roots, fruits, and other wild plants. And in horticultural groups they cultivated crops such as corn, beans, and squash. Women were also typically responsible for cooking, preserving foods, and making household utensils and furnishings. In addition, they built and maintained dwellings, such as earth or bark lodges and tepees, and associated household facilities like storage pits, benches, mats, wooden racks, and scaffolds. In groups that moved on a seasonal basis, women were often responsible for transporting all household goods from one location to the next.

Male activities in many groups centered on hunting and warfare. After the hunts, Indian women played an important role in processing the hides of deer or buffalo into clothing, blankets, floor coverings, tepees, or trade goods; preserving the meat; and manufacturing a variety of bone implements from the remains of the animals.

Indian societies differed in their definitions of which tasks were appropriate for women or men and in their degree of flexibility or rigidity. In some groups people would be ridiculed and shamed for engaging in tasks inappropriate for their gender, while other groups were more tolerant. Sometimes men and women performed separate, but complementary tasks. Among the Iroquois, for example, men cleared the fields so women could plant them. In other cases men and women performed the same tasks but the work was still segregated on the basis of sex. For example, many Plains Indian tribes divided the task of tanning hides according to the animal, some being assigned exclusively to women, others to men.

These differences shaped the relationships among women and between women and men. Societies with a clear sexual division of labor and cooperative modes of production, for example, encouraged gender solidarity. The Pawnee, a Plains society, lived in lodges large enough for several families, or about fifty people. Women shared cooking responsibilities among themselves, alternating between those on the north and those on the south sides of the lodge. Among the Hidatsa, another Plains

group, female labor was organized by the household of female kin while male activities, ranging from individual vision quests to sporadic hunting parties, were organized by age and by village. Groups of female kin built and maintained their homes, gathered seeds and edible plants, raised crops, and processed the meat and skins of animals killed by the men.[3]

In Iroquois society, where men were frequently away for prolonged periods of time, women farmed in a highly organized way. A white woman adopted in 1758 by the Seneca (one of the six tribes of the Iroquois Confederacy) described their work:

In the summer season, we planted, tended, and harvested our corn, and generally had all of our children with us; but had no master to oversee or drive us, so that we could work as leisurely as we pleased. . . . We pursued our farming business according to the general custom of Indian women, which is as follows: In order to expedite their business, and at the same time enjoy each other's company, they all work together in one field, or at whatever job they may have on hand. In the spring, they choose an old active squaw to be their driver and overseer, when at labor, for the ensuing year. She accepts the honor, and they consider themselves bound to obey her.

When the time for planting arrives, and the soil is prepared, the squaws are assembled in the morning, and conducted into a field where each plants one row. They then go into the next field and plant once across, and so on till they have gone through the tribe.[4]

As they gathered, cultivated, and produced food, tools, and housing, some women also actively participated in trade. Algonkian women on the Atlantic coast traded with whites from the earliest days. In 1609 John Juet, Henry Hudson's first mate, recorded an incident in New York Harbor: ''There came eight and twentie Canoes full of men, women and children to betray us: but we saw their intent, and suffered none of them to come aboord us. . . . They brought with them Oysters and Beanes, whereof we bought some.''[5] In later years many observers noted both transactions with women and the high proportion of trade goods that were particularly interesting to women. Far to the northwest, on the Alaskan coast, the Tlingit built their economy on fishing for plentiful salmon and on trading with neighboring groups. Tlingit women not only dried and processed the salmon but they were also entrusted with managing and dispensing the family wealth. White traders were continually struck by the skill and sophistication of these women, who frequently stepped in to cancel unwise deals made by their husbands. These shrewd dealings paid off in that society where status could be gained by impressive displays of gift-giving.[6]

Religious myths and rituals offered women additional sources of power and status in their villages and tribes as they reflected in a symbolic realm the relations between people and nature.[7] In most North American Indian creation myths, females played critical roles as mediators between supernatural powers and earth. Many horticultural societies ritually celebrated the seasonal powers of Earth Mother—whose body produced the sacred foods of corn, beans, and squash. Groups primarily oriented to hunting more frequently conceptualized sacred powers as male, but in some cases the Keeper of the Game appeared as a woman. She observed humans' failures to address proper ritual prayers to the spirits of the animals and to treat the animal world on which they depended with proper respect; she could also inflict punishments of disease and famine.

American Indians perceived their world as sacred and alive. Power and mystery infused all living things, inspiring awe and fear. Women, like men, sought spiritual understanding and power by engaging in individual quests for visions. Quests involved a period of seclusion, fasting, and performance of prescribed rituals. Women's quests drew on the fasting and seclusion accompanying menstruation.

In most societies menstruating women were believed to be dangerously powerful, capable of harming crops or hunts and draining the spiritual powers of men. To avoid such harm they withdrew to menstrual huts outside the villages. Did women interpret this experience in terms of pollution and taboo, seeing it as a banishment, as many observers assumed? More likely they welcomed the occasional respite from daily responsibilities as an opportunity for meditation, spiritual growth, and the company of other women. The power that visions conferred allowed some women to serve as herbalists, midwives, medicine women, and shamans.

Marriage practices in some societies granted women considerable control in choosing their partners. In others, marriages were arranged by elders (often women) as a means of building economic alliances through kinship. Divorce, on the other hand, was common and easy to accomplish. A woman could simply leave her husband or, if the house was hers, she could order him out on grounds of sterility, adultery, laziness, cruelty, or bad temper. Women's autonomy often had a further sexual dimension: Although the male-dominated groups prized female chastity, most Indian groups encouraged sexual expressiveness and did not enforce strict monogamy. Female power in marital and sexual relations could also be shaped by the proximity of a woman to her own kin.

Women's political power was rooted in kinship relations and economics. The scale of clan and village life meant that people knew one another primarily through kinship designators (daughter, husband, mother's brother, grandmother), and in many cases the most important level of sociopolitical organization was the local kin group. It seems likely that female power was most salient at the level of the village group, where it would shape many facets of daily life. In many tribes, however, there were some (often transitory or temporary) public forums, such as a council of elders, where decisions could be made for the community as a whole. Women held proportionately few of these public roles, but a recent reevaluation of ethnographic evidence shows that despite most scholars' belief that women had no significant political roles, there were numerous female chiefs, shamans, and traders.[8]

Iroquois women represented the apex of female political power. The land was theirs; the women worked it cooperatively and controlled the distribution of all food whether originally procured by women or by men. This gave them essential control over the economic organization of their tribe; they could withhold food at any point—in the household, the council of elders, war parties, or religious celebrations.[9] The Iroquois institutionalized female power in the rights of matrons, or older women, to nominate council elders and to depose chiefs. As one missionary wrote: "They did not hesitate, when the occasion required, to 'knock off the horns' as it was technically called, from the head of a chief and send him back to the ranks of the

Their rype corne.

Their greene corne.

Corne newly sprong.

Their sitting at meate.

The place of solemne prayer.

The house wherin the Tombe of their Herounds standeth.

SECOTON

A Ceremony in their prayers w[i]
strange iestures and songs dansing
about posts caruod on the topps
lyke mens faces.

This drawing depicts the settlement of Secoton, the home of the Algonquin woman pictured on page 24. The Secoton system of successive planting is illustrated by, from top to bottom, a field of ripe corn, a field of green corn, and newly planted corn. (Courtesy of the British Museum. See also Paul Hulton, America 1585: The Complete Drawings of John White *[Chapel Hill: University of North Carolina Press and British Museum Publications, 1984], pp. 66–67)* warriors. The original nomination of the chiefs also always rested with them."[10] When the council met, the matrons would lobby with the elders to make their views known. Though women did not sit in formal or public positions of power, as heads of households they were empowered *as a group*. This, in turn, reflected their considerable autonomy within their households.[11]

GENDER AND CHANGE: THE IMPACT OF EUROPEAN CONTACT

When Europeans began to invade the Americas in the 1500s, the most devastating assault on Indian life initially came from the unseen bacteria and viruses Europeans brought with them. Within a century raging epidemics of typhoid, diphtheria, influenza, measles, chicken pox, whooping cough, tuberculosis, smallpox, scarlet fever, strep, and yellow fever reduced the population of Mexico to only 5 to 10 percent of its former level of 25 million. The population of the northern areas which later became the United States suffered similar fates.[12]

As cultural, economic, and military contacts grew, the differences between women and men in each group began to change. In some cases women appropriated new sources of wealth and power; in others they lost both skills and autonomy. These various changes were shaped by the sexual division of labor in indigenous cultures, the demographic composition of European colonizers, and the nature of the economic relations between Indians and Europeans.

For example, when the Aztec empire fell before the superior military technology of the Spanish, women were booty in the military victory. The demographic facts of a dense Indian population and Spanish conquerors who were almost exclusively male shaped a continuing sexual interaction between Spanish men and Indian women. Seeking stability, the Spanish soon began to encourage marriages with Christianized Indian women. These Indian mothers of the mestizo (mixed-bloods) were historically stigmatized both by a racial caste system and by association with illegitimacy. Nevertheless, they fashioned for their children a new culture blending Christianity and the Spanish language with cultural concepts and practices from their Indian heritage. Contemporary

Mexican culture is the result of their creative survival.[13]

On the Atlantic coast of North America, by contrast, English colonizers emigrated in family groups, and sexual liaisons with Indians were rare. Algonkian Indian women quickly seized the opportunity to trade for European goods such as metal kettles, tools, and needles and put them to use in their daily work. Although quick to appropriate European technology, they and their people actively resisted European domination. They fought back militarily, politically, and culturally. One key form of resistance was the Indian insistence on continuing women's prominent roles in politics, religious ritual, and trade despite the inability of Englishmen to recognize or deal with them.[14]

The impact of Europeans was more indirect for inland Indians. The European market for furs represented an opportunity for tribes eager to procure European trade goods. In all likelihood the men's increased emphasis on hunting and warfare sharpened the separation of men's and women's lives. The Iroquois, for example, quickly became dependent on trade goods and lost traditional crafts such as making pottery, stone axes, knives, and arrowheads. Yet by the 1640s they had depleted the beaver supply and had to compete with neighboring tribes for hunting grounds. One result of their longer and longer hunting expeditions was that the village itself became a female space. As hunters, traders, and fighters, men had to travel most of the year while women stayed at home, maintaining villages and cornfields generation after generation.[15] One consequence, then, of the fur trade in the first two centuries after contact was increased power for Iroquois women as they controlled local resources and local affairs.

Lacking a similar strong base in highly productive local agriculture, however, women in other tribes did not gain the power and influence that Iroquois women did. Among the Montagnais-Naskapi in the upper St. Lawrence valley, the fur trade gradually shifted the economic balance toward dependence on income provided by the men's trap lines or wages.[16] In some tribes, polygamy increased when a single hunter could provide more carcasses than a single woman could process.[17]

One group of Indian women—those who married fur traders—created an altogether new cultural and economic pattern. European fur traders, principally the French and later the English and Dutch, were almost exclusively male. As they traveled thousands of miles inland, traders depended on the Indians for their immediate survival and for long-term trade relations; thus, they began to marry Indian women. Indeed, Indian women provided the knowledge, skills, and labor that made it possible for many traders to survive in an unfamiliar environment. On the basis of such relationships, over the course of two centuries a fur trade society emerged, bound together by economics, kinship, rituals, and religion.[18]

Essentially traders adopted an indigenous way of life. Indian women prepared hides, made clothing and moccasins; manufactured snowshoes; prepared and preserved foods such as pemmican—a buffalo meat and fat mixture that could be carried on long trips; caught and dried fish; and gathered local fruits and vegetables such as wild rice, maple sugar, and berries. Stories abound of trading posts saved from starvation by the fishing or gathering or snaring skills of Indian women.

Indian women's ability to dress furs, build canoes, and travel in the wilderness rendered them invaluable to traders. A Chipewyan guide argued that the Hudson's Bay Company's failed expeditions were caused by a lack of women:

> in case they meet with success in hunting, who is to carry the produce of their labour? Women . . . also pitch our tents, make and mend our clothing, keep us warm at night; and, in fact, there is no such thing as travelling any considerable distance, or for any length of time, in this country, without their assistance.[19]

Indian women were active participants in the trade itself: They served as interpreters on whose linguistic and diplomatic abilities much depended. They trapped small animals and sold their pelts, as did many of their sisters who remained in traditional Indian society.

There is considerable evidence that some marriages between Indian women and fur traders resulted in long-lasting and apparently caring alliances. William McNeil, ship captain for the Hudson's Bay Company, mourned the loss of his wife Haida in childbirth: "The deceased has been a good and faithful partner for me for twenty years and we had twelve children together . . . [she] was a most kind mother

to her children, and no Woman could have done her duty better, although an Indian."[20]

Despite their importance, many Indian women involved in the fur trade were exploited. As guides or as wives, they lived in a social and economic structure organized around the needs of male European traders.[21] When they decided to return to Europe, traders were notorious for abandoning wives of many years, sometimes simply passing them on to their successors. Such practices contributed to the increased reluctance of Indian women to have any relations with white men. According to observers in the early nineteenth century, the fertility of traders' wives, who commonly had eight to twelve children, was sharply higher than that of traditional Indian women, who bore only four children on average. Traders did not observe traditional practices that restricted fertility, such as lengthy hunting expeditions and ritually prescribed abstinence. And unlike their traditional sisters who had virtual control over their offspring, traders' wives experienced the assertion of patriarchal authority most painfully when their children—especially their sons—were sent away to receive a "civilized education."[22]

The daughters of such marriages eventually replaced Indian women as the wives of traders. Their mothers' training in language and domestic skills and their ongoing relations with Indian kin fitted them to continue the role of "women-in-between" and their marriages settled into more permanent, lifelong patterns. At the same time, these mixed-blood, or metis, daughters lacked many of the sources of power and autonomy of their Indian mothers. They were less likely to choose their marriage partners and they married at a much younger age. Also, they did not have strong kinship networks to which to escape if their marriages proved unhappy or abusive. The absorption of European norms meant a far more polarized notion of men's public and women's private spheres along with the explicit subordination of women in both. The ultimate burden for the Indian wives of European traders came with the arrival of increased numbers of white women to the wilderness in the nineteenth century. Indian and mixed-blood wives experienced a growing racial prejudice that was not abated by even the highest degree of acculturation.[23]

The fur trade collapsed in the middle of the nineteenth century, as did the society that had grown up around it. Sizable towns in the Great Lakes region were populated by metis people who spoke a common language used in trade, shared the Catholic religion, and grounded their lives in the economics of the fur trade. The disappearance of the fur trade and the emergence of reservation policies in the United States forcing persons of Indian descent to register as Indians defined out of existence a people whose unique culture was built on the lives and activities of Indian "women-in-between."

By contrast, in the sixteenth and seventeenth centuries a very different set of circumstances strengthened the influence of women in some tribes on the Great Plains while marginalizing their power in others. These changes were less a product of trading relationships than of new technologies and economic possibilities inadvertently introduced by Europeans. Navaho women, for example, owned and managed livestock, enabling them to develop broad social and economic powers and a position of high prestige based on their economic independence. Sheep and goats, originally introduced by Spanish explorers, rapidly became the principal livestock, greatly expanding women's resources.[24]

Farther north, the introduction of horses in the early 1700s transformed the technology of hunting and, therefore, the Indians' way of life on the Plains.[25] Nomadic tribes previously had traveled slowly, depending principally on women's gathering for subsistence and engaging in highly organized collective hunts that often failed. Early in the eighteenth century, however, Plains tribes gained access to horses descended from those brought by early Spanish explorers. Horses enabled bands of hunters to range over a far wider territory and transformed buffalo hunting. An individual hunter could ride into a herd, choose as prey the largest rather than the weakest animals, and shoot his arrows at point-blank range. The consequence for the material life of Plains people was sudden, unprecedented wealth: more meat protein than they could consume, with plentiful hides for tepees, clothing, and finally, for trade.

More individualized hunting styles placed a premium on skill and prowess while encouraging the accumulation of wealth. The fact that a single hunter could easily supply several women with hides to dress and meat to cure encouraged polygamy. And the chronic shortage of horses led to institutionalized raiding and continuous intertribal warfare. The lifestyle that emerged under such circumstances has become in some respects the center of American mythology about the Indian. Mythical images of warlike braves galloping across the Plains in full headdress or engaging in rituals like the famed sundance leave little place for Indian women except as passive squaws waiting in the background.

The myths themselves reflect the heightened emphasis on male domination and concurrent loss of female power that accompanied the social and economic revolution brought by the use of horses. Certainly men's and women's life experiences diverged substantially. Frequently women traveled with hunting parties, charged with the care of tepees, children, food preparation, and clothing manufacture, as well as the processing of the huge carcasses. Though the women continued to do the bulk of the work, the romance and daring of war and hunting dominated the ritual life of the group. Male bonding grew with such ritual occasions and the development of military societies.[26]

By the nineteenth century the Lakota culture had incorporated an emphasis on sexual differences into all aspects of daily life. Cultural symbols sharply emphasized the distinction between aggressive maleness and passive femaleness. The sexual division of labor defined these differences concretely.[27] Extreme distinctions in demeanor, personality, and even language flowed from this rigid division. Men went on vision quests, directed religious rituals, and served as shamans and medicine men. Though women were economically dependent, their work remained essential to group survival, and their importance found ritual expression in female societies and in some women's individual visions that gave them access to sacred powers. The most important female society was made up of quill and beadwork specialists devoted to the mythic Double Woman Dreamer. The Lakota believed that dreams of the Double Woman caused women to behave in aggressive masculine ways: "They possessed the power to cast spells on men and seduce them. They were said to be very promiscuous, to live alone, and on occasion to perform the Double Woman Dreamer ceremony publically."[28]

The Double Woman Dreamer enabled the Lakota and other Plains Indians to incorporate specific social roles for women whose behavior violated feminine norms. Another was the widespread role of a "warrior woman" or "manly hearted woman" who acted as a man in both hunting and warfare. The manly hearted woman is a parallel role to the male "berdache," a man who could assume the dress and roles of a woman and was presumed to have special powers. Thus, although women lost both economic and cultural power as Plains tribes began using horses to hunt, to some degree women and men could move outside the boundaries of strictly defined feminine and masculine roles.

This fluidity allowed a few women quite literally to live the lives of men. In some societies manly hearted women were noticed very young and raised with extreme favoritism and license. In others the shift in gender roles received validation at a later age through dreams or visions. A trader on the Upper Missouri River told the story of one such woman, a member of the Gros Ventres captured at the age of 12.

> Already exhibiting manly interests, her adopted father encouraged these inclinations and trained her in a wide variety of male occupational skills. Although she dressed as a woman throughout her life, she pursued the role of a male in her adult years. She was a proficient hunter and chased big game on horseback and on foot. She was a skilled warrior, leading many successful war parties. In time, she sat on the council and ranked as the third leading warrior in a band of 160 lodges. After achieving success in manly pursuits, she took four wives whose hide-processing work brought considerable wealth to her lodge.[29]

WHAT THE EUROPEANS THOUGHT THEY SAW

At the time of the American Revolution, the existence of Indian societies, and in particular the highly democratic Iroquois Confederacy, provided for white Americans a living proof of the possibility of self-rule. Their virtues furnished a useful contrast to the corruption and tyranny against which Americans saw themselves struggling. For example, Thomas Jefferson wrote that the Europeans "have divided their nations into two classes, wolves and sheep." But for the Indians, "controls are in their manners and their moral sense of right and wrong." As a result, Indians "enjoy . . . an infinitely greater degree of happiness than those who live under European governments."[30]

What the founding fathers did not explore, however, was that the Iroquois model included considerably more political and economic power for women than any Europeans considered possible. Many white observers overlooked the cultural complexity of Indian societies and the great range of women's economic, social, and religious roles. From the sixteenth to the nineteenth century both male and female writers persisted in describing Indian women—if they described them at all—as slaves, degraded and abused. A sixteenth-century Jesuit outlined the many tasks of Montagnais-Naskapi women, contrasted them with the observation that "the men concern themselves with nothing but the more laborious hunting and waging of war," and concluded that "their wives are regarded and treated as slaves."[31] An English fur trader, exploring the Canadian forests in the 1690s, described the status of Cree women: "Now as for a woman they do not so much mind her for they reckon she is like a Slead dog or Bitch when she is living & when she dies they think she departs to Eternity but a man they think departs to another world & lives again."[32]

Similarly, Europeans failed to comprehend women's political power. Early contacts with the coastal Algonkians, for example, produced elaborate descriptions of villages, tribes, and occasional confederacies headed by "chiefs" or "kings." Because Europeans looked for social organizations similar to the cities and states they knew, they could not imagine that the most significant political and economic unit of these people was the matrilineal-matrilocal clan in which women had considerable power and autonomy.[33]

What these observers saw was a division of labor in which women performed many tasks that European culture assigned to men. They were especially outraged to see women chopping wood, building houses, carrying heavy loads, and engaging in agriculture—jobs that in their view constituted the very definition of manly work. Missionaries, for example, persistently defined their goal as civilizing the

Indians, by which they meant not only urging them to accept Christian doctrine and sacraments but also to adopt a way of life based on female domesticity and male-dominated, settled agriculture. Not surprisingly, their ideas met sharp resistance.

Iroquois women by the late eighteenth century, for example, were eager to obtain information about the agricultural practices of Quaker missionaries, but they wanted to use it themselves. When Quakers insisted on teaching men, the women ridiculed them as transvestites. "If a Man took hold of a Hoe to use it the Women would get down his gun by way of derision & would laugh & say such a warrior is a timid woman."[34]

In the long run, the Iroquois example held deep implications not only for self-rule but also for an inclusive democracy that sanctioned female participation. The latter, however, was something that revolutionary founding fathers could not fathom. Their definitions of "public" and "private," "masculine" and "feminine" did not allow them to see the more fluid, democratic, and simply *different* realities of Indian life. Yet over the course of American history, an understanding of public, political life built on an inclusive definition of citizenship proved to be a powerful idea, one capable of subverting even the ancient hierarchies of gender.

NOTES

1. Louis Hennepin, *A Description of Louisiana*, trans. John Gilmary Shea (New York: John G. Shea, 1880), pp. 278–80, in *The Colonial and Revolutionary Periods*, vol. 2 of *Women and Religion in America*, ed. Rosemary Radford Reuther and Rosemary Skinner Keller (San Francisco: Harper & Row, 1983), pp. 20–21.

2. See Carolyn Niethammer, *Daughters of the Earth: The Lives and Legends of American Indian Women* (New York: Collier Books, 1977); Ferdinand Anton, *Women in Pre-Columbian America* (New York: Abner Scham, 1973); and Gary B. Nash, *Red, White, and Black: The Peoples of Early America* (Englewood Cliffs, N.J.: Prentice-Hall, 1974). . . .

3. Janet D. Spector, "Male/Female Task Differentiation among the Hidatsa: Toward the Development of an Archeological Approach to the Study of Gender," in *The Hidden Half: Studies of Plains Indian Women*, ed. Patricia Albers and Beatrice Medicine (Washington, D.C.: University Press of America, 1983), pp. 77–99.

4. James Seaver, *Life of Mary Jemison: Deh-he-wa-mis* (1880), pp. 69–71, quoted in Judith Brown, "Economic Organization and the Position of Women among the Iroquois," *Ethnohistory* 17 (1970):151–67, quote on p. 158. . . .

5. Quoted in Robert Grumet, "Sunksquaws, Shamans, and Tradeswomen: Middle Atlantic Coastal Algonkian Women during the 17th and 18th Centuries," in *Women and Colonization: Anthropological Perspectives*, ed. Mona Etienne and Eleanor Leacock (New York: Praeger, 1980), p. 57.

6. Laura F. Klein, "Contending with Colonization: Tlingit Men and Women in Change," in Etienne and Leacock, *Women and Colonization*, pp. 88–108.

7. This section draws heavily on Jacqueline Peterson and Mary Druke, "American Indian Women and Religion," in Reuther and Keller, *Women and Religion*, pp. 1–41; see also Niethammer, *Daughters*, chap. 10.

8. Grumet, "Sunksquaws, Shamans, and Tradeswomen," pp. 43–62; see also Niethammer, *Daughters*, chap. 6.

9. Brown, "Economic Organization"; Diane Rothenberg, "The Mothers of the Nation: Seneca Resistance to a Quaker Intervention," in Etienne and Leacock, *Women and Colonization*, pp. 66–72.

10. Quoted in Brown, "Economic Organization," p. 154.

11. . . . [S]ee Elizabeth Tooker, "Women in Iroquois Society," in *Extending the Rafters: Interdisciplinary Approaches to Iroquois Studies*, ed. Michael K. Foster, Jack Campisi, and Marianne Mithun (Albany: State University of New York Press, 1984), pp. 109–23; . . . and Daniel K. Richter, "War and Culture: the Iroquois Experience," *William and Mary Quarterly* 40 (1983):528–59.

12. . . . See Henry Dobyns, "Estimating Aboriginal American Population: An Appraisal of Techniques with a New Hemispheric Estimate," *Current Anthropology* 7 (1966):395–412; . . . and Russell Thornton, *American Indian Holocaust and Survival: A Population History since 1492* (Norman: University of Oklahoma Press, 1987); . . .

13. See June Nash, "Aztec Women: The Transition from Status to Class in Empire and Colony," in Etienne and Leacock, *Women and Colonization*, pp. 134–48.

14. Niethammer, *Daughters*, chaps. 5–6.

15. Anthony F. C. Wallace, *The Death and Rebirth of the Seneca* (New York: Alfred A. Knopf, 1970), p. 28.

16. Leacock, "Montagnais Women and the Jesuit Program for Colonization," in Etienne and Leacock, *Women and Colonization*, p. 27. . . .

17. . . . See Carol Devens, "Separate Confrontations: Gender as a Factor in Indian Adaptation to European Colonization in New France," *American Quarterly* 38 (1986):461–80.

18. See Sylvia Van Kirk, *"Many Tender Ties": Women in Fur Trade Society in Western Canada, 1700–1850* (Winnipeg: Watson & Dwyer, 1980); Jennifer S. Brown, *Strangers in the Blood: Fur Trade Company Families in Indian Country* (Vancouver: University of British Columbia Press,1980); . . .

19. Quoted in Van Kirk, *"Many Tender Ties,"* p. 63.

20. Ibid., p. 33.

21. Ibid., p. 88.

22. Ibid., chap. 4.

23. [Ibid.,] . . . p. 145. See also chaps. 5–10.

24. Niethammer, *Daughters,* pp. 127–29.

25. Alan Klein, "The Political-Economy of Gender: A 19th Century Plains Indian Case Study," in Albers and Medicine, *The Hidden Half,* pp. 143–73; Niethammer, *Daughters,* pp. 111–18.

26. See Klein, "The Political-Economy of Gender."

27. See, for example, quote from Geo. Sword, *Manuscript Writings of Geo Sword,* vol. 1 (ca. 1909), quoted in Raymond J. DeMallie, "Male and Female in Traditional Lakota Culture," in Albers and Medicine, *The Hidden Half,* p. 238.

28. Ibid., pp. 241–47, quote from p. 245; also Niethammer, *Daughters,* pp. 132–37.

29. In Beatrice Medicine, "Warrior Women—Sex Role Alternatives for Plains Indian Women," in Albers and Medicine, *The Hidden Half,* p. 273, see also pp. 267–80.

30. Thomas Jefferson quoted in Bruce Johnasen, *Forgotten Founders: Benjamin Franklin, the Iroquois and the Rationale for the American Revolution* (Ipswich, Mass.: Gambit, 1982), pp. 112, 114.

31. Quoted in Leacock, "Mantagnais Women," in Etienne and Leacock, *Women and Colonization,* p. 27.

32. Quoted in Van Kirk, *"Many Tender Ties,"* p. 17.

33. Grumet, "Sunksquaws, Shamans, and Tradeswomen."

34. "Journal of William Allinson of Burlington" (1809) quoted in Rothenberg, "Mothers of the Nation," in Etienne and Leacock, *Women and Colonization,* p. 77.

LAUREL THATCHER ULRICH
The Ways of Her Household

One of the greatest barriers to an accurate assessment of women's role in the community has been the habit of assuming that what women did was not very important. Housekeeping has long been women's work, and housework has long been regarded as trivial. Laurel Thatcher Ulrich shows, however, that housekeeping can be a complex task and that real skill and intelligence might be exercised in performing it. The services housekeepers perform, in traditional as well as contemporary America, are an important part of the economic arrangements that sustain the family and need to be taken into account when describing any community or society. Note the differences Ulrich finds between rural and urban women, and between middle-class and impoverished women.

By English tradition, a woman's environment was the family dwelling and the yard or yards surrounding it. Though the exact composition of her setting obviously depended upon the occupation and economic status of her husband, its general outlines were surprisingly similar regardless of where it was located. The difference between an urban "houselot" and a rural "homelot" was not as dramatic as one might suppose.

If we were to draw a line around the housewife's domain, it would extend from the kitchen and its appendages, the cellars, pantries, brewhouses, milkhouses, washhouses, and butteries which appear in various combinations in household inventories, to the exterior of the house, where, even in the city, a mélange of animal and vegetable life flourished among the straw, husks, clutter, and muck. Encircling the pigpen, such a line would surround

Excerpted from "The Ways of Her Household," chap. 1 of *Good Wives: Image and Reality in the Lives of Women in Northern New England, 1650–1750* by Laurel Thatcher Ulrich (New York: Alfred A. Knopf, 1982). Copyright © 1980, 1982 by Laurel Thatcher Ulrich. Condensed and reprinted by permission of A. A. Knopf. Notes have been renumbered and edited.

the garden, the milkyard, the well, the hen-house, and perhaps the orchard itself—though husbands pruned and planted trees and eventually supervised the making of cider, good housewives strung their wash between the trees and in season harvested fruit for pies and conserves.

The line demarking the housewife's realm would not cross the fences which defined outlying fields of Indian corn or barley, nor would it stretch to fishing stages, mills, or wharves, but in berry or mushroom season it would extend into nearby woods or marsh and in spells of dearth or leisure reach to the shore. Of necessity, the boundaries of each woman's world would also extend into the houses of neighbors and into the cartways of a village or town. Housewives commanded a limited domain. But they were neither isolated nor self-sufficient. Even in farming settlements, families found it essential to bargain for needed goods and services. For prosperous and socially prominent women, interdependence took on another meaning as well. Prosperity meant charity, and in early New England charity meant personal responsibility for nearby neighbors. . . .

. . . For most historians, as for almost all antiquarians, the quintessential early American woman has been a churner of cream and a spinner of wool. Because home manufacturing has all but disappeared from modern housekeeping, many scholars have assumed that the key change in female economic life has been a shift from "production" to "consumption," a shift precipitated by the industrial revolution.[1] This is far too simple, obscuring the variety which existed even in the preindustrial world. . . .

. . . Beatrice Plummer, Hannah Grafton, and Magdalen Wear lived and died in New England in the years before 1750. One of them lived on the frontier, another on a farm, and a third in town. Because they were real women, however, and not hypothetical examples, the ways of their households were shaped by personal as well as geographic factors. A careful examination of the contents of their kitchens and chambers suggests the varied complexity as well as the underlying unity in the lives of early American women.

Let us begin with Beatrice Plummer of Newbury, Massachusetts.[2] Forgetting that death brought her neighbors into the house on January 24, 1672, we can use the probate inventory which they prepared to reconstruct the normal pattern of her work.

With a clear estate of £343, Francis Plummer had belonged to the "middling sort" who were the church members and freeholders of the Puritan settlement of Newbury. As an immigrant of 1653, he had listed himself as a "linnen weaver," but he soon became a farmer as well.[3] At his death, his loom and tackling stood in the "shop" with his pitchforks, his hoes, and his tools for smithing and carpentry. Plummer had integrated four smaller plots to form one continuous sixteen-acre farm. An additional twenty acres of salt marsh and meadow provided hay and forage for his small herd of cows and sheep. His farm provided a comfortable living for his family, which at this stage of his life included only his second wife, Beatrice, and her grandchild by a previous marriage. . . .

The house over which Beatrice presided must have looked much like surviving dwellings from seventeenth-century New England, with its "Hall" and "Parlor" on the ground floor and two "chambers" above. A space designated in the inventory only as "another Roome" held the family's collection of pots, kettles, dripping pans, trays, buckets, and earthenware. . . . The upstairs chambers were not bedrooms but storage rooms for foodstuffs and out-of-season equipment. The best bed with its bolster, pillows, blanket, and coverlet stood in the parlor; a second bed occupied one corner of the kitchen, while a cupboard, a "great chest," a table, and a backless bench called a "form" furnished the hall. More food was found in the "cellar" and in the "dairy house," a room which may have stood at the coolest end of the kitchen lean-to.[4]

The Plummer house was devoid of ornament, but its contents bespeak such comforts as conscientious yeomanry and good huswifery afforded. On this winter morning the dairy house held four and a half "flitches" or sides of bacon, a quarter of a barrel of salt pork, twenty-eight pounds of cheese, and four pounds of butter. Upstairs in a chamber were more than twenty-five bushels of "English" grain—barley, oats, wheat, and rye. (The Plummers apparently reserved their Indian corn, stored in another location, for their animals.) When made into malt by a village specialist, barley would become the basis for beer. Two bushels of malt were already stored in the house. The oats might appear in a variety of dishes, from plain breakfast porridge to "flummery," a gelatinous dish flavored with spices and dried fruit.[5] But the wheat and rye were almost certainly reserved for bread and pies. The fine hair sieves stored with the grain in the hall chamber suggest that Beatrice Plummer was particular about her baking, preferring a finer flour than came directly from the miller. A "bushell of pease & beans" found near the grain and a full barrel of cider in the cellar are the only vegetables and fruits listed in the inventory, though small quantities of pickles, preserves, or dried herbs might have escaped notice. Perhaps the Plummers added variety to their diet by trading some of their abundant supply of grain for cabbages, turnips, sugar, molasses, and spices. . . .

Since wives were involved with early-morning milking, breakfast of necessity featured prepared foods or leftovers—toasted bread, cheese, and perhaps meat and turnips kept from the day before, any of this washed down with cider or beer in winter, with milk in summer. Only on special occasions would there be pie or doughnuts. Dinner was the main meal of the day. Here a housewife with culinary aspirations and an ample larder could display her specialities. After harvest Beatrice Plummer might have served roast pork or goose with apples, in spring an eel pie flavored with parsley and winter savory, and in summer a leek soup or gooseberry cream; but for ordinary days the most common menu was boiled meat with whatever "sauce" the season provided—dried peas or beans, parsnips, turnips, onions, cabbage, or garden greens. A heavy pudding stuffed into a cloth bag could steam atop the vegetables and meat. The broth from this boiled dinner might reappear at supper as "pottage" with the addition of minced herbs and some oatmeal or barley for thickening. Supper, like breakfast, was a simple meal. Bread, cheese, and beer were as welcome at the end of a winter day as at the beginning. . . .

Preparing the simplest of these meals required both judgment and skill. . . . The most basic of the housewife's skills was building and regulating fires—a task so fundamental that it must have appeared more as habit than craft. Summer and winter, day and night, she kept a few brands smoldering, ready to stir into flame as needed. The cavernous fireplaces of early New England were but a century removed from the open fires of medieval houses, and they retained some of the characteristics of the latter. Standing inside one of these huge openings today, a person can see the sky above. Seventeenth-century housewives *did* stand in their fireplaces, which were conceived less as enclosed spaces for a single blaze than as accessible working surfaces upon which a number of small fires might be built. Preparing several dishes simultaneously, a cook could move from one fire to another, turning a spit, checking the state of the embers under a skillet, adjusting the height of a pot hung from the lugpole by its adjustable trammel. The complexity of firetending, as much as anything else, encouraged the one-pot meal.[6]

The contents of her inventory suggest that Beatrice Plummer was adept not only at roasting, frying, and boiling but also at baking, the most difficult branch of cookery. Judging from the grain in the upstairs chamber, the bread which she baked was "maslin," a common type made from a mixture of wheat and other grains, usually rye. She began with the sieves stored nearby, carefully sifting out the coarser pieces of grain and bran. Soon after supper she could have mixed the "sponge," a thin dough made from warm water, yeast, and flour. Her yeast might have come from the foamy "barm" found on top of fermenting ale or beer, from a piece of dough saved from an earlier baking, or even from the crevices in an unwashed kneading trough. Like fire-building, bread-making was based upon a self-perpetuating chain, an organic sequence which if once interrupted was difficult to begin again. Warmth from the banked fire would raise the sponge by morning, when Beatrice could work in more flour, knead the finished dough, and shape the loaves, leaving them to rise again.

Even in twentieth-century kitchens with standardized yeast and thermostatically controlled temperatures, bread dough is subject to wide variations in consistency and behavior. In a drafty house with an uncertain supply of yeast, bread-making was indeed "an art, craft, and mystery." Not the least of the problem was regulating the fire so that the oven was ready at the same time as the risen loaves. Small cakes or biscuits could be baked in a skillet or directly on the hearth under an upside-down pot covered with coals. But to produce bread in any quantity required an oven. Before 1650 these were frequently constructed in dooryards, but in the last decades of the century they were built into the rear of the kitchen fireplace, as Beatrice Plummer's must have been. Since her oven would have had no flue, she would have left the door open once she kindled a fire inside, allowing the smoke to escape through the fireplace chimney. Moving about her kitchen, she would have kept an eye on this fire, occasionally raking the coals to distribute the heat evenly, testing periodically with her hand to see if the oven had reached the right temperature. When she determined that it had, she would have scraped out the coals and inserted the bread—assuming that it had risen enough by this time or had not risen too much and collapsed waiting for the oven to heat.[7]

Cooking and baking were year-round tasks. Inserted into these day-by-day routines were seasonal specialities which allowed a housewife to bridge the dearth of one period with the bounty of another. In the preservation calendar, dairying came first, beginning with the first calves of early spring. In colonial New England cows were all-purpose creatures, raised for meat as well as for milk. Even in new settlements they could survive by browsing on rough land; their meat was a hedge against famine. But only in areas with abundant meadow (and even there only in certain months) would they produce milk with sufficient butterfat for serious dairying.[8] Newbury was such a place.

We can imagine Beatrice Plummer some morning in early summer processing the milk which would appear as cheese in a January breakfast. Slowly she heated several gallons with rennet dried and saved from the autumn's slaughtering. Within an hour or two the curd had formed. She broke it, drained off the whey, then worked in a little of her own fresh butter. Packing this rich mixture into a mold, she turned it in her wooden press for an hour or more, changing and washing the cheesecloth frequently as the whey dripped out. Repacking it in dry cloth, she left it in the press for another thirty or forty hours before washing it once more with whey, drying it, and placing it in the cellar or dairy house to age. As a young girl she would have learned from her mother or a mistress the importance of thorough pressing and the virtues of cleanliness. . . .

The Plummer inventory gives little evidence of the second stage of preservation in the housewife's year, the season of gardening and

gathering which followed quickly upon the dairy months. But there is ample evidence of the autumn slaughtering. Beatrice could well have killed the smaller pigs herself, holding their "hinder parts between her legs," as one observer described the process, "and taking the snout in her left hand" while she stuck the animal through the heart with a long knife. Once the bleeding stopped, she would have submerged the pig in boiling water for a few minutes, then rubbed it with rosin, stripped off the hair, and disemboweled it. Nothing was lost. She reserved the organ meats for immediate use, then cleaned the intestines for later service as sausage casing. Stuffed with meat scraps and herbs and smoked, these "links" were a treasured delicacy. The larger cuts could be roasted at once or preserved in several ways.[9] . . .

Fall was also the season for cider-making. The mildly alcoholic beverage produced by natural fermentation of apple juice was a staple of the New England diet and was practically the only method of preserving the fruit harvest. With the addition of sugar, the alcoholic content could be raised from five to about seven percent, as it usually was in taverns and for export. . . .

Prosaic beer was even more important to the Plummer diet. Although some housewives brewed a winter's supply of strong beer in October, storing it in the cellar, Beatrice seems to have been content with "small beer," a mild beverage usually brewed weekly or bi-weekly and used almost at once. Malting—the process of sprouting and drying barley to increase its sugar content—was wisely left to the village expert. Beatrice started with cracked malt or grist, processing her beer in three stages. "Mashing" required slow steeping at just below the boiling point, a sensitive and smelly process which largely determined the success of the beverage. Experienced brewers knew by taste whether the enzymes were working. If it was too hot, acetic acid developed which would sour the finished product. The next stage, "brewing," was relatively simple. Herbs and hops were boiled with the malted liquid. In the final step this liquor was cooled and mixed with yeast saved from last week's beer or bread. Within twenty-four hours—if all had gone well—the beer was bubbling actively.[10]

. . . A wife who knew how to manage the ticklish chemical processes which changed milk into cheese, meal into bread, malt into beer, and flesh into bacon was a valuable asset, though some men were too churlish to admit it. After her husband's death, Beatrice married a man who not only refused to provide her with provisions, but insisted on doing his own cooking. He took his meat "out of ye pickle" and broiled it directly on the coals, and when she offered him "a cup of my owne Sugar & Bear," he refused it. When the neighbors testified that she had been a dutiful wife, the Quarterly Court fined him for "abusive carriages and speeches." Even the unhappy marriage that thrust Beatrice Plummer into court helps to document the central position of huswifery in her life.[11] . . .

Beatrice Plummer represents one type of early American housewife. Hannah Grafton represents another.[12] Chronology, geography, and personal biography created differences between the household inventories of the two women, but there are obvious similarities as well. Like Beatrice Plummer, Hannah Grafton lived in a house with two major rooms on the ground floor and two chambers above. At various locations near the gound-floor rooms were service areas—a washhouse with its own loft or chamber, a shop, a lean-to, and two cellars. The central rooms in the Grafton house were the "parlour," with the expected featherbed, and the "kitchen," which included much of the same collection of utensils and iron pots which appeared in the Plummer house. Standing in the corner of the kitchen were a spade and a hoe, two implements useful only for chipping away ice and snow on the December day on which the inventory was taken, though apparently destined for another purpose come spring. With a garden, a cow, and three pigs, Hannah Grafton clearly had agricultural responsibilities, but these were performed in a strikingly different context than on the Plummer farm. The Grafton homelot was a single acre of land standing just a few feet from shoreline in the urban center of Salem.[13]

Joshua Grafton was a mariner like his father before him. His estate of £236 was modest, but he was still a young man and he had firm connections with the seafaring elite who were transforming the economy of Salem. When he died late in 1699, Hannah had three living children—Hannah, eight; Joshua, six; and Priscilla, who was just ten months.[14] This young family

used their space quite differently than had the Plummers. The upstairs chambers which served as storage areas in the Newbury farmhouse were sleeping quarters here. In addition to the bed in the parlor and the cradle in the kitchen, there were two beds in each of the upstairs rooms. One of these, designated as "smaller," may have been used by young Joshua. It would be interesting to know whether the mother carried the two chamber pots kept in the parlor upstairs to the bedrooms at night or whether the children found their way in the dark to their parents' sides as necessity demanded. But adults were probably never far away. Because there are more bedsteads in the Grafton house than members of the immediate family, they may have shared their living quarters with unmarried relatives or servants.

Ten chairs and two stools furnished the kitchen, while no fewer than fifteen chairs, in two separate sets, crowded the parlor with its curtained bed. The presence of a punch bowl on a square table in the parlor reinforces the notion that sociability was an important value in this Salem household. Thirteen ounces of plate, a pair of gold buttons, and a silverheaded cane suggest a measure of luxury as well—all of this in stark contrast to the Plummers, who had only two chairs and a backless bench and no discernible ornamentation at all. Yet the Grafton house was only slightly more specialized than the Newbury farmhouse. It had no servants' quarters, no sharp segregation of public and private spaces, no real separation of sleeping, eating, and work. A cradle in the kitchen and a go-cart kept with the spinning wheels in the upstairs chamber show that little Priscilla was very much a part of this workaday world.

How then might the pattern of Hannah Grafton's work have differed from that of Beatrice Plummer? Certainly cooking remained central. Hannah's menus probably varied only slightly from those prepared in the Plummer kitchen, and her cooking techniques must have been identical. But one dramatic difference is apparent in the two inventories. The Grafton house contained no provisions worth listing on that December day when Isaac Foot and Samuel Willard appeared to take inventory. Hannah had brewing vessels, but no malt; sieves and a meal trough, but no grain; and a cow, but no cheese. What little milk her cow gave in

winter probably went directly into the children's mugs. Perhaps she would continue to
breast-feed Priscilla until spring brought a
more secure supply.... Trade, rather than
manufacturing or agriculture, was the dominant motif in her meal preparations.

In colonial New England most food went
directly from processer or producer to consumer. Joshua may have purchased grain or
flour from the mill near the shipbuilding center
called Knocker's Hole, about a mile away from
their house. Or Hannah may have eschewed
bread-making altogether, walking or sending a
servant the half-mile to Elizabeth Haskett's
bakery near the North River. Fresh meat for the
spits in her washhouse may have come from
John Cromwell's slaughterhouse on Main
Street near the Congregational meetinghouse,
and soap for her washtubs from the soap-boiler
farther up the street near the Quaker meeting-
house.[15] Salem, like other colonial towns, was
laid out helter-skelter, with the residences of
the wealthy interspersed with the small houses
of carpenters or fishermen. Because there was
no center of retail trade, assembling the ingredients of a dinner involved many transactions.
Sugar, wine, and spice came by sea; fresh lamb,
veal, eggs, butter, gooseberries, and parsnips
came by land. Merchants retailed their goods
in shops or warehouses near their wharves and
houses. Farmers or their wives often hawked
their produce door to door.[16] ...

In such a setting, trading for food might
require as much energy and skill as manufacturing or growing it. One key to success was
simply knowing where to go. Keeping abreast
of the arrival of ships in the harbor or establishing personal contact with just the right
farmwife from nearby Salem village required
time and attention. Equally important was the
ability to evaluate the variety of unstandard-
ized goods offered. An apparently sound
cheese might teem with maggots when cut.[17]
Since cash was scarce, a third necessity was the
establishment of credit, a problem which ultimately devolved upon husbands. But petty
haggling over direct exchanges was also a feature of this barter economy.

Hannah Grafton was involved in trade on
more than one level. The "shop" attached to
her house was not the all-purpose storage shed
and workroom it seems to have been for Francis Plummer. It was a retail store, offering door
locks, nails, hammers, gimlets, and other hard-

ware as well as English cloth, pins, needles,
and thread. As a mariner, Joshua Grafton may
well have sailed the ship which brought these
goods to Salem. In his absence, Hannah was
not only a mother and a housewife but, like
many other Salem women, a shopkeeper as
well.

There is another highly visible activity in
the Grafton inventory which was not immediately apparent in the Plummer's—care of
clothing. Presumably, Beatrice Plummer
washed occasionally, but she did not have a
"washhouse." Hannah did. The arrangement
of this unusual room is far from clear. On December 2, 1699, it contained two spits, two
"bouldishes," a gridiron, and "other things."
Whether those other things included washtubs,
soap, or a beating staff is impossible to determine. ...

But on any morning in December the
washhouse could ... have been hung with the
family wash. Dark woolen jackets and petticoats went from year to year without seeing a
kettle of suds, but linen shifts, aprons, shirts,
and handkerchiefs required washing. Laundering might not have been a weekly affair in most
colonial households, but it was a well-defined
if infrequent necessity even for transient seamen and laborers. One can only speculate on
its frequency in a house with a child under a
year. When her baby was only a few months
old, Hannah may have learned to hold little
Priscilla over the chamber pot at frequent intervals, but in early infancy, tightly wrapped in
her cradle, the baby could easily have used five
dozen "clouts" and almost as many "belly
bands" from one washing to another. Even
with the use of a "pilch," a thick square of flan-
nel securely bound over the diaper, blankets
and coverlets occasionally needed sudsing as
well.[18]

Joshua's shirts and Hannah's own aprons
and shifts would require careful ironing. Hannah's "smoothing irons" fitted into their own
heaters, which she filled with coals from the
fire. As the embers waned and the irons cooled,
she would have made frequent trips from her
table to the hearth to the fire and back to the
table again. At least two of these heavy instruments were essential. A dampened apron
could dry and wrinkle while a single flatiron
replenished its heat.

As frequent a task as washing was sewing.
Joshua's coats and breeches went to a tailor, but

his shirts were probably made at home. Certainly Hannah stitched and unstitched the tucks which altered Priscilla's simple gowns and petticoats as she grew. The little dresses which the baby trailed in her go-cart had once clothed her brother. Gender identity in childhood was less important in this society than economy of effort. It was not that boys were seen as identical to girls, only that all-purpose garments could be handed from one child to another regardless of sex, and dresses were more easily altered than breeches and more adaptable to diapering and toileting. At eight years of age little Hannah had probably begun to imitate her mother's even stitches, helping with the continual mending, altering, and knitting which kept this growing family clothed.[19]

In some ways the most interesting items in the Grafton inventory are the two spinning wheels kept in the upstairs chamber. Beatrice Plummer's wheel and reel had been key components in an intricate production chain. The Plummers had twenty-five sheep in the fold and a loom in the shed. The Graftons had neither. Children—not sheep—put wheels in Hannah's house. The mechanical nature of spinning made it a perfect occupation for women whose attention was engrossed by young children. This is one reason why the ownership of wheels in both York and Essex counties had a constancy over time unrelated to the ownership of sheep or looms. In the dozen inventories taken in urban Salem about the time of Joshua Grafton's death, the six non-spinners averaged one minor child each, the six spinners had almost four. Instruction at the wheel was part of the almost ritualistic preparation mothers offered their daughters.[20] Spinning was a useful craft, easily picked up, easily put down, and even small quantities of yarn could be knitted into caps, stockings, dishcloths, and mittens.

. . . a cluster of objects in the chamber over Hannah Grafton's kitchen suggests a fanciful but by no means improbable vignette. Imagine her gathered with her two daughters in this upstairs room on a New England winter's day. Little Priscilla navigates around the end of the bedstead in her go-cart while her mother sits at one spinning wheel and her sister at the other. Young Hannah is spinning "oakum," the coarsest and least expensive part of the flax. As her mother leans over to help her wind the uneven thread on the bobbin, she catches a troublesome scent from downstairs. Have the turnips caught on the bottom of the pot? Has the maid scorched Joshua's best shirt? Or has a family servant returned from the wharf and spread his wet clothes by the fire? Hastening down the narrow stairs to the kitchen, Hannah hears the shop bell ring. Just then little Priscilla, left upstairs with her sister, begins to cry. In such pivotal but unrecorded moments much of the history of women lies hidden.

The third inventory can be more quickly described.[21] Elias Wear of York, Maine, left an estate totaling £92, of which less than £7 was in household goods—including some old pewter, a pot, two bedsteads, bedding, one chest, and a box. Wear also owned a saddle, three guns, and a river craft called a gundalow. But his wealth, such as it was, consisted of land (£40) and livestock (£36). It is not just relative poverty which distinguished Elias Wear's inventory from that of Joshua Grafton or Francis Plummer. Every settlement in northern New England had men who owned only a pot, a bed, and a chest. Their children crowded in with them or slept on straw. These men and their sons provided some of the labor which harvested barley for farmers like Francis Plummer or stepped masts for mariners like Joshua Grafton. Their wives and their daughters carded wool or kneaded bread in other women's kitchens. No, Elias Wear was distinguished by a special sort of frontier poverty.

His father had come to northern New England in the 1640s, exploring and trading for furs as far inland in New Hampshire as Lake Winnipesaukee. By 1650 he had settled in York, a then hopeful site for establishing a patrimony. Forty years later he died in the York Massacre, an assault by French and Indians which virtually destroyed the town, bringing death or captivity to fully half of the inhabitants. Almost continuous warfare between 1689 and 1713 created prosperity for the merchant community of Portsmouth and Kittery, but it kept most of the inhabitants of outlying settlements in a state of impecunious insecurity.[22]

In 1696, established on a small homestead in the same neighborhood in which his father had been killed, Elias Wear married a young widow with the fitting name of Magdalen. When their first child was born "too soon," the couple found themselves in York County court

owning a presentment for fornication. Although New England courts were still sentenc-
ing couples in similar circumstances to "nine
stripes a piece upon the Naked back," most of
the defendants, like the Wears, managed to pay
the not inconsequential fine. The fifty-nine shillings which Elias and Magdalen pledged the
court amounted to almost half of the total value
of two steers. A presentment for fornication
was expensive as well as inconvenient, but it
did not carry a permanent onus. Within seven
years of their conviction Elias was himself serving on the "Jury of Tryalls" for the county,
while Magdalen had proved herself a dutiful
and productive wife.[23]

Every other winter she gave birth, producing four sons—Elias, Jeremiah, John, and
Joseph—in addition to the untimely Ruth. A
sixth child, Mary, was just five months old
when her father met his own death by Indians
in August of 1707 while traveling between their
Cape Neddick home and the more densely settled York village. Without the benefits of a cradle, a go-cart, a spinning wheel, or even a secure supply of grain, Magdalen raised these six
children. Unfortunately, there is little in her inventory and nothing in any other record to
document the specific strategies which she
used, though the general circumstances of her
life can be imagined.

Chopping and hauling for a local timber
merchant, Elias could have filled Magdalen's
porridge pot with grain shipped from the port
of Salem or Boston. During the spring corn
famine, an almost yearly occurrence on the
Maine frontier, she might have gone herself
with other wives of her settlement to dig on the
clam flats, hedging against the day when relief
would come by sea.[24] Like Beatrice Plummer
and Hannah Grafton, she would have spent
some hours cooking, washing, hoeing cabbages, bargaining with neighbors, and, in season, herding and milking a cow. But poverty,
short summers, and rough land also made
gathering an essential part of her work. We
may imagine her cutting pine splinters for
lights and "cattails" and "silkgrass" for beds.
Long before her small garden began to produce, she would have searched out a wild "sal-
let" in the nearby woods, in summer turning
to streams and barrens for other delicacies congenial to English taste—eels, salmon, berries,
and plums. She would have embarked on such

excursions with caution, however, remembering the wives of nearby Exeter who took their
children into the woods for strawberries "without any Guard" and narrowly avoided capture.[25] . . .

. . . The Wears probably lived in a single-
story cottage which may or may not have been
subdivided into more than one room. A loft
above provided extra space for storage or
sleeping. With the addition of a lean-to, this
house could have sheltered animals as well as
humans, especially in harsh weather or in periods of Indian alarm. Housing a pig or a calf
in the next room would have have simplified
Magdalen's chores in the winter. If she managed to raise a few chickens, these too would
have thrived better near the kitchen fire.[26]

Thus, penury erased the elaborate de-
marcation of "houses" and "yards" evident in
yeoman inventories. It also blurred distinctions
between the work of a husbandman and the
work of his wife. At planting time and at harvest Magdalen Wear undoubtedly went into
the fields to help Elias, taking her babies with
her or leaving Ruth to watch them as best she
could.[27] A century later an elderly Maine
woman bragged that she "had dropped corn
many a day with two governors: a judge in her
arms and a general on her back."[28] None of the
Wear children grew up to such prominence,
but all six of them survived to adulthood and
four married and founded families of their
own. Six children did not prevent Magdalen
Wear from remarrying within two years of her
husband's death. Whatever her assets—a
pleasant face, a strong back, or lifetime possession of £40 in land—she was soon wed to the
unmarried son of a neighboring millowner.[29]

Magdalen Wear, Hannah Grafton, and Beatrice
Plummer were all "typical" New England
housewives of the period 1650–1750. Magdalen's iron pot represents the housekeeping
minimum which often characterized frontier
life. Hannah's punch bowl and her hardware
shop exemplify both the commerce and the
self-conscious civilization of coastal towns.
Beatrice's brewing tubs and churn epitomize
home manufacturing and agrarian self-sufficiency as they existed in established villages.
Each type of housekeeping could be found
somewhere in northern New England in any
decade of the century. Yet these three women

should not be placed in rigidly separate categories. Wealth, geography, occupation, and age determined that some women in any decade would be more heavily involved in one aspect of housekeeping than another, yet all three women shared a common vocation. Each understood the rhythms of the seasons, the technology of fire-building, the persistence of the daily demands of cooking, the complexity of home production, and the dexterity demanded from the often conflicting roles of housekeeper, mother, and wife.

The thing which distinguished these women from their counterparts in modern America was not, as some historians have suggested, that their work was essential to survival. "Survival," after all, is a minimal concept. Individual men and women have never needed each other for mere survival but for far more complex reasons, and women were *essential* in the seventeenth century for the very same reasons they are essential today—for the perpetuation of the race. . . . Nor was it the narrowness of their choices which really set them apart. Women in industrial cities have lived monotonous and confining lives, and they may have worked even harder than early American women. The really striking differences are social.

. . . [T]he lives of early American housewives were distinguished less by the tasks they performed than by forms of social organization which linked economic responsibilities to family responsibilities and which tied each woman's household to the larger world of her village or town.

For centuries the industrious Bathsheba has been pictured sitting at a spinning wheel— "She layeth her hands to the spindle, and her hands hold the distaff." Perhaps it is time to suggest a new icon for women's history. Certainly spinning was an important female craft in northern New England, linked not only to housework but to mothering, but it was one enterprise among many. Spinning wheels are such intriguing and picturesque objects, so resonant with antiquity, that they tend to obscure rather than clarify the nature of female economic life, making home production the essential element in early American huswifery and the era of industrialization the period of crucial change. Challenging the symbolism of the wheel not only undermines the popular stereotype, it questions a prevailing emphasis in women's history.

An alternate symbol might be the pocket. In early America a woman's pocket was not attached to her clothing, but tied around her waist with a string or tape. (When "Lucy Locket lost her pocket, Kitty Fisher found it.") Much better than a spinning wheel, this homely object symbolizes the obscurity, the versatility, and the personal nature of the housekeeping role. A woman sat at a wheel, but she carried her pocket with her from room to room, from house to yard, from yard to street. The items which it contained would shift from day to day and from year to year, but they would of necessity be small, easily lost, yet precious. A pocket could be a mended and patched pouch of plain homespun or a rich personal ornament boldly embroidered in crewel. It reflected the status as well as the skills of its owner. Whether it contained cellar keys or a paper of pins, a packet of seeds or a baby's bib, a hank of yarn, or a Testament, it characterized the social complexity as well as the demanding diversity of women's work.

NOTES

1. [See] William H. Chafe, *Women and Equality: Changing Patterns in American Culture* (New York: Oxford University Press, 1977), p. 17; . . . and Nancy F. Cott, *The Bonds of Womanhood* (New Haven and London: Yale University Press, 1977), p. 21.

2. Unless otherwise noted, the information which follows comes from the Francis Plummer will and inventory, *The Probate Records of Essex County* (hereafter *EPR*) (Salem, Mass.: Essex Institute, 1916–1920), II:319–22.

3. Joshua Coffin, *A Sketch of the History of Newbury, Newburyport, and West Newbury* (Boston, 1845; Hampton, N.H.: Peter E. Randall, 1977), p. 315.

4. Abbott Lowell Cummings, *The Framed Houses of Massachusetts Bay, 1625–1725* (Cambridge, Mass., and London: Harvard University Press, 1979), pp. 29–32.

5. Darrett B. Rutman, *Husbandmen of Plymouth* (Boston: Beacon Press, 1967), pp. 10–11. . . . *Records and Files of the Quarterly Courts of Essex County, Massachusetts* (hereafter *ECR*) (Salem, Mass.: Essex Institute, 1911–1975), III:50; . . . Massachusetts Historical Society (hereafter MHS) *Collections,* 5th Ser., I:97; and Jay Allen Anderson, "A Solid Sufficiency: An Ethnography of Yeoman Foodways in Stuart England" (Ph.D. diss., University of Pennsylvania, 1971), pp. 171, 203–04, 265, 267, 268.

6. Cummings, *Framed Houses,* pp. 4, 120–22; . . . Jane Carson, *Colonial Virginia Cookery* (Charlottesville: University Press of Virginia, 1968), p. 104; . . .

7. Carson, *Colonial Virginia Cookery*, pp. 104–06.

8. Anderson, "Solid Sufficiency," pp. 63, 65, 118; . . . New Hampshire Historical Society *Collections*, V (1837), p. 225.

9. Anderson, "Solid Sufficiency," pp. 99–108, 120–32.

10. Sanborn C. Brown, *Wines and Beers of Old New England* (Hanover, N.H.: University Press of New England, 1978). . . .

11. *ECR*, IV:194–95, 297–98.

12. Unless otherwise noted, the information which follows comes from the Joshua Grafton will and inventory, Manuscript Probate Records, Essex County Probate Court, Salem, Mass. (hereafter Essex Probate), vol. CCCVII, pp. 58–59.

13. "Part of Salem in 1700," pocket map in James Duncan Phillips, *Salem in the Seventeenth Century* (Boston: Houghton Mifflin, 1933), H-6.

14. Sidney Perley, *The History of Salem, Massachusetts* (Salem, 1924), I:435, 441.

15. Phillips, *Salem in the Seventeenth Century*, pp. 328, 314, 318, 317; and James Duncan Phillips, *Salem in the Eighteenth Century* (Boston: Houghton Mifflin, 1937), pp. 20–21.

16. [See] Karen Friedman, "Victualling Colonial Boston," *Agricultural History* XLVII (July 1973): 189–205, and . . . Benjamin Coleman, *Some Reasons and Arguments Offered to the Good People of Boston and Adjacent Places, for the Setting Up Markets in Boston* (Boston, 1719), pp. 5–9.

17. . . . *The Salem Witchcraft Papers*, ed. Paul Boyer and Stephen Nissenbaum (New York: Da Capo Press, 1977), I:117–29.

18. [See] . . . e.g., *Province and Court Records of Maine* (hereafter *MPCR*) (Portland: Maine Historical Society, 1928–1975), IV:205–06; . . . and Essex Probate, CCCXXI:96. . . .

19. Susan Burrows Swan, *Plain and Fancy: American Women and Their Needlework, 1700–1850* (New York: Holt, Rinehart and Winston, 1977), pp. 18–19, 34–38.

20. "Letter-Book of Samuel Sewall," MHS *Collections*, 6th Ser., I:19. . . .

21. Unless otherwise noted, the information which follows comes from the Elias Wear will and inventory, Manuscript Probate Records, York County Probate Court, Alfred, Me., . . . II:26.

22. Charles Clark, *The Eastern Frontier* (New York: Alfred A. Knopf, 1970), pp. 67–72.

23. *MPCR*, IV:91–92, 175, 176, 206, 263, 307, 310.

24. Maine Historical Society *Collections*, IX:58–59, 457, 566; MHS *Collections*, 6th Ser., I:126–65, 182–84, 186–89; . . .

25. Cotton Mather, *Decennium Luctuosum* (Boston, 1699), reprint Charles H. Lincoln, ed., *Narratives of the Indian Wars* (New York: Charles Scribner's Sons, 1913), pp. 266–67.

26. Richard M. Candee, "Wooden Buildings in Early Maine and New Hampshire: A Technological and Cultural History, 1600–1720" (Ph.D. diss., University of Pennsylvania, 1976), pp. 18, 42–48. . . .

27. . . . MHS *Proceedings* (1876), p. 129. Also see *ECR*, II:372–73, 22, 442; . . .

28. Sarah Orne Jewett, *The Old Town of Berwick* (Berwick, Me.: Old Berwick Historical Society, 1967), n.p., . . .

29. Sybil Noyes, Charles Thornton Libby, and Walter Goodwin Davis, *A Genealogical Dictionary of Maine and New Hampshire* (Portland, Me.: Southworth-Anthoensen Press, 1928), pp. 726, 729.

DOCUMENT: *The Trial of Anne Hutchinson, 1637*

"What law have I broken?"

The Antinomian heresy threw the Puritan colony of Massachusetts Bay into turmoil for years and forced its leaders to reconsider the nature of their experiment. Antinomians placed greater emphasis on religious feeling than did orthodox Puritans. They tended to be suspicious *(anti)* of law *(nomos)* or formal rules and came close to asserting that individuals had access to direct revelation from the Holy Spirit. They criticized ministers who seemed to argue that it was possible to *earn* salvation by good deeds rather than leaving it to God freely to decide who was to be saved by their faith, a distinction between the "covenant of works" and a "covenant of faith," which they thought separated authentic Puritans from ones who remained too close to the Anglican Church. The close relationship between church and state in Massachusetts Bay meant that challenge to the ministers was quickly interpreted as challenge to established authority of all kinds.

The leader of the dissenters was Anne Hutchinson, a woman who had come to the colony in 1634, four years after its founding, and who commanded great respect for her competence as a midwife. At meetings held in her home after Sunday church services she summarized, discussed, and criticized ministers' sermons. The meetings became very popular; soon she was holding separate gatherings for men as well as for women. Women who followed Hutchinson were often those who respected her medical knowledge and also shared her criticisms of the ministers. The men who came to the meetings were often those who were critical of the Puritan leadership on political and economic as well as religious grounds. Rumor spread that criticism of the governor and council as well as ministers was voiced in the Hutchinson home, and she was challenged, first by a convocation of ministers and then, in November 1637, by the General Court of the Colony. Her trial was conducted by the governor of the colony, John Winthrop. He was joined in his questioning by the deputy governor and other members of the legislature; at the end they handed down the very heavy sentence of banishment from the colony.

Hutchinson's secular trial before the General Court was followed by an examination before a board of ministers, who handed down the heaviest sentence in their arsenal, excommunication. When Hutchinson was held up to public ridicule and exiled, explicit dissent by women was firmly squelched in the Puritan community. In Winthrop's memoir of the events, published in 1644, miscarriages suffered by Hutchinson and her closest

Excerpted from "Examination of Mrs. Anne Hutchinson before the court at Newton, 1637," in David D. Hall, ed., *The Antinomian Controversy, 1636–1638: A Documentary History* (Middletown, Conn.: Wesleyan University Press, 1968), pp. 312–16. Copyright © 1968 by David D. Hall. Reprinted by permission of the editor. Notes have been renumbered.

colleague, Mary Dyer, were offered as evidence of God's "displeasure against their opinions and practises, as clearly as if he had pointed with his finger, in causing the two fomenting women in the time of the height of the Opinions to produce out of their wombs, as before they had out of their braines, such monstrous births as no Chronicle . . . hardly ever recorded the like."*

Hutchinson and her husband fled to Rhode Island, where Roger Williams offered toleration to dissenters; several years later they moved on to the forests of what is now Westchester County, north of New York City. Hutchinson died at the hands of Indians in 1643.

In reading this excerpt from Anne Hutchinson's trial in 1637, note the extent to which criticisms of her religious and political behavior merge with the complaint that she is challenging gender roles. Note also the shrewdness with which Hutchinson defends her actions; at one point she challenges Winthrop that if he thinks it "not lawful for me to teach women . . . why do you call me to teach the court?"

NOVEMBER 1637

THE EXAMINATION OF MRS. ANN HUTCHINSON
AT THE COURT AT NEWTOWN

Mr. Winthrop, governor. Mrs. Hutchinson, you are called here as one of those that have troubled the peace of the commonwealth and the churches here; you are known to be a woman that hath had a great share in the promoting and divulging of those opinions that are causes of this trouble, and to be nearly joined not only in affinity and affection with some of those the court had taken notice of and passed censure upon, but you have spoken divers things as we have been informed very prejudicial to the honour of the churches and ministers thereof, and you have maintained a meeting and an assembly in your house that hath been condemned by the general assembly as a thing not tolerable nor comely in the sight of God nor fitting for your sex, and notwithstanding that was cried down you have continued the same, therefore we have thought good to send for you to understand how things are, that if you be in an erroneous way we may reduce you that so you may become a profitable member here among us, otherwise (if you be obstinate in your course that then the court may take such course that you may trouble us no further) therefore I would intreat you to express whether you do not hold and assent in practice to those opinions and factions that

have been handled in court already, that is to say, whether you do not justify Mr. Wheelwright's sermon and the petition.

Mrs. Hutchinson. I am called here to answer before you but I hear no things laid to my charge.

Gov. I have told you some already and more I can tell you.

Mrs. H. Name one, Sir.

Gov. Have I not named some already?

Mrs. H. What have I said or done?

Gov. Why for your doings, this you did harbour and countenance those that are parties in this faction that you have heard of.

Mrs. H. That's matter of conscience, Sir.

Gov. Your conscience you must keep or it must be kept for you. . . . Say that one brother should commit felony or treason and come to his other brother's house, if he knows him guilty and conceals him he is guilty of the same. It is his conscience to entertain him, but if his conscience comes into act in giving countenance and entertainment to him that hath broken the law he is guilty too. So if you do countenance those that are transgressors of the law you are in the same fact.

Mrs. H. What law do they transgress?

Gov. The law of God and of the state.

Mrs. H. In what particular?

Gov. Why in this among the rest, whereas the Lord doth say honour thy father and thy mother.

---

*John Winthrop, *A Short Story of The Rise, Reign, and Ruine of the Antinomians, Familists & Libertines,* in David D. Hall, ed. *The Antinomian Controversy, 1636–1638: A Documentary History* (Middletown, Conn.: Wesleyan University Press, 1968), p. 214.

Mrs. H. Ey Sir in the Lord.

Gov. This honour you have broke in giving countenance to them. . . .

Mrs. H. What law have I broken?

Gov. Why the fifth commandment.

Mrs. H. I deny that for [Mr. Wheelwright] saith in the Lord.

Gov. You have joined with them in the faction.

Mrs. H. In what faction have I joined with them?

Gov. In presenting the petition[1]. . . .

Mrs. H. But I had not my hand to the petition.

Gov. You have councelled them.

Mrs. H. Wherein?

Gov. Why in entertaining them.

Mrs. H. What breach of law is that Sir?

Gov. Why dishonouring of parents.

Mrs. H. But put the case Sir that I do fear the Lord and my parents, may not I entertain them that fear the Lord because my parents will not give me leave?

Gov. If they be the fathers of the commonwealth, and they of another religion, if you entertain them then you dishonour your parents and are justly punishable.

Mrs. H. If I entertain them, as they have dishonoured their parents I do.

Gov. No but you by countenancing them above others put honor upon them.

Mrs. H. I may put honor upon them as the children of God and as they do honor the Lord.

Gov. We do not mean to discourse with those of your sex but only this; you do adhere unto them and do endeavour to set forward this faction and so you do dishonour us.

Mrs. H. I do acknowledge no such thing neither do I think that I ever put any dishonour upon you.

Gov. Why do you keep such a meeting at your house as you do every week upon a set day?

Mrs. H. It is lawful for me so to do, as it is all your practices and can you find a warrant for yourself and condemn me for the same thing? [I]t was in practice before I came therefore I was not the first.

Gov. For this, that you appeal to our practice you need no confutation. If your meeting had answered to the former it had not been offensive, but I will say that there was no meeting of women alone, but your meeting is of an-other sort for there are sometimes men among you.

Mrs. H. There was never any man with us.

Gov. Well, admit there was no man at your meeting and that you was sorry for it, there is no warrant for your doings, and by what warrant do you continue such a course?

Mrs. H. I conceive there lyes a clear rule in Titus, that the elder women should instruct the younger[2] and then I must have a time wherein I must do it.

Gov. All this I grant you, I grant you a time for it, but what is this to the purpose that you Mrs. Hutchinson must call a company together from their callings to come to be taught of you?

Mrs. H. Will it please you to answer me this and to give me a rule for then I will willingly submit to any truth. If any come to my house to be instructed in the ways of God what rule have I to put them away?

Gov. But suppose that a hundred men come unto you to be instructed will you forbear to instruct them?

Mrs. H. As far as I conceive I cross a rule in it.

Gov. Very well and do you not so here?

Mrs. H. No Sir for my ground is they are men.

Gov. Men and women all is one for that, but suppose that a man should come and say Mrs. Hutchinson I hear that you are a woman that God hath given his grace unto and you have knowledge in the word of God I pray instruct me a little, ought you not to instruct this man?

Mrs. H. I think I may.—Do you think it not lawful for me to teach women and why do you call me to teach the court?

Gov. We do not call you to teach the court but to lay open yourself.

Mrs. H. I desire you that you would then set me down a rule by which I may put them away that come unto me and so have peace in so doing.

Gov. You must shew your rule to receive them.

Mrs. H. I have done it.

Gov. I deny it because I have brought more arguments than you have.

Mrs. H. I say, to me it is a rule.

Mr. Endicot. You say there are some rules unto you. I think there is a contradiction in your own words. What rule for your practice do you bring, only a custom in Boston.

Mrs. H. No Sir that was no rule to me but if you look upon the rule in Titus it is a rule to me. If you convince me that it is no rule I shall yield.

Gov. ... [T]his rule crosses that in the Corinthians.[3] But you must take it in this sense that elder women must instruct the younger about their business, and to love their husbands and not to make them to clash.

Mrs. H. I do not conceive but that it is meant for some publick times.

Gov. Well, have you no more to say but this?

Mrs. H. I have said sufficient for my practice.

Gov. Your course is not to be suffered for, besides that we find such a course as this to be greatly prejudicial to the state, besides the occasion that it is to seduce many honest persons that are called to those meetings and your opinions being known to be different from the word of God may seduce many simple souls that resort unto you, besides that the occasion which hath come of late hath come from none but such as have frequented your meetings, so that now they are flown off from magistrates and ministers and this since they have come to you, and besides that it will not well stand with the commonwealth that families should be neglected for so many neighbours and dames and so much time spent, we see no rule of God for this, we see not that any should have authority to set up any other exercises besides what authority hath already set up and so what hurt comes of this you will be guilty of and we for suffering you.

Mrs. H. Sir I do not believe that to be so.

Gov. Well, we see how it is we must therefore put it away from you, or restrain you from maintaining this course.

Mrs. H. If you have a rule for it from God's word you may.

Gov. We are your judges, and not you ours and we must compel you to it.

Mrs. H. If it please you by authority to put it down I freely let you for I am subject to your authority.

NOTES

1. The petition the Antinomian party presented to the General Court in March 1637.

2. Titus 2.3, 4, 5.

3. 1 Corinthians 14.34, 35.

CAROL F. KARLSEN

The Devil in the Shape of a Woman: The Economic Basis of Witchcraft

Puritan ministers stressed the equality of each soul in the eyes of God and the responsibility of each believer to read the Bible. They urged women as well as men toward literacy and taking responsibility for their own salvation. One distinguished minister, Cotton Mather, writing at the end of the seventeenth century, observed that since women came close to the experience of death in repeated childbirth, their religiosity was likely to be greater than that of men. In being "helpmeets" to their husbands, women were

Excerpted from "The Economic Basis of Witchcraft," chap. 3 of *The Devil in the Shape of a Woman: Witchcraft in Colonial New England* by Carol F. Karlsen (New York: W. W. Norton, 1987). Copyright © 1987 by Carol F. Karlsen. Condensed and reprinted by permission of the author and W. W. Norton & Co., Inc. Notes have been revised and renumbered and tables renumbered.

encouraged to strengthen their ability to be competent and capable. There was much in Puritan thought that could be appealing to women.

But, as we have seen in the case of Anne Hutchinson, the Puritan community was unforgiving to women who failed to serve the needs of godly men in their strictly hierarchical community. Lurking in their imagination—as it lurked throughout the Judeo-Christian tradition—was the cautionary biblical story of Eve, who, by her disobedience, brought evil into the world. (Puritans paid no attention to other elements of that complicated tale: Eve's disobedience, after all, was in quest of Knowledge; the biology of birth is reversed, with Eve emerging from Adam's body.) Witchcraft prosecutions were endemic throughout the Puritan colonies in America and exploded into the famous outbreak in Salem, Massachusetts, in 1692, during which nearly 200 people, three-quarters of them women, were accused, and 20 people, nearly three-quarters of them women, were executed. Carol Karlsen argues that an older view of women as a necessary evil had been only superficially superseded by a new view of women as a necessary good.

Anthropologists have long understood that communities define as witches people whose behavior enacts the things the community most fears; witchcraft beliefs, wrote Monica Hunter Wilson, are "the standardized nightmare of a group, and . . . the comparative analysis of such nightmares . . . [is] one of the keys to the understanding of society.* If the most cherished values of the Puritan community were hierarchy and order, then it was an easy step to the condemnation of those who did not accept—or in some cases could not accept—their place in it. In what ways do the women described in the following essay fail to fit the values of the Puritan community?

Most observers now agree that witches in the villages and towns of late sixteenth- and early seventeenth-century England tended to be poor. They were not usually the poorest women in their communities, one historian has argued; they were the "moderately poor." Rarely were relief recipients suspect; rather it was those just above them on the economic ladder, "like the woman who felt she ought to get poor relief, but was denied it."[1] This example brings to mind New England's Eunice Cole, who once berated Hampton selectmen for refusing her aid when, she insisted, a man no worse off than she was receiving it.[2]

Eunice Cole's experience also suggests the difficulty in evaluating the class position of the accused. Commonly used class indicators such as the amount of property owned, yearly income, occupation, and political offices held are almost useless in analyzing the positions of women during the colonial period. While early New England women surely shared in the material benefits and social status of their fathers, husbands, and even sons, most were economically dependent on the male members of their families throughout their lives. Only a small proportion of these women owned property outright, and even though they participated actively in the productive work of their communities, their labor did not translate into financial independence or economic power. Any income generated by married women belonged by law to their husbands, and because occupations open to women were few and wages meager, women alone could only rarely support themselves. Their material condition, moreover, could easily change with an alteration in their marital status. William Cole, with an estate at his death of £41 after debts, might be counted among the "moderately poor," as might Eunice Cole when he was alive. But the refusal of the authorities to recognize the earlier transfer of this estate from husband to wife ensured, among other things, that as a widow Eunice Cole was among the poorest of New England's poor. . . .

Despite conceptual problems and sparse evidence, it is clear that poor women, both the destitute and those with access to some resources, were surely represented, and very probably overrepresented, among the New England accused. Perhaps 20 percent of accused

*Quoted in Karlsen, p. 181.

women . . . were either impoverished or living at a level of bare subsistence when they were accused.[3] Some, like thirty-seven-year-old Abigail Somes, worked as servants a substantial portion of their adult lives. Some supported themselves and their families with various kinds of temporary labor such as nursing infants, caring for sick neighbors, taking in washing and sewing, or harvesting crops. A few, most notably Tituba, the first person accused during the Salem outbreak, were slaves. Others, like the once-prosperous Sarah Good of Wenham and Salem, and the never-very-well-off Ruth Wilford of Haverhill, found themselves reduced to abject poverty by the death of a parent or a change in their own marital status.[4] Accused witches came before local magistrates requesting permission to sell family land in order to support themselves, to submit claims against their children or executors of their former husbands' estates for nonpayment of the widow's lawful share of the estate, or simply to ask for food and fuel from the town selectmen. Because they could not pay the costs of their trials or jail terms, several were forced to remain in prison after courts acquitted them. The familiar stereotype of the witch as an indigent woman who resorted to begging for her survival is hardly an inaccurate picture of some of New England's accused.

Still, the poor account for only a minority of the women accused. Even without precise economic indicators, it is clear that women from all levels of society were vulnerable to accusation. . . . Wives, daughters, and widows of "middling" farmers, artisans, and mariners were regularly accused, and (although much less often) so too were women belonging to the gentry class. The accused were addressed as Goodwife (or Goody) and as the more honorific Mrs. or Mistress, as well as by their first names.

Prosecution was a different matter. Unless they were single or widowed, accused women from wealthy families—families with estates valued at more than £500—could be fairly confident that the accusations would be ignored by the authorities or deflected by their husbands through suits for slander against their accusers. Even during the Salem outbreak, when several women married to wealthy men were arrested, most managed to escape to the safety of other colonies through their husbands' influence. Married women from moderately well-off families—families with estates valued at between roughly £200 and £500—did not always escape prosecution so easily, but neither do they seem, as a group, to have been as vulnerable as their less prosperous counterparts. When only married women are considered, women in families with estates worth less than £200 seem significantly overrepresented among *convicted* witches—a pattern which suggests that economic position was a more important factor to judges and juries than to the community as a whole in its role as accuser.[5]

Without a husband to act on behalf of the accused, wealth alone rarely provided women with protection against prosecution. Boston's Ann Hibbens, New Haven's Elizabeth Godman, and Wethersfield's Katherine Harrison, all women alone, were tried as witches despite sizable estates. In contrast, the accusations against women like Hannah Griswold of Saybrook, Connecticut, Elizabeth Blackleach of Hartford, and Margaret Gifford of Salem, all wives of prosperous men when they were accused, were simply not taken seriously by the courts.[6] . . .

Economic considerations, then, do appear to have been at work in the New England witchcraft cases. But the issue was not simply the relative poverty—or wealth—of accused witches or their families. It was the special position of most accused witches vis-à-vis their society's rules for transferring wealth from one generation to another. To explain why their position was so unusual, we must turn first to New England's system of inheritance.

Inheritance is normally thought of as the transmission of property at death, but in New England, as in other agricultural societies, adult children received part of their father's accumulated estates prior to his death, usually at the time they married.[7] Thus the inheritance system included both pre-mortem endowments and post-mortem distributions. While no laws compelled fathers to settle part of their estates on their children as marriage portions, it was customary to do so. Marriages were, among other things, economic arrangements, and young people could not benefit from these arrangements unless their fathers provided them with the means to set up households and earn their livelihoods. Sons' portions tended to be land, whereas daughters commonly received movable goods and/or money. The exact value of these endowments varied according to a father's wealth and inclination, but it appears that as a general rule the father of the young woman settled on the couple roughly half as much as the father of the young man.[8]

Custom, not law, also guided the distribution of a man's property at his death, but with two important exceptions. First, a man's widow, if he left one, was legally entitled "by way of dower" to one-third part of his real property, "to have and injoy for term of her natural life." She was expected to support herself with the profits of this property, but since she held only a life interest in it, she had to see that she did not "strip or waste" it.[9] None of the immovable estate could be sold, unless necessary for her or her children's maintenance, and then only with the permission of the court. A man might will his wife more than a third of his real property—but not less. Only if the woman came before the court to renounce her dower right publicly, and then only if the court approved, could this principle be waived. In the form of her "thirds," dower was meant to provide for a woman's support in widowhood. The inviolability of dower protected the widow from the claims of her children against the estate and protected the community from the potential burden of her care.

The second way in which law determined inheritance patterns had to do specifically with intestate cases.[10] If a man died without leaving a will, several principles governed the division of his property. The widow's thirds, of course, were to be laid out first. Unless "just cause" could be shown for some other distribution, the other two-thirds were to be divided among the surviving children, both male and female.[11] A double portion was to go to the eldest son, and single portions to his sisters and younger brothers. If there were no sons, the law stipulated that the estate was to be shared equally by the daughters. In cases where any or all of the children had not yet come of age, their portions were to be held by their mother or by a court-appointed guardian until they reached their majorities[12] or married. What remained of the widow's thirds at her death was to be divided among the surviving children, in the same proportions as the other two-thirds.

Although bound to conform to laws concerning the widow's thirds, men who wrote wills were not legally required to follow the principles of inheritance laid out in intestate cases. Individual men had the right to decide

for themselves who would ultimately inherit their property. . . . [T]he majority seem to have adhered closely (though not always precisely) to the custom of leaving a double portion to the eldest son. Beyond that, New England men seem generally to have agreed to a system of partible inheritance, with both sons and daughters inheriting.

When these rules were followed, property ownership and control generally devolved upon men. Neither the widow's dower nor, for the most part, the daughter's right to inherit signified more than *access to* property. For widows, the law was clear that dower allowed for "use" only. For inheriting daughters who were married, the separate but inheritance-related principle of coverture applied. Under English common law, "feme covert" stipulated that married women had no right to own property—indeed, upon marriage, "the very being or legal existence of the woman is suspended."[13] Personal property which a married daughter inherited from her father, either as dowry or as a post-mortem bequest, immediately became the legal possession of her husband, who could exert full powers of ownership over it. A married daughter who inherited land from her father retained title to the land, which her husband could not sell without her consent. On her husband's death such land became the property of her children, but during his life her husband was entitled to the use and profits of it, and his wife could not devise it to her children by will.[14] The property of an inheriting daughter who was single seems to have been held "for improvement" for her until she was married, when it became her dowry.[15]

This is not to say that women did not benefit when they inherited property. A sizable inheritance could provide a woman with a materially better life; if single or widowed, inheriting women enjoyed better chances for an economically advantageous marriage or remarriage. But inheritance did not normally bring women the independent economic power it brought men.

The rules of inheritance were not always followed, however. In some cases, individual men decided not to conform to customary practices; instead, they employed one of several legal devices to give much larger shares of their estates to their wives or daughters, many times for disposal at their own discretion. Occasionally, the magistrates themselves allowed the estate to be distributed in some other fashion. Or, most commonly, the absence of male heirs in families made conformity impossible. In all three exceptions to inheritance customs, but most particularly the last, the women who stood to benefit economically also assumed a position of unusual vulnerability. They, and in many instances their daughters, became prime targets for witchcraft accusations.

Consider first the experience of witches who came from families without male heirs. . . . [T]hese histories begin to illuminate the subtle and often intricate manner in which anxieties about inheritance lay at the heart of most witchcraft accusations.

KATHERINE HARRISON

Katherine Harrison first appears in the Connecticut colonial records in the early 1650s, as the wife of John Harrison, a wealthy Wethersfield landowner.[16] Her age is unknown[17] and her family background is obscure. We know that she called John, Jonathan, and Josiah Gilbert, three prominent Connecticut Valley settlers, her cousins, but her actual relationship to them is ambiguous.[18] . . . She may have been the daughter or niece of Lydia Gilbert, who was executed as a witch in Hartford in 1654, but we can be reasonably certain only that the two women were members of the same Connecticut family.[19] . . .

It has been said that Katherine Harrison was first tried as a witch in October 1668.[20] If so, then she must have been acquitted, because she was indicted in the Court of Assistants in Hartford on 25 May 1669, on the same charge.[21] The jury was unable to agree upon a verdict, however, and the court adjourned to the next session. Meantime, Harrison was supposed to remain in jail, but for some reason she was released in the summer or early fall, and she returned home to Wethersfield. Shortly thereafter, thirty-eight Wethersfield townsmen filed a petition, complaining that "shee was suffered to be at libertie," since she "was lately prooved to be Deaply guiltie of *suspicion* of Wichcrafte" and that "the Juerie (the greater part of them) judged or beleaved that she was guilty of such high crimes" and "ought to be put to death." Among the petition's signers were several of the town's most prominent citizens, including John Blackleach, Sr., who had "taken much

paines in the prosecution of this cause from the beginninge," and John Chester, who was then involved in a legal controversy with Harrison concerning a parcel of land.[22] When the Court of Assistants met again in October, all of the jury members found her guilty of witchcraft.[23]

The Hartford magistrates, however, were reluctant to accept the verdict. Perhaps remembering how accusations had gotten out of hand during the Hartford outbreak seven years before, they put Harrison back in prison and appealed to local ministers for advice on the use of evidence. The response was ambiguous enough to forestall execution.[24] At a special session of the Court of Assistants the following May, the magistrates reconsidered the verdict, determined that they were not able to concur with the jury "so as to sentance her to death or to a longer continuance in restraynt," and ordered Harrison to pay her fees and leave the colony for good.[25]

If witnesses testifying against her in her 1669 trial can be believed, Katherine Harrison's neighbors had suspected that she was a witch sixteen or eighteen years earlier. Elizabeth Simon deposed that as a single woman, Harrison was noted to be "a great or notorious liar, a Sabbath breaker and one that told fortunes"—and that her predictions frequently came to pass. Simon was also suspicious of Harrison for another reason: because she "did often spin so great a quantity of fine linen yarn as the said Elizabeth did never know nor hear of any other woman that could spin so much."[26] Other witnesses testified to the more recent damage she did to individuals and their property. Harrison was also a healer, and although many of her neighbors called upon her skills, over the years some of them came to suspect her of killing as well as curing.[27] Or so they said in 1668–69; she was not formally accused of any witchcraft crimes until after her husband's death.

John Harrison had died in 1666, leaving his wife one of the wealthiest, if not *the* wealthiest woman in Wethersfield. In his will he bequeathed his entire estate of £929 to his wife and three daughters. Rebecca, age twelve, was to have £60, and his two younger daughters, eleven-year-old Mary and nine-year-old Sarah, were to have £40 each. The remaining £789 was to go to his widow.[28] Unlike many widows in colonial New England, Katherine Harrison chose not to remarry. Instead she lived alone, managing her extensive holdings herself, with the advice and assistance of her Hartford kinsman, Jonathan Gilbert.

In October 1668, not long after her adversaries began gathering their witchcraft evidence against her, Harrison submitted a lengthy petition to "the Fathers of the Comonweale" asking for relief for the extensive vandalism of her estate since her husband's death. Among other damage, she spoke of oxen beaten and bruised to the point of being "altogether unserviceable"; of a hole bored into the side of her cow; of a three-year-old heifer slashed to death; and of the back of a two-year-old steer broken. Her corn crop was destroyed, she said, "damnified with horses, they being staked upon it," and "30 poles of hops cutt and spoyled." Twelve of her relatives and neighbors, she said, including Jonathan and Josiah Gilbert, could testify to the damage done. The response of the court went unrecorded, but there is no indication that provision was made for the "due recompense" Harrison requested or that her grievances were even investigated.[29]

The Court of Assistants also seems to have been unsympathetic to another petition Harrison submitted in the fall of 1668, in which she complained that the actions of the magistrates themselves were depleting her estate.[30] Indeed, the local court had recently fined her £40 for slandering her neighbors, Michael and Ann Griswold—a fine greatly in excess of the normal punishment in such cases.[31] The exact circumstances of the incident are unknown, but the Griswolds were among Harrison's witchcraft accusers, and she apparently considered Michael Griswold central in the recruiting of additional witnesses against her, for she said that "the sayd Michael Griswold would Hang her though he damned a thousand soules," adding that "as for his own soule it was damned long agoe." Griswold, a member of Wethersfield's elite, but not as wealthy as Harrison, sued her for these slanderous remarks and for calling his wife Ann "a savadge whore."[32] Besides levying the fine, the court ordered Harrison to confess her sins publicly.[33] She made the required confession, but she appealed the exorbitant fine.

Harrison's petition, which she filed within the month, was a peculiar mixture of justification for her actions, concession to the magistrates' insistence on deference in women, determination in her convictions, and desperation in her attempt to salvage her estate. Acknowledging herself to be "a female, a weaker vessell, subject to passion," she pleaded as the source of her frustration and anger the vicious abuse to which she had been subjected since her husband's death. She admitted her "corruption," but pointed out that it was well known that she had made "a full and free confession of [her] fault" and had offered "to repaire the wound that [she] had given to [the Griswolds'] names by a plaster as broad as the sore, at any time and in any place where it should content them." At the same time, she indicted Michael Griswold for being less interested in the reparation of his name than in her estate and did not hesitate to call the fine oppressive, citing the laws of God and the laws of the commonwealth as providing "that noe mans estate shal be deminished or taken away by any colony or pretence of Authority" in such an arbitrary manner. In her final statements, however, she returned to a more conciliatory stance: "I speake not to excuse my fault," she said, "but to save my estate as far as Righteousness will permit for a distressed Widow and Orphanes."[34]

Fear of losing her estate is a recurring theme in the records of Harrison's life during this period. Almost immediately after her husband's death in 1666, she petitioned the court to change the terms of her husband's will. Arguing that the bequests to the children were "inconsiderate" (by which she probably meant inconsiderable), she asked that the magistrates settle on her eldest daughter £210, and £200 on each of her younger daughters, reserving the house and lot for herself during her lifetime.[35] Since her husband had left her full ownership of most of his estate, she could simply have given her daughters larger portions, but she must have felt that the court's sanction rendered the inheritances less vulnerable. Several months later, she appealed directly to Connecticut's governor, John Winthrop, Jr., requesting that Hartford's John and Jonathan Gilbert, and John Riley of Wethersfield, be appointed overseers of her estate.[36] Winthrop must not have granted her request, because in 1668 Harrison signed over the rest of the estate she had inherited from her husband to her daughters and appointed Jonathan and John Gilbert her daughters' guardians.[37] By the following year, her neighbors reported, she had "disposed of great part of her estate to others in trust."[38]

In June 1670, Katherine Harrison moved to Westchester, New York, to begin her life anew. Her reputation for witchcraft followed her, however, in the form of a complaint, filed in July by two of her new neighbors, that she had been allowed to resettle in Westchester. Noting that suspicion of her in Connecticut "hath given some cause of apprehension" to the townspeople, in order to "end their jealousyes and feares" a local New York magistrate told her to leave the jurisdiction.[39] Harrison refused. Before any action could be taken against her, her eldest daughter was fortuitously betrothed to Josiah Hunt, a son of Thomas Hunt, one of the men who had protested her presence in Westchester. The elder Hunt became a supporter and appeared in court on her behalf, with his son and three other influential men. Though she was required to give security for her "Civill carriage and good behaviour," the General Court of Assizes in New York ordered "that in regard there is nothing appears against her deserving the continuance of that obligacion shee is to bee releast from it, and hath Liberty to remain in the Towne of Westchester where shee now resides, or any where else in the Government during her pleasure."[40]

Evidently Harrison continued to live with recurring witchcraft suspicion, but after 1670 there is no further evidence of official harassment.[41] Early in 1672, she reappeared in Hartford to sue eleven of her old Connecticut Valley neighbors, in most cases for debt, and to release her "intrusted overseer" Jonathan Gilbert from his responsibilities for her estate (although he continued to act as guardian to her two younger daughters).[42] A month later, she signed at least some of her remaining Wethersfield land over to Gilbert.[43] After that, she fades from view. She may have returned to Connecticut for good at that time, for some evidence suggests that she died at Dividend, then an outlying section of Wethersfield, in October 1682.[44]

SUSANNA MARTIN

Born in England in 1625, Susanna North was the youngest of three daughters of Richard North. Her mother died when Susanna was young and her father subsequently remarried. The family migrated to New England in or just prior to 1639, the year in which Richard North was listed as one of the first proprietors of Salisbury, Massachusetts. Susanna's sister Mary had married Thomas Jones and was living in Gloucester by 1642. Of her sister Sarah we know only that she married a man named Oldham, had a daughter named Ann, and died before the child was grown. In August 1646, at the age of twenty-one, Susanna married George Martin, a Salisbury man whose first wife had recently died. In June of the following year, she gave birth to her son Richard, the first of nine children. One of these children, a son, died in infancy.[45] . . .

Early in 1668, less than a year after the birth of her last child, Susanna Martin's father died, leaving a modest estate of about £150. As the only surviving children, the then fortythree-year-old Susanna and her sister Mary anticipated receiving a major portion of the property, to posses either immediately or after the death of their stepmother, Ursula North. They were disappointed. According to the will probated shortly after he died, Richard North had voided all previous wills and written a new one—*nearly two decades* before his death. In this document, dated January 1649, he left all but £22 of his estate directly to his wife. Twentyone pounds was to be divided among Mary Jones, Susanna Martin, and Ann Bates (Sarah Oldham's daughter). Susanna's share was 20 shillings and the cancellation of a £10 debt George Martin owed his father-in-law. Listed as witnesses to this will were Thomas Bradbury of Salisbury and Mary Jones's daughter, Mary Winsley.[46] But the will raised problems. In 1649, Ann Bates was still Ann Oldham (she did not marry Francis Bates until 1661) and the Mary Winsley listed as witness to the will was still Mary Jones, at most eleven or twelve years old when it was allegedly written.[47] Despite the obvious irregularities, Thomas Bradbury and Mary Winsley attested in court that this was indeed Richard North's last will and testament.

Whether Susanna Martin and her sister saw or protested this will when it was probated cannot be determined. Susanna, at least, may have had more pressing concerns on her mind. In April 1669, a bond of £100 was posted for her appearance at the next Court of Assistants "upon suspicion of witchcraft." That was the same day that George Martin sued William Sargent for slandering his wife. According to George Martin, Sargent had not only said that Susanna "was a witch, and he would call her witch," but also accused her of having "had a child" while still single and of "wringing its neck" shortly after. George Martin also sued William Sargent's brother Thomas for saying "that his son George Marttin was a bastard and that Richard Marttin was Goodwife Marttin's imp."[48] . . .

Meanwhile, the magistrates bound Susanna Martin over to the higher court to be tried for witchcraft. Although the records have not survived, she must have been acquitted, because several months later she was at liberty. In October 1669, George Martin was again bound for his wife's appearance in court, not for witchcraft this time but for calling one of her neighbors a liar and a thief.[49]

By April 1671, George and Susanna Martin (Susanna's sister Mary Jones would later join them) were involved in what would become protracted litigation over the estate of Susanna's father. Ursula North had died a month or two before, leaving a will, dated shortly after her husband's death, that effectively disinherited her two stepdaughters by awarding them 40 shillings apiece. She left the rest of the original North estate first to her grandaughter, Mary Winsley, and secondarily to Mary and Nathaniel Winsley's only child, Hepzibah.[50]

The exact sequence of the numerous court hearings that followed is less clear. Evidently, Susanna and George Martin initiated legal proceedings against Mary and Nathaniel Winsley in April 1671, for unwarranted possession of the North estate. . . . In October 1672, the General Court responded, giving Susanna Martin liberty to sue for her inheritance a second time at the local level.

In April 1673, the recently widowed Mary Jones and George Martin, acting for his wife, sued Nathaniel Winsley "for withholding the inheritance of housing, lands and other estate . . . under color of a feigned or confused writing like the handwriting of Mr. Thomas Bradbury and seemingly attested by him, and Mary Winsly." The court declared the case nonsuited, and again Susanna Martin appealed to the General Court, requesting that the case be reheard at the local level. The General Court consented in May 1673, and the following October, Susanna and George Martin instituted proceedings against the Winsleys for the third time. Again the county court decided for the defendants, and the Martins appealed to the Court of Assistants. For a while it looked as though things were finally going their way. The higher court, which "found for the plaintiff

there being no legall prooffe of Richard North's will," ordered that "the estate the said North left be left to the disposall of the county court." . . .

[In 1674] Susanna, George, and Mary appealed a final time to the General Court, this time for "a hearing of the whole case" by the highest court itself. The magistrates agreed to hear the case, remitting the usual court fees, as they had done before, on the basis of Susanna's pleas of poverty. But in October 1674, after "perusall of what hath binn heard and alleadged by both parties," the court found for Nathaniel Winsley.[51] In what Susanna Martin and Mary Jones believed was a flagrant miscarriage of justice, they had lost what they considered their rightful inheritances.

For almost the next two decades, Susanna Martin's name rarely appears in the public records of the colony. Her sister Mary died in 1682, followed by her husband George in 1686.[52] Early in 1692, she was again accused of witchcraft, this time by several of the possessed females in Salem. They claimed that her apparition "greviously afflected" them, urging them to become witches themselves. Summoned before the court as witnesses against her were eleven men and four women, all old neighbors of the now sixty-seven-year-old widow.[53]

Unnerved by neither the agonies of the possessed or the magistrates' obvious belief in her guilt, Martin insisted that she was innocent. To Cotton Mather, she "was one of the most impudent, scurrilous, wicked Creatures in the World," who had the effrontery to claim "that she had lead a most virtuous and holy life."[54] Years of living as a reputed witch had left Martin well-versed on the subject of the Devil's powers. "He that appeared in sam[uel]s shape, a glorifyed saint," she said, citing the Bible in her own defense, "can appear in any ones shape." She laughed at the fits of her young accusers, explaining: "Well I may at such folly." When asked what she thought the possessed were experiencing, she said she did not know. Pressed to speculate on it, she retorted: "I do not desire to spend my judgment upon it" and added (revealing what must have been her long-standing opinion of the magistrates' bias), "my thoughts are my own, when they are in, but when they are out they are anothers."[55] . . .

Susanna Martin was found guilty of witchcraft and was one of five women executed on 19 July 1692. One week later, another Salisbury woman was indicted on the same charge. She was Mary Bradbury, the now elderly wife of the man Susanna Martin believed had written her father's "will" nearly twenty-five years before. Mary Bradbury was sentenced to hang too, but friends helped her to escape. No explicit connection between the accusations of the two women is discernible. Rumors circulated, however, that because Thomas Bradbury had friends in positions of authority, there had been little real effort to capture his fugitive wife.[56] . . .

These . . . short histories . . . suggest the diverse economic circumstances of witches in early New England. . . . The . . . women featured in these histories were either (1) daughters of parents who had no sons (or whose sons had died), (2) women in marriages which brought forth only daughters (or in which the sons had died), or (3) women in marriages with no children at all. These patterns had significant economic implications. Because there were no legitimate male heirs in their immediate families, each of these . . . women stood to inherit, did inherit, or were denied their apparent right to inherit substantially larger portions of their fathers' or husbands' accumulated estates than women in families with male heirs. Whatever actually happened to the property in question—and in some cases we simply do not know—these women were aberrations in a society with an inheritance system designed to keep property in the hands of men.

These . . . cases also illustrate fertility and mortality patterns widely shared among the families of accused witches. A substantial majority of New England's accused females were women without brothers, women with daughters but no sons, or women in marriages with no children at all (see Table 1). Of the 267 accused females, enough is known about 158 to identify them as either having or not having brothers or sons to inherit: only 62 of the 158 (39 percent) did, whereas 96 (61 percent) did not. More striking, *once accused*, women without brothers or sons were even more likely than women with brothers or sons to be tried, convicted, and executed: women from families without male heirs made up 64 percent of the females prosecuted, 76 percent of those who

were found guilty, and 89 percent of those who were executed.

These figures must be read with care, however, for two reasons. First, eighteen of the sixty-two accused females who *had* brothers or sons to inherit were themselves daughters and granddaughters of women who did not. It appears that these eighteen females, most of whom were young women or girls, were accused because their neighbors believed that their mothers and grandmothers passed their witchcraft on to them. Therefore they form a somewhat ambiguous group. Since they all had brothers to inherit, it would be inaccurate to exclude them from this category in Table 1, yet including them understates the extent to which inheritance-related concerns were at issue in witchcraft accusations. At the same time, the large number of cases in which the fertility and mortality patterns of witches' families are unknown (109 of the 267 accused females in New England) makes it impossible to assess precisely the proportion of women among the accused who did not have brothers or sons.

Table 2 helps clarify the point. It includes as a separate category the daughters and granddaughters of women without brothers or sons and incorporates the cases for which this information is unknown. Although inclusion of the unknowns renders the overall percentages meaningless, this way of representing the available information shows clearly the particular vulnerability of women without brothers or sons. Even if *all* the unknown cases involved women from families *with* male heirs—a highly unlikely possibility—women from families without males to inherit would still form a majority of convicted and executed witches. Were

TABLE 1. Female Witches by Presence or Absence of Brothers or Sons, New England, 1620–1725 (A)

Action	Women without Brothers or Sons		Women with Brothers or Sons		Total
Accused	96	(61%)	62	(39%)	158
Tried	41	(64%)	23	(36%)	64
Convicted	25	(76%)	8	(24%)	33
Executed	17	(89%)	2	(11%)	19

TABLE 2. Female Witches by Presence or Absence of Brothers or Sons, New England, 1620–1725 (B)

Action	Women without Brothers or Sons		Daughters and Granddaughters of Women without Brothers or Sons		Women with Brothers or Sons		Unknown Cases		Total
Accused	96	(36%)	18	(7%)	44	(16%)	109	(41%)	267
Tried	41	(48%)	6	(7%)	17	(20%)	22	(26%)	86
Convicted	25	(56%)	0	(0%)	6	(13%)	12	(27%)	45
Executed	17	(61%)	0	(0%)	2	(7%)	9	(32%)	28

the complete picture visible, I suspect that it would not differ substantially from that presented earlier in Table 1—which is based on data reflecting 60 percent of New England's witches and which indicates that women without brothers and sons were more vulnerable than other women at all stages of the process.

Numbers alone, however, do not tell the whole story. More remains to be said about what happened to these inheriting or potentially inheriting women, both before and after they were accused of witchcraft.

It was not unusual for women in families without male heirs to be accused of witchcraft shortly after the deaths of fathers, husbands, brothers, or sons. Katherine Harrison [and] Susanna Martin . . . exemplify this pattern. So too does elderly Ann Hibbens of Boston, whose execution in 1656 seems to have had a profound enough effect on some of her peers to influence the outcome of subsequent trials for years to come. Hibbens had three sons from her first marriage, all of whom lived in England; but she had no children by her husband William Hibbens, with whom she had come to Massachusetts in the 1630s. William died in 1654; Ann was brought to trial two years later. Although her husband's will has not survived, he apparently left a substantial portion (if not all) of his property directly to her: when she wrote her own will shortly before her execution, Ann Hibbens was in full possession of a £344 estate, most of which she bequeathed to her sons in England.[57]

Similarly, less than two years elapsed between the death of Gloucester's William Vinson and the imprisonment of his widow Rachel in 1692. Two children, a son and a daughter, had been born to the marriage, but the son had died in 1675. Though William Vinson had had four sons (and three daughters) by a previous marriage, the sons were all dead by 1683. In his will, which he wrote in 1684, before he was certain that his last son had been lost at sea, William left his whole £180 estate to Rachel for her life, stipulating that she could sell part of the lands and cattle if she found herself in need of resources. After Rachel's death, "in Case" his son John "be Living and returne home agayne," William said, most of the estate was to be divided between John and their daughter Abigail. If John did not return, both shares were to be Abigail's.[58] . . .

In other cases, many years passed between the death of the crucial male relative and the moment when a formal witchcraft complaint was filed.

. . . Mary English of Salem was charged with witchcraft seven years after she came into her inheritance. Her father, merchant William Hollingworth, had been declared lost at sea in 1677, but at that time Mary's brother William was still alive. Possibly because the younger William was handling the family's interests in other colonies, or possibly because the father's estate was in debt for more than it was worth, the magistrates gave the widow Elinor Hollingworth power of attorney to salvage what she could. With her "owne labor," as she put it, "but making use of other mens estates," the aggressive and outspoken Mistress Hollingworth soon had her deceased husband's debts paid and his wharf, warehouse, and tavern solvent again.[59] She had no sooner done so, however, than she was accused of witchcraft by the wife of a Gloucester mariner.[60] Though the magistrates gave little credence to the charge at the time, they may have had second thoughts later. In 1685, her son William died, and Elinor subsequently conveyed the whole Hollingworth estate over to Mary English, who was probably her only surviving child.[61]

Elinor Hollingworth had died by 1692, but Mary English was one of the women cried out upon early in the Salem outbreak. Her husband, the merchant Philip English, was accused soon after. Knowing their lives were in grave danger, the Englishes fled to the safety of New York. But as one historian of witchcraft has pointed out, flight was "the legal equivalent of conviction."[62] No sooner had they left than close to £1200 of their property was confiscated under the law providing attainder for witchcraft.[63]

Not all witches from families without male heirs were accused of conspiring with the Devil *after* they had come into their inheritances. On the contrary, some were accused prior to the death of the crucial male relative, many times before it was clear who would inherit. . . . [O]ne of these women . . . was Martha Corey of Salem, who was accused of witchcraft in 1692 while her husband was still alive. Giles Corey had been married twice before and had several daughters by the time he married the widow Martha Rich, probably in the 1680s. With no sons to inherit, Giles's substantial land holdings would, his neighbors might have assumed, be passed on to his wife and daughters. Alice Parker, who may have been Giles's daughter from a former marriage, also came before the magistrates as a witch in 1692, as did Giles himself. Martha Corey and Alice Parker maintained their innocence and were hanged. Giles Corey, in an apparently futile attempt to preserve his whole estate for his heirs, refused to respond to the indictment. To force him to enter a plea, he was tortured: successively heavier weights were placed on his body until he was pressed to death.[64]

What seems especially significant here is that most accused witches whose husbands were still alive were, like their counterparts who were widows and spinsters, over forty years of age—and therefore unlikely if not unable to produce male heirs. Indeed, the fact that witchcraft accusations were rarely taken seriously by the community until the accused stopped bearing children takes on a special meaning when it is juxtaposed with the anomalous position of inheriting women or potentially inheriting women in New England's social structure.

Witches in families without male heirs

sometimes had been dispossessed of part or all of their inheritances before—sometimes long before—they were formally charged with witchcraft. Few of these women, however, accepted disinheritance with equanimity. Rather, like Susanna Martin, they took their battles to court, casting themselves in the role of public challengers to the system of male inheritance. In most instances, the authorities sided with their antagonists. . . .

. . . The property of women in families without male heirs was vulnerable to loss in a variety of ways, from deliberate destruction by neighbors (as Katherine Harrison experienced) to official sequestering by local magistrates. In nearly every case, the authorities themselves seem hostile or at best indifferent to the property claims of these women. One final example deserves mention here, not only because it indicates how reluctant magistrates were to leave property in the control of women, but because it shows that the property of convicted witches was liable to seizure even without the benefit of an attainder law.

Rebecca Greensmith had been widowed twice before her marriage to Nathaniel Greensmith. Her first husband, Abraham Elsen of Wethersfield, had died intestate in 1648, leaving an estate of £99. After checking the birth dates of the Elsens' two children, three-year-old Sarah and one-year-old Hannah, the court initially left the whole estate with the widow. When Rebecca married Wethersfield's Jarvis Mudge the following year, the local magistrates sequestered the house and land Abraham Elsen had left, worth £40, stating their intention to rent it out "for the Use and Benefit of the two daughters."[65] The family moved to New London shortly after, but Jarvis Mudge died in 1652 and Rebecca moved with Hannah and Sarah to Hartford. Since Rebecca was unable to support herself and her two daughters, the court allowed her to sell the small amount of land owned by her second husband (with whom she had had no children) "for the paing of debts and the Bettering the Childrens portyons."[66]

Sometime prior to 1660, Rebecca married Nathaniel Greensmith. During the Hartford outbreak, Rebecca came under suspicion of witchcraft. After Nathaniel sued his wife's accuser for slander, Nathaniel himself was named. Both husband and wife were convicted and executed.[67]

Respecting Nathaniel's £182 estate, £44 of which was claimed by the then eighteen-year-old Sarah and seventeen-year-old Hannah Elsen, the court ordered the three overseers "to preserve the estate from Waste" and to pay "any just debts," the only one recorded being the Greensmiths' jail fees. Except for allowing the overseers "to dispose of the 2 daughters," presumably to service, the magistrates postponed until the next court any decision concerning the young women's portions. First, however, they deducted £40 to go "to the Treasurer for the County."[68] No reason was given for this substantial appropriation and no record of further distribution of the estate has survived.

Aside from these many women who lived or had lived in families without male heirs, there were at least a dozen other witches who, despite the presence of brothers and sons, came into much larger shares of estates than their neighbors would have expected. In some cases, these women gained full control over the disposition of property. We know about these women because their fathers, husbands, or other relatives left wills, because the women themselves wrote wills, or because male relatives who felt cheated out of their customary shares fought in the courts for more favorable arrangements.

Grace Boulter of Hampton, one of several children of Richard Swain, is one of these women. Grace was accused of witchcraft in 1680, along with her thirty-two-year-old daughter, Mary Prescott. Twenty years earlier, in 1660, just prior to his removal to Nantucket, Grace's father had deeded a substantial portion of his Hampton property to her and her husband Nathaniel, some of which he gave directly to her.[69]

Another witch in this group is Jane James of Marblehead, who left an estate at her death in 1669 which was valued at £85. While it is not clear how she came into possession of it, the property had not belonged to her husband Erasmus, who had died in 1660, though it did play a significant role in a controversy between her son and son-in-law over their rightful shares of both Erasmus's and Jane's estates. Between 1650 and her death in 1669, Jane was accused of witchcraft at least three times by her Marblehead neighbors. . . .[70]

Looking back over the lives of these many women—most particularly those who did not have brothers or sons to inherit—we begin to understand the complexity of the economic dimension of New England witchcraft. Only rarely does the actual trial testimony indicate that economic power was even at issue. Nevertheless it is there, recurring with a telling persistence once we look beyond what was explicitly said about these women as witches. Inheritance disputes surface frequently enough in witchcraft cases, cropping up as part of the general context even when no direct link between the dispute and the charge is discernible, to suggest the fears that underlay most accusations. No matter how deeply entrenched the principle of male inheritance, no matter how carefully written the laws that protected it, it was impossible to insure that all families had male offspring. The women who stood to benefit from these demographic "accidents" account for most of New England's female witches.

The amount of property in question was not the crucial factor in the way these women were viewed or treated by their neighbors, however. Women of widely varying economic circumstances were vulnerable to accusation and even to conviction. Neither was there a direct line from accuser to material beneficiary of the accusation: others in the community did sometimes profit personally from the losses sustained by these women . . . , but only rarely did the gain accrue to the accusers themselves. Indeed, occasionally there was no direct temporal connection: in some instances several decades passed between the creation of the key economic conditions and the charge of witchcraft; the charge in other cases even anticipated the development of those conditions.

Finally, inheriting or potentially inheriting women were vulnerable to witchcraft accusations not only during the Salem outbreak, but from the time of the first formal accusations in New England at least until the end of the century. . . . The Salem outbreak created only a slight wrinkle in this established fabric of suspicion. If daughters, husbands, and sons of witches were more vulnerable to danger in 1692 than they had been previously, they were mostly the daughters, husbands, and sons of inheriting or potentially inheriting women. As the outbreak spread, it drew into its orbit increasing numbers of women, "unlikely" witches in that they were married to well-off and influential men, but familiar figures to some of their neighbors nonetheless. What the impoverished Sarah Good had in common with Mary Phips, wife of Massachusetts's governor, was what Eunice Cole had in common with Katherine Harrison. . . . However varied their backgrounds and economic positions, as women without brothers or women without sons, they stood in the way of the orderly transmission of property from one generation of males to another.

NOTES

1. Alan Macfarlane, *Witchcraft in Tudor and Stuart England: A Regional and Comparative Study* (New York, 1970), pp. 149–51. See also Keith Thomas, *Religion and the Decline of Magic* (New York, 1971), pp. 457, 520–21, 560–68.

2. See Trials for Witchcraft in New England (unpaged), dated 5 September 1656 (manuscript volume, Houghton Library, Harvard University, Cambridge, Mass.).

3. Relying on very general indicators (a married woman who worked as a servant, a widow whose husband had left an estate of £39, and so forth), I was able to make rough estimates about the economic position of 150 accused women. Twenty-nine of these women seem to have been poor. Until we have a more detailed picture of women's lives in the seventeeth century, however, and better ways of conceptualizing women's class experience, we cannot know the extent to which poor women were overrepresented among the accused.

4. For Abigail Somes, see *The Salem Witchcraft Papers: Verbatim Transcripts of the Legal Documents of the Salem Witchcraft Outbreak of 1692*, 3 vols., ed. Paul Boyer and Stephen Nissenbaum (New York, 1977), 3: 733–37 (hereafter cited as *Witchcraft Papers*). For Tituba, see *Witchcraft Papers* 3:745–57. Documents relating to Ruth Wilford are in *Witchcraft Papers* 2:459; 3:961; *The Probate Records of Essex County, Massachusetts, 1635–1681*, 3 vols. (Salem, 1916–20), 3:93–95 (hereafter cited as *Essex Probate Records*).

5. Most families in seventeenth-century New England had estates worth less than £200. However, since only a very small proportion of convicted witches who were married seem to have come from families with estates worth *more* than £200, it seems reasonable to conclude that married women from families with less than £200 estates were overrepresented among the accused. Nearly all of the convictions of married women from families with estates worth more than £200 occurred during the Salem outbreak. . . .

In the minds of many New Englanders, possession of a £200 estate distinguished a family "of quality" from other colonists and therefore seems a reasonable dividing line between the majority of colonists and their "betters." The £500 estate dividing line between the "prosperous" and the "wealthy" is more arbitrary, but it seems to fit with general colonial conceptions.

6. For accusations against Hannah Griswold and Margaret Gifford, see Norbert B. Lacy, "The Records of the Court of Assistants of Connecticut, 1665–1701" (M.A. thesis, Yale University, 1937), pp. 6–7 (hereafter cited as "Conn. Assistants Records"); and *Records and Files of the Quarterly Courts of Essex County, Massachusetts*, 9 vols. (Salem, 1912–75), 7:405; 8:23 (hereafter cited as *Essex Court Records*).

7. This discussion of the inheritance system of seventeenth-century New England is drawn from the following sources: *The Book of the General Lawes and Libertyes Concerning the Inhabitants of the Massachusetts*, ed. Thomas G. Barnes (facsimile from the 1648 edition, San Marino, Calif., 1975); *The Colonial Laws of Massachusetts. Reprinted from the Edition of 1672, with the Supplements through 1686*, ed. William H. Whitmore (Boston, 1887); John D. Cushing, comp., *The Laws and Liberties of Massachusetts, 1641–91: A Facsimile Edition*, 3 vols. (Wilmington, Del., 1976); *Massachusetts Province Laws, 1692–1699*, ed. John D. Cushing (Wilmington, Del., 1978); *New Hampshire Probate Records; Essex Probate Records; A Digest of the Early Connecticut Probate Records*, vol. 1, ed. Charles W. Manwaring (Hartford, 1904) (hereafter cited as *Conn. Probate Records*); Marylynn Salmon, *Women and the Law of Property in Early America* (Chapel Hill, 1986); George L. Haskins, "The Beginnings of Partible Inheritance in the American Colonies," in *Essays in the History of American Law*, ed. David H. Flaherty (Chapel Hill, 1969); Edmund S. Morgan, *The Puritan Family: Religion and Domestic Relations in Seventeenth-Century New England* (1944; reprint New York, 1966).

8. See Morgan, *The Puritan Family*, pp. 81–82.

9. Barnes, *The Book of the General Lawes*, pp. 17–18. Although historians have generally assumed that one-third of the personal estate was for the widow's own disposing, it is not clear to what extent this was actually the case in Massachusetts over the course of the seventeenth century.

10. Since only a small proportion of men left wills during the colonial period, intestacy law played a significant role in determining inheritance practices. See Salmon, *Women and the Law of Property*, p. 141.

11. Barnes, *The Book of the General Lawes*, p. 53.

12. Young women officially came of age in New England when they reached 18; young men when they reached 21.

13. William Blackstone, *Commentaries on the Laws of England*, 4 vols. (Oxford, 1765–69), 1:433.

14. Once widowed, a woman who inherited land from her father (or who had bought land with her husband in both of their names) could make a will of her own, as could a single woman who came into possession of land. Although these were significant property rights for women, in New England few women were in a position to claim them. See Salmon, *Women and the Law of Property*, pp. 144–45 and passim.

15. Evidence suggests that in seventeenth-century New England, daughters of fathers who died relatively young (and possibly most sons) did not normally come into their inheritances until they married. If daughters had received their shares when they came of age, we would expect to find probate records for single women who died before they had

the opportunity to marry. Though there are many existing intestate records and wills for single men who died in early adulthood, I have located only one record involving a young, single woman.

16. Wethersfield Land Records (manuscript volume, Town Clerk's Office, Town Hall, Wethersfield, Conn.) 1:19, 38.

17. Given the ages of her children, Katherine Harrison had to have been between her late twenties and her mid-fifties when she was first accused of witchcraft in 1668. I suspect that she was in her forties.

18. See Wethersfield Land Records 2:149; Katherine Harrison to John Winthrop, Jr., undated letter (probably early 1667), and Katherine Harrison's Testimony, undated document (probably October 1669), in the Winthrop Papers, Massachusetts Historical Society, Boston (hereafter cited as Winthrop Papers); and Gilbert Collection, Wethersfield Historical Society Archives, Wethersfield, Conn. (hereafter cited as Gilbert Collection).

19. Samuel Wyllys Papers: Depositions on Cases of Witchcraft, Assault, Theft, Drunkenness and Other Crimes, Tried in Connecticut, 1663–1728 (manuscript volume, Archives, History and Genealogy Unit, Connecticut State Library, Hartford, doc. 15) (hereafter cited as Wyllys Papers).

20. See Sherman W. Adams and Henry R. Stiles, *The History of Ancient Wethersfield*, 2 vols. (New York, 1904), 1:682; and Lacy, "Conn. Assistants Records," p. 12.

21. Lacy, "Conn. Assistants Records," p. 13.

22. Petition for the Investigation of Katherine Harrison, Recently Released after Imprisonment, Signed by John Chester and Thirty-Eight Other Citizens of Wethersfield (Manuscript Collections, Connecticut Historical Society, Hartford [hereafter cited as Petition for the Investigation of Katherine Harrison]) (emphasis mine). See also Order about Katherine Harrison's Land, in the Winthrop Papers; Records of the Colony of Connecticut, Connecticut Colonial Probate Records, County Court, vol. 56, 1663–77 (Archives, History and Genealogy Unit, Connecticut State Library, Hartford, 56:79–81 (hereafter cited as Connecticut Colonial Probate Records); *The Public Records of the Colony of Connecticut*, 15 vols., ed. J. H. Trumbull and Charles J. Hoadly (Hartford, 1850–1890) [hereafter cited as *Conn. Records*], 2:118.

23. Lacy, "Conn. Assistants Records," pp. 13–14, 18–19.

24. "The Answers of Some Ministers to the Questions Propounded to Them by the Honored Magistrates," dated 20 October 1669, Samuel Wyllys Papers, Supplement: Depositions on Cases of Witchcraft Tried in Connecticut, 1662–1693, photostat copies of original documents from the Wyllys Papers, Annmary Brown Memorial, Brown University Library, Providence, R.I. (manuscript volume, Archives, History and Genealogy Unit, Connecticut State Library, Hartford, Conn.), p. 18 (hereafter cited as Wyllys Papers Supplement).

25. Lacy, "Conn. Assistants Records," p. 23. See also *Conn. Records* 2:132.

26. Wyllys Papers Supplement, p. 11.

27. Depositions submitted against Harrison in 1668 and 1669 are in the Wyllys Papers, docs. 6–17; Wyllys Papers Supplement, pp. 46–63. . . . For Harrison's response to these accusations, see Katherine Harrison's Testimony, Winthrop Papers.

28. Manwaring, *Conn. Probate Records* 1:206.

29. "A Complaint of Severall Greevances of the Widdow Harrison's," Wyllys Papers Supplement, p. 53.

30. "The Declaration of Katherine Harrison in Her Appeal to This Court of Assistants," dated September 1668, in Connecticut Archives, Crimes and Misdemeanors, 1st ser. (1662–1789) (manuscript volume, Archives, History and Genealogy Unit, Connecticut State Library, Hartford), vol. 1 (pt. 1):34 (hereafter cited as Crimes and Misdemeanors).

31. Connecticut Colonial Probate Records 56:80.

32. Ibid., pp. 78–79. For the Griswolds as accusers, see Katherine Harrison's Testimony, Winthrop Papers.

33. Connecticut Colonial Probate Records 56:80.

34. "The Declaration of Katherine Harrison," Crimes and Misdemeanors, 1 (pt. 1):34.

35. Manwaring, *Connecticut Probate Records*, p. 206.

36. Katherine Harrison to John Winthrop, Jr., "Letter," Winthrop Papers.

37. Wethersfield Land Records 2:149.

38. Petition for the Investigation of Katherine Harrison.

39. See "The Cases of Hall and Harrison," in *Narratives of the Witchcraft Cases, 1648–1706*, ed. Charles Lincoln Burr (New York, 1914), pp. 48–49.

40. Ibid., pp. 48–52.

41. See Samuel D. Drake, *Annals of Witchcraft in New England* (New York, 1869), pp. 133–34.

42. Connecticut Colonial Probate Records 56:118; Wethersfield Land Records 2:249.

43. Wethersfield Land Records 2:210.

44. See Gilbert Collection.

45. See Joseph Merrill, *History of Amesbury, Including the First Seventeen Years of Salisbury, to the Separation of 1654; and Merrimac, From Its Incorporation in 1876* (Haverhill, Mass., 1880), pp. 11–13, 28; *Vital Records of Salisbury, Massachusetts, to the End of the Year 1849* (Topsfield, Mass., 1915), pp. 151, 415.

46. *Essex Probate Records* 2:125–27.

47. James Savage, *A Genealogical Dictionary of the First Settlers of New England*, 4 vols. (Boston, 1860–62), 1:138; 4:483.

48. See *Essex Court Records* 4:129, 133.

49. *Essex Court Records* 4:184, 187, 239.

50. *Essex Probate Records* 2:223–24.

51. See *Records of the Governor and Company of the Massachusetts Bay in New England*, 6 vols., ed. Nathaniel B. Shurtleff (Boston, 1853–54), 5:6, 26–27.

52. Savage, *Genealogical Dictionary* 2:566. . . . When he died, George Martin left an estate valued at £75, most of which he left to Susanna "during her Widowhood."

53. See *Witchcraft Papers* 2:549–79.

54. Cotton Mather, *The Wonders of the Invisible World* (1693; facsimile of the 1862 London edition, Ann Arbor, Mich., 1974), p. 148.

55. *Witchcraft Papers* 2:551.

56. *Witchcraft Papers* 1:115–29.

57. Ann Hibbens' will is reprinted in *New England Historical and Genealogical Register,* vol. 6 (1852), pp. 287–88.

58. See *Witchcraft Papers* 3:880–81.

59. *Essex Probate Records* 3:191–93.

60. *Essex Court Records* 7:238.

61. *New England Historical and Genealogical Register,* vol. 3 (1849), p. 129.

62. Marion L. Starkey, *The Devil in Massachusetts* (New York, 1949), p. 185.

63. *Witchcraft Papers* 3:988–91.

64. For Martha and Giles Corey and Alice Parker, see *Witchcraft Papers* 1:239–66; 2:623–28, 632–33; 3:985–86, 1018–19.

65. Manwaring, *Conn. Probate Records* 1:7–8.

66. *Records of the Particular Court of Connecticut, 1639–1663, Collections of the Connecticut Historical Society,* vol. 22 (1928), p. 119.

67. Ibid., p. 258.

68. Manwaring, *Conn. Probate Records* 1:121–22.

69. Norfolk Deeds (manuscript volume, Registry of Deeds, Essex County Courthouse, Salem, Mass.), 1:116, 154.

70. *Essex Probate Records* 1:314–16; 2:160; *Essex Court Records* 1:199, 204, 229; 2:213; 3:292, 342, 413.

DOCUMENTS: *Service and Servitude*

"According to the condition of the mother . . ."

Slavery and the slave trade to the Americas had long been established by the Spanish and the Dutch when Virginians bought their first African slaves in 1619. In an era in which white working people often sold their labor for a term of years, African workers seem at first to have been treated not very differently from white indentured servants. But by the 1640s, Africans were increasingly treated as property. Although white women servants were not generally required to do field labor, slave women were. Slave children, denied all education, were also forced to work earlier than their white counterparts. By the 1660s, slavery was clearly established in Virginia law, and subsequently masters were given great latitude in their dealings with slaves. A law of 1669, for example, exonerated masters who killed rebellious slaves while administering "correction" on the grounds that no master would *intentionally* destroy his own property.

All slaves were their masters' property, subject to the domination of white male heads of households who controlled their work, their diet, their living conditions, and their punishments. Slave women were additionally vulnerable; they had no defense against violation or rape.

How to interpret the status of children whose fathers were white and whose mothers were black? Might they make a claim for free status or support from their free parent? Could white fathers be obliged to take responsibility for such children? In Spanish colonies in South America, a complex system of godparenting made it possible for white fathers to maintain a wide variety of relationships with their mixed-blood children.

The Virginia Law of 1662 established a different set of rules for the English colony; Maryland passed a similar statute two years later. How does the 1662 law challenge traditional English inheritance practices? What do the two sections of the law reveal about how Virginia legislators wished to shape interracial sexual relations? What are the implications of the law for children whose fathers were free black men and whose mothers were enslaved?

WHEREAS some doubts have arrisen whether children got by any Englishman upon a negro woman should be slave or free, *Be it therefore enacted and declared by this present grand assembly,* that all children borne in this country shalbe held bond or free only according to the condition of the mother, *And* that if any chris-tian shall committ fornication with a negro man or woman hee or shee soe offending shall pay double the [usual] fines. . . .*

*NOTE: The usual fine for fornication was 500 pounds of tobacco.

Laws of Virginia, Act XII, December 1662, in William Waller Hening, *The Statutes at Large: Being a Collection of All the Laws of Virginia, from the First Session of the Legislature, in the Year 1619,* 13 vols. (New York: R & W & G Bartow, 1823), 2:170.

"For prevention of that abominable mixture . . ."

The system of slavery relied heavily on marking differences of status (slave or free)—by visible bodily difference (black or white). Free blacks and enslaved mulattoes undermined the simplicity of these signals, displaying in their very beings the fact that it was power, not nature, that placed any particular individual in one status or another. By the late seventeenth century, Virginia and Maryland attempted to punish interracial sexual relations, even among free men and women. What relationships does the Virginia law of 1691 make illegal? What does it prescribe for interracial children? Why did the legislators think the law would be self-enforcing? A restatement of the statute in 1705 also punished ministers for officiating at interracial marriages.

[1691] . . . for prevention of that abominable mixture and spurious issue which hereafter may encrease in this dominion, as well by negroes, mulattoes, and Indians intermarrying with English, or other white women, as by their unlawfull accompanying with one another, *Be it enacted* . . . that . . . whatsoever English or other white man or woman being free shall intermarry with a negroe, mulatto or Indian man or woman bond or free shall within three months after such marriage be banished and removed from this dominion forever. . . .

And be it further enacted . . . That if any English woman being free shall have a bastard child by any negro or mulatto, she pay the sume of fifteen pounds sterling, within one moneth after such bastard child shall be born, to the Church wardens of the parish . . . and in default of such payment she shall be taken into the possession of the said Church wardens and disposed of for five yeares, and the said fine of fifteen pounds, or whatever the woman shall be disposed of for, shall be paid, one third part to their majesties . . . and one other third part to the use of the parish . . . and the other third part to the informer, and that such bastard child be bound out as a servant by the said Church wardens untill he or she shall attaine the age of thirty yeares, and in case such English woman that shall have such bastard child be a servant, she shall be sold by the said church wardens, (after her time is expired that she ought by law to serve her master) for five yeares, and the money she shall be sold for divided as is before appointed, and the child to serve as aforesaid.

[1705] *And be it further enacted*, That no minister of the church of England, or other minister, or person whatsoever, within this colony and dominion, shall hereafter wittingly presume to marry a white man with a negro or mulatto woman; or to marry a white woman with a negro or mulatto man, upon pain of forfeiting or paying, for every such marriage the sum of ten thousand pounds of tobacco; one half to our sovereign lady the Queen . . . and the other half to the informer. . . .

Assembly of Virginia, Act XVI, April 1691, in William Waller Henning, *The Statutes at Large: Being a Collection of All the Laws of Virginia, from the First Session of the Legislature, in the Year 1619*, 13 vols. (New York: 1823), vol. 3, pp. 86–87; and Assembly of Virginia, Chap. XLIX, Sec. XX, October 1705 in Henning, vol. 3, p. 453.

Elizabeth Sprigs, "The deplorable Condition your poor Betty endures . . ."

British America was "the land of the . . . unfree," observes historian Philip Morgan. Some 90 percent of the nearly three million persons who arrived in the mainland and island colonies in the seventeenth and eighteenth centuries were unfree laborers. Many of these people were slaves, but approximately 500,000 were indentured—contracted to service for a set number of years.* Relatively few became apprentices, with the expectation of learning a trade; many had signed contracts with ship captains in return for passage to America. The captain, in turn, could sell the contracts; the servants would be set to labor for a period of years to any work their master chose.

We know virtually nothing about Elizabeth Sprigs, whose cry of distress is printed below. She seems to have fled the home of her father, a tinsmith in London; she may have labored in the household of Richard Crosses in or near Baltimore.

Honred Father   Maryland Sept'r 22'd 1756. My being for ever banished from your sight, will I hope pardon the Boldness I now take of troubling you with these, my long silence has been purely owing to my undutifullness to you, and well knowing I had offended in the highest Degree, put a tie to my tongue and pen, for fear I should be extinct from your good Graces and add a further Trouble to you, but too well knowing your care and tenderness for me so long as I retain my Duty to you, induced me once again to endeavour if possible, to kindle up that flame again. O Dear Father, belive what I am going to relate the words of truth and sincerity, and Ballance my former bad Conduct [to] my sufferings here, and then I am sure you'll pitty your Destress [ed] Daughter, What we unfortunat English People suffer here is beyond the probability of you in England to Conceive, let it suffice that I one of the unhappy Number, am toiling almost Day and Night, and very often in the Horses drug-gery, with only this comfort that you Bitch you do not halfe enough, and then tied up and whipp'd to that Degree that you'd not serve an Annimal, scarce any thing but Indian Corn and Salt to eat and that even begrudged nay many Neagroes are better used, almost naked no shoes nor stockings to wear, and the comfort after slaving dureing Masters pleasure, what rest we can get is to rap ourselves up in a Blanket and ly upon the Ground, this is the deplorable Condition your poor Betty endures, and now I beg if you have any Bowels of Compassion left show it by sending me some Relief, Clothing is the principal thing wanting, which if you should condiscend to, may easely send them to me by any of the ships bound to Baltimore Town Patapsco River Maryland, and give me leave to conclude in Duty to you and Uncles and Aunts, and Respect to all Friends
Honred Father
Your undutifull and Disobedient Child
Elizabeth Sprigs

---

*Philip Morgan, "Bound Labor: The British and Dutch Colonies," in *Encyclopedia of the North American Colonies,* ed. Jacob Ernest Cooke, 3 vols. (New York, 1993), 2:17–32.

Elizabeth Sprigs to John Sprigs, in White Cross Street near Cripple Gate, London. Public Record Office, London, High Court of Admiralty, 301, 258, no. 106, printed in Isabel M. Calder, ed., *Colonial Captivities, Marches and Journeys* (New York: Macmillan, 1935), pp. 151–52.

CORNELIA HUGHES DAYTON
Taking the Trade: Abortion and Gender Relations in an Eighteenth-Century New England Village

Some pregnancies end spontaneously, probably because of an abnormality in the fetus or in the way it is implanted in the womb. Colonial Americans made little distinction between spontaneous and induced abortion; no law attempted to regulate the practice. Efforts to end pregnancies by the use of herbs like savin were generally understood to be efforts to "restore" the regular menstrual cycle.

In the course of the eighteenth century, male physicians were increasingly involved with midwifery, a practice that had been monopolized by women. Men were also more likely than women midwives to use instruments; indeed only men were trained in the use of the first forceps. In the following essay, Cornelia Hughes Dayton carefully reconstructs the narrative of the abortion and death of Sarah Grosvenor in a Connecticut village in 1742. How does Dayton interpret the meaning of abortion for Sarah Grosvenor and her friends? If it was not illegal, why did they seek to keep it secret? In what ways does Dayton think that relations between young women and young men changed in the mid-eighteenth century? In what ways does Dayton think that relations between young people and their parents changed? How was the memory of Sarah Grosvenor's death transmitted in the histories of the town?

In 1742 in the village of Pomfret, perched in the hills of northeastern Connecticut, nineteen-year-old Sarah Grosvenor and twenty-seven-year-old Amasa Sessions became involved in a liaison that led to pregnancy, abortion, and death. Both were from prominent yeoman families, and neither a marriage between them nor an arrangement for the support of their illegitimate child would have been an unusual event for mid-eighteenth-century New England. Amasa Sessions chose a different course; in consultation with John Hallowell, a self-proclaimed "practitioner of physick," he coerced his lover into taking an abortifacient. Within two months, Sarah fell ill. Unbeknownst to all but Amasa, Sarah, Sarah's sister Zerviah, and her cousin Hannah, Hallowell made an attempt to "Remove her Conseption" by a "manual opperation." Two days later Sarah miscarried, and her two young relatives secretly buried the fetus in the woods. Over the next month, Sarah struggled against a "Malignant fever" and was attended by several physicians, but on September 14, 1742, she died.[1]

Most accounts of induced abortions among seventeenth- and eighteenth-century whites in the Old and New Worlds consist of only a few lines in a private letter or court record book; these typically refer to the taking of savin or pennyroyal—two common herbal abortifacients. While men and women in diverse cultures have known how to perform abortions by inserting an instrument into the uterus, actual descriptions of such operations are extremely rare for any time period. Few accounts of abortions by instrument have yet been uncovered for early modern England, and I know of no other for colonial North America.[2] Thus the historical fragments recording events in a small New England town in 1742 take on

Excerpted from "Taking the Trade: Abortion and Gender Relations in an Eighteenth-Century New England Village" by Cornelia Hughes Dayton in *William and Mary Quarterly*, 3rd Ser., 48 (1991):19–49.

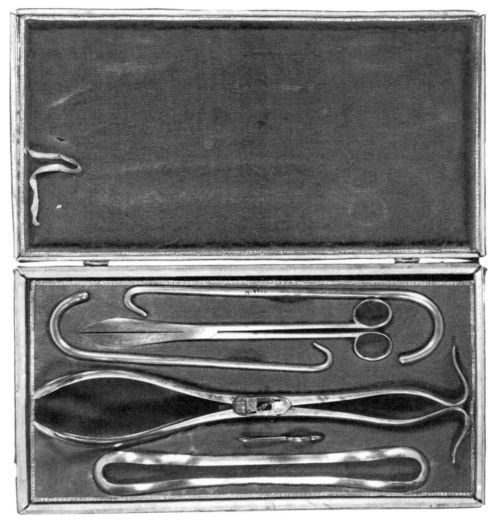

Obstetrical Instruments Case, ca. 1780.
The case includes forceps, a double lever, two double blunt hooks, and a perforator. Perhaps no technological invention in traditional America had more direct connection to women's lives than these. Hooks were used to dismember and remove a fetus that had died during delivery. Skillfully employed, forceps could be lifesaving. Professional training in the use of instruments was monopolized by male physicians, to whom the middle class turned in the late eighteenth and early nineteenth centuries. Advances in medical technology were accompanied by the exclusion of midwives from advanced training and, increasingly, from the birthing room itself. (Division of Medical Sciences, National Museum of American History, Smithsonian Institution)

an unusual power to illustrate how an abortion was conducted, how it was talked about, and how it was punished.

We know about the Grosvenor-Sessions case because in 1745 two prominent Windham County magistrates opened an investigation into Sarah's death. Why there was a three-year gap between that event and legal proceedings, and why justices from outside Pomfret initiated the legal process, remain a mystery. In November 1745 the investigating magistrates offered their preliminary opinion that Hallowell,

Amasa Sessions, Zerviah Grosvenor, and Hannah Grosvenor were guilty of Sarah's murder, the last three as accessories. From the outset, Connecticut legal officials concentrated not on the act of abortion per se, but on the fact that an abortion attempt had led to a young woman's death.[3]

The case went next to Joseph Fowler, king's attorney for Windham County. He dropped charges against the two Grosvenor women, probably because he needed them as key witnesses and because they had played cover-up roles rather than originating the scheme. A year and a half passed as Fowler's first attempts to get convictions against Hallowell and Sessions failed either before grand juries or before the Superior Court on technical grounds. Finally, in March 1747, Fowler presented Hallowell and Sessions separately for the "highhanded Misdemeanour" of attempting to destroy both Sarah Grosvenor's health and "the fruit of her womb."[4] A grand jury endorsed the bill against Hallowell but rejected a similarly worded presentment against Sessions. At Hallowell's trial before the Superior Court in Windham, the jury brought in a guilty verdict and the chief judge sentenced the physician to twenty-nine lashes and two hours of public humiliation standing at the town gallows. Before the sentence could be executed, Hallowell managed to break jail. He fled to Rhode Island; as far as records indicate, he never returned to Connecticut. Thus, in the end, both Amasa Sessions and John Hallowell escaped legal punishment for their actions, whereas Sarah Grosvenor paid for her sexual transgression with her life.

Nearly two years of hearings and trials before the Superior Court produced a file of ten depositions and twenty-four other legal documents. This cache of papers is extraordinarily rich, not alone for its unusual chronicle of an abortion attempt, but for its illumination of the fault lines in Pomfret dividing parents from grown children, men from women, and mid-eighteenth-century colonial culture from its seventeenth-century counterpart.

The depositions reveal that in 1742 the elders of Pomfret, men and women alike, failed to act as vigilant monitors of Sarah Grosvenor's courtship and illness. Instead, young, married householders—kin of Sarah and Amasa—pledged themselves in a conspiracy of silence to allow the abortion plot to unfold undetected. The one person who had the opportunity to

play middleman between the generations was Hallowell. A man in his forties, dogged by a shady past and yet adept at acquiring respectable connections, Hallowell provides an intriguing and rare portrait of a socially ambitious, rural medical practitioner. By siding with the young people of Pomfret and keeping their secret, Hallowell betrayed his peers and elders and thereby opened himself to severe censure and expulsion from the community.

Beyond depicting generational conflict, the Grosvenor-Sessions case dramatically highlights key changes in gender relations that reverberated through New England society in the eighteenth century. One of these changes involved the emergence of a marked sexual double standard. In the mid-seventeenth century, a young man like Amasa Sessions would have been pressured by parents, friends, or the courts to marry his lover. Had he resisted, he would most likely have been whipped or fined for the crime of fornication. By the late seventeenth century, New England judges gave up on enjoining sexually active couples to marry. In the 1740s, amid shifting standards of sexual behavior and growing concern over the evidentiary impossibility of establishing paternity, prosecutions of young men for premarital sex ceased. Thus fornication was decriminalized for men, but not for women. Many of Sarah Grosvenor's female peers continued to be prosecuted and fined for bearing illegitimate children. Through private arrangements, and occasionally through civil lawsuits, their male partners were sometimes cajoled or coerced into contributing to the child's upkeep.[5]

What is most striking about the Grosvenor-Sessions case is that an entire community apparently forgave Sessions for the extreme measures he took to avoid accountability for his bastard child. Although he initiated the actions that led to his lover's death, all charges against him were dropped. Moreover, the tragedy did not spur Sessions to leave town; instead, he spent the rest of his life in Pomfret as a respected citizen. Even more dramatically than excusing young men from the crime of fornication, the treatment of Amasa Sessions confirmed that the sexually irresponsible activities of men in their youth would not be held against them as they reached for repute and prosperity in their prime.

The documents allow us to listen in on the quite different responses of young men and women to the drama unfolding in Pomfret.

Sarah Grosvenor's female kin and friends, as we shall see, became preoccupied with their guilt and with the inevitability of God's vengeance. Her male kin, on the other hand, reacted cautiously and legalistically, ferreting out information in order to assess how best to protect the Grosvenor family name. The contrast reminds us yet again of the complex and gendered ways in which we must rethink conventional interpretations of secularization in colonial New England.

Finally, the Grosvenor case raises more questions than it answers about New Englanders' access to and attitudes toward abortion. If Sarah had not died after miscarriage, it is doubtful that any word of Sessions's providing her with an abortifacient or Hallowell's operation would have survived into the twentieth century. Because it nearly went unrecorded and because it reveals that many Pomfret residents were familiar with the idea of abortion, the case supports historians' assumptions that abortion attempts were far from rare in colonial America.[6] We can also infer from the case that the most dangerous abortions before 1800 may have been those instigated by men and performed by surgeons with instruments.[7] But both abortion's frequency and the lineaments of its social context remain obscure. . . .

Perhaps the most intriguing question centers on why women and men in early America acted *covertly* to effect abortions when abortion before quickening was legal. The Grosvenor case highlights the answer that applies to most known incidents from the period: abortion was understood as blameworthy because it was an extreme action designed to hide a prior sin, sex outside of marriage.[8] Reading the depositions, it is nearly impossible to disentangle the players' attitudes toward abortion itself from their expressions of censure or anxiety over failed courtship, illegitimacy, and the dangers posed for a young woman by a secret abortion. Strikingly absent from these eighteenth-century documents, however, is either outrage over the destruction of a fetus or denunciations of those who would arrest "nature's proper course." Those absences are a telling measure of how the discourse about abortion would change dramatically in later centuries.

THE NARRATIVE

Before delving into the response of the Pomfret community to Sarah Grosvenor's abortion and death, we need to know just who participated in the conspiracy to cover up her pregnancy and how they managed it. . . .

The chronicle opens in late July 1742 when Zerviah Grosvenor, aged twenty-one, finally prevailed upon her younger sister to admit that she was pregnant. In tears, Sarah explained that she had not told Zerviah sooner because "she had been taking [the] trade to remove it."[9] "Trade" was used in this period to signify stuff or goods, often in the deprecatory sense of rubbish and trash. The *Oxford English Dictionary* confirms that in some parts of England and New England the word was used to refer to medicine. In Pomfret trade meant a particular type of medicine, an abortifacient, thus a substance that might be regarded as "bad" medicine, as rubbish, unsafe and associated with destruction. What is notable is that Sarah and Zerviah, and neighboring young people who also used the word, had no need to explain to one another the meaning of "taking the trade." Perhaps only a few New Englanders knew how to prepare an abortifacient or knew of books that would give them recipes, but many more, especially young women who lived with the fear of becoming pregnant before marriage, were familiar with at least the *idea* of taking an abortifacient.

Sarah probably began taking the trade in mid-May when she was already three-and-a-half-months pregnant.[10] It was brought to her in the form of a powder by Amasa.[11] Sarah understood clearly that her lover had obtained the concoction "from docter hollowel," who conveyed "directions" for her doses through Amasa. Zerviah deposed later that Sarah had been "loath to Take" the drug and "Thot it an Evil," probably because at three and a half months she anticipated quickening, the time from which she knew the law counted abortion an "unlawful measure."[12] At the outset, Sarah argued in vain with Amasa against his proposed "Method." Later, during June and July, she sometimes "neglected" to take the doses he left for her, but, with mounting urgency, Amasa and the doctor pressed her to comply. "It was necessary," Amasa explained in late July, that she take "more, or [else] they were afraid She would be greatly hurt by what was already done." To calm her worries, he assured her that "there was no life [left] in the Child" and that the potion "would not hurt her." Apparently, the men hoped that a few more doses would provoke a miscarriage, thereby expelling the dead fetus and restoring Sarah's body to its natural balance of humors.

Presumably, Hallowell decided to operate in early August because Sarah's pregnancy was increasingly visible, and he guessed that she was not going to miscarry. An operation in which the fetus would be removed or punctured was now the only certain way to terminate the pregnancy secretly.[13] To avoid the scrutiny of Sarah's parents, Hallowell resorted to a plan he had used once before in arranging a private examination of Sarah. Early one afternoon he arrived at the house of John Grosvenor and begged for a room as "he was weary and wanted Rest." John, Sarah's thirty-one-year-old first cousin, lived with his wife, Hannah, and their young children in a homestead only a short walk down the hill but out of sight of Sarah's father's house. While John and Hannah were busy, the physician sent one of the little children to fetch Sarah.

The narrative of Sarah's fateful meeting with Hallowell that August afternoon is best told in the words of one of the deponents. Abigail Nightingale had married and moved to Pomfret two years earlier, and by 1742 she had become Sarah's close friend. Several weeks after the operation, Sarah attempted to relieve her own "Distress of mind" by confiding the details of her shocking experience to Abigail. Unconnected to the Grosvenor or Sessions families by kinship, and without any other apparent stake in the legal uses of her testimony, Abigail can probably be trusted as a fairly accurate paraphraser of Sarah's words.[14] If so, we have here an unparalleled eyewitness account of an eighteenth-century abortion attempt.

This is how Abigail recollected Sarah's deathbed story:

On [Sarah's] going down [to her cousin John's], [Hallowell] said he wanted to Speake with her alone; and then they two went into a Room together; and then sd. Hallowell told her it was necessary that something more should be done or else she would Certainly die; to which she replyed that she was afraid they had done too much already, and then he told her that there was one thing more that could easily be done, and she asking him what it was; he said he could easily deliver her. but she said she was afraid there was life in the Child, then he asked her how long she had felt it; and she replyed about a fortnight; then he said that was impossible or could not be or ever would; for that the trade she had taken had or would prevent it; and that the alteration she felt Was owing to what she had taken. And he

farther told her that he verily thought that the Child grew to her body to the Bigness of his hand, or else it would have Come away before that time. and that it would never Come away, but Certainly Kill her, unless other Means were used.[15] On which she yielded to his making an Attempt to take it away; charging him that if he could percieve that there was life in it he would not proceed on any Account. And then the Doctor openning his portmantua took an Instrument out of it and Laid it on the Bed, and she asking him what it was for, he replyed that it was to make way; and that then he tryed to remove the Child for Some time in vain putting her to the Utmost Distress, and that at Last she observed he trembled and immediately perceived a Strange alteration in her body and thought a bone of the Child was broken; on which she desired him (as she said) to Call in some body, for that she feared she was a dying, and instantly swooned away.

With Sarah's faint, Abigail's account broke off, but within minutes others, who would testify later, stepped into the room. Hallowell reacted to Sarah's swoon by unfastening the door and calling in Hannah, the young mistress of the house, and Zerviah, who had followed her sister there. Cold water and "a bottle of drops" were brought to keep Sarah from fainting again, while Hallowell explained to the "much Surprized" women that "he had been making an Attempt" to deliver Sarah. Despite their protests, he then "used a further force upon her" but did not succeed in "Tak[ing] the Child . . . away." Some days later Hallowell told a Pomfret man that in this effort "to distroy hir conception" he had "either knipt or Squeisd the head of the Conception." At the time of the attempt, Hallowell explained to the women that he "had done so much to her, as would Cause the Birth of the Child in a Little time." Just before sunset, he packed up his portmanteau and went to a nearby tavern, where Amasa was waiting "to hear [the outcome of] the event." Meanwhile, Sarah, weak-kneed and in pain, leaned on the arm of her sister as the young women managed to make their way home in the twilight.

After his attempted "force," Hallowell fades from the scene, while Zerviah and Hannah Grosvenor become the key figures. About two days after enduring the operation, Sarah began to experience contractions. Zerviah ran to get Hannah, telling her "she Tho't . . . Sarah would be quickly delivered." They returned to find Sarah, who was alone "in her Father's Chamber," just delivered and rising from the chamber pot. In the pot was "an Untimely birth"—a "Child [that] did not Appear to have any Life In it." To Hannah, it "Seemed by The Scent . . . That it had been hurt and was decaying," while Zerviah later remembered it as "a perfect Child," even "a pritty child." Determined to keep the event "as private as they Could," the two women helped Sarah back to bed, and then "wr[ap]ed . . . up" the fetus, carried it to the woods on the edge of the farmstead, and there "Buried it in the Bushes."

. . . [A]bout ten days after the miscarriage, Sarah grew feverish and weak. Her parents consulted two college-educated physicians who hailed from outside the Pomfret area. Their visits did little good, nor were Sarah's symptoms—fever, delirium, convulsions—relieved by a visit from Hallowell, whom Amasa "fetcht" to Sarah's bedside. In the end, Hallowell, who had decided to move from nearby Killingly to more distant Providence, washed his hands of the case. A few days before Sarah died, her cousin John "went after" Hallowell, whether to bring him back or to express his rage, we do not know. Hallowell predicted "that She woul[d] not live."

Silence seems to have settled on the Grosvenor house and its neighborhood after Sarah's death on September 14. It was two and a half years later that rumors about a murderous abortion spread through and beyond Pomfret village, prompting legal investigation. The silence, the gap between event and prosecution, the passivity of Sarah's parents—all lend mystery to the narrative. But despite its ellipses, the Grosvenor case provides us with an unusual set of details about one young couple's extreme response to the common problem of failed courtship and illegitimacy. To gain insight into both the mysteries and the extremities of the Grosvenor-Sessions case, we need to look more closely at Pomfret, at the two families centrally involved, and at clues to the motivations of the principal participants. Our abortion tale, it turns out, holds beneath its surface a complex trail of evidence about generational conflict and troubled relations between men and women.

THE POMFRET PLAYERS

In 1742 the town of Pomfret had been settled for just over forty years. Within its central neighborhood and in homesteads scattered over rugged, wooded hillsides lived probably no more than 270 men, women, and children.[16] During the founding decades, the fathers of Sarah and Amasa ranked among the ten leading householders; Leicester Grosvenor and Nathaniel Sessions were chosen often to fill important local offices.

Grosvenor, the older of the two by seven years, had inherited standing and a choice farmstead from his father, one of the original six purchasers of the Pomfret territory. When the town was incorporated in 1714, he was elected a militia officer and one of the first selectmen. He was returned to the latter post nineteen times and eventually rose to the highest elective position—that of captain—in the local trainband. Concurrently, he was appointed many times throughout the 1710s and 1720s to ad hoc town committees, often alongside Nathaniel Sessions. But unlike Sessions, Grosvenor went on to serve at the colony level. Pomfret freemen chose him to represent them at ten General Assembly sessions between 1726 and 1744. Finally, in the 1730s, when he was in his late fifties, the legislature appointed him a justice of the peace for Windham County. Thus, until his retirement in 1748 at age seventy-four, his house would have served as the venue for petty trials, hearings, and recordings of documents. After retiring from public office, Grosvenor lived another eleven years, leaving behind in 1759 an estate worth over £600.[17]

Nathaniel Sessions managed a sizable farm and ran one of Pomfret's taverns at the family homestead. Town meetings were sometimes held there. Sessions was chosen constable in 1714 and rose from ensign to lieutenant in the militia—always a step behind Leicester Grosvenor. He could take pride in one exceptional distinction redounding to the family honor: in 1737 his son Darius became only the second Pomfret resident to graduate from Yale College, and before Sessions died at ninety-one he saw Darius elected assistant and then deputy governor of Rhode Island.[18]

The records are silent as to whether Sessions and his family resented the Grosvenors, who must have been perceived in town as more prominent, or whether the two families . . . enjoyed a close relationship that went sour for some reason *before* the affair between Sarah and Amasa. Instead, the signs (such as the cooperative public work of the two fathers, the visits back and forth between the Grosvenor and Sessions girls) point to a long-standing friendship and dense web of interchanges between the families. Indeed, courtship and marriage between a Sessions son and a Grosvenor daughter would hardly have been surprising.

What went wrong in the affair between Sarah and Amasa is not clear. Sarah's sisters and cousins knew that "Amasy" "made Sute to" Sarah, and they gave no indication of disapproving. The few who guessed at Sarah's condition in the summer of 1742 were not so much surprised that she was pregnant as that the couple "did not marry." It was evidently routine in this New England village, as in others, for courting couples to post banns for their nuptials soon after the woman discovered that she was pregnant.

Amasa offered different answers among his Pomfret peers to explain his failure to marry his lover. When Zerviah Grosvenor told Amasa that he and Sarah "had better Marry," he responded, "That would not do," for "he was afraid of his parents . . . [who would] always make their lives [at home] uncomfortable." Later, Abigail Nightingale heard rumors that Amasa was resorting to the standard excuse of men wishing to avoid a shotgun marriage—denying that the child was his.[19] Hallowell, with whom Amasa may have been honest, claimed "the Reason that they did not marry" was "that Sessions Did not Love her well a nough for [he] saith he did not believe it was his son and if he Could Cause her to gitt Red of it he would not Go near her again." Showing yet another face to a Grosvenor kinsman after Sarah's death, Amasa repented his actions and extravagantly claimed he would "give All he had" to "bring Sarah . . . To life again . . . and have her as his wife."

The unusual feature of Amasa's behavior was not his unwillingness to marry Sarah, but his determination to terminate her pregnancy before it showed. Increasing numbers of young men in eighteenth-century New England weathered the temporary obloquy of abandoning a pregnant lover in order to prolong their bachelorhood or marry someone else. What drove Amasa, and an ostensibly reluctant Sarah, to resort to abortion? Was it fear of their fathers? Nathaniel Sessions had chosen Amasa as the son who would remain on the family farm and care for his parents in their old age. An ill-timed marriage could have disrupted these plans and threatened Amasa's inheritance.[20] For his part, Leicester Grosvenor may have made it clear to his daughter that he

would be greatly displeased at her marrying before she reached a certain age or until her older sister wed. Rigid piety, an authoritarian nature, an intense concern with being seen as a good household governor—any of these traits in Leicester Grosvenor or Nathaniel Sessions could have colored Amasa's decisions.

Perhaps it was not family relations that proved the catalyst but Amasa's acquaintance with a medical man who boasted about a powder more effective than the herbal remedies that were part of women's lore. Hallowell himself had fathered an illegitimate child fifteen years earlier, and he may have encouraged a rakish attitude in Amasa, beguiling the younger man with the promise of dissociating sex from its possible consequences. Or the explanation may have been that classic one: another woman. Two years after Sarah's death, Amasa married Hannah Miller of Rehoboth, Massachusetts. Perhaps in early 1742 he was already making trips to the town just east of Providence to see his future wife.[21]

What should we make of Sarah's role in the scheme? It is possible that she no longer loved Amasa and was as eager as he to forestall external pressures toward a quick marriage. However, Zerviah swore that on one occasion before the operation Amasa reluctantly agreed to post banns for their nuptials and that Sarah did not object.[22] *If* Sarah was a willing and active participant in the abortion plot all along, then by 1745 her female kin and friends had fabricated and rehearsed a careful and seamless story to preserve the memory of the dead girl untarnished.

In the portrait drawn by her friends, Sarah reacted to her pregnancy and to Amasa's plan first by arguing and finally by doing her utmost to protect her lover. She may have wished to marry Amasa, yet she did not insist on it or bring in older family members to negotiate with him and his parents. Abigail Nightingale insisted that Sarah accepted Amasa's recalcitrance and only pleaded with him that they not "go on to add sin to sin." Privately, she urged Amasa that there was an alternative to taking the trade—a way that would enable him to keep his role hidden and prevent the couple from committing a "Last transgression [that] would be worse then the first." Sarah told him that "she was willing to take the sin and shame to her self, and to be obliged never to tell whose Child it was, and that she did not doubt but that if she humbled her self on her Knees to her Father he would take her and her Child home." Her lover, afraid that his identity would become known, vetoed her proposal.[23]

According to the Pomfret women's reconstruction, abortion was not a freely chosen and defiant act for Sarah. Against her own desires, she reluctantly consented in taking the trade only because Amasa "So very earnestly perswaided her." In fact, she had claimed to her friends that she was coerced; he "would take no denyal." Sarah's confidantes presented her as being aware of her options, shrinking from abortion as an unnatural and immoral deed, and yet finally choosing the strategy consistent with her lover's vision of what would best protect their futures. Thus, if Amasa's hubris was extreme, so too was Sarah's internalization of those strains of thought in her culture that taught women to make themselves pleasing and obedient to men.

While we cannot be sure that the deponents' picture of Sarah's initial recoil and reluctant submission to the abortion plot was entirely accurate, it is clear that once she was caught up in the plan she extracted a pledge of silence from all her confidantes. Near her death, before telling Abigail about the operation, she "insist[ed] on . . . [her friend's] never discovering the Matter" to anyone. Clearly, she had earlier bound Zerviah and Hannah on their honor not to tell their elders. Reluctant when faced with the abortionist's powder, Sarah became a leading co-conspirator when alone with her female friends.

One of the most remarkable aspects of the Grosvenor-Sessions case is Sarah and Amasa's success in keeping their parents in the dark, at least until her final illness. If by July Sarah's sisters grew suspicious that Sarah was "with child," what explains the failure of her parents to observe her pregnancy and to intervene and uncover the abortion scheme? Were they negligent, preoccupied with other matters, or willfully blind? . . .

In terms of who knew what, the events of summer 1742 in Pomfret apparently unfolded in two stages. The first stretched from Sarah's discovery of her pregnancy by early May to some point in late August after her miscarriage. In this period a determined, collective effort by Sarah and Amasa and their friends kept their elders in the dark.[24] When Sarah fell seriously ill from the aftereffects of the abortion attempt

and miscarriage, rumors of the young people's secret activities reached Leicester Grosvenor's neighbors and even one of the doctors he had called in. It is difficult to escape the conclusion that by Sarah's death in mid-September her father and stepmother had learned of the steps that had precipitated her mortal condition and kept silent for reasons of their own.

Except for Hallowell, the circle of intimates entrusted by Amasa and Sarah with their scheme consisted of young adults ranging in age from nineteen to thirty-three. Born between about 1710 and 1725, these young people had grown up just as the town attracted enough settlers to support a church, militia, and local market. They were second-generation Pomfret residents who shared the generational identity that came with sitting side by side through long worship services, attending school, playing, and working together at children's tasks. By 1740, these sisters, brothers, cousins, courting couples, and neighbors, in their visits from house to house—sometimes in their own households, sometimes at their parents'—had managed to create a world of talk and socializing that was largely exempt from parental supervision.[25] In Pomfret in 1742 it was this group of young people in their twenties and early thirties, *not* the cluster of Grosvenor matrons over forty-five, who monitored Sarah's courtship, attempted to get Amasa to marry his lover, privately investigated the activities and motives of Amasa and Hallowell, and, belatedly, spoke out publicly to help Connecticut juries decide who should be blamed for Sarah's death.

That Leicester Grosvenor made no public move to punish those around him and that he avoided giving testimony when legal proceedings commenced are intriguing clues to social changes underway in New England villages in the mid-eighteenth century. Local leaders like Grosvenor, along with the respectable yeomen whom he represented in public office, were increasingly withdrawing delicate family problems from the purview of their communities. Slander, illegitimacy, and feuds among neighbors came infrequently to local courts by midcentury, indicating male householders' growing preference for handling such matters privately.[26] Wealthy and ambitious families adopted this ethic of privacy at the same time that they became caught up in elaborating their material worlds by adding rooms and acquir-

ing luxury goods.[27] . . . But all the fine accoutre-
ments in the world would not excuse Justice
Grosvenor from his obligation to govern his
household effectively. Mortified no doubt at his
inability to monitor the young people in his extended family, he responded, ironically, by extending their conspiracy of silence. The best
way for him to shield the family name from
scandal and protect his political reputation in
the county and colony was to keep the story of
Sarah's abortion out of the courts.

THE DOCTOR

John Hallowell's status as an outsider in Pomfret and his dangerous, secret alliance with the
town's young adults may have shaped his destiny as the one conspirator sentenced to suffer
at the whipping post. Although the physician
had been involved in shady dealings before
1742, he had managed to win the trust of many
patients and a respectable social standing.
Tracking down his history . . . tells us something of the uncertainty surrounding personal
and professional identity before the advent of
police records and medical licensing boards. It
also gives us an all-too-rare glimpse into the
fashion in which an eighteenth-century country doctor tried to make his way in the world.

Hallowell's earliest brushes with the law
came in the 1720s. In 1725 he purchased land
in Killingly, a Connecticut town just north of
Pomfret and bordering both Massachusetts and
Rhode Island. Newly married, he was probably
in his twenties at the time. Seven months before
his wife gave birth to their first child, a sixteen-
year-old Killingly woman charged Hallowell
with fathering her illegitimate child. Using the
alias Nicholas Hallaway, he fled to southeastern Connecticut, where he lived as a "transient" for three months. He was arrested and
settled the case by admitting to paternity and
agreeing to contribute to the child's maintenance for four years.[28]

Hallowell resumed his life in Killingly.
Two years later, now referred to as "Dr.," he
was arrested again; this time the charge was
counterfeiting. Hallowell and several confederates were hauled before the governor and
council for questioning and then put on trial
before the Superior Court. Although many Killingly witnesses testified to the team's suspect
activities in a woodland shelter, the charges

against Hallowell were dropped when a key
informer failed to appear in court.[29]

Hallowell thus escaped conviction on a serious felony charge, but he had been tainted by
stories linking him to the criminal subculture
of transient, disorderly, greedy, and manually
skilled men who typically made up gangs of
counterfeiters in eighteenth-century New England.[30] After 1727 Hallowell may have given
up dabbling in money-making schemes and
turned to earning his livelihood chiefly from
his medical practice. Like two-thirds of the
male medical practitioners in colonial New England, he probably did not have college or apprentice training, but his skill, or charm, was
not therefore necessarily less than that of any
one of his peers who might have inherited a
library of books and a fund of knowledge from
a physician father. All colonial practitioners, as
Richard D. Brown reminds us, mixed learned
practices with home or folk remedies, and no
doctor had access to safe, reliable pharmaco-
logical preparations or antiseptic surgical procedures.[31]

In the years immediately following the
counterfeiting charge, Hallowell appears to
have made several deliberate moves to portray
himself as a sober neighbor and reliable physician. At about the time of his second marriage, in 1729, he became a more frequent attendant at the Killingly meetinghouse, where
he renewed his covenant and presented his first
two children for baptism. He also threw himself into the land and credit markets of northeastern Connecticut, establishing himself as a
physician who was also an enterprising yeoman and a frequent litigant.[32]

These activities had dual implications. On
the one hand, they suggest that Hallowell epitomized the eighteenth-century Yankee citizen—a man as comfortable in the courtroom
and countinghouse as at a patient's bedside; a
man of restless energy, not content to limit his
scope to his fields and village; a practical, ambitious man with a shrewd eye for a good
deal.[33] On the other hand, Hallowell's losses to
Boston creditors, his constant efforts to collect
debts, and his farflung practice raise questions
about the nature of his activities and medical
practice. He evidently had clients not just in
towns across northeastern Connecticut but also
in neighboring Massachusetts and Rhode Island. Perhaps rural practitioners normally

traveled extensively, spending many nights away from their wives and children. It is also possible, however, either that Hallowell was forced to travel because established doctors from leading families had monopolized the local practice or that he chose to recruit patients in Providence and other towns as a cover for illicit activities.[34] Despite his land speculations and his frequent resort to litigation, Hallowell was losing money. In the sixteen years before 1742, his creditors secured judgments against him for a total of £1,060, while he was able to collect only £700 in debts.[35] The disjunction between his ambition and actual material gains may have led Hallowell in middle age to renew his illicit money-making schemes. By supplying young men with potent abortifacients and dabbling in schemes to counterfeit New England's paper money, he betrayed the very gentlemen whose respect, credit, and society he sought.

What is most intriguing about Hallowell was his ability to ingratiate himself throughout his life with elite men whose reputations were unblemished by scandal. Despite the rumors that must have circulated about his early sexual dalliance, counterfeiting activities, suspect medical remedies, heavy debts, and shady business transactions, leading ministers, merchants, and magistrates welcomed him into their houses. . . .

Lacking college degree and family pedigree, Hallowell traded on his profession and his charm to gain acceptability with the elite. In August 1742 he shrewdly removed himself from the Pomfret scene, just before Sarah Grosvenor's death. In that month he moved, possibly without his wife and children, to Providence, where he had many connections. Within five years, Hallowell had so insinuated himself with town leaders such as Stephen Hopkins that fourteen of them petitioned for mitigation of what they saw as the misguided sentence imposed on him in the Grosvenor case.[36]

Hallowell's capacity for landing on his feet, despite persistent brushes with scandal, debt, and the law, suggests that we should look at the fluidity of New England's eighteenth-century elite in new ways.[37] What bound sons of old New England families, learned men, and upwardly mobile merchants and professionals in an expanded elite may partly have been a reshaped, largely unspoken set of values

shared by men. We know that the archetype for white New England women as sexual beings was changing from carnal Eve to resisting Pamela and that the calculus of accountability for seduction was shifting blame solely to women.[38] But the simultaneous metamorphosis in cultural images and values defining manhood in the early and mid-eighteenth century has not been studied. The scattered evidence we do have suggests that, increasingly, for men in the more secular and anglicized culture of New England, the lines between legitimate and illegitimate sexuality, between sanctioned and shady business dealings, and between speaking the truth and protecting family honor blurred. Hallowell's acceptability to men like minister Ebenezer Williams and merchant Stephen Hopkins hints at how changing sexual and moral standards shaped the economic and social alliances made by New England's male leadership in the 1700s.

WOMEN'S TALK AND MEN'S TALK

If age played a major role in determining who knew the truth about Sarah Grosvenor's illness, gender affected how the conspiring young adults responded to Sarah's impending death and how they weighed the issue of blame. Our last glimpse into the social world of eighteenth-century Pomfret looks at the different ways in which women and men reconstructed their roles in the events of 1742.

An inward gaze, a strong consciousness of sin and guilt, a desire to avoid conflict and achieve reconciliation, a need to confess—these are the impulses expressed in women's intimate talk in the weeks before Sarah died. The central female characters in the plot, Sarah and Zerviah Grosvenor, lived for six weeks with the daily fear that their parents or aunts might detect Sarah's condition or their covert comings and goings. Deposing three years later, Zerviah represented the sisters as suffering under an intensifying sense of complicity as they had passed through two stages of involvement in the concealment plan. At first, they were passive players, submitting to the hands of men. But once Hallowell declared that he had done all he could, they were left to salvage the conspiracy by enduring the terrors of a first delivery alone, knowing that their failure to call in the older women of the family resembled the decision made by women who committed infanticide.[39] While the pain and shock of miscarrying a five-and-one-half-month fetus through a possibly lacerated vagina may have been the experience that later most grieved Sarah, Zerviah would be haunted particularly by her stealthy venture into the woods with Hannah to bury the shrouded evidence of miscarriage.[40]

The Grosvenor sisters later recalled that they had regarded the first stage of the scheme—taking the trade—as "a Sin" and "an Evil" not so much because it was intended to end the life of a fetus as because it entailed a protracted set of actions, worse than a single lie, to cover up an initial transgression: fornication. According to their religion and the traditions of their New England culture, Sarah and Zerviah knew that the proper response to the sin of "uncleanness" (especially when it led to its visible manifestation, pregnancy) was to confess, seeking to allay God's wrath and cleanse oneself and one's community. Dire were the consequences of hiding a grave sin, so the logic and folklore of religion warned.[41] Having piled one covert act upon another, all in defiance of her parents, each sister wondered if she had not ventured beyond the pale, forsaking God and in turn being forsaken. . . .

. . . [V]isions of judgment and of their personal accountability to God haunted Sarah and Zerviah during the waning days of summer— or so their female friends later contended. Caught between the traditional religious ethic of confession, recently renewed in revivals across New England, and the newer, status-driven cultural pressure to keep moral missteps private, the Grosvenor women declined to take up roles as accusers. By focusing on their own actions, they rejected a portrait of themselves as helpless victims, yet they also ceded to their male kin responsibility for assessing blame and mediating between the public interest in seeing justice done and the private interests of the Grosvenor family. Finally, by trying to keep the conspiracy of silence intact and by allowing Amasa frequent visits to her bedside to lament his role and his delusion by Hallowell, Sarah at once endorsed a policy of private repentance and forgiveness *and* indicated that she wished her lover to be spared eventual public retribution for her death.

Talk among the men of Pomfret in the weeks preceding and following Sarah's death centered on more secular concerns than the preoccupation with sin and God's anger that ran through the women's conversations. Neither Hallowell nor Sessions expressed any guilt or sense of sin, as far as the record shows, *until* Sarah was diagnosed as mortally ill.[42] Indeed, their initial accounts of the plot took the form of braggadocio, with Amasa (according to Hallowell) casting himself as the rake who could "gitt Red" of his child and look elsewhere for female companionship, and Hallowell boasting of his abortionist's surgical technique to Sarah's cousin Ebenezer. Later, anticipating popular censure and possible prosecution, each man "Tried to Cast it" on the other. The physician insisted that "He did not do any thing but What Sessions Importuned him to Do," while Amasa exclaimed "That he could freely be Strip[p]ed naked provided he could bring Sarah . . . To life again . . . , but Doct Hollowell had Deluded him, and Destroyed her."[43] While this sort of denial and buck-passing seems very human, it was the antithesis of the New England way—a religious way of life that made confession its central motif. The Grosvenor-Sessions case is one illustration among many of how New England women continued to measure themselves by "the moral allegory of repentance and confession" while men, at least when presenting themselves before legal authorities, adopted secular voices and learned self-interested strategies.[44]

For the Grosvenor men—at least the cluster of Sarah's cousins living near her—the key issue was not exposing sin but protecting the family's reputation. In the weeks before Sarah died, her cousins John and Ebenezer each attempted to investigate and sort out the roles and motives of Amasa Sessions and John Hallowell in the scheme to conceal Sarah's pregnancy. Grilled in August by Ebenezer . . . , Hallowell revealed that "Sessions had bin Interseeding with him to Remove her Conseption." On another occasion, . . . Hallowell was more specific. He "[did] with her [Sarah] as he did . . . because Sessions Came to him and was So very earnest . . . and offered him five pounds if he would do it." "But," Hallowell boasted, "he would have twenty of[f] of him before he had done."[45]. . .

John and Ebenezer, deposing three or four years after these events, did not . . . explain why they did not act immediately to have charges brought against the two conspirators.

Perhaps these young householders were loath to move against a male peer and childhood friend. More likely, they kept their information to themselves to protect John's wife, Hannah, and their cousin Zerviah from prosecution as accessories. They may also have acted, in league with their uncle Leicester, out of a larger concern for keeping the family name out of the courts. Finally, it is probable that the male cousins, partly because of their own complicity and partly because they may have believed that Sarah had consented to the abortion, simply did not think that Amasa's and Hallowell's actions added up to the murder of their relative.

Three years later, yet another Grosvenor cousin intervened, expressing himself much more vehemently than John or Ebenezer ever had. In 1742, John Shaw at age thirty-eight may have been perceived by the younger Grosvenors as too old—too close to the age when men took public office and served as grand jurors— to be trusted with their secret. Shaw seems to have known nothing of Sarah's taking the trade or having a miscarriage until 1745 when "the Storys" suddenly surfaced. Then Hannah and Zerviah gave him a truncated account. Shaw reacted with rage, realizing that Sarah had died not of natural causes but from "what Hallowell had done," and he set out to wring the truth from the doctor. Several times he sought out Hallowell in Rhode Island to tell him that "I could not look upon him otherwise Than [as] a Bad man Since he had Destroyed my Kinswoman." When Hallowell countered that "Amasa Sessions . . . was the Occasion of it," Shaw's fury grew. "I Told him he was like old Mother Eve When She said The Serpent beguild her; . . . [and] I Told him in my Mind he Deserved to dye for it."

Questioning Amasa, Shaw was quick to accept his protestations of sincere regret and his insistence that Hallowell had "Deluded" him. Shaw concluded that Amasa had never "Importuned [Hallowell] . . . to lay hands on her" (that is, to perform the manual abortion). Forged in the men's talk about the Grosvenor-Sessions case in 1745 and 1746 appears to have been a consensus that, while Amasa Sessions was somewhat blameworthy "as concerned in it," it was only Hallowell—the outsider, the man easily labeled a quack—who deserved to be branded "a Man of Death." Nevertheless, it was the stories of *both* men and women that ensured the fulfillment of a doctor's warning to

Hallowell in the Leicester Grosvenor house just before Sarah died: "The Hand of Justice [will] Take hold of [you] sooner or Later."[46]

THE LAW

The hand of justice reached out to catch John Hallowell in November 1745. . . . *Something* had caused Zerviah and Hannah Grosvenor to break their silence. Zerviah provided the key to the puzzle, as she alone had been present at the crucial series of incidents leading to Sarah's death. The only surviving account of Zerviah's belated conversion from silence to public confession comes from the stories told by Pomfret residents into the nineteenth century. In Ellen Larned's melodramatic prose, the "whispered" tale recounted Zerviah's increasing discomfort thus: "Night after night, in her solitary chamber, the surviving sister was awakened by the rattling of the rings on which her bed-curtains were suspended, a ghostly knell continuing and intensifying till she was convinced of its preternatural origin; and at length, in response to her agonized entreaties, the spirit of her dead sister made known to her, 'That she could not rest in her grave till her crime was made public.'"[47]

Embellished as this tale undoubtedly is, we should not dismiss it out of hand as a Victorian ghost story. In early modern English culture, belief persisted in both apparitions and the supernatural power of the guiltless victim to return and expose her murderer.[48] Zerviah in 1742 already fretted over her sin as an accomplice, yet she kept her pledge of silence to her sister. It is certainly conceivable that, after a lapse of three years, she could no longer bear the pressure of hiding the acts that she increasingly believed amounted to the murder of her sister and an unborn child. Whether Zerviah's sudden outburst of talk in 1745 came about at the urging of some Pomfret confidante, or perhaps under the influence of the revivals then sweeping Windham County churches, or indeed because of her belief in nightly visitations by her dead sister's spirit, we simply cannot know.[49]

The Pomfret meetinghouse was the site of the first public legal hearing into the facts behind Sarah Grosvenor's death. We can imagine that townsfolk crowded the pews over the course of two November days to watch two prominent county magistrates examine a string of witnesses before pronouncing their preliminary judgment. The evidence, they concluded, was sufficient to bind four people over for trial at the Superior Court: Hallowell, who in their opinion was "Guilty of murdering Sarah," along with Amasa Sessions, Zerviah Grosvenor, and Hannah Grosvenor as accessories to that murder.[50] The inclusion of Zerviah and Hannah may have been a ploy to pressure these crucial, possibly still reluctant, witnesses to testify for the crown. When Joseph Fowler, the king's attorney, prepared a formal indictment in the case eleven months later, he dropped all charges against Zerviah and Hannah. Rather than stand trial, the two women traveled frequently during 1746 and 1747 to the county seat to give evidence against Sessions and Hallowell.

The criminal process recommenced in September 1746. A grand jury empaneled by the Superior Court at its Windham session first rejected a presentment against Hallowell for murdering Sarah "by his Wicked and Diabolical practice." Fowler, recognizing that the capital charges of murder and accessory to murder against Hallowell and Sessions were going to fail before jurors, changed his tack. He presented the grand jury with a joint indictment against the two men not for outright murder but for endangering Sarah's health by trying to "procure an Abortion" with medicines and "a violent manual opperation"; this time the jurors endorsed the bill. When the Superior Court trial opened in November, two attorneys for the defendants managed to persuade the judges that the indictment was faulty on technical grounds. However, upon the advice of the king's attorney that there "appear reasons vehemently to suspect" the two men "Guilty of Sundry Heinous Offenses" at Pomfret four years earlier, the justices agreed to bind them over to answer charges in March 1747.[51]

Fowler next moved to bring separate indictments against Hallowell and Sessions for the "highhanded misdemeanour" of endeavoring to destroy Sarah's health "and the fruit of her womb." This wording echoed the English common law designation of abortion as a misdemeanor, not a felony or capital crime. A newly empaneled grand jury of eighteen county yeomen made what turned out to be the pivotal decision in getting a conviction: they returned a true bill against Hallowell and rejected a similarly worded bill against Sessions.[52] Only Hallowell, "the notorious physician," would go to trial.[53]

On March 20, 1747, John Hallowell stepped before the bar for the final time to answer for the death of Sarah Grosvenor. He maintained his innocence, the case went to a trial jury of twelve men, and they returned with a guilty verdict. The Superior Court judges, who had discretion to choose any penalty less than death, pronounced a severe sentence of public shaming and corporal punishment. Hallowell was to be paraded to the town gallows, made to stand there before the public for two hours "with a rope visibly hanging about his neck," and then endure a public whipping of twenty-nine lashes "on the naked back."[54]

Before the authorities could carry out this sentence, Hallowell escaped and fled to Rhode Island. From Providence seven months after his trial, he audaciously petitioned the Connecticut General Assembly for a mitigated sentence, presenting himself as a destitute "Exile." As previously noted, fourteen respected male citizens of Providence took up his cause, arguing that this valued doctor had been convicted by prejudiced witnesses and hearsay evidence and asserting that corporal punishment was unwarranted in a misdemeanor case. While the Connecticut legislators rejected these petitions, the language used by Hallowell and his Rhode Island patrons is yet another marker of the distance separating many educated New England men at mid-century from their more God-fearing predecessors. Never mentioning the words "sin" or "repentance," the Providence men wrote that Hallowell was justified in escaping the lash since "every Person is prompted [by the natural Law of Self-Preservation] to avoid Pain and Misery."[55]

In the series of indictments against Hallowell and Sessions, the central legal question became who had directly caused Sarah's death. To the farmers in their forties and fifties who sat as jurors, Hallowell clearly deserved punishment. By recklessly endangering Sarah's life he had abused the trust that heads of household placed in him as a physician.[56] Moreover, he had conspired with the younger generation to keep their dangerous activities secret from their parents and elders.

Several rationales could have been behind the Windham jurors' conclusion that Amasa Sessions ought to be spared the lash. Legally, they could distinguish him from Hallowell as not being *directly* responsible for Sarah's death. Along with Sarah's male kin, they dismissed the evidence that Amasa had instigated the scheme, employed Hallowell, and monitored all of his activities. Perhaps they saw him as a native son who deserved the chance to prove himself mature and responsible. They may have excused his actions as nothing more than a misguided effort to cast off an unwanted lover. Rather than acknowledge that a culture that excused male sexual irresponsibility was responsible for Sarah's death, the Grosvenor family, the Pomfret community, and the jury men of the county persuaded themselves that Sessions had been ignorant of the potentially deadly consequences of his actions.

MEMORY AND HISTORY

No family feud, no endless round of recriminations followed the many months of deposing and attending trials that engaged the Grosvenor and Sessions clans in 1746 and 1747. Indeed, as Sarah and Amasa's generation matured, the ties between the two families thickened. . . . In 1775 Amasa's third son, and namesake, married sixteen-year-old Esther Grosvenor, daughter of Sarah's brother, Leicester, Jr.[57]

It is clear that the Grosvenor clan was not willing to break ranks with their respectable yeoman neighbors and heap blame on the Sessions family for Sarah's death. It would, however, be fascinating to know what women in Pomfret and other Windham County towns had to say about the outcome of the legal proceedings in 1747. Did they concur with the jurors that Hallowell was the prime culprit, or did they, unlike Sarah Grosvenor, direct their ire more concertedly at Amasa, insisting that he too was "a Bad man"? Several decades later, middle-class New England women would organize against the sexual double standard. However, Amasa's future career tells us that female piety in the 1740s did not instruct Windham County women to expel the newly married, thirty-two-year-old man from their homes.[58]

Amasa, as he grew into middle age in Pomfret, easily replicated his father's status. He served as militia captain in the Seven Years' War, prospered in farming, fathered ten children, and lived fifty-seven years beyond Sarah

Grosvenor. His handsome gravestone, inscribed with a long verse, stands but twenty-five feet from the simpler stone erected in 1742 for Sarah.

After his death, male kin remembered Amasa fondly; nephews and grandsons recalled him as a "favorite" relative, "remarkably capable" in his prime and "very corpulent" in old age. Moreover, local story-telling tradition and the published history of the region, which made such a spectacular ghost story out of Sarah's abortion and death, preserved Amasa Sessions's reputation unsullied: the *name* of Sarah's lover was left out of the tale.[59]

If Sarah Grosvenor's life is a cautionary tale in any sense for us in the late twentieth century, it is as a reminder of the historically distinctive ways in which socialized gender roles, community and class solidarity, and legal culture combine in each set of generations to excuse or make invisible certain abuses and crimes against women. The form in which Sarah Grosvenor's death became local history reminds us of how the excuses and erasures of one generation not unwittingly become embedded in the narratives and memories of the next cultural era.

NOTES

1. The documentation is found in the record books and file papers of the Superior Court of Connecticut: *Rex* v. *John Hallowell et al.,* Superior Court Records, Book 9, pp. 113, 173, 175, and Windham County Superior Court Files, box 172, Connecticut State Library, Hartford. Hereafter all loose court papers cited are from *Rex* v. *Hallowell,* Windham County Superior Court Files, box 172, unless otherwise indicated. . . .

2. . . . On the history of abortion practices see . . . Angus McLaren, *Reproductive Rituals: The Perception of Fertility in England from the Sixteenth Century to the Nineteenth Century* (London, 1984), chap. 4; Linda Gordon, *Woman's Body, Woman's Right: A Social History of Birth Control in America* (New York, 1976), pp. 26–41, 49–60. . . .

For specific cases indicating use of herbal abortifacients in the North American colonies, see Julia Cherry Spruill, *Women's Life and Work in the Southern Colonies* (New York, 1972: orig. pub. Chapel Hill, N.C., 1938), pp. 325–26; Roger Thompson, *Sex in Middlesex: Popular Mores in a Massachusetts County, 1649–1699* (Amherst, Mass., 1986), pp. 11, 24–26, 107–8, 182–83. I have found two references to the use of an abortifacient in colonial Connecticut court files.

3. Abortion before quickening (defined in the early modern period as the moment when the mother first felt the fetus move) was not viewed by the En-

glish or colonial courts as criminal. No statute law on abortion existed in either Britain or the colonies. To my knowledge, no New England court before 1745 had attempted to prosecute a physician or other conspirators for carrying out an abortion.

On the history of the legal treatment of abortion in Europe and the United States see McLaren, *Reproductive Rituals,* chap. 5; Gordon, *Woman's Body, Woman's Right,* chap. 3; James C. Mohr, *Abortion in America: The Origins and Evolution of National Policy, 1800–1900* (New York, 1978); Michael Grossberg, *Governing the Hearth: Law and the Family in Nineteenth-Century America* (Chapel Hill, N.C., 1985), chap. 5; and Carroll Smith-Rosenberg, "The Abortion Movement and the AMA, 1850–1880," in *Disorderly Conduct: Visions of Gender in Victorian America* (New York, 1985), pp. 217–244.

4. Indictment against John Hallowell, Mar. 1746/47.

5. The story of the decriminalization of fornication for men in colonial New England is told most succinctly by Carol F. Karlsen, *The Devil in the Shape of a Woman: Witchcraft in Colonial New England* (New York, 1987), pp. 194–96, 198–202, 255. Laurel Thatcher Ulrich describes a late eighteenth-century Massachusetts jurisdiction in *A Midwife's Tale: The Life of Martha Ballard, Based on Her Diary, 1785–1812* (New York, 1990), 147–60. . . . A partial survey of fornication prosecutions in the Windham County Court indicates that here, too, the local JPs and annually appointed grand jurymen stopped prosecuting men after the 1730s. The records for 1726–31 show that fifteen men were prosecuted to enjoin child support and twenty-one single women were charged with fornication and bastardy, while only two women brought civil suits for child maintenance. Nearly a decade ahead, in the three-year period 1740–42, *no* men were prosecuted while twenty-three single women were charged with fornication and ten women initiated civil paternity suits.

6. For a recent summary of the literature see Brief for American Historians as *Amicus Curiae* Supporting the Appellees 5–7, *William L. Webster et al.* v. *Reproductive Health Services et al.,* 109 S. Ct. 3040 (1989).

7. In none of the cases cited in n. 2 above did the woman ingesting an abortifacient die from it. . . .

8. Married women may have hidden their abortion attempts because the activity was associated with lewd or dissident women.

9. Deposition of Zerviah Grosvenor. [All direct quotations from witnesses come from Depositions (see n. 1).] . . . Hallowell's trade may have been an imported medicine or a powder he mixed himself, consisting chiefly of oil of savin, which could be extracted from juniper bushes found throughout New England.

10. So her sister Zerviah later estimated. . . .

11. After she was let into the plot, Zerviah more than once watched Amasa take "a paper or powder out of his pockett" and insist that Sarah "take Some of it." . . .

12. . . . "Unlawful measure" was Zerviah's phrase for Amasa's "Method." Concerned for Sarah's well-being, she pleaded with Hallowell not to give her sister "any thing that should harm her"; De-

position of Zerviah Grosvenor. At the same time, Sarah was thinking about the quickening issue. She confided to a friend that when Amasa first insisted she take the trade, "she [had] feared it was too late". . . .

13. Hallowell claimed that he proceeded with the abortion in order to save Sarah's life. If the powder had had little effect and he knew it, then this claim was a deliberate deception. On the other hand, he may have sincerely believed that the potion had poisoned the fetus and that infection of the uterine cavity had followed fetal death. Since healthy babies were thought at that time to help with their own deliveries, Hallowell may also have anticipated a complicated delivery if Sarah were allowed to go to full term—a delivery that might kill her. . . .

14. Hearsay evidence was still accepted in many eighteenth-century Anglo-American courts. . . . Sarah's reported words may have carried special weight because in early New England persons on their deathbeds were thought to speak the truth.

15. Twentieth-century obstetrical studies show an average of six weeks between fetal death and spontaneous abortion; J Robert Willson and Elsie Reid Carrington, eds., *Obstetrics and Gynecology,* 8th ed. (St. Louis, Mo., 1987), p. 212. Hallowell evidently grasped the link between the two events but felt he could not wait six weeks, either out of concern for Sarah's health or for fear their plot would be discovered.

16. I am using a list of forty heads of household in the Mashamoquet neighborhood of Pomfret in 1731, presuming five persons to a household, and assuming a 2.5 percent annual population growth. See Ellen D. Larned, *History of Windham County, Connecticut* (Worcester, Mass., 1874), vol. I, p. 342, and Bruce C. Daniels, *The Connecticut Town: Growth and Development, 1635–1790* (Middletown, Conn., 1979), pp. 44–51. Pomfret village had no central green or cluster of shops and small house lots around its meetinghouse. No maps survive for early Pomfret apart from a 1719 survey of proprietors' tracts. See Larned, *History of Windham County* (1976 ed.), I, foldout at p. 185.

17. . . . Larned, *History of Windham County,* I:200–202, 208–9, 269, 354, 343–44. . . .

18. Larned, *History of Windham County,* I:201, 204, 206, 208–9, 344; Ellen D. Larned, *Historic Gleanings in Windham County, Connecticut* (Providence, R. I., 1899), pp. 141, 148–49. . . .

19. . . . Contradicting Amasa's attempt to disavow paternity were both his investment in Hallowell's efforts to get rid of the fetus and his own ready admission of paternity privately to Zerviah and Sarah.

20. Two years later, in Feb. 1744 (nine months before Amasa married), the senior Sessions deeded to his son the north part of his own farm for a payment of £310. Amasa, in exchange for caring for his parents in their old age, came into the whole farm when his father died in 1771. Pomfret Land Records, III:120; Estate Papers of Nathaniel Sessions, 1771, Pomfret Probate District. On the delay between marriage and "going to housekeeping" see Ulrich, *A Midwife's Tale,* pp. 138–44.

21. Francis G. Sessions, comp, *Materials for a History of the Sessions Family in America* (Albany, N.Y.,

1890), p. 60; Pomfret Vit. Rec., I:29. All vital and land records cited hereafter are found in the Barbour Collection, Connecticut State Library.

22. The banns never appeared on the meeting-house door. . . .

23. . . . I have argued elsewhere that this is what most young New England women in the eighteenth century did when faced with illegitimacy. Their parents did not throw them out of the house but instead paid the cost of the mother and child's upkeep until she managed to marry. Dayton, "Women Before the Bar: Gender, Law and Society in Connecticut, 1710–1790" (Ph.D. diss., Princeton Univ., 1986), pp. 163–80.

24. In Larned's account, the oral legend insisted that Hallowell's "transaction" (meaning the abortion attempt) and the miscarriage were "utterly unsuspected by any . . . member of the household" other than Zerviah. *History of Windham County.* I:363.

25. The famous "bad books" incident that disrupted Jonathan Edwards's career in 1744 involved a similar group of unsupervised young adults ages twenty-one to twenty-nine. See Patricia J. Tracy, *Jonathan Edwards, Pastor: Religion and Society in Eighteenth-Century Northampton* (New York, 1980), pp. 160–64. The best general investigation of youth culture in early New England is Thompson's *Sex in Middlesex*, pp. 71–96. . . .

26. Helena M. Wall, *Fierce Communion: Family and Community in Early America* (Cambridge, Mass., 1990); Bruce H. Mann, *Neighbors and Strangers: Law and Community in Early Connecticut* (Chapel Hill, N.C., 1987).

27. . . . For recent studies linking consumption patterns and class stratification see . . . T. H. Breen, " 'Baubles of Britain': The American and Consumer Revolutions of the Eighteenth Century," *Past and Present* 119 (May 1988):73–104. . . .

28. Killingly Land Records, II:139; *Rex v. John Hallowell and Mehitable Morris,* Dec. 1726, Windham County Court Records, Book I:43, and Windham County Court Files, box 363. . . .

29. Hallowell was clearly the mastermind of the scheme, and there is little doubt that he lied to the authorities when questioned. . . . The case is found in Charles Hoadley, ed., *Public Records of the Colony of Connecticut,* 15 vols. (Hartford, Conn., 1873), vol. VII, p. 118.

30. The authority on counterfeiting in the colonies is Kenneth Scott . . . *Counterfeiting in Colonial America* [(New York, 1957),] esp. pp. 125, 35, 10, 36. See also Scott's more focused studies, *Counterfeiting in Colonial Connecticut* (New York, 1957) and *Counterfeiting in Colonial Rhode Island* (Providence, R.I., 1960).

For an illuminating social profile of thieves and burglars who often operated in small gangs, see Daniel A. Cohen, "A Fellowship of Thieves: Property Criminals in Eighteenth-Century Massachusetts," *Journal of Social History* XXII (1988):65–92.

31. Richard D. Brown, "The Healing Arts in Colonial and Revolutionary Massachusetts: The Context for Scientific Medicine," in Publications Col. Soc. Mass., *Medicine in Colonial Massachusetts 1620–1820* (Boston, 1980), esp. pp. 40–42. . . .

32. Between 1725 and 1742, Hallowell was a party to twenty land sales and purchases in Killingly. . . .

33. For example, in early 1735 Hallowell made a £170 profit from the sale of a sixty-acre tract with mill and mansion house that he had purchased two months earlier. Killingly Land Rec., IV:26, 36.

34. For a related hypothesis about the mobility of self-taught doctors in contrast to physicians from established medical families see Christianson, "Medical Practitioners of Massachusetts," in Col. Soc. Mass., *Medicine in Colonial Massachusetts,* p. 61. . . .

35. These figures apply to suits in the Windham County Court record books, 1727–42. Hallowell may, of course, have prosecuted debtors in other jurisdictions.

36. The petition's signers included Hopkins, merchant, assembly speaker, and Superior Court justice, soon to become governor; Daniel Jencks, judge, assembly delegate, and prominent Baptist; Obadiah Brown, merchant and shopkeeper; and George Taylor, justice of the peace, town schoolmaster, and Anglican warden. Some of the signers stated that they had made a special trip to Windham to be "Earwitnesses" at Hallowell's trial. . . .

37. For discussions of the elite see Jackson Turner Main, *Society and Economy in Colonial Connecticut* (Princeton, N.J., 1985), esp. pp. 317–66. . . .

38. Laurel Thatcher Ulrich, *Good Wives: Image and Reality in the Lives of Women in Northern New England, 1650–1750* (New York, 1982), pp. 103–5, 113–17.

39. See Ulrich, *Good Wives,* pp. 195–201. . . .

40. Burying the child was one of the key dramatic acts in infanticide episodes and tales, and popular beliefs in the inevitability that "murder will out" centered on the buried corpse. . . . For more on "murder will out" in New England culture, see David D. Hall, *Worlds of Wonder, Days of Judgment: Popular Religious Belief in Early New England* (New York, 1989), pp. 176–78. . . .

41. Hall, *Worlds of Wonder,* pp. 172–78.

42. . . . Abigail Nightingale recalled a scene when Sarah "was just going out of the world." She and Amasa were sitting on Sarah's bed, and Amasa "endeavour[ed] to raise her up &c. He asked my thought of her state &c. and then leaning over her used these words: poor Creature, I have undone you[!]"; Deposition of Abigail Nightingale.

43. . . . For discussions of male and female speech patterns and the distinctive narcissistic bravado of men's talk in early New England, see Robert St. George, " 'Heated' Speech and Literacy in Seventeenth-Century New England," in David Grayson Allen and David D. Hall, eds., *Seventeenth-Century New England,* Publications of the Colonial Society of Massachusetts, LXIII (Boston, 1984), pp. 305–15. . . .

44. On the centrality of confession see Hall, *Worlds of Wonder,* pp. 173, 241. . . . On the growing gap between male and female piety in the eighteenth century see Mary Maples Dunn, "Saints and Sisters: Congregational and Quaker Women in the Early Colonial Period," *American Quarterly* XXX (1978):582–601. . . .

45. Deposition of Ebenezer Grosvenor; Deposition of John Grosvenor.

46. . . . Shaw here was reporting Dr. [Theodore?] Coker's account of his confrontation with Hallowell during Sarah's final illness. . . .

47. Larned reported that, according to "the legend," the ghostly visitations ceased when "Hallowell fled his country." *History of Windham County,* I:363.

48. For mid-eighteenth-century Bristol residents who reported seeing apparitions and holding conversations with them see Jonathan Barry, "Piety and the Patient: Medicine and Religion in Eighteenth Century Bristol," in Roy Porter, ed., *Patients and Practitioners: Lay Perceptions of Medicine in Pre-Industrial Society* (Cambridge, 1985), p. 157.

49. None of the depositions produced by Hallowell's trial offers any explanation of the three-year gap between Sarah's death and legal proceedings. . . .

50. Record of the Inferior Court held at Pomfret, Nov. 5–6, 1745. . . .

51. Indictment against Hallowell, Sept. 4, 1746; Indictment against Hallowell and Sessions, Sept. 20, 1746: Pleas of Hallowell and Sessions before the adjourned Windham Superior Court, Nov. [18], 1746; Sup. Ct. Rec., bk. 12, pp. 112–17, 131–33.

52. Sup. Ct. Rec., bk. 12, pp. 173, 175; Indictment against John Hallowell, Mar. 1746/47; *Rex* v. *Amasa Sessions,* Indictment, Mar. 1746/47, Windham Sup. Ct. Files, box 172. See William Blackstone, *Commentaries on the Laws of England* (Facsimile of 1st ed. of 1765–69) (Chicago, 1979), I:125–26, IV:198.

53. Larned, *History of Windham County,* I:363.

54. Even in the context of the inflation of the 1740s, Hallowell's bill of costs was unusually high: £110.2s6d. Sessions was hit hard in the pocketbook too; he was assessed £83.14s.2d. in costs.

55. Petition of John Hallowell, Oct. 1747, Conn. Archives, Crimes and Misdemeanors, Ser. I, IV:108. . . .

56. Note Blackstone's discussion of the liability of "a physician or surgeon who gives his patient a portion . . . to cure him, which contrary to expectation kills him." *Commentaries,* IV:197.

57. Pomfret Vit. Rec., II:67.

58. Carroll Smith-Rosenberg, "Beauty, the Beast and the Militant Woman: A Case Study in Sex Roles and Social Stress in Jacksonian America," *American Quarterly* XXIII (1971):562–84. . . .

59. Sessions, *Sessions Family,* pp. 31, 35; Larned, *History of Windham County,* I:363–64.

"The ladies going about for money exceeded everything . . ."

This broadside of 1780 announced a women's campaign to raise contributions for patriot soldiers. Organized and led by Esther DeBerdt Reed, wife of the president of Pennsylvania, and by Benjamin Franklin's daughter Sarah Franklin Bache, the campaign was large and effective. "Instead of waiting for the Donations being sent the ladys of each Ward go from dore to dore and collect them," wrote one participant. Collecting contributions this way invited confrontation. One loyalist wrote to her sister, "Of all absurdities, the ladies going about for money exceeded everything; they were so extremely importunate that people were obliged to give them something to get rid of them."* The campaign raised $300,000 in paper dollars in inflated war currency. Rather than let George Washington merge it with the general fund, the women insisted on using it to buy materials for making shirts so that each soldier might know he had received an extraordinary contribution from the women of Philadelphia. The broadside itself is an unusually explicit justification for women's intrusion into politics.

On the commencement of actual war, the Women of America manifested a firm resolution to contribute . . . to the deliverance of their country. Animated by the purest patriotism, they are sensible of sorrow at this day, in not offering more than barren wishes for the success of so glorious a Revolution. They aspire to render themselves more really useful; and this sentiment is universal from the north to the south of the Thirteen United States. Our ambition is kindled by the fame of those heroines of antiquity, who have rendered their sex illustrious, and have proved to the universe, that, if the weakness of our Constitution, if opinion and manners did not forbid us to march to glory by the same paths as the Men, we should at least equal, and sometimes surpass them in our love for the public good. I glory in all that which my sex has done great and commendable. I call to mind with enthusiasm and with admiration, all those acts of courage, of constancy and patriotism, which history has transmitted to us: The people favoured by Heaven, preserved from destruction by the virtues, the zeal and the resolution of Deborah, of Judith, of Esther! The fortitude of the mother of the Macchabees, in giving up her sons to die before her eyes: Rome saved from the fury of a victorious enemy by the efforts of Volumnia, and other Roman Ladies: So many famous sieges where the Women have been seen forgetting the weakness of their sex, building new walls, digging trenches with their feeble hands, furnishing arms to their defenders, they themselves darting the missile weapons on the enemy, resigning the ornaments of their apparel, and their fortune, to fill the public treasury, and to hasten the deliverance of their country; bury-

*Mary Morris to Catharine Livingston, June 10 [1780], Ridley Family Papers, Massachusetts Historical Society, Boston; Anna Rawle to Rebecca Rawle Shoemaker, June 30, 1780, in *Pennsylvania Magazine of History and Biography* 35 (1911):398.

Excerpted from *The Sentiments of an American Woman* ([Philadelphia]: John Dunlap, 1780).

DEBORAH SAMPSON

Drawn by Joseph Stone Framingham 1797.

Women like Sarah Osborn, who served in an informal quartermaster corps, were not the only women on or near Revolutionary War battlefields. In 1782, Deborah Sampson, who was already notable in her community of Middleborough, Massachusetts for her height and strength, adopted men's clothing and the name of Robert Shurtleff. She enlisted for service with the Fourth Massachusetts Regiment. Like many young women from impoverished families, Deborah Sampson had been bound out to domestic service as a young teenager; when her term was up she taught school briefly in Middleborough, and joined the First Baptist Church there. She was expelled from the church before her enlistment. She served with her regiment in New York and possibly in Pennsylvania until she was wounded at a battle near Tarrytown, New York.

After her return to Massachusetts, she married and bore three children, but the fame of her exploits persisted. After a fictionalized biography was published by Herman Mann, she went on a wide-ranging speaking tour, perhaps the first American woman to undertake such an enterprise, and applied for the pensions to which her wartime service entitled her. These were awarded slowly and grudgingly, and she died impoverished in 1827. (Joseph Stone, "Deborah Sampson Garrett," oil on paper, courtesy of the Rhode Island Historical Society)

ing themselves under its ruins; throwing themselves into the flames rather than submit to the disgrace of humiliation before a proud enemy.

Born for liberty, disdaining to bear the irons of a tyrannic Government, we associate ourselves to the grandeur of those Sovereigns, cherished and revered, who have held with so much splendour the scepter of the greatest States, The Batildas, the Elizabeths, the Maries, the Catharines, who have extented the empire of liberty, and contented to reign by sweetness and justice, have broken the chains of slavery, forged by tyrants in times of ignorance and barbarity. . . .

We know that at a distance from the theatre of war, if we enjoy any tranquility, it is the fruit of your watchings, your labours, your dangers. . . . Who, amongst us, will not renounce with the highest pleasure, those vain ornaments, when she shall consider that the valiant defenders of America will be able to draw some advantage from the money which she may have laid out in these. . . . The time is arrived to display the same sentiments which animated us at the beginning of the Revolution, when we renounced the use of teas, however agreeable to our taste, rather than receive them from our persecutors; when we made it appear to them that we placed former necessaries in the rank of superfluities, when our liberty was interested; when our republican and laborious hands spun the flax, prepared the linen intended for the use of our soldiers; when [as] exiles and fugitives we supported with courage all the evils which are the concomitants of war. . . .

Sarah Osborn, "The bullets would not cheat the gallows . . ."

Sarah Osborn was eighty-one years old when Congress made it possible for dependent survivors of Revolutionary war veterans to claim their pensions. She testified to her own service as well as to her husband's in the following deposition, sworn before the Court of Common Pleas in Wayne County, New Jersey, in 1837. Osborn's husband was a commissary guard; like many thousands of women, Osborn traveled with him, cooking and cleaning for troops at a time when there was no formal quartermaster corps and in which cleanliness was virtually the only guard against disease. Her account tells of working when the army was at West Point in 1780; of the long expedition south, marching proudly on horseback into Philadelphia, and then continuing to Yorktown. Osborn is the only one of the "women of the army" who has left us a narrative of her experiences. At Yorktown she brought food to soldiers under fire. When she told George Washington that she did not fear the bullets because they "would not cheat the gallows," she was conveying her understanding that her challenge to royal authority was congruent with his; if the soldiers risked being hanged for treason, so would she.

[In the march to Philadelphia in 1781?] Deponent was part of the time on horseback and part of the time in a wagon. Deponent's . . . husband was still serving as one of the commissary's guard. . . . They continued their march to Philadelphia, deponent on horseback through the streets. . . . Being out of bread, deponent was employed in baking the afternoon and evening

Excerpted from John C. Dann, ed., *The Revolution Remembered: Eyewitness Accounts of the American Revolution* (Chicago: University of Chicago Press, 1980), pp. 240–45.

. . . they continued their march . . . [at Baltimore she] embarked on board a vessel and sailed . . . until they had got up the St. James River as far as the tide would carry them. . . . They . . . marched for Yorktown. . . . Deponent was on foot. . . . Deponent took her stand just back of the American tents, say about a mile from the town, and busied herself washing, mending, and cooking for the soldiers, in which she was assisted by the other females; some men washed their own clothing. She heard the roar of the artillery for a number of days. . . . Deponent's . . . husband was there throwing up entrenchments, and deponent cooked and carried in beef, and bread, and coffee (in a gallon pot) to the soldiers in the entrenchment.

On one occasion when deponent was thus employed carrying in provisions, she met General Washington, who asked her if she "was not afraid of the cannonballs?"

She replied, "No, the bullets would not cheat the gallows," that "It would not do for the men to fight and starve too."

They dug entrenchments nearer and nearer to Yorktown every night or two till the last. While digging that, the enemy fired very heavy till about nine o'clock next morning, then stopped, and the drums from the enemy beat excessively. Deponent was a little way off in Colonel Van Shaick's or the officers' marquee and a number of officers were present. . . .

The drums continued beating, and all at once the officers hurrahed and swung their hats, and deponent asked them, "What is the matter now?"

One of them replied, "Are not you soldier enough to know what it means?"

Deponent replied, "No."

They then replied, "The British have surrendered."

Deponent, having provisions ready, carried the same down to the entrenchments that morning, and four of the soldiers whom she was in the habit of cooking for ate their breakfasts.

Deponent stood on one side of the road and the American officers upon the other side when the British officers came out of the town and rode up to the American officers and delivered up [their swords, which the deponent] thinks were returned again, and the British officers rode right on before the army, who marched out beating and playing a melancholy tune, their drums covered with black handkerchiefs and their fifes with black ribbands tied around them, into an old field and there grounded their arms and then returned into town again to await their destiny. . . . The British general at the head of the army was a large, portly man, full face, and the tears rolled down his cheeks as he passed along.

Rachel Wells, "I have Don as much to Carrey on the Warr as maney . . ."

Rachel Wells was probably sixty-five years old when she wrote the following words. She had bought loan office certificates from the state of New Jersey during the Revolution: subsequently she had moved to Philadelphia, but returned to Bordentown, New Jersey, after the war. In an effort to curb speculation, the New Jersey legislature decided that only state residents had a claim on interest payments; Rachel Wells's claim on her money was turned down because she had not been in the state at the war's end in 1783. She appealed directly to the Continental Congress. Although her petition was tabled, it re-

Rachel Wells, Petition to Congress, May 18, 1786, Microfilm Papers of the Continental Congress, National Archives, Washington, D.C., microfilm M247, roll 56, item 42, vol. 8, pp. 354–55.

mains—despite its bad spelling—as perhaps the most moving witness to the Revolution left to us by a woman. What did Rachel Wells think had been her contribution to the Revolution? What did she think the government owed to her?

To the Honnorabell Congress I rachel do make this Complaint Who am a Widow far advanced in years & Dearly have ocasion of ye Interst for that Cash I Lent the States. I was a Sitisen in ye jersey when I Lent ye State a considerable Sum of Moneys & had I justice dun me it mite be Suficant to suporte me in ye Contrey whear I am now, near burdentown. I Leved hear then . . . but Being . . . so Robd by the Britans & others i went to Phila to try to get a Living . . . & was There in the year 1783 when our assembley was pleasd to pas a Law that No one Should have aney Interest that Livd out of jearsey Stats . . .

Now gentelmen is this Liberty, had it bin advertised that he or She that Moved out of the Stat should Louse his or her Interest you mite have sum plea against me. But I am Innocent Suspected no Trick. I have Don as much to Carrey on the Warr as maney that Sett now at ye healm of government. . . . your asembly Bor-

rowed £300 in gould of me jest as the Warr Comencd & Now I Can Nither git Intrust nor principall Nor Even Security. . . . My dr Sister . . . wrote to me to be thankfull that I had it in my Power to help on the Warr which is well enough but then this is to be Considerd that others gits their Intrust & why then a poor old widow to be put of[f]. . . . I hartely pity others that ar in my Case that Cant Speak for themselves. . . .

god has Spred a plentifull table for us & you gentelmen are ye Carvers for us pray forgit Not the Poor weaklings at the foot of the Tabel ye poor Sogers has got Sum Crumbs That fall from their masters tabel. . . . Why Not Rachel Wells have a Littel intrust?

if She did not fight She threw in all her mite which bought ye Sogers food & Clothing & Let Them have Blankets & Since that She has bin obligd to Lay upon Straw & glad of that. . . .

LINDA K. KERBER
The Republican Mother

The years of the early republic (1776–1820) were a time of profound social and political change. Rebellion against England meant that throughout America there was a major reconsideration of political relationships, culminating in the Declaration of Independence, new state constitutions, and the federal Constitution. Male political leaders redefined the relationship of the individual to the state. They rarely explored what the new relationship of women to the state might be, though they left some important questions open: women were citizens and alien women could become naturalized citizens; the qualifications for suffrage were framed in terms of "persons." But full political identity was also based on a willingness to take up arms for the republic, and for this role women

A revised version of " 'Why Should Girls Be Learnd or Wise?' Education and Intellect in the Early Republic" and "The Republican Mother: Female Political Imagination in the Early Republic," chaps. 7 and 9 of *Women of the Republic: Intellect and Ideology in Revolutionary America* (Chapel Hill: University of North Carolina Press, for the Institute of Early American History and Culture, 1980; paperback ed., New York: W. W. Norton, 1986).

were thought biologically unfit. Even more important, full political autonomy was assumed to involve control of enough property so that one was not vulnerable to economic pressure by a master or employer, yet married women could not control property. They were denied suffrage in large part because it was thought that to give women a vote was, in practice, to give a double vote to their husbands. (On the other hand, a substantial minority of adult women at any given moment were single or widowed and *did* control their own property; political theorists ignored their presence.)

Those who articulated the ideology of Republican Motherhood sought to draw together the political, biological, and economic reality experienced by free white women and to redefine the role of women in the new post-Revolutionary era in a way that reflected realistically the constraints of their lives but also emphasized that women, too, were part of a deeply radical republican experiment. What features of this ideology were conservative? What features were radical? What elements of the ideology of Republican Motherhood persist into our own time?

When women looked back to the years of the Revolution, what did they remember? Several themes were repeated with great frequency. The war had been a nightmare. It had frightened people and disrupted lives. It had been a time when women had chosen political identities, prided themselves on their loyalism or on their patriotism, and performed services for the government of their choice. Women who had survived the war had been strong and courageous, but the republic had offered only the most grudging response to their sacrifices, as Rachel Wells had discovered.

Americans did not choose to explore with much rigor the socially radical implications of their republican ideology. For example, only haltingly did a few develop the obvious anti-slavery implications of egalitarian rhetoric. Nor did they explore very deeply the implications of female citizenship; the Revolution and the republic that followed were thought to be men's work. "To be an adept in the art of Government," Abigail Adams observed to her husband, "is a prerogative to which your Sex lay almost an exclusive claim."[1] Women were left to invent their own political character. They devised their own interpretation of what the Revolution had meant to them as women, and they began to invent an ideology of citizenship that merged the domestic domain of the pre-industrial woman with the new public ideology of individual responsibility and civic virtue. They did this in the face of severe ridicule, responding both to the anti-intellectual complaint that educating women served no practical purpose and to the conservative complaint that women had no political significance.

Memories of the Revolution, as they appear in postwar fiction, suggest some of the lessons women drew from the wartime experience. An early exploration of women's political options appears in Mercy Otis Warren's verse play *The Ladies of Castile*, written shortly after the close of the war. The play concerns two women of contrasting temperaments caught up in a civil war in Spain that, Warren makes clear in her introduction, is meant to be a metaphor for the Revolutionary War in America. The soft and delicate Louisa introduces herself with the words, "I wander wilder'd and alone / Like some poor banish'd fugitive . . . I yield to grief"; while the determined Maria, wife of the leader of the rebellion, announces in her opening scene, "Maria has a bolder part to act— / I scorn to live upon ignoble terms." The message of *The Ladies of Castile* is simple and obvious. Even in the exigencies of war, women must control themselves and their options. The Louisas of the world do not survive revolutions; the Marias—who take political positions, make their own judgment of the contending sides, and risk their lives— emerge stronger and in control. "A soul, inspir'd by freedom's genial warmth," says Maria, "expands—grows firm—and by resistance, strong."[2]

The experience of war had given words like *independence* and *self-reliance* personal as well as political overtones. As the song played at Yorktown had it, the world could turn upside down: the rich could quickly become poor, wives might suddenly have to manage the family economy, women might even shoulder a gun. Revolutionary experience taught that it was useful to be prepared for a wide range of unusual possibilities; political theory taught that republics rested on the virtue and intelligence of their citizens. The stability and competence on which republican government relied required a highly literate and politically sophisticated constituency. Maintaining the republic was an educational as well as a political challenge.

Warren was joined in her demand for self-reliance by Judith Sargent Murray, of Salem, Massachusetts, whose essays provide the most fully developed articulation of the idea that political independence should be the catalyst for female autonomy. When the Revolution ended, she published a prescient argument calling for the strengthening of what she called "Self-Complacency in Female Bosoms." She decried the tradition of educating middle-class girls for an upwardly mobile marriage by encouraging fashion, flirtatiousness, and charm. Lacking a strong and positive sense of their own identity, Murray complained, young women had no personal resources to give them confidence, and so they rushed into marriages to establish their social status.[3] Eight years later, widowed and remarried, she developed this theme at great length in a series of newspaper essays in which she emphasized the need for an education for competence. "I would give my daughters every accomplishment which I thought proper," she wrote,

and, to crown all, I would early accustom them to habits of industry and order. They should be taught with precision the art economical; they should be enabled to procure for themselves the necessaries of life; independence should be placed within their grasp.... THE SEX should be taught to depend on their own efforts, for the procurement of an establishment in life.[4]

The model republican woman was competent and confident. She could resist the vagaries of fashion; she was rational, benevolent, independent, self-reliant. Nearly every writer who described this paragon prepared a list of role models, echoing the pantheon of heroines admired by the fundraising women of Philadelphia in 1780. There were women of the ancient world, like Cornelia, the mother of the Gracchi; rulers like Elizabeth of England and the Empress Catherine the Great of Russia; and a long list of British intellectuals: Lady Mary Wortley Montagu, Hannah More, Mary Wollstonecraft, and the historian Catharine Macau-

lay. Those who believed in these republican models demanded that their presence be recognized and endorsed and that a new generation of young women be urged to find in them patterns for their own behavior. "I expect to see our young women forming a new era in female history," Murray wrote.[5]

Other Americans made demands for the direct participation of women in public affairs. There is the well-known comment by Abigail Adams, which her husband jokingly turned away, that women ought to have the right to participate in the new system of government, for "all men would be tyrants if they could." All her life Abigail Adams was a shrewd commentator on the political scene, assuming as active an obligation to judge good and evil as if she were called upon annually to vote. But she was known, of course, only in a circle that, though relatively large, remained private. In *Alcuin,* the Philadelphia novelist Charles Brockden Brown sneered at the "charming system of equality and independence" that denied women a part in the choice of the governors, but the circulation of his novel was small. The distinguished Virginia jurist St. George Tucker admitted that laws neither respected nor favored females, but he made the concession in a single footnote in a three-volume work.[6]

Expressions of women's desire to play a frankly political role were regularly camouflaged in satire, a device that typically makes new ideas and social criticism seem less threatening and more palatable. In 1791, for example, a New Jersey newspaper published a pair of semiserious satires in which women discuss the politics of excise taxes and national defense. "Roxana" expresses a feminist impatience:

In fifty quarto volumes of ancient and modern history, you will not find fifty illustrious female names; heroes, statesmen, divines, philosophers, artists, are all of masculine gender. And pray what have they done during this long period of usurpation? . . . They have written ten thousand unintelligible books. . . . They have been cutting each other's throats all over the globe.[7]

Some years later, the students at Sarah Pierce's famous school for girls in Litchfield, Connecticut, prepared a "Ladies Declaration of Independence" for July Fourth. Alongside the frivolous phrasing is some earnest comment on the unfilled promises of the republic. Less than ten years after that Elizabeth Cady Stanton would use the same technique. "When in the

Course of Human Events," the Litchfield declaration begins,

> it becomes necessary for the Ladies to dissolve those bonds by which they have been subjected to others, and to assume among the self styled Lords of Creation that separate and equal station to which the laws of nature and their *own talents* entitle them, a decent respect to the opinions of mankind requires, that they should declare the causes which impel them to the separation.
>
> We hold these truths to be self evident. That all *mankind* are created equal.

The Litchfield women wished to change "social relations." They complained about men who "have undervalued our talents, and disparaged our attainments; they have combined with each other, for the purpose of excluding us from all participation in Legislation and in the administration of Justice; . . . [they have declared] themselves invested with power to act & legislate for us in all cases whatsoever."[8]

To accept an openly acknowledged role for women in the public sector was to invite extraordinary hostility and ridicule. Although neither political party took a consistent position on the matter, hostility to the political participation of women seems to have been particularly acute in Federalist circles. It is no accident that it was a Republican periodical that first reprinted Mary Wollstonecraft's *Vindication of the Rights of Woman.* "It is said by one of the federalist papers," remarked the Republican *Register* of Salem, Massachusetts, that

> "Women have no business to speak about politicks and that a woman meddling in politicks is like a monkey in a china ware shop, where he can't do any good but may do a great deal of mischief." On our part we are of a contrary opinion, we can see no reason why, with the same evidence before them, they cannot judge on politicks or any other subject equally with men—On many subjects they certainly are better judges.[9]

Some counterarguments developed a life of their own, appearing and reappearing under different disguises. Among these the most persistent was that linking female intellectual activity and political autonomy to an unflattering masculinity. "From all we read, and all we observe, we are authorized in supposing that there is a *sex of soul,*" announced the Boston minister John Gardiner. "Women of masculine minds, have generally masculine manners. . . . Queen Elizabeth understood Latin and Greek, swore with the fluency of a sailor, and boxed the ears of her courtiers. . . . Mrs. Macaulay, the author of a dull democratic history, at a tolerably advanced age, married a boy." A "mild, dove-like temper is so necessary to Female beauty, is so natural a part of the sex," reflected Parson Mason Locke Weems wistfully. "A masculine air in a woman frightens us."[10]

When women addressed political issues, the attacks were similar. A good example of this response appears in a newspaper letter written in 1790 by a Marylander who signed as "Philanthropos." Warning against literal interpretations of the phrase "All mankind are born equal," "Philanthropos" thought the principle of equality could be "taken in too extensive a sense, and might tend to destroy those degrees of subordination which nature seems to point out," including the subordination of women to men. "However flattering the path of glory and ambition may be, a woman will have more commendation in being the mother of heroes, than in setting up, Amazon-like, for a heroine herself." The reasons he offered in support of the continued exclusion of women from "political bustle and anxiety" were of three sorts. Women, involved as they were with domestic cares, had no time for politics. Women were inept at politics; behind every queen lurked male advisers and guiding the well-known political vigor of Quaker women was a peculiar and distasteful view of the nature of the universe. But if women were inept, they were also somehow too effective.

> A Female Orator, in haranguing an Assembly, might like many crafty politicians, keep her *best argument* for last, and would then be sure of the victory—Men would be exposed to temptations too great for their strength, and those who could resist a bribe, offered in the common way, might reasonably yield to what it would be hardly possible for a *man* to refuse.

Although the political woman was thus thought to be sexually aggressive, "famous" women of the past were, however, "generally deficient in those charms which it is the peculiar lot of the fair sex to excel in." "Philanthropos" ended with the familiar argument that so long as virtuous women had private opportunity to influence men and to "mould our minds," they ought not regret "their exclusion from the perplexity and tumult of a political life."[11]

Mary Wollstonecraft had borne one illegitimate daughter (Fanny Imlay) and lived with William Godwin before marrying him; after marriage she maintained lodgings in another house so that she could be free to write. Once her life history became generally known, it could be used to link political feminism to aggressive sexuality, as the Federalist Timothy Dwight did in his bitter "Morpheus" essays, which ran in a Boston newspaper in 1802. In an early dream sequence in "Morpheus," Wollstonecraft has arrived in America and sets out to teach its inhabitants wisdom.

> Women . . . are entitled to all the rights, and are capable of all the energies, of men. I do not mean merely mental energies. If any dispute remained on this subject, I have removed it entirely by displaying, in my immortal writings, all the mental energy of LOCKE and BACON. I intend bodily energies. They can naturally run as fast, leap as high, and as far, and wrestle, scuffle, and box with as much success, as any of the . . . other sex.
>
> That is a mistake (said an old man just before her.)
>
> It is no mistake, (said the Female Philosopher.)
>
> . . . Why then, (said the senior again) are women always feebler than men?
>
> Because (said MARY) they are educated to be feeble; and by indulgence . . . are made poor, puny, baby-faced dolls; instead of the *manly women*, they ought to be.
>
> *Manly women!* (cried the wag). Wheu! a manly woman is a hoyden, a non descript.
>
> Am I a hoyden (interrupted MARY, with spirit.)
>
> You used to be a strumpet.

Wollstonecraft tells him that she was not a strumpet but a sentimental lover, "too free to brook the restraints of marriage." Her interlocutor responds, "We call them strumpets here, Madam—no offense, I hope," and then argues that when a woman claims the rights of men and the character of a manly woman, she necessarily forgoes what he calls women's "own rights" to "refined consideration." The implication is that Wollstonecraft can be insulted with impunity. "Still, (said the senior) you ought to remember that she is a woman. *She* ought to remember it (said the young man.)" Thus political behavior, like abstract thought, continued to be specifically proscribed as a threat to sensual attractiveness. "*Cupid* is a timid, playful child, and is fright-

ened at the helmet of Minerva," observed Maria Edgeworth.[12]

Only the Republican Mother was spared this hostility. The concept was a variant of the argument for the improved education of women that republicans like Judith Sargent Murray and Wollstonecraft herself had demanded. It defended education for women not only for their autonomy and self-realization but also so that they could be better wives and better mothers for the next generation of virtuous republican citizens—especially sons. In a widely reprinted speech, "Thoughts upon Female Education," originally given at the new Young Ladies Academy of Philadelphia, the physician and politician Benjamin Rush addressed the issue directly: "The equal share that every citizen has in the liberty and the possible share he may have in the government of our country make it necessary that our ladies should be qualified to a certain degree, by a peculiar and suitable education, *to concur in instructing their sons in the principles of liberty and government.*"[13] The Republican Mother was an educated woman who could be spared the criticism normally directed at the intellectually competent woman because she placed her learning at her family's service.

The Republican Mother's life was dedicated to the service of civic virtue. She educated her sons for it; she condemned and corrected her husband's lapses from it. It was commonly believed that republican government was fragile and rested on the presence of virtuous citizens. The creation of those virtuous citizens required wives and mothers who were well informed, "properly methodical," and free of "invidious and rancorous passions." It was perhaps more than mere coincidence that the word *virtue* was derived from the Latin word for *man*, with its connotations of virility. Political action seemed somehow inherently masculine. Virtue in a woman seemed to require another theater for its display. To that end theorists created a mother who had a political purpose and argued that her domestic behavior had a direct political function in the republic.

This constellation of ideas and the republican rhetoric that made it convincing appear at great length in the Columbia College commencement oration of 1795 entitled "Female Influence." Behind the flowery language lurks a social and political message.

Let us then figure to ourselves the accomplished woman, surrounded by a sprightly band, from the babe that imbibes the nutritive fluid, to the generous youth just ripening into manhood.... Let us contemplate the mother distributing the mental nourishment to the fond smiling circle, by means proportionate to their different powers of reception, watching the gradual openings of their minds, and studying their various turns of temper; see, under her cultivating hand, reason assuming the reins of government, and knowledge increasing gradually to her beloved pupils.... the Genius of Liberty hovers triumphant over the glorious scene.... Yes, ye fair, the reformation of a world is in your power.... Contemplate the rising glory of confederated America. Consider that your exertions can best secure, increase, and perpetuate it. The solidity and stability of the liberties of your country rest with you; since Liberty is never sure, 'till Virtue reigns triumphant.... Already may we see the lovely daughters of Columbia asserting the importance and the honour of their sex. "Let us" ... say they ... "assiduously employ our influence over the men, in promoting their happiness and the best interests of society." ... Begin then, ye fair! ... It rests with you to make this retreat [from the corruptions of Europe] doubly peaceful, doubly happy, by banishing from it those crimes and corruptions, which have never yet failed of giving rise to tyranny, or anarchy. While you thus keep our country virtuous, you maintain its independence.[14]

Defined this way, the educated woman ceased to threaten the sanctity of marriage; the intellectual woman need not be masculine. In this awkward and, in the 1790s, still only vaguely expressed fashion, the traditional womanly virtues were endowed with a political purpose. "Let the ladies of a country be educated properly," Rush said, "and they will not only make and administer its laws, but form its manners and character."[15]

The ideology of Republican Motherhood was deeply ambivalent. Those who opposed women in politics were challenged by the proposal that women could—and should—play a political role through influencing their husbands and raising patriotic children. The Republican Mother was to encourage in her sons civic interest and participation. She was to educate both sons and daughters and guide them in the paths of morality and virtue. She was to take advantage of the "authority" invested in her by love and courtship to "mould the taste, the manners, and the conduct" of her admirers and her husband. But she was not to tell her male friends and relatives for

whom to vote. She was a citizen but not really a constituent.

On the one hand, Republican Motherhood was a progressive ideology. Women were redefined as more than "helpmates" to their husbands. Within the dynamic relationships of the private family—between husbands and wives, mothers and children—it allocated an assertive role to women. In the past, Western political theory had rarely contemplated the role of women in the civic culture. A political community that now accepted women as political actors would have to eliminate the assumption that the world of women is separate from the empire of men. The ideology of Republican Motherhood seemed to accomplish what the Enlightenment had not by identifying the intersection of the woman's private domain and the public order.

The notion that a mother can perform a political function represents the recognition that a citizen's political socialization takes place at an early age, that the family is a basic part of the system of political communication, and that patterns of family authority influence the general political culture. Most premodern political societies—and even some fairly modern democracies—maintained unarticulated, but nevertheless very firm, social restrictions that isolated the family's domestic world from politics. The willingness of the American woman to overcome this ancient separation brought her into the all-male political community.[16] In this sense Republican Motherhood was a very important, even revolutionary invention. It altered the female domain in which most women had always lived out their lives; it justified women's absorption and participation in the civic culture. Women had the major role in developing this formulation, women who had learned from the exigencies of the Revolution that the country needed Marias, not Louisas. Those who shared the vision of the Republican Mother usually insisted upon better education, clearer recognition of women's economic contributions, and a strong political identification with the republic. The ideology was strong enough to rout "Philanthropos" and "Morpheus" by redefining female political behavior as valuable rather than abnormal, as a source of strength to the republic rather than an embarrassment. The ideology would be revived as a rallying point for many twentieth-century women reformers of the progressive era who saw their commitment to honest politics, efficient urban sanitation, and pure food and drug laws as an extension of their responsibilities as mothers.

But Republican Motherhood legitimized only a minimum of political sophistication and interest. Women were expected to be content to perform their narrow political role permanently and were not expected to wish for fuller participation. Just as planters claimed that democracy in the antebellum South rested on the economic base of slavery, so egalitarian society was said to rest on the moral base of deference among a class of people—women—who would devote their efforts to service by raising sons and disciplining husbands to be virtuous citizens of the republic. The learned woman, who might very well wish to make choices as well as to influence attitudes, was a visible threat to this arrangement. Women were to contain their political judgments within their homes and families; they were not to bridge the world outside and the world within.

In this sense restricting women's politicization was one of a series of conservative choices that Americans made in the postwar years as they avoided the full implications of their own Revolutionary radicalism. In America responsibility for maintaining public virtue was channeled into domestic life. By these decisions Americans may well have been spared the agony of the French cycle of revolution and counterrevolution, which spilled more blood and produced a political system more retrogressive than had the American war. Nevertheless the impact of this choice was to delay the resolution of matters of particular concern to women—the continuation of coverture, for example, the inability of married women to control their own earnings, the right to judgment by a jury of their peers.

When the war was over, Judith Sargent Murray predicted "a new era in female history."[17] That new era remained to be created by women, fortified by their memories and myths of female strength during the trials of war, politicized by their resentment of male legislators slighting issues of greatest significance to women. But it could not be created until the inherent paradox of Republican Motherhood was resolved, until the world was not separated into a woman's realm of domesticity and nurture and a man's world of politics and intellect. The promises of the republic had yet to be fulfilled; remembering the Revolution helped to keep confidence alive. "Yes, gentle-

men," said Elizabeth Cady Stanton to the New York legislature in 1854, "in republican America . . . we, the daughters of the revolutionary heroes of '76 demand at your hands the redress of our grievances—a revision of your State constitution—a new code of laws."[18] Stanton would wrestle throughout her own career with the contradictory demands of domesticity and civic activism. The ambivalent relationship between motherhood and citizenship would be one of the most lasting, and most paradoxical, legacies of the Revolutionary generation.

NOTES

1. Abigail Adams to John Adams, May 9, 1776, *Adams Family Correspondence,* ed. L. H. Butterfield (Cambridge, Mass., 1963), 1:404.

2. Mercy Otis Warren, *The Ladies of Castile,* in her *Poems, Dramatic and Miscellaneous* (Boston, 1790), pp. 100, 125–26, 144, 162–64.

3. Judith Sargent Murray, "Self-Complacency in Female Bosoms," *Gentlemen and Ladies Town and Country Magazine* (Oct. 1784), pp. 251–52.

4. Murray's essays were reprinted in a collected edition entitled *The Gleaner* (Boston, 1798). These comments appear in 1:167, 168.

5. Ibid., 3:189.

6. Abigail Adams to John Adams, Mar. 31, 1776, *Adams Family Correspondence,* 1:370; Charles Brockden Brown, *Alcuin: A Dialogue* (1798), ed. Lee R. Edwards (New York, 1971), p. 33; St. George Tucker, ed., *Blackstone's Commentaries, With Notes of Reference, to the Constitution and Laws, of the Federal Government of the United States, and of the Commonwealth of Virginia,* vol. 1 (Philadelphia, 1803).

7. *Burlington* (N.J.) *Advertiser,* Feb. 1, 1791.

8. Miss Pierce's School Papers, 1839, Litchfield Historical Society, Litchfield, Conn.

9. *Register* (Salem, Mass.), Oct. 4, 1802.

10. *New-England Palladium,* Sept. 18, 1801; Mason Locke Weems, *Hymen's Recruiting Serjeant; or, The New Matrimonial Tatoo, for Old Bachelors* (Philadelphia, 1800).

11. *Virginia Gazette and Alexandria Advertiser,* Apr. 22, 1790.

12. *Mercury & New-England Palladium,* Mar. 1, 1802; Maria Edgeworth, *Letters for Literary Ladies* (Georgetown, D.C., 1810), p. 22.

13. Benjamin Rush, "Thoughts upon Female Education . . ." (1787), in *Essays on Education in the Early Republic,* ed. Frederick Rudolph (Cambridge, Mass., 1965), pp. 25–40.

14. *New York Magazine,* May 1795, pp. 301–5.

15. Rush, "Thoughts upon Female Education," p. 36.

16. See Gabriel Almond and Sidney Verba, *The Civic Culture* (Princeton, 1963), pp. 377–401.

17. Murray, *Gleaner,* 3:189.

18. Elizabeth Cady Stanton, Susan B. Anthony, and Matilda Joslyn Gage, eds., *History of Woman Suffrage,* vol. 1 (New York, 1881), p. 595.

Women at textile machinery in a New England mill, approximately 1850. (Courtesy of International Museum of Photography at George Eastman House)

IIA

Industrializing America
1820–1880

To Americans who lived through it, the Civil War was the most traumatic experience of the nineteenth century. The years from 1830 to 1860 have come to be called the *antebellum* period, as though their importance derives from what they preceded rather than what they encompassed. Other familiar labels—the Jacksonian era, the Rise of the Common Man, Freedom's Ferment—suggest the difficulty historians have had in characterizing the period.

In these years the American economy was transformed by the industrial revolution. Railroads and steamboats linked distant parts of the country and simplified economic interaction; during the Civil War the control of transportation networks would be an important ingredient in the North's success. The cotton gin ensured the profitability of the crop and reinforced the system of slave labor in the South. Steam-powered spinning and weaving equipment was placed in northern factories and tended by a new class of wage workers. The distinctive economies of North and South fostered a political dialogue that became increasingly acerbic over the years. The position of legislators on issues as disparate as tariffs or free speech could be linked to the economic interests of their sections and to the distinctive regional cultures. By 1860 institutions that had helped connect the two cultures—political parties, churches, economic networks—had broken down completely.

It has been relatively easy for historians to see that economic and political developments affected men's lives. The right to vote and hold office was extended to virtually every white man, whether or not he held property; after the Civil War it was extended to black men as well. Congress was a national forum for debate among male political leaders; by the 1850s speeches made there were rapidly diffused to the public by cheap newspapers, printed by newly efficient presses and distributed by railroads throughout the nation. A host of new careers opened to men as politicians, journalists, teachers, capitalists, physicians, and reformers. The expansion of the physical boundaries of the country, by treaty and by war, opened new frontiers and created new opportunities for farmers, merchants, civic promoters, and land speculators.

When we look at these developments through women's eyes, we find that women's lives also changed markedly. The transportation revolution, for example, had special significance for women. Single women rarely traveled in the colonial period; long trips meant nights in unfamiliar taverns and lodging houses where accommodations were uncertain and safety could not be assured. The railroad changed that. The women who traveled to raise funds for abolition societies and women's seminaries could not have played that role a century before. After the Civil War Elizabeth Cady Stanton and Susan B. Anthony traveled a regular lyceum circuit throughout the North and Midwest, speaking on behalf of women's rights.

Improvements in the printing technology and distribution of newspapers meant that women as well as men were no longer dependent on local sources of information and political guidance. Even if one's town lacked a temperance society or an abolitionist organization, one could still subscribe to a temperance or abolitionist newspaper. A person who did so was reaching out, past the local notables—ministers, politicians, lawyers—who had shaped opinion in the colonial period, to make contact with a larger political community. Abolition newspapers like the *National Anti-Slavery Standard* (which was, for a time, edited by a woman, Lydia Maria Child) and women's rights newspapers like *Una* or *The Revolution* could come straight to a woman's mailbox, enlarging her political world.

Although women could travel more freely and read more widely, in other ways the new industrial economy constrained their lives. As Gerda Lerner has pointed out, many of the new opportunities for men came in a form that closed options for women. When additional men were granted suffrage, for example, "women's political status, while legally unchanged, . . . deteriorated relative to the advances made by men."[1] When new medical schools offered formal training only to men, "the process of professionalization . . . proceeded in such a way as to institutionalize an exclusion of women. . . . The status differential between male and female practitioners was more obviously disadvantageous and underscored women's marginality."[2]

The historian David Potter urged us to ask whether established generalizations about the past apply to women as accurately as they apply to men. We often find that they do not. Several traditional pictures must be refocused. For example, the great religious revival of the early part of the century is often described as though it affected both men and women with equal force. But careful examination of church records has suggested that women were already church members when the revival began; the new recruits were most likely to be sons and husbands of women who had long since been "saved." Seen in this light, the Second Great Awakening may be better understood as an occasion on which women acted as a catalyst for church recruitment.[3]

Although the experience of slavery has received fresh attention from historians, the distinctive experience of female slaves has been little examined. Deborah Gray White's work makes it clear that work roles on the plantation were defined by gender as well as by race. Women were especially vulnerable to sexual exploitation and to debilitating chronic ailments incidental to childbearing. The research of Michael P. Johnson has shown that excessive labor requirements affected not only the slave women but their unborn children.[4]

In free households female work—including taking in boarders, washing their clothes, and cooking for them—might account for as much income as working-class husbands gained from their own employment. If the husband's work was seasonal or erratic, the steady income from taking in boarders could be crucial to the family's survival. The story of the work done by women who took in boarders ought not to be relegated to the obligatory chapters on "home and family life." As Jeanne Boydston demonstrates, all housework is central to the history of American labor.

Traditional interpretations of industrialization require refinement. Familiar accounts are likely to ignore the dependence of early mills on women for their labor force, yet even Alexander Hamilton recognized that a crucial factor in the development of new factories was that their owners could count on a steady supply of female workers at low rates of pay. Women were among the first self-conscious laborers in America. They were also among the poorest. Christine Stansell's study of New York working women and children shows that the "feminization of poverty" long predated the twentieth century.

Viewed through women's eyes, antebellum America looks different. The common school movement looms even larger than in traditional accounts. As Kathryn Kish Sklar's essay suggests, the story of the building of public schools does not begin and end with Horace Mann and Henry Barnard. The work of Emma Willard and Catharine Beecher also requires attention. A history of education in antebellum America needs to explain how the great gap in literacy between men and women was closed during those years, and it must also find room for the large number of women who worked, even briefly, as schoolteachers at wage rates so low that planners could think it feasible to construct enough classrooms to educate every child in America.

The frontier has traditionally been treated as a metaphor for unbounded opportunity. But the experience of married women in the trans-Mississippi West was likely to be one of hardship encountered at the urging of their husbands, not out of their own initiative and choice.

Finally, in the middle years of the nineteenth century women pressed at the limits of the ways in which nonvoting citizens could influence the political order. In antislavery petition campaigns, in lobbying to persuade legislatures to reform laws dealing with married women's property rights and child custody, in responding to the crisis of the Civil War, in pressing charges against former Confederates who tried physically to intimidate them, in volunteering as teachers for freedmen's schools, women expressed political opinions and sought to shape political events. Some, like Catharine Beecher and Sarah Josepha Hale, began to formulate an interpretation of the republican community that suggested women could play an important part in it without voting; others, like Elizabeth Cady Stanton and Sojourner Truth, insisted that women's political rights ought to be the same as those of men.[5] But whatever particular solutions they proposed, whether suffragist or not, the way in which women's citizenship was displayed was a significant element on the American political scene.

NOTES

1. Gerda Lerner, *The Majority Finds Its Past: Placing Women in History* (New York, 1979), p. 18.
2. Ibid., p. 20.
3. David Potter, "American Women and the American Character" (1962), in *History and American Society: Essays of David M. Potter*, ed. Don E. Fehrenbacher (New York, 1979), p. 279; Mary P. Ryan, "A Woman's

Awakening: Evangelical Religion and the Families of Utica, New York, 1800–1840," *American Quarterly* 30 (1978):602–23. See also her *Cradle of the Middle Class: The Family in Oneida County, New York, 1790–1865* (Cambridge, 1981).

4. Michael P. Johnson, "Smothered Slave Infants: Were Slave Mothers at Fault?" *Journal of Southern History* 47 (1981):493–520.

5. For Sojourner Truth's politics, see Carleton Mabee, *Sojourner Truth: Slave, Prophet, Legend* (New York, 1993), esp. chap. 15.

DOCUMENTS: *The Testimony of Slave Women*

Maria Perkins, "I am quite heartsick . . ."

Because masters understood the connection between literacy and rebelliousness, slaves were rarely taught to read and write. This anguished letter from Maria Perkins is unusual because it was written by an enslaved woman. We do not know whether Perkins's husband Richard managed to persuade his master to buy her and keep the family together. If a trader did buy Maria Perkins or her child, the likelihood of permanent separation was great. Scottsville, mentioned in the letter, is a small town near Charlottesville; Staunton is some forty miles away.

Charlottesville, Oct. 8th, 1852
Dear Husband   I write you a letter to let you know my distress   my master has sold albert to a trader on Monday court day and myself and other child is for sale also and I want you to let [me] hear from you very soon before next cort if you can   I don't know when   I don't want you to wait till Christmas   I want you to tell dr Hamelton and your master if either will buy me they can attend to it know and then I can go afterwards. I don't want a trader to get me   they asked me if I had got any person to buy me and I told them no   they took me to the court houste too   they never put me up   a man buy the name of brady bought albert and is gone I don't know where   they say he lives in Scottesville   my things is in several places some is in staunton and if I should be sold I don't know what will become of them   I don't expect to meet with the luck to get that way till I am quite heartsick   nothing more   I am and ever will be your kind wife Maria Perkins.

Maria Perkins to Richard Perkins, October 8, 1852, Ulrich B. Phillips Collection, Yale University Library, New Haven.

Rose, "Look for some others for to 'plenish de earth"

Letters like Maria Perkins's are very rare. Most firsthand evidence of the experience of being a slave comes from narratives prepared by ex-slaves after they were free. Some accounts were published by abolitionist societies before the Civil War; some people were interviewed by agents of the Freedmen's Bureau after the war. A large group of elderly

Manuscript Slave Narrative Collection, Federal Writers' Project, 1941, vol. 17, Texas Narratives, part 4, pp. 174–78, Library of Congress, Washington, D.C.

ex-slaves was interviewed in the 1930s as part of the Federal Writers' Project. One of these speakers we know only as Rose.

Abolitionists shrilly accused masters of breeding slaves as they did cattle. Masters denied these charges and claimed that high birth rates among slave women should be taken as evidence of high levels of nutrition and of good treatment. In Brazil, for example, where the treatment of slaves was much more brutal, fewer children survived. There was some truth in this defense. But slave women lacked the normal legal protections against rape, and, as Rose's moving narrative shows, the line between "forced breeding" and "strong encouragement" could be a very thin one.

What I say am de facts. If I's one day old, I's way over 90, and I's born in Bell County, right here in Texas, and am owned by Massa William Black. He owns mammy and pappy, too. Massa Black has a big plantation but he has more niggers dan he need for work on dat place, 'cause he am a nigger trader. He trade and buy an sell all de time.

Massa Black am awful cruel and he whip de cullud folks and works 'em hard and feed dem poorly. We'uns have for rations de cornmeal and milk and 'lasses and some beans and peas and meat once a week. We'uns have to work in de field every day from daylight till dark and on Sunday we'uns do us washin'. Church? Shucks, we'uns don't know what dat mean.

I has de correct mem'randum of when de war start. Massa Black sold we'uns right den. Mammy and pappy powerful glad to get sold, and dey and I is put on de block with 'bout ten other niggers. When we'uns gits te de tradin' block, dere lots of white folks dere what come to look us over. One man shows de intres' in pappy. Him named Hawkins. He talk to pappy and pappy talk to him and say, "Dem my woman and chiles. Please buy all of us and have mercy on we'uns." Massa Hawkins say, "Dat gal am a likely lookin' nigger, she am portly and strong, but three am more dan I wants, I guesses."

De sale start and 'fore long pappy a put on de block. Massa Hawkins wins de bid for pappy and when mammy am put on de block, he wins de bid for her. Den dere am three or four other niggers sold befo' my time comes. Den massa Black calls me to de block and de auction man say, "What am I offer for dis portly, strong young wench. She's never been 'bused and will make de good breeder."

I wants to hear Massa Hawkins bid, but him say nothin'. Two other men am biddin' 'gainst each other and I sho' has de worryment. Dere am tears comin' down my cheeks 'cause I's bein' sold to some man dat would make sep'ration from my mammy. One man bids $500 and de auction man ask, "Do I hear more? She am gwine at $500.00." Den someone say, $525.00 and de auction man say, "She am sold for $525.00 to Massa Hawkins." Am I glad and 'cited! Why, I's quiverin' all over.

Massa Hawkins takes we'uns to his place and it am a nice plantation. Lots better am dat place dan Massa Black's. Dere is 'bout 50 niggers what is growed and lots of chillen. De first thing massa do when we'uns gits home am give we'uns rations and a cabin. You mus' believe dis nigger when I says dem rations a feast for us. Dere plenty meat and tea and coffee and white flour. I's never tasted white flour and coffee and mammy fix some biscuits and coffee. Well, de biscuits was yum, yum, yum to me, but de coffee I doesn't like.

De quarters am purty good. Dere am twelve cabins all made from logs and a table and some benches and bunks for sleepin' and a fireplace for cookin' and de heat. Dere am no floor, jus' de ground.

Massa Hawkins am good to he niggers and not force 'em work too hard. Dere am as much diff'ence 'tween him and old Massa Black in de way of treatment as 'twixt de Lawd and de devil. Massa Hawkins 'lows he niggers have reason'ble parties and go fishin', but we'uns am never tooken to church and has no books for larnin'. Dere am no edumcation for de niggers.

Dere am one thing Massa Hawkins does to me what I can't shunt from my mind. I knows he don't do it for meanness, but I allus holds it 'gainst him. What he done am force me to live with dat nigger, Rufus, 'gainst my wants.

After I been at he place 'bout a year, de

massa come to me and say, "You gwine live with Rufus in dat cabin over yonder. Go fix it for livin'." I's 'bout sixteen year old and has no larnin', and I's jus' igno'mus chile. I's thought dat him mean for me to tend de cabin for Rufus and some other niggers. Well, dat am start de pestigation for me.

I's took charge of de cabin after work am done and fixes supper. Now, I don't like dat Rufus, 'cause he a bully. He am big and 'cause he so, he think everybody do what him say. We'uns has supper, den I goes here and dere talkin', till I's ready for sleep and den I gits in de bunk. After I's in, dat nigger come and crawl in de bunk with me 'fore I knows it. I says, "What you mean, you fool nigger?" He say for me to hush de mouth. "Dis am my bunk, too," he say.

"You's teched in de head. Git out," I's told him, and I puts de feet 'gainst him and give him a shove and out he go on de floor 'fore he knows what I's doin'. Dat nigger jump up and he mad. He look like de wild bear. He starts for de bunk and I jumps quick for de poker. It am 'bout three feet long and when he comes at me I let him have it over de head. Did dat nigger stop in he tracks? I's say he did. He looks at me steady for a minute and you's could tell he thinkin' hard. Den he go and set on de bench and say, "Jus wait. You thinks it am smart, but you's am foolish in de head. Dey's gwine larn you somethin'."

"Hush yous big mouth and stay 'way from dis nigger, dat all I wants," I say, and jus' sets and hold dat poker in de hand. He jus' sets, lookin' like de bull. Dere we'uns sets and sets for 'bout an hour and den he go out and I bars de door.

De nex' day I goes to de missy and tells her what Rufus wants and missy say dat am de massa's wishes. She say, "Yous am de portly gal and Rufus am de portly man. De massa wants you-uns for to bring forth portly chillen."

I's thinkin' 'bout what de missy say, but say to myse'f, "I's not gwine live with dat Rufus." Dat night when him come in de cabin, I grabs de poker and sits on de bench and says, "Git 'way from me, nigger, 'fore I busts yous brains out and stomp on dem." He say nothin' and git out.

De nex' day de massa call me and tell me, "Woman, I's pay big money for you and I's done dat for de cause I wants you to raise me chillens. I's put yous to live with Rufus for dat purpose. Now, if you doesn't want whippin' at de stake, yous do what I wants."

I thinks 'bout massa buyin' me offen de block and savin' me from bein' sep'rated from my folks and 'bout bein' whipped at de stake. Dere it am. What am I's to do? So I 'cides to do as de massa wish and so I yields.

When we'uns am given freedom, Massa Hawkins tells us we can stay and work for wages or share crop de land. Some stays and some goes. My folks and me stays. We works de land on shares for three years, den moved to other land near by. I stay with my folks till they dies.

If my mem'radum am correct, it am 'bout thirty year since I come to Fort Worth. Here I cooks for white folks till I goes blind 'bout ten year ago.

I never marries, 'cause one 'sperience am 'nough for dis nigger. After what I does for de massa, I's never wants no truck with any man. De Lawd forgive dis cullud woman, but he have to 'scuse me and look for some others for to 'plenish de earth.

DEBORAH GRAY WHITE
The Nature of Female Slavery

There was much in the slave experience that men and women shared. Denied any legal ability to control the conditions of their lives, both men and women labored according to their masters' demands. Both women and men were vulnerable to brutal punishment and to the separation of families; both men and women had no choice but to accept marginal food and clothing. They were part of the productive system of the master's economy (usually, but not always, an agricultural one).

But women also did reproductive work. By this we mean not only the actual bearing and nurturing of children but the domestic work within slave quarters that fed husbands, fathers, and children and gave them the strength to persevere at the productive work of the plantation. As childbearing women they were physically vulnerable in ways that men were not; indeed as the work of Michael P. Johnson (to which Deborah White refers) has shown, slaves suffered a heavy proportion of deaths due to Sudden Infant Death Syndrome because of the malnutrition and overwork of mothers. In the lives of slave women, economics and biology intersected in complex and sorrowful ways.

Considering both physical and psychological factors, in what ways was the experience of enslaved women different from that of enslaved men?

> Slavery is terrible for men: but it is far more terrible for women. Superadded to the burden common to all, *they* have wrongs, and sufferings, and mortifications peculiarly their own.[1]

The images of African-American women that grew out of the slavery era reflect the fact that black males and females did not experience slavery the same way. For both sexes the broad outline of racial oppression was similar, as was the general way in which the race resisted and survived. However, within the institution of racial slavery there were two systems, one for women, the other for men. This was due, in part, to the different expectations that slave owners had of male and female slaves. Different expectations gave rise to different responsibilities, and these responsibilities often defined the life chances of the male or female slave. . . .

Male and female slavery was different from the very beginning. . . . women did not generally travel the middle passage in the holds of slave ships but took the dreaded journey on the quarter deck. According to the 1789 Report of the Committee of the Privy Council the female passage was further distinguished from that of males in that women and girls were not shackled. The slave trader William Snelgrave mentioned the same policy: "We couple the sturdy Men together with Irons; but we suffer the Women and children to go freely about."[2]

This policy had at least two significant consequences for black women. First, they were more easily accessible to the criminal whims and sexual desires of seamen, and few attempts were made to keep the crew members of slave ships from molesting African women. As one slaver reported, officers were permitted to indulge their passions at pleasure and were "sometimes guilty of such brutal excesses as disgrace human nature."[3]

Although white masters seem to have hesitated to require field work of indentured white women servants, they felt no hesitancy in requiring enslaved women to work in the fields at heavy labor. In this rare eyewitness testimony, Benjamin Henry Latrobe's watercolor documents the practice in late eighteenth-century Virginia. He gave it the ironic title "An Overseer doing his duty." Watercolor, ink, and ink wash on paper, 1798. Papers of Benjamin Henry Latrobe. (Courtesy of the Collection of the Maryland Historical Society, Baltimore)

Conversely, African women were occasionally able to incite and/or assist slave insurrections that occurred at sea. For instance, in 1721 the crew on board the *Robert* was stunned when they were attacked by a woman and two men intent on gaining their freedom. Before they were subdued by the captain and other crew members, the slaves, including the woman, had killed several sailors and wounded many others. In his investigation into the mutiny, Captain Harding reflected on the near success of the slaves and found that they had been assisted by the woman "who being more at large, was to watch the proper Opportunity." The woman had served as a lookout and alerted the leader as to the number of sailors on deck. She had also stolen all the weapons used in the mutiny. For her exceptional

participation she paid dearly: "The Woman he hoisted up by the Thumbs, whipp'd, and slashed her with Knives before the other Slaves till she died."[4]

In another incident, in 1785, the captain of a Bristol slaver was attacked by a group of women who tried to throw him overboard. When he was rescued by his crew the women threw themselves down the hatchway. Some died from the injuries incurred in their desperate plunge. Others starved themselves to death. Nine years earlier a similar incident had occurred aboard the Rhode Island vessel the *Thames.* As reported by Dr. Bell, the physician on board, two women aided thirty-two men and two boys in their attempt at mutiny. In a letter to his employer, John Fletcher of London, Bell indicated that the women played a limited role only because the revolt had been so spontaneous that the men did not have time to consult and plan with the women. "Had the women assisted them, in all probability your property here at this time would have been small."[5]

It would seem that a primary reason for allowing women to go without irons was the natural assumption that women could be overpowered. However, since seventeenth- and eighteenth-century merchants and captains were convinced that "prime male slaves generally sell best in any market," slavers crammed the holds full of men and brought women almost as an afterthought. . . .

Therefore, for most of the seventeenth century and for at least the first third of the eighteenth, the system of slavery relied mostly upon black males. This was the case in both the Chesapeake and Carolina regions. For the period from 1658 to 1730 black men in colonial Maryland outnumbered women by roughly one and one half to one. Indeed, the entire Chesapeake area had many more slave men than women. In Surry County, Virginia, the ratio was about 145 men to 100 women in the 1670s and 1680s, and rose to over two to one in the 1690s and 1700s. In South Carolina, too, men outnumbered women. In 1720 in St. George's Parish the sex ratio was 129 to 100. A sample of slaves taken from inventories in 1730 and 1731 revealed that on sizable plantations throughout the colony slave men outnumbered slave women 180 to 100.[6]

The uneven sex ratio clearly made colonial slavery different for black men and women; it was much harder for a man to find a wife than for a woman to find a husband. Until about 1730 a significant number of men could expect to die without ever having had a spouse, and because plantations were small it was likely that many of those with wives had had to seek them in other plantations and therefore did not live with them. On colonial plantations both married and unmarried men lived together in small groups. In short, the emphasis that white colonialists put on muscle and brawn in the development of their plantation systems made early colonial slavery very lonely and desolate for men.

The situation was different for the bonded woman. Few went without husbands and even though plantations were small the preponderance of men made it likely that a woman would be able to live with her spouse. Nevertheless, many women had husbands on plantations other than their own, and these women lived with their children and raised them without the daily company of their husbands.[7]

These sex-segregated living arrangements did have some imperfect analogs in the African experience. Like their American counterparts, seventeenth- and eighteenth-century West African women usually did not raise small children with the help of their husbands, but raised them alone or with the assistance of other women. While West African men lived with their spouses in the same compound, and couples were free to come together at will, they did not share the same hut or area of the compound. But in Africa segregated living arrangements flowed from the corporate nature of the family and from a belief in the inherent differences of the sexes. The Africans' definition of family extended far beyond parents and children, or the nuclear family, to aunts, uncles, and grandparents. Since a husband and wife did not alone compose a family there was no reason for them to reside alone together. A woman's duty was to bear and raise small children, a duty that was hers alone. In colonial North America the African woman was separated from the cultural foundations and environment that had lent meaning to sex-segregated living and independent child rearing in Africa, but the demographics of slave settlement caused such living and rearing patterns to persist in a not too dissimilar form.

Slavers separated the black woman from most of what had lent meaning to her life. In Africa, her primary role had been motherhood, yet in the early years of plantation settlement she figured in some plantation building as a means of keeping male slaves content. Between 1763 and 1783 Britain attempted to establish a plantation colony in East Florida modeled after that of South Carolina. The slaves involved in this endeavor were mostly men. Correspondence among the governor, his overseer, and those assisting in the undertaking reveals a concern that women be purchased and transported forthwith lest the men become dissatisfied and run away. Thus, the Earl of Egmont wrote that the slaves could not be happy and content without each having a wife. This, he wrote, "will greatly tend to keep them at home and to make them Regular."[8]

The use of black female labor in the fields tended to make farming profitable for seventeenth-century Virginia planters. Although some Virginia white women did field work, this was generally assumed to be a temporary state of affairs and therefore no taxes were levied on their labor. No such assumption was made about the field labor of black women. In fact, in 1629, in colonial Virginia, a tax was levied on any person who worked in the ground, and subsequent laws defined those subject to taxation as black and white male servants and "negro women at age of sixteen years." Because the cost of a female slave was less than that of a male slave, female slave labor was cheaper than male slave labor, particularly when planters applied to black women the same tax-exempt status that applied to white female servants. Naturally, Virginia planters did just that, necessitating another series of laws, passed between 1662 and 1672, reiterating that tithes were to be paid on all field workers including black women.[9]

Surprisingly, slaveholders were slow to appreciate the economic value of the slave woman's procreative ability, but by the middle of the eighteenth century most slave owners, especially those with twenty or more slaves, had come to realize the potential benefits. Thomas Nairne, an eighteenth-century South Carolina planter, expected bondwomen to do the same work as his male slaves. They would, he thought, clear, plant and hoe three acres of land in six months. Besides doing field work he expected them to have children, and thus, by natural means increase the slave population. In 1732, Nairne estimated that the yearly advantage from this increase would be 540 British pounds.[10]

Although many planters made similar calculations, they did not move to increase the number of female slaves through importation. In the years prior to the American Revolution, the female slave population grew more as a result of natural increase than by importation. It was not until sometime between 1730 and 1750 that the sex ratio evened out. The first African-American women began childbearing earlier than their African mothers, and thus had more children, including more females, than their mothers. The second generation also had more children than the first, and on, and on until the ratio was even.[11]

Although a one to one sex ratio was achieved slowly, the consequences were astounding. First, the presence of an even slave sex ratio made American slavery unique in the Western Hemisphere. Everywhere else that

slavery reared its ugly head, black men composed the overwhelming majority of the labor force. A related consequence was the creation by North American slaves of monogamous families. In Latin America and the Caribbean black men lived in barracklike environments and had far fewer opportunities to establish long-lasting emotional relationships with black women.[12] Taken together, these two facts suggest that North American male slaves had a more balanced life than their Caribbean or South American counterparts. However, the Earl of Egmont's request for wives to make men more "regular" suggests that powerless North American male slaves were more easily manipulated, because their spouses and children could be held hostage and compelled to answer for their transgressions. Black women, unfortunately, proved to be mirrors for black men. Each time the former was abused, the latter's own helplessness was reflected.[13]

For black women the consequences of the even sex ratio were also severe. Once slaveholders realized that the reproductive function of the female slave could yield a profit, the manipulation of procreative sexual relations became an integral part of the sexual exploitation of female slaves. Few of the calculations made by masters and overseers failed to take a slave woman's childbearing capacity into account. This was particularly true after Congress outlawed the overseas slave trade in 1807. The slave woman's "marital" status, her work load, her diet all became investment concerns of slaveholders, who could maximize their profits if their slave women had many children.

It was little consolation for slave women; in fact, they may not have even realized that when slaveholders put a premium on female slave childbearing, slaveholders unwittingly supplied another thread of continuity between Africa and North America. As noted, in the seventeenth and eighteenth centuries many first-generation African slave women raised their children without a lot of male assistance, much as they had done in Africa. In all likelihood this helped preserve that part of African culture that put emphasis on motherhood, and the African mother probably passed it on to her daughters. When mid-eighteenth-century slaveholders made female slave childbearing their desired goal and acted on that goal, they reinforced a cultural attitude which for African-American women now had roots in both Africa and North America. The nature and conditions of black motherhood in Africa and the North American South obviously differed because the motivations of Africans, African-Americans, and slaveholders were different. But for the purpose of our current discussion it is important to note the continuity. . . .

In the one hundred years after 1750 the American black population, 90 percent of which was enslaved, was notable for, among other things, its fertility. In the pre–Civil War period black women were very prolific. According to demographers the crude birthrate exceeded fifty per one thousand, meaning that each year more than one fifth of the black women in the 15–44 age cohort bore a child.[14] This statistic indicates a major functional difference between male and female bondage. Male slavery centered mostly around the work that black men did for whites. Female slavery had much to do with work, but much of it was concerned with bearing, nourishing, and rearing children whom slaveholders needed for the continual replenishment of their labor force. This does not mean that work and childbearing were always kept in perfect balance. The extent to which the slave owner consciously emphasized one or the other ultimately depended on his needs. In antebellum America, these were often determined by the region of the country in which he was settled. The lower black fertility rates in the lower and newer regions of the south (Alabama, Mississippi, Louisiana, and Texas) may be an indication that female labor in the fields superseded childbearing in importance. In both the upper and lower South, however, slave owners attended to the proverbial bottom line by striving to maximize profits. Few ignored the important role that natural increase played in the realization of that goal.

Meanwhile, the responsibilities of childbearing and child care seriously circumscribed the female slave's life. The limits were reflected in patterns of female resistance. Studies of fugitive slaves reveal that their ranks were not swelled with women. Seventy-seven percent of the runaways advertised in colonial South Carolina during the 1730s were men. This pattern persisted throughout the century. South Carolina was by no means unique. The 1,500 newspaper advertisements published in Williamsburg, Richmond, and Fredericksburg, Virginia, from 1736 to 1801 evince much the same pattern. Of the runaways whose sex could be discerned 1,138 were men, while only 142 were

women. The same pattern existed in antebellum Huntsville, Alabama, where, between 1820 and 1860, of the 562 fugitives advertised, 473 were listed as male and only 87 as female. In North Carolina from 1850 to 1860, only 19 percent of the runaway ads described women. In 1850, 31.7 percent of the runaways advertised for in New Orleans newspapers were women.[15]

Some of the reasons why women were underrepresented in the fugitive population had to do with childbearing. Most runaways were between sixteen and thirty-five years old.[16] A woman of this age was either pregnant, nursing an infant, or had at least one small child to care for. While all that men between sixteen and thirty-five could count on was hard work and severe punishment if they angered the master or overseer, it was during these years that many slave women got their best care. Slave owners were less likely to insist on a full day's heavy workload when the laborer involved was a pregnant woman.

Also important in understanding why females ran away less frequently than men is the fact that women tended to be more concerned with the welfare of their children, and this limited their mobility. Fugitive men loved their offspring, but unlike the runaway male, the slave woman who left her children behind could not be certain that they would be given the best possible care. A father could not provide for a suckling infant because "in dem days no bottle was given to no baby under a year old." Moreover, since women and small children were often sold as a group, a father was more likely to be sold away from his children. Sometimes the children of runaway mothers were lucky enough to have an aunt or grandmother on the same or nearby plantation, and sometimes a father or uncle cared for the child. But, for those fugitive women who left children in slavery, the physical relief which freedom brought was limited compensation for the anguish they suffered. Of the same one hundred fifty-one fugitive women advertised for in the 1850 New Orleans newspapers, none was listed as having run away without her children.[17]

This, of course, was no secret to slaveholders and probably accounts for the casual attitude many masters and overseers had about female runaways. For years the Flint family's hold upon Linda Brent's children kept her from fleeing. In her narrative Brent explained: "I was certain my children were to be put in their power, in order to give them a stronger hold on me." Similarly, in 1838 a slave named Clarissa was sent to Philadelphia even though there was some concern about her running away once she reached free territory. Mrs. Trigg, her mistress, had few qualms because Clarissa's husband and children remained in Kentucky.[18]

Women could probably have escaped more often if they could have done so with their husbands and offspring, but children, in particular, made the journey more difficult than it already was and increased the chances of capture. For instance, although Josiah Henson successfully reached Cincinnati with his wife and children he had to carry his two stout toddlers most of the way and listen to their cries of hunger and exhaustion at night. Henry Bibb also tried to escape with his family but was unsuccessful. With his wife, Malinda, and small child, he started on his journey north, but a pack of blood-thirsty canines and patrollers put a stop to his quest for freedom. For Bibb, the difficulties of escaping with a wife and child proved insurmountable, and although he regretted his capture he was actually relieved. Some time later he escaped, but without Malinda or his child.[19] . . .

If women in the company of men encountered insurmountable difficulties, imagine the problems encountered by women and children escaping alone. For conductors and directors of the Underground Railroad, fugitive women with children were a tremendous source of anxiety. William Still, the chairman of the Vigilance Committee of the Philadelphia Underground Railroad, was always nervous about transporting women with children since they stood a greater chance of being caught. "Females," he wrote, "undertook three times the risk of failure that males are liable to." William Penn, who worked with the Underground Railroad, also expressed apprehension. Speaking of two women, both of whom had two children, he noted: "none of these can walk so far or so fast as scores of *men* that are constantly leaving."[20] . . .

The few women who ran away did so for a variety of reasons. Some escaped with men and many left for the same reasons as men—cruel treatment or the fear of it, fear of sale or sale of a loved one, or just the desire to be free. Not surprisingly, for many women it was the children, or more properly, the fear of losing them, that provided the incentive to flee. The desperation of some slave mothers was captured in Harriet Beecher Stowe's fictionalized account of the escape to freedom by Eliza Harris and her son across the ice floes of the Ohio River. Many took the heart-rending tale of Eliza's flight as evidence of Stowe's vivid imagination, but actually Stowe described in fiction what was a real life episode for a few women. One such woman was a Kentucky slave who feared that her two little girls were to be sold away from her. Surviving only on fruits and green corn she managed to cross the river. The odds were formidable even when there was no river to cross. For instance, there was the Maryland slave named Maria who with the help of the Underground Railroad escaped in 1859 with all *seven* of her children.[21]

Many female fugitives were much less fortunate than Maria and had to leave some of their children behind. . . .

. . . A Maryland slave woman named Vina was forced to choose which of her children would be free and which would remain enslaved. She fled to New Jersey to meet her husband with her two daughters after having consigned her two small sons "into the hands of God." The journey still proved to be too much for her; she left one of them on a lonely road to be retrieved by her husband. The story of Mary Montgomery is especially heartbreaking. Although sickly, Mary had a nursing infant at her breast. According to Christopher Nichols, a successful fugitive, Mary had been given conflicting work orders by the overseer and master. Unable to satisfy both she "took to the woods" and disappeared. "It was said that she got to the North, but nobody knew." Mary Montgomery did what few other bondwomen did; she left her suckling infant behind to die for lack of nourishment.[22]

Such desperate decisions inevitably induced emotional trauma and psychological torment. At age twenty-seven, when she fled to Pennsylvania to escape the sexual overtures of her master, Linda Brent made a decision similar to Mary Montgomery's. She knew her grandmother would keep a watchful eye on her son and daughter. However, she feared her mistress's vengeance would put them in danger of severe punishment, even sale. The advice she sought and was given served only to confuse her and increase her anxiety. From her friend and accomplice, Betty, she received encouragement to escape: "Lors, chile! What's you crying 'bout? Dem young uns vil kill you dead. Don't be so chick'n hearted! If you does, you vil nebber git thro' dis world." But, her grandmother, who, unlike childless Betty, had helped raise three generations of black children, admonished: "Stand by your own children, and suffer with them till death. Nobody respects a mother who forsakes her children; and if you leave them, you will never have a happy moment."[23]

Truancy seems to have been the way many slave women reconciled their desire to flee and their need to stay. Studies of female runaways demonstrate that females made the most likely truants because they were more concerned about breaking family ties. Benjamin Johnson of Georgia remembered that "sometimes de women wouldn't take it an' would run away an' hide in de woods. Sometimes dey would come back after a short stay an' den again dey would have to put de hounds on dere trail to bring dem back home." Short-term absences of this sort were not mere flights of fancy. Truants were often no less angry, resentful, and frightened than their fugitive brethren who chose to flee to the North. If anything they were more frightened of the unknown to the North than of the certainties they left behind. However, this frightful ambivalence did not keep them from shouldering substantial risk. Thus we find cases such as that of a St. Simon's woman who, after being severely beaten by her master, found the rattlesnakes of the South Carolina rice swamps more comforting than her own cabin. Sickness induced by hunger finally forced her back to her plantation.[24] . . .

Such behavior was not unique to the nineteenth century. As early as 1710 Virginian William Byrd recorded a case of truancy that had a tragic ending. One of his slave women ran away on June 25, 1710, and was found on June 28, only to disappear again two days later. She was recovered again on July 8, but ran away again on the fifteenth. Three weeks later she turned up again, but in November she disappeared and was soon found dead.[25]

Motherhood structured the slave woman's behavior, but so too did the female slave work experience. The division of labor on most plantations conferred greater mobility on male than on female slaves. Few of the chores performed by bondwomen took them off the plantation.

Usually masters chose their male slaves to assist in the transportation of crops to market, and the transport of supplies and other materials to the plantation. More male than female slaves were artisans and craftsmen, and this made it more difficult to hire a female slave than a male slave. Fewer bondwomen therefore had a chance to vary their work experience. As a consequence, more men than women were able to test their survival skills under different circumstances.

Another factor affecting slave mobility was the "abroad marriage," a marriage between slaves who resided at different locations. When "abroad" spouses visited each other, usually once a week, it was most often the husband who traveled to the wife. All in all, it was female bondage, more than male bondage, that meant being tied to the immediate environment of the plantation or farm. This was a liability when it came to running away. The would-be female fugitive, including the domestic who conceivably had more polished verbal and language skills than the field slave, had to consider her unfamiliarity with the surrounding countryside before fleeing. She also had to consider how conspicuous a lone black woman or group of black women would be in a countryside infrequently traveled by such humanity. Some female fugitives overcame this last impediment by disguising themselves as males.[26] However, the small number of female runaways indicates that more bondwomen than bondmen just "stayed put."

This does not mean that they did not resist enslavement or sexual exploitation. As historians have been quick to point out, the dearth of large-scale slave revolts suggests that in the United States slave resistance often manifested itself in intransigent behavior. If resistance in the United States was seldom politically oriented, consciously collective, or violently revolutionary, it was generally individualistic and aimed at maintaining what the slaves, master, and overseer had, in the course of their relationships, perceived as an acceptable level of work, shelter, food, punishment, and free time. Slaves may have thought about overthrowing the system of slavery but the odds against them were so overwhelming that the best most could hope for was survival with a modicum of dignity. Slave resistance was aimed at maintaining what seemed to all concerned to be the status quo.

Bondwomen, like bondmen, were adept in inventing schemes and excuses to get their own way. After her mistress died, Alcey, the cook on the Burleigh plantation in Virginia, decided she no longer wanted to work in the kitchen. When her request to be transferred to the field was ignored, she found another way to make her desire known. "She systematically disobeyed orders and stole or destroyed the greater part of the provisions given to her for the table." When that failed "she resolved to show more plainly that she was tired of the kitchen": "Instead of getting chickens for dinner from the coop, as usual, she unearthed from some corner an old hen that had been sitting for six weeks and served her up as a fricassee!" Alcey achieved her objective and was sent to the field the following day without even so much as a reprimand.[27] . . .

Some bondwomen were more direct in their resistance. Some murdered their masters, some were arsonists, and still others refused to be whipped. Overseers and masters learned which black women and men they could whip, and which would not be whipped. Sometimes they found out the hard way. Equipped with a whip and two healthy dogs, an Alabama overseer tied a woman named Crecie to a stump with intentions of beating her. To his pain and embarrassment she jerked the stump out of the ground, grabbed the whip, and sent the overseer running. Women fought back despite severe consequences. An Arkansas overseer decided to make an example of a slave woman named Lucy "to show the slaves that he was impartial." Lucy, however, was not to be made an example of. According to her son, "she jumped on him and like to tore him up." Word got around that Lucy would not be beaten. She was sold, but she was never again whipped.[28]

Slave women also sometimes violently resisted sexual exploitation. Since Southern laws did not recognize the rape of a black woman as a crime, often the only recourse slave women had was to fight off their assailants. When Jermain Loguen's mother was attacked she picked up a stick and dealt her would-be rapist a blow that sent him staggering. She stood her ground even as he rebounded with a knife, and finally she knocked him out cold.[29] . . .

Bondwomen used dissembling tactics and force much as bondmen did. It was probably safe to assume that women chose violent resistance, particularly that which involved fist-

icuffs, less often than did men. However, it should also be remembered that such resistance was not really a viable option for bondmen, either. A bullet through the head, a jail cell, a merciless whipping, and/or sale was the likely fate of any slave, male or female, who demonstrated aggressive behavior, even in self-defense.

A less overt form of resistance involved the use of poison and this suited women because they officiated as cooks and nurses on the plantation. As early as 1755 a Charleston slave woman was burned at the stake for poisoning her master, and in 1769 a special issue of the *South Carolina Gazette* carried the story of a slave woman who had poisoned her master's infant child. No one will ever know how many slave owners and members of their families were poisoned. The slave's objective was not to get caught because punishment was sure and swift. A case in point was recorded by Mary Chesnut in her diary. A friend of hers told her the story of a man named Dr. Keitt who was chronically ill. Dr. Keitt's friend suggested to him that his slaves were perhaps trying to kill him: Dr. Keitt promised to be prudent and to come the next day. As soon as his friend left, a Negro woman brought him a cup of tea. As he stirred it, a white powder became evident, settled in the bottom of the cup. In a moment he believed what his friend had suspected. He dashed the tea in her face. "You ungrateful beast, I believe you are trying to poison me." Next morning, he was found with his throat cut from ear to ear. It was found that the woman, in league with two male slaves, was putting a poison in Dr. Keitt's coffee every morning and when discovered they murdered him outright. Interestingly enough, and consistent with female runaway statistics, the men successfully escaped but the woman was caught and hanged.[30]

Perhaps the most important difference between male and female slave resistance was the greater propensity of women to feign illness in order to gain a respite from their work or to change the nature of their work altogether. This strategy was feasible precisely because childbearing was the primary expectation that slave owners had of slave women. The perpetuation of the institution of slavery, as nineteenth-century Southerners knew it, rested on the slave woman's reproductive capacity. In an age when women's diseases were still shrouded in mystery, getting the maximum amount of work from women of childbearing age while remaining confident that no damage was done to their reproductive organs was a guessing game that few white slave owners wanted to play or could afford to lose. A Virginia planter summed up the "problem" when he complained of the "liability of women, especially to disorders and irregularities which cannot be detected by exterior symptoms, but which may be easily aggravated into serious complaints." He further explained that women were rendered "nearly valueless" for work because of the ease with which they could impose upon their owners. His frustration was obvious as he told Frederick Olmsted that "they don't come to the field and you go to the quarters and ask the old nurse what's the matter and she says, 'Oh, she's not ... fit to work sir'; and ... you have to take her word for it that something or other is the matter with her, and you dare not set her to work; and so she will lay up till she feels like taking the air again, and plays the lady at your expense."[31] Although few slave women were given as much latitude as this planter suggested, they did sometimes "play the lady" and get away with it.

By the time Olmsted heard this complaint slave women had been engaging in such behavior for some time. On Landon Carter's eighteenth-century Virginia plantation, this form of resistance was raised to an art. Although Carter was certain that Mary faked her fits, her violent and uncontrollable howls always got the better of him, and she spent a good deal of time away from the fields. Another woman, named Sarah, laid up for *eleven* months before delivering her infant. She, no doubt, "played the lady" at Carter's expense, and even tried to do it again during her next pregnancy. To her chagrin she met a wiser Landon Carter who was determined not to let her get away with it. Sarah was determined, too, and proved to be as good at truancy as she was at feigning illness. Although "big with child" she took to the woods and stayed over a week.[32] ...

The case of Maria, one of President James Polk's slaves, is particularly revealing. Since Polk spent a good deal of time away from his plantations, they were run by overseers with the aid of a few of his close friends. With the exception of Eophraim Beanland, all of Polk's overseers had trouble with Maria, who was al-

ways complaining of some malady. Maria began pleading illness in May 1839, significantly, after the strict Beanland was replaced by the more indulgent George Bratton. At that time, Bratton wrote to Polk that "she had bin in bad helth since the first of march and is likely not to be able to do any sirvice." Bratton died that year and was replaced by John Garner who also had difficulty making Maria work. In June 1840, Garner informed Polk that Maria "has spels onste a month very bad." A week later he explained in greater detail that "she is in a very bad condishon every thre or fore weks, so very bad onst this spring she was thone into fits of spasms." Maria's health continued to keep her from the fields and finally she was reassigned to the house where she was taught to weave. She was particularly good at weaving and Garner soon reported that "Marier aperes to enjoy as good helth at present as any person." In fact, Maria had such a miraculous recovery, and became so good at weaving that she informed Polk that she had increased her worth by at least thirty dollars.[33]

Maria was "fortunate" because many slave masters refused to accept even obvious illness as an excuse to lay off work. James Mercer, for instance, had a strict formula for judging illness: "No woman was allowed to 'lay up' unless her illness was accompanied by a fever." Some masters insisted on giving the "patient" a thorough examination before excusing her from work. After sending his slave, Caroline, to the fields in spite of her protestations, a Mississippi Valley planter claimed: "We have to be sharp with them; if we were not, every negro on the estate would be abed."[34]

The subject of feigning illness is as difficult for the historian as it was for the planter. Was Maria actually ill, or was she deceiving the overseers? The description of her complaint suggests a menstrual disorder but she could also have been quite an actress. Whatever we conclude we must not overlook the important point that Maria's behavior, feigned or otherwise, is what landed her the easier weaver's job. This case, and the many like it, suggest that while slave owners had a vested interest in keeping pregnant women healthy, the relatively better care expectant mothers received was as much a result of the pressure slave women exerted as of self-serving benevolence extended by slave owners and overseers. If slave women frequently "played the lady," as the Virginia planter argued, it was only after they risked a lot to be treated humanely.

Data on slave illness on Southern plantations reveal that plantations were havens for disease, and that slaves were indeed plagued by sickness. Slaves suffered and often died from pneumonia, diarrhea, cholera, and smallpox. The slave diet was high in calories but suffered from dangerously low levels of protein and other nutrients. Lean meats, poultry, eggs, milk, and grain products other than corn—foods needed to help the human immune system produce antibodies to fight off infections—were only sporadically seen on most slaves' plates. In addition, most slaves did not get nearly enough fruits and vegetables. Blindness, sore eyes, skin irritations, rickets, toothaches, pellagra, beriberi, and scurvy were among the many afflictions that resulted from vitamin deficiencies caused by the monotonous daily servings of rice, fat-back, corn meal, and salt pork.[35]

Slave women suffered from these illnesses as well as from those associated with the menstrual cycle and childbirth. According to Todd Savitt, Virginia bondwomen probably lost more time from work for menstrual pain, discomfort, and disorders than for any other cause. Among the menstrual maladies were amenorrhea (lack of menstrual flow), abnormal bleeding between cycles (sometimes caused by benign and malignant tumors), and abnormal discharges (resulting from such conditions as gonorrhea, tumors, and prolapsed uterus). Although the 1850 mortality statistics for Virginia indicate that slave women were slightly less likely than white women to die from complications of pregnancy, bondwomen suffered during childbirth. Convulsions, retention of placenta, ectopic pregnancy, breech presentation, premature labor, and uterine rigidity were among the difficulties they faced. Birthing was complicated further by the unsanitary practices of midwives and physicians who delivered a series of children in the course of a day without washing their hands, thereby triggering outbreaks of puerperal (child bed) fever. These infections of the reproductive organs were often fatal.[36]

Still it is difficult to ascertain whether bondwomen who claimed to be ill were actually sick or whether they were practicing a kind of passive resistance. They certainly had more leverage in the realm of feigning illness than men, but they also perhaps had more reason than men to be ill. This does not mean that women were more disadvantaged than black men in this regard. It does suggest, however, that their health experiences were radically different. Although women may have had a less healthy day-to-day existence they could generally expect to outlive their male counterparts, probably because men were engaged usually in heavier and more dangerous work. On the average, antebellum black women out-lived their men by two years. This average varied depending on the state. In Louisiana in 1850, for instance, at birth a black male could expect to live about twenty-nine years, while a black female had a life expectancy of about thirty-four years. At age thirty the life expectancy of a Louisiana black male was approximately another twenty-seven years. The thirty-year-old black woman could expect to live for another thirty-one years.[37]

If it is hard to differentiate real sickness from passive resistance it is almost impossible to determine whether slave women practiced birth control and abortion. These matters were virtually exclusive to the female world of the quarters, and when they arose they were attended to in secret and were intended to remain secret. Some Southern whites were certain that slave women knew how to avoid pregnancy as well as how to deliberately abort a pregnancy. When Daph, a woman on the Ferry Hill plantation in Virginia, miscarried twins in 1838 the overseer reported that Daph took some sort of abortifact to bring about the miscarriage. Suspicions about slave abortions ran high enough to spur public comment. In an essay entitled "On the Susceptibility of the Caucasian and African Races to the Different Classes of Disease," Dr. E. M. Pendleton claimed that planters regularly complained of whole families of women who failed to have any children. A Tennessee physician, Dr. John H. Morgan, said of slave women that "often they will attempt to bring all the aids into requisition that they can ascertain that will increase the parturient effort, either by medicine, violent exercise, or by external and internal manipulations." Morgan was relatively certain that black females declined the use of mechanical implements to effect miscarriage but he was convinced they used abortifacients. Among those he listed were the herbs of tansy and rue, the roots and seed of the cotton plant, pennyroyal, cedar berries, and camphor, either in gum or spirits.[38]

The suspicions of planters on this account were not without foundation. For example, an 1869 South Carolina court case revealed that a slave woman sold as "unsound" and barren in 1857 had three children *after* emancipation. In another instance, a bondwoman refused to have children because her master forced her to marry someone she did not like. After she was sold and found someone of her own choosing, she had ten children. Sarah Shaw of Missouri remembered that when her father was sold away, her master compelled her mother to take a new husband. Her mother complied but she was determined not to have any more children. "Mama said she would never marry a man and have children so she married my step-father Trattle Barber, because she knew he had a disease and could not be a father."[39]

The record on self-imposed sterility and self-induced miscarriages is ambiguous. Strenuous work might have been the culprit in many cases involving barrenness or abortion. For example, on the Ball rice plantations in South Carolina, from 1760 to 1865, the months of greatest hoeing and weeding activity—May, June, and July—produced the smallest number of conceptions resulting in a birth.[40] Several physicians, including Doctors Morgan and Pendleton, made the connection between the bonded woman's work regimen and sterility and miscarriages. Dr. Morgan thought that slave fertility would be higher if, among other things, female field hands were not so "exposed" during menstruation and pregnancy: "When by proper care and attention during these periods, in the way of moderate labor, good clothing etc., they are much more thrifty and fruitful."[41]

The jury will have to remain out on whether slave women were guilty of practicing birth control and abortion, but some reasons why they might have been guilty as accused should be considered. Certainly, they had reason not to want to bear and nurture children who could be sold from them at a slave master's whim. They had ample cause to want to deny whites the satisfaction of realizing a profit on the birth of their children. But they also had as much reason as any antebellum woman,

white or free black, to shun pregnancy and childbirth. As long as obstetrics had not yet evolved into a science, childbirth was dangerous. We would also be remiss if we did not at least suppose that a few abortions were motivated by attempts to hide teenage pregnancy or marital infidelity. Black women were slaves but they were also human.

The entire subject of feigned illness, sterility, deliberate and nondeliberate miscarriages illustrates some of the ways in which female slavery was different from male slavery; at the same time it raises interesting points of comparison between antebellum black and white women. Although black women did considerably more heavy labor than white women, on a diet with less nutritional value, their fertility rates were usually similar to or higher than that of Southern white women. One explanation offered for the symmetry revolves around the natural immunity blacks have to malaria, or more specifically, the greater susceptibility of whites to this disease, which destroys male sperm by elevating male scrotal temperature. It has been argued that had not malaria been so devastating to whites, black fertility would not have compared so favorably, given the deprivation under which slave women functioned.[42] Historians have also observed that some white women of this period, particularly of the middle and upper classes, feigned illness or pretended to be very delicate in order to avoid sexual intercourse that could result in an unwanted pregnancy. There seems to be no evidence to confirm or deny that slave women did the same. It is truly ironic, though, that while slave women probably shared with white women a natural fear of childbirth, slave women had to feign illness to ease the burden of work in order to make bearing a child easier. Some female slaves even got pregnant in order to avoid backbreaking field labor. The plight of both groups of women was unenviable but on the average white women were much more successful in avoiding pregnancies than black women. The white birthrate declined throughout the nineteenth century and continued to do so well into the twentieth century. The black birthrate did not begin to show a significant decline until the very end of the nineteenth century.[43] Throughout the antebellum period especially, the incentives to have children were greater for black than for white women. Although they showed much concern, planters had little to worry about when it came to the rate of slave reproduction.

Did slave infanticide pose a serious threat? Probably not. There were some cases where mothers were accused of murdering their children, and a few women may have done so. In 1830 a North Carolina slave woman was convicted of murdering her own child. A year later a Missouri slave was accused of poisoning and smothering her infant, and in 1834, Elizabeth, one of James Polk's slaves, was said to have smothered her newborn. No one will ever know what drove these women to kill their infants, if they did. Some whites thought slave women lacked maternal feelings, yet a few women who killed their children claimed to have done so because of their intense concern for their offspring. Thus, an Alabama woman killed her child because her mistress continually abused it. In confessing her guilt, she claimed that her master was the father of the child, and that her mistress knew it and treated it so cruelly that she had to kill it to save it from further suffering. Another woman killed her newborn because she knew that the master had plans to sell the baby, the same way he had sold her three older children. Years later Lou Smith recalled the incident: "When her fourth baby was born and was about two months old, she just studied all the time about how she would have to give it up, and one day she said, 'I just decided I'm not going to let Old Master sell this baby; he just ain't going to do it.' She got up and give it something out of a bottle, and pretty soon it was dead."[44]

These cases represent atypical behavior on the part of slave mothers. Runaway and truancy data suggest mothers cared dearly for their children, and recent historical and medical research suggests that many children who supposedly were suffocated by a mother were actually victims of what today is known as Sudden Infant Death Syndrome (SIDS) or "crib death." According to Michael P. Johnson the 1850 census showed that of the victims of suffocation 82 percent were slaves. The 1860 census showed a similar high percentage of slave deaths due to suffocation. Johnson estimates that between 1790 and 1860 smothering was reported to be responsible for the deaths of over sixty thousand slave infants. Most white Southerners attributed these deaths to the carelessness of slave mothers who rolled onto them while sleeping, deliberately murdered them, or otherwise provided insufficient care. Johnson and Savitt, however, argue that recent medical discoveries suggest that "crib death"—the sudden death of any infant or young child who does not have a history of illness and whose postmortem examination fails to demonstrate an identifiable cause of death—was probably responsible for the majority of such slave infant deaths. Statistics compiled by Johnson show that most "smothered" slave infants died in the winter months, and a significant number were between two and four months old. Modern day physicians have pinpointed the peak age period for "crib death" victims to be between two and four months, and have found that more infants succumb between October and March than in any other time period. In addition, a disproportionately high number of today's victims come from low socioeconomic groups, infants of women who are not likely to get good prenatal care.[45] Therefore, we can suppose that some of the infant deaths that planters attributed to infanticide and some that whites blamed on maternal carelessness were actually due to causes which even today baffle medical experts. We might also suppose that it was easier and cheaper for planters to malign slave women than to thoroughly investigate infant slave deaths and that, based on findings linking prenatal care and nutrition to SIDS, it was the planters who fed pregnant women too little and worked them too hard who were more responsible for "smothered infants" than the women who subsequently bore the guilt and blame.

Female slave bondage was not better or worse, or more or less severe, than male bondage, but it was different. From the very beginning of a woman's enslavement she had to cope with sexual abuse, abuse made legitimate by the conventional wisdom that black women were promiscuous Jezebels. Work assignments also structured female slave life so that women were more confined to the boundaries of the plantation than were men. The most important reason for the difference between male and female bondage, however, was the slave woman's childbearing and child care responsibilities. These affected the female slave's pattern of resistance and figured prominently in her general health.

NOTES

1. Linda Brent, *Incidents in the Life of a Slave Girl,* Lydia Maria Child, ed. (New York: Harcourt Brace Jovanovich, 1973 [1860]), p. 79.

2. Elizabeth Donnan, ed., *Documents Illustrative of the History of the Slave Trade to America,* 4 vols. (Washington, D.C.: Carnegie Institute of Washington, 1930), 2:595, 353.

3. Charles H. Nichols, *Many Thousand Gone: The Ex-Slaves' Account of Their Bondage and Their Freedom* (Bloomington: Indiana University Press, 1963), p. 9; George Francis Dow, *Slave Ships and Slaving* (Salem, Mass.: Marine Research Society, 1927), p. 145.

4. Donnan, ed., *Slave Trade,* 2:266.

5. Helen T. Catterall, ed., *Judicial Cases Concerning American Slavery and the Negro,* 5 vols. (Washington, D.C.: Carnegie Institute of Washington, 1936), 1:19; Donnan, ed., *Slave Trade,* 3:323.

6. Russell R. Menard, "The Maryland Slave Population, 1658 to 1730: A Demographic Profile of Blacks in Four Countries," *William and Mary Quarterly* 32 (January 1975):33; Allan Kulikoff, "The Beginnings of the Afro-American Family in Maryland," in *The American Family in Social-Historical Perspective,* Michael Gordon, ed., 2nd ed. (New York: St. Martin's, 1978), p. 446; Peter H. Wood, *Black Majority: Negroes in Colonial South Carolina from 1670 through the Stono Rebellion* (New York: Norton, 1974), p. 160....

7. See Kulikoff, "The Beginnings of the Afro-American Family," pp. 446–48; Menard, "The Maryland Slave Population," p. 354....

8. Daniel C. Littlefield, *Rice and Slaves: Ethnicity and the Slave Trade in Colonial South Carolina* (Baton Rouge: Louisiana State University Press, 1981), pp. 63–65.

9. William Waller Hening, ed., *The Statutes at Large, Being a Collection of all the Laws of Virginia* (Richmond: Samuel Pleasants, 1823), 1:144, 242, 292, 454; ibid., 2:170, 187, 296.

10. Thomas Nairne, *A Letter from South Carolina Giving an Account of the Soil, Air, Products, Trade, Government, Laws, Religion, People, Military Strength, etc. of that Province* (London: J. Clarke, 1732), pp. 50–60.

11. Edmund S. Morgan, *American Slavery, American Freedom: The Ordeal of Colonial Virginia* (New York: Norton, 1975), pp. 295–315; ... Allan Kulikoff, "A 'Prolifick' People: Black Population Growth in the Chesapeake Colonies, 1700–1790," *Southern Studies,* 16(4) (Winter 1977):398–414.

12. See ... Carl N. Degler, *Neither Black Nor White: Slavery and Race Relations in Brazil and the United States* (New York: Macmillan, 1971), pp. 61–67....

13. See Henry Bibb, *Narrative of the Life and Adventures of Henry Bibb, An American Slave,* in *Puttin' On Ole Massa,* Gilbert Osofsky, ed. (New York: Harper & Row, 1969) (hereafter cited as Osofsky, ed., *Ole Massa*), pp. 74, 80, 81; William Wells Brown, *A Fugitive Slave,* in Osofsky, ed., *Ole Massa,* pp. 180, 213....

14. Reynolds Farley, *Growth of the Black Population: A Study of Demographic Trends* (Chicago: Markham, 1970), pp. 21, 34....

15. Wood, *Black Majority,* p. 244; ... Gerald W. Mullin, *Flight and Rebellion: Slave Resistance in Eighteenth-Century Virginia* (London: Oxford University Press, 1972), p. 40. James Sellers, *Slavery in Alabama* (University, Ala.: University of Alabama Press, 1950), p. 292; Eugene Genovese, *Roll, Jordan, Roll: The World The Slaves Made* (New York: Random House, 1974), p. 798; Judith Kelleher Schafer, "New Orleans Slavery in 1850 as Seen in Advertisements," *Journal of Southern History* 46 (February 1981):43....

16. Kenneth Stampp, *The Peculiar Institution: Slavery in the Ante-Bellum South* (New York: Random House, 1956), p. 110; Genovese, *Roll, Jordan, Roll,* p. 648....

17. ... See Kenneth F. Kipple and Virginia Himmelstieb King, *Another Dimension to the Black Diaspora: Diet, Disease, and Racism* (Cambridge: Cambridge University Press, 1981), p. 97; ... Schafer, "New Orleans Slavery," p. 47.

18. Brent, *Incidents in the Life of a Slave Girl,* p. 97; Catterall, ed., *Judicial Cases,* 1:411.

19. Josiah Henson, *Autobiography of the Reverend Josiah Henson,* in *Four Fugitive Slave Narratives* (Reading, Mass.: Addison Wesley, 1969), p. 60; Bibb, in Osofsky, ed., *Ole Massa,* pp. 126–28.

20. William Still, *The Underground Railroad: A Record of Facts, Authentic Narratives, Letters, etc.* (Philadelphia: Porter and Coates, 1872), pp. 50, 188.

21. Harriet Beecher Stowe, *Uncle Tom's Cabin* (New York: Washington Square Press, 1962 [1852]), p. 74; Levi Coffin, *Reminiscences of Levi Coffin* (Cincinnati: Robert Clarke, 1898), pp. 147–49, 114; Marion Gleason McDougall, *Fugitive Slaves [1619–1865]* (New York: Bergman, 1967 [1891]), p. 47; Still, *Underground Railroad,* pp. 68, 264....

22. Still, *Underground Railroad,* p. 158; Benjamin Drew, *The Refugee: A North-Side View of Slavery,* in *Four Fugitive Slave Narratives,* p. 49.

23. Brent, *Slave Girl,* pp. 93, 104....

24. Mullin, *Flight and Rebellion,* pp. 103–4, 187; Wood, *Black Majority,* p. 241; Catterall, ed., *Judicial Cases,* 5:220; ... Frances Anne Kemble, *Journal of a Residence on a Georgian Plantation,* John A. Scott, ed. (New York: Knopf, 1961), pp. 215–16.

25. William Byrd, *The Secret Diary of William Byrd of Westover, 1709–1712,* Louis B. Wright and Marion Tinling, eds. (Richmond, Va.: Dietz, 1941), pp. 196, 197, 199, 202, 205, 206, 215, 257....

26. .... See Still, *Underground Railroad,* p. 182....

27. Susan Dabney Smedes, *Memorials of a Southern Planter,* Fletcher M. Greene, ed. (New York: Knopf, 1965), p. 180....

28. Frederick Law Olmsted, *The Cotton Kingdom,* David Freeman Hawke, ed. (New York: Bobbs-Merrill, 1971), p. 153; Olmsted, *A Journey in the Seaboard Slave States* (New York: Dix and Edwards, 1856), p. 194; B. A. Botkin, ed., *Lay My Burden Down: A Folk History of Slavery* (Chicago: University of Chicago Press, 1945), pp. 174, 175....

29. Rev. J. W. Loguen, *The Rev. J. W. Loguen as a Slave and as a Free Man* (Syracuse, N.Y.: by the author, 1859), pp. 20–21.

30. Joshua Coffin, ed., *An Account of Some of the Principal Slave Insurrections ...* (New York: American

Anti-Slavery Society, 1860), reprinted in *Slave Insurrections: Selected Documents* (Westport, Conn.: Negro Universities Press), p. 15; *South Carolina Gazette*, August 1, 1769; C. Vann Woodward, ed., *Mary Chesnut's Civil War* (New Haven: Yale University Press, 1981), pp. 218–19.

31. Olmsted, *Seaboard Slave States*, p. 190.

32. Landon Carter, *The Diary of Colonel Landon Carter of Sabine Hall, 1752–1778*, Jack P. Greene, ed., 2 vols. (Charlottesville: Virginia Historical Society, 1965), 2:604, 610, and 1:371–72.

33. John Spencer Bassett, ed., *The Southern Plantation Overseer as Revealed in His Letters* (Northampton, Mass.: Southworth, 1925), pp. 35, 59, 77, 119, 139, 142, 144, 150, 151, 156, 157.

34. See Mullin, *Flight and Rebellion*, p. 55; Frederick Law Olmsted, *A Journey through the Back Country, 1853–1854* (New York: Putnam's Sons, 1907), p. 79.

35. Leslie Howard Owens, *This Species of Property: Slave Life and Culture in the Old South* (Oxford: Oxford University Press, 1976), pp. 50–69. . . .

36. Todd L. Savitt, *Medicine and Slavery: The Diseases and Health Care of Blacks in Antebellum Virginia* (Urbana: University of Illinois Press, 1978), pp. 115, 119–20.

37. Farley, *Growth of the Black Population*, p. 33. . . .

38. Fletcher M. Greene, ed., *Ferry Hill Plantation Journal*, in *The James Sprunt Studies in History and Political Science* (Chapel Hill: University of North Carolina Press, 1961), pp. 25–56; E. M. Pendleton, "On the Susceptibility of the Caucasian and African Races to the Different Classes of Diseases," *Southern Medical Reports* (1949 [1856]), 2:338; John H. Morgan, "An Essay on the Production of Abortion among Our Negro Population," *Nashville Journal of Medicine and Surgery* (August 1860), 19:117–18. . . .

39. Catterall, ed., *Judicial Cases*, 2:475; Botkin, ed., *Lay My Burden Down*, pp. 130–31; George P. Rawick, ed., *The American Slave: A Composite Autobiography*, 19 vols. (Westport, Conn.: Greenwood Press, 1972), Mo., 10(7):135.

40. Cheryll Ann Cody, "Slave Demography and Family Formation: A Community Study of the Ball Family Plantation, 1720–1896" (Ph.D. diss., University of Minnesota, 1982), pp. 122–23.

41. Morgan, "Essay on the Production of Abortion," pp. 117, 122.

42. Kipple and King, *Diet, Disease, and Racism*, p. 65. . . .

43. Farley, *Growth of the Black Population*, p. 57; Linda Gordon, *Woman's Body, Woman's Right: A Social History of Birth Control in America* (New York: Penguin, 1976), p. 48.

44. Catterall, ed., *Judicial Cases*, 2:59, 5:139; Bassett, ed., *Plantation Overseer*, p. 59; Olmsted, *Seaboard Slave States*, p. 601; Rawick, ed., *American Slave*, Ok., 6:302.

45. Michael P. Johnson, "Smothered Slave Infants: Were Slave Mothers at Fault?" *Journal of Southern History* 47(4) (November 1981):495–509; Savitt, *Medicine and Slavery*, pp. 122–27. . . .

JOHN MACK FARAGHER
The Midwestern Farming Family, 1850

The folklore of rural America suggests that farm people understood intuitively that female work was central to the domestic economy even if the full extent of women's labors were little appreciated. Male farmers spoke of the need to marry a "good strong woman," and folk songs expressed the same understanding. "There was an old man who lived in the woods," runs one song, who wagers that

> he could do more work in one day
> Than his wife could do in three.

Excerpted from "The Midwestern Farming Family, 1850," chap. 2 of *Women and Men on the Overland Trail* by John Mack Faragher (New Haven: Yale University Press, 1979). Copyright © 1979 by Yale University Press. Reprinted by permission of the author and the publisher. Notes have been renumbered and edited, tables omitted, and cross-references adjusted.

She leaves him with a list of her tasks and goes off to do his plowing. When the farmer tries to do her work, he comes to grief; even milking presents unforeseen difficulties:

> But Tiny hitched, and Tiny switched,
> And Tiny she cocked her nose,
> And Tiny she gave the old man such a kick
> That the blood ran down to his toes.

By the time the song ends the old man is swearing

> by all of the stars in heaven
> That his wife could do more work in one day
> Than he could do in seven.*

As long as anyone could remember, farmers had ordered their lives by work patterns strictly defined by gender. Historians and anthropologists can now see that both sorts of tasks were central to the maintenance of the economic health of the family farm. As John Mack Faragher shows, what was missing was a convenient set of measures for female productivity; in the absence of these, women's work tended to be undervalued.

The dominant paradigm of farm life was the cycle: the recurrence of the days and seasons, the process of growth and reproduction.[1] Hand-power technology did not deceive men into thinking they could overcome nature; their goal was to harmonize man's needs with natural forces as best they could. The length of the working day, for example, was largely determined by the hours of sunlight. Candles and grease lamps were common but expensive, and the hearth's flickering light was too dim for more than a little work after dark.[2] So most work was largely confined to daylight: up and at work by dawn, nights for sleeping. And keeping with this daily round, midwesterners told time by the movements of the sun, not the clock. There was a variety of time phrases so rich they nearly matched the clock in refinement; the hours before sunrise, for example, were distinguished thus: long before day, just before day, just comin' day, just about daylight, good light, before sunup, about sunup, and finally, sunup. Each period of the day was similarly divided.[3]

The seasons imposed the same kind of rule as the sun. The farm's work demands were primarily shaped by the seasons, each quarter calling upon husbandman and housewife to perform appointed tasks. The farming year opened in mid-March when thaws called the tenants outside. Land had to be cleared, drained, manured, and plowed, fields sown, gardens planted. Sheep, grown woolly, needed washing and shearing, geese plucking. In the hardwood stands farmers might spend a few days collecting and rendering maple sap, or searching out and hiving bees.

As the sun approached summer solstice, the work load increased with the day's length. The corn needed cultivation and hilling until it was strong enough to compete successfully with the weeds and "laid by" till harvest. There was hay to make, garden crops to nurture, gather, and replant, and often a winter wheat crop to harvest and thresh. In August, with the corn laid by and harvest coming, men took the opportunity for a respite; these were the dog days when "onery" farmers took long naps and "progressive" farmers mended fences. But August was soon overwhelmed by the frantic pace of September's harvest. Summer grain had to be cut, bound, and shocked within a critically short period, the corn picked, the last round of garden vegetables safely packed away in cold storage while still fresh.

Days continued to shorten, but after harvest the pace of work slowed as well. Still the grain needed threshing, the corn husking and cribbing, there was perhaps fruit to pick, dry, or preserve in a variety of ways, possibly pickles and kraut to make. These and other activities prepared the way for the winter: sowing

*Jean Ritchie, *The Swapping Song Book* (Oxford, 1952), pp. 54–55. Copyright © 1952 Jean Ritchie, Geordie Music Publishing Co. Suggested by Laura Becker, Clemson University.

the winter wheat, making firewood, daubing the cracks in old cabins, barns, and outbuildings, banking dirt around foundations to keep out some of the cold, and butchering enough hogs for salted and smoked meat until the spring again provided a larder of milk, eggs, and poultry.

Summer's activity was counterbalanced by winter's leisure. The daily chores of the farm—tending livestock, hauling wood and water, the domestic routine—continued. There were also numerous tasks to keep an industrious farmer busy: fences to mend, manure to haul and spread, trees to girdle and later fell, roads to maintain. But there was comparatively little opportunity for productive activity in the winter, aside from work in the woodlot. So winter months were occupied with general farm repair and improvement, visiting neighbors, trading the surpluses that summer's labor had produced. In late winter farmers would begin to plan the plantings of the next season, setting out planting dates in traditional fashion by carefully determining with the farm almanac the timing of the phases of the moon and the rising and falling of astrological signs.

Encouraged by their subordination to the natural world, the people of the Midwest held to a traditional animistic conception of the universe: the inanimate world was infused with will, feeling, and spirit. "The world was a huge kaleidoscope, whose bewildering pieces fell by the twist of analogy or contrast into beautifully logical patterns of form, direction, texture, quality, process—patterns to cover everything that might happen, from evening to evening and from spring to spring." As William Oliver, an English visitor and resident of Illinois in the 1840s, wrote, "There is a good deal of superstition or belief in witchcraft, omens, lucky times, etc." The world could be best understood by analogy (if an animal disturbed the afterbirth, that baby would take on some trait of the beast) or contrast (cold hands, warm heart) or the rule of "firsts" (if a woman cries on her wedding day she will cry throughout her married life). Many of the beliefs were employed in a half-embarrassed way, perhaps pulled out only in times of emergencies like sickness, death, disaster; others were the stock-in-trade of midwestern life.[4]

The cycle of the seasons encouraged a traditional view of work as well. Work was the expenditure of human energy to meet given tasks. When wheat was ready for harvesting, for example, men would readily work fifteen-hour days to bring it in before the precious grain was shed on the ground. On the other hand, when seasonal demands slackened, as in winter, a man might quit early without qualms, and few worried when a winter storm closed in the family for a few days. The persistent pace of modern labor, measured not by natural cycles but by the clock, was almost unknown to midwesterners. By the same token, work was understood not as the opposite of leisure but as life's requirement for all creatures, regardless of sex or age. Men, women, and children would share life's burdens. "The rule was," William Howells remembered of his farm life, "that whoever had the strength to work, took hold and helped."[5]

The common work of the farm was, then, divided among family members, but the principal division of work was by sex. Men and women worked in different areas, skilled at different tasks, prepared and trained for their work in different ways. In an economy based on the family unit, women and men in midwestern society achieved common goals by doing different jobs.

Sex and gender is a foundation of individual and social identity in all human societies. As Michael Banton puts it, gender roles "are related so closely to the performance of most other roles that the sex of a party can be concealed only in the most restricted situations."[6] The differences of sex are the starting place for gender roles: each person is given a polar label, either man or woman. Sex implies general natural potentials and limitations, to be sure, but the biological distinctions alone have never been sufficient social determinants of distinctive gender roles; sex differences have always had to be elaborated by patterned cultural forms. "Natural features are never translated directly into social ones. They are always dressed in cultural clothing."[7]

If gender roles are essentially cultural constructions, it follows that the notion of what constitutes the masculine and the feminine will vary greatly from one culture to another and from one time to another. Men and women play their gender roles according to a cultural script outlining the appropriate activities and tasks (the sexual division of labor) as well as the attitudes and personality (the character) of the two sexes. People appear most obviously in society and history as players of their gender roles.[8]

For historians (as well as other social scientists), the proper place to begin an understanding of gender roles is by reconstructing and examining the customary ways in which men and women divided the work of society among themselves.[9] This priority makes methodological sense if for no other reason than because outward behavior is what historians can best determine, and broad areas of behavioral uniformity suggest the presence of roles. These patterns then establish a context of human action for the evaluation of what men and women thought.[10] Such an approach employs an active, concrete concept of gender roles: gender roles are social regularities observed in what men and women do and the ways they think and feel about what they do, as well as how and why they do what they do. In this study both behavioral and attitudinal facts must be derived from the same subjective source—the diaries and recollections. But even with such documents of personal experience the behavioral regularities are readily exposed and pieced together to form a whole pattern.

The functional principles of the general divisions of work by sex on the midwestern farm were quite clear and quite strict in application. In only a few areas did the work of men and women overlap. Most clearly, men were occupied with the heaviest work. First, they had responsibility for work with the broadax. If the family was taking up new wooded ground—as many Oregon emigrants would be doing, for example—the land had to be cleared. Frequently a farmer would gird the trees with his ax the first season to kill foliage, felling trees and removing stumps in the following winters. Logrolling, when the men of the neighborhood joined together to clear a field belonging to one of them, was a common late-winter social event for men. Construction, including making fences, was also a male job, as was the ongoing work in the family woodlot. Wood was chopped, hauled and stacked, or dumped near the house.

Men also controlled work with the plow. For new land a breaking plow, drawn by several yoke of oxen, was often needed, especially in prairie sod. Working improved acres was easier, but still hard, heavy work. And within the limitations of available labor and marketability, men were usually itching to put new land to the plow, so the plow was associated with work of the heaviest sort and understood to be male. Work in the cleared and plowed fields, where grain or corn grew, also fell to male control and supervision. Men plowed in spring or winter, sowed their wheat broadcast (until the 1850s), and planted their corn in hills. Men and boys harrowed and weeded until harvest, when they picked the corn together and cooperated in bringing in the wheat, men cradling and boys binding. Fieldwork kept men extremely busy. Two mature men on fifty acres of corn and wheat land spent three-quarters of the whole growing season plowing, planting, and harvesting, exclusive of any other work.[11]

There was plenty of other work to do. Men were responsible for upkeep and repair of tools, implements, and wagons and care of the draft animals, the oxen, mules, or horses. Hogs and sheep, both pretty much allowed to roam, were herded, fed, and tended by men and boys. Finally, men were responsible for cleanup and maintenance of the barn, barnyard, fields, and woodlot. This meant ditching and trenching, innumerable repairs on all the things that could—and did—break, laying down straw and hay, and hauling manure.[12]

Less important in fact, but work which nonetheless played an important role in male thinking, was hunting. For the early pioneers game provided most of the protein in the family diet. By mid-century those pioneer days had passed in the Midwest. But the rifle remained in its central place over the door or mantel long after the emergencies that might call it out had gone the way of the forests. Hunting remained, if only as an autumn sport or shooting match, a central aspect of male identity. "Even farmers," says Buley, "at certain seasons felt a peculiar restlessness."[13] The hunting legacy had one practical consequence for male work loads: men had primary responsibility for slaughtering and butchering large farm animals. Indeed, when hogs ran wild, they were sometimes picked off by rifle shot. Hunting was the male activity that most embodied men's self-conceived role—keystone of the hearth, defender of the household, and main provider.

In fact, women were more centrally involved in providing subsistence for the farm family than men. Nearly all the kinds of food consumed by farm families were direct products of women's work in growing, collecting, and butchering. An acre or so of improved land near the house was set aside for the domestic garden. After husbands had plowed the plot, farm women planted their gardens. Housewives began setting out onions and potatoes in early April, following up later that month by planting lettuce, beets, parsnips, turnips, and carrots in the garden, tomatoes and cabbages in window boxes indoors. When danger of late frosts had passed, the seedlings were moved outside and set out along with May plantings of cucumbers, melons, pumpkins, and beans. Women also frequently laid down a patch of buckwheat and a garden of kitchen and medicinal herbs—sage, peppers, thyme, mint, mustard, horseradish, tansy, and others.[14]

The garden required daily attention. At first the seedlings needed hand watering. Then crops required cultivation, and the everlasting battle against weeds began. Garden harvesting could commence in late April and was a daily chore throughout the summer, supplying fresh vegetables for the family table.

Wives and daughters were also traditionally responsible for the care of henhouse and dairy. After a dormant winter, poultry came alive in the spring. The farm-wise woman carefully kept enough chickens to produce both eggs for the kitchen and to set hens for a new flock of spring roasters. From late spring to late fall the family feasted regularly on fresh-killed rooster, selected and usually butchered by the housewife. Daughters and young boys gathered the eggs that were another mainstay of the summer diet. Women's responsibility for the henhouse extended even to cleaning out the manure by the bucket load.[15]

Cows were sheltered in whatever served as a barn, and men's general supervision there relieved women of having to shovel the stalls. But women milked, tended, and fed the animals. The milking and the manufacture of butter and cheese was one of their central tasks. Cows were milked first thing in the morning and the last thing at night; housewives supervised the milking but parceled the job out to children as soon as they were able. Boys, however, with their father's sanction would rebel from milking; "the western people of the early days entertained a supreme contempt for a man who attended to the milking."[16] Making

good butter was a matter of pride among farm women. The churn had to be operated with patience and persistence if the butter was to come.

> Come butter, come;
> Come butter, come;
> Little Johnny's at the gate,
> Waiting for his buttered cake.
> Come butter, come.[17]

The meter marked the up and down of the churn. When it had come, the butter was packed into homemade, hand-decorated molds, and pounds of it consumed each week. Cheesemaking was less general; ripened cheeses were the product of a minority. Nearly all women, however, were trained in the manufacture of cottage cheese and farmer's cheese. Dairy production was especially important to the household and central to the definition of women's work. In 1839 a Springfield, Illinois newspaper reprinted with horror a report that New England women were pressuring their husbands to take over the milking.[18]

There were some areas of food production where women's and men's operations overlapped, but these were the exceptions. When hogs were butchered in fall, men from several farms might work together; it was mainly when it became necessary to supplement the meat supply that women helped men to slaughter and dress the animal. In any event, women were always a part of the butchering, there to chop the scraps and odd pieces into sausage, prepare the hams for curing, and cook the ribs immediately. At other social and almost ritual occasions of food preparation— making cider or apple butter, rendering maple sugar—men and women regularly worked side by side. All of the work of the orchard was often a joint project.

The sexes also sometimes combined their energies during planting. If not preoccupied with field planting, men might help to set out garden seed. More likely, however, field planting would fall behind the schedule set by zodiac or moon, and men called their womenfolk out to help. Women most often assisted in the cornfield. "Tarpley made a furrow with a single-shovel plow drawn by one horse," Iowa farm woman Elmira Taylor remembered of the 1860s. "I followed with a bag of seed corn and dropped two grains of seed each step forward." A farmer with no sons worked his daughters in the fields at planting time without a second thought.[19]

Food preparation was, of course, women's work, and by all reports midwestern men kept women busy by consuming great quantities at mealtime.[20] Wives were responsible for preparing three heavy meals a day; most farm wives spent their entire mornings cooking and tried to save afternoons for other work. Included in the daily midwestern diet were two kinds of meat, eggs, cheese, butter, cream (especially in gravies), corn in one or more forms, two kinds of bread, three or four different vegetables from the garden or from storage, several kinds of jellies, preserves, and relishes, cake or pie, and milk, coffee, and tea. Making butter and cheese were only two of the innumerable feminine skills needed to set the farm table. . . .

Women cooked on the open hearth, directly over the coals; it was low, backbreaking work that went on forever; a pot of corn mush took from two to six hours with nearly constant stirring.[21] Cast-iron, wood-burning cook stoves were available in Illinois in the mid-1840s, and by 1860 most midwestern women had been given the opportunity to stand and cook.[22] The next great improvement in domestic technology was the general introduction of running water in close proximity to the kitchen. But throughout the antebellum Midwest, water had to be carried to the house, sometimes from quite a distance, and that invariably was women's work. Domestic work—housecleaning, care of the bedding, all the kitchen work, in addition to responsibility for decorating and adding a "woman's touch"—was a demanding task under the best of circumstances, and farms offered far from the best. The yard between the kitchen and barn was always covered with enough dung to attract hordes of summer houseflies. In those days before screen doors kitchens were infested; men and women alike ignored the pests. In wet months the yard was a mess of mud, dung, and castoff water, constantly tracked into the house. A cleanly wife had to be a constant worker.

A farmer was said to be a jack-of-all-trades. But women's work outdistanced men's in the sheer variety of tasks performed. In addition to their production of food, women had complete responsibility for all manufacture, care, and repair of family clothing. During the first half of the nineteenth century, domestic manufacture gave way to industrial production of thread and cloth, but in the Midwest, from 1840 to 1860, while home manufactures declined, they remained an important activity for women. On the Taylor homestead in southeastern Iowa, for example, the assessed valuation of household manufactures declined from $73 in 1850 to $50 in 1860, but this marked a decline, not an end to the use of the wheel and loom: in 1861 Elmira Taylor spun her own wool, took it to a mill to be carded, and wove it into cloth throughout the winter on her mother-in-law's loom.[23]

Midwestern homespun was mostly of flax and wool, supplemented by a little homegrown cotton or purchased cotton thread. A few sheep and a quarter-acre of flax were enough to supply the largest family. Farm wives sowed flax in March, harvested it in June (replanting immediately with a sterile-soil crop like potatoes), and prepared it that summer by soaking and sun-drying it to rot the outer coating.[24] Men lent a hand by crushing the flax on the flax break to remove the inner fibers and washing and shearing the sheep, but from that point it was a woman's operation. Spinning wheels were in universal use; each household required separate wheels for wool and flax. Wheels were precision tools, but families could get them rather cheaply from the wheelwright, and according to William Oliver, "spinning wheels and a loom are very general items in a farmer's establishment."[25] Wool had first to be carded into lean bunches, then spun on the great wheel; the spinner paced back and forth, whirling the wheel with her right hand, manipulating the wool and guiding the yarn on the spindle with her left. Two miles of yarn, enough for two to four yards of woven wool, required pacing over four miles, a full day's work. An excellent spinner, sitting at the smaller flax wheel, could spin a mile of linen thread in a day.[26]

The yarn was woven into wool and linen cloth or more commonly combined into durable linsey-woolsey on homemade looms. If cotton was available it was woven with wool warp to make jean. The giant loom dominated cramped living quarters when in use; it was knocked down and put away when weaving was completed.[27] The cloth still had to be shrunk and sized (fulled)—a job usually put out to the fulling mill if one were nearby—and dyed, sometimes from home dyes, but increasingly with commercial dyes bought at local stores. Nearly all farm clothing was cut from this cloth. Coarser tow cloth, made from the short-fiber, darker parts of the flax, was used for toweling, bandage, menstrual cloth, rags, or rough field clothing. Pillows and mattresses were made of tow and stuffed with the down women collected from the geese and ducks in their charge. The finest homespun, the pure linen bleached scores of times till it reached its characteristic color, was reserved for coverlets, tablecloths, appliqué, and stitchery. For their annual clothing a family of four would require a minimum of forty yards of cloth, or at least two full weeks at the wheel and loom for an experienced housewife. This work was, of course, spread throughout the available time, and one could expect to find women spinning or weaving at almost any time of the day, at every season of the year.[28]

Itinerant weavers first made their appearance in the Midwest during the 1840s, their Jacquard looms offering what seemed incredible detail in patterns. For most farm families, however, everyday cloth remained home-produced until the general availability of low-cost factory-produced dry goods. It was during the commercial shift in midwestern agriculture that family looms and then wheels gave way to cheap commercial cloth. Until the Civil War, however, a good deal of all midwestern clothing, and most clothing on emigrant backs, was homespun.

Every wife was a tailor, fitting and cutting cloth for her own slip-on dresses and those of her daughter, her son's and husband's blouses and pantaloons, and the tow shirts of the younger ones. If there was "boughten" cloth available—cotton or woolen broadcloth, gingham or calico—it was used for dress-up clothing, home-tailored of course. Socks, mittens, and caps were knit for winter wear, but every adult went sockless and children barefoot in summer. Underclothes were not manufactured or worn, for they were considered an unnecessary extravagance.[29]

Women were personally involved in clothing manufacture, from sowing the flax seed to sewing the garment. Homespun "could not be lightly cast aside after so much toil and patience, on account of being slightly or considerably worn."[30] So worn pants and shirts were continually mended, garments too worn to be used saved for patches, and every scrap of every kind of cloth that passed through the house was saved for that special purpose it would one day find. As an old Kentucky woman remembered,

> You see you start out with just so much caliker; you don't go to the store and pick it out and buy it, but the neighbors will give you a piece here and a piece there, and you will have a piece left every time you cut out a dress, and you take what happens to come and that's predestination. But when it comes to cuttin' out why you're free to choose your patterns. You can give the same kind o' pieces to two persons, and one will be a *Nine Patch* and one'll make a *Wild Goose Chase* and there'll be two quilts made out o' the same kind of pieces, and jest as different as they can be, and that is just the way with livin'. The Lord sends in the pieces, but we can cut 'em out and put 'em together pretty much to suit ourselves.[31]

Sewing was the consummate feminine skill, a domestic necessity but one practiced and refined until in the hand of many it achieved the status of an art form. Girls were taught to sew before they were taught to read, and started on a four- or nine-patch quilt cover as soon as they could hold a needle. Coverlets, counterpanes, crocheted samplers, and most especially the elaborate patchwork or appliqué front pieces for quilts were the highest expression of the material culture of women. With patchwork, appliqué, and quilt stitchery, utility was a secondary consideration; these were primarily modes of creative artistry for women. One farm woman testified to the importance of this avenue for her: "I would have lost my mind if I had not had my quilts to do."[32]

On a more mundane level, clothes had to be washed, and women made their own soap for both the clothes and the family who wore them. Women loaded hardwood ashes into the ash hopper, poured water over, and collected the lye in the trough below. They boiled kitchen fats and grease, added the lye, and if everything was going well the soap would "come" after long, hot hours of stirring. They poured the hot soap into molds or tubs and stored it. Soapmaking was a big, all-day job, done only two or three times a year.[33] Monday, by all accounts, was the universal washday. Rainwater was used for washing, or alternately a little lye was added to soften well water. The water was heated in the washtub over hearth or stove, soap added, and clothes were pounded against a washboard, then rinsed, wrung out by hand, and hung. The lye, harsh soap, and hot water chapped and cracked the skin; women's hands would often break open and bleed into the tub. In the winter, the clothes were hung outside where sore, wet hands would freeze painfully, or inside, draped over chairs or lines, steaming up the windows and turning the whole place clammy. Ironing and mending were also allocated one day each week.

To women fell a final task. Women bore the children and nursed them for at least the first few months, and in this they worked completely alone. Even after weaning, farm women remained solely responsible for the supervision of young children; both boys and girls were under their mother's supervision until the boys were old enough to help with the fieldwork, at about ten years, at which time they came under their father's guidance. Girls, of course, remained apprenticed to the housewife's craft. Farm mothers put their charges to work "almost as soon as they could walk," and although they could not contribute materially until they were five or six, the correct work attitude had by then been instilled.[34] There was plenty that children could do around the garden, dairy, and henhouse; they watered, fed the animals, collected eggs, milked, hauled water, weeded, and performed innumerable other chores that housewives could never have finished but for the work of their children.

Midwestern farm mothers had relatively large families. The mean family size in the Midwest in 1850 was 5.7.[35] Mean family size of the overland emigrants in this study was a little less, 5.0, mainly because there were so many newlyweds; otherwise the size of emigrant families was very typical of the population at large. The mean size of emigrating families in their full childbearing phase was 7.6. In her lifetime, then, a farm woman could expect to raise five or six children of her own. These children helped significantly with the burden of farm work, but not without the expenditure of a great deal of physical and emotional energy by their mothers.

To determine the full occupations of women, their total work load, we must consider the social effects of childbearing as well as childrearing. Miscarriages, stillbirths, birth accidents, and infant mortality took a terrible toll on the energies and spirit of women. Counting infant deaths alone, one in five children died before its fifth birthday, and prenatal losses were at least as high.[36] Childbirth certainly was a central experience for farm women. It was no occasional or unique event but occurred with demanding regularity. To assess women's reproductive burdens fairly we can measure women's fertility. The mean age of marriage for emigrant men and women was 25.1 and 20.5, respectively. Some women, of course, married earlier than the average and were pregnant before their twentieth birthdays. The peak childbearing years were from age twenty to thirty-five, during which time emigrant women bore over four out of five of their children. Fertility declined precipitously after thirty-five as a combined effect of lowered male and female fecundity, although some mothers continued to bear children into their late forties.

Let us translate abstract fertility into the real terms of farm women's lives: childbearing had to be a dominant fact. Over half the emigrant women gave birth to their first child within their first year of marriage, another quarter the second year, and fully 98 percent by the end of the third. Thereafter a mean of 29.0 months intervened between births throughout a woman's twenties and thirties. For their most vital years farm women lived under the dictatorial rule of yet another cycle, a two-and-a-half-year cycle of childbirth, of which nineteen or twenty months were spent in advanced pregnancy, infant care, and nursing. Until her late thirties, a woman could expect little respite from the physical and emotional wear and tear of nearly constant pregnancy or suckling.

Given the already burdensome tasks of women's work, the additional responsibilities of the children were next to intolerable. Women must have searched for some way of limiting the burden. It is possible that mothers introduced their babies to supplemental feeding quite early and encouraged children's independence in order to free themselves from the restrictions of nursing, which had to seriously limit their capacity to work.[37] There is almost no mention of child-feeding practices in the literature, but there are some indirect indications that babies were soon consuming "bread, corn, biscuits and pot-likker" right along with their parents. On the other hand, there was a prevalent old wives' notion that prolonged nursing was a protection against conception. To achieve a twenty-nine-month cycle without practicing some form of self-conscious family limitation, women would have had to nurse for at least a year.[38]

Short of family planning there was no easy choice for women in the attempt to reduce the burden of child care. Other groups had practiced family limitation before this time, but the need for labor may have been a mitigating factor here. It comes as no surprise, then, that as soon as it was possible, children were pretty much allowed and encouraged to shift for themselves, to grow as they might, with relatively little parental or maternal involvement in the process. We will find children little mentioned in overland diaries and reminiscences.

By no means were men the "breadwinners" of this economy. Both women and men actively participated in the production of family subsistence. Indeed, women were engaged in from one-third to one-half of all the food production of the farm, the proportions varying with regional and individual differences.[39] Of the farm staples—meat, milk, corn, pumpkins, beans, and potatoes—women produced the greater number as a product of their portion of the division of labor. Women were also likely to be found helping men with their portion at peak planting time. To this must be added the extremely important work of clothing manufacture, all the household work, and the care of the children. To be sure, men and women alike worked hard to make their farms produce. But one cannot avoid being struck by the enormousness of women's work load.

In 1862, in its first annual report, the Department of Agriculture published a study by Dr. W. W. Hall on the condition of farm women. "In plain language," Hall proclaimed, "in the civilization of the latter half of the nineteenth century, a farmer's wife, as a general rule, is a laboring drudge. . . . It is safe to say, that on three farms out of four the wife works harder, endures more, than any other on the place; more than the husband, more than the 'farm hand,' more than the 'hired help' of the kitchen."[40] In his recommendations for improvements in women's condition, Hall's report supplements our view of farm work. The practice of many farmers of letting their wives cut the firewood and haul the water, especially in the cold of winter, needed correction. Men should be responsible for providing a root cel-

lar for potatoes and other vegetables, otherwise wives were compelled to go out in the cold "once or twice every day, to leave a heated kitchen, and most likely with thin shoes, go to the garden with a tin pan and a hoe, to dig them out of the wet ground and bring them home in slosh or rain." Equally perilous for women were the extremes of heat and cold encountered in washing and hanging the winter laundry; men were stronger and should take that job. "The truth is, it perils the life of the hardiest persons, while working over the fire in cooking or washing, to step outside the door of the kitchen for an instant, a damp, raw wind may be blowing, which coming upon an inner garment throws a chill or the clamminess of the grave over the whole body in an instant of time." . . .

Hall lamented the lack of attention to women's needs and recommended to men that they adopt a more sympathetic attitude. "There are 'seasons' in the life of women which, as to some of them, so affect the general system, and the mind also, as to commend them to our warmest sympathies. . . . Some women, at such times, are literally insane. . . ." Husbands had to be patient and affectionate or risk driving their wives to a "lunatic's cell." In addition, a man should realize that his wife loved finery and beauty and should supply her "according to his ability, with the means of making her family and home neat, tasteful and tidy." Hall reminded the farmer that "his wife is a social being; that she is not a machine, and therefore needs rest, and recreation, and change." If hands were to be hired perhaps help in the kitchen was worth considering. Women should be allowed to get out of the house once in a while to do a little visiting with other people; in fact, it was a good idea for both husband and wife to dress up and step out for the day now and then. . . .

Hall's report was a mixture of constructive suggestions and temporizing platitudes; it is unlikely that many farmers or farm women ever saw, let alone heeded, its advice.[41] In the end it is more important for what it suggests concerning the working relations of husbands and wives than for its proposed reforms. Hall implicitly leveled a harsh indictment against farmers: that they were insensitive to the work load of their wives and drove women past reasonable limits; that they did not comprehend the natural or psychological needs of their

wives; that they refused to give women the respect and authority that was their due. Hall attributed the problem to calculations of profit
and loss which ignored social and emotional
needs (although he made his appeal to men on
the very same basis: "no man will ever lose in
the long run").

The report adds depth to what we have
thus far seen and suggests that the division of
labor was structured in favor of men, that it
exploited women, and that it was perpetuated,
in part, by a masculine attitude of superiority.
Daniel Drake, who visited the Midwest in the
late 1830s, concluded that the farmer's wife
was one who "surrounded by difficulties or
vexed with hardships at home, provided with
no compensation for what she has left behind,
pines away, and wonders that her husband can
be so happy when she is so miserable."[42] The
true inequity in the division of labor was
clearly expressed in the aphorism "A man may
work from sun to sun, but a woman's work is
never done." The phrase has a hollow ring to
us today, but it was no joke to farm women,
who by all accounts worked two to three hours
more each day than the men, often spinning,
weaving, or knitting late into the dark evening
hours.

There are some areas of women's participation in farm life that suggest a higher status.
Cross-cultural studies indicate that the respon-
siblity for exchanging goods and services with
persons outside the family tends to confer family power and prestige. "The relative power of
women is increased if women both contribute
to subsistence *and also* have opportunities for
extra domestic distribution and exchange of
valued goods and services."[43] In the Midwest,
the products of dairy, henhouse, garden, and
loom were often the only commodities successfully exchanged for other family necessities.
Powder, glass, dyes, crockery, coffee, tea, store
cloth, metal utensils, and sugar were bought on
credit from the local merchant; butter, cheese,
eggs, vegetables, homespun, and whiskey were
the main items offered in trade to pay the tab.[44]

However, while it was true that women
traded, the proceeds were not credited to them
individually, but to the family in general. Commodity exchange in corn and grain surpluses,
on the other hand, was most frequently used
for male economic pursuits: paying off the farm
mortgage, speculating in new lands, and as in-

novations in technology became available, experimenting with new farm equipment. Men's
product was for male use; women's product
was for the family. It has been claimed that
"there was no doubt of her equality in those
days because she showed herself equally capable in all the tasks of their life together, and
she was proud to know that this was true. Her
position and dignity and age-old strength was
that of the real help-mate in everything that
touched the welfare of the family and the
home." From a modern perspective equal work
may seem a first step toward sexual equality,
but the question of power is not only a question
of what people do but also of the recognition
they are granted for what they do and the authority that recognition confers. There is little
evidence to suggest that men, for their part,
gave women's work a second thought. That it
was a woman's lot to work that hard was simply taken for granted.[45]

Indeed, one theme of midwestern folksongs was the lament of the husband wronged
by the wife who refused to perform her appointed tasks.

> Come all you wary bachelors,
> Come listen unto me
> Come all you wary bachelors,
> Who married once would be.
>
> Before my wife was married
> She was a dainty dame.
> She could do all kinds of cunjer work,
> Like butter, cheese an' cream.
>
> She'd weed her father's oats an' flax
> And milk the cows I know;
> And when she would return at night
> She could spin a pound of tow.
>
> But since my wife got married,
> Quite worthless she's become.
> An' all that I can say of her
> She will not stay at home.
>
> She will wash herself, an' dress herself,
> An' a-visiting she will go;
> An' that's the thing she'd rather do
> In place of spinning tow.[46]

One looks in vain for evidence of songs that
sang the praises of women's diligence. Even
the woman accomplished at all of her duties
was likely to fall short in male estimation.

> She could wash and she could brew,
> She could cut and she could sew,

But alas and alas! she was dumb,
  dumb, dumb.
  . . . .

She could card and she could spin,
She could do most anything,
But alas and alas! she was dumb,
  dumb, dumb.

She was pretty, she was smart,
An' she stole away my heart,
But alas, in the door she was dumb,
  dumb, dumb.[47]

Men and women were locked into productive harmony. The farm could not exist without the cooperative labor of both sexes. Yet men gave women minimal recognition for their work. Women, fully equal in production, were not granted the status of equality.

Despite its interdependence, the character of men's and women's work was essentially different. Woman's work was dominated by the omnipresent awareness of the immediate usefulness of her product, be it milk, cabbage, eggs, or flax. Whatever processing was required she herself performed. Her view was inward, to her household and family. For them she was not simply to provide food and clothing and keep up the house, but to do these things with imagination and care: by gardening industriously, by preserving, drying, and storing to overcome the limitations of nature, by preparing the season's fare with distinction, by dyeing, bleaching, and cutting clothes in ways to please, and by keeping not only a clean but a well-appointed house. The joys of women's work lay in the satisfaction of accomplishment—of bread well made, butter nicely molded, quilts intended for heirlooms—and in the variety of skills each woman had to master. Women who worked up to this standard were good wives; those who failed on these counts were cast in male folklore as improvident slatterns.[48]

Men, for their part, worked long, monotonous, solitary hours at a single pursuit in the fields, plowing row after row, hoeing hill after hill. Hamilton remembered work in the cornfield: "Usually you cultivated the corn with a hired man or two. But you each had your own 'land,' maybe two dozen rows each was working on, a row at a time. So you did not pass close as the two or three crossed and recrossed the fields, stopping, uncovering corn, pulling

cockleburrs."[49] Such work would produce, it was hoped, quantities of staple grain great enough to sustain the family and provide a surplus, but there was little satisfaction in the immediate labor. The flavor of male work was quantitative: acres, fields, bushels—all measured a man's work. Neither the corn nor the grain was immediately consumable but required processing; the connection between production and consumption—the full cycle of work—was not embodied in a man's own activity. The cyclical nature of farm women's work might allow her to see in a flowering field of blue flax the linen for next summer's chemise. For men the fields would yield not usable, tangible articles—bread or hominy—but bushels; quantities, not things.

On the self-sufficient farm, or farms approaching self-sufficiency, the character of men's work was a powerful link between the field and the house. The housewife converted the corn to hominy, the grain to bread, while the farmer looked on: only woman could realize the product of man. But the somewhat abstract nature of men's work enabled them to envision another mode within which they were not dependent upon their wives to fulfill their labor. The market could connect men's work to a larger social process and remunerate them in the tokens of commerce. In order to qualify as social labor, work had to have this characteristic: to be able to reach out and connect the family to the larger social world. Women's work, always cyclical, always looking inward, did not qualify; it was hidden by domestic draperies. Men's work, even in the precommercial Midwest, encouraged a kind of economic vision women could not ordinarily achieve.

NOTES

1. The following section is based on numerous sources, but see especially Logan Esarey, *The Indiana Home* (Crawfordsville, Ind.: R. E. Banta, 1943); Rodney Loehr, "Minnesota Farmers' Diaries," *Minnesota History* 18 (1937):284–97; Eric Sloan, *Seasons of America Past* (New York: Wilfred Funk, 1958); Henry C. Taylor, *Tarpleywick: A Century of Iowa Farming* (Ames: Iowa State University Press, 1970); and Carl Hamilton, *In No Time at All* (Ames: Iowa State University Press, 1975).

2. Kerosene lamps came into wide use during the early 1860s; Evadene Burris, "Keeping House on

the Minnesota Frontier," *Minnesota History* 14 (1933): 265–67.

3. W. O. Rice, "The Pioneer Dialect of Southern Illinois," *Dialect Notes* 2 (1902):233.

4. Frank R. Kramer, *Voices in the Valley: Mythmaking and Folk Belief in the Shaping of the Middle West* (Madison: University of Wisconsin Press, 1964), p. 107; . . . William Oliver, *Eight Months in Illinois* (Chicago: W. M. Hill, 1924; original ed. 1843), p. 71; Kramer, *Voices in the Valley*, p. 70. . . .

5. William Cooper Howells, *Recollections of Life in Ohio from 1813–1840* (Cincinnati: Robert Clarke, 1895), p. 157.

6. Michael P. Banton, *Roles: An Introduction to the Study of Social Relations* (London: Tavistock Publications, 1965), p. 71. . . .

7. Ibid.

8. . . . See Thomas C. Cochran, "The Historian's Use of Social Role," in Louis Gottschalk, ed., *Generalization in the Writing of History* (Chicago: University of Chicago Press, 1963), pp. 103–4.

9. . . . The best work on gender roles continues to be done in anthropology. For an excellent symposium of recent work, see Reyna R. Reiter, ed., *Toward an Anthropology of Women* (New York: Monthly Review Press, 1975).

10. . . . For a historical and structural discussion of the origins of men's and women's work, . . . [see] M. Kay Martin and Barbara Voorhies, *Female of the Species* (New York: Columbia University Press, 1975); . . . Reiter, ed., *Toward an Anthropology of Women;* and . . . Heidi Hartmann, "Capitalism, Patriarchy, and Job Segregation by Sex," *Signs* 1, no. 3, pt. 2 (1976): 137–69. . . .

11. Calculated from figures in R. C. Buley, *The Old Northwest Pioneer Period, 1815–1840* (Indianapolis, 1950), I:182.

12. Men were responsible for cleaning the privy. Most farms had outhouses used by women and children but disdained by men as effeminate. Ibid., I:223.

13. Ibid., I:153, 319.

14. Ibid., I:217–18; Marjorie Caroline Taylor, "Domestic Arts and Crafts in Illinois (1800–1860)," *Journal of the Illinois State Historical Society* 33 (1940): 294. . . .

15. Oliver, *Eight Months*, pp. 109–10; Hamilton, *In No Time*, p. 163.

16. . . . Buley, *Old Northwest*, I:216–17.

17. For American variations of this traditional English chant, see Chuck Perdue, "Come Butter Come: A Collection of Churning Chants from Georgia," *Foxfire* 3 (1966):20–24, 65–72.

18. Buley, *Old Northwest*, I:392.

19. Taylor, *Tarpleywick*, p. 15; . . .

20. . . . [See] Buley, *Old Northwest*, I:218–21; Evadene A. Burris, "Frontier Food," *Minnesota History* 14 (1933):378–92; Burris, "Keeping House"; . . .

21. Taylor, "Domestic Arts," p. 287; Charles Beneulyn Johnson, *Illinois in the Fifties* (Champaign, Ill.: Flanigan-Pearson, 1918), pp. 18 ff.; . . .

22. Samuel Willard, "Personal Reminiscences of Life in Illinois, 1830–1850." *Transactions of the Illinois State Historical Society* 11 (1906):80; Evadene A. Burris, "Furnishing the Frontier Home," *Minnesota History* 15 (1934):192; . . .

23. Taylor, *Tarpleywick*, pp. 9, 13. For general studies, see Rolla Milton Tryon, *Household Manufactures in the United States, 1640–1860* (Chicago: University of Chicago Press, 1917); . . .

24. Howells, *Recollections*, p. 123.

25. Oliver, *Eight Months*, pp. 89–90. . . .

26. Jared Van Wagenen, Jr., *The Golden Age of Homespun* (Ithaca: Cornell University Press, 1953), pp. 264–65; . . .

27. Johnson, *Illinois*, p. 16.

28. Van Wagenen, *Golden Age of Homespun*, pp. 264–65; Sloan, *Seasons of America*, p. 118; . . .

29. Buley, *Old Northwest*, I:201–10; Margaret Gilbert Mackey and Louise Pickney Sooy, *Early California Costumes, 1769–1847* (Stanford: Stanford University Press, 1932), pp. 101–10.

30. Wiley Britton, *Pioneer Life in Southwestern Missouri* (Kansas City: Smith-Grieves Company, 1929), p. 130.

31. Aunt Jane (of Kentucky), quoted in Elizabeth Wells Robertson, *American Quilts* (New York: Studio Publications, 1948), pp. 59–60.

32. . . . Patricia Mainardi, "Quilts: The Great American Art," *Radical America* 7 (1973):39–40; . . .

33. Soapmaking, Buley reports, was the last domestic manufacture to pass from the farm household; *Old Northwest*, I:223. . . .

34. Vance Randolph, *The Ozarks: An American Survival of Primitive Society* (New York: Vanguard Press, 1931), p. 59.

35. *Compendium of the Eleventh Census; 1890: Part I—Population* (Washington, D.C.: Government Printing Office, 1893), p. 866.

36. Grabill estimates an age-specific infant (0–5) mortality of 220 out of 1,000 live births for the nineteenth century as a whole; W. H. Grabill, C. V. Kiser, and P. K. Whelpton, *The Fertility of American Women* (New York: John Wiley, 1958), p. 379.

37. S. B. Nerlove, "Women's Workload and Infant Feeding Practices: A Relationship with Demographic Implications," *Ethnology* 13 (1974):207–14; establishes that in societies where women contribute significantly to the production of subsistence, mothers tend to introduce their babies to supplemental food earlier than mothers in other societies. . . .

38. Buley, *Old Northwest*, I:310. Lactation does indeed have the effect of prolonging postpartum amenorrhea and delaying ovulation. Lactation beyond a year, however, by which time the infant must be receiving its essential protein from supplemental sources, has little continued effect in delaying the menses. . . .

39. Using the scale employed by Nerlove, "Women's Workload," pp. 208–10. . . .

40. Dr. W. W. Hall, "Health of Farmer's Families," in *Report of the Commissioner of Agriculture for the Year 1862* (Washington, D.C.: Government Printing Office, 1863), pp. 462–63. All subsequent quotations from ibid., pp. 462–70, passim.

41. The following all document the same situation for farm women in the first quarter of the twentieth century: Randolph, *The Ozarks*, pp. 41–43; . . . Edward B. Mitchell, "The American Farm Woman As She Sees Herself," in U.S. Department of Agriculture, *Yearbook of Agriculture, 1914* (Washing-

ton, D.C.: Government Printing Office, 1915), pp. 311–18; U.S. Department of Agriculture, "The Needs of Farm Women," Reports nos. 103–6 (Washington, D.C.: Government Printing Office, 1905).

42. Daniel Drake, quoted in Harriet Martineau, *Retrospect of Western Travel* (London: Saunders and Otley, 1838), 3:224.

43. Friedl, *Women and Men,* pp. 8, 135.

44. Of these, only whiskey was a male product. Buley, *Old Northwest,* I:235; Taylor, *Tarpleywick,* p. 14; Hamilton, *In No Time,* pp. 46, 168.

45. Mitchell, "American Farm Woman," p. 314; Mary Meek Atkeson, *The Woman on the Farm* (New York: Century, 1924), pp. 4–5.

46. "The Wife Who Wouldn't Spin Tow," Vance Randolph, *Ozark Folksongs,* 4 vols. (Columbia: State Historical Society of Missouri, 1946–1950), 1:123–24.

47. "The Scolding Wife," Paul G. Brewster, "Some Folk Songs from Indiana," *Journal of American Folk Lore* 57 (1944):282–83; Mary O. Eddy, *Ballads and Songs from Ohio* (New York: J. J. Angustin, 1939), p. 214; last verse supplied in another version, "The Dumb Wife Cured," Randolph, *Ozark Folksongs,* 3: 119.

48. Randolph, *The Ozarks,* p. 42.

49. Hamilton, *In No Time,* p. 73.

CHRISTINE STANSELL

Women, Children, and the Uses of the Streets: Class and Gender Conflict in New York City, 1850–1860

As John Mack Faragher shows, rural life involved hard work and insecurities—not only the unpredictability of the weather but the difficulties of paying debts and the loneliness that came with being far from friends and neighbors. The insecurities of urban life for working people could be even more severe. By the 1830s, the conditions of the urban poor had begun to command attention: in Philadelphia, Mathew Carey published a landmark investigation of the lives of working women. In many cities groups of middle-class reformers tried to help with food, clothing, and religious consolation. But as Christine Stansell shows, this "help" could involve intrusion into the patterns of family relationships.

How did middle-class women define the role of the mother? In what ways was this definition different from the way working-class mothers understood their role? What parallels does Stansell draw between conditions in New York City in the 1850s and today?

On a winter day in 1856, an agent for the Children's Aid Society (CAS) of New York encountered two children out on the street with market baskets. Like hundreds he might have seen, they were desperately poor—thinly dressed and barefoot in the cold—but their cheerful countenances struck the gentleman, and he stopped to inquire into their circumstances. They explained that they were out gathering bits of wood and coal their mother could burn for fuel and agreed to take him home to meet her. In a bare tenement room, bereft of heat,

Excerpted from "Women, Children, and the Uses of the Streets: Class and Gender Conflict in New York City, 1850–1860" by Christine Stansell, in *Feminist Studies,* 8 (1982):309–35. Copyright © 1982 by Feminist Studies, Inc. Reprinted by permission of the publisher, Feminist Studies, Inc., c/o Women's Studies Program, University of Maryland, College Park, Maryland 20742. Notes have been renumbered and edited.

furniture, or any other comforts, he met a "stout, hearty woman" who, even more than her children, testified to the power of hardihood and motherly love in the most miserable circumstances. A widow, she supported her family as best she could by street peddling; their room was bare because she had been forced to sell her clothes, furniture, and bedding to supplement her earnings. As she spoke, she sat on a pallet on the floor and rubbed the hands of the two younger siblings of the pair from the street. "They were tidy, sweet children," noted the agent, "and it was very sad to see their chilled faces and tearful eyes." Here was a scene that would have touched the heart of Dickens, and seemingly many a chillier mid-Victorian soul. Yet in concluding his report, the agent's perceptions took a curiously harsh turn.

> Though for her pure young children too much could hardly be done, in such a woman there is little confidence to be put . . . it is probably, some cursed vice has thus reduced her, and that, if her children be not separated from her, she will drag them down, too.[1]

Such expeditions of charity agents and reformers into the households of the poor were common in New York between 1850 and 1860. So were such harsh and unsupported judgments of working-class mothers, judgments which either implicitly or explicitly converged in the new category of the "dangerous classes." In this decade, philanthropists, municipal authorities, and a second generation of Christian evangelicals, male and female, came to see the presence of poor children in New York's streets as a central element of the problem of urban poverty. They initiated an ambitious campaign to clear the streets, to change the character of the laboring poor by altering their family lives, and, in the process, to eradicate poverty itself. They focused their efforts on transforming two elements of laboring-class family life, the place of children and the role of women.

There was, in fact, nothing new about the presence of poor children in the streets, nor was it new that women of the urban poor should countenance that presence. For centuries, poor people in Europe had freely used urban public areas—streets, squares, courts, and marketplaces—for their leisure and work. For the working poor, street life was bound up not only with economic exigency, but also with childrearing, family mortality, sociability, and neighborhood ties. In the nineteenth century, the crowded conditions of the tenements and the poverty of great numbers of metropolitan laboring people made the streets as crucial an arena as ever for their social and economic lives. As one New York social investigator observed, "In the poorer portions of the city, people live much and sell mostly out of doors."[2]

How, then, do we account for this sudden flurry of concern? For reformers like the agent from the CAS, street life was antagonistic to ardently held beliefs about childhood, womanhood and, ultimately, the nature of civilized urban society. The middle class of which the reformers were a part was only emerging, an economically ill-defined group, neither rich nor poor, just beginning in the antebellum years to assert a distinct cultural identity. Central to its self-conception was the ideology of domesticity, a set of sharp ideas and pronounced opinions about the nature of a moral family life. The sources of this ideology were historically complex and involved several decades of struggles by women of this group for social recognition, esteem, and power in the family. Nonetheless, by midcentury, ideas initially developed and promoted by women and their clerical allies had found general acceptance, and an ideology of gender had become firmly embedded in an ideology of class. Both women and men valued the home, an institution which they perceived as sacred, presided over by women, inhabited by children, frequented by men. The home preserved those social virtues endangered by the public world of trade, industry, and politics; a public world which they saw as even more corrupting and dangerous in a great city like New York.[3]

Enclosed, protected, and privatized, the home and the patterns of family life on which it was based thus represented to middle-class women and men a crucial institution of civilization. From this perspective, a particular geography of social life—the engagement of the poor in street life rather than in the enclave of the home—became in itself evidence of parental neglect, family disintegration, and a pervasive urban social pathology. Thus in his condemnation of the impoverished widow, the CAS agent distilled an entire analysis of poverty and a critique of poor families: the presence of her children on the streets was synonymous with a corrupt family life, no matter how disguised it might be. In the crusade of such mid-Victorian reformers to save poor children from their parents and their class lie the roots of a long history of middle-class intervention in working-class families, a history which played a central part in the making of the female American working class.

Many historians have shown the importance of antebellum urban reform to the changing texture of class relations in America, its role in the cultural transformations of urbanization and industrialization.[4] Confronted with overcrowding, unemployment, and poverty on a scale theretofore unknown in America, evangelical reformers forged programs to control and mitigate these pressing urban problems, programs which would shape municipal policies for years to come. Yet their responses were not simply practical solutions, the most intelligent possible reactions to difficult circumstances; as the most sensitive historians of reform have argued, they were shaped by the world view, cultural affinities, conceptions of gender, class prejudices, and imperatives of the reformers themselves. Urban reform was an interaction in which, over time, both philanthropists and their beneficiaries changed. In their experience with the reformers, the laboring poor learned—and were forced—to accommodate themselves to an alien conception of family and city life. Through their work with the poor, the reformers discovered many of the elements from which they would forge their own class and sexual identity, still ill-defined and diffuse in 1850; women, particularly, strengthened their role as dictators of domestic and familial standards for all classes of Americans. The reformers' eventual triumph in New York brought no solutions to the problem of poverty, but it did bring about the evisceration of a way of urban life and the legitimation of their own cultural power as a class.

The conflict over the streets resonated on many levels. Ostensibly the reformers aimed to rescue children from the corruptions and dangers of the city streets; indeed the conscious motives of many, if not all, of these well-meaning altruists went no further. There were many unquestioned assumptions, however, on which their benevolent motives rested, and it is in examining these assumptions that we begin to see the challenge which these middle-class people unwittingly posed to common practices of the poor. In their cultural offensive, reformers

sought to impose on the poor conceptions of childhood and motherhood drawn from their own ideas of domesticity. In effect, reformers tried to implement their domestic beliefs through reorganizing social space, through creating a new geography of the city. Women were especially active; while male reformers experimented, through a rural foster home program, with more dramatic means of clearing the streets, middle-class ladies worked to found new working-class homes, modeled on their own, which would establish a viable alternative to the thoroughly nondomesticated streets. Insofar as the women reformers succeeded, their victory contributed to both the dominance of a class and of a specific conception of gender. It was, moreover, a victory which had enduring and contradictory consequences for urban women of all classes. In our contemporary city streets, vacated, for the most part, of domestic life yet dangerous for women and children, we see something of the legacy of their labors.

CHILDREN'S USES OF THE STREETS

Unlike today, the teeming milieu of the New York streets in the mid-nineteenth century was in large part a children's world. A complex web of economic imperatives and social mores accounted for their presence there, a presence which reformers so ardently decried. Public life, with its panoply of choices, its rich and varied texture, its motley society, played as central a role in the upbringing of poor children as did private, domestic life in that of their more affluent peers. While middle-class mothers spent a great deal of time with their children (albeit with the help of servants), women of the laboring classes condoned for their offspring an early independence—within bounds—on the streets. Through peddling, scavenging, and the shadier arts of theft and prostitution, the streets offered children a way to earn their keep, crucial to making ends meet in their households. Street life also provided a home for children without families—the orphaned and abandoned—and an alternative to living at home for the especially independent and those in strained family circumstances.

Such uses of the streets were dictated by exigency, but they were also intertwined with patterns of motherhood, parenthood, and childhood. In contrast to their middle- and upper-class contemporaries, the working poor did not think of childhood as a separate stage of life in which girls and boys were free from adult burdens, nor did poor women consider mothering to be a full-time task of supervision. They expected their children to work from an early age, to "earn their keep" or to "get a living," a view much closer to the early modern conceptions which Philippe Ariès describes in *Centuries of Childhood*.[5] Children were little adults, unable as yet to take up all the duties of their elders, but nonetheless bound to do as much as they could. To put it another way, the lives of children, like those of adults, were circumscribed by economic and familial obligations. In this context, the poor expressed their care for children differently than did the propertied classes. Raising one's children properly did not mean protecting them from the world of work; on the contrary, it involved teaching them to shoulder those heavy burdens of labor which were the common lot of their class, to be hardworking and dutiful to kin and neighbors. By the same token, laboring children gained an early autonomy from their parents, an autonomy alien to the experience of more privileged children. But there were certainly generational tensions embedded in these practices: although children learned independence within the bounds of family obligation, their self-sufficiency also led them in directions that parents could not always control. When parents sent children out to the streets, they could only partially set the terms of what the young ones learned there.

Street selling, or huckstering, was one of the most common ways for children to turn the streets to good use. Through the nineteenth century, this ancient form of trade still flourished in New York alongside such new institutions of mass marketing as A. T. Stewart's department store. Hucksters, both adults and children, sold all manner of necessities and delicacies. In the downtown business and shopping district, passers-by could buy treats at every corner: hot sweet potatoes, bake-pears, teacakes, fruit, candy, and hot corn. In residential neighborhoods, hucksters sold household supplies door to door: fruits and vegetables in season, matchsticks, scrub brushes, sponges, strings, and pins. Children assisted adult hucksters, went peddling on their own, and worked in several low-paying trades which were their special province: crossing-sweeping for girls;

errandrunning, bootblacking, horseholding and newpaperselling for boys.[6] . . .

Younger children, too, could earn part of their keep on the streets. Scavenging, the art of gathering useful and salable trash, was the customary chore for those too small to go out streetselling. Not all scavengers were children; there were also adults who engaged in scavenging full-time, ragpickers who made their entire livelihoods from "all the odds and ends of a great city."[7] More generally, however, scavenging was children's work. Six- or seven-year-olds were not too young to set out with friends and siblings to gather fuel for their mothers. Small platoons of these children scoured neighborhood streets, ship and lumber yards, building lots, demolished houses, and the precincts of artisan shops and factories for chips, ashes, wood, and coal to take home or peddle to neighbors. . . .

The economy of rubbish was intricate. As children grew more skilled, they learned how to turn up other serviceable cast-offs. "These gatherers of things lost on earth," a journal had called them in 1831. "These makers of something out of nothing."[8] Besides taking trash home or selling it to neighbors, children could peddle it to junk dealers, who in turn vended it to manufacturers and artisans for use in industrial processes. Rags, old rope, metal, nails, bottles, paper, kitchen grease, bones, spoiled vegetables, and bad meat all had their place in this commercial network. The waterfront was especially fruitful territory: there, children foraged for loot which had washed up on the banks, snagged in piers, or spilled out on the docks. . . . Old rope was shredded and sold as oakum, a fiber used to caulk ships. Whole pieces of hardware—nails, cogs, and screws—could be resold: broken bits went to iron- and brass-founders and coppersmiths to be melted down; bottles and bits of broken glass, to glassmakers.[9] . . . The waterfront also yielded trash which could be used at home rather than vended: tea, coffee, sugar, and flour spilled from sacks and barrels, and from the wagons which carried cargo to nearby warehouses.[10]

By the 1850s, huckstering and scavenging were the only means by which increasing numbers of children could earn their keep. A decline in boys' positions as artisans' apprentices and girls' positions as domestic servants meant that the streets became the most accessible employer of children. Through the 1840s, many artisan masters entirely rearranged work in their shops to take advantage of a labor market glutted with impoverished adults, and to survive within the increasingly cutthroat exigencies of New York commerce and manufacturing. As a result, apprenticeship in many trades had disappeared by 1850. Where it did survive, the old perquisites, steady work and room and board, were often gone: boys' work, like that of the adults they served, was irregular and intermittent.[11]

There were analogous changes in domestic service. Until the 1840s, girls of the laboring classes had easily found work as servants, but in that decade, older female immigrants, whom employers preferred for their superior strength, crowded them out of those positions. By the early 1850s, domestic service was work for Irish and German teenagers and young women. In other industrial centers, towns like Manchester and Lowell, children moved from older employments into the factories; New York, however, because of high ground rents and the absence of sufficient water power, lacked the large establishments which gave work to the young in other cities.[12] Consequently, children and adolescents, who two generations earlier would have worked in more constrained situations, now flooded the streets.

The growth of the street trades meant that increasing numbers of children worked on their own, away from adult supervision. This situation magnified the opportunities for illicit gain, the centuries-old pilfering and finagling of apprentices and serving-girls. When respectable parents sent their children out to scavenge and peddle, the consequences were not always what they intended: these trades were an avenue to theft and prostitution as well as to an honest living. Child peddlers habituated household entryways, with their hats and umbrellas and odd knickknacks, and roamed by shops where goods were often still, in the old fashion, displayed outside on the sidewalks.[13] And scavenging was only one step removed from petty theft. The distinction between gathering spilled flour and spilling flour oneself was one which small scavengers did not always observe. Indeed, children skilled in detecting value in random objects strewn about the streets, the seemingly inconsequential, could as easily spot value in other people's property. . . . Thefts against persons, pickpocketing and mugging, belonged to another province, that of the professional child criminal.

Not all parents were concerned about their children's breaches of the law. Reformers were not always wrong when they charged that by sending children to the streets, laboring-class parents implicitly encouraged them to a life of crime. The unrespectable poor did not care to discriminate between stolen and scavenged goods, and the destitute could not afford to. . . .

As scavenging shaded into theft, so it also edged into another street trade, prostitution. The same art of creating commodities underlay both. In the intricate economy of the streets, old rope, stray coal, rags, and sex all held the promise of cash, a promise apparent to children who from an early age learned to be "makers of something out of nothing." For girls who knew how to turn things with no value into things with exchange value, the prostitute's act of bartering sex into money would have perhaps seemed daunting, but nonetheless comprehensible. These were not professional child prostitutes; rather, they turned to the lively trade in casual prostitution on occasion or at intervals to supplement other earnings. One encounter with a gentleman, easy to come by in the hotel and business district, could bring the equivalent of a month's wages in domestic service, a week's wages seamstressing, or several weeks' earnings huckstering. Such windfalls went to pay a girl's way at home or, more typically, to purchase covertly some luxury—pastries, a bonnet, cheap jewelry, a fancy gown—otherwise out of her reach.

Prostitution was quite public in antebellum New York. It was not yet a statutory offense, and although the police harassed streetwalkers and arrested them for vagrancy, they had little effect on the trade. Consequently, offers from men and inducements from other girls were common on the streets, and often came a girl's way when she was out working. This is the reason a German father tried to prevent his fourteen-year-old daughter from going out scavenging when she lost her place in domestic service. "He said, 'I don't want you to be a rag-picker. You are not a child now—people will look at you—you will come to harm,'" as the girl recounted the tale.[14] The "harm" he feared was the course taken by a teenage habitué of the waterfront in whom William Bell, police inspector of second-hand shops, took a special interest in 1851. After she rejected his offer of a place in service, he learned from a junk shop proprietor that, along with scavenging around the docks, she was "in the habit of going aboard the Coal Boats in that vicinity and prostituting herself."[15] Charles Loring Brace, founder of the CAS, claimed that "the life of a swill-gatherer, or coal-picker, or chiffonier [ragpicker] in the streets soon wears off a girl's modesty and prepares her for worse occupation," while Police Chief George Matsell accused huckster-girls of soliciting the clerks and employees they met on their rounds of counting houses.[16]

While not all girls in the street trades were as open to advances as Brace and Matsell implied, their habituation to male advances must have contributed to the brazenness with which some of them could engage in sexual bartering. Groups of girls roamed about the city, sometimes on chores and errands, sometimes only with an eye for flirtations, or being "impudent and saucy to men," as the parents of one offender put it.[17] In the early 1830s, John R. McDowall, leader of the militant Magdalen Society, had observed on fashionable Broadway "females of thirteen and fourteen walking the streets without a protector, until some pretended gentleman gives them a nod, and takes their arm and escorts them to houses of assignation."[18] McDowall was sure to exaggerate, but later witnesses lent credence to his description. In 1854, a journalist saw nearly fifty girls soliciting one evening as he walked a mile up Broadway, while diarist George Templeton Strong referred to juvenile prostitution as a permanent feature of the promenade in the early 1850s: "no one can walk the length of Broadway without meeting some hideous troop of ragged girls."[19] But despite the entrepreneurial attitude with which young girls ventured into prostitution, theirs was a grim choice, with hazards which, young as they were, they could not always foresee. Nowhere can we see more clearly the complexities of poor children's lives in the public city. The life of the streets taught them self-reliance and the arts of survival, but this education could also be a bitter one.

The autonomy and independence which the streets fostered through petty crime also extended to living arrangements. Abandoned children, orphans, runaways, and particularly independent boys made the streets their home: sleeping out with companions in household ar-

eas, wagons, marketplace stalls, and saloons. In June 1850, the *Tribune* noted that the police regularly scared up thirty or forty boys sleeping along Nassau and Ann streets; they included boys with homes as well as genuine vagabonds.[20] . . .

Reformers like Matsell and the members of the CAS tended to see such children as either orphaned or abandoned, symbols of the misery and depravity of the poor. Their perception, incarnated by writers like Horatio Alger in the fictional waifs of sentimental novels, gained wide credibility in nineteenth-century social theory and popular thought. Street children were essentially "friendless and homeless," declared Brace. "No one cares for them, and they care for no one."[21] His judgment, if characteristically harsh, was not without truth. If children without parents had no kin or friendly neighbors to whom to turn, they were left to fend for themselves. . . . But the testimony garnered by reformers about the "friendless and homeless" young should also be taken with a grain of salt. The CAS, a major source of these tales, was most sympathetic to children who appeared before the agents as victims of orphanage, desertion, of familial cruelty; accordingly, young applicants for aid sometimes presented themselves in ways which would gain them the most favor from philanthropists. . . .

Not surprisingly, orphanage among the poor was a far more complex matter than reformers perceived. As Carol Groneman has shown, poor families did not disintegrate under the most severe difficulties of immigration and urbanization.[22] In the worst New York slums, families managed to keep together and to take in those kin and friends who lacked households of their own. Orphaned children as well as those who were temporarily parentless—whose parents, for instance, had found employment elsewhere—typically found homes with older siblings, grandparents, and aunts. The solidarity of the laboring-class family, however, was not as idyllic as it might seem in retrospect. Interdependence also bred tensions which weighed heavily on children, and in response, the young sometimes chose—or were forced—to strike out on their own. Step-relations, so common in this period, were a particular source of bad feelings. . . . If natural parents died, step-parents might be particularly forceful about sending children "on their own hook." . . .

Moreover, the difficulties for all, children and adults, of finding work in these years of endemic underemployment created a kind of half-way orphanage. Parents emigrating from New York could place their boys in apprenticeships which subsequently collapsed and cast the children on their own for a living. . . . Similarly, adolescents whose parents had left them in unpleasant or intolerable situations simply struck out on their own. . . . Thus a variety of circumstances could be concealed in the category of the street "orphan."

All these customs of childhood and work among the laboring poor were reasons for the presence of children, girls and boys, in the public life of the city, a presence which reformers passionately denounced. Children and parents alike had their uses for the streets. For adults, the streets allowed their dependents to contribute to their keep, crucial to making ends meet in the household economy. For girls and boys, street life provided a way to meet deeply ingrained family obligations. This is not to romanticize their lives. If the streets provided a way to meet responsibilities, it was a hard and bitter, even a cruel one. Still, children of the laboring classes lived and labored in a complex geography, which reformers of the poor perceived only as a stark tableau of pathology and vice.

To what degree did their judgments of children redound on women? Although reformers included both sexes in their indictments, women were by implication more involved. First, poverty was especially likely to afflict women.[23] To be the widow, deserted wife, or orphaned daughter of a laboring man, even a prosperous artisan, was to be poor; female self-support was synonymous with indigence. The number of self-supporting women, including those with children, was high in mid-century New York: in the 1855 census report for two neighborhoods, nearly 60 percent of six hundred working women sampled had no adult male in the household. New York's largest charity reported in 1858 that it aided 27 percent more women than men.[24] For women in such straits, children's contributions to the family income were mandatory. As a New York magistrate had written in 1830: "of the children brought before me for pilfering, nine out of ten are those whose fathers are dead, and who live with their mothers."[25] Second, women were more responsible than men for children, both

from the perspective of reformers and within the reality of the laboring family. Mothering, as the middle class saw it, was an expression of female identity, rather than a construction derived from present and past social conditions. Thus the supposedly neglectful ways of laboring mothers reflected badly not only on their character as parents, but also on their very identity as women. When not depicted as timid or victimized, poor women appeared as unsavory characters in the annals of reformers: drunken, abusive, or, in one of the most memorable descriptions, "sickly-looking, deformed by over work . . . weak and sad-faced."[26] Like prostitutes, mothers of street children became a kind of half-sex in the eyes of reformers, outside the bounds of humanity by virtue of their inability or unwillingness to replicate the innate abilities of true womanhood.

REFORMERS AND FAMILY LIFE

In the 1850s, the street activities of the poor, especially those of children, became the focus of a distinct reform politics in New York. The campaign against the streets, one element in a general cultural offensive against the laboring classes which evangelical groups had carried on since the 1830s, was opened in 1849 by Police Chief Matsell's report to the public on juvenile delinquency. In the most hyperbolic rhetoric, he described a "deplorable and growing evil" spreading through the streets. "I allude to the constantly increasing number of vagrants, idle and vicious children of both sexes, who infest our public thoroughfares."[27] Besides alerting New York's already existing charities to the presence of the dangerous classes, Matsell's exposé affected a young Yale seminarian, Charles Loring Brace, just returned from a European tour and immersed in his new vocation of city missionary. Matsell's alarmed observations coalesced with what Brace had learned from his own experiences working with boys in the city mission. Moved to act, Brace in 1853 founded the CAS, a charity which concerned itself with all poor children, but especially with street "orphans." Throughout the 1850s, the CAS carried on the work Matsell had begun, documenting and publicizing the plight of street children.[28] In large measure because of its efforts, the "evil" of the streets became a central element in the reform analysis of poverty and a focus of broad concern in New York.

Matsell, Brace, and the New York philan-thropists with whom they associated formed—like their peers in other Northeastern cities—a closely connected network of secular and moral reformers. By and large, these women and men were not born into New York's elite, as were those of the generation who founded the city's philanthropic movement in the first decades of the century. Rather, they were part of an emerging middle class, typically outsiders to the ruling class, either by birthplace or social status.[29] Although much of the ideology which influenced reformers' dealings with the poor is well known, scholars have generally not ex-plored the extent to which their interactions with the laboring classes were shaped by de-veloping ideas of gentility: ideas, in turn, based upon conceptions of domestic life. Through their attempts to recast working-class life within these conceptions, this still-inchoate class sharpened its own vision of urban culture and its ideology of class relations. Unlike phi-lanthropists in the early nineteenth century, who partook of an older attitude of tolerance to the poor and of the providential inevitability of poverty, mid-Victorians were optimistic that poverty could be abolished by altering the character of their almoners as workers, citizens, and family members. The reformers of the streets were directly concerned with the latter. In their efforts to teach the working poor the virtues of the middle-class home as a means of self-help, they laid the ideological and pro-grammatic groundwork for a sustained inter-vention in working-class family life.

What explains the sudden alarm about the streets at midcentury? The emergence of street life as a target of organized reform was partly due to the massive immigrations of those years, which created crises of housing, unemploy-ment, and crime. The influx of Irish and Ger-man immigrants in the 1840s greatly increased the presence of the poor in public areas. Thousands of those who arrived after 1846 wandered through the streets looking for hous-ing, kin, work, or, at the least, a spot to shelter them from the elements. A news item from 1850 reported a common occurrence.

Six poor women with their children, were dis-covered Tuesday night by some police officers, sleeping in the alleyway, in Avenue B, between 10th and 11th streets. When interrogated they said they had been compelled to spend their nights wherever they could obtain any shelter.

They were in a starving condition, and without the slightest means of support.[30]

Indeed, severe overcrowding in the tenements meant that more of the poor strayed outside, particularly in hot weather. . . .

The existence of the new police force, or-ganized in 1845, also aggravated the reformers' sense of crisis by broadening their notions of criminal behavior. The presence of these new agents of mediation between the poor and the propertied shed light on a milieu which there-tofore had been closed to the genteel. Indeed, the popularization of the idea of the dangerous classes after 1850 was partly due to publicized police reports and to accounts written by jour-nalists who accompanied the police on their rounds. The "vicious" activities of the laboring classes were elaborated in such reports as Mat-sell's, published in pamphlet form for philan-thropic consumption, and novelists' and jour-nalists' exposés like those of Ned Buntline and Charles Dickens's description of Five Points in his *American Notes*.

The police also seem to have enforced pro-hibitions on street life with their own def-initions of juvenile crime. Because conceptions of vagrancy depended on whether the police considered the child's presence in the streets to be legitimate, it is possible that some of the high number of juvenile commitments—about two thousand a year[31]—can be attributed to conflicting notions of the proper sphere of chil-dren. Brace was struck by the drama of chil-dren, police, and mothers in Corlear's Hook (now the Lower East Side). The streets teemed with

wild ragged little girls who were flitting about . . . some with baskets and poker gathering rags, some apparently seeking chances of stealing. . . . The police were constantly arresting them as "va-grants," when the mothers would beg them off from the good-natured justices, and promise to train them better in the future.[32]

As for petty larceny, that at least some of the arrests were due to an ambiguity about what constituted private property was testified to by one New York journalist. The city jail, he wrote, was filled, along with other malefactors, "with young boys and girls who have been caught asleep on cellar doors or are suspected of the horrible crime of stealing junk bottles and old iron!"[33] As children's presence in the public realm became inherently criminal, so did the gleaning of its resources. The distinction between things belonging to no one and things belonging to someone blurred in the minds of propertied adults as well as propertyless children.

There were, then, greater numbers of children in the New York streets after 1845, and their activities were publicized as never before. Faced with an unprecedented crisis of poverty in the city, reformers fastened on their presence as a cause rather than a symptom of impoverishment. The reformers' idea that the curse of poor children lay in the childrearing methods of their parents moved toward the center of their analysis of the etiology of poverty, replacing older notions of divine will.[34] In the web of images of blight and disease which not only reflected but also shaped the midcentury understanding of poverty, the tenement house was the "parent of constant disorders, and the nursery of increasing vices," but real parents were the actual agents of crime.[35] In opposition to the ever more articulate and pressing claims of New York's organized working men, this first generation of "experts" on urban poverty averred that familial relations rather than industrial capitalism were responsible for the misery which any clear-headed New Yorker could see was no transient state of affairs. One of the principal pieces of evidence of "the ungoverned appetites, bad habits, and vices"[36] of laboring-class parents was the fact that they sent their offspring out to the streets to earn their keep.

The importance of domesticity to the reformers' own class identity fostered this shift of attention from individual moral shortcomings to the family structure of a class. For these middle-class city dwellers, the home was not simply a place of residence; it was a focus of social life and a central element of class-consciousness, based on specific conceptions of femininity and childrearing. There, secluded from the stress of public life, women could devote themselves to directing the moral and ethical development of their families. There, protected from the evils of the outside world, the young could live out their childhoods in innocence, freed from the necessity of labor, cultivating their moral and intellectual faculties.[37]

From this vantage point, the laboring classes appeared gravely deficient. When charity visitors, often ladies themselves, entered the households of working people, they saw a domestic sparseness which contradicted their deepest beliefs about what constituted a morally sustaining family life.[38] "[Their] ideas of domestic comfort and standard of morals, are far below our own," wrote the Association for Improving the Condition of the Poor (AICP).[39] The urban poor had intricately interwoven family lives, but they had no *homes*. Middle-class people valued family privacy and intimacy: among the poor, they saw a promiscuous sociability, an "almost fabulous gregariousness."[40] They believed that the moral training of children depended on protecting them within the home; in poor neighborhoods, they saw children encouraged to labor in the streets. The harshness and intolerance with which midcentury reformers viewed the laboring classes can be partly explained by the disparity between these two ways of family life. . . . The AICP scoffed at even using the word: "Homes . . . if it is not a mockery to give that hallowed name to the dark, filthy hovels where many of them dwell."[41] To these middle-class women and men, the absence of home life was not simply due to the uncongenial physical circumstances of the tenements, nor did it indicate the poor depended upon another way of organizing their family lives. Rather, the homelessness of this "multitude of half-naked, dirty, and leering children"[42] signified an absence of parental love, a neglect of proper childrearing which was entwined in the habits and values of the laboring classes.

THE CHILDREN'S AID SOCIETY

Although Brace shared the alarm and revulsion of reformers like Matsell at the "homelessness" of the poor, he also brought to the situation an optimistic liberalism, based upon his own curious and ambiguous uses of domesticity. In his memoirs of 1872, looking back on two decades of work with the New York laboring classes, Brace took heart from the observation that the absence of family life so deplored by his contemporaries actually operated to stabilize American society. Immigration and continual mobility disrupted the process by which one generation of laboring people taught the next a cultural identity, "that continuity of influence which bad parents and grandparents exert." . . . "The mill of American life, which grinds up so many delicate and fragile things, has its uses, when it is turned on the vicious fragments of the lower strata of society."[43]

It was through the famed placing-out system that the CAS turned the "mill of American life" to the uses of urban reform. The placing-out program sent poor city children to foster homes in rural areas where labor was scarce. With the wages-fund theory, a common Anglo-American liberal reform scheme of midcentury which proposed to solve the problem of metropolitan unemployment by dispersing the surplus of labor, the society defended itself against critics' charges that "foster parents" were simply farmers in need of cheap help, and placing-out, a cover for the exploitation of child labor.[44] At first, children went to farms in the nearby countryside, as did those the city bound out from the Almshouse, but in 1854 the society conceived the more ambitious scheme of sending parties of children by railroads to the far Midwest: Illinois, Michigan, and Iowa. By 1860, 5,074 children had been placed out.[45]

At its most extreme, the CAS only parenthetically recognized the social and legal claims of working-class parenthood. The organization considered the separation of parents and children a positive good, the liberation of innocent, if tarnished, children from the tyranny of unredeemable adults. Here, as in so many aspects of nineteenth-century reform, the legacy of the Enlightenment was ambiguous: the idea of childhood innocence it had bequeathed, socially liberating in many respects, also provided one element of the ideology of middle-class domination.[46] Since the CAS viewed children as innocents to be rescued and parents as corrupters to be displaced, its methods depended in large measure on convincing children themselves to leave New York, with or without parental knowledge or acquiescence. Street children were malleable innocents in the eyes of the charity, but they were also little consenting adults, capable of breaking all ties to their class milieu and families. To be sure, many parents did bring their children to be placed out, but nonetheless, the society also seems to have worked directly through the children.[47] . . .

Placing-out was based on the thoroughly middle-class idea of the redeeming influence of the Protestant home in the countryside.[48] There, the morally strengthening effects of labor, mixed with the salutary influences of domesticity and female supervision, could re-

mold the child's character. Thus domestic ideology gave liberals like Brace the theoretical basis for constructing a program to resocialize the poor in which force was unnecessary. Standards of desirable behavior could be internalized by children rather than beaten into them, as had been the eighteenth-century practice. With home influence, not only childrearing but the resocialization of a class could take the form of subliminal persuasion rather than conscious coercion.[49]

Earlier New York reformers had taken a different tack with troublesome children. In 1824, the Society for the Reformation of Juvenile Delinquents had established an asylum, the House of Refuge, to deal with juvenile offenders. As in all the new institutions for deviants, solitary confinement and corporal punishment were used to force the recalcitrant into compliance with the forces of reason.[50] But Brace thought the asylum, so prized by his predecessors, was impractical and ineffectual. Asylums could not possibly hold enough children to remedy the problem of the New York streets in the 1850s; moreover, the crowding together of the children who were incarcerated only reinforced the habits of their class.[51] The foster home, however, with its all-encompassing moral influence, could be a more effective house of refuge. "We have wished to make every kind of religious family, who desired the responsibility, an Asylum or a Reformatory Institution . . . by throwing about the wild, neglected little outcast of the streets, the love and gentleness of home."[52] The home was an asylum, but it was woman's influence rather than an institutional regimen that accomplished its corrections.

This is an overview of the work of the CAS, but on closer examination, there was also a division by sex in the organization, and domesticity played different roles in the girls' and boys' programs. The emigrants to the West seem to have been mostly boys: they seem to have been more allured by emigration than were girls, and parents were less resistant to placing out sons than daughters. "Even as a beggar or pilferer, a little girl is of vastly more use to a wretched mother than her son," the society commented. "The wages of a young girl are much more sure to go to the pockets of the family than those of a boy."[53] Brace's own imagination was more caught up with boys than girls; his most inventive efforts were directed at them. Unlike most of his contemporaries, he appreciated the vitality and tenacity of the street boys; his fascination with the Western scheme came partly from the hope that emigration would redirect their toughness and resourcefulness, "their sturdy independence,"[54] into hearty frontier individualism.[55] Similarly, the agents overseeing the foster home program were men, as were the staff members of the society's much-touted Newsboys' Lodging-House, a boardinghouse where, for a few pennies, news boys could sleep and eat. The Lodging-House, was, in fact, a kind of early boys' camp, where athletics and physical fitness, lessons in entrepreneurship (one of its salient features was a savings bank), and moral education knit poor boys and gentlemen into a high-spirited but respectable masculine camaraderie.[56]

Women were less visible in the society's literature, their work less well-advertised, since it was separate from Brace's most innovative programs. The women of the CAS were not paid agents like the men, but volunteers who staffed the girls' programs: a Lodging-House and several industrial schools. The work of the women reformers was, moreover, less novel than that of the men. Rather than encouraging girls to break away from their families, the ladies sought the opposite: to create among the urban laboring classes a domestic life of their own. They aimed to mold future wives and mothers of a reformed working class: women who would be imbued with a belief in the importance of domesticity and capable of patterning their homes and family lives on middle-class standards.

Yet it was this strategy of change, rather than Brace's policy of fragmentation, which would eventually dominate attempts to reform working-class children. The ladies envisioned homes which would reorganize the promiscuously sociable lives of the poor under the aegis of a new, "womanly" working-class woman. In the CAS industrial schools and Lodging-House, girls recruited off the streets learned the arts of plain sewing, cooking, and housecleaning, guided by the precept celebrated by champions of women's domestic mission that "nothing was so honorable as industrious *house-work*."[57] These were skills which both prepared them for waged employment in seamstressing and domestic service and outfitted them for homes of their own: as the ladies proudly attested after several years of work, their students entered respectable married life as well as honest employment. "Living in homes reformed through their influence,"[58] the married women carried on their female mission, reformers by proxy.

Similarly, the women reformers instituted meetings to convert the mothers of their students to a new relationship to household and children. Classes taught the importance of sobriety, neat appearance, and sanitary housekeeping: the material basis for virtuous motherhood and a proper home. Most important, the ladies stressed the importance of keeping children off the streets and sending them to school. Here, they found their pupils particularly recalcitrant. Mothers persisted in keeping children home to work and cited economic reasons when their benefactresses upbraided them. The CAS women, however, considered the economic rationale a pretense for the exploitation of children and the neglect of their moral character. "The larger ones were needed to 'mind' the baby," lady volunteers sardonically reported, "or go out begging for clothes . . . and the little ones, scarcely bigger than the baskets on their arms, must be sent out for food, or chips, or cinders."[59] The Mothers' Meetings tried, however unsuccessfully, to wean away laboring women from such customary practices to what the ladies believed to be a more nurturant and moral mode of family life: men at work, women at home, children inside.

In contrast to the male reformers, the women of the society tried to create an intensified private life within New York itself, to enclose children within tenements and schools rather than to send them away or incarcerate them in asylums. There is a new, optimistic vision of city life implied in their work. With the establishment of the home across class lines, a renewed city could emerge, its streets free for trade and respectable promenades, and emancipated from the inconveniences of pickpockets and thieves, the affronts of prostitutes and hucksters, the myriad offenses of working-class mores and poverty. The "respectable" would control and dominate public space as they had never before. The city would itself become an asylum on a grand scale, an environment which embodied the eighteenth-century virtues of reason and progress, the nineteenth-century virtues of industry and domesticity. And as would befit a city for the middle class, boundaries between public and private life would be clear: the public space of the metropolis would be the precinct of men, the private space of the home, that of women and children.

In the work of the CAS female volunteers lie the roots of the Americanization campaign which, half a century later, reshaped the lives of so many working-class immigrants. The settlement houses of turn-of-the-century New York would expand the mothers' classes and girls' housekeeping lessons into a vast program of nativist assimilation. Female settlement workers would assure immigrant mothers and daughters that the key to decent lives lay in creating American homes within the immigrant ghettoes: homes that were built on a particular middle-class configuration of possessions and housekeeping practices and a particular structure of family relations. And, as in the 1850s, the effort to domesticate the plebeian household would be linked to a campaign to clear the streets of an ubiquitous, aggressive, and assertive working-class culture.

Neither the clearing of the streets nor the making of the working-class home were accomplished at any one point in time. Indeed, these conflicts still break out in Manhattan's poor and working-class neighborhoods. Today, in the Hispanic *barrios* of the Upper West and Lower East sides and in black Harlem, scavenging and street huckstering still flourish. In prosperous quarters as well, where affluent customers are there for the shrewd, the battle continues between police on the one hand, hucksters and prostitutes on the other. Indeed, the struggle over the streets has been so ubiquitous in New York and other cities in the last 150 years that we can see it as a structural element of urban life in industrial capitalist societies. As high unemployment and casualized work have persisted in the great cities, the streets have continued to contain some of the few resources for the poor to make ends meet. At the same time, the social imagination of the poor, intensified by urban life, has worked to increase those resources. All the quick scams— the skills of the con men, street musicians, beggars, prostitutes, peddlers, drug dealers, and pickpockets—are arts of the urban working poor, bred from ethnic and class traditions and the necessities of poverty.

Neither is the conflict today, however, identical to the one which emerged in the 1850s. The struggle over the streets in modern New York takes place in a far different context, one defined by past victories of reformers and municipal authorities. Vagrancy counts against children are now strengthened by compulsory school legislation; child labor laws prohibit most kinds of child huckstering; anti-peddling laws threaten heavy fines for the unwary. Most important, perhaps, the mechanisms for "placing out" wandering children away from "negligent" mothers are all in place (although the wholesale breakdown of social services in New York has made these provisions increasingly ineffectual, creating a new problem in its wake). The street life of the working poor survives in pockets, but immeasurably weakened, continually under duress.

In more and more New York neighborhoods, the rich and the middle class can walk untroubled by importunate prostitutes, beggars, and hucksters. The women gossiping on front stoops, the mothers shouting orders from upstairs windows, and the housewife habitués of neighborhood taverns have similarly disappeared, shut away behind heavily locked doors with their children and television sets. New York increasingly becomes a city where a variant of the nineteenth-century bourgeois vision of respectable urban life is realized. "NO LOITERING / PLAYING BALL / SITTING / PLAYING MUSIC ON SIDEWALKS IN FRONT OF BUILDINGS," placards on the great middle-class apartment houses warn potential lingerers. The sidewalks are, indeed, often free of people, except for passers-by and the doormen paid to guard them. But as Jane Jacobs predicted so forcefully two decades ago, streets cleared for the respectable have become free fields for predators. The inhabitants of modern-day New York, particularly women and children, live in a climate of urban violence and fear historically unprecedented save in wartime. In the destruction of the street life of the laboring poor, a critical means of creating urban communities and organizing urban space has disappeared. As the streets are emptied of laboring women and children, as the working-class home has become an ideal, if not a reality, for ever-widening sectors of the population, the city of middle-class hopes becomes ever more bereft of those ways of public life which once mitigated the effects of urban capitalism.

NOTES

1. Children's Aid Society (hereafter referred to as CAS), *Third Annual Report* (New York, 1856), pp. 26–27.

2. Virginia Penny, *The Employments of Women* (Boston, 1863), p. 317.

3. ... [S]ee Carroll Smith-Rosenberg, *Religion and the Rise of the American City: The New York City Mission Movement, 1812–1870* (Ithaca, N.Y.: Cornell University Press, 1971); and ... Mary Ryan, *Cradle of the Middle Class* (Cambridge: Cambridge University Press, 1981).

4. ... [See] Thomas Bender, *Toward an Urban Vision: Ideas and Institutions in Nineteenth-Century America* (Lexington: University Press of Kentucky, 1975); and Paul Boyer, *Urban Masses and Moral Order in America, 1820–1920* (Cambridge, Mass.: Harvard University Press, 1978).

5. Philippe Ariès, *Centuries of Childhood: A Social History of Family Life* (New York: Random House, 1965).

6. Penny, *Employments of Women*, pp. 133–34, 143–44, 150–52, 168, 421, 473, 484; ... CAS, *First Annual Report* (1854), pp. 23–24, *Seventh Annual Report* (1860), p. 16.

7. Charles L. Brace, *The Dangerous Classes of New York and Twenty Years' Work among Them* (New York, 1872), pp. 152–53.

8. *New York Mirror* 9 (1831):119, quoted in the I.N.P. Stokes Collection, New York Public Library, New York, p. 461.

9. Brace, *Dangerous Classes*, pp. 152–53; ... Solon Robinson, *Hot Corn: Life Scenes in New York Illustrated* (New York, 1854), p. 207; ... See also Sean Wilentz, "Crime, Poverty and the Streets of New York City: The Diary of William H. Bell 1850–51," *History Workshop* 7 (Spring 1979):126–55.

10. See also *New York Daily Tribune*, 16 March 1850.

11. Sean Wilentz, *Chants Democratic: New York City and the Rise of the American Working Class* (New York: Oxford University Press, 1983). ...

12. Victor S. Clark, *History of Manufactures in the United States*, 3 vols. (New York: McGraw-Hill Book Company, 1929), 1:351. For the lack of children's factory employment, see CAS, *Seventh Annual Report* (1860), p. 7.

13. ... David R. Johnson, "Crime Patterns in Philadelphia, 1840–70," in *The Peoples of Philadelphia: A History of Ethnic Groups and Lower Class Life, 1790–1940*, ed. Allen F. Davis and Mark H. Haller (Philadelphia, 1973).

14. Brace, *Dangerous Classes*, p. 120.

15. Bell Diary, 10 June 1851, in Wilentz, "Crime, Poverty, and the Streets of New York City," p. 147.

16. Brace, *Dangerous Classes*, p. 154; "Semi-Annual Report of the Chief of Police," *Documents of the Board of Aldermen*, vol. 17, part 1 (1850), p. 63.

17. House of Refuge Papers, Case Histories, New York State Library, Albany, vol. 1, case no. 61.

18. John R. McDowall, *Magdalen Facts* (New York, 1832), p. 53.

19. Allan Nevins and Milton Halsey Thomas, eds., *The Diary of George Templeton Strong*, 2 vols. (New York: The Macmillan Company, 1952), 2:57 (entry for 7 July 1851).

20. *New York Daily Tribune*, 3 June 1850.

21. Brace, *Dangerous Classes*, p. 91.

22. Carol Groneman (Pernicone), "The 'Bloudy Ould Sixth': A Social Analysis of a New York City Working-Class Community in the Mid-Nineteenth Century" (Ph.D. diss., University of Rochester, 1973).

23. See my essay "Origins of the Sweatshop," in *Working-Class America: Essays in the New Labor History*, ed. Michael Frish and Daniel Walkowitz (Urbana: University of Illinois Press, 1982), for an extended treatment of this point.

24. New York State Census, 1855, Population Schedules, Ward 4, Electoral district 2, and Ward 17, Electoral district 3, MSS at County Clerk's Office, New York City; Association for Improving the Condition of the Poor, *Fifteenth Annual Report* (New York, 1858), p. 38.

25. Letter reprinted in Mathew Carey, "Essays on the Public Charities of Philadelphia," *Miscellaneous Essays* (Philadelphia, 1830), p. 161.

26. CAS, *Third Annual Report* (1856), p. 27.

27. "Semi-Annual Report," p. 58.

28. Miriam Z. Langsam, *Children West: A History of the Placing-Out System in the New York Children's Aid Society* (Madison, Wis., 1964).

29. Boyer, *Urban Masses*, stresses the role of charity work in providing status and fellowship for newcomers to the city. ... See Emma Brace, ed., *The Life of Charles Loring Brace ... Edited by His Daughter* (New York, 1894); "George W. Matsell," *Palimpsest* 5 (July 1924):237–48.

30. *New York Daily Tribune*, 4 July 1850.

31. From "Reports of Commitments to First District Prison published in Commissioners of the Almshouse," *Annual Reports* (1850–60).

32. Brace, *Dangerous Classes*, p. 145.

33. George C. Foster, *New York in Slices; By an Experienced Carver* (New York, 1849), p. 20.

34. Smith-Rosenberg, *Religion and the Rise of the American City*, pp. 3, 29.

35. New York Assembly, *Report of the Select Committee Appointed to Examine into the Condition of Tenant Houses in New-York and Brooklyn*, Assembly doc. 205, 80th sess., 1857, p. 12.

36. CAS, *Third Annual Report* (1856), p. 29.

37. The best works on nineteenth-century domesticity are Nancy F. Cott, *The Bonds of Womanhood: 'Woman's Sphere' in New England, 1780–1835* (New Haven: Yale University Press, 1977); Ann Douglas, *The Feminization of American Culture* (New York: Avon, 1978); Kathryn Kish Sklar, *Catharine Beecher: A Study in American Domesticity* (New Haven: Yale University Press, 1973).

38. Here I strongly disagree with the view of the sisterly relations between women charity workers and their almoners presented in Barbara Berg, *The Remembered Gate: Origins of American Feminism—the Women and the City, 1800–1860* (New York: Oxford University Press, 1975).

39. Association for Improving the Condition of the Poor, *Thirteenth Annual Report* (1856), p. 23.

40. New York Assembly, *Report of the Select Committee*, p. 20.

41. Association for Improving the Condition of the Poor, *Fourteenth Annual Report* (1857), p. 21.

42. CAS, *Third Annual Report* (1856), p. 4.

43. Brace, *Dangerous Classes*, pp. 46–47.

44. CAS, *Sixth Annual Report* (1859), p. 9.

45. Figures are from Langsam, *Children West*, p. 64.

46. Michael Foucault has most forcefully analyzed this ambiguity. See *Madness and Civilization: A History of Insanity in the Age of Reason* (New York: Random House, 1973).

47. See the appendices in CAS, *Annual Reports* (1854–60).

48. CAS, *Third Annual Report* (1856), p. 8.

49. This is similar to the shift in criminal law from corporal punishment to the more enlightened environmental techniques of the penitentiary. See Michael Ignatieff, *A Just Measure of Pain: The Penitentiary in the Industrial Revolution, 1750–1850* (New York: Pantheon, 1978).

50. Ibid.

51. CAS, *First Annual Report* (1854), p. 7; *Second Annual Report* (1855), p. 5. See also Boyer, *Urban Masses*, pp. 94–95.

52. CAS, *Second Annual Report* (1855), p. 5.

53. CAS, *Fifth Annual Report* (1858), p. 17.

54. Brace, *Dangerous Classes*, p. 100.

55. See Boyer, *Urban Masses*, pp. 94–107; and Brace, *Dangerous Classes*, pp. 98–99.

56. Brace, *Dangerous Classes*, pp. 99–105.

57. CAS, *Ninth Annual Report* (1862), p. 13. See also *First Annual Report* (1854), pp. 7, 9.

58. CAS, *Tenth Annual Report* (1863), p. 23; *Seventh Annual Report* (1860), p. 8.

59. CAS, *Eleventh Annual Report* (1864), p. 28.

JEANNE BOYDSTON
The Pastoralization of Housework

Having read fiction and advice literature directed to women in the years before the Civil War, in 1966 the historian Barbara Welter identified a pervasive stereotype, which she called the "Cult of True Womanhood." Women were encouraged to cultivate the virtues of domesticity, piety, purity, and submissiveness. Home was referred to as women's "proper sphere" and understood to be a shelter from the outside world in which men engaged in hard work and cutthroat competition. Other historians agreed that men's and women's spheres of activity were separated and suggested that this separation was somehow linked to the growth of capitalism and industrialization in the same period. Historian Gerda Lerner argued that stressing the shelter of home was a way by which middle-class women distinguished themselves from mill girls, and so maintained class boundaries.

How does Jeanne Boydston describe the relationship between home and work in antebellum America? How does she describe the relationship between women's work and men's work? What does she think were the uses of the ideology of separate spheres?

In the colonial period, family survival had been based on two types of resources: the skills of the wife in housewifery, and the skills and property of the husband in agriculture. Both sets of skills involved the production of tangible goods for the family—such items as furnishings, food, and fabrics. Both were likely to involve some market exchange, as husbands sold grain and wives sold eggs or cheese, for example. And both involved services directly to the household. By the early nineteenth century, however, husbands' contributions to their households were focused disproportionately on market exchange—on the cash they brought into the family—while their direct activities in producing both goods and services for the family had vastly decreased.

The meaning of this shift has often been

misread, interpreted as an indication that households were no longer dependent on goods and services provided from within but had instead become reliant upon the market for their survival. . . . [But] consumerism was sharply curtailed by the amount of available cash. Choices constantly had to be made: to purchase a new cloak or try to refurbish the old one for another season, to hire a woman to help with the wash or lay aside some money to buy a house. In these patterns of mundane decisions lay the essential economic character of antebellum households: they were in fact "mixed economies"—economic systems that functioned on the bases of both paid and unpaid labor and were dependent upon both. They required paid labor for the cash to purchase some goods and services. Equally, they depended on unpaid labor in the household to process those commodities into consumable form and to produce other goods and services directly without recourse to the cash market. . . .

[The] antebellum era was the last period during which most adult women shared the experience of having been, at some point in their lives, *paid* household workers. To an extent never repeated, even middle-class wives were likely to have worked as hired "help" in their youth. . . . [It is therefore possible to make a rough calculation] of the cost to a family to replace the unpaid labor of the wife by purchasing it on the market. . . .[1]

In northeastern cities in 1860, a woman hired both to cook and to do the laundry earned between $3 and $4 a week. Seamstresses and maids averaged two-and-a-half dollars a week. On the market, caring for children was at the lower end of the pay scale, seldom commanding more than $2 a week. If we assume that a woman did the full work of a hired cook and child's nurse, and also spent even an hour a day each sewing and cleaning (valued at about three cents an hour apiece), the weekly price of her basic housework would approximate $4.70. Even if we reduce this almost by half to $3 a week (to allow for variations in her work schedule and for the presence of assistance of some sort), taken at an average, this puts the price of a wife's basic housework at about $150 dollars a year. . . .[2]

To this should be added the value of goods a wife might make available within the family for free or at a reduced cost. Among poorer households, this was the labor of scavenging. A rag rug found among the refuse was worth half a dollar in money saved, an old coat, several dollars. Flour for a week, scooped from a broken barrel on the docks, could save the household almost a dollar in cash outlay.[3] In these ways, a wife with a good eye and a quick hand might easily save her family a dollar a week—or $50 or so over the course of the year. In households with more cash, wives found other ways to avoid expenditures. By shopping carefully, buying in bulk, and drying or salting extra food, a wife could save ten to fifty percent of the family food budget . . . this could mean a savings of from 40 cents to over $2 a week. Wives who kept kitchen gardens or chickens . . . could . . . produce food worth a quarter a week (the price of ¼ bushel of potatoes in New York in 1851).[4]

But there was also the cash that working-class wives brought into the household, by their needlework, or vending, or by taking in boarders, running a grocery or a tavern from her kitchen, or working unpaid in her husband's trade. A boarder might pay $4 a week into the family economy. Subtracting a dollar and a half for food and rent, the wife's labor-time represented $2.50 of that amount, or $130 a year. . . .[5]

The particular labor performed by a given woman depended on the size and resources of her household. . . . Yet we can estimate a general market price of housework by combining the values of the individual activities that made it up: perhaps $150 for cooking, cleaning, laundry, and childrearing; another $50 or so saved through scavenging or careful shopping, another $50 or so in cash brought directly into the household. This would set the price of a wife's labor-time among the laboring poor at roughly $250 a year beyond maintenance. . . . In working-class households with more income, where the wife could focus her labor on money-saving and on taking in a full-time boarder, that price might reach over $500 annually. . . . These shifts in the nature of a wife's work, and in the value of that work, as a husband's income increased seems not to have been entirely lost on males, who advised young men that if they meant to get ahead, they should "get married". . . .[6]

But husbands were not the sole beneficiaries of the economic value of housework, or of its unique invisibility. Employers were enabled by the presence of this sizeable but un-counted labor in the home to pay both men and women wages which were, in fact, below the level of subsistence. The difference was critical to the development of industrialization in the antebellum Northeast. . . .[7] Occasionally, mill owners acknowledged that the wages they paid did not cover maintenance. One agent ad-mitted: "So long as they can do my work *for what I choose to pay them*, I keep them, getting out of them all I can. . . . [H]ow they fare out-side my walls I don't know, nor do I consider it my business to know. They must look out for themselves. . . ."[8]

Even when employers paid high enough salaries to provide present security for a family, they seldom provided either the income or the job security to ensure a household's well-being against the erratic boom-and-bust cycles of business and the unemployment consequent upon those cycles. . . . Women's unremuner-ated labor in the household provided the needed "safety net," enabling middle-class families to maintain some degree of both ma-terial stability and healthfulness in a volatile economic environment. . . . Put simply, a wife was a good investment for a man who wanted to get ahead.

THE PASTORALIZATION OF HOUSEWORK

The culture of the antebellum Northeast rec-ognized the role of wives in the making of con-tented and healthy families. Indeed, the years between the War of 1812 and the Civil War were a period of almost unabated celebration of women's special and saving domestic mis-sion. "Grant that others besides woman have responsibilities at home. . . ." wrote the Rever-end Jesse Peck in 1857, "[s]till we fully accord the supremacy of domestic bliss to the wife and mother. . . ."[9]

As recent historians have recognized, this glorification of wife and motherhood was at the heart of one of the most compelling and widely shared belief systems of the early nineteenth century: the ideology of gender spheres. An elaborate set of intellectual and behavioral con-ventions, the doctrine of gender spheres ex-pressed a worldview in which both the order-liness of daily social relations and the larger organization of society derived from and de-pended on the preservation of an all-encom-passing gender division of labor. Conse-quently, in the conceptual and emotional universe of the doctrine of spheres, males and females existed as creatures of naturally and essentially different capacities. As the Provi-dence-based *Ladies Museum* explained in 1825:

> Man is strong—woman is beautiful. Man is dar-ing and confident—woman is diffident and un-assuming. Man is great in action—woman i[n] suffering. Man shines abroad—woman at home. Man talks to convince—woman to persuade and please. Man has a rugged heart—woman a soft and tender one. Man prevents misery—woman relieves it. Man has science—woman taste. Man has judgment—woman sensibility. Man is a being of justice—woman of mercy.

These "natural" differences of temperament and ability were presumed to translate into dif-ferent social roles and responsibilities for men and women. Clearly intended by the order of nature to "shine at home," Woman was deemed especially ill-equipped to venture into the world of nineteenth-century business, where "cunning, intrigue, falsehood, slander, [and] vituperative violence" reigned and where "mercy, pity, and sympathy, are vagrant fowls." . . .[10]

. . . the ideology of gender spheres was partly a response to the ongoing chaos of a changing society—an intellectually and emo-tionally comforting way of setting limits to the uncertainties of early industrialization. . . . The traits that presumably rendered Woman so de-fenseless against the guiles and machinations of the business world not only served to con-fine her to the home as her proper sphere but made her presence there crucial for her family, especially for her husband. Even the most en-thusiastic boosters of economic expansion agreed that the explosive opportunism of an-tebellum society created an atmosphere too heady with competition and greed to engender either social or personal stability. However great his wisdom or strong his determination, to each man must come a time

> when body, mind, and heart are overtaxed with exhausting labor; when the heavens are overcast, and the angry clouds portend the fearful storm; when business schemes are antagonized, thwarted by stubborn matter, capricious man, or an inauspicious providence; when coldness, jeal-ousy, or slander chills his heart, misrepresents his motives, or attacks his reputation; when he looks

with suspicion on all he sees, and shrinks from the frauds and corruptions of men with instinctive dread. . . . [11]

Whatever the proclivities or ambitions of individual women, the presumed contrasts between the sexes permitted Woman-in-the-abstract to be defined as the embodiment of all that was contrary to the values and behaviors of men in the marketplace, and thus, to the marketplace itself. Against its callousness, she offered nurturance. Against its ambition, she pitted her self-effacement and the modesty of her needs. Against its materialism, she held up the twin shields of morality and spiritual solace. If business was a world into which only men traveled and where they daily risked losing their souls, then wherever Woman was, was sanctuary. And Woman was in the Home.

The contrast between Man and Woman melted easily into a contrast between "workplace" and "home" and between "work" as Man engaged in it and the "occupations" of Woman in the home. Most writers of prescriptive literature did acknowledge that women were involved in activities of some sort in their households. For example, T. S. Arthur worried that a woman would be unable to keep the constant vigilance required to be a good mother if she also had to attend to "the operations of the needle, the mysteries of culinary science, and all the complicated duties of housekeeping." His language is revealing, however: housework consisted of "mysteries" and "duties"; it was a different order of activity from the labor that men performed. Indeed, some observers cautioned that the wife and mother should deliberately stay clear of employments which might seem to involve her in the economy. . . . William Alcott was among this group. Noting that a woman ". . . has duties to perform to the sick and to the well—to the young and to the aged; duties even to domestic animals," Alcott nevertheless cautioned that "[v]ery few of these duties are favorable to the laying up of much property, and some are opposed to it. So that while we commend industry—of the most untiring kind, too—we would neither commend nor recommend strong efforts to lay up property." The advice was not only consistent with, but reflected a critical aspect of the ideology of spheres: to the extent that workers in the household identified themselves with the labor of the marketplace, the function of the home as a place of psychological refuge would be undermined.[12]

Thus, the responsibilities of wives in their households were generally described in the prescriptive literature less as purposeful activities required and ordered by the welfare of their individual families than as emanations of an abstract but shared Womanhood. As Daniel C. Eddy explained:

Home is woman's throne, where she maintains her royal court, and sways her queenly authority. It is there that man learns to appreciate her worth, and to realize the sweet and tender influences which she casts around her; there she exhibits the excellences of character which God had in view in her creation.

Underscoring the essentially passive nature of women's functions, Eddy concluded: "Her life should be a calm, holy, beautiful walk. . . ."[13]

. . . The consequence of this conflation of ideology with behavior was to obscure both the nature and the economic importance of women's domestic labor. It was not only Woman-in-the-abstract who did not labor in the economy, but also, by extension, individual women. It was not only Woman-in-the-abstract, but presumably, real women who guided the ongoing functions of the home through the effortless "emanations" of their very being, providing for the needs of their families without labor, through their very presence in the household. As romantic narrative played against lived experience, the labor and economic value of housework ceased to exist in the culture of the antebellum Northeast. It became work's opposite: a new form of leisure. . . .

William Alcott's description of the wife's labors in *The Young Wife* provides a striking illustration of the pastoralization of housework in descriptions of the antebellum home:

Where is it that the eye brightens, the smile lights up, the tongue becomes flippant, the form erect, and every motion cheerful and graceful? Is it at home? Is it in doing the work of the kitchen? Is it at the wash-tub—at the oven—darning a stocking—mending a coat—making a pudding? Is it in preparing a neat table and table cloth, with a few plain but neat dishes? Is it in covering it with some of nature's simple but choice viands? Is it in preparing the room for the reception of an absent companion? Is it in warming and lighting the apartments at evening, and waiting, with female patience, for his return from his appointed labor? Is it in greeting him with all her heart on his arrival?[14]

Clearly, Alcott was quite familiar with the types of work performed by women in their own families, and his description is all the more interesting on this account: cooking, baking, washing clothes, mending and darning, serving meals, building fires, attending to lamps—it is a surprisingly accurate catalogue. It is also incomplete, of course. Missing from this picture is the making of the soap that the wash might be done, the lugging and heating of the water, the tiresome process of heating and lifting cast-iron irons, the dusting and sweeping of rooms, the cleaning of the stove, and the making of the stocking and the coat now in need of repair.

Even the domestic tasks which Alcott acknowledges, however, are not to be contemplated as true work, a point which is made explicit in his identification of only the husband's employments as "labor." With "labor," indeed, the wife's activities have no truck, for there is no labor here to perform. . . . the food appears virtually as a gift of nature, and the compliant fires and lamps seem to light and tend themselves. . . . All is ordered, and the ordering of it is not only *not* burdensome or tiring, but the certain vehicle of good health and a cheerful disposition. Far from labor, housework is positively regenerating. . . .

The pastoralization of housework, with its emphasis on the sanctified home as an emanation of Woman's nature, required the articulation of a new way of seeing (or, more exactly, of *not* seeing) women as actors, capable of physical exertion. Most specifically, this applied to women as laborers, but the "magical extraction" of physical activity from the concept of Womanhood in fact proceeded in much larger terms and was most apparent in the recurrent celebrations of female "influence." Typically invoked as the female counterpart to the presumably *male* formal political power,[15] the concept of indirect womanly "influence" supplanted notions of women as direct agents, and thus as laborers. [In an article entitled "Woman's Offices and Influences," J. H. Agnew argued that] the contrast between presumably male "power" (physical as well as moral)

and female "influence" could be drawn quite explicitly:

> We may stand in awe, indeed, before the exhibition of *power,* whether physical or moral, but we are not won by them to the love of truth and goodness, while *influence* steals in upon our hearts, gets hold of the springs of action, and leads us into its own ways. It is the *inflowing* upon others from the nameless traits of character which constitute woman's idiosyncracy. Her heart is a great reservoir of love, the water-works of moral influence, from which go out ten thousand tubes, conveying the ethereal essences of her nature, and diffusing them quietly over the secret chambers of man's inner being.

Woman does not herself *act.* Rather, she "gets hold of the springs of action." An idiosyncrasy in the human order, she is not so much a physical as an ethereal being. Agnew concluded: "Let man, then, exercise power; woman exercise influence. By this she will best perform her offices, discharge her duties." It is the crowning touch on the pastoralization of housework: the home is not the setting of labor, but of "offices" and "duties." Therefore, what is required for the happy home is not a worker, but rather "a great reservoir of love."[16]

The pastoralization of household labor became a common feature of antebellum literature, both private and published. . . . [It] shaped much of the fiction of the period. In a piece entitled "The Wife" (published in the *Ladies' Literary Cabinet* in July of 1819 and included in *The Sketch Book* the following year), Washington Irving described the plight of a young couple forced by the husband's disastrous speculations to give up their fashionable life in the city and move to a modest country cottage. One might anticipate numerous headaches and a good deal of hard work in such a move, especially for the wife, but such was not the case for Irving's "Wife." Mary goes out to the cottage to spend the day "superintending its arrangement," but the substance of that process remains a mystery, for the packing and unpacking, cleaning, hanging of curtains, arranging of furniture, putting away of dishes, sorting of clothes, and adjusting of new domestic equipment which one might expect to be required under such circumstances remain undisclosed in the text. Indeed, all we learn is that, when next encountered by the narrator, Mary "'seems in better spirits than I have ever known.'" Transformed into a creature who is far more sylvan nymph than human female, Mary greets her husband and the narrator "singing, in a style of the most touching simplicity.... Mary came tripping forth to meet us; she was in a pretty rural dress of white, a few wild flowers were twisted in her fine hair, a fresh bloom was on her cheek, her whole countenance beamed with smile—I have never seen her look so lovely." To complete the pastoral scene, nature has obligingly provided "'a beautiful tree behind the cottage'" where the threesome picnic on a feast of wild strawberries and thick sweet cream.[17] ...

In both its briefer and its more extended forms in fiction and in exposition, in prescription and in proscription, the pastoralization of housework permeated the culture of the antebellum Northeast. Often, it was expressed simply as a truism, as when the Reverend Hubbard Winslow reminded his Boston congregation that "[t]he more severe manual labors, the toils of the fields, the mechanics, the cares and burdens of mercantile business, the exposures and perils of absence from home, the duties of the learned professions devolve upon man...." [H]e considered women's occupations to be of a "more delicate and retired nature." That same year, the shocked and angered Congregational clergy of Massachusetts drew upon the same assumptions and the same imagery of Womanhood to denounce the abolitionist activities of Sarah and Angelina Grimké. Reminding their female congregants that "the power of woman is in her dependence," the clergy spoke of the "unobtrusive and private" nature of women's "appropriate duties" and directed them to devote their energies to "those departments of life that form the character of individuals" and to embodying "that modesty and delicacy which is the charm of domestic life...."[18]

As we have seen, working class husbands appear to have embraced the view that paid labor was economically superior to unpaid labor. They shared, too, a tendency to pastoralize the labor of their wives. The speeches of early labor activists, for example, frequently invoked both the rhetoric of the ideology of spheres and pastoral images of the household, implying a sharp contrast between "the odious, cruel, unjust and tyrannical system" of the factory, which "compels the operative Mechanic to exhaust his physical and mental powers," with the presumably rejuvenating powers of the home. Discouraging women from carrying their labor "beyond the home," working men called upon women to devote themselves to improving the quality of life within their families.... [A]s William Sylvis put it, it was the proper work of woman "to guide the tottering footsteps of tender infancy in the paths of rectitude and virtue, to smooth down the wrinkles of our perverse nature, to weep over our shortcomings, and make us glad in the days of our adversity, ..."[19]

African-American newspapers of the antebellum Northeast also reflected and reaffirmed the pastoral conventions of women's domestic labor. *The Rights of All* compared women to ornamental creatures of nature, "as various in decorations as the insects, the birds, and the shells...." In 1842, *The Northern Star and Freeman's Advocate* approvingly reprinted an article from the *Philadelphia Temperance Advocate* in which wives were described as deities "who preside over the sanctities of domestic life, and administer its sacred rights...." That this perception ill fit the experiences of those female readers whose home was also their unpaid workplace, as well as those women who worked for money in someone else's home, appears not to have disturbed the paper's editors. Rather than as a worker, Woman was represented as a force of nature—and presumably one intended for man's special benefit: "The morning star of our youth—the day star of our manhood—the evening star of our age."[20]

For both middle-class and working-class men, the insecurities of income-earning during the antebellum period struck at the very heart of their traditional roles as husbands and fathers. Particularly since the late eighteenth century, manhood had been identified with wage-earning—with the provision of the cash necessary to make the necessary purchases of the household. In the context of the reorganization of paid work in the antebellum Northeast, the growing dependency of households on cash, and the roller-coaster business cycles against which few families could feel safe, that identification faced almost constant challenge. And as it was challenged, it intensified.

By the antebellum period, the late-eighteenth century association of manhood with wage-earning had flowered into the cult of the male "breadwinner." A direct response to the unstable economic conditions of early industrialization, this association crossed the lines of the emerging classes, characterizing the self-perceptions and social claims of both laboring and middle-class men.

Among laboring men, the identification of manhood with wage-earning melded easily with the traditional emphasis on the "manliness" of the crafts. . . . General Trades' Union leader Ely Moore warned that the unchecked industrial avarice of employers would create a class of "breadless and impotent" workers. When they struck for higher wages in 1860, the shoemakers of Massachusetts linked the encroachments of capital with an attack upon their manhood; in the "Cordwainers' Song," they called upon each other to "stand for your rights like men" and "Resolve by your fathers' graves" to emerge victorious and "like men" to "hold onto the last!"[21] Gender also provided the language for belittling the oppressor, for working men often expressed their rage—and reaffirmed the importance of their own manhood—by impugning the masculinity of their employers. The "Mechanic" sneered at "[t]he employers and those who hang on their skirts."[22]

In the midst of the upheavals of the antebellum economy, however, it was not only employers who threatened the old artisan definitions of manhood. Because an entire way of life was being undermined, so the dangers seemed to arise from everywhere in the new social order—including from wage-earning women themselves. In fact, women seldom directly imperiled men's jobs. The young women who went to Lowell were entering an essentially new industry. Moreover, in their families and hired out on an individual basis, carding, spinning, fulling, and even, to some extent, weaving had long been a part of women's work. . . .

But if wage-earning women did not directly challenge men's jobs, their very presence in the new paid labor force may have underscored the precariousness of men's position as wage-earners. Particularly given the post-Revolutionary emphasis on the importance of women's remaining in the home to cultivate the private virtues, females who were visible as outworkers and operatives may have seemed to bespeak an "unnaturalness" in so-ciety—an inability of wage-earning men to establish proper households. Like the witches of the seventeenth century, wage-earning women became symbols of the threats posed to a particular concept of manhood—in this instance, a concept that identified male claims to authority and power with the status of sole wage-earner. As they grappled with the precariousness of their own positions, laboring-class men focused their anxieties on the women who were their wives, daughters, and sisters, as well as on the men who were their employers.

They expressed these anxieties in two forms. First, wage-earning men complained that women were taking jobs—and thus the proper masculine role—away from men. An 1836 report of the National Trades Union charged that because women's wages were so low, a woman's "efforts to sustain herself and family are actually the same as tying a stone around the neck of her natural protector, Man, and destroying him with the weight she has brought to his assistance." Not uncommonly, working men suggested that women did not really need to work for money and castigated "the girl, or the woman, as the case may be, who being in a condition to live comfortably at home by proper economy" selfishly took work from the truly needy. In 1831, the *Working Man's Advocate* called upon "those females who . . . are not dependent on their labor for a living" to withdraw from paid work so that men might have the jobs.[23]

At the same time, working men organized to call for "the family wage"—a wage packet for the male "breadwinner" high enough to permit his wife and children to withdraw from paid work. As Martha May has pointed out, the family wage "promised a means to diminish capitalists' control over family life, by allowing workingmen to provide independently for their families." But the demand for the family wage also signalled the *gendering* of the emerging class system, and, in this, the gendering of early industrial culture. Identifying the husband as the proper and "natural" wage-earner, the family wage ideal reinforced a distinctive male claim to the role of "breadwinner." By nature, women were ill-suited to wage-earning, many laboring-class men insisted. The National Trades' Union called attention to Women's "physical organization" and "moral sensibilities" as evidence of her unfitness for paid labor, and the anonymous "mechanic" focused on "the fragile character of a girl's constitution, [and] her peculiar liability to sickness."[24] Presumably, only men had the constitution for regular, paid labor.

It is tempting to see in the antebellum ideology of spheres a simple extension of the Puritan injunction to wives to be keepers at home and faithful helpmates to men. Certainly, the two sets of beliefs were related. The colonists brought with them a conviction that men and women were socially different beings, so created by God and so designated in the order of nature. Both were meant to labor, but they were meant to labor at different tasks. Perhaps even more important, they were meant to occupy quite different stations in social life and to exercise quite different levels of control over economic life. . . . "Labor" may have been a gender-neutral term in colonial culture, but "authority" and "property" were masculine concepts, while "dependence" and "subordination" were clearly feminine conditions. . . .

The origins of the antebellum gender culture were as much in the particular conditions of early industrialization as in the inherited past, however. . . . [T]he specific character of the nineteenth-century gender culture was dictated less by transformations in women's experience than by tranformations in men's. To be sure, the principle of male dominance persisted into the nineteenth century. . . . Social power in the antebellum Northeast rested increasingly on the ability to command the instruments of production and to accumulate and reinvest profits. From these activities wives were legally barred, as they were from formal political processes that established the ground rules for the development of industrial capitalism. While most men were also eliminated from the contest on other grounds (race, class, and ethnicity, primarily), one had to be male to get into the competition at all. . . .

With the demise of the artisan system, and so of a man's hopes to pass along a trade to his sons, the practical grounds on which a laboring man might lay claim to the role of male head-of-household had altered. Increasingly, it was less his position as future benefactor of the next generation than his position as the provider of the present generation (that is, the "breadwinner") that established a man's familial authority.

For men of the emerging middle class, the stakes were equally high but somewhat differ-ent. Many of these were the sons and grandsons of middling farmers, forebears who, while not wealthy, had established their adulthood through the ownership of land, and whose role within the family had been centrally that of the "father." Their power residing in their control of inheritance to the next generation—these were men who might have been described with some degree of accuracy as "patriarchs." But by the second decade of the nineteenth century middling farms throughout much of the Northeast were scarcely capable of supporting the present generation; much less were they sizeable or fertile enough to establish patriarchal control of the family. Simultaneously, the emergence of an increasingly industrialized and urbanized society rendered the inheritance of land a less useful and less attractive investment in the future for sons. Even successful businessmen and professionals experienced diminishing control over their sons' economic futures. A son might still read the law with his father, but new law schools, like medical schools, foreshadowed the time when specialized education, rather than on-the-job training with his father or his father's friends, would offer a young man the best chance for success. . . .

Early industrialization preserved the principle of male dominance, then, but in a new form: the "husband" replaced the "father." Men claimed social authority—and indeed exercised economic control—not because they owned the material resources upon which subsequent generations would be founded, but because they owned the resources upon which the present generations subsisted. More important, they had established hegemony over the definition of those resources. In the gender culture of the antebellum Northeast, subsistence was purchased by wages—and men were the wage-earners.

Early industrialization had simultaneously redefined the paradigm that guided the social and economic position of women. . . . [T]he paradigm of womanhood shifted from "goodwife" to "mother"—that is, from "worker" to "nurturer." . . . [W]hatever cultural authority women gained as "mothers" was at the direct cost of a social identity in the terms that counted most in the nineteenth century—that is, as workers. As Caroline Dall noted in 1860, most Americans cherished "that old idea, that all men support all women. . . ."

Dall recognized this to be "an absurd fiction," but it was a fiction with enormous social consequences. Even when women did enter paid work, their preeminent social identity as "mothers" (in distinct contrast to "workers") made their status as producers in the economy suspect: the predisposition to consider women "unfit" helped to justify underpaying them.[25]

In all of this, the pastoralization of housework implicitly reinforced both the social right and the power of husbands and capitalists to claim the surplus value of women's labor, both paid and unpaid. It accomplished this by rendering the economic dimension of the labor invisible, thereby making pointless the very question of exploitation: one cannot confiscate what does not exist. Since the ideology of spheres made the non-economic character of housework a simple fact of nature, few observers in the antebellum Northeast felt compelled to argue the point.

The ideology of spheres did not affect all women in the same way, of course. Insisting that the domestic ideal was founded in the nature of Woman (and not in the nature of society), prescriptive writers saw its embodiments everywhere—from the poorest orphan on the streets, to the mechanic's daughter, to the merchant's wife. But their models transparently were meant to be the women of the emerging middle class. It was, after all, in the middle classes that women had presumably been freed from the necessity for labor that had characterized the colonial helpmate; there, that mothers and wives had supposedly been enabled to express their fullest capacities in the service of family formation. In celebrations of middle-class "Motherhood" lay the fullest embodiments of the marginalization of housewives as workers.

But if middle-class women were encased in the image of the nurturant (and nonlaboring) mother, working-class women found that their visible inability to replicate that model worked equally hard against them. As historian Christine Stansell has vividly demonstrated, the inability (or unwillingness) of working-class women to remain in their homes—that is, their need to go out into the streets, as vendors, washerwomen, prostitutes, or simply as neighbors helping a friend out—provided the excuse for a growing middle-class intrusion into working-class households, as reformers claimed that women who could not (or did not

wish to) aspire to middle-class standards were defined as poor mothers.[26]

In addition to its specific implications for women, the ideology of spheres, and the pastoralization of housework which lay at the heart of that ideology, both represented and supported larger cultural changes attendant upon the evolution of early industrial capitalism. The transition of industrialization was not purely material: it was ideological as well, involving and requiring new ways of viewing the relationship of labor to its products and of the worker to his or her work. In its denial of the economic value of one form of labor, the pastoralization of housework signalled the growing devaluation of labor in general in industrial America. Artisans were discovering, and would continue to discover, what housewives learned early in the nineteenth century: as the old skills were debased, and gradually replaced by new ones, workers' social claims to the fruits of their labor would be severely undercut. Increasingly, productivity was attributed, not to workers, but to those "most wonderful machines."[27] It was in part against such a redefinition that the craft workers of New York and the shoemakers of Lynn, Massachusetts, struggled.[28]

The denial of the economic value of housework was also one aspect of a tendency, originating much earlier but growing throughout the eighteenth and nineteenth centuries, to draw ever-finer distinctions between the values of different categories of labor, and to elevate certain forms of economic activity to a superior status on the grounds of the income they produced. As with housework, these distinctions were rarely founded on the actual material value of the labor in question. Rather, they were based on contemporary levels of power and wealth, and served to justify those existing conditions. An industrialist or financier presumably deserved to earn very sizeable amounts of money, because in accumulating capital he had clearly contributed more labor and labor of a more valuable kind to society than had, for example, a drayman or a foundry worker. . . .

Finally, the ideology of spheres functioned to support the emergence of the wage system necessary to the development of industrial capitalism. The success of the wage system depends upon a number of factors—among them the perception of money as a neutral index of economic value and the acceptance of the wage as representing a fair "livelihood." The devaluation of housework was a part of a larger process of obscuring the continuation of and necessity for barter-based exchanges in the American economy. In this, it veiled the reliance of the family on resources other than those provided through paid labor and heightened the visibility of the wage as the source of family maintenance.

But how did women respond to the growing devaluation of their contributions as laborers in the family economy? . . . [I]n their private letters and diaries, wives quietly offered their own definition of what constituted the livelihood of their families, posing their own perception of the importance of conservation and stewardship against the cash-based index of the marketplace and easily integrating the family's periodic needs for extra cash into their understanding of their own obligations.

Nevertheless, among the public voices affirming that Woman was meant for a different sphere than Man, and that the employments of Woman in the home were of a spiritual rather than an economic nature, were the voices of many women. In *Woman in America*, for example, Mrs. A. J. Graves declared: ". . . home is [woman's] appropriate sphere of action; and . . . whenever she neglects these duties, or goes out of this sphere . . . she is deserting the station which God and nature have assigned to her." Underscoring the stark contrast between Woman's duties in the household and Man's in "the busy and turbulent world," Graves described the refuge of the home in terms as solemn as any penned by men during the antebellum period: ". . . our husbands and our sons . . . will rejoice to return to its sanctuary of rest," she averred, "there to refresh their wearied spirits, and renew their strength for the toils and conflicts of life."[29]

Graves was not unusual in her endorsement of the ideology of spheres and of the pastoralization of housework. Even those women who most championed the continuing importance of women's household labor often couched that position in the language of spheres. No one more graphically illustrates this combination than Catharine Beecher, at once probably the most outspoken defender of the importance of women's domestic labor *and* one of the chief proponents of the ideology of female domesticity. . . . Beecher was clear and insistent that housework was hard work, and she did not shrink from suggesting that its demands and obligations were very similar to men's "business." In her *Treatise on Domestic Economy*, Beecher went so far as to draw a specific analogy between the marriage contract and the wage labor contract:

> No woman is forced to obey any husband but the one she chooses for herself; nor is she obliged to take a husband, if she prefers to remain single. So every domestic, and every artisan or laborer, after passing from parental control, can choose the employer to whom he is to accord obedience, or, if he prefers to relinquish certain advantages, he can remain without taking a subordinate place to any employer.

Nevertheless, Beecher regularly characterized women's work in the home as the occupation merely of administering "the gentler charities of life," a "mission" chiefly of "self-denial" to "lay up treasures, not on earth, but in heaven." This employment she contrasts with the "toils" of Man, to whom was "appointed the out-door labor—to till the earth, dig the mines, toil in the foundries, traverse the ocean, transport the merchandise, labor in manufactories, construct houses . . . and all the heavy work. . . ."[30]

Beecher's apparently self-defeating endorsement of a view that ultimately discounted the value of women's labor arose from many sources, not the least of which was her own identification with the larger middle-class interests served by the ideology of spheres. Beecher enjoyed the new standing afforded middle-class women by their roles as moral guardians to their families and to societies, and based much of her own claim to status as a woman on the presumed differences between herself and immigrant and laboring-class women. For example, she ended an extended discussion of "the care of Servants" in *The American Woman's Home* with the resigned conclusion that "[t]he mistresses of American families, whether they like it or not, have the duties of missionaries imposed upon them by that class from which our supply of domestic servants is drawn."[31]

But, also like many women in antebellum America, Catharine Beecher was sharply aware of the power difference between males and females. It was a theme to which she constantly returned in her writings, especially in her discussions of women's rights. . . . In her *Essay on Slavery and Abolitionism,* Beecher was quite explicit about the reasons why a woman might cloak herself and her positions in the language of dependency and subordination:

> [T]he moment woman begins to feel the promptings of ambition, or the thirst for power, her aegis of defence is gone. All the sacred protection of religion, all the generous promptings of chivalry, all the poetry of romantic gallantry, depend upon woman's retaining her place as dependent and defenceless, and making no claims. . . .

It was much the same point that Elizabeth Ellet would later make in her *The Practical Housekeeper:* since men had many more alternatives than women, the smart woman made it her "policy" to create an appearance of domestic serenity.[32]

But it would be a mistake to read women's endorsement of the pastoralization of housework purely as a protective strategy. Women were not immune from the values of their communities, and many wives appear to have shared the perception of the larger society that their work had separated from the economic life of the community and that it was, in fact, not really work at all.

Those misgivings were nowhere more evident than in the letter that Harriet Beecher Stowe wrote to her sister-in-law, Sarah Beecher, in 1850. It was the first opportunity Harriet had had to write since the Stowes had moved to Brunswick, Maine, the spring before. Since her arrival with the children, she explained, she had "made two sofas—or lounges—a barrel chair—divers bedspreads—pillowcases—pillows—bolsters—matresses . . . painted rooms . . . [and] revarnished furniture." She had also laid a month-long siege at the landlord's door, lobbying him to install a new sink. Meanwhile, she had given birth to her eighth child, made her way through the novels of Sir Walter Scott, and tried to meet the obligations of her increasingly active career as an author—all of this while also attending to the more mundane work of running a household: dealing with tradespeople, cooking, and taking care of the children. From delivery bed to delivery cart, downstairs to the kitchen, upstairs to the baby, out to a neighbor's, home to stir the stew, the image of Stowe flies through these pages like the specter of the sorcerer's apprentice.

Halfway through the letter, Stowe paused. "And yet," she confided to her sister-in-law, "I am constantly pursued and haunted by the idea that I don't do anything."[33] It is a jarring note in a letter—and a life—so shaped by the demands of housework. That a skilled and loving mother could impart dignity and a sense of humane purpose to a family otherwise vulnerable to the degradations of the marketplace, Stowe had no doubt. But was that really "work"? She was less certain. In that uncertainty, to borrow Daniel Eddy's words, lay "a world of domestic meaning"—for housewives of the antebellum era, and for women since.

Notes

1. See Luisella Goldschmidt-Clermont, *Unpaid Work in the Household: A Review of Economic Evaluation Methods* (Geneva, 1982).

2. See Edgar Martin, *The Standard of Living in 1860: American Consumption Levels on the Eve of the Civil War* (Chicago, 1942), p. 177; and Faye Dudden, *Serving Women: Household Service in Nineteenth-Century America* (Middletown, Conn., 1983), p. 149.

3. This is calculated on the basis of an average weekly budget for a working-class family of five, as itemized in the New York *Daily Tribune,* May 27, 1851. See also Martin, *Standard of Living,* p. 122.

4. The New York *Daily Tribune,* May 27, 1851.

5. Martin, *Standard of Living,* p. 168.

6. Grant Thorburn, *Sketches from the Note-book of Lurie Todd* (New York, 1847), p. 12.

7. See Alice Kessler-Harris and Karen Brodlin Sacks, "The Demise of Domesticity in America," *Women, Households, and the Economy,* ed. Lourdes Beneria and Catherine R. Stimpson (New Brunswick, N.J., 1987), p. 67.

8. Quoted in Norman Ware, *The Industrial Worker, 1840–1860: The Reaction of American Industrial Society to the Advance of the Industrial Revolution* (New York, 1924; reprinted Gloucester, Mass., 1959), p. 77.

9. Jesse T. Peck, *The True Woman; or, Life and Happiness at Home and Abroad* (New York, 1857), p. 245.

10. *The Ladies Museum,* July 16, 1825, p. 3; Henry Ward Beecher, *Lectures to Young Men, on Various Important Subjects* (Boston, 1846), pp. 87, 91.

11. Peck, *The True Woman,* pp. 242–43.

12. *The Mother's Rule; or, The Right Way and the Wrong Way,* ed. T. S. Arthur (Philadelphia, 1856), p. 261; William A. Alcott, *The Young Wife, or, Duties of Woman in the Marriage Relation* (Boston, 1837), p. 149.

13. Daniel C. Eddy, *The Young Woman's Friend; or the Duties, Trials, Loves, and Hopes of Woman* (Boston, 1857), p. 23.

14. Alcott, *The Young Wife,* pp. 84–85.

15. For an excellent discussion of the concept of female "influence," see Lori D. Ginzburg, *Women and the Work of Benevolence: Morality and Politics in the Northeastern United States, 1820–1885* (New Haven, Conn., 1990).

16. J. H. Agnew, "Women's Offices and Influence," *Harper's New Monthly Magazine* 17:no. 3 (Oct. 1851):654–57, quote on p. 657.

17. Washington Irving, "The Wife," *Ladies Literary Cabinet*, July 4, 1819, pp. 82–84. Quotations are from Washington Irving, *The Sketch Book of Geoffrey Crayon, Gent.* (New York, 1961), pp. 34–36.

18. "Pastoral Letter of the Massachusetts Congregationalist Clergy" (1837) in *Up From the Pedestal: Selected Writings in the History of American Feminism*, ed. Aileen S. Kraditor (Chicago, 1968), pp. 51–52; Reverend Hubbard Winslow, *A Discourse Delivered in the Bowdoin Street Church* (Boston, 1837), p. 8.

19. *The Man*, May 13, 1835; *Life, Speeches, Labors, and Essays of William H. Sylvis*, ed. James C. Sylvis (Philadelphia, 1872), p. 120.

20. *The Rights of All*, June 12, 1829; *The Northern Star and Freeman's Advocate*, Dec. 8, 1842, and Jan. 2, 1843.

21. Moore is quoted in Sean Wilentz, *Chants Democratic: New York City and the Rise of the American Working Class, 1788–1850* (New York, 1986), p. 239. The "Cordwainers' Song" is printed in Alan Dawley, *Class and Community: The Industrial Revolution in Lynn* (Cambridge, Mass., 1976), pp. 82–83.

22. "A Mechanic," *Elements of Social Disorder: A Plea for the Working Classes in the United States* (Providence, R.I., 1844), p. 96.

23. Quoted in John Andrews and W. D. P. Bliss, *A History of Women in Trade Unions*, vol. 10 of *Report on Condition of Woman and Child Earners in the United States*, Senate Doc. 645, 61st Cong., 2d Sess. (Washington, D.C., 1911; reprint ed. New York, 1974), p. 48; "Mechanic," *Elements of Social Disorder*, p. 45; *Working Man's Advocate*, June 11, 1831.

24. Martha May, "Bread Before Roses: American Workingmen, Labor Unions and the Family Wage," in *Women, Work, and Protest: A Century of U.S.*

Women's Labor History, ed. Ruth Milkman (Boston, 1985), p. 4; vol. 6 of *A Documentary History of American Industrial Society*, ed. John R. Commons et al. (New York, 1958), p. 281; "Mechanic," *Elements of Social Disorder*, p. 42.

25. Caroline Dall, *"Woman's Right to Labor"; or, Low Wages and Hard Work* (Boston, 1860), p. 57.

26. Christine Stansell, *City of Women: Sex and Class in New York, 1789–1860* (New York, 1986), pp. 193–216.

27. The phrase is from the title of Judith McGaw's study, *Most Wonderful Machine: Mechanization and Social Change in Berkshire Papermaking, 1801–1885* (Princeton, 1987).

28. See Wilentz, *Chants Democratic;* and Dawley, *Class and Community*, cited in n. 21 above.

29. Mrs. A. J. Garves, *Women in America: Being an Examination into the Morals and Intellectual Condition of American Female Society* (New York, 1841), p. 156.

30. Catharine E. Beecher, *A Treatise on Domestic Economy, for the Use of Young Ladies at Home, and at School* (Boston, 1841), p. 26; Beecher, *An Essay on Slavery and Abolitionism, with Reference to the Duty of American Females* (Philadelphia, 1837), p. 128; Catharine E. Beecher and Harriet Beecher Stowe, *The American Woman's Home, or Principles of Domestic Science* (Hartford, Conn., 1975), p. 19.

31. Beecher and Stowe, *The American Woman's Home*, p. 327.

32. Beecher, *Essay on Slavery and Abolitionism*, pp. 101–2; *The Practical Housekeeper; a Cyclopaedia of Domestic Economy*, ed. Mrs. [Elizabeth] Ellet (New York, 1857), p. 17.

33. Harriet Beecher Stowe to Sarah Buckingham Beecher, Dec. 17 [1850], The Schlesinger Library, Radcliffe College, Cambridge, Mass.

"She complained of the hours for labor being too many . . ."

The textile factories of the first wave of industrialization might not have been built at all had their owners not believed they could count on a steady supply of cheap female labor. The history of industrialization as it affected both men and women needs to be understood in the context of the segmented labor market that women entered. Women were a major part of the first new work force that was shaped into "modern" work patterns: long, uninterrupted hours of labor in a mechanized factory with little or no room for individual initiative.

One of the earliest mill towns was Lowell, Massachusetts, where factory owners began recruiting young, unmarried women to work in six textile mills in 1823. Rural young women already toiled at home at farm labor and also at "outwork," goods that could be made at home and sold for cash. Compared to the work they had done at home, mill work at first seemed to pay well and to offer new opportunities. The Lowell mills developed a system of boardinghouses, which assured families that girls would live in wholesome surroundings. Letters sent home and fiction published by young women in the first wave of employment often testified to their pride in the financial independence that their new work brought.

Work in the mills was strictly segregated by sex: men were supervisors and skilled mechanics; women attended the spinning and weaving machinery. Women's wages ranged from one-third to one-half that of men; the highest-paid woman generally earned less than the lowest-paid man. Employers responded to economic downturns in the 1830s by adjusting their expenses. Women's wages in the Lowell mills dropped; piece rates forced increases in production without increases in pay. Mills established stricter discipline: those who were insubordinate were fired, workers who did not fulfill their year-long contracts were blacklisted. But boardinghouse life meant that the factory women developed strong support networks; when their wages were cut and work hours lengthened in the 1830s, those who lived together came together in opposition to the owners and staged some of the earliest industrial strikes in American history. In 1836, 1,500 women walked out in protest, claiming their inheritance as "Daughters of the Revolution." One manifesto stated: "As our fathers resisted unto blood the lordly avarice of the

Excerpted from "The First Official Investigation of Labor Conditions in Massachusetts," in vol. 8 of *A Documentary History of American Industrial Society*, ed. John R. Commons, Ulrich B. Phillips, Eugene A. Gilmore, Helen L. Sumner, and John B. Andrews (Cleveland, 1910), pp. 133–142.

British ministry, so we, their daughters, never will wear the yoke which has been prepared for us."*

In January 1845, led by the indomitable worker Sarah Bagley, the Female Labor Reform Association organized a petition drive throughout the region, which forced the Massachusetts legislature to hold the first public hearings on industrial working conditions ever held in the United States. On February 13, 1845, Eliza Hemmingway and Sarah Bagley had their chance to testify. What did they think it was important for the legislators to know?

. . . The first petitioner who testified was Eliza R. Hemmingway. She had worked 2 years and 9 months in the Lowell Factories . . . Her employment is weaving—works by the piece. . . . and attends one loom. Her wages average from $16 to $23 a month exclusive of board. She complained of the hours for labor being too many, and the time for meals too limited. In the summer season, the work is commenced at 5 o'clock, a.m., and continued till 7 o'clock, p.m., with half an hour for breakfast and three quarters of an hour for dinner. During eight months of the year, but half an hour is allowed for dinner. The air in the room she considered not to be wholesome. There were 293 small [oil] lamps and 61 large lamps lighted in the room in which she worked, when evening work is required. These lamps are also lighted sometimes in the morning. About 130 females, 11 men, and 12 children (between the ages of 11 and 14) work in the room with her . . . The children work but 9 months out of 12. The other 3 months they must attend school. Thinks that there is no day when there are less than six of the females out of the mill from sickness. Has known as many as thirty. She herself, is out quite often, on account of sickness. . . .

She thought there was a general desire among the females to work but ten hours, regardless of pay. . . . She knew of one girl who last winter went into the mill at half past 4 o'clock, a.m. and worked till half past 7 o'clock, p.m. She did so to make more money. She earned from $25 to $30 per month. There is always a large number of girls at the gate wishing to get in before the bell rings. . . . They do this to make more wages. A large number come to Lowell to make money to aid their parents who are poor. She knew of many cases where married women came to Lowell and worked in the mills to assist their husbands to pay for their farms. . . .

Miss Sarah G. Bagley said she had worked in the Lowell Mills eight years and a half . . . She is a weaver, and works by the piece. . . . She thinks the health of the operatives is not so good as the health of females who do housework or millinery business. The chief evil, so far as health is concerned, is the shortness of time allowed for meals. The next evil is the length of time employed—not giving them time to cultivate their minds. . . . She had presented a petition, same as the one before the Committee, to 132 girls, most of whom said that they would prefer to work but ten hours. In a pecuniary point of view, it would be better, as their health would be improved. They would have more time for sewing. Their intellectual, moral and religious habits would also be benefited by the change. . . .

On Saturday the 1st of March, a portion of the Committee went to Lowell to examine the mills, and to observe the general appearance of the operatives. . . . [The Committee concluded:] Not only is the interior of the mills kept in the best order, but great regard has been paid by many of the agents to the arrangement of the enclosed grounds. Grass plats have been laid out, trees have been planted . . . everything in and about the mills, and the boarding houses appeared, to have for its end, health and comfort. . . . The [average hours of work per day throughout the year was 11½; the workday was longest in April, when it reached 13½ hours].

*Thomas Dublin, *Women at Work* (New York, 1979), p. 98.

MARY H. BLEWETT
The Sexual Division of Labor and the Artisan Tradition

The women of the Lowell mills entered the industrial work force directly, leaving their parents' homes to work in factories. But for many women the entry into the industrial work force was more gradual. As Mary Blewett shows, women who were the wives and daughters of shoemakers did industrial work in their own kitchens.

What difference did it make that women worked in the kitchen when their husbands worked in the shop? At first women received no wages but contributed their labor to the family economy; what difference did it make when they received wages and contributed those wages to the family economy? What differences does Blewett find between the "factory girls" who, like the women at the Lowell mills, entered the shoe factories directly, and the women who continued to work in their homes? Explain the issues that faced shoebinding women who worked at home when, during the strike of 1860, they had to choose between an alliance based on class and an alliance based on gender.

"The artisan, not the debased proletariat, fathered the labour movement. . . . The working class was born, not in the factory, but in the [artisan] workshop," wrote historian Bryan Palmer in 1976.[1] . . . [I]n this conception of the working class . . . [women] are invisible as workers and as a gender.

. . . The artisan's workshop was indeed a male world. [Many historians] . . . assume that the experience of female members of artisan families who were drawn into preindustrial production was indistinguishable from male experience. Labor historians regard the artisan workshop as the center of preindustrial political and cultural life and the source of the ideology and consciousness of the American working class. Such an assumption underestimates the importance of changes in the sexual division of labor within a craft of skilled male artisans, such as the New England shoemakers in the late eighteenth century. These artisans came to view women shoe workers as persons in separate and immutable gender categories that defined both their work and their relationship to the family and to artisan life. The

artisan tradition fostered the sexual division of labor and perpetuated the preindustrial patterns of work and life that shaped the family wage system of the nineteenth century. Gender categories made it difficult for male artisans to regard women as fellow workers, include them in the ideology and politics based on their work culture, or see in the experience of working women what awaited all workers under industrialization. The failure of male artisans to perceive or accommodate the interests of the women involved in shoe production weakened their ability to resist the reorganization of work by early industrial capitalism.[2]

Women in eighteenth-century New England shoemaking families were recruited to new work as a result of a shift in the control of profits when markets expanded after 1780 and production increased. Before this expansion, women had contributed as "helpmeets" to the family economy in ways tied to their domestic duties: by boarding apprentices and journeymen and by spinning flax into shoe thread. A cutoff of British imports during the American Revolution stimulated efforts to secure tariff protection and create new domestic markets. Merchants began to supply capital in the form of raw materials (tanned leather) to workers in artisan shops and marketed the finished shoes in towns and cities along the Atlantic seaboard. Since merchant control over raw materials and access to markets meant merchant control of profits, artisan masters borrowed money if they could to purchase their own leather. Those shoemakers who owned no leather divided up the work among the men in their shops and augmented their own income by recruiting (unpaid) female members of their families to sew shoe uppers. Robert Gilman, traveling through Essex County in 1797, observed the early involvement of women in shoemaking work: "In our way to Salem we passed through a number of pretty little villages one of which, Lynn, is scarcely inhabited by any but shoemakers. . . . The women work also and we scarcely passed a house where the trade was not carried on."[3]

The male head of the shoemaking family assigned and controlled work on shoes in both the home and the shop. The merchant capitalists welcomed the new potential for production, but they paid no wages directly to women workers and did not supervise them. Direction of work remained in the hands of male artisans. Women simply added this new chore to their traditional household labor. The recruitment of women to shoe production was a carefully controlled assignment of work designed to fit women's role in family life and maintain gender relationships in the family, while preserving the artisan system as a training ground for the craft and part of the process of male gender formation. Apprentices continued to learn their craft as shoemakers and find their place in the gender hierarchy of the shoe shop by performing services and running errands for the master and journeymen. Women in shoemaking families were recruited to do only a small part of the work—the sewing of the upper part of the shoe—and not to learn the craft itself. They were barred from apprenticeships and group work and isolated from the center of artisan life: the shoe shop.

The new work assigned to women in shoemaking families took on social connotations appropriate to female gender. "Shoebinding," a new word for this sexual division of labor, became a category of women's work in the early nineteenth century. The activity, combined with domestic chores and child care, took place in the kitchen. The shoebinder did not straddle a shoemaker's bench. She used a new tool, the shoe clamp, which rested on the floor and accommodated her long skirt and apron while providing a flexible wooden holder for leather pieces. The binder held the clamp tightly between her knees, freeing her hands to use her awl and needle. The use of women expanded production, met the needs of both capitalist and artisan, and threatened no change in the traditional patterns of gender and craft formation. The sexual division of labor guaranteed the subordination of women by separating the work of shoebinding from additional knowledge of the craft and by maintaining separate workplaces for men and women. These patterns survived the transformation of shoe production into the factory system at midcentury and constituted a fundamental social dimension of industrial work.

As shoebinders worked in their kitchens, the demands of the artisan shop intruded upon and shaped their time. The binding of uppers by shoemakers' wives and daughters was essential to the timing and pace of the work of shoemakers. Women's work in the home combined both task labor (their domestic duties) and timed labor: the erratic but compelling need to keep all the men in the shoe shop supplied with sewn shoe uppers. One historian of shoework in nineteenth-century Lynn described the process:

> Then there would be a little delay, perhaps, until a shoe was bound, with which to start off the new lot. But generally, before the "jour" got his "stock" seasoned, one or two "uppers" were ready, and enough were usually bound ahead to keep all hands at work. And so, now and then, the order would be heard—"Come John, go and see if your mother has got a shoe bound: I'm already to last it."[4]

Shoebinders remained, however, socially and physically isolated from the group life of the shop. The collective nature of men's work in the artisan shop supported a militant tradition of resistance to the reorganization of production in early industrialization, but this tradition did not mirror the experience of women workers.

Binders in shoemaking families earned no wages before 1810 but simply contributed their labor to the family economy. However, the capacity of women to bind uppers for the shoe shop while also performing all kinds of domestic tasks had its limits. The domestic setting of shoebinding contradicted the increasing demands by merchant capitalists for production, but the recruitment of additional women outside the shoemaking family required some kind of a payment for their labor. After 1810, shoebinding, while still performed by hand in the home, gradually shifted to part-time outwork paid in goods (often in the new factory-made cotton textiles) and later in wages. Women's work on shoes came to be increasingly dissociated from the family labor system and done more and more by female workers outside of shoemaking families. As a result, the merchant capitalist or shoe boss assumed responsibility for hiring female workers, including those in shoemaking families, and directed their work from a central shop; his authority replaced that of shoemaking husbands and fathers.[5]

The shift in the coordination of the work process out of the hands of shoemakers and into the hands of the shoe boss represented a decline in the ability of male artisans to control their work. As shoebinding moved onto the wage labor market, its character as women's work without craft status kept wages low. These wages became part of the family wage, earnings pooled in the family's interests by its members. In New England shoemaking, the male artisan contributed the primary source of family income; it was supplemented by the much lower wages of shoebinders.

By the 1830s, shoebinders in Massachusetts outnumbered female operatives in cotton textile factories. Women shoe workers still combined sewing uppers with household tasks, a situation that continued to limit their productivity and to characterize their work as part time, intermittent, and poorly paid. In order to expand production, shoe bosses built networks of rural female outworkers in eastern Massachusetts and southern New Hampshire. This recruitment of rural New England women undercut the strikes against low wages that occurred among shoebinders in the early 1830s in the shoe towns of Essex County. The objective conditions of shoebinding—performed in isolation from group work and combined with domestic tasks—discouraged collective activity.[6]

Artisan shoemakers in Essex County burst into labor activity in the 1840s, organizing with other workers into workingmen's associations. They sought to include women in their activities but offered no way in which shoebinders as workers could associate themselves ideologically or strategically with the artisan protest societies. Rebellious shoemakers saw women as persons whose lives were defined primarily by family and morality. In 1844 the editor of *The Awl*, the newspaper of the Lynn Cordwainers' Society, cast women's support of labor protest in moral terms: "Thank heaven our movement is not a political one. If it were, it would not be warmed into life by the bright sunshine of woman's smiles, nor enriched by the priceless dower of her pure affections. But as it is strictly a moral enterprise, it opens to her willing heart a wide field of usefulness."[7] Oblivious of the implications of the domestic setting of shoebinding and offering no solutions for the problems that isolated outworkers faced in dealing with shoe bosses, artisan shoemakers received little support from shoebinders in the 1840s.

The expansion of markets in the developing West and the South created new demands for increased production in the early 1850s. The adaptation of the Singer sewing machine in 1852 to stitch light leather solved many of the problems of low productivity and coordination of production which characterized shoebinding as outwork. Capitalists had already centralized cutting and finishing operations in central shops, to which they added sewing machines run first by hand cranks or foot treadles and then by steam power in 1858. Because the Singer Company marketed its machines exclusively to garment manufacturers rather than immediately developing the market for home sewing machines, the initial unfamiliarity of Essex County women with the sewing machine in the early 1850s provoked some organized resistance by shoebinders, who feared that machine operations would destroy their work:

> In 1853 . . . the first stitching machine was brought into [Haverhill]. A Mr. Pike was the first operator and so many people came from far and near to see how the great curiosity worked, that the firm was obliged to keep the factory doors locked. The women were fully excited as the men, and some of them shook their fists in Mr. Goodrich's face telling him that he was destroying their means of livelihood.[8]

Manufacturers, especially in Lynn, responded by training young women as stitchers on machines in central shops and leasing machines to women who chose to work at home. A new female factory work force was recruited from local families, but by 1860 sizable numbers of native-born, young, single New England women, once the source of industrial workers for the textile factories of the Merrimack Valley, were seeking employment in the shoe shops of eastern Massachusetts. As machine operators in steam-powered factories, they came under the direct control of their employers and the time discipline of industrial work. However, factory work offered women new opportunities for full-time employment, higher wages (three times those of homeworkers) and group work, an experience that contrasted sharply with their situation as outworkers.

The mechanization of women's work and the productivity of factory stitchers changed the composition of the work force throughout the shoe industry. One factory girl working full time at her machine replaced eleven shoebinders. As a result, the number of women employed in shoe work decreased quickly in the 1850s. But higher productivity by women workers in factories stimulated the demand for additional male workers; by contemporary estimates, one sewing machine operator could supply enough work for twenty shoemakers. The new male recruits had little craft knowledge or artisan experience; they were rural migrants, Irish and German immigrants, and country shoemakers who resided in the villages and towns of eastern Massachusetts and southern New Hampshire. As a result, the sex ratio of men and women in the Lynn shoe industry sharply reversed in the 1850s from 63 percent females and 37 percent males in 1850 to 40 percent females and 60 percent males in 1860. Wages for female factory operatives rose by 41 percent between 1852 and 1860, but wages fell for female homeworkers, unable to keep up with the productivity of centralized sewing machine operations. (Men's wages increased by only 10 percent and were severely cut during the depression of 1857.)[9] The mechanization of women's work intensified the hard conditions of all outworkers.

Intense competition among shoe manufacturers, the recruitment of large numbers of male outworkers, and the collapse of market demand for shoes in 1857 brought a crisis to the shoe industry of New England and precipitated in 1860 the largest demonstration of labor protest by American workers before the Civil War. The manufacturers blamed low wages on the laws of supply and demand, while male shoeworkers reasserted the moral and political values of the artisan tradition. The ideological emphasis on the brotherhood of the craft inherent in artisan culture prevented divisions between the new male recruits and more experienced shoemakers. The target of the strikers was the emerging factory system and the threat of mechanization and centralization to the preindustrial family wage system based on outwork. The new female factory workers seemed an alien group, while those who remained outside factory walls reaffirmed family, craft, and community values.

Significant divisions surfaced among shoe workers over the objectives of the 1860 strike in Lynn, the principal shoe town of Essex County.[10] Factory girls, realizing the power of their strategic location as machine operators in centralized production, sought increases in wages for all women workers. Their productivity on steam-powered machinery was the key to shutting down the largest manufacturers in Lynn and preventing them from sending machine-sewn uppers and leather stock by express teams to country shoemakers. This tactic powerfully aided the cause of the shoemakers' regional strike. Identifying themselves with female homeworkers, the factory girls proposed a coalition to raise wages for both categories of women's work: homework and factory work. Many of the factory girls lived as boarders in the households of Lynn families but had relatively little connection with the community or its artisan culture. Their leader, twenty-one-year-old Clara H. Brown of Medford, Massachusetts, boarded with another factory stitcher in the household of a Lynn shoemaker. However, living with a young shoemaker and his wife and infant son did not deter Clara Brown from speaking for the interests of the factory girls, and it may have inspired her vision of an alliance of women working at home and in the factory.

The factory girls insisted that their proposed coalition represented the interests of *all* women workers in Lynn. They were in effect proposing an alternative to the family wage as the objective of the strike. An alliance based on gender would protect working women wherever the location of their work or whatever their marital status, and would offer homeworkers a vital and powerful link with female workers in the new factories. For example, the wage demands voted by the women strikers in 1860 included prices for homework high enough to offset the customary costs to homeworkers of furnishing their own thread and lining material, a practice that cut earnings. In return, the factory girls could anticipate that when they married, they too could do shoe work at home for decent wages. They also tried to organize machine stitchers in the shoe factories of other towns. For these new industrial workers, it was just as important to increase women's wages as it was to increase men's wages during the strike. Their support of female homeworkers offered a bridge between preindustrial patterns of work for women and the factory system. Three times during the early meetings held by home and factory workers, the majority of striking women voted for the gender alliance.

Some female homeworkers, however, identified their interests with the men of the Lynn strike committee, who sought to protect the preindustrial family wage system and decentralized work. Shoemakers, who controlled the strike committees in each New England town, sought—as they had in the 1840s—to organize women's support for the strike on the basis of female moral stature and loyalty to family interests. In addition, the men's strike committee in Lynn insisted that wage increases for men were primary. Male workers opposed efforts to raise wages for women, fearing that an increase in the wages of female factory workers might promote a centralization of all stitching operations and thereby entirely eliminate women's work in the home and its supplemental earnings. For striking shoemakers and their allies among the female homeworkers, the best protection for the family wage lay in obtaining higher wages for men's work while defending homework for women. Implicit in their defense of the family wage was the subordinated role of women's contribution to family income.

The shoemakers of Lynn and their female allies seized control of the women's strike meetings and ended the emerging coalition of women shoeworkers. They ignored the votes at the women's strike meetings, substituted a wage proposal written by homeworkers, and circulated this altered wage list in Lynn for the signatures of strikers. The factory girls confronted the betrayal of their leadership at a tumultuous meeting on March 2, 1860. Above the uproar, Clara Brown angrily demanded to know who had dared to change the women's strike objectives. During the long debate, disgruntled homeworkers characterized the factory operatives as "smart girls," motivated by selfish individualism and the desire for lavish dress, an urge "to switch a long-tailed skirt."[11] In vain, Clara Brown tried to rally the supporters of the women's alliance. She emphasized the power of the machine operatives, who as industrial workers could obtain higher wages for all women workers: "For God's sake, don't act like a pack of fools. We've got the bosses where we can do as we please with 'em. If we won't work our machines, and the out-of-town girls won't take the work, what can the bosses do?"[12] The issue had become a test of loyalty: to the family wage or to the possibility of an alliance among female workers. Swayed by pressure from the leaders and supporters of the men's strike committee and their arguments for the family wage, the majority of women strikers at the March 2 meeting reversed themselves, voted against the factory girls, and agreed to march with the male strikers in a giant procession through the streets of Lynn on March 7. One of the banners carried by the striking women indicated their acceptance of moral and family values as primary to their role in labor protest: "Weak in physical strength but strong in moral courage, we dare to battle for the right, shoulder to shoulder with our fathers, husbands and brothers."[13]

The well-known sketches of women's participation in the Lynn strike of 1860 which appeared in *Frank Leslie's Illustrated Newspaper* depict the triumph of the artisan cause and the family wage but obscure the conflict among the women shoeworkers. The factory girls dropped out of the strike, which went on another two months but ended without a resolution of the wage issue.

The Lynn shoe workers in 1860 had failed to see the strategic potential for labor protest of female factory workers, ignored and opposed their articulated interests, and refused to recognize the implications for women of the mechanization and centralization of their work. The artisans of Lynn and their female allies fought in the 1860 strike to defend the traditions and ideology of preindustrial culture and decentralized production for men and women. This strategy cut off the new female factory work force from contributing to labor protest. The failure of the alliance among women shoe workers meant a continuation of the family wage system in which women workers were subordinated to male wage earners and divided from each other by marital status and the location of their work. The perceptions that shoemakers had developed of work and gender in the early nineteenth century made it difficult for them to regard women as fellow workers outside of family relationships, to include them as equals in the ideology and politics built on artisan life, or to represent the interests of female factory workers. The experiences of these women workers in centralized production symbolized what awaited all workers as capitalism in the New England shoe industry moved toward the factory system.

While male artisans defended their craft and its traditions between 1780 and 1860, women workers experienced the cutting edge of change in the reorganization of production: a sexual division of labor that denied women craft status; the separation of women's work from the family labor system; the loss of control over the coordination of work by artisans; the development of the family wage system; the isolation and vulnerability of the individual shoebinder in the outwork system; and the mechanization and centralization of work. The submersion of women's work experience within artisan culture in the new labor history has obscured the penetration of home life and household production by early industrial capitalism and has sustained the illusion of the home as a refuge from the marketplace. Artisan culture prevented men from perceiving the circumstances and accommodating the interests of women as workers, and thus weakened their ability to challenge the reorganization of production in early industrialization. The patriarchal ideology of artisan culture and the sex structuring of labor in the New England shoe industry worked together to prevent women workers from contributing to the most vital tradition of collective protest among the workers of early nineteenth-century New England.

Notes

1. Bryan D. Palmer, "Most Uncommon Common Men: Craft and Culture in Historical Perspective," *Labour/Le Travailler* 1 (1976):14.

2. For an overall discussion of the political and ideological implications of the sexual division of labor in shoe production, see Mary H. Blewett, "Work, Gender and the Artisan Tradition in New England Shoemaking, 1780–1860," *Journal of Social History* 17 (1983):221–48. . . .

3. George F. Dow, ed., *Two Centuries of Travel in Essex County* (Topsfield, Mass., 1921), p. 182. . . .

4. David Newhall Johnson, *Sketches of Lynn; or, The Changes of Fifty Years* (Lynn, Mass., 1880), p. 331. . . .

5. Among the account books that illustrate the shift of shoebinders' work out of the family labor system are those at the Lynn Historical Society, . . . and at the Old Sturbridge Village Archives. . . .

6. In 1837, 15,366 women worked as shoebinders, while 14,759 worked in cotton textile factories (Massachusetts, Secretary of the Commonwealth, *Statistical Information Relating to Certain Branches of Industry in Massachusetts for the Year Ending 1837* [Boston, 1837]). . . .

7. "Woman," *The Awl* 21 December 1844. Women shoe workers had already claimed a moral *and* political role for women in labor protest in the early 1830s. By 1845, 18,678 women in Massachusetts were working as shoebinders, compared with 14,407 in cotton textile factories: in 1855, 32,826 women worked on shoes and 22,850 in textile factories. Shoe work was part-time work performed in the home: textile work was full-time work in factories (Massachusetts, Secretary of the Commonwealth, *Statistics of the Condition and Production of Certain Branches of Industry in Massachusetts* [Boston, 1845, 1855]).

8. Philip C. Swett, "History of Shoemaking in Haverhill, Massachusetts," MS, Haverhill Public Library, pp. 16–17.

9. Sex ratios and wage increases are based on the schedules for Lynn in the federal census of manufacture for 1850 and 1860 and on the statistics of industry for Massachusetts in 1855. . . . Helen L. Sumner noted the high productivity of the machine operators in relation to the shoemakers after the introduction of the sewing machine (*History of Women in Industry in the United States* [Washington, D.C., 1910], p. 172).

10. The regional shoe strike in 1860 has had attention from labor historians, but the role of women in the strike has had little systematic analysis. The most detailed account is in Philip S. Foner, *Women and the American Labor Movement: From Colonial Times to the Eve of World War I* (New York, 1979), pp. 90–97. . . .

11. *New York Times*, 6 Mar. 1860.

12. *New York Times*, 6 Mar. 1860. For a detailed analysis of the strike, see chap. 5 in Mary H. Blewett, *Men, Women, and Work: A Study of Class, Gender, and Protest in the Nineteenth-Century New England Shoe Industry* (Urbana, Ill., 1989).

13. *Bay State* (Lynn), 8 Mar. 1860. Marxist feminists have debated whether the family wage served the interests of patriarchy or served the ability of working-class families to resist exploitation by employers. See Heidi Hartmann, "The Unhappy Marriage of Marxism and Feminism: Towards a More Progressive Union," *Capital and Class* 8 (1979):1–43; and Jane Humphries, "Class Struggle and the Persistence of the Working-Class Family," *Cambridge Journal of Economics* 1 (1979):241–58. The two models appear to have operated in conflict during the Lynn strike in 1860.

KATHRYN KISH SKLAR
Catharine Beecher: Transforming the Teaching Profession

In the following essay Kathryn Kish Sklar describes the merger of economic and ideological concerns in the career of Catharine Beecher. By publicizing the appropriateness of teaching as a career for women, Beecher facilitated the entry of many women into the profession. In the process she also developed her own career, traveling widely, speaking in public frequently, and publishing popular books. Beecher made use of the familiar ideology that stressed women's "natural" docile and nurturing qualities and has been called the "Cult of True Womanhood." It was said, for example, that women had a duty to be teachers because their natural role as mothers suited them to the care of young children.

Within a single generation women replaced men in the ranks of teachers and were entrusted with classes that included boys as well as girls. It has been estimated that approximately one out of five white women in antebellum Massachusetts was a schoolteacher at some time in her life. Once the profession of teaching was "feminized" it would remain so; in 1970 more than 85 percent of the nation's elementary school teachers were women.

For the next decade and a half Catharine Beecher maintained the pace of life that she began in the summer of 1843. She sought out people ... who were either themselves wealthy or could open doors to the wealth of other evangelical individuals and groups. She toured constantly in both East and West, raising funds, seeking sites for schools and seminaries, and recruiting teachers to occupy them. Her *Treatise [on Domestic Economy]* made her nationally known, and her frequent speaking tours kept her immediately in the public view. By the end of the 1840s she was one of the most widely known women in America.

Over the course of the decade, as she met with greater and greater success in promoting the primacy of women in American education, Catharine's public and private lives converged. Finally she had found a role commensurate with her personal needs and desires, and much of her achievement during this decade may

have arisen from that congruence. As she traveled about the country advocating a special role for her sex, she became the living embodiment of that role. This new consistency in Catharine's life lent conviction to her activities and greatly enhanced her powers of persuasion. . . .

Catharine returned to Cincinnati in the fall of 1843. . . . She spent the winter striving to create a national organization to promote "the cause of popular education, and as intimately connected with it, the elevation of my sex by the opening of a profession for them as educators of the young." All that winter and spring she corresponded with prominent individuals in the East and West, soliciting their endorsement of such an organization.[1] . . .

. . . in the winter of 1845 she visited almost every major city in the East, delivering a standard speech and organizing local groups of church women to collect and forward funds and proselytize her views.[2]

Catharine's addresses were subsequently published in three volumes by Harpers. The first was entitled *The Evils Suffered by American Women and American Children: The Causes and the Remedy;* it was followed by *The Duty of American Women to Their Country;* and lastly, by *An Address to the Protestant Clergy of the United States.* These addresses clarified the ideas Catharine had evolved over the course of the last two decades. Now however like a practiced evangelist she played expertly upon the feelings and fears of her audience and ultimately brought them to commit themselves to her vision of a nation redeemed by women. The full meaning of Catharine's exhortation was not revealed until halfway through her addresses. First she gained her audiences' sympathy for the sufferings of masses of American children under cruel teachers and in degenerate environments. She quoted from several reports to state legislatures that described "the comfortless and dilapidated buildings, the un-hung doors, broken sashes, absent panes, stilted benches, gaping walls, yawning roofs, and muddy moldering floors," of contemporary schools and "the self-styled teachers, who lash and dogmatize in these miserable tenements of humanity." Many teachers were "low, vulgar, obscene, intemperate," according to one report to the New York State legislature, "and utterly incompetent to teach anything good."[3]

To remedy this situation Catharine then proposed a national benevolent movement, similar to the temperance movement or the missionary boards, to raise money for teachers and schoolrooms. Yet Catharine's plan went even beyond the contemporary benevolent models. Her chief goal was to "elevate and dignify" her sex, and this goal was inextricably bound to her vision of a more consolidated society. The united effort of women in the East, combined with the moral influence of women in the West, would create homogeneous national institutions, Catharine asserted. The family, the school, and the social morality upon which these institutions were based would everywhere be similar. Sectional and ethnic diversities would give way to national unity as the influence of women increased.

To make her image of a unified society more understandable to her audience, she explained that it was a Protestant parallel to the Catholic pattern of close interaction between social and religious forms. Protestant women should have the same social support for their religious and moral activities as Catholic nuns received from their society. She related the stories of many women she had known who were willing to sacrifice themselves to socially ameliorative efforts, but who had been rebuffed by public opinion and restricted to quiet domestic lives. "Had these ladies turned Catholic and offered their services to extend that church, they would instantly have found bishops, priests, Jesuits and all their subordinates at hand, to counsel and sustain; a strong *public sentiment* would have been created in their favor; while abundant funds would have been laid at their feet," she said.[4] Her plan envisioned a similar kind of cultural support for Protestant women. A web of interlocking social institutions, including the family, the school, and the church, would form a new cultural matrix within which women would assume a central role.

The ideological basis of Catharine's social theory was self-denial. The Catholic church's employment of self-denying women initially attracted Catharine to it as a model for her own plan. Yet Catharine emphasized that her notion of self-denial was different from the Catholic one. The Catholics had "a selfish and ascetic self-denial, aiming mainly to save *self* by inflictions and losses," Catharine said, whereas she advocated self-denial not as the means of personal salvation, but as the means of social cohesion.[5] . . . Self-denial was an inclusive virtue that could be practiced by wealthy and poor, converted and unconverted, by persons of all ages and both sexes. As the ideological basis of a national morality it was especially congenial to Catharine since women could be both the embodiment and the chief instructors of self-denial. It made possible an expanded cultural role for women as the exemplars and the teachers of a national morality.

To support this cultural role for women Catharine advocated three corollary ideas, each of which pointed toward a more consolidated American society. First, she said, women should abolish class distinctions among themselves and form one united social group. Catharine Beecher had earlier defended class distinctions as a part of the natural order of God's universe, but such divisions were no longer endorsed in her public writings. This change in her views was prompted in part by a visit she made to Lowell, Massachusetts, where she went to look for teachers. Catharine did not believe the Lowell owners' claims that factory work was a means of self-improvement for the women operatives. She concluded that at Lowell and in New York City women were deliberately exploited. "Work of all kinds is got from poor women, at prices that will not keep soul and body together," Catharine wrote, "and then the articles thus made are sold for prices that give monstrous profits to the capitalist, who thus grows rich on the hard labors of our sex."[6] Rather than participate in this kind of class exploitation, Catharine suggested women should donate their services to the cause of education. Although they might still be poor, their economic sacrifice would transcend class lines and benefit the whole nation instead of a self-interested class of businessmen.

While economic factors oppressed working-class women, social custom suppressed upper-class women. "The customs and prejudices of society forbid" educated young women from engaging in socially useful employments. Their sufferings were just as keen as those of working-class women, Catharine said, the only difference being that their spirits were starved instead of their bodies. "A little working of muslin and worsted, a little light reading, a little calling and shopping, and a great deal of the high stimulus of fashionable amusement, are all the ailment their starving spirits find," Catharine wrote. "The influence and the principle of *caste*," she maintained, must cease to operate on both these groups. Her solution was to secure "a proper education for all classes, and make productive labor honorable, by having all classes engage in it."[7]

The specific labor Catharine endorsed for both groups was teaching. Working-class women should leave the factories and seize the opportunity to go to the West as missionary teachers. Their places in the factories should be taken by men. Upper-class women, Catharine said, should do whatever they could to contribute to the "proper education" of American children. Whether by teaching themselves, or by raising funds, or by supervising schools in their community, all well-to-do women could do some productive labor for education. By their efforts, moreover, the public attitude toward the teaching profession could be

changed. Teaching is regarded "as the most wearying drudgery, and few resort to it except from necessity," Catharine said, but by elevating the teaching profession into a "true and noble" one, and by making it the special "profession of a woman," women would be freed from the caste principles that suppressed them and enter into a new casteless, but elevated condition.[8] In effect Catharine would eliminate the extremes of class identity and fortify a middle-class social order.

The second corollary to the new social role Catharine described for women was that of fostering the nation's social conscience. Young women teachers in the West would be in the vanguard of settlement, and from them the character of the place would take its shape. "Soon, in all parts of our country, in each neglected village, or new settlement, the Christian female teacher will quietly take her station, collecting the ignorant children around her, teaching them habits of neatness, order and thrift; opening the book of knowledge, inspiring the principles of morality, and awakening the hope of immortality," she said.[9] . . . Catharine cited several examples of western settlement where the female teacher preceded the minister. Thus she asserted that a woman could be chiefly responsible for setting the moral tone of the community. A community could coalesce around women rather than the church.

The promotion of national unity was a third aspect of the new social role Catharine was defining for women. The special esteem in which American women were held meant that their united actions would have a nationwide effect. "It is the pride and honour of our country," she said, "that woman holds a commanding influence in the domestic and social circle, which is accorded to the sex in no other nation, and such as will make her wishes and efforts, if united for a benevolent and patriotic object, almost omnipotent." Women thus had the power to shape the character of the whole nation, and that character, Catharine said, would be one of a united nation rather than a collection of sections.[10] . . .

At the end of each address Catharine presented to her audience her plan for practical action. A committee of clergymen led by [Calvin] Stowe would, as soon as sufficient funds were raised for a salary, "appoint one man who shall act as an agent," giving his full time to the organization. The committee would also appoint "a Board of Managers, consisting of men from each of the principal Protestant denominations from each of the different sections of the country." In addition, local committees of women would raise funds "to aid in educating and locating missionary teachers." In the West such committees could aid in providing schools for those sent out. In both places the committees could publicize the cause. Lastly Catharine revealed how "every woman who feels an interest in the effort can contribute at least a small sum to promote it" by immediately purchasing Catharine's *Treatise on Domestic Economy* and her *Domestic Receipt Book,* since half the profits from the sale of these books was to be given to the cause.[11]

Catharine Beecher apparently misled her audience when she claimed that "the copyright interest in these two works is held by a board of gentlemen appointed for the purpose." Her original contract with Harper & Brothers, still preserved by Harper & Row, gave Catharine full control of the profits and did not mention a "board of gentlemen." Catharine's contract gave her 50 percent of the net profits, so she was correct in representing to her audience the fact that only half the price went to the publisher. But when she said that "Half the profits (after paying a moderate compensation to the author for the time and labour of preparing them, the amount to be decided by the above gentlemen) will be devoted to this object," she misrepresented the flow of power and profit between herself and the "gentlemen." For neither Stowe nor any of the other named Cincinnati clergymen would have been capable of questioning Catharine's use of the money that came to her from Harpers. Catharine had a reputation in her family of being "clever" to deal with financially, and it was extremely unlikely that Calvin Stowe would have crossed swords with his sister-in-law on financial issues. Later, when a salaried agent was found for the organization, he received his funds from the money he himself raised, not from the profits of Catharine's books.

Catharine's tactics in presenting herself and her cause to the public made her an enormously successful publicist. She sent circulars signed by Calvin Stowe to county newspapers and small-town clergymen throughout the East and West, asking for the names of women who might be willing to serve as missionary teachers and for the names of towns and villages where such teachers would be welcomed. The Catholic analogy and the ideology of self-denial made her efforts newsworthy, and to make the work of county editors easier she dispatched articles, such as the one entitled "Education at the West—Sisters of Charity," for newspapers to print alongside Stowe's circular.[12] The primary targets for Catharine's fund-raising efforts were the local groups of church women she organized in every city and town she visited.[13] She asked each group to make at least a hundred-dollar donation, this being the amount necessary to train and locate one teacher.

Catharine's efforts gained the endorsement of the most prominent American educators. Horace Mann, Henry Barnard, Thomas Burrowes, Samuel Lewis, and Gorham Abbot lent their support, and with each new endorsement by a national figure, Catharine's local fund-raising became more successful.[14] Catharine's tactic in each city was to plead her cause with the town's most eminent personage and, having gained his or her endorsement, to use it to build a substantial and active local committee. In this way she even drew into her cause those who traditionally opposed evangelical projects and especially opposed the Beecher family. . . .

By the spring of 1846 Catharine had delivered her addresses in most of the major cities of the East. Everywhere she called upon women to "save" their country from ignorance and immorality, and everywhere women responded. In Boston the Ladies Society for Promoting Education at the West donated several thousand dollars over the course of the decade to Catharine Beecher and her cause, and in other cities similar groups of women were organized by her into active proponents of her ideas on women and education. She corresponded with these groups constantly, relating her recent advances in other cities and exhorting her followers on to greater efforts. In a typical five-week period early in 1846 Catharine spoke in Pittsburgh, Baltimore, Washington, D.C., Philadelphia, New York City, Troy, Albany, and Hartford. She retraced her steps often, sometimes staying only one night in a place—long enough to deliver a public speech, encourage her old supporters, and welcome new ones. She traveled like a candidate for political office, moving quickly from one city to another, thereby promoting a large amount of newspaper coverage of her arrivals and departures.[15] . . .

In Albany in the spring of 1847 and in Hartford in the fall Catharine collected two groups of thirty-five young women for one month's training before they were sent to locations . . . in the West. The local women's committees provided room and board for Catharine and her young women. Catharine lectured the prospective teachers on how to meet all the difficulties that were to face them in the West: how to overcome the lack of books and proper schoolrooms; how to train children to good moral habits "when all domestic and social influences tend to weaken such habits"; how to impart spiritual training "without giving occasion for sectarian jealousy and alarm"; and how to preserve their health "from the risks of climate and dangers of overexertion and excessive care." Catharine also lectured on the ways in which they could influence the community outside the schoolroom. They learned how to teach "the laws of health by the aid of simple drawings on the blackboard so that the children could copy them on slates to take home and explain to their parents," and how to teach certain branches of "domestic economy" so that parents would "be willing to adopt these improvements." Most of all they learned how to be moral examples that the rest of the community could imitate.[16]

Most of the seventy young women were New Englanders; only three came from New York and one from Pennsylvania. More than half of them went to Illinois and Indiana, seven crossed the Mississippi into Iowa, and a few went to Wisconsin, Michigan, Kentucky, and Tennessee. Each of them was expected to act as "a new source of moral power" in her community, and the reports they made at the end of the year revealed how seriously they took this charge.[17] . . .

The letters Catharine received from these teachers testified to the effectiveness of her training and to the tenacity of purpose she instilled. One woman went West to join a constituency that had migrated from North Carolina, Tennessee, and Germany and was met with a log cabin classroom holding forty-five pupils ranging in age from six to eighteen, and

a community of hostile parents. "They seem desirous to have their children educated, but they differed so much about almost every thing, that they could not build a schoolhouse," she wrote Catharine.

> I was told, when I came, that they would not pay a teacher for more than three months in a year. At first, they were very suspicious, and watched me narrowly; but, through the blessing of my heavenly Father, I have gained their good will and confidence, so that they have provided me a good frame schoolhouse, with writing-desks and a blackboard, and they promise to support me all the year around.

Having proved herself in their eyes, she succeeded next in drawing both parents and children to a Sunday school. Then, because the nearest church was seven miles away and the people did not go to it, she persuaded them "to invite the nearest clergyman to preach" in her schoolhouse the next Sunday. This New England woman, though unused to frontier conditions, decided to stay on in the place even though she had to board "where there are eight children and the parents and only two rooms in the house," and she went without simple amenities such as candles and a place to bathe.[18] . . . Developments shaping the teaching profession at this precise moment made the field especially receptive to Catharine Beecher's view that it properly belonged to women. Although female teachers began to replace men in some eastern states in the 1830s, the utility of that shift was not apparent to most state and local boards of education until 1840. What had begun as an improvised economic measure had by then proved to be a pedagogic as well as a fiscal improvement, and as these obvious benefits were discovered by state and local boards of education from 1840 to 1880, women gradually replaced their male predecessors in the teaching profession. By 1888, 63 percent of American teachers were women, and in cities women constituted 90 percent of the teaching force.[19]

Although it is impossible to measure completely Catharine Beecher's impact on the profession, her publicizing in behalf of women did at least facilitate an otherwise confused transition period in the nation's schools. For the traditionally higher value attached to male labor blinded many communities to the advantages of female teachers, and as late as 1850 the state of Indiana viewed the female teacher as the exception rather than the rule.[20] The West was, on the whole, slower to employ women as teachers, perhaps because it attracted ample numbers of ambitious men who, typically, would teach for a brief period or even a few years before locating more lucrative commercial employment.[21] These male teachers were usually paid twice as much as female teachers, and a male teacher frequently brought fewer pedagogic talents to the job than a woman. In New York, one of the earliest states to shift to women teachers, the state board of regents in 1838 still assumed that teachers should be male, and they failed to approve the governor's request that normal schools be attached to female academies because they concluded that men, rather than women, needed the normal training.[22] Therefore it was far from obvious to the American public that teaching was a woman's profession.

On the other hand the shift to women teachers was well enough along by 1843 to provide a solid factual basis for Catharine Beecher's claims on their behalf. In Massachusetts, the first state to promote the employment of women as teachers, women outnumbered men three to two in 1837 and two to one in 1842.[23] Many school districts had since the 1820s routinely employed women to teach the summer session, although they believed men were needed to "manage" the older boys present at the winter school session. Some New York districts learned in the 1820s that they could, with the state subsidy of half a teacher's salary, employ a woman to teach full-time and thus not have to bear any of the cost themselves.[24] As a leading educator pointed out later in the century, "the effective reason" women were employed in schools was that they were "cheaper than men." If they had not been cheaper, "they would not have replaced nine-tenths of the men in American public schools."[25]

The need for such educational economies became more critical in the 1830s and 1840s, when immigration and internal migration increased the population of many areas, but did not immediately increase the tax base. By reducing the school costs by hiring women, a district could accommodate its larger numbers of children without taxing itself at a higher rate.[26]

Three basic assumptions were used to justify these lower salaries for women: women, unlike men, did not have to support a family; women were only working temporarily until they married; and the free workings of the economic marketplace determined cheaper salaries for women. Women do not "expect to accumulate much property by this occupation; if it affords them a respectable support and a situation where they can be useful, it is as much as they demand," wrote the state superintendent of Ohio in 1839. He therefore urged "those counties who are in the habit of paying men for instructing little children" to hire women since "females would do it for less than half the sum and generally much better than men can."[27]

Catharine chose to exploit the short-term gains that these discriminatory practices brought to women, and her publicity on behalf of female teachers emphasized their willingness to work for less money. "To make education universal, it must be moderate in expense," Catharine wrote in a petition to Congress in 1853 for free normal schools for female teachers, "and women can afford to teach for one-half, or even less, the salary which men would ask, because the female teacher has only to sustain herself; she does not look forward to the duty of supporting a family, should she marry; nor has she the ambition to amass a fortune." Catharine also insisted that women's employment as teachers would not create a "celibate class" of women, but that their employment was only temporary, and would in fact prepare them to be better wives and mothers. By defining teaching as an extension of the duties of the home, Catharine presented her idea in a form most likely to gain widespread public support. "It is ordained by infinite wisdom, that, as in the family, so in the social state, the interests of young children and of women are one and the same," Catharine insisted.[28]

Since the profession had lower pay and status than most men qualified to teach could get elsewhere, since the economics of education called for even lower pay in the 1830s and 1840s, and since the schoolroom could be seen as functionally akin to the home, both public sentiment and economic facts supported Catharine Beecher's efforts to redefine the gender of the American teacher.

NOTES

1. Catharine Beecher, *Educational Reminiscences and Suggestions* (New York, 1874), p. 101. Hereafter cited as CB, *Reminiscences.* . . .

2. CB, "Memoranda," 3 Oct. 1844 to 7 June 1845, Beecher-Stowe Collection, Radcliffe College, Cambridge, Mass.

3. CB, *The Evils Suffered by American Women and American Children: The Causes and the Remedy* (New York, 1846), p. 29.

4. CB, *An Address to the Protestant Clergy of the United States* (New York, 1846), p. 29.

5. Ibid., pp. 22–23; CB, *The Evils Suffered*, p. 16.

6. CB, "Memoranda," 29 Nov. to 4 Dec. 1844; CB, *The Evils Suffered*, pp. 6–9.

7. CB, *The Evils Suffered*, pp. 11–14.

8. Ibid., p. 11.

9. Ibid., pp. 9–10.

10. Ibid., p. 11.

11. CB, *The Duty of American Women to Their Country* (New York, 1845), pp. 112–31.

12. CB to Judge Lane, 26 July 1845, Ebenezer Lane Papers, Rutherford B. Hayes Library, Fremont, Ohio. . . .

13. CB, *Reminiscences*, p. 115.

14. Samuel Lewis was the state superintendent of schools for Ohio; Gorham Abbot, the brother of Jacob Abbot, was the director of a fashionable school for girls in New York City. CB also appealed to Rufus Choate, then the director of the Smithsonian Institution, and Mrs. James K. Polk, the nation's first lady, for their endorsements. See CB to The Hon. Rufus Choate, 29 Aug. 1846, Harriet Beecher Stowe Collection, Clifton Waller Barrett Library, University of Virginia; CB to Mrs. James K. Polk [1847], Hillhouse Family Papers, box 27, Sterling Memorial Library.

15. CB, "Memoranda," 21 Mar. to 27 Apr. 1846. Charles H. Foster, *An Errand of Mercy, The Evangelical*

United Front, 1790–1837 (Chapel Hill, 1960), p. 136, describes the traditional support New England women gave to education. . . .

16. William Slade, "Circular to the Friends of Popular Education in the United States," 15 May 1847, Increase Lapham Papers, State Historical Society of Wisconsin, Madison.

17. *First Annual Report of the General Agent of the Board of National Popular Education* (Hartford, 1848), pp. 15, 22–26.

18. CB, *The True Remedy for the Wrongs of Women* (Boston, 1851), pp. 163, 167.

19. Thomas Woody, *A History of Women's Education in the United States* (New York, 1929), 1:499.

20. Richard G. Boone, *A History of Education in Indiana* (New York, 1892), p. 142.

21. Michael Katz, *The Irony of Early School Reform: Innovation in Mid-Nineteenth Century Massachusetts* (Cambridge, Mass., 1968), pp. 57–58. . . .

22. Elsie Garland Hobson, "Educational Legislation and Administration in the State of New York from 1772 to 1850," *Supplementary Educational Monographs* 3, no. 1 (Chicago, 1918), p. 75.

23. Woody, *History of Women's Education*, 1:497.

24. Hobson, "Educational Legislation," p. 66.

25. . . . Charles William Eliot, "Wise and Unwise Economy in Schools," *Atlantic Monthly*, no. 35 (June 1875):715, quoted in Katz, *Irony of Early School Reform*, p. 58.

26. Katz, *Irony of Early School Reform*, pp. 56–58.

27. Woody, *History of Women's Education*, 1:491.

28. Petition appeared in *Godey's Lady's Book* (January 1853): 176–77. . . .

CARROLL SMITH-ROSENBERG

The Female World of Love and Ritual: Relations Between Women in Nineteenth-Century America

Women's associations with each other have traditionally been ignored by historians. One reason for this has been a fascination with public life; only women who were powerful in the same fashion as men or whose lives were intertwined with the lives of powerful men attracted the historical spotlight. The world of women was treated as wholly private or domestic, encompassing only family responsibilities. Women's diaries and letters were used primarily as a source of illustrative anecdote.

Carroll Smith-Rosenberg has read the letters and diaries of women in a strikingly original way. She evaluates nineteenth-century American society in much the same way an anthropologist might observe a distant culture. She describes relations between women as intellectually active, personally rewarding, mutually supportive, and socially creative. Smith-Rosenberg offers a radically new account of the relationship between the sexes in Victorian America. What revision does she suggest ought to be made in our traditional understanding of Victorian sexuality?

The female friendship of the nineteenth century, the long-lived, intimate, loving friendship between two women, is an excellent example of the type of historical phenomena which most historians know something about, which few have thought much about, and which virtually no one has written about.[1] It is one aspect of the female experience which consciously or unconsciously we have chosen to ignore. Yet an abundance of manuscript evidence suggests that eighteenth- and nineteenth-century women routinely formed emotional ties with other women. Such deeply felt, same-sex friendships were casually accepted in American society. Indeed, from at least the late eighteenth through the mid-nineteenth century, a female world of varied and yet highly structured relationships appears to have been an essential aspect of American society. These relationships ranged from the supportive love of sisters, through the enthusiasms of adolescent girls, to sensual avowals of love by mature women. It was a world in which men made but a shadowy appearance.[2]

Defining and analyzing same-sex relationships involves the historian in deeply problematical questions of method and interpretation. This is especially true since historians, influenced by Freud's libidinal theory, have discussed these relationships almost exclusively within the context of individual psychosexual developments or, to be more explicit, psychopathology.[3] Seeing same-sex relationships in terms of a dichotomy between normal and abnormal, they have sought the origins of such apparent deviance in childhood or adolescent trauma and detected the symptoms of "latent" homosexuality in the lives of both those who later became "overtly" homosexual and those who did not. Yet theories concerning the nature and origins of same-sex relationships are frequently contradictory or based on questionable or arbitrary data. In recent years such hypotheses have been subjected to criticism both from within and with-

out the psychological professions. Historians who seek to work within a psychological framework, therefore, are faced with two hard questions: Do sound psychodynamic theories concerning the nature and origins of same-sex relationships exist? If so, does the historical datum exist which would permit the use of such dynamic models?

I would like to suggest an alternative approach to female friendships—one which would view them within a cultural and social setting rather than from an exclusively individual psychosexual perspective. Only by thus altering our approach will we be in the position to evaluate the appropriateness of particular dynamic interpretations. Intimate friendships between men and men and women and women existed in a larger world of social relations and social values. To interpret such friendships more fully they must be related to the structure of the American family and to the nature of sex-role divisions and of male-female relations both within the family and in society generally. The female friendship must not be seen in isolation; it must be analyzed as one aspect of women's overall relations with one another. The ties between mothers and daughters, sisters, female cousins and friends, at all stages of the female life cycle constitute the most suggestive framework for the historian to begin an analysis of intimacy and affection between women. Such an analysis would not only emphasize general cultural patterns rather than the internal dynamics of a particular family or childhood; it would shift the focus of the study from a concern with deviance to that of defining configurations of legitimate behavioral norms and options.[4]

This analysis will be based upon the correspondence and diaries of women and men in thirty-five families between the 1760s and the 1880s. These families, though limited in number, represented a broad range of the American middle class, from hard-pressed pioneer families and orphaned girls to daughters of the intellectual and social elite. It includes families from most geographic regions, rural and urban, and a spectrum of Protestant denominations ranging from Mormon to orthodox Quaker. Although scarcely a comprehensive sample of America's increasingly heterogeneous population, it does, I believe, reflect accurately the literate middle class to which the historian working with letters and diaries is necessarily bound. It has involved an analysis of many thousands of letters written to women friends, kin, husbands, brothers, and children at every period of life from adolescence to old age. Some collections encompass virtually entire life spans; one contains over 100,000 letters as well as diaries and account books. It is my contention that an analysis of women's private letters and diaries which were never intended to be published permits the historian to explore a very private world of emotional realities central both to women's lives and to the middle-class family in nineteenth-century America.[5]

The question of female friendships is peculiarly elusive; we know so little or perhaps have forgotten so much. An intriguing and almost alien form of human relationship, they flourished in a different social structure and amidst different sexual norms. Before attempting to reconstruct their social setting, therefore, it might be best first to describe two not atypical friendships. These two friendships, intense, loving, and openly avowed, began during the women's adolescence and, despite subsequent marriages and geographic separation, continued throughout their lives. For nearly half a century these women played a central emotional role in each other's lives, writing time and again of their love and of the pain of separation. Paradoxically to twentieth-century minds, their love appears to have been both sensual and platonic.

Sarah Butler Wister first met Jeannie Field Musgrove while vacationing with her family at Stockbridge, Massachusetts, in the summer of 1849.[6] Jeannie was then sixteen, Sarah fourteen. During two subsequent years spent together in boarding school, they formed a deep and intimate friendship. Sarah began to keep a bouquet of flowers before Jeannie's portrait and wrote complaining of the intensity and anguish of her affection.[7] Both young women assumed nom de plumes, Jeannie a female name, Sarah a male one; they would use these secret names into old age.[8] They frequently commented on the nature of their affection: "If the day should come," Sarah wrote Jeannie in the spring of 1861, "when you failed me either through your fault or my own, I would forswear all human friendship, thenceforth." A few months later Jeannie commented: "Gratitude is a word I should never use toward you. It is perhaps a misfortune of such intimacy and love that it makes one regard all kindness as a matter of course, as one has always found it, as natural as the embrace in meeting."[9]

Sarah's marriage altered neither the frequency of their correspondence nor their desire to be together. In 1864, when twenty-nine, married, and a mother, Sarah wrote to Jeannie: "I shall be entirely alone [this coming week]. I can give you no idea how desperately I shall want you. . . ." After one such visit Jeannie, then a spinster in New York, echoed Sarah's longing: "Dear darling Sarah! How I love you & how happy I have been! You are the joy of my life. . . . I cannot tell you how much happiness you gave me, nor how constantly it is all in my thoughts. . . . My darling how I long for the time when I shall see you. . . ." After another visit Jeannie wrote: "I want you to tell me in your next letter, to assure me, that I am your dearest. . . . I do not doubt you, & I am not jealous but I long to hear you say it once more & it seems already a long time since your voice fell on my ear. So just fill a quarter page with caresses & expressions of endearment. Your silly Angelina." Jeannie ended one letter: "Goodbye my dearest, dearest lover—ever your own Angelina." And another, "I will go to bed . . . [though] I could write all night—A thousand kisses—I love you with my whole soul—your Angelina."

When Jeannie finally married in 1870 at the age of thirty-seven, Sarah underwent a period of extreme anxiety. Two days before Jeannie's marriage Sarah, then in London, wrote desperately: "Dearest darling—How incessantly have I thought of you these eight days— all today—the entire uncertainty, the distance, the long silence—are all new features in my separation from you, grievous to be borne. . . . Oh Jeannie. I have thought & thought & yearned over you these two days. Are you married I wonder? My dearest love to you wherever and *who*ever you are."[10] Like many other women in this collection of thirty-five families, marriage brought Sarah and Jeannie physical separation; it did not cause emotional distance.

Although at first they may have wondered how marriage would affect their relationship, their affection remained unabated throughout their lives, underscored by their loneliness and their desire to be together.[11]

During the same years that Jeannie and Sarah wrote of their love and need for each other, two slightly younger women began a similar odyssey of love, dependence and—ultimately—physical, though not emotional, separation. Molly and Helena met in 1868 while both attended the Cooper Institute School of Design for Women in New York City. For several years these young women studied and explored the city together, visited each other's families, and formed part of a social network of other artistic young women. Gradually, over the years, their initial friendship deepened into a close intimate bond which continued throughout their lives. The tone in the letters which Molly wrote to Helena changed over these years from "My dear Helena," and signed "your attached friend," to "My dearest Helena," "My Dearest," "My Beloved," and signed "Thine always" or "thine Molly."[12]

The letters they wrote to each other during these first five years permit us to reconstruct something of their relationship together. As Molly wrote in one early letter:

> I have not said to you in so many or so few words that I was happy with you during those few so incredibly short weeks but surely you do not need words to tell you what you must know. Those two or three days so dark without, so bright with firelight and contentment within I shall always remember as proof that, for a time, at least—I fancy for quite a long time—we might be sufficient for each other. We know that we can amuse each other for many idle hours together and now we know that we can also work together. And that means much, don't you think so?

She ended: "I shall return in a few days. Imagine yourself kissed many times by one who loved you so dearly."

The intensity and even physical nature of Molly's love was echoed in many of the letters she wrote during the next few years, as, for instance in this short thank-you note for a small present: "Imagine yourself kissed a dozen times my darling. Perhaps it is well for you that we are far apart. You might find my thanks so expressed rather overpowering. I have that delightful feeling that it doesn't matter much what I say or how I say it, since we shall meet so soon and forget in that moment that we were ever separated. . . . I shall see you soon and be content."[13]

At the end of the fifth year, however, several crises occurred. The relationship, at least in its intense form, ended, though Molly and Helena continued an intimate and complex relationship for the next half-century. The exact nature of these crises is not completely clear, but it seems to have involved Molly's decision not to live with Helena, as they had originally planned, but to remain at home because of parental insistence. Molly was now in her late twenties. Helena responded with anger and Molly became frantic at the thought that Helena would break off their relationship. Though she wrote distraught letters and made despairing attempts to see Helena, the relationship never regained its former ardor—possibly because Molly had a male suitor.[14] Within six months Helena had decided to marry a man who was, coincidentally, Molly's friend and publisher. Two years later Molly herself finally married. The letters toward the end of this period discuss the transition both women made to having male lovers—Molly spending much time reassuring Helena, who seemed depressed about the end of their relationship and with her forthcoming marriage.[15]

It is clearly difficult from a distance of 100 years and from a post-Freudian cultural perspective to decipher the complexities of Molly and Helena's relationship. Certainly Molly and Helena were lovers—emotionally if not physically. The emotional intensity and pathos of their love becomes apparent in several letters Molly wrote Helena during their crisis: "I wanted so to put my arms round my girl of all the girls in the world and tell her . . . I love her as wives do love their husbands, as *friends* who have taken each other for life—and believe in her, as I believe in my God. . . . If I didn't love you do you suppose I'd care about anything or have ridiculous notions and panics and behave like an old fool who ought to know better. I'm going to hang on to your skirts. . . . You can't get away from [my] love." Or as she wrote after Helena's decision to marry: "You know dear Helena, I really was in love with you. It was a passion such as I had never known until I saw you. I don't think it was the noblest way to love you." The theme of intense female love was one Molly again expressed in a letter she wrote to the man Helena was to marry: "Do you know sir, that until you came along I believe that she loved me almost as girls love their lovers. *I know I loved her so.* Don't you wonder that I can stand the sight of you." This was in a letter congratulating them on their forthcoming marriage.[16]

The essential question is not whether these women had genital contact and can therefore be defined as heterosexual or homosexual. The twentieth-century tendency to view human love and sexuality within a dichotomized universe of deviance and normality, genitality and platonic love, is alien to the emotions and attitudes of the nineteenth century and fundamentally distorts the nature of these women's emotional interaction. These letters are significant because they force us to place such female love in a particular historical context. There is every indication that these four women, their husbands and families—all eminently respectable and socially conservative—considered such love both socially acceptable and fully compatible with heterosexual marriage. Emotionally and cognitively, their heterosocial and their homosocial worlds were complementary.

One could argue, on the other hand, that these letters were but an example of the romantic rhetoric with which the nineteenth century surrounded the concept of friendship. Yet they possess an emotional intensity and a sensual and physical explicitness that is difficult to dismiss. Jeannie longed to hold Sarah in her arms; Molly mourned her physical isolation from Helena. Molly's love and devotion to Helena, the emotions that bound Jeannie and Sarah together, while perhaps a phenomenon of nineteenth-century society, were not the less real for their Victorian origins. A survey of the correspondence and diaries of eighteenth- and nineteenth-century women indicates that Molly, Jeannie, and Sarah represented one very real behavioral and emotional option socially available to nineteenth-century women.

This is not to argue that individual needs, personalities, and family dynamics did not have a significant role in determining the nature of particular relationships. But the scholar must ask if it is historically possible and, if possible, important, to study the intensely individual aspects of psychosexual dynamics. Is it not the historian's first task to explore the social structure and the world view which made intense and sometimes sensual female love both a possible and an acceptable emotional option? From such a social perspective a new and quite different series of questions suggests itself. What emotional function did such female love serve? What was its place within the hetero- and homosocial worlds which women jointly inhabited? Did a spectrum of love-object choices exist in the nineteenth century across which some individuals, at least, were capable of moving? Without attempting to answer these questions it will be difficult to understand either nineteenth-century sexuality or the nineteenth-century family.

Several factors in American society between the mid-eighteenth and the mid-nineteenth centuries may well have permitted women to form a variety of close emotional relationships with other women. American society was characterized in large part by rigid gender-role differentiation within the family and within society as a whole, leading to the emotional segregation of women and men. The roles of daughter and mother shaded imperceptibly and ineluctably into each other, while the biological realities of frequent pregnancies, childbirth, nursing, and menopause bound women together in physical and emotional intimacy. It was within just such a social framework, I would argue, that a specifically female world did indeed develop, a world built around a generic and unself-conscious pattern of single-sex or homosocial networks. These supportive networks were institutionalized in social conventions or rituals which accompanied virtually every important event in a woman's life, from birth to death. Such female relationships were frequently supported and paralleled by severe social restrictions on intimacy between young men and women. Within such a world of emotional richness and complexity devotion to and love of other women became a plausible and socially accepted form of human interaction.

An abundance of printed and manuscript sources exists to support such a hypothesis. Etiquette books, advice books on child rearing, religious sermons, guides to young men and young women, medical texts, and school curricula all suggest that late eighteenth- and most nineteenth-century Americans assumed the existence of a world composed of distinctly male and female spheres, spheres determined by the immutable laws of God and nature.[17] The unpublished letters and diaries of Americans during this same period concur, detailing the existence of sexually segregated worlds inhabited by human beings with different values, expectations, and personalities. Contacts between men and women frequently partook of a formality and stiffness quite alien to twentieth-century America and which today we tend to define as "Victorian." Women, however, did not form an isolated and oppressed subcategory in male society. Their letters and diaries indicate that women's sphere had an essential integrity and dignity that grew out of women's shared experiences and mutual affection and that, despite the profound changes which affected American social structure and institutions between the 1760s and the 1870s, retained a constancy and predictability. The ways in which women thought of and interacted with each other remained unchanged. Continuity, not discontinuity, characterized this female world. Molly Hallock's and Jeannie Field's words, emotions, and experiences have direct parallels in the 1760s and the 1790s.[18] There are indications in contemporary sociological and psychological literature that female closeness and support networks have continued into the twentieth century—not only among ethnic and working-class groups but even among the middle class.[19]

Most eighteenth- and nineteenth-century women lived within a world bounded by home, church, and the institution of visiting—that endless trooping of women to each other's homes for social purposes. It was a world inhabited by children and by other women.[20] Women helped each other with domestic chores and in times of sickness, sorrow, or trouble. Entire days, even weeks, might be spent almost exclusively with other women.[21] Urban and town women could devote virtually every day to visits, teas, or shopping trips with other women. Rural women developed a pattern of more extended visits that lasted weeks and sometimes months, at times even dislodging husbands from their beds and bedrooms so that dear friends might spend every hour of every day together.[22] When husbands traveled, wives routinely moved in with other women, invited women friends to teas and suppers, sat together sharing and comparing the letters they had received from other close women friends. Secrets were exchanged and cherished, and the husband's return at times viewed with some ambivalence.[23]

Summer vacations were frequently organized to permit old friends to meet at water spas or share a country home. In 1848, for example, a young matron wrote cheerfully to her husband about the delightful time she was having with five close women friends whom she had invited to spend the summer with her; he remained at home alone to face the heat of Philadelphia and a cholera epidemic.[24] Some ninety years earlier, two young Quaker girls commented upon the vacation their aunt had taken alone with another woman; their remarks were openly envious and tell us something of the emotional quality of these friendships: "I hear Aunt is gone with the Friend and wont be back for two weeks, fine times indeed I think the old friends had, taking their pleasure about the country . . . and have the advantage of that fine woman's conversation and instruction, while we poor young girls must spend all spring at home. . . . What a disappointment that we are not together. . . ."[25]

Friends did not form isolated dyads but were normally part of highly integrated networks. Knowing each other, perhaps related to each other, they played a central role in holding communities and kin systems together. Especially when families became geographically mobile women's long visits to each other and their frequent letters filled with discussions of marriages and births, illness and deaths, descriptions of growing children, and reminiscences of times and people past provided an important sense of continuity in a rapidly changing society.[26] Central to this female world was an inner core of kin. The ties between sisters, first cousins, aunts, and nieces provided the underlying structure upon which groups of friends and their network of female relatives clustered. Although most of the women within this sample would appear to be living within isolated nuclear families, the emotional ties between nonresidential kin were deep and binding and provided one of the fundamental existential realities of women's lives.[27] Twenty years after Parke Lewis Butler moved with her husband to Louisiana, she sent her two daughters back to Virginia to attend school, live with their grandmother and aunt, and be integrated back into Virginia society.[28] The constant letters between Maria Inskeep and Fanny Hampton, sisters separated in their early twenties when Maria moved with her husband from New Jersey to Louisiana, held their families together, making it possible for their daughters to feel a part of their cousins' network of friends and interests.[29] The Ripley daughters, growing up in western Massachusetts in the early 1800s, spent months each year with their mother's sister and her family in distant Boston; these female cousins and their network of friends exchanged gossip-filled letters and gradually formed deeply loving and dependent ties.[30]

Women frequently spent their days within the social confines of such extended families. Sisters-in-law visited each other and, in some families, seemed to spend more time with each other than with their husbands. First cousins cared for each other's babies—for weeks or even months in times of sickness or childbirth. Sisters helped each other with housework, shopped and sewed for each other. Geographic separation was borne with difficulty. A sister's absence for even a week or two could cause loneliness and depression and would be bridged by frequent letters. Sibling rivalry was hardly unknown, but with separation or illness the theme of deep affection and dependency reemerged.[31]

Sisterly bonds continued across a lifetime. In her old age a rural Quaker matron, Martha Jefferis, wrote to her daughter Anne concerning her own half-sister, Phoebe: "In sister Phoebe I have a real friend—she studies my comfort and waits on me like a child. . . . She is exceedingly kind and this to all other homes (set aside yours) I would prefer—it is next to being with a daughter." Phoebe's own letters confirmed Martha's evaluation of her feelings. "Thou knowest my dear sister," Phoebe wrote, "there is no one . . . that exactly feels [for] thee as I do, for I think without boasting I can truly say that my desire is for thee."[32]

Such women, whether friends or relatives, assumed an emotional centrality in each other's lives. In their diaries and letters they wrote of the joy and contentment they felt in each other's company, their sense of isolation and despair when apart. The regularity of their correspondence underlies the sincerity of their words. Women named their daughters after one another and sought to integrate dear friends into their lives after marriage.[33] As one

young bride wrote to an old friend shortly after her marriage: "I want to see you and talk with you and feel that we are united by the same bonds of sympathy and congeniality as ever."[34] After years of friendship one aging woman wrote of another: "Time cannot destroy the fascination of her manner . . . her voice is music to the ear. . . ."[35] Women made elaborate presents for each other, ranging from the Quakers' frugal pies and breads to painted velvet bags and phantom bouquets.[36] When a friend died, their grief was deeply felt. Martha Jefferis was unable to write to her daughter for three weeks because of the sorrow she felt at the death of a dear friend. Such distress was not unusual. A generation earlier a young Massachusetts farm woman filled pages of her diary with her grief at the death of her "dearest friend" and transcribed the letters of condolence other women sent her. She marked the anniversary of Rachel's death each year in her diary, contrasting her faithfulness with that of Rachel's husband who had soon remarried.[37]

These female friendships served a number of emotional functions. Within this secure and empathetic world women could share sorrows, anxieties, and joys, confident that other women had experienced similar emotions. One mid-nineteenth-century rural matron in a letter to her daughter discussed this particular aspect of women's friendships: "To have such a friend as thyself to look to and sympathize with her—and enter into all her little needs and in whose bosom she could with freedom pour forth her joys and sorrows—such a friend would very much relieve the tedium of many a wearisome hour. . . ." A generation later Molly more informally underscored the importance of this same function in a letter to Helena: "Suppose I come down . . . [and] spend Sunday with you quietly," she wrote Helena ". . . that means talking all the time until you are relieved of all your latest troubles, and I of mine. . . ."[38] These were frequently troubles that apparently no man could understand. When Anne Jefferis Sheppard was first married, she and her older sister Edith (who then lived with Anne) wrote in detail to their mother of the severe depression and anxiety which they experienced. Moses Sheppard, Anne's husband, added cheerful postscripts to the sisters' letters—which he had clearly not read—remarking on Anne's and Edith's contentment. Theirs was an emotional world to which he had little access.[39]

This was, as well, a female world in which hostility and criticism of other women were discouraged, and thus a milieu in which women could develop a sense of inner security and self-esteem. As one young woman wrote to her mother's longtime friend: "I cannot sufficiently thank you for the kind unvaried affection & indulgence you have ever shown and expressed both by words and actions for me. . . . Happy would it be did all the world view me as you do, through the medium of kindness and forbearance."[40] They valued each other. Women, who had little status or power in the larger world of male concerns, possessed status and power in the lives and worlds of other women.[41]

An intimate mother-daughter relationship lay at the heart of this female world. The diaries and letters of both mothers and daughters attest to their closeness and mutual emotional dependency. Daughters routinely discussed their mother's health and activities with their own friends, expressed anxiety in cases of their mother's ill health and concern for her cares.[42] Expressions of hostility which we would today consider routine on the part of both mothers and daughters seem to have been uncommon indeed. On the contrary, this sample of families indicates that the normal relationship between mother and daughter was one of sympathy and understanding.[43] Only sickness or great geographic distance was allowed to cause extended separation. When marriage did result in such separation, both viewed the distance between them with distress.[44] Something of this sympathy and love between mothers and daughters is evident in a letter Sarah Alden Ripley, at age sixty-nine, wrote her youngest and recently married daughter: "You do not know how much I miss you, not only when I struggle in and out of my mortal envelop and pump my nightly potation and no longer pour into your sympathizing ear my senile gossip, but all the day I muse away, since the sound of your voice no longer rouses me to sympathy with your joys or sorrows. . . . You cannot know how much I miss your affectionate demonstrations."[45] A dozen aging mothers in this sample of over thirty families echoed her sentiments.

Central to these mother-daughter relations is what might be described as an apprenticeship system. In those families where the daughter followed the mother into a life of traditional domesticity, mothers and other older women carefully trained daughters in the arts of housewifery and motherhood. Such training undoubtedly occurred throughout a girl's childhood but became more systematized, almost ritualistic, in the years following the end of her formal education and before her marriage. At this time a girl either returned home from boarding school or no longer divided her time between home and school. Rather, she devoted her energies on two tasks: mastering new domestic skills and participating in the visiting and social activities necessary to finding a husband. Under the careful supervision of their mothers and of older female relatives, such late-adolescent girls temporarily took over the household management from their mothers, tended their young nieces and nephews, and helped in childbirth, nursing, and weaning. Such experiences tied the generations together in shared skills and emotional interaction.[46]

Daughters were born into a female world. Their mother's life expectations and sympathetic network of friends and relations were among the first realities in the life of the developing child. As long as the mother's domestic role remained relatively stable and few viable alternatives competed with it, daughters tended to accept their mother's world and to turn automatically to other women for support and intimacy. It was within this closed and intimate female world that the young girl grew toward womanhood.

One could speculate at length concerning the absence of that mother-daughter hostility today considered almost inevitable to an adolescent's struggle for autonomy and self-identity. It is possible that taboos against female aggression and hostility were sufficiently strong to repress even that between mothers and their adolescent daughters. Yet these letters seem so alive and the interest of daughters in their mothers' affairs so vital and genuine that it is difficult to interpret their closeness exclusively in terms of repression and denial. The functional bonds that held mothers and daughters together in a world that permitted few alternatives to domesticity might well have created a source of mutuality and trust absent in societies where greater options were available for daughters than for mothers. Furthermore, the extended female network—a daughter's close ties with her own older sisters, cousins, and aunts—may well have permitted a diffusion and a relaxation of mother-daughter identification and so have aided a daughter in her struggle for identity and autonomy. None of these explanations are mutually exclusive; all may well have interacted to produce the degree of empathy evident in those letters and diaries.

At some point in adolescence, the young girl began to move outside the matrix of her mother's support group to develop a network of her own. Among the middle class, at least, this transition toward what was at the same time both a limited autonomy and a repetition of her mother's life seemed to have most frequently coincided with a girl's going to school. Indeed education appears to have played a crucial role in the lives of most of the families in this study. Attending school for a few months, for a year, or longer, was common even among daughters of relatively poor families, while middle-class girls routinely spent at least a year in boarding school.[47] These school years ordinarily marked a girl's first separation from home. They served to wean the daughter from her home, to train her in the essential social graces, and, ultimately, to help introduce her into the marriage market. It was not infrequently a trying emotional experience for both mother and daughter.[48]

In this process of leaving one home and adjusting to another, the mother's friends and relatives played a key transitional role. Such older women routinely accepted the role of foster mother; they supervised the young girl's deportment, monitored her health and introduced her to their own network of female friends and kin.[49] Not infrequently women, friends from their own school years, arranged to send their daughters to the same school so that the girls might form bonds paralleling those their mothers had made. For years Molly and Helena wrote of their daughters' meeting and worried over each other's children. When Molly finally brought her daughter east to school, their first act on reaching New York was to meet Helena and her daughters. Elizabeth Bordley Gibson virtually adopted the daughters of her school chum, Eleanor Custis Lewis. The Lewis daughters soon began to write Elizabeth Gibson letters with the salutation "Dearest Mama." Eleuthera DuPont, attending boarding school in Philadelphia at roughly the same time as the Lewis girls, developed a parallel relationship with her moth-

er's friend, Elizabeth McKie Smith. Eleuthera went to the same school and became a close friend of the Smith girls and eventually married their first cousin. During this period she routinely called Mrs. Smith "Mother." Indeed Eleuthera so internalized the sense of having two mothers that she casually wrote her sisters of her "Mamma's" visits at her "mother's" house—that is, at Mrs. Smith's.[50]

Even more important to this process of maturation than their mother's friends were the female friends young women made at school. Young girls helped each other overcome homesickness and endure the crises of adolescence. They gossiped about beaux, incorporated each other into their own kinship systems, and attended and gave teas and balls together. Older girls in boarding school "adopted" younger ones, who called them "Mother."[51] Dear friends might indeed continue this pattern of adoption and mothering throughout their lives; one woman might routinely assume the nurturing role of pseudomother, the other the dependency role of daughter. The pseudomother performed for the other woman all the services which we normally associate with mothers; she went to absurd lengths to purchase items her "daughter" could have obtained from other sources, gave advice and functioned as an idealized figure in her "daughter's" imagination. Helena played such a role for Molly, as did Sarah for Jeannie. Elizabeth Bordley Gibson bought almost all Eleanor Parke Custis Lewis's necessities—from shoes and corset covers to bedding and harp strings—and sent them from Philadelphia to Virginia, a procedure that sometimes took months. Eleanor frequently asked Elizabeth to take back her purchases, have them redone, and argue with shopkeepers about prices. These were favors automatically asked and complied with. Anne Jefferis Sheppard made the analogy very explicitly in a letter to her own mother written shortly after Anne's marriage, when she was feeling depressed about their separation: "Mary Paulen is truly kind, almost acts the part of a mother and trys to aid and *comfort me,* and also to *lighten my new cares.*"[52]

A comparison of the references to men and women in these young women's letters is striking. Boys were obviously indispensable to the elaborate courtship ritual girls engaged in. In these teenage letters and diaries, however, boys appear distant and warded off—an effect produced both by the girl's sense of bonding and by a highly developed and deprecatory whimsy. Girls joked among themselves about the conceit, poor looks or affectations of suitors. Rarely, especially in the eighteenth and early nineteenth centuries, were favorable remarks exchanged. Indeed, while hostility and criticism of other women were so rare as to seem almost tabooed, young women permitted themselves to express a great deal of hostility toward peer-group men.[53] When unacceptable suitors appeared, girls might even band together to harass them. When one such unfortunate came to court Sophie DuPont she hid in her room, first sending her sister Eleuthera to entertain him and then dispatching a number of urgent notes to her neighboring sister-in-law, cousins, and a visiting friend who all came to Sophie's support. A wild female romp ensued, ending only when Sophie banged into a door, lacerated her nose, and retired, with her female cohorts, to bed. Her brother and the presumably disconcerted suitor were left alone. These were not the antics of teenagers but of women in their early and mid-twenties.[54]

Even if young men were acceptable suitors, girls referred to them formally and obliquely: "The last week I received the unexpected intelligence of the arrival of a friend in Boston," Sarah Ripley wrote in her diary of the young man to whom she had been engaged for years and whom she would shortly marry. Harriet Manigault assiduously kept a lively and gossipy diary during the three years preceding her marriage, yet did not once comment upon her own engagement nor indeed make any personal references to her fiancé—who was never identified as such but always referred to as Mr. Wilcox.[55] The point is not that these young women were hostile to young men. Far from it; they sought marriage and domesticity. Yet in these letters and diaries men appear as an other or out group, segregated into different schools, supported by their own male network of friends and kin, socialized to different behavior, and coached to a proper formality in courtship behavior. As a consequence, relations between young women and men frequently lacked the spontaneity and emotional intimacy that characterized the young girls' ties to each other.

Indeed, in sharp contrast to their distant relations with boys, young women's relations with each other were close, often frolicsome, and surprisingly long lasting and devoted. They wrote secret missives to each other, spent long solitary days with each other, curled up together in bed at night to whisper fantasies and secrets.[56] In 1862 one young woman in her early twenties described one such scene to an absent friend: "I have sat up to midnight listening to the confidences of Constance Kinney, whose heart was opened by that most charming of all situations, a seat on a bedside late at night, when all the household are asleep & only oneself & one's confidante survive in wakefulness. So she has told me all her loves and tried to get some confidences in return but being five or six years older than she, I know better. . . ."[57] Elizabeth Bordley and Nelly Parke Custis, teenagers in Philadelphia in the 1790s, routinely secreted themselves until late each night in Nelly's attic, where they each wrote a novel about the other.[58] Quite a few young women kept diaries, and it was a sign of special friendship to show their diaries to each other. The emotional quality of such exchanges emerges from the comments of one young girl who grew up along the Ohio frontier:

> Sisters CW and RT keep diaries & allow me the inestimable pleasure of reading them and in turn they see mine—but O shame covers my face when I think of it; theirs is so much better than mine, that every time. Then I think well now I *will* burn mine but upon second thought it would deprive me the pleasure of reading theirs, for I esteem it a very great privilege indeed, as well as very improving, as we lay our hearts open to each other, it heightens our love & helps to cherish & keep alive that sweet soothing friendship and endears us to each other by that soft attraction.[59]

Girls routinely slept together, kissed and hugged each other. Indeed, while waltzing with young men scandalized the otherwise flighty and highly fashionable Harriet Manigault, she considered waltzing with other young women not only acceptable but pleasant.[60]

Marriage followed adolescence. With increasing frequency in the nineteenth century, marriage involved a girl's traumatic removal from her mother and her mother's network. It involved, as well, adjustment to a husband, who, because he was male came to marriage with both a different world view and vastly different experiences. Not surprisingly, marriage was an event surrounded with supportive, almost ritualistic, practices. (Weddings are one of the last female rituals remaining in twentieth-century America.) Young women routinely spent the months preceding their marriage almost exclusively with other women—at neighborhood sewing bees and quilting parties or in a round of visits to geographically distant friends and relatives. Ostensibly they went to receive assistance in the practical preparations for their new home—sewing and quilting a trousseau and linen—but of equal importance, they appear to have gained emotional support and reassurance. Sarah Ripley spent over a month with friends and relatives in Boston and Hingham before her wedding; Parke Custis Lewis exchanged visits with her aunts and first cousins throughout Virginia.[61] Anne Jefferis, who married with some hesitation, spent virtually half a year in endless visiting with cousins, aunts, and friends. Despite their reassurance and support, however, she would not marry Moses Sheppard until her sister Edith and her cousin Rebecca moved into the groom's home, met his friends, and explored his personality.[62] The wedding did not take place until Edith wrote to Anne: "I can say in truth I am entirely willing thou shouldst follow him even away in the Jersey sands believing if thou are not happy in thy future home it will not be any fault on his part. . . ."[63]

Sisters, cousins, and friends frequently accompanied newlyweds on their wedding night and wedding trip, which often involved additional family visiting. Such extensive visits presumably served to wean the daughter from her family of origin. As such they often contained a note of ambivalence. Nelly Custis, for example, reported homesickness and loneliness on her wedding trip. "I left by my Beloved and revered Grandmamma with sincere regret," she wrote Elizabeth Bordley. "It was sometime before I could feel reconciled to traveling without her." Perhaps they also functioned to reassure the young woman herself, and her friends and kin, that though marriage might alter it would not destroy old bonds of intimacy and familiarity.[64]

Married life, too, was structured about a host of female rituals. Childbirth, especially the birth of the first child, became virtually a *rite de passage*, with a lengthy seclusion of the woman before and after delivery, severe restrictions on her activities, and finally a dramatic reemergence.[65] This seclusion was supervised by moth-

ers, sisters, and loving friends. Nursing and weaning involved the advice and assistance of female friends and relatives. So did miscarriage.[66] Death, like birth, was structured around elaborate unisexed rituals. When Nelly Parke Custis Lewis rushed to nurse her daughter who was critically ill while away at school, Nelly received support, not from her husband, who remained on their plantation, but from her old school friend, Elizabeth Bordley. Elizabeth aided Nelly in caring for her dying daughter, cared for Nelly's other children, played a major role in the elaborate funeral arrangements (which the father did not attend), and frequently visited the girl's grave at the mother's request. For years Elizabeth continued to be the confidante of Nelly's anguished recollections of her lost daughter. These memories, Nelly's letters make clear, were for Elizabeth alone. "Mr. L. knows nothing of this," was a frequent comment.[67] Virtually every collection of letters and diaries in my sample contained evidence of women turning to each other for comfort when facing the frequent and unavoidable deaths of the eighteenth and nineteenth centuries.[68] While mourning for her father's death, Sophie DuPont received elaborate letters and visits of condolence—all from women. No man wrote or visited Sophie to offer sympathy at her father's death.[69] Among rural Pennsylvania Quakers, death and mourning rituals assumed an even more extreme same-sex form, with men or women largely barred from the deathbeds of the other sex. Women relatives and friends slept with the dying woman, nursed her, and prepared her body for burial.[70]

Eighteenth- and nineteenth-century women thus lived in emotional proximity to each other. Friendships and intimacies followed the biological ebb and flow of women's lives. Marriage and pregnancy, childbirth and weaning, sickness and death involved physical and psychic trauma which comfort and sympathy made easier to bear. Intense bonds of love and intimacy bound together those women who, offering each other aid and sympathy, shared such stressful moments.

These bonds were often physical as well as emotional. An undeniably romantic and even sensual note frequently marked female relationships. This theme, significant throughout the stages of a woman's life, surfaced first during adolescence. As one teenager from a struggling pioneer family in the Ohio Valley wrote in her diary in 1808: "I laid with my dear R[ebecca] and a glorious good talk we had until about 4[A.M.]—O how hard I do *love* her. . . ."[71] Only a few years later Bostonian Eunice Callender carved her initials and Sarah Ripley's into a favorite tree, along with a pledge of eternal love, and then waited breathlessly for Sarah to discover and respond to her declaration of affection. The response appears to have been affirmative.[72] A half-century later urbane and sophisticated Katherine Wharton commented upon meeting an old school chum: "She was a great pet of mine at school & I thought as I watched her light figure how often I had held her in my arms—how dear she had once been to me." Katie maintained a long intimate friendship with another girl. When a young man began to court this friend seriously, Katie commented in her diary that she had never realized "how deeply I loved Eng and how fully." She wrote over and over again in that entry: "Indeed I love her!" and only with great reluctance left the city that summer since it meant also leaving Eng with Eng's new suitor.[73]

Peggy Emlen, a Quaker adolescent in Philadelphia in the 1760s, expressed similar feelings about her first cousin, Sally Logan. The girls sent love poems to each other (not unlike the ones Elizabeth Bordley wrote to Nellie Custis a generation later), took long solitary walks together, and even haunted the empty house of the other when one was out of town. Indeed Sally's absences from Philadelphia caused Peggy acute unhappiness. So strong were Peggy's feelings that her brothers began to tease about her affection for Sally and threatened to steal Sally's letters, much to both girls' alarm. In one letter that Peggy wrote the absent Sally she elaborately described the depth and nature of her feelings: "I have not words to express my impatience to see My Dear Cousin, what would I not give just now for an hours sweet conversation with her, it seems as if I had a thousand things to say to thee, yet when I see thee, everything will be forgot thro' joy. . . . I have a very great friendship for several Girls yet it dont give me so much uneasiness at being absent from them as from thee. . . . [Let us] go and spend a day down at our place together and there unmolested enjoy each others company."[74]

Sarah Alden Ripley, a young, highly educated woman, formed a similar intense relationship, in this instance with a woman somewhat older than herself. The immediate bond of friendship rested on their atypically intense scholarly interests, but it soon involved strong emotions, at least on Sarah's part. "Friendship," she wrote Mary Emerson, "is fast twining about her willing captive the silken hands of dependence, a dependence so sweet who would renounce it for the apathy of self-sufficiency?" Subsequent letters became far more emotional, almost conspiratorial. Mary visited Sarah secretly in her room, or the two women crept away from family and friends to meet in a nearby woods. Sarah became jealous of Mary's other young friends. Mary's trips away from Boston also thrust Sarah into periods of anguished depression. Interestingly, the letters detailing their love were not destroyed but were preserved and even reprinted in a eulogistic biography of Sarah Alden Ripley.[75]

Tender letters between adolescent women, confessions of loneliness and emotional dependency, were not peculiar to Sarah Alden, Peggy Emlen, or Katie Wharton. They are found throughout the letters of the thirty-five families studied. They have, of course, their parallel today in the musings of many female adolescents. Yet these eighteenth- and nineteenth-century friendships lasted with undiminished, indeed often increased, intensity throughout the women's lives. Sarah Alden Ripley's first child was named after Mary Emerson. Nelly Custis Lewis's love for and dependence on Elizabeth Bordley Gibson only increased after her marriage. Eunice Callender remained enamored of her cousin Sarah Ripley for years and rejected as impossible the suggestion by another woman that their love might some day fade away.[76] Sophie DuPont and her childhood friend, Clementina Smith, exchanged letters filled with love and dependency for forty years while another dear friend, Mary Black Couper, wrote of dreaming that she, Sophie, and her husband were all united in one marriage. Mary's letters to Sophie are filled with avowals of love and indications of ambivalence toward her own husband. Eliza Schlatter, another of Sophie's intimate friends, wrote to her at a time of crisis: "I wish I could be with you present in the body as well as the mind & heart—I would turn your *good husband out of bed*—and snuggle into you and we would have a long talk like old times in Pine St.—I want to tell you so many things that are not *writable*. . . ."[77]

Such mutual dependency and deep affection is a central existential reality coloring the world of supportive networks and rituals. In the case of Katie, Sophie, or Eunice—as with Molly, Jeannie, and Sarah—their need for closeness and support merged with more intense demands for a love which was at the same time both emotional and sensual. Perhaps the most explicit statement concerning women's lifelong friendships appeared in the letter abolitionist and reformer Mary Grew wrote about the same time, referring to her own love for her dear friend and lifelong companion, Margaret Burleigh. Grew wrote, in response to a letter of condolence from another woman on Burleigh's death: "Your words respecting my beloved friend touch me deeply. Evidently . . . you comprehend and appreciate, as few persons do . . . the nature of the relation which existed, which exists, between her and myself. Her only surviving niece . . . also does. To me it seems to have been a closer union than that of most marriages. We know there have been other such between two men and also between two women. And why should there not be. Love is spiritual, only passion is sexual."[78]

How then can we ultimately interpret these long-lived intimate female relationships and integrate them into our understanding of Victorian sexuality? Their ambivalent and romantic rhetoric presents us with an ultimate puzzle: the relationship along the spectrum of human emotions between love, sensuality, and sexuality.

One is tempted, as I have remarked, to compare Molly, Peggy, or Sophie's relationships with the friendships adolescent girls in the twentieth century routinely form—close friendships of great emotional intensity. Helene Deutsch and Clara Thompson have both described these friendships as emotionally necessary to a girl's psychosexual development. But, they warn, such friendships might shade into adolescent and postadolescent homosexuality.[79]

It is possible to speculate that in the twentieth century a number of cultural taboos evolved to cut short the homosocial ties of girlhood and to impel the emerging women of thirteen or fourteen toward heterosexual relationships. In contrast, nineteenth-century American society did not taboo close female relationships but rather recognized them as a so-

cially viable form of human contact—and, as such, acceptable throughout a woman's life. Indeed it was not these homosocial ties that were inhibited but rather heterosexual leanings. While closeness, freedom of emotional expression, and uninhibited physical contact characterized women's relationships with each other, the opposite was frequently true of male-female relationships. One could thus argue that within such a world of female support, intimacy, and ritual it was only to be expected that adult women would turn trustingly and lovingly to each other. It was a behavior they had observed and learned since childhood. A different type of emotional landscape existed in the nineteenth century, one in which Molly and Helena's love became a natural development.

Of perhaps equal significance are the implications we can garner from this framework for the understanding of heterosexual marriages in the nineteenth century. If men and women grew up as they did in relatively homogeneous and segregated sexual groups, then marriage represented a major problem in adjustment. From this perspective we could interpret much of the emotional stiffness and distance that we associate with Victorian marriage as a structural consequence of contemporary sex-role differentiation and gender-role socialization. With marriage both women and men had to adjust to life with a person who was, in essence, a member of an alien group.

I have thus far substituted a cultural or psychosocial for a psychosexual interpretation of women's emotional bonding. But there are psychosexual implications in this model which I think it only fair to make more explicit. Despite Sigmund Freud's insistence on the bisexuality of us all or the recent American Psychiatric Association decision on homosexuality, many psychiatrists today tend explicitly or implicitly to view homosexuality as a totally alien or pathological behavior—as totally unlike heterosexuality. I suspect that in essence they may have adopted an explanatory model similar to the one used in discussing schizophrenia. As a psychiatrist can speak of schizophrenia and of a borderline schizophrenic personality as both ultimately and fundamentally different from a normal or neurotic personality, so they also think of both homosexuality and latent homosexuality as states totally different from heterosexuality. With this rapid dichotomous model of assumption, "latent homosexuality'' becomes the indication of a disease in progress—seeds of a pathology which belie the reality of an individual's heterosexuality.

Yet at the same time we are well aware that cultural values can affect choices in the gender of a person's sexual partner. We, for instance, do not necessarily consider homosexual-object choice among men in prison, on shipboard or in boarding schools a necessary indication of pathology. I would urge that we expand this relativistic model and hypothesize that a number of cultures might well tolerate or even encourage diversity in sexual and nonsexual relations. Based on my research into this nineteenth-century world of female intimacy, I would further suggest that rather than seeing a gulf between the normal and the abnormal we view sexual and emotional impulses as part of a continuum or spectrum of affect gradations strongly affected by cultural norms and arrangements, a continuum influenced in part by observed and thus learned behavior. At one end of the continuum lies committed heterosexuality, at the other uncompromising homosexuality; between, a wide latitude of emotions and sexual feelings. Certain cultures and environments permit individuals a great deal of freedom in moving across this spectrum. I would like to suggest that the nineteenth century was such a cultural environment. That is, the supposedly repressive and destructive Victorian sexual ethos may have been more flexible and responsive to the needs of particular individuals than those of mid-twentieth century.

Notes

1. The most notable exception to this rule is now eleven years old: William R. Taylor and Christopher Lasch, ''Two 'Kindred Spirits': Sorority and Family in New England, 1839–1846,'' *New England Quarterly* 36 (1963):25–41. . . . I do not . . . accept the Taylor-Lasch thesis that female friendships developed in the mid-nineteenth century because of geographic mobility and the breakup of the colonial family. I have found these friendships as frequently in the eighteenth century as in the nineteenth and would hypothesize that the geographic mobility of the mid-nineteenth century eroded them as it did so many other traditional social institutions. . . .

2. I do not wish to deny the importance of women's relations with particular men. Obviously, women were close to brothers, husbands, fathers, and sons. However, there is evidence that despite such closeness relationships between men and women differed in both emotional texture and frequency from those between women. . . . I have discussed some aspects of male-female relationships in two articles: ''Puberty to Menopause: The Cycle of Femininity in Nineteenth-Century America,'' *Feminist Studies* 1 (1973):58–72, and, with Charles Rosenberg, ''The Female Animal: Medical and Biological Views of Women in 19th Century America,'' *Journal of American History* 59 (1973):331–56.

3. See Freud's classic paper on homosexuality, ''Three Essays on the Theory of Sexuality,'' in *The Standard Edition of the Complete Psychological Works of Sigmund Freud*, trans. James Strachey (London: Hogarth Press, 1953), 7:135–72. The essays originally appeared in 1905. . . .

4. . . . [S]ee Charles Rosenberg, ''Sexuality, Class and Role,'' *American Quarterly* 25 (1973):131–53.

5. See, e.g., the letters of Peggy Emlen to Sally Logan, 1768–72, Wells Morris Collection, Box 1, Historical Society of Pennsylvania; and the Eleanor Parke Curtis Lewis Letters, Historical Society of Pennsylvania, Philadelphia.

6. Sarah Butler Wister was the daughter of Fanny Kemble and Pierce Butler. In 1859 she married a Philadelphia physician, Owen Wister. The novelist Owen Wister is her son. Jeannie Field Musgrove was the half-orphaned daughter of constitutional lawyer and New York Republican politician David Dudley Field. Their correspondence (1855–98) is in the Sarah Butler Wister Papers, Wister Family Papers, Historical Society of Pennsylvania.

7. Sarah Butler, Butler Place, S.C., to Jeannie Field, New York, Sept. 14, 1855.

8. See, e.g., Sarah Butler Wister, Germantown, Pa., to Jeannie Field, New York, Sept. 25, 1862, Oct. 21, 1863; or Jeannie Field, New York, to Sarah Butler Wister, Germantown, July 3, 1861, Jan. 23 and July 12, 1863.

9. Sarah Butler Wister, Germantown, to Jeannie Field, New York, June 5, 1861, Feb. 29, 1864; Jeannie Field to Sarah Butler Wister, Nov. 22, 1861, Jan. 4 and June 14, 1863.

10. Sarah Butler Wister, London, to Jeannie Field Musgrove, New York, June 18 and Aug. 3, 1870.

11. See, e.g., two of Sarah's letters to Jeannie: Dec. 21, 1873, July 16, 1878.

12. This is the 1868–1920 correspondence between Mary Hallock Foote and Helena, a New York friend (the Mary Hallock Foote Papers are in the Manuscript Division, Stanford University). . . . In many ways these letters are typical of those women wrote to other women. Women frequently began letters to each other with salutations such as ''Dearest,'' ''My Most Beloved,'' ''You Darling Girl,'' and signed them ''tenderly'' or ''to my dear dear sweet friend, good-bye.''. . . She was by no means unique. See, e.g., Annie to Charlene Van Vleck Anderson, Appleton, Wis., June 10, 1871, Anderson Family Papers, Manuscript Division, Stanford University; Maggie to Emily Howland, Philadelphia, July 12, 1851, Howland Family Papers, Phoebe King Collection, Friends Historical Library, Swarthmore College; Mary Jane Burleigh to Emily Howland, Sherwood, N.Y., Mar. 27, 1872, Howland Family Papers, Sophia Smith Collection, Smith College; Mary Black Couper to Sophia Madeleine DuPont, Wilmington, Del.: n.d. [1834] (two let-

ters), Samuel Francis DuPont Papers, Eleutherian Mills Foundation,Wilmington, Del. . . . in general the correspondence (1838–49) between Rebecca Biddle of Philadelphia and Martha Jefferis, Chester County, Pa., Jefferis Family Correspondence, Chester County Historical Society, West Chester, Pa.; Phoebe Bradford Diary, June 7 and July 13, 1832, Historical Society of Pennsylvania; . . . the Sarah Alden Ripley Correspondence, Schlesinger Library, Radcliffe College; . . . Anne Sterling Biddle Family Papers, Friends Historical Society, Swarthmore College; Harriet Manigault Wilcox Diary, Aug. 7, 1814, Historical Society of Pennsylvania; . . . Mrs. O. J. Wister and Miss Agnes Irwin, eds., *Worthy Women of Our First Century* (Philadelphia: J. B. Lippincott & Co., 1877), p. 195.

13. Mary Hallock [Foote] to Helena, n.d. [1869–70], n.d. [1871–72], Folder 1, Mary Hallock Foote Letters, . . .

14. Mary Hallock [Foote] to Helena, Sept. 15 and 23, 1873, n.d. [Oct. 1873], Oct. 12, 1873.

15. Mary Hallock [Foote] to Helena, n.d. [Jan. 1874], n.d. [Spring 1874].

16. Mary Hallock [Foote] to Helena, Sept. 23, 1873; Mary Hallock [Foote] to Richard, Dec. 13, 1873. Molly's and Helena's relationship continued for the rest of their lives. . . .

17. . . . [S]ee Barbara Welter, ''The Cult of True Womanhood: 1820–1860,'' *American Quarterly* 18 (Summer 1966):151–74; Anne Firor Scott, *The Southern Lady: From Pedestal to Politics, 1830–1930* (Chicago: University of Chicago Press, 1970), chaps. 1–2; Smith-Rosenberg and Rosenberg.

18. See, e.g., the letters of Peggy Emlen to Sally Logan, 1768–72. . . .

19. See, [e.g.,] Elizabeth Botts, *Family and Social Network* (London: Tavistock Publications, 1957); . . .

20. This pattern seemed to cross class barriers. . . . See Ann McGrann, Philadelphia, to Sophie M. DuPont, Philadelphia, July 3, 1834, Sophie Madeleine DuPont Letters, Eleutherian Mills Foundation.

21. [See, e.g.,] Harriet Manigault Diary, June 28, 1814, and passim; . . .

22. [See, e.g.,] . . . Ann Sterling Biddle Papers, passim, . . .

23. [See, e.g.,] Phoebe Bradford Diary, Jan. 13, Nov. 16–19, 1832, Apr. 26 and May 7, 1833; . . .

24. Lisa Mitchell Diary, 1860s, passim, Manuscript Division, Tulane University; . . . Jeannie McCall, Cedar Park, to Peter McCall, Philadelphia, June 30, 1849, McCall Section, Cadwalader Collection, Historical Society of Pennsylvania.

25. Peggy Emlen to Sally Logan, May 3, 1769.

26. For a prime example of this type of letter, see Eleanor Parke Custis Lewis to Elizabeth Bordley Gibson, passim; . . .

27. Place of residence is not the only variable significance in characterizing family structure. Strong emotional ties and frequent visiting and correspondence can unite families that do not live under one roof. . . .

28. Eleanor Parke Custis Lewis to Elizabeth Bordley Gibson, Apr. 20 and Sept. 25, 1848.

29. Maria Inskeep to Fanny Hampton Correspondence, 1823–60, Inskeep Collection, Tulane University Library.

30. Eunice Callender, Boston, to Sarah Ripley [Stearns], Sept. 24 and Oct. 29, 1803, Feb. 16, 1805, Apr. 29 and Oct. 9, 1806, May 26, 1810.

31. Sophie DuPont filled her letters to her younger brother Henry (with whom she had been assigned to correspond while he was at boarding school) with accounts of family visiting (see, e.g., Dec. 13, 1827, Jan. 10 and Mar. 9, 1828, Feb. 4 and Mar. 10, 1832). . . . Mary B. Ashew Diary, July 11 and 13, Aug. 17, Summer and Oct. 1858. . . .

32. Martha Jefferis to Anne Jefferis Sheppard, Jan. 12, 1845; Phoebe Middleton to Martha Jefferis, Feb. 22, 1848. . . .

33. Rebecca Biddle to Martha Jefferis, 1838–49, passim; Martha Jefferis to Anne Jefferis Sheppard, July 6, 1846; Anne Jefferis Sheppard to Rachael Jefferis, Jan. 16, 1865; Sarah Foulke Farquhar [Emlen] Diary, Sept. 22, 1813, Friends Historical Library, Swarthmore College; . . .

34. Sarah Alden Ripley to Abba Allyn, n.d. . . .

35. Phoebe Bradford Diary, July 13, 1832.

36. Mary Hallock [Foote] to Helena, Dec. 23 [1868 or 1869]; Phoebe Bradford Diary, Dec. 8, 1832; Martha Jefferis and Anne Jefferis Sheppard letters, passim.

37. Martha Jefferis to Anne Jefferis Sheppard, Aug. 3, 1849; Sarah Ripley [Stearns] Diary, Nov. 12, 1808, Jan. 8, 1811. . . .

38. Martha Jefferis to Edith Jefferis, Mar. 15, 1841; Mary Hallock Foote to Helena, n.d. [1874–75?]; . . .

39. Anne Jefferis Sheppard to Martha Jefferis, Sept. 29, 1841.

40. Frances Parke Lewis to Elizabeth Bordley Gibson, Apr. 29, 1821.

41. [See, e.g.,] Mary Jane Burleigh, Mount Pleasant, S.C., to Emily Howland, Sherwood N.Y., Mar. 27, 1872, Howland Family Papers; . . .

42. [See, e.g.,] Harriet Manigault Diary, Aug. 15, 21, and 23, 1814, Historical Society of Pennsylvania; . . .

43. Mrs. S. S. Dalton, ''Autobiography'' (Circle Valley, Utah, 1876), pp. 21–22, Bancroft Library, University of California, Berkeley; Sarah Foulke Emlen Diary, Apr. 1809; Louisa G. Van Vleck, Appleton, Wis., to Charlena Van Vleck Anderson, Göttingen, n.d. [1875], . . .

44. Abigail Brackett Lyman, Boston, to Mrs. Abigail Brackett (daughter to mother), n.d. [1797], June 3, 1800; Sarah Alden Ripley wrote weekly to her daughter, Sophy Ripley Fisher, after the latter's marriage (Sarah Alden Ripley Correspondence, passim); Phoebe Bradford Diary, Feb. 25, 1833, passim, 1832–33; Louisa G. Van Vleck to Charlena Van Vleck Anderson, Dec. 15, 1873, July 4, Aug. 15 and 29, Sept. 19, and Nov. 9, 1875. . . . Daughters evidently frequently slept with their mothers—into adulthood (Harriet Manigault [Wilcox] Diary, Feb. 19, 1815; Eleanor Parke Custis Lewis to Elizabeth Bordley Gibson, Oct. 10, 1832). Daughters also frequently asked mothers to live with them and professed delight when they did so. . . . We did find a few exceptions to this mother-daughter felicity (M. B. Ashew Diary, Nov. 19, 1857, Apr. 10 and May 17, 1858). Sarah Foulke Emlen was at first very hostile to her stepmother (Sarah Foulke Emlen Diary, Aug. 9, 1807, but they later developed a warm supportive relationship.

45. Sarah Alden Ripley to Sophy Thayer, n.d. [1861].

46. [See, e.g.,] Mary Hallock Foote to Helena [Winter 1873] (no. 52); Jossie, Stevens Point, Wis., to Charlena Van Vleck [Anderson], Appleton, Wis., Oct. 24, 1870; Pollie Chandler, Green Bay, Wis., to Charlena Van Vleck [Anderson], Appleton, n.d. [1870]; Eleuthera DuPont to Sophie DuPont, Sept. 5, 1829; . . .

47. . . . Sarah Foulke Emlen Journal, Sarah Ripley Stearns Diary, Mrs. S. S. Dalton, "Autobiography."

48. Maria Revere to her mother [Mrs. Paul Revere], June 13, 1801, Paul Revere Papers, Massachusetts Historical Society. In a letter to Elizabeth Bordley Gibson, Mar. 28, 1847, Eleanor Parke Custis Lewis from Virginia discussed the anxiety her daughter felt when her granddaughters left home to go to boarding school. . . .

49. . . . [See, e.g.,] the letters and diaries of three generations of Manigault women in Philadelphia: Mrs. Gabrielle Manigault, her daughter, Harriet Manigault Wilcox, and granddaughter, Charlotte Wilcox McCall. . . . Mrs. Henry Middleton, Charleston, S.C., to Mrs. Gabrielle Manigault, n.d. [mid 1800s]; Harriet Manigault Diary, vol. 1; Dec. 1, 1813, June 28, 1814; Charlotte Wilcox McCall Diary, vol. 1, 1842, passim. All in Historical Society of Philadelphia.

50. Frances Parke Lewis, Woodlawn, Va., to Elizabeth Bordley Gibson, Philadelphia, Apr. 11, 1821, Lewis Correspondence; Eleuthera DuPont, Philadelphia, to Victorine DuPont Bauday, Brandywine, Dec. 8, 1821, Jan. 31, 1822; Eleuthera DuPont, Brandywine, to Margaretta Lammont [DuPont], Philadelphia, May 1823.

51. [See, e.g.,] Sarah Ripley Stearns Diary, Mar. 9 and 25, 1810; Peggy Emlen to Sally Logan, Mar. and July 4, 1769; . . . Deborah Cope, West Town School, to Rest Cope, Philadelphia, July 9, 1828, Chester County Historical Society, West Chester, Pa.; . . .

52. Anne Jefferis Sheppard to Martha Jefferis, Mar. 17, 1841.

53. [See, e.g.,] Peggy Emlen to Sally Logan, Mar. 1769, Mount Vernon, Va.; . . .

54. Sophie M. DuPont and Eleuthera DuPont, Brandywine, to Victorine DuPont Bauday, Philadelphia, Jan. 25, 1832.

55. Sarah Ripley [Stearns] Diary and Harriet Manigault Diary, passim.

56. [See, e.g.,] Sophie Madeleine DuPont to Eleuthera DuPont, Dec. 1827; Clementina Beach Smith to Sophie Madeleine DuPont, Dec. 26, 1828; Sarah Faulke Emlen Diary, July 21, 1808, Mar. 30, 1809; . . .

57. Jeannie Field, New York, to Sarah Butler Wister, Germantown, Apr. 6, 1862.

58. Elizabeth Bordley Gibson, introductory statement to the Eleanor Parke Custis Lewis Letters [1850s], Historical Society of Pennsylvania.

59. Sarah Foulke [Emlen] Diary, Mar. 30, 1809.

60. Harriet Manigault Diary, May 26, 1815.

61. Sarah Ripley [Stearns] Diary, May 17 and Oct. 2, 1812; Eleanor Parke Custis Lewis to Elizabeth Bordley Gibson, Apr. 23, 1826; . . .

62. Anne Jefferis to Martha Jefferis, Nov. 22 and 27, 1840, Jan. 13 and Mar. 17, 1841; Edith Jefferis, Greenwich, N.J., to Anne Jefferis, Philadelphia, Jan. 31, Feb. 6 and Feb. 1841.

63. Edith Jefferis to Anne Jefferis, Jan. 31, 1841.

64. Eleanor Parke Custis Lewis to Elizabeth Bordley, Nov. 4, 1799. . . .

65. [See, e.g.,] Mary Hallock to Helena DeKay Gilder [1876] (no. 81); n.d. (no. 83), Mar. 3, 1884; Mary Ashew Diary, vol. 2, Sept.–Jan. 1860; . . .

66. [See, e.g.,] Fanny Ferris to Anne Biddle, Nov. 19, 1811; Eleanor Parke Custis Lewis to Elizabeth Bordley Gibson, Nov. 4, 1799, Apr. 27, 1827; . . .

67. Eleanor Parke Custis Lewis to Elizabeth Bordley Gibson, Oct.–Nov. 1820, passim.

68. [See, e.g.,] Emily Howland to Hannah, Sept. 30, 1866; Emily Howland Diary, Feb. 8, 11, and 27, 1880; Phoebe Bradford Diary, Apr. 12 and 13, and Aug. 4, 1833; . . .

69. Mary Black [Couper] to Sophie Madeleine DuPont, Feb. 1827 [Nov. 1, 1834], Nov. 12, 1834, two letters [late Nov. 1834]; Eliza Schlatter to Sophie Madeleine DuPont, Nov. 2, 1834.

70. For a few of the references to death rituals in the Jefferis papers see: Martha Jefferis to Anne Jefferis Sheppard, Sept. 28, 1843, Aug. 21 and Sept. 25, 1844, Jan. 11, 1846, Summer 1848, passim; . . . This is not to argue that men and women did not mourn together. Yet in many families women aided and comforted women and men, men. . . .

71. Sarah Foulke [Emlen] Diary, Dec. 29, 1808.

72. Eunice Callender, Boston, to Sarah Ripley [Stearns], Greenfield, Mass., May 24, 1803.

73. Katherine Johnstone Brinley [Wharton] Journal, Apr. 26, May 30, and May 29, 1856, Historical Society of Pennsylvania.

74. A series of roughly fourteen letters written by Peggy Emlen to Sally Logan (1768–71) has been preserved in the Wells Morris Collection, Box 1, Historical Society of Pennsylvania (see esp. May 3 and July 4, 1769, Jan. 8, 1768).

75. . . . The eulogistic biographical sketch appeared in Wister and Irwin (n. 12 above). . . .

76. See Sarah Alden Ripley to Mary Emerson, Nov. 19, 1823. Sarah Alden Ripley routinely, and one must assume ritualistically, read Mary Emerson's letters to her infant daughter, Mary. Eleanor Parke Custis Lewis reported doing the same with Elizabeth Bordley Gibson's letters, passim. Eunice Callender, Boston, to Sarah Ripley [Stearns], Oct. 19, 1808.

77. Mary Black Couper to Sophie M. DuPont, Mar. 5, 1832. The Clementina Smith–Sophie DuPont correspondence is in the Sophie DuPont Correspondence. The quotation is from Eliza Schlatter, Mount Holly, N.J., to Sophie DuPont, Brandywine, Aug. 24, 1834. . . .

78. Mary Grew, Providence, R.I., to Isabel Howland, Sherwood, N.Y., Apr. 27, 1892, Howland Correspondence, Sophia Smith Collection, Smith College.

79. Helena Deutsch, *Psychology of Women* (New York: Grune & Stratton, 1944), 1: chaps. 1–3; Clara Thompson, *On Women*, ed. Maurice Green (New York: New American Library, 1971).

JUDITH WALZER LEAVITT
Under the Shadow of Maternity

During the centuries before reliable fertility control measures made it possible for women to set limits on reproduction, most married women and many unmarried women had to bear the physical and psychological burden of repeated pregnancies, childbirths, and postpartum recoveries. The cost in terms of time, energy, dreams, and bodies was high. While the biological act of maternity set real constraints on women's lives, it also created powerful bonds among women as they coped with the experience of childbirth. Focusing on the legitimate fears surrounding that experience, Judith Walzer Leavitt examines the supports that women provided each other during the many years when birth occurred in the home and women remained in charge of it.

As medicine became more professional, it also became more strictly segregated by gender. Despite a few unenthusiastic efforts to teach the newest obstetric techniques to midwives, women were denied access to training in the newest medical skills. Because male physicians were more likely than midwives to be trained in the use of forceps and, after the middle of the nineteenth century, anesthesia, they were often present at home births. Their presence, especially in the early nineteenth century, did not necessarily mean better results; Martha Ballard, who delivered more than eight hundred infants on the Maine frontier between 1785 and 1812, had as good a record of infant and maternal survival as existed in urban hospitals in 1920, and a considerably better record than her male competitors in her own time.*

Leavitt argues that even when male physicians supervised home births, the traditional control exercised by the birthing woman, her mother and sisters, and her woman friends continued; women did not lose their ability to make decisions during the course of the birth process until birth was moved to hospitals in the twentieth century. Ironically, the scientific developments that led to less painful childbirths also increased the dependence of women on male physicians. Death rates in birth did not decline sharply until the invention of antibiotics in the mid-1930s.

In 1846 a young woman in Warren, Pennsylvania, gave birth to a son and soon after was taken with "sinking spells." Her female friends and relatives were there to help her; they took encouragement when she appeared better and consoled each other when she fell into a stupor.

A woman who was with her during these days wrote to a mutual friend, describing the scene around Mary Ann Ditmer's bed.

> Oh my beloved Girl—You may imagine our sorrow, for you too must weep with us—How can I

---

*The Diary of Martha Moore Ballard, ed. Laurel Thatcher Ulrich (New York: A. A. Knopf, 1990).

tell you: I cannot realize myself—Mary Ann will soon cease to be among the living—and numbered with the dead. . . . Elizabeth, it was such a scene that is hard to be described—L and I remained until the afternoon. Mrs. Mersel came and relieved us, also Mrs. Whalen came. We took a few hours sleep and returned—She had requested us to remain as long as she lived—there was every indication of a speedy termination of her suffering—Mary had come over—Mrs. N remained to watch . . . all thought she was dying—She was very desirous of living till day light—She thought she might have some hope if she could stand it until morning—She retained her sense perfectly—She begged us to be active and not be discouraged that she might live yet—that life was so sweet—how she clung to it—Elizabeth I would wish you might be spared such a sight—we surrounded her dying bed—Each one diligent to keep life and animation in the form of one they so much loved and who at that very time was kept alive with stimulating medicines and wine—I cannot describe it for o my God the horrors of that night will ever remain in the minds of those who witnessed it—our hearts swelled at the sight.[1]

Mary Ann lingered a few days, during which time she bestowed rings and locks of hair upon her friends so they might remember her; she made her peace with God and provided for her child. Then she died. Her story, both in its recognition of the childbirth-related dangers to women's lives and in its revelations of women helping women, represents a reality visited upon countless numbers of American women in the eighteenth and nineteenth centuries, and it is a reality with supreme significance for understanding women's lives. . . .

During most of American history, women's anticipation of the possibility of dying or of being permanently injured during childbirth influenced their life expectations and experiences. But women's responses to their repeated and dangerous confinements suggest, instead of resignation to their difficulties, an active participation in shaping events in America's birthing rooms. . . . Women used the strengths and help of other women to face their problems, and in their unity developed coping mechanisms that were illustrative of what I think can be called a feminist impulse embedded within traditional women's experiences. . . . [F]eminist inclinations and the collective behavior they fostered developed out of the basic and shared experiences of women's bodies at times when

those bodies seemed most confining and difficult. In this sense, feminism, women grasping control and working together to overcome their commonly experienced burdens, can arise out of the very essence of biological femaleness and reside alongside the most traditional part of women's experiences. . . .

Underlying the shadow of maternity most significantly were high fertility rates. At the turn of the nineteenth century, American women bore an average of seven children before their fertile years ended. This implies considerably more than seven pregnancies, because many terminated before term. For many groups in the expanding American population, rates remained high throughout the nineteenth century. . . . [W]ithin the context of limited choices over conception, [p]regnancy, birth, and postpartum recovery occupied a significant portion of most women's adult lives, and the ensuing motherhood defined a major part of women's identity.

Take, for example, the life of Mary Vial Holyoke, who married into a prominent New England family in 1759. In 1760, after ten months of marriage, she gave birth to her first baby. Two years later, her second was born. In 1765 she was again "brought to bed" of a child. Pregnant immediately again, she bore another child in 1766. The following year she delivered her fifth, and in one more year delivered her sixth. Free from pregnancy and childbirth in 1769, she gave birth again in 1770. During the next twelve years, she bore five more children. The first twenty-three years of Mary Vial Holyoke's married life, the years of her youth and vigor, were spent pregnant or recovering from childbirth. Because only three of her twelve children lived to adulthood, she withstood, also, frequent tragedies. She devoted her body and her life to procreation throughout her reproductive years. Mary Holyoke had more pregnancies and suffered more child deaths than her average contemporary, and she presents a poignant example of the extreme physical trials women endured. Mary Holyoke had little choice in her frequent pregnancies: her life reveals how the biological capacity of women to bear children historically has translated into life's destiny for individual women.[2]

Mary Holyoke's experience became less common in nineteenth-century America, especially among white women, as fertility rates declined. By 1900, white women, showing the ability to cut their fertility in half over the century, averaged 3.56 children. Historians and demographers trying to understand this decline have suggested that as much as 75 percent of the dropping fertility rate can be explained by active fertility control, including abortion and birth control techniques. Some people seem to have succeeded in asserting partial control over the size of their families, but it is important to keep in mind that the fertility declines demographers have identified with nineteenth-century America apply only to white native-born women; immigrant and black women continued to have babies in larger numbers.[3]

Fertility rates explain only part of the impact of childbirth on women's lives. Maternity cast a shadow greater than its frequent repetition alone could have caused. Maternity, the creation of new life, carried with it the ever-present possibility of death. The shadow that followed women through life was the fear of the ultimate physical risk of bearing children. Young women perceived that their bodies, even when healthy and vigorous, could yield up a dead infant or could carry the seeds of their own destruction. As Cotton Mather had warned at the beginning of the eighteenth century, and as American women continued to believe, conception meant "your *Death* has Entered into you." Nine months' gestation could mean nine months to prepare for death. A possible death sentence came with every pregnancy.[4]

Many women spent considerable time worrying and preparing as if they would not survive their confinements. During Nannie Stillwell Jackson's pregnancy in 1890, she wrote in her diary: "I have not felt well today am afraid I am going to be sick I went up to Fannies a little while late this evening & was talking to her, & I told her to see after Lizzie & Sue [other children] if I was to die & not to let me be buried here . . . & I want Lizzie & Sue to have *everything that is mine,* for no one has as good a rite [sic] to what I have as they have."[5] A pregnant Clara Clough Lenroot confided in her diary in 1891: "It occurs to me that *possibly* I may not live. . . . I wonder if I should die, and leave a little daughter *behind* me, they would name her 'Clara.' I should like to have them." Three days later she again was worrying. "If I shouldn't live I wonder what they will do with the baby! I should want Mama and Bertha [sister] to have the bringing up of it, but I should

want Irvine [husband] to see it every day and love it so much, and I should want it taught to love him better than anyone else in the world." With the successful termination of the birth, Clara's husband wrote in his wife's diary, "Dear Clara, 'mama and Bertha' won't have to take care of your baby, thank God." He continued, "Everything is all right, but at what cost. My poor wife, how you have suffered, and you have been so brave. . . . I have seen the greatest suffering this day that I have ever known or ever imagined. . . ."[6]

Women and family members were not the only ones who anticipated maternal death. Many physicians who attended parturients through the fearful hours of labor and delivery . . . brooded on mortality. In the 1870s, Dr. James S. Bailey of Albany, New York, pondered the sometimes sudden and unexplained deaths of women following childbirth. He wrote: "To see a female, apparently in vigorous health until the period of accouchement, suddenly expire from some unforeseen accident, which is beyond the control of the attending physician, is well calculated to fill the mind with alarm and gloomy forebodings" and make it impossible "while attending a case of confinement, to banish the feeling of uncertainty and dread as to the result of cases which seemingly are terminating favorably. . . ."[7]

Fears of confinement's dangers [also] permeated society. The extent to which social fears about maternal deaths reflected a reality of high death rates is almost impossible for historians to determine with any degree of confidence. Perhaps more valuable to our understanding of the reality of maternal death is the observation that most women seemed to know or know of other women who had died in childbirth. One woman, for example, wrote that her friend "died as she has expected to" as a result of childbirth as had six other of their childhood friends. Early in the twentieth century approximately 1 mother died for each 154 live births. If women delivered, let us estimate, an average of five live babies, these statistics can mean that over their reproductive years, one of every thirty women might be expected to die in childbirth. In another early-twentieth-century calculation, one of every seventeen men claimed they had a mother or sister who had died as the immediate results of childbirth.[8] . . .

In the past, the shadow of maternity extended beyond the possibility and fear of death. Women knew that if procreation did not kill them or their babies, it could maim them for life. Postpartum gynecological problems—some great enough to force women to bed for the rest of their lives, others causing milder disabilities—hounded the women who did not succumb to their labor and delivery. For some women, the fears of future debility were more disturbing than fears of death. Vesicovaginal and rectovaginal fistulas (holes between the vagina and either the bladder or the rectum caused by the violence of childbirth or by instrument damage), which brought incontinence and constant irritation to sufferers; unsutured perineal tears of lesser degree, which may have caused significant daily discomforts; major infections; and general weakness and failure to return to prepregnant physical vigor threatened young women in the prime of life. Newly married women looking forward to life found themselves almost immediately faced with the prospect of permanent physical limitations that could follow their early and repeated confinements.

Chicago physician Henry Newman believed that the "normal process of reproduction [is] a formidable menace to the afterhealth of the parous woman."[9] Lacerations—tears in the perineal tissues—probably caused the greatest postpartum trouble for women. The worst of these, the fistulas, which led to either urine or feces constantly leaking through the vaginal opening without the possibility of control, were, in the words of one sympathetic doctor, "the saddest of calamities, entailing . . . endless suffering upon the poor patient . . . death would be a welcome visitor."[10] Women who had to live with this condition sat sick and alone as long as they lived unless they were one of the beneficiaries of Dr. J. Marion Sims's operation in the second half of the century. Their incontinence made them unpleasant companions, and even their loved ones found it hard to keep them constant company.[11]

More frequent and less debilitating, but still causing major problems for many women, were tears in the vaginal wall or cervix that might have led to prolapsed uterus, uncomfortable sexual intercourse, or difficulties with future deliveries. One physician noted that "the wide-spread mutilation . . . is so common, indeed, that we scarcely find a normal perineum after childbirth."[12] Most perineal lacerations probably were minor and harmless; but if severe ones were not adequately repaired,

women might suffer from significant postpartum discomfort. Women complained most frequently of a prolapsed uterus. This displacement of the womb downwards, sometimes even through the vaginal opening, often resulted from lacerations or postpartum relaxation and consequent elongation of the ligaments. One physician noted that fallen womb is often a temporary condition, but he also found it quite common: "Any woman subject to ill turns, lassitude, and general debility will tell you that not unfrequently upon these occasions she is sensible of a falling of the womb."[13] The condition caused misery for women. Albina Wight's sister Eliza, to give just one example from the 1870s, had a difficult delivery that was followed by prolapse. Six weeks following one of her sister's confinements, Albina recorded: "Eliza is sick yet can only walk across the room and that overdoes her. She has falling of the Womb. poor girl." Eliza's medical treatment by "a calomel doctor" who gave her "blue pills" did not help. Five months following the delivery she could only "walk a few steps at a time and cannot sit up all day." A second doctor predicted that "it will be a long time before she will get around again."[14]

The typical treatment for this common female ailment was the use of a pessary, a mechanical support for the uterus inserted into the vagina and left there as long as necessary. Pessaries themselves often led to pelvic inflammations and pain for the women whose conditions they were designed to alleviate. In the opinion of one physician,

> I think it is indisputable that a pessary allowed to remain for a very short period will invariably produce irritation, and if continued longer, will produce almost as certainly, ulceration. I have removed many pessaries that have produced ulceration; one in particular, hollow and of silver gilt, was completely honey combed by corrosion, its interior filled with exuviae of the most horrible offensiveness, the vagina ulcerated through into the bladder, producing a vesico-vaginal fistula, and into the rectum, producing a recto-vaginal fistula; the vagina in some portion obliterated by adhesive inflammation and numerous fistulae made through the labia and around the mons veneris for the exit of the various discharges.[15]

Uterine displacements puzzled physicians and pained women throughout the nineteenth century. A midcentury physician noted that anteflexion, an abnormal forward curvature of the uterus that seemed not amenable to pessary correction, "is the dread of almost every physician, and the constant, painful perplexity of many a patient." He told of his recent case:

> In the winter of 1863, I was consulted by a young lady from a distant part of the State, on account of a disease from which she had suffered for nearly four years. She had received the advice of many a physician of high and low degree—had worn the ring pessary—the globe pessary—the horseshoe pessary—the double S pessary and the intra-uterine stem pessary—and the common sponge. . . . The patient gave a history of frequent inflammation of the uterus and ovaries, and there appeared to be quite strong adhesions binding the womb in its assumed place. She had had too frequent menstruation—profuse and intolerably painful—frequent and painful micturition [urination].

The physician inserted his "modified" ring pessary and reported that "the patient went to her home after a few weeks entirely relieved from all bad symptoms."[16]

In the last half of the nineteenth century, physicians reported increased incidence of perineal and cervical lacerations and their accompanying gynecological problems, attributed by many observers to increased use of forceps and other interventions in physician-directed deliveries. If it is true that physicians' interventions caused problems for women in this period . . . , it is also the case that physicians became increasingly adept at repairing the problems. The medical journals are filled with case studies of women whose badly managed deliveries had caused them problems, which could then be fixed by superior medical care. . . .

Women who had already had children were more likely than first-time mothers to worry about the possible aftereffects of labor and delivery. They remembered how long it took them the first time to recover from the birth, they remembered how they had suffered, and they were particularly loath to repeat the ordeal. As one woman wrote about her second pregnancy: "I confess I had dreaded it with a dread that every mother must feel in repeating the experience of child-bearing. I could only think that another birth would mean another pitiful struggle of days' duration, followed by months of weakness, as it had been before."[17]

Apart from their concern about resulting death and physical debility, women feared pain and suffering during the confinement itself. They worried about how they would bear up under the pain and stress, how long the confinement might last, and whether trusted people would accompany them through the ordeal. The short hours between being a pregnant woman and becoming a mother seemed, in anticipation, to be interminably long, and they occupied the thoughts and defined the worries of multitudes of women. . . . Surviving a childbirth did not allow women to forget its horrors. Lillie M. Jackson, recalling her 1905 confinement, wrote: "While carrying my baby, I was so miserable. . . . I went down to death's door to bring my son into the world, and I've never forgotten. Some folks say one forgets, and can have them right over again, but today I've not forgotten, and that baby is 36 years old."[18] Too many women shared with Hallie Nelson her feelings upon her first birth: "I began to look forward to the event with dread—if not actual horror." Even after Nelson's successful birth, she "did not forget those awful hours spent in labor."[19]

Regardless of the particular fear that women carried along with their swelling uteruses, the end result was similar for all of them. The prospect of often repeated motherhood promised hardship and anxiety. As Hannah Whitall Smith wrote in her diary in 1852:

> I am very unhappy now. The trial of my womanhood which to me is so very bitter has come upon me again. When my little Ellie is 2 years old she will have a little sister or brother. And this is the end of all my hopes, my pleasing anticipations, my returning youthful joyousness. Well, it is a woman's lot and I must try to become resigned and bear it in patience and *silence* and not make my home unhappy because I am so. But oh, how hard it is.[20]

Many women walked with Hannah Smith under the shadow of maternity, experiencing repeated and agonizing births in unrelenting succession with no relief throughout their fertile years. . . . The childbirth experience was, of course, heavily influenced by cultural and economic conditions, the particular time and place in which women lived, and their socioeconomic class or ethnic group. But much of the meaning of childbirth for women was determined not by the particulars of the event, but by what women shared with each other by virtue of their common biological experience.

With all the horrors and dangers and worries, women could have easily given up hopes of improving their childbirth experiences or their hard domestic prospects. And no doubt some women did merely resign themselves to lives of invalidism and deprivation. But what comes through the written record much more strongly are the positive aspects of the experience that women chose to emphasize, the caring ways in which they tried to help each other, and the simple fact that women were able to change the childbirth experience for themselves in significant ways throughout the nineteenth century.

Let us examine first the cooperative nature of the labor and delivery experience. Throughout American history up until the twentieth century, when childbirth moved to the hospital, most women gave birth at home with the help of their female friends and relatives. . . . When possible, sisters and cousins and mothers came to help the parturient through the ordeal of labor and delivery, and close friends and neighbors joined them around the birthing bed. One woman who described her 1866 confinement wrote: "A woman that was expecting had to take good care that she had plenty fixed to eat for her neighbors when they got there. There was no telling how long they was in for. There wasn't no paying these friends so you had to treat them good." To this women's world, husbands, brothers, or fathers could gain only temporary entrance. In an 1836 account, the new father was invited in to see his wife and new daughter, and then: "But Mrs. Warren, who was absolute in this season of female despotism, interposed, and the happy father was compelled, with reluctant steps, to quit the spot."[21] . . .

Women went to considerable sacrifice to help their birthing relatives and friends, interrupting their lives to travel long distances and frequently staying months before and after delivery to do the household chores. When relatives were not available, neighbors stayed for the labor and delivery and brought food and kept up with washing and other domestic duties. The women's network that developed at least in part through the strong attachments formed across the childbirth bed had long-lasting effects on women's lives. When women had suffered the agonies of watching their friends die, when they had helped a friend recover from a difficult delivery, or when they had participated in a successful birthing they developed a closeness that lasted a lifetime. Surviving life's traumas together made the crises bearable and produced important bonds that continued to sustain other parts of women's lives. "It was as if mothers were members of a sorority and the initiation was to become a mother," Marilyn Clohessy wrote.[22] Nannie Jackson's female support network offers one example of the importance of good friends. Her diary, only one year of which survives, is a litany of friends helping each other. Her best friend was Fannie, who lived one-half mile away; Nannie and Fannie visited each other daily, and sometimes, two, three, and four times a day. Once, during the eighth month of her third pregnancy, Nannie visited her friend three times in one evening and her husband got angry. But, Nannie noted, "I just talk to Fannie & tell her my troubles because it seems to help me to bear it better when she knows about it. I shall tell her whenever I feel like it."[23] Indeed, in this diary fragment, there is evidence of significant rebellion against her husband's wishes and her strong reliance on her relationship with Fannie. When Nannie was confined, Fannie stayed over with her for four nights. But Fannie is only the most important in a long list of close friends. Nannie, who was white, visited daily with many other women, both white and black, cooking special things for them, sharing the limited family resources, helping them with sewing projects, sitting up with them when they were sick, helping out at births, arranging funerals. These women, whose economically limited lives left nothing for outside entertainment or expense, found rich resources within their own group.

Perhaps more significant . . . was the very real support friends could provide during times of crisis. During labor and delivery, when a woman might not be able to stand up for herself she could rely on her women friends to do her talking for her. . . . The collectivity of women gathered around the birthing bed made sure that birth attendants were responsive to their wishes. They made decisions about when and if to call physicians to births that midwives were attending; they gave or withheld permission for physicians' procedures; and they created the atmosphere of female support in a room that might have contained both women and men. The result of women's seeming lack of control over biological imperatives was in fact increased control and the ability to influence events.

The power that the friends had did not necessarily result in better care for the parturient, but it does indicate a level of support that the birthing woman could count on. Dr. E. L. Larkins of Terre Haute, Indiana, believed that pressures from these other birth attendants led physicians to poor practices. "The sympathy of attending friends, coupled with the usual impatience of the woman from her suffering, will too often incite even the physician, against his better judgment, to resort to means to hasten labor, resulting in disaster which time and patience would have avoided."[24] But from the birthing women's point of view, this network of women supporting each other through this difficult ordeal assisted them in getting through a situation in which they felt so powerless. One woman concluded that "the most important thing is not to be left alone and to know that someone is there who cares and will help you when the going gets rough."[25] Through their social network, women were able to keep control over childbirth despite the presence and authority of male physicians.

I cannot quantify my findings to say what percentage of women found the kind of support that Nannie Jackson and others developed. Nor can I determine to what extent these friendship networks might have worked better among the middle classes. I can say that I have found them across class and ethnic lines, in the rural areas and in the cities, in the beginning of the nineteenth century and at its end. I am not positing a universal experience. I'm sure that there were countless women who underwent their severest suffering virtually alone or accompanied only by their husbands, with whom they may not have been able to share their deepest feelings. I understand that unremitting poverty took its toll on many suffering women who could not develop even the outlines of a support network. I think, also, that some rich women stood outside a meaningful network of friends, isolated perhaps by their status and background. But personal accounts of childbirth by women and birth attendants suggest that the birth experience was crucial in creating the social dimensions of most women's lives distinct from other socioeconomic factors. Anita McCormick Blaine, living an affluent life in Chicago at the end of the nineteenth century, shared in many respects the birth experience of Nannie Jackson, living in impoverished rural Arkansas at the same time. They both needed,

sought, and got the help of their close women friends at the crucial time of their confinements. Although it is certainly true that Blaine had more advantages and more choice in the particulars of the birth experience, to both women the female context in which they delivered their babies was crucial to a successful experience. The biological female experience of giving birth provided women with some of their worst moments and some of their best ones, and the good and the bad were experiences that all women could share with each other.

Despite the very real changes in the technical and physical experience of birth during the nineteenth century, women's perceptions of its dangers and methods of dealing with those dangers within a female-centered protective environment remained very much the same during the course of the time that birth remained in women's homes. When birth moved to the hospital for the majority of American women in the twentieth century, women lost their domestic power base and with it lost certain controls that they had traditionally held. This is the change, as I argue elsewhere, that took away women's traditional controls over childbirth and caused a basic transformation in women's birth experiences.[26]

The silver lining in maternity's shadow that accompanied the crisis of childbirth during the home birth period—women actively helping each other shape their childbirth experiences—enabled women to find each other, to learn to give solace and support, and to receive them back in turn. . . . Although the fears and dangers of childbirth followed women, the experience itself opened up new vistas and created practical and emotional bonds beyond the family that sustained them throughout the rest of their lives. Participating together in the function of procreation led women to share with each other some other aspects of their lives in close intimacy. This "female world of love and ritual,"[27] as Carroll Smith-Rosenberg so aptly called it, with its strong emotional and psychological supports and its ability to produce real change in women's lives, was in large part created around women's shared biological moments including repeated confinements and procreative death and debility fears. The valley of the shadow of birth gave women the essence of a good life at the same time it contributed to a strict definition of that life's boundaries. In uniting women, it ultimately provided the ability for women to stretch the boundaries of their world.

NOTES

1. Jane Savine (?) of Warren, Pennsylvania, to Elizabeth Gordon of Cleveland, Ohio, 26 Feb. 1846; see also letter of 10 Mar. 1846, in Elizabeth Gordon Correspondence, Wisconsin State Historical Society Archives, Madison, Wisconsin.

2. *The Holyoke Diaries, 1709–1856*, Introduction and annotations by George Francis Dow (Salem, Mass.: Essex Institute, 1911).

3. Warren C. Sanderson, "Quantitative Aspects of Marriage, Fertility, and Family Limitation in Nineteenth-Century America: Another Application of the Coale Specifications," *Demography* 11 (August 1979): 339–58; Ansley J. Coale and Melvin Zelnik, *New Estimates of Fertility and Population in the United States: A Study of Annual White Births from 1855 to 1960 and of Completeness of Enumeration in the Censuses from 1880 to 1960* (Princeton: Princeton University Press, 1963). . . .

4. Cotton Mather, chap. 53, "Retired Elizabeth: A Long tho' no very Hard, Chapter for A Woman whose Travail approaches with Remedies to Abate the Sorrows of Childbearing" (1710), in *The Angel of Bethesda* (Barre, Mass.: American Antiquarian Society, 1972), pp. 235–48; quotations from p. 237.

5. Margaret Jones Bolsterli, ed., entry for July 1890, in *Vinegar Pie and Chicken Bread: A Woman's Diary of Life in the Rural South, 1890–1891* (Fayetteville: University of Arkansas Press, 1982), p. 38.

6. Clara Clough Lenroot, Journals and Diaries, pt. 1, 1891 to 1929, edited by her daughter, Katherine F. Lenroot, typescript (May 1969) in family hands. . . .

7. James S. Bailey, "Cases Illustrating Some of the Causes of Death Occurring Soon after Childbirth," *New York State Medical Society Transactions*, 1872, pp. 121–29; quotation from p. 121. . . .

8. The use of the figure five births per married woman in the United States is not far off the mark, and may in fact be low, given that the 3.56 recorded average includes only white and mostly native-born women. The Northwestern Mutual Life Insurance Company recorded that of 10,000 applicants for life insurance, "one man in every 17.3 who applied for insurance had a mother or sister or both who died from the immediate effects of childbirth." . . . The quotation is Anne Lesley, in Susan Inches Lesley, *Recollections of My Mother* (Boston: Press of George H. Ellis, 1889), p. 306.

9. Henry Parker Newman, "Prolapse of the Female Pelvic Organs," *Journal of the American Medical Association* 21 (2 Sept. 1893):335.

10. S. D. Gross, "Lacerations of the Female Sexual Organs Consequent upon Parturition: Their Causes and Their Prevention," *Journal of the American Medical Association* 3 (1884):337–38.

11. J. Marion Sims developed the surgical repair of the vesicovaginal fistula through his experiments on slave women in the 1840s; it gathered adherents in the second half of the nineteenth century and relieved many women of their suffering.

12. J. O. Malsbery, "Advice to the Prospective Mother: Assistance during Her Confinement and Care for a Few Days Following," *Journal of the American Medical Association* 28 (15 May 1897):932.

13. Augustus K. Gardner, "On the Use of Pessaries," *Transactions of the American Medical Association* 15 (1865):110.

14. Albina Wight Diary, vol. 11: entries of 20 Aug., 6 and 9 Oct. 1873; 18 Jan. 1874. . . .

15. Gardner, ["Pessaries,"] p. 113.

16. Homer O. Hitchcock, "A Modified Ring Pessary for the Treatment and Cure of Anteflexion and Anteversion of the Uterus," *Transactions of the American Medical Association* 15 (1865):103–06.

17. Agnes Just Reid, *Letters of Long Ago* (Caldwell, Idaho: Caxton Printers, 1936), p. 24.

18. Lillie M. Jackson, *Fanning the Embers* (Boston: Christopher Publishing House, 1966), pp. 90–91.

19. Hallie F. Nelson, *South of the Cottonwood Tree* (Broken Bow, Neb.: Purcells, 1977), p. 173.

20. This diary entry is all the more poignant because it influenced two generations in this family. Hannah Whitall Smith's niece, M. Carey Thomas, found the journal and was so moved by it that she copied it into her own diary in 1878. Marjorie Housepian Dobkin, ed., *The Making of a Feminist: Early Journals and Letters of M. Carey Thomas* (Kent, Ohio: Kent State University Press, 1979). Hannah Smith's diary entry was dated 20 Dec. 1852, and Thomas copied it on 1 Sept. 1878, p. 149.

21. Malinda Jenkins, *Gambler's Wife: The Life of Malinda Jenkins*, as told in conversation to Jessie Lilienthal (Boston: Houghton Mifflin Co., 1933), p. 48; Elizabeth Elton Smith, *The Three Eras of Woman's Life* (New York: Harper & Brothers, 1836), p. 85.

22. Marilyn Clohessy to the author, 9 Sept. 1983, in response to author's query in the *New York Times Book Review*.

23. Entry of 27 June 1890, Bolsterli, p. 35.

24. E. L. Larkins, "Care and Repair of the Female Perineum," *Journal of the American Medical Association* 32 (11 Feb. 1899):284.

25. Clohessy to the author.

26. Discussed in "Alone among Strangers: Childbirth Moves to the Hospital" (Paper delivered at the American Historical Association Annual Meeting, San Francisco, December 1983); and Leavitt, *Brought to Bed: Birthing Women and Their Physicians in America, 1750–1950* (New York: Oxford University Press, 1988).

27. Carroll Smith-Rosenberg, "The Female World of Love and Ritual: Relations between Women in Nineteenth-Century America," *Signs* 1 (1975):1–29.

JAMES C. MOHR
Abortion in America

If we observe nineteenth-century society through women's eyes, surely no statistic was as significant as the one that marked the decline in the average number of children borne by each woman. Childbirth was a time of terror; as James C. Mohr shows, many women sought actively to control the number of times they faced it. When unsuccessful in avoiding pregnancies, they attempted to abort them. The methods of the times were dangerous, but until the 1840s the women were rarely censured by the community if fetal movement had not been felt. The vigorous attack on abortion after 1840 may well have been a response to the growing willingness of married women to attempt it. After 1840 an act that had been dealt with in a biological context was given ideological overtones. What does the debate on abortion policy reveal about public attitudes toward women and their place in the family and in society? How had attitudes changed since Sarah Grosvenor's time? (see pp. 68–81).

ABORTION IN AMERICA
1800–1825

In the absence of any legislation whatsoever on the subject of abortion in the United States in 1800, the legal status of the practice was governed by the traditional British common law as interpreted by the local courts of the new American states. For centuries prior to 1800 the key to the common law's attitude toward abortion had been a phenomenon associated with normal gestation known as quickening. Quickening was the first perception of fetal movement by the pregnant woman herself. Quickening generally occurred near the midpoint of gestation, late in the fourth or early in the fifth month, though it could and still does vary a good deal from one woman to another. The common law did not formally recognize the existence of a fetus in criminal cases until it had quickened. After quickening, the expulsion and destruction of a fetus without due cause was considered a crime, because the fetus itself had manifested some semblance of a separate existence: the ability to move. The crime was

qualitatively different from the destruction of a human being, however, and punished less harshly. Before quickening, actions that had the effect of terminating what turned out to have been an early pregnancy were not considered criminal under the common law in effect in England and the United States in 1800.[1]

Both practical and moral arguments lay behind the quickening distinction. Practically, because no reliable tests for pregnancy existed in the early nineteenth century, quickening alone could confirm with absolute certainty that a woman really was pregnant. Prior to quickening, each of the telltale signs of pregnancy could, at least in theory, be explained in alternative ways by physicians of the day. Hence, either a doctor or a woman herself could take actions designed to restore menstrual flow after one or more missed periods on the assumption that something might be unnaturally "blocking" or "obstructing" her normal cycles, and if left untreated the obstruction would wreak real harm upon the woman. Medically, the procedures for removing a blockage were the same as those for inducing an early abortion. Not until the obstruction moved could either a physician or a woman, regardless of their suspicions, be completely certain that it was a "natural" blockage—a pregnancy—rather than a potentially dangerous situation. Morally, the question of whether or not a fetus was "alive" had been the subject of philosophical and religious debate among honest people for at least 5000 years. The quickening doctrine itself appears to have entered the British common law tradition by way of the tangled disputes of medieval theologians over whether or not an impregnated ovum possessed a soul.[2] The upshot was that American women in 1800 were legally free to attempt to terminate a condition that might turn out to have been a pregnancy until the existence of that pregnancy was incontrovertibly confirmed by the perception of fetal movement.

An ability to suspend one's modern preconceptions and to accept the early nineteenth century on its own terms regarding the distinction between quick and unquick is absolutely crucial to an understanding of the evolution of abortion policy in the United States. However doubtful the notion appears to modern readers, the distinction was virtually universal in America during the early decades of the nineteenth century and accepted in good faith. Perhaps the strongest evidence of the tenacity and universality of the doctrine in the United States was the fact that American courts pointedly sustained the most lenient implications of the quickening doctrine even after the British themselves had abandoned them. . . .

Because women believed themselves to be carrying inert non-beings prior to quickening, a potential for life rather than life itself, and because the common law permitted them to attempt to rid themselves of suspected and unwanted pregnancies up to the point when the potential for life gave a sure sign that it was developing into something actually alive, some American women did practice abortion in the early decades of the nineteenth century. One piece of evidence for this conclusion was the ready access American women had to abortifacient information from 1800 onward. A chief source of such information was the home medical literature of the era.

Home medical manuals characteristically contained abortifacient information in two different sections. One listed in explicit detail a number of procedures that might release "obstructed menses" and the other identified a number of specific things to be avoided in a suspected pregnancy because they were thought to bring on abortion. Americans probably consulted William Buchan's *Domestic Medicine* more frequently than any other home medical guide during the first decades of the nineteenth century.[3] Buchan suggested several courses of action designed to restore menstrual flow if a period was missed. These included bloodletting, bathing, iron and quinine concoctions, and if those failed, "a tea-spoonful of the tincture of black hellebore [a violent purgative] . . . twice aday in a cup of warm water." Four pages later he listed among "the common causes" of abortion "great evacuations [and] vomiting," exactly as would be produced by the treatment he urged for suppressed menses. Later in pregnancy a venturesome, or desperate, woman could try some of the other abortion inducers he ticked off: "violent exercise; raising great weights; reaching too high; jumping, or stepping from an eminence; strokes [strong blows] on the belly; [and] falls."[4] . . .

Like most early abortion material, Buchan's . . . advice harked back to almost primordial or instinctual methods of ending a pregnancy. Bloodletting, for example, was evidently thought to serve as a surrogate period; it was hoped that bleeding from any part of the body might have the same flushing effect upon the womb that menstrual bleeding was known to have. This primitive folk belief lingered long into the nineteenth century, well after bleeding was abandoned as medical therapy in other kinds of cases, and it was common for abortionists as late as the 1870s to pull a tooth as part of their routine.[5] . . .

In addition to home medical guides and health manuals addressed to women, abortions and abortifacient information were also available in the United States from midwives and midwifery texts.[6] . . .

Herbal healers, the so-called Indian doctors, and various other irregular practitioners also helped spread abortifacient information in the United States during the early decades of the nineteenth century. Their surviving pamphlets, of which Peter Smith's 1813 brochure entitled "The Indian Doctor's Dispensary" is an example, contained abortifacient recipes that typically combined the better-known cathartics with native North American ingredients thought to have emmenagogic properties. For "obstructed menses" Smith recommended a concoction he called "Dr. Reeder's chalybeate." The key ingredients were myrrh and aloes, combined with liquor, sugar, vinegar, iron dust, ivy, and Virginia or seneca snakeroot.[7] A sweet-and-sour cocktail like that may or may not have induced abortion, but must certainly have jolted the system of any woman who tried one. . . .

Finally, and most importantly, America's regular physicians, those who had formal medical training either in the United States or in Great Britain or had been apprenticed under a regular doctor, clearly possessed the physiological knowledge and the surgical techniques necessary to terminate a pregnancy by mechanical means. They knew that dilation of the cervix at virtually any stage of gestation would generally bring on uterine contractions that would in turn lead to the expulsion of the contents of the uterus. They knew that any irritation introduced into the uterus would have the same effect. They knew that rupturing the amniotic sac, especially in the middle and later months of pregnancy, would usually also induce contractions and expulsion, regardless of whether the fetus was viable. Indeed, they were taught in their lecture courses and in their textbooks various procedures much more complex than a simple abortion, such as in utero decapitation and fetal pulverization, processes they were instructed to employ in lieu of the even more horribly dangerous Caesarean section. Like the general public, they knew the drugs and herbs most commonly used as abortifacients and emmenagogues, and also like the general public, they believed such preparations to have been frequently effective.[8] . . .

This placed great pressure on physicians to provide what amounted to abortion services early in pregnancy. An unmarried girl who feared herself pregnant, for example, could approach her family doctor and ask to be treated for menstrual blockage. If he hoped to retain the girl and her family as future patients, the physician would have little choice but to accept the girl's assessment of the situation, even if he suspected otherwise. He realized that every member of his profession would testify to the fact that he had no totally reliable means of distinguishing between an early pregnancy, on the one hand, and the amenorrhea that the girl claimed, on the other. Consequently, he treated

for obstruction, which involved exactly the same procedures he would have used to induce an early abortion, and wittingly or unwittingly terminated the pregnancy. Regular physicians were also asked to bring to a safe conclusion abortions that irregulars or women themselves had initiated. . . . And through all of this the physician might bear in mind that he could never be held legally guilty of wrongdoing. No statutes existed anywhere in the United States on the subject of abortion, and the common law . . . considered abortion actionable only after a pregnancy had quickened. No wonder then that Heber C. Kimball, recalling his courtship with a woman he married in 1822, claimed that she had been "taught . . . in our young days, when she got into the family way, to send for a doctor and get rid of the child"; a course that she followed.[9]

In summary, then, the practice of aborting unwanted pregnancies was, if not common, almost certainly not rare in the United States during the first decades of the nineteenth century. A knowledge of various drugs, potions, and techniques was available from home medical guides, from health books for women, from midwives and irregular practitioners, and from trained physicians. Substantial evidence suggests that many American women sought abortions, tried the standard techniques of the day, and no doubt succeeded some proportion of the time in terminating unwanted pregnancies. Moreover, this practice was neither morally nor legally wrong in the eyes of the vast majority of Americans, provided it was accomplished before quickening.

The actual number of abortions in the United States prior to the advent of any statutes regulating its practice simply cannot be known. But an equally significant piece of information about those abortions can be gleaned from the historical record. It concerns the women who were having them. Virtually every observer through the middle of the 1830s believed that an overwhelming percentage of the American women who sought and succeeded in having abortions did so because they feared the social consequences of an illegitimate pregnancy, not because they wanted to limit their fertility per se. The doctor who uncovered the use of snakeroot as an abortifacient, for example, related that in all of the many instances he heard about "it was taken by women who had indulged in illegitimate love. . . ."[10]

In short, abortion was not thought to be a means of family limitation in the United States, at least on any significant scale, through the first third of the nineteenth century. This was hardly surprising in a largely rural and essentially preindustrial society, whose birthrates were exceeding any ever recorded in a European nation.[11] One could, along with medical student [Thomas] Massie, be less than enthusiastic about such an "unnatural" practice as abortion, yet tolerate it as the "recourse . . . of the victim of passion . . . the child of nature" who was driven by "an unrelenting world" unable to forgive any "deviation from what they have termed virtue."[12] Consequently, Americans in the early nineteenth century could and did look the other way when they encountered abortion. Nothing in their medical knowledge or in the rulings of their courts compelled them to do otherwise, and, as Massie indicated, there was considerable compassion for the women involved. It would be nearly midcentury before the perception of who was having abortions for what reasons would begin to shift in the United States, and that shift would prove to be one of the critical developments in the evolution of American abortion policy.

A final point remains to be made about abortion in the United States during the first decades of the nineteenth century. Most observers appeared to consider it relatively safe, at least by the medical standards of the day, rather than extremely dangerous. . . . This too must have reassured women who decided to risk an abortion before quickening. According to the lecture notes of one of his best students, Walter Channing told his Harvard classes that abortion could be troublesome when produced by external blows, because severe internal hemorrhage would be likely, but that generally considered, "abortion [was] not so dangerous as commonly supposed."[13]

The significance of these opinions lay less in whether or not they were accurate than in the fact that writers on abortion, including physicians, saw no reason to stress the dangers attendant to the process. Far from it. They were skeptical about poisons and purgatives, but appear to have assessed physically induced abortions as medically acceptable risks by the standards of the day, especially if brought on during the period of pregnancy when both popular belief and the public courts condoned them anyhow. Here again was a significant

early perception that would later change. That change, like the shift in the perception of who was having abortions for what purposes, would also have an impact on the evolution of American abortion policy. . . .

THE SOCIAL CHARACTER OF ABORTION IN AMERICA 1840–1880

Before 1840 abortion was perceived in the United States primarily as a recourse of the desperate, especially of the young woman in trouble who feared the wrath of an overexacting society. After 1840, however, evidence began to accumulate that the social character of the practice had changed. A high proportion of the women whose abortions contributed to the soaring incidence of that practice in the United States between 1840 and 1880 appeared to be married, native-born, Protestant women, frequently of middle- or upper-class status. The data came from disparate sources, some biased and some not, but in the end proved compelling.

Even before the availability of reliable evidence confirmed that the nation's birthrates were starting to plummet, observers noticed that abortion more and more frequently involved married women rather than single women in trouble. Professor Hugh L. Hodge of the University of Pennsylvania, one of the first physicians in the United States to speak out about abortion in anything approaching a public forum, lectured his introductory obstetrics students in 1839 that abortion was fast becoming a prominent feature of American life. Hodge still considered women trying "to destroy the fruit of illicit pleasure" to be the ones most often seeking abortions, but he alerted his students to the fact that "married women, also, from the fear of labor, from indisposition to have the care, the expense, or the trouble of children, or some other motive" were more and more frequently requesting "that the embryo be destroyed by their medical attendant." Hodge attributed a good deal of this activity to the quickening doctrine, which allowed "women whose moral character is, in other respects, without reproach; mothers who are devoted, with an ardent and self-denying affection, to the children who already constitute[d] their family [to be] perfectly indifferent respecting the foetus in the utero."[14] . . .

Opinion was divided regarding the social status of the women who accounted for the great upsurge of abortion during the middle period of the nineteenth century. While most observers agreed "all classes of society, rich and poor" were involved to some extent, many thought that the middle and upper classes practiced abortion more extensively than the lower classes.[15] The Michigan State Medical Society in 1859 declared that abortion "pervade[d] all ranks" in that state.[16] The Medical Society of Buffalo pointed out that same year "now we have ladies, yes, *educated and refined ladies*" involved as well.[17] On the other hand, court cases revealed at least a sprinkling of lower-class women, servant girls, and the like. . . .

Although the going price for an abortion varied tremendously according to place, time, practitioner, and patient, abortions appear to have been generally quite expensive. Regular physicians testified repeatedly throughout the period that the abortion business was enormously lucrative. Those doctors pledged not to perform abortions bitterly resented men like the Boston botanic indicted for manslaughter in an abortion case in 1851, who posted $8000 bond and returned to his offices, at a time when the average university professor in the United States earned under $2000 per year.[18] . . .

When women turned from regulars to the commercial abortionists, the prices were still not cheap. Itinerants and irregulars generally tried to charge whatever they judged the traffic would bear, which could vary anywhere from $5 to $500. During the 1840s, for example, Madame Restell charged $5 for an initial visit and diagnosis, then negotiated the price of the operation "according to the wealth and liberality of the parties." In a case for which she was indicted in 1846 she asked a young woman about "her beau's circumstances" before quoting a figure, and then tried to get $100 when she found out the man was a reasonably successful manufacturer's representative. The man thought that was too costly, and only after extensive haggling among go-betweens was a $75 fee agreed upon.[19] . . .

Despite the apparent gradual leveling of prices, however, the abortion business remained a profitable commercial venture well into the 1870s. Anthony Comstock, the single-minded leader of a massive anti-obscenity campaign launched in the United States during the 1870s, kept meticulous and extensive records of all of the people he helped arrest while operating as a special agent of the Post Office Department. Between 1872 and 1880 Comstock and his associates aided in the indictment of 55 persons whom Comstock identified as abortionists. The vast majority were very wealthy and posted large bonds with ease. . . .

. . . abortion entered the mainstream of American life during the middle decades of the nineteenth century. While the unmarried and the socially desperate continued to have recourse to it as they had earlier in the century, abortion also became highly visible, much more frequently practiced, and quite common as a means of family limitation among white, Protestant, native-born wives of middle- and upper-class standing. These dramatic changes, in turn, evoked sharp comment from two ideologically opposed groups in American society, each of which either directly or indirectly blamed the other for the shift in abortion patterns. On one side of the debate were the antifeminists, led by regular physicians, and on the other side were the nation's feminists. Both groups agreed that abortion had become a large-scale and socially significant phenomenon in American life, but they disagreed over the reasons why.

Before examining the two chief explanations put forward by contemporaries for the striking shifts in the incidence and the character of abortion in the United States after 1840, two observations may be worth making. First, it is never easy to understand why people do what they do even in the most straightforward of situations; it is nearly impossible to know with certainty the different reasons, rational and irrational, why people in the past might have taken such a psychologically loaded action as the termination of a suspected pregnancy. Second, most participants on both sides of the contemporary debate over why so many American women began to practice abortion after 1840 actually devoted most of their attention to the question of why American women wanted to limit their fertility. This confirmed that abortion was important between 1840 and 1880 primarily as a means of family limitation, but such discussions offer only marginal help in understanding why so many American women turned to abortion itself as a means toward that end.

Cultural anthropologists argue that abortion has been practiced widely and frequently in preindustrial societies at least in part because "it is a woman's method [of limiting fertility] and can be practiced without the man's knowledge."[20] This implies a sort of women's conspiracy to limit population, which would be difficult to demonstrate in the context of nineteenth-century America. Nonetheless, there is some evidence, though it must be considered carefully, to suggest that an American variant of this proposition may have been at least one of the reasons why abortion became such a common form of family limitation in the United States during the period. A number of physicians, as will become evident, certainly believed that one of the keys to the upsurge of abortion was the fact that it was a uniquely female practice, which men could neither control nor prevent. . . .

Earlier in the century observers had alleged that the tract literature and lectures of the women's rights movement advocated family planning and disseminated abortifacient information.[21] In 1859 Harvard professor Walter Channing reported the opinion that "women for whom this office of foeticide, unborn-child-killing, is committed, are *strong-minded*," and no later writer ever accused them of being weak-minded.[22] . . .

The most common variant of the view that abortion was a manifestation of the women's rights movement hinged upon the word "fashion." Over and over men claimed that women who aborted did so because they cared more about scratching for a better perch in society than they did about raising children. They dared not waste time on the latter lest they fall behind in the former. Women, in short, were accused of being aggressively self-indulgent. Some women, for example, had "the effrontery to say boldly, that they have neither the time nor inclination to nurse babies"; others exhibited "self-indulgence in most disgusting forms"; and many of the women practicing abortion were described as more interested in "selfish and personal ends" or "fast living" than in the maternity for which God had supposedly created them.[23] . . . For this reason, some doctors urged that feticide be made a legal ground for divorce.[24] A substantial number of writers between 1840 and 1880, in other words, were willing to portray women who had abortions as domestic subversives. . . .

Notwithstanding the possibility that recourse to abortion sometimes reflected the rising consciousness of the women who had them, and notwithstanding the fact that some males, especially regular physicians, were distinctly uneasy about the practice because of what its ultimate effects upon the social position of women might be, the relationship between abortion and feminism in the nineteenth century nevertheless remained indirect and ironical. This becomes evident when the arguments of the feminists themselves are analyzed. One of the most forceful early statements of what subsequently became the feminist position on abortion was made in the 1850s in a volume entitled *The Unwelcome Child*.[25] The author, Henry C. Wright, asserted that women alone had the right to say when they would become pregnant and blamed the tremendous outburst of abortion in America on selfishly sensual husbands. Wright's volume was more interesting than other similar tracts, however, because he published a large number of letters from women detailing the circumstances under which they had sought abortions.

One of Wright's letters was from a woman who had her first abortion in 1841, because her one-year-old firstborn was sick and her husband was earning almost nothing. She "consulted a lady friend, and by her persuasion and assistance, killed" the fetus she was carrying. When she found herself pregnant again shortly thereafter she "consulted a physician. . . . He was ready with his logic, his medicines and instruments, and told me how to destroy it. After experimenting on myself three months, I was successful. I killed my child about five months after conception." She steeled herself to go full term with her next pregnancy and to "endure" an addition to her impoverished and unhappy household. When pregnant again she "employed a doctor, to kill my child, and in the destruction of it . . . ended my power to be a mother." The woman's point throughout, however, was that abortion "was most repulsive" to her and her recourse to it "rendered [her] an object of loathing to [her]self." Abortion was not a purposeful female conspiracy, but an undesirable necessity forced by thoughtless men. As this woman put it: "I was the veriest slave alive."[26] . . .

The attitudes expressed by Wright's correspondents in the 1840s and 1850s became the basis of the official position of American feminists toward abortion after the Civil War. As

Elizabeth Cady Stanton phrased it, the practice was one more result of "the degradation of woman" in the nineteenth century, not of woman's rising consciousness or expanding opportunities outside the home.[27] . . . The remedy to the problem of abortion in the United States, in their view, was not legalized abortion open to all but *"the education and enfranchisement of women"* which would make abortion unnecessary in a future world of egalitarian respect and sexual discretion.[28] In short, most feminists, though they agreed completely with other observers that abortion was endemic in America by midcentury, did not blame the increase on the rising ambitions of women but asserted with Matilda E. J. Gage "that this crime of 'child murder,' 'abortion,' 'infanticide,' lies at the door of the male sex."[29] The *Woman's Advocate* of Dayton, Ohio, put it even more forcefully in 1869: "Till men learn to check their sensualism, and leave their wives free to choose their periods of maternity, let us hear no more invectives against women for the destruction of prospective unwelcome children, whose dispositions, made miserable by unhappy ante-natal conditions, would only make their lives a curse to themselves and others."[30] . . .

Despite the blame and recrimination evoked by the great upsurge of abortion in the United States in the nineteenth century, some of which was directed at women and some at men, it appears likely that most decisions to use abortion probably involved couples conferring together, not just men imposing their wills or women acting unilaterally, and that abortion was the result of diffuse pressures, not merely the rising consciousness of women or the tyrannical aggressions of men. American men and women wanted to express their sexuality and mutual affections, on the one hand, and to limit their fertility, on the other. Abortion was neither desirable nor undesirable in itself, but rather one of the few available means of reconciling and realizing those two higher priorities. And it seems likely that the man and woman agreed to both of those higher priorities in most instances, thus somewhat mooting in advance the question of which one was more responsible for the decisions that made abortion a common phenomenon in mid-nineteenth-century America.[31]

Court records provide one source of evidence for the mutuality of most abortion decisions. Almost every nineteenth-century abortion case that was written up, whether in the popular press, in medical journals, or in the official proceedings of state supreme courts, involved the agreement of both the man and the woman. There is no record of any man ever having sued any woman for aborting his child. . . .

Perhaps the best evidence for the likely mutuality of most abortion decisions is contained in the diary that Lester Frank Ward, who later became one of America's most famous sociologists, kept as a newlywed in the 1860s. Though Ward was unique in writing down the intimate decisions that he and his wife had to make, the couple seemed otherwise typical young Americans, almost as Tocqueville might have described them, anxious for further education and ambitious to get ahead quickly. Both Ward and his wife understood that a child would overburden their limited resources and reduce the probability of ever realizing either their individual goals of self-improvement or their mutual goals as a couple. They avoided pregnancy in pre-marital intercourse, then continued to avoid it after their marriage in August 1862. Not until early in 1864 did Lizzie Ward become pregnant. In March, without consulting her husband, she obtained "an effective remedy" from a local woman, which made her very sick for two days but helped her to terminate her pregnancy. She probably took this action after missing three or four periods; it was still early enough in gestation that her husband did not realize she was pregnant but late enough that lactation had begun. Ward noted in his diary that "the proof" she had been pregnant was "the milk" that appeared after the abortion.[32]

Anti-feminists might have portrayed Lizzie Ward's action as diabolical, a betrayal of duty. Feminists might have viewed it as the only recourse open to a female who wanted both to further her own education and to remain on good terms with an ambitious spouse who would certainly have sacrificed his wife's goals to child-rearing, while he pursued his own. But the decision was really the result of a pre-existing consensus between the two of them. Though Ward had not been party to the process in a legal or direct sense, which may go some distance toward confirming the role of abortion as a more uniquely female method of family limitation than contraception, he was clearly delighted that his wife was "out of danger" and would not be having a child. After this brush with family responsibility, the Wards tried a number of new methods of contraception, which they presumably hoped would be more effective than whatever they had been using to avoid pregnancy before Lizzie had to resort to abortion. These included both "pills" and "instruments." Not until the summer of 1865, after Ward had obtained a decent job in Washington, did the couple have a baby.[33]

Abortion had been for the Wards what it apparently also was for many other American couples: an acceptable means toward a mutually desirable end, one of the only ways they had to allow themselves both to express their sexuality and affection toward each other with some degree of frequency and to postpone family responsibilities until they thought they were better prepared to raise children. The line of acceptability for most Americans trying to reconcile these twin priorities ran just about where Lizzie Ward had drawn it. Infanticide, the destruction of a baby after its birth, was clearly unacceptable, and so was abortion after quickening, though that was a much grayer area than infanticide. But abortion before quickening, like contraception itself, was an appropriate and legally permissible method of avoiding unwanted children. And it had one great advantage, as the Wards learned, over contraception: it worked. As more and more women began to practice abortion, however, and as the practice changed from being invisible to being visible, from being quantitatively insignificant to being a systematic practice that terminated a substantial number of pregnancies after 1840, and from being almost entirely a recourse of the desperate and the socially marginal to being a commonly employed procedure among the middle and upper classes of American society, state legislators decided to reassess their policies toward the practice. Between 1840 and 1860 law-makers in several states began to respond to the increase of abortion in American life.

NOTES

1. The quickening doctrine went back to the thirteenth century in England.... On quickening in the common law see Cyril C. Means, Jr., "The Law of New York concerning Abortion and the Status of the Foetus, 1664–1968: A Case of Cessation of Constitutionality," *New York Law Forum* XIV, no. 3 (Fall 1968): 419–426.

2. Ibid., pp. 411–19, and John T. Noonan, Jr., "An Almost Absolute Value in History," in John T. Noonan, Jr., ed., *The Morality of Abortion* (Cambridge, Mass., 1970), pp. 1–59....

3. ... Buchan's volume was published in Philadelphia as early as 1782, where it went through many editions.... This remarkably successful book continued to be reprinted in America through 1850.

4. Buchan, *Domestic Medicine,* pp. 400, 403–4.

5. See, for example, Frederick Hollick, *Diseases of Women, Their Causes and Cure Familiarly Explained: With Practical Hints for Their Prevention, and for the Preservation of Female Health: For Every Female's Private Use* (New York, 1849), p. 150....

6. ... [See] George Ellington, *The Women of New York, or the Under-World of the Great City* (New York, 1869), pp. 399–400.

7. Peter Smith, "The Indian Doctor's Dispensary, Being Father Peter Smith's Advice Respecting Diseases and Their Cure; Consisting of Prescriptions for Many Complaints: And a Description of Medicines, Simple and Compound, Showing Their Virtues and How to Apply Them," [1813] reproduced in J. U. Lloyd, ed., *Bulletin of the Lloyd Library of Botany, Pharmacy and Materia Medica* (1901), Bull. #2, Reproduction Series #2, pp. 46–47.

8. John Burns, *Observations on Abortion: Containing an Account of the Manner in Which It Takes Place, the Causes Which Produce It, and the Method of Preventing or Treating It* (Troy, N.Y., 1808), pp. 73–81....

9. Heber C. Kimball in the *Journal of Discourses,* 26 vols. (Liverpool, 1857), V:91–92.

10. Thomas Massie, "An Experimental Inquiry into the Properties of the Polygala Senega," in Charles Caldwell, ed., *Medical Theses,* ... (Philadelphia, 1806), p. 203.

11. ... William Petersen's widely used *Population* (New York, 3rd ed., 1975), p. 15, labels [the U.S. population from 1800 to 1830 as] the "underdeveloped" type and identifies its characteristics as a mixed economy, high fertility rates, falling mortality rates, and very high rates of population growth.

12. Massie, "Polygala Senega," p. 204.

13. John G. Metcalf, student notebooks written while attending Dr. Walter Channing's lectures of midwifery at Harvard Medical School, 1825–1826 (Countway Library, Harvard Medical School), entry for Dec. 27, 1825....

14. Hugh L. Hodge in Francis Wharton and Moreton Stillé, *Treatise on Medical Jurisprudence* (Philadelphia, 1855), p. 270.

15. "Report on Criminal Abortion," *Transactions of the American Medical Association* XII (1859):75.

16. E. P. Christian, "Report to the State Medical Society on Criminal Abortions," *Peninsular & Independent Medical Journal* II:135.

17. "Criminal Abortions," *Buffalo Medical Journal and Monthly Review* XIV (1859):249.

18. *Boston Medical and Surgical Journal* XLIV, no. 14 (May 7, 1851):288.... Worthington Hooker, *Physician and Patient* ... (New York, 1849), passim, and especially pp. 405–8. The estimate on income is from Colin B. Burke, "The Quiet Influence" (Ph.D. diss,

Washington University of St. Louis, 1973):69, Table 2.19.

19. A Physician of New-York, *Trial of Madame Restell, For Producing Abortion on the Person of Maria Bodine, . . .* (New York, 1847), pp. 3–4, 10.

20. Kingsley Davis and Judith Blake, "Social Structure and Fertility: An Analytical Framework," *Economic Development and Cultural Change* IV, no. 3 (April 1956):230.

21. Hooker, *Physician and Patient*, p. 93; James Reed, *From Private Vice to Public Virtue: The Birth Control Movement and American Society since 1830* (New York, 1978), chaps. 1–5.

22. Walter Channing, "Effects of Criminal Abortion," *Boston Medical and Surgical Journal* LX (Mar. 17, 1859):135.

23. E. M. Buckingham, "Criminal Abortion," *Cincinnati Lancet & Observer* X (Mar. 1867):141; Channing, "Effects of Criminal Abortion," p. 135; J. C. Stone, "Report on the Subject of Criminal Abortion," *Transactions of the Iowa State Medical Society* I (1867):29; J. Miller, "Criminal Abortion," *The Kansas City Medical Record* I (Aug. 1884):296.

24. [See] H. Gibbons, Sr., "On Feticide," *Pacific Medical and Surgical Journal* (San Francisco) XXI, no. 3 (Aug. 1879): 97–111; . . .

25. Henry C. Wright, *The Unwelcome Child; or, the Crime of an Undesigned and Undesired Maternity* (Boston, 1860). The volume was copyrighted in 1858.

26. Ibid., pp. 65–69.

27. E[lizabeth] C[ady] S[tanton], "Infanticide and Prostitution," *Revolution* I, no. 5 (Feb. 5, 1868):65.

28. Ibid. For the same point reiterated see "Child Murder," in ibid. I, no. 10 (Mar. 12, 1868):146–47. . . .

29. Ibid. I, no. 14 (Apr. 9, 1868):215–16.

30. E. V. B., "Restellism, and the N.Y. Medical Gazette," *Woman's Advocate* (Dayton, Ohio) I, no. 20 (Apr. 8, 1869):16. . . .

31. Carl N. Degler is one of those who have argued persuasively that nineteenth-century American women were very much aware of their own sexuality and desirous, morality books notwithstanding, of expressing it: "What Ought To Be and What Was: Women's Sexuality in the Nineteenth Century," *American Historial Review* LXXIX, no. 5 (Dec. 1974):1467–90.

32. Lester Ward, *Young Ward's Diary*, Bernhard J. Stern, ed. (New York, 1935), p. 140.

33. Ibid., pp. 150, 152–53, 174.

DOCUMENT: *Married Women's Property Acts*

Keziah Kendall, "What I have suffered, I cannot tell you"

We know nothing more about "Keziah Kendall" than what she revealed in this letter, which historians Dianne Avery and Alfred S. Konefsky discovered among the papers of Simon Greenleaf, a prominent Harvard law professor. It has not been possible to locate the author in the usual places—tax lists, land records, church lists—but whether the name is real or fictional, the issues addressed in the letter are authentic. "Kendall" had been dismayed by what she heard when she attended a public lyceum lecture on women's rights given by Greenleaf early in 1839. At a time when the legal disabilities of inherited common law were increasingly being questioned—in Massachusetts, the abolitionists Sarah and Angelina Grimke had only recently delivered a forthright series of lectures on the rights of women—Greenleaf devoted his lecture to the claim that American women were well protected by American law as it stood. He argued that excluding women from politics saved society from "uproar" and impropriety; that constraints on married women's use of their property was merely a technicality because in a happy marriage all property became part of "a common fund . . . it can make but little difference . . . by whose name it is called." And he insisted that except for "restriction in *political* matters" there were no significant "distinctions between the legal rights of unmarried women, and of men."

"Keziah Kendall" was unpersuaded. The farm that she and her sisters inherited was a substantial one; she and her sisters were wealthy rural women. Describing her own anxieties as the older sister of a flighty girl and her own tragic ordeal as the fiancée of a man with high ethical commitments, "Kendall" demanded that Greenleaf offer another lecture, acknowledging the "legal wrongs" of women.

What are "Kendall's" objections to the law as she experienced it? What connections does she draw between paying taxes, voting, and officeholding? Why does she blame Massachusetts property law for her fiancé's death? Why is she worried about her sister's forthcoming marriage?

Keziah Kendall to Simon Greenleaf   [1839?]
I take the liberty to write to you on the subject of the Lyceum lecture you delivered last Feb. but as you are not acquainted with me I think I will introduce myself. My name is Kezia Ken-dall. I live not many miles from Cambridge, on a farm with two sisters, one older, one younger than myself. I am thirty two. Our parents and only brother are dead—we have a good es-tate—comfortable house—nice barn, garden,

Excerpted from Dianne Avery and Alfred S. Konefsky, "The Daughters of Job: Property Rights and Women's Lives in Mid-Nineteenth-Century Massachusetts," *Law and History Review* X (Fall 1992):323–56. This essay is dedicated to the memory of Mary Joe Frug. Notes have been edited and renumbered.

orchard &c and money in the bank besides. Jemima is a very good manager in the house, keeps everything comfortable—sees that the milk is nicely prepared for market—looks after everything herself, and rises before day, winter and summer,—but she never had any head for figures, and always expects me to keep all accounts, and attend to all business concerns. Keranhappuck, (who is called Kerry) is quite young, only nineteen, and as she was a little girl when mother died, we've always petted her, and let her do as she pleased, and now she's courted. Under these circumstances the whole responsibility of our property, not less than twenty five thousand dollars rests upon me. I am not over fond of money, but I have worked hard ever since I was a little girl, and tried to do all in my power to help earn, and help save, and it would be strange if I did not think more of it than those who never earned anything, and never saved anything they could get to spend, and you know Sir, there are many such girls nowadays. Well—our milkman brought word when he came from market that you were a going to lecture on the legal rights of women, and so I thought I would go and learn. Now I hope you wont think me bold when I say, I did not like that lecture much. I dont speak of the manner, it was pretty spoken enough, but there was nothing in it but what every body knows. We all know about a widow's thirds,[1] and we all know that a man must maintain his wife, and we all know that he must pay her debts, if she has any—but I never heard of a yankee woman marrying in debt. What I wanted to know, was good reasons for some of those laws that I cant account for. I do hope if you are ever to lecture at the Lyceum again, that you will give us some. I must tell my story to make you understand what I mean. One Lyceum lecture that I heard in C. stated that the Americans went to war with the British, because they were taxed without being represented in Parliament. Now we are taxed every year to the full amount of every dollar we possess—town, county, state taxes—taxes for land, for movables, for money and all. Now I dont want to go representative or any thing else, any more than I do to be a "constable or a sheriff," but I have no voice about public improvements, and I dont see the justice of being taxed any more than the "revolutionary heroes" did. You mention that woman here, are not treated like heathen and Indian women—

we know that—nor do I think we are treated as Christian women ought to be, according to the Bible rule of doing to others as you would others should do unto you. I am told (not by you) that if a woman dies a week after she's married that her husband takes all her personal property and the use of her real estate as long as he lives[2]—if a man dies his wife can have her thirds—*this* does not come up to the Gospel rule. Now the young fellow that is engaged to our Kerry, is a pleasant clever fellow, but he is not quite one and twenty, and I dont s'pose he ever earned a coat in his life. Uncle told me there was a way for a woman to have her property trustee'd,[3] and I told it to Kerry—but she, poor girl has romantic notions owing to reading too many novels,[4] and when I told her of it, she would not hear of such a thing—"What take the law to keep my property away from James before I marry him—if it was a million of dollars he should have it all." So you see I think the law is in fault here—to tell you the truth I do not think young men are near so careful about getting in debt as girls, and I have known more than one that used their wife's money to pay off old scores. . . . I had rather go to my mantua maker[5] to borrow twenty dollars if I needed it, than to the richest married woman I know.

Another thing I have to tell you—when I was young I had a lover, Jos. Thompson, he went into business in a neighboring town, and after a year or two while I was getting the wedding things—Joe failed, he met with misfortunes that he did not expect,—he could have concealed it from me and married, but he did not—he was honorable, and so we delayed. He lived along here two or three years, and tried all he could to settle with his creditors, but some were stiff and held out, and thought by and by we would marry, and they should get my property. Uncle said he knew if we were married, there were those who would take my cattle and the improvement of my land. Joseph used to visit me often those years, but he lost his spirits and he could not get into business again, and he thought he must go to sea. I begged him not to, and told him we should be able to manage things in time, but he said no— he must try his luck, and at least get enough to settle off old scores, and then he would come here and live and we would make the best of what I had. We parted—but it pleased God he should be lost at sea. What I have suffered, I cannot tell you. Now Joe was no sailor when I engaged with him, and if it had been a thing known that I should always have a right to keep possession of my own, he need never have gone to sea, and we might have lived happily together, and in time with industry and economy, he might have paid off all. I am one that cant be convinced without better reasons than I have heard of, that woman are dealt with by the "gospel rule." There is more might than right in such laws as far as I can see—if you see differently, do tell us next time you lecture. Another thing—you made some reflections upon women following the Anti's. . . . Women have joined the Antislavery societies, and why? women are kept for slaves as well as men—it is a common cause, deny the justice of it, who can! To be sure I do not wish to go about lecturing like the Misses Grimkie, but I have not the knowledge they have, and I verily believe that if I had been brought up among slaves as they were, and knew all that they know, and felt a call from humanity to speak, I should run the venture of your displeasure, and that of a good many others like you.[6] I told Uncle that I thought your lecture was a onesided thing— and he said, "why Keziah, Squire Greenleaf is an advocate, not a judge, you must get him to take t'other side next time." Now I have taken this opportunity to ask you to give us a remedy for the "legal wrongs" of women, whenever you have a chance. The fathers of the land should look to these things—who knows but your daughter may be placed in the sad situation I am in, or the dangerous one Kerry is in. I hear you are a good man, to make it certain— do all the good you can, and justify no wrong thing.

Yours with regard
Keziah Kendall.

NOTES

1. She is, of course, referring to a widow's dower rights. (See "The Law of Domestic Relations" p. 564.)

2. ["Kendall"] was correct in her understanding of a husband's rights in his wife's personal property if she should die as early as "a week after she's married." But under the common law he would not inherit a life interest in her real estate unless they were parents of a child.

3. This is a reference to the equitable device of placing the woman's property in a trust before marriage for the purpose of avoiding the husband's common law rights in her property as well as protecting it from the husband's creditors. Under the trust agreement, the trustee would be obligated to manage the property for the benefit of the married woman.

4. ["Kendall"] shared a widely held distrust of romantic novels.

5. In the early republic, mantua makers [i.e., skilled dressmakers] were often economically independent women.

6. ["Kendall"] is probably referring here to the "Pastoral Letter" issued by the Congregationalist ministers in the summer of 1837 denouncing the public lecturing of the Grimke sisters.

JUDITH WELLMAN

The Seneca Falls Women's Rights Convention: A Study of Social Networks

---

As Keziah Kendall's words suggest, many people in the 1830s and 1840s had begun to criticize the way American law and custom defined gender relations. The 1848 *Declaration of Sentiments* (see p. 567) gathered scattered complaints into a manifesto and offered an

Excerpted from "The Seneca Falls Women's Rights Convention: A Study of Social Networks" by Judith Wellman in *Journal of Women's History* 3 (1991):9–37. Copyright © 1991 by the *Journal of Women's History*. Reprinted by permission of the author and publisher. Notes have been edited and renumbered.

agenda for change that would shape a women's rights movement for at least three-quarters of a century. But the *Declaration* itself has its own history, emerging out of specific social conditions in western New York state, out of political and religious arguments, and out of the personal experiences of the men and women who wrote its words and signed their names to it.

Judith Wellman traces the immediate history of the Seneca Falls Convention. Her careful research has enabled her to tell us the class position, religious affiliation, kin relations, and political sympathies of many of the signers. Although the initiative and imagination of Elizabeth Cady Stanton herself does much to account for the form of the final document, what other elements help explain the timing and content of the Seneca Falls Convention and the *Declaration*? Note the participation of Daniel Anthony, whose daughter, Susan, would soon become Stanton's colleague in women's rights activism. That partnership would last all their lives.

How many of the political demands of the *Declaration* can be connected to public political issues already being debated in the state legislature and in political parties? How was the recruitment to the convention shaped by arguments within local churches? Why did the authors of the *Declaration* adopt the rhetoric of the era of the American Revolution, two generations before their time?

Shortly after 11:00 A.M. on the bright, sunlit morning of July 19, 1848, Elizabeth Cady Stanton walked to the front of the Wesleyan Chapel in Seneca Falls, New York. The time had come to take public action, to inaugurate, as Stanton later recalled, "the greatest rebellion the world has ever seen." She was so nervous, she remembered, that she "wanted to abandon all her principles" and run away. But she did not, and the first women's rights convention of modern North America began.[1]

For the next two days, perhaps three hundred people met in the Wesleyan Chapel to discuss not only the "social, civil, and religious condition and rights of woman" but also women's political rights, especially the right to vote. When the meeting was over, one hundred people (sixty-eight women and thirty-two men) had signed the Declaration of Sentiments, which was patterned after the Declaration of Independence, and asserted "that all men and women are created equal; they they are endowed by their Creator with certain inalienable rights; that among these are life, liberty, and the pursuit of happiness. . . ." Just as the colonists had brought charges against King George, so the signers at Seneca Falls brought charges against the men of America, against an establishment that legitimized male authority, denied women political rights (including the right to vote), gave husbands the power even to beat their wives, discriminated against women in

employment, education, and property ownership, and took from women a sense of self-respect and of confidence in their own abilities.[2]

By using the Declaration of Independence as their model, women's rights advocates at Seneca Falls drew immediate public attention to their cause, and they initiated a new, activist phase of the women's rights movement. As the historian Ellen Carol DuBois has argued, "For many years before 1848, American women had manifested considerable discontent with their lot. . . . Yet women's discontent remained unexamined, implicit, and above all, disorganized. . . . The women's rights movement crystallized these sentiments into a feminist politics . . . [and] began a new phase in the history of feminism." . . .[3]

This is the story of the one hundred signers of the Declaration of Sentiments. Who were they? And why did they sign a document that they agreed was "of the kind called radical"? . . .[4]

In 1888, Frederick Douglass, then editor of the *North Star* in Rochester, New York, and himself one of the signers, provided us a clue . . . at the fortieth anniversary of the convention, held by the International Council of Women in Washington, D.C.; [he said]

Then who were we, for I count myself in, who did this thing? We were few in numbers, moderate in resources, and very little known in the world. The most that we had to commend us, was a firm conviction that we were in the right, and a firm faith that the right must ultimately prevail.[5]

For Douglass, it was shared values rather than a shared relationship to material resources that brought these women's rights advocates together at Seneca Falls. One value, that of equality, was central to all of their lives. "All men and women are created equal," they had affirmed. So we might hypothesize that the networks that linked the signers would reflect egalitarian values. . . .[6]

. . . [T]hose who signed the Seneca Falls Declaration of Sentiments were . . . very ordinary people. Only five of them—Frederick Douglass, Lucretia and James Mott, Martha Wright, and Stanton herself—ever became figures of national importance. Why did these relatively obscure people take such an early and unequivocal stand for women's rights? . . .

Beyond the simple act of signing the Declaration of Sentiments itself, few of these signers left any record of what shaped and sustained their egalitarian ideals. They did, however, leave imprints of their basic values on the social institutions in which they lived out their daily lives. . . .

. . . [T]hree major reform organizations linked these signers into value-oriented networks long before they knew about the Seneca Falls convention. These networks were composed of (1) legal reformers, who worked to implement the right of married women to own property and who also raised the question of political rights for women; (2) political abolitionists, who helped form the emerging Free Soil party; and (3) Quaker abolitionists, who supported Garrisonian abolitionism. . . .

Three networks, three events, three concerns. How did these develop? How did they coalesce in the summer of 1848 to motivate one hundred people to sign the Seneca Falls Declaration of Sentiments? . . .

ELIZABETH CADY STANTON

Elizabeth Cady Stanton was clearly the main organizer of the convention, and understanding her own story is key to understanding why the convention occurred in the first place. . . .

Three months before Stanton's eleventh birthday, in August 1826, her oldest brother, Eleazer, came home from Union College to die.

Three more brothers died in infancy or early childhood, leaving Stanton's parents—Daniel and Margaret Cady—with six girls but no living sons. Daniel Cady never fully recovered, and he rebuffed Elizabeth's efforts to be as good as the sons he had lost. "I taxed every power," she remembered in her autobiography, "hoping some day to hear my father say: 'Well, a girl is as good as a boy, after all.' But he never said it."[7]

A few months later, Elizabeth's sister, Tryphena, married Edward Bayard, and the newly wedded couple became surrogate parents for the remaining Cady children. Edward and his brother, Henry, studied law with Daniel Cady, Elizabeth's father, and she began to spend much of her time in her father's law office. With the revision of New York State's laws in 1828, the legal position of married women was suddenly clouded with doubt, and Daniel Cady's law students liked to tease Elizabeth about her powerlessness under the law. Contacts she made in her father's office would connect her with a significant network of legal reformers.

As she grew, Stanton began to spend considerable time with her cousin and his wife, Gerrit and Nancy Smith, at their home in Peterboro, New York. . . . One of the most famous was Henry B. Stanton, abolitionist orator and organizer. Against her father's wishes, Elizabeth married Henry in May 1840. Through Gerrit Smith and Henry Stanton, Elizabeth made important contacts among a second major network, that of political abolitionists.

On their honeymoon, Elizabeth and Henry attended the World Anti-Slavery convention in London. By refusing to seat women delegates, antislavery males unwittingly transformed their meeting into an episode in the development of the women's rights movement. As Stanton recalled:

> The action of this convention was the topic of discussion, in public and private, for a long time, and . . . gave rise to the movement for women's political equality both in England and the United States. As the convention adjourned, the remark was heard on all sides, "It is about time some demand was made for new liberties for women."[8]

Most important for Stanton was her introduction to Lucretia Mott and the circle of Quaker abolitionist women from Philadelphia. As an older woman, an abolitionist, and an accomplished public speaker, Mott represented "a new world of thought" to Stanton. She also connected Stanton to another wing of the antislavery movement, those who emphasized not political action but moral suasion. Often called Garrisonians after William Lloyd Garrison, perhaps the most vocal proponent of this view, these abolitionists embraced total equality for all people, "the *equal brotherhood* of the entire Human Family, without distinction of color, sex, or clime." It may have been in London that Elizabeth began to call herself a Garrisonian. Shortly afterward, she began to subscribe to the *Liberator*, Garrison's newspaper, and she continued to do so, in her own name, until the paper went out of existence.[9]

In 1840, just before the London meeting, political abolitionists had split with moral suasionist Garrisonians at the annual meeting of the American Anti-Slavery Society. They were never to be reconciled. Stanton, however, would maintain strong ties with both groups— with the political abolitionists through her husband, Henry, and her cousin, Gerrit Smith, and with the moral suasionists through her new mentor, Lucretia Mott.

All three of these networks—the legal reformers Stanton had met through her father's law office, the political abolitionists she knew so well through her husband, and the Garrisonian abolitionists that she herself belonged to and that she had come to know through Mott— came together in Stanton's life in the summer of 1848.

Stanton would be ready to take public action with these three networks in 1848, in part because of deeply disturbing events in her own personal life. Stanton had moved to Seneca Falls from Boston, and the change was both dramatic and depressing. With her husband almost always away from home, she struggled to maintain herself and her three rambunctious sons with little household help. Their house was on the outskirts of the village, in an Irish working-class neighborhood, overlooking the Seneca Turnpike, the Seneca and Cayuga Canal, and the mills along the Seneca River. Her life was made even more difficult when her children and servants all developed malaria. As she recalled, "Cleanliness, order, the love of the beautiful and artistic, all faded away in the struggle to accomplish what was absolutely necessary from hour to hour." . . . Increasingly frustrated, increasingly angry, Stanton tried to make sense of her feelings. She thought about

cooperative housekeeping and about the advantages of Fourierist communities. . . . [She probably] suffered either a miscarriage or a still birth. . . . She was a woman in a state of siege.[10] At that critical point in her life, events outside her control would rouse her neighbors to organized action. The passage of the Married Women's Property Act in April 1848, the formation of the Free-Soil party, and the organization of dissident Quakers into the Congregational Friends in June 1848 set the stage to help Stanton transform her personal problems into political action through a convention for the rights of women.

BACKGROUND INFLUENCES

Although national in its impact, the Seneca Falls convention was local in its origins. Of the eighty-three known signers, 69 percent of them came either from Seneca Falls or the neighboring town of Waterloo. So many people attended the convention from Waterloo, in fact, that one newspaper called the meeting the "Waterloo Female Convention." A few people came from other townships in Seneca County, and a few more arrived from as far away as Rochester (forty miles west of Seneca Falls), Wayne County (just north of Seneca Falls), or Syracuse (forty miles east). Only three came from farther distances, and these were all on visits to relatives in central New York.[11]

In the 1840s, upstate New York, like the whole northeastern United States, was changing rapidly. Both Seneca Falls and Waterloo . . . lay on the country's major east–west transportation route, developed first as the Seneca Turnpike, then as the Erie Canal (connected to Seneca County by the Seneca and Cayuga Canal), and finally as a major rail route. Local industries epitomized the early industrial revolution. The 43-foot waterfall from which Seneca Falls took its name provided abundant waterpower for mills and factories. Four miles west, Waterloo's woolen factory sustained production from the mid-1830s.

By the 1840s, Seneca Falls found itself economically in transition. Strongly affected by the depression of 1837, the town lost its older economy, which was based on milling local wheat into flour for eastern markets, as wheat production moved farther west. Local entrepreneurs had begun to manufacture both pumps and textiles, but these industries would not provide a dependable economic base until the 1850s.

Economic change eroded stable social institutions and challenged basic values of community cohesion. At the same time, it offered opportunities. On the one hand, signers of the Declaration of Sentiments were secure enough in their basic economic, social, and cultural positions to be willing to take risks. On the other hand, they found themselves on the shifting sands of change, where risk was not only possible but necessary. A complex mix—different for different signers—of personal characteristics, economic status, and family patterns set the stage for the involvement of these individuals in reform. By themselves, these elements do not explain why the signers became women's rights activists. They did, however, provide a context that promoted the growth of women's rights activism.[12]

Gender, for example, was an important variable but not a definitive one. Two-thirds of the signers were women. Whether or not men should sign the Declaration of Sentiments was, in fact, one of only two topics that occasioned disagreement at the convention.[13] . . .

Age did not link the signers, who ranged from fourteen-year-old Susan Quinn, the youngest signer, to sixty-eight-year-old George W. Pryor, the oldest. Their mean age was 38.7 years old.[14]

Ethnicity, race, and place of birth were also contributing but not defining factors. In race and ethnicity, the majority of signers reflected the majority of the surrounding population: they were native-born European Americans. Only one known signer, Frederick Douglass, was African American. Only one, Susan Quinn, was of Irish descent. Most had been born in New York State, New England, or Pennsylvania.[15]

Wealth, too, provided a context but not a cause for reform. According to the 1850 census, signers' families did, on average, own more property than did nonsigners' families. Variation among signers' families was so great, however, that wealth alone does not adequately distinguish the signers from the ordinary population. Excluding the four richest signatories from our calculations, the average value of property held by signers' families was $2,051. The average value of property held by non-signing families in Seneca Falls and Waterloo, in contrast, was $1,117. (Seneca Falls had by far

the lowest average amount of property ownership, with $869 per family, compared to $2,915 in Waterloo. . . .[16]

Occupations also provide clues about the relationship of signers to one another and to a new economic order. . . . Those who worked in manufacturing certainly had to confront directly the possibility of dramatic changes in the way they earned their living. In fact, 39.6 percent of signers lived in households that derived their main income from manufacturing. Only 30.2 percent were involved in farming and 30.2 percent in services or trade. In Seneca Falls, most signers (55.2 percent) lived in manufacturing households. . . .[17]

Other signers, although they listed their occupations as farmers or as professionals, derived at least part of their income from industrialization. Richard P. Hunt, for example, told the census taker that he was a farmer. He did, indeed, own several farms in Waterloo, but he was also the major investor in the Waterloo woolen factory and one of the owners of Waterloo's main business district. Elisha Foote, a lawyer, specialized in patent law and himself held several patents. . . .[18]

Family networks give us another important clue about the relationship of these signers to other people. Almost half the identifiable signers (and perhaps almost two-thirds of the total) attended the convention with at least one other family member. Wives and husbands came together. Mothers brought their daughters, and fathers brought sons. Sisters and brothers came together, and so, in some cases, did uncles and cousins.[19]

. . . Some families did argue among themselves about women's rights. Henry Stanton, for example, refused to attend the convention at all. But many of the signers (including Stanton herself, who brought Harriet Cady Eaton, her sister, and Daniel Cady Eaton, her nephew) could count on at least one other family member to lend support. Women's rights may have divided some families, but it brought others together in a common cause.

. . . [T]hese family patterns lead us to suspect that husbands and wives had important ties not only with each other but with their own parents and siblings. While many husbands and wives signed the Declaration together, many women and men also signed the Declaration with members of their birth families. Sometimes these family relationships became very complicated. Richard P. Hunt, for example, signed not only with his wife, Jane, but with two sisters (Lydia Mount and Hannah Plant) and with Lydia's daughter, Mary E. Vail. . . .

Clearly, these signers valued their ties with sisters, brothers, parents, and children as much as those with husbands and wives. Links with their families of origin balanced marital relationships and provided women with a large network of support of "significant others." In spite of legal theory and emerging popular opinion, wives in this group did not define themselves solely by their relationship to their husbands.

Finally, for many signers, home was not simply a private place. It was also a public place, part of the world of work and of social interaction beyond the nuclear family. Many signers incorporated non-family members into their households, including apprentices, servants, boarders, and children. . . . The emerging distinction between women (whose place was in the home) and men (who worked outside the home) was blurred for these signers. Families and households were not peripheral to public activity but the very basis of community life itself.

All of these factors—sex, age, race and ethnicity, wealth and work, family and household—set the stage for the involvement of these people in the Seneca Falls convention. But these were contributing factors, not defining ones. I believe that the convention happened when and where it did primarily because these signers were linked together into three value-oriented networks and because Elizabeth Cady Stanton herself mobilized people in all three groups to create the Seneca Falls women's rights convention.

WOMEN AND LEGAL REFORM IN NEW YORK STATE

The first network emerged from a statewide debate about the legal rights of women in New York State. For almost two decades before the Seneca Falls convention, this debate was so widespread and so intertwined with fundamental questions of American identity that it engaged people at a grass-roots level all across New York State. And it framed the debate about women's rights in the language of the Declaration of Independence. Did the phrase "all men are created equal" include women? Were women, indeed, citizens? In effect, the debate over legal rights for married women provided a dress rehearsal for the Seneca Falls convention itself.[20]

In Seneca Falls, legal reform found its most ardent advocate in Ansel Bascom, lawyer, abolitionist, legal reformer, and temperance man. Bascom did not sign the Declaration of Sentiments. He was a candidate for Congress in 1848 and perhaps did not want to commit himself to such a radical position. He did, however, attend the women's rights meeting, and he took a very active part in the discussion.[21]

Stanton herself formed a second member of this legal reform network. As a child, she had listened to her father and her father's law students debate women's legal rights. She had lobbied in Albany for legal reform in the 1840s. And she contributed in her own special way to the Declaration of Sentiments by emphasizing women's citizenship rights, especially the right of all women—married or single—to vote, which she articulated in terms of the statewide debate about women and the law.

Discussions about women's legal rights undoubtedly affected other signers, too. Elisha Foote, for example, a Seneca Falls lawyer and one of Stanton's father's former law students, quite likely took an active part. So, probably, did men such as Charles Hoskins and Jacob P. Chamberlain, who were politically aware, interested in questions of equality, financially well off, and worried about the future of their several daughters. . . .[22]

Two questions about legal rights for women roused considerable attention in New York State. The first was the right of married women to own property. The second concerned the right of women as citizens to participate in a democratic government. Particularly, should women be allowed to vote? Under the broad umbrella of republican rhetoric that dominated political discourse from the Revolution to the Civil War, these two questions, of property rights and citizenship rights, although often debated separately, were integrally intertwined. Only those with some material investment in the body politic, some argued, should be given a voice in public affairs. Such investment could be property ownership (which led to the payment of taxes) or militia service. As long as women were subject to neither, the rationale for denying them the vote remained intact. If laws were changed to allow married women to own property in their own names, then the whole legal and philosophical scaffolding of resistance to women's political power collapsed. As George Geddes, one of the supporters of a married women's property act, realized, such legislation raised "the whole question of woman's proper place in society, in the family and everywhere."[23]

New York State's citizens had publicly debated the question of women's rights at least since the 1821 state constitutional convention. There, opponents of universal male suffrage (i.e., of voting rights for all males, regardless of property ownership or race) argued that citizenship rights did not necessarily include voting rights. Over and over again, they used the exclusion of women from voting rights (as well as the exclusion of children, native Americans, foreigners, paupers, and felons) as a rationale for denying suffrage to others, including black males and white males without property. If women could legitimately be disfranchised, why could not others be excluded as well?[24]

In 1828, the question of married women's rights emerged in full force. Under the old law, based on English common law, wealthy New York families could protect property rights for their wives and married daughters by means of legal trusts, administered through equity courts. Many New Yorkers, however, viewed equity courts as fortresses of privilege for the wealthy. After 1828, New York State's Revised Statutes [cast in doubt] any sure protection for the right of married women to own property.

By the mid-1830s, considerable support existed across the state for a law protecting married women's right to own property. Men from wealthy families pushed for such a law most vigorously. They, after all, had most to lose, either to profligate sons-in-law or to ill-fated business ventures. Women's rights advocates, however, added their own small voice for reform. In 1836, Ernestine Rose, who was Polish American and Jewish, circulated a petition urging the passage of the married women's property act promoted by Thomas Herttell, a Democratic assemblyman from New York City. Although only six women signed this petition, it marked the first time that women themselves had taken public action for legal reform.[25]

Nowhere did the argument for full rights for women emerge more clearly than in a speech given in the late 1830s or early 1840s before the lyceum in Ogdensburg, New York. Arguing strenuously for married women's property rights, the author also raised the prospect both of the right to vote and the right to hold office. The Declaration of Independence provided the key. "THAT ALL ARE CREATED FREE AND EQUAL; THAT THEY ARE ENDOWED BY THEIR CREATOR WITH CERTAIN UNALIENABLE RIGHTS; THAT AMONG THESE ARE LIFE, LIBERTY, AND THE PURSUIT OF HAPPINESS—is acknowledged to be the fundamental doctrine upon which this Republic is founded," the author asserted. Furthermore, this idea "is freedom's golden rule. . . . None should ever be allowed to restrict its universality. Women, as well as men, are entitled to the full enjoyment of its practical blessings." Clearly, women were citizens of this Republic, "amenable to the constitution and laws." Yet,

> would any man be denominated free who was deprived of a representation in the government, under which he lived, who was thus disfranchised and had no voice in the affairs of his country? . . . He would be called a slave. Such, I blush for my country to say it—such is the degraded condition of women, in this boasted land of liberty. . . . Is this slavish condition of women compatible with the doctrine that all are created free and equal? . . .[26]

Discussion of women's rights—both property rights and political rights—reached a crescendo in 1846, when New York State called a new constitutional convention. The convention opened up once more the question of suffrage. Who should be allowed to vote in the State of New York? Should illiterates? Foreigners? Blacks? Even women? The issue seemed especially pressing because of recent unsuccessful efforts to legalize equal rights to suffrage for blacks in New York State.[27]

. . . At least three petitions (from Albany, Jefferson, and Wyoming counties, New York) asked for women's suffrage. Jefferson County petitioners argued, for example, that

> the present government of this state has widely departed from the true democratic principles upon which all just governments must be based by denying to the female portion of the community the right of suffrage and any participation in forming the government and laws under which they live, and to which they are amenable, and by imposing upon them burdens of taxation, both

directly and indirectly, without admitting them the right of representation. . . .[28]

No taxation without representation constituted so powerful an argument that the convention could not entirely ignore it. Yet there was little sentiment in favor of doing anything about it. . . .

In April 1848, the New York State legislature again addressed the problem of married women's property rights. Again, they were prodded by petitions from citizens. One in particular revealed the importance of revolutionary rhetoric and grass-roots commitment in sustaining support for women's rights. In March 1848, forty-four "ladies" (married, as they were clear to assert), petitioned the legislature from the towns of Darien and Covington in Genesee and Wyoming counties, New York. Their petition argued, with potent sarcasm:

> That your Declaration of Independence declares, that governments derive their just powers from the consent of the governed. And as women have never consented to, been represented in, or recognized by this government, it is evident that in justice no allegiance can be claimed from them. . . .[29]

Perhaps inspired (or shamed) by such rhetoric, the New York State legislature did pass its first married women's property act just one month later, in April 1848. In creating a supportive climate for the Seneca Falls women's rights convention, discussion of the legal rights of women was extremely important. Passage of the Married Women's Property Act helped legitimize more radical action and prompted Stanton herself to promote women's right to vote. As Stanton noted, the Married Women's Property Act "encouraged action on the part of women, as the reflection naturally arose that, if the men who make the laws were ready for some onward step, surely the women themselves should express interest in legislation."[30]

FREE-SOIL ORGANIZATION

Passage of the Married Women's Property Act in April 1848 was the first major event in 1848 to set the stage for the Seneca Falls convention. Two more key events followed. Both occurred in June. Both linked local people to larger concerns. Both involved value-oriented networks,

and both reflected major disruptions in those networks. One (in Seneca Falls) ripped apart political allegiances. It was the growth, in the late spring and early summer of 1848, of the new Free-Soil party. The other (in Waterloo and beyond) mirrored a profound break in religious ties, when a group of Quaker abolitionists split away from the Genesee Yearly Meeting (Hicksite) to form the nucleus of the new Congregational or Progressive Friends. Both splits led directly to a confrontation over questions about equality in American life.

Both also involved people who were part of Elizabeth Cady Stanton's own personal circle. The Free-Soil movement drew support from men (and the women who had married these men) whom Stanton had met in her father's law office, as well as from political abolitionists she had met through her husband, Henry. The Quaker controversy deeply affected Friends who were linked to Lucretia Mott, Stanton's mentor and friend.

Political institutions in Seneca Falls were profoundly strained by debates surrounding the nomination of presidential candidates in 1848. Discussion centered on one question: Should slavery be allowed in the territories? In New York State, the question hit the Democratic party, already under stress from a decade of bickering, with particular force.[31] At a meeting in Syracuse in September 1847, the radical Barnburner wing of the party stalked out in anger when the conservative Hunkers refused to support resolutions against the extension of slavery. In May 1848, the national Democratic convention nominated Lewis Cass for president. For the Barnburners, now joined by former president Martin Van Buren, that was the last straw. They called a Barnburner state convention, to meet at Utica on June 22. Joined by antislavery Whigs and by men from the Liberty party, these dissident Democrats formed the nucleus of a new Free-Soil party, which would be organized formally at Buffalo in August. Championing "free soil, free labor, free men," they would rally behind Martin Van Buren for president.[32]

Electors in Seneca Falls found themselves swept into this national confrontation. On June 13, in preparation for the Utica meeting, 196 voters published an invitation in the *Seneca County Courier* to the "freemen of Seneca Falls" to meet in the Wesleyan Chapel to consider "the course of action which existing circumstances require of Northern Freemen." Chaired by Jacob Chamberlain, owner of a local flour mill, the attendees of the June 15 meeting agreed that slavery was "the chiefest curse and foulest disgrace" in America. The author of these stern resolutions? Ansel Bascom.[33]

Henry Stanton, too, leaped into the fight with gusto. He teamed up with Bascom to stump the state for the Free-Soil party. And he was one of 102 local delegates to the Buffalo Free-Soil convention, held in August.[34]

Old party issues were insignificant compared to the pressing need to find a presidential candidate who would restrict slavery. Such sentiments allied Seneca Falls Free-Soilers with the party's abolitionist wing. Nationally, many Free-Soil adherents supported the party not from antislavery principles but as a way to keep the west for whites only. People in Seneca Falls, however, considered slavery a moral evil and hoped the new party would strike a mortal blow against it.[35]

Some of them would go even further. They would take the idea of equality seriously enough to consider not only rights for black and white males but also for women. They would attend the Seneca Falls women's rights convention and would sign its Declaration of Sentiments.

... Of the twenty-six separate families of signers of the Declaration of Sentiments identifiable from Seneca Falls, eighteen of them also included a Free-Soil advocate. In Seneca Falls, not all Free-Soilers were women's rights advocates. But 69.2 percent of the households of women's rights advocates (compared to only 21.2 percent of nonsigners' households) were affiliated with the Free-Soilers.[36]

CONGREGATIONAL FRIENDS

Organizing for the Free-Soil party, combined with public discussion over women's legal rights, prepared citizens in Seneca Falls for the women's rights convention. Meanwhile, in Waterloo, four miles west of Seneca Falls, a different kind of excitement prevailed at just the same time.... [In June 1848 t]he Genesee Yearly Meeting of Friends, held at Farmington, in Ontario County, opened calmly enough, in spite of the heat. But tense disputes, left over from the year before, soon broke the Sabbath peace. On Sunday, June 11, the meeting house was filled to overflowing. Several speakers,

"not very talented," as one observer commented, made the audience restive before Lucretia Mott rose and delivered an impressive sermon.[37]

... Disagreements were acrimonious and fundamental. Partly they centered on slavery. Conservative Quakers objected to the antislavery activities of many of their fellow Friends. Especially they did not want to open Quaker meeting houses for public discussion of abolitionism....

Partly the disagreements involved the question of proper authority. Did essential authority reside within each individual person and then within each individual meeting? Or did the meeting of ministers and elders, along with quarterly and yearly meetings, have special power to determine the actions of local (i.e., monthly) meetings? ...

For the Genesee Yearly Meeting, both these questions came to a head in June 1848.... About two hundred Friends ("something towards half," according to one observer) walked out, unhappy with what they felt was a manipulative and unfair action.[38]

With strong support from Quakers in Waterloo, Rochester, and Wayne County, these dissidents adjourned to a three-day conference of their own, held June 14–16.... Daniel Anthony, one of the few contemporaries to leave a detailed comment on the split, wrote to his daughter, Susan, that those who had left the "shriveled up nutshell" of the Genesee Yearly Meeting were those "who take the liberty of holding up to view the wickedness of War—Slavery—Intemperance—Hanging & c" and "who are of the opinion that each individual should have a right to even think as well as act for himself & in his own way to assist in rooling [sic] on the wheel of reform."[39]

Daniel Anthony reported, a month after the meeting, that "in Rochester they have commenced a new Meeting under the dictation of neither Priest deacon nor Elder."[40] We can assume that dissident Friends in the Waterloo area, affiliated with the Junius Monthly Meeting (after the original name of the township that once included Waterloo), did the same, for in Waterloo lived one of the main organizers of the walkout.... Thomas McClintock....

The McClintock family (Thomas and Mary Ann and their four children) had come to Waterloo by canal in 1837. Thomas ran a drugstore on Main Street, where, in a business block constructed by his brother-in-law, Richard P. Hunt, McClintock sold goods "free from the labor of slaves." Hunt also rented the family a comfortable brick house just behind the store.[41]

... As Quakers and as abolitionists, they took leadership roles in their own meeting. From 1839 to 1843, ... [Thomas] was ... clerk of the Genesee Yearly Meeting. Mary Ann was assistant clerk of the Women's Yearly Meeting. The whole family signed abolitionist petitions, helped organize antislavery fairs, and hosted antislavery lecturers.

When the split in the Genesee Yearly Meeting came in June 1848, Thomas was one of those who walked out. In the fall, this group would meet again. They would call themselves the Congregational Friends, and they would adopt a new form of organization. Men and women would meet together, not separately, as in traditional Quaker meetings. No person was to be subordinate to another. There were to be no ministers and no hierarchy of meetings. They were not to be tied to creeds or rituals, and they need not agree with one another on points of doctrine. They would focus instead on practical philanthropy....

In mid-July, these Friends would become the single largest group to sign the Seneca Falls Declaration of Sentiments. At least twenty-three signers were affiliated with this wing of Friends. Most of them (nineteen) came from the Junius Monthly Meeting at Waterloo. One signer, Rhoda Palmer, remembered, in fact, that "every member" of that meeting attended the women's rights convention.[42]

Just as the Free-Soilers of Seneca Falls had broken out of traditional political parties, so had the Waterloo Quakers broken away from their traditional religious affiliation. Both had split away over issues of equality. Both did so in dramatic and emotionally wrenching ways.

In late June and early July, both groups were in the process of self-definition. They had many questions: Who were their members? What did they believe? In particular, how far did they want to carry this idea of equality?

THE RESULTS OF LOCAL AGITATION

At this critical juncture, in the midst of excitement caused by the Free-Soilers and the Congregational Friends, Lucretia Mott came with her sister, Martha Wright, to meet with Quaker women at the home of Jane and Richard Hunt. Elizabeth Cady Stanton was also invited.

There, Stanton "poured out," as she remembered, "the torrent of my long-accumulating discontent, with such vehemence and indignation that I stirred myself, as well as the rest of the party, to do and dare anything." That evening, they wrote the call for a women's rights convention and published it on Tuesday, July 11, in the *Seneca County Courier*. Area newspapers (the *North Star* and the *Ovid Bee*, for example) printed the call in their own editions on Friday, July 14.[43]

Local people, concerned about women's legal rights, agitated about deep changes in their own institutional affiliations, and willing in this time of trial and transformation to expand their own boundaries, considered the purposes of the women's rights convention to be, as Stanton later remembered, "timely, rational and sacred." A core group of legal reformers, Free-Soilers, and Congregational Friends found the Declaration of Sentiments sensible, a logical extension of their own beliefs in ideals of liberty, equality, and independence.

But what about Elizabeth Cady Stanton? Can she still be called the convention's main organizer? Indeed she can. The convention would not have happened at all without her. Before the women's rights convention, Free-Soilers and advocates of legal reform in Seneca Falls had few identifiable contacts with the Congregational Friends of Waterloo and central New York. Stanton, however, knew leaders in all three movements. She knew Ansel Bascom, champion of legal reform. Among the Free-Soilers, she could count as friends not only Jacob Chamberlain (president of the June 13 Free-Soil meeting and Stanton's neighbor), and Charles Hoskins (secretary of that meeting and fellow attender of the Episcopal Church), but also her own husband, Henry. Finally, Stanton gained credibility among the Quakers of Waterloo, first, by her long-standing friendship with Lucretia Mott and, second, by her introduction to the McClintocks, who wholeheartedly endorsed her convention plans. Stanton persuaded these leaders to come to the convention. They, in turn, would attract their followers. She would become what network theorists call a broker, bringing together three networks at a critical juncture in their own development.[44]

Stanton willingly played this position, not because she wanted primarily to promote the Free-Soil party or Congregational Friends, nor even because she wanted to take up the challenge posed to women by passage of the Married Women's Property Act, to act on their own behalf. Instead, Stanton's most powerful motivation emerged from the stresses of her own personal life in 1848. The move to Seneca Falls, Henry's frequent absences, the lack of trained household help, and her family's sickness threatened to overwhelm her. Other women might have become depressed. Not Elizabeth Cady Stanton. Instead, she used her energy to enlist legal reformers, Free-Soilers, and Congregational Friends into a battle against social structures that oppressed women, rather than against individual oppressors.

People across the country reacted to the Seneca Falls convention. Many observers ridiculed the whole idea. The New York *Evening Post* squealed incredulously that the convention "had seriously resolved that all men and women are created equal!" Women's rights, said the *Mechanic's Advocate*, were "impracticable, uncalled for, and unnecessary," "a monstrous injury to all mankind," while *The Religious Recorder* of Syracuse simply dismissed it as "excessively silly."[45]

A few, however, endorsed women's rights with enthusiasm. "Success to the cause in which they have enlisted," cheered O.C.W. in the Herkimer *Freeman*. "Railroad speed to the ends they would accomplish!" The Rochester *National Reformer* encouraged continued agitation. "To the ladies we say," wrote editor George W. Cooper, "act—agitate—bid high, you will not get, in this age, more than you demand."[46]

It had been the genius of the convention's organizers, however, to couch their demands in terms of the Declaration of Independence. Americans found it difficult to repudiate the document upon which their nation had been founded. Many, therefore, would have agreed with Horace Greeley, the influential editor of the *New York Tribune*. Greeley, always logical, had to admit the justice of the cause, for

> when a sincere republican is asked to say in sober earnest, what adequate reason he can give for refusing the demand of women to an equal participation with men in political rights, he must answer, None at all.... However unwise and mistaken the demand, it is but the assertion of a natural right, and as such must be conceded.[47]

By using the language of the Declaration of Independence, the Seneca Falls Declaration of Sentiments reached deep into the culture and conscience of many Americans. Although it may have been a historical accident that Stanton found herself in Seneca Falls in 1848, she seized the moment of agitation over married women's property rights, of political turmoil among the Free-Soilers, and of religious divisions among the Quakers to turn her personal vision into what would become a major political movement.

NOTES

1. For references to weather, see Mary A. Bull, "Woman's Rights and 'Other Reforms' in Seneca Falls," *Seneca Falls Reville*, July 9, 1880, and manuscript diary of Jefferson Palmer, Montezuma, July 1848, in Seneca Falls Historical Society. Quotations about the convention are in *History of Woman Suffrage*, vol. 1 (New York: Fowler and Wells, 1881), p. 68. . . .

2. Call to the convention, *Seneca County Courier*, July 11, 1848; *Report of the Woman's Rights Convention Held at Seneca Falls, N.Y., July 19th and 20th, 1848* (Rochester: John Dick at North Star, 1848). . . . Eleanor Flexner, *Century of Struggle: The Woman's Rights Movement in the United States* (Cambridge, Mass.: Harvard University Press, 1959), p. 76, notes that three hundred people attended the convention. . . . This is corroborated by calculations derived from the size of the Wesleyan Methodist Church building itself and from the arrangement of seats within it.

3. Ellen DuBois, *Feminism and Suffrage: The Emergence of an Independent Women's Movement in America, 1848–1869* (Ithaca: Cornell University Press, 1978), p. 21.

4. John Dick at the *North Star* office in Rochester printed a list of one hundred signers in the *Report of the Woman's Rights Convention*. This list may or may not contain the names of all those who originally signed the Declaration of Sentiments. In her autobiography, Stanton remembered that "so pronounced was the popular voice against us, in the parlor, press, and pulpit, that most of the ladies who had attended the convention and signed the declaration, one by one, withdrew their names and influence and joined our persecutors." *Eighty Years and More* reprint (New York: Schocken Books, 1971), p. 149. No manuscript of the Declaration has ever been found, and we do not know whether the printed list duplicates the original or omits those signers who later withdrew their names. . . .

5. Frederick Douglass, *Report on the International Council of Women* (Washington, D.C.: Rufus H. Darby, 1888), p. 329.

6. For discussions of these issues, see, for example (listed in chronological order), Alma Lutz, *Created Equal: A Biography of Elizabeth Cady Stanton* (New York: John Day, 1940); Eleanor Flexner, *Century of Struggle*; Gerda Lerner, *The Grimke Sisters from South Carolina* (Boston: Houghton Mifflin, 1967); Ross Evans Paulson, *Women's Suffrage and Prohibition: A Comparative Study of Equality and Social Control* (Glenview, Ill.: Scott, Foresman, 1973). . . . Lois Banner, *Elizabeth*

Cady Stanton: A Radical for Woman's Rights (Boston: Little, Brown, 1980). . . . Nancy Hewitt, *Women's Activism and Social Change, Rochester, New York, 1822–1872* (Ithaca: Cornell University Press, 1984).

7. Stanton, *Eighty Years,* chap. 2.

8. Ibid., p. 82.

9. Ibid., p. 83; Minutes of Seventh Annual Meeting of the American Anti-Slavery Society, May 12–15, 1840, in Garrison Papers, Boston Public Library; *Liberator* subscription list, Garrison Papers, Boston Public Library. . . .

10. Stanton, *Eighty Years,* p. 47. Stanton's last living child, Gerrit, had been born in Sept. 1845; her next child, Theodore, would arrive on Feb. 10, 1851. . . .

11. Data on residence comes primarily from the 1850 federal census. . . .

12. The following brief analysis is based on preliminary results of a detailed statistical study, now under way, of all the residents of Seneca Falls and Waterloo in 1850, comparing the signers of the Declaration of Sentiments with the nonsigners in those two townships.

13. People signed the declaration in two groups, female and male, so we know the sex of the signers, even if no other information is available. . . .

14. Seneca Falls had the youngest average age, with 37.5; Waterloo had the oldest, with 41.

15. The sixteen signers about whom we have no reliable information may, of course, have been either black or foreign born. Seneca Falls had only twenty-four black residents in 1850 (.5 percent of the population), and Waterloo had sixty-one (1.7 percent). Of the 1,473 households in Seneca Falls in 1850, 196 of them (13.3 percent) were headed by Irish-born residents. Source: [*U.S. Census for 1850*].

16. Fifty-five signers' families appeared in the 1850 census. Average value of real estate for these families was $3,720. But these figures obscure considerable variation, both from family to family and from place to place. Overall, almost half (47.3 percent) of the signers' families held no property at all in 1850, varying from 64.3 percent in Waterloo to 59.3 percent in Seneca Falls to 7.1 percent elsewhere in central New York. Four families, in contrast, owned more than $15,000 of real estate. Those families of signers who owned more than $15,000 worth of property included the Hunts from Waterloo ($40,000), the father of S. D. Tillman, from Seneca Falls ($25,000), Martha Wright's family in Auburn ($20,000). . . .

17. Information about occupations comes primarily from the 1850 census. For our purposes, this census has a major defect: it did not list occupations for women. Some of the women signers may also have been textile workers. . . .

18. Information about Elisha Foote's patents comes from *Appleton's Cyclopedia of American Biography* (New York, 1887), v. 2:495. . . .

19. At least 47 percent of the signers (and perhaps as many as 62.7 percent) attended with at least one other family member. Sources: *U.S. Census for 1850* and family genealogies.

20. For a more detailed discussion of debate over legal reform, see Norma Basch, *In the Eyes of the Law: Women, Marriage, and Property in Nineteenth-Century New York* (Ithaca: Cornell University Press, 1982); and Marylynn Salmon, *Women and the Law of Property in Early America* (Chapel Hill: University of North Carolina Press, 1986). . . .

21. Information on Bascom comes from many sources, including scattered copies of *The Memorialist,* a legal reform paper published by Bascom in Seneca Falls.

22. Martha Wright to Lucretia Mott, Mar. 11, 1841, in Garrison Papers, Smith College.

23. Geddes to Matilda Joslyn Gage, Nov. 25, 1880, in Stanton, Anthony, and Gage, eds., *History of Woman Suffrage,* I:65.

24. For examples of the debate, see Nathaniel H. Carter and William L. Stone, *Reports of the Proceedings and Debates of the Convention of 1821* (Albany: E. and E. Hosford, 1821), pp. 181, 190, 191, 248–49, 278. . . .

25. Basch, *In the Eyes of the Law,* pp. 115–19.

26. *Lecture Delivered Before the Ogdensburg Lyceum on the Political Rights of Women* (Ogdensburg, N.Y.: Tyler and James, 1837). This may have been delivered by Democratic politician and judge John Fine. . . . Angelina Grimke, for example, came right to the point in her *Appeal to the Women of the Nominally Free States* (Boston: Isaac Knapp, 1838): "Are we aliens because we are women?" she asked. "Are we bereft of citizenship because we are the mothers, wives, and daughters of a mighty people?" (p. 19). . . .

27. Phyllis Field, *Politics of Race in New York: The Struggle for Black Suffrage in the Civil War Era* (Ithaca: Cornell University Press, 1982). . . .

28. William G. Bishop and William H. Attree, *Report of the Debates and Proceedings of the Convention for the Revision of the Constitution of the State of New York* (Albany: Bishop and Attree, 1846), p. 646.

29. *New York Assembly Documents,* Mar. 15, 1848, no. 129:1–2. . . .

30. Theodore Stanton and Harriet Stanton Blatch, eds., *Elizabeth Cady Stanton as Revealed in Her Letters, Diary and Reminiscences,* 2 vols. (New York: Harper & Bros., 1992), I:149.

31. Judah Ginsberg, "The Tangled Web: The New York Democratic Party and the Slavery Controversy, 1844–1860," Ph.D. dissertation, University of Wisconsin, 1974, chap. 4.

32. Richard Sewall, *Ballots for Freedom: Anti-Slavery Politics in the United States, 1837–1860* (New York: Norton, 1976), pp. 145–69.

33. *Seneca County Courier,* June 13, 1848, and June 16, 1848.

34. Ibid., Aug. 4, 1848.

35. Sewall, *Ballots for Freedom,* pp. 160, 170–201, discusses the racial stance of Free-Soilers in general; Dwight Lowell Dumond, *Antislavery: The Crusade for Freedom in America,* reprint (New York: Norton, 1966), p. 304.

36. I identified Free-Soil advocates as those who signed one or more of three Free-Soil lists in the *Seneca County Courier* (June 13, Aug. 4, or Aug. 18, 1848).

37. For a thoughtful and detailed analysis of Quakers who attended the Seneca Falls convention from Rochester and of differences between evangelical and Hicksite Quaker activism, see Nancy Hewitt, "Feminist Friends," *Feminist Studies* 12 (Spring 1986): 27–49. . . . Information about this meeting comes in bits and pieces from several sources. Most important is A. Day Bradley, "Progressive Friends in Michigan

and New York," *Quaker History* 52 (Autumn 1963): 95–101; John J. Cornell, *Autobiography* (Baltimore: Lord Baltimore Press, 1906), p. 22; Katharine Anthony, *Susan B. Anthony* (Garden City, N.Y.: Doubleday, 1954), pp. 92–93. . . .

38. . . . Daniel Anthony to Susan B. Anthony, July 16, 1848, in Anthony Papers, Schlesinger Library, Radcliffe.

39. Daniel Anthony to Susan B. Anthony, July 16, 1848, Anthony Papers, Schlesinger Library.

40. Ibid.

41. Material on the McClintocks comes from John Becker, *History of Waterloo* (Waterloo: Waterloo Library and Historical Society, 1948), p. 135; Thomas McClintock, *Observations on the Articles Published in the Episcopal Recorder*. . . . (New York: Isaac T. Hopper, 1837); Ruth Ketring Nuermberger, *The Free-Produce Movement* (Durham, N.C.: Duke University Press, 1942), p. 14. . . .

42. Interview with Rhoda Palmer in *Geneva Daily Times*, Mar. 17, 1915; Lucretia Mott to Elizabeth Cady Stanton, July 16, 1848, in Stanton Papers, Library of Congress. . . .

43. Stanton, *Eighty Years*, p. 148.

44. Ronald S. Burt, "Models of Network Structure," *Annual Review of Sociology* 6 (1980):91, fn. 8, identifies a broker as one who is "the only connection between two subgroups of actors."

45. *Evening Post*, Aug. 12, 1848, quoted in Terpstra, "The 1848 Seneca Falls Women's Rights Convention," p. 46; *Mechanic's Advocate*, [n.d.] quoted in *History of Woman Suffrage* I:803. . . .

46. *Herkimer Freeman*, as reprinted in the *Liberator*, Sept. 22, 1848; *National Reformer*, Aug. 10, 1848, in Alma Lutz notes, Vassar College.

47. *New York Tribune*, n.d., quoted from Alma Lutz notes, Vassar College.

NELL IRVIN PAINTER
Sojourner Truth's Defense of the Rights of Women (as reported in 1851; rewritten in 1863)

Sojourner Truth (ca. 1797–1883) is often equated with the phrase "ar'n't I a woman?" which symbolizes black women in American history and strong women of any race. Truth, who was born a slave named Isabella in New York's Hudson River Valley, was emancipated by state law in 1827, moved to New York City in 1828, worked in private households to gain her living, became an unorthodox Methodist, and made a reputation as an exhorter. In 1843 divine inspiration directed her to take the name Sojourner Truth and become an itinerant preacher. Addressing outdoor camp meetings on Long Island and up the Connecticut River Valley, she reached the utopian Northampton [Massachusetts] Association in the winter of 1843–1844, where she settled and met abolitionists like William Lloyd Garrison and Frederick Douglass.

In 1845 Douglass published his first autobiography, which became a best-seller in England and the United States and inspired Sojourner Truth. Unlike Douglass, Truth was illiterate, and she dictated her narrative to Olive Gilbert, a teacher from Connecticut. In 1850 Truth paid to have *The Narrative of Sojourner Truth* published and began traveling the reform lecture circuit, speaking against slavery and for women's rights. Wherever she appeared she sold her *Narrative*, which provided her material support.

A women's rights convention in Akron, Ohio, in 1851 furnished Truth an opportunity to address a sympathetic gathering and sell books. The 1851 report by one of Truth's close associates in the Salem *Antislavery Bugle* runs like this:

> One of the most unique and interesting speeches of the Convention was made by Sojourner Truth, an emancipated slave. It is impossible to transfer it to paper, or convey any adequate idea of the effect it produced upon the audience. Those only can appreciate it who saw her powerful form, her whole-souled, earnest gestures, and listened to

Sojourner Truth (ca. 1797–1883) is better known in the twentieth century for words she did not utter—"ar'n't I a woman?"—than for her fierce and exemplary insistence on asserting her rights to speak and act publicly and to religious expression. (The Schomburg Center for Research in Black Culture, The New York Public Library, Astor, Lenox and Tilden Foundations)

her strong and truthful tones. She came forward to the platform and addressing the President said with great simplicity:

May I say a few words? Receiving an affirmative answer, she proceeded; I want to say a few words about this matter. I am a woman's rights. [sic] I have as much muscle as any man, and can do as much work as any man. I have plowed and reaped and husked and chopped and mowed, and can any man do more than that? I have heard much about the sexes being equal; I can carry as much as any man, and can eat as much too, if I can get it. I am as strong as any man that is now. As for intellect, all I can say is, if a woman have

a pint and man a quart—why cant she have her little pint full? You need not be afraid to give us our rights for fear we will take too much,—for we cant take more than our pint'll hold. The poor men seem to be all in confusion, and dont know what to do. Why children, if you have woman's rights give it to her and you will feel better. You will have your own rights, and they wont be so much trouble. I cant read, but I can hear. I have heard the bible and have learned that Eve caused man to sin. Well if woman upset the world, do give her a chance to set it right side up again. The Lady has spoken about Jesus, how he never spurned woman from him, and she was right.

When Lazarus died, Mary and Martha came to him with faith and love and besought him to raise their brother. And Jesus wept—and Lazarus came forth. And how came Jesus into the world? Through God who created him and woman who bore him. Man, where is your part? But the women are coming up blessed be God and a few of the man are coming up with them. But man is in a tight place, the poor slave is on him, woman is coming on him, and he is surely between a hawk and a buzzard.

The same newspaper also ran a report of the speech given by Frances Dana Gage (1808–1884), who chaired the convention. Gage was a lecturer, journalist, and poet who published mainly in the antislavery and feminist press. A more radical feminist and abolitionist than Harriet Beecher Stowe, Gage was less well known. In 1851 Gage used Sojourner Truth as a character called Winna in a story she serialized in a feminist newspaper, but she did not describe Truth's 1851 speech until a good deal later. In the meanwhile, Truth continued speaking and selling her books.

In the nineteenth century, as today, authors commonly asked celebrities for blurbs to use as advertisement. After the phenomenal success of *Uncle Tom's Cabin* in 1851–1852 made Harriet Beecher Stowe famous, Truth visited her to request a blurb, which was forthcoming. In subsequent years, Stowe mentioned Truth to her friends privately, but she did not publish anything until the 1860s. Once the Emancipation Proclamation and the acceptance of black men into the Union Army made the Civil War into an acknowledged struggle over slavery, "the Negro" became a popular topic of discourse; then Stowe tapped into her recollections of Truth to shape an essay in the *Atlantic Monthly*, one of the most respectable periodicals of the time. "Sojourner Truth, the Libyan Sibyl" appeared in April 1863.

The publication of Stowe's article inspired Gage to write her own essay and invent the phrase, "ar'n't I a woman?" As long as the values of consumers of journalism were more attuned to the sentimentalism of Stowe than the radicalism of Gage, Stowe's "Libyan Sibyl" remained more popular, but at the end of the nineteenth century, the balance began to tip in Gage's favor.

Susan B. Anthony (Gage's friend since the 1850s) and Elizabeth Cady Stanton included Gage's report, not Stowe's, in *The History of Woman Suffrage*, where woman suffragists found a figure of Sojourner Truth that was useful against antagonists. In the mid-twentieth century American tastes changed, rejecting Stowe's quaint little exotic and embracing Gage's bold feminist. The 1851 report of Truth's speech, however, still seems too moderate to be useful as symbolism, even though it captures the historic—as opposed to the emblematic—Sojourner Truth. At least for the time being, a symbol rather than an individual black woman's utterance is what American culture demands.

Mary C. Vaughan, "We would act as well as endure . . ."

Temperance was a more popular reform movement among women than abolition and probably accounted for more recruits to the women's rights cause. Alcohol was widely drunk in the early republic; the national per capita consumption in 1830 was twice what it would be in 1990. Temperance reformers were the first to speak publicly and explicitly about a link between excessive drinking and domestic violence. In an era in which it was difficult for women to speak publicly about sexual matters and particularly about rape, incest, and prostitution, temperance provided a rhetoric in which it was possible to address domestic violence. Temperance speakers and columnists in temperance newspapers publicized major cases of wife beating; sometimes they called for legislation on behalf of battered women. By the 1850s women temperance reformers had tired of calling for repentance on the part of abusive fathers and husbands and were urging legal reform to enable the drunkard's wife to free herself and her children from his control. "The very survival of a drunkard's wife," observed historian Elizabeth Pleck, "depended on a woman's rights—her right to custody of her children, her right to her own earnings, and her right to secure a divorce." In the 1850s, Tennessee and Georgia made wife beating a misdemeanor, the first states in the country to do so.

Mary Vaughan's speech at an Albany, New York temperance meeting suggests some of the issues to which women responded that led them from a concern about alcoholism and domestic violence to a demand for women's rights. Which sex does Vaughan think is most likely to abuse alcohol? Whom does she think most requires protection? Note that, at the end of her address, Vaughan mentions "the true woman." What does Vaughan imply are the characteristics of a "true woman"?

January 28, 1852

We have met to consider what we, as women, can do and may do, to forward the temperance reform. We have met, because, as members of the human family, we share in all the sufferings which error and crime bring upon the race, and because we are learning that our part in the drama of life is something beside inactive suffering and passive endurance. We would act as well as endure; and we meet here to-day because many of us have been trying to act, and we would combine our individual experiences, and together devise plans for the future, out of which shall arise well-based hopes of good results to humanity. We are aware that this proceeding of ours, this calling together of a body of women to deliberate publicly upon plans to carry out a specified reform, will rub rather harshly upon the mould of prejudice, which has gathered thick upon the common mind.

. . . There are plenty of women, as well as men, who can labor for reforms without ne-

Excerpted from Mary C. Vaughan, Address, Daughters of Temperance Assembly, in *History of Woman Suffrage*, edited by Elizabeth Cady Stanton, Susan B. Anthony, and Matilda Joslyn Gage, vol. 1 (New York: Fowler & Wells, 1881), pp. 476–78.

glecting business or duty. It is an error that clings most tenaciously to the public mind, that because a part of the sex are wives and mothers and have absorbing duties, that all the sex should be denied any other sphere of effort. To deprive every unmarried woman, spinster, or widow, or every childless wife, of the power of exercising her warm sympathies for the good of others, is to deprive her of the greatest happiness of which she is capable; to rob her highest faculties of their legitimate operation and reward; to belittle and narrow her mind; to dwarf her affections; to turn the harmonies of her nature to discord; and, as the human mind must be active, to compel her to employ hers with low and grovelling thoughts, which lead to contemptible actions.

There is no reform in which woman can act better or more appropriately than temperance. I know not how she can resist or turn aside from the duty of acting in this; its effects fall so crushingly upon her and those whose interests are identical with her own; she has so often seen its slow, insidious, but not the less surely fatal advances, gaining upon its victim; she has seen the intellect which was her dearest pride, debased; the affections which were her life-giving springs of action, estranged; the children once loved, abused, disgraced and impoverished; the home once an earthly paradise, rendered a fit abode for lost spirits; has felt in her own person all the misery, degradation, and woe of the drunkard's wife; has shrunk from revilings and cowered beneath blows; has

labored and toiled to have her poor earnings transferred to the rum-seller's ill-gotten hoard; while her children, ragged, fireless, poor, starving, gathered shivering about her, and with hollow eyes, from which all smiles had fled, begged vainly for the bread she had not to bestow. Oh! the misery, the utter, hopeless misery of the drunkard's wife!

. . . We account it no reason why we should desist, when conscience, an awakened sense of duty, and aroused heart-sympathies, would lead us to show ourselves something different than an impersonation of the vague ideal which has been named, Woman, and with which woman has long striven to identify herself. A creature all softness and sensibility, who must necessarily enjoy and suffer in the extreme, while sharing with man the pleasures and the ills of life; bearing happiness meekly, and sorrow with fortitude; gentle, mild, submissive, forbearing under all circumstances; a softened reflex of the opinions and ideas of the masculines who, by relationship, hold mastery over her; without individualism, a mere adjunct of man, the chief object of whose creation was to adorn and beautify his existence, or to minister to some form of his selfishness. This is nearly the masculine idea of womanhood, and poor womanhood strives to personify it. But not all women. This is an age of iconoclasms; and daring hands are raised to sweep from its pedestal, and dash to fragments, this false image of woman. We care not how soon, if the true woman but takes its place.

A. S. Hitchcock, "Young women particularly flock back & forth . . ."

Early in the Civil War, before the Emancipation Proclamation, the Union Army occupied the Sea Islands off the coast of Georgia; plantation owners fled and the army established base camps there. Although the Union forces expected former slaves to continue to work on their old plantations as contract laborers, freedpeople believed that the end of slavery should mean that they could travel freely and that they could choose other ways of supporting themselves.

How did the Union officials interpret the movement of women around the Islands?

A. S. HITCHCOCK, ACTING GENERAL SUPERINTENDENT OF CONTRABANDS TO PROVOST MARSHAL GENERAL OF THE DEPARTMENT OF THE SOUTH, AUGUST 25, 1864
In accordance with a request made by you at this office . . . concerning measures to be instituted to lessen the number of idle & dissolute persons hanging about the central Posts of the Department & traveling to & from between them . . . I write this note. . . .

Had I the control of the negroes the first thing I would endeavor to do, & the thing I think of most importance to be done, is to Keep all the people possible on the farms or plantations at *honest steady* labor. As one great means to this end, I would make it as difficult as possible for them to get to the centres of population.—Young women particularly flock back & forth by scores to Hilton Head, to Beaufort, to the country simply to while away their time, or constantly to seek some new excitement, or what is worse to live by lasciviousness. . . . I would allow no peddling around camps whatsoever. . . . All rationing I would stop utterly, & introduce the poor house system, feeding none on any pretense who would not go to the place provided for all paupers to live. . . . All

persons out of the poor house and running from place to place to beg a living I would treat as vagabonds, & also all persons, whether in town or on plantations, white or black, who lived without occupation should either go to the poor house or be put in a place where they *must work*—a work house or chain gang, & if women where they could wash iron & scrub for the benefit of the public. . . .

SEPTEMBER 6, 1864
GENERAL ORDERS NO. 130
Hilton Head, S.C. . . . The practice of allowing negro women to wander about from one plantation to another, and from one Post or District to another, on Government transports, for no other purpose than to while away their time, or visit their husbands serving in the ranks of the Army, is not only objectionable in every point of view, both to the soldiers and to themselves, but is generally subversive of moral restraint, and must be discontinued at once. All negro women, in future found wandering in this manner, will be immediately arrested, and compelled to work at some steady employment on the Plantations.

Excerpted from *Freedom: A Documentary History of Emancipation 1861–1867*, edited by Ira Berlin, Joseph P. Reidy, and Leslie S. Rowland, Ser. I, vol. 3 (Cambridge, Engl.: Cambridge University Press, 1990), pp. 316–17.

Roda Ann Childs, "I was more dead than alive. . . ."

The Civil Rights Act of 1866 was designed to protect freedmen; even before the passage of the Fourteenth Amendment, it promised "citizens of every race and color . . . full and equal benefit of all laws and proceedings for the security of person and property, as is enjoyed by white citizens. . . ." But the statute had been passed only over the veto of President Andrew Johnson, who denied that the states of the Confederacy had forfeited all civil rights and privileges by their rebellion. The Freedmen's Bureau was charged with protecting the rights of former slaves and assisting their transition to a market economy; it accomplished much, but it was always underfunded and understaffed, and many of its staff members were themselves deeply skeptical of freedpeople.

In a political climate marked by struggle between Congress and the President, the Ku Klux Klan and other vigilantes who wanted to intimidate freedpeople and take vengeance for their own defeat in war seized their opportunity. Not until 1871 did Congress pass the Ku Klux Klan Act, prescribing fines and imprisonment for those who went in disguise to terrorize others. The congressional committee that conducted a traveling inquiry into "the Condition of Affairs in the Late Insurrectionary States" filled a twelve-volume report. Its testimony of violence and intimidation, in excruciating detail, makes it clear that Roda Ann Childs's experience was replicated throughout the South.

Roda Ann Childs made her way to a Freedman's Bureau agent in Griffin, Georgia, to swear this affidavit; she signed it with her mark. There is no evidence that her case was pursued. What clue does she offer for why she was a target for mob violence?

[*Griffin, Ga.*] Sept. 25, 1866 Rhoda Ann Childs came into this office and made the following statement:

"Myself and husband were under contract with Mrs. Amelia Childs of Henry County, and worked from Jan. 1, 1866, until the crops were laid by, or in other words until the main work of the year was done, without difficulty. Then, (the fashion being prevalent among the planters) we were called upon one night, and my husband was demanded; I Said he was not there. They then asked where he was. I Said he was gone to the water mellon patch. They then Seized me and took me Some distance from the house, where they 'bucked' me down across a log, Stripped my clothes over my head, one of the men Standing astride my neck, and beat me across my posterior, two men holding my legs. In this manner I was beaten until they were tired. Then they turned me parallel with the log, laying my neck on a limb which projected from the log, and one man placing his foot upon my neck, beat me again on my hip and thigh. Then I was thrown upon the ground on my back, one of the men Stood upon my breast, while two others took hold of my feet and stretched My limbs as far apart as they could, while the man Standing upon my breast applied the Strap to my private parts until fatigued into stopping, and I was more dead than alive. Then a man, Supposed to be an ex-confederate Soldier, as he was on crutches, fell

Excerpted from *Freedom: A Documentary History of Emancipation 1861–1867*, edited by Ira Berlin, Joseph P. Reidy, and Leslie S. Rowland, Ser. II (Cambridge, Engl.: Cambridge University Press, 1982), pp. 807–8.

upon me and ravished me. During the whipping one of the men ran his pistol into me, and Said he had a hell of a mind to pull the trigger, and Swore they ought to Shoot me, as my husband had been in the 'God damned Yankee Army,' and Swore they meant to kill every black Son-of-a-bitch they could find that had ever fought against them. They then went back to the house, Seized my two daughters and beat them, demanding their father's pistol, and upon failure to get that, they entered the house and took Such articles of clothing as Suited their fancy, and decamped. There were concerned in this affair eight men, none of which could be recognized for certain.

her
Roda Ann × Childs
mark

Susan B. Anthony, "Guaranteed to us and our daughters forever"

The capstone of the celebration of the Centennial was a public reading of the Declaration of Independence in Independence Square, Philadelphia, by a descendant of a signer, Richard Henry Lee. Elizabeth Cady Stanton, who was then president of the National Woman Suffrage Association, asked permission to present silently a women's protest and a written Declaration of Rights. The request was denied. "Tomorrow we propose to celebrate what we have done the last hundred years," replied the president of the official ceremonies, "not what we have failed to do."

Led by suffragist Susan B. Anthony, five women appeared at the official reading, distributing copies of their declaration. After this mildly disruptive gesture they withdrew to the other side of Independence Hall, where they staged a counter-Centennial and Anthony read the following address. Compare it to the Declaration of Sentiments (document 2 in Essential Documents) of twenty-eight years before. Note the splendid oratorical flourish of the final paragraph.

July 4, 1876

While the nation is buoyant with patriotism, and all hearts are attuned to praise, it is with sorrow we come to strike the one discordant note, on this one-hundredth anniversary of our country's birth. When subjects of kings, emperors, and czars, from the old world join in our national jubilee, shall the women of the republic refuse to lay their hands with benedictions on the nation's head? Surveying America's exposition, surpassing in magnificence those of London, Paris, and Vienna, shall we not rejoice at the success of the youngest rival among the nations of the earth? May not our hearts, in unison with all, swell with pride at our great achievements as a people; our free speech, free press, free schools, free church, and the rapid progress we have made in material wealth, trade, commerce and the inventive arts? And we do rejoice in the success, thus far, of our experiment of self-government. Our faith is firm and unwavering in the broad principles of human rights proclaimed in 1776, not only as abstract truths, but as the corner stones of a republic. Yet we cannot forget, even in this glad hour, that while all men of every race, and clime, and condition, have been invested with the full rights of citizenship under our hospitable flag, all women still suffer the degradation of disfranchisement.

The history of our country the past hundred years has been a series of assumptions and usurpations of power over woman, in direct opposition to the principles of just government, acknowledged by the United States as its foundation. . . .

And for the violation of these fundamental principles of our government, we arraign our rulers on this Fourth day of July, 1876,—and these are our articles of impeachment:

Bills of attainder have been passed by the introduction of the word "male" into all the State constitutions, denying to women the right of suf-

Excerpted from Susan B. Anthony, Declaration of Rights for Women by the National Woman Suffrage Association, in *History of Woman Suffrage*, edited by Elizabeth Cady Stanton, Susan B. Anthony, and Matilda Joslyn Gage, vol. 3 (Rochester, N.Y.: Susan B. Anthony, 1886), pp. 31–34.

"All my future plans are based on you as a coadjutor," wrote Elizabeth Cady Stanton to Susan B. Anthony in 1865. *"Yes, our work is one, we are one in aim and sympathy. . . ."* This photograph was taken c. 1870, midway through their career-long partnership, and not long before their collaborative work on the Centennial Address. In this picture Stanton is approximately 55 years old, Anthony approximately 50. (Photograph courtesy of the Smithsonian Institution)

frage, and thereby making sex a crime—an exercise of power clearly forbidden in article 1, sections 9, 10, of the United States constitution. . . .

The right of trial by a jury of one's peers was so jealously guarded that States refused to ratify the original constitution until it was guaranteed by the sixth amendment. And yet the women of this nation have never been allowed a jury of their peers—being tried in all cases by men, native, and foreign, educated and ignorant, virtuous and vicious. Young girls have been arraigned in our courts for the crime of infanticide; tried, convicted, hanged—victims, perchance, of judge, jurors, advocates—while no woman's voice could be heard in their defense. . . .

Taxation without representation, the immediate

cause of the rebellion of the colonies against Great Britain, is one of the grievous wrongs the women of this country have suffered during the century. Deploring war, with all the demoralization that follows in its train, we have been taxed to support standing armies, with their waste of life and wealth. Believing in temperance, we have been taxed to support the vice, crime and pauperism of the liquor traffic. While we suffer its wrongs and abuses infinitely more than man, we have no power to protect our sons against this giant evil. . . .

Unequal codes for men and women. Held by law a perpetual minor, deemed incapable of self-protection, even in the industries of the world, woman is denied equality of rights. The fact of sex, not the quantity or quality of work, in most cases, decides the pay and position; and because of this injustice thousands of fatherless girls are compelled to choose between a life of shame and starvation. Laws catering to man's vices have created two codes of morals in which penalties are graded according to the political status of the offender. Under such laws, women are fined and imprisoned if found alone in the streets, or in public places of resort, at certain hours. Under the pretense of regulating public morals, police officers seizing the occupants of disreputable houses, march the women in platoons to prison, while the men, partners in their guilt, go free. . . .

Representation of woman has had no place in the nation's thought. Since the incorporation of the thirteen original States, twenty-four have been admitted to the Union, not one of which has recognized woman's right of self-government. On this birthday of our national liberties, July Fourth, 1876, Colorado, like all her elder sisters, comes into the Union with the invidious word "male" in her constitution. . . .

The judiciary above the nation has proved itself but the echo of the party in power, by upholding and enforcing laws that are opposed to the spirit and letter of the constitution. When the slave power was dominant, the Supreme Court decided that a black man was not a citizen, because he had not the right to vote; and when the constitution was so amended as to make all persons citizens, the same high tribunal decided that a woman, though a citizen, had not the right to vote. Such vacillating interpretations of constitutional law unsettle our faith in judicial authority, and undermine the liberties of the whole people.

These articles of impeachment against our rulers we now submit to the impartial judgment of the people. To all these wrongs and oppressions woman has not submitted in silence and resignation. From the beginning of the century, when Abigail Adams, the wife of one president and mother of another, said, "We will not hold ourselves bound to obey laws in which we have no voice or representation," until now, woman's discontent has been steadily increasing, culminating nearly thirty years ago in a simultaneous movement among the women of the nation, demanding the right of suffrage. In making our just demands, a higher motive than the pride of sex inspires us; we feel that national safety and stability depend on the complete recognition of the broad principles of our government. Woman's degraded, helpless position is the weak point in our institutions today; a disturbing force everywhere, severing family ties, filling our asylums with the deaf, the dumb, the blind; our prisons with criminals, our cities with drunkenness and prostitution; our homes with disease and death. It was the boast of the founders of the republic, that the rights for which they contended were the rights of human nature. If these rights are ignored in the case of one-half the people, the nation is surely preparing for its downfall. Governments try themselves. The recognition of a governing and a governed class is incompatible with the first principles of freedom. Woman has not been a heedless spectator of the events of this century, nor a dull listener to the grand arguments for the equal rights of humanity. From the earliest history of our country woman has shown equal devotion with man to the cause of freedom, and has stood firmly by his side in its defense. Together they have made this country what it is. Woman's wealth, thought and labor have cemented the stones of every monument man has reared to liberty.

And now, at the close of a hundred years, as the hour-hand of the great clock that marks the centuries points to 1876, we declare our faith in the principles of self-government; our full equality with man in natural rights; that woman was made first for her own happiness, with the absolute right to herself—to all the opportunities and advantages life affords for her complete development; and we deny that dogma of the centuries, incorporated in the codes of all nations—that woman was made for man—her best interests, in all cases, to be sacrificed to his will. We ask of our rulers, at this hour, no special privileges, no special legislation. We ask justice, we ask equality, we ask that all the civil and political rights that belong to citizens of the United States, be guaranteed to us and our daughters forever.

This photograph of a young woman, nonchalantly posed atop the framing of a Chicago skyscraper in 1920, conveys both personal daring and a challenge to gender roles. (Photograph by Connie Colliers, courtesy of the Bettman Archive)

II_B

Industrializing America
1880–1920

Americans triumphantly celebrated the end of the nineteenth century. They had secured sectional unity between North and South and the benefits of continental expansion. The industrial revolution, dominated by the vision and organizational genius of a few hard-driving, ruthless entrepreneurs, had transformed a wilderness into a new landscape, crisscrossed by railroads and telegraph and telephone lines and dotted with foundries, factories, and mills. Sprawling cities and industrial centers lured native and immigrant alike with the promise of a new job and a fresh start. As the urban population increased from 15 million in 1880 to 45 million in 1910, America's farmers expanded their output not only to feed this nation's teeming cities but those of Europe as well. American technology provided its own "miracles." The Brooklyn Bridge, upon completion in 1883, was the longest suspension bridge in the world. Serving thousands of daily commuters between Brooklyn and Manhattan, it stood as a symbol not only of the technological achievements of the American people but of the emergence of a new nation—industrial, urban, and ethnically diverse.

Maturing as an economic power in an age of imperialism, America was fast becoming an international power as well. Competing with Europe in a worldwide quest for new trade outlets, the United States picked up new territories along with new markets. Acquisition of Alaska (1867) was followed by involvement in—and ultimately annexation of—Samoa (1872) and Hawaii (1898). After a "splendid little war" with Spain, this nation was left with Puerto Rico, Guam, and the Philippines. Eager to protect strategic interests in the Pacific, the United States acquired the right to construct an interoceanic canal to be owned by the new country of Panama but under American control. The Panama Canal, another triumph of American engineering, was one of many developments portending this nation's willingness to intervene in the affairs of other nations to the south in order to establish hemispheric dominance and protect American investments.

The economic expansion that had enabled, and indeed encouraged, this former British colony to create its own imperial system did not occur painlessly. The populist movement of the 1890s, for example, expressed the anger of agrarians who attacked the injustices of an economic system that victimized farmers while benefiting industrial, railroad, and banking interests. The growing socialist movement was but one expression of workers' discontent with an industrial order in which 5 percent of the population owned nearly half the nation's property while more than a third of its 76 million people in 1910 lived below the poverty line. Living conditions were no better than working conditions for the millions trapped in the poverty and misery of teeming urban ghettos. Cities, ill prepared to cope with rapid population growth, were governed inadequately and often dishonestly by politicians whose base of support lay in wards populated by immigrants inexperienced with American politics and grateful for services provided by the "machine."

Attempting to steer a middle course between radicalism and reaction, many Americans at the turn of the century turned to progressivism, participating in a multifaceted coalition of reformers that included insurgent intellectuals and university professors, Christian "social gospelers," women activists, investigative reporters, business and professional men, farmers, and laborers. A diverse lot dedicated to a variety of goals, progressives generally agreed on certain basic propositions. Government, particularly at the local and state level, must be made more democratic, honest, and efficient; monopolies must be controlled and big business made more responsive to the public interest; natural resources must be used more rationally; social conditions must be made more just and humane and the environment in which people lived and worked made safer. Extending to international affairs this same concern for order and reform, they agreed that in the wake of World War I the postwar world created must be progressive as well. Although their efforts to meet the needs of this new urban, industrial society were sometimes contradictory and not always successful, progressives laid the foundations of the modern welfare state.

Technology, industrialization, immigration, urbanization, domestic reform and international involvement: these were the developments shaping American life between 1880 and 1920, and they involved women as well as men. Women, many from southern and eastern Europe, moved to cities, seeking there some measure of economic survival and family stability. Women worked on farms and in factories, some emerging as populist agitators, socialist activists, and labor organizers. Women also became progressives and pacificists, serving in the vanguard of those struggling for economic and social justice and international peace.

Historians have customarily acknowledged these women with little more than a cursory nod toward such figures as Mary Elizabeth Lease, the populist orator who urged farmers "to raise less corn and more hell"; Mary Harris ("Mother") Jones, the fiery labor agitator who became a symbol of defiance wherever strikers gathered; and, of course, Jane Addams, the humanitarian reformer whose settlement house work made her a relentless foe of political corruption and economic exploitation. Although historians usually include women's winning the vote among progressive achievements, they have been reluctant to examine the ways in which men and women differed in their experiences of industrial work and technological change. Even in studying reform most historians of progressivism have focused on males, whether as business, professional, or political elites or as working-class voters. Suppose, however, we reverse this emphasis, exploring progressivism as one example of the way in which the inclusion of women's experience prompts a refocusing of what we know about this much studied era in American reform.

We should begin by reversing the relation of women reformers to progressivism. Instead of focusing on them as part of a reform coalition, let us, for the moment, view progressivism as part of women's history, looking especially at the way in which women steadily moved from the domestic into the public sphere, in the process changing both. The first stage of that process we can locate in the early years of the republic when women as "Republican Mothers" assumed a role that made their domestic domain of education and nurture into a schoolroom for the next generation of virtuous citizens. This acknowledgment of the mother's private domain as a public trust helped to establish women— in the ideal, at least—as public persons with public responsibilities, even if exercised within the privacy of the family. At an ever-accelerating pace between 1820 and 1880— the dates are approximations—women expanded that role into what might be called "Reformist Motherhood." Instead of influencing the public domain indirectly through the lives of their sons, women began to extend their role as nurturer and teacher of morals from the domestic sphere into the public sphere through church, missionary, and moral reform groups. Women sought to make the world conform more strictly to values taught in the home—sexual responsibility and restraint for men as well as women, self-discipline for those who used strong drink, charity and rehabilitation for those who were entrapped by poverty and crime, sympathy and justice for African-Americans.

Between 1880 and 1920 a new role developed that might be called "Political Motherhood." Increasing numbers of women joined the Woman's Christian Temperance Union (WCTU), the Young Women's Christian Association (YWCA), the settlement house movement, the General Federation of Women's Clubs, the National Association of Colored Women, the Children's Aid Society, the National Child Labor Committee, the National Consumers' League, the Pure Food Association, and a host of others. (By 1920, for example, the WCTU had 800,000 members, the General Federation of Women's Clubs nearly one million.) Through these organizations and related activities, women enlarged still further their sphere in public life where once only men had acted. They worked to protect industrial workers, especially women and children, to clean up local politics as well as unsanitary slaughterhouses and polluted water supplies, to promote health, education, social welfare, and mental hygiene. Even big business was no longer "off limits" to women, as Ida Tarbell proved when she exposed the corrupt practices used by John D. Rockefeller to create his oil empire. In their rejection of an individualism that, in the hands of such men, had become exploitative, and in their willingness to use government at all levels to create a more humane, caring community, women were thinking and acting in ways that were quintessentially progressive.

In transforming women's sphere from the private, family-oriented world of domesticity into the formerly male world of politics and public policy, a major change was occurring. The "womanhood" identified with "mothering" was becoming less a biological fact—giving birth to children—and more a political role with new ideological dimensions. The traditional word *motherhood* was being reshaped so as to justify women's assuming new, ever-more-public responsibilities. Women now clearly meant to transform the domestic housekeeping responsibilities of their grandmothers into an attack on the worst abuses of an urban, industrial society. The household now included market-place and city hall.

Viewed in this context, prohibition, a progressive reform often regarded as a political aberration, can be seen as the logical extension of women's traditional concern for those women and children who were so often the victims of alcohol-related abuse. Indeed, such protection seemed as necessary and as logical as legislation abolishing child labor or limiting the hours of working women whose health as potential mothers would affect the health of the next generation. In this context, too, suffrage marks the final step in the movement out of the domestic sphere into the political sphere. That women should justify the need to vote in terms of their domestic responsibilities, a justification criticized by some historians, becomes quite consistent. That, too, must be viewed as part of a long process in which the drive to enlarge women's sphere came through gradual transfor-mation of ideals identified with an older domesticity into a new and broader sense of responsibility appropriate for a public sphere itself changing under the impact of indus-trialization, immigration, and urbanization.

What, then, have we accomplished through this exercise of taking women out of the progressive coalition and putting progressivism into women's history? We discover first of all that female reformers were not merely one group among many in the progressive coalition. Women's perspective quite as much as their participation gave progressivism much of its ideological direction as well as its momentum. Indeed, we can even say that the progressive perspective was, in large part, the appropriation by male reformers of those ideas most intimately associated with the social perspective of women, almost literally the application to society of moral issues nurtured in women's domain. The significance of this achievement is understood, however, only when we include women's experience as basic, *not incidental*, to how we view the past. Refocusing history is, to be sure, a complicated task, but this one example—women and progressivism—suggests how we may begin to view afresh the first two decades of the twentieth century.

ELSA BARKLEY BROWN

Maggie Lena Walker and the Independent Order of Saint Luke: Advancing Women, Race, and Community in Turn-of-the-Century Richmond

In the aftermath of the Civil War, Radical Republicans in Congress were successful in securing amendments to the Constitution that guaranteed newly emancipated slaves their freedom, citizenship, and the franchise. They were unsuccessful in passing legislation to provide the land that would have given freedmen an economic base in the impoverished South. By the turn of the century, even these gains were being eroded throughout the region as racism increased, lynchings became commonplace, and laws disfranchising and segregating African-Americans appeared on the statute books. Fighting these reverses, black leaders redoubled their efforts. Many followed the lead of Booker T. Washington, who emphasized the importance of economic advancement through hard work and self-help.

The mutual benefit societies that were an example of this organizational impulse were not unique to African-Americans. Commonplace throughout the United States in the nineteenth century, especially in immigrant communities, they allowed working people to set aside small sums of money that could be used to cover the cost of burials and other emergencies. A few subsequently developed into full-fledged banks and insurance companies. Most, however, were more modest enterprises that combined economic aid with social and political activities.

"By the turn of the century," writes historian Anne F. Scott, "there were associations of some sort in nearly every black community, North and South, in cities, towns and villages. . . . When the NAACP got underway after 1908, various observers remarked that most of its local work was performed by women. In one way or another organized black women touched every area of life, from home to politics."* One such society, the Independent Order of Saint Luke, flourished in Richmond, Virginia, under the leadership of a remarkable woman, Maggie Lena Walker, who became the first female bank president in the United States. A staunch suffragist as well as an entrepreneur, Walker refused to separate women's issues from race issues. Like many black female activists, past as well as present, she believed that racism and sexism had to be fought simultaneously and that black women must organize to fight both.

---

*Anne Firor Scott, "Most Invisible of All: Black Women's Voluntary Associations," *Journal of Southern History* LVI (1990):16–17.

In the first decades of the twentieth century Maggie Lena Walker repeatedly challenged her contemporaries to "make history as Negro women." Walker (1867–1934) was born and educated in Richmond, Virginia, graduating from Colored Normal School in 1883. During her school years she assisted her widowed mother in her work as a washerwoman and cared for her younger brother. Following graduation she taught in the city's public schools and took courses in accounting and sales. Required to stop teaching when she married Armstead Walker, a contractor, her coursework had well prepared her to join several other black women in founding an insurance company, the Woman's Union. Meanwhile, Walker, who had joined the Independent Order of Saint Luke at the age of fourteen, rose through the ranks to hold several important positions in the order and, in 1895, to organize the juvenile branch of the order. In addition to her Saint Luke activities, Walker was a founder or leading supporter of the Richmond Council of Colored Women, the Virginia State Federation of Colored Women, the National Association of Wage Earners, the International Council of Women of the Darker Races, the National Training School for Girls, and the Virginia Industrial School for Colored Girls. She also helped direct the National Association for the Advancement of Colored People, the Richmond Urban League, and the Negro Organization Society of Virginia.[1]

Walker is probably best known today as the first woman bank president in the United States. She founded the Saint Luke Penny Savings Bank in Richmond, Virginia, in 1903. Before her death in 1934 she oversaw the reorganization of this financial institution as the present-day Consolidated Bank and Trust Company, the oldest continuously existing black-owned and black-run bank in the country. The bank, like most of Walker's activities, was the outgrowth of the Independent Order of Saint Luke, which she served as Right Worthy Grand Secretary for thirty-five years.

The Independent Order of Saint Luke was one of the larger and more successful of the many thousands of mutual benefit societies that have developed throughout Africanamerican communities since the eighteenth century. These societies combined insurance functions with economic development and social and political activities. As such they were important loci of community self-help and racial solidarity. Unlike the Knights of Pythias and its female auxiliary, the Courts of Calanthe, societies like the Independent Order of Saint Luke had a nonexclusionary membership policy; any man, woman, or child could join. . . .

Founded in Maryland in 1867 by Mary Prout, the Independent Order of Saint Luke began as a women's sickness and death mutual benefit association. By the 1880s it had admitted men and had expanded to New York and Virginia. At the 1899 annual meeting William M. T. Forrester, who had served as Grand Secretary since 1869, refused to accept reappointment, stating that the order was in decline, having only 1,080 members in fifty-seven councils, $31.61 in the treasury, and $400.00 in outstanding debts. Maggie Lena Walker took over the duties of Grand Worthy Secretary at one-third of the position's previous salary.[2]

According to Walker, her "first work was to draw around me *women*." In fact, after the executive board elections in 1901, six of the nine members were women: Walker, Patsie K. Anderson, Frances Cox, Abigail Dawley, Lillian H. Payne, and Ella O. Waller.[3] Under their leadership the order and its affiliates flourished. The order's ventures included a juvenile department, an educational loan fund for young people, a department store, and a weekly newspaper. Growing to include over 100,000 members in 2,010 councils and circles in twenty-eight states, the order demonstrated a special commitment to expanding the economic opportunities within the black community, especially those for women.

It is important to take into account Walker's acknowledgment of her female colleagues. Most of what we know about the Order of Saint Luke highlights Walker because she was the leader and spokeswoman and therefore the most visible figure. She was able, however, to function in that role and to accomplish all that she did not merely because of her own strengths and skills, considerable though they were, but also because she operated from the strength of the Saint Luke collective as a whole and from the special strengths and talents of the inner core of the Saint Luke women in particular. . . .

The women of Saint Luke expanded the

role of women in the community to the political sphere through their leadership in the 1904 streetcar boycott and through the *St. Luke Herald*'s pronouncements against segregation, lynching, and lack of equal educational opportunities for black children. Walker spearheaded the local struggle for women's suffrage and the voter registration campaigns after the passage of the Nineteenth Amendment. In the 1920 elections in Richmond, fully 80 percent of the eligible black voters were women. The increased black political strength represented by the female voters gave incentive to the growing movement for independent black political action and led to the formation of the Virginia Lily-Black Republican Party. Walker ran on this ticket for state superintendent of public instruction in 1921.[4] Thus Walker and many other of the Saint Luke women were role models for other black women in their community activities as well as their occupations.

Undergirding all of their work was a belief in the possibilities inherent in the collective struggle of black women in particular and of the black community in general. Walker argued that the only way in which black women would be able "to avoid the traps and snares of life" would be to "band themselves together, organize, ... put their mites together, put their hands and their brains together and make work and business for themselves."[5]

The idea of collective economic development was not a new idea for these women, many of whom were instrumental in establishing the Woman's Union, a female insurance company founded in 1898. Its motto was The Hand That Rocks the Cradle Rules the World. But unlike nineteenth-century white women's rendering of that expression to signify the limitation of woman's influence to that which she had by virtue of rearing her sons, the idea as these women conceived it transcended the separation of private and public spheres and spoke to the idea that women, while not abandoning their roles as wives and mothers, could also move into economic and political activities in ways that would support rather than conflict with family and community. Women did not have to choose between the two spheres; in fact, they necessarily had to occupy both. Indeed, these women's use of this phrase speaks to their understanding of the totality of the task that lay ahead of them as black women. It ne-

gates, for black women at least, the public/private dichotomy.

Saint Luke women built on tradition. A well-organized set of institutions maintained community in Richmond: mutual benefit societies, interwoven with extended families and churches, built a network of supportive relations.[6] The families, churches, and societies were all based on similar ideas of collective consciousness and collective responsibility. Thus, they served to extend and reaffirm notions of family throughout the black community. Not only in their houses but also in their meeting halls and places of worship, they were brothers and sisters caring for each other. The institutionalization of this notion of family cemented the community. Community/family members recognized that this had to be maintained from generation to generation; this was in part the function of the juvenile branches of the mutual benefit associations. The statement of purpose of the Children's Rosebud Fountains, Grand Fountain United Order of True Reformers, clearly articulated this:

> Teaching them . . . to assist each other in sickness, sorrow and afflictions and in the struggles of life; teaching them that one's happiness greatly depends upon the others. . . . Teach them to live united. . . . The children of different families will know how to . . . talk, plot and plan for one another's peace and happiness in the journey of life.
>
> Teach them to . . . bear each other's burdens . . . to so bind and tie their love and affections together that one's sorrow may be the other's sorrow, one's distress be the other's distress, one's penny the other's penny.[7]

Through the Penny Savings Bank the Saint Luke women were able to affirm and cement the existing mutual assistance network among black women and within the black community by providing an institutionalized structure for these activities. The bank recognized the meager resources of the black community, particularly black women. In fact, its establishment as a *penny* savings bank is an indication of that. Many of its earliest and strongest supporters were washerwomen, one of whom was Maggie Walker's mother. And the bank continued throughout Walker's leadership to exercise a special commitment to "the small depositor."[8]

In her efforts Walker, like the other Saint Luke women, was guided by a clearly understood and shared perspective concerning the relationship of black women to black men, to the black community, and to the larger society. This was a perspective that acknowledged individual powerlessness in the face of racism and sexism and that argued that black women, because of their condition and status, had a right—indeed, according to Walker, a special duty and incentive—to organize. She argued, "Who is so helpless as the Negro woman? Who is so circumscribed and hemmed in, in the race of life, in the struggle for bread, meat and clothing as the Negro woman?"[9] . . .

Walker was determined to expand opportunities for black women. In fulfilling this aim she challenged not only the larger society's notions of the proper place of blacks but also those in her community who held a limited notion of women's proper role. Particularly in light of the increasing necessity to defend the integrity and morality of the race, a "great number of men" and women in Virginia and elsewhere believed that women's clubs, movements "looking to the final exercise of suffrage by women," and organizations of black professional and business women would lead to "the decadence of home life."[10] Women involved in these activities were often regarded as "pullbacks, rather than home builders." Maggie Walker countered these arguments, stressing the need for women's organizations, saying, "Men should not be so pessimistic and down on women's clubs. They don't seek to destroy the home or disgrace the race."[11] In fact, the Richmond Council of Colored Women, of which she was founder and president, and many other women's organizations worked to elevate the entire black community, and this, she believed, was the proper province of women.

In 1908 two Richmond men, Daniel Webster Davis and Giles Jackson, published *The Industrial History of the Negro Race of the United States*, which became a textbook for black children throughout the state. The chapter on women acknowledged the economic and social achievements of black women but concluded that "the Negro Race Needs Housekeepers . . . wives who stay at home, being supported by their husbands, and then they can spend time in the training of their children."[12] Maggie Walker responded practically to those who held such ideas: "The bold fact remains that there are more women in the world than men; . . . if each and every woman in the land was

allotted a man to marry her, work for her, support her, and keep her at home, there would still be an army of women left uncared for, unprovided for, and who would be compelled to fight life's battles alone, and without the companionship of man."[13] Even regarding those women who did marry, she contended, "The old doctrine that a man marries a woman to support her is pretty nearly thread-bare today." Only a few black men were able to fully support their families on their earnings alone. Thus many married women worked, "not for name, not for glory and honor—but for bread, and for [their] babies."[14]

The reality was that black women who did go to work outside the home found themselves in a helpless position. "How many occupations have Negro Women?" asked Walker. "Let us count them: Negro women are domestic menials, teachers and church builders." And even the first two of these, she feared, were in danger. As Walker perceived it, the expansion of opportunities for white women did not mean a corresponding expansion for black women; instead, this trend might actually lead to an even greater limitation on the economic possibilities for black women. She pointed to the fact that white women's entry into the tobacco factories of the city had "driven the Negro woman out," and she, like many of her sisters throughout the country, feared that a similar trend was beginning even in domestic work.[15]

In fact, these economic realities led members of the Order of Saint Luke to discuss the development of manufacturing operations as a means of giving employment and therefore "a chance in the race of life" to "the young Negro woman." In 1902 Walker described herself as "consumed with the desire to hear the whistle on our factory and see our women by the hundreds coming to work."[16] It was this same concern for the economic status of black women that led Walker and other Saint Luke women to affiliate with the National Association of Wage Earners (NAWE), a women's organization that sought to pool the energies and resources of housewives, professionals, and managerial, domestic, and industrial workers to protect and expand the economic position of black women. The NAWE argued that it was vital that all black women be able to support themselves.[17] Drawing on traditional stereotypes in the same breath with which she defied them, Walker contended that it was in the self-interest of black men to unite themselves with these efforts to secure decent employment for black women: "Every dollar a woman makes, some man gets the direct benefit of same. Every woman was by Divine Providence created for some man; not for some man to marry, take home and support, but for the purpose of using her powers, ability, health and strength, to forward the financial . . . success of the partnership into which she may go, if she will. . . . [W]hat stronger combination could ever God make—than the partnership of a business man and a business woman."[18]

By implication, whatever black women as a whole were able to achieve would directly benefit black men. In Walker's analysis family is a reciprocal metaphor for community: family is community and community is family. But this is more than rhetorical style. Her discussions of relationship networks suggest that the entire community was one's family. Thus Walker's references to husbands and wives reflected equally her understandings of male/female relationships in the community as a whole and of those relationships within the household. Just as all family members' resources were needed for the family to be well and strong, so they were needed for a healthy community/family.

In the process of developing means of expanding economic opportunities in the community, however, Walker and the Saint Luke women also confronted white Richmond's notions of the proper place of blacks. While whites found a bank headed by a "Negress" an interesting curiosity, they were less receptive to other business enterprises. In 1905 twenty-two black women from the Independent Order of Saint Luke collectively formed a department store aimed at providing quality goods at more affordable prices than those available in stores outside the black community, as well as a place where black women could earn a living and get a business education. The Saint Luke Emporium employed fifteen women as salesclerks. While this may seem an insignificant number in comparison to the thousands of black women working outside the home, in the context of the occupational structure of Richmond these women constituted a significant percentage of the white-collar and skilled working-class women in the community. In 1900 less than 1 percent of the employed black women in the city were either clerical or skilled work-

ers. That number had quadrupled by 1910, when 222 of the more than 13,000 employed black women listed their occupations as typists, stenographers, bookkeepers, salesclerks, and the like. However, by 1930 there had been a reduction in the numbers of black women employed in clerical and sales positions. This underscores the fact that black secretaries and clerks were entirely dependent on the financial stability of black businesses, and in this regard the Independent Order of Saint Luke was especially important. With its fifty-five clerks in the home office, over one-third of the black female clerical workers in Richmond in the 1920s worked for this order. The quality of the work experience was significantly better for these women as compared to those employed as laborers in the tobacco factories or as servants in private homes. They worked in healthier, less stressful environments and, being employed by blacks, they also escaped the racism prevalent in most black women's workplaces. Additionally, the salaries of these clerical workers were often better than those paid even to black professional women, that is, teachers. While one teacher, Ethel Thompson Overby, was receiving eighteen dollars a month as a teacher and working her way up to the top of the scale at forty dollars, a number of black women were finding good working conditions and a fifty-dollar-per-month paycheck as clerks in the office of the Independent Order of Saint Luke. Nevertheless, black women in Richmond, as elsewhere, overwhelmingly remained employed in domestic service in the years 1890–1930.[19]

Located on East Broad Street, Richmond's main business thoroughfare, the Saint Luke Emporium met stiff opposition from white merchants. When the intention to establish the department store was first announced, attempts were made to buy the property at a price several thousand dollars higher than that which the Order of Saint Luke had originally paid. When that did not succeed, an offer of ten thousand dollars cash was made to the order if it would not start the emporium. Once it opened, efforts were made to hinder the store's operations. A white Retail Dealers' Association was formed for the purpose of crushing this business as well as other "Negro merchants who are objectionable . . . because they compete with and get a few dollars which would otherwise go to the white merchant." Notices were sent to wholesale merchants in the city warning them not to sell to the emporium at the risk of losing all business from any of the white merchants. Letters were also sent to wholesale houses in New York City with the same warning. These letters charged that the emporium was underselling the white merchants of Richmond. Clearly, then, the white businessmen of Richmond found the emporium and these black women a threat; if it was successful, the store could lead to a surge of black merchants competing with white merchants and thus decrease the black patronage at white stores. The white merchants' efforts were ultimately successful: the obstacles they put in the way of the emporium, in addition to the lack of full support from the black community itself, resulted in the department store's going out of business seven years after its founding. Though its existence was short-lived and its demise mirrors many of the problems that black businesses faced from both within and without their community, the effort demonstrated the commitment of the Order of Saint Luke to provide needed services for the community and needed opportunities for black women.

Maggie Walker's appeals for support of the emporium show quite clearly the way in which her notions of race, of womanhood, and of community fused. Approximately one year after the opening of the emporium, Walker called for a mass gathering of men in the community to talk, in part, about support for the business. Her speech, "Beniah's Valour; An Address for Men Only," opened with an assessment of white businessmen's and officials' continuing oppression of the black community. In her fine rhetorical style she queried her audience. "Hasn't it crept into your minds that we are being more and more oppressed each day that we live? Hasn't it yet come to you, that we are being oppressed by the passage of laws which not only have for their object the degradation of Negro manhood and Negro womanhood, but also the destruction of all kinds of Negro enterprises?" Then, drawing upon the biblical allegory of Beniah and the lion, she warned, "There is a lion terrorizing us, preying upon us, and upon every business effort which we put forth. The name of this insatiable lion is PREJUDICE. . . . The white press, the white pulpit, the white business associations, the legis-lature—all . . . the lion with whom we contend daily . . . in Broad Street, Main Street and in every business street of Richmond. Even now . . . that lion is seeking some new plan of attack."[20]

Thus, she contended, the vital question facing their community was how to kill the lion. And in her analysis, "the only way to kill the Lion is to stop feeding it." The irony was that the black community drained itself of resources, money, influence, and patronage to feed its predator. As she had many times previously, Walker questioned the fact that while the white community oppressed the black, "the Negro . . . carries to their bank every dollar he can get his hands upon and then goes back the next day, borrows and then pays the white man to lend him his own money." So, too, black people patronized stores and other businesses in which white women were, in increasing numbers, being hired as salesclerks and secretaries while black women were increasingly without employment and the black community as a whole was losing resources, skills, and finances. Walker considered such behavior racially destructive and believed it necessary to break those ties that kept "the Negro . . . so wedded to those who oppress him." The drain on the resources of the black community could be halted by a concentration on the development of a self-sufficient black community. But to achieve this would require the talents of the entire community/family. It was therefore essential that black women's work in the community be "something more tangible than elegant papers, beautifully framed resolutions and pretty speeches." Rather, "the exercising of every talent that God had given them" was required in the effort to "raise . . . the race to higher planes of living."[21]

The Saint Luke women were part of the Negro Independence Movement that captured a large segment of Richmond society at the turn of the century. Disillusioned by the increasing prejudice and discrimination in this period, which one historian has described as the nadir in U.S. race relations, black residents of Richmond nevertheless held on to their belief in a community that they could collectively sustain.[22] As they witnessed a steady erosion of their civil and political rights, however, they were aware that there was much operating against them. In Richmond, as elsewhere, a sys-

tem of race and class oppression including segregation, disfranchisement, relegation to the
lowest rungs of the occupational strata, and enforcement of racial subordination through intimidation was fully in place by the early twentieth century. In Richmond between 1885 and
1915 all blacks were removed from the city
council; the only predominantly black political
district, Jackson Ward, was gerrymandered out
of existence; the state constitutional convention
disfranchised the majority of black Virginians;
first the railroads and streetcars, and later the
jails, juries, and neighborhoods were segregated; black principals were removed from the
public schools and the right of blacks to teach
was questioned; the state legislature decided to
substitute white for black control of Virginia
Normal and College and to strike "and College" from both name and function; and numerous other restrictions were imposed. As attorney J. Thomas Hewin noted, he and his
fellow black Richmonders occupied "a peculiar
position in the body politic":

> He [the Negro] is not wanted in politics, because
> his presence in official positions renders him ob-
> noxious to his former masters and their descen-
> dants. He is not wanted in the industrial world as
> a trained handicraftsman, because he would be
> brought into competition with his white brother.
> He is not wanted in city positions, because posi-
> tions of that kind are always saved for the ward-
> heeling politicans. He is not wanted in State and
> Federal offices, because there is an unwritten law
> that a Negro shall not hold an office. He is not
> wanted on the Bench as a judge, because he
> would have to pass upon the white man's case
> also. Nor is he wanted on public conveyances, be-
> cause here his presence is obnoxious to white peo-
> ple.[23]

Assessing the climate of the surrounding society in 1904, John Mitchell, Jr., editor of the
Richmond Planet, concluded, "This is the beginning of the age of conservatism."[24] The
growing movement within the community for
racial self-determination urged blacks to depend upon themselves and their community
rather than upon whites: to depend upon their
own inner strengths, to build their own institutions, and thereby to mitigate the ways in
which their lives were determined by the white
forces arrayed against them. Race pride, self-
help, racial cooperation, and economic development were central to their thinking about

their community and to the ways in which they
went about building their own internal support
system in order to be better able to struggle
within the majority system.

The Saint Luke women argued that the development of the community could not be
achieved by men alone, or by men on behalf of
women. Only a strong and unified community
made up of both women and men could wield
the power necessary to allow black people to
shape their own lives. Therefore, only when
women were able to exercise their full strength
would the community be at its full strength,
they argued. Only when the community was at
its full strength would they be able to create
their own conditions, conditions that would allow men as well as women to move out of their
structural isolation at the bottom of the labor
market and to overcome their political im-
potence in the larger society. The Saint Luke
women argued that it was therefore in the self-
interest of black men and of the community as
a whole to support expanded opportunities for
women.

Their arguments redefined not only the
roles of women but also the roles and notions
of manhood. A strong "race man" traditionally
meant one who stood up fearlessly in defense
of the race. In her "Address for Men" Walker
argued that one could not defend the race unless one defended black women. Appealing to
black men's notions of themselves as the protectors of black womanhood, she asked on behalf of all her sisters for their "FRIENDSHIP, . . .
LOVE, . . . SYMPATHY, . . . PROTECTION, and . . .
ADVICE": "I am asking you, men of Richmond,
. . . to record [yourselves] as . . . the strong race
men of our city. . . . I am asking each man in
this audience to go forth from this building, determined to do valiant deeds for the Negro
Women of Richmond." And how might they
offer their friendship, love, and protection; how
might they do valiant deeds for Negro womanhood? By supporting the efforts of black
women to exercise every talent; by "let[ting]
woman choose her own vocation, just as man
does his"; by supporting the efforts then underway to provide increased opportunities—
economic, political, and social—for black
women.[25] Once again she drew upon traditional notions of the relationship between men
and women at the same time that she countered those very notions. Black men could play

the role of protector and defender of womanhood by protecting and defending and aiding women's assault on the barriers generally imposed on women.[26] Only in this way could they really defend the race. Strong race consciousness and strong support of equality for black women were inseparable. Maggie Walker and the other Saint Luke women therefore came to argue that an expanded role for black women within the black community itself was an essential step in the community's fight to overcome the limitations imposed upon the community by the larger society. Race men were therefore defined not just by their actions on behalf of black rights but by their actions on behalf of women's rights. The two were inseparable.

This was a collective effort in which Walker believed black men and black women should be equally engaged. Therefore, even in creating a woman's organization, she and her Saint Luke associates found it essential to create space within the structure for men as well. Unlike many of the fraternal orders that were male or female only, the Order of Saint Luke welcomed both genders as members and as employees. Although the office force was all female, men were employed in the printing department, in field work, and in the bank. Principal offices within the order were open to men and women. Ten of the thirty directors of the emporium were male; eight of the nineteen trustees of the order were male. The Saint Luke women thus strove to create an equalitarian organization, with men neither dominant nor auxiliary. Their vision of the order was a reflection of their vision for their community. In the 1913 Saint Luke Thanksgiving Day celebration of the order, Maggie Walker "thank[ed] God that this is a *woman's* organization, broad enough, liberal enough, and unselfish enough to accord equal rights and equal opportunity to men."[27]

Only such a community could become self-sustaining, self-sufficient, and independent, could enable its members to live lives unhampered by the machinations of the larger society, and could raise children who could envision a different world in which to live and then could go about creating it. The women in the Order of Saint Luke sought to carve a sphere for themselves where they could practically apply their belief in their community

and in the potential that black men and women working together could achieve, and they sought to infuse that belief into all of black Richmond and to transmit it to the next generation.

The Saint Luke women challenged notions in the black community about the proper role of women; they challenged notions in the white community about the proper place of blacks. They expanded their roles in ways that enabled them to maintain traditional values of family/community and at the same time move into new spheres and relationships with each other and with the men in their lives. To the larger white society they demonstrated what black men and women in community could achieve. This testified to the idea that women's struggle and race struggle were not two separate phenomena but one indivisible whole. "First by practice and then by precept" Maggie Lena Walker and the Saint Luke women demonstrated in their own day the power of black women discovering their own strengths and sharing them with the whole community.[28] . . .

NOTES

1. Although there exists no scholarly biography of Walker, information is available in several sources. See Sadie Daniel St. Clair, "Maggie Lena Walker," in *Notable American Women, 1607–1960* (Cambridge, Mass.: Harvard University Press, Belknap, 1971), pp. 530–31; . . . and Rayford Logan, "Maggie Lena Walker," in *Dictionary of American Negro Biography*, ed. Rayford W. Logan and Michael R. Winston (New York: Norton, 1982), pp. 626–27; Sallie Chandler, "Maggie Lena Walker (1867–1934): An Abstract of Her Life and Activities," 1975 Oral History Files, Virginia Union University Library, Richmond, Va., 1975; Maggie Lena Walker Papers, Maggie L. Walker National Historic Site, Richmond, Va. (hereafter cited as MLW Papers). . . .

2. *50th Anniversary—Golden Jubilee Historical Report of the R.W.G. Council I. O. St. Luke, 1867–1917* (Richmond, Va.: Everett Waddey, 1917), pp. 5–6, 20 (hereafter cited as *50th Anniversary*).

3. Maggie L. Walker, "Diary," Mar. 6, 1928, MLW Papers; . . . *50th Anniversary*, p. 26.

4. The high proportion of female voters resulted from whites' successful efforts to disfranchise the majority of black male voters, as well as the enthusiasm of women to exercise this new right; see, e.g., *Richmond News-Leader* (Aug.–Oct. 1920); *Richmond Times-Dispatch* (Sept.–Oct. 1920). . . . However, black women soon found themselves faced with the same obstacles to political rights as confronted black men.

5. M. L. Walker, "Addresses," 1909, MLW Papers, cited in Celia Jackson Suggs, "Maggie Lena

Walker," *TRUTH: Newsletter of the Association of Black Women Historians* 7 (Fall 1985):6.

6. Some of the societies had only women members, including some that were exclusively for the mutual assistance of single mothers. For an excellent discussion of the ties among the societies, families, and churches in Richmond, see Peter J. Rachleff, *Black Labor in the South: Richmond, Virginia, 1865–1890* (Philadelphia: Temple University Press, 1984).

7. W. P. Burrell and D. E. Johnson, Sr., *Twenty-Five Years History of the Grand Fountain of the United Order of True Reformers, 1881–1905* (Richmond, Va.: Grand Fountain, United Order of True Reformers, 1909), pp. 76–77.

8. Saint Luke Penny Savings Bank records; . . . Consolidated Bank and Trust Company, Richmond, Va.; *Cleveland Plain Dealer* (June 28, 1914), in Peabody Clipping File, Collis P. Huntington Library, Hampton Institute, Hampton, Va. (hereafter cited as Peabody Clipping File), no. 88, vol. 1. . . .

9. This analysis owes much to Cheryl Townsend Gilkes's work on black women, particularly her . . . " 'Holding Back the Ocean with a Broom': Black Women and Community Work," in *The Black Woman,* ed. LaFrances Rodgers-Rose (Beverly Hills, Calif.: Sage, 1980). . . .

10. The prevailing turn-of-the-century stereotype of black women emphasized promiscuity and immorality; these ideas were given prominence in a number of publications, including newspapers, periodicals, philanthropic foundation reports, and popular literature. The attacks by various segments of the white community on the morality of black women and the race at the turn of the century are discussed in Beverly Guy-Sheftall, " 'Daughters of Sorrow': Attitudes toward Black Women, 1880–1920" (Ph.D. diss., Emory University, 1984), pp. 62–86; Darlene Clark Hine, "Lifting the Veil, Shattering the Silence: Black Women's History in Slavery and Freedom," in *The State of Afro-American History: Past, Present, and Future,* ed. Darlene Clark Hine (Baton Rouge: Louisiana State University Press, 1986), pp. 223–49, esp. pp. 234–38; . . .

11. Charles F. McLaurin, "State Federation of Colored Women" (n.p., Nov. 10, 1908), Peabody Clipping File, no. 231, vol. 1; Chandler (n. 1 above), pp. 10–11.

12. Daniel Webster Davis and Giles Jackson, *The Industrial History of the Negro Race of the United States* (Richmond: Virginia Press, 1908), p. 133. . . .

13. M. L. Walker, "Speech to Federation of Colored Women's Clubs," Hampton, Va., July 14, 1912, MLW Papers.

14. M. L. Walker, "Speech to the Negro Young People's Christian and Educational Congress," Convention Hall, Washington, D.C., Aug. 5, 1906, MLW Papers.

15. . . . [See] M. L. Walker, "Speech to the Federation of Colored Women's Clubs." These ideas,

however, were a central theme in Walker's speeches and were repeated throughout the years. . . .

16. Excerpts from speech given by M. L. Walker at 1901 annual Saint Luke convention, *50th Anniversary,* p. 23; and "Our Mission" (n. 15 above).

17. Container 308, Nannie Helen Burroughs Papers, Manuscript Division, Library of Congress.

18. M. L. Walker, "Speech to Federation of Colored Women's Clubs" (n. 13 above).

19. In 1900, 83.8 percent of employed black women worked in domestic and personal service; in 1930, 76.5 percent. U.S. Bureau of the Census, *Twelfth Census of the United States Taken in the Year 1900, Population Part 1* (Washington, D.C.: Census Office, 1901), *Thirteenth Census of the United States Taken in the Year 1910,* vol. 4: *Population 1910—Occupation Statistics* (Washington, D.C.: Government Printing Office, 1914), p. 595, and *Fifteenth Census of the United States: Population,* vol. 4: *Occupations, by States* (Washington, D.C.: Government Printing Office, 1933); Benjamin Brawley, *Negro Builders and Heroes* (Chapel Hill: University of North Carolina Press, 1937), pp. 267–72; U.S. Bureau of the Census, *Fourteenth Census of the United States Taken in the Year 1920,* vol. 4: *Population 1920—Occupations* (Washington, D.C.: Government Printing Office, 1923). . . .

20. M. L. Walker, "Beniah's Valour: An Address for Men Only," Saint Luke Hall, Mar. 1, 1906, MLW Papers.

21. Chandler (n. 1 above), p. 30; *New York Age* (June 22, 1909), Peabody Clipping File, no. 231, vol. 1.

22. Rayford W. Logan, *The Betrayal of the Negro from Rutherford B. Hayes to Woodrow Wilson* (New York: Collier, 1965; originally published in 1954 as *The Negro in American Life and Thought: The Nadir*).

23. J. Thomas Hewin, "Is the Criminal Negro Justly Dealt with in the Courts of the South?" in *Twentieth Century Negro Literature, or a Cyclopedia of Thought on the Vital Topics Relating to the American Negro,* ed. D. W. Culp (Toronto: J. L. Nichols, 1902), pp. 110–11.

24. *Richmond Planet* (Apr. 30, 1904).

25. M. L. Walker, "Beniah's Valour: An Address for Men Only" (n. 20 above); *New York Age* (June 22, 1909). . . .

26. W.E.B. DuBois, who explored extensively the connection between race struggle and women's struggle in "The Damnation of Women," also challenged men's traditional roles, . . . *Darkwater, Voices from within the Veil* (New York: Harcourt, Brace, & Howe, 1920), p. 165.

27. M. L. Walker, "Saint Luke Thanksgiving Day Speech," City Auditorium, Mar. 23, 1913, MLW Papers. . . .

28. M. L. Walker, "Address—Virginia Day Third Street Bethel AME Church," Jan. 29, 1933, MLW Papers.

DAVID M. KATZMAN
Seven Days a Week: Domestic Work

For women who needed to work outside the home, domestic service has always been one of the limited job options available. Housekeeping was, after all, presumed to be "women's work." By 1900 over one-third of the wage-earning women in this country were employed as domestics or waitresses. Many were either immigrants or the daughters of immigrants from Europe; others were African-Americans. The lot of such women was not easy, especially in the years before the invention of the labor-saving appliances that became common fixtures in middle-class households by 1920. Note the number of tasks expected of a domestic in a single-servant household, the long hours, the low pay, the necessity of always being at the "beck and call" of the mistress, and the lack of time of one's own. Because of these factors, many women of European background left domestic service for jobs in factories or shops, leaving black women—victims of even greater discrimination—to form a larger proportion of domestic workers.

The best way of illustrating the daily and weekly cycles is to follow a general household worker through a part of her week's work. Inez Godman recorded her activities on a typical workday in 1901. She worked in a Northern home, doing all the work except the wash. She had negotiated a 75¢-a-week reduction in wages to $2.75 in return for her mistress hiring the wash out. Godman began work on a Wednesday afternoon and immediately prepared the dinner. Apparently no time was allotted for her to adjust to her new work and living environment. Wearing the apron and cap provided her, she served the meal. After cleaning up the kitchen and dining room, she prepared bread dough; her mistress had become "weary of baker's stuff." At 9:00 P.M. she was through for the day.[1]

On Thursday she rose at 6:00 A.M. and served breakfast an hour later. By 9:30 A.M. the kitchen and dining room had been cleaned, and her weekly chores began. She spent two hours cleaning the sitting room. "Everything had to be carried into the adjoining room, and there was much china and bric-a-brac," she wrote. The carpet had to be moved, and each slat of the Venetian blinds wiped clean. Twice she had to go to the kitchen to check the bread she was baking (it had risen overnight), and five times she had to answer the doorbell. Lunch required an hour of preparation, and she served her mistress at one. Already she had worked seven hours: "I was thankful for a chance to sit, and dawdled over my lunch for half an hour." By 2:30 P.M. the kitchen and dining room were clean again, and her mistress suggested Godman clean the kitchen floor. Afterwards, she rested in her room from 3:20 to 4:00 P.M. At 4:00 she had to go downstairs to heat the oven and begin the evening meal. "Dinner was a complex meal," she explained, "and coming at night when I was tired was always something of a worry. To have the different courses ready at just the right moment, to be sure that nothing burned or curdled while I was waiting on the table, to think quickly and act calmly; all this meant weariness."[2]

The alternation of the daily and weekly chores continued during each day. On Friday after breakfast she cleaned the halls, stairs, vestibule, and bathroom: "It was heavy work, for the halls were carpeted with moquette, but I sat

Excerpted from "Household Work," chap. 3 of *Seven Days a Week: Women and Domestic Service in Industrializing America* by David M. Katzman (New York: Oxford University Press, 1978). Copyright © 1978 by Oxford University Press. Reprinted by permission. Notes have been renumbered.

on the stairs as I swept them with a whisk broom, thus saving my feet." Before lunch she had gone to the market, then returned and made the midday meal. After cleaning the kitchen and dining room and doing the weekly cleaning of the refrigerator, she wearily climbed to her room. She passed her mistress, who "sat with a flushed face still sewing." She offered to help, and her mistress responded: "I don't know how to rush sewing but I wish to wear this skirt to-morrow, and if you *would* do it I would like to rest." Godman finished it in half an hour. She still had another hour of rest, since she was cooking fish for dinner and would not have to light the oven. She could rest until 4:30. She was rewarded for doing the skirt; her employer gave her Saturday evening off, since she was going out to dinner.[3]

Sunday was filled with daily chores, but Godman was pressed for time because she had to help her mistress dress for church. She rushed and managed to finish by 2:00 P.M. so she could attend a Sunday school class. That night she served a light supper and managed to retire at 8:00 P.M. On Monday morning she cleaned the dining room, polished silver, did the marketing, and baked bread. Since guests were invited to dinner that evening she worked straight through her afternoon break, and did not finish cleaning up until 10:00 P.M. Monday had turned into a sixteen-hour workday, including time for meals. The laundress came on Tuesday, and Godman spent all afternoon plus all day Wednesday and part of Thursday between her daily chores and ironing. But Thursday began a new weekly cycle. Wisely her mistress went out for lunch that first week so Godman could complete the ironing and clean the sitting room without having to make lunch and clean up. She finished the ironing at 11:00 A.M. Thursday and then went to the sitting room. She simply rested there for an hour, then cleaned the room in just twenty minutes. Though she thought it looked clean, she knew it was not thoroughly done. Each week she failed to complete the ironing on Wednesday;

it was physically impossible for her. The result was that Thursday was "a hard day, for my lady did not go out to luncheon after that first week, and with her in the house I could not slight the work nor stop to rest. Every Thursday night I was ready to collapse."[4]

Inez Godman's full workdays are typical. Daily chores for the maid-of-all-work included lighting fires (in stoves, for hot water, in winter fireplaces or furnaces), preparing and serving meals and cleaning up, making beds, doing light dusting, sweeping or scrubbing front steps and porch, answering the doorbell, and running errands. The weekly cycle, dominated by washing, ironing, and heavy cleaning, was more physically demanding. A typical week would begin with washing on Monday, ironing on Tuesday, and mending on Wednesday. On Thursday the dining room would be thoroughly cleaned, including the polishing of silver and glass. On Friday the house would be swept and the windows cleaned. Saturday would entail major housecleaning—the kitchen, cellar, and rooms not cleaned thoroughly on other days—and then perhaps breadbaking. Repetition of tasks made the work monotonous, but the complaint heard most seemed to be that of physical fatigue and tiredness. Over and over again women mentioned how they often collapsed in bed at the end of the day, too tired to read or even take a bath. "If one of the twelve labors of Hercules had been to solve the servant girl problem," one servant wrote, "he never would have had the reputation he has."[5]

NOTES

1. Inez A. Godman, "Ten Weeks in a Kitchen," *Independent* LIII (Oct. 17, 1901):2459.
2. Ibid., p. 2460.
3. Ibid.
4. Ibid., p. 2461.
5. Catherine Owen, *Progressive Housekeeping: Keeping House Without Knowing How, and Knowing How to Keep House Well* (Boston and New York, 1896), p. 14; "A Servant Girl's Letter," *Independent* LIV (Jan. 2, 1902):37.

DOCUMENT: *Working for Wages*

Pauline Newman, "We fought and we bled and we died. . . ."

One of the earliest industries in which women found employment was the garment industry. Based in New York City—the port of entry for millions of immigrants—the industry provided countless married women with piecework to take back to dimly lit tenements where they often enlisted the help of grandmothers and children. By the end of the nineteenth century much of the work had been transferred to sweatshops notorious for their low wages and squalid working conditions. Later the work was done in small factories such as the Triangle Shirtwaist Factory. This building became the scene of one of the great industrial tragedies in New York City's history. Although the factory contained several elevators and two staircases, the eight-story wooden building had no sprinkler system; the doors to the fire escapes were locked to prevent outdoor relaxation. When fire broke out in 1911, five hundred employees—many of them young Jewish and Italian women—were trapped behind locked doors. Some jumped to their death; others burned or asphyxiated inside. Altogether the fire claimed the lives of 146 women. Viewing their charred bodies on the street, one reporter recalled that some of these same women had gone on strike only the year before to demand decent wages, more sanitary working conditions, and safety precautions.

One of the strikers was Pauline Newman, who had worked at the Triangle Factory until she became an organizer for the International Ladies Garment Workers Union (ILGWU). Its educational director until her death in 1986, Newman conveys in this brief account a sense of what it was like to be a garment worker in the early twentieth century. She also expresses the indomitable spirit of these early women organizers who carried on a tradition established by their predecessors in the Lowell mills.

A cousin of mine worked for the Triangle Shirtwaist Company and she got me on there in October of 1901. It was probably the largest shirtwaist factory in the city of New York then. They had more than two hundred operators, cutters, examiners, finishers. Altogether more than four hundred people on two floors. The fire took place on one floor, the floor where we worked. You've probably heard about that. But that was years later.

We started work at seven-thirty in the morning, and during the busy season we worked until nine in the evening. They didn't pay you any overtime and they didn't give you anything for supper money. Sometimes they'd give you a little apple pie if you had to work very late. That was all. Very generous.

What I had to do was not really very difficult. It was just monotonous. When the shirtwaists were finished at the machine there were

Adapted from "Pauline Newman," in *American Mosaic: The Immigrant Experience in the Words of Those Who Lived It,* edited by Joan Morrison and Charlotte Fox Zabusky (New York: E. P. Dutton, 1980), pp. 9–14. Copyright © 1980 by Joan Morrison and Charlotte Fox Zabusky. Reprinted by permission of the publisher.

some threads that were left, and all the young-sters—we had a corner on the floor that resem-bled a kindergarten—we were given little scis-sors to cut the threads off. It wasn't heavy work, but it was monotonous, because you did the same thing from seven-thirty in the morn-ing till nine at night.

Well, of course, there were [child labor] laws on the books, but no one bothered to enforce them. The employers were always tipped off if there was going to be an inspection. "Quick," they'd say, "into the boxes!" And we children would climb into the big boxes the finished shirts were stored in. Then some shirts were piled on top of us, and when the inspector came—no children. The factory always got an okay from the inspector, and I suppose some-one at City Hall got a little something, too.

The employers didn't recognize anyone working for them as a human being. You were not allowed to sing. Operators would have liked to have sung, because they, too, had the same thing to do and weren't allowed to sing. We weren't allowed to talk to each other. Oh, no, they would sneak up behind if you were found talking to your next colleague. You were admonished: "If you keep on you'll be fired." If you went to the toilet and you were there longer than the floor lady thought you should be, you would be laid off for half a day and sent home. And, of course, that meant no pay. You were not allowed to have your lunch on the fire escape in the summertime. The door was locked to keep us in. That's why so many people were trapped when the fire broke out.

My pay was $1.50 a week no matter how many hours I worked. My sisters made $6.00 a week; and the cutters, they were skilled work-ers, they might get as much as $12.00. The em-ployers had a sign in the elevator that said: "If you don't come in on Sunday, don't come in on Monday." You were expected to work every day if they needed you and the pay was the same whether you worked extra or not. You had to be there at seven-thirty, so you got up at five-thirty, took the horse car, then the elec-tric trolley to Greene Street, to be there on time. . . .

I stopped working at the Triangle Factory during the strike in 1909 and I didn't go back. The union sent me out to raise money for the strikers. I apparently was able to articulate my feelings and opinions about the criminal con-ditions, and they didn't have anyone else who could do better, so they assigned me. And I was successful getting money. After my first speech before the Central Trade and Labor Council I got front-page publicity, including my picture. I was only about fifteen then. Everybody saw it. Wealthy women were curious and they asked me if I would speak to them in their homes. I said I would if they would contribute to the strike, and they agreed. So I spent my time from November to the end of March up-state in New York, speaking to the ladies of the Four Hundred [the elite of New York's society] and sending money back. . . .

We didn't gain very much at the end of the strike. I think the hours were reduced to fifty-six a week or something like that. We got a 10 percent increase in wages. I think that the best thing that the strike did was to lay a foundation on which to build a union. There was so much feeling against unions then. The judge, when one of our girls came before him, said to her: "You're not striking against your employer, you know, young lady. You're striking against God," and sentenced her to two weeks on Blackwell's Island, which is now Welfare Is-land. And a lot of them got a taste of the club. . . .

After the 1909 strike I worked with the un-ion, organizing in Philadelphia and Cleveland and other places, so I wasn't at the Triangle Shirtwaist Factory when the fire broke out, but a lot of my friends were. I was in Philadelphia for the union and, of course, someone from here called me immediately and I came back. It's very difficult to describe the feeling because I knew the place and I knew so many of the girls. The thing that bothered me was the em-ployers got a lawyer. How anyone could have *defended* them!—because I'm quite sure that the fire was planned for insurance purposes. And no one is going to convince me otherwise. And when they testified that the door to the fire es-cape was open, it was a lie! It was never open. Locked all the time. One hundred and forty-six people were sacrificed, and the judge fined Blank and Harris seventy-five dollars!

Conditions were dreadful in those days. But there was something that is lacking today and I think it was the devotion and the belief. We *believed* in what we were doing. We fought and we bled and we died. Today they don't have to.

You sit down at the table, you negotiate

with the employers, you ask for 20 percent, they say 15, but the girls are working. People are working. They're not disturbed, and when the negotiations are over they get the increases. They don't really have to fight. Of course, they'll belong to the union and they'll go on strike if you tell them to, but it's the inner faith that people had in those days that I don't see today. It was a terrible time, but it was interesting. I'm glad I lived then.

Even when things were terrible, I always had that faith. . . . Only now, I'm a little discouraged sometimes when I see the workers spending their free hours watching television—trash. We fought so hard for those hours and they waste them. We used to read Tolstoy, Dickens, Shelley, by candlelight, and they watch the "Hollywood Squares." Well, they're free to do what they want. That's what we fought for.

ALICE KESSLER-HARRIS
Where Are the Organized Women Workers?

Because so many wage-earning women in the early twentieth century were young, single women who regarded their work as a temporary necessity until rescued by marriage, male labor leaders—and historians—usually assumed that women workers had little interest in joining unions. Alice Kessler-Harris explores this assumption and other barriers to the organization of women workers. She demonstrates with particular effectiveness how unionization was inhibited by fears of job competition on the part of male workers and the conviction of male trade unionists and employers alike that woman's proper place of work was in the home. She also calls attention to the ambivalent position of women like Rose Schneiderman, who had the difficult task of mediating between working women and middle-class reformers. The result, Kessler-Harris points out, was not only the division of the working class on the basis of gender but the perpetuation of an underclass of workers whose experience with wage work is still characterized by "sex typing" that limits job options, by low pay whatever the job involved, and by the absence of significant union membership.

"The Organization of Women," wrote Fannia Cohn, an officer of the International Ladies Garment Workers Union to William Green, newly elected president of the American Federation of Labor, "is not merely a moral question, but also an economic one. Men will never be certain with their conditions unless the conditions of the millions of women are improved."[1] Her letter touched a home truth and

yet in 1925, the year in which Cohn's letter was written, the A. F. of L., after nearly forty years of organizing, remained profoundly ambivalent about the fate of more than eight million wage-earning women.

During these four decades of industrial growth, the women who worked in the industrial labor force had not passively waited to be organized. Yet their best efforts had been tinged with failure. Figures for union members are notoriously unreliable, and estimates fluctuate widely. But something like 3.3 percent of the women who were engaged in industrial occupations in 1900 were organized into trade unions. As low as that figure was, it was to decline even further. Around 1902 and 1903 trade union membership among women began to decrease, reaching a low of 1.5 percent in 1910. Then, a surge of organization among garment workers lifted it upwards. A reasonable estimate might put 6.6 percent of wage-earning women into trade unions by 1920. In a decade that saw little change in the relative proportion of female and male workers, the proportion of women who were trade union members quadrupled, increasing at more than twice the rate for trade union members in general. Even so, the relative numbers of wage-earning women who were trade union members remained tiny. One in every five men in the industrial workforce belonged to a union, compared to one in every fifteen women. Although more than 20 percent of the labor force was female, less than 8 percent of organized workers were women. And five years later, when Fannia Cohn was urging William Green to pay attention to female workers, these startling gains had already been eroded.[2]

Figures like these have led historians of the working class to join turn-of-the-century labor organizers in lamenting the difficulty of unionizing female workers. Typically, historians argue that the traditional place of women in families, as well as their position in the workforce, inhibited trade unionism. Statistical overviews suggest that these arguments have much to be said for them. At the turn of the century, most wage-earning women were young temporary workers who looked to marriage as a way to escape the shop or factory. Eighty-five percent of these women were unmarried and nearly half were under twenty-five years old. Most women worked at traditionally hard-to-organize unskilled jobs: a third were domestic servants and almost one quarter worked in the garment and textile industries. The remainder were scattered in a variety of industrial and service jobs, including the tobacco and boot and shoe industries, department stores, and laundries. Wage-earning women often came from groups without a union tradition: about one-half of all working women were immigrants or their daughters who shared rural

backgrounds. In the cities, that figure sometimes climbed to 90 percent.[3]

For all these reasons, women in the labor force unionized with difficulty. Yet the dramatic fluctuations in the proportions of organized working women testify to their potential for organization. And the large numbers of unions in which the proportion of women enrolled exceeded their numbers in the industry urge us to seek further explanations for the small proportions of women who actually became union members.[4]

No apparent change either in the type of women who worked or in the structure of jobs explains the post-1902 decline in the proportion of unionized women. On the contrary, several trends would suggest the potential for a rise in their numbers. The decline began just at the point when union membership was increasing dramatically after the devastating depression of 1893–1897. The proportion of first-generation immigrant women who were working dropped after the turn of the century only to be matched by an increase in the proportion of their Americanized daughters who worked. Married women entered the labor force in larger numbers suggesting at once a more permanent commitment to jobs and greater need for the security unions could provide. Large declines in the proportion of domestic workers reduced the numbers of women in these isolated low-paying, and traditionally hard-to-organize jobs. At the same time, increases in office and clerical workers, department store clerks, and factory operatives, offered fertile areas for promoting unionization among women. Strenuous organizing compaigns by and among women in all these areas achieved few results.

Although cultural background, traditional roles, and social expectations hindered some unionizing efforts, they were clearly not insurmountable barriers. Given a chance, women were devoted and successful union members, convinced that unionism would serve them as it seemed to be serving their brothers. In the words of a seventeen-year-old textile worker, "We all work hard for a mean living. Our boys belong to the miners' union so their wages are better than ours. So I figured that girls must have a union. Women must act like men, ain't?"[5] In the garment workers union where women were the majority of members, they often served as shop "chairladies" and reached positions of minor importance in the union structure. Faige Shapiro recalled how her union activity began at the insistence of a business agent but quickly became an absorbing interest. In these unions, women arrested on picket lines thought highly enough of the union to try to save it bail money by offering to spend the night in jail before they returned to the line in the morning.[6]

In mixed unions, women often led men in militant actions. Iowa cigar makers reported in 1899 that some striking men had resumed work, while the women were standing pat.[7] Boot and shoe workers in Massachusetts were reported in 1905 to be tough bargainers. "It is harder to induce women to compromise," said their president, "they are more likely to hold out to the bitter end . . . to obtain exactly what they want."[8] The great uprising of 1909 in which 20,000 women walked out of New York's garment shops occurred over the objections of the male leadership, striking terror into the hearts of Jewish men afraid "of the security of their jobs."[9] Polish "spool girls" protesting a rate cut in the textile mills of Chicopee, Massachusetts, refused their union's suggestion that they arbitrate and won a resounding victory. Swedish women enrolled in a Chicago Custom Clothing Makers local, lost a battle against their bosses' attempts to subdivide and speed up the sewing process when the United Garment Workers union, largely male, agreed to the bosses' conditions. The bosses promptly locked out the women forcing many to come to terms and others to seek new jobs.[10] At the turn of the century, female garment workers in San Francisco and tobacco strippers, overall and sheepskin workers, and telephone operators in Boston ran highly successful sex-segregated unions.[11]

If traditional explanations for women's failure to organize extensively in this period are not satisfying, they nevertheless offer clues to understanding the unionization process among women. They reveal the superficiality of the question frequently asked by male organizers and historians alike: "Why don't women organize?" and they encourage us to adopt economist Theresa Wolfson's more sensitive formulation: "Where are the organized women workers?"[12] For when we stop asking why women have not organized themselves, we are led to ask how women were, and are, kept out of unions.

The key to this question lies, I think, in looking at the function that wage-earning women have historically played in the capitalist mode of production. Most women entered the labor force out of economic necessity. They were encouraged by expanding technology and the continuing division of labor which in the last half of the nineteenth century reduced the need for skilled workers and increased the demand for cheap labor. Like immigrant men, and blacks today, women formed a large reservoir of unskilled workers. But they offered employers additional advantages. They were often at the mercy of whatever jobs happened to be available in the towns where their husbands or fathers worked, and they willingly took jobs that offered no access to upward mobility. Their extraordinarily low pay and exploitative working conditions enabled employers to speed up the process of capital accumulation. Their labor was critical to industrial expansion, yet they were expected to have few job-related aspirations and to look forward instead to eventual marriage. Under these circumstances, employers had a special incentive to resist unionization among women. As John Andrews, writing in the 1911 Report on the Condition of Women and Child Wage Earners, put it: ". . . the moment she organizes a union and seeks by organization to secure better wages she diminishes or destroys what is to the employer her chief value."[13]

If the rising numbers of working women are any gauge, women for the most part nicely filled the expectations of employers. Traditional social roles and the submissive behavior expected of women with primary attachments to home and family precisely complemented the needs of their bosses. To those women whose old world or American family norms encouraged more aggressive and worldly behavior—Russian Jews, for example—unionization came easier. Yet, for the most part, women fought on two fronts: against the weight of tradition and expectation, and against employers. If that were not enough, there was yet a third battlefront.

Unionists, if they thought about it at all, were well aware of women's special economic role. Samuel Gompers, head of the American Federation of Labor, editorialized in 1911 that some companies had "taken on women not so much to give them work as to make dividends fatter."[14] In a competitive labor market unionists tended to be suspicious of women who worked for wages and to regard them as potentially threatening to men's jobs. "Every woman employed," wrote an editor in the A. F. of L. journal, *American Federationist,* "displaces a man and adds one more to the idle contingent that are fixing wages at the lowest limit."[15]

Since employers clearly had important economic incentives for hiring women, male trade unionists felt they had either to eliminate that incentive, or to offer noneconomic reasons for restricting women's labor-force participation. In the early 1900s they tried to do both. In order to reduce the economic threat, organized labor repeatedly affirmed a commitment to unionize women wage earners and to extract equal pay for them. Yet trade unionists simultaneously argued that women's contributions to the home and their duties as mothers were so valuable that women ought not to be in the labor force at all. Their use of the home-and-motherhood argument had two negative effects: it sustained the self-image on which the particular exploitation of women rested, and it provided employers with a weapon to turn against the working class as a whole.

Buttressed by the grim realities of exploitative working conditions and the difficulties of caring for children while working ten or more hours a day, and supported by well-intentioned social reformers, the argument to eliminate women from the work force, in the end, held sway. It was, of course, impossible to achieve, so the A. F. of L. continued to organize women and to demand equal pay for equal work. But genuine ambivalence tempered its efforts. The end result was to divide the working-class firmly along gender lines and to confirm women's position as a permanently threatening underclass of workers who finally resorted to the protection of middle-class reformers and legislators to ameliorate intolerable working conditions. The pattern offers us some lessons about what happens to the work force when one part of it attacks another.

The published sources of the A. F. of L. reveal some of the attitudes underlying A. F. of L. actions, and I have focused attention on these because I want to illustrate not only how open and prevalent the argument was, but because the A. F. of L.'s affiliated unions together constituted the largest body of collective working-class opinion. We have amassed enough

evidence by now to know that the A. F. of L. was a conservative force whose relatively privileged members sacrificed the larger issues of working-class solidarity for a piece of the capitalist pie. In the creation of what labor economist Selig Perlman called "a joint partnership of organized labor and organized capital," the Federation cooperated extensively with corporation-dominated government agencies, sought to exclude immigrants, and supported an imperialist foreign policy.[16] Its mechanisms for dealing with the huge numbers of women entering the labor force are still unclear. Yet they are an integral part of the puzzle surrounding the interaction of ideological and economic forces in regulating labor market participation.

In the period from 1897 to 1920, the A. F. of L. underwent dramatic expansion. It consolidated and confirmed its leadership over a number of independent unions, including the dying Knights of Labor. Membership increased from about 265,000 members in 1897 to more than four million by 1920, and included four-fifths of all organized workers. In the same period, the proportion of women working in the industrial labor force climbed rapidly. Rapid and heady expansion offered a golden opportunity for organizers. That they didn't take advantage of it is one of the most important facts in the history of labor organizing in America.

Union leaders were sure that women did not belong in the workforce. Anxious about losing jobs to these low-paid workers, they tried instead to drive women out of the labor force. "It is the so-called competition of the unorganized defenseless woman worker, the girl and the wife, that often tends to reduce the wages of the father and husband," proclaimed Samuel Gompers.[17] And the *American Federationist* was filled with tales of men displaced by women and children. "One house in St. Louis now pays $4 per week to women where men got $16," snapped the journal in 1896. "A local typewriter company has placed 200 women to take the place of unorganized men," announced an organizer in 1903.[18]

The Federation's fear had some basis. In the late nineteenth and early twentieth century, new technology and techniques of efficiency pioneered by Frederick Taylor eroded the control and the jobs of skilled workmen, replacing

them with managerial experts and the unskilled and semiskilled. Skilled members of the
A. F. of L. who might appropriately have directed their anger at the way technology was
being manipulated, lashed out instead at
women who dared to work. Gompers offers a
good example. In an article published in 1904,
he declared, "The ingenuity of man to produce
the world's wealth easier than ever before, is
utilized as a means to pauperize the worker, to
supplant the man by the woman and the
woman by the child. . . ."[19] Some of the least
appropriate bitterness was expressed by
Thomas O'Donnell, secretary of the National
Spinners Union whose constituency, once
largely female, had been replaced by men after
the Civil War. The advent of simple electric-
powered machinery caused him to complain
that "the manufacturers have been trying for
years to discourage us by dispensing with the
spinning mule and substituting female and
child labor for that of the old time skilled spinners. . . ."[20]

Real anxieties about competition from
women stimulated and supported rationali-
zations about woman's role as wife and
mother. Working men had argued even before
the Civil War that women belonged at home,
and both the harsh conditions of labor and the
demands of rearing a family supported their
contention. But the women who worked for
wages in the early 1900s were overwhelmingly
single, and often supported widowed mothers
and younger siblings with their meager pay.
An argument that could have been used to improve conditions for all workers was directed
at eliminating women from the work force entirely. By the early 1900s it had become an irre-
pressible chorus. "The great principle for
which we fight," said the A. F. of L.'s treasurer
in 1905, "is opposed to taking . . . the women
from their homes to put them in the factory and
the sweatshop."[21] "We stand for the principle,"
said another A. F. of L. member, "that it is
wrong to permit any of the female sex of our
country to be forced to work, as we believe that
the man should be provided with a fair wage
in order to keep his female relatives from going
to work. The man is the provider and should
receive enough for his labor to give his family
a respectable living."[22] And yet a third proclaimed, "Respect for women is apt to decrease
when they are compelled to work in the factory
or the store. . . . More respect for women brings

less degeneration and more marriages . . . if
women labor in factories and similar institutions they bring forth weak children who are
not educated to become strong and good citizens."[23] No language was too forceful or too
dramatic. "The demand for female labor,"
wrote an official of the Boston Central Labor
Union in 1897, is "an insidious assault upon the
home . . . it is the knife of the assassin, aimed
at the family circle."[24] The *American Federationist* romanticized the role of women's jobs at
home, extolling the virtues of refined and
moral mothers, of good cooking and even of
beautiful needlework and embroidery.[25]

These sentiments did not entirely prevent
the A. F. of L. from attempting to unionize
women. Gompers editorialized on the subject
in 1904: "We . . . shall bend every energy for
our fellow workmen to organize and unite in
trade unions; to federate their effort without regard to . . . sex."[26] Yet the limited commitment
implied by the wish that women would get out
of the work force altogether was tinged with
the conviction and perhaps the hope that
women would, in the end, fail. The Federation's first female organizer, Mary Kenny, had
been appointed as early as 1892. But the Federation had supported her only half-heartedly
and allowed her position to expire when she
gave up the job to marry. It was 1908 before the
organization appointed another woman, Annie
Fitzgerald, as full-time organizer. While Gompers and others conceded the "full and free opportunity for women to work whenever and
wherever necessity requires," Gompers did not
address himself to the problem of how to determine which women were admissible by
these standards, and his actions revealed that
he thought their numbers relatively few.[27] The
A. F. of L. repeatedly called for an end to
discriminatory pay for women and men:
"Equal compensation for equal service performed."[28] The demand was a double-edged
sword. While it presumably protected all
workers from cheap labor, in the context of the
early 1900s labor market it often functioned to
deprive women of jobs. The Boston Typographical Union, noted one observer, saw "its
only safety in maintaining the principle of
equal pay for men and women. . . ."[29] Officials
must have been aware that equal compensation
for women often meant that employers would
as soon replace them with men. It was no
anomaly, then, to find an A. F. of L. organizer

say of his daughters in 1919 that though he had "two girls at work [he] ... wouldn't think of having them belong to a labor organization."[30]

When the A. F. of L. did organize women, its major incentive was often the need to protect the earning power of men. Women were admitted to unions after men recognized them as competitors better controlled from within than allowed to compete from without. "It has been the policy of my associates and myself," wrote Gompers in 1906, "to throw open wide the doors of our organization and invite the working girls and working women to membership for their and our common protection."[31] *American Federationist* articles that began with pleas that women stay out of the work force concluded with equally impassioned pleas to organize those who were already in it. Alice Woodbridge, writing in 1894, concluded an argument that women who worked for wages were neglecting their duties to their "fellow creatures" with the following statement: "It is to the interest of both sexes that women should organize ... until we are well organized there is little hope of success among organizations of men."[32] The A. F. of L. officially acknowledged competition as a primary motivation for organizing women in 1923. "Unorganized they constitute a menace to standards established through collective action. Not only for their protection, but for the protection of men ... there should be organization of all women...."[33]

These were not of course the only circumstances of which men suspended their hostility toward women's unions. Occasionally in small towns female and male unions in different industries supported each other against the hostile attacks of employers. Minersville, Pennsylvania miners, for example, physically ousted railroad detectives who tried to break up a meeting of female textile workers.[34] The women in this case were the daughters, sisters and sweethearts of miners. Far from competing with men for jobs, women were helping to support the same families as the miners. Similarly, women and men in newly established industries could cooperate more effectively in unionizing together. The garment industry saw parallel but equally effective organization among its various branches. Though female organizers complained bitterly of the way they were treated, male leadership depended on the numerical majority of female workers to bargain

successfully with employers and did not deny women admission. Yet, even here, union leadership successfully eliminated "home work" without offering to the grossly underpaid and often needy female workers who did it a way of recouping their financial losses.

Occasional exceptions notwithstanding, the general consequence of union attitudes toward women was to isolate them from the male work force. Repeatedly women who organized themselves into unions applied for entry to the appropriate parent body only to be turned down or simply ignored. Pauline Newman, who had organized and collected dues from a group of candy makers in Philadelphia, in 1910 offered to continue to work with them if the International Bakery and Confectionery Workers union would issue a charter. The International stalled and put them off until the employers began to discharge the leaders and the group disintegrated.[35] Waitresses in Norfolk, Virginia, suffered a similar fate. Mildred Rankin, who requested a charter for a group of fifteen, was assured by the local A. F. of L. organizer that she was wasting her time. "The girls were all getting too much money to be interested," was his comment on denying the request.[36] New York's International Typographical Union refused to issue female copyholders a charter on the grounds that they were insufficiently skilled. When the group applied to the parent A. F. of L. for recognition, they were refused on the grounds that they were within the ITU's jurisdiction. The Women's Trade Union League got little satisfaction when it raised this issue with the A. F. of L.'s executive council the following year. Though the Federation had agreed to issue charters to black workers excluded from all-white unions, it refused to accord the same privilege to women. The parent body agreed only to "take up the subject with the trade unions and to endeavor to reach an understanding" as far as women were concerned.[37]

A strong union could simply cut women out of the kinds of jobs held by unionized men. This form of segmenting the labor market ran parallel to, and sometimes contradicted the interests of employers who would have preferred cheap labor. A Binghamton, New York printing establishment, for example, could not hire women linotype operators because "the men's union would not allow it."[38] The technique was as useful for excluding racial minorities as it was for restricting women.[39] Like appeals to racist beliefs, arguments based on the natural weakness of women worked well as a rationale, as the following examples will indicate. Mary Dreier, then President of the New York Chapter of the Women's Trade Union League, recalled a union of tobacco workers whose leaders refused to admit women because "they could only do poor sort of work . . . , because women had no colour discrimination."[40] A Boston metal polishers union refused to admit women. "We don't want them," an official told a Women's Bureau interviewer. "Women can only do one kind of work while men can polish anything from iron to gold and frame the smallest part to the largest," and besides, he added, "metal polishing is bad for the health."[41]

Women were often excluded from unions in less direct but equally effective ways. The International Retail Clerks Union charged an initiation fee of $3, and dues of 50¢ a month. Hilda Svenson, a local organizer in 1914, complained that she had been unable to negotiate a compromise with the International. "We want to be affiliated with them," she commented, "but on account of the dues and initiation fee we feel it is too high at the present time for the salaries that the girls in New York are getting."[42] Sometimes union pay scales were set so high that the employer would not pay the appropriate wage to women. Joining the union could mean that a female printer would lose her job, so women simply refused to join.

Though the A. F. of L. supported its few female organizers only half-heartedly, male organizers complained of the difficulty of organizing women. Social propriety hindered them from talking to women in private or about moral or sanitary issues. Women felt keenly the absence of aid. When the Pennsylvania State Federation of Labor offered to finance the Philadelphia Womens' Trade Union League's program for organizing women, its secretary pleaded with Rose Schneiderman to take the job. "We have never had a wise head to advise, or an experienced worker," she wrote.[43]

But even membership in a union led by men guaranteed little to women. Such well-known tactics as locating meetings in saloons, scheduling them at late hours, and ridiculing women who dared to speak deprived women of full participation. And unions often deliberately sabotaged their female members. Fifteen hundred female street railway conductors and ticket agents, dues-paying members of New York City's Amalgamated Street Workers Union, complained in 1919 that their brother union members had supported a reformers' bill to deprive them of their jobs. When the women discovered they had been betrayed they resigned from the union and formed their own organization sending women throughout the state to Albany "to show them that they . . . were able to take care of their own health and morals." To no avail. Eight hundred of the 1500 women lost their jobs and the remaining 700 continued to work only at reduced hours.[44] Supporting union men was not likely to benefit women either. Mary Anderson, newly appointed head of the Women's Bureau, got a frantic telegram from a WTUL organizer in Joliet, Illinois, early in 1919. The women in a Joliet steel plant who, in return for the promise of protection, had supported unionized men in a recent strike, were fighting desperately for jobs that the union now insisted they give up. The company wanted to retain the women, but union men argued the work was too heavy for them.[45]

As the idea of home-and-motherhood was used to exclude women from unions, so it enabled unionized workers to join legislatures and middle-class reformers in restricting women's hours and regulating their working conditions through protective labor legislation. The issue for the Federation's skilled and elite corps of male workers was clearly competiton. Their wives did not work for wages, and most could afford to keep their daughters outside the marketplace. In an effort to preserve limited opportunity, they attacked fellow workers who were women, attempting to deny them access to certain kinds of jobs. Abused by employers who valued women primarily for their "cheap labor," women were isolated by male workers who were afraid their wages and their jobs would fall victim to the competition. Arguments used by male workers may have undercut their own positions, confirming the existence of a permanent underclass of workers and locking men psychologically and economically into positions of sole economic responsibility for their families. Appeals to morality and to the duties of motherhood obscured the economic issues involved, encouraging women and men alike to see women as impermanent workers whose major commitment would be to families and not to wage earning. Women would, therefore, require the special protection of the state for their presumably limited wage-earning lives.

The argument reached back at least as far as the 1880s and it was firmly rooted in the idea that the well-being of the state depended on the health of future mothers. But the line between the interests of the state and those of working men was finely drawn, and occasionally a protagonist demonstrated confusion about the issue. A few examples will illustrate the point. The cigar maker, Adolph Strasser, testifying before a Congressional Committee in 1882, concluded a diatribe against the number of women entering the trade with a plea to restrict them. "Why?" asked his questioner. "Because," replied Strasser, "I claim that it is the duty of the government to protect the weak and the females are considered among the weak in society."[46] Nearly forty years later, a Women's Bureau investigator reported that the Secretary of the Amalgamated Clothing Workers Union, fearful that women were taking jobs from men, had argued that women were "going into industry so fast that home life is very much in danger, not to mention the propagation of the race."[47] As the idea spread, it took on new forms, leading a Boston streetcar union secretary to acknowledge that "he would not care to see [women] employed as conductors. . . . It coarsened [them] to handle rough crowds on cars."[48] But in more sophisticated form, the argument for protective legislation appeared as a patriotic appeal to enlightened national self-interest. "Women may be adults," argued one A. F. of L. columnist in 1900, "and why should we class them as children? Because it is to the interest of all of us that female labor should be limited so as not to injure the motherhood and family life of a nation."[49] Sometimes pleas were more dramatic. In a piece entitled, "The Kingdom of God and Modern Industry," Ira Howerth, a sociologist writing for the *American Federationist,* asserted:

The highest courts in some of our states declare that a law limiting the hours of labor for these women is unconstitutional. It may be so, but if it is so, so much the worse for the state. The state or nation that permits its women to stunt their bodies and dwarf their minds by overexertion in insanitary [sic] stores and mills and factories is thereby signing its own death warrant. For the degeneracy of women is the degeneracy of the race. A people can never be any better than its mothers.[50]

Gompers, as well as other Federation officials, at first opposed the idea of legislation. But in the period following World War I, their attitudes changed, perhaps as a result of what seemed like an enormous increase in the number of women in the industrial labor force. The A. F. of L. encouraged the Department of Labor to set up a Women's Bureau to defend the interests of wage-earning women.[51] The Bureau, on investigation, found that many union officials viewed unionization and protective legislation as alternate means to the same goal: better working conditions. Sara Conboy, United Textile Workers official and a WTUL activist, told a Women's Bureau interviewer that she believed in "legislation to limit long hours of work for women where and when the union [was] not strong enough to limit hours."[52] Some unionized workers thought legislation surer and faster or remarked that it was more dependable than possible untrustworthy union leaders. A. J. Muste, then secretary of the Amalgamated Textile Workers Union of America, preferred unionization, but was said to have believed that legislation did not hinder organization and might be essential in industries with many women and minors.[53] But some women union leaders were not so sanguine. Fannia Cohn of the International Ladies Garment Workers Union only reluctantly acquiesced to the need for protective legislation. "I did not think the problem of working women could be solved in any other way than the problem of working men and that is through trade union organization," she wrote in 1927, "but considering that very few women are as yet organized into trade unions, it would be folly to agitate against protective legislation."[54] Cohn laid the problems of female workers on the absence of organization.

In any event, exclusion from unions merely confirmed the discomfort many women felt about participating in meetings. Italian and Southern families disliked their daughters going out in the evenings. Married and self-supporting women and widows had household duties at which they spent after-work hours. Women who attended meetings often participated reluctantly. They found the long discussions dull and were often intimidated by the preponderance of men. Men, for their part, resented the indifference of the women and further excluded them from leadership roles, thereby discouraging more women from attending. Even fines failed to spark attendance. Some women preferred to pay them rather than to go to the meeting.[55]

Self-images that derived from a paternalistic society joined ethnic ties in hindering unionization. Wage-earning women, anxious to marry, were sometimes reluctant to join unions for what they felt would be a temporary period. Occasionally, another role conflict was expressed: "No nice girl would belong to one," said one young woman.[56] An ILG organizer commented that most women who did not want to join a union claimed that "the boss is good to us and we have nothing to complain about and we don't want to join the union."[57] A woman who resisted unionization told an organizer that she knew "that $6 a week is not enough pay but the Lord helps me out. He always provides . . . I won't ever join a union. The Lord doesn't want me to."[58] A recent convert to unionism apologized for her former reticence. She had always scabbed because church people disapproved of unions. Moreover she and her sister had only with difficulty, she told an organizer, overcome their fear of the Italian men who were organizing their factory.[59]

Exceptions to this pattern occurred most often among women whose ethnic backgrounds encouraged both wage labor and a high level of social consciousness, as in the American Jewish community, for example. Young Jewish women constituted the bulk of the membership of the International Ladies Garment Workers Union in the period from 1910 to 1920. Their rapid organization and faithful tenure is responsible for at least one quarter of the increased number of unionized women in the second decade of the twentieth century. And yet, they were unskilled and semiskilled workers, employed in small, scattered shops, and theoretically among the least organizable workers. These women, unionized at their own initiative, formed the backbone of the ILGWU, which had originally been directed toward organizing the skilled, male, cutters in the trade.

As it became clear to many laboring women that unionists would offer them little help, many women turned to such middle-class

allies as the Women's Trade Union League. Established in 1905, the WTUL, an organization founded by female unionists and upper-middle-class reformers, offered needed financial and moral support for militant activity. Its paternalistic and benevolent style was not unfamiliar to women and those who came from immigrant families seemed particularly impressed with its Americanizing aspects. Young immigrant girls spoke with awe of the "fine ladies" of the WTUL and did not object to the folk-dancing classes that were part of the Chicago League's program.[60] But help from these nonwage-earning women came at a price. Working women who became involved in the WTUL moved quickly from working-class militance to the search for individual social mobility through vocational training, legislation, and the social refinements that provided access to better-paying and rapidly increasing clerical and secretarial jobs. Rose Schneiderman illustrates this syndrome well. Beginning as a fiery organizer of the hat and cap makers, she moved through the WTUL to become Secretary of the New York State Department of Labor. Like the WTUL, which had begun by organizing women into trade unions, she began in the 1920s to devote herself to attaining protective legislation, even borrowing some of the arguments used by men who did not wish women to compete with them.

By this time many working women were themselves moving in the direction of legislative solutions to exploitative working conditions. It seemed to be the most accessible solution to the problems of exploitation. Female workers interviewed by the Women's Bureau at first felt that both women and men should be included in any legislation. Later, they asked that office workers be exempted.[61] Other women acquiesced reluctantly. "I have always been afraid," wrote a supervisor in a Virginia silk mill, "that if laws were made discriminating for women, it would work a hardship upon them." By 1923 she had changed her mind: ". . . it would in time raise the entire standard rather than make it hard for women."[62] As women came to accept the necessity for legislation, they, like men, saw it as an alternative to unionization and rationalized its function in terms of their female "roles." A Women's Bureau agent noted of the reactions to a 48-hour law passed in Massachusetts that "the girls felt that legislation establishing a 48-hour week

Rose Schneiderman addresses a street rally in New York. (Courtesy Brown Brothers)

was more 'dignified' and permanent than one obtained through the union as it was not so likely to be taken away."[63] By the mid-1920s only business and professional women remained staunchly opposed to protective legislation.

Within this framework of trade-union ambivalence and the real need for wage-earning women for some form of protection, employers who were particularly anxious that women not unionize pressed their advantage. Using crude techniques, rationalized by the home-and-motherhood argument, they contributed more than their share toward keeping women out of unions. In the small businesses in which women most often worked, employers used a variety of techniques to discourage organization, some of them familiar to men. Department store employees whose union membership became known were commonly fired. Many stores had spy systems so that employees could not trust their coworkers. Blacklists were common. A representative of the year-old retail clerks union testifying before a Congressional Committee in 1914 was afraid even to reveal the number of members in her union.

Owners of New York's garment shops, fighting a losing battle by 1910, nevertheless frequently discharged employees who were thought to be active organizers or union members.[64]

Other tactics were no more subtle. Employers often played on ethnic and racial tensions in order to prevent women from unionizing. Rose Schneiderman, who formed the Hat and Cap Makers Union in 1903, fought against bosses who urged immigrant workers to stick to the "American shop"—a euphemism for an antiunion shop. Jewish owners sometimes hired only Italian workers who were thought to be less prone to unionization than Jews.[65] Others hired "landsmen" from the same old country community, hoping that fraternal instincts might keep them from striking. Blacks were played off against whites. Waitresses picketing Knab's restaurant in Chicago were met with counterpickets paid by the employers. A representative of the waitresses union reported indignantly that the employer "placed colored pickets on the street, colored women who wore signs like this 'Gee, I ain't mad at nobody and nobody ain't mad at Knab.'" When the nonunion pickets attracted a crowd, police moved in and arrested the union members. The women were further discouraged by trials engineered by employers who had previously given "every policeman a turkey free."[66]

Police routinely broke up picket lines and outdoor union meetings. Women who were accused of obstructing traffic or were incited into slapping provocateurs were arrested. More importantly, women who might have been interested in unionization were intimidated by police who surrounded open air meetings or by department store detectives who mingled obtrusively with potential recruits. Department store owners diverted workers from street meetings by locking all but one set of doors or sending trucks, horns honking full blast, to parade up and down the street in which a meeting was scheduled.[67]

Small employers formed mutual assistance associations to help them resist their employees' attempts to unionize. The Chicago Restaurant Keepers Association, for example, denied membership to any "person, firm or corporation . . . having signed agreements with any labor organization."[68] Garment manufacturers in both New York and Chicago created protective associations to combat what they called "the spreading evil of unionism."[69] In small towns, the power of town officials was called into play. Ann Washington Craton, organizing textile workers in Minersville, Pennsylvania, was warned by the town burgess: "You are to let our girls alone . . . Mr. Demsky will shut the factory down rather than have a union. . . . The town council brought this factory here to provide work for worthy widows and poor girls. We don't intend to have any trouble about it."[70]

Employers justified continued refusal to promote women or to offer them access to good jobs on the grounds that women's major contribution was to home and family. When they were challenged with the argument that bad working conditions were detrimental to that end, they responded slowly with paternalistic amelioration of the worst conditions and finally by acquiescing to protective labor legislation. Often concessions to workers were an effort to undercut mounting union strength, as for example when department store owners voluntarily closed their shops one evening a week. Some employers introduced welfare

work in their factories, providing social workers, or other women, to help smooth relationships between them and their female employees. Mutual benefit associations, sometimes resembling company unions, were a more familiar tactic. Though they were presumably cooperative and designed to incorporate input from workers, membership in them was compulsory and dues of ten to twenty-five cents per month were deducted from wages. In return employees got sickness and health benefits of varying amounts but only after several months of continuous employment. A 1925 investigation of one widely publicized cooperative association operated by Filene's department store in Boston revealed that in all its twelve years, only store executives had ever served on its board of directors.[71]

Manufacturers seemed to prefer legislation regulating the hours and conditions of women's work to seeing their workers join unions. One, for example, told the Women's Bureau of the Department of Labor that a uniform 48-hour week for women would equalize competition and would, in any event, only confirm existing conditions in some shops. Some went even further hoping for federal legislation that would provide uniform standards nationwide.[72]

When occasionally employers found it in their interests to encourage unionism they did so in return for certain very specific advantages. One of these was the union label. In the garment industry the label on overalls in certain parts of the country assured higher sales. To acquire the right to use it, some employers rushed into contracts with the United Garment Workers and quite deliberately urged their workers into the union.[73] New York garment manufacturers negotiated a preferential union shop, higher wages, and shorter hours with the ILGWU in return for which the union agreed to discipline its members and to protect employers against strikes. The garment manufacturers' protective association urged employers to "make every effort to increase the membership in the union so that its officers may have complete control of the workers and be enabled to discipline them when necessary."[74] Southern textile mill owners, otherwise violently opposed to unions, were similarly interested in the disciplinary functions of unionism. They would, an observer reported, modify their opposition "if the purposes of the union were to improve the educational, moral and social conditions of the workers."[75]

In general, however, employers made valiant attempts to keep women out of unions. The paternalism, benevolence, and welfare they offered in compensation were supported by other sectors of their society, including the trade unions. Middle-class reformers and government investigators had long viewed the harsh conditions under which women worked as detrimental to the preservation of home and family, and government regulation or voluntary employer programs seemed to many an adequate alternative. Unions played into this competitive structure adopting the home-and-motherhood argument to restrict women's labor-force participation. In the process they encouraged women to see their interests apart from those of male workers.

Limited labor-force opportunities, protective labor legislation and virtual exclusion from labor unions institutionalized women's isolation from the mainstream of labor. Not accidentally, these tendencies confirmed traditional women's roles, already nurtured by many ethnic groups and sustained by prevailing American norms. Together they translated into special behavior on the part of female workers that isolated them still further from male workers and added up to special treatment as members of the labor force.

In acquiescing, women perhaps bowed to the inevitable, seeking for themselves the goals of employers who preferred not to see them in unions, of male workers who hoped thereby both to limit competition and to share in the advantages gained, and of middle-class reformers who felt they were helping to preserve home and motherhood. Echoing labor union arguments of twenty years earlier, Women's Bureau head Mary Anderson defended protective legislation in 1925 on the grounds that such laws were necessary to conserve the health of the nation's women.[76]

A final consequence for women was to lead them to search for jobs in non-sex-stereotyped sectors of the labor market. Employers' needs in the rapidly expanding white-collar sector led women increasingly toward secretarial and clerical work. Vocational education to train women for office jobs, teaching,

and social work expanded rapidly in the early twentieth century. Working women rationalized these jobs as steps up the occupational ladder; state and local governments and employers provided financial aid; and middle-class women launched a campaign to encourage women to accept vocational training.[77] It took an astute union woman like Fannia Cohn to see what was happening. She drew a sharp line between her own function as educational director of the International Ladies Garment Workers Union and the functions of the new schools. Her hope was to train women to be better union members, not to get them out of the working class.

The parallel development of protective legislation and vocational education confirmed for many working women their marginal positions in the labor force, positions they continued to rationalize with obeisance to marriage and the family. As Alice Henry said of an earlier group of female wage-earners, "They did not realize that women were within the scope of the labor movement."[78] Fannia Cohn understood what that meant. That hard-headed and clear-sighted official of the ILGWU prefaced a call for a revolution in society's view of women with a plea for an end to competition between working women and men. Because it was destructive for all workers, she argued, "this competition must be abolished once and for all, not because it is immoral, yes inhuman, but because it is impractical, it does not pay."[79] But in the first two decades of the twentieth century, the moral arguments prevailed—releasing some women from some of the misery of toil, but simultaneously confirming their place in those jobs most conducive to exploitation.

NOTES

Abbreviations: WB/NA: Women's Bureau Collection, Record Group no. 86, National Archives; CIR: Final Report and Testimony of the Commission on Industrial Relations, Senate Documents, vol. 21, 64th Congress, 1st session, vol. 3, 1914; AF: American Federationist.

1. Fannia Cohn to William Green, Mar. 6, 1925. Fannia Cohn collection, New York Public Library, Box. 4.

2. . . . Leo Volman, The Growth of American Trade Unions, 1880–1923 (New York: National Bureau of Economic Research, 1923), chap. 5, estimates that about 40 percent of organized women were in the three garment industry unions: ILGWU, Amalgamated Clothing Workers, and United Garment Work-

ers, unions that had been either literally or virtually nonexistent before 1910. See [also] Alice Henry, *Women and the Labor Movement* (New York: George Doran, 1923), chap. 4, . . .

3. . . . Such occupations as taking in boarders, homework, and working on husbands' farms or in family businesses are not counted by census takers. Including these legitimate forms of labor would create drastic upward revisions in the proportion of working women, but we have no way of knowing by how much. . . .

4. John Andrews and W.D.P. Bliss, *History of Women in Trade Unions*, Report on the Condition of Women and Child Wage Earners in the U.S. (Washington, D.C.: G.P.O., 1911).

5. Ann Blankenhorn, miscellaneous notes, chap. 2, p. 12, file no. 23, box no. 1, Ann Craton Blankenhorn collection, Archives of Labor History, Wayne State University. . . .

6. Interview with Faigele Shapiro, Aug. 6, 1964. Amerikaner Yiddishe Geschichte Bel-pe, YIVO, pp. 2, 7.

7. *AF* 6 (Nov. 1899):228.

8. Quoted in Andrews and Bliss, *History of Women in Trade Unions*, p. 173.

9. New York Women's Trade Union League, *Report of the Proceedings*, 4th Annual Conference of Trade Union Women, Oct. 9, 10, 1926, p. 18.

10. Vera Shlakman, *Economic History of a Factory Town: A Study of Chicopee, Massachusetts*, Smith College Studies in History, vol. 20, no. 1–4 (Oct. 1934–July 1935), p. 216; . . .

11. Andrews and Bliss, *History of Women in Trade Unions*, p. 168; Massachusetts Women's Trade Union League, *The History of Trade Unionism among Women in Boston* (Boston: WTUL, n.d., but c. 1907), pp. 22, 23.

12. Theresa Wolfson, "Where Are the Organized Women Workers?" *AF* 32 (June 1925):455–57.

13. Andrews and Bliss, *History of Women in Trade Unions*, p. 151.

14. *AF* 17 (Nov. 1911), p. 896. . . .

15. Eva McDonald Valesh, "Women and Labor," *AF* 3 (Feb. 1896):222.

16. Selig Perlman, *A History of Trade Unionism in the U.S.* (New York: Macmillan, 1923), p. 166. . . .

17. Samuel Gompers, "Should the Wife Help Support the Family?" *AF* 13 (Jan. 1906):36. . . .

18. "Mainly Progressive," *AF* 3 (Mar. 1896):16; "What Our Organizers Are Doing," *AF* 10 (Apr. 1903):370.

19. Editorial, *AF* 11 (July 1904):584.

20. "Trade Union History," *AF* 9 (Nov. 1902):871.

21. John Safford, "The Good That Trade Unions Do," part 1, *AF* 9 (July 1902):353, 358; "Talks on Labor," *AF* 12 (Nov. 1905):846.

22. William Gilthorpe, "Advancement," *AF* 17 (Oct. 1910):847.

23. Safford, "The Good That Trade Unions Do," part 2, *AF* 9 (August 1902):423.

24. Edward O'Donnell, "Women as Breadwinners: The Error of the Age," *AF* 4 (Oct. 1897):186. . . .

25. Safford, "The Good That Trade Unions Do," part 1, pp. 357–58.

26. Gompers, "Should the Wife Help Support the Family?" p. 36.

27. Ibid. . . .

28. Women's Labor Resolution, *AF* 5 (Jan. 1899):220; "Talks on Labor," *AF* 10 (June 1903):477.

29. Massachusetts, WTUL, *History of Trade Unionism Among Women in Boston*, p. 13; . . .

30. Mildred Rankin to Mrs. Raymond Robins, Mar. 30, 1919, Margaret Dreier Robins Collection, University of Florida, Gainesville, Florida. . . .

31. Gompers, "Should the Wife Help Support the Family?" p. 36.

32. Alice Woodbridge, "Women's Labor," *AF* 1 (Apr. 1894):66–67; . . .

33. WTUL Action of Policies, pp. 3, 8, box 4, accession no. 55A556, WB/NA: Proceedings of the A. F. of L. convention, 1923. . . .

34. Blankenhorn manuscript notes, chap. 4, p. 17, box 1, file no. 24. . . .

35. Pauline Newman, interview, undated, Amerikaner Yiddisher Geschichte Bel-pe, p. 21, YIVO. . . .

36. Mildren Rankin to Mrs. Raymond Robins, Mar. 30, 1919, Robins papers.

37. Gladys Boone, *The Women's Trade Unions League, in Great Britain and the U.S.A.* (New York: Columbia University Press, 1942), p. 167; Alice Henry, *Women in the Labor Movement* (New York: Doran, 1923):102.

38. Interview with Vail Ballou Press, Effects of Legislation: Night Work Schedule, New York, NA/WB.

39. See for example Rankin to Robins, Mar. 30, 1919; . . .

40. New York Women's Trade Union League, *Report of the Proceedings*, 4th Conference, p. 14.

41. Undated interviews, unions, for Bulletin no. 65, NA/WB.

42. Testimony of Hilda Svenson, C.I.R., p. 2307; the testimony was taken in June 1914.

43. Florence Sanville to Rose Schneiderman, Nov. 28, 1917, Rose Schneiderman collection. Tamiment Institute library, box A 94. . . .

44. Testimonies, box 15, accession no. 51A101, WB/NA. The women had been hired when the war broke out.

45. Emma Steghagen to Mary Anderson, Jan. 15, 1919, WTUL Action on Policies, accession no. 55A556, WB/WA.

46. United States Education and Labor Committee, *Report Upon the Relations Between Capital and Labor* (Washington, D.C., G.P.O., 1882), 1:453. . . .

47. Interview with Mr. Salerno, Amalgamated Clothing Workers, interviews, unions, accession no. 51A101, WB/NA.

48. Interview with Mr. Hurley, July 1919, Women Street Car Conductors, accession no. 51A101, WB/NA.

49. Sir Lyon Playfair, "Children and Female Labor," *AF* 7 (Apr. 1900):103. . . .

50. Ira Howerth, "The Kingdom of God in Modern Industry," *AF* 14 (Aug. 1907):544.

51. Mary Anderson, "The Federal Government Recognizes Problems of Women in Industry," *AF* 32 (June 1925):453.

52. Individual interviews, Massachusetts, Apr. 12, 1920, accession no. 51A101, WB/NA. . . .

53. Individual interviews, Massachusetts and New Jersey, accession no. 51A101, WB/NA. . . .

54. Fannia Cohn to Dr. Marion Phillips, Sept. 13, 1927, Fannia Cohn Collection, box 4.

55. Interviews with Tony Salerno, Amalgamated Clothing Workers Union and Hat and Cap Makers Local 7, Boston, individual interviews, unions, accession no. 51A101, WB/NA. . . .

56. Lizzie Swank Holmes, "Women Workers of Chicago," *AF* 12 (Aug. 1905):507–10; . . .

57. Shapiro, p. 25.

58. *Justice* (Apr. 19, 1919):2.

59. Blankenhorn manuscript notes, chap. 13, p. 4, box 1, file 25.

60. For example, see Mary Dreier, address to New York WTUL in *Report of the Proceedings,* 4th conference, 1926, p. 14. . . .

61. Individual interviews, California, effects of legislation, accession no. 51A101, WB/NA.

62. Quoted in a letter from Mary Van Kleeck to Mary Anderson, Feb. 2, 1923, Mary Van Kleeck collection, Smith College, unsorted.

63. Breman and O'Brien, individual interviews, Massachusetts, accession no. 51A101, WB/NA. . . .

64. Sylvia Shulman, testimony, CIR, pp. 2285, 2292; Hilda Svenson, testimony, CIR, pp. 2311, 2317; Elizabeth Dutcher, testimony, CIR, p. 2392. Exceptions sometimes occurred in small western towns where workers would not patronize nonunion stores. . . .

65. Rose Schneiderman with Lucy Goldthwaite, *All for One* (New York: Paul Erickson, 1967):59; Shapiro, p. 9.

66. Elizabeth Maloney testimony, CIR, pp. 3246–47. . . .

67. Agnes Nestor, testimony, CIR, p. 3389; Elizabeth Dutcher testimony, CIR, p. 2405.

68. Elizabeth Maloney testimony, CIR, p. 3245.

69. Leon Stein, *The Triangle Fire* (Philadelphia: J. P. Lippincott, 1952); Nestor, CIR, p. 3382.

70. Blankenhorn, manuscript notes, chap. 4, p. 17, file 24, box 1.

71. Nestor, CIR, p. 3382; Svenson, CIR, pp. 3382 and . . . p. 2308, reveal the degree to which this was an attempt to undercut union strength; . . .

72. See Cambridge Paper Box Company, Long Hour Day Schedule, accession no. 51A101, WB/NA.

73. Andrews and Bliss, *History of Women in Trade Unions,* p. 169.

74. U.S. Department of Labor, Bureau of Labor Statistics, Bulletin no. 145, 1914, p. 37.

75. *The Cotton Textile Industry,* Report on the Condition of Women and Child Wage Earners, vol. 1, (Washington, D.C.: G.P.O., 1910), p. 608.

76. Mary Anderson, "Industrial Standards for Women," *AF* 32 (July 1925):21.

77. See Massachusetts WTUL, *History of Trade Unionism Among Women in Boston,* pp. 7, 32; New York WTUL, *Report of the Proceedings,* 4th Conference, p. 21.

78. Henry, *Women and the Labor Movement,* p. 108.

79. Typescript of "Complete Equality Between Men and Women," from the December 1917 issue of the *Ladies Garment Worker,* Fannia Cohn Collection, box. 7.

KATHY PEISS

Putting on Style: Working Women and Leisure in Turn-of-the-Century New York

The daily round of toil faced by young wage-earning women inspired both militant efforts to improve working conditions, as Alice Kessler-Harris demonstrated, and an intense quest for escape. The leisure activities providing that escape are explored with a discerning eye by Kathy Peiss. What similarities exist between the behavior of adolescent girls at the turn of the century and their contemporary counterparts? What evidence does she provide of an emerging consumer culture as well as a youth culture? How does dress continue to serve as a means of expression and a source of family conflict?

In the twentieth century, youth is regarded as a distinctive stage of life, a time of self-expression and experimentation before the experience of marriage, children, and work. Clearly applicable to middle-class teen-agers, who can nurture a separate culture in high schools and colleges,[1] this notion of youth may not seem relevant to the working-class adolescents of 1900, who felt the pinch of financial responsibility at an early age and subordinated individual desires to the family's survival. Nevertheless, working-class youth spent much of their leisure apart from their families and enjoyed greater social freedom than their parents or married siblings, especially married women. . . .

For single women in New York . . . the search for pleasure in public forms of recreation was shaped not only by long-standing patterns of culture and social organization but by new conditions of family life, work, and commercialized leisure in the city. . . . Not content with quiet recreation in the home, they sought adventure in dance halls, cheap theaters, amusement parks, excursion boats, and picnic grounds. Putting on finery, promenading the streets, and staying late at amusement resorts became an important cultural style for many working women. Entrepreneurs sought ways to increase female participation in commercialized recreation, encouraging women's fancy dress, slangy speech, and provocative public behavior. . . . These cultural forms were not simply imposed on working-class female consumers by the emergent entertainment industry, however, but were developed and articulated as well by the young women themselves. This process is most apparent in two noncommercial forms of recreation, the streets and social clubs, which working-class youth colonized as their own social spaces.

SOCIAL LIFE IN THE STREETS

The city streets were public conduits of sociability and free expression for all working-class people, avenues for protest, celebration, and amusement. Still, children and young people claimed ownership of the streets, despite intensified efforts by police and reformers to eradicate unruly revelry and unsanctioned behavior from the mid-century onward. . . . [Al-
though w]orking-class girls were more supervised than boys, . . . the streets offered countless diversions. . . . "We shared the life of the street," Sophie Ruskay recalled, "unhampered by our parents who were too busy to try to mold us into a more respectable pattern."[2] Even when saddled with minding a younger sibling, girls could still play sidewalk games, chat with friends, revel in the city's sights and sounds, or gather around itinerant musicians to try out their dancing skill. Girls did not form their own gangs, but some of the more adventurous joined in the boys' fun, roaming the streets and playing tricks on passers-by. As one study noted, "individual girls are frequently attached to boys' gangs and are sometimes real factors in the gang-government."[3] More important, the streets were alternative environments that taught children a repertoire of manners and mores they did not learn in school. Attitudes toward sexuality, marriage, and women's work were conveyed in street games and rhymes.[4]

In their teens, young women and men used the streets as a place to meet the other sex, to explore nascent sexual feelings, and carry on flirtations, all outside the watchful eyes and admonitions of parents. "Doing nothing"—small talk, scuffling, joking, and carrying on—was infused with meaning for working-class youth. With no supervision but the cop on the beat, young women could be unladylike and unrestrained on street corners and in doorways. To Maureen Connelly, an Irish immigrant to the Yorkville section of Manhattan, "fun was standing at the door with boys and girls and kidding around—this was a big thing in our life—until the policeman came and chased us."[5] Some adolescent girls, whom parents and reformers labelled "tough," spent their evenings on street corners and in alleys and gang hangouts until late at night. More respectable young women might promenade the local commercial streets or parks in a group or with a gentleman friend, enjoying the walk, window-shopping, and chatting. Each working-class neighborhood had its place to be seen: Eighth Avenue, with its gaudy movie houses and flashing lights drew crowds of West Side Irish, German, and native-born youth; the Bowery, Grand Street, and 14th Street attracted the inhabitants of the lower East Side; and First

Avenue near 72nd Street was known as the Czech Broadway to its promenaders.[6]

SOCIAL CLUBS

The streets offered uninhibited space for youth activity; social clubs and amusement societies offered an organizational structure. . . . Young women's involvement in social and pleasure clubs varied. Some joined clubs that functioned like the lodges and associations of older working-class men. The Roumanian Young Folks' Social Club and the Independent Bukowmaer Young Men's and Young Ladies' Benefit Society were typical *landsmanschaft* organizations of the lower East Side. These proffered mutual assistance, sick benefits, and burial plots while encouraging immigrant youth to remain close to their traditional cultures through sociable gatherings. . . . More often, youth organizations tended to be oriented toward amusement and mixed-sex sociability rather than mutual aid, education, or political action. Significantly, social clubs were often called "pleasure clubs" by their patrons, to differentiate them from the more serious-minded lodges and benefit societies. . . .

Organizing social clubs was a simple task. "You get together a number of people, you know, youngsters, . . . in the neighborhood and you just open up a social club," recalled Rachel Levin, who lived in the lower East Side. "We set . . . up our own programs," observed Ida Schwartz, a Russian-born milliner who joined a club when she was seventeen. "We made an organization, and we had a little dues, and then we used to make affairs and you made dances and met people, like young people do."[7] . . .

Schwartz noted that her club was comprised of men and women from school and work, whose friendship often led to marriage: "We were about twenty couples, and then of course when we got older, we were married . . . among the girls."[8] To parents, allowing a daughter to step out with the crowd was more acceptable than permitting her to go out alone on a date. Young women too sought safety in numbers. Around the time that she graduated eighth grade and entered the workforce, Maureen Connelly joined the Friends of Irish Freedom, an ostensibly political organization, but one which, she noted, "was more social than anything else." The group had meetings every Friday night, followed by a dance, which was "the highlight of our lives." She had little in-

terest in what they did for Ireland, but "most of the girls joined—and of course you didn't go with a boy when you were seventeen. They were there and we danced with them and laughed about them, but you didn't take them serious."[9] . . . Reformer Belle Israels summed up the attitude of many [other] working girls when she noted, "No amusement is complete in which *he* is not a factor."[10] At the same time, it would be misleading to view the consciousness of most young women solely in terms of a desire for marriage and to argue that their leisure activities simply affirmed the world of their fathers, a traditional patriarchal order.

Ambiguously, young women marked out their leisure time not only as an opportunity for romantic entanglement but also as a sphere of autonomy and assertion. The Bachelor Girls Social Club, composed of female mail order clerks at Siegel-Cooper, addressed this paradox when they were accused by several male coworkers of being "manhaters" and of "celebrat[ing] Washington's Birthday without even thinking of a man." The club heatedly responded: "No, we are not married, neither are we men haters, but we believe in woman's rights, and we enjoy our independence and freedom, notwithstanding the fact that if a fair offer came our way we might not [sic] consider it."[11] Young women's desire for social freedom and its identification with leisure activities spilled over into behavior unsanctioned by parents and neighbors, as well as middle-class reformers. Clubs, for example, could be gathering places for sexual experimentation. A club member familiar with the organizational life of young East Siders reported to the University Settlement that "in all [clubs] 'they have kissing all through pleasure time, and use slang language,' while in some they 'don't behave nice between young ladies.'" Similarly the street corners and doorways were spaces for kissing, hugging, and fondling, free and easy sexual behavior "which seem[s] quite improper to the 'up-towner,'" but was casually accepted by working-class youth.[12]

CLOTHING, STYLE, AND LEISURE

Streets and social clubs, as well as such commercial forms of amusement as dance halls and theaters, became the spaces in which young women could carve out a cultural style expressing these complex and often contradictory values. It was in leisure that women played with identity, trying on new images and roles, appropriating the cultural forms around them—clothing, music, language—to push at the boundaries of immigrant, working-class life. This public presentation of self was one way to comment upon and mediate the dynamics of urban life and labor—poverty and the magnet of upward mobility, sexual assertion and the maintenance of respectability, daughterly submission and the attractions of autonomy and romance, the grinding workday and the glittering appeal of urban nightlife.

Promenading the streets and going places with the crowd, young working-class women "put on style." Dress was a particularly potent way to display and play with notions of respectability, allure, independence, and status and to assert a distinctive identity and presence. Genteel reformers noted with concern the tendency of young working women to present an appearance fraught with questionable moral and social connotations. Mary Augusta LaSelle lamented the use of low decolletage, gauze stockings, high-heeled shoes, freakish hats, and hair dressed with "rats" and "puffs," or artificial hair pieces—"in too many cases a fantastic imitation of the costly costumes of women of large incomes."[13] To such middle-class observers, working women were seeking upward mobility, dressing like their betters in order to marry into a higher class. This interpretation, while not without foundation, obscures the more complex role of fashion and style in the social life of working women.

Proper clothing in working-class culture traditionally helped to define respectability. As Lillian Betts observed of the workingman, "He, with the mother, has one standard—clothes."[14] Among laboring families hard pressed for income, dress divided itself into two types, work clothes and Sunday clothes. Work clothing necessarily varied with the requirements of job and employer, from the crisp white aprons and caps of waitresses to the hand-me-down garments worn by factory hands. Sunday clothes, however, were visible displays of social standing and self-respect in the rituals of church-going, promenading, and visiting. Appropriate attire was a requirement of social participation. Elena and Gerda Nakov, two impoverished needlewomen, considered "their clothing [to be] so poor that they were ashamed to go out on Sunday—when everybody else put on 'best dresses'—and would sit in their room all

day."[15] For newly arrived immigrants, changing one's clothes was the first step in securing a new status as an American. When Rose Pasternak landed at Castle Garden, her brother took her directly to a hat store: "They said in this country you don't go to work without a hat."[16]

Clothing was only the palpable aspect of competing cultural styles among young working-class women. Patterns of speech, manners, levels of schooling, attitudes toward self-improvement, and class consciousness differentiated groups of women beyond the obvious divisions of ethnicity and religion. In workshops, stores, clubs, and dance halls, observers noted the cliquishness of adolescent girls around these considerations. In the moralistic language of one reform committee, "The several floors of a large factory often mean as many degrees of respectability or demoralization" among working women.[17] Journalist Mary Gay Humphreys described the New York girls of the 1890s who took themselves seriously as independent and thoughtful workers, and reflected this view in their public style. Women strikers in a thread-mill, for example, linked fashion—wearing bonnets—to their sense of American identity and class consciousness, contrasting their militancy to Scottish scabs who wore shawls on their heads. Believing in the labor movement's ideology of self-improvement, organization, and workers' dignity, these women devoted their leisure to lectures, evening school, political meetings, and union dances. While they sewed their own ball gowns and loved display, they also agreed that ribbons were a "foolish extravagance."[18]

For other young women, dress became a cultural terrain of pleasure, expressiveness, romance, and autonomy. "A girl must have clothes if she is to go into high society at Ulmer Park or Coney Island or the theatre," explained Sadie Frowne, a sixteen-year-old garment worker. "A girl who does not dress well is stuck in a corner, even if she is pretty." Similarly, Minnie saved her earnings in order to "'blow herself' to an enormous bunch of new hair, which had transformed her from what she called 'a back number' to 'something dead swell.'" As another working woman succinctly put it, "If you want to get any notion took of you, you gotta have some style about you."[19]

Stylish clothing—a chinchilla coat, a beaded wedding dress, a straw hat with a willow plume—was an aspect of popular culture that particularly tugged at women's desires. Maria Cichetti lovingly remembers hats and the sense of being "dressed": "They were so beautiful, those hats. . . . They were so rich. A woman looked so dressed, you know, in the back, with the bustle. . . . I wanted to grow up to wear earrings and hats and high heels."[20] . . . To be stunningly attired at the movies, balls, or entertainments often counted more in the working woman's calculations than having comfortable clothes and shoes for the daily round of toil.

The fashions such young women wore often displayed aristocratic pretensions. Grand Street clothing stores cheaply produced the styles found in exclusive establishments. Working women read the fashion columns, and many could observe wealthy women in department stores and the streets for inspiration in their dressmaking. . . . Significantly, [working] women did not imitate *haute couture* directly, but adapted and transformed such fashion in creating their own style. While they could ill afford the fine cloth or exquisite decorations of the wealthy woman's dress, there was no purely economic reason why they chose to wear flashy colors, gaudy hats, and cosmetics. Indeed, imitation of "ladies of leisure" might involve admiring the style of prostitutes as well as socialites. As Ruth Rosen has argued, much of the appearance of twentieth-century women, including their use of make-up and wigs, was common among prostitutes before becoming accepted by "respectable" females.[21] In the promiscuous spaces of the streets, theaters, and dance halls, prostitutes provided a cultural model both fascinating and forbidden to other young working-class women. Tantalized by the fine dress, easy life, sexual expressiveness, and apparent independence, while carefully marking the boundary between the fallen and respectable, a working woman might appropriate parts of the prostitute's style as her own. So-called "tough girls," as Lillian Wald described the assertive and rowdy working girls of her community, played with the subculture of prostitution: "Pronounced lack of modesty in dress was one of several signs; . . . their dancing, their talk, their freedom of manner, all combined to render them conspicuous."[22] . . .

Putting on style seemed to fly in the face of the daily round of toil and family obligation—an assertive flash of color and form that belied some of the realities of everyday life. Yet this mode of cultural expression, linked to the pleasures of the streets, clubs, and dance halls, was closely shaped by the economic and social relations of working-class life. Maintaining style on the streets, at dance halls, or at club functions was an achievement won at other costs—going without food, sewing into the night to embellish a hat or dress, buying on installment, leaving school early to join the workforce, and forcing confrontations within the working-class family.

THE FAMILY ECONOMY AND CONFLICT OVER LEISURE

. . . Most young women negotiated leisure within the dynamics of the family economy, which was both a strategy for survival and a working-class cultural ideal. In an industrial system dominated by low-paying unskilled and semiskilled jobs, the inadequacy of men's wages necessitated the economic contribution of daughters, sons, and wives, thus reinforcing the interdependency of family members. In a 1914 study, for example, the typical working-class family of five contained three wage-earners.[23] . . . Custom demanded that daughters contribute all or a substantial part of their earnings to the family. In 1888, 72 percent of female factory workers interviewed gave all their earnings, and this figure remained relatively unchanged into the 1910s, when three-quarters to four-fifths handed their pay envelopes over to their parents unopened.[24] . . . While daughters may have accepted the family claim to their wages and work, struggles often ensued over their access to and use of leisure time. Participation in social life, parental supervision, spending money, and clothing were common issues of conflict. As wage-earners and contributors to the family, they sought to parlay their newfound status toward greater autonomy in their personal lives.

In an example of this familial drama, Louisa, a young woman living in a West Side Irish neighborhood around 1910, discovered that working in a candy factory for five dollars a week gave her power within the family. Her economic contribution enabled her to claim the privilege of going to dance halls, staying out late with men, and purchasing extravagant suits and hats. Social investigator Ruth True observed of Louisa that "the costume in which she steps out so triumphantly has cost many bitter moments at home. She has gotten it by force, with the threat of throwing up her job." Her distraught mother decried such undutiful behavior: "She stands up and answers me back. An' she's comin' in at 2 o'clock, me not knowin' where she has been. Folks will talk, you know, an' it ain't right fer a girl."[25] Indeed, a bargain was struck in many families, with daughters bartering their obedience in turning over wages for the freedom to come and go as they pleased. . . .

Family controversy over young women's leisure was compounded by the problem of space and privacy in tenement apartments, where the "parlor" served as kitchen, dining room, and bedroom. New York housing ranged from abysmal rear tenements to "new law" apartments with indoor plumbing and adequate ventilation, but overcrowding remained a dominant characteristic of working-class neighborhoods. Dumbbell tenements, the prevailing housing type between 1879 and 1901, usually contained several apartments per floor, in a five- to seven-story walk-up. In 1900, an average of eight families lived in each tenement house, and the mean size of households was 4.3 individuals, usually crowded into two or three rooms. Although housing conditions improved after 1900 with the construction of new law tenements, families still had to contend with small rooms and, often, the presence of boarders. Consequently, "privacy could be had only in public," and young people sought the streets, clubs, and halls in order to nurture intimate relationships.[26]

Contention over leisure, social freedom, and dating was also heightened by the inevitable cultural conflicts between the American-born or educated youth and their immigrant parents, who clung to Old World traditions. . . . Sadie Frowne, a young garment worker, observed that immigrant women criticized her for spending her income on fashionable clothes: "Those who blame me are the old country people who have old-fashioned notions, but the people who have been here a long time know better."[27] . . . [O]ne young East Sider asked . . . in an advice column: "Is it a sin to use face powder? Shouldn't a girl look beautiful? My father does not want me to use face powder. Is it a sin?"[28] . . .

RECREATION AND THE "WOMAN ADRIFT"

Although most adolescent working-class women lived at home, a sizable number—as many as sixty-eight thousand in 1910—lived alone, lodging in boardinghouses or renting rooms.[29] Style and amusement were important aspects of their lives as well, but the "woman adrift," as she was called, experienced the culture of the streets, clubs, and dance halls in a different context from those who resided at home. Women who lived outside families trod a fine line between asserting independence and guarding respectability in their everyday lives. Many chose to live with relatives or board in the houses of strangers rather than risk their reputations living alone. Foreign-born women especially tended to seek a room with a "Missus," occupying a passageway or sharing a folding bed in the parlor at night. . . .

[Other] young women sought lodging in commercial rooming houses and apartments for greater social freedom, in order to come and go as they pleased. . . . Rooms were small, bleak, and cold, and houses usually lacked public parlors or reception rooms where women could socialize with their friends. Moreover, women entertaining men ran the gauntlet between landladies' disapproving stares and the knowing glances of male boarders. For boardinghouse keepers concerned with decency, "the most commonly used device is the rule that one may entertain only 'steadies' in one's room. . . . The working girl who numbers among her acquaintances more than one man is looked upon askance." Thus women combatted the loneliness of the furnished room by seeking out the movie houses, dance halls, cafes, and even saloons as places of rendezvous, diversion, conviviality, and courtship.[30]

Whether they lived at home or alone, young women's notion of a "good time" was intimately linked to the public spaces of the streets, clubs, and commercial amusement resorts. Clearly not all women could pursue these forms of leisure activities. With tiring labor and few resources, many had little opportunity to enter the social whirl. "When the girls get home they're too tired to do anything," observed one bookbinder, a statement confirmed by female workers in restaurants, garment shops, and other businesses.[31] Family responsibilities kept others at home. . . . The demands of the family economy often left women dependent on unsavory men for amusements, an arrangement many rejected. Commented a working girl who gave her weekly wages to her mother, "We have not the money for pretty clothes to attract the boys who would really care for us and of course we have no money to pay for our own amusement, and as a result we stay at home." Some obviously craved the world of popular amusements to which they could not belong. "Never have I been to a moving picture show or taken out," lamented Celia, a young immigrant. "The excursions that leave the pier make me jealous sometimes. . . . Only to be out like everybody else!"[32] Within the varieties of working-class cultural experience, Celia's words suggest that those who could indulge in the city's cheap amusements stood out as a model for other young working women.

NOTES

1. See, e.g., Paula S. Fass, *The Damned and the Beautiful: American Youth in the 1920's* (New York, 1977).

2. Irving Howe and Kenneth Libo, *How We Lived: A Documentary History of Immigrant Jews in America* (New York, 1979), p. 54.

3. Collier and Barrows, *City Where Crime Is Play* (New York, Jan. 1914), p. 20; John W. Martin, "Social Life in the Street," in University Settlement Society of New York, *Report* (New York, 1899), p. 23; Frederick A. King, "Influences in Street Life," in University Settlement Society of New York, *Report* (New York, 1900), p. 29.

4. Percy Stickney Grant, "Children's Street Games," *Survey* 23 (13 Nov. 1909):235; Cary Goodman, *Choosing Sides: Playground and Street Life on the Lower East Side* (New York, 1979).

5. Tape IV-12 (side B), New York City Immigrant Labor History Collection of the City College Oral History Project, Robert F. Wagner Archives, Tamiment Institute Library, New York University; also [Russell Sage Foundation,] *Boyhood and Lawlessness* (New York, 1914), pp. 155–56; Ruth S. True, *The Neglected Girl* (New York, 1914), pp. 62–63. . . .

6. True, *Neglected Girl*, pp. 66–67; Transcript K-3, p. 13, Immigrant Labor History Collection; King, "Street Life," p. 32.

7. Tapes I-1 (transcript) and I-117 (side B), Immigrant Labor History Collection; Herbert Asbury, *The Gangs of New York* (1927; reprint New York, 1970), p. 269; Belle L. Mead, "The Social Pleasures of East Side Jews," (M.A. thesis, Columbia University, 1904), p. 6; *University Settlement Studies* 2, no. 2 (1906):20; New York State Bureau of Labor Statistics, *Eighteenth Annual Report* (Albany, N.Y., 1900), p. 294.

8. Tape I-117 (side B), Immigrant Labor History Collection.

9. Tape IV-12 (side A), Immigrant Labor History Collection.

10. Belle Lindner Israels, "The Way of the Girl," *Survey* 22 (3 July 1909):486.

11. *Thought and Work*, May 1906, p. 8. . . .

12. Martin, "Social Life in the Street," p. 23; King, "Street Life," p. 30. . . .

13. Mary Augusta LaSelle, *The Young Woman Worker* (Boston, 1914), pp. 91, 89; Helen S. Campbell, *Prisoners of Poverty: Women Wage-Earners, Their Trades and Their Lives* (1887; reprint Westport, Conn., 1970), p. 175; Helen Campbell et al., *Darkness and Daylight, or Lights and Shadows of New York Life* (Hartford, Conn., 1897), p. 257.

14. Lillian W. Betts, *The Leaven in a Great City* (New York, 1902), p. 258. . . .

15. Sue Ainslie Clark and Edith Wyatt, *Making Both Ends Meet: The Income and Outlay of New York Working Girls* (New York, 1911), p. 143; New York Factory Investigating Commission, *Fourth Report*, vol. 4, p. 1528.

16. Tape I-132 (side A), Immigrant Labor History Collection. For the male case, see Abraham Cahan, *The Rise of David Levinsky* (1917; reprint New York, 1960), p. 101.

17. [New York] State Charities Aid Association, Standing Committee on the Elevation of the Poor in Their Homes, *Moral Elevation of Girls: Suggestions Relating to Preventive Work* (New York, 1885), p. 21. . . .

18. Mary Gay Humphreys, "The New York Working Girl," *Scribner's* 20 (Oct. 1896):504, 502–503.

19. Sadie Frowne, "The Story of a Sweatshop Girl," in *Workers Speak: Self Portraits*, ed. Leon Stein and Philip Taft (New York, 1971), p. 118; Clara E. Laughlin, *The Work-a-Day Girl: A Study of Some Present-day Conditions* (New York, 1913), pp. 14, 136. . . .

20. Tape II-31 (side A), Immigrant Labor History Collection.

21. Ruth Rosen, *The Lost Sisterhood: Prostitution in America, 1900–1918* (Baltimore and London, 1982), p. 107.

22. Lillian D. Wald, *The House on Henry Street* (1915; reprint New York, 1971), p. 190.

23. New York Factory Investigating Commission, *Fourth Report*, vol. 4, pp. 1491–94. . . .

24. U.S. Bureau of Labor, *Working Women in Large Cities: Fourth Annual Report of the Commissioner of Labor, 1888* (Washington, D.C., 1889), pp. 340–42; U.S. Senate, *Report on the Condition of Woman and Child Wage-Earners in the United States, Vol. 5: Wage-Earning Women in Stores and Factories* (S. 645, 61st Cong., 2d sess.; Washington, D.C., 1910), p. 15; New York Factory Investigating Commission, *Fourth Report*, vol. 5, p. 2562.

25. True, *Neglected Girl*, pp. 54–55.

26. Samuel Chotzinoff, *A Lost Paradise* (New York, 1955), p. 81. . . .

27. Wald, *House on Henry Street*, p. 197; Frowne, "Sweatshop Girl," p. 118. . . .

28. Howe and Libo, *How We Lived*, p. 147; Isaac Metzker, ed., *A Bintel Brief* (New York, 1972), p. 14. . . .

29. Esther Packard, *A Study of Living Conditions of Self-Supporting Women in New York City* (New York, 1915), p. 40.

30. Packard, *Self-Supporting Women*, pp. 51, 52 (quote), 72, 84–85; U.S. Bureau of Labor, *Boarding Homes and Clubs for Working Women*, by Mary S. Fer-

gusson (Bulletin no. 15; Washington, D.C., 1898), p. 142; Mary K. Maule, "What Is a Shopgirl's Life?" *World's Work* 14 (Sept. 1907); 9314; U.S. Bureau of Labor, *Working Women in Large Cities*, p. 32; Clark and Wyatt, *Making Both Ends Meet*, p. 21.

31. Mary Van Kleeck, *Women in the Bookbinding Trade* (New York, 1913), p. 152; Consumer's League of New York City, *Behind the Scenes in a Restaurant: A Study of 1017 Women Restaurant Employees* (n.p.,

1916), p. 16; Clark and Wyatt, *Making Both Ends Meet*, p. 132.

32. "Letter from a Working Girl," in New York State Bureau of Labor Statistics, *Third Annual Report* (Albany, N.Y., 1885), p. 158; Thomas H. Russell, *The Girl's Fight for a Living* (Chicago, 1913), p. 163; New York Factory Investigating Commission, *Fourth Report*, vol. 4, p. 1700.

DOCUMENTS: *Struggling for Educational Opportunities*

Zitkala-Ša, ". . . This semblance of civilization"

Education has long been regarded as a key to the upward economic and social mobility inherent in the American dream. School was (and is) also a means of instructing "outsiders" in the values and behavior of the dominant culture. Although the early settlers of the original thirteen colonies were, in fact, the "outsiders," they and their descendants regarded Amerindians as such. Because Euroamericans measured all other cultures by their own, federal officials and missionaries alike thought *all* women should conform in their behavior and dress to the standard set by white middle-class women. Amerindian women were regarded with great consternation because the work they did was judged unsuitable and the leisure behavior they engaged in viewed as immoral. Although they were perceived as "backward," many Indian women in fact enjoyed greater responsibilities and economic independence than did their Euroamerican counterparts.

While Indian women may have had reason to welcome some aspects of modernization, the process of acculturation was often traumatic, as this account of a Sioux Indian girl, Zitkala-Ša, makes clear. Zitkala-Ša, as Gertrude Simmons Bonnin, went on to have an active career as an author and reformer.* To what extent did her mother anticipate that the experience at the mission school would be difficult? What evidence is there to suggest that she herself was involved in the process of acculturation?

The first turning away from the easy, natural flow of my life occurred in an early spring. It was in my eighth year; in the month of March, I afterward learned. At this age I knew but one language, and that was my mother's native tongue.

From some of my playmates I heard that two paleface missionaries were in our village. They were from that class of white men who wore big hats and carried large hearts, they said. Running direct to my mother, I began to question her why these two strangers were among us. She told me, after I had teased much, that they had come to take away Indian boys

and girls to the East. My mother did not seem to want me to talk about them. But in a day or two, I gleaned many wonderful stories from my playfellows concerning the strangers.

"Mother, my friend Judéwin is going home with the missionaries. She is going to a more beautiful country than ours; the palefaces told her so!" I said wistfully, wishing in my heart that I too might go.

Mother sat in a chair, and I was hanging on her knee. Within the last two seasons my big brother Dawée had returned from a three years' education in the East, and his coming back influenced my mother to take a farther

*Bonnin's interesting life is described at length by Mary E. Young in *Notable American Women, 1607–1950: A Biographical Dictionary*, ed. Edward T. James, Janet Wilson James, and Paul Boyer (Cambridge, Mass., 1971) 1:198–200.

Excerpted from "Impressions of an Indian Childhood," "The School Days of an Indian Girl," and "An Indian Teacher among Indians" by Zitkala-Ša, *Atlantic Monthly* 85 (January, February, and March 1900):45–47, 186–87, and 386.

step from her native way of living. First it was a change from the buffalo skin to the white man's canvas that covered our wigwam. Now she had given up her wigwam of slender poles, to live, a foreigner, in a home of clumsy logs.

Judéwin had told me of the great tree where grew red, red apples; and how we could reach out our hands and pick all the red apples we could eat. I had never seen apple trees. I had never tasted more than a dozen red apples in my life; and when I heard of the orchards of the East, I was eager to roam among them. The missionaries smiled into my eyes, and patted my head. I wondered how mother could say such hard words against them.

"Mother, ask them if little girls may have all the red apples they want, when they go East," I whispered aloud, in my excitement.

The interpreter heard me, and answered: "Yes, little girl, the nice red apples are for those who pick them; and you will have a ride on the iron horse if you go with these good people."

I had never seen a train, and he knew it.

"Mother, I'm going East! I like big red apples, and I want to ride on the iron horse! Mother, say yes!" I pleaded.

My mother said nothing. The missionaries waited in silence; and my eyes began to blur with tears, though I struggled to choke them back. The corners of my mouth twitched, and my mother saw me.

"I am not ready to give you any word," she said to them. "Tomorrow I shall send you my answer by my son."

With this they left us. Alone with my mother, I yielded to my tears, and cried aloud, shaking my head so as not to hear what she was saying to me. This was the first time I had ever been so unwilling to give up my own desire that I refused to harken to my mother's voice.

There was a solemn silence in our home that night. Before I went to bed I begged the Great Spirit to make my mother willing I should go with the missionaries.

The next morning came, and my mother called me to her side. "My daughter, do you still persist in wishing to leave your mother?" she asked.

"Oh, mother, it is not that I wish to leave you, but I want to see the wonderful Eastern land," I answered. . . .

. . . My brother Dawée came for mother's decision. I dropped my play, and crept close to my aunt.

"Yes, Dawée, my daughter, though she does not understand what it all means, is anxious to go. She will need an education when she is grown, for then there will be fewer real Dakotas, and many more palefaces. This tearing her away, so young, from her mother is necessary, if I would have her an educated woman. The palefaces, who owe us a large debt for stolen lands, have begun to pay a tardy justice in offering some education to our children. But I know my daughter must suffer keenly in this experiment. For her sake, I dread to tell you my reply to the missionaries. Go, tell them that they may take my little daughter, and that the Great Spirit shall not fail to reward them according to their hearts."

Wrapped in my heavy blanket, I walked with my mother to the carriage that was soon to take us to the iron horse. I was happy. I met my playmates, who were also wearing their best thick blankets. We showed one another our new beaded moccasins, and the width of the belts that girdled our new dresses. Soon we were being drawn rapidly away by the white man's horses. When I saw the lonely figure of my mother vanish in the distance, a sense of regret settled heavily upon me. I felt suddenly weak, as if I might fall limp to the ground. I was in the hands of strangers whom my mother did not fully trust. I no longer felt free to be myself, or to voice my own feelings. The tears trickled down my cheeks, and I buried my face in the folds of my blanket. Now the first step, parting me from my mother, was taken, and all my belated tears availed nothing.

Having driven thirty miles to the ferry-boat, we crossed the Missouri in the evening. Then riding again a few miles eastward, we stopped before a massive brick building. I looked at it in amazement, and with a vague misgiving, for in our village I had never seen so large a house. Trembling with fear and distrust of the palefaces, my teeth chattering from the chilly ride, I crept noiselessly in my soft moccasins along the narrow hall, keeping very close to the bare wall. I was as frightened and bewildered as the captured young of a wild creature.

The first day in the land of apples was a bitter-cold one; for the snow still covered the ground, and the trees were bare. A large bell rang for breakfast, its loud metallic voice crashing through the belfry overhead and into our sensitive ears. The annoying clatter of shoes on bare floors gave us no peace. The constant clash of harsh noises, with an undercurrent of many voices murmuring an unknown tongue, made a bedlam within which I was securely tied. And though my spirit tore itself in struggling for its lost freedom, all was useless.

A paleface woman, with white hair, came up after us. We were placed in a line of girls who were marching into the dining room. These were Indian girls, in stiff shoes and closely clinging dresses. The small girls wore sleeved aprons and shingled hair. As I walked noiselessly in my soft moccasins, I felt like sinking to the floor, for my blanket had been stripped from my shoulders. I looked hard at the Indian girls, who seemed not to care that they were even more immodestly dressed than I, in their tightly fitting clothes. While we marched in, the boys entered at an opposite door. I watched for the three young braves who came in our party. I spied them in the rear ranks, looking as uncomfortable as I felt. . . .

. . . Late in the morning, my friend Judéwin gave me a terrible warning. Judéwin knew a few words of English; and she had overheard the paleface woman talk about cutting our long, heavy hair. Our mothers had taught us that only unskilled warriors who were captured had their hair shingled by the enemy. Among our people, short hair was worn by mourners, and shingled hair by cowards!

We discussed our fate some moments, and when Judéwin said, "We have to submit, because they are strong," I rebelled.

"No, I will not submit! I will struggle first!" I answered.

I watched my chance, and when no one noticed I disappeared. I crept up the stairs as quietly as I could in my squeaking shoes,—my moccasins had been exchanged for shoes. Along the hall I passed, without knowing whither I was going. Turning aside to an open door, I found a large room with three white beds in it. The windows were covered with dark green curtains, which made the room very dim. Thankful that no one was there, I directed my steps toward the corner farthest from the door. On my hands and knees I crawled under the bed, and cuddled myself in the dark corner.

From my hiding place I peered out, shuddering with fear whenever I heard footsteps near by. Though in the hall loud voices were calling my name, and I knew that even Judéwin was searching for me, I did not open my mouth to answer. Then the steps were quickened and the voices became excited. The sounds came nearer and nearer. Women and girls entered the room. I held my breath, and watched them open closet doors and peep behind large trunks. Some one threw up the curtains, and the room was filled with sudden light. What caused them to stoop and look under the bed I do not know. I remember being dragged out, though I resisted by kicking and scratching wildly. In spite of myself, I was carried downstairs and tied fast in a chair.

I cried aloud, shaking my head all the while until I felt the cold blades of the scissors against my neck, and heard them gnaw off one of my thick braids. Then I lost my spirit. Since the day I was taken from my mother I had suffered extreme indignities. People had stared at me. I had been tossed about in the air like a wooden puppet. And now my long hair was shingled like a coward's! In my anguish I moaned for my mother, but no one came to comfort me. Not a soul reasoned quietly with me, as my own mother used to do; for now I was only one of many little animals driven by a herder. . . .

. . . Now, as I look back upon the recent past, I see it from a distance, as a whole. I remember how, from morning till evening, many specimens of civilized peoples visited the Indian school. The city folks with canes and eyeglasses, the countrymen with sunburnt cheeks and clumsy feet, forgot their relative social ranks in an ignorant curiosity. Both sorts of these Christian palefaces were alike astounded at seeing the children of savage warriors so docile and industrious.

As answers to their shallow inquiries they received the students' sample work to look upon. Examining the neatly figured pages, and gazing upon the Indian girls and boys bending over their books, the white visitors walked out of the schoolhouse well satisfied: they were educating the children of the red man! They were paying a liberal fee to the government employees in whose able hands lay the small forest of Indian timber.

In this fashion many have passed idly through the Indian schools during the last decade, afterward to boast of their charity to the North American Indian. But few there are who have paused to question whether real life or long-lasting death lies beneath this semblance of civilization.

Mary Antin, "I walked on air for . . . I was a *student* now"

Education was also a means of acculturation for the millions of immigrant children who came to this country between 1880 and 1920. Predominantly southern or eastern Europeans, they were set apart by differences of religion as well as language—many were Catholic or Jewish. Mary Antin (the name has been Anglicized), a young Jewish girl from the Russian town of Polotzk, communicates in the following account her enormous yearning for education and her boundless enthusiasm for her new home.

That the public school of Chelsea, Massachusetts, provided happier memories for Mary Antin than did the missionary school for Zitkala-Ša can be explained in part by the greater sensitivity of Antin's teachers. Equally important was the fact that Antin was able to remain with her family and within her ethnic community. The process of acculturation was also made easier by the fact that her father, who had preceded his family to Boston, was eager to embrace things American. More important, he attached a high value to education, as did most Jews, although, as among other ethnic groups, greater sacrifices were likely to be made on behalf of sons than daughters. That this should be the case is not surprising given the greater earning potential of males. What neither essay reveals fully is the extent to which, in a period of intense racial and ethnic prejudice, many "old-stock" Americans believed that education for such girls should serve only to prepare them for domestic service in their own homes or the homes of others, irrespective of individual aspirations and abilities. How important was it to Mary Antin's educational development that her father did *not* share that assumption? In what ways was he supportive of her?

Father himself conducted us to school. He would not have delegated that mission to the President of the United States. He had awaited the day with impatience equal to mine, and the visions he saw as he hurried us over the sun-flecked pavements transcended all my dreams. Almost his first act on landing on American soil, three years before, had been his application for naturalization. He had taken the remaining steps in the process with eager promptness, and at the earliest moment allowed by the law, he became a citizen of the United States. It is true that he had left home in search of bread for his hungry family, but he went blessing the necessity that drove him to America. The boasted freedom of the New World meant to him far more than the right to reside, travel, and work wherever he pleased; it meant the freedom to speak his thoughts, to throw off the shackles of superstition, to test his own fate, unhindered by political or religious tyranny. . . .

. . . His struggle for a bare living left him no time to take advantage of the public evening school; but he lost nothing of what was to be learned through reading, through attendance at public meetings, through exercising the rights of citizenship. Even here he was hindered by a natural inability to acquire the English language. In time, indeed, he learned to read, to follow a conversation or lecture; but he never learned to write correctly, and his pro-

Excerpted from "The Promised Land" and "Initiation," chaps. 9 and 10 of *The Promised Land* by Mary Antin (Boston: Houghton Mifflin, 1912).

Medical Examination at Ellis Island. "The day of the emigrants' arrival in New York was the nearest earthly likeness to the final day of Judgment, when we have to prove our fitness to enter Heaven." The words were those of a sympathetic journalist who shared the anxiety-ridden experience awaiting immigrants at the port of entry, usually Ellis Island. Failing the medical test could mean deportation. (Courtesy of Brown Brothers)

nunciation remains extremely foreign to this day.

If education, culture, the higher life were shining things to be worshipped from afar, he had still a means left whereby he could draw one step nearer to them. He could send his children to school, to learn all those things that he knew by fame to be desirable. The common school, at least, perhaps high school; for one or two, perhaps even college! His children should be students, should fill his house with books and intellectual company; and thus he would walk by proxy in the Elysian Fields of liberal learning. As for the children themselves, he knew no surer way to their advancement and happiness.

So it was with a heart full of longing and hope that my father led us to school on that first day. He took long strides in his eagerness, the rest of us running and hopping to keep up. . . .

I was not a bit too large for my little chair and desk in the baby class, but my mind, of course, was too mature by six or seven years for the work. So as soon as I could understand what the teacher said in class, I was advanced to the second grade. This was within a week after Miss Nixon took me in hand. But I do not mean to give my dear teacher all the credit for my rapid progress, nor even half the credit. I shall divide it with her on behalf of my race and my family. I was Jew enough to have an aptitude for language in general, and to bend my mind earnestly to my task; I was Antin enough to read each lesson with my heart, which gave me an inkling of what was coming next, and so carried me along by leaps and bounds. As for the teacher, she could best explain what theory she followed in teaching us foreigners to read. . . .

There were about half a dozen of us beginners in English, in age from six to fifteen. Miss Nixon made a special class of us, and aided us so skilfully and earnestly in our endeavors to "see-a-cat," and "hear-a-dog-bark," and "look-at-the-hen," that we turned over page after page of the ravishing history, eager to find out how the common world looked, smelled, and tasted in the strange speech. The teacher knew just when to let us help each other out with a word in our own tongue,—it happened that we were all Jews,—and so, working all together, we actually covered more ground in a lesson than the native classes, composed entirely of the little tots. . . .

Whenever the teachers did anything special to help me over my private difficulties, my gratitude went out to them, silently. . . . Dear Miss Carrol, of the second grade, would be amazed to hear what small things I remember, all because I was so impressed at the time with her readiness and sweetness in taking notice of my difficulties.

Says Miss Carrol, looking straight at me:
"If Johnnie has three marbles, and Charlie has twice as many, how many marbles has Charlie?"

I raise my hand for permission to speak.
"Teacher, I don't know vhat is tvice."

Teacher beckons me to her, and whispers to me the meaning of the strange word, and I am able to write the sum correctly. It's all in the day's work with her; with me, it is a special act of kindness and efficiency. . . .

If I was eager and diligent, my teachers did not sleep. As fast as my knowledge of English allowed, they advanced me from grade to grade, without reference to the usual schedule of promotions. My father was right, when he often said, in discussing my prospects, that ability would be promptly recognized in the public schools. Rapid as was my progress, on account of the advantages with which I started, some of the other "green" pupils were not far behind me; within a grade or two, by the end of the year. . . .

This is the document, copied from an educational journal, a tattered copy of which lies in my lap as I write—treasured for fifteen years, you see, by my vanity.

EDITOR "PRIMARY EDUCATION":—
This is the uncorrected paper of a Russian child twelve years old, who had studied English only four months. She had never, until September, been to school even in her own country and has heard English spoken *only* at school. I shall be glad if the paper of my pupil and the above explanation may appear in your paper.
CHELSEA, MASS.   M. S. DILLINGHAM

SNOW
Snow is frozen moisture which comes from the clouds.

Now the snow is coming down in feather-flakes, which makes nice snowballs. But there is still one kind of snow more. This kind of snow is called snow-crystals, for it comes down in little curly balls. These snow-crystals aren't quiet as good for snow-balls as feather-flakes, for they (the snow-crystals) are dry: so they can't keep together as feather-flakes do.

The snow is dear to some children for they like sleighing.

As I said at the top—the snow comes from the clouds.

Now the trees are bare, and no flowers are to see in the fields and gardens, (we all know why) and the whole world seems like asleep without the happy birds songs which left us till spring. But the snow which drove away all these pretty and happy things, try, (as I think) not to make us at all unhappy; they covered up the branches of the trees, the fields, the gardens and houses, and the whole world looks like dressed in a beautiful white—instead of green—dress, with the sky looking down on it with a pale face.

And so the people can find some joy in it, too, without the happy summer.

MARY ANTIN

. . . So here was my teacher, the moment she saw that I could give a good paraphrase of her talk on "Snow," bent on finding out what more I could do. One day she asked me if I had ever written poetry. I had not, but I went home and tried. I believe it was more snow, and I know it was wretched. . . . But Miss Dillingham was not discouraged. She saw that I had no idea of metre, so she proceeded to teach me. We repeated miles of poetry together, smooth lines that sang themselves, mostly out of Longfellow. Then I would go home and write—oh, about the snow in our back yard!—but when Miss Dillingham came to read my verses, they limped and they lagged and they dragged, and there was no tune that would fit them.

At last came the moment of illumination: I saw where my trouble lay. I had supposed that my lines matched when they had an equal number of syllables, taking no account of accent. Now I knew better; now I could write poetry! The everlasting snow melted at last, and the mud puddles dried in the spring sun, and the grass on the common was green, and still I wrote poetry! . . .

Making fair allowance for my youth, retarded education, and strangeness to the language, it must still be admitted that I never wrote good verse. But I loved to read it. My half-hours with Miss Dillingham were full of delight for me, quite apart from my new-born ambition to become a writer. What, then, was my joy, when Miss Dillingham, just before locking up her desk one evening, presented me with a volume of Longfellow's poems! It was a thin volume of selections, but to me it was a bottomless treasure. I had never owned a book before. The sense of possession alone was a source of bliss, and this book I already knew and loved. And so Miss Dillingham, who was my first American friend, and who first put my name in print, was also the one to start my library. . . .

About the middle of the year I was promoted to the grammar school. Then it was that I walked on air. For I said to myself that I was a *student* now, in earnest, not merely a schoolgirl learning to spell and cipher. I was going to learn out-of-the-way things, things that had nothing to do with ordinary life—things to *know*. When I walked home afternoons, with the great big geography book under my arm, it seemed to me that the earth was conscious of my step. Sometimes I carried home half the books in my desk, not because I should need them, but because I loved to hold them; and also because I loved to be seen carrying books. It was a badge of scholarship, and I was proud of it. I remembered the days in Vitebsk when I used to watch my cousin Hirshel start for school in the morning, every thread of his student's uniform, every worn copybook in his satchel, glorified in my envious eyes. And now I was myself as he: aye, greater than he; for I knew English, and I could write poetry. . . .

How long would you say, wise reader, it takes to make an American? By the middle of my second year in school I had reached the sixth grade. When, after the Christmas holidays, we began to study the life of Washington, running through a summary of the Revolution, and the early days of the Republic, it seemed to me that all my reading and study had been idle until then. The reader, the arithmetic, the song book, that had so fascinated me until now, became suddenly sober exercise books, tools wherewith to hew a way to the source of inspiration. When the teacher read to us out of a big book with many bookmarks in it, I sat rigid with attention in my little chair, my hands tightly clasped on the edge of my desk; and I painfully held my breath, to prevent sighs of disappointment escaping, as I saw the teacher skip the parts between bookmarks. When the class read, and it came my turn, my voice shook and the book trembled in my hands. I could not pronounce the name of George Washington without a pause. Never had I prayed, never had I chanted the songs of David, never had I called upon the Most Holy, in such utter reverence and worship as I repeated the simple sentences of my child's story of the patriot. I gazed with adoration at the portraits of George and Martha Washington, till I could see them with my eyes shut. . . .

On the day of the Washington celebration I recited a poem that I had composed in my enthusiasm. But "composed" is not the word. The process of putting on paper the sentiments that seethed in my soul was really very discomposing. I dug the words out of my heart, squeezed the rhymes out of my brain, forced the missing syllables out of their hiding-places in the dictionary. . . .

When I had done, I was myself impressed with the length, gravity, and nobility of my poem. My father was overcome with emotion as he read it. His hands trembled as he held the paper to the light, and the mist gathered in his eyes. My teacher, Miss Dwight, was plainly astonished at my performance, and said many kind things, and asked many questions; all of which I took very solemnly, like one who had been in the clouds and returned to earth with a sign upon him. When Miss Dwight asked me to read my poem to the class on the day of celebration, I readily consented. It was not in me to refuse a chance to tell my schoolmates what I thought of George Washington. . . .

I can laugh now at the impossible metres, the grandiose phrases, the verbose repetitions of my poem. . . .

> He whose courage, will, amazing
>   bravery,
>   Did free his land from a despot's rule,
> From man's greatest evil, almost slavery,
>   And all that's taught in tyranny's school,
>
> Who gave his land its liberty,
>   Who was he?
>
> 'T was he who e'er will be our pride,
>   Immortal Washington,
> Who always did in truth confide,
>   We hail our Washington!

The best of the verses were no better than these, but the children listened. They had to. Presently I gave them news, declaring that Washington

> Wrote the famous Constitution;
>   sacred's the hand
> That this blessed guide to man had
>   given, which says, "One
> And all of mankind are alike,
>   excepting none."

This was received in respectful silence, possibly because the other Fellow Citizens were as hazy about historical facts as I at this point. "Hurrah for Washington!" they understood, and "Three cheers for the Red, White, and Blue!" was only to be expected on that occasion. But there ran a special note through my poem—a thought that only Israel Rubinstein or Beckie Aronovitch could have fully understood, besides myself. For I made myself the spokesman of the "luckless sons of Abraham," saying—

> Then we weary Hebrew children at last
>   found rest
> In the land where reigned Freedom,
>   and like a nest
> To homeless birds your land proved to
>   us, and therefore
> Will we gratefully sing your praise
>   evermore. . . .

If I had been satisfied with my poem in the first place, the applause with which it was received by my teachers and schoolmates convinced me that I had produced a very fine thing indeed. So the person, whoever it was,—perhaps my father—who suggested that my tribute to Washington ought to be printed, did not find me difficult to persuade. When I had achieved an absolutely perfect copy of my verses, at the expense of a dozen sheets of blue-ruled note paper, I crossed the Mystic River to Boston and boldly invaded Newspaper Row. . . .

When the paper with my poem in it arrived, the whole house pounced upon it at once. . . . It occupied a gratifying amount of space, and was introduced by a flattering biographical sketch of the author—the *author!*—the material for which the friendly editor had artfully drawn from me during that happy interview. And my name, as I had prophesied, was at the bottom!

When the excitement in the house had subsided, my father took all the change out of the cash drawer and went to buy up the "Herald." He did not count the pennies. He just bought "Heralds," all he could lay his hands on, and distributed them gratis to all our friends, relatives, and acquaintances; to all who could read, and to some who could not. For weeks he carried a clipping from the "Herald" in his breast pocket, and few were the occasions when he did not manage to introduce it into the conversation. He treasured that clipping as for years he had treasured the letters I wrote him from Polotzk.

M. Carey Thomas, "The passionate desire of women . . . for higher education . . ."

The way Americans have viewed intellectual activity among women tells us a great deal about what they believed to be woman's proper role. By the late nineteenth and early twentieth centuries a slightly higher proportion of girls than boys were attending school, and girls were increasing their lead over boys in the upper age group. College, however, was another matter. Families that sent sons to college as a matter of course might understandably be reluctant to extend that same opportunity to their daughters when medical experts warned that too much exposure to the "impedimenta of libraries" could leave young female graduates incapable of performing their normal reproductive functions.

M. Carey Thomas conveys with particular effectiveness the yearnings of the young college-bound women of her generation. When she later became president of Bryn Mawr College, one of several elite women's colleges founded in the latter half of the nineteenth century, she strongly disagreed with those who argued that the primary purpose of a woman's education was to prepare her for marriage and motherhood. Insisting that the Bryn Mawr student enter college with the same qualifications in Greek, Latin, and mathematics required of her male counterpart at Harvard or Yale, Thomas expected Bryn Mawr graduates to lead lives as productive, economically independent women, finding, as did men, "their greatest happiness in congenial work."* Note her insistence on the importance of having women scholars who could serve as role models for their students.

The passionate desire of women of my generation for higher education was accompanied thruout its course by the awful doubt, felt by women themselves as well as by men, as to whether women as a sex were physically and mentally fit for it. I think I can best make this clear to you if I refer briefly to my own experience. I cannot remember the time when I was not sure that studying and going to college were the things above all others which I wished to do. I was always wondering whether it could be really true, as every one thought, that boys were cleverer than girls. Indeed, I cared so much that I never dared to ask any grown-up person the direct question, not even my father or mother, because I feared to hear the reply. I remember often praying about it, and begging God that if it were true that because I was a girl I could not successfully master Greek and go to college and understand things to kill me at once, as I could not bear to live in such an unjust world. When I was a little older I read the Bible entirely thru with passionate eagerness because I had heard it said that it proved that women were inferior to men. Those were not the days of the higher criticism. I can remember weeping over the account of Adam and Eve because it seemed to me that the curse pronounced on Eve might imperil girls' going to college; and to this day I can never read many parts of the Pauline epistles without feeling again the sinking of the heart with which I used

*M. Carey Thomas, "The Future of Women's Higher Education," in *Mount Holyoke College: The Seventy-Fifth Anniversary* (South Hadley, Mass., 1913), p. 104.

Excerpted from "Present Tendencies in Women's College and University Education" by M. Carey Thomas, in *Educational Review* 30 (1908):64–85.

to hurry over the verses referring to women's keeping silence in the churches and asking their husbands at home. . . .

It was not to be wondered at that we were uncertain in those old days as to the ultimate result of women's education. Before I myself went to college I had never seen but one college woman. I had heard that such a woman was staying at the house of an acquaintance. I went to see her with fear. Even if she had appeared in hoofs and horns I was determined to go to college all the same. But it was a relief to find this Vassar graduate tall and handsome and dressed like other women. When, five years later, I went to Leipzig to study after I had been graduated from Cornell, my mother used to write me that my name was never mentioned to her by the women of her acquaintance. I was thought by them to be as much of a disgrace to my family as if I had eloped with the coachman. Now, women who have been to college are as plentiful as blackberries on summer hedges. Even my native city of Baltimore is full of them, and women who have in addition studied in Germany are regarded with becoming deference by the very Baltimore women who disapproved of me.

During the quarter of the century of the existence of the Association of Collegiate Alumnae [now American Association of University Women] two generations of college women have reached mature life, and the older generation is now just passing off the stage. We are therefore better prepared than ever before to give an account of what has been definitely accomplished, and to predict what will be the tendencies of women's college and university education in the future.

The curriculum of our women's colleges has steadily stiffened. Women, both in separate, and in coeducational colleges, seem to prefer the old-fashioned, so-called disciplinary studies. They disregard the so-called accomplishments. I believe that to-day more women than men are receiving a thoro college education, even altho in most cases they are receiving it sitting side by side with men in the same college lecture rooms.

The old type of untrained woman teacher has practically disappeared from women's colleges. Her place is being taken by ardent young women scholars who have qualified themselves by long years of graduate study for advanced teaching. Even the old-fashioned untrained matron, or house-mother, is swiftly being replaced in girls' schools, as well as in women's colleges, by the college-bred warden or director.

We did not know when we began whether women's health could stand the strain of college education. We were haunted in those early days by the clanging chains of that gloomy little specter, Dr. Edward H. Clarke's *Sex in Education.* With trepidation of spirit I made my mother read it, and was much cheered by her remark that, as neither she, nor any of the women she knew, had ever seen girls or women of the kind described in Dr. Clarke's book, we might as well act as if they did not exist. Still, we did not *know* whether colleges might not produce a crop of just such invalids. Doctors insisted that they would. We women could not be sure until we had tried the experiment. Now we have tried it, and tried it for more than a generation, and we know that college women are not only not invalids, but that they are better physically than other women in their own class of life. We know that girls are growing stronger and more athletic. Girls enter college each year in better physical condition. For the past four years I have myself questioned closely all our entering classes, and often their mothers as well. I find that an average of sixty per cent. enter college absolutely and in every respect well, and that less than thirty per cent. make, or need to make, any periodic difference whatever in exercise, or study, from year's end to year's end. This result is very different from that obtained by physicians and others writing in recent magazines and medical journals. These alarmists give grewsome statistics from high schools and women's colleges, which they are very careful not to name. Probably they are investigating girls whose general hygienic conditions are bad. . . .

We are now living in the midst of great and, I believe on the whole beneficent, social changes which are preparing the way for the coming economic independence of women. Like the closely allied diminishing birth rate, but unlike the higher education of women, this great change in opinion and practise seems to have come about almost without our knowledge, certainly without our conscious coöperation. The passionate desire of the women of my generation for a college education seems, as we study it now in the light of coming events, to have been a part of this greater movement.

In order to prepare for this economic independence, we should expect to see what is now taking place. Colleges for women and college departments of co-educational universities are attended by ever-increasing numbers of women students. In seven of the largest western universities women already outnumber men in the college departments.

A liberal college course prepares women for their great profession of teaching. College women have proved to be such admirably efficient teachers that they are driving other women out of the field. Until other means of self-support are as easy for women as teaching, more and more women who intend to teach will go to college. Such women will elect first of all the subjects taught by women in the high schools, such as Latin, history, and the languages. They will avoid chemistry, physics, and other sciences which are usually taught by men. Until all women become self-supporting, more women than men will go to college for culture, especially in the west, and such women will tend to elect the great disciplinary studies which men neglect because they are intrinsically more difficult and seem at first sight less practical. For these obvious reasons certain college courses are therefore already crowded by women and almost deserted by men in many of the coeducational universities.

And just because women have shown such an aptitude for a true college education and such delight in it, we must be careful to maintain it for them in its integrity. We must see to it that its disciplinary quality is not lowered by the insertion of so-called practical courses which are falsely supposed to prepare for life. Women are rapidly coming to control women's college education. It rests with us to decide whether we shall barter for a mess of pottage the inheritance of the girls of this generation which the girls of my generation agonized to obtain for themselves and for other girls. . . .

I believe also that every women's college ought to maintain . . . a graduate school of philosophy of the highest grade. . . .

. . . The highest service which colleges can render to their time is to discover and foster imaginative and constructive genius. Such genius unquestionably needs opportunity for its highest development. This is peculiarly the case with women students. As I watch their gallant struggles I sometimes think that the very stars in their courses are conspiring against them. Women scholars can assist women students, as men can not, to tide over the first discouragements of a life of intellectual reunification. Ability of the kind I am speaking of is, of course, very rare, but for this reason it is precious beyond all other human products. . . .

The time has now come for those of us who are in control of women's education to bend ourselves to the task of creating academic conditions favorable for the development of this kind of creative ability. We should at once begin to found research chairs for women at all our women's colleges, with three or four hours a week research teaching and the rest of the time free for independent investigation. We should reserve all the traveling fellowships in our gift for women who have given evidence, however slight, of power to do research work. We should bring pressure on our state universities to give such women opportunities to compete for professors' chairs. In the four women suffrage states this can be accomplished in the twinkling of an eye: it will only be necessary for women's organizations to vote for university regents with proper opinions. The Johns Hopkins University situated in conservative Baltimore has two women on its academic staff who are lecturing to men. Why can not all chairs in the arts departments of universities, that is, in the college and school of philosophy, be thrown open to the competition of women? This is the next advance to be made in women's education—the last and greatest battle to be won.

SARAH DEUTSCH

Hispanic Village Women on the Southwest Frontier

The expansion of the boundaries of the United States, through treaty and through war, was accompanied by the movement of people of European ancestry onto new terrain. The highly developed system of railroads that crisscrossed the West in the nineteenth century was not only a neutral form of transportation; it also represented the intrusion of industrial technology into rural space. For some people this meant opportunity; for others it meant disruption.

State boundaries are abstractions; lines on maps. Sarah Deutsch argues that what mattered to people who lived there at the turn of the twentieth century was the "regional community" of northern New Mexico and southern Colorado. The rhythm of life in Chicano villages since the eighteenth century had involved men migrating for work and returning home again. Villages were sustained by women in their traditional ways of life and work. When this ebb and flow of village life was disrupted by "federal land appropriations and Anglo incursions," Hispanic communities proved stunningly resilient.

Although comparisons across time and space are risky, can you compare the traditional work and roles among the Hispanic women Deutsch describes and the New England women studied by Laurel Ulrich (pp. 37–45)? Why did Anglo census takers list fewer Hispanic women with occupations than did Hispanic census takers? What differences can you see in property relations in marriage governed by traditional Roman law and those governed by the law of the United States in the late nineteenth century? What choices did Hispanic women make about the elements of modern society that they would embrace? What constraints governed Hispanic village women's lives? Like Carol Karlsen (pp. 50–62), Deutsch suggests that belief in witchcraft is one way in which people hold "disruptive elements . . . at bay." Do you agree?

Looking back on a New Mexico village of the early twentieth century, Luisa Torres recalled:

> I watched my maternal grandparents a lot. . . . On the day that my grandmother was seventy, I saw her open the doors of her little adobe house. It was a spring day and there were millions of orange and black butterflies around the corn plants; my grandmother ran towards the butterflies and gathered so many of them in her apron that she flew up in the air, while she laughed contentedly. I wanted to know all that my grandmother knew.

Like many grandmothers of the time, Luisa's grandmother knew particularly about medicinal plants, "remedios."[1] But in wanting to know all that her grandmother knew, Luisa was expressing more than a desire to share in the knowledge of herbal medicine. . . . [I]n the Hispanic heartland's communal villages, women had their own world. . . .

This world of village women has scarcely appeared in the historical literature of Chicanos except as overgeneralized and stereotyped images of submissive, cloistered, and powerless women. The focus has been on a rigidly patriarchal ideology, articulated only by those peripheral to or outside this world, by the Hispanic elite or Anglo observers of the time, or by later authors imposing views derived from other sites and times. . . .

At the center of the family stood Hispanic women, and they dared not move beyond it, or so runs the common wisdom. According to this wisdom, sexual divisions and the separate women's world served to keep women subordinate, cloistered, and protected within the family. But the family was more complex than a woman's kingdom or her prison. An examination of village women's lives as daughters, wives, mothers, and widows reveals more subtle nuances regarding their status, even within the realm of family.

At age eight or nine, the separate women's world began. Before that, villagers expected boys and girls to behave in much the same way and share the same chores. But after their first Communion, they could dance at "bailes" and learn adult tasks. By age sixteen, girls had received enough training from their mothers or grandmothers to be ready for marriage.[2] At this crucial stage, the village insisted on monitoring male/female relations. Unmarried males as well as females found that "almost the only recognized means of contact" outside their own homes and away from their families was the informal ritual of the village dance.[3] Adolescent girls went out always accompanied, whether by mother, aunt, little sister, grandmother, or, later, a number of girlfriends.[4] So between fiestas and weddings, the young men used their earnings to sponsor dances in the hope of finding a mate.

At dances, women and children seated themselves on benches around the walls, and men stood outside the dance hall except when requesting a dance or dancing. Conversation was theoretically forbidden between unmarried partners, but acquaintance from a dance could lead to a courtship conducted through furtive letters if the parties were literate, by studiously fortuitous visits with the family, or by communication through siblings. Sometimes secret engagements resulted.[5] Even for adolescents, the distance between theory and reality permitted a degree of autonomy.

Village girls more often than boys were the targets of warning stories which depicted the dire and often supernatural consequences of walking out with mysterious strangers.[6] But these stories did not simply reflect a double standard. They told of village mores; the young man was never a local village youth, the girl was always in her grandmother's care. The tales reveal as much about expectations for village boys and the trials of elderly widowed grandmothers raising none-too-submissive young girls, as they reveal about definitions of female virtue. And reality was often more lenient. Of the family and the village, it was only Jesusita Aragon's grandmother who never forgave her the two illegitimate children Jesusita had while under her roof. The children's father escaped equal shame only because Jesusita, who did not want to marry him, refused to identify him.[7] . . .

When a village youth decided to make a public offer of marriage, he required the consensual participation of a panoply of villagers, male and female. He had his father, or occasionally his mother, and a godparent visit the girl's parents and leave a written offer.[8] The girl's father and mother discussed the matter and sent for the "madrina," the godmother. The madrina acted as an intermediary between the parents and the girl, who was "at liberty to accept or refuse." Women within the family were acknowledged to have a mind of their own, and not socially forbidden to exercise it. Both the boy and the girl communicated through their parents and grandparents. Age determined one's actions more than sex.

The groom or his family provided the wedding, trousseau, and reception, which helps to explain why males tended to marry later than females.[9] But this was not a purchase of the bride by the groom's family. The bride often brought property into the marriage; the new couple was equally likely to live with the bride's as with the groom's parents, and after the wedding ceremony the "entregada de los novios" symbolized the giving of the groom to the bride's family and the bride to the groom's.[10] The marriage created not just binary ties, but networks.

In a rigidly patriarchal society, one would expect consistent and sizable age differences between spouses, but in the villages there were no strong norms as to age difference in first marriage. Women tended to marry between the ages of fifteen and twenty-one, men between nineteen and twenty-six. But every village had women who had married younger men as well as the occasional woman married to a man twenty years older than she.

Lack of strict norms regarding age at marriage, of course, is hardly proof that marriages were not rigidly patriarchal. But there is other evidence. In the northern New Mexico and southern Colorado villages, molestation of women and wife-whipping were considered punishable crimes and cause for divorce. In 1903, for example, a Hispanic man in a Hispanic southern Colorado county was arrested merely for quarreling with his wife.[11] . . .

Property relations in marriage testified to this lack of rigid stratification. That husband and wife shared rights in property acquired during marriage was the rule for Hispanic families long before it became so for Anglos, as was equal inheritance by sons and daughters.[12] Unlike early agricultural settlers in the eastern United States, at death Hispanic men tended to leave the bulk of their property to their wives rather than to their daughters or sons. This pattern created a number of widowed females in almost every village who were more than titular heads of household. These women were listed in the census as general farmers who owned their own land and used the labor of their married and unmarried children, or planted the land themselves. This inheritance norm was strong enough for a Señora Martinez in southern Colorado to contest the disposition of her husband's estate even though in this case all the property had been in his name. She claimed a right to half the property "because," she explained in 1900, "all know that I worked as much as my husband and spent less than he and our son. My husband always told me that for my work half was for me, that it was not owed me except that I had earned it."[13] . . .

When women did enter marriage with their own property, particularly women who were better-off than average, they often quite consciously kept the property separate from their husband's and managed it themselves. John Lawrence's Hispanic wife let her sheep out on partido contracts separately from his sheep, and Cleofas Jaramillo noted that her "husband had borrowed the money from [her] and had never paid it back" when he died unexpectedly.[14] Less wealthy women joined their husbands in taking out mortgages and partido contracts, but affixed their name separately.

These women also participated, with or without their husbands, as heirs in land-grant litigation. And one woman, "of her own separate means," added a few hogs and chickens valued at $150 to an estate the total value of which was only $700. A married couple's identity of interest was a desirable but not always assumed state in these Hispanic villages.

Even an unhappily married Hispanic woman, however, when asked why she had married, responded, "Where else could I have gone?" The norm in the villages was a household headed by a married couple.[15] Women, even propertied women, would not want to grow old in the village alone. Marriage provided a means to integrate the individual once more into the group and to perpetuate that integration through children. In villages as interdependent for labor and subsistence as the Hispanic communal villages of New Mexico, such reinforced networking was crucial to ensure mutuality and harmony. Whether male or female, the individual found that multiplying the ties to the group increased his or her security, and remarriage after widowhood was common for both sexes.[16]

Widowed women nonetheless engaged actively in business enterprises and defended their interests in court beyond the traditional geographic bounds of Hispanic women's activities, the village. They bought, homesteaded, or rented land, or entered and continued business on their own or with their children. As widows, their role as head of the family made the enlarged scope legitimate. Since these women had often retained the management of their own property throughout their marriage [unlike, for example, the colonial New England women described on p. 51] . . . what was new was less the nature of the activities than their occasional location outside the village.[17]

Widows were not the only women who broke the bounds of women's usual behavior with impunity. So, too, did midwives. Indisputably in the women's realm alone was childbirth. And the partera, the midwife, stood at the apex of the community of women, and at the same time transcended it. As a key figure in the community she had no male equivalent and was not bound by many of the strictures which applied to male/female interactions. When the men came to fetch the partera for childbirth, none cast aspersions on her for traveling alone with a man even for thirty miles.

The midwives themselves recognized a danger "because," as Jesusita Aragon admitted, "sometimes you go out when you don't know the guy who comes to get you, and you don't know if you can trust him or not. But," she concluded, "you have to go, and any hour night or day."[18] Both men and women realized the village relied on children to perpetuate itself, and that in the partera's hands lay the well-being of mother and child. . . .

The mode and ritual of payment were also significant and reinforced communal values. In contrast to the set fees of Anglo male doctors, the compensations "were called gifts, because they were free-will offerings," a WPA investigator discovered in the 1930s.[19] Like curanderas (herbal healers), when the patient "asked how much was owed her—they knew she would not charge them—she would reply that it was nothing, 'just what you want to give me.'" As neither curanderas nor parteras could refuse to treat destitute villagers, the recompense varied from a value of fifty cents to a maximum of ten dollars, and was almost always in kind.[20] The villagers never lost sight of the personal nature, the community aspect, of midwifery and health care, and except among rich and Anglicized families, the busy, impersonal, non-communicative, and very expensive doctors could not compete.[21] As midwife Susana Archuleta explained, "you can't look at midwifery in terms of dollar signs. You have to be sympathetic."[22] . . .

The midwife's specialized knowledge and vital function gave her a respected place in the community as a whole. It was not just that her calling exempted her from certain mores. According to one observer:

> The midwife was the only type of leader in a village community except for the men who were politically inclined, and, of course, except for the religious teachers. People would go to the midwife because there was no other leader.[23]

For women, the midwife became "a general counselor."[24] But the men, too, recognized her importance and took pains to assure her contentedness in the village. Mothers and fathers often chose the partera as godmother to the children she delivered, creating a multitude of connections to bind her to village families. In a communal society where illiteracy was common, respect depended on knowledge, character, and function. Parteras combined the

three in high order, and although their authority had its base in the community of women, it was not limited to that community. . . .

In addition to the community of family, women shared in the larger community of the village. . . . They . . . entered the community as women and as individuals, unmediated by family, particularly in religion and production. Indeed, women not only shared in the community, they were instrumental in creating it, socially and physically, and in sustaining it.

As girls played "comadres," or co-mothers, in the dusty soil near the house, promising to choose each other as "madrina" or godmother for their children, they pledged, as one woman recalled, "not to quarrel, or be selfish with each other.[25] Between Hispanic women, the comadre relationship was among the most significant of relations. The natural mother and the comadre, natural father and copadre, shared the parenting, but co-parents' ideas on child-raising prevailed in any dispute. They named the child, sponsored the christening, acted as surrogate chaperones, consulted on the choice of a mate for the child, and were the only witnesses at the child's wedding. The parents usually asked the wife's parents to be co-parents for the first child, and the husband's for the second, and then other relatives and friends. In this way, the comadre relationship created a dense network of care and obligations in the village.

Besides reinforcing close relations and fostering a special relationship between grandmother and granddaughter, the madrina relationship provided insurance. The grandmother/madrina frequently ended up raising her godchild, sometimes because the mother had died and the widowed father had married a woman who did not want the extra child, or, as one Anglo observer put it, because "the grandparents must have some children to be with and work for them in old age." From their grandmothers these girls learned such skills as healing and midwifery, and in turn they provided lifelong care and devotion. Sometimes the girls were their grandmothers' only companions. The madrina system worked to ensure companionship, to prevent isolation, and to provide care.

The clustered settlement pattern so chaotic to Anglo eyes further fostered the sense of neighborhood created by networks of co-parents and other relatives. It encouraged cooperative labor and aid in difficulties such as illness, and provided mutual benefits and responsibilities which "neighborhood" implied. Many married children built houses on their parents' land, often attached to their parents' house. Occasionally entire plazas or village squares were enclosed. Butchering, house raising, harvesting, and funerals became community-wide social events for both men and women.

As in other agricultural communities, however, women had more of a hand in creating the neighborhood than men did. Their daily visiting, sustaining social networks, far exceeded that of the men. Observers in one village home counted as many as fourteen different visitors in a single afternoon. Women also maintained the links with kin in other villages; wives went on visits for weeks at a time, traveling sometimes with the whole family, other times alone.

These neighborhood and kin networks provided temporary or permanent care for children whose own parents could not support the extra mouths. They provided farm labor in case of old age, illness, or widowhood; employment (in exchange for food and services) for widowed mothers or their children, or children living with destitute grandparents; and temporary homes for children in villages with schools. In maintaining community ties, women ensured the cohesiveness of the village as well as the welfare of themselves and their families.

Women maintained the community through their participation in religion, also, although the most visible sign of Hispanic Catholicism in northern New Mexico was the widespread male religious society known as the Penitentes. The Penitentes, with their mutual benefits aspects and flagellant practices, involved the entire village, members and nonmembers, in their Holy Week rituals.[26] . . .

In Penitente functions, women acted mainly as auxiliaries, but they had their own answer to the male-dominated Holy Week. They had the month of May, which was devoted to Mary. During the month many women met daily for prayer meetings, and in some villages they gathered twice daily. Women led a procession carrying an image of Mary from house to house and conducting prayers. . . .

The importance these Hispanics attributed to Mary provided a basis and legitimation for woman's role in what has often seemed a male-dominated church. Where the tangible symbol of that male dominance, the priest, appeared monthly at best, there was little to enforce a subordinate role for women. Indeed, in many villages a local woman, usually an older woman or one prominent for some other reason, led services in the weeks between priestly visits. Most of the villagers, male and female, attended.[27] Religion in the Hispanic villages was clearly the property of both sexes.[28] . . .

In their productive work, as in religion and in the family, women achieved an autonomous base and, simultaneously, integration into the village. Both mutuality and parallelism characterized the sexual division of labor here as well. . . .

Perhaps the most fundamental work of women, the one most obviously allied to maintenance, centered around food in all its stages: production, processing, provision, and exchange. Hispanic women were responsible for the garden, a plot of irrigated land usually close to the house. As loss of land led to a decline in livestock, the garden grew in significance. Women controlled this land, and planted, weeded, irrigated, and harvested such items as melons, chili, onions, garlic, native tobacco, sweet corn, green beans, radishes, and pumpkins with or without the help of men. Often a widow who had no other land survived on the produce of her garden. Where families owned a few goats and chickens, these too fell under the care of the women or the children under their supervision, and produced eggs and milk from which women made cheese. The garden provided Hispanic women with an autonomous base, a source of subsistence independent of but not in competition with men. In addition, women's participation in the essential production phase of food—though they also helped process men's crops and livestock—legitimized their participation in ownership and minimized status differences between sexes. . . .

The effort and time involved in processing, the vagaries of the harvest, and the love of the land which had produced it for generations, as well as its life-giving properties, imbued food at times with a symbolic significance. Cooking was usually simple. Once the foods were all milled or dried, a single pot of beans, vegetables, and occasionally meat would be put on the fire and would serve as the day's meals. On special occasions, the women gathered to bake bread. It was not the cooking itself, but what women did with the food after it was cooked that mattered. . . . The significance . . . involved the definition of female virtue, as is best revealed by a Hispanic midwife's story.

The midwife had come to deliver a child and found the labor lasting an unusually long time. Exhausted, she went to borrow something from a neighbor and there discovered the apparent reason for the difficult birth. It seemed the woman ate her meals standing in her doorway, but gave nothing away. Children who were hungry asked for bread and stood watching her eat, but to no avail. The midwife concluded that the mother was so stingy the child did not want to be born to her, so the midwife took the woman's wheat flour (considered a luxury and kept for feast days) and made a large number of tortillas. Then she had the mother-to-be call in all the children she could find and dispense the tortillas with her own hands. The child was finally born, and the woman became very generous.[29]

Food was a woman's own product, the disposal of which she controlled, and her treatment of it defined her character both as a woman (one worthy to be a mother) and as a member of a communal village. . . . This definition of virtue did not preclude either the men or the women from producing food for exchange. One woman "sold" her cheese "to the village people who did not have cows or goats of their own." She sold it within an informal women's network; mothers sent their children for it and bought it "not for money, but traded" for "flour, cornmeal, and sometimes a bar of home made soap." In addition, women paid church dues with hens and, when they could, children's school fees with their produce. Trading for cash, however—outside the village almost by definition and certainly outside a woman's network—usually remained in the hands of either married men or widows.

The allocation of dealing with outsiders to men was at least in part a legacy of bad roads, inadequate transportation, and women needing to stay near their children in the village. Just as women processed some of men's produce, men sold some of women's cash crops, such as chili peppers or goat kids. But food re-

mained distinct from other products, and there were separate requirements for its legitimate sale. It was more like village land, whose preferred buyers were always relatives, than like, for example, weavings or sheep. . . .

Women had a hand more literally, also, in the construction of the community. While men made adobes and built the basic structure of the houses, women plastered them each fall, inside and out, with plaster made by mixing burnt and ground rock with water, and they built their own fireplaces and outdoor ovens. Plastering was usually a communal event, both for individual homes and for community structures. In 1911 at Embudo, New Mexico, forty women joined together to plaster the new school and build two fireplaces. In 1901 at San Pablo, Colorado, the village women working on the church divided their services among child care, kitchen work, and plastering. This was not work strictly within the home, nor work strictly for their own family. Plastering involved women as members in their own right of a larger community, in a service which required work both inside and outside the home, and it allowed them a share in shaping the village environment.

Much of this women's economy of production and exchange has remained invisible to historians, made so less by its unsalaried and often informal nature than by male recorders and census takers. It is highly significant that in the 1910 census for Rio Arriba County, whereas male or Anglo female enumerators listed ten females with occupations for every one hundred males in communities they covered, Sophie Archuleta, a public school teacher in Truchas whose father was a general farmer, whose mother was a seamstress, and whose sister and brother performed labor on the home farm, listed seventy-nine females with occupations for every one hundred males.[30] To Hispanic women, their own work was highly visible and, in terms of value, on a par with that of the men.

But even the basic outlines of acceptable women's work had always depended more on the composition of the family than on sexual norms. Anthropologists Paul Kutsche and John Van Ness noted that within the household, tasks were divided by sex and age "in a marked but not rigid fashion," adding that "the division of labor is not absolute. If age and sex distribution in a family, or illness, or jobs away from home, makes it inconvenient to go by custom, then anyone does anything without stigma."[31] Men could wash, cook, and iron; women could build fences, hoe corn, plant fields, and herd and shear sheep.... As men increasingly migrated for labor, both women's work and the traditional, flexible sexual division of labor were increasingly exploited, and their prior existence eased the transition to a migratory community whether or not the norms changed.

Both Anglos and Hispanics noted the relatively rapid spread of "bedsteads, tables, chairs, sewing machines, and cooking stoves" into Hispanic homes between 1880 and 1900, and that the men's newly available wage labor paid for it. They noted the technological cross-cultural contact, but gave less notice to the concomitant extension of women's work. . . .

That women often enjoyed the new technology, in particular the cookstoves, is not in dispute. In 1901, two women were sufficiently attached to a single cookstove to bring the case to court. But the alterations in women's labor were not limited to their work within the home. In most villages, the women's gardens lay closer to the home than the men's grain fields did, so that the women could tend the children and the garden at one time. When the men left the village for wage labor each spring, gathering at the local store with their families and bedding and departing "moist-eyed" for the railroad station, the women were left with the care of the men's crops. In the 1930s, Cordova resident Lorin Brown reflected back on this "new order":

> There was no abandonment of the land; rather a new order saw the women taking charge of the planting of crops aided in part by their children and men too old to seek work outside the valley.... During the long summers, the women tended their gardens and fields with perhaps more care than even their menfolk might have done.

When the men returned with the summer's wages, they found they needed to purchase only sugar, coffee, salt, and possibly some white flour and clothing. Women were moving from a shared position at the village center as village producer, to sole tenancy of that position.

Not everyone found that ends met easily. In an increasingly cash-dependent economy, some women found the new pattern required them to go even further afield, beyond adopting the men's farm work. Whether because of declining fertility of home fields, an early or late frost, loss of land, or other reasons, wives and daughters even of farmers found themselves working as seamstresses and laundresses away from home. Their cash income supplemented whatever the men's crops brought. In isolated Truchas, many of the nine out of sixteen laundresses who worked away from home were daughters and wives of landowning farmers. To an even greater degree did the wives of those wage earners (usually sawmill, railroad, or farm laborers) who had moved off the land permanently and now lived in rented housing in the villages, perform wage labor either in or away from the home.[32] . . .

Within the villages, subtle shifts occurred in the nature of women's work. For the most part plastering had been performed for exchange or as community service, though it was acknowledged as a skill if not an art. By 1910, however, census records show that some women had become professionals, making their living by plastering. Similar trends emerged in sewing, weaving, and later, mattress-making. By 1910, Chimayo held fourteen men and twenty women whose primary occupation was weaving; none had been so listed in 1880.[33] Women were crossing the fine line between the traditional provision of labor for others for the maintenance of community and the newer trend of providing the same services within the community for maintenance of self.

There were other departures from the communal norm which did not necessarily originate with the renewed Anglo activity of the 1880s but were exacerbated by it. For example, between 1895 and 1905, Hispanic men brought seven divorce cases and Hispanic women brought six into Rio Arriba County's district court; from 1905 to 1910, the men brought seven and the women thirteen, more than keeping pace with the increase in population.[34] By 1913, in the court's June term alone there were fourteen Hispanic divorces; eight of them brought by men.[35] . . .

According to the census records almost every village had at least one Hispanic divorced person, usually female, and there were frequently more. . . . Usually these women lived alone as heads of households with their children and occasionally a widowed mother or grandmother.[36]. . . Sometimes the divorced women owned property. If it were a farm, and they had grown sons, life could continue more or less in its old patterns. But if it were only a house, which was far more often the case, and particularly if the children were young, the women had to enter the cash sector, which usually meant work as poorly paid washerwomen inside or outside the home. . . .

Divorce and separation were . . . acceptable when either partner deviated from the norms of mutual support and respect, but such disruptions in the network of village life could not be encouraged. One woman who left an abusive husband and eventually moved to Cordova became "Tia Lupe" (Aunt Lupe), to the whole village, providing healing and counseling services and receiving fuel and other compensation, but she lived there alone.[37] Divorced women and men may not have been shunned by the community, but neither were they fully reincorporated through, for example, a return to their landowning parents. Many parents lacked the resources to maintain the enlarged household. . . .

In these less than perfectly harmonious communal villages, also, lived single women with illegitimate children.[38] In the late 1930s, Daniel Valdez commented, "this is common throughout the Valley. Every year brings a score of illegitimate babies with it. This is no more common now than it was a generation past."[39] Illegitimacy was not the product of cultural breakdown or of a new modernism, but a long-term phenomenon of an agricultural society. But length of tradition did not necessarily mean smooth acceptance, and the increasingly dominant cash economy placed extra burdens on unwed mothers. . . . While most illegitimate children seem to have been accepted by the community, there were husbands who refused to recognize them, and mothers whose washing work could not support them or who fostered them to couples who abused them. Perhaps these are the children who fell through the social net of the northern Hispanic villages and landed in St. Vincent's Orphans' Home for girls in Sante Fe, which had forty-seven Hispanic girls in 1909, and 116 (at least 23 from Rio Arriba County alone) in 1913. Of the fifty-nine Hispanic women in the New Mexico State Penitentiary between 1884 and 1917, nine were separated wives, three were single women, and two were widows. Forty-two had been charged

with sexually related crimes, including thirty-seven cases of adultery. Of the forty-two women charged, ten were laundresses, seven seamstresses, seven servants, two laborers, and one was a farmer. It is a measure of the difficulty of these women's lives that of the eight who gave reasons for their "crime," two listed desertion by husband, five claimed "necessity," and only one claimed "love."

There was another set of women who found no comfortable place in village society. These were the "brujas" or witches. . . . Divorced people and witches existed not simply as eccentric individuals, but as individuals unattached and possibly even hostile to the dense and vital network of family relations that sustained the community.

Ironically, belief in witchcraft could operate to ensure tolerance of a certain degree of eccentricity. New Mexico's Writers' Project investigators in the 1930s found that "brujas were taken for granted by all. The men as well as the women believed in brujas, and were careful not to offend anyone they were not sure of." Eccentric behavior in these cases was safest dealt with politely. As with witchcraft elsewhere, in New Mexico these beliefs also provided a forum for the relief of social tensions, as when Hispanics told Charles Briggs, "all *Indios* are witches."[40] Witches in New Mexico could be either male or female, but they were usually female, and in a classic juxtaposition of good woman/bad woman, the color blue, associated with Mary, was used to protect against witches, while "I go without God and without the Holy Virgin" was the incantation which allowed witches to fly.[41]

According to historian Marc Simmons, it was only after Hispanics realized that the United States courts would not hear witchcraft cases that vigilante-style reprisals occurred. In 1844, a woman near Chimayo "was taken from her lonely adobe hut by three roughs . . . and murdered," apparently for suspected dealings with the devil; and in 1882 a woman from Abiquiu was whipped until near death by the henchmen of her supposed victim.[42] Those suspected of witchcraft in the villages tended to be older women, usually of somewhat mysterious origins, women, whether widowed or never married, who lived alone with few if any kinship ties to the villagers.[43] The village women's fear of growing old alone which led them to adopt and foster small children thus had far more than economic or even affectional roots, and the loss of ties to the village had more than economic consequences.

Some of these village tensions were less a sign of cultural breakdown or even of the adjustment to the new economic context than a witness to the perpetual distance between the ideal aspired to and the reality in any society, and to the perceived fragility of the corporate community. They represented the ways in which villagers had long dealt with elements that threatened the family economy and communal virtues, elements potentially too disharmonious to incorporate safely into their small mutually dependent society of one hundred to five hundred people. Into this pattern of dealing with village tensions they thrust the newer tensions, the potential problems, caused by the adaptation to the regional community and the Anglo-dominated larger economy: the professionalization of former services, the cash-dependent widows. As they held the disruptive elements of Anglo society at bay, beyond the village, the villagers also relegated their own disruptive elements, including witches and divorcées, to the village periphery if not beyond. . . .

NOTES

1. Luisa Torres, "Palabras de Una Viejita/The Words of an Old One," *El Palacio* 84 (Fall 1978):12. . . .

2. Antonio Goubaud-Carrera, "Food Patterns and Nutrition in Two Spanish-American Communities" (Master's thesis, University of Chicago, 1943): 59.

3. Olen Leonard, *The Role of the Land Grant in the Social Organization and Social Processes of a Spanish American Village in New Mexico* (1943, reprint ed. Albuquerque, 1970), p. 70.

4. Annette Thorp, "Chana," WPA [Works Project Administration] 5.5.52, no. 71, NMHL [New Mexico Historical Library, Santa Fe]; Grace Farrell, "Home-making with the 'Other Half' Along Our International Border," *Journal of Home Economics* 21 (June 1929):416. . . .

5. Nan Elsasser et al., *Las Mujeres: Conversations from a Hispanic Community* (Old Westbury, N.Y., 1979), p. 9. . . .

6. Thorp, "Satan and the Girl," WPA 5.5.53, no. 4, NMHL.

7. Fran Leeper Buss, *La Partera: Story of a Midwife* (Ann Arbor, 1980).

8. . . . Illiterate parents often left a squash; the way in which it was returned signified a positive or negative response.

9. Thorp, "Weddings," WPA 5.5.52, no. 67, NMHL.

10. . . . Re: property, see, for example, Cleofas Jaramillo, *Romance of a Little Village Girl* (San Antonio, 1955), p. 131. She had a herd of sheep in her own right, which she continued to hold as such, given her by her father. . . .

11. See RACo. Records [Rio Arriba County, New Mexico], Criminal and Civil Docket, vols. D, E; Reception Book 1887–1912; and Juez de Paz Record Book, Abiquiu, NMSRCA [New Mexico State Records Center and Archives, Santa Fe]; Dorothy Woodward, "The Penitentes of New Mexico" (Ph.D. dissertation, Yale University, 1935):281; WPA files and John Lawrence Diary, 16 Apr. 1903, WHC [Western Historical Collections, University of Colorado, Boulder]. On fathers refusing daughters' choice in marriage, see, for example, "Manuela," WPA files, 11, pp. 275ff, NMSRCA. See also Mirande and Enriquez, p. 116.

12. Wayne Moquin, with Charles Van Doren, eds., *A Documentary History of the Mexican Americans* (New York, 1971), p. 268. . . . On Hispanic versus Anglo marital property law, see . . . Joan Jensen, who warns against romanticizing this community property practice in " 'I've Worked, I'm Not Afraid of Work': Farm Women in New Mexico, 1920–1940," *NMHR* [*New Mexico Historical Review*] 61 (Jan. 1986): 30.

13. Mrs. J. B. Martinez to Vigil, 24 Jan. 1900, Vigil Family Collection, Box 1, WHC (my translation). . . .

14. John Lawrence Diary, 5 Nov. 1901 and 27 Oct. 1901; Jaramillo, p. 131.

15. For example, of El Rito's 117 households in 1880, only 9 were headed by women; in 1900, 16 of 120; and in 1910, 18 of 164. Respectively, 6, 16, and 17 of these were widows; 2, 1, and 3 were single women; and 1, 1, 0 were divorcées. Ms. Census [Manuscript Census of the United States], RACo. 1880, 1900, 1910. . . .

16. As few single males as single females headed households. Ms. Census, RACo. 1880, 1900, 1910.

17. For example, Laurel Ulrich, *Goodwives: Image and Reality in the Lives of Women in Northern New England 1650–1750* (New York, 1982), p. 50. Similar to the environment Ulrich describes is the personal nature of business transactions within the community.

18. . . . Curanderas were also exempt from this sexual taboo and could treat men alone and go to widowers' homes and give, for example, massages, see John Lawrence Diary, 2 Dec. 1907.

19. Lou Sage Batchen, "La Curandera," *El Palacio* 18 (Spring 1975):22.

20. Thorp, "Curandera."

21. . . . Doctors charged, in addition to their set fees, one dollar each mile traveled, which added up rapidly as there were only four doctors in New Mexico north of Santa Fe in this period.

22. Elsasser et al., 41.

23. Buss, App. I: Rackley, 116.

24. Buss, 6–7.

25. . . . "Co-parent" is a more accurate translation of the duties of the comadre or madrina than "godparent". . . .

26. Lorin Brown (Lorenzo de Cordova), *Echoes of the Flute* (Santa Fe, 1972), p. 22.

27. John Burma, *Spanish Speaking Groups in the United States* (Durham, 1954), p. 24. . . .

28. Men and women also sat separately at religious services, and fiestas had both a mayordomo and a mayordama. . . .

29. "Parteras," WPA 5.5.53, no. 8, NMHL.

30. Ms. Census, RACo. 1910.

31. Paul Kutsche and John Van Ness, *Cañones: Values, Crisis and Survival in a Northern New Mexico Community* (Albuquerque, 1984), p. 35.

32. Ms. Census, RACo. 1910. In Chama, nine women did washing, three did odd job labor, three took in lodgers, and six did housework. . . .

33. Ms. Census, RACo. New Mexico and Las Animas County, Colorado, 1880, 1900, 1910. . . .

34. Divorce thus seems more common than legend would have it. . . .

35. RACo. Criminal and Civil Docket, District Court, June 1913. . . .

36. Ms. Census, RACo. 1910; see, for example, a Vallecitos divorcée whose father was a farmer. She was twenty-four with two children. . . .

37. "Tia Lupe", pp. 96–102, WPA.

38. Ms. Census, RACo. 1910, Chama, Cebolla, and Canjilon. There were also women living apart from their husbands. . . .

39. Daniel Valdez, *A History of the San Luis Valley* (Alamosa, 1930).

40. . . . In the 1930s, a Spanish Colonial Arts store manager who employed Hispanic spinners on the premises found that a new, relatively young Hispanic woman became the target of such accusations because she spun so much faster than her older co-workers. See Sarah Nestor, *The Native Market of the Spanish New Mexican Craftsmen, Santa Fe 1933–1940* (Santa Fe, 1978), p. 23.

41. Marc Simmons, *Witchcraft in the Southwest* (Flagstaff, 1974), pp. 36, 41–42, 56, for examples of male witches or sorcerers, and pp. 2, 40 for the rest.

42. *New Mexican Review*, 8 Sept. 1884, and *Santa Fe Daily New Mexican*, 2 Oct. 1882, cited in ibid., pp. 36–38.

43. . . . Cleofas Jaramillo, *Shadows of the Past* (Santa Fe, 1941, pp. 99, 102; Marta Weigle, *Spiders and Spinsters: Women and Mythology* (Albuquerque, 1982), pp. 41–42 on the particular vulnerability of spinsters. . . .

PEGGY PASCOE

Home Mission Women, Race, and Culture: The Case of Native "Helpers"

The population of the United States became more ethnically diverse in the late nineteenth century. In a largely Protestant nation, the beliefs of Catholic Chicanos in New Mexico or Chinese in San Francisco could seem as exotic as the beliefs of Hindus in India or Shinto in Japan. Protestant churches initiated "home missions" to offer the mixture of social service and religious proselytizing that they offered abroad, and recruited Protestant women to staff them. Many of the women, like Donaldina Cameron, who headed the Chinese Mission Home in San Francisco, made real sacrifices in their lives in order to serve.

The forms of these missions varied. In the Hispanic villages of New Mexico, where state legislatures resisted spending money on public education, Protestant women missionaries who came to establish schools were often welcomed. In the city of San Francisco,

Excerpted from "Home Mission Women, Race, and Culture: The Case of 'Native Helpers,'" chap. 4 of *Relations of Rescue: The Search for Female Moral Authority in the American West, 1874–1939* by Peggy Pascoe (New York: Oxford University Press, 1990). Copyright © 1990 by Peggy Pascoe. Reprinted by permission of the author and Oxford University Press, Inc. Notes have been renumbered and edited.

where impoverished Chinese immigrant women were often coerced into arranged marriages or even into prostitution, home missions could provide desperately needed shelter.

In New Mexico, villagers found that the same missionaries who dedicated themselves to offering health care and education also challenged traditional customs, foods, and relationships. Targets of missionary attentions varied greatly in their responses. Sometimes they resented these attentions, sometimes they resisted them. But sometimes, as Peggy Pascoe reports in the following essay, they enthusiastically welcomed the intrusion of missionaries on traditional power relationships within families and communities, choosing gender solidarity over family solidarity.

Consider the life choices of Tien Fu Wu. What elements of the Chinese Mission Home might she have found empowering? What aspects of the mission might she have found patronizing?

On a visit to the East Coast, Tien Fu Wu, an assistant at the Chinese Mission Home in San Francisco, took time to check in on a former resident, Ah Ho, who was married and living in Boston. As Wu reported to Mission Home matron Donaldina Cameron, she found Ah Ho "thin and frail and well worn out with her nest of babies." Wu informed Cameron that Ah Ho "wept and told me her family troubles, and I tried to comfort her the best way I could."[1] Maddie, another Mission Home resident who accompanied Wu, was also distressed by Ah Ho's condition. Maddie lamented that "it is dreadful how our dear [friend] is hemmed in on all sides . . . she isn't free even in her own home." Ah Ho's husband, she charged, was "stubborn as a mule [and] . . . so Chinesey about letting his wife go out" that it made her "most thankful that I haven't a man to boss me about."[2]

Wu stewed over Ah Ho's predicament all day, and finally returned later that night to confront her husband. "I began to lecture him as if he were my boy," she told Cameron, "[and told him] that he must be more thoughtful and kinder to his wife. . . . I tried hard to impress upon him to be more sensible and considerate of his wife by not having any more children." Although Wu was aware that she was skating on thin ice in lecturing a husband (rather than a young boy), she defended her actions. She told Cameron that "I really didn't care whether it was a delicate situation or not. I feel strongly that poor Ah Ho ought to be protected in some way or another."[3]

Tien Fu Wu was one of a handful of ethnic minority women who had been selected by home mission women to serve as trusted assistants referred to a *native helpers,* a term that suggests the mixture of fascination and condescension with which mission women regarded them. By all accounts the most enthusiastic of home mission converts, native helpers wrapped themselves in the mantle of female moral authority and dedicated themselves to implanting the values of Victorian women's culture in their own communities.

To Protestant home mission women, native helpers were living proof of the transforming power of female moral authority. For this reason, home mission women lavished attention on them, making them the centerpieces of mission public relations efforts by telling and retelling their life stories. Historians have for the most part ignored these relatively abundant historical sources. To those accustomed to late–twentieth-century conventions of race and ethnicity, which focus attention on the members of minority groups who champion ethnic solidarity, such women can only be a bit of an embarrassment, evidence of the power of white efforts to assimilate peoples of other races—in other words, classic Uncle Toms.[4] In terms of these conventions, Tien Fu Wu would have done better to defend Ah Ho and her husband against the incursions of white missionaries than to defend Ah Ho against her husband.

But, as Ah Ho's situation indicates, such an analysis would not take adequate account of power differences based on gender.[5] Although only a small percentage of the ethnic minority women who came into contact with home mission women became native helpers, by exploring the lives of those who did, we can begin to understand the interaction between the ideology of female moral authority and nineteenth-century ideas about race and culture.

HOME MISSION WOMEN AND NINETEENTH-CENTURY IDEAS ABOUT RACE AND CULTURE

Modern scholars of race relations usually distinguish between race, a biological classification, and culture, a more diffuse set of attitudes, values, and traditions unrelated to biology, closer to what we nowadays term *ethnicity* than to race.[6] But because such a distinction rests on twentieth-century intellectual developments, it is of limited use to historians trying to understand Victorian race relations. To be sure, a handful of nineteenth-century doctors promoted a theory of "scientific racism" that depended largely on a biologically determined concept of race, but such fine distinctions were lost on most nineteenth-century Americans. At least until the first decades of the twentieth century, the concepts we call race and culture were fused in the popular mind, the differences between them only dimly perceived.[7] As late as 1897, one native helper, Omaha Indian Susan LaFlesche, could speak of the different "races" of "Swedes, Irish, Danes, Dutch, and Indians" with none of the confusion such a statement would cause for modern readers.[8]

In late–nineteenth-century America, to conflate race and culture in order to speak of different "races" was not to suggest equality between them; for Victorian evolutionary theory posited a distinct hierarchy of racial development ranging from the "primitive" to the "civilized."[9] Victorians would have said that only the highest group, the "civilized," showed "culture." To them, culture was not a rough synonym for society; rather, to have culture was to display one's standing at the apex of evolution by adhering to Victorian standards of morality. In such a scheme, culture and civilization were assumed to be the sole property of white middle-class Americans; other races, classes, and (what we would call) cultures were considered both morally and physically inferior.[10]

Historians disagree on the extent to which Protestant missionaries adhered to this Victorian racial hierarchy and its accompanying ideology, the set of ideas we have come to call "racialism" to distinguish it from twentieth-century racism. Some historians celebrate the potential for equality in the Protestant belief that people of all colors could—and should—

be brought under the umbrella of Christianity; others consider missionaries the shock troops of American ethnocentrism.[11] Both the celebrators and the critics have a point, but neither grasps the central importance of the ideology of female moral authority in shaping the racial attitudes of Protestant missionary women.

What stands out on examination of these racial attitudes is the extent to which home mission women challenged racial biological determinism. This challenge was in large part an outgrowth of missionary experience with native helpers. Because Protestant women were eager to convince Americans that Tien Fu Wu and her peers were models of Victorian morality, they argued that race should be no barrier to educational opportunity or to participation in religious activities.

Home mission challenges to racial biological determinism rested on several justifications—scriptural, environmental, and even evolutionary—each intended to prove that nonwhite women could become exemplars of Victorian female values. Determined to show that "mind and morals are not olive, or white, or black," some home mission women chanted the Biblical verse, "He has made of one blood all the nations of the earth."[12] Others stressed that social environment, not biological race, determined individual development. Taunted by those who believed that Chinese children were incapable of learning, one home mission woman in San Francisco responded with the flat statement that "environment means everything to the children of every race and nation."[13] . . .

The strength of these convictions can be seen in the educational programs of the Chinese Mission Home. Mission Home officials encouraged all residents to excel in their studies; good students who adopted the Victorian values of piety and purity were sent on for advanced schooling. A core of these students became *de facto* ambassadors of integration, because Protestant women fought for their admission to Bible schools and business colleges—in one case, even to Stanford University—composed of predominantly white student bodies.[14]

These challenges to racial determinism put home mission women in an anomalous position *vis-à-vis* their Victorian contemporaries. On the one hand, their defense of Chinese . . . women set missionaries apart from the general context of late-Victorian social thought. The ideology of female moral authority stressed universal bonds between women; expressed in high hopes for native helpers, it nurtured home mission challenges to racial determinism. Perhaps the best measure of the home mission challenge is the vehemence of the opposition it aroused. Missionaries at the Chinese Mission Home, for example, found it impossible to forget one woman who had declined their invitation to attend a meeting with the comment, "I'd rather see all the Chinese women heaped in a pile—*and set fire to.*"[15] They sensed strong intolerance even among "those who call themselves Christians."[16] They never ran out of opponents, from those who advocated Chinese exclusion in the 1880s, to the "buy and employ American" advocates of the 1930s. Yet, despite this opposition, Protestant women maintained their belief in racial malleability. They held to their ideals into the twentieth century, ignoring both the revival of neo-Lamarckian racialism, and the heyday of scientific racism (exemplified by anthropometry, eugenics, and IQ tests) that culminated in the immigration restriction campaigns of the 1920s.[17]

Yet the same Protestant women who challenged distinctions made according to biological race maintained distinctions according to culture. Native helpers were expected to display Victorian piety and purity, but they were also encouraged to retain ties to the culture of their original communities. . . . It is important to avoid the temptation to lump all the activities of home mission women into the oversimplified cateory of "assimilation."

At the Chinese Mission Home in San Francisco, for example, missionaries hedged the assimilation of residents by expressing a desire that residents retain what they termed, so revealingly, "all that is *good* of Chinese tradition and custom."[18] They provided Chinese food for residents; they also put together a small museum to display Chinese artifacts. All Home residents took Chinese language classes, even though some of those born in the United States were less than enthusiastic about doing so. "My Chinese lessons are very difficult," wrote one such woman to a friend outside the Home. "I wouldn't take [the class] if it wasn't required."[19]

Furthermore, white officials insisted on retaining Chinese stylistic touches in the clothes Mission Home residents wore, from the dark skirts and white saams they wore every day, to the distinctive collars and fastenings added to their wedding dresses.[20] As a result, one visitor to the Home in 1887 commented that "the only Americanism I could discover was that some of the girls had banged their hair."[21] In 1902, Mrs. E. V. Robbins described the attitude of white mission women during a visit to an official at the Chinese legation in Washington, D.C. When the minister commented on the "American" clothes worn by Choi Qui, a Home resident brought with the group, missionaries told him (perhaps a little defensively) that she was wearing them for the first time, and "this by the request of the man she is to marry." "We keep them in their own costumes, and supply them with their own food," explained Robbins, "deeming it wise not to detach them from their own people."[22]. . .

Some white missionaries developed strong personal fascinations for their "adopted" cultures.[23]. . . Donaldina Cameron, matron of the Chinese Mission Home, was equally proud of her own Scots ancestry and her dedication to the Chinese, "among whom," she once remarked, "I have lived for twenty five years, and whom as a nation I love."[24] Her delight when Mission Home residents redecorated her rooms in Chinese style overcame her reluctance to accept personal gifts. Years later, a part of her much-loved Chinese print bedspread was framed and displayed on a wall in the Mission Home. Cameron lived in the Mission Home from her mid-twenties until national mission officials forced her to retire after she turned sixty-five. She left then only with a deep sense of personal loss, no longer quite at home in white American society.

Neither the missionary challenge to biological determinism nor matrons' fascination for their "adopted" cultures allowed home mission women to overcome all of the racialism inherent in Victorian social thought. Just beneath the surface of their calls for the education and fair treatment of ethnic minority women ran a persistent theme of racialist moral judgment. Nevertheless, the extent to which his racialism was expressed was shaped by the ideology of female moral authority. Protestant women held their Victorian concept of womanhood so dear that they focused their complaints about Chinese culture primarily on its challenges to Victorian female piety and purity. . . . Although they were quick to cast aspersions on women who publicly challenged their goals, in general they relied on depictions of unfortunate women as innocent victims of predatory men to resist the tendency to label women as immoral. Their experience with native helpers concentrated this dynamic by strengthening their belief that most ethnic minority women were natural advocates of purity and piety.

Home mission women had, however, very little equivalent experience with ethnic minority men. When they lapsed into racialist rhetoric, they usually aimed their remarks at minority men. Because their Victorian conception of gender roles led them to see men in general as sexually aggressive creatures in need of female restraint, their complaints about ethnic minority men were reinforced by their gender consciousness. And when moralistic racialism was combined with Victorian assumptions about the nature of men, Protestant women were capable of sounding like the most extreme racists.

Consider, for example, the words of Donaldina Cameron, who, in a moment of exasperation at the tenacity of Chinatown procurers, railed that "the Chinese themselves will never abolish the hateful practice of buying and selling their women like so much merchandise, it is born in their blood, bred in their bone and sanctioned by the government of their native land."[25] Such a statement was hardly typical; Cameron spent most of her life defending Chinese women immigrants from stereotyping, sensationalism, and ideas of racial determinism. It is, however, revealing, because it suggests the limitations of the missionary challenge to biological determinism rooted in the Victorian ideology of female moral authority. Protestant women assumed that just under the surface of every ethnic minority woman was a pure, pious Christian woman waiting to emerge; but they routinely suspected the intentions of ethnic minority men, even those who professed Christian belief. In this sense, the gendered assumptions of Protestant women conditioned them to defend most ethnic minority women but condemn most ethnic minority men.

As the experiences of native helpers . . . show, some ethnic minority women joined in the condemnations. Because the ideology of female moral authority could be used to challenge the social vulnerability of ethnic minority women, it held great appeal for native helpers. Donaldina Cameron may have been outraged at Chinese immigrant slaveholders, but Tien Fu Wu was so furious with Ah Ho's husband that she swept past Cameron's demurrals and went out of her way to lecture him to respect female purity. Maddie, the Chinese American girl who accompanied her, expressed indignation, too. Revealing the links between home mission ideology and Victorian racial hierarchies, Maddie charged that Ah Ho's husband was too "Chinesey," asked Cameron "never again [to] marry any of our girls to unchristian men," and said she was relieved that she didn't have "a man to boss me about."[26] Despite her complaints, Ah Ho saw a different reason for her husband's behavior. "The American teachers are so kind and want me to go often to church," she wrote to Donaldina Cameron, "but the Chinese people here gossip so much about women going out that my husband does not approve of my going out very much."[27] As her comments suggest, missionaries and native helpers developed a sharp critique of behavior that many Chinese immigrants considered entirely ordinary.

Like the Victorian Protestant women who ran home mission projects, native helpers defended women in the name of Victorian female values. Unlike them, native helpers had to confront in their own lives the conflict between the Victorian ideology of female moral authority and the distinctly different ideals maintained by ethnic minority communities. . . .

Ah Tsun was a home mission "success" story, the first in the history of the Chinese Mission Home in San Francisco. Ah Tsun entered the Home in 1877 at the age of sixteen, fleeing from her "owner," who, after bringing her into the country disguised as a boy (a ruse to evade immigration officials), planned to sell her into prostitution. Shortly after entering the Home, she was arrested on charges of grand larceny, a ploy slaveowners used to regain control of prostitutes by convincing police officers that they had stolen clothes or jewelry found in their possession—and regarded by them as legitimate payments or gifts. After two court trials, Ah Tsun was acquitted and released to the custody of the Mission Home.[28] . . . She touched the hearts of Home board members by announcing at their annual meeting: "I wish to tell you that I love this home, and am happy here. When my time for staying has expired, with your permission, I still wish to remain. I do not wish to marry and leave the Home. I love Jesus and pray to him each day for a clean and new heart."[29] Although she did, after turning down several proposals, eventually marry and leave the Home, her words were nonetheless prophetic, for she retained strong ties to home mission women.

Her marriage to Chinese Christian Ngo Wing in 1884 evoked a great deal of ambivalence among Mission Home officials who regretted losing her services as Home interpreter, organist, and prayer leader. They reminded themselves, however, that "we cannot travel the road with them [after they leave the Home], nor do they need us, as they need to travel it themselves to their own destination. We can only take the stones of stumbling out of the way. . . ."[30] Mission women tried to do just that by establishing the new bride in a nearby residence selected so that the handful of "Christian girls who had married from the Home might feel that they were secure from molestation."[31] In her new home Ah Tsun Wing busied herself with housework, child-rearing, and proselytizing; she reported regularly to mission women on her evangelistic activities.

Neither Wing's Victorian morality nor her mission-selected residence saved her from local toughs who stoned the house during anti-Chinese disturbances in 1885. Although Mission officials tracked down her harassers and told them "that these Chinese women had rights that were as dear as our own, and were entitled to the same protection as American women," they seem to have made little impression on the toughs.[32] Partly to escape such disturbances, Wing entered a Bible school in Canton, China, where she remained for two years. On her return to San Francisco, she completed her professional education by spending a few months in the Golden Gate Kindergarten Training School.

By now a widow who needed work, Ah Tsun Wing found her best hope of employment within the mission system. She enrolled her children in the Mission's Occidental School for Chinese children (a parallel project operated outside the Mission Home), and began work as a kindergarten teacher, Mission Home assistant, and Sunday school leader. The first native helper to come out of the Chinese Mission Home, she would remain associated with it for more than forty years, from 1894 until her retirement in 1935.[33]

Just about the time that Ah Tsun Wing started to work for the Chinese Mission Home, Tien Fu Wu entered the institution. Wu had been brought to the United States as a child of six after her father, reduced to poverty through gambling debts, sold her to an agent. In California, the young girl was transferred from person to person until she ended up in the hands of a woman who abused her with hot iron tongs. When someone reported her condition to Mission workers, they located her and took her to the Mission Home.[34]

Once away from her abusers, Wu was, as she later remembered, a "happy-go-lucky tom boy" who had a tumultuous adolescence in the Mission Home. She remembered years later that on one occasion she held her head out the window of her room in a vain attempt to contract pneumonia and die so that she could return to haunt the matron who had reprimanded her for some minor offense. In her late teens, however, she had a change of heart and converted to Christianity.[35]

Wu attributed her conversion to a single incident that occurred one night as she sat beside matron Donaldina Cameron at the deathbed of Cameron's interpreter Yuen Qui. Wu had volunteered to help Cameron because she was attracted to Yuen Qui, "in spite of the fact" that she was a "quiet student, a seamstress and a reader." Wu remembered that "when Miss Cameron saw [Yuen Qui die], she absolutely broke down. I felt very sorry for her and was convinced of the great loss. So I offered to help her in the rescue work." This decision, she later remarked, saved her from leading a "selfish and worldly life."[36] It was the personal connection she felt with Cameron, based on Cameron's grief at Yuen Qui's death, that laid the basis for Wu's lifelong dedication to home mission work.

By 1905, Wu had completed the course at the Mission Home school to the satisfaction of Mission workers, who reported that she had been "of such assistance as a dear elder daughter may become to the burdened mother of a large family."[37] She was able to continue her education because of a benefactor, Mr. Coleman, who had attended a Philadelphia lecture about the San Francisco rescue work. Coleman visited San Francisco in 1905 and invited Wu to join a party of evangelical guests at his country house at New Hampshire. After she told him she needed more education to hone her skills as Mission Home interpreter, he offered to pay for further schooling. As a result, she spent four years at the Stevens' School in Germantown, Pennsylvania, and two years at the Toronto Bible School.[38]

In 1911, Wu returned to the Mission Home to work as Donaldina Cameron's helper, a job that involved assisting in rescues and appearing in court as Cameron's interpreter. She saved her salary until she could afford to return to China and search for her long-lost relatives. Unable to locate them, she decided that "I must come back to help Cameron House because they had helped to rear me."[39] . . .

The emotional bonds they shared with mission women, the educations they gained, and the praise they received for their exemplary behavior were formative experiences that inspired trust in the benevolence of home mission women. Adopting the central tenets of Victorian women's culture, native helpers dedicated themselves to extending Victorian conceptions of female purity and piety to their own communities. Their task required them to weld the ideology of female moral authority onto their own distinct cultures. . . .

Yet, even while native helpers pledged themselves to defend their peoples, the universalizing thrust of the ideology of female moral authority distanced them from their own communities by challenging conventional arrangements of gender power in those communities. In the case of San Francisco's Chinatown, Chinese immigrant men who made their money from prostitutes reserved special ire for native helpers, whose work threatened their livelihoods. Since it was part of Wu's job to assist Donaldina Cameron in rescuing prostitutes from San Francisco brothels, she frequently had to face brothel owners in court. After one of these incidents, an angry Chinese man tried to intimidate Wu by writing her a letter that indicates slaveowners' hostility toward her. "Tien Fook, stinking sow," he wrote, "now you are interpreter in the Mission Home and have the backing of the Home so you even dare to arrest a family girl." After accusing her (incorrectly) of being a prostitute, the letter threatened that "you have overreached yourself and in so doing negroes, dogs, and thunder will come after you."[40] Mission women deemed the rest of the letter "too vile to translate."

This viciousness from the men who profited from organized prostitution might have been expected; but criticism was also forthcoming from Chinese immigrants not directly involved with the trade. Thus, after one troubled Chinese woman fled to the Mission Home for assistance, her father-in-law wrote to tell her, "you made a mistake by going to the Mission Home because good women do not enter there. . . . I am afraid that you have surely lost your reputation by going into the Mission Home."[41] Many other immigrants shared his opinion. Chinese Mission workers like Ah Tsun Wing, who taught for many years in the missionary group's Occidental School, had to dissociate the school from the Mission Home for fear that Chinese merchant parents would not let young children attend if missionaries acknowledged the connection between the two.[42]

Attitudes like these cut at the very heart of Protestant mission work. In choosing native helpers, white women assumed that reinforcing Victorian female moral authority was a viable strategy for commanding community respect. But, given the precepts of the Chinese gender system, Chinese immigrants found it only too easy to discredit native helpers as immoral women who had "overreached" themselves. When Chinese immigrants saw native helpers as threats to (rather than exemplars of) morality, they inadvertently revealed the Victorian bias of the search for female moral authority.

As native helpers were to discover, the lip-service Americans paid to white mission home women was based, not only on claims to female moral authority, but also on the operation of the Victorian racial hierarchy. Although white mission women, too, received threatening letters from Chinese opponents, writers took care to be much more polite in addressing them. Given the white dominance in American society, Chinese vice operators who offended white women risked reprisals from Victorians eager to defend the purity of white womanhood, the cultural symbol used to justify, among other things, the widespread lynching of blacks in the American South. Under these circumstances, slaveowners saved their strongest barbs for Chinese native helpers, and native helpers' determination to fight against prostitution set them apart from a significant segment of their Chinese immigrant communities. . . . Yet their efficacy as agents of community change depended on their holding to home mission goals without losing ties to their own communities. When the gap between the two seemed unbridgeable, native helpers faced difficult choices.

Native helpers at the Chinese Mission Home found little scope to maneuver within their own communities and only minimal opportunities to work in white-owned businesses. Despite their educational achievements, those who sought employment outside the Mission Home faced blatant discrimination. Many white employers took racial boundaries for granted to such an extent that they refused to hire Chinese women regardless of their qualifications. Even those who managed to find jobs found little security in them. One such woman, Ah Tye Leung, a Mission Home interpreter, was appointed Assistant Matron when the Angel Island Immigration Station opened in 1910. Since her appointment put her in a position to intercede between immigration officials and Chinese women immigrants, Home officials were delighted. They optimistically quoted a minister who told them that "if [Leung's appointment] was the only result of the work of the [Chinese Mission Home] Board, it was enough." As they saw it, it was "splendid . . . to know we shall have a dear Christian girl to do this work among heathen women."[43] Their high hopes, however, evaporated when Leung married a white immigration worker. Both were fired for this affront to white racial sensibilities.[44] As her experience indicates, even the best-prepared native helper was vulnerable to racism of the most arbitrary sort. The female moral authority that had been the backbone of mission training could ensure them neither the respect of their own communities nor acceptance by white Americans.

Faced with obstacles like these, Ah Tsun Wing and Tien Fu Wu chose to remain within the mission system. Their decisions allowed them to retain the emotional bonds they had formed with mission officials and to use their skills in paid employment. While in the Mission Home, they were insulated from the most blatant forms of racism. Nonetheless, they were never allowed to hold substantial authority within that institution either. Tien Fu Wu, for example, worked as "interpreter and general supervisor of girls" at the Chinese Mission Home from 1911 through the 1930s, during which period she was Superintendent Donaldina Cameron's closest confidante. Yet Mission Home residents referred to Wu as "auntie" rather than as "mother," the term used to describe Donaldina Cameron.[45] In a mission system in which authority rested in claims to

motherhood, the distinction was significant. It helped to pave the way for another, much more telling, slight.

When Cameron began to think about retirement in 1934, some Presbyterian officials proposed Wu to be her replacement, but others assumed she would not be interested in the post. Belatedly consulted for her opinion, Wu formally declined consideration, saying that she was not adequately prepared for the job and that she was more interested in assisting Cameron or working with children than in shouldering the supervisory duties of administering the Home. "I am," she wrote, "of the same opinion as I told Miss Cameron before, that an American person should be the head of this work."[46] She based her conclusion in part on her belief that judges were prejudiced against her because she was Chinese, an opinion supported by accounts of her treatment by court officials.[47] Wu's demurral suggests her recognition that, in white-dominated American society, a white woman would hold more influence with the power structure than Wu could command. In the end, the job went to Lorna Logan, a white woman who had begun her work at the Home only two years earlier. Unlike Wu, Logan could not speak Chinese.

Wu recognized—and chafed at—the limitations of her authority within the Mission Home. Her relations with Donaldina Cameron were affectionate, not to say adoring, but she had no such emotional ties to Lorna Logan. To Logan, Wu made her resentment clear. A dozen years later, Logan told Presbyterian officials that "[Wu] has been increasingly unhappy here, partly because we have disagreed on some points of policy, and partly because she feels that she is not given the status she should have."[48]. . .

Wu stayed on at the Mission Home until her own retirement. In 1952, she moved into a cottage next door to Cameron's Palo Alto home, and the two women shared both their daily lives and their memories of rescue work until Cameron's death in 1968.[49] Matrons and native helpers formed bonds between women across socially drawn racial boundaries; these bonds, along with employment in the mission system, shielded trusted assistants from the worst of the racism prevalent in American society outside the institutions. . . . [Yet] because white missionary women were unable to transcend Victorian "racial" hierarchies, trusted assistants grew into "native helpers" rather than full-fledged colleagues, and never held autonomous authority in mission circles. . . .

By the 1920s, missionary work [itself was losing its attraction both to women who in the past had become home missionaries and to those who were native helpers.] . . . In Victorian America, a missionary career was one of the few professional jobs open to women; furthermore, it combined the appeal of exoticism with the social authority of speaking for Protestant America. By the turn of the century, however, the kind of ambitious young women who might earlier have become missionaries were increasingly attracted to business, government, social work, or academia.[50]

NOTES

1. Tien Fu Wu to Donaldina Cameron, June 13, 1915, about Ah Ho (psuedonym), file #269, Cameron House files, San Francisco, California [CH].

2. Maddie (pseudonym) to Donaldina Cameron, June 10, 1915, file #269, CH.

3. Tien Fu Wu to Donaldina Cameron, June 13, 1915, file #269, CH.

4. Milton Gordon, *Assimilation in American Life: The Role of Race, Religion, and National Origins* (New York: Oxford University Press, 1964).

5. Micaela di Leonardo, *The Varieties of Ethnic Experience: Kinship, Class, and Gender among California Italian-Americans* (Ithaca: Cornell University Press, 1984), p. 221.

6. Barbara Fields, "Ideology and Race in American History," in J. Morgan Kousser and James McPherson, eds., *Region, Race, and Reconstruction: Essays in Honor of C. Vann Woodward* (New York: Oxford University Press, 1982), pp. 143–78; Karen Blu, *The Lumbee Problem: The Making of an American Indian People* (London: Cambridge University Press, 1980), p. 7.

7. Robert Berkhofer, *The White Man's Indian: Images of the American Indian from Columbus to the Present* (New York: Alfred A. Knopf, 1978), pp. 55–61; Reginald Horsman, *Race and Manifest Destiny: The Origins of American Racial Anglo-Saxonism* (Cambridge: Harvard University Press, 1981).

8. "News From Dr. Picotte," *Bulletin* (Feb. 1897).

9. Thomas Gossett, *Race: The History of an Idea in America* (Dallas: Southern Methodist Press, 1963), chap. 7; George Stocking, *Race, Culture, and Evolution: Essays in the History of Anthropology* (Chicago: University of Chicago Press, 1982), chap. 6.

10. Daniel Joseph Singal, *The War Within: From Victorian to Modernist Thought in the South, 1919–1945* (Chapel Hill: University of North Carolina Press, 1982), p. 5; Henry May, *The End of American Innocence: A Study of the First Years of Our Own Time, 1912–1917* (New York: Alfred A. Knopf, 1959).

11. Francis Prucha, "Scientific Racism and Indian Policy," in Francis Prucha, *Indian Policy in the United States* (Lincoln: University of Nebraska Press, 1981); Robert Seager II, "Some Denominational Reactions to Chinese Immigration to California, 1856–1892," *Pacific Historical Review* 28 (Feb. 1959):59–66.

12. *Occidental Board Bulletin* (May 1, 1902):3–4; *Occident* (Apr. 27, 1887):11.

13. *Far West* (Mar. 1908):6.

14. Victor Low, *The Unimpressible Race: A Century of Educational Struggle by the Chinese in San Francisco* (San Francisco: East/West, 1982), p. 96; Charles Wollenberg, *All Deliberate Speed: Segregation and Exclusion in California Schools, 1855–1975* (Berkeley: University of California Press, 1976), pp. 28–47.

15. *Occident* (Oct. 27, 1877).

16. Woman's Foreign Missionary Society, *Annual Report* (1887):34; Woman's Foreign Missionary Society, Occidental Board (WFMS-OBo), *Annual Report* (1889):34.

17. Frederick Hoxie, *A Final Promise: The Campaign to Assimilate the Indians, 1880–1920* (Lincoln: University of Nebraska Press, 1984), pp. 115–45; John Higham, *Strangers in the Land: Patterns of American Nativism, 1860–1925* (New York: Atheneum, 1978), chaps. 6–11.

18. Grace King, "Presbyterian Chinese Mission Home," MS report for California State Board of Charities and Corrections, November–December 1919, p. 3, Cadwallader Papers, San Francisco Theological Seminary, San Anselmo, California (SFTS): emphasis mine.

19. Resident to friend, Sept. 23, 1927, file #158, CH.

20. Ethel Higgins to resident's mother, Oct. 24, 1928, file #174, CH; *Women and Missions* 5 (1928–29): 184–85.

21. *Woman's Work* (July 1887):169.

22. *Occidental Board Bulletin* (Feb. 1, 1902):4.

23. Sarah Deutsch, *No Separate Refuge: Culture, Class, and Gender on an Anglo-Hispanic Frontier in the American Southwest, 1880–1940* (New York: Oxford University Press, 1987), pp. 63–86; Helen Bannan, "Newcomers to Navajoland: Transculturation in the Memoirs of Anglo Women, 1900–1945," *New Mexico Historical Review* 59 (Apr. 1984):165–85.

24. Donaldina Cameron to Grace Abbott, Mar. 30, 1923, 1923 correspondence file, CH.

25. Woman's Occidental Board of Foreign Missionary Society [WOBFM], *Annual Report* (1904):53.

26. Maddie (pseudonym) to Donaldina Cameron, June 10, 1915, file #269, CH.

27. Ah Ho (pseudonym) to Donaldina Cameron, ibid.

28. Woman's Foreign Missionary Society, Occidental Branch [WFMS-OBr], *Annual Report* (1878): 9–10.

29. *Occident* (Nov. 13, 1878):6.

30. Ibid. (Jan. 30, 1884):7.

31. WFMS-OBo, *Annual Report* (1886):43–44.

32. Ibid.

33. *Occident* (Feb. 20, 1889):11, (Oct. 28, 1897):13; WOBFM, *Annual Report* (1889):49, (1891):48, (1920): 22–23.

34. WOBFM, *Annual Report* (1894):38–39; Victor Nee and Brett de Bary Nee, *Longtime Californ': A Documentary Study of an American Chinatown* (New York: Pantheon Books, 1971), pp. 84–87.

35. "Tien Wu," clipping, Donaldina Cameron file, SFTS.

36. *MS* (Jan. 1934); Tien Fu Wu biographical file #2, Presbyterian Office of History, Philadelphia, Pennsylvania [POH].

37. WOBFM, *Annual Report* (1905):64.

38. *Pacific Presbyterian* (Aug. 10, 1905):14; WOBFM, *Annual Report* (1912):57–58; Nee and Nee, *Longtime Californ'*, p. 89.

39. Nee and Nee, *Longtime Californ'*, p. 86; WOBFM, *Annual Report* (1917):35.

40. "Translation of letter received by Miss Wu," Dec. 14, 1914, file #44, CH.

41. Letter from resident's father-in-law, file #167, CH.

42. *Occident* (June 30, 1886):11.

43. *Far West* (Mar. 1910):2; Mrs. E. V. Robbins, *How Do the Chinese Girls,* (n.p., n.d.); WOBFM, *Annual Report* (1910):28 and 62; (1911):32.

44. Him Mark Lai et al., *Island: Poetry and History of Chinese Immigrants on Angel Island, 1910–1940* (San Francisco: HOC-DOI, 1980), p. 16; Shih-Shan Henry Tsai, *The Chinese Experience in America* (Bloomington: Indiana University Press, 1986), p. 98.

45. "Tien Wu," clipping, Donaldina Cameron file, SFTS.

46. Edna Voss to Donaldina Cameron, Aug. 21, 1934; Edna Voss to Tien FJ Wu, Aug. 7, 1934, Tien Fu Wu biographical file #2, POH.

47. Nee and Nee, *Longtime Californ'*, pp. 89–90.

48. Lorna Logan to Katharine Gladfelter, Feb. 26, 1948, Tien Fu Wu biographical file #1, POH.

49. "Tien Wu," clipping, Donaldina Cameron file, SFTS; Nee and Nee, *Longtime Californ'*, p. 83; Milfred Crowl Martin, *Chinatown's Angry Angel: The Story of Donaldina Cameron* (Palo Alto: Pacific Books, 1977), pp. 282–93.

50. Barbara Welter, " 'She Hath Done What She Could'," *American Quarterly* 30 (Winter 1978):624–38; R. Pierce Beaver, *All Loves Excelling: American Protestant Women in World Mission* (Grand Rapids: Wm. B. Eerdmans, 1968), chaps. 2–3, 6; Lois Boyd and R. Douglas Brackenridge, *Presbyterian Women in America: Two Centuries of A Quest for Status* (Westport: Greenwood Press, 1983), chap. 4.

DOCUMENTS: *Working for Economic and Racial Justice*

Florence Kelley, "I arrived at Hull House, . . . [and] discovered the . . . sweating system."

Hull House was a pioneering social settlement, established in Chicago in 1889 by twenty-nine-year-old Jane Addams. In the years to come it would be the model for settlement houses in cities all across America, staffed by women and men who shared Addams's vision and were caught up in the excitement of developing the new field of professional social service. They represented, as we have suggested in our introduction to this section, a distinctive female component in American progressivism.

In the following account, Florence Kelley describes her first encounter with the women of Hull House. It was no accident that Kelley was drawn to this novel institution or that she was soon put in charge of the Chicago inquiry into sweated labor. Preparation for a career as a reformer had begun as a young girl when her father, a Republican congressman from Pennsylvania, shared with her his voluminous library, his commitment to female suffrage, and his own concern over the economic exploitation that accompanied the industrial development he believed so essential to America. Further preparation occurred at Cornell, one of the few co-ed institutions in the country, where Kelley wrote her thesis on legislation affecting women and children. Denied permission to enroll in law school at the University of Pennsylvania because of her sex, she went to Switzerland for further study at the University of Zurich. There her passion for economic and social justice was reinforced by contact with Marxism and young radicals in the student body. Returning home in 1886, Kelley began five years later at Hull House a distinguished career as an advocate for legislation protecting women and children from exploitation in the workplace.

On a snowy morning between Christmas 1891 and New Year's 1892, I arrived at Hull House, Chicago, a little before breakfast time, and found there Henry Standing Bear, a Kickapoo Indian, waiting for the front door to be opened. It was Miss Addams who opened it, holding on her left arm a singularly unattractive, fat, pudgy baby belonging to the cook, who was behindhand with breakfast. Miss Addams was a little hindered in her movements by a super-energetic kindergarten child, left by its mother while she went to a sweatshop for a bundle of cloaks to be finished.

We were welcomed as though we had been invited. We stayed, Henry Standing Bear as helper to the engineer several months, when he returned to his tribe; and I as a resident seven happy, active years until May 1, 1899, when I returned to New York City to enter upon work in which I have since been engaged as secretary of the National Consumers' League.

I cannot remember ever again seeing Miss Addams hold a baby, but that first picture of her gently keeping the little Italian girl back from charging out into the snow, closing the

Excerpted from "I Go to Work" by Florence Kelley, in *Survey* 58, no. 5 (June 1, 1927):271–74.

door against the blast of wintry wind off Lake Michigan, and tranquilly welcoming these newcomers, is as clear today as it was at that moment.

Henry Standing Bear had been camping under a wooden sidewalk which surrounded a vacant lot in the neighborhood, with two or three members of his tribe. They had been precariously employed by a vendor of a hair improver, who had now gone into bankruptcy leaving his employees a melancholy Christmas holiday. Though a graduate of a government Indian school, he had been trained to no way of earning his living and was a dreadful human commentary upon Uncle Sam's treatment of his wards in the Nineties.

At breakfast on that eventful morning, there were present Ellen Gates Starr, friend of many years and fellow-founder of Hull-House with Jane Addams; Jennie Dow, a delightful young volunteer kindergartner, whose good sense and joyous good humor found for her unfailing daily reward for great physical exertion. She spent vast energy visiting the homes of her Italian pupils, persuading their mothers to remove at least two or three times during the winter their layers of dresses, and give them a thorough sponge-bath in the sympathetic and reassuring presence of their kindergartner. Mary Keyser, who had followed Miss Addams from the family home in Cedarville and throughout the remainder of her life relieved Miss Addams of all household care. This was a full-time professional job where such unforeseen arrivals as Henry Standing Bear's and mine were daily episodes in the place which Miss Addams' steadfast will has made and kept, through war and peace, a center of hospitality for people and for ideas.

Julia Lathrop, then recently appointed county visitor for Cook County for those dependent families who received outdoor relief in money or in kind, was mentioned as away for the holidays with her family at Rockford, Illinois. Miss Lathrop, later a member of the Illinois State Board of Charities and from 1912 to 1921 through its first nine creative years, chief of the Children's Bureau at Washington, was then and is now a pillar of Hull-House. Two others of the permanent group were Edward L. Burchard, for many years curator of the Field Museum; and Anna Farnsworth, an agreeable woman of leisure and means, happy to be hostess-on-call to some and all who appeared at the front door from breakfast until

midnight seven days a week. That was before the squalid, recent social convention had been set up, according to which everyone, however abundant and well assured her income, must earn her own living or be censured as a parasite. Miss Farnsworth's gracious gifts of free time and abundant good-will for counseling perplexed immigrants, finding comfortable quarters for old people who could do little work but not fend for themselves in the labor market, providing happy Saturdays in the parks for little groups of school children whose mothers worked away from home, were among the Settlement's early enrichments of the neighborhood life.

Reaching Hull-House that winter day was no small undertaking. The streets between car-track and curb were piled mountain high with coal-black frozen snow. The street cars, drawn by horses, were frequently blocked by a fallen horse harnessed to a heavily laden wagon. Whenever that happened, the long procession of vehicles stopped short until the horse was restored to its feet or, as sometimes occurred, was shot and lifted to the top of the snow, there to remain until the next thaw facilitated its removal.

Nor were these difficulties in the way of travel minimized by free use of the telephone. In all weathers and through all depths of snow and slush and sleet, we used to navigate across Halsted Street, the thirty-miles-long thoroughfare which Hull-House faced, to a drug store where we paid ten cents a call, stood throughout the process, and incidentally confided our business to the druggist and to any English-speaking neighbors who might happen in.

A superb embodiment of youth in the Mississippi Valley was Mary Kenney. Born in Keokuk, Iowa, of Irish immigrant parents, she had moved with her mother to a nearby brick tenement house, a distinguished three-story edifice in that region of drab one- and two-story frame cottages, in order to be a close neighbor to Hull-House and participate in its efforts to improve industrial conditions. Her volunteer work was with self-supporting, wage-earning young women whom she hoped to form into powerful, permanent trade unions. Tall, erect, broad-shouldered, with ruddy face and shining eyes, she carried hope and confidence whithersoever she went. Her rich Irish voice and friendly smile inspired men, women and children alike to do what she wished. Her undertakings prospered and throve.

A highly skilled printer, she was employed by a company which gave preference to union employees. As a numberer she earned fourteen dollars a week, supporting herself and her lovely old mother on that wage. Hers was the initiative in making of the brick tenement a cooperative house for working girls known as the Jane Club, a large part of the success of which was for many years due to the gentle sweetness of Mrs. Kenney, who mothered the cooperators as though they had been her own.

Although this was an entirely self-governed undertaking, Miss Addams was elected year after year an honorary director, having underwritten the experiment from the beginning. Later a friend of the Settlement, as a first step towards an endowment, paid for a building planned for the convenience of the cooperators, the rent going to Hull-House. This became a model for the Eleanor Clubs and countless other cooperative home clubs for self-supporting women scattered over the great city and growing with its growth during the past quarter century. . . .

In my first year at Hull-House, Carroll D. Wright, U.S. commissioner of commerce and labor, in charge of a federal study of the slums of great cities, entrusted me with the Chicago part of the enquiry. With a group of schedule men under my guidance, we canvassed a square mile extending from Hull-House on the west to State Street on the east, and several long blocks south. In this area we encountered people of eighteen nationalities.

Hull-House was, we soon discovered, surrounded in every direction by home-work carried on under the sweating system. From the age of eighteen months few children able to sit in high chairs at tables were safe from being required to pull basting threads. In the Hull-House kindergarten children used with pleasure blunt, coarse needles for sewing bright silk into perforated outlines of horses, dogs, cats, parrots and less known creatures on cards. They did this in the intervals between singing, modeling and playing active games. At home they used equally coarse sharp needles for sewing buttons on garments. The contrast was a hideously painful one to witness, especially when the children fell asleep at their work in the homes.

Out of this inquiry, amplified by Hull-House residents and other volunteers, grew the volume published under the title Hull-House Maps and Papers. One map showed the distribution of the polyglot peoples. Another exhibited their incomes (taken by permission from the federal schedules) indicated in colors, ranging from gold which meant twenty dollars or more total a week for a family, to black which was five dollars or less total family income. There was precious little gold and a superabundance of black on that income map!

The discoveries as to home work under the sweating system thus recorded and charted in 1892 (that first year of my residence) led to the appointment at the opening of the legislature of 1893, of a legislative commission of enquiry into employment of women and children in manufacture, for which Mary Kenney and I volunteered as guides. Because we knew our neighborhood, we could and did show the commissioners sights that few legislators had then beheld; among them unparalleled congestion in frame cottages which looked decent enough, though drab and uninviting, under their thick coats of soft coal soot. One member of the Commission would never enter any sweatshop, but stood in the street while the others went in, explaining that he had young children and feared to carry them some infection.

This Commission had been intended as a sop to labor and a sinecure, a protracted junket to Chicago, for a number of rural legislators. Our overwhelming hospitality and devotion to the thoroughness and success of their investigation, by personally conducted visits to sweatshops, though irksome in the extreme to the lawgivers, ended in a report so compendious, so readable, so surprising that they presented it with pride to the legislature. We had offered it to them under the modest title, Memorandum for Legislative Commission of 1893. They renamed it. The subject was a new one in Chicago. For the press the sweating system was that winter a sensation. No one was yet blasé.

With backing from labor, from Hull-House, from the Henry Demarest Lloyds and their numberless friends, the Commission and the report carried almost without opposition a bill applying to manufacture, and prescribing a maximum working day not to exceed eight hours for women, girls and children, together with child labor safeguards based on laws then existing in New York and Ohio, and quite advanced. There was a drastic requirement in the interest of the public health that tenement houses be searched for garments in process of manufacture, and goods found exposed in homes to contagious disease be destroyed on the spot. Owners of goods produced under the sweating system were required to furnish to the inspectors on demand complete lists of names and addresses of both contractors and home workers.

The bill created a state factory inspection department on which was conferred power, with regard to tenement-made goods found in infected premises, unique in this country in 1893. Illinois changed, at a single stride, from no legislation restricting working hours in manufacture for men, women or children, by day, by night, or by the week, to a maximum eight-hour-day for girls and for women of all ages, in all branches of manufacture. . . .

. . . When the new law took effect, and its usefulness depended upon the personnel pre-scribed in the text to enforce it, Governor Alt-geld offered the position of chief inspector to Mr. Lloyd, who declined it and recommended me. I was accordingly made chief state inspec-tor of factories, the first and so far as I know, the only woman to serve in that office in any state. . . .

My first effort to apply the penalty for em-ploying children below the age of sixteen years without the prescribed working paper, led me to the office of the district attorney for Cook County. This was a brisk young politician with no interest whatever in the new law and less in the fate of the persons for whose benefit it ex-isted. The evidence in the case I laid before him was complete. An eleven-year-old boy, ille-gally engaged to gild cheap picture frames by means of a poisonous fluid, had lost the use of his right arm, which was paralyzed. There was no compensation law and no prohibition of work in hazardous occupations. There was only a penalty of twenty dollars for employing a child without the required certificate. The young official looked at me with impudent sur-prise and said in a tone of astonishment:

"Are you calculating on *my* taking this case?"

I said: "I thought you were the district at-torney."

"Well," he said, "suppose I am. You bring me this evidence this week against some little two-by-six cheap picture-frame maker, and how do I know you won't bring me a suit against Marshall Field next week? Don't count on me. I'm overloaded. I wouldn't reach this case inside of two years, taking it in its order."

That day I registered as a student in the Law School of Northwestern University for the approaching fall term, and received in June, 1894, a degree from that University whose graduates were automatically empowered to practice before the Supreme Court of Illinois. Credit was given for my reading law with Fa-ther in Washington in 1882, my study in Zu-rich, and one year in the senior class in Chi-cago. The lectures were given in the evening and did not interfere with my administrative work.

Ida B. Wells, "Nobody . . . believes the old thread bare lie"

Ida B. Wells was born in Holly Springs, Mississippi, to enslaved parents on July 16, 1862. After the Civil War her parents remained in Holly Springs, where her father's work as

Excerpted from "The Reason Why the Colored American Is Not in the World's Columbian Exposition" (1893), "Southern Horrors: Lynch Law in All Its Phases" (1892), and "A Red Record: Tabulated Statistics and Alleged Cases of Lynchings in the United States, 1892–1893–1894" (1895) by Ida B. Wells-Barnett, in *Selected Works of Ida B. Wells-Barnett* edited by Trudier Harris (New York: Oxford University Press, 1991), pp. 17–19, 74–79, 145, and 226–32.

a carpenter gave them hopes of rising into the middle class. Ida was educated in schools supported by the American Missionary Association; by the age of 16 she was studying at Shaw University [later Rust College] in Holly Springs. When both parents and a younger sibling died in the yellow fever epidemic of 1878, sixteen-year-old Ida refused to let her sisters and brothers be divided among relatives. She supported them by her work as a schoolteacher for six years. In 1883 she moved to Memphis, where a thriving black community seemed to offer more opportunities.

Railroad facilities in an increasingly segregated South were allocated in overlapping categories of race, class, and gender. When twenty-two-year-old Ida B. Wells bought a ticket for the "ladies" car on a Chesapeake and Ohio train in May 1884 and refused to exchange her seat for one in the "colored" car, where men and women sat together, she was physically pulled off the train. She sued the railroad and won. But she could not collect the $500 damages she was awarded; the state supreme court reversed the decision in 1887. She could not pursue the case all the way to the U.S. Supreme Court, but another challenge to segregation on public conveyances—*Plessy* v. *Ferguson*—would be lost in 1896, when the Supreme Court ruled that "separate but equal" facilities were enough to satisfy the "equal protection" clause of the Fourteenth Amendment.

When Wells wrote an account of her experience for a black-owned Memphis newspaper, she was asked to write more; when, in 1891, she criticized inadequate black schools and segregated education, she was fired from her teaching job. After that she would support herself by journalism. She was an editor of the Memphis *Free Speech* when three friends, young black struggling businessmen, were lynched. Wells's editorials denouncing the lynching urged the black community to move out of Memphis, urged whites of good will to control mob rule, and denounced the claim that black men deserved lynching because they threatened white women's virtue, arguing that the real threat was the economic challenge a middle-class black community could pose to white competitors.

Wells's editorials put her in grave personal danger. She extended her editorials into powerful pamphlets and speeches publicizing the scale of mob violence in America. Between 1892 and 1895, years in which lynching was at its height but presidents and Congress refused to act and newspapers trivialized its horrors, Wells carried on a vigorous campaign demanding that the nation, which called itself democratic, cease encouraging mob rule. During this period she moved to Chicago and married Ferdinand Barnett; they had four children. For the rest of her life Wells-Barnett worked for social justice for African Americans. Among her Chicago activities were the organization of an activist women's club and the Negro Fellowship League, a settlement house for migrant men. She also worked for woman suffrage, founding the first black women's suffrage association in Illinois and directly challenging white women's organizations to accept black women as colleagues.

Among Ida B. Wells's most bitter writings was her pamphlet distributed at the Chicago Columbian Exposition of 1893, which contrasted the beauty of the nation's presentation of itself at the world's fair against the terror with which all black Americans daily lived. She was bitterly disappointed in the refusal of the largest women's reform organization of her time, the Women's Christian Temperance Union, and its long-term president, Frances Willard, to denounce lynching and to help create a multiracial women's movement against violence.

The selections that follow are taken from several pamphlets written between 1892 and 1895, the years of her most vigorous journalism. Most of the people lynched were men; most of the lynchers were men. On what grounds does Wells argue that white women were often complicit in lynching? Why does she think Frances Willard refused to support her attack?

Lynch law flourishes most largely in the states which foster the convict lease system, and is brought to bear mainly against the Negro. The first fifteen years of his freedom he was murdered by masked mobs for trying to vote. Public opinion having made lynching for that cause unpopular, a new reason is given to justify the murders of the past 15 years. The Negro was first charged with attempting to rule white people, and hundreds were murdered on that pretended supposition. He is now charged with assaulting or attempting to assault white women. This charge, as false as it is foul, robs us of the sympathy of the world and is blasting the race's good name.

The men who make these charges encourage or lead the mobs which do the lynching. They belong to the race which holds Negro life cheap, which owns the telegraph wires, newspapers, and all other communication with the outside world. They write the reports which justify lynching by painting the Negro as black as possible, and those reports are accepted by the press associations and the world without question or investigation. The mob spirit has increased with alarming frequency and violence. Over a thousand black men, women and children have been thus sacrificed the past ten years. Masks have long since been thrown aside and the lynchings of the present day take place in broad daylight. The sheriffs, police and state officials stand by and see the work well done. The coroner's jury is often formed among those who took part in the lynching and a verdict, "Death at the hands of parties unknown to the jury" is rendered. As the number of lynchings have increased, so has the cruelty and barbarism of the lynchers. Three human beings were burned alive in civilized America during the first six months of this year (1893). Over one hundred have been lynched in this half year. They were hanged, then cut, shot and burned.

The following table published by the Chicago *Tribune* January, 1892, is submitted for thoughtful consideration.

1882,	52	Negroes murdered by mobs			
1883,	39	"	"	"	"
1884,	53	"	"	"	"
1885,	77	"	"	"	"
1886,	73	"	"	"	"
1887,	70	"	"	"	"
1888,	72	"	"	"	"
1889,	95	"	"	"	"
1890,	100	"	"	"	"
1891,	169	"	"	"	"

Of this number

269	were	charged	with	rape.
253	"	"	"	murder.
44	"	"	"	robbery.
37	"	"	"	incendiarism.
4	"	"	"	burglary.
27	"	"	"	race prejudice.
13	"	"	"	quarreling with white men.
10	"	"	"	making threats.
7	"	"	"	rioting.
5	"	"	"	miscegenation.
32	"	"	"	no reasons given.

This table shows . . . that only one-third of nearly a thousand murdered black persons have been even charged with the crime of outrage. This crime is only so punished when white women accuse black men, which accusation is never proven. The same crime committed by Negroes against Negroes, or by white men against black women is ignored even in the law courts. . . .

. . . Will Lewis, an 18 year old Negro youth was lynched at Tullahoma, Tennessee, August, 1891, for being "drunk and saucy to white folks."

The women of the race have not escaped the fury of the mob. In Jackson, Tennessee, in the summer of 1886, a white woman died of poisoning. Her black cook was suspected, and as a box of rat poison was found in her room, she was hurried away to jail. When the mob had worked itself to the lynching pitch, she was dragged out of jail, every stitch of clothing torn from her body, and she was hung in the public courthouse square in sight of everybody. Jackson is one of the oldest towns in the State, and the State Supreme Court holds its sittings there; but no one was arrested for the deed—not even a protest was uttered. The husband of the poisoned woman has since died a raving maniac, and his ravings showed that he, and not the poor black cook, was the poisoner of his wife. . . .

. . . In 1892 there were 241 persons lynched. . . . Of this number 160 were of Negro descent. Four of them were lynched in New York, Ohio and Kansas; the remainder were murdered in the South. Five of this number were females. . . .

. . . A lynching equally as cold-blooded took place in Memphis, Tennessee, March 1892. Three young colored men in an altercation at their place of business, fired on white men in self-defense. They were imprisoned for three days, then taken out by the mob and horribly shot to death. Thomas Moss, Will Stewart and Calvin McDowell were energetic business men who had built up a flourishing grocery business. This business had prospered and that of a rival white grocer named Barrett had declined. Barrett led the attack on their grocery which resulted in the wounding of three white men. For this cause were three innocent men barbarously lynched, and their families left without protectors. Memphis is one of the leading cities of Tennessee, a town of seventy-five thousand inhabitants! No effort whatever was made to punish the murderers of these three men. It counted for nothing that the victims of this outrage were three of the best known young men of a population of thirty thousand colored people of Memphis. They were the officers of the company which conducted the grocery. Moss being the President, Stewart the Secretary of the Company and McDowell the Manager. Moss was in the Civil Service of the United States as letter carrier, and all three were men of splendid reputation for honesty, integrity and sobriety. But their murders, though well known, have never been indicted, were not even troubled with a preliminary examination.

[In an editorial for *Free Speech,* May 21, 1892, Wells wrote:]

["]Nobody in this section of the country believes the old thread bare lie that Negro men rape white women. If Southern white men are not careful, they will over-reach themselves and public sentiment will have a reaction; a conclusion will then be reached which will be very damaging to the moral reputation of their women."

"The Daily Commercial" [a white-owned newspaper] of Wednesday following, May 25th, contained the following . . . [editorial]:

"Those negroes who are attempting to make the lynching of individuals of their race a means for arousing the worst passions of their kind are playing with a dangerous sentiment. The negroes may as well understand that there is no mercy for the negro rapist and little patience with his defenders. A negro organ printed in this city, in a recent issue publishes the following atrocious paragraph: 'Nobody in this section of the country believes the old thread-bare lie that negro men rape white women. . . .

"The fact that a black scoundrel is allowed to live and utter such loathsome and repulsive calumnies is a volume of evidence as to the wonderful patience of Southern whites. But we have had enough of it.

"There are some things that the Southern white man will not tolerate, and the obscene intimations of the foregoing have brought the writer to the very outermost limit of public patience. We hope we have said enough.". . .

Acting upon this advice, the leading citizens met in the Cotton Exchange Building the same evening, and threats of lynching were freely indulged, not by the lawless element upon which the deviltry of the South is usually saddled—but by the leading business men, in the leading business centre. Mr. Fleming, the business manager and owning a half interest the "Free Speech," had to leave town to escape the mob, and was afterwards ordered not to return; letters and telegrams sent me in New York where I was spending my vacation advised me that bodily harm awaited my return. Creditors took possession of the office and sold the outfit, and the "Free Speech" was as if it had never been.

The editorial in question was prompted by the many inhuman and fiendish lynchings of Afro-Americans which have recently taken place and was meant as a warning. Eight lynched in one week and five of them charged with rape! The thinking public will not easily believe freedom and education more brutalizing than slavery, and the world knows that the crime of rape was unknown during four years of civil war, when the white women of the South were at the mercy of the race which is all at once charged with being a bestial one.

Since my business has been destroyed and I am an exile from home because of that editorial, the issue has been forced, and as the writer of it I feel that the race and the public generally should have a statement of the facts as they exist. They will serve at the same time as a defense for the Afro-American Samsons who suffer themselves to be betrayed by white Delilahs. . . .

. . . [T]here are many white women in the South who would marry colored men if such an act would not place them at once beyond the pale of society and within the clutches of the law. The miscegenation laws of the South only operate against the legitimate union of the races; they leave the white man free to seduce all the colored girls he can, but it is death to the colored man who yields to the force and advances of a similar attraction in white women. White men lynch the offending Afro-American, not because he is a despoiler of virtue, but because he succumbs to the smiles of white women.

. . . The Southern white man says that it is impossible for a voluntary alliance to exist between a white woman and a colored man, and therefore, the fact of an alliance is a proof of force. In numerous instances where colored men have been lynched on the charge of rape, it was positively known at the time of lynching, and indisputably proven after the victim's death, that the relationship sustained between the man and woman was voluntary and clandestine, and that in no court of law could even the charge of assault have been successfully maintained. . . .

MISS WILLARD'S ATTITUDE

. . . [I]n her Annual Address to the W. C. T. U. Convention at Cleveland, November 5, 1894, . . . Miss [Frances] Willard said:

> The zeal for her race of Miss Ida B. Wells, a bright young colored woman, has, it seems to me, clouded her perception. . . . It is my firm belief that in the statements made by Miss Wells concerning white women having taken the initiative in nameless acts between the races she has put an imputation upon half the white race in this country that is unjust, and, save in the rarest exceptional instances, wholly without foundation. . . .

[Wells:]

What I have said and what I now repeat—in answer to her first charge—is, that colored men have been lynched for assault upon women, when the facts were plain that the re-lationship between the victim lynched and the alleged victim of his assault was voluntary, clandestine and illicit. For that very reason we maintain, that, in every section of our land, the accused should have a fair, impartial trial, so that a man who is colored shall not be hanged for an offense, which, if he were white, would not be adjudged a crime. . . .

. . . It has been said that the Women's Christian Temperance Union, the most powerful organization of women in America, was misrepresented by me while I was in England. . . .

. . . When asked what concerted action had been taken by churches and great moral agencies in America to put down Lynch Law, I was compelled in truth to say that no such action had occurred, that pulpit, press and moral agencies in the main were silent and for reasons known to themselves, ignored the awful conditions which to the English people appeared so abhorrent. Then the question was asked what the great moral reformers like Miss Frances Willard and Mr. [Dwight] Moody had done to suppress Lynch Law and again I answered—nothing. That Mr. Moody had never said a word against lynching in any of his trips to the South, or in the North either, so far as was known, and that Miss Willard's only public utterance on the situation had condoned lynching and other unjust practices of the South against the Negro. When proof of these statements was demanded, I sent a letter containing a copy of the New York Voice, Oct. 23, 1890, in which appeared Miss Willard's own words of wholesale slander against the colored race and condonation of Southern white people's outrages against us. My letter in part reads as follows:

> But Miss Willard, the great temperance leader, went even further in putting the seal of her approval upon the southerners' method of dealing with the Negro. In October, 1890, the Women's Christian Temperance Union held its national meeting at Atlanta, Georgia. It was the first time in the history of the organization that it had gone south for a national meeting, and met the southerners in their own homes. They were welcomed with open arms. The governor of the state and the legislature gave special audiences in the halls of state legislation to the temperance workers. They set out to capture the northerners to their way of seeing things, and without troubling to hear the Negro side of the question, these temperance people accepted the white man's story of the problem

with which he had to deal. State organizers were appointed that year, who had gone through the southern states since then, but in obedience to southern prejudices have confined their work to white persons only....

... [T]he question was submitted to Miss Willard: "What do you think of the race problem ...?"

Said Miss Willard: "Now, as to the 'race problem' ... I am a true lover of the southern people—have spoken and worked in, perhaps, 200 of their towns and cities; have been taken into their love and confidence at scores of hospitable firesides ... Going South, a woman, a temperance woman, and a Northern temperance woman—three great barriers to their good will yonder—I was received by them with a confidence that was one of the most delightful surprises of my life. I think we have wronged the South, though we did not mean to do so. The reason was, in part, that we have irreparably wronged ourselves by putting no safeguards on the ballot box at the North that would sift out alien illiterates. They rule our cities today; the saloon is their palace, and the toddy stick their sceptre. It is not fair that they should vote, nor is it fair that a plantation Negro, who can neither read nor write, whose ideas are bounded by the fence of his own field and the price of his own mule, should be en-

trusted with the ballot. We ought to have put an educational test upon that ballot from the first. The Anglo-Saxon race will never submit to be dominated by the Negro so long as his altitude reaches no higher than the personal liberty of the saloon, and the power of appreciating the amount of liquor that a dollar will buy.... Would-be demagogues lead the colored people to destruction. Half-drunken white roughs murder them at the polls, or intimidate them so that they do not vote. But the better class of people must not be blamed for this.... The problem on their hands is immeasurable. The colored race multiplies like the locusts of Egypt. The grog-shop is its center of power. 'The safety of woman, of childhood, of the home, is menaced in a thousand localities at this moment, so that the men dare not go beyond the sight of their own rooftree.'["] ...

... Here we have Miss Willard's words in full, condoning fraud, violence, murder, at the ballot box; rapine, shooting, hanging and burning; for all these things are done and being done now by the Southern white people. She does not stop there, but goes a step further to aid them in blackening the good name of an entire race.... These utterances ... are to be found in full in the Voice of October 23, 1890, a temperance organ published at New York city.

BLANCHE WIESEN COOK
Female Support Networks and Political Activism: Lillian Wald, Crystal Eastman, Emma Goldman

---

In her passion to create a more just and humane society, Florence Kelley was typical of a remarkable generation of female reformers and radicals. As a divorcée (she had married in Zurich) and the mother of three children, she did not typify her many colleagues who, like Jane Addams, were single and childless. Writing about those women in the 1950s, historian Ray Ginger strongly suggested that exciting, useful, and important as their work might be, it was ultimately best understood as a compromise "that helped to reconcile so many brilliant women to an unmarried, childless, career-cloistered life."* This last phrase may tell us more about the assumptions of its author and popular attitudes of the 1950s than it does of the way Jane Addams viewed her own life. Did *she* think her career was a compromise, valuable primarily as consolation for a marriage and children she could not have?

The sensitive essay that follows reflects a very different interpretation of the choices Addams and her friends made. It is a particularly good example of the way in which historians' interpretations may be shaped by the cultural climate in which they write; virtually all of the material Blanche Wiesen Cook uses was available to Ray Ginger.

What does Cook mean by the phrase "female support networks"? To what extent does her interpretation extend the suggestion made in the last paragraph of Carroll Smith-Rosenberg's essay "The Female World of Love and Ritual" (part IIA)? How does Cook evoke private lives in order to point toward a more precise understanding of the ways in which these women built public careers?

In Vera Brittain's *Testament of Friendship*, the biography of her beloved friend Winifred Holtby, the British activist and author wrote that

> From the days of Homer the friendships of men have enjoyed glory and acclamation, but the friendships of women, in spite of Ruth and Naomi, have usually been not merely unsung, but mocked belittled and falsely interpreted. . . .[1]

Part of the problem is general in scope and involves a distorted vision of the historian's craft that is no longer operable. Historians of my generation were trained to believe that the proper study of our past should be limited to the activities of great men—the wars of kings, the hero's quest for power. We were taught that the personal was separate from the political and that emotions were irrelevant to history.

Recent history and the movements of the sixties, the decade of our professional maturing, have revealed the absurdity of that tradition. It has become clear that in history, no less than in life, our personal choices and the nature of our human relationships were and remain inseparable from our political, our public efforts. Once the personal impact of such confined historical perspective emerged, the need for revision became clear.

In my own work, ten years of work on the historical peace movement—studies that included such significant women as Lillian Wald,

Jane Addams, Crystal Eastman, and Emma Goldman—I had focused entirely on women's political contributions. I wrote about their programs for social justice and their opposition to international war. Nothing else. Whenever I came across a love letter by Lillian Wald, for example, I would note "love letter," and move on.

This paper is the result of a long overdue recognition that the personal is the political: that networks of love and support are crucial to our ability as women to work in a hostile world where we are not in fact expected to survive. And it comes out of a recognition that frequently the networks of love and support that enable politically and professionally active women to function independently and intensively consist largely of other women.

LILLIAN WALD, CRYSTAL EASTMAN, EMMA GOLDMAN, JANE ADDAMS

Beyond their commitment to economic and social change and their opposition to America's entrance into World War I, Lillian Wald, Crystal Eastman, Emma Goldman, and Jane Addams had very little in common. They are of different generations, represent contrary political solutions, and in private lives reflect a broad range of choice. Yet all four women expanded the narrow contours of women's role and all four left a legacy of struggle against poverty and discrimination.

*Ray Ginger, *Altgeld's America* (New York, 1958), p. 139.

Jane Addams and Lillian Wald were progressive social reformers. The most famous of the settlement-house crusaders, Wald created the Henry Street Settlement and Visiting Nurse Service in New York while Addams founded Hull-House in Chicago.

Crystal Eastman, a generation younger than Addams and Wald, was an attorney and journalist who investigated labor conditions and work accidents. In 1907 she authored New York State's first workman's compensation law, which became the model for most such laws in the United States. One of the three founders of Alice Paul's Congressional Union for suffrage, Eastman was a socialist and radical feminist who believed in "free love."

More outspoken and less respectful of authority than Addams and Wald, Eastman nevertheless worked closely with them in the peace movement. Wald was president of the American Union Against Militarism, the parent organization of the American Civil Liberties Union, and Eastman was its executive secretary. Addams was president of the Woman's Peace Party (renamed the Women's International League for Peace and Freedom), and Eastman, also one of its founders, was president of the New York branch. Their differences of temperament and tactics tell us much about the nature of the women's movement during the rapidly changing era of World War I.[2]

Emma Goldman was outside their company, but always in the vanguard of their activity. Addams, Wald, and Eastman worked to improve immigrant and labor conditions. Goldman, an anarchist immigrant worker, sought to recreate society. They worked within the law to modify it. Goldman worked without the law to replace it with anarchist principles of voluntary communism.

Goldman frequently visited the Nurses' Settlement on Henry Street and liked Lillian Wald and her co-workers, particularly Lavinia Dock, well enough. She thought them "women of ideals, capable of fine, generous deeds." But she disapproved of their work and feared that their activities created "snobbery among the very people they were trying to help." Although Jane Addams was influenced by anarchist writings, Goldman regarded her even more critically. She thought Addams an elitist snob.[3]

Emma Goldman's work with Crystal Eastman on behalf of birth control, the legalization of prostitution, and free speech in wartime was also dissatisfying. They agreed on more issues: but when Eastman and her circle were on the same picket line or in the same park distributing birth-control literature with Goldman and her allies, only Goldman's group would be arrested. That was the nature of class in America.

Wald, Eastman, and Addams worked to keep America out of war through the American Union Against Militarism (AUAM). They dined at the White House with Wilson and his advisors. They hired professional lobbyists to influence Congress. Goldman worked through the Anti-Militarist League and spoke throughout the United States on the capitalist nature of war and the cruelties of the class system. When she was arrested, the Civil Liberties Bureau of the AUAM defended her; but the members of the AUAM were not themselves arrested. Goldman's wartime activities resulted in her deportation. Wald and Addams received commendations from the government because, in addition to their anti-war work, they allowed their settlement houses to be used as conscription centers.[4]

As different as their political visions and choice of strategies were, Addams and Wald, Eastman and Goldman were dedicated to a future society that guaranteed economic security and the full development of individual potential for women and men on the basis of absolute equality. Reformists, socialist, anarchist, all four women made contributions toward progressive change that are today being dismantled. The playgrounds, parks, and school lunch facilities they built are falling apart all over America because of lack of funding and a callous disregard for the needs of our country's children. The free-speech and human-rights issues they heralded are today facing a reawakened backlash that features the needs of "national security" and a fundamentalist Christianity that seems more appropriate to the seventeenth century.

THE HISTORICAL DENIAL OF LESBIANISM

The vigor and strength of these four women, born daughters in a society that reared daughters to be dependent and servile, cannot be explained without an understanding of their support networks and the nature of their private lives. Their lifestyles varied as dramatically as did their public activities from the prescribed norm of "wife-mother in obedient service to husband-father" that their culture and their era valued above all.

Of the four women, only Emma Goldman relied predominantly on men for emotional sustenance and political support. Although she was close to many anarchist and radical women, there were few with whom she had intimate and lasting relations. The kind of communal and noncompetitive intimacy of the settlement houses or the younger feminist movement Crystal Eastman was associated with was never a feature of Goldman's life.

Yet throughout her life, Goldman wrote, she "longed for a friend of my own sex, a kindred spirit with whom I could share the innermost thoughts and feelings I could not express to men. . . . Instead of friendship from women I had met with much antagonism, petty envy and jealousy because men liked me." There were exceptions, and Goldman listed them in her autobiography. But basically, she concluded, "there was no personal, intimate point of contact."[5]

Like Goldman, Crystal Eastman was also surrounded by men who shared her work, her vision, and her commitment to social change. Unlike Goldman, she had a feminist support group as well. Her allies consisted of her husband (particularly her second husband, Walter Fuller), her brother Max, and the women who were her friends, many of them from childhood and Vassar until her early death in 1928. Eastman's comrades were the "new women" of Greenwich Village. Radical feminists and socialists, they considered men splendid lovers and friends, but they believed that women needed the more egalitarian support of other women. For Crystal Eastman and her associates this was not only an emotional choice, it was a political necessity.

Jane Addams and Lillian Wald were involved almost exclusively with women who remained throughout their lives a nurturing source of love and support. Henry Street and Hull House were staffed by their closest friends, who, night and day, made possible their unrelenting schedules.

In the past, historians tended to ignore the crucial role played by the networks of love and support that have been the very sources of strength that enabled political women to function. Women's friendships were obscured and

trivialized. Whether heterosexual or homosexual, the private lives of political women were declared beyond the acceptable boundaries of historical inquiry. As a result, much of our history and the facts that define our heritage have been removed from our consciousness. Homophobia, a bigotry that declares woman-loving women an evil before God or a mental disease or both, has served to erase the very aspects of our history that would have enabled us to deal healthfully with what has been for most lesbians an isolating and cruel experience. Homophobia has also erased a variety of role-models whose existence would tend to obliterate crude and dehumanizing stereotypes. . . .

This denial has persisted over time. The figures that serve as the frontispiece for Dolores Klaich's book *Woman + Woman* symbolize the problem. We see a sculpture, dated c. 200 B.C., of two women in a tender and erotic embrace. It has been called by the curators of the British Museum, "Women Gossiping."

Similarly, companionate women who have lived together all their adult lives have been branded "lonely spinsters." When their letters might reveal their love, their papers have often been rendered unavailable.* Interpreting Freud through a Victorian prism and thinking it enlightened, male historians have concluded that the settlement-house reformers were asexual women who sublimated their passionate energies into their work. Since they were not recognizably "dykes" on the order of Radclyffe Hall or Gertrude Stein, and they always functioned too successfully to be called "sick," the historical evidence was juggled to deny the meaning of their lifestyles altogether.

So, for example, William O'Neill can refer to the 40-year relationship between Mary Rozet Smith and Jane Addams as that of "spouse-surrogates" and then conclude: "Finally, one suspects the very qualities that led [Addams] to reject the family claim prevented her from experiencing the human reality that she celebrated in her writings and defied convention to encounter. She gave her time, money, and tal-

---

*See Dolores Klaich, *Woman + Woman: Attitudes Toward Lesbianism* (Morrow, 1974). The recently successful pressure to open the Mary E. Woolley Papers at Mt. Holyoke is a case in point. The famous college president lived with the chairwoman of the English Department, Jeannette Marks, for many years. They were lovers. When that fact was discovered their papers were closed.

ents entirely to the interests of the poor. . . . In a sense she rejected the personal claims upon her, . . . and remained largely untouched by the passionate currents that swirled around her. The crowning irony of Jane Addams's life, therefore, was that she compromised her intellect for the sake of human experiences which her nature prevented her from having. Life, as she meant the term, forever eluded her.'"[6]

Allen Davis observes a different phenomenon. "It would be easy to misunderstand," Davis writes, the friendship and affection between Jane Addams and her early companion Ellen Gates Starr. Quoting Gordon Haight, Davis concludes: " 'The Victorian conception of love between those of the same sex cannot be fairly understood by an age steeped in Freud—where they say only beautiful friendship, the modern reader suspects perversion.' '"[7]

It is important to understand the language here. We are being told that, since Jane Addams was a conventional lady with pearls, her intense "romantic attachments" to other women could not possibly by suspected of "perversion." As a result, the perfectly ordinary nature of women's differing sexual preferences has been denied expression. Without information and history, we have become ignorant of the range of our choices. Repression and conformity have been fostered and an entire generation of activist and passionate women branded by historians, on no evidence whatsoever, as "asexual."

Our prejudices are such that it has been considered less critical—kinder, even—to label a woman "asexual" rather than "lesbian." . . .

More sensitive than most male historians, Allen Davis notes that although the romantic words and the love letters "can be easily misinterpreted," what is important is "that many unmarried women drew warmth and strength from their supportive relationships with other women." But he concludes that "whether or not these women were actually lesbians is essentially irrelevant."[8]

If we lived in a society where individual choice and the diversity of our human rhythms were honored, the actuality of lesbianism would in fact be irrelevant. But we live in a society where children are taken away from lesbian mothers, where teachers are fired for bedroom activities, where in June 1976 the Supreme Court endorsed the imprisonment of consenting adults for homosexual relations, and where as I sit typing this paper—in June 1977—the radio annouces that Dade County, Florida, by a vote of 2:1, has supported Anita Bryant's hate campaign against homosexuals.

Such legal and social manifestations of bigotry and repression have been reinforced and are validated by the historical rejection and denial of diversity in general and of independent and alternative lifestyles among women in particular. It is the very conventionality of women like Jane Addams and Lillian Wald that is significant. Not until our society fully accepts as moral and ordinary the wide range of personal choice will differences be "essentially irrelevant."

As I think about Anita Bryant's campaign to "Save Our Children" from homosexuality, my thoughts turn to Lillian Wald, who insisted that every New York City public school should have a trained nurse in residence and who established free lunch programs for the city's school children. My thoughts then turn to Jane Addams, who, in an essay called, "Women, War and Babies," wrote:

> As women we are the custodians of the life of the ages and we will no longer consent to its reckless destruction. We are particularly charged with the future of childhood, the care of the helpless and the unfortunate, and we will no longer endure without protest that added burden of maimed and invalid men and poverty-stricken women and orphans which war places on us.
>
> We have builded by the patient drudgery of the past the basic foundations of the home and of peaceful industry; we will no longer endure that hoary evil which in an hour destroys or tolerate that denial of the sovereignty of reason and justice by which war and all that makes for war today render impotent the idealism of the race.[9]

And in the wake of the first mid-twentieth-century American vote to discriminate against an entire group of people,[10] my thoughts turn again to Lillian Wald and Jane Addams, who campaigned for the creation of the United States Children's Bureau. That bureau set up programs thoughout the United States to care for battered wives and battered children; it crusaded against child labor and for humane child care.[11] Yet Anita Bryant would demand that we save our children from Jane Addams if Anita Bryant knew that Jane Addams slept in the same house, in the same room, in the same bed with Mary Rozet Smith for 40 years. (And when they travelled, Addams even wired ahead to order a large double bed for their hotel room.)

Because difference arouses fear and condemnation, there are serious methodological problems involved in writing about women who, for political and economic reasons, kept their private lives as secret as possible. The advent of the homosexual "closet" at the end of the nineteenth century was not accidental. Oscar Wilde had, after all, been released from prison on 19 May 1897. In addition to the criminal stigma now attached to homosexuality, a sudden explosion of "scientific" publications on "sexual disorders" and "perversions" appeared at the turn of the century. Nancy Sahli, historian and archivist, reports that in the first series of 16 volumes of the *Index Catalogue of the Library of the Surgeon General's Office, U.S. Army*, covering the years 1740 to 1895, only one article ("A Case of Man-Impersonation") dealt specifically with lesbians. In the second series, published between 1896 and 1916, there were over 90 books and 566 articles listed that related to women's "perversions," "inversions," and "disorders."[12]

Secrecy is not a surprising response to this psychoanalytic assault. How then, male historians continually ask, do you know these women were lesbians? Even if we were to assume that Addams and Smith never in 40 years in the same bed touched each other, we can still argue that they were lesbians because they chose each other. Women who love women, who choose women to nurture and support and to create a living environment in which to work creatively and independently, are lesbians.

It may seem elementary to state here that lesbians cannot be defined simply as women who practice certain physical rites together. Unfortunately, the heterosexist image—and sometimes even the feminist image—of the lesbian is defined by sexual behavior alone, and sexual in the most limited sense. It therefore seems important to reiterate that physical love between women is one expression of a whole range of emotions and responses to each other that involves all the mysteries of our human nature. Women-related women feel attraction, yearning, and excitement with women. Nobody and no theory has yet explained why for some women, despite all cultural conditioning

and societal penalties, both intellectual and emotional excitement are aroused in response to women.

LILLIAN WALD

Besides, there *is* evidence of these women's lesbianism. Although Lillian Wald's two volumes of memoirs are about as personal as her entry in *Who's Who Among American Women*, her letters underscore the absurdity of a taxi conversation that Mabel Hyde Kittredge reported to Wald after a meeting at Henry Street:

> *First man:*   Those women are really lonely.
> *Second man:*   Why under the sun are they lonely?
> *First man:*   Any woman is lonely without a man.

Unlike Jane Addams, Lillian Wald seems not to have had one particular "great friend," and the chronology of the women in her life, with their comings and goings, is impossible to follow. There are gaps and surprises throughout over 150 boxes of correspondence. But all of Lillian Wald's companions appear to have been friends for life.

Wald's basic support group consisted of the long-term residents of Henry Street, Ysabella Waters, Anne Goodrich, Florence Kelley, Helene MacDowell, and Lavinia L. Dock. They worked together on all projects, lived and vacationed together for over 50 years, and, often in company with the women of Hull House, travelled together to Europe, Japan, Mexico, and the West Indies.

But the letters are insufficient to tell us the specifics of her life. There are turmoils that we will probably never know anything about—upheavals that result, for example, in a 10-year hiatus in Wald's correspondence with Lavinia Dock. This hiatus, combined with the fact that in November 1915, after 20 years, "Docky" moved out of the Henry Street Settlement and, in an icy and formal note of March 1916, even resigned from the Henry Street Corporation, remains unexplained. There is also the puzzling fact that Dock, the ardent suffragist, feminist and socialist, a pioneer of American nursing education and organization, appears to be R. L. Duffus' major source of information—beyond Wald herself—for his 1938 biography, *Lillian Wald: Neighbor and Crusader*. The first letter to appear in the collection after Dock's 1916 resignation is dated 1925 and implies that the two women have not had a long-term falling out at all:

> why-dear-I was imagining you radiating around the town telling about Mexico and here you are in the hospital just like any commonplace person—oh dear oh dear! . . . Dearest I would scrape up some money if you need—you have often done the same for me . . . and I am not telling anyone that you are ill and in the hospital for I know how you would dislike being thought just a mere mortal. . . .[13]

It is clear from another letter that Dock went to New York to be with Wald during her first operation. She wrote Wald's nurse that she was so relieved the tumor turned out to be benign that "for the first time my knees wobbled as I went down the steps to go to the train. . . ." The next week Dock wrote to Wald: "Dearest— I'm not sure whether to give you letters yet so I haven't written before and just send this line to tell you that you do your illnesses and recoveries in the same dazzling form and with the same vivacity and originality as all your other deeds; With Love/Ever yours/Docky."

Why then did Dock leave? Was there a personal reason? A new lover? An old anger? Or was it connected with the political differences that emerged between them in 1915 when Wald became more absorbed by antimilitarist activities and Dock, also a pacifist, joined the radical suffragist movement of Alice Paul's Congressional Union? All the evidence indicates that the only significant differences between these women at this time were political. Their lives were dedicated to work each regarded as just and right. When they disagreed so intensively that they could no longer support and nurture each other's activities, they temporarily parted. . . .

During the war, while Wald was meeting with President Wilson and being as conciliatory as possible on behalf of the peace movement, Dock and the militant suffragists were infuriating official Washington, getting themselves arrested, and generally aggravating the very people Wald was attempting to persuade—and for a different purpose.

Dock considered Paul's Congressional Union "fresh-young-glorious." She wrote to Paul in June 1915: "Pay no attention to criticism. Go right ahead with your splendid daring and resourcefulness of youth." Dock reacted furiously to criticism that the

Congressional Union's confrontational tactics not only harmed the suffrage movement but threatened the peace movement. And Lillian Wald was one of the leading critics of such tactics. On this issue they disagreed utterly. Dock was adamant: "And what is this terrible burden of responsibility and anxiety now resting on the American Men's President? Is it arising from anything women have done or are going to do? Not at all. . . . I can't see it—surely there could be no more appropriate moment for women to press forward with their demand for a voice—women—who are at this moment going on errands of peace—and who are being called a national menace for doing so—followed wherever he goes, by the demand which, so long as it remains unanswered shows a painful insincerity in those rounded and sonorous paragraphs on American ideals and American freedom that he utters so eloquently. . . ."[14]

Five months after this exchange, Lavinia Dock moved permanently out of her Henry Street home of 20 years. I have not yet found one correspondence between her and Wald that deals with the event. And all Wald says about Dock in *Windows on Henry Street* is that "Everyone admired her, none feared her, though she was sometimes very fierce in her denunciations. Reputed a man-hater, we knew her as a lover of mankind."

WALD'S OTHER SUPPORT NETWORK

There were two other categories of women close to Wald and the settlement. The first consisted of affluent women such as Irene and Alice Lewisohn and Rita Morgenthau. Younger than Wald, they admired her and regarded her as a maternal figure. She in turn nurtured their spirits, supported their ambitions, and provided them with sustaining and secure friendship. They, together with Wald's "friend of friends" Jacob Schiff, contributed tirelessly and abundantly to Henry Street. The Lewisohns founded the Neighborhood Playhouse and supported the famous music and dance education projects that continue to this day. They were also coworkers in the Woman's Peace Party and the American Union Against Militarism. On occasion they travelled with Wald. And they wrote numerous letters of affection and devotion to their dear "Lady Light." Alice Lewisohn frequently signed her letters "Your

Baby Alice." One letter from Irene, conveying love and gratitude after a trip the Lewisohn sisters took with Ysabella Waters and Wald, is replicated in the collection by scores of others:

> Why attempt to tell a clairvoyant all that is in one's mind? You know even better than I what those months of companionship with you and Sister Waters have meant. For way and beyond even the joys of our wanderings I have some memories that are holier by far than temples or graves or blossoms. A fireside romance and a moonlight night are among the treasures carefully guarded. . . . As an offering for such inspirations, I am making a special vow to be and to do. . . . Much of my heart to you!

Wald's closest friend among the younger nonresidents appears to have been Rita Wallach Morgenthau, who generally signed her letters with love from "Your Daughter," "Your Foolish Daughter," or "Your Spoiled Child." However much Wald may have spoiled her "adoptive daughters," the very fact of her nurturing presence helped establish the nature of their life's work; and their work focused on social change and the education, dance, and theatre programs they created. . . .[15]

All of Wald's friends and correspondents wrote of how she inspired them, fired their imaginations, and directed their lives to greater heights of consciousness and activity. Lavinia Dock referred to this quality in a letter to Duffus for his biography of Wald: "She believed absolutely in human nature and as a result the best of it was shown to her. People just naturally turned their best natures to her scrutiny and developed what she perceived in them, when it had been dormant and unseen in them before. I remember often being greatly impressed by this inner vision that she had. . . ."[16]

The last group of women involved with Wald and the settlement differed basically from the other two. Although they also served as residents or volunteered their time to Henry Street, they were "society women" perhaps more interested in Wald than in social change. Such long-term residents as Dock, Waters, and MacDowell, and Wald's younger friends, Morgenthau and the Lewisohns, supported Wald emotionally and politically and shared collectively in all her interests. The society women, however, attempted to possess or monopolize Wald, lamented that her activities kept her from them, and were finally rebuffed in what

must have been thoroughly specific terms. Generally they fell into that trap that Margaret Anderson defined so well: "In real love you want the other person's good. In romantic love you want the other person."[17]

Lillian Wald had structured her life to avoid becoming anybody's possession. While she did get involved in emotional enthusiasms, as soon as the woman involved sought to redirect her priorities Wald's enthusiasm evaporated.

The clearest representatives of the society group were Mabel Hyde Kittredge and Helen Arthur. Both women were rich "uptowners" who spent many years "downtown." Both were highly educated, hardworking, and demanding. Both devoted their time to good works, in large part because their friendship with Wald encouraged them to think politically, and not because social change was their life's commitment. But they were loyal. Kittredge, for example, evidently left Henry Street because Wald encouraged her to do so. Yet she continued to be involved in settlement activities, helped organize the free lunch program in public schools in 1908, and founded the Association of Practical Housekeeping Centers that operated as a subsidiary organization for many years.

To understand Lillian Wald fully, it is necessary to deal with her relationship with Mabel Hyde Kittredge. Kittredge's demands seem on occasion outrageous, and her biases are transparent. Yet it is clear that for a time Wald was not only smitten by this lady, but relied upon her for comfort and trusted her deeply.

A Park Avenue socialite who frequently played bridge whist all night after she had played in a golf tournament all day, Kittredge was the daughter of Reverend Abbot E. Kittredge of the prominent Madison Avenue Church. After she had lived at Henry Street for several years, she wrote to Wald on 28 April 1904 that she understood Wald's objections to what appears to have been a moment of flagrant ethnic bigotry: "I believe that I will never again say 'my people and *your* people.' It may be that even though I have no prejudice I have used words and expressions that have done something to keep the lines drawn between the two peoples. . . ."

Whatever her views, it appears that when Wald was troubled she turned for a time to Kittredge. In a long letter of tender assurance and sensible advice to Wald concerning a bereaved friend, Kittredge wrote:

> ... I seemed to hold you in my arms and whisper all this.... If you want me to stay all night tomorrow night just say so when you see me.... Please dont feel that I keep before me the signs of sorrow that you trusted me enough to let me see—of the things of Thursday evening that are consciously with me are first the fact that in a slight degree I can share with you the pain that you suffer. Then I can hear you say "I love you"—and again and again I can see in your eyes the strength, and the power and the truth that I love but the confidence in yourself not there. All this I have before me—never a thought of weakness because you dared to be human. Why dear I knew that you were human before Thursday night—I think though that our love never seemed quite so real a thing before then. Good night.

But after 1904 most of Kittredge's letters became competitive—Kittredge *vs.* humanity in their claims on Wald's attentions. Wald evidently reserved one night in the week for Kittredge and then occasionally cancelled their date, infuriating her friend:

> Just because you have reformed on Tuesday night—I havent got to give you entirely to humanity. I am human too and tonight I'd keep you up until—well later than Miss MacDowell would approve of—if I had you....

On a similar evening Kittredge wrote that she had just done two very sensible things, not telephoned to say good night and torn up a whiny letter:

> But what business has a great grown woman like myself to sit up in her nightclothes and write nothings.... I am getting altogether too close to you Lady Wald—or is it ... all those doors that you have pushed open for me? Half open-dear-just half open. And then I come up here and grow hungry for more knowledge.... And I feel that my strength ends and love you so.... I can feel your arms around me as you say I really must go.

When Wald cancelled a visit to Kittredge at Monmouth Beach, she wrote: "And so the verdict has gone forth—I can't have you.... But even you must want the ocean at times instead of Henry Street...."

Wald did want the ocean at times. More than that, she sought the relaxation and comfort of Kittredge's friendship. During a business trip that was evidently particularly hectic,

Wald wrote to Kittredge from Chattanooga that she looked forward to long, quiet, cosy evenings on the back porch. Kittredge replied that Wald's letter "was a real life-giving thing." But she no longer believed that Wald would actually make such free time possible and wrote: "When Lady Lillian is that cosy time to be? Miss MacDowell says not after midnight and your humanity world would not let me have you before. 'Long evenings on the back porch'—it sounds fine—and improbable...."

Eventually Kittredge's jealousy extended from humanity in general to the residents of Henry Street in particular:

> If you think that I wasnt damned mad today it is simply that I have inherited so much self-control and sweetness from my minister parent that the fact was hidden....
>
> There are times when to know that Miss Clark is standing behind one curtain, Miss MacDowell behind another and to feel an endless lot of people forever pressing the door or presenting unsigned papers makes me lack that perfect sympathy with "work for others" as exemplified by a settlement. No wonder I am called "one of your crushes." ... It is kiss and run or run without kissing—there really isnt time for anything else....

After what appears to have been for Kittredge a particularly difficult Christmas season, she gave up entirely the competition for Wald's affections:

> These may be "Merry" days but they starve one to death as far as any satisfaction in calm, every day loving and talking goes.... I would very much like to meet you on a desert island or a farm where the people cease from coming and the weary are at rest—will the day ever come? Or is that white ring, those long, lazy drives, the quiet and the yellow trees only a lost dream? And yet you love me—the plant on my table tells me so. The new coffee tray tells me so ... and a look that I see in your eyes makes me sure....

Refusing to participate, evidently for the first time, in Henry Street's Christmas festivities, Kittredge wrote that she was

> ... not loveless nor lonely, I am free and strong and alive and awfully happy—But someway as I think back over this year, I believe that I needed you—it may be as much as the others ... I know that it would be a loss out of my life if my thoughts of you, my love for you and my confidence in you were taken away—I don't believe they ever could be less than they are tonight....[18]

Judging from the letters, whatever gap the loss of Mabel Hyde Kittredge's friendship may have opened Wald seems to have filled by that summer. Wald vacationed through August and September 1906 with another society woman, Helen Arthur, an attorney and director of the research department of the Woman's Municipal League. Helen Arthur seems to have been more spontaneous and less complaining than Kittredge; and she had a sense of humor. . . .

Arthur was also more dependent on Wald, and in this relationship Wald's maternal aspects were more evident. She coaxed Arthur out of repeated depressions, encouraged her law practice, managed her finances, and kept her bankbook so that she would not overspend. This last made Arthur pout, especially during one Christmas season when she wrote to Wald that she tried to buy "exactly 28 presents for $10 worth of currency without visiting the 5 and 10 cent store which is, I regret to say, not on the Consumer's League list! If you were at 265 Henry Street—I should hold you up for my bankbook—What's vacation money compared to Christmas toys—Surely it is more blessed to give than to receive interest on deposits! Couldn't you be an old dear and let me rob it for a month? Please, mommy."

When Wald travelled, Arthur wrote long newsy letters about her law cases and activities; but they all concluded or began with a note of despair that her good mother had left her sad or naughty "son" all alone: "Such a strange feeling—no one to telephone me no 'Hello-de-e-ar' to listen for—Rainy horrid day outside and a lonesome atmosphere within. . . ." At another time she wrote "I am as near blue tonight as green can ever get and if I just had my nicest mommy to snuggle up to and talk it out straight for her son, I'd feel less like a disbarred judge. . . . Couldnt you write me a note and tell me—something?"

Eventually, Wald's busy schedule resulted in disappointments, cancelled dates, loneliness for Arthur, and what must have been for Wald familiar letters of discontent:

> Dearest, nothing could have relieved the gloom of this day except the presence of the one person her secretary notified me not to expect. . . . Now that I am being severely left alone—I have much time to spend in my own room—the walls of which formerly saw . . . me only from 2 until 7 a.m. . . . I've put you—the dear old you in your silver frame on my desk and close to me when I

write and I shoved my decanter and cigarette case to the other side—if I had you, the real you instead of one-ten-thousandth part of you I might shove the unworthy things way off—Summertime has spoiled the judge who longs to get back to your comfortable lap and the delights of kicking her pajammaed legs in peace and comfort instead of being solicitously hustled from your room at 10 o'clock. . . .

In another letter, Arthur, like so many others, expressed her desire to live up to Wald's expectations of her: "If only I could pull out of my easy ways—the pleasant vices which hinder me so. . . ." But her physical longing for Wald was equally powerful. The two combined to explain Wald's magnetism: "If only August and September, 1906 were all the year round for me, but their memories stay by and perhaps some day you'll be proud of your small judge. . . . I think so often of the hundreds who remember you with affection and of the tens who openly adore you and I appreciate a little what it all means and I'm grateful to think that your arms have been close around me and that you did once upon a time, kiss me goodnight and even good morning, and I am your lonesome little/Judge."

Arthur, more than many others, was genuinely mindful of Wald's time and her emotional needs. On 30 January 1907, she wrote that "Little by little there is being brought in upon me, the presumption of my love for you—the selfishness of its demands, the triviality of its complaints—and more slowly still, is coming the realization of what it ought to bring to you and what I mean it shall. . . ."[19]

Whatever special friend came or went in Lillian Wald's life, the women of Henry Street, the residents who called themselves her "steadies," were the mainstay of her support. The women in Wald's communal family served each other as well as society. There was nothing self-sacrificing about that community: It was a positive choice. For Wald it was the essential key to her life—and the only aspect of her personal life about which she wrote clearly. On the 40th anniversary of the settlement, Wald wrote: "I came with very little program of what could or should be done. I was perhaps conscious only of a passionate desire to have people, who had been separated and who for various causes were not likely to come together, know each other that they might sympathize and understand the problems and difficulties of each other. I made no sacrifices. My friend Mary Brewster [the first coworker at Henry Street] and I were engrossed in the edifice which was taking form and in which my friends and I might dwell together."[20]

Wald and her friends lived together for over 50 years. At the end, during long years of pain and poor health, she was surrounded by love and support. After her first operation, Mabel Hyde Kittredge wrote to Wald that "at least you must feel that this is a world full of friends and love and sympathy. I hope all the bread you ever cast upon any waters has come back fresh and lovely and so much as to be a surprise. . . ." On the morning of her death, Lillian Wald turned to her nurse and said, "I'm a very happy woman . . . because I've had so many people to love, and so many to love me."[21]

The letters in the Wald collections document only a fragment of her life, and they raise as many questions as they answer. Because we can never know the intimate details of people's lives if they are censored, withheld, or destroyed, we are confined to the details we have. But the details we have make it abundantly clear that Lillian Wald lived in a homosocial world that was also erotic. Her primary emotional needs and desires were fulfilled by women. She was woman-supported, woman-allied. Once that has been established, it becomes entirely unnecessary to pursue evidence of a specific variety of genital contact. Beyond a certain point, we get into fairly small-minded questions of technique. Since society's presumption of heterosexuality stops short of any inquiry as to what the husband and wife do atop their conjugal bed, it is only to indulge our prejudices that we demand "evidence" of lesbianism from conventional or famous women. Insistence on genital evidence as proof for a lesbian identity derives from a male model that has very little to do with the love, support, and sensuality that exist among women.

EMMA GOLDMAN

Emma Goldman wrote vividly about the difficulties faced by people who attempt to express themselves in harmony with their own nature. In a 1906 essay, "The Child and Its Enemies," she wrote that society employs all its forces to mould out of all our human differences a thing of dehumanized, patterned regularity: "Every institution . . . , the fam-

ily, the state, our moral codes, sees in every strong, beautiful uncompromising personality a deadly enemy." Every effort is made, from earliest infancy, "to cramp human emotion and originality of thought" in order to create "a patient work slave, professional automaton, tax-paying citizen, or righteous moralist." To that end, all the child's questions "are met with narrow, conventional, ridiculous replies mostly based on falsehoods." Thus uniformity and order, rather than "eternal change, thousandfold variation, continual innovation," have become the hallmarks of our culture.

The full implications of our brutally deforming institutions were clear to Goldman: "Since every effort in our educational life seems to be directed toward making of the child a being foreign to itself, it must of necessity produce individuals foreign to one another. . . ."[22]

Urged to deny the secrets within our natures and to reject the differences of others, we are taught to be fearful of ourselves and contemptuous of others. Separated from ourselves and isolated from each other, we are encouraged to huddle together for comfort under the socially acceptable banners of racism, sexism, classism, and homophobia. While people are called "human resources" in advanced industrial societies, we are discouraged from seeing the ways in which we are all connected. We are thus rendered powerless and immobilized by our prejudices. This is not an accident.

Ardent feminists and fiercely independent, Emma Goldman and Crystal Eastman depended on men for the comradeship and pleasure Lillian Wald and Jane Addams sought from women. Far more specific about their sexual orientations, Eastman and Goldman wrote about their private lives and their commitment to free love. They made it clear that they refused to be trapped by conventional or legal arrangements such as marriage.

Both were, in the larger sense, maternal women. Crystal Eastman considered the status of the unmarried mother and decided to get married largely for the sake of the two children she would have. Emma Goldman nurtured all her friends and associates. According to Kate Richards O'Hare, Emma Goldman while in prison was, above all, "the tender cosmic mother."

Contrary to popular notions of "free love" as promiscuous and amoral, Goldman's long-term relations with the men she loved—Sasha Berkman, Ed Brady, Ben Reitman, Max Baginsky, and Hippolyte Havel—were nurturing and tender on her part and devoted and supportive on theirs. They worked for her and cared for her. Ed Brady enabled her to go to Europe to study. Ben Reitman, her manager, served as her "advance man"; he raised money for *Mother Earth* and arranged her speaking tours. These men did not possess her, control her, dominate her, or expect from her more than she would give freely because she loved them as a free woman.

Free love, for Emma Goldman and Crystal Eastman meant simply love given freely to the lover of one's choice. Both rejected the notion that love was a limited commodity. They believed that it was an undefinable sentiment that expanded in proportion to the number of people who evoked it. Possession and jealousy were anathema to them. They rejected the notion that women were love objects to be married into the service and control of men.

Despite the clarity of their writings, their views were frequently misunderstood. The refusal of Eastman and Goldman to separate the personal from the political, their contempt for sham and hypocrisy, and their unfaltering openness about the most intimate subjects horrified their contemporaries. Among the social reformers with whom Crystal Eastman worked, she acquired a reputation as a reckless revolutionary. Her attitudes on free love and her frank affirmation of women's right to physical sexuality appeared hedonistic and horrible. A frequent contributor to feminist journals, her attitudes and behavior—notably her "affairs," divorce, and remarriage were perceived as scandalous. After years of leadership in the peace movement, as founder and president of the Woman's Peace Party of New York and as executive director of the American Union Against Militarism, she was blocked from attending the second meeting at the Hague in 1919 by a committee chaired by Jane Addams, specifically because of Eastman's radical socialism and her espousal of free love.[23]

The reaction of the older social-reform women such as Jane Addams to Crystal Eastman's lifestyle is not explained by the simple fact that the sword of bigotry is many-edged. The failure of Jane Addams and most social-reform women to analyze traditional assumptions about marriage and sexuality is another byproduct of the societal pressure that kept alternative lifestyles of any kind in the closet for so many years. The settlement-house women were supplicants to the rich on behalf of the poor. Steadfast about their priorities, they frequently made political decisions which were not in harmony with their lives and which locked them into a conservative public position regarding such issues as sexuality.

CRYSTAL EASTMAN'S VISION

Emma Goldman was adamant in her opposition to marriage, which she considered an economic arrangement. Since a wife's body is "capital to be exploited and manipulated, she came to look on success as the size of her husband's income." For Goldman marriage was the very antithesis of love. Why, she asked, should two people who love each other get married? Marriage is an arbitrary, mercenary, legal tie; while it does not bind, it fetters. Only love is free. Love for Emma was "the strongest and deepest element in all life; . . . love, the freest, the most powerful moulder of human destiny; how can such an all-compelling force be synonymous with that poor State-and-Church begotten weed, marriage?"[24]

Although Crystal Eastman shared Goldman's views on marriage, she married twice. But she was not limited or stifled in these marriages and arranged them to suit both her work and her emotional needs. According to one of her closest friends, Jeannette Lowe, Crystal Eastman was free—"You would not believe how free she was."[25] Vigorous and bold, Crystal Eastman discarded her first marriage with alacrity and then sought to revolutionize the institution. In her own life she extended the contours of marriage beyond recognition. During the first years of her second marriage, she and her husband, her brother Max, and several of their friends lived communally.

After the war she, her two children, and her husband, Walter Fuller, lived in England "under two roofs" as ordinary lovers. "He keeps a change of clothes and all the essentials for night and morning comfort at my house, as might a favorite and frequent guest." They phoned each other daily and often met for the theatre or dinner or at a friend's house. After the evening's entertainment they decided, "like married lovers," whether to part on the street or go home together. "Marriage under two roofs makes room for moods." As for the children, "without a scowling father around for breakfast, the entire day began cheerfully. . . ."

Crystal Eastman was, above all, a feminist. She considered the true feminist the most radical member of society. The true feminist, Eastman wrote, begins with the knowledge "that the vast majority of women as well as men are without property, and are of necessity bread and butter slaves under a system which allows the very sources of life to be privately owned by a few, and she counts herself a loyal soldier in the working-class army that is marching to overthrow that system." But she had no illusions about where men in that army placed women. "If we should graduate into communism tomorrow . . . man's attitude to his wife would not be changed." For Eastman, the creation of a communistic society based on sex equality was a task of the organized feminist movement.[26]

Unlike Emma Goldman, who lived almost exclusively among men, Crystal Eastman always had a feminist support group of considerable importance to her life. She was supported by women with whom she had deep and lasting relations: many of the ardent suffragists of the Congressional Union, her friends from Vassar who worked with her in the Woman's Peace Party of New York and who were part of her communal family in Greenwich Village. On several occasions she lived with one or more of these friends, and her experiences enabled her to write in "Now We Can Begin":

> Two business women can "make a home" together without either one being over-burdened or over-bored. It is because they both know how and both feel responsible.
>
> But it is a rare man who can marry one of them and continue the home-making partnership. Yet if there are no children, there is nothing essentially different in the combination. Two self-supporting adults decide to make a home together: if both are women it is a pleasant partnership, more fun than work; if one is a man, it is almost never a partnership—the woman simply adds running the home to her regular outside job. Unless she is very strong, it is too much for her, she gets tired and bitter over it, and finally perhaps gives up her outside work and condemns herself to the tiresome half-job of housekeeping for two.

Crystal Eastman evidently solved that problem for herself by spending her summers in the south of France with Jeannette Lowe and their children, leaving her husband under his separate roof and in his separate country.

Throughout the postwar years Eastman had planned to write a book about women. But in 1928, one year after returning to New York to look for new work, she died of a kidney ailment. She was 47 years old, and her death came as a shock to her friends. Claude McKay wrote: "Crystal Eastman was a great-hearted woman whose life was big with primitive and exceptional gestures. She never wrote that Book of Woman which was imprinted on her mind. She was poor, and fettered with a family. She had a grand idea for a group of us to go off to write in some quiet corner of the world, where living was cheap and easy. But it couldn't be realized. And so life was cheated of one contribution about women that no other woman could write."[27]

EMMA GOLDMAN AND WOMEN

Emma Goldman's lack of a feminist support group did not affect her adversely until the postwar years. Before and during the war she was surrounded by her anarchist comrades and Ben Reitman. But even then her friends found Reitman distasteful and tended to admonish Goldman for her choice of lovers. Sasha Beckman in particular hated Reitman because he was not dedicated to the revolution, anarchism, or even social change. Margaret Anderson thought that the "fantastic" Dr. Reitman was not "so bad if you could hastily drop all your ideas as to how human beings should look and act. . . ." But Emma loved him and wrote that he "gave without measure or restraint. His best years, his tremendous zest for work, he had devoted to me. It is not unusual for a woman to do as much for the man she loves. Thousands of my sex had sacrificed their own talents and ambitions for the sake of the man. But few men had done so for women. Ben was one of the few; he had dedicated himself completely to my interests."[28] . . .

. . . Before the war Goldman idealized heterosexual relations. In many of her writings she scorned the bourgeois American feminists whose "narrow puritanical vision banished man as a disturber and doubtful character out of their emotional life. . . ." In a March 1906 essay, "The Tragedy of Woman's Emancipation," she argued that the "greatest shortcoming" of the feminist movement was "its narrow respectabilities which produce an emptiness in woman's soul that will not let her drink from the fountain of life." In September 1915 she published a similar editorial in *Mother Earth* by one "R.A.P.," who argued that "American feminists are the exponents of a new slavery," which denied sexual activity, encouraged inhibition, and crusaded against the "sexual victimization of virtuous females by some low, vulgar male." R.A.P. judged the bourgeois feminist movement classist and hypocritical and of "no interest except as an amusing and typical instance of feminine intellectual homosexuality."[29]

This is not to imply that Emma Goldman was homophobic in any intellectual or traditional sense. On the contrary, she was the only woman in America who defended homosexuality in general and the [rights] of Oscar Wilde in particular. Although she was absolute about a person's right to sexual choice, she felt a profound ambivalence about lesbianism as a lifestyle. She believed that "the body, in all its splendid sensuality, had to be reclaimed from the repressive hands of the prudes and the philistines." When she was criticized by her comrades for dealing with such "unnatural themes as homosexuality," thereby increasing the difficulties of the already misunderstood anarchist movement, she persisted. "I minded the censors of my own ranks as little as I did those in the enemy's camp." Censorship from her comrades had, she wrote, "the same effect on me as police persecution; it made me . . . more determined to plead for every victim, be it of social wrong or of moral prejudice."[30]

There is even some evidence that Goldman may have experimented with a woman herself. The 1912 letters of an anarchist worker, Almeda Sperry, to Goldman are very one-sided. They consist in part of affirmations of passionate love by Sperry and apparent rebuffs by Goldman. These do not deter Sperry, who evidently luxuriated for a time in a state of unrequited yearning: "God how I dream of you! You say that you would like to have me near you always if you were a man, or if you felt as I do. I would not if I could. . . ." In response to Goldman's queries about Sperry's feelings toward men, she replies: "If you mean have I ever loved a man I will frankly say that I never *saw* a man. No, I have never deeply loved any man." Sperry was, however, married, and several letters refer to her affection for her husband.

Then, in the summer of 1912, the letters take a different turn. Sperry thanks Goldman for addressing her with terms of endearment, and . . . she tells Goldman to know, just before she sleeps, that "I kiss your body with biting kisses—I inhale the sweet pungent odor of you and you plead with me for relief." A month later Sperry refers to the week they spent together after all in the country:

> Dearest, I have been flitting about from one thing to another . . . to quell my terrible longing for you . . . I am . . . seized with a fire that races over my body in recurrent waves. My last thoughts at night are of you . . . and that hellish alarm clock is losing some of its terrors for me for my first waking thoughts are of you.
>
> Dear, that day you were so kind to me and afterwards took me in your arms, your beautiful throat, that I kissed with a reverent tenderness. . . .
>
> Do you know, sweet cherry-blossom, that my week with you has filled me with such an energy, such an eagerness to become worthy of your friendship, that I feel that I must either use my intensity toward living up to my best self or ending it all quickly in one last, grand debauch. . . .
>
> How I wish I [were] with you on the farm! You are so sweet in the mornings—your eyes are like violets and you seem to forget, for a time, the sorrows of the world. And your bosom—ah, your sweet bosom, unconfined.[31]

There is nothing simple about Goldman's attitude toward lesbianism. She never refers to Almeda Sperry, and it is impossible to know the significance of this correspondence in her life. Her absolute commitment to personal liberty and her total respect for individual choice prompted Magnus Hirschfeld, a leading homosexual rights advocate in Germany and the founder of the Humanitarian Committee, organized in 1897, to write that Goldman was the "only human being of importance in America to carry the issue of homosexual love to the broadest layers of the public."[32]

But in a long article in the 1923 Yearbook of Hirschfeld's committee, Goldman criticizes an earlier article on Louise Michel in puzzling terms. Goldman reaffirms her political commitment to free sexual choice and affirms her disinterest in "protecting" Louise Michel from the charge of lesbianism. "Louise Michel's service to humanity and her great work of social liberation are such that they can be neither enlarged nor reduced, whatever her sexual habits were." Then follows a long tirade against minorities who claim for themselves all the earth's significant people, and a longer analysis of why it would be "nonsensical" to assume that Louise Michel was a lesbian. In an ultimately vague and paradoxical paragraph, Goldman concludes: "In short, Louise Michel was a complete woman, free of all the prejudices and traditions which for centuries held women in chains and degraded them to household slaves and objects of sexual lust. The new woman celebrated her resurrection in the figure of Louise, the woman capable of heroic deeds but one who remains a woman in her passion and in her love."[33]

It appears that, in Goldman's mind, to be a lesbian was an absolute right, and nothing nasty about it. But it was also to be rendered somehow less a woman.

EMMA GOLDMAN IN EXILE

In the long years of Emma Goldman's exile, years made lonelier by her political isolation, she wrote a series of letters that explored the difficulties and the pain of being a free and independent woman without a support group that provided emotional nurturance as well as a shared vision of the work to be done. After two years of disappointment in Soviet Russia, Goldman travelled back and forth between England, France, and Germany, seeking to rebuild her shattered life and attempting to convince her friends on the left that her critical analysis of the Soviet experiment was correct. In these letters she revealed the toll on her spirit taken by her personal loneliness and her political isolation. Also revealed is the brutal double standard to which even advanced women in progressive anarchist circles are subjected if their friendships are limited to men. On 28 May 1925 she wrote to Berkman:

> I agree with you that both men and women need some person who really cares. The woman needs it more and finds it impossible to meet anyone when she has reached a certain age. That is her tragedy.... I think in the case of one who gave out so much in her life, it is doubly tragic not to have anyone, to really be quite alone.... I am consumed by longing for love and affection for some human being of my own.[34] ...

As Goldman looked back over her life while in exile, even the good times seemed bit-

ter. In a heartbreaking letter to Sasha she deals with the sexist double standard of her closest comrades:

> Where did you ever get the idea that I suspected you of being jealous of Ben in any sexual sense.... What I did suspect—more than that what I knew—was that you are a prig who constantly worries about what the comrades will say and how it will affect the movement when you yourself lived your life to suit yourself, I mean as far as women are concerned. It was painful to me, at the time, as it has been on many other occasions, to see you fly the movement in the face a hundred times and then condemn me for doing the same.... Do I mean to deny Ben's faults? Of course not, my dear.... I knew Ben inside and out two weeks after we went on tour; I not only knew but loathed his sensational ways, his bombast, his braggadocio, and his promiscuity, which lacked the least sense of selection. But above all that there was something large, primitive, unpremeditated, and simple about Ben which had terrific charm. Had you and the other friends concerned in my salvation recognized this ... instead of writing to the university to find out about his medical degree (which the boy never could forget).... Ben would not have become a renegade.... The trouble with you was ... as with all our comrades, you are a puritan at heart....
>
> I have been too long in the movement not to know how narrow and moral it is, how unforgiving and lacking in understanding toward everyone different from them.... You will repeat your objections to Ben were because ... "he did not belong in our ranks." All right, but what were your objections to Arthur Swenson? He never was in our ranks. Why did you treat him like a dog after he came to Berlin? Why did you fail to understand the terrific turmoil the boy created in my being? ... Of course it is nonsense to say that the attitude of men and women in their love to younger people is the same.... It is nothing of the kind.... Hundreds of men marry women much younger than themselves; they have circles of friends; they are accepted by the world. Everyone objects, resents, in fact dislikes a woman who lives with a younger man; they think her a goddamned fool; no doubt she is that, but it is not the business or concern of friends to make her look and feel like a fool....

In another letter Emma tried to console Sasha after the sudden departure of his former lover Fitzie. Secretary of the Provincetown Players, Eleanor Fitzgerald had been Sasha's companion until his arrest during World War I. In 1928 she arrived at St. Tropez to be with Djuna Barnes and to visit Berkman. Although the events are unclear, Goldman's letters of explanation for Fitzie's behavior over several years formulate her own reflections on the struggle of women to be liberated: "Here we have been worrying about who should meet Fitzie, then that crazy Djuna kidnaps her. Damned fool. . . . Really, the Lesbians are a crazy lot. Their antagonism to the male is almost a disease with them. I simply cant bear such narrowness. . . ."

By implication, Goldman denied that Fitzie's affair with Barnes might have been a positive choice. To understand Fitzie, Goldman wrote, it was necessary to understand that all her relations with men had been disastrous. Her tragedy "is the tragedy of all emancipated women, myself included. We are still rooted in the old soil, though our visions are of the future and our desire is to be free and independent. . . . It is a longing for fulfillment which very few modern women find because most men too are rooted in the old tradition. They too want the woman as wife and mother in the old sense, and the new medium has not yet been devised, I mean the way of being wife, mother, friend and yet retain one's complete freedom. Will it ever? . . ."[35]

Emma Goldman doubted it. Ultimately she even doubted that women could enjoy real satisfaction even physically with men. After a lifetime of celebrating woman's absolute right to full sexual pleasure, there is something intensively poignant about a letter to Dr. Samuel D. Schmalhausen in which she implied that all through the years the pleasure she received from the men she loved had been inadequate. Schmalhausen had written *Woman's Coming of Age,* and on 26 January 1935 Goldman wrote that ever since her "intellectual awakening" she had had the same thought. Namely,

> that the sex of the man lasts from the moment of its dominant motivation to its climax. After that the brute has done of his share. The brute can go to sleep. Not so the woman. The climax of the embrace, far from leaving her relaxed or stupefied as it does the man, raises all her sensibilities to the highest pitch. All her yearning for love, affection, tenderness becomes more vibrant and carries her to ecstatic heights. At that moment she needs the understanding of and communion with her mate perhaps more than the physical. But the brute is asleep and she remains in her own world far removed from him. I know this from my personal experience and experiences of scores of

women who have talked freely with me. I am certain that the cause for the conflict between the sexes which continues to exist regardless of woman's emancipation is due to the differences in quality of the sex embrace. Perhaps it will always be that way. Certainly I find very few men who have the same need, or who know how to minister that of the woman's. Naturally, I felt elated to read your analysis . . . which actually expresses what I have felt and voiced for well nigh 45 years. . . .[36]

Despite anger, isolation, and disappointment, Emma Goldman remained active and enthusiastic to the end of her life. After her despondent years in London, several friends presented her with a cottage on St. Tropez: "Georgette LeBlanc, Margaret Anderson, Peggy Guggenheim, Lawrence Vail and many others came for an hour or a day to discuss serious matters or in jolly company." Life in St. Tropez, Goldman wrote, restored her health and her "fighting spirit." It was there that she decided to write her memoirs, tour Canada, and cable friends in the United States for loans to continue her important work, now focused mainly in Spain.[37] But she never found the one great friend who could understand her empty places, and she never acknowledged the value of feminist alliances for active women whose very activity, depths of passion, and committed independence alienated them from the men with whom they worked and struggled.

Lillian Wald, Jane Addams, Crystal Eastman, and Emma Goldman all had visions of social change and economic justice that, 60 years later, we have yet to see fulfilled. They lived as they did at a time when, as Vera Brittain noted, women were programmed to monopolize their husbands, dominate their sons, possess their daughters, and make fetishes of their kitchens and shrines of their homes. These four women present a range of choices and affinities that were charged with courage, experiment, fulfillment, and intensity. In viewing women of the past it has been a common practice to assume that feminists, spinsters, woman-related women, and most women engaged in social reform were asexual, self-denying, and puritanical, sublimating their sexual passions in their work. Even today the myth persists that women unattached to men are lonely, bitter, and without community; that women who are political activists working with men can function effectively without a support network of women. In the lives of Wald, Addams, and Eastman, we see clearly the energy and strength they received from feminist networks. Crystal Eastman's feminism drew upon and allowed her to appreciate the woman-identification of her lesbian friends. On the other hand, despite Emma Goldman's intellectual and political identification with the oppressed, including women and homosexuals, she never did understand or identify with the feminist movement, and she never did find a friend of her own sex, "a kindred spirit with whom she could share her innermost thoughts and feelings."

For Jane Addams and Lillian Wald, service to humanity and leadership in public life were constantly refueled by their female support communities and by personal relationships with women who gave them passionate loyalty and love. The power of communities of independent women, and of the love between individual women, expressed not only sensually but in a range of ways, is part of the history that has been taken from us by heterosexist culture. To recognize this history is to recognize our own personal forces of energy and courage and the power to change.

NOTES

1. See Vera Brittain, *Testament of Friendship: The Story of Winifred Holtby* (Macmillan, 1947), p. 2. . . .

2. See Blanche Wiesen Cook, "Democracy in Wartime: Antimilitarism in England and the United States, 1914–1918," *American Studies* (Spring 1972), reprinted in Charles Chatfield, ed., *Peace Movements in America* (Schocken Books, 1973), pp. 39–57; Cook, "Woodrow Wilson and the Antimilitarists, 1914–1918" (unpublished Ph.D. diss., The Johns Hopkins University, 1970); and Cook, ed., *Toward the Great Change: Crystal and Max Eastman on Feminism, Antimilitarism and Revolution* (Garland Publishing, 1976).

3. Emma Goldman, *Living My Life*, Vol. I (Dover Reprint, 1970), pp. 160, 375, passim.

4. Blanche Wiesen Cook, "The Woman's Peace Party: Collaboration and Non-Cooperation," *Peace and Change* (Fall 1972), pp. 36 ff.

5. Goldman, *Living My Life*, pp. 157–160.

6. William O'Neill, *Everyone Was Brave: Feminism in America* (Quadrangle, 1969), p. 120.

7. Allen Davis, *American Heroine: The Life and Legend of Jane Addams* (Oxford University Press, 1973), p. 46.

8. Davis, *American Heroine*, p. 91.

9. Jane Addams, "Women, War, and Babies" (31 July 1915), reprinted in Allen Davis, ed., *Jane Addams on Peace, War and International Understanding, 1895–1932* (Garland Publishing, 1976).

10. George Will, "How Far Out of the Closet?" *Newsweek*, 3 May 1977, p. 92.

11. For information about the U.S. Children's Bureau, see Nancy P. Weiss, "The Children's Bureau: A Case Study of Women's Voluntary Networks," an unpublished paper presented at the Berkshire Conference on the History of Women, 10 June 1976, Bryn Mawr.

12. See Nancy Sahli's unpublished paper, "Changing Patterns of Sexuality and Female Interaction in Nineteenth-Century America," presented at the Berkshire Conference, 11 June 1976, pp. 12–13.

13. Lillian Wald's correspondence is divided between the New York Public Library and Columbia University. See Dock to Wald, 27 Apr. 1925; 10 May 1925; 10 Mar. 1916, Columbia University.

14. Lavinia Dock's correspondence with the Congressional Union is in the Woman's Party Papers, Library of Congress. See especially Dock to Paul, 8 Sept. 1914, tray 1, box 6; 28 June 1915, New York, tray 1, box 6; Dock to C.U., 22 May 1915, tray 1, box 5.

15. Irene Lewisohn to Dear Lady Light, n.d., Wald Papers, Columbia. This probably refers to a round-the-world trip that lasted six months (1910). . . .

16. Dock to Duffus, 28 May 1936, in R. L. Duffus, *Lillian Wald* (Macmillan, 1938), pp. 346–347.

17. Margaret Anderson, *The Fiery Fountains* (Horizon Press, 1969 [1951]), p. 84.

18. Mabel Hyde Kittredge to Wald, 28 April 1904; all Kittredge letters, Wald Papers, Columbia.

19. Helen Arthur's correspondence with Wald is generally undated between 1906 and 1908. Ibid.

20. Wald quoted in Duffus, *Lillian Wald*, p. 55.

21. Kittredge to Wald, 11 May 1925, Wald Papers, Columbia; George V. Alger, Oral History, Columbia, pp. 251–52; Allen Reznick, "Lillian Wald: The Years at Henry Street" (unpublished Ph.D. diss., University of Wisconsin, 1973), p. ii.

22. Emma Goldman, "The Child and Its Enemies," *Mother Earth* (April 1906):107–9.

23. A long correspondence to block Eastman's participation at The Hague may be found in the Balch and Addams Papers at the Swarthmore College Peace Collection; see especially Lucia Ames Mead to Emily Green Balch, Balch Papers. . . .

24. See Richard Drinnon, *Rebel in Paradise: A Biography of Emma Goldman* (University of Chicago Press, 1961), pp. 149–51; and Goldman, "Marriage and Love," in Alix Shulman, ed., *Red Emma Speaks* (Vintage, 1972), pp. 158 ff. . . .

25. Jeannette Lowe to author, 27 Mar. 1973.

26. Crystal Eastman, "Marriage under Two Roofs" (1923); "Feminists Must Fight" (1924); and "Now We Can Begin" (1920)—all reprinted in Cook, *Toward the Great Change*.

27. Claude McKay, *A Long Way from Home* (Harcourt, 1970 [1935]), pp. 154–55.

28. Margaret Anderson, *My Thirty Years' War* (Corici, Friede, 1930), pp. 54–55; Goldman, *Living My Life*, Vol. II, p. 694.

29. Goldman, "The Tragedy of Woman's Emancipation," *Mother Earth* (No. 3, 1906):9–18 (reprinted

in *Red Emma Speaks*); R.A.P., "Feminism in America," *Mother Earth* (Feb. 1915), pp. 392–94.

30. Goldman, *Living My Life*, Vol. 1, p. 555.

31. See Sperry to Goldman in Jonathan Katz, *Gay American History* (Crowell, 1976), pp. 523–30.

32. John Lauritsen and David Thorstad, *The Early Homosexual Rights Movement, 1864–1935* (Times Change Press, 1974), pp. 36–37.

33. Katz, *Gay History*, pp. 376–80.

34. Richard and Anna Maria Drinnon, eds., *Nowhere At Home: Letters From Exile of Emma Goldman and Alexander Berkman* (Schocken Books, 1975), p. 128.

35. Ibid., pp. 132–33, p. 86.

36. Goldman to Dr. Samuel Schmulhausen, 26 Jan. 1935, Goldman Papers, Labadie Collection, University of Michigan.

37. Goldman, *Living My Life*, Vol. II, pp. 985–86; see also Goldman to Margaret Anderson, ed., *The Little Review Anthology* (Horizon Press, 1953), p. 363.

SUZANNE LEBSOCK

Woman Suffrage and White Supremacy: A Virginia Case Study

Enfranchisement of women is part of many histories: the history of suffrage, of Progressivism, of mass movements, of race relations, and of women. It is a story bound up with defense of privilege and fear of reform. Antisuffragists included in their number women as well as men. Yet despite conservative attacks on suffrage as a major innovation that would undermine traditional gender boundaries by permitting women to enter the male world of politics, some historians have accused suffragists of diverting attention from women's "real" problems to the ritual of casting a ballot. Because suffrage did not prove to be the emancipatory tool advocates of the ballot had hoped, such an interpretation is understandable.

Yet we should not ignore the sharp challenge to tradition that occurred when women, by the millions, mobilized to demand the ballot both as an equal right and as an instrument of change. If women could do little about their subordinate status within the family in the nineteenth century, they could, as historian Ellen Du Bois has pointed out, *bypass* the family. They could focus on the public sector, making their demands not indirectly as an extension of their roles as wives and mothers, but directly as individuals, as citizens, and as voters. Winning the vote was essential to establishing the principle that women's rights were "public" and that citizenship was not limited by sex.

Suffrage, however, was never only about whether women should vote; it was also about which people should vote. Northern suffragists had to deal with fears that giving the ballot to women would enlarge the immigrant vote. Ida B. Wells's bitter exchange with Frances Willard [p. 303] suggests something of the challenge southern suffragists faced. They were asking for the expansion of the ballot at precisely the time southern

Excerpted from "Woman Suffrage and White Supremacy: A Virginia Case Study" by Suzanne Lebsock, in *Visible Women: New Essays in American Activism*, edited by Nancy Hewitt and Suzanne Lebsock (Urbana: University of Illinois Press, 1993), pp. 62–100. Copyright © by the author and University of Illinois Press. Condensed and reprinted by permission of University of Illinois Press. Notes have been edited and renumbered.

politicians were restricting it in the interests of white supremacy. How Virginia suffragists responded to this challenge is the focus of the following essay.

> I think that as women we should be most prayerfully careful lest, in the future, women—whether coloured women or white women who are merely poor—should be able to say that we had betrayed their interests and excluded them from freedom.
>
> Mary Johnston to Lila Meade Valentine, 1913

This letter from the novelist Mary Johnston to the president of Virginia's Equal Suffrage League was remarkable.[1] It was remarkable in its attention to poor women and women of color, an intriguing contrast to the gross and overt racism that prevailed among white Virginians—and to the bigotry and elitism we have come to expect from white southern suffragists. Even more remarkable was the way in which race and class figured in Johnston's sense of history in the making. Johnston foresaw a day when privileged suffragists would be harshly judged if they sold out black women and the white poor to press their own claims to the vote.

Mary Johnston proved to be right, although not specifically for Virginia. Virginia suffragists have escaped judgment because their existence has simply been erased. Despite the fact that contemporary newspapers were filled with suffrage news, editorials, debates, and jokes, and despite the rich archival sources that have been available for decades, no study of the Virginia woman suffrage movement has ever been published.[2] Nor does woman suffrage appear prominently in the standard Virginia political histories of the period.

The woman suffrage movement at large, meanwhile, has come in for a good deal of criticism, both for the white leaders' shabby treatment of African American suffragists and for the willingness of many prominent white suffragists to exploit racist arguments when it seemed advantageous to do so. Suffragists from all parts of the country were implicated in such behavior.[3] The South, however, has landed in its usual spot, with southern suffragists assigned primary responsibility for the movement's racist thought and policy. Indeed, the southern woman suffrage movement has achieved its greatest fame as a purveyor of white supremacy. . . .

But . . . [w]hat happens when we move to the context in which the southern suffragists actually operated, the arena of local and state politics? And what happens when we open the stage to a wider range of southern characters?

The plot, first of all, gets thicker . . . [H]ow important were white supremacist arguments relative to other kinds? . . . To the degree that white supremacy did inform the woman suffrage debates, who was responsible for it, and what sort of damage did it do? . . . [H]ow might the evidence generated by these debates advance the larger project of understanding of how gender and race have operated simultaneously in our past?

As befits a complicated story, the answers will make more sense after the evidence is put forward, but some conclusions can be offered here. . . . In the beginning, race was scarcely mentioned. By 1915 the antisuffragists succeeded in making white supremacy *an* issue, arguing that woman suffrage would doom a large part of Virginia to black control at the polls. In the last two years of the campaign, the antis succeeded in making white supremacy an issue of considerable importance. The principal actors in the story of woman suffrage and white supremacy, in other words, were the antisuffragists. The antis introduced the white supremacy issue; as time went on they pressed it with increasing intensity and disregard for truth; and they refused to give it up, even after the Nineteenth Amendment was ratified. Responsibility for the white supremacist dimensions of the woman suffrage debates rests squarely on the shoulders of the antis.

It rests more ambiguously on the white suffragists, whose behavior needs to be examined bifocally. With one lens trained on the egalitarian standards of the present, it is possible to make a substantial list of ways in which the white suffragists failed to measure up. From first to last, the white suffragists saw white supremacy as a bogus issue, and they countered with a strategy of denial, arguing in most instances that white supremacy was simply not in danger and thus should not stand in the way of votes for women. They did not disavow white supremacy itself, and this by present standards must be judged a failure of major proportions. At the same time, we need a second lens for distance, to focus and clarify the standards and practicalities of southern politics in the early twentieth century. By local white

standards (of which the antis' poisonous po-
lemics were a good example), the suffragists'
strategy of denial was a moderate approach. To
understand just how low the antis would go
does not excuse the suffragists, but it helps us
locate them on a political spectrum that would
have been meaningful to white southerners at
the time.

Understanding the depths of the antisuffragists' unremitting bigotry also helps us locate black Virginians in the woman suffrage
controversy. To resume the theatrical metaphor, there were numerous black characters on
stage, but none of them had speaking parts. After the antisuffragists linked woman suffrage
to the demise of white supremacy, there was
nothing an African American could say that
would help the woman suffrage cause. The apparent consequence was a black stance that
stressed deeds over words. Once the Nineteenth Amendment was ratified, African
Americans in the cities organized voter registration drives among women. Until that time,
they tended to keep their own counsel. . . .

From 1870 on, Virginia women had made sporadic attempts to form woman suffrage organizations,[4] but not until 1909 was the first sustained organization founded. The timing was
important, for in 1909, when the Equal Suffrage
League of Virginia was launched, the political
momentum in Virginia was decidedly undemocratic. The new century had opened with
a resolute, relentless, and successful effort to
destroy black political power. The central
achievement of this movement was the constitution of 1902, written with the explicit purpose
of disfranchising black men. A great many
lower-class whites were also disfranchised—
enough to arouse suspicions that the constitutional convention's unspoken purpose was to
demolish the Republican party. The 1902 constitution, in any case, threatened to disfranchise
so many whites that the framers did not dare
submit it to the voters. They simply promul-
gated it as the supreme law of the commonwealth.[5]

In one stroke, the Virginia electorate was
cut in half, and the number of eligible black
voters was radically reduced, from about
147,000 to roughly 21,000. The stage was set for
the triumph of a Democratic party machine
dedicated to white supremacy, minimal gov-

ernment, and keeping itself in power. But even
though the machine—or "the Organization,"
as its leaders preferred to call it—had succeeded in winning control of the state, the men
who ran the state felt they could never do
enough to secure their position. Despite the virtual elimination of black men as a force in Virginia elections, race baiting was still a campaign commonplace. Both parties, moreover,
moved to eliminate any residual black influence from within their ranks. The Democrats
saw to it that no blacks could vote in their pri-
maries. The desperate white Republicans, who
had traditionally relied on substantial black
support, tried to purge their remaining black
members, hoping in that way to attract white
defectors from the Democrats.[6] This was bigotry that did not quit.

Given this context, the most striking feature of race issues in the debates over woman
suffrage was the infrequency with which they
were raised. From January 1912, when woman
suffrage was brought before the Virginia legislature for the first time, to March 1920, when
the legislature defeated woman suffrage for the
last time, the *Richmond Times-Dispatch* published more than four hundred letters to the
editor (pro and con) regarding votes for
women. Eight percent of those letters made explicit mention of the race question. In the same
period, the *Times-Dispatch* printed more than
two hundred editorials (mostly con) on woman
suffrage. Only 4 percent of them explicitly
mentioned the alleged menace of the black
voter—and this in a newspaper in which racist
insults were standard fare.

Other hunting grounds yield even less in
the way of white supremacist arguments.
There was nothing about race in the special suffrage edition of the *Richmond News Leader* published in 1914, nor was there anything about
black votes in the suffragists' own shortlived
newspaper, the *Virginia Suffrage News*. The
Times-Dispatch reported on all the annual conventions of the Equal Suffrage League of Virginia and printed dozens of routine summaries
of speeches delivered at meetings of the Equal
Suffrage League of Richmond. If anyone
breathed a word about race, it was not reported
here. Finally, in the archives of the Norfolk
Equal Suffrage League there is a paper listing
planks in the antisuffrage platform, and they
are labeled "Stock arguments we had to meet

over & over." None of them concerned white supremacy.[7]

The great bulk of woman suffrage propaganda, both pro and anti, conveyed the same arguments that predominated in the rest of the country—a phenomenon abetted by the fact that both sides bought leaflets in bulk from national headquarters. Suffragists contended the vote was a natural right; antis countered it was a privilege. Suffragists and antis went back and forth about whether the vote would make women better mothers and what the vote would do to, or for, the home. They debated whether women could do more for reform with the vote or without it—interestingly many antis shared the suffragists' assumption that women *should* work for reform—and in that connection the two sides offered differing interpretations of legislation enacted in states where women already had the vote. They wrangled over the question of whether women really wanted the vote and whether it mattered whether women wanted it. They fought over the question of whether woman suffrage was inevitable.

The entry of the United States into World War I provided more grist for both mills. Suffragists contended that women had earned the vote by their prodigious war service, and they repeatedly cited the recommendation of Virginia-born President Woodrow Wilson that women be enfranchised as a war measure. To antis, Wilson's recommendation was evidence that he had lived away from Virginia for too long. They dusted off the ancient argument that only those who could fight should be able to vote. And increasingly they resorted to guilt by association, accusing suffragists of being cozy with socialists, anarchists, and Bolsheviks. All these arguments came straight from the national book, and together they accounted for most of the ink and oratory devoted to woman suffrage in Virginia. . . .

Before proceeding with this story, it would be helpful to identify the protagonists. Unless otherwise specified, *suffragists* refers to activists in the Equal Suffrage League of Virginia.[8] All were women, all were white, and they tended to be members of socially prominent (though not always wealthy) families. A high proportion of them lived in Richmond. There were local leagues in most of the larger towns, however, and there were pockets of suffrage

activity in all kinds of places. Although officers of both state and local leagues were female, they sought allies among men and won the support of labor leaders, some liberal clergymen, a few public officials, and a very occasional newspaper editor. There were black advocates of woman suffrage as well, but for reasons that will become apparent, they rarely spoke within the hearing of white people.

The antisuffragists are in some ways more difficult to identify than the suffragists and in other ways easier. The Virginia Association Opposed to Woman Suffrage organized in 1912, when woman suffrage first came before the General Assembly. Like the Equal Suffrage League, this association was centered in Richmond, and it was made up of prominent white women, who (unlike the suffragists) took care to list the names of their prominent husbands. Their workings, however, were very shadowy. If they kept papers, they have never come to light, and it is thus impossible to know how much of the political work of antisuffrage was actually accomplished by the Virginia Association. Certainly there were legions of powerful Virginians who were willing to speak against woman suffrage, quite independently of any group organized specifically for that purpose. For these reasons, *antisuffragists,* or *antis,* in this essay refers not only to the leaders of the antisuffrage association but also to a congeries of Virginians who went on public record against votes for women. [Virtually all of the antis were white.] Altogether the antisuffrage forces were a formidable group, counting among them most of Virginia's newspaper editors, several well-known clergymen and writers, Virginia's governors, its U.S. senators, almost all the men Virginians sent to the U.S. House of Representatives, and most members of the General Assembly. . . .

. . . In the . . . early days of the suffrage campaign, Virginians for the first time in the history of the commonwealth engaged in a serious, vigorous, extended, and highly publicized debate about the status of women and the relation of women to the polity. The discussion crescendoed early in 1912 and again in 1914, when the General Assembly was in session. In both sessions the woman suffrage amendment was trounced; in 1912 the House vote was 12 to 85, and the amendment failed again in 1914 by a vote of 13 to 74. The leaders of the Equal

Suffrage League took what comfort they could from the fact that their cause was still young, and they resolved to make a better showing in the next legislature by dint of diligent organizing, district by district.

During these early debates, white supremacist arguments were sporadic and few, and the suffragists ignored them. In 1913, for example, the *Times-Dispatch* printed a letter from William Watts Parker. Parker was an elderly physician who had opinions on just about everything, and for decades he had been firing them off to the newspapers. In this instance he identified woman suffrage as the cause of interracial marriages. "Look at the thousands of marriages in the North and West of white women and negroes, and getting worse every day!" Parker's rantings about the New Woman were by this time legendary, and the suffragists apparently paid no attention.[9] . . .

. . . As long as racist attacks on woman suffrage remained scattered, the suffragists avoided answering in kind. In 1915, however, antisuffragists gave their argument a sharper focus and brought it closer to home. This time the suffragists took the bait, and the relationship of woman suffrage to white supremacy entered a new phase.

The key document was an editorial by Alfred Williams in the *Richmond Evening Journal.* Williams invoked "figures and facts," "actual facts," and multiple "hard facts," all of which boiled down to the single "hard fact" that "twenty-nine counties of Virginia would be condemned by woman suffrage to colored rule and five others would be in serious peril of it with woman suffrage." The figures came from the census of 1910; Williams arranged them in a neat column and reasoned that wherever black females outnumbered white, woman suffrage would result in black rule. Williams contrasted his alleged facts with the desires of the suffragists, who as women could not be expected to understand practical politics and who would likely "fall back on the traditional conclusive feminine argument 'because.' " "No other argument," Williams continued, ". . . is quite so convincing or fascinating as that word 'because,' accompanied by some pouting of alluring and scarlet lips—especially if there be dimples by way of re-enforcement." But facts had to be faced. Otherwise, Williams concluded, "the Democratic party and white rule

in Virginia will be swinging on a mighty thin line."[10]

Clearly the antis thought they could score with this argument. Williams's editorial found its way into other Virginia newspapers, and it was reprinted as a broadside for distribution in other southern states.[11] The suffragists decided they had to respond. They wrote letters to editors, and for the first time they published a flyer on the alleged "menace to white supremacy.". . . The suffragists' central contention was that white supremacy was not endangered and therefore not an issue. In two-thirds of Virginia's counties, there were white majorities. In the counties with black majorities, the voting qualifications in the state constitution would apply to women as they already applied to men. The constitution provided for a cumulative poll tax. The constitution also required a literacy test; here the suffragists pointed out that the black illiteracy rate was 22 percent, compared with 8 percent among whites. There was a further provision in the constitution that had never even been used. If whites in a particular county believed themselves in danger of losing their electoral majority, they could petition for a special act of the legislature imposing an additional requirement that voters own property worth $250. That act would apply only to the county that petitioned for it. Since this had never yet been deemed necessary, the suffragists had a hard time believing white supremacy was in jeopardy.

Indeed, the suffragists saw white supremacy as a bogus issue—and they said so in their private correspondence as consistently as they did in their public pronouncements. Lila Meade Valentine, president of the Equal Suffrage League, called the white supremacy scare "nonsense," "the last stand of the antis.". . . Mary Johnston wrote, "If it wasn't the negro woman (Poor soul!) it would be something else—any thing or everything—far-fetchedness wouldn't matter."[12] Farfetchedness, as we shall see, in fact did not matter to the antis. It did matter to the suffragists, who relied on careful preparation and authoritative texts. "Do not have a public debate on this subject until you are thoroughly posted by some good constitutional lawyer," wrote Valentine to Townsend. "By all means keep a copy of the Va. Constitution close at hand."[13]

By such means the suffragists hoped to settle the white supremacy question once and for all. "We are in the last stages of a controversy about the negro vote," came the inside word from headquarters, "and feel much indebted to Mr. Alfred Williams, editor of the Richmond Journal, for attacking us."[14] The antis, however, were not about to let the white supremacy issue die. In January 1916 the General Assembly again convened in regular session, and for the first time white supremacy was prominent in a legislative debate on woman suffrage.

Hugh White of Rockbridge led the charge. . . . "Every argument for woman suffrage, warned Mr. White, is also an argument for negro suffrage." Another newspaper reported White's comments thus: "He said equal suffrage rights would mean equal race rights, and would tend to a reversal to barbarism, since it would strip woman of her refinement." While he was at it, White contributed his bit to the male antis' stock of observations on female appearance: "Where equal suffrage prevails women have wrinkles and lines in their faces, he said, and have hawk-like faces."[15]

The woman suffrage resolution did surprisingly well in the 1916 session, losing in the House by the relatively close vote of 40 to 52. It is not clear why. Certainly the suffragists had worked hard. Lila Meade Valentine had made personal appearances all over the state, organizing new local leagues and rejuvenating older ones. By 1916 almost every town in Virginia with more than twenty-five hundred residents had a suffrage league. Suffragists were supplying suffrage news to more than forty newspapers. In any case, the leaders of the Equal Suffrage League were jubilant to have come so far in so short a time; they called the House vote "our victorious defeat."[16]

Little did they know that 40 to 52 was the best woman suffrage would ever do in Virginia (at least until 1952, when the General Assembly at last roused itself and ratified the Nineteenth Amendment). Woman suffrage did not come to a vote in the legislature again until 1919, and by that time a great deal had changed. First, there was World War I and in its wake a red scare, a season of deadly racial violence, and a surge of hope for a new world order. All of this provided material for the ongoing suffrage debate. Second, at the urging of the National American Woman Suffrage Association, the Equal Suffrage League of Virginia lined up be-

hind Carrie Chapman Catt's "Winning Plan." That meant quietly putting aside the campaign for a state woman suffrage amendment and joining in a highly disciplined national campaign for the passage of an amendment to the U.S. Constitution. Nothing could have made the antisuffragists happier. Here was an opportunity to divert the debate from woman suffrage itself to the hallowed ground of states' rights. The antis took full advantage of the opportunity and in so doing moved questions about race closer to the center of the debate.

As the suffragists pointed out, the federal amendment—commonly called the Anthony Amendment—did not directly enfranchise anyone. It merely stated that citizens could not be denied the vote on the basis of sex, and it gave Congress the power to enforce that principle. Careful antisuffragists thus argued that the danger of the woman suffrage amendment lay in its power as a precedent. If the federal government was allowed to interfere with the state's power to define its electorate in one way, it might be more likely to interfere with the state's powers in yet other ways. It might, for example, opt for enforcement of the Fifteenth Amendment (which denied states the power to deny citizens the vote on the basis of race). It might impose universal suffrage. It had happened before, during Reconstruction. What was to stop it from happening again?

As a rule, however, the antisuffragists were not careful. By June 1919, when suffrage forces at last pushed the Anthony Amendment through the U.S. Senate, the *Times-Dispatch* was arguing that the amendment would directly enfranchise millions of black women. Significantly, the *Times-Dispatch* also warned that woman suffrage would spell the end of school segregation and every other form of Jim Crow legislation. This was a marked departure from the antis' earlier tendency to construe white supremacy narrowly, that is, as a matter of numerical superiority at the polls. Late in 1919 and in 1920, as the Anthony Amendment was presented to the Virginia General Assembly for ratification, the antis' rhetoric grew ever more global and apocalyptic. Woman suffrage would mean black supremacy in politics and, as the president of the Virginia Association Opposed to Woman Suffrage wrote, "racial social equality and the intermarriage of whites and blacks."[17] Woman suffrage, moreover, was already responsible for the race riots that racked the country in 1919. "Race rioting in Arkansas," one anti told the State Democratic Committee, "is the direct result of equal suffrage. . . ." Woman suffrage, another anti claimed, "means race and sex war!"[18] . . .

The . . . Anthony Amendment came before the Virginia House of Delegates, and it was trounced. This was more than a defeat. It was a resounding defeat, meant to echo across the nation. The deed was done by means of a resolution that declared the federal amendment "an unwarranted, unnecessary, undemocratic and dangerous interference with the rights reserved to the States," and it called upon "our sister States of the Union" to join in resistance to all such measures.[19] Although the vote was not close—61 to 21—the suffragists pressed on, hoping the General Assembly would come around once it became clear that ratification was inevitable. As Lila Meade Valentine wrote to the state senator from Fauquier, "How will the women of Virginia feel should they owe their political liberty to the men of other states, instead of to Virginians?" The senator was not moved, nor were most of his colleagues. In 1920 the Virginia House approved a resolution rejecting the Anthony Amendment 62 to 22, while the Senate vote was 24 to 10. The General Assembly then completed its work on woman suffrage by passing the "machinery" bill. The bill stipulated that should the federal amendment be ratified by action of other states, the voting restrictions then in force for Virginia men would be applied to women as well.

Was it racism that defeated woman suffrage in Virginia? There is no clear answer to this question. On the one hand, the antis did exploit white anxieties to the hilt, and in the final months of the campaign suffragists could occasionally be found expressing the private opinion that "our worst stumbling block" was fear of the black voter.[20] On the other hand, the Virginia General Assembly had already demonstrated its willingness to thwart feminist aspirations, quite apart from any controversies about race relations or states' rights. The campaign for a state-supported "coordinate college" for women had commanded the support of almost every white women's organization in the state. It went without saying that this college would admit white students only, but it too was rejected in one legislative session after

another.[21] If anything in Virginia was ever overdetermined, it was opposition to women's rights.

What is clear is that the antisuffragists' willingness to voice and exploit racist feeling had profound effects on the terms of the debate. For their part, the antis as a group were willing to say anything that might strengthen their cause; there were no minimal standards of either decency or truthfulness to which they held themselves or anyone else. The range of responses available to white suffragists and to African Americans was consequently narrow. The white suffragists, unwilling to get in the gutter with the antis, opted for a complex politics of distance and denial. Black Virginians were almost completely silenced.

One further example of antisuffrage tactics will help clarify the suffragists' options. After 1918 the antisuffragists increasingly expanded their accusations beyond the realm of electoral politics and into the equally explosive territory of "social equality." Carrie Chapman Catt, who came to Richmond in 1920 to address the General Assembly, was subjected to the full treatment. Catt was the president of the National American Woman Suffrage Association (NAWSA), and in her long career as a suffragist she had said many different things to many sorts of audiences. In recent years she has been routinely chastised by historians for using nativist and racist appeals for woman suffrage.[22] She arrived in Richmond, however, to find the House chamber blanketed with leaflets entitled "The 'Three Immediate Women Friends' of the Anthony Family." A portrait of Catt was followed by a portrait of Anna Howard Shaw, the former president of NAWSA, which was in turn placed beside a portrait of "Mrs. R. Jerome Jeffrey (Negro)." Mrs. Jeffrey, the caption explained, was "Often 'Guest in Anthony Home' with Mrs. Shaw and Mrs. Carrie Chapman Catt, President of National Woman Suffrage Association, to which all Southern Suffragettes belong." Completing the leaflet's front page were two quotations in large type. From Catt: "Suffrage Democracy Knows no Bias of Race, Color, Creed, or Sex." From Susan B. Anthony: "Look not to Greece or Rome for heroes, nor to Jerusalem or Mecca for saints, but for all the higher virtues of heroism, let us WORSHIP the black man at our feet."[23]

Let it be emphasized that the antis assumed these quotations and associations to be self-evidently devastating to the suffrage cause. If a woman suffragist suggested that votes for women would or should empower any black women (to say nothing of black men), she played right into the hands of the antis. So did any white suffragist who associated with black people or organizations on a footing of anything like equality.

This was the context for the Equal Suffrage League's complicity in NAWSA's 1919 decision on the application of a federation of black women's organizations for cooperating membership. When the Northeastern Federation of Women's Clubs first applied for affiliation, NAWSA tried to persuade them to withdraw their application. That failing, NAWSA headquarters polled its own executive council, which included Lila Meade Valentine. In a private letter Valentine recommended against acceptance of the application, in the process producing the most explicit extant statement of the Equal Suffrage League's stance on race politics. "As I understand it," Valentine wrote, "the National is organized for the purpose of securing the right of suffrage for all women. I believe that all women, white or black, who meet the qualifications for suffrage in any State should have that right," Valentine continued, and then she turned practical politician:

> but in working to secure that right, we should exercise common sense, and not complicate our efforts and add to the difficulties of the task by injecting elements of discord. As you know, the negro is the one remaining argument against suffrage in the Southern States and our work in behalf of the federal amendment, already meeting great opposition because of that element, would be rendered immeasurably more difficult by admitting a large body of negro women to membership in the National at this time. This is not a matter of principle but of expediency, and I trust that the National Board will see fit to regard it as such. . . .[24]

. . . Expediency prevailed, the Northeastern Federation was denied cooperating membership in NAWSA, and we are left with a set of questions about how to evaluate the white suffragists' decisions—not only their rejection of the Northeastern Federation but their entire strategy of denial.

It might be helpful to further clarify their options. In Virginia the power was on the side of white supremacy, and given the antis' willingness to exploit any resonances between woman suffrage and black suffrage, white woman suffragists were presented with a stark choice: they could distance their cause from the aspirations of black Virginians and thereby preserve some chance of victory, or they could acknowledge the legitimate interests of black women and doom their movement to certain failure. To put it another way, they could deny that white supremacy was in danger, or they could hush up and go home.

There was also a third road, a road not taken: they could have attempted to outbait the antis. One ironic development in the twisted history of antisuffrage thinking was that to argue that woman suffrage was dangerous, the antis had to pay tribute to the potential good citizenship of black women, at the same time disparaging the character of black men. "We have managed the men," said the *Newport News Daily Press,* "but could we manage the women? It is a different proposition. We believe that most of the women would qualify, and we further believe that they would persuade many of the men to qualify; and pay their poll taxes for them if need be." The *Winchester Evening Star* printed a similar prediction: "The negro woman, as a rule, is ahead of the negro man. She is the wage-earner, and as such has the rule over the more indolent negro man. He may stay away from the polls, but she won't." An antisuffrage legislator claimed that black women would "face twenty-five shotguns" to vote.[25]

Given this line of argument, the most effective counterattack available to the white suffragists was the defamation of the black woman's character. The culture of early twentieth-century America abounded with negative stereotypes of black women, and it would have been easy for the suffragists to deploy them, to paint black women as ignorant or irresponsible, as lazy or loose.[26] But this the suffragists did not do, either publicly or in their letters to one another. When in the last months of the campaign the antis succeeded in making race a "stumbling block" to woman suffrage, the suffragists could have blamed Virginia's black population. Instead, they placed the blame where it belonged, on the antisuffragists.

The white suffragists, in other words, occupied a middling place—a far cry from the theoretical egalitarianism that currently dominates feminism but also well removed from the shrieking racism of the antis. That middle ground bears further exploration. I have so far emphasized the constraints on the Equal Suffrage League, constraints imposed by the tactics of the antis and by the conservatism that prevailed among Virginia's voters and legislators. It is important to recognize, however, that the suffragists had some rhetorical latitude. They spoke on street corners and from automobiles, they handed out fliers by the hundreds, they fed news to the press, and although they failed to carry the day for woman suffrage, they contributed to the shape of the political universe in which all Virginians moved. How, in matters respecting race, do we evaluate those contributions?

The first thing to remember is that the white suffragists typically did not talk about race at all; it takes a certain intellectual agility to hold on to that fact while simultaneously attempting to evaluate the racialist arguments they did make. Meanwhile, if we are going to make moral judgments—and how can we not?—it would seem worthwhile to devise standards that are explicit and appropriate to the compromised situation in which the suffragists found themselves. For example, were their claims true or at least plausible? Second, did the suffragists accommodate white supremacy in a minimalist way, or did they pander to it or in some other way legitimate it? Third, did they leave open the possibility that black women might vote in significant numbers, or did they tend to foreclose that possibility? . . .

The suffragists' primary argument with respect to race . . . was one of denial: woman suffrage would not endanger whites' control of the ballot box. In its original form this was a strictly defensive argument that rendered no judgment on the justice of white supremacy itself. Thus in 1915, in response to the antis' charges that woman suffrage would subject some thirty counties to black rule, the Equal Suffrage League issued a small pamphlet called *Voting Qualifications in Virginia*, which was nothing if not matter of fact. "As these laws restrict the negro man's vote," the pamphlet explained, "it stands to reason that they will also restrict the negro woman's vote."[27]

But what a difference a few words could make. Early in 1916 the Equal Suffrage League issued a new flier, presumably for the benefit of the General Assembly then in session. *Equal Suffrage and the Negro Vote* repeated the argu-

ments of the earlier pamphlet but with some brief additions. Most important was the final sentence: "We are secure from negro domination now—then, even more."[28] These ten words put an entirely different stamp on the suffragists' constitutional argument. They promised that woman suffrage would actually increase the margin of white voting strength; they implied that white supremacy was a good thing; and the use of "we" placed the Equal Suffrage League squarely within the community of whites who had an interest in maintaining white supremacy.

It is not surprising that such phrases should appear in a literature manufactured for the purpose of neutralizing the antis' allegations about the dangers woman suffrage posed to white supremacy. More surprising were statements to the effect that with woman suffrage, voting qualifications would and should operate in ways that were race blind. Mary Pollard Clarke put the question in 1915: "Does not everybody agree in this enlightened age that the educated, property-holding negro should have a chance to vote? Can any white man or white woman claim the right of citizenship for himself or herself and deny it to the negro man or woman of intelligence and attainment?"[29] This formulation was evidently too liberal for public consumption and apparently did not appear in print again. Subsequent statements about the evenhandedness of the law—and the consequent irrelevance of race—tended to be phrased negatively, in terms of the groups that would not qualify to vote. As Adèle Clark asserted in a broadside of 1919, voting qualifications "will operate to eliminate the illiterate and irresponsible women of both races, as they now eliminate the illiterate and irresponsible men of both races."[30] . . .

All of which adds urgency to the question, What did the white suffragists *really* think? Not one of these articulate women left a document that tells. It may be that they did not know. The politics of denial had two dimensions. One, as we have repeatedly seen, was the belief that white supremacy was a bogus issue, stirred up by the antis to camouflage the real issues at stake in the campaign. The second dimension of denial grew out of the first: having decided from the beginning that race was not a genuine issue, the suffragists excused themselves from grappling with it in any thoughtful way. Lila Meade Valentine believed in the "principle" that black women should be able to vote where they met the state qualifications. But what should those qualifications be? Because they were women, the suffragists were exempted from struggling with that question, which for the time being had been settled by the framers of the 1902 constitution. Because the suffragists were white in a time of declining black political power, they could agitate for the vote without ever having to explain themselves to black Virginians. The suffragists operated in a zone in which they were immune from the necessity of articulating principle—a reminder, if one is needed, of how both the spoken and the unspoken can be conditioned by political circumstance.

This was even more acutely the case for African Americans. In the North and West there was substantial black support for woman suffrage—and also enough opposition to make for lively debate within black communities.[31] In Virginia, however, the tactics of the antis put blacks in an impossible position, one that made taking a public stand, whether advocacy or opposition, extremely awkward. To oppose woman suffrage in public was to align oneself with the white antis and their boundless exploitation of the race issue. A black person who supported woman suffrage, meanwhile, could only damage the cause by saying so; recall Hugh White waving *The Crisis* about during his antisuffrage peroration in the House of Delegates.

There was the further consideration that woman suffrage was unlikely to make a dramatic difference in the power of the black electorate. The *Planet*, Richmond's African American weekly, made the point in 1919, shortly after the General Assembly torpedoed the Anthony Amendment: "White folks down here are opposing woman suffrage because colored women will have the right to vote. They argue that the preponderance of colored women in some counties will show itself at the polls. We used to think so too, but a bitter experience has taught us otherwise." Even the votes of whites were discounted (or miscounted) if they went against the interests of the dominant party, the *Planet* went on. "The talk about majority rule is a joke and the colored folks of the Southland know it," said the *Planet*. " 'Quit your kidding.' "[32]

From this tough-minded critique, one might extrapolate a certain lukewarmness on the subject of votes for women. This, however, is a guess. The (male) editors of Virginia's black newspapers printed occasional woman suffrage news, and they sometimes commented on the behavior of the protagonists. On the justice or wisdom of woman suffrage itself, however, the black press took no position.[33]

As for the opinions of Virginia's black women, we have only a few tantalizing clues. In 1912 the National Association of Colored Women held its biennial convention in Hampton, Virginia. In the course of addressing the convention on "Woman and Business," Maggie Lena Walker, the Richmond banker, insurance executive, and community leader, injected a single sentence on behalf of woman suffrage. Women were rebelling against their unjust wages, Walker asserted, "yet Capital is deaf—and will never hear their cries, until the women force Capital to hear them at the ballot box, and to be just and honest to them as to the men." The *Southern Workman*, the magazine published by Hampton Institute, praised the speech but did not report its slant on woman suffrage.[34] A small news item in the *Richmond Planet* suggests that Walker had company. In 1916 the *Planet* reported the outcome of a women's basketball game between two teams of black public school teachers; the contest was billed as the Feminists vs. the Suffragists.[35]

. . . [T]he suffragists' argument on the simplest level turned out to be true. Votes for women, as we shall soon see, did not empower black Virginians as a group; woman suffrage did not operate on so dramatic a scale. Black women in Virginia cities, however, were quite willing to engage in the politics of the smaller gain, to attempt to use the vote for whatever it might prove to be worth.

Woman suffrage came to Virginia in 1920, after thirty-six other states ratified the Nineteenth Amendment to the U.S. Constitution. Ratification was completed in late August; in Virginia, women were given one month to register to vote in the November elections. . . .

In the course of this first registration period, black women, white suffragists, and the defeated antisuffragists all revealed themselves more fully. With the Nineteenth Amendment ratified, it was no longer necessary for black Virginians to be so quiet or for white suffragists to be so cautious. Nor should it have been necessary for the antis to continue to beat the

drums of white supremacy. The antis, however, were not improved by defeat; in the registration scenes of September 1920, they found
new occasions for setting off racist alarms. This
was largely in response to the initiatives of
black women, who organized voter registration campaigns and qualified in impressive
numbers in several cities. . . .

The record of the white suffragists, meanwhile, was mixed. Having invested a great deal
in the argument that woman suffrage would
not endanger white supremacy, the suffragists
felt vindicated by the final outcome. In the end
the overall voting power of black people in Virginia did not increase, and that seems to have
been all right with the white suffragists. At the
same time, a number of suffragists turned up
among the South's most forward-thinking
white people. In the early 1920s small groups
of white southerners joined with black leaders,
together arguing that social progress depended
on greater justice for black people and on
greater contact and frank discussions between
the representatives of the two races. In the Virginia wing of this fledgling interracial movement, a high proportion of the white women
had been active in the Equal Suffrage League
of Virginia.

When the registration books were opened
in early September, Virginia women initially
presented themselves in modest numbers.
With about two weeks to go, however, observers in many parts of the state reported surges
of applicants. . . . "Swamped by a rush of
women voters, both white and colored," the
News Leader reported, "Central Registrar William S. Woodson threw up his hands this
morning and called for help." A second room
and a deputy were found so that the crowd
could be segregated. "It was impossible for
Central Registrar Woodson to supervise so
many, and as a result the whole throng, white
and colored, were milling about giving each
other aid, suggestion and instructions, regardless of the plain provision of the constitution."
Despite the confusion, 276 women were registered that day.[36]

The real rush was yet to come. . . . The accelerated pace of registration was made possible in part by the appointment of three white
women deputies to handle white applicants.
After the deputies were sworn in, Maggie
Walker [and other black activists] pressed one
official after another to have black deputies appointed as well, . . . but to no avail.[37] The reg-

istration line for blacks would continue to
move more slowly than that for whites, both
because of the shortage of personnel and because black women's applications were more
frequently challenged. Consequently, black
women were more likely than whites to find
themselves still waiting when registration was
shut down for the day. . . . When all the paper-
work was complete, the total registration of the
black women of Richmond was 2,410. The total
for white women was 10,645.[38]

A casual reader of the newspapers might
have concluded that the numbers were just the
reverse. As soon as the organization of Richmond's black women began to show results,
some white newspapers turned to distortion.
"NEGRO WOMEN CONTINUE TO OUTNUMBER
WHITE IN ATTEMPTING TO QUALIFY," screamed
the headline of the *Richmond News Leader*. The
article itself said that three-quarters of the reg-
istrants that day were white. Newspapers in
other parts of the state nevertheless picked up
the hysterical headline. . . . "More Negro
Women Than White," said the *Index-Appeal* of
Petersburg. . . . [T]he *Roanoke World News* said
black women were qualifying "in far greater
numbers" than were whites; and the *Norfolk
Virginian-Pilot* supplied a ratio of three to one.[39]

Where the newspapers left off, the Democratic party began. . . . At the very center of the
party's pitch to white women was white supremacy. As the chairman of the Richmond
City Democratic Committee phrased it, "It is
the duty of every woman who regards the
domination of the white race as essential to the
welfare of the Southland to qualify for the ballot. . . ."[40] The officials of the party were assisted
by the Virginia Association Opposed to
Woman Suffrage, whose president called for
conservative women to qualify "in view of the
fact that colored women are registering in large
numbers. . . ."[41]

Registration figures . . . make it plain . . .
that the forces of white supremacy were highly
resilient in the face of woman suffrage. Everywhere in Virginia, white women were able to
register in greater numbers than black women,
both absolutely and relatively. Male dominance proved almost as durable. Nowhere did
women emerge as the majority of registered
voters, even though women were a numerical
majority in many Virginia cities.

Within these general patterns there were
some interesting variations. For both black and
white women, urban residence made a big dif-

ference. In most rural counties the proportion of black women who registered was 5 percent or less of the black adult female population; the comparable figure for white women was anywhere from about 8 percent to 20 percent. Both groups did much better in the cities. In Richmond, for example, the 2,410 black women who registered represented 12.5 percent of the black adult female population; the comparable figure for white women was 26.8 percent.[42]

The reasons for this urban–rural difference are not hard to figure out. Citizens newly eligible to register to vote are most likely to actually register when shown the ropes by someone who already knows how it's done. Organizing a voter registration campaign was easier in town, where the population was dense, communications were speedy, and networks of organizations stood ready to be mobilized. The law also favored the urban citizen. Virginia lawmakers had intentionally made the registration process complicated. One had to locate the county or city treasurer, pay one's poll tax, and then proceed with receipt in hand to find the registrar. In the largest cities, this was not usually difficult; the registrar was required to sit for thirty days in a centrally located public building. In the country, registration was handled in local precincts by registrars who were required to sit for only one day out of the thirty-day registration period. They were not required to announce when that day might be or where they might be located. As Adèle Clark later recalled, "Our rural women had a lot of trouble running all over the county trying to catch the registrars, who were out plowing or fishing or doing various things."[43] Once the registrar was located, he had considerable latitude in deciding whether a given applicant was indeed literate; applicants were required to record a number of facts about themselves without prompting from anyone.

Obviously these factors could be manipulated to encourage some applicants and discourage others; in a rural district, all the registrar had to do to defeat a black woman's effort to register was to pretend he wasn't home when he saw her coming down the road. There is no hard evidence on exactly how it was done, but it could hardly have been coincidental that black women's registration rates tended to be lowest in the most heavily black counties. . . .

By the same token, black women's registration rates were higher where the total number of blacks in the population was relatively small and where competition between Democrats and Republicans was keen enough to encourage the Republican leaders to cultivate their black constituencies. . . .

Even with these relatively high rates of black registration, however, the white majority was slightly larger than it had been. The Equal Suffrage League had argued all along that woman suffrage was no threat to white supremacy; this had been their central, unifying contention with respect to race. When actual registration figures became available, the white suffragists were thoroughly vindicated. At the same time, the suffragists' old strategy of denial became obsolete. By late September it was clear that there would be some black women voters in Virginia and that there would be significant concentrations of them in several cities. . . .

. . . White suffragists like Adèle Clark and Nora Houston felt compelled to make some sort of effort to reach their counterparts in black Richmond, and before long they were joined by a number of their suffrage colleagues in a more systematic movement for interracial cooperation. Of the thirty-four white women who were identified as leaders in the interracial movement of the 1920s, more than one-third had been active in the Equal Suffrage League. The antis were nowhere to be found. None of the women who were publicly identified as antisuffragists before 1920 appeared after 1920 on the rosters of Virginia's interracial organizations.[44]

In organizations like the Urban League and the Women's Section of the Commission on Interracial Cooperation, black and white women pursued a wide-ranging agenda for social action. They worked on health, recreation, housing, and education. They condemned new white supremacist groups like the revived Ku Klux Klan and the Anglo Saxon Leagues. They spoke out against lynching and the sexual exploitation of black women.[45]

In these endeavors they were sometimes joined by organizations that remained exclusively white. In September 1921 the Virginia League of Women Voters, the successor organization to the Equal Suffrage League, passed a resolution "Strongly Condemning Organizations That Breed Class, Race, or Religious Hatred."[46] "But we never had the nerve to enroll the Negro women in the League of Women Voters," as Adèle Clark confessed. "I've always regretted it, but we just couldn't bring the middle-of-the-road thinkers to the point of bringing the Negro women in."[47]

In the 1920s, as before, the white woman suffragists negotiated a middling course. After 1920 that course included significant and open cooperation with leading black Virginians, who in turn challenged the white women to enlarge their democratic vision. Virginia's Janie Porter Barrett, for example, joined other southern black club women in 1921 in asking "that white women, for the protection of their homes as well as ours indicate their sanction of the ballot for all citizens as representing government by the sober, reasoned and deliberate judgment of all the people."[48] That far the white suffragists were unwilling to go. The interracial movement took up many issues, and suffragists like Adèle Clark and Lucy Randolph Mason did some quiet citizenship work among black women.[49] The whites as a group, however, would not risk open advocacy of greater voting rights for black people.

It is important that we hold this failing firmly in mind. If one of the functions of history is to serve as social criticism—and for feminists, as self-criticism—it is essential to take a long look at the suffragists' failures, to measure their motives and actions against what we conceive to be ideal feminist practice. It will not do to stop here, however. In feminist scholarship there is a tendency to beam most of our attention on the advocates of women's rights, from whom we expect much, while their adversaries, from whom we expect little, get off the hook. I am suggesting that we pay more attention to the adversaries and to the specific and evolving political worlds in which the woman suffragists and their opponents did daily battle.

. . . [Yet] we also need to . . . acknowledge modest achievements even while . . . [acknowledging] vast failures. Virginia was a bastion of white supremacy in 1919, and black women had no voice in formal politics. By the end of 1920 Virginia was still a bastion of white supremacy, but several thousand black women had achieved the dignity of citizenship, they had acquired a new instrument of resistance, and a select few had gained new channels into national political councils, chiefly through the Republican party.[50] In some cases they were able to seize the moment and push beyond the vote itself. In 1921, for example, Maggie Walker ran for state office; she ran for superintendent of public instruction on an all-black ticket of

dissident Republicans.[51] The "Lily Blacks" could not hope to win, but Walker's candidacy forced everyone who read the news to cope at least momentarily with the image of a black woman seeking high office. Before 1920 putting Walker on the ticket would not have even been thinkable. In its immediate results, woman suffrage made electoral politics more inclusive. That is more than can be said for anything else in Virginia politics for many decades.

NOTES

1. Mary Johnston to Lila Meade Valentine, Jan. 5, 1913, Lila Meade Valentine Papers, Virginia Historical Society, Richmond, Va.

2. There are, however, a few published biographical treatments of woman suffrage leaders. . . . Marjorie Spruill Wheeler, *New Women of the New South: The Leaders of the Woman Suffrage Movement in the Southern States* (New York: Oxford University Press, 1993), deals at length with Lila Meade Valentine and Mary Johnston. See also Wheeler's recent "Mary Johnston, Suffragist," *Virginia Magazine of History and Biography* 100 (Jan. 1992):99–188. There are two biographical articles on Valentine: [Elizabeth Dabney-Coleman], "Genteel Crusader," *Virginia Cavalcade* 4 (Autumn 1954):29–32; Lloyd C. Taylor, Jr., "Lila Meade Valentine: The FFV as Reformer," *Virginia Magazine of History and Biography* 70 (Oct. 1962):471–87. . . . Suzanne Lebsock, *Virginia Women, 1600–1945: "A Share of Honour"* (Richmond: Virginia State Library, 1987), gives a brief history of the woman suffrage movement, placing it in the context of other women's reform causes of the period.

3. Aileen S. Kraditor, *Up from the Pedestal: Selected Writings in the History of American Feminism* (Chicago: Quadrangle Books, 1968), pp. 253–65; Gerda Lerner, *Black Women in White America: A Documentary History* (New York: Pantheon Books, 1972), p. 321; Rosalyn Terborg-Penn, "Discrimination against Afro-American Women in the Woman's Movement, 1830–1920," in *The Afro-American Woman: Struggles and Images*, ed. Sharon Harley and Rosalyn Terborg-Penn (Port Washington, N.Y.: Kennikat Press, 1978), pp. 17–27; Angela Y. Davis, *Women, Race and Class* (New York: Random House, 1981), pp. 70–86; Paula Giddings, *When and Where I Enter: The Impact of Black Women on Race and Sex in America* (New York: William Morrow, 1984), pp. 159–70; Barbara Hilkert Andolsen, *"Daughters of Jefferson, Daughters of Bootblacks": Racism and American Feminism* (Macon, Ga.: Mercer University Press, 1986).

4. Elizabeth Cady Stanton, Susan B. Anthony, and Matilda Joslyn Gage, eds., *History of Woman Suffrage*, vol. 3 (Rochester, N.Y.: Susan B. Anthony, 1886), pp. 823–24; Susan B. Anthony and Ida Husted Harper, *History of Woman Suffrage*, vol. 4 (Rochester, N.Y.: Susan B. Anthony, 1902), pp. 964–66. . . .

5. Andrew Buni, *The Negro in Virginia Politics, 1902–1965* (Charlottesville: University Press of Virginia, 1967), pp. 13–19; J. Morgan Kousser, *The Shaping of Southern Politics: Suffrage Restriction and the Establishment of the One-Party South* (New Haven, Conn.: Yale University Press, 1974), pp. 171–81. . . .

6. Buni, *The Negro in Virginia Politics*, pp. 24–93, gives the fullest account.

7. *Richmond News Leader*, May 2, 1914. The papers of the Norfolk Equal Suffrage League are located in the Virginia Woman Suffrage Collection in the Virginia State Library and Archives, Richmond, Va. . . .

8. The Equal Suffrage League was affiliated with the National American Woman Suffrage Association. A small group of Virginians affiliated with NAWSA's rival organization, the Congressional Union [CU]. . . .

9. *Richmond Times-Dispatch*, April 23, 1913. An earlier controversy over allowing Virginia women to practice medicine and law had prompted Parker to write *The Woman's Place, Her Position in the Christian World, The Problem Considered under Four Grand Heads—Woman Outstripped by Man, Even in Domestic Handiwork* (Richmond: n.p., 1892).

10. Broadside in the Virginia Woman Suffrage Collection.

11. See, for example, the *Newport News Daily Press*, May 6, 1915. The broadside was headlined "Virginia Warns Her People Against Woman Suffrage—Twenty-Nine Counties would Go Under Negro Rule—Over Sixty Counties in the State of Georgia—The Entire State of Mississippi—What of Your State? Isn't It About Time for Reflecting Men and Women to Think—And Act?" Virginia Woman Suffrage Collection.

12. Lila Meade Valentine to Jessie E. Townsend, Apr. 10, 1915 (Valentine wrote two letters to Townsend dated Apr. 10; "nonsense" appears in one and "last stand" appears in the other), Virginia Woman Suffrage Collection; Jessie Townsend to Alice O. Taylor, Apr. 13, 1915, Adèle Clark Papers. . . .

13. Valentine to Townsend, Apr. 10, 1915 (as above, each of the two April 10 letters contains one of the quotations), Virginia Woman Suffrage Collection.

14. Alice O. Taylor to Jessie E. Townsend, Apr. 16, 1915, Adèle Clark Papers.

15. *Richmond Times-Dispatch*, Feb. 19, 1916; *Newport News Daily Press*, Feb. 19, 1916. . . .

16. [?] to Mrs. B. M. Hagan, Mar. 8, 1916, Adèle Clark Papers.

17. Mary Mason Anderson Williams, letter to the editor, *Richmond Times-Dispatch*, Sept. 2, 1919.

18. *Richmond Times-Dispatch*, Feb. 11 and 21, 1920.

19. Virginia, *Journal of the House of Delegates of Virginia* (Richmond: Superintendent of Public Printing, 1919), p. 158. . . .

20. Headquarters Secretary [Ida M. Thompson] to National American Woman Suffrage Association, Dec. 20, 1918, Adèle Clark Papers. A letter from a suffragist in Warrenton to state headquarters made a similar point: "The greatest stumbling block here is the vote of the Negro woman. . . . It is most important here." Susie F. H. Hilleary to Lila Meade Valentine, Oct. 5, 1919, Adèle Clark Papers.

21. Anne Hobson Freeman, "Mary Munford's Fight for a College for Women Coordinate with the University of Virginia," *Virginia Magazine of History and Biography* 78 (Oct. 1970):481–91.

22. Robert Booth Fowler, *Carrie Catt: Feminist Politician* (Boston: Northeastern University Press, 1986), pp. 83–90; Mari Jo Buhle and Paul Buhle, eds.,

The Concise History of Woman Suffrage: Selections from the Classic Work of Stanton, Anthony, Gage, and Harper (Urbana: University of Illinois Press, 1978), pp. 312–13; Andolsen, "*Daughters of Jefferson*," pp. 21–44.

23. The leaflet is preserved in the Virginia Woman Suffrage Collection.

24. Lila Meade Valentine to Justina L. Wilson, Feb. 17, 1919, Adèle Clark Papers. The story at the national level is told by Giddings, *When and Where I Enter*, pp. 161–62.

25. *Newport News Daily Press*, May 6, 1915; *Winchester Evening Star*, Mar. 19, 1918. Clippings containing all these quotations were found in the Virginia Woman Suffrage Collection. . . .

26. On the devaluation of black women and attempts to counter it, see Beverly Guy-Sheftall, *Daughters of Sorrow: Attitudes toward Black Women, 1880–1920* (Brooklyn: Carlson Publishing, 1990), esp. chap. 3.

27. Equal Suffrage League of Virginia, *Voting Qualifications in Virginia*. The pamphlet was undated, but a ledger in the Adèle Clark Papers indicates that it was initially ordered from the printer on Apr. 15, 1915.

28. The flier can be found in the Virginia Woman Suffrage Collection. The flier itself is undated, but the ledger in the Adèle Clark Papers indicates it was first ordered from the printer on Jan. 19, 1916.

29. Unidentified newspaper clipping, Mary Pollard Clarke Scrapbook, Clarke Family Papers, Virginia Historical Society. A typescript version signed by Mary Pollard Clarke and dated Dec. 19, 1915, can be found in box 1, Roberta Wellford Papers, University of Virginia. Since this article also contains the text of *Equal Suffrage and the Negro Vote*, it is reasonable to assume that Mary Pollard Clarke was the pamphlet's author.

30. *Richmond Times-Dispatch*, Dec. 21, 1919. The same statement, indeed the entire letter, was reprinted as a broadside, "Reply to Thomas Nelson Page on the Federal Women Suffrage Amendment," Virginia Woman Suffrage Collection. . . . The article continued, "This is a white man's country and always will be, and can he be less generous than to allow his negro brother or sister the reward of citizenship which he or she has attained under the laws which the state has made?" The use of "brother" and "sister" is especially interesting in an article claiming that the grant of the vote to all black men during Reconstruction was a "crime," that woman suffrage will increase white supremacy, and that white women, outnumbering black women and men, will "raise greatly the educational and moral standard of the voters."

31. Rosalyn M. Terborg-Penn, "Afro-Americans in the Struggle for Woman Suffrage" (Ph.D. diss., Howard University, 1977), p. 275; Guy-Sheftall, *Daughters of Sorrow*, pp. 99–130.

32. *Richmond Planet*, Sept. 20, 1918.

33. The *Norfolk Journal and Guide* shared the *Planet's* contempt for the antis: on July 29, 1922, the *Journal and Guide* summed up the antis' position: "Rather than enfranchise *some* black women, they said, we would keep the suffrage from *all* white women." For blacks, the *Journal and Guide* went on, this was "humiliating exploitation.". . .

34. Maggie Lena Walker, "Woman in Business," typescript, 5, Maggie Walker House, Richmond, Va.; William Anthony Aery, "National Association of Colored Women," *Southern Workman* 41 (Sept. 1912):537.

35. *Richmond Planet,* Feb. 28, 1916.

36. Maggie Lena Walker Diary, Sept. 12–23, 1920, Maggie Walker House; *Richmond News Leader,* Sept. 17, 1920. The *Richmond Evening Journal,* Sept. 25, 1920, reported that the black wing of the Republican party, under the direction of Mrs. E. L. Dixon-Bryan, had been organizing women in a house-to-house canvass since April.

The statistics were taken from the running tallies printed in the *Richmond News Leader* and the *Richmond Times-Dispatch,* Sept. 17–Oct. 4, 1920.

37. The text of the petition was given in the *Richmond Evening Journal,* Sept. 23, 1920, which reported the signatories as Mrs. E. L. D. Bryan, Mrs. Bettie G. Cousins, Mrs. Margaret R. Johnson, Mrs. Lizzie E. Davis, Mrs. Sylvia L. Mitchell Scott, Giles B. Jackson, and Mrs. Ora Brown Stokes. On Walker's efforts, see Maggie Walker Diary, Sept. 20, 1920; and *Richmond Times-Dispatch,* Sept. 21, 1920.

38. The 2,410 black women registered slightly exceeded the number of black men registered (2,401); 2,410 was 12.5 percent of the black female population aged twenty-one and up. The 10,645 white women registered compared with 28,148 white men registered: 10,645 was 26.8 percent of the white female population aged twenty-one and up. Among black men above the age of twenty, 14.8 percent were registered. Among white men above the age of twenty, 79.4 percent were registered. Registration figures for all groups are from the *Richmond News Leader,* Nov. 27, 1920. Population figures are from the Bureau of the Census, *Fourteenth Census of the United States Taken in the Year 1920,* vol. 2. *Population 1920* (Washington, D.C.: Government Printing Office, 1922), p. 357.

39. . . . The *Newport News Daily Press* had made a similar maneuver on September 8 in its report on the progress of registration locally. The headline read "Colored Women Ahead in Rush for Ballot," while the article itself went on to say that 122 white women and 36 black women had qualified so far.

40. *Richmond News Leader,* Sept. 18, 1920.

41. The quotation from Rorer James was taken from the *Bedford Bulletin,* Sept. 30, 1920. . . .

42. Registration figures for Richmond come from the *Richmond News Leader,* Nov. 27, 1920. Population figures are from *Fourteenth Census,* vol. 2, 357, and so specify actual numbers of women and men.

43. Adèle Clark Interview, p. 20.

44. Names of members of the Women's Section of the Virginia State Committee on Interracial Cooperation were listed in the *Richmond Planet,* Dec. 3, 1921. I am grateful to John Kneebone for additional names that appeared in the Commission on Interracial Cooperation Papers, microfilm, reel 55, frames 505, 1416, 1478. Other feeders for interracial work included the Protestant churches; at least four of the thirty-four white women activists were lay leaders in the Baptist, Methodist, or Presbyterian churches. For help in identifying them, I thank John Kneebone, Brent Tarter, and Sandra Treadway of the *Dictionary of Virginia Biography* Project, Virginia State Library and Archives.

45. *Richmond Planet,* Dec. 3, 1921.

46. *Norfolk Journal and Guide,* Sept. 3, 1921.

47. Adèle Clark Interview, pp. 21–22.

48. *Southern Negro Women and Race Cooperation* (n.p.: Southeastern Federation of Negro Women's Clubs, 1921), pp. 6–7 [pamphlet located in the Maggie Walker House].

49. Adèle Clark Interview, p. 22. For the obvious reasons, there is not much written evidence about these efforts. Maggie Walker made a cryptic note after having been contacted by Adèle Clark: "Call from Miss Clarke, white,—political leader—to plan the study of citizenship." Maggie Walker Diary, Nov. 20, 1920.

50. On the political initiatives of black women nationally, see Evelyn Brooks Higginbotham, "In Politics to Stay: Black Women Leaders and Party Politics in the 1920s," in *Women, Politics, and Change,* ed. Louise A. Tilly and Patricia Gurin (New York: Russell Sage Foundation, 1990), pp. 199–220.

51. *Richmond Planet,* Sept. 10 and Nov. 5, 1921.

DOCUMENT: Controlling Reproduction

Margaret Sanger, "I resolved that women should have knowledge of contraception. . . ."

Nowhere does gender matter more than in the area of reproduction. The contrast between the high fertility of newly arriving immigrants and the low birth rate among old-stock Americans around the turn of the century prompted such leaders as Theodore Roosevelt to lament "race suicide" and to exhort women of the "proper sort" to perform their maternal functions in the selfless fashion dictated by time and tradition. Viewed through women's eyes, however, these population trends looked different, as this selection on the beginnings of the birth control movement dramatically illustrates. While a few radicals such as Emma Goldman saw contraception as a means of liberating women by restoring to them control over their own bodies and thereby lessening their economic dependence on men, it was Margaret Higgins Sanger whose name would become most closely linked with the crusade for birth control.

The factors that propelled Sanger—always a complex personality—to leadership were many. One of eleven children, she helped bury her mother, who died of tuberculosis. Young Margaret, however, was convinced that it was the passion of her father who lived to be eighty which was the real cause of her mother's death. A nursing career also shaped Sanger's thinking, as the following account suggests. Arrested under the Comstock Law (p. 574) for publication of a newspaper advocating contraception, she fled in 1914 to England with her husband and three children. There she met the famous British psychologist and sex expert, Havelock Ellis, who further convinced her that sexual experience should be separated from reproduction, enabling couples to enhance the quality of their sexual relationship. Returning to New York, the Sangers continued their activities on behalf of birth control. The opening of the Brownsville clinic in 1916, recounted here, resulted in still further confrontation with authorities. The hunger strike of Sanger's sister, Ethel Byrne, a nurse at the clinic, was followed by Sanger's own trial. Convicted of "maintaining a public nuisance," she was sentenced to thirty days in the workhouse. Ever the iconoclast and rebel, she gave talks to other inmates on sex hygiene when the matrons were out of sight. Divorcing William Sanger, she subsequently married a wealthy oil man who contributed liberally to the American Birth Control League, which she founded in 1921.

Important financial aid would also come in later years from the wealthy feminist Katherine McCormick, who shared Sanger's commitment to research in contraception.

Margaret Sanger, following a decision by the New York Court of Appeals in 1918. Although the court upheld her conviction, it interpreted the law in question more broadly, allowing physicians to provide contraceptives to married women "to cure or prevent (venereal) disease." (Photograph courtesy of Planned Parenthood Federation of America, Inc.)

In the early 1950s McCormick provided funds for experiments in endocrinology that led to the development of the birth control pill. At a time when few scientists thought an oral contraceptive was possible, the insistence of Sanger and McCormick that every woman had the right to control her own body helped bring about a major breakthrough in medical technology. In 1960 "the pill" became available to the public. The timing was propitious, for it coincided with a period of sexual liberation that, while proving in some respects to be a mixed blessing for women, also coincided with new recognition of the intensity of their sexual drive and capacity for sexual pleasure.

Although Sanger saw the development of an oral contraceptive as another victory in a long and difficult struggle for reproductive freedom, others viewed the birth control movement differently. Arguments that limiting family size could not only free women's energies for social reform but prevent the world's poor from producing children they were unable to care for met with opposition from women themselves in the early years of Sanger's crusade. Some feared that birth control would contribute to promiscuity; others feared it would deny women the dignity that was theirs by virtue of motherhood. The Roman Catholic Church was unrelenting in its opposition, maintaining that the use of contraceptives is a sin. Among groups in the self-styled profamily movement of the present, Sanger is still being angrily attacked. Her contribution to the lives of modern American women remains a matter of political debate. Birth control is not only a technical way of spacing and limiting children so as to benefit both mother and child but is part of a larger debate about the extent to which women should be able to control their own reproductive lives.

AWAKENING AND REVOLT

Early in the year 1912 I came to a sudden realization that my work as a nurse and my activities in social service were entirely palliative and consequently futile and useless to relieve the misery I saw all about me. . . .

It is among the mothers here that the most difficult problems arise—the outcasts of society with theft, filth, perjury, cruelty, brutality oozing from beneath.

Ignorance and neglect go on day by day; children born to breathe but a few hours and pass out of life; pregnant women toiling early and late to give food to four or five children, always hungry; boarders taken into homes where there is not sufficient room for the family; little girls eight and ten years of age sleeping in the same room with dirty, foul smelling, loathsome men; women whose weary, pregnant, shapeless bodies refuse to accommodate themselves to the husbands' desires find husbands looking with lustful eyes upon other women, sometimes upon their own little daughters, six and seven years of age.

In this atmosphere abortions and birth become the main theme of conversation. On Saturday nights I have seen groups of fifty to one hundred women going into questionable offices well known in the community for cheap abortions. I asked several women what took place there, and they all gave the same reply: a quick examination, a probe inserted into the uterus and turned a few times to disturb the fertilized ovum, and then the woman was sent home. Usually the flow began the next day and often continued four or five weeks. Sometimes an ambulance carried the victim to the hospital for a curetage, and if she returned home at all she was looked upon as a lucky woman.

This state of things became a nightmare with me. There seemed no sense to it all, no reason for such waste of mother life, no right to exhaust women's vitality and to throw them on the scrap-heap before the age of thirty-five.

Everywhere I looked, misery and fear stalked—men fearful of losing their jobs, women fearful that even worse conditions might come upon them. The menace of another pregnancy hung like a sword over the head of every poor woman I came in contact with that year. The question which met me was always the same: What can I do to keep from it? or, What can I do to get out of this? Sometimes they talked among themselves bitterly.

"It's the rich that know the tricks," they'd say, "while we have all the kids." Then, if the women were Roman Catholics, they talked about "Yankee tricks," and asked me if I knew what the Protestants did to keep their families down. When I said that I didn't believe that the rich knew much more than they did I was laughed at and suspected of holding back information for money. They would nudge each other and say something about paying me before I left the case if I would reveal the "secret." . . .

I heard over and over again of their desperate efforts at bringing themselves "around"—drinking various herb-teas, taking drops of turpentine on sugar, steaming over a chamber of boiling coffee or of turpentine water, rolling down stairs, and finally inserting slippery-elm sticks, or knitting needles, or shoe hooks into the uterus. I used to shudder with horror as I heard the details and, worse yet, learned of the conditions *behind the reason* for such desperate actions.

. . . Each time I returned it was to hear that Mrs. Cohen had been carried to a hospital but had never come back, that Mrs. Kelly had sent the children to a neighbor's and had put her head into the gas oven to end her misery. Many of the women had consulted midwives, social workers and doctors at the dispensary and asked a way to limit their families, but they were denied this help, sometimes indignantly or gruffly, sometimes jokingly; but always knowledge was denied them. Life for them had but one choice: either to abandon themselves to incessant childbearing, or to terminate their pregnancies through abortions. Is it any wonder they resigned themselves hopelessly, as the Jewish and Italian mothers, or fell into drunkenness, as the Irish and Scotch? The latter were often beaten by husbands, as well as by their sons and daughters. They were driven and cowed, and only as beasts of burden were allowed to exist. . . .

They claimed my thoughts night and day. One by one these women, with their worried, sad, pensive and aging faces would marshal themselves before me in my dreams, sometimes appealingly, sometimes accusingly. I could not escape from the facts of their misery,

neither was I able to see the way out of their problems and their troubles. . . .

Finally the thing began to shape itself, to become accumulative during the three weeks I spent in the home of a desperately sick woman living on Grand Street, a lower section of New York's East Side.

Mrs. Sacks was only twenty-eight years old; her husband, an unskilled worker, thirty-two. Three children, aged five, three and one, were none too strong nor sturdy, and it took all the earnings of the father and the ingenuity of the mother to keep them clean, provide them with air and proper food, and give them a chance to grow into decent manhood and womanhood.

Both parents were devoted to these children and to each other. The woman had become pregnant and had taken various drugs and purgatives, as advised by her neighbors. Then, in desperation, she had used some instrument lent to her by a friend. She was found prostrate on the floor amidst the crying children when her husband returned from work. Neighbors advised against the ambulance, and a friendly doctor was called. The husband would not hear of her going to a hospital, and as a little money had been saved in the bank a nurse was called and the battle for that precious life began.

. . . The three-room apartment was turned into a hospital for the dying patient. Never had I worked so fast, so concentratedly as I did to keep alive that little mother. . . .

. . . July's sultry days and nights were melted into a torpid inferno. Day after day, night after night, I slept only in brief snatches, ever too anxious about the condition of that feeble heart bravely carrying on, to stay long from the bedside of the patient. With but one toilet for the building and that on the floor below, everything had to be carried down for disposal, while ice, food and other necessities had to be carried three flights up. It was one of those old airshaft buildings of which there were several thousands then standing in New York City.

At the end of two weeks recovery was in sight, and at the end of three weeks I was preparing to leave the fragile patient to take up the ordinary duties of her life, including those of wifehood and motherhood. . . .

But as the hour for my departure came nearer, her anxiety increased, and finally with trembling voice she said: "Another baby will finish me, I suppose."

"It's too early to talk about that," I said, and resolved that I would turn the question over to the doctor for his advice. When he came I said: "Mrs. Sacks is worried about having another baby."

"She well might be," replied the doctor, and then he stood before her and said: "Any more such capers, young woman, and there will be no need to call me."

"Yes, yes—I know, Doctor," said the patient with trembling voice, "but," and she hesitated as if it took all of her courage to say it, "*what* can I do to prevent getting that way again?"

"Oh ho!" laughed the doctor good naturedly, "You want your cake while you eat it too, do you? Well, it can't be done." Then, familiarly slapping her on the back and picking up his hat and bag to depart, he said: "I'll tell you the only sure thing to do. Tell Jake to sleep on the roof!"

With those words he closed the door and went down the stairs, leaving us both petrified and stunned.

Tears sprang to my eyes, and a lump came in my throat as I looked at that face before me. It was stamped with sheer horror. I thought for a moment she might have gone insane, but she conquered her feelings, whatever they may have been, and turning to me in desperation said: "He can't understand, can he?—he's a man after all—but you do, don't you? You're a woman and you'll tell me the secret and I'll never tell it to a soul."

She clasped her hands as if in prayer, she leaned over and looked straight into my eyes and beseechingly implored me to tell her something—something *I really did not know.* . . .

I had to turn away from that imploring face. I could not answer her then. I quieted her as best I could. She saw that I was moved by the tears in my eyes. I promised that I would come back in a few days and tell her what she wanted to know. The few simple means of limiting the family like *coitus interruptus* or the condom were laughed at by the neighboring women when told these were the means used by men in the well-to-do families. That was not believed, and I knew such an answer would be swept aside as useless were I to tell her this at such a time. . . .

The intelligent reasoning of the young mother—how to *prevent* getting that way again—how sensible, how just she had been— yes, I promised myself I'd go back and have a long talk with her and tell her more, and perhaps she would not laugh but would believe that those methods were all that were really known.

But time flew past, and weeks rolled into months. . . . I was about to retire one night three months later when the telephone rang and an agitated man's voice begged me to come at once to help his wife who was sick again. It was the husband of Mrs. Sacks, and I intuitively knew before I left the telephone that it was almost useless to go.

. . . I arrived a few minutes after the doctor, the same one who had given her such noble advice. The woman was dying. She was unconscious. She died within ten minutes after my arrival. It was the same result, the same story told a thousand times before—death from abortion. She had become pregnant, had used drugs, had then consulted a five-dollar professional abortionist, and death followed.

The doctor shook his head as he rose from listening for the heart beat. . . . The gentle woman, the devoted mother, the loving wife had passed on leaving behind her a frantic husband, helpless in his loneliness, bewildered in his helplessness as he paced up and down the room, hands clenching his head, moaning "My God! My God! My God!"

The Revolution came—but not as it has been pictured nor as history relates that revolutions have come. . . .

After I left that desolate house I walked and walked and walked; for hours and hours I kept on, bag in hand, thinking, regretting, dreading to stop; fearful of my conscience, dreading to face my own accusing soul. At three in the morning I arrived home still clutching a heavy load the weight of which I was quite unconscious.

. . . As I stood at the window and looked out, the miseries and problems of that sleeping city arose before me in a clear vision like a panorama: crowded homes, too many children; babies dying in infancy; mothers overworked; baby nurseries; children neglected and hungry—mothers so nervously wrought they could not give the little things the comfort nor care they needed; mothers half sick most of their lives—"always ailing, never failing"; women made into drudges; children working in cellars; children aged six and seven pushed into the labor market to help earn a living; another baby on the way; still another; yet another; a baby born dead—great relief; an older child dies—sorrow, but nevertheless relief—insurance helps; a mother's death—children scattered into institutions; the father, desperate, drunken; he slinks away to become an outcast in a society which has trapped him.

. . . There was only one thing to be done: call out, start the alarm, set the heather on fire! Awaken the womanhood of America to free the motherhood of the world! I released from my almost paralyzed hand the nursing bag which unconsciously I had clutched, threw it across the room, tore the uniform from my body, flung it into a corner, and renounced all palliative work forever.

I would never go back again to nurse women's ailing bodies while their miseries were as vast as the stars. I was now finished with superficial cures, with doctors and nurses and social workers who were brought face to face with this overwhelming truth of women's needs and yet turned to pass on the other side. They must be made to see these facts. I resolved that women should have knowledge of contraception. They have every right to know about their own bodies. I would strike out—I would scream from the housetops. I would tell the world what was going on in the lives of these poor women. I *would* be heard. No matter what it should cost. *I would be heard.* . . .

I announced to my family the following day that I had finished nursing, that I would never go on another case—and I never have.

I asked doctors what one could do and was told I'd better keep off that subject or Anthony Comstock would get me. I was told that there were laws against that sort of thing. This was the reply from every medical man and woman I approached. . . .

A "PUBLIC NUISANCE"

The selection of a place for the first birth control clinic was of the greatest importance. No one could actually tell how it would be received in any neighborhood. I thought of all the possible difficulties: The indifference of women's organizations, the ignorance of the workers themselves, the resentment of social agencies, the opposition of the medical profession. Then there was the law—the law of New York State.

Section 1142 was definite. It stated that *no one* could give information to prevent conception to *anyone* for any reason. There was, however, Section 1145, which distinctly stated that physicians (*only*) could give advice to prevent conception for the cure or prevention of disease. I inquired about the section, and was told by two attorneys and several physicians that this clause was an exception to 1142 referring only to venereal disease. But anyway, as I was not a physician, it could not protect me. Dared I risk it?

I began to think of the doctors I knew. Several who had previously promised now refused. I wrote, telephoned, asked friends to ask other friends to help me find a woman doctor to help me demonstrate the need of a birth control clinic in New York. None could be found. No one wanted to go to jail. No one cared to test out the law. Perhaps it would have to be done without a doctor. But it had to be done; that I knew.

Fania Mindell, an enthusiastic young worker in the cause, had come on from Chicago to help me. Together we tramped the streets on that dreary day in early October, through a driving rainstorm, to find the best location at the cheapest terms possible . . .

Finally at 46 Amboy Street, in the Brownsville Section of Brooklyn, we found a friendly landlord with a good place vacant at fifty dollars a month rental; and Brownsville was settled on. It was one of the most thickly populated sections. It had a large population of working class Jews, always interested in health measures, always tolerant of new ideas, willing to listen and to accept advice whenever the health of mother or children was involved. I knew that here there would at least be no breaking of windows, no hurling of insults into our teeth; but I was scarcely prepared for the popular support, the sympathy and friendly help given us in that neighborhood from that day to this. . . .

With a small bundle of handbills and a large amount of zeal, we fared forth each morning in a house-to-house canvass of the district in which the clinic was located. Every family in that great district received a "dodger" printed in English, Yiddish and Italian. . . .

Women of every race and creed flocked to the clinic with the determination not to have any more children than their health could stand or their husbands could support. Jews and Christians, Protestants and Roman Catholics alike made their confessions to us, whatever they may have professed at home or in the church. Some did not dare talk this over with their husbands; and some came urged on by their husbands. Men themselves came after work; and some brought timid, embarrassed wives, apologetically dragging a string of little children. . . .

When I asked a bright little Roman Catholic woman what she would say to the priest when he learned that she had been to the Clinic, she answered indignantly: "It's none of his business. My husband has a weak heart and works only four days a week. He gets twelve dollars, and we can barely live on it now. We have enough children."

Her friend, sitting by, nodded a vigorous approval. "When I was married," she broke in, "the priest told us to have lots of children, and we listened to him. I had fifteen. Six are living. Nine baby funerals in our house. I am thirty-six years old now. Look at me! I look sixty."

As I walked home that night, I made a mental calculation of fifteen baptismal fees, nine funeral expenses, masses and candles for the repose of nine little souls, the physical suffering of the mother, and the emotional suffering of both parents; and I asked myself, "Was it fair? Is this the price of Christianity?" . . .

Ethel Byrne, who is my sister and a trained nurse, assisted me in advising, explaining, and demonstrating to the women how to prevent conception. As all of our 488 records were confiscated by the detectives who later arrested us for violation of the New York State law, it is difficult to tell exactly how many more women came in those days to seek advice; but we estimate that it was far more than five hundred. As in any new enterprise, false reports were maliciously spread about the clinic; weird stories without the slightest foundation of truth. We talked plain talk and give plain facts to the women who came there. We kept a record of every applicant. All were mothers; most of them had large families.

It was whispered about that the police were to raid the place for abortions. We had no fear of that accusation. We were trying to spare mothers the necessity of that ordeal by giving them proper contraceptive information. . . .

The arrest and raid on the Brooklyn clinic was spectacular. There was no need of a large force of plain clothes men to drag off a trio of decent, serious women who were testing out a law on a fundamental principle. My federal ar-

rest, on the contrary, had been assigned to intelligent men. One had to respect the dignity of their mission; but the New York city officials seem to use tactics suitable only for crooks, bandits and burglars. We were not surprised at being arrested, but the shock and horror of it was that a *woman*, with a squad of five plain clothes men, conducted the raid and made the arrest. A woman—the irony of it!

I refused to close down the clinic, hoping that a court decision would allow us to continue such necessary work. I was to be disappointed. Pressure was brought upon the landlord, and we were dispossessed by the law as a "public nuisance." In Holland the clinics were called "public utilities."

When the policewoman entered the clinic with her squad of plain clothes men and announced the arrest of Miss Mindell and myself (Mrs. Byrne was not present at the time and her arrest followed later), the room was crowded to suffocation with women waiting in the outer room. The police began bullying these mothers, asking them questions, writing down their names in order to subpoena them to testify against us at the trial. These women, always afraid of trouble which the very presence of a policeman signifies, screamed and cried aloud. The children on their laps screamed, too. It was like a panic for a few minutes until I walked into the room where they were stampeding and begged them to be quiet and not to get excited. I assured them that nothing could happen to them, that I was under arrest but they would be allowed to return home in a few minutes. That quieted them. The men were blocking the door to prevent anyone from leaving, but I finally persuaded them to allow these women to return to their homes, unmolested though terribly frightened by it all.

. . . The patrol wagon came rattling through the streets to our door, and at length Miss Mindell and I took our seats within and were taken to the police station. . . .

HUNGER STRIKE

Out of that spectacular raid, which resulted in an avalanche of nation-wide publicity in the daily press, four separate and distinct cases resulted:

Mrs. Ethel Byrne, my sister, was charged with violating Section 1142 of the Penal Code, designed to prevent dissemination of birth control information.

Miss Fania Mindell was charged with having sold an allegedly indecent book entitled "What Every Girl Should Know" written by Margaret Sanger.

I was charged with having conducted a clinic at 46 Amboy Street, Brooklyn, in violation of the same section of the Penal Code.

Having re-opened the clinic, I was arrested on a charge of "maintaining a public nuisance," in violation of Section 1530 of the Penal Code.

The three of us were held for trial in the Court of Special Sessions, with bail fixed at $500 each. This meant that our cases would be decided by three judges appointed by the Mayor and not by a jury. . . .

My sister was found guilty, and on January 22 she was sentenced to thirty days in the Workhouse. A writ of habeas corpus as a means of suspending sentence during appeal was refused by Supreme Court Justice Callahan. She spent the night in jail.

Ethel Byrne promptly declared a hunger strike. I knew that she would not flinch. Quiet, taciturn, with a will of steel hidden by a diffident air, schooled by her long training as a professional nurse, she announced briefly that she would neither eat, drink, nor work until her release. Commissioner of Correction Burdette G. Lewis promptly announced that she would be permitted to see no one but her attorney.

While the newspapers were reporting—always on the front page—the condition of the hunger striker, plans were hastened for a monster mass meeting of protest, to be held in Carnegie Hall. Helen Todd acted as chairman, and Dr. Mary Halton was an additional speaker. The hall was crowded by a huge audience of all classes. The women patients of the Brownsville clinic were given places of honor on the platform. The salvos of applause which greeted me showed that intelligent opinion was strongly behind us, and did much to give me the courage to fight with renewed strength for the immediate release of Ethel Byrne.

This meeting was acclaimed by the press as a "triumph of women, for women, by women." The meeting was said to have struck the right note—that of being instructive and persuasive, instead of agitational.

In the meantime, Ethel Byrne's refusal to eat and drink was crowding all other news off the front pages of the New York papers. Her defiance was sharpening the issue between self-respecting citizens and the existing law, which was denounced on every street corner as hypocritical. In the subway crowds, on street-corners, everywhere people gathered, the case was discussed. "They are imprisoning a woman for teaching physiological facts!" I heard one man exclaim. . . .

"It makes little difference whether I starve or not," she replied, through her attorney, "so long as this outrageous arrest calls attention to the archaic laws which would prevent our telling the truth about the facts of life. With eight thousand deaths a year in New York State from illegal operations on women, one more death won't make much difference."

All this served to convince the now panic-stricken Mr. Lewis [Commissioner of Correction in charge of Blackwell's Island] that Mrs. Byrne was different, after all, from the alcoholics and drug addicts who had given him his previous experience, and with whom he had gallantly compared her. When she had gone 103 hours without food, he established a precedent in American prison annals. He ordered her forcibly fed. She was the first woman so treated in this country. . . .

The truth was that Mrs. Byrne was in a critical condition after being rolled in a blanket and having milk, eggs and a stimulant forced into her stomach through a rubber tube. I realized this as soon as I heard that she was "passive under the feeding." Nothing but loss of strength could have lessened the power of her resistance to such authority. Nothing but brutality could have reduced her fiery spirit to acquiescence. I was desperate; torn between admiration for what she was doing and misery over what I feared might be the result.

On January 31st, a committee headed by Mrs. Amos Pinchot, Jessie Ashley and myself went to Albany for the purpose of asking Governor Whitman to appoint a commission to investigate birth control and make a report to the state legislature. Governor Whitman, a wise, fair, intelligent executive and statesman, received us, and listened to our exposition of the economic and moral necessity for birth control; the medical theory behind its justification. He promised to consider appointing the commission. During the interview Miss Jessie Ashley introduced the subject of Mrs. Byrne's treatment on Blackwell's Island and the anxiety we felt about her condition. We tried to make him see the outrage committed by the state in making anyone suffer for so just a cause. The Governor offered Mrs. Byrne a pardon on condition that she would not continue to disseminate birth control information. . . .

When we left Albany that day, I had the promise of a provisional pardon for Mrs. Byrne, but best of all I had in my purse a letter from the Governor to the authorites at Blackwell's Island authorizing me to see her. I was shocked and horrified when, in the late afternoon of February 1st, I saw my sister. She was lying semi-conscious on a cot in a dark corner of the prison cell. . . .

There was not time to inform her of the conditions of her pardon, and moreover she was too ill to face the question. I still believe that I was right in accepting the conditions which the Governor imposed. There was no other course. I saw that she was dangerously ill, that nothing further was to be gained by her keeping on, and that her death would have been a terrible calamity. Her life was what mattered to me, regardless of her future activities. . . .

At any rate, by the time she was released the subject was a burning issue. Newspapers which previously had ignored the case, had to mention a matter important enough to bring the Governor of the State from Albany to New York.

LOIS W. BANNER
Menopause and Its Meaning

The importance of childbirth, accompanied by its physical hazards, which Judith Walzer Leavitt has described (pp. 184–91), long dominated women's lives. Indeed, in the centuries before medical advances increased the life span of both sexes, most women did not live long after their childbearing years were over. For many women, the infertility that came with aging was welcome.

Yet aging often had complex negative connotations as well. Unlike Asian or American Indian cultures, Euroamericans rarely honored the wisdom and experiences of the elderly. Sexuality in older women was regarded as dangerous. Witchcraft traditions, as Carol Karlsen and Sarah Deutsch have suggested, often targeted older women who lacked male protectors.

As the expectation for companionship within even a paternalistic marriage grew among the middle class in the early nineteenth century, more positive attitudes developed toward aging women, so long as their sexuality remained contained in marriage. Between 1880 and 1920, menopause assumed new importance. How menopause has been viewed—whether positively or negatively—is the subject of the following essay.

In what ways can negative definitions of menopause evoke earlier images of aging women? Do you see parallels between the medicalization of childbirth described by Leavitt and the medicalizaion of menopause?

Excerpted from "The Twentieth Century: Menopause and Its Meaning," chap. 8 of *In Full Flower: Aging Women, Power, and Sexuality: A History* by Lois W. Banner (New York: Vintage Books, 1992). Copyright © 1992 by Lois W. Banner. Reprinted by permission of the author and Alfred A. Knopf, Inc. Notes have been renumbered and edited.

In 1911 *The Dangerous Age,* a novel by Danish author Karin Michaelis, was published. It quickly became an international best-seller. A work of popular fiction (although of debatable aesthetic merit), its widespread readership nonetheless indicated Michaelis's sensitivity to public interests. The novel tells the story of Elsie Lindtner, a woman in her mid-forties, who has divorced her wealthy husband, taken a younger lover, and then alone gone to live on a remote island. What seems initially to be a story of middle-aged liberation, however, quickly turns into an indictment . . . of her supposed mental irrationality produced by menopause. In Michaelis's exposition, Lindtner is undergoing "the dangerous age." "The dangerous age," according to Michaelis, is that period in women's lives between the ages of forty and fifty when most women's menstrual cycle stops and their reproductive years end. During this decade, Lindtner declares, "we are all more or less mad."[1]

As the novel progresses, most of Lindtner's middle-aged women friends suffer emotional breakdowns. Some alternate between mania and depression; some leave their husbands. Some become obsessive; one woman cleans her house over and over again. Another is institutionalized and treated surgically. (The nature of the treatment is obscure, although it sounds as though it involves a hysterectomy, a surgical procedure sometimes used in this era for female mental imbalance.). . . "What is the use of all these discussions and articles about the equality of the sexes, so long as we women are at times the slaves of an inevitable necessity?" queries Lindtner.[2]

In 1912 appeared *Women's Share in Social Culture,* by American writer Anna Garlin Spencer. Published one year after *The Dangerous Age,* this work of popular sociology contains what reads like a rebuttal to Michaelis. Spencer drew from contemporary evidence that women lived longer than men and were more vital in older years to assert that menopause afforded women a "second youth." In her view the menstrual cycle caused mood swings, and its end improved mental health. "When the climacteric of middle life is reached, nature gives a fresh start and a fresh balance of power." Further, relieved from childbearing, women could turn toward personal or social goals. And their experience as homemakers and mothers could translate into effectiveness in other activities.

"All that has gone into the sacrificial service to family life," wrote Spencer, "may add a peculiar flavor and a special wisdom to personal achievement or to enlarged social service."[3]

The differing opinions of Michaelis and Spencer in the 1910s reflect two divergent opinions about menopause which have continued throughout the twentieth century. The first opinion has been that menopause is an illness, bringing a breakdown of body and mind. The second has been that menopause initiates a time of strength for women, a regrouping before entry into what Margaret Mead in the 1950s called a period of "post-menopausal zest."[4]. . .

In the late-nineteenth- and early-twentieth-century Progressive era, advice books and magazine articles as well as technical and popular medical writings foregrounded Spencer's liberatory point of view. After World War I, however, although the optimistic sentiments were still to be found, they were overwhelmed by a cacophony of voices asserting that menopause equaled illness. The negative views reached a nadir in the 1950s with the ubiquity of the Freudian interpretation, especially articulated by the American psychoanalyst, Helene Deutsch. They continue to the present in medical views that all menopausal women need to take the hormone estrogen. . . .

The topic of menopause connects with the ongoing feminist debate over the relative importance of biology and of culture in producing behavior. For like sexuality or gender, other primary areas of human self-identification, menopause is a physical experience conditioned by cultural constructions of its meaning. Triggered by hormonal changes, menopause produces a physical symptomology; most women experience some of the symptoms, which seem to have remained fairly standard over time. (Heat flashes, weight gain, a growth in facial hair, a decrease in the size of the uterus, and a drying of vaginal tissue are the most common experiences.) The issue becomes the extent of symptoms experienced by individual women and in the general population of women as well as the extent to which cultural signals can operate to magnify the symptoms— or to ameliorate them.

Survey data suggest that cultural signals are key to both the perception and the experience of menopause. From rudimentary nineteenth-century surveys to sophisticated recent ones, the data show that although almost all women experience some menopausal symptoms, only a small minority suffer severe symptoms. Yet doctors, drawing their illustrations from a patient population, identify the severe symptoms they encounter with the entire population of menopausal women and define all women undergoing menopause as requiring medical attention. The "medicalization" of menopause has been a consistent theme throughout the twentieth century; in the final analysis it may be more for the benefit of doctors than for the women they treat.[5]

Throughout the twentieth century, a major debate regarding aging women has focused on menopause. The debate has been international, carried on especially in medical journals but also, to a lesser extent, in popular periodicals. The central issues in this debate have been two. The first issue has been the extent to which menopause is an illness, producing physiological distress and mental disorder. The second, evident through the 1950s, was whether menopausal women invariably fell in love with young men. Once again sexuality became key to definitions of women's aging. . . .

Between 1890 and 1920 a vigorous woman's rights movement spearheaded progressive changes for women. Women entered the work force and the professions; many legal discriminations were removed; formerly forbidden areas of sports and leisure opened up to them. . . . Newspapers and novels celebrated "the New Woman." This widely used phrase came to represent the new opportunities for women.[6]

But the "New Woman" was not only a young woman: older women also were included. What one observer called "the renaissance of the middle aged" was widely chronicled by the day's press, especially in the United States. New opportunities for aging women to leave the confines of home and family stimulated a new cultural imagery regarding them. For example, aging unmarried women, previously denigrated as unwanted spinsters, now were joined by "bachelor women," who lived in glamorous cities. Indeed, the powerful nineteenth-century negative stereotyping of the unmarried aging woman was now considerably muted.

"Old maids no longer exist!" declaimed one author. . . . "The woman of fifty who only a few years ago would have been sent to the ranks of dowagers and grandmothers, today is celebrated for distinctive charm and beauty, ripe views, disciplined intellect, cultivated and manifold gifts."[7] . . .

The liberatory sentiments regarding aging women in this era extended to the medical community. In these years medical researchers produced a large literature concluding that most women experienced little discomfort during menopause. In 1880 Dr. A. Arnold, a Baltimore medical school professor, contended that all recent medical studies of menopause reported no pathology associated with it. In 1897 Andrew Currier, in his oft-cited work on menopause, called the negative view a "hoary" tradition with no basis in fact. In 1900 Dr. Mary Dixon Jones, writing in the *Medical Record*, angrily called categorizing menopause as a "dangerous period" a "libel on the natural formation of one half of the human race."[...]

A new conceptualization of menstruation initiated the new views about menopause. By the late nineteenth century doctors discovered that menstruation was not simply a purging of the blood (the accepted viewpoint for centuries). Rather, experimentation showed that it was connected to the cyclical production of the ovum and thus directly to conception. Older ideas about menstruation's purgative benefit were now revised, and many physicians came to view the menstrual flow as an unfortunate failure in bodily processes designed to build up a fetus. With this new negative attitude toward menstruation, menopause could be viewed positively, as a regrouping of body forces away from childbirth toward other kinds of maternal, generative ends.[8] . . .

The advent of the nineteenth-century birth control consciousness which resulted by the end of the century in a greatly reduced birthrate, especially in France and the United States, also encouraged a positive evaluation of menopause. With the impetus to limit births a popular reality (even though in opposition to state policy), menopause could be viewed positively for its birth control potential. . . . Better diet and medical advances such as successful gynecological surgery for women to correct debilitating conditions like prolapsed uterus, previously a common condition resulting from childbirth, put aging in a more positive light.[9] The prospect for women of having to live many years with chronic illness, even in middle age, was fading. Moreover, statistics in census data and in such indices as life insurance actuarial tables were demonstrating the strength of women's life span.[10] What had often been the case now became apparent: if women could survive childbirth, they would live longer than men. . . .

Declining rates of childbirth plus the lessened risk of death in childbirth also enhanced women's perception of the entire life cycle. And, by the late nineteenth century middle-class women began to bear children at earlier ages and to cluster their childbearing in the early years of their marriages rather than throughout their procreative years. With the last child in school as early as their mid-thirties, they had the expectation of spending some years without domestic and child-care responsibilities. Thus they could develop a stronger sense of self or embark on philanthropic activities in this age of reform attention.[11]

As early as 1870 popular writer Fanny Fern noted the changes in the perception of women's life cycle. She traced the origins of these changes to the impact of the woman's rights movement and to the sense of vigor generated in women through leaving home for work. . . . As older women left the home to participate in voluntary activities or to take up careers, their forcefulness brought a different perception of all older women. In the 1890s and 1900s feminist leaders like Elizabeth Cady Stanton, Susan B. Anthony, and Frances Willard remained active campaigners until well into their sixties. Mary Baker Eddy, a founder of the Christian Science Church, entered her vocation as teacher and healer in 1866 at the age of forty-five; she led the organized church until into her seventies. With regard to her experience of menopause, Elizabeth Cady Stanton, drawing on the contemporary liberatory view, described it as an empowering force. Her "vital forces," formerly contained in her reproductive organs, wrote Stanton, were now "flowing" to her brain, prompting her to leave her family for many months a year to pursue a career as a lecturer.[12]

Jane Addams was fifty-two and still active at Hull House when she seconded Theodore Roosevelt's nomination as the Progressive Party presidential candidate in 1912. Julia Lathrop became head of the Children's Bureau that same year, when she was fifty-four. In 1914, at the age of forty-seven, Lillian Wald became president of the American Union Against Militarism. She had never worked harder, states a biographer, and, as she wrote to a friend, she had never felt better.[13] Frances Perkins became FDR's Secretary of Labor in 1933 when she was fifty-two. . . . One presumes that these women were menopausal or post-menopausal when they undertook these activities.

The career and reform involvements of older women in this era furthered women's positive definition of menopause and aging. But a group of actresses especially advanced the claims of older women to beauty.

Perhaps the most famed female performer of international reputation was the French actress Sarah Bernhardt. Bernhardt continued her popular tours of the United States even when in her sixties. . . . "Thousands of women," wrote Mary Roberts Coolidge, "have seen Madame Sara [sic] Bernhardt, when long past middle age, play L'Aiglon, the part of a youth of nineteen; and many more thousands have read the interviews in which she explained how she kept her youthful figure by muscular activity and hygienic living." Bernhardt, Coolidge asserted, was a major model for women's positive aging.[14]

Aging women's access to more positive definitions of their later life-cycle development was also related to the rise of a more sophisticated business culture, motivated toward creating and exploiting consumption needs. Victorian codes about appropriate public behavior for women and older prohibitions on women's use of cosmetics were breaking down at the same time that cosmetic companies were expanding their markets and beauty parlors were increasing in numbers. Given the financial resources of aging women, they constituted a prime market for commercial beauty promoters. As early as 1888 Elizabeth Lynn Linton noted that the "kohl for the eyelids," the "eaux noire, brun, et chatain, which dyes the hair any shade," as well as the "rouge of eight shades" were being used mainly by the "femme passé" trying to make herself look young. (According to Linton, this woman was especially motivated by the desire to attract a young male companion.) It was no accident that Vogue magazine in the 1890s and 1900s published many articles about the new possibilities for aging women and praised their new access to youthful standards of appearance.[15] Yet the commercialization of aging women's appearance, with commercialism's focus on youth and sexuality, fed into strains of negativity about aging—and about menopause. . . .

Other orientations during the Progressive era [also] countered the positive trends for aging women. Many doctors, for example, contested the optimistic view of menopause to assert that it was a serious illness requiring medical attention: menopausal symptoms . . . [indicated] a body in disorder, . . . [a forerunner of] diseases of aging like cancer. . . . Many posited a similarity between menarche and menopause, suggesting that a similar physical and mental disequilibrium characterized both. With proof of the connection between menstruation and procreation, gynecologists as new medical specialists refurbished older ideas about the power of women's reproductive organs to present them as a unified, albeit delicate, system determining female character.

Michaelis's presentation of menopause as producing insanity resonated in the views of many gynecologists. Drawing on misperceptions standard for centuries, many gynecologists posited a direct linkage between the uterus and the brain. (Such a belief would result in the term "hysterectomy" for the removal of the uterus and ovaries, referencing the mental condition of hysteria and its presumed connection to female reproductive organs.) And such beliefs were extended to aging women. "Involutional melancholia" and "climacteric insanity" were terms used as early as 1865 in diagnoses of disturbed menopausal patients. By late century special diagnostic categories were reserved for menopausal spinsters: "old maid's insanity" was the term occasionally used. . . .[16]

Medical arguments may have a scientific basis, but they are influenced by cultural valuations and individual biases. In the first instance, developments in medicine as a profession probably played a role in the genesis and spread of these negative appraisals of menopause. In this era the medical profession was growing both in numbers of practitioners and in organizational structure. (The same process was also occurring in other professions like business and law.) The expanding medical profession focused on increasing the patient population: given their financial resources and vague symptoms, menopausal women were a potentially large client group. At the same time that doctors took over childbirth from mid-

wives, they expanded the newly established field of gynecology to include menopausal women. The "medicalization of menopause" was entirely to their benefit.[17]

Moreover, women's movement into the professions during the Progressive era threatened both male control of those professions and of the larger male public sphere of which the professions were a part. Historians have often interpreted the medical arguments advanced during these decades in opposition to women's entry into college as in actuality a response to this development's implied challenge to the male public sphere.[18] Similarly, one might argue that negative medical definitions of menopause constituted another set of quasi-scientific explanations given to prevent another (and even potentially more powerful) group of women from leaving the home to challenge male public authority. . . .

By the last decades of the nineteenth century, notions that aging women possessed an inappropriate sexuality also began to appear. By 1900 sexologists like Havelock Ellis issued charges of lesbianism against unmarried career women and reformers. They declared heterosexuality to be the proper human orientation and hinted that women's friendships easily became sexual, thereby challenging the claims of women's superior morality and undermining the legitimacy of their separate bonding networks.[19] They went further. They posited that aging women were driven by a prurient sexual drive which could propel them into deviant, destructive behavior.

In his important 1905 chapters on women in *Studies in the Psychology of Sex*, a work repeatedly reprinted over the next decades, Havelock Ellis included fulsome references to pre-nineteenth-century writers' estimations of women as highly sexed. He drew from the French tradition of valorizing older women to contend that the sexual drive in women is especially strong at older ages. Indeed, he averred, strong sexual passion sometimes does not appear in women until after the menopause.[20]

Yet he viewed the appearance of this drive as problematic. In the first instance he saw it as the major cause of "old maid's insanity." In this case a heightened desire for heterosexual intercourse drove women without sexual experience to desire any men who were kind to them, even though these men had no interest in them.

(Usually, Ellis asserted, the unfortunate men were clergymen.) In his estimation, aging women's prurient sexual desire could take additional forms. He cited numerous cases of older women, especially servant women, who he contended had seduced younger men, sometimes the boys who were their charges. And he continued by asserting that girls' interest in boys was mere curiosity, "but it is pathology when expressed by older women." To him these instances of seduction proved that women were more sexually aggressive than men and that their sexual aggression was dangerous. He concluded his discussion of aging women's sexuality with the assertion that the incidences of male rape were vastly overstated. A real problem, in his opinion, lay in the uncontrollable sexuality of older women and their desire for young men.[21] . . .

Aging women's dangerous sexuality, in the schema of many sexologists and others, had to be controlled. Centuries before, such a conception had contributed to the persecution of aging women as witches. In the modern era, the perceptions of evil were more attenuated and the attempts at containment were nowhere as severe. They primarily produced a good deal of rhetoric against women's participation in social reform and woman's rights activities. Yet parallels can be drawn. The rhetoric was successful in casting doubt on feminist involvement and women's individual independence. In extreme cases, the identification of menopause with madness could bring hospitalization. When repackaged by Freud in a new "scientific" formulation, these ideas indicated that menopause was not a time of increasing vitality but rather a time for retrenchment, for dealing with an inevitable illness in women's lives. . . .

The identification of menopause with illness continues to the present. In our own era have appeared ever new ailments, like osteoporosis, to make menopause an illness and not an experience. And estrogen is routinely prescribed for all the symptoms of menopause, while many doctors maintain that all women, no matter their symptomology, should take estrogen as they age.[22] . . .

Much recent literature on menopause suggests that, like the experience of pregnancy and birth, that of menopause is highly individualistic and that each woman experiences it differently. Much depends on self-image and on life-style, as well as on biological tendencies.

Women with a positive self-image and with an affirmative attitude toward aging experience less severe menopausal symptoms. Exercise and healthy diet can also be important; in the management of specific symptoms like heat flashes positive results have been registered with vitamin therapy and acupuncture.[23]

How then ought we to approach menopause? Should we continue to hide any acknowledgment of its occurrence, silently passing through what we still call, in words freighted with life-cycle significance, "the change of life"? Should women, by their silence, allow the medical profession to assert, by default, the predominating voice in the definition of menopause? . . .

As a life-cycle experience, menopause can be viewed in terms of its own definition. But it is also encased . . . by the broader situation of aging. And, in contemporary times, aging has become of substantial interest. For demographic dispensations have created the possibility of a longer life span for more individuals, especially for more women, than ever before in history. Complex in individualized experience, menopause has had many meanings over the course of the twentieth century. The new developments in aging may once again shift the definitional boundaries of menopause, as it becomes even more a midlife experience in what is a long life.

NOTES

1. Karin Michaelis, *The Dangerous Age* (New York: John Lane, 1911), pp. 49–89.

2. Ibid., pp. 49, 58.

3. Anna Garlin Spencer, *Woman's Share in Social Culture* (New York: Mitchell Kennerley, 1912), p. 231.

4. Cf. Margaret Mead, typescript, "Woman in a Post-Industrial Society," Margaret Mead Papers, Library of Congress.

5. Edward Tilt, *The Change of Life in Health and Disease* (London: Churchill, 1857); Mary Dixon Jones, "Insanity, Its Causes: Is There a Correlation of the Sexual Function with Insanity and Crime?" *Medical Record* (1900):925–37.

6. Lois W. Banner, *Women in Modern America: A Brief History* (New York: Harcourt Brace Jovanovich, 1984); Patricia Branca, *Women in Europe Since 1750* (New York: St. Martin's Press, 1978).

7. Ruth Freeman and Patricia Klaus, "Blessed or Not? The New Spinster in England and the United States in the Late Nineteenth and Early Twentieth Centuries," *Journal of Family History* 9 (Winter 1984):394–413; Grace M. Johnston, "The New Old Maid," *Woman Beautiful* 2 (May 1909):68; Mrs. Wilson Woodrow, "The Woman of Fifty," *Cosmopolitan* 34 (March 1903):505.

8. Sarah J. Stage, *Female Complaints: Lydia Pinkham and the Business of Women's Medicine* (New York: W. W. Norton, 1979).

9. A prolapsed uterus involves the breakdown of the muscles holding the uterus in place. The condition produces the potential for the uterus to "fall" into the vagina, in extreme cases extending outside of the genital region and the body cavity.

10. Cf. John Stockton Hough, *Longevity; Or, the Relative Variability of the Sexes, Particularly with Regard to the Relative Liability of the Inheritance of Certain Transmitted Diseases. Considered in Relation to the Selection of Life Insurance Risks, with a View of Exhibiting the Unjustice of the Practice of Charging Higher Rates for Women* (New York, 1873).

11. Peter G. Filene, *Him/Her/Self: Sex Roles in Modern America* (Baltimore: Johns Hopkins University Press, 1984), p. 11.

12. Lois W. Banner, *Elizabeth Cady Stanton: A Radical for Woman's Right* (Boston: Little, Brown, 1979), pp. 109–10.

13. Robert H. Bremner, "Lillian Wald," in Edward T. James, ed., *Notable American Women* (Cambridge: Belknap Press of Harvard University Press, 1971), p. 528.

14. Mary Roberts Coolidge, *Why Women Are So* (New York: Holt, 1912), p. 127.

15. Elizabeth Lynn Linton, *Modern Woman* (New York: Worthington, 1888), pp. 351–53; Kathy Peiss, "Making Faces: The Cosmetics Industry and the Cultural Construction of Gender, 1890–1930," *Genders* 7 (Spring 1990):143–69.

16. Carroll Smith-Rosenberg, "Puberty to Menopause: The Cycle of Femininity in Nineteenth-Century America," in Smith-Rosenberg, *Disorderly Conduct: Visions of Gender in Victorian America* (New York: Alfred A. Knopf, 1985), pp. 182–96; Peter N. Stearns, "Old Women: Some Historical Observations," *Journal of Family History* 5 (Spring 1980):44–57.

17. Cf. Regina Markell Morantz-Sanchez, *Sympathy and Science: Women Physicians in American Medicine* (New York: Oxford University Press, 1985).

18. Cf. Miriam Lewin, "The Victorians, the Psychologists, and Psychic Birth Control," in Miriam Lewin, *In the Shadow of the Past: Psychology Portrays the Sexes: A Social and Intellectual History* (New York: Columbia University Press, 1984), pp. 50–51.

19. Carroll Smith-Rosenberg, "The New Woman as Androgyne: Social Disorder and Gender Crisis, 1870–1936," in Smith-Rosenberg, *Disorderly Conduct*, p. 265; Lilliam Faderman, *Odd Girl and Twilight Lovers: A History of Lesbian Life in Twentieth Century America* (New York: Columbia University Press, 1991), pp. 37–61.

20. Havelock Ellis, *Studies in the Psychology of Sex: The Sexual Impulse in Women [1905]* (New York: Random House, 1942), p. 243.

21. Ibid., pp. 242–45; Havelock Ellis, *Man and Woman: A Study of Human Secondary Characteristics* (New York: Charles Scribner's Sons, 1908), pp. 224–25.

22. Judith Posner, "It's All in Your Head: Feminist and Medical Models of Menopause (Strange Bedfellows)," *Sex Roles* 5 (1979):179–94; Robert Wilson, *Forever Feminine* (New York: M. Evans, 1966).

23. Helena Harris, "A Critical View of Three Psychoanalytic Positions on Menopause," in Ruth Formanek, ed., *The Meanings of Menopause: Historical, Medical, and Clinical Perspectives* (Hillsdale: Analytical Press, 1990), p. 75.

A sixteen-year-old girl leads children's march to the courthouse in Greenwood, Alabama, 1965. "You think we have problems in Greenwood? We can't even have a peaceful march to our courthouse to talk about them." (Photography © by Bob Fitch. See Worth Long et al., We'll Never Turn Back *[Washington, D.C.: Smithsonian Performing Arts, 1980], p. 68)*

III

Modern America
1920–1990

The years between 1920 and 1990 have, in the main, been years of crisis. Domestically, innovations in technology, management, and marketing transformed an industrial nation into a consumer society. But consumption did not automatically bring the good life that advertisers promised. In the early years after World War I Americans were plagued by tensions that erupted into strikes, attacks upon radicals, and indiscriminate accusations of communism. The climate of suspicion and anxiety brought out the uglier aspects of American society—the Ku Klux Klan enjoyed a brief rebirth. Conflict between generations underscored anxiety over the continuing erosion of Victorian moral standards. Although elements of progressivism persisted, successive Republican administrations pursued policies designed primarily to benefit American corporations on the assumption that the prosperity of the few would bring prosperity to the many. Whether the assumption was true or not, the collapse of corporate America brought collapse to all after the stock market crash of 1929.

The resulting depression crippled industry and left 20 percent of the labor force unemployed. In 1932, after the Hoover administration had failed to produce recovery, voters turned to Franklin Delano Roosevelt and the Democrats. Promising a "new deal" at a time when people were homeless and starving, Roosevelt launched a program of economic recovery and reform, much of it improvised, not all of it successful, and some of it far less radical and extensive than many critics had wished. The result, however, was that in its efforts to cope with economic disaster, the Roosevelt administration redefined the responsibility of the federal government to its citizens. Relief and work programs were provided, unemployment compensation and minimum wages and hours legislation passed, old-age pensions introduced, individual savings accounts insured, farm prices supported, farm ownership encouraged, farm and home mortgages guaranteed, rural houses electrified, and regional development and soil conservation promoted. The welfare state had arrived. Presidents of both parties would subsequently expand it, designing their own programs to benefit the American people. In the process other changes accelerated by international crises occurred: growth in the power of the presidency, in the size of the federal bureaucracy, and in the level of government spending.

If domestic events had occupied the attention of most Americans in previous years, Nazi aggression and Japan's attack upon Pearl Harbor in 1941 thrust their country into a new international role. Mobilized for total war along conventional lines, Americans were psychologically unprepared for their entry into the new atomic age as citizens of the strongest industrial and military power in world history. The implications of these new developments were scarcely understood when tensions between the United States and its former ally, the USSR, escalated into a "cold" war. The expansion of Russian hegemony in eastern Europe and the victory of Chinese communists in a bloody civil war convinced key policy makers that this nation would have to pursue a vigorous policy to "contain" communism throughout the world. If historians cannot agree on the process that led to cold war, they can agree that the persistent confrontations between East and West during the 1950s profoundly affected American life. Viewing North Korea's invasion of South Korea as proof of Russia's drive for world domination and convinced that the credibility of "containment" was at stake, the Truman administration sent troops to check communist aggression. In the United States there was another kind of warfare. Fearing domestic subversion, anticommunists during the McCarthy era purged government, organized labor, the entertainment industry, and schools and universities of communists—real and alleged. Dissent had become tantamount to disloyalty. By the mid-1950s it was axiomatic to some Americans that any critique of American foreign policy or American society—even if justified—was communist inspired. It was not surprising, therefore, that in the 1960s and 1970s blacks and women who wished to improve their social position should be accused of leftist and un-American sympathies. Many Americans, however, weary of conflict and crisis, had long since sought refuge in suburban privatism and the affluent consumerism of the postwar years.

The election of John Fitzgerald Kennedy in 1960 promised energy and optimism. The succeeding years exemplified both, but not in the manner anticipated. Blacks refused to be intimidated any longer by appeals to "gradualism" or threats of violence. They forced white America to address domestic problems too long deferred; they also provided insight, tactics, rhetoric, and impetus to a resurgent feminist movement. Through the vivid images conveyed to them by television, Americans faced a new and disorderly world. Blacks, Chicanos, Indians, students, women, and protesters against the Vietnam War—all confronted the nation in its living rooms. America seemed to be disintegrating. Convinced that protest had become anarchy, middle America elected Richard M. Nixon in 1968 and again in 1972. But the candidate of "law and order" became the president who put himself above the law. His successors tried to repair the damage done the nation's highest office. In some measure, they succeeded. However, they also faced overwhelming economic problems. These became so grave that the American people would elect a conservative to the presidency in 1980 and reelect him in 1984—one whose "old-fashioned values" kept him from supporting an amendment to give women equal rights under the Constitution. The time of social reform was over. The expansive mood of the 1960s disintegrated in the face of anxiety over unemployment, inflation, rising energy costs, and declining productivity. Foreign relations were no consolation. There were the embarrassment of Vietnam and the danger of Soviet aggression, the weakening ties with our allies, and a greater interdependence of the industrial nations and the Third World. Looking ahead to the remaining years of the century, a distinguished historian observed that this nation's vaunted capacity for self-renewal would be "sorely tested." Few would disagree, even after the demise of the Cold War in 1990.[1]

Recounting these successive decades in traditional fashion suggests the difficulty of specifying the impact on women's experience. During an era when international developments assumed increasing importance, women were simply not part of the inner councils that debated issues of national security. Women were, of course, included in other aspects of historical experience. As shoppers in the 1920s, they purchased new consumer goods. As unemployed laborers and as wives and daughters of unemployed laborers and dispossessed farmers, they shared the economic problems of the Depression; as members of the Roosevelt administration, they shared in the search for solutions. As industrial workers and as members of the armed forces during World War II, women filled critical jobs in a time of labor shortages and contributed to an allied victory. We can even incorporate women into the Washington drama of the McCarthy era, recognizing that women were among the victims of repressive practices and also among the critics of the practitioners. Margaret Chase Smith was one of the first senators to denounce the "'know-nothing suspect everything' attitudes" that had transformed the Senate into a "forum of hate and character assassination."[2] The women participating in Women Strike for Peace also played a role in discrediting the inquisition, as Amy Swerdlow demonstrates in her account of their confrontation with the House Un-American Activities Committee.

Including women, even in this cursory fashion, requires recognition of differing experiences that are gender related. Two examples come immediately to mind. The first concerns the differing experience of male and female industrial workers employed during World War II. For working-class men wartime jobs provided a foundation on which to build a secure future in a postwar era of full employment. For working-class women the jobs were only a temporary bonus that they forfeited to returning veterans. Although no long-term study exists to support firm conclusions, there is reason to believe that many of the women who lost their jobs were heads of households. Some may have found low-paying jobs as clerical workers, beauticians, waitresses, or domestics, but in 1947 the increases in the number of women listed as unemployed—as actively seeking work— may have "foreshadow[ed] the great shift among poor women onto unemployment and later welfare rolls." One need not push that hypothesis further to conclude that wartime industrial employment could constitute economically a new beginning—or an end— depending on gender.

A second example concerns participation in the protest movements that shattered the complacency of the affluent society, transforming the 1960s into a decade of self-criticism and turmoil. Two groups in the vanguard of the struggle were the Student Nonviolent Coordinating Committee (SNCC), part of the militant wing of the civil rights movement, and the Students for a Democratic Society (SDS), an organization of the New Left. Both attracted young white women who shared with their male counterparts a commitment to equality. But while men in these organizations often assumed leadership roles, women found themselves functioning in traditional fashion as housekeepers and sexual partners. That this should be so in movements dedicated to radical change, and above all to equality, seemed an inconsistency of such magnitude that women began to organize on their own behalf.

Including women's experience, even as it differed significantly from that of men, does not in itself refocus history, although it does remind us that attention only to public events and international relations can divert us from understanding how most people lived. The process of refocusing history can occur successfully only when we have a fuller understanding of the way gender has affected *all* aspects of human life. We know, for example, that technological developments have been basic to the development of a modern economy. Yet we have only begun to probe the way in which gender has affected technological development. In the garment industry, women have long been employed as seamstresses, sewing being work women have traditionally done and therefore not a skill to command high wages. Men have been employed at higher pay as cutters and pressers. In part because of gender-related wage differentials, little technological change has occurred in sewing since the invention of the sewing machine, according to Ruth Schwartz Cowan.[3] Yet substantial change has occurred in the ancillary process of cutting and pressing. If the relationship between gender, the price of labor, and technological innovation has eluded us in the past, it need not do so in the future. The situation of women sewing-machine operators is but one area in which scholarship informed by the insights of contemporary feminism has begun to capture a larger portion of historical reality. As feminist scholars—male as well as female—restore women to history, comparing both the differences and similarities in the experiences of both sexes and valuing the experience of both, we can begin to refocus history. We must search then for a new paradigm that will enable us to find a past in which, as Gerda Lerner suggests, both *"men and women are the measure of significance."*[4]

NOTES

1. William E. Leuchtenburg, *A Troubled Feast: American Society since 1945* (New York, 1973), p. 270.
2. *Congressional Record,* 96 (June 1, 1950):7894–95.
3. Ruth Schwartz Cowan, "From Virginia Dare to Virginia Slims: Women and Technology in American Life," *Technology and Culture* 20 (1979):51–63.
4. Gerda Lerner, *The Majority Finds Its Past: Placing Women in History* (New York, 1979), p. 180.

NANCY F. COTT

Equal Rights and Economic Roles: The Conflict Over the Equal Rights Amendment in the 1920s

The vote achieved, former suffragists turned their attention to sex-based discrimination in the law. The proper strategy, as in suffrage, seemed to be a constitutional amendment affirming equal rights; men and women would have to be treated under the law as equals and as individuals. Suffragists who had struggled to pass legislation shortening hours and improving working conditions for women in industry had achieved that goal only because the Supreme Court was prepared to regard women as a special class of workers in need of governmental protection because of their childbearing role. [See *Muller* v. *Oregon*, p. 576.] An equal rights amendment would invalidate sex-based labor laws, they feared, since comparable protection would not be extended to men. The ensuing debate was a critical one creating deep and lasting divisions. Unable to agree on a unified agenda for four decades, veterans of the first women's movement expended energy in internal conflict, thereby diluting their political effectiveness. Not surprisingly women's issues made little headway until the 1960s.

The debate over ERA was critical not only because of its long-term consequences, but because it highlighted differing views within feminism of the social significance of gender and the meaning of equality. Does equality require that men and women have the "same" rights and be subject to the "same" treatment or does equality require "different" rights? How should the law treat the difference created by women's unique reproductive system? With these questions in mind, Nancy Cott carefully assesses the initial debate over ERA, making clear the assumptions and limitations inherent in the arguments of each side.

THE CONFLICT OVER THE EQUAL RIGHTS AMENDMENT IN THE 1920s

Campaigning for ratification of the Equal Rights Amendment during the 1970s, feminists who found it painful to be opposed by other groups of women were often unaware that the first proposal of that amendment in the 1920s had likewise caused a bitter split between women's groups claiming, on both sides, to represent women's interests. The 1920s conflict itself echoed some earlier ideological and tac-

tical controversies. One central strategic question for the women's rights movement in the late nineteenth century had concerned alliances: should proponents of "the cause of woman" ally with advocates for the rights for freed slaves, with temperance workers, or labor reformers, or a political party, or none of them? At various times different women leaders felt passionately for and against such alliances, not agreeing on what they meant for the breadth of the women's movement and for the priority assigned to women's issues.[1] The 1920s contest over the equal rights amendment reiterated that debate insofar as the National Woman's Party, which proposed the ERA, took a "single-issue" approach, and the opposing women's organizations were committed to maintaining multiple alliances. But in even more striking ways than it recapitulated nineteenth-century struggles the 1920s equal rights conflict also predicted lines of fracture of the later twentieth-century women's movement. The advantages or compromises involved in "multi-issue" organizing are matters of contemporary concern, of course. Perhaps more important, the 1920s debate brought into sharp focus (and left for us generations later to resolve) the question whether "equal rights"—a concept adopted, after all, from the male political tradition—matched women's needs. The initial conflict between women over the ERA set the goal of enabling women to have the same opportunities and situations as men *against* the goal of enabling women freely to be different from men without adverse consequences. As never before in nineteenth-century controversies, these two were seen as competing, even mutually exclusive, alternatives.

The equal rights amendment was proposed as a legal or civic innovation but the intrafeminist controversy it caused focused on the economic arena. Indeed, the connection between economic and political subordination in women's relation to men has been central in women's rights advocacy since the latter part of the nineteenth century. In the Western political tradition, women were historically excluded from political initiatives because they were defined as dependent—like children and slaves—and their dependence was read as fundamentally economic. Nineteenth-century advocates, along with the vote, claimed women's "right to labor," by which they meant the right for women to have their labor recognized, and diversified. They emphasized that women, as human individuals no less than men, had the right and need to use their talents to serve society and themselves and to gain fair compensation. Influential voices such as Charlotte Perkins Gilman's at the turn of the century stressed not only women's service but the necessity and warrant for women's economic independence. Gilman argued simultaneously that social evolution made women's move "from fireside to factory" inevitable, and also

that the move ought to be spurred by conscious renovation of outworn tradition.

By the 1910s suffragists linked political and economic rights, and connected the vote with economic leverage, whether appealing to industrial workers, career women or housewives. They insisted on women's economic independence in principle and defense of wage-earning women in fact. Since the vast majority of wage-earning women were paid too little to become economically independent, however, the two commitments were not identical and might in practice be entirely at odds.[2] The purpose to validate women's existing economic roles might openly conflict with the purpose to throw open economic horizons for women to declare their own self-definition. These tensions introduced by the feminist and suffrage agitation of the 1910s flashed into controversy over the equal rights amendment in the 1920s.

The ERA was the baby of the National Woman's Party, yet not its brainchild alone. As early as 1914, a short-lived New York City group called the Feminist Alliance had suggested a constitutional amendment barring sex discrimination of all sorts. Like the later NWP, the Feminist Alliance was dominated by highly educated and ambitious women in the arts and professions, women who believed that "equal rights" were their due while they also aimed to rejuvenate and reorient thinking about "rights" around female rather than only male definition. Some members of the Feminist Alliance surely joined the NWP, which emerged as the agent of militant and political action during the final decade of the suffrage campaign.[3]

A small group (engaging perhaps 5 percent of all suffragists), the NWP grew from the Congressional Union founded by Alice Paul and Lucy Burns in 1913 to work on the federal rather than the state-by-state route to woman suffrage. Through the 'teens it came to stand for partisan tactics (opposing all Democrats because the Democratic administration had not passed woman suffrage) and for flamboyant, symbolic, publicity-generating actions—large parades, pickets in front of the White House, placards in the Congress, hunger-striking in jail, and more. It gained much of its energy from leftwing radical women who were attracted to its wholesale condemnation of gender inequality and to its tactical adaptations from the labor movement; at the same time, its imperious tendency to work from the top down attracted crucial financial and moral support from some very rich women. When the much larger group, the National American Woman Suffrage Association, moved its focus to a constitutional amendment in 1916, that was due in no little part (although certainly not solely), to the impact of the NWP. Yet while imitating its aim, NAWSA's leaders always hated and resented the NWP, for the way it had horned in on the same pro-suffrage turf while scorning the NAWSA's traditional nonpartisan, educative strategy. These resentments festered into deep and long-lasting personal conflicts between leaders of the two groups.

Just after the 19th Amendment was ratified in August of 1920, the NWP began planning a large convention at which its members would decide whether to continue as a group and, if so, what to work for. The convention, held six months later and tightly orchestrated by chairman Alice Paul, brushed aside all other suggestions and endorsed an ongoing program to "remove all remaining forms of the subjection of women," by means of the elimination of sex discrimination in law.[4] At the outset, NWP leaders seemed unaware that this program of "equal rights" would be much thornier to define and implement than "equal suffrage" had been. They began surveying state legal codes, conferring with lawyers, and drafting numerous versions of equal rights legislation and amendments at the state and federal levels.

Yet the "clean sweep" of such an approach immediately raised a problem: would it invalidate sex-based labor legislation—the laws regulating women's hours, wages, and conditions of work, that women trade unionists and reformers had worked to establish over the past thirty years? The doctrine of "liberty of contract" between employer and employed had ruled court interpretations of labor legislation in the early twentieth century, stymying state regulation of the wages and hours of male workers. State regulation for women workers, espoused and furthered by many women in the NWP, had been made possible only by differentiating female from male wage-earners on the basis of physiology and reproductive functions. Now members of the NWP had to grapple with the question whether such legislation was sex "discrimination," hampering women workers in the labor market. Initially, there was

a great deal of sentiment within the NWP, even voiced by Alice Paul herself, that efforts at equal rights legislation should not impair existing sex-based protective labor legislation. However, there was also contrary opinion, which Paul increasingly heeded; by late November 1921 she had come to believe firmly that "enacting labor laws along sex lines is erecting another handicap for women in the economic struggle." Some NWP affiliates were still trying to draft an amendment that would preserve special labor legislation, nonetheless, and continued to introduce equal rights bills with "safeguards" in some states through the following spring.[5]

Meanwhile women leaders in other organizations were becoming nervous and distrustful of the NWP's intentions. Led by the League of Women Voters (successor to the NAWSA), major women's organizations in 1920 formed a national lobbying group called the Women's Joint Congressional Committee. The LWV was interested in eliminating sex discrimination in the law, but more immediately concerned with the extension of sex-based labor legislation. Moreover, the LWV had inherited NAWSA's hostility to Alice Paul. The first president of the LWV, Maud Wood Park, still smarted from the discomfiture that NWP picketing tactics had caused her when she headed the NAWSA's Congressional Committee from 1916 to 1920.[6] Other leading groups in the Women's Joint Congressional Committee were no less suspicious of the NWP. The National Women's Trade Union League since the mid-1910s had concentrated its efforts on labor legislation to protect women workers. Florence Kelley, director of the National Consumers' League, had been part of the inner circle of the NWP during the suffrage campaign, but on the question of protective labor laws her priorities diverged. She had spent three decades trying to get state regulation of workers' hours and conditions, and was not about to abandon the gains achieved for women.[7]

In December 1921, at Kelley's behest, Paul and three other NWP members met for discussion with her and leaders of the League of Women Voters, the National Women's Trade Union League, the Woman's Christian Temperance Union, and the General Federation of Women's Clubs. All the latter objected to the new constitutional amendment now formulated by the NWP: "No political, civil or legal disabilities or inequalities on account of sex, or on account of marriage unless applying alike to both sexes, shall exist within the United States or any place subject to their jurisdiction." Paul gave away no ground, and all left feeling that compromise was unlikely. Each side already thought the other intransigent, though in fact debate was still going on within the NWP.[8]

By mid-1922 the National Consumers' League, the LWV, and the Women's Trade Union League went on record opposing "blanket" equal rights bills, as the NWP formulations at both state and federal levels were called. About the same time, the tide turned in the NWP. The top leadership accepted as definitive the views of Gail Laughlin, a lawyer from Maine, who contended that sex-based labor legislation was not a lamented loss but a positive harm. "If women can be segregated as a class for special legislation," she warned, "the same classification can be used for special restrictions along any other line which may, at any time, appeal to the caprice or prejudice of our legislatures." In her opinion, if "protective" laws affecting women were not abolished and prohibited, "the advancement of women in business and industry will be stopped and women relegated to the lowest, worst paid labor."[9] Since NWP lobbyists working at the state level were making little headway, a federal constitutional amendment appeared all the more appealing. In November 1923, at a grand conference staged in Seneca Falls, New York, commemorating the seventy-fifth anniversary of Elizabeth Cady Stanton's Declaration of Sentiments, the NWP announced new language: "Men and women shall have equal rights throughout the United States and every place subject to its jurisdiction." The constitutional amendment was introduced into Congress on December 10, 1923.[10]

In the NWP view, this was the logical sequel to the 19th Amendment. There were so many different sex discriminations in state codes and legal practices—in family law, labor law, jury privileges, contract rights—that only a constitutional amendment seemed effective to remove them. The NWP took the language of liberal individualism, enshrined the catchphrase of "equal rights," to express its feminism. As Alice Paul saw it, what women as a gender group shared was their subordination and inequality to men as a whole; the legal

structure most clearly expressed this subordination and inequality, and therefore was the logical point of attack. The NWP construed this agenda as "purely feminist," that is, appealing to women as women, uniting women around a concern common to them regardless of the other ways in which they might differ. Indeed, at its founding postsuffrage convention the NWP leadership purposely bypassed issues it saw as less "pure," including birth control, the defense of black women's voting rights in the South, and pacifism, which were predictably controversial among women themselves.

The NWP posited that women could and would perceive self-interest in "purely" gender terms. Faced by female opponents, its leaders imagined a fictive or abstract unity among women rather than attempting to encompass women's real diversity. They separated the proposal of equal rights from other social and political issues and effects. Although the campaign for equal rights was initiated in a vision of inclusiveness—envisioned as a stand that all women could take—it devolved into a practice of exclusiveness. The NWP's "appeal for conscious sex loyalty" (as a member once put it) went out to members of the sex who could subordinate identifications and loyalties of class, ethnicity, race, religion, politics, or whatever else to a "pure" sense of themselves as women differentiated from men. That meant principally women privileged by the dominant culture in every way except that they were female.[11]

In tandem with its lobbying for an equal rights amendment, the NWP presented its opposition to sex-based labor legislation as a positive program of "industrial equality." It championed women wage-earners who complained of "protective" legislation as restrictive, such as printers, railroad conductors, or waitresses hampered by hours limitation, or cleaning women fired and replaced by men after the passage of minimum-wage laws. Only a handful of working-class women rose to support for the ERA, however.[12] Mary Anderson, former factory worker herself and since 1919 the director of the U.S. Women's Bureau, which was founded to guide and assist women workers, threw her weight into the fight against the amendment. Male trade unionists—namely leaders of the American Federation of Labor— also voiced immediate opposition to the NWP aims, appearing at the very first U.S. Senate subcommittee hearings on the equal rights amendment. Male unionists or class-conscious workers in this period put their faith in collective bargaining and did not seek labor legislation for themselves, but endorsed it for women and child workers. This differentiation derived partly from male workers' belief in women's physical weakness and veneration of women's "place" in the home, partly from presumptions about women workers being difficult to organize, and also from the aim to keep women from competing for men's jobs. Male unionists tended to view wage-earning women first as women—potential or actual wives and mothers—and only secondarily as workers. For differing reasons women and men in the labor movement converged in their support of sex-based legislation: women because they saw special protection necessary to defend their stake in industry and in union organizations, limited as it was; men to hold at bay women's demands for equal entry into male-controlled union jobs and organizations.[13]

The arguments against the equal rights amendment offered by trade unionists and by such women's organizations as the League of Women Voters overlapped. They assumed that an equal rights amendment would invalidate sex-based labor laws or, at least, destine them for protracted argument in the courts, where judges had shown hostility to any state regulation of employer prerogatives. They insisted that the greatest good for the greatest number was served by protective labor laws. If sex-based legislation hampered some—as the NWP claimed, and could be shown true, for instance, in the case of women linotypists, who needed to work at night—then the proper tactic was to exempt some occupations, not to eliminate protective laws whole. They feared that state welfare legislation in place, such as widows' pensions, would also be at risk. They contended that a constitutional amendment was too undiscriminating an instrument: objectionable sex discriminations such as those concerning jury duty, inheritance rights, nationality, or child custody would be more efficiently and accurately eliminated by specific bills for specific instances. Sometimes, opponents claimed that the ERA took an unnecessarily federal approach, overriding states' rights, although here they were hardly consistent for many of them were at the same time advocating a constitutional amendment to prohibit child labor.

Against the ERA, spokeswomen cited evidence that wage-earning women wanted and valued labor legislation and that male workers, too, benefitted from limits on women's hours in factories where men and women worked at interdependent tasks. Before hours were legally limited, "we were 'free' and 'equal' to work long hours for starvation wages, or free to leave the job and starve!" WTUL leader Pauline Newman bitterly recalled. Dr. Alice Hamilton, pioneer of industrial medicine, saw the NWP as maintaining "a purely negative program, . . . holding down in their present condition of industrial slavery hundreds of thousands of women without doing anything to alleviate their lot."[14] Trade-unionist and Women's Bureau colleagues attacked the NWP's vision as callously class-biased, the thoughtless outlook of rich women, at best relevant to the experience of exceptional skilled workers or professionals. They regularly accused the NWP of being the unwitting tool (at best) or the paid servant of rapacious employers, although no proof of the latter was ever brought forward. They heard in the NWP program the voice of the ruling class and denounced the equal rights amendment as "class" legislation, by and for the bourgeoisie.[15]

Indeed, at the Women's Bureau Conference on Women in Industry in 1926, the NWP's opposition to sex-based labor legislation was echoed by the president of the National Association of Manufacturers, who declared that the "handful" of women in industry could take care of themselves and were not served by legislative "poultices." In this controversy, the positions also lent themselves to, and inevitably were colored by, male "allies" whose principal concerns dealt less with women's economic or legal protection or advancement than political priorities of their own. At the same conference the U.S. Secretary of Labor appointed by President Coolidge took the side of sex-based protective legislation, proclaiming that "The place fixed for women by God and Nature is a great place," and "wherever we see women at work we must see them in terms of motherhood." What he saw as the great danger of the age was the "increasing loss of the distinction between manliness and true femininity."[16]

Often, ERA opponents who supported sex-based labor legislation—including civic-minded middle-class women, social welfare reformers, government officials, and trade union men—appeared more concerned with workingwomen's motherhood than with economic justice. "Women who are wage earners, with one job in the factory and another in the home have little time and energy left to carry on the fight to better their economic status. They need the help of other women and they need labor laws," announced Mary Anderson. Dr. Hamilton declared that "the great inarticulate body of working women . . . are largely helpless, . . . [and] have very special needs which unaided they cannot attain. . . ."[17] Where NWP advocates had before their eyes women who were eager and robust, supporters of protective legislation saw women overburdened and vulnerable. The former claimed that protective laws penalized the strong; the latter claimed that the ERA would sacrifice the weak. The NWP looked at women as individuals and wanted to dislodge gender differentiation from the labor market. Their opponents looked at women as members of families—daughters, wives, mothers, and widows with family responsibilities—and believed that the promise of "mere equality" did not sufficiently take those relationships into account. The one side tacitly positing the independent professional woman as the paradigm, the other presuming the doubly burdened mother in industry or service, neither side distinguished nor addressed directly the situation of the fastest-growing sector of employed women, in white-collar jobs. At least half of the female labor force—those in manufacturing and in domestic and personal service—worked in taxing, menial jobs with long hours, unpleasant and often unhealthy conditions, very low pay, and rare opportunities for advancement. But in overall pattern women's employment was leaving these sectors and swelling in clerical, managerial, sales, and professional areas. White-collar workers were fewer than 18 percent of all women employed in 1900, but the proportion more than doubled by 1920 and by 1930 was 44 percent.[18]

The relation of sex-based legislation to women workers' welfare was more ambiguous and complicated than either side acknowledged. Such laws immediately benefitted far larger numbers of employed women than they hindered, but the laws also had a negative impact on women's overall economic opportunities, both immediately and in the long term. Sex segregation of the labor market was a very significant factor. In industries monopolizing women workers, where wages, conditions, and hours were more likely to be substandard, protective legislation helped to bring things up to standard. It was in more desirable crafts and trades more unusual for women workers, where skill levels and pay were likely to be higher—that is, where women needed to enter in order to improve their earnings and economic advancement—that sex-based protective legislation held women back. There, as a contemporary inquiry into the issue said, "the practice of enacting laws covering women alone appears to discourage their employment, and thereby fosters the prejudice against them." The segregation of women into low-paid, dead-end jobs that made protective laws for women workers necessary, was thus abetted by the legislation itself.[19]

By 1925, all but four states limited workingwomen's hours; eighteen states prescribed rest periods and meal hours; sixteen states prohibited night work in certain occupations; and thirteen had minimum wage regulations. Such regulation was passed not only because it served women workers, but also because employers, especially large corporate employers, began to see benefits in its stabilization of the labor market and control of unscrupulous competition. Although the National Association of Manufacturers, fixed on "liberty of contract," remained opposed, large employers of women accepted sex-based labor legislation on reasoning about "protection of the race," or could see advantages for themselves in it, or both. A vice-president of Filene's, a large department store in Boston, for instance, approved laws regulating the hours, wages, and conditions of women employees because "economies have been effected by the reduction of labor turnover; by reduction of the number of days lost through illness and accidents; and by increase in the efficiency of the working force as well as in the efficiency of management." He appreciated the legislation's maintaining standards as to hours, wages, and working conditions "throughout industry as a *whole,* thus preventing selfish interests from indulging in unfair competition by the exploitation of women. . . ."[20]

While the anti-ERA side was right in the utilitarian contention that protective laws meant the greatest good to the greatest number of women workers (at least in the short run), the pro-ERA side was also right that such laws hampered women's scope in the labor market and sustained the assumption that employment advantage was not of primary concern to women. Those who advocated sex-based laws were looking at the labor market as it was, trying to protect women in it, but thereby contributing to the perpetuation of existing inequalities. They envisaged wage-earning women as veritable beasts of burden. That group portrait supplanted the prior feminist image of wage-earning women as a vanguard of independent female personalities, as equal producers of the world's wealth. Its advocates did not see that their conception of women's needs helped to confirm women's second-class position in the economy. On the other hand, the ERA advocates who opposed sex-based "protections" were envisioning the labor market as it might be, trying to ensure women the widest opportunities in that imagined arena, and thereby blinking at existing exploitation. They did not admit to the vulnerabilities that sex-based legislation addressed, while they overestimated what legal equality might do to unchain women from the economic stranglehold of the domestic stereotype.

Women on both sides of the controversy, however, saw themselves as legatees of suffragism and feminism, intending to defend the value of women's economic roles, to prevent economic exploitation of women and to open the doors to economic opportunity. A struggle over the very word feminism, which the NWP had embraced, became part of the controversy. For "us even to use the word feminist," contended Women's Trade Union League leader Ethel Smith, "is to invite from the extremists a challenge to our authenticity." Detractors in the WTUL and Women's Bureau called the NWP "ultra" or "extreme" feminists. Mary Anderson considered herself "a good feminist" but objected that "over-articulate theorists were attempting to solve the working women's problems on a purely feministic basis with the working women's own voice far less adequately heard." Her own type of feminist was moderate and practical, Anderson declared; the others, putting the "woman question" above all other questions, were extreme and abstract. The bitterness was compounded by a conflict of personalities and tactics dragged on from the suffrage years. Opponents of the ERA, deeply resenting having to oppose something called equal rights, maligned the NWP as "pernicious," women who "discard[ed] all ethics

and fair play," an "insane crowd" who espoused "a kind of hysterical feminism with a slogan for a program."[21] Their critiques fostered public perception of feminism as a sectarian and impracticable doctrine unrelated to real life and blind to injustices besides sex inequality. By the end of the 1920s women outside the NWP rarely made efforts to reclaim the term feminist for themselves, and the meaning of the term was depleted.

Forced into theorizing by this controversy, not prepared as philosophers or legal theorists, spokeswomen on either side in the 1920s were grappling with definitions of women's rights as compared to men's that neither the legal nor economic system was designed to accommodate. The question whether equality required women to have the same rights as men, or different rights, could not be answered without delving into definitions. Did "equality" pertain to opportunity, treatment, or outcome?[22] Should "difference" be construed to mean separation, discrimination, protection, privilege— or assault on the very standard that the male was the human norm?[23]

Opponents of the ERA believed that sex-based legislation was necessary because of women's biological and social roles as mothers. They claimed that "The inherent differences are permanent. Women will always need many laws different from those needed by men"; "Women as such, whether or not they are mothers present or prospective, will always need protective legislation"; "The working mother is handicapped by her own nature."[24] Their approach stressed maternal nature and inclination as well as conditioning, and implied that the sexual division of labor was eternal.

The NWP's approach, on the other hand, presupposed that women's differentiation from men in the law and the labor market was a particular, social-historical, and not necessary or inevitable construction. The sexual division of labor arose from archaic custom, enshrined in employer and employee attitudes and written in the law. The NWP approach assumed that wives and mothers as well as unencumbered women would want and should have open access to jobs and professions. NWP proponents imagined that the sexual division of labor (in the family and the marketplace) would change if women would secure the same rights as men and have free access to wage-earning. Their view made a fragile potential into a necessary fact. They assumed that women's wage-earning would, by its very existence, challenge the sexual division of labor, and that it would provide the means for women's economic independence—although neither of these tenets was necessarily being realized.

Wage-earning women's experience in the 1910s and 1920s, as documented by the Women's Bureau, showed that the sexual division of labor was budged only very selectively and marginally by women's gainful employment. Most women's wages did not bring them economic independence; women earned as part of a plan for family support (as men did, though that was rarely stressed). Contrary to the NWP's feminist visions, in those places in the nation where the highest proportions of wives and mothers worked for pay, the sexual division of labor was most oppressively in place. To every child growing up in the region of Southern textile and tobacco mills, where wives and mothers worked more "jobs" at home and in the factory than any other age or status group—and earned less—the sexual division of labor appeared no less prescriptive and burdensome than it had before women earned wages.[25]

Critiques of the NWP and its ERA as "abstract" or "extreme" or "fanatical" represented the gap between feminist tenets and harsh social reality as an oversight of the NWP, a failure to adjust their sights. Even more sympathetic critics, such as one Southern academic, asked rhetorically, "Do the feminists see in the tired and haggard faces of young waitresses, who spend seventy hours a week of hard work in exchange for a few dollars to pay for food and clothing, a deceptive mask of the noble spirit within?" She answered herself, "Surely it is not an increasing army of jaded girls and spent women that pours every day from factory and shop that the leaders of the feminist movement seek. But the call for women to make all labor their province can mean nothing more. They would free women from the rule of men only to make them greater slaves to the machines of industry."[26] Indeed, the exploitation of female service and industrial workers at "cheap" wages cruelly parodied the feminist notion that gainful employment represented an assertion of independence (just as the wifely duties required of a secretary parodied the feminist expectation that wage-earning would challenge the sexual division of labor and reopen defini-

tions of feminity). What such critics were observing was the distance between the potential for women's wage-earning to challenge the sexual division of labor, and the social facts of gender and class hierarchy that clamped down on that challenge.

Defenders of sex-based protective legislation, trying to acknowledge women's unique reproductive endowments and social obligations, were grappling with problems so difficult they would still be present more than half a century later. Their immediate resolution was to portray women's "difference" in merely customary terms. "Average American women prefer to make a home for husbands and children to anything else," Mary Anderson asserted in defense of her position. "They would rather fulfill this normal function than go into the business world."[27] Keeping alive a critique of the class division of wealth, protective legislation advocates lost sight of the need to challenge the very sexual division of labor that was the root of women's "handicap" or "helplessness." As compared to the NWP's emphasis on the historical and social construction of gender roles, advocates of sex-based protective legislation echoed customary public opinion in proposing that motherhood and wage-earning should be mutually exclusive. They easily found allies among such social conservatives as the National Council of Catholic Women, whose representatives testified against the ERA because it "seriously menaced . . . the unity of the home and family life" and contravened the "essential differences in rights and duties" of the two sexes which were the "result of natural law." Edging into plain disapproval of mothers of young children who earned, protective legislation supporters became more prescriptive, less flexible, than wage-earning mothers themselves, for whom cash recognition of their labor was very welcome. "Why should not a married woman work [for pay], if a single one does?" demanded a mill worker who came to the Southern Summer School for Women Workers. "What would men think if they were told that a married man should not work? If we women would not be so submissive and take everything for granted, if we would awake and stand up for our rights, this world would be a better place to live in, at least it would be better for the women. . . ."[28]

The onset of the Depression in many ways worsened the ERA controversy, for the one side thought protective legislation all the more crucial when need drove women to take any jobs available, and the other side argued that protective legislation prevented women from competing for what jobs there were. In the 1930s it became clear that the labor movement's and League of Women Voters' opposition to the equal rights amendment ran deeper than concern for sex-based legislation as an "entering wedge." The Fair Labor Standards Act of 1938 mandated wages and hours regulation for all workers, and the U.S. Supreme Court upheld it in 1941; but the labor movement and the LWV still opposed the ERA. Other major women's organizations, however—most importantly the National Federation of Business and Professional Women's Clubs and the General Federation of Women's Clubs—and the national platforms of both the Republican [Party] and the Democratic Party endorsed the ERA by 1944.[29]

We generally learn "winners'" history—not the history of lost causes. If the ERA passed by Congress in 1972 had achieved ratification by 1982, perhaps historians of women would read the trajectory of the women's movement from 1923 to the present as a steady upward curve, and award the NWP unqualified original insight. The failure of the ERA this time around (on new, but not unrelated, grounds) compels us to see the longer history of equal rights in its true complexity.[30] The ERA battle of the 1920s seared into memory the fact of warring outlooks among women while it illustrated the inevitable intermeshing of women's legal and political rights with their economic situations. If the controversy testified to the difficulty of protecting women in the economic arena while opening opportunities to them, even more fundamentally the debate brought into question the NWP's premise that the articulation of sex discrimination—or the call for equal rights—would arouse all women to mobilize as a group. What kind of a group were women when their occupational and social and other loyalties were varied, when not all women viewed "women's" interests, or what constituted sex "discrimination," the same way? The ideological dimensions of that problem cross-cut both class consciousness and gender identity. The debate's intensity, both then and now, measured how fundamental was the revision needed if policies and practices of economic and civic life deriving from a male norm

were to give full scope to women—and to women of all sorts.

NOTES

1. A good introduction to the issue of alliances in the nineteenth-century women's movement, and an essential text on the mid-ninteenth-century split, is Ellen Carol DuBois, *Feminism and Suffrage: The Emergence of an Independent Women's Movement, 1848–1869* (Ithaca, N.Y.: Cornell, 1978).

2. See Leslie Woodcock Tentler, *Wage-Earning Women: Industrial Work and Family Life in the U.S., 1900–1930* (New York: Oxford University Press, 1979), chap. 1, on industrially employed women's wages, keyed below subsistence.

3. On feminists in the final decade of the suffrage campaign, see Nancy F. Cott, *The Grounding of Modern Feminism* (New Haven: Yale University Press, 1987), pp. 23–66.

4. For more detailed discussion of the February 1921 convention, see Nancy F. Cott, "Feminist Politics in the 1920s: The National Woman's Party," *Journal of American History* 71, no. 1 (June 1984).

5. Paul to Jane Norman Smith, Nov. 29, 1921, folder 110, J. N. Smith Collection, Schlesinger Library (hereafter SL). See NWP correspondence of Feb.–Mar. 1921 in the microfilm collection "The National Woman's Party, 1913–1974" (Microfilm Corp. of America), reels #5–7 (hereafter NWP with reel no.), and Cott, *Grounding,* pp. 66–74, 120–25, for more detail.

In Wisconsin, prominent NWP suffragist Mabel Raef Putnam put together a coalition which successfully lobbied through the first state equal rights bill early in 1921. This legislation granted women the same rights and privileges as men *except for* "the special protection and privileges which they now enjoy for the general welfare." . . .

6. Maud Wood Park, *Front Door Lobby,* ed. Edna Stantial (Boston: Beacon Press, 1960), p. 23.

7. Historians' treatments of women's organizations' differing views on the ERA in the 1920s include William N. O'Neill, *Everyone Was Brave* (Chicago: Quadrangle, 1969), pp. 274–94; J. Stanley Lemons, *The Woman Citizen: Social Feminism in the 1920s* (Urbana: University of Illinois Press, 1973), pp. 184–99; William Chafe, *The American Woman: Her Changing Social, Economic and Political Roles* (New York: Oxford University Press, 1972), pp. 112–32; Sheila M. Rothman, *Woman's Proper Place: A History of Changing Ideals and Practices, 1870 to the Present* (New York: Basic Books, 1978), pp. 153–65; Susan Becker, *Origins of the Equal Rights Amendment: American Feminism between the Wars* (Westport, Conn.: Greenwood Press, 1981), pp. 121–51; Alice Kessler-Harris, *Out to Work: A History of Wage-Earning Women in the U.S.* (New York: Oxford University Press, 1982), pp. 194–95, 205–12; Judith Sealander, *As Minority Becomes Majority* (Westport, Conn.: Greenwood Press, 1983). Fuller documentation of my reading of both sides can be found in Cott, *Grounding,* pp. 122–29 and accompanying notes.

8. "Conference on So-Called 'Equal Rights' Amendment Proposed by the National Woman's

Party Dec. 4, 1921," ts. NWTUL Papers, microfilm reel 2. . . .

9. NWP National Council minutes, Dec. 17, 1921, Feb. 14, 1922, Apr. 11, 1922, NWP #114. To the NWP inner circle Laughlin's point was borne out by a 1923 ruling in Wisconsin, where, despite the Equal Rights Bill, the attorney general declined to strike down a 1905 law which prohibited women from being employed in the state legislature. He likened the prohibition to an hours-limitation law, because legislative service required "very long and often unreasonable hours." Alice Paul read his decision as "an extremely effective argument against" drafting equal rights bills with exemptions for sex-based protective legislation. Anita L. Pollitzer to Mrs. Jane Norman Smith, Jan. 5, 1922, folder 110, and Paul to Jane Norman Smith, Feb. 20, 1923, folder 111, J. N. Smith Coll.

10. National Council Minutes, June 19, 1923, NWP #114. Before 1923 the ERA went through scores of drafts, recorded in part F, NWP #116. Versions akin to the suffrage amendment—e.g., "Equal rights with men shall not be denied to women or abridged on account of sex or marriage . . ."—were considered in 1922, but not until 1943 was the amendment introduced into Congress in the form "Equality of rights under the law shall not be denied or abridged by the United States or by any state on account of sex," modeled on the Nineteenth Amendment, which in turn was modeled on the Fifteenth Amendment.

11. Quotation from Edith Houghton Hooker, Editor's Note, *Equal Rights* (the NWP monthly publication), Dec. 22, 1928, p. 365. See Cott, *Grounding,* pp. 75–82.

12. The two most seen on NWP platforms were Josephine Casey, a former ILGWU organizer, suffrage activist, later a bookbinder, and Mary Murray, a Brooklyn Railway employee who had resigned from her union in 1920 to protest its acceptance of laws prohibiting night work for women.

13. Kessler-Harris, *Out to Work,* 200–5; and "Problems of Coalition-Building: Women and Trade Unions in the 1920s," in *Women, Work and Protest,* ed. Ruth Milkman (Boston: Routledge and Kegan Paul, 1985), esp. p. 132.

14. . . . More extensive documentation of the debate can be found in the notes in Cott, *Grounding,* pp. 325–26.

15. Kessler-Harris, *Out to Work,* pp. 189–94, reveals ambivalent assessments of labor legislation by ordinary wage-earning women.

16. Printed release from the National Association of Manufacturers, "Defend American Womanhood by Protecting Their Homes, Edgerton Tells Women in Industry," Jan. 19, 1926, in folder 1118, and ts. speech by James Davis, U.S. Secretary of Labor, Jan. 18, 1926, in folder 1117, Box 71, Mary Van Kleeck Collection, Sophia Smith Collection, Smith College.

17. Mary Anderson, "Should There Be Labor Laws for Women? Yes," *Good Housekeeping,* Sept. 1925. . . .

18. See Valerie K. Oppenheimer, *The Female Labor Force in the U.S.* (Westport, Conn.: Greenwood Press, 1976), pp. 3, 149; Lois Scharf, *To Work and to Wed* (Westport, Conn.: Greenwood Press, 1980), pp. 15–16; Winifred Wandersee, *Women's Work and Fam-*

ily Values 1920–1940 (Cambridge Mass.: Harvard, 1981), p. 85, 89.

19. Elizabeth F. Baker, "At the Crossroads in the Legal Protection of Women in Industry," *Annals of the American Academy of Political and Social Science* 143 (May 1929):277. . . .

Recently historians have stressed the regressive potential of sex-based protective laws. See . . . Nancy Schrom Dye, *As Equals and as Sisters: Feminism, Unionism and the Women's Trade Union League of New York* (Columbia: University of Missouri Press, 1980), pp. 159–60; Olive Banks, *Faces of Feminism: A Study of Feminism as a Social Movement* (New York: St. Martin's, 1981), p. 115; Judith A. Baer, *The Chains of Protection: The Judicial Response to Women's Labor Legislation* (Westport, Conn.: Greenwood Press, 1978). . . .

20. T. K. Cory to Mary Wiggins, Nov. 10, 1922, folder 378, Consumers' League of Mass. Coll., SL. See n. 16, above.

21. Ethel M. Smith, "What Is Sex Equality and What Are the Feminists Trying to Accomplish?" *Century Monthly Magazine* 118 (May 1929):96. . . . Mary Anderson, *Woman at Work: The Autobiography of Mary Anderson as Told to Mary N. Winslow* (Minneapolis: University of Minnesota Press, 1951), p. 168.

22. There is a valuable discussion of differing meanings for "equality" between the sexes in Jean Bethke Elshtain, "The Feminist Movement and the Question of Equality," *Polity* 7 (Summer 1975):452–77.

23. This is, of course, the set of issues that has preoccupied feminist lawyers in the 1980s. For a sense of the recent debate, see, e.g., Wendy Williams, "The Equality Crisis: Some Reflections on Culture, Courts, and Feminism," *Women's Rights Law Reporter* 7, no. 3 (Spring 1982):175–200; Nadine Taub, "Will Equality Require More Than Assimilation, Accommodation or Separation from the Existing Social Structure?" *Rutgers Law Review* 37 (1985):825–44; Lucinda Finley, "Transcending Equality Theory: A Way out of the Maternity and the Workplace Debate," *Columbia Law Review* 86, no. 6 (Oct. 1986):1118–82; and Joan Williams, "Deconstructing Gender," *Michigan Law Review* 87, no. 4 (Feb. 1989):797–845.

24. Florence Kelley, "Shall Women Be Equal before the Law?" (debate with Elsie Hill), *Nation* 114 (Apr. 12, 1922):421. . . .

25. Dolores Janiewski, *Sisterhood Denied: Race, Gender and Class in a New South Community* (Philadelphia: Temple University Press, 1985), pp. 30–32, 127–50; Table 26 (p. 134) shows less than 40% of Durham women above age 12 engaged only in unpaid housework.

26. Guion G. Johnson, "Feminism and the Economic Independence of Woman," *Journal of Social Forces* 3 (May 4, 1925):615; cf. Tentler, *Wage-Earning Women,* esp. pp. 25, 45–46, and Wandersee, *Women's Work,* on motivations and psychological results of women's wage-earning.

27. Mary Anderson quoted in unidentified newspaper clipping, Nov. 25, 1925, in folder 349, Bureau of Vocational Information Collection, SL. Cf. Ethel Smith's objection that the NWP's feminism required that "men and women must have exactly the same things, and be treated in all respects as if they were alike," as distinguished from her own view that

"men and women must each have the things best suited to their respective needs, which are not all the time, nor in all things, alike." Smith, "What Is Sex Equality?", p. 96.

28. National Council of Catholic Women testimony at U.S. Congress (House of Representatives) subcommittee of Committee on the Judiciary, hearings, 1925, quoted in Robin Whittemore, "Equality vs. Protection: Debate on the Equal Rights Amendment, 1923–1937" (M.A. thesis, Boston University, 1981), p. 19; mill worker quoted in Mary Frederickson, "The Southern Summer School for Women Workers," *Southern Exposure* 4 (Winter 1977):73. See also Maurine Greenwald, "Working-Class Feminism and the Family Wage Ideal: The Seattle Debate on Married Women's Right to Work, 1914–1920," *Journal of American History* 76, no. 1 (June 1989):118–49.

29. For the history of the NWP in the 1930s and 1940s see Becker, *Origins of the Equal Rights Amendment.* On the initiatives of the National Federation of Business and Professional Women and other groups to forward the equal rights amendment, see Lemons, *Woman Citizen,* pp. 202–4, and the papers of Lena Madesin Phillips and Florence Kitchelt at SL.

30. Jane L. Mansbridge's astute analysis, *Why We Lost the ERA* (Chicago: University of Chicago Press, 1986), is essential reading on the failed 1970s campaign for ratification.

BLANCHE WIESEN COOK

Eleanor Roosevelt as Reformer, Feminist, and Political Boss

Despite the divisions over an equal rights amendment, many women who had been enthusiastic reformers, suffragists, and feminists continued their political activism during the 1920s. Few did so more effectively than Eleanor Roosevelt.

A woman of limitless energy, compassion, and humanitarian zeal, Eleanor Roosevelt was the most active and controversial First Lady in the nation's history. A fascinating figure, her ability to change never ended. She began her adult life a shy, insecure woman who had imbibed the racism and anti-Semitism of the privileged world to which she was born. She ended her life a feminist and a political champion of civil rights, civil liberties, social justice, and world peace—a woman whose activism was played out on a world stage.

This transformation was well underway by the 1920s. Indeed, it had been accelerated when Franklin Delano Roosevelt was paralyzed by polio in 1921 and Eleanor began serving as his representative in the political arena. But as Blanche Cook makes clear in the following essay, Eleanor was no mere surrogate. A political activist, she was a shrewd analyst of the political scene whose observations remain timely. At the end of the twentieth century, political observers continue to seek remedies to women's prolonged political marginality. Even if women repeat the gains made in the 1992 Congressional elections each election year, it will take another seventy-four years before parity is achieved in Congress.

What did ER think women needed to do in order to make their votes meaningful? What advice did she give to those who wished to see women achieve numerical parity as officeholders? How did she respond to those who distrusted political activity in a

Excerpted from "ER, Political Boss," chap. 14 of *Eleanor Roosevelt: Volume One, 1884–1933* by Blanche Wiesen Cook (New York: Viking, 1992). Copyright © 1992 by Blanche Wiesen Cook. Reprinted by permission of the author and Viking Penguin, a division of Penguin Books, USA, Inc. Notes have been renumbered and edited.

woman as unfeminine? What advice do you think she would offer to those who seek real political power in the interests of social justice?

Eleanor Roosevelt began her career as the foremost political woman of the twentieth century convinced that women and men enter politics for different reasons: Men enter politics to pursue their own careers; women are motivated by a desire to change society, to improve the daily conditions of life. Impressed by the women she worked with, she came to believe that women's public activities would determine America's national future. Not a prewar suffragist herself, she fully appreciated the suffragists' century of struggle, and the grass-roots strategy that ultimately triumphed.

She believed that fundamental change required active and committed women who were willing to go door to door, block by block, and educate people on an individual basis about the real needs and conditions of society. She saw the need for newsletters and information bulletins. ER was one of the first women activists to relize that little would be achieved without a mimeograph machine, and persuaded New York's League of Women Voters to purchase one on 3 October 1922.[1] Above all, ER understood that information and organization required local clubs and political centers, a network of women active in every town and village connected to one another through meetings, debates, round-table discussions, luncheons, dinner parties, and personal friendships.

During the 1920s, there were four centers of political power for women in New York State: the League of Women Voters, . . . the Women's Trade Union League (WTUL), . . . the Women's Division of the New York State Democratic Committee, . . . and the Women's City Club, an umbrella organization dedicated to social reform and municipal affairs. Most of the two thousand members of the club were professional women—attorneys, physicians, educators, consumer activists, unionists, businesswomen, writers, artists, advertising agents, architects, engineers, printers, accountants, volunteer activists, saleswomen, office workers, and bankers—and many of them were active also in the WTUL and the League of Women Voters. Here ER met and worked with every activist political woman in New York—social workers like Lillian Wald, Mary (Molly)

Dewson, and Mary Simkhovitch; labor reformers such as Frances Perkins and Belle Moskowitz; Marie Jennie Howe, the Unitarian minister who created the women's social club Heterodoxy.

There were many and labyrinthine connections.[2] But a small number of women really pulled the network together. They served on the governing councils of each organization and decided on policy and strategy. ER rapidly became a leader of this group, which was made up largely of her own circle of Democratic women. She helped to raise funds, edited newsletters, moderated panels, participated in debates, presented information, toured the state on behalf of candidates and causes, and represented New York at national conventions of political women. To pursue the women's agenda, for six years ER, Nancy Cook, Marion Dickerman, Elinor Morgenthau, and Caroline O'Day went "Trooping for Democracy." In every weather and in every season, they toured New York State in their Democratic blue roadster, which they had bought together, or in O'Day's chauffeured Packard. They toured every county to demand an expanded public-housing program, improved sanitation and sewerage control, frequent and comfortable public transit, new parks and public playgrounds, school lunches and nursing facilities, unemployment insurance, workers' compensation, occupational-safety-and-health legislation, the eight-hour day, protective laws for women workers, mandatory-education laws, child-labor legislation, pure food-and-milk legislation, the right of women to serve on juries, and equal representation of women on all committees of the Democratic Party. . . .

Throughout the 1920s, articles about ER and her political work appeared almost weekly in *The New York Times*. She was the subject of news accounts, columns, editorials, profiles in the Sunday *Magazine* section, and letters to the editor. Her public appearances were national news. . . . [However] in her memoirs ER called the chapter devoted to the 1920s, the decade of the most robust political activity she undertook on her own, "Private Interlude."[3] Since she could hardly have meant by that an absorption in private or domestic affairs, one must conclude that this period in her life seemed in retrospect private in the sense that it was hers to do with as she pleased. She neither campaigned for FDR [who was recuperating from polio] nor served as his surrogate. He was preoccupied with recovery; she was preoccupied with politics. She became famous not as FDR's wife, but as a major political force to be reckoned with.

Yet, the more she achieved, the more she was acclaimed and celebrated in her own right, the more she sought to reassure FDR that she was doing it all for him. On 6 February 1924, for example, ER wrote him a long, rambling letter full of detail about her activities. But she concluded by reminding her husband that she was merely his temporary stand-in.[4] She had been asked to sponsor or attend several memorial services for President Wilson, who died on 3 February. She agreed, though she understood they only wanted FDR's name. She aimed neither to compete with her husband nor to upstage him. Only slowly and with considerable reluctance did ER admit that she was genuinely pleased by her public activities. Much more often she professed a selfless lack of interest in her own work and her own career, and thereby contributed to our distorted image of her public self. While she was First Lady, she wrote that she was pushed into politics reluctantly—and solely in support of her husband. She never acknowledged her own joy in the game, or her own skills at manipulating the cards. . . .

[For example] in her 6 February 1924 letter to FDR where she minimized her activities, she reported that she, Caroline O'Day, and Nancy Cook had been to a "remarkable dinner" of "600 women from Albany and nearby and all workers!" They saw Governor Al Smith, who asked them to lobby for his new reform program, and ER spent several days in Albany, working out the details. But there was still one piece of additional news, she noted almost as an afterthought: Cordell Hull, the Democratic Party's National Committee chairman in 1924, had invited ER—currently finance chair of the Women's Division—to head a platform committee for women to present their demands at the June convention in New York. She was delighted, though she gave no hint of that to FDR: "I'm up to my eyes in work for the convention preparations and trying to raise our budget which is going to be an endless job." ER even

rejected FDR's praise for her work, the words of which are now lost along with most of his correspondence during this period: "You need not be proud of me dear. I'm only being active till you can be again. . . .[5]

When one considers the disparity between ER's denial and the reality of her daily activities, one pauses to wonder what motivated her decision to trivialize both her work and her commitment to it. Her need to minimize her efforts and to reassure her husband that she was in fact no threat, and no competition to his primary place in the political arena, is a sturdy testimony to the proverbial double standard that was and remains the burden of political women. . . .

ER was embattled on several fronts in 1924. On 9 April, she wrote FDR that she wished he were at home to advise her "on the fight I'm putting up on a delegate and 2 alternates at large." The fight was classic: Would the female or male party leaders get to name the women delegates? Forty-nine county chairwomen had already selected and endorsed their representatives when Tammany boss Charles Murphy claimed it his privilege to name the delegates. ER, resolute and ready for a fight, wrote: "I imagine it is just a question of which [Murphy] disliked most—giving me my way or having me give the papers a grand chance for a story by telling [all] at the women's dinner . . . and by insisting on recognition on the floor of the convention & putting the names in nomination!" Clearly, ER had already decided to do full battle: "There's one thing I'm thankful for—I haven't a thing to lose and for the moment you haven't either."[6]

The New York Times featured ER's fight for women's equality at the state convention in an article titled "Women Are in Revolt." It was the "only inharmonious note" of the convention: the women supported Smith, but demanded their right to choose their own representatives. "Mrs. Franklin D. Roosevelt . . . slated to be one of the four delegates-at-large, led the fight for the women." She said:

> We have now had the vote for four years, and some very ardent suffragists seem to feel that instead of gaining in power the women have lost. . . .
>
> I have been wondering whether it occurs to the women as a whole that, if they expect to gain the ends for which they fought, it is not going to be sufficient simply to cast a ballot. . . . They must

gain for themselves a place of real equality and the respect of the men. . . . The whole point in women's suffrage is that the Government needs the point of view of all its citizens and the women have a point of view which is of value to the Government. . . .[7]

ER was in the vanguard of those feminists who protected and promoted women's issues and the equal representation of women within the party's committees. She demanded that women be represented on county committees "in equal numbers" and be listed among those nominated for office in all primary elections. . . .

ER's efforts were victorious. She was named chair of a committee that negotiated the women's right to name their own delegates and alternates. Their meetings with Smith and other party leaders "established a precedent," and ER felt encouraged: "We go into the campaign feeling that our party has recognized us as an independent part of the organization."

But it was only a preliminary victory. The women's political movement had become a significant element within the Democratic Party. It was feminist and bold. And the entrenched male power brokers hated it. They sought at every turn to set up roadblocks, brake its momentum, and destroy it. A daily and nasty battle ensued, fought meanly and through subterfuge. For example, women who finally achieved membership status on a committee often found the doors to the meetings locked, or the meetings moved to secret places. Other apparent victories were no sooner announced than betrayed.

In March 1924, the Democratic National Committee proudly announced that it was "the first political group to seek women's views on important questions of peculiar interest to them so that these social legislation planks as incorporated in the national Democratic platform may represent their ideas." And, with considerable public relations fanfare, the leadership announced it had asked Eleanor Roosevelt to chair the women's platform committee.[8]

ER agreed, and determined to base the recommendations for needed social-welfare legislation on the "requests of all women's organizations in the country." She appointed a panel of activist experts. . . . The committee endorsed the League of Nations, and called for the creation of a federal department of educa-

tion, equal pay for women workers, and the ratification of the child-labor amendment. It called for a forty-eight-hour workweek, wages commensurate with the cost of living and health care, the creation of employment bureaus and the means to ensure "healthy and safe working conditions."

But in June, their three months' effort was rudely rebuffed by the Resolutions Committee at the convention. For hours ER and her coworkers sat outside the locked doors of the all-male Resolutions Committee and waited to be heard. At dawn the men voted twenty-two to eighteen, for the third and last time, to reaffirm their refusal even to hear the women's proposals. ER wrote that at the convention of 1924 she saw "for the first time where the women stood when it came to a national convention. I shortly discovered that they were of very little importance. They stood outside the door of all important meetings and waited." She spent most of her time during the deadlocked, heat-filled convention—every day the temperature topped one hundred degrees Fahrenheit—trying to seem calm. "I sat and knitted, suffered with the heat and wished it would end." One day, [comedian] Will Rogers noticed ER and asked: "Knitting in the names of the future victims of the guillotine?" ER was tempted to respond that she was "ready to call any punishment down on the heads of those who could not bring the convention to a close."[9]

The 1924 convention was a setback for the women, and a disaster for the Democrats. But for the Roosevelts 1924 represented another turning point. Both ER and FDR were widely perceived as the most significant contributors to the Democratic convention. The women's political community acknowledged ER as a major leader. Personally, she was informed and toughened by her new understanding of the way male bastions of power actually worked. And during the convention, FDR's reputation as a national figure soared. In fact, the only bright moment of the divided and frequently violent convention—a convention dominated by Al Smith and his chief opponent, William Gibbs McAdoo, who was now frankly associated with the Ku Klux Klan—occurred when FDR presented the nominating speech for Smith. [Although Smith lost the presidential nomination,] . . . ER agreed to help run Al Smith's campaign for re-election as New York's governor—against Republican nominee Theodore Roosevelt, Jr.

ER's willingness to support Al Smith in the face of the continued rebuffs and indignities experienced by the organized political women throughout 1924 was more than a testimony to her belief that Smith was serious about social reform. It was a demonstration of her own conviction that women needed to work systematically and earnestly within the power structure if they were to achieve political change. Votes for women could be rendered meaningless unless women organized to take over specific areas of party activity, specific areas of real power. Now was the time "to prove our strength and demand respect."[10]

ER appreciated that this meant working under duress with frequently hostile allies, who would attempt to undermine every victory. She spoke directly of male hostility to women in politics. In an interview in *The New York Times* published on 20 April 1924, she described male contempt for politically involved women. Men would say: "You are wonderful. I love and honor you. . . . Lead your own life, attend to your charities, cultivate yourself, travel when you wish, bring up the children, run your house. I'll give you all the freedom you wish and all the money I can but—leave me my business and politics." This, ER urged, women must not allow. "Women must get into the political game and stay in it." Women together must build up new institutions of alternative power "from the inside."[11]

She had seconded Smith's nomination at the New York State convention with vigor, and with a thrust at her cousin TR, Jr., that finally and forever alienated the two branches of the family. How could Smith not win, she asserted, since the Republicans, by their useless nomination of TR, "did everything to help him"? She campaigned throughout the state in an extraordinary vehicle rigged up with a steam-spouting teapot to signify TR, Jr.'s involvement in the Teapot Dome scandal. [The scandal involved the transfer of oil-rich public lands to private oil companies by the Secretary of the Interior, Albert B. Fall. The Wyoming land called Teapot Dome was sold to Harry Sinclair. Although Fall went to prison, the national oil reserves remained in the hands of Sinclair and other developers.] In county after county she systematically dismissed her cousin as a reasonably nice "young man whose public service

record shows him willing to do the bidding of his friends." . . .[12]

ER was delighted by Smith's victory, and entirely pleased with the success of her "rough stunt."[13] Indeed, she was so proud of the teapot, which was of her own design, that she drove it to Connecticut, evidently to give her Aunt Bye a glimpse of what the fuss was all about. Aunt Bye was frankly dismayed by her niece's unseemly display of raw political muscle: "Alas and lackaday! Since politics have become her choicest interest all her charm has disappeared, and the fact is emphasized by the companions she chooses to bring with her. . . ."[14]

However much ER's political vigor, new friends, and public prominence might disturb the older members of her family, she herself greeted every new controversy with verve. Eleanor Roosevelt had become a feminist [as well as a politician.] She fought for women's rights steadfastly and with determination; she championed equality in public and private matters; and she herself used the word "feminist." But during the 1920s, the bitterly divisive Equal Rights Amendment ripped the women's movement apart, obscuring for decades the full dimensions of historical feminism—and ER's leadership role with it. . . .

The ERA-protectionist division resulted from a conflicting understanding of what was possible in an unrestrained capitalist economy. In 1923, despite years of progressive action, there was still no limitation on the number of hours or the conditions of work for women *or* men; and ER and the protectionist feminists—all of whom wanted protective legislation for all—sincerely believed that it was possible to achieve a fair and just administration of a forty-eight-hour workweek by demanding it for women *first*. Equal-rights feminists sincerely believed that shorter hours for women first would result in the loss of jobs for women, who were not as valued as men workers and were not paid on a par with them, and who were therefore required by economic need to work longer hours merely to survive. Although both sides agreed that women worked in a brutal economy that achieved profits by demanding the longest possible hours for the least possible pay, the battle between them raged in bitter tones of acrimony. The protectionists believed the ERA women were elitists and careerists who cared only for privileged and professional women and were ignorant of and unconcerned about the poor. The ERA activists believed the protectionists were old-fashioned reformers who refused to see that, until women were acknowledged equal in law, all reforms to protect women were frauds that could only work against them. . . .

Eleanor Roosevelt too tended to consider the ERA proponents self-serving aristocrats who cared little and understood less about the needs of the poor. She was drawn toward the vision of reform created by that earlier generation of community activists, unionists, and radicals led by Florence Kelley, Jane Addams, Lillian Wald, Rose Schneiderman, and Dr. Alice Hamilton, [who] regarded the ERA as a fantasy that endangered their life's work. . . .

As Eleanor Roosevelt's influence grew, and as her confidence increased, she threw herself into a range of social initiatives aimed at strengthening government protection for women and children. She fought for the Child Labor Amendment, increased support for the Children's Bureau and the Women's Bureau, and worked to raise state matching funds for the $1.25-million Sheppard-Towner Act to establish maternity and pediatric clinics and a health-care program for mothers and infants. A great victory for social feminists, who had campaigned for years to decrease the grim rate of infant mortality in the United States, the Sheppard-Towner Act was attacked as "Sovietism," and a dangerous precedent leading to birth control and governmental programs of "social hygiene." ER and Narcissa Vanderlip were among the leaders of New York's crusade to raise the enabling funds.

To charges that the law was unconstitutional and not economical, Vanderlip countered: "If it is constitutional to use federal funds to save hogs from cholera, and cows from tuberculosis, it is constitutional to use them to save babies and their mothers from death."[15]

Every issue involving women was of concern to ER. . . . She called for equal political education for girls and for boys, and noted with pride that "Girls nowadays may be rivals of their brothers in school, sports, and business." But ER lamented they "lag behind in a knowledge and interest in government." She gave as examples her own daughter, Anna, and Governor Smith's daughter Emily, whom she had

overheard complaining that politics dominated their fathers' conversations. ER contrasted this attitude with the one that prevailed among "flappers of politically prominent families in England. British daughters not only take a keen interest in their fathers' careers but go out to help in the political battle." She cited the good works of Ishbel MacDonald and Megan Lloyd George in particular, and concluded that, if "our American girls are not to be left behind, something must be done to stimulate their interest in civic responsibilities." She thought that daughters of politicians should at least want to be able "to outtalk their fathers."[16]

Eleanor Roosevelt's own sense of responsibility took her beyond strong words to vigorous deeds. In 1926, she made headline news when she participated in a mass picket demonstration of three hundred women in support of striking paper-box makers. Eight notable women "of prominence" were arrested for ignoring a police order "to move on," and charged with "disorderly conduct," including ER, Margaret Norrie, Mrs. Samuel Bens, Marion Dickerman, Evelyn Preston, and Dorothy Kenyon.[17]

ER was proud of the achievements of women. She honored their daring and their vision. She considered women flyers marvelously courageous, and she promoted women in flight. She herself wanted to fly, and she did. . . .[18] Her friend Amelia Earhart gave her preliminary lessons, and ER actually took and passed the physical examination. But FDR persuaded her that he had sufficient worries without her flying above the clouds at top speed. FDR's opposition to flying was genuine. In 1920, he was horrified when his mother flew from London to Paris, and asked her never to go aloft again. Evidently both women acquiesced to his fear; but ER always regretted not becoming a pilot, because, she said, she liked to be in control of her own mobility.

Increasingly, ER's interests became international [ist as well as feminist and reformist]. [In 1923, Edward Bok, the former publisher of *Ladies' Home Journal*, had offered a prize of $50,000 to a practical plan that would allow the United States to do its share to preserve world peace without making compulsory the nation's involvement in any future European wars. ER had agreed to serve on the prize committee at the request of Esther Lape, a college professor, journalist, researcher, and publicist whom she much admired. The winning plan recommended the United States' immediate adherence to the Permanent Court of Internal Justice and cooperation with (though not membership in) the League of Nations. When Bok, Lape, ER, and their allies proceeded to promote U.S. entrance into the World Court, Senate isolationists charged them with being a tool of foreign radicals who were trying to manipulate public opinion and legislative action. Investigation by the FBI, the first of many, did not deter ER. She continued to work for the League and for U.S. entrance into the World Court.] In October 1927, she hosted a meeting of four hundred women at Hyde Park to launch a women's peace movement and support the Kellogg-Briand Treaty to outlaw war.... For the next ten years, ER was to be one of the most prominent antiwar women in the United States, associated with both Jane Addams's Women's International League for Peace and Freedom, and Carrie Chapman Catt's National Conference on the Cause and Cure of War. ER [also] devoted considerable space in the *Women's Democratic News* to issues of war and peace.... Wherever she went, or whatever her announced topic, whenever ER spoke as the decade of the 1920s drew to a close, she spoke at least in part about world peace. Long before the war clouds gathered her message was urgent: "The time to prepare for world peace is during the time of peace and not during the time of war."[19]

By 1928, the year FDR ran for governor of New York, Eleanor Roosevelt had become a major political force. For six years, she had served as finance chair of women's activities of the New York Democratic State Committee. She was vice-chair of the Woman's City Club of New York, chair of the Non-Partisan Legislative Committee, editor and treasurer of the *Women's Democratic News*, a member of the board of directors of the Foreign Policy Association and the City Housing Corporation. In fact, in 1928, ER was one of the best-known and highest-ranking Democrats in the United States. She was named director of the Bureau of Women's Activities of the Democratic National Committee, and in July asked to head a Woman's Advisory Committee to develop Al Smith's presidential campaign organization.

In 1928, ER held, therefore, the most powerful positions ever held by a woman in party politics. In matters of "turfing," which we now

recognize as more than symbolic, she demanded and received equality for the women political organizers: Their offices had the same floor space their male counterparts had, and equal comfort. There were windows, carpets, plants; the accommodations were light and airy. *The New York Times* reported that the space allotted to women in the national headquarters of the Democratic party was "said to be the largest headquarters ever occupied by a women's political organization." ER's rooms and those of John J. Raskob, then Democratic national chairman, were "identical in size and location."[20]

Throughout the 1920s ER worked to ensure that this equality involve more than floor space. In September 1926, after a bitter struggle for equal representation for women within the New York State Democratic Party, the party convention elected Caroline O'Day vice-chair of the State Committee, and women were voted equal representation with men in 135 of 150 Assembly districts....[21] But she quickly realized that equal representation had as yet very little to do with equal power. Increasingly distressed by the manipulations of her male colleagues, ER argued that women needed to take tougher, more direct measures.

In April 1928, she published a boldly feminist article in *Redbook*. "Women Must Learn to Play the Game as Men Do" was a battle cry that urged women to create their own "women bosses" in order to achieve real power:

> Women have been voting for ten years. But have they achieved actual political equality with men? No ... In small things they are listened to; but when it comes to asking for important things they generally find they are up against a blank wall....
>
> Politically, as a sex, women are generally "frozen out" from any intrinsic share of influence....
>
> The machinery of party politics has always been in the hands of men, and still is. Our statesmen and legislators are still keeping in form as the successors of the early warriors [who gathered] around the camp-fire plotting the next day's attack....[22]

ER's tone was outraged and unrelenting: Women went into politics with high hopes and specific intentions. They were courted and wooed. But when they demanded and expected real power, they were rebuffed....

Although only a few years before ER had

contended that women did not go into politics for personal gain, or the customary party reward for their work, by 1928 she expressed dismay that the hardworking women who devoted their time and energy to the political game continued to go unrewarded: "Men who work hard in party politics are always recognized, or taken care of in one way or another. Women, most of whom are voluntary workers . . . are generally expected to find in their labor its own reward. . . ."

Then there was the matter of political office. Party leaders "will ask women to run for office now and then, sometimes because they think it politic and wise to show women how generous they are, but more often because they realize in advance their ticket cannot win in the district selected. Therefore they will put up a woman, knowing it will injure the party less to have a woman defeated, and then they can always say it was her sex that defeated her. Where victory is certain, very rarely can you get a woman nominated. . . ."

ER was proud of the many women throughout the United States who had been elected to public office. . . . But, ER asked: "Does this indicate any equal recognition or share in political power?" She answered with a resounding no: There were instead infinite "examples . . . of women who were either denied a nomination or who were offered it only when inevitable defeat stared the party leaders in the face." ER suggested a reason for this situation: Public men dislike women in public life. "Beneath the veneer of courtesy and outward show of consideration universally accorded women, there is a widespread male hostility—age-old perhaps—against sharing with them any actual control."

To alter this, she urged women to "elect, accept and back" women bosses on every level of party management, in "districts, counties and states. Women must organize just as men organize." ER did not believe in a separate woman's party. "A woman's ticket could never possibly succeed. And to crystalize the issues on the basis of sex-opposition would only further antagonize men, congeal their age-old prejudices, and widen the chasm of existing differences." Rather, within the party, women needed to select, promote, and elect women bosses to positions of leadership and authority—where they could, with equality and independence and above all the assurance that they had the backing of their women's constit-

uency, fight it out with the men who routinely denied power to women.

ER was aware that the word "boss" might "shock sensitive ears." She did not mean by "boss" some sleazy and easy-to-buy politician, but, rather, a "high-minded leader." And she chose the word deliberately, "as it is the word men understand." She explained in detail her conviction that, "if women believe they have a right and duty in political life today, they must learn to talk the language of men. They must not only master the phraseology, but also understand the machinery which men have built up through years of practical experience. Against the men bosses there must be women bosses who can talk as equals, with the backing of a coherent organization of women voters behind them."

Tough-minded and direct, ER was also critical of women who refused to take the business of politics seriously or to consider their own political work a matter of fundamental urgency and significance: "If we are still a negligible factor, ignored and neglected, we must be prepared to admit in what we have ourselves failed." ER believed that too many women refused to work; to take themselves and their visions seriously; and too many women lacked knowledge and refused to "take the pains to study history, economics, political methods or get out among human beings." . . .

ER explained, in conclusion, that women could only achieve real power by serious organization, unlimited study, endless work. Male hostility to women was only partly responsible for women's failure to achieve power. Women seemed to ER reluctant to claim power. She dismissed the attitude of those women who professed "to be horrified at the thought of women bosses bartering and dickering in the hard game of politics with the men." ". . . [But] politics cannot be played from the clouds," [she insisted.] She understood that the task was hard and that the role of women in public life was difficult. Women's lives, to begin with, ER noted, were always "full of interruptions." There were the home, the children, the meals to prepare, the dinner parties to arrange. She was aware of the double standards and the double-job burdens. And so, she argued, women have to be more organized, more methodical, and, yes, more hardworking than men. She was adamant: "Women must learn to play the game as men do."

ER's earlier years in Albany and Washington, and her lifelong association with politicians and their ways, had accustomed her to the vagaries and strategies of power. Silence on the sidelines never achieved a thing, and was always interpreted as consent. The more she spoke out, the more she recognized her impact. She was ready to become—indeed, had already become—the very "political boss" about whom she wrote.

ER's *Redbook* article hit the stands with rather a splash. It resulted in several *New York Times* articles, including a *Magazine* interview by S. J. Woolf, "A Woman Speaks Her Political Mind," . . . [which] was entirely favorable to ER, [but] revealed an ever-present double standard: ER was a mother, a teacher, and a homemaker, Woolfe wrote, who never allowed her public or political activities to

> interfere with her devotion to her home, nor has she sacrificed her private life in any respect to her public activities. She is the mother of five children and their upbringing has been her first consideration. She believes that a woman fitted to serve her community or her country can show that fitness best in the management of her own home. . . .
>
> Mrs. Roosevelt is tall and has an engaging smile. There is something about that smile that is reminiscent of her illustrious uncle, while the droop in the outer corner of her eyes likewise reminds one of the former President. There is nothing about her that marks her as a woman in public life. Her manner is that of the young suburban mother. She is the strongest argument that could be presented against those who hold that by entering politics a woman is bound to lose her womanliness and her charm.
>
> She is the type of mother . . . interested in civic betterment, who believes that that finds its beginning in the home.[23]

Woolf's article was a clear indication of what was expected of ER if she were to maintain credibility and acceptance as a woman in public life. Among her colleagues and friends, she might depart from such prescriptions. But publicly ER understood and always worked within the limitations of her time and her marriage. Publicly she denied to the end of her life that she ever had, or ever wanted, real political power. She acknowledged that she worked for those issues that she believed in, but not once did she profess to enjoy the game. She never publicly acknowledged that it satisfied her own interests, served her own needs, or that she delighted even in the rough-and-tumble of the deals and battles. Nevertheless, she did express

dismay whenever she or other women were bypassed or blithely ignored and men took credit for their efforts and ideas. And she hated it when she was given no specific job to do, or was not encouraged to participate in a way she deemed appropriate. . . . [Her dilemma was reflected in her response to the 1928 election when Al Smith finally ran for president and her husband for governor of New York.]

ER's initial response to Smith's defeat and FDR's victory was complex. For over nine months, she had worked daily and imaginatively for the Smith campaign. ER hated to lose. It was not merely Smith's personal loss, or her own, but the continued defeat on the national level of all the social programs she championed. . . . ER was eager to continue the battle, but in terms of her own work, she considered FDR's victory a mixed blessing. She feared that FDR's election to office meant that she would have to withdraw from public life. To reporters, her remarks were restrained, even ungracious: "If the rest of the ticket didn't get in, what does it matter?" "No, I am not excited about my husband's election. I don't care. What difference can it make to me?"[24] In retrospect, she wondered if she had "really wanted Franklin to run. I imagine I accepted his nomination and later his election as I had accepted most of the things that had happened in life thus far; one did whatever seemed necessary and adjusted one's personal life to the developments in other people's lives."[25]

There was in 1928 no accepted place for a political wife, except in the background. ER had grown accustomed to a different role. She was a publisher, an editor, a columnist; she debated on the radio and before large audiences; her opinions were forthright and specific. She had a following, and people relied on her views and depended on her leadership. . . . There was no turning back. Yet neither was there any precedent for this new reality. History presented no other couple similarly equal in spirit, commitment, and ambition—giant personalities, powerful egos, inspiring and commanding presences. Was ER seriously meant to become again the dutiful wife at home with the children, . . . while her husband and all their friends were engaged in the work she most enjoyed? It was impossible. She could not abide the thought. She resented even contemplating it. And so the Roosevelt partnership departed yet again from tradition. . . . She would do it all—she would be the governor's wife, and she would pursue her own agenda.

NOTES

1. New York League of Women Voters, *Weekly News*, 22 Oct. 1922.

2. Elizabeth Israels Perry, "Training for Public Life: ER and Women's Political Networks in the 1920s," and Susan Ware, "ER and Democratic Politics: Women in the Postsuffrage Era," both in *Without Precedent: The Life and Career of Eleanor Roosevelt*, eds. Joan Hoff-Wilson and Marjorie Lightman (Bloomington: Indiana University Press, 1984), pp. 28–45, 46–60.

3. Eleanor Roosevelt, *This I Remember* (New York: Harper & Brothers, 1949), p. 32.

4. ER to FDR, 6 Feb. 1924, Franklin Delano Roosevelt Library [FDRL].

5. Ibid.

6. ER to FDR, 9 April 1924, FDRL.

7. *New York Times*, 15 April 1924.

8. Ibid., 31 March 1924.

9. Ibid., 11 June 1924 and 23 June, 1924. Also Eleanor Roosevelt, *This Is My Story* (New York: Garden City Publishing Company, 1937), pp. 354–55.

10. *New York Times*, 14 April 1924.

11. Interview with ER by Rose Feld, Ibid., 20 April 1924.

12. *New York Times*, 27 Sept. 1924.

13. ER, *This I Remember*, pp. 31–32.

14. Anna Roosevelt Cowles to Corinne Alsop, Alsop Family papers, Houghton; quoted in Geoffrey C. Ward, *A First-Class Temperament: The Emergence of Franklin Roosevelt* (New York: Harper & Row, 1989), p. 701n.

15. Vanderlip on Sheppard-Towner, quoted in Hilda R. Watrous, *Narcissa Cox Vanderlip*, League of Women Voters' pamphlet (New York: Foundation for Citizenship Education, 1982), p. 31.

16. *New York Times*, 26, 27 May 1927.

17. *New York Times*, 9 Dec. 1926.

18. *New York Times*, 1, 6 June 1929.

19. *New York Times*, 15 Oct. 1927; 8 Dec. 1927; 2 Nov. 1929.

20. *New York Times*, 19 July 1928; 4 Aug. 1928.

21. *New York Times*, 28 Sept. 1926.

22. For this quotation and those in the following paragraphs, see "Women Must Learn to Play the Game as Men Do," *Redbook* (April 1928):71–72ff.

23. *New York Times Magazine*, 8 April 1928.

24. Quoted in Joseph P. Lash, *Eleanor and Franklin* (New York: W. W. Norton, 1971), p. 320.

25. ER, *This I Remember*, p. 46.

JOAN JACOBS BRUMBERG

Fasting Girls: The Emerging Ideal of Slenderness in American Culture

Although anorexia nervosa is generally considered a modern disease, appetite control has long been an important dimension of female experience. Joan Jacobs Brumberg's pioneering study of anorexia nervosa traces changing cultural pressure on women to control their appetite. Exploring the links between food and femininity in the nineteenth century, Brumberg found that by 1890 thinness had become a way in which young privileged women could distance themselves from their working-class counterparts. More important, food preferences and thin bodies also sent moral and aesthetic messages. The young woman whose frail, delicate frame demonstrated her rejection of all carnal appetites more closely approached the Victorian ideal of femininity than did her more robust counterpart whose heavier physique signaled sexual craving. The twentieth century brought additional pressures to control body weight, according to Brumberg, with the development of scientific nutrition and the standard sizing of clothes. By 1920, fat had become a moral issue. Combined with social changes having to do with food and sexuality occurring in the 1960s, the stage was set for the epidemic of eating disorders evident in the 1980s and 1990s.

Within the first two decades of the twentieth century, even before the advent of the flapper, the voice of American women revealed that the female struggle with weight was under way and was becoming intensely personal. As early as 1907 an *Atlantic Monthly* article described the reaction of a woman trying on a dress she had not worn for over a year: "The gown was neither more [n]or less than anticipated. But I . . . *the fault was on me* . . . I was more! Gasping I hooked it together. The gown was hopeless, and I . . . I am fat."[1] . . . By the twentieth century . . . overweight in women was not only a physical liability, it was a character flaw and a social impediment.

Early in the century elite American women began to take body weight seriously as fat became an aesthetic liability for those who followed the world of haute couture. Since the mid-nineteenth century wealthy Americans—the wives of J. P. Morgan, Cornelius Vanderbilt, and Harry Harkness Flagler, for instance—had traveled to Paris to purchase the latest creations from couturier collections such as those on view at Maison Worth on the famed rue de la Paix. The couturier was not just a dressmaker who made clothes for an individual woman; rather, the couturier fashioned "a look" or a collection of dresses for an abstraction—the stylish woman. In order to be stylish and wear couturier clothes, a woman's body had to conform to the dress rather than the dress to the body, as had been the case when the traditional dressmaker fitted each garment.[2] . . .

In 1908 the world of women's fashion was revolutionized by Paul Poiret, whose new silhouette was slim and straight. . . . Almost immediately women of style began to purchase new kinds of undergarments that would make Poiret's look possible; for example, the traditional hourglass corset was cast aside for a rubber girdle to retract the hips.

After World War I the French continued to set the fashion standard for style-conscious American women. In 1922 Jeanne Lanvin's chemise, a straight frock with a simple bateau neckline, was transformed by Gabrielle Chanel into the uniform of the flapper. Chanel dropped the waistline to the hips and began to expose more of the leg: in 1922 she moved her hemlines to midcalf, and in 1926–27 the ideal hem was raised to just below the knee. In order to look good in Chanel's fashionable little dress, its wearer had to think not only about the appearance of her legs but about the smoothness of her form.[3] Women who wore the flapper uniform turned to flattening brassieres constructed of shoulder straps and a single band of material that encased the body from chest to waist. In 1914 a French physician commented on the revised dimensions of women's bodies: "Nowadays it is not the fashion to be corpulent; the proper thing is to have a slight, graceful figure far removed from embonpoint, and *a fortiori* from obesity. For once, the physician is called upon to interest himself in the question of feminine aesthetics."[4]

The slenderized fashion image of the French was picked up and promoted by America's burgeoning ready-to-wear garment industry.[5] Stimulated by the popularity of the Gibson girl and the shirtwaist craze of the 1890s, ready-to-wear production in the United States accelerated in the first two decades of the twentieth century. Chanel's chemise dress was a further boon to the garment industry. Because of its simple cut, the chemise was easy to copy and produce, realities that explain its quick adoption as the uniform of the 1920s. According to a 1923 *Vogue,* the American ready-to-wear industry successfully democratized French fashion: "Today, the mode which originates in Paris is a factor in the lives of women of every rank, from the highest to the lowest."[6]

In order to market ready-to-wear clothing, the industry turned in the 1920s to standard sizing, an innovation that put increased emphasis on personal body size and gave legitimacy to the idea of a normative size range. For women, shopping for ready-to-wear clothes in the bustling department stores of the early twentieth century fostered heightened concern about body size.[7] With a dressmaker, every style was theoretically available to every body; with standard sizing, items of clothing could be identified as desirable, only to be rejected on the grounds of fit. (For women the cost of altering a ready-made garment was an "add-on"; for men it was not.) Female figure flaws became a source of frustration and embarrassment, not easily hidden from those who accompanied the shopper or from salesclerks. Experiences in department-store dressing rooms created a host of new anxieties for women and girls who could not fit into stylish clothing. . . .

Ironically, standard sizing created an unexpected experience of frustration in a marketplace that otherwise was offering a continually expansive opportunity for gratification via purchasable goods. Because many manufacturers of stylish women's garments did not make clothing in large sizes, heavy women were at the greatest disadvantage. In addition to the moral [disgrace] of overweight, the standardization of garment production precluded fat women's participation in the mainstream of fashion. This situation became worse as the century progressed. Fashion photography was professionalized, a development that paralleled the growth of modern advertising, and models became slimmer both to compensate for the distortions of the camera and to accommodate the new merchandising canon—modern fashion was best displayed on a lean body.[8]

The appearance in 1918 of America's first best-selling weight-control book confirmed that weight was a source of anxiety among women and that fat was out of fashion. *Diet and Health with a Key to the Calories* by Lulu Hunt Peters was directed at a female audience and based on the assumption that most readers wanted to lose rather than gain weight. . . . "You should know and also use the word calorie as frequently, or more frequently, than you use the words foot, yard, quart, gallon and so forth. . . . Hereafter you are going to eat calories of food. Instead of saying one slice of bread, or a piece of pie, you will say 100 calories of bread, 350 calories of pie."[9]

Peters' book was popular because it was personal and timely. Her 1918 appeal was related to food shortages caused by the exigen-

cies of the war in Europe. Peters told her readers that it was "more important than ever to reduce" and recommended the formation of local Watch Your Weight Anti-Kaiser Classes. "There are hundreds of thousands of individuals all over America who are hoarding food," she wrote. "They have vast amounts of this valuable commodity stored away in their own anatomy." In good-humored fashion Peters portrayed her own calorie counting as both an act of patriotism and humanitarianism:

> I am reducing and the money that I can save will help keep a child from starving . . . [I am explaining to my friends] that for every pang of hunger we feel we can have a double joy, that of knowing we are saving worse pangs in some little children, and that of knowing that for every pang we feel we lose a pound. A pang's a pound the world around we'll say.[10]

But Peters showed herself to be more than simply an informative and patriotic physician. Confessing that she once weighed as much as 200 pounds, the author also understood that heavy women were ashamed of their bulk and unlikely to reveal their actual weight. Peters observed that it was not a happy situation for fat women. "You are viewed with distrust, suspicion, and even aversion," she told her overweight readers. . . .

Peters' book was among the first to articulate the new secular credo of physical denial: modern women suffered to be beautiful (thin) rather than pious. Peters' language and thinking reverberated with references to religious ideas of temptation and sin. For the modern female dieter, sweets, particularly chocolate, were the ultimate temptation. Eating chocolate violated the morality of the dieter and her dedication to her ideal, a slim body. Peters joked about her cravings ("My idea of heaven is a place with me and mine on a cloud of whipped cream") but she was adamant about the fact that indulgence must ultimately be paid for. "If you think you will die unless you have some chocolate creams [go on a] *debauch*," she advised. " 'Eat 10 or so' but then *repent* with a 50-calorie dinner of bouillon and crackers." (Italics added.)[11]

Although the damage done by chocolate creams could be mediated by either fasting or more rigid dieting, Peters explained that there was a psychological cost in yielding to the temptation of candy or rich desserts. Like so many modern dieters, Peters wrote about the issue of guilt followed by redemption through parsimonious eating: "Every supposed pleasure in sin [eating] will furnish more than its equivalent of pain [dieting]." But appetite control was not only a question of learning to delay gratification, it was also an issue of self-esteem. "You will be tempted quite frequently, and you will have to choose whether you will enjoy yourself hugely in the twenty minutes or so that you will be consuming the excess calories, or whether you will dislike yourself cordially for the two or three days you lose by your lack of will power." For Peters dieting had as much to do with the mind as with the body. "There is a great deal of psychology to reducing," she wrote astutely.[12] In fact, with the popularization of the concept of calorie counting, physical features once regarded as natural—such as appetite and body weight—were designated as objects of conscious control. The notion of weight control through restriction of calories implied that . . . overweight control through restriction of calories implied that overweight resulted solely from lack of control; to be a fat woman constituted a failure of personal morality.

The tendency to talk about female dieting as a moral issue was particularly strong among the popular beauty experts, that is, those in the fashion and cosmetics industry who sold scientific advice on how to become and stay beautiful. Many early-twentieth-century beauty culturists, including Grace Peckham Murray, Helena Rubenstein, and Hazel Bishop, studied chemistry and medical specialties such as dermatology. The creams and lotions they created, as well as the electrical gadgets they promoted, were intended to bring the findings of modern chemistry and physiology to the problem of female beauty. Nevertheless, women could not rely entirely on scientifically achieved results. The beauty experts also preached the credo of self-denial: to be beautiful, most women must suffer.

Because they regarded fat women as an affront to their faith, some were willing to criminalize as well as medicalize obesity. In 1902 *Vogue* speculated, "To judge by the efforts of the majority of women to attain slender and sylph-like proportions, one would fancy it a crime to be fat." By 1918 the message was more distinct: "There is one crime against the modern ethics of beauty which is unpardonable; far better it is to commit any number of petty crimes than to be guilty of the sin of growing fat." By 1930 there was no turning back. Helena Rubenstein, a high priestess of the faith, articulated in *The Art of Feminine Beauty* the moral and aesthetic dictum that would govern the lives of subsequent generations of women: "An abundance of fat is something repulsive and not in accord with the principles that rule our conception of the beautiful.[13] . . .

In adolescence fat was considered a particular liability because of the social strains associated with that stage of life. In the 1940s articles with titles such as "What to Do about the Fat Child at Puberty," "Reducing the Adolescent," and "Should the Teens Diet?" captured the rising interest in adolescent weight control.[14] Women's magazines, reflecting the concerns of mothers anxious to save their daughters from social ostracism, for the first time promoted diets for young girls. According to the *Ladies' Home Journal:* "Appearance plays too important a part in a girl's life not to have her grow up to be beauty-conscious. Girls should be encouraged to take an interest in their appearance when they are very young."[15] . . . Adolescent weight control was also promoted by popular magazines hoping to sell products to young women. . . . *Seventeen's* adoption of the cause of weight control confirmed that slimness was a critical dimension of adolescent beauty and that a new constituency, high school girls, was learning how to diet. From 1944 [when it was founded] to 1948, *Seventeen* had published a full complement of articles on nutrition but almost nothing on weight control. Following the mode of earlier home economists and scientific nutritionists, the magazine had presented basic information about food groups and the importance of each in the daily diet; balance but not calories had been the initial focus. In 1948, however, *Seventeen* proclaimed overweight a medical problem and began educating its young readers about calories and the psychology of eating. Adolescent girls were warned against using eating as a form of emotional expression (do not "pamper your blues" with food) and were given practical tips on how to avoid food bingeing. No mention was made of the new "diet pills" (amphetamines) introduced in the 1930s for clinical treatment of obesity. Instead, teenagers were encouraged to go on "sensible" and "well-rounded" diets of between 1,200 and 1,800 calories. By the 1950s advertisements for "diet foods" such as Ry-Krisp were offering assistance as they told the readership "Nobody

Loves a Fat Girl."[16] Girls, much as adult women, were expected to tame the natural appetite.

Although adolescent girls were consistently warned against weight reduction without medical supervision, dieting was always cast a worthwhile endeavor with transforming powers. "Diets can do wonderful things. When dispensed or approved by your physician . . . all you have to do is follow whither the chart leads."[17] The process of metamorphosis from fat to thin always provided a narrative of uplift and interest. "The Fattest Girl in the Class" was the autobiographical account of Jane, an obese girl who, after suffering the social stigma associated with teenage overweight, went on a diet and found happiness.[18] Being thin was tied to attractiveness, popularity with the opposite sex, and self-esteem—all primary ingredients in adolescent culture. Nonfiction accounts of "make-overs" became a popular formula in all the beauty magazines of the postwar period and provided a tantalizing fantasy of psychological and spiritual transformation for mature and adolescent women alike.[19]

The popularization of adolescent female weight control in the postwar era is a prime component of the modern dieting story and a critical factor in explaining anorexia nervosa as we know it today. . . . Since the 1960s the dieting imperative has intensified in two noticeable and important ways. . . . First, the ideal female body size has become considerably slimmer. After a brief flirtation with full-breasted, curvaceous female figures in the politically conservative postwar recovery of the 1950s, our collective taste returned to an ideal of extreme thinness and an androgynous, if not childlike, figure.[20] A series of well-known studies point to the declining weight since the 1950s of fashion models, Miss America contestants, and *Playboy* centerfolds.[21] Neither bosoms, hips, nor buttocks are currently in fashion as young and old alike attempt to meet the new aesthetic standard. A Bloomingdale's ad posits, "Bean lean, slender as the night, narrow as an arrow, pencil thin, get the point?"[22] It is appropriate to recall Annette Kellerman who, at 5 feet 3¾ inches and 137 pounds, epitomized the body beautiful of 1918. Obviously, our cultural tolerance for body fat has diminished over the intervening years.

Second, notably since the middle to late 1970s, a new emphasis on physical fitness and athleticism has intensified cultural pressures on the individual for control and mastery of the body. For women this means that fitness has been added to slimness as a criterion of perfection.[23] Experts on the subject, such as Jane Fonda, encourage women to strive for a lean body with musculature. The incredible popularity among women of aerobics, conditioning programs, and jogging does testify to the satisfactions that come with gaining physical strength through self-discipline, but it also expresses our current urgency about the physical body. Many who are caught up in the exercise cult equate physical fitness and slimness with a higher moral state. . . . Compulsive exercising and chronic dieting have [thus] been joined as twin obsessions. . . . [In the] 1980s clinical reports and autobiographical statements show a clear-cut pattern of anorexic patients who exercise with ritualistic intensity. How much one runs and how little one eats is the prevailing moral calculus in present-day anorexia nervosa. . . .

The proliferation of diet and exercise regimens in the past decade, although an important context for understanding the increase in anorexia nervosa, is not the whole story. For a more complete explanation we must turn to some other recent social changes, keeping in mind that no one factor has caused the contemporary problem. Rather, it is the nature of our economic and cultural environment, interacting with individual and family characteristics, which exacerbates the social and emotional insecurities that put today's young women at increasing risk for anorexia nervosa. Two very basic social transformations are relevant to the problem: one has to do with food; the other, with new expectations between the sexes.

Since World War II, and especially in the last two decades, middle-class Americans have experienced a veritable revolution in terms of how and what we eat, as well as how we think about eating.[24] The imperatives of an expanding capitalist society have generated extraordinary technological and marketing innovations, which in turn have transformed food itself, expanded our repertoire of foods, and affected the ways in which we consume them. Even though much contemporary food is characterized by elaborate processing and conservation techniques that actually reduce and flatten distinctive textures and flavors, the current array of food choices seems to constitute an endless smorgasbord of new and different tastes. [Since] the 1980s an individual in an urban center looking for a quick lunch [has been] able to choose from tacos with guacamole and salsa, hummus and falafel in pita, sushi, tortellini, quiche, and pad thai—along with more traditional "American" fare such as hamburgers. Thirty years ago this diversified international menu was as unknown to most Americans as were many of the food products used to create it. . . . As a consequence of [the expansion of our food repertoire], we are faced with an abundance of food which, in our obesophobic society, necessitates ever greater self-control. . . . It is no wonder, then, that we talk so incessantly about food and dieting.

The food revolution is a matter of ideas and manners as much as technology and markets. . . . In our society food is chosen and eaten not merely on the basis of hunger. It is a commonplace to observe that contemporary advertising connects food to sociability, status, and sexuality. In an affluent society, in particular, where eating appears to involve considerable individual choice, food is regarded as an important analogue of the self.

In the 1960s, for example, many young people in the counterculture gave up goods associated with their bourgeois upbringing and turned instead to a diet of whole grains, unprocessed foods, and no meat. This new diet made a statement about personal and political values and became a way of separating one generation from another. . . . In the 1980s, the extent to which the choice of cuisine dominates and defines the sophisticated life-style [among well-to-do urbanites] is reflected in a recent *New Yorker* cartoon, which shows a young professional couple after a dinner party given by friends. In complete seriousness they say to each other, "We could get close with David and Elizabeth if they didn't put béarnaise sauce on everything."[25] The anorectic is obviously not alone in her use of food and eating as a means of self-definition. There are many others who internalize the dictum "You are what you eat"—or, for that matter, what you don't eat.[26]

Along with the expansion of our food repertoire and our extraordinary attention to food selection, the eating context has changed. Eating is being desocialized. In American society today, more and more food is being consumed away from the family table or any other fixed center of sociability. This process began in the postwar period with the introduction of convenience foods and drive-in restaurants, precursors of the fast-food chains that now constitute a $45-billion-a-year industry. . . . Americans [now] eat everywhere—in the classroom; in theaters, libraries, and museums; on the street; at their desks; on the phone; in hot tubs; in cars while driving. . . . Signs saying "no food and drink," infrequent in other parts of the world, adorn our public buildings, a clear sign of our pattern of vagabond eating.[27]

On college and university campuses, where eating disorders are rampant, the situation is exaggerated. By the early 1970s most undergraduate students were no longer required to take any sit-down meals at fixed times in college dormitories. . . . Typically, students frequent a series of university cafeterias or commercial off-campus restaurants where they can obtain breakfast, lunch, or dinner at any time of the day. Some campus food plans allow unlimited amounts, a policy that fuels the behavior of the bulimic: "I used to go to Contract, eat a whole bunch of stuff, go to the bathroom, throw it up, come back, eat again, throw it up, eat again."[28] In addition, the availability of nearly any kind of food at any time contributes to a pattern of indiscriminate eating. Traditions of food appropriateness—that is, that certain foods are eaten at particular times of the day or in a certain sequence—disappear in this unstructured climate. Thus, an ice-cream cone, a carbonated soft drink, and a bagel constitute an easy popular "meal" that may be eaten at any time of day. Most colleges and the surrounding communities have made provisions to gratify student appetites no matter what the hour. Snack bars and vending machines adorn nearly every free alcove in classroom buildings and residence halls; pizza and Chinese food are delivered hot in the middle of the night.

In a setting where eating is so promiscuous, it is no wonder that food habits become problematic. This is not to say that our universities, on their own, generate eating-disordered students. They do, however, provide fertile ground for those who carry the seeds of disorder with them from home. In the permissive and highly individualized food environment of the post-1970 college or university, overeating and undereating become distinct possibilities.[29]

For those young women with either incip-

ient or pronounced anorexia nervosa, the unstructured college life . . . often accentuates the
anorectic's physical and emotional problems.
[As one young anorectic explained]:

> I don't know any limits here at all. At home, I
> have my mom dishing out my food . . . But when
> I'm here it's a totally different story—I can't tell
> portion size at all. I always get so afraid after-
> wards, after eating. Oh my God did I eat that
> much or this much? So I just pass things up al-
> together and don't eat.[30]

The anorectic's preoccupation with appetite control is fueled by incessant talk about
dieting and weight even among friends and associates who eat regularly. Diet-conscious female students report that fasting, weight control, and binge eating are a normal part of life
on American college campuses.[31] . . . In our
obesophobic society women struggle with food
because, among other things, food represents
fat and loss of control. For a contemporary
woman to eat heartily, energetically, and happily is usually problematic (and, at best, occasional). As a result, some come to fear and hate
their own appetite; eating becomes a shameful
and disgusting act, and denial of hunger becomes a central facet of identity and personality. . . .

Among adolescents concerned with the
transition to adulthood, an intense concern
with appetite control and the body [also] operates in tandem with increasing anxiety over
sexuality and the implications of changing sex
roles. For sex is the second important arena of
social change that may contribute to the rising
number of anorectics. There are, in fact, some
justifiable social reasons why contemporary
young women fear adult womanhood. The
"anorexic generations," particularly those born
since 1960, have been subject to a set of insecurities that make heterosexuality an anxious
rather than a pleasant prospect. Family insecurity, reflected in the frequency of divorce,
and changing sex and gender roles became
facts of life for this group in their childhood. . . .
Although there is no positive correlation between divorced families and anorexia nervosa,
family disruption is part of the world view of
the anorexic generations. Its members understand implicitly that not all heterosexual relationships have happy endings.

As a consequence of these social changes,
some young women are ambivalent about

commitments to men and have adopted an
ideal of womanhood that reflects the impact of
post-1960 feminism. Although they generally
draw back from an explicitly feminist vocabu-
lary, most undergraduate women today desire
professional careers of their own without forsaking the idea of marriage and a family. A
1985 study of college women by sociologist
Mirra Komarovsky reveals that finding one's
place in the world of work has become essential
for personal dignity in this generation—yet a
career without marriage was the choice of only
2 percent of the sample.[32] Convinced that individuality can be accommodated in marriage,
these young women are interested in heterosexuality, but admit that "relationships with
guys" are difficult even in college. Komarovsky describes conflict over dating rituals (who
takes the initiative and who pays), decision
making as a couple, intellectual rivalries, and
competition for entrance into graduate school.
Unlike Mother, who followed Dad to graduate
school and supported him along the way, today's undergraduate—whether she is a declared feminist or not—wants her own professional career both as a ticket to the good life
and as a protection for herself in case of divorce.

Sexual activity also requires an extraordinary degree of self-protection in the modern
world of AIDS. While premarital sex is acceptable (if not desirable), it is an understandable
source of worry among female undergradu-
ates. An advertisement in a 1986 issue of Ms.,
aimed at selling condoms to young women,
captured the current ambivalence about the
physical side of heterosexuality: "Let's face it,
sex these days can be risky business, and you
need all the protection you can get. Between
the fear of unplanned pregnancy, sexually
transmitted diseases, and the potential side effects of many forms of contraception, it may
seem like sex is hardly worth the risk anymore."[33] For some students the unprecedented
privacy and freedom of modern university life
generates as much fear as pleasure. It bears repeating that clinical materials suggest an *absence* [emphasis is the editor's] of sexual activity on the part of anorectics.

Even though feminine dependency is no
longer in fashion, these same young women
combine traditional expectations with a quest
for equity and power. To be brainy and beautiful; to have an exciting $75,000-a-year job; to

nurture two wonderful children in consort with a supportive but equally high-powered husband—these are the personal ambitions of many in the present college generation. In order to achieve this level of personal and social perfection, young women must be extremely demanding of themselves: there can be no distracting personal or avocational detours—they must be unrelenting in the pursuit of goals. The kind of personal control required to become the new Superwoman (a term popularized by columnist Ellen Goodman)[34] parallels the single-mindedness that characterizes the anorectic. In sum, the golden ideal of this generation of privileged young women and their most distinctive pathology appear to be flip sides of the same record.

My assertion that the post-1960 epidemic of anorexia nervosa can be related to recent social change in the realm of sexuality [and gender roles] is not an argument for turning back the clock. . . . [H]istorical investigation demonstrates that anorexia nervosa was latent in the economic and emotional milieu of the bourgeois family as early as the 1950s. It makes little sense to think a cure will be achieved by putting women back in the kitchen, reinstituting sit-down meals on the nation's campuses, or limiting personal and professional choices to what they were in the Victorian era. On the basis of the best current research on anorexia nervosa, we must conclude that the disease develops as a result of the intersection of external and internal forces in the life of an individual. External forces such as those described here do not, by themselves, generate psychopathologies, but they do give them shape and influence their frequency.

In the confusion of this transitional moment, when a new future is being tentatively charted for women but gender roles and sexuality are still constrained by tradition, young women on the brink of adulthood are feeling the pain of social change most acutely.[35] They look about for direction, but find little in the way of useful experiential guides. What parts of women's tradition do they want to carry into the future? What parts should be left behind? These are difficult personal and political decisions, and most young women are being asked to make them without benefit of substantive education in the history and experience of their sex. In effect, our young women are being chal-

lenged and their expectations raised without a simultaneous level of support for either their specific aspirations or for female creativity in general.

Sadly, the cult of diet and exercise is the closest thing our secular society offers women in terms of a coherent philosophy of the self.[36] This being the case, anorexia nervosa is not a quirk and the symptom choice is not surprising. When personal and social difficulties arise, a substantial number of our young women become preoccupied with their bodies and control of appetite. Of all the messages they hear, the imperative to be beautiful and good, by being thin, is still the strongest and most familiar. Moreover, they are caught, often at a very early age, in a deceptive cognitive trap that has them believing that body weight is entirely subject to their conscious control. Despite feminist influences on the career aspirations of the present college-age generation, little has transpired to dilute the basic strength of this powerful cultural prescription that plays on both individualism and conformity. The unfortunate truth is that even when she wants more than beauty and understands its limitations as a life goal, the bourgeois woman still expends an enormous amount of psychic energy on appetite control as well as on other aspects of presentation of the physical self.

And what of the future? . . .

We can expect to see eating disorders continue, if not increase, among young women in those postindustrial societies where adolescents tend to be under stress. For both young men and young women, vast technological and cultural changes have made the transition to adulthood particularly difficult by transforming the nature of the family and community and rendering the future unpredictable. According to psychologist Urie Bronfenbrenner and others, American adolescents are in the worst trouble: we have the highest incidence of alcohol and drug abuse among adolescents of any country in the world; we also have the highest rate of teenage pregnancy of any industrialized nation; and we appear to have the most anorexia nervosa.[37]

Although the sexually active adolescent mother and the sexually inactive adolescent anorectic may seem to be light-years apart, they are linked by a common, though unarticulated, understanding. For adolescent women the body is still the most powerful paradigm regardless of social class. Unfortunately, a sizable number of our young women—poor and privileged alike—regard their body as the best vehicle for making a statement about their identity and personal dreams. This is what unprotected sexual intercourse and prolonged starvation have in common. Taken together, our unenviable preeminence in these two domains suggests the enormous difficulty involved in making the transition to adult womanhood in a society where women are still evaluated primarily in terms of the body rather than the mind.

Notes

1. "On Growing Fat," *Atlantic Monthly* (Mar. 1907):430–31.

2. Jo Ann Olian, *The House of Worth: The Gilded Age, 1860–1918* (New York: Museum of the City of New York, 1982); Jane Beth Abrams, "The Thinning of America: The Emergence of the Ideal of Slenderness in American Popular Culture, 1870–1930," B.A. thesis, Harvard University, 1983, chap. 2.

3. Michael Batterberry and Ariane Batterberry, *Mirror Mirror: A Social History of Fashion* (New York: Holt, Rinehart and Winston, 1977), pp. 289–97; Diane DeMarly, *The History of Haute Couture, 1850–1950* (New York: Holmes & Meier, 1980), pp. 81–83.

4. P. Rostaine, "How to Get Thin," *Medical Press and Circular* 149 (Dec. 23, 1914):643–44.

5. Stuart Ewen and Elizabeth Ewen, *Channels of Desire: Mass Images and the Shaping of American Consciousness* (New York: McGraw-Hill, 1982), pt. 4; Claudia Kidwell and Margaret C. Christman, *Suiting Everyone: The Democratization of Clothing in America* (Washington, D.C.: Smithsonian Institution Press, 1974).

6. *Vogue* (Jan. 1, 1923):63.

7. Lois W. Banner, *American Beauty* (New York: Random House, 1983), p. 262; Ewen and Ewen, *Channels of Desire*, pp. 193–98.

8. Banner, *American Beauty*, p. 287; Anne Hollander, *Seeing through Clothes* (New York: Viking Press, 1975).

9. Lulu Hunt Peters, *Diet and Health with a Key to the Calories* (Chicago: The Reilly & Britton Company, 1918), pp. 24, 39.

10. Ibid., pp. 12, 104, 110.

11. Ibid., pp. 85, 94.

12. ibid., pp. 85, 93, 94.

13. "On Her Dressing Table," *Vogue* (Apr. 24, 1902):413, ibid. (July 1, 1918):78.

14. Mildred H. Bryan, "Don't Let Your Child Get Fat!" *Hygeia* 15 (1937):801–3; G. D. Schultz, "Forget That Clean-Plate Bogey!" *Better Homes and Gardens* 21 (Sept. 1942):24.

15. Louise Paine Benjamin, "I Have Three Daughters," *Ladies Homes Journal* 57 (June 1940):74.

16. "You'll Eat It Up at Noon," *Seventeen* (Sept. 1946):21–22; Irma M. Phorylles, "The Lost Waist-

line," ibid. (Mar. 1948):124; "Overweight?" ibid. (Aug. 1948):184.

17. Ibid.

18. "Fattest Girl in the Class," ibid. (Jan. 1948):21–22.

19. "Psychology of Dieting," *Ladies' Home Journal* (Jan. 1965):66.

20. Banner, *American Beauty*, pp. 283–85.

21. David M. Garner et al., "Cultural Expectations of Thinness in Women," *Psychology Reports* 47 (1980):483–91.

22. Rita Freedman, *Beauty Bound* (Lexington: Lexington Books, 1986), p. 150.

23. "Coming on Strong: The New Ideal of Beauty," *Time* (Aug. 30, 1983):71–77.

24. William Chafe, *The Unfinished Journey: America since World War II* (New York: Oxford University Press, 1986).

25. *New Yorker* (July 21, 1986):71.

26. "What's Your Food Status Because the Way You Live Has a Lot to Do with the Way You Eat," *Mademoiselle* (Sept. 1985):224–26; "Food as Well as Clothes, Today, Make the Man—As a Matter of Life and Style," *Vogue* (June 1985):271–73.

27. "Severe Growing Pains for Fast Food," *Business Week* (Mar. 22, 1985):225.

28. Greg Foster and Susan Howerin, "The Quest for Perfection: An Interview with a Former Bulimic," *Iris: A Journal about Women* [Charlottesville, Va.] (1986):21.

29. Before they even arrive on campus, during their senior year in high school and the summer before entering college, many girls began to talk about the "freshmen 10 or 15." This is the weight gain predicted as a result of eating starchy institutional food and participating in late-night food forays with friends.

30. Elizabeth Greene, "Support Groups Forming for Students with Eating Disorders," *Chronicle of Higher Education* (Mar. 5, 1986):1, 30.

31. K. A. Halmi, J. R. Falk, and E. Schwartz, "Binge-Eating and Vomiting: A Survey of a College Population," *Psychological Medicine* 11 (1981):697–706; R. L. Pyle et al., "The Incident of Bulimia in Freshman College Students," *International Journal of Eating Disorders* 2, 3 (1983):75–86.

32. Mirra Komarovsky, *Women in College: Shaping the New Feminine Identities* (New York: Basic Books, 1985), pp. 89–92, 225–300.

33. *Ms.* (Sept. 1986):n.p. The condom is called Mentor.

34. Ellen Goodman, *Close to Home* (New York: Fawcett Crest, 1979).

35. In *Theories of Adolescence* (New York: Random House, 1962), R. E. Muuss wrote: "Societies in a period of rapid transition create a particular adolescent period; the adolescent has not only the society's problem to adjust to but his [or her] own as well" (p. 164).

36. My view of this issue complements ideas presented in Robert Bellah et al., *Habits of the Heart: Individualism and Commitment in American Life* (New York: Harper & Row, 1986).

37. These data are synthesized in Urie Bronfenbrenner, "Alienation and the Four Worlds of Childhood," *Phi Delta Kappan* (Feb. 1986):434.

RUTH SCHWARTZ COWAN

The "Industrial Revolution" in the Home: Household Technology and Social Change in the Twentieth Century

The industrial technology that changed factory work also changed housework; the washing machine replaced the washtub just as the power loom replaced the handloom. Yet the impact of changing household technology on household workers has been little explored. In the following essay Ruth Schwartz Cowan examines how housework changed with the introduction of a variety of laborsaving appliances and the aggressive use of advertising designed to promote their sale. What emerges is a job that has changed in structure. Less burdensome physically, housework became no less time consuming as new duties were added and the work itself invested with new expectations and greater emotional content. What Cowan describes, in part, is the transition from the nineteenth-century mistress of the household who directed a servant's work to the twentieth-century middle-class housewife who, as jane-of-all-trades—laundress, scrub woman, gardener, nursemaid, chauffeur, and cook—was expected to find self-fulfillment in housework. What does this assumption suggest about the role of ideology as well as technology in defining work? What has happened to Henrietta Rodman's vision of "the grand domestic revolution" that technology and the "professionalization" of housework would bring about? In what sense is the individual housewife more isolated than ever?

When we think about the interaction between technology and society, we tend to think in fairly grandiose terms: massive computers invading the workplace, railroad tracks cutting through vast wildernesses, armies of women and children toiling in the mills. These grand visions have blinded us to an important and rather peculiar technological revolution which has been going on right under our noses: the technological revolution in the home. This revolution has transformed the conduct of our daily lives, but in somewhat unexpected ways. The industrialization of the home was a process very different from the industrialization of other means of production, and the impact of that process was neither what we have been led to believe it was nor what students of the other industrial revolutions would have been led to predict.

Some years ago sociologists of the functionalist school formulated an explanation of the impact of industrial technology on the modern family. Although that explanation was not empirically verified, it has become almost universally accepted.[1] Despite some differences in emphasis, the basic tenets of the traditional interpretation can be roughly summarized as follows:

Before industrialization the family was the basic social unit. Most families were rural, large, and self-sustaining; they produced and processed almost everything that was needed for their own support and for trading in the marketplace, while at the same time performing a host of other functions ranging from mutual protection to entertainment. In these pre-industrial families women (adult women, that is) had a lot to do, and their time was almost entirely absorbed by household tasks. Under industrialization the family is much less important. The household is no longer the focus of production; production for the marketplace and production for sustenance have been removed to other locations. Families are smaller and they are urban rather than rural. The number of social functions they perform is much reduced, until almost all that remains is consumption, socialization of small children, and tension management. As their functions diminished, families became atomized; the social bonds that had held them together were loosened. In these postindustrial families women have very little to do, and the tasks with which they fill their time have lost the social utility that they once possessed. Modern women are in trouble, the analysis goes, because modern families are in trouble; and modern families are in trouble because industrial technology has either eliminated or eased almost all their former functions, but modern ideologies have not kept pace with the change. The results of this time lag are several: some women suffer from role anxiety, others land in the divorce courts, some enter the labor market, and others take to burning their brassieres and demanding liberation.

This sociological analysis is a cultural artifact of vast importance. Many Americans believe that it is true and act upon that belief in various ways: some hope to reestablish family solidarity by relearning lost productive crafts—baking bread, tending a vegetable garden—others dismiss the women's liberation movement as "simply a bunch of affluent housewives who have nothing better to do with their time." As disparate as they may seem, these reactions have a common ideological source—the standard sociological analysis of the impact of technological change on family life.

As a theory this functionalist approach has much to recommend it, but at present we have very little evidence to back it up. Family history is an infant discipline, and what evidence it has produced in recent years does not lend credence to the standard view.[2] Phillippe Ariès has shown, for example, that in France the ideal of the small nuclear family predates industri-

alization by more than a century.[3] Historical demographers working on data from English and French families have been surprised to find that most families were quite small and that several generations did not ordinarily reside together; the extended family, which is supposed to have been the rule in preindustrial societies, did not occur in colonial New England either.[4] Rural English families routinely employed domestic servants, and even very small English villages had their butchers and bakers and candlestick makers; all these persons must have eased some of the chores that would otherwise have been the housewife's burden.[5] Preindustrial housewives no doubt had much with which to occupy their time, but we may have reason to wonder whether there was quite as much pressure on them as sociological orthodoxy has led us to suppose. The large rural family that was sufficient unto itself back there on the prairies may have been limited to the prairies—or it may never have existed at all (except, that is, in the reveries of sociologists).

Even if all the empirical evidence were to mesh with the functionalist theory, the theory would still have problems, because its logical structure is rather weak. Comparing the average farm family in 1750 (assuming that you knew what that family was like) with the average urban family in 1950 in order to discover the significant social changes that had occurred is an exercise rather like comparing apples with oranges; the differences between the fruits may have nothing to do with the differences in their evolution. Transferring the analogy to the case at hand, what we really need to know is the difference, say, between an urban laboring family of 1750 and an urban laboring family 100 and then 200 years later, or the difference between the rural nonfarm middle classes in all three centuries, or the difference between the urban rich yesterday and today. Surely in each of these cases the analyses will look very different from what we have been led to expect. As a guess we might find that for the urban laboring families the changes have been precisely the opposite of what the model predicted; that is, that their family structure is much firmer today than it was in centuries past. Similarly, for the rural nonfarm middle class the results might be equally surprising; we might find that married women of that class rarely did any housework at all in 1890 because they had farm girls as servants, whereas in 1950 they bore the full brunt of the work themselves. I could go on, but the point is, I hope, clear: in order to verify or falsify the functionalist theory it will be necessary to know more than we presently do about the impact of industrialization on families of similar classes and geographical locations.

With this problem in mind I have, for the purposes of this initial study, deliberately limited myself to one kind of technological change affecting one aspect of family life in only one of the many social classes of families that might have been considered. What happened, I asked, to middle-class American women when the implements with which they did their everyday household work changed? Did the technological change in household appliances have any effect upon the structure of American households, or upon the ideologies that governed the behavior of American women, or upon the functions that families needed to perform? Middle-class American women were defined as actual or potential readers of the better-quality women's magazines, such as the *Ladies' Home Journal, American Home, Parents Magazine, Good Housekeeping,* and *McCall's.*[6] Nonfictional material (articles and advertisements) in those magazines was used as a partial indicator of some of the technological and social changes that were occurring.

The *Ladies' Home Journal* has been in continuous publication since 1886. A casual survey of the nonfiction in the *Journal* yields the immediate impression that that decade between the end of World War I and the beginning of the depression witnessed the most drastic changes in patterns of household work. Statistical data bear out this impression. Before 1918, for example, illustrations of homes lit by gaslight could still be found in the *Journal;* by 1928 gaslight had disappeared. In 1917 only one-quarter (24.3 percent) of the dwellings in the United States had been electrified, but by 1920 this figure had doubled (47.4 percent—for rural nonfarm and urban dwellings), and by 1930 four-fifths of all households had been electrified.[7] If electrification had meant simply the change from gas or oil lamps to electric lights, the changes in the housewife's routines might not have been very great (except for eliminating the chore of cleaning and filling oil lamps);

but changes in lighting were the least of the changes that electrification implied. Small electric appliances followed quickly on the heels of the electric light, and some of those augured much more profound changes in the housewife's routine.

Ironing, for example, had traditionally been one of the most dreadful household chores, especially in warm weather when the kitchen stove had to be kept hot for the better part of the day; irons were heavy and they had to be returned to the stove frequently to be reheated. Electric irons eased a good part of this burden.[8] They were relatively inexpensive and very quickly replaced their predecessors; advertisements for electric irons first began to appear in the ladies' magazines after the war, and by the end of the decade the old flatiron had disappeared; by 1929 a survey of 100 Ford employees revealed that ninety-eight of them had the new electric irons in their homes.[9]

Data on the diffusion of electric washing machines are somewhat harder to come by; but it is clear from the advertisements in the magazines, particularly advertisements for laundry soap, that by the middle of the 1920s those machines could be found in a significant number of homes. The washing machine is depicted just about as frequently as the laundry tub by the middle of the 1920s; in 1929, forty-nine out of those 100 Ford workers had the machines in their homes. The washing machines did not drastically reduce the time that had to be spent on household laundry, as they did not go through their cycles automatically and did not spin dry; the housewife had to stand guard, stopping and starting the machine at appropriate times, adding soap, sometimes attaching the drain pipes, and putting the clothes through the wringer manually. The machines did, however, reduce a good part of the drudgery that once had been associated with washday, and this was a matter of no small consequence.[10] Soap powders appeared on the market in the early 1920s, thus eliminating the need to scrape and boil bars of laundry soap.[11] By the end of the 1920s Blue Monday must have been considerably less blue for some housewives—and probably considerably less "Monday," for with an electric iron, a washing machine, and a hot water heater, there was no reason to limit the washing to just one day of the week.

Like the routines of washing the laundry, the routines of personal hygiene must have been transformed for many households during the 1920s—the years of the bathroom mania.[12] More and more bathrooms were built in older homes, and new homes began to include them as a matter of course. Before the war most bathroom fixtures (tubs, sinks, and toilets) were made out of porcelain by hand; each bathroom was custom-made for the house in which it was installed. After the war industrialization descended upon the bathroom industry; cast iron enamelware went into mass production and fittings were standardized. In 1921 the dollar value of the production of enameled sanitary fixtures was $2.4 million, the same as it had been in 1915. By 1923, just two years later, that figure had doubled to $4.8 million; it rose again, to $5.1 million, in 1925.[13] The first recessed, double-shell cast iron enameled bathtub was put on the market in the early 1920s. A decade later the standard American bathroom had achieved its standard American form: the recessed tub, plus tiled floors and walls, brass plumbing, a single-unit toilet, an enameled sink, and a medicine chest, all set into a small room which was very often 5 feet square.[14] The bathroom evolved more quickly than any other room of the house; its standardized form was accomplished in just over a decade.

Along with bathrooms came modernized systems for heating hot water: 61 percent of the homes in Zanesville, Ohio, had indoor plumbing with centrally heated water by 1926, and 83 percent of the homes valued over $2,000 in Muncie, Indiana, had hot and cold running water by 1935.[15] These figures may not be typical of small American cities (or even large American cities) at those times, but they do jibe with the impression that one gets from the magazines: after 1918 references to hot water heated on the kitchen range, either for laundering or for bathing, become increasingly difficult to find.

Similarly, during the 1920s many homes were outfitted with central heating; in Muncie most of the homes of the business class had basement heating in 1924; by 1935 Federal Emergency Relief Administration data for the city indicated that only 22.4 percent of the dwellings valued over $2,000 were still heated by a kitchen stove.[16] What all these changes meant in terms of new habits for the average housewife is somewhat hard to calculate; changes there must have been, but it is difficult to know whether those changes produced an overall saving of labor and/or time. Some chores were eliminated—hauling water, heating water on the stove, maintaining the kitchen fire—but other chores were added—most notably the chore of keeping yet another room scrupulously clean.

It is not, however, difficult to be certain about the changing habits that were associated with the new American kitchen—a kitchen from which the coal stove had disappeared. In Muncie in 1924, cooking with gas was done in two out of three homes; in 1935 only 5 percent of the homes valued over $2,000 still had coal or wood stoves for cooking.[17] After 1918 advertisements for coal and wood stoves disappeared from the Ladies' Home Journal; stove manufacturers purveyed only their gas, oil, or electric models. Articles giving advice to homemakers on how to deal with the trials and tribulations of starting, stoking, and maintaining a coal or a wood fire also disappeared. Thus it seems a safe assumption that most middle-class homes had switched to the new method of cooking by the time the depression began. The change in routine that was predicated on the change from coal or wood to gas or oil was profound; aside from the elimination of such chores as loading the fuel and removing the ashes, the new stoves were much easier to light, maintain, and regulate (even when they did not have thermostats, as the earliest models did not).[18] Kitchens were, in addition, much easier to clean when they did not have coal dust regularly tracked through them; one writer in the Ladies' Home Journal estimated that kitchen cleaning was reduced by one-half when coal stoves were eliminated.[19]

Along with new stoves came new foodstuffs and new dietary habits. Canned foods had been on the market since the middle of the nineteenth century, but they did not become an appreciable part of the standard middle-class diet until the 1920s—if the recipes given in cookbooks and in women's magazines are a reliable guide. By 1918 the variety of foods available in cans had been considerably expanded from the peas, corn, and succotash of the nineteenth century; an American housewife with sufficient means could have purchased almost any fruit or vegetable and quite a surprising array of ready-made meals in a can—from Heinz's spaghetti in meat sauce to Purity Cross's lobster à la Newburg. By the middle of the 1920s home canning was becoming a lost art. Canning recipes were relegated to the back pages of the women's magazines; the business-class wives of Muncie reported that, while their mothers had once spent the better part of the summer and fall canning, they themselves rarely put up anything, except an occasional jelly or batch of tomatoes.[20] In part this was also due to changes in the technology of marketing food; increased use of refrigerated railroad cars during this period meant that fresh fruits and vegetables were in the markets all year round at reasonable prices.[21] By the early 1920s convenience foods were also appearing on American tables: cold breakfast cereals, pancake mixes, bouillon cubes, and packaged desserts could be found. Wartime shortages accustomed Americans to eating much lighter meals than they had previously been wont to do; and as fewer family members were taking all their meals at home (businessmen started to eat lunch in restaurants downtown, and factories and schools began installing cafeterias), there was simply less cooking to be done, and what there was of it was easier to do.[22]

Many of the changes just described—from hand power to electric power, from coal and wood to gas and oil as fuels for cooking, from one-room heating to central heating, from pumping water to running water—are enormous technological changes. Changes of a similar dimension, either in the fundamental technology of an industry, in the diffusion of that technology, or in the routines of workers, would have long since been labeled an "industrial revolution." The change from the laundry tub to the washing machine is no less profound than the change from the hand loom to the power loom; the change from pumping water to turning on a water faucet is no less destructive of traditional habits than the change from manual to electric calculating. It seems odd to speak of an "industrial revolution" connected with housework, odd because we are talking about the technology of such homely things, and odd because we are not accustomed to thinking of housewives as a labor force or of housework as an economic commodity—but

despite this oddity, I think the term is altogether appropriate.

In this case other questions come immediately to mind, questions that we do not hesitate to ask, say, about textile workers in Britain in the early nineteenth century, but we have never thought to ask about housewives in America in the twentieth century. What happened to this particular work force when the technology of its work was revolutionized? Did structural changes occur? Were new jobs created for which new skills were required? Can we discern new ideologies that influenced the behavior of the workers?

The answer to all of these questions, surprisingly enough, seems to be yes. There were marked structural changes in the work force, changes that increased the work load and the job description of the workers that remained. New jobs were created for which new skills were required; these jobs were not physically burdensome, but they may have taken up as much time as the jobs they had replaced. New ideologies were also created, ideologies which reinforced new behavioral patterns, patterns that we might not have been led to expect if we had followed the sociologists' model to the letter. Middle-class housewives, the women who must have first felt the impact of the new household technology, were not flocking into the divorce courts or the labor market or the forums of political protest in the years immediately after the revolution in their work. What they were doing was sterilizing baby bottles, shepherding their children to dancing classes and music lessons, planning nutritious meals, shopping for new clothes, studying child psychology, and hand stitching color-coordinated curtains—all of which chores (and others like them) the standard sociological model has apparently not provided for.

The significant change in the structure of the household labor force was the disappearance of paid and unpaid servants (unmarried daughters, maiden aunts, and grandparents fall in the latter category) as household workers—and the imposition of the entire job on the housewife herself. Leaving aside for a moment the question of which was cause and which effect (did the disappearance of the servant create a demand for the new technology, or did the new technology make the servant obsolete?), the phenomenon itself is relatively easy to document. Before World War I, when illustrators in the women's magazines depicted women doing housework, the women were very often servants. When the lady of the house was drawn, she was often the person being served, or she was supervising the serving, or she was adding an elegant finishing touch to the work. Nursemaids diapered babies, seamstresses pinned up hems, waitresses served meals, laundresses did the wash, and cooks did the cooking. By the end of the 1920s the servants had disappeared from those illustrations; all those jobs were being done by housewives—elegantly manicured and coiffed, to be sure, but housewives nonetheless.

If we are tempted to suppose that illustrations in advertisements are not a reliable indicator of structural changes of this sort, we can corroborate the changes in other ways. Apparently, the illustrators really did know whereof they drew. Statistically the number of persons throughout the country employed in household service dropped from 1,851,000 in 1910 to 1,411,000 in 1920, while the number of households enumerated in the census rose from 20.3 million to 24.4 million.[23] In Indiana the ratio of households to servants increased from 13.5/1 in 1890 to 30.5/1 in 1920, and in the country as a whole the number of paid domestic servants per 1,000 population dropped from 98.9 in 1900 to 58.0 in 1920.[24] The business-class housewives of Muncie reported that they employed approximately one-half as many woman-hours of domestic service as their mothers had done.[25]

In case we are tempted to doubt these statistics (and indeed statistics about household labor are particularly unreliable, as the labor is often transient, part-time, or simply unreported), we can turn to articles on the servant problem, the disappearance of unpaid family workers, the design of kitchens, or to architectural drawings for houses. All of this evidence reiterates the same point: qualified servants were difficult to find; their wages had risen and their numbers fallen; houses were being designed without maid's rooms; daughters and unmarried aunts were finding jobs downtown; kitchens were being designed for housewives, not for servants.[26] The first home with a kitchen that was not an entirely separate room was designed by Frank Lloyd Wright in 1934.[27] In 1937 Emily Post invented a new character for her etiquette books: Mrs. Three-in-One, the woman who is her own cook, waitress, and hostess.[28]

There must have been many new Mrs. Three-in-Ones abroad in the land during the 1930s.

As the number of household assistants declined, the number of household tasks increased. The middle-class housewife was expected to demonstrate competence at several tasks that previously had not existed at all. Child care is the most obvious example. The average housewife had fewer children than her mother had had, but she was expected to do things for her children that her mother would never have dreamed of doing: to prepare their special infant formulas; sterilize their bottles, weigh them every day, see to it that they ate nutritionally balanced meals, keep them isolated and confined when they had even the slightest illness, consult with their teachers frequently, and chauffeur them to dancing lessons, and evening parties.[29] There was very little Freudianism in this new attitude toward child care: mothers were not spending more time and effort on their children because they feared the psychological trauma of separation, but because competent nursemaids could not be found, and the new theories of child care required constant attention from well-informed persons—persons who were willing and able to read about the latest discoveries in nutrition, in the control of contagious diseases, or in the techniques of behavioral psychology. These persons simply had to be their mothers.

Consumption of economic goods provides another example of the housewife's expanded job description; like child care, the new tasks associated with consumption were not necessarily physically burdensome, but they were time consuming, and they required the acquisition of new skills.[30] Home economists and the editors of women's magazines tried to teach housewives to spend their money wisely. The present generation of housewives, it was argued, had been reared by mothers who did not ordinarily shop for things like clothing, bed linens, or towels; consequently modern housewives did not know how to shop and would have to be taught. Furthermore, their mothers had not been accustomed to the wide variety of goods that were now available in the modern marketplace; the new housewives had to be taught not just to be consumers, but to be informed consumers.[31] Several contemporary observers believed that shopping and shopping wisely were occupying increasing amounts of housewives' time.[32]

Several of these contemporary observers also believed that standards of household care changed during the decade of the 1920s.[33] The discovery of the "household germ" led to almost fetishistic concern about the cleanliness of the home. The amount and frequency of laundering probably increased, as bed linen and underwear were changed more often, children's clothes were made increasingly out of washable fabrics, and men's shirts no longer had replaceable collars and snap cuffs.[34] Unfortunately all these changes in standards are difficult to document, being changes in the things that people regard as so insignificant as to be unworthy of comment; the improvement in standards seems a likely possibility, but not something that can be proved.

In any event we do have various time studies which demonstrate somewhat surprisingly that housewives with conveniences were spending just as much time on household duties as were housewives without them—or, to put it another way, housework, like so many other types of work, expands to fill the time available. A study comparing the time spent per week in housework by 288 farm families and 154 town families in Oregon in 1928 revealed 61 hours spent by farm wives and 63.4 hours by town wives; in 1929 a U.S. Department of Agriculture study of families in various states produced almost identical results.[35] Surely if the standard sociological model were valid, housewives in towns, where presumably the benefits of specialization and electrification were most likely to be available, should have been spending far less time at their work than their rural sisters. However, just after World War II economists at Bryn Mawr College reported the same phenomenon: 60.55 hours spent by farm housewives, 78.35 hours by women in small cities, 80.57 hours by women in large ones—precisely the reverse of the results that were expected.[36] A recent survey of time studies conducted between 1920 and 1970 concludes that the time spent on housework by nonemployed housewives has remained remarkably constant throughout the period.[37] All these results point in the same direction: mechanization of the household meant that time expended on some jobs decreased, but also that new jobs were substituted, and in some cases—notably laundering—time expenditures for old jobs increased because of higher standards. The advantages of mechanization may be somewhat more dubious than they seem at first glance.

As the job of the housewife changed, the connected ideologies also changed; there was a clearly perceptible difference in the attitudes that women brought to housework before and after World War I.[38] Before the war the trials of doing housework in a servantless home were discussed and they were regarded as just that—trials, necessary chores that had to be got through until a qualified servant could be found. After the war, housework changed: it was no longer a trial and a chore, but something quite different—an emotional "trip." Laundering was not just laundering, but an expression of love; the housewife who truly loved her family would protect them from the embarrassment of tattletale gray. Feeding the family was not just feeding the family, but a way to express the housewife's artistic inclinations and a way to encourage feelings of family loyalty and affection. Diapering the baby was not just diapering, but a time to build the baby's sense of security and love for the mother. Cleaning the bathroom sink was not just cleaning, but an exercise of protective maternal instincts, providing a way for the housewife to keep her family safe from disease. Tasks of this emotional magnitude could not possibly be delegated to servants, even assuming that qualified servants could be found.

Women who failed at these new household tasks were bound to feel guilt about their failure. If I had to choose one word to characterize the temper of the women's magazines during the 1920s, it would be "guilt." Readers of the better-quality women's magazines are portrayed as feeling guilty a good lot of the time, and when they are not guilty they are embarrassed: guilty if their infants have not gained enough weight, embarrassed if their drains are clogged, guilty if their children go to school in soiled clothes, guilty if all the germs behind the bathroom sink are not eradicated, guilty if they fail to notice the first signs of an oncoming cold, embarrassed if accused of having body odor, guilty if their sons go to school without good breakfasts, guilty if their daughters are unpopular because of old-fashioned, or unironed, or—heaven forbid—dirty dresses. In earlier times women were made to feel guilty if they abandoned their children or were too free with their affections. In the years after

World War I, American women were made to feel guilty about sending their children to school in scuffed shoes. Between the two kinds of guilt there is a world of difference.

Let us return for a moment to the sociological model with which this essay began. The model predicts that changing patterns of household work will be correlated with at least two striking indicators of social change: the divorce rate and the rate of married women's labor force participation. That correlation may indeed exist, but it certainly is not reflected in the women's magazines of the 1920s and 1930s; divorce and full-time paid employment were not part of the life-style or the life pattern of the middle-class housewife as she was idealized in her magazines.

There were social changes attendant upon the introduction of modern technology into the home, but they were not the changes that the traditional functionalist model predicts; on this point a close analysis of the statistical data corroborates the impression conveyed in the magazines. The divorce rate was indeed rising during the years between the wars, but it was not rising nearly so fast for the middle and upper classes (who had, presumably, easier access to the new technology) as it was for the lower classes. By almost every gauge of socioeconomic status—income, prestige of husband's work, education—the divorce rate is higher for persons lower on the socioeconomic scale— and this is a phenomenon that has been constant over time.[39]

The supposed connection between improved household technology and married women's labor force participation seems just as dubious, and on the same grounds. The single socioeconomic factor which correlates most strongly (in cross-sectional studies) with married women's employment is husband's income, and the correlation is strongly negative; the higher his income, the less likely it will be that she is working.[40] Women's labor force participation increased during the 1920s but this increase was due to the influx of single women into the force. Married women's participation increased slightly during those years, but that increase was largely in factory labor—precisely the kind of work that middle-class women (who were, again, much more likely to have laborsaving devices at home) were least likely

to do.[41] If there were a necessary connection between the improvement of household technology and either of these two social indicators, we would expect the data to be precisely the reverse of what in fact has occurred: women in the higher social classes should have fewer functions at home and should therefore be more (rather than less) likely to seek paid employment or divorce.

Thus for middle-class American housewives between the wars, the social changes that we can document are not the social changes that the functionalist model predicts; rather than changes in divorce or patterns of paid employment, we find changes in the structure of the work force, in its skills, and in its ideology. These social changes were concomitant with a series of technological changes in the equipment that was used to do the work. What is the relationship between these two series of phenomena? Is it possible to demonstrate causality or the direction of that causality? Was the decline in the number of households employing servants a cause or an effect of the mechanization of those households? Both are, after all, equally possible. The declining supply of household servants, as well as their rising wages, may have stimulated a demand for new appliances at the same time that the acquisition of new appliances may have made householders less inclined to employ the laborers who were on the market. Are there any techniques available to the historian to help us answer these questions?

In order to establish causality, we need to find a connecting link between the two sets of phenomena, a mechanism that, in real life, could have made the causality work. In this case a connecting link, an intervening agent between the social and the technological changes, comes immediately to mind: the advertiser— by which term I mean a combination of the manufacturer of the new goods, the advertising agent who promoted the goods, and the periodical that published the promotion. All the new devices and new foodstuffs that were being offered to American households were being manufactured and marketed by large companies which had considerable amounts of capital invested in their production: General Electric, Procter & Gamble, General Foods, Lever Brothers, Frigidaire, Campbell's, Del

Monte, American Can, Atlantic & Pacific Tea—these were all well-established firms by the time the household revolution began, and they were all in a position to pay for national advertising campaigns to promote their new products and services. And pay they did; one reason for the expanding size and number of women's magazines in the 1920s was no doubt the expansion in revenues from available advertisers.[42]

Those national advertising campaigns were likely to have been powerful stimulators of the social changes that occurred in the household labor force; the advertisers probably did not initiate the changes, but they certainly encouraged them. Most of the advertising campaigns manifestly worked, so they must have touched upon areas of real concern for American housewives. Appliance ads specifically suggested that the acquisition of one gadget or another would make it possible to fire the maid, spend more time with the children, or have the afternoon free for shopping.[43] Similarly, many advertisements played upon the embarrassment and guilt which were now associated with household work. Ralston, Cream of Wheat, and Ovaltine were not themselves responsible for the compulsive practice of weighing infants and children repeatedly (after every meal for newborns, every day in infancy, every week later on), but the manufacturers certainly did not stint on capitalizing upon the guilt that women apparently felt if their offspring did not gain the required amounts of weight.[44] And yet again, many of the earliest attempts to spread "wise" consumer practices were undertaken by large corporations and the magazines that desired their advertising; mail-order shopping guides, "product-testing" services, pseudoinformative pamphlets, and other such promotional devices were all techniques for urging the housewife to buy new things under the guise of training her in her role as skilled consumer.[45]

Thus the advertisers could well be called the "ideologues" of the 1920s, encouraging certain very specific social changes—as ideologues are wont to do. Not surprisingly, the changes that occurred were precisely the ones that would gladden the hearts and fatten the purses of the advertisers; fewer household servants meant a greater demand for labor- and time-saving devices; more household tasks for women meant more and more specialized products that they would need to buy; more guilt and embarrassment about their failure to succeed at their work meant a greater likelihood that they would buy the products that were intended to minimize that failure. Happy, full-time housewives in intact families spend a lot of money to maintain their households; divorced women and working women do not. The advertisers may not have created the image of the ideal American housewife that dominated the 1920s—the woman who cheerfully and skillfully set about making everyone in her family perfectly happy and perfectly healthy—but they certainly helped to perpetuate it.

The role of the advertiser as connecting link between social change and technological change is at this juncture simply a hypothesis, with nothing much more to recommend it than an argument from plausibility. Further research may serve to test the hypothesis, but testing it may not settle the question of which was cause and which effect—if that question can ever be settled definitively in historical work. What seems most likely in this case, as in so many others, is that cause and effect are not separable, that there is a dynamic interaction between the social changes that married women were experiencing and the technological changes that were occurring in their homes. Viewed this way, the disappearance of competent servants becomes one of the factors that stimulated the mechanization of homes, and this mechanization of homes becomes a factor (though by no means the only one) in the disappearance of servants. Similarly, the emotionalization of housework becomes both cause and effect of the mechanization of that work; and the expansion of time spent on new tasks becomes both cause and effect of the introduction of time-saving devices. For example, the social pressure to spend more time in child care may have led to a decision to purchase the devices; once purchased, the devices could indeed have been used to save time—although often they were not.

If one holds the question of causality in abeyance, the example of household work still has some useful lessons to teach about the general problem of technology and social change. The standard sociological model for the impact of modern technology on family life clearly needs some revision: at least for middle-class nonrural American families in the twentieth century, the social changes were not the ones that the standard model predicts. In these families the functions of at least one member, the housewife, have increased rather than decreased and the dissolution of family life has not in fact occurred.

Our standard notions about what happens to a work force under the pressure of technological change may also need revision. When industries become mechanized and rationalized, we expect certain general changes in the work force to occur: its structure becomes more highly differentiated, individual workers become more specialized, managerial functions increase, and the emotional context of the work disappears. On all four counts our expectations are reversed with regard to household work. The work force became less rather than more differentiated as domestic servants, unmarried daughters, maiden aunts, and grandparents left the household and as chores which had once been performed by commercial agencies (laundries, delivery services, milkmen) were delegated to the housewife. The individual workers also became less specialized; the new housewife was now responsible for every aspect of life in her household, from scrubbing the bathroom floor to keeping abreast of the latest literature in child psychology.

The housewife is just about the only unspecialized worker left in America—a veritable jane-of-all-trades at a time when the jacks-of-all-trades have disappeared. As her work became generalized the housewife was also proletarianized: formerly she was ideally the manager of several other subordinate workers; now she was idealized as the manager and the worker combined. Her managerial functions have not entirely disappeared, but they have certainly diminished and have been replaced by simple manual labor; the middle-class, fairly well educated housewife ceased to be a personnel manager and became, instead, a chauffeur, charwoman, and short-order cook. The implications of this phenomenon, the proletarianization of a work force that had previously seen itself as predominantly managerial, deserve to be explored at greater length than is possible here, because I suspect that they will explain certain aspects of the women's liberation movement of the 1960s and 1970s which have previously eluded explanation: why, for ex-

ample, the movement's greatest strength lies in social and economic groups who seem, in the surface at least, to need it least—women who are white, well-educated, and middle-class.

Finally, instead of desensitizing the emotions that were connected with household work, the industrial revolution in the home seems to have heightened the emotional context of the work, until a woman's sense of self-worth became a function of her success at arranging bits of fruit to form a clown's face in a gelatin salad. That pervasive social illness, which Betty Friedan characterized as "the problem that has no name," arose not among workers who found that their labor brought no emotional satisfaction, but among workers who found that their work was invested with emotional weight far out of proportion to its own inherent value: "How long," a friend of mine is fond of asking, "can we continue to believe that we will have orgasms while waxing the kitchen floor?"

NOTES

1. For some classic statements of the standard view, see W. F. Ogburn and M. F. Nimkoff, *Technology and the Changing Family* (Cambridge, Mass., 1955); Robert F. Winch, *The Modern Family* (New York, 1952); and William J. Goode, *The Family* (Englewood Cliffs, N.J., 1964).

2. This point is made by Peter Laslett in "The Comparative History of Household and Family," in *The American Family in Social Historical Perspective*, ed. Michael Gordon (New York, 1973), pp. 28–29.

3. Phillippe Ariès, *Centuries of Childhood: A Social History of Family Life* (New York, 1960).

4. See Laslett, pp. 20–24; . . .

5. Peter Laslett, *The World We Have Lost* (New York, 1965), passim.

6. For purposes of historical inquiry, this definition of middle-class status corresponds to a sociological reality, although it is not, admittedly, very rigorous. Our contemporary experience confirms that there are class differences reflected in magazines, and this situation seems to have existed in the past as well. . . .

7. *Historical Statistics of the United States, Colonial Times to 1957* (Washington, D.C., 1960), p. 510.

8. The gas iron, which was available to women whose homes were supplied with natural gas, was an earlier improvement on the old-fashioned flatiron, but this kind of iron is so rarely mentioned in the sources that I used for this survey that I am unable to determine the extent of its diffusion.

9. Hazel Kyrk, *Economic Problems of the Family* (New York, 1933), p. 368, reporting a study in *Monthly Labor Review* 30 (1930):1209–52.

10. Although this point seems intuitively obvious, there is some evidence that it may not be true. Studies of energy expenditure during housework have indicated that by far the greatest effort is expended in hauling and lifting the wet wash, tasks which were not eliminated by the introduction of washing machines. In addition, if the introduction of the machines served to increase the total amount of wash that was done by the housewife, this would tend to cancel the energy-saving effects of the machines themselves.

11. Rinso was the first granulated soap; it came on the market in 1918. . . .

12. I take this account, and the term, from Robert S. Lynd and Helen M. Lynd, *Middletown: A Study in Contemporary American Culture* (New York, 1929), p. 97. . . . The rural situation was quite different from the urban; the President's Conference on Home Building and Home Ownership reported that in the late 1920s, 71 percent of the urban families surveyed had bathrooms, but only 33 percent of the rural families did. . . .

13. The data above came from Siegfried Giedion, *Mechanization Takes Command* (New York, 1948), pp. 685–703.

14. For a description of the standard bathroom see Helen Sprackling, "The Modern Bathroom," *Parents Magazine* 8 (Feb. 1933):25.

15. *Zanesville, Ohio and Thirty-six Other American Cities* (New York, 1927), p. 65. Also see Robert S. Lynd and Helen M. Lynd, *Middletown in Transition* (New York, 1936), p. 537. Middletown is Muncie, Indiana.

16. Lynd and Lynd, *Middletown*, p. 96, and *Middletown in Transition*, p. 539.

17. Lynd and Lynd, *Middletown*, p. 98, and *Middletown in Transition*, p. 562.

18. On the advantages of the new stoves, see *Boston Cooking School Cookbook* (Boston, 1916), pp. 15–20; and Russell Lynes, *The Domesticated Americans* (New York, 1957), pp. 119–20.

19. "How To Save Coal While Cooking," *Ladies' Home Journal* 25 (Jan. 1908):44.

20. Lynd and Lynd, *Middletown*, p. 156.

21. Ibid.; see also "Safeway Stores," *Fortune* 26 (Oct. 1940):60.

22. Lynd and Lynd, *Middletown*, pp. 134–35, 153–54.

23. *Historical Statistics*, pp. 16, 77.

24. For Indiana data, see Lynd and Lynd, *Middletown*, p. 169. For national data, see D. L. Kaplan and M. Claire Casey, *Occupational Trends in the United States, 1900–1950*, U.S. Bureau of the Census Working Paper no. 5 (Washington, D.C., 1958), table 6. . . .

25. Lynd and Lynd, *Middletown*, p. 169.

26. On the disappearance of maiden aunts, unmarried daughters, and grandparents, see Lynd and Lynd, *Middletown*, pp. 25, 99, 110; Edward Bok, "Editorial," *American Home* 1 (Oct. 1928):15; . . . .

27. Giedion, p. 619. . . .

28. Emily Post, *Etiquette: The Blue Book of Social Usage*, 5th ed. rev. (New York, 1937), p. 823.

29. This analysis is based upon various child-care articles that appeared during the period in the *Ladies' Home Journal, American Home,* and *Parents Magazine.* . . .

30. John Kenneth Galbraith has remarked upon the advent of woman as consumer in *Economics and the Public Purpose* (Boston, 1973), pp. 29–37.

31. . . . On consumer education see, for example, "How to Buy Towels," *Ladies' Home Journal* 45 (Feb. 1928):134; "Buying Table Linen," *Ladies' Home Journal* 45 (Mar. 1928):43; . . .

32. See, for example, Lynd and Lynd, *Middletown*, pp. 176, 196; and Margaret G. Reid, *Economics of Household Production* (New York, 1934), chap. 13.

33. See Reid, pp. 64–68; and Kyrk, p. 98.

34. See advertisement for Cleanliness Institute—"Self-respect thrives on soap and water," *Ladies' Home Journal* 45 (Feb. 1928):107. On changing bed linen, see "When the Bride Goes Shopping," *American Home* 1 (Jan. 1928):370. . . .

35. As reported in Kyrk, p. 51.

36. Bryn Mawr College Department of Social Economy, *Women During the War and After* (Philadelphia, 1945); and Ethel Goldwater, "Woman's Place," *Commentary* 4 (Dec. 1947):578–85.

37. JoAnn Vanek, "Keeping Busy: Time Spent in Housework, United States, 1920–1970" (Ph.D. diss., University of Michigan, 1973).

38. This analysis is based upon my reading of the middle-class women's magazines between 1918 and 1930. For detailed documentation see my paper "Two Washes in the Morning and a Bridge Party at Night: The American Housewife between the Wars," *Women's Studies* 3 (1976):147–72. . . .

39. For a summary of the literature on differential divorce rates, see Winch, p. 706; and William J. Goode, *After Divorce* (New York, 1956), p. 44. . . .

40. For a summary of the literature on married women's labor force participation, see Juanita Kreps, *Sex in the Marketplace: American Women at Work* (Baltimore, 1971), pp. 19–24.

41. Valerie Kincaid Oppenheimer, *The Female Labor Force in the United States*, Population Monograph Series, no. 5 (Berkeley, 1970), pp. 1–15; and Lynd and Lynd, *Middletown*, pp. 124–27.

42. On the expanding size, number, and influence of women's magazines during the 1920s, see Lynd and Lynd, *Middletown*, pp. 150, 240–44.

43. See, for example, the advertising campaigns of General Electric and Hotpoint from 1918 through the rest of the decade of the 1920s; both campaigns stressed the likelihood that electric appliances would become a thrifty replacement for domestic servants.

44. The practice of carefully observing children's weight was initiated by medical authorities, national and local governments, and social welfare agencies, as part of the campaign to improve child health which began about the time of World War I.

45. These practices were ubiquitous. *American Home,* for example, which was published by Doubleday, assisted its advertisers by publishing a list of informative pamphlets that readers could obtain; devoting half a page to an index of its advertisers; specifically naming manufacturer's and list prices in articles about products and services; allotting almost one-quarter of the magazine to a mail-order shopping guide which was not (at least ostensibly) paid advertisement; and as part of its editorial policy, urging its readers to buy new goods.

Women used suffrage for a wide range of political expressions. Here women of the Ku Klux Klan parade down Pennsylvania Avenue in 1928. (Photograph courtesy of the National Archives)

JACQUELYN DOWD HALL

Disorderly Women: Gender and Labor Militancy in the Appalachian South

For many women the workplace included factory or mill as well as home. Factories in the 1920s were rent by strikes as workers whose wages were already low tried to cope with innovations designed to increase productivity. Southern textile mills, always the employer of large numbers of women, were especially vulnerable.

Excerpted from "Disorderly Women: Gender and Labor Militancy in the Appalachian South" by Jacquelyn Dowd Hall, in *Journal of American History* 73 (1986):354–82. Copyright © 1986 by Jacquelyn Dowd Hall. Condensed and reprinted by permission of the author. Notes have been renumbered and edited.

Jacquelyn Dowd Hall focuses on one of the many strikes exploding across the South in that tumultuous decade, exploring female activism in an essay that calls into question old stereotypes about southern workers as individualistic, docile, and "hard to organize." In this important study, Hall illuminates the distinctive style of collective action that the women of Elizabethton, Tennessee, employed and the self-concepts and family networks on which that style relied.

The rising sun "made a sort of halo around the crown of Cross Mountain" as Flossie Cole climbed into a neighbor's Model T and headed west down the gravel road to Elizabethton, bound for work in a rayon plant. Emerging from Stoney Creek hollow, the car joined a caravan of buses and self-styled "taxis" brimming with young people from dozens of tiny communities strung along the creek branches and nestled in the coves of the Blue Ridge Mountains of East Tennessee. The caravan picked up speed as it hit paved roads and crossed the Watauga River bridge, passing beneath a sign advertising the county seat's new-found identity as a "City of Power." By the time Cole reached the factory gate, it was 7:00 A.M., time to begin another ten-hour day as a reeler at the American Glanzstoff plant.[1]

The machines whirred, and work began as usual. But the reeling room stirred with anticipation. The day before, March 12, 1929, all but seventeen of the 360 women in the inspection room next door had walked off their jobs. Now they were gathered at the factory gate, refusing to work but ready to negotiate. When 9:00 A.M. approached and the plant manager failed to appear, they broke past the guards and rushed through the plant, urging their co-workers out on strike. By 1:40 P.M. the machines were idle and the plant was closed.

The Elizabethton conflict rocked Carter County and made national headlines. Before March ended, the spirit of protest had jumped the Blue Ridge and spread through the Piedmont. Gastonia, Marion, and Danville saw the most bitter conflicts, but dozens of towns were shocked by an unexpected workers' revolt.[2]

The textile industry has always been a stronghold of women's labor, and women were central to these events. They were noted by contemporaries, sometimes as leaders, more often as pathetic mill girls or as "Amazons" providing comic relief.[3] In historical renditions they have dropped out of sight. The result has been thin description: a one-dimensional view

of labor conflict that fails to take culture and community into account.

Elizabethton, of course, is not unusual in this regard. Until recently, historians of trade unionism, like trade unionists themselves, neglected women, while historians of women concentrated on the Northeast and the middle class. There were few scholarly challenges to the assumption that women workers in general and southern women in particular were "hard to organize" and that women as family members exercised a conservative pull against class cohesion. Instances of female militancy were seen and not seen.[4] Because they contradicted conventional wisdom, they were easily dismissed.

Recent scholarship has revised that formulation by unearthing an impressive record of female activism. But our task is not only to describe and celebrate but also to contextualize, and thus to understand. In Elizabethton the preindustrial background, the structure of the work force and the industry, the global forces that impinged on local events—these particularities of time and place conditioned women's choices and shaped their identities. Equally important was a private world traditionally pushed to the margins of labor history. Female friendships and sexuality, cross-generational and cross-class alliances, the incorporation of new consumer desires into a dynamic regional culture—these too energized women's participation. Women in turn were historical subjects, helping to create the circumstances from which the strike arose and guiding by their actions the course the conflict took.

With gender at the center of analysis, unexpected dimensions come into view. Chief among them is the strike's erotic undercurrent, its sexual theme. The activists of Elizabethton belonged to a venerable tradition of "disorderly women," women who, in times of political upheaval, embody tensions that are half-conscious or only dimly understood.[5] Beneath the surface of a conflict that pitted workers and farmers against a new middle class in the town lay an inner world of fantasy, gender ideology, and sexual style.

The melding of narrative and analysis that follows has two major goals. The first is a fresh reading of an important episode in southern labor history, employing a female angle of vision to reveal aspects of the conflict that have been overlooked or misunderstood. The second is a close look at women's distinctive forms of collective action, using language and gesture as points of entry to a culture.

The Elizabethton story may also help to make a more general point. Based as it is on what Michel Foucault has termed "local" or "subjugated" knowledge, that is, perceptions that seem idiosyncratic, naive, and irrelevant to historical explanation, this study highlights the limitations of conventional categories.[6] The women of Elizabethton were neither traditionalists acting on family values nor market-oriented individualists, neither peculiar mountaineers nor familiar modern women. Their irreverence and inventiveness shatter stereotypes and illuminate the intricacies of working-class women's lives.

In 1925 the J. P. Bemberg Company of Barmen, Germany, manufacturer of high-quality rayon yarn by an exclusive stretch spinning process, began pouring the thick concrete floors of its first United States subsidiary. Three years later Germany's leading producer of viscose yarn, the Vereinigte Glanzstoff Fabriken, A.G., of Elberfeld opened a jointly managed branch nearby. A post–World War I fashion revolution, combined with protective tariffs, had spurred the American rayon industry's spectacular growth. As one industry publicist put it, "With long skirts, cotton stockings were quite in order; but with short skirts, nothing would do except sheer, smooth stockings. . . . It was on the trim legs of post-war flappers, it has been said, that rayon first stepped out into big business." Dominated by a handful of European giants, the rayon industry clustered along the Appalachian mountain chain. By World War II, over 70 percent of American rayon production took place in the southern states, with 50 percent of the national total in Virginia and Tennessee alone.[7]

When the Bemberg and Glanzstoff companies chose East Tennessee as a site for overseas expansion, they came to a region that has occupied a peculiar place in the American economy and imagination. Since its "discovery" by local-color writers in the 1870s, southern Appalachia has been seen as a land "where time stood still." Mountain people have been romanticized as "our contemporary ancestors" or maligned as "latter-day white barbarians." Central to both images is the notion of a people untouched by modernity. In fact, as a generation of regional scholars has now made clear, the key to modern Appalachian history lies not in the region's isolation but in its role as a source of raw materials and an outlet for investment in a capitalist world economy.[8]

Frontier families had settled the fertile Watauga River Valley around Elizabethton before the Revolution. Later arrivals pushed farther up the mountains into the hollows carved by fast-falling creeks. Stoney Creek is the oldest and largest of those creek-bed communities. Here descendants of the original settlers cultivated their own small plots, grazed livestock in woods that custom held open to all, hunted and fished in an ancient hardwood forest, mined iron ore, made whiskey, spun cloth, and bartered with local merchants for what they could not produce at home.

In the 1880s East Tennessee's timber and mineral resources attracted the attention of capitalists in the United States and abroad, and an era of land speculation and railroad building began. The railroads opened the way to timber barons, who stripped away the forests, leaving hillsides stark and vulnerable to erosion. Farmers abandoned their fields to follow the march of the logging camps. Left behind, women and children did their best to pick up the slack.[9] But by the time Carter County was "timbered out" in the 1920s, farm families had crept upward to the barren ridge lands or grown dependent on "steady work and cash wages." Meanwhile, in Elizabethton, the county seat, an aggressive new class of bankers, lawyers, and businessmen served as brokers for outside developers, speculated in land, invested in homegrown factories, and looked beyond the hills for their standards of "push, progress and prosperity."[10]

Carter County, however, lacked Appalachia's grand prize: The rush for coal that devastated other parts of the mountains had bypassed that part of East Tennessee. Nor had county farmers been absorbed into the cotton kingdom, with its exploitative credit system and spreading tenancy. To be sure, they were increasingly hard pressed. As arable land disappeared, farms were divided and redivided. In 1880 the average rural family had supported itself on 140 acres of land; by 1920 it was making do on slightly more than 52 acres. Yet however diminished their circumstances, 84.5 percent still owned their own land.[11] The economic base that sustained traditional expectations of independence, production for use, and neighborly reciprocity tottered but did not give way.

The coming of the rayon plants represented a coup for Elizabethton's aspiring businessmen, who wooed investors with promises of free land, tax exemptions, and cheap labor. But at first the whole county seemed to share the boomtown spirit. Men from Stoney Creek, Gap Creek, and other mountain hamlets built the cavernous mills, then stayed on to learn the chemical processes that transformed the cellulose from wood pulp and cotton linters (the short fibers that remain on cotton seeds after longer, spinnable fibers are removed) into "artificial silk." Women vied for jobs in the textile division where they wound, reeled, twisted, and inspected the rayon yarn. Yet for all the excitement it engendered, industrialization in Carter County retained a distinctly rural cast. Although Elizabethton's population tripled (from 2,749 in 1920 to 8,093 in 1930), the rayon workers confounded predictions of spectacular urban growth, for most remained in the countryside, riding to work on chartered buses and trains or in taxis driven by neighbors and friends.

Women made up approximately 37 percent of the 3,213 workers in the mills. Most were under twenty-one, but many were as young as twelve, or more commonly, fourteen. By contrast, the work force contained a large proportion of older, married men. Those men, together with a smaller number of teenage boys, dominated the chemical division, while young women processed the finished yarn.[12]

Whether married or single, town- or country-bred, the men who labored in the rayon plants followed in the footsteps of fathers, and sometimes grandfathers, who had combined farming with a variety of wage-earning occupations. To a greater extent than we might expect, young women who had grown up in Elizabethton could also look to earlier models of gainful labor. A search of the 1910 manuscript census found 20 percent (97/507) of women

aged fourteen and over in paid occupations. The largest proportion (29.6 percent) were cooks and servants. But close behind were women in what mountain people called "public work": wage-earning labor performed outside a household setting. For rayon workers from the countryside it was a different story. Only 5.2 percent of adult women on Stoney Creek were gainfully employed (33/638). Nineteen of these were farmers. The rest—except for one music teacher—were servants or washerwomen.[13]

These contrasts are telling, and from them we can surmise two things. The first is that industrialization did not burst upon a static, conflict free "traditional" world. The women who beat a path to the rayon plants came from families that had already been drawn into an economy where money was a key to survival. The second is that the timber industry, which attracted Carter County's men, undermined its agricultural base, and destroyed its natural resources, created few opportunities for rural women. No wonder that farm daughters in the mills counted their blessings and looked on themselves as pioneers.

Whether they sought work out of family need or for more individualistic reasons, these "factory girls" saw their jobs as a hopeful gamble rather than a desperate last resort, and they remembered the moment with astounding precision. "I'll never forget the day they hired me at Bemberg," said Flossie Cole. "We went down right in front of it. They'd come out and they'd say, 'You and you and you,' and they'd hire so many. And that day I was standing there and he picked out two or three more and he looked at me and he said, 'You.' It thrilled me to death." She worked 56 hours that week and took home $8.16.[14]

Such pay scales were low even for the southern textile industry, and workers quickly found their income eaten away by the cost of commuting or of boarding in town. When the strike came it focused on the issue of Glanzstoff women's wages, which lagged behind those at the older Bemberg plant. But workers had other grievances as well. Caustic chemicals were used to turn cellulose into a viscous fluid that was then forced through spinnerets, thimble-shaped nozzles pierced with tiny holes. The fine, individual streams coagulated into rayon filaments in an acid bath. In the chemical division men waded through water and acid, ex-

posed all day to a lethal spray. Women labored
under less dangerous conditions, but for longer
hours and less pay. Paid by the piece, they
complained of rising production quotas and
what everyone referred to as "hard rules."[15]

Women in particular were singled out for
petty regulations, aimed not just at extracting
labor but at shaping deportment as well. They
were forbidden to wear makeup; in some departments they were required to purchase uniforms. Most galling of all was company surveillance of the washroom. According to Bessie
Edens, who was promoted to "forelady" in the
twisting room, "men could do what they
wanted to in their own department," but
women had to get a pass to leave the shop
floor. "If we went to the bathroom, they'd follow us," Flossie Cole confirmed, "'fraid we'd
stay a minute too long." If they did, their pay
was docked; one too many trips and they lost
their jobs.[16]

Complaints about the washroom may
have had other meanings as well. When asked
how she heard that a strike was brewing, Nettie Reece cited "bathroom gossip."[17] As the
company well knew, the women's washroom,
where only a forelady, not a male supervisor
could go, might serve as a communications
center, a hub of gossip where complaints were
aired and plans were formulated.

The German origins of the plant managers
contributed to the tension. Once the strike began, union organizers were quick to play on
images of an "imported Prussian autocracy."
The frontier republicanism of the mountains
shaded easily into post–World War I Americanism as strikers demanded their rights as
"natural-born American citizens" oppressed
by a "latter day industrialism." In that they had
much in common with other twentieth-century
workers, for whom the democratic values articulated during the war became a rallying cry
for social justice at home. The nationality of the
managers helped throw those values into sharp
relief.[18]

The strike came on March 12, 1929, led by
women in Glanzstoff inspection department,
by what one observer called "girls in their
teens [who] decided not to put up with the
present conditions any longer." The county
court immediately issued injunctions forbid-
ding all demonstrations against the company.
When strikers ignored the injunctions, the governor sent in the National Guard. The strikers

secured a charter from the American Federation of Labor's United Textile Workers union
(UTW). Meeting in a place called the Tabernacle, built for religious revivals, they listened
to a Baptist preacher from Stoney Creek warn:
"The hand of oppression is growing on our
people. . . . You women work for practically
nothing. You must come together and say that
such things must cease to be." Each night more
workers "came forward" to take the union
oath.[19]

Meanwhile, UTW and Federal Conciliation Service officials arrived on the scene. On
March 22 they reached a "gentlemen's agreement" by which the company promised a new
wage scale for "good girl help" and agreed not
to discriminate against union members. The
strikers returned to work, but the conflict was
far from over. Higher paychecks never materialized; union members began losing their
jobs. On April 4 local businessmen kidnapped
two union organizers and ran them out of
town. Eleven days later the workers responded
with what most observers agreed was a "spontaneous and complete walkout."[20]

This time the conflict quickly escalated.
More troops arrived, and the plants became
fortresses, with machine guns on the rooftops
and armed guardsmen on the ground. The
company sent buses manned by soldiers farther up the hollows to recruit new workers and
escort them back to town. Pickets blocked narrow mountain roads. Houses were blown up;
the town water main was dynamited. An estimated 1,250 individuals were arrested in confrontations with the National Guard.[21]

As far as can be determined, no women
were involved in barn burnings and dynamit-
ings—what Bessie Edens referred to as "the
rough . . . stuff" that accompanied the second
strike. Men "went places that we didn't go,"
explained Christine Galliher. "They had big
dark secrets . . . the men did." But when it came
to public demonstrations women held center
stage. At the outset "hundreds of girls" had
ridden down main street "in buses and taxis,
shouting and laughing at people who watched
them from windows and doorsteps." Now they
blocked the road at Gap Creek and refused soldiers' orders that they walk twelve miles to jail
in town. "And there was one girl that was awful tough in the bunch. . . . She said, 'No, by
God. We didn't walk out here, and we're not
walking back!' And she sat her hind end down

in the middle of the road, and we all sat down with her. And the law used tear gas on us! . . . And it nearly put our eyes out, but we still wouldn't walk back to town." In Elizabethton after picket duty, women marched down the "Bemberg Highway . . . draped in the American flag and carrying the colors"—thereby forcing the guardsmen to present arms each time they passed. Inventive, playful, and shrewd, the women's tactics encouraged a holiday spirit. They may also have deflected violence and garnered community support.[22]

Laughter was among the women's most effective weapons. But beneath high spirits the terms of battle had begun to change. Local organizers were hobbled by a national union that lacked the resources and commitment to sustain the strike. Instead of translating workers' grievances into a compelling challenge, the UTW pared their demands down to the bone. On May 26, six weeks after the strike began, the union agreed to a settlement that made no mention of wages, hours, working conditions, or union recognition. The company's only concession was a promise not to discriminate against union members. The workers were less than enthusiastic. According to one reporter, "It took nine speeches and a lot of question answering lasting two and a half hours to get the strikers to accept the terms."[23]

The press, for the most part, greeted the settlement as a workers' victory, or at least a satisfactory resolution of the conflict. Anna Weinstock, the first woman to serve as a federal conciliator, was credited with bringing the company to the bargaining table and was pictured as the heroine of the event. "SETTLED BY A WOMAN!" headlined one journal. "This is the fact that astounds American newspaper editors." "Five feet five inches and 120 pounds of femininity; clean cut, even features"—and so on, in great detail. Little was made of Weinstock's own working-class origins. She was simply a "new woman," come to the rescue of a backward mountain folk. The strikers themselves dropped quickly from view.[24]

From the outside, the conflict at Elizabethton looked like a straightforward case of labor-management strife. But it appeared quite different from within. Everyone interviewed put the blame for low wages on an alliance between the German managers and the "leading citizens" of the town. Preserved in the oral tradition is the story of how the "town fathers" promised the company a supply of cheap and unorganized labor. Bessie Edens put it this way: They told the company that "women wasn't used to working, and they'd work for almost nothing, and the men would work for low wages. That's the way they got the plant here." In this version of events the strike was part of a long-term struggle, with development-minded townspeople on one side and workers, farmers, and country merchants on the other.[25]

Workers' roots in the countryside encouraged resistance and helped them to mobilize support once the strike began. "These workers have come so recently from the farms and mountains . . . and are of such independent spirit," Alfred Hoffman observed, "that they 'Don't care if they do lose their jobs' and cannot be scared." Asked by reporters what would happen if strike activity cost them their jobs, one woman remarked, "I haven't forgotten how to use a hoe," while another said, "We'll go back to the farm."[26] Such threats were not just bravado. High levels of farm ownership sustained cultural independence. Within the internal economy of families, individual fortunes were cushioned by reciprocity; an orientation toward subsistence survived side by side with the desire for cash and store-bought goods.

Stoney Creek farmers were solidly behind the sons and daughters they sent to the factories, as were the small shopkeepers who relied on farmers for their trade. In county politics Stoney Creekers had historically marshaled a block vote against the town. In 1929 Stoney Creek's own J. M. Moreland was county sheriff, and he openly took the strikers' side. A strike leader in the twisting room ran a country store and drove his working neighbors into town. "That's why he was pretty well accepted as their leader," said a fellow worker. "Some of them were cousins and other relations. Some of them traded at his store. Some of them rode in his taxi. All intertwined."[27]

The National Guard had divided loyalties. Parading past the plants, the strikers "waved to and called the first names of the guardsmen, for most of the young men in uniforms [were friends of] the men and girls on strike." Even when the local unit was fortified by outside recruits, fraternizing continued. Nettie Reece, like a number of her girlfriends, met her future husband that way; she saw him on the street and "knew that was mine right there." Some guardsmen went further and simply refused to serve. "The use of the National Guard here was the dirtiest deal ever pulled," one protested. "I turned in my equipment when I was ordered to go out and patrol the road. I was dropped from the payroll two weeks later."[28]

In this context of family- and community-based resistance, women had important roles to play. Farm mothers nurtured the strikers' independence simply by cleaving to the land, passing on to their children a heritage at odds with the values of the new order and maintaining family production as a hedge against the uncertainties of a market economy. But the situation of farm mothers had other effects as well, and it would be a mistake to push the argument for continuity too far. As their husbands ranged widely in search of wage labor, women's work intensified while their status—now tied to earning power—declined. The female strikers of Elizabethton saw their mothers as resourceful and strong but also as increasingly isolated and hard pressed. Most important, they no longer looked to their mothers' lives as patterns for their own.[29]

The summer after the strike, Bessie Edens attended the Southern Summer School for Women Workers, a workers' education project in North Carolina, where she set the group on its ear with an impassioned defense of women's rights:

> It is nothing new for married women to work. They have always worked.... Women have always worked harder than men and always had to look up to the man and feel that they were weaker and inferior.... If we women would not be so submissive and take every thing for granted, if we would awake and stand up for our rights, this world would be a better place to live in, at least it would be better for the women.
>
> Some girls think that as long as mother takes in washings, keeps ten or twelve boarders or perhaps takes in sewing, she isn't working. But I say that either one of the three is as hard work as women could do. So if they do that at home and don't get any wages for it, why would it not be all right for them to go to a factory and receive pay for what they do?

Edens had been the oldest of ten children. She had dreamed of going to nursing school, but her poverty-stricken parents had opposed her plan. At fifteen, she had gone to work as a ser-

vant. "Then I'd come back when Momma had a baby and wait on her, and help if she needed me in any way." Asked fifty years later about a daughter's place on a hardscrabble farm, Edens replied: "The girls were supposed to do housework and work in the fields. They were supposed to be slaves."[30]

Bessie Edens was unusual in her articulation of a working-class feminism. But scattered through the life histories written by other students are echoes of her general themes. Read in the context of farm daughters' lives—their first-hand exposure to rural poverty, their yearnings for a more expansive world—these stories reflect the "structure of feeling" women brought to the rayon plants and then to the picket line and union hall.[31] Women such as Edens, it seems, sensed the devaluation of women's handicraft labor in the face of cheap consumer goods. They feared the long arm of their mothers' fate, resented their fathers' distant authority, and envied their brothers' exploits away from home. By opting for work in the rayon plants, they struck out for their own place in a changing world. When low wages, high costs, and autocratic managers affronted their dignity and dashed their hopes, they were the first to revolt.

The Elizabethton story thus presents another pattern in the female protest tradition. In coal-mining communities a rigid division of labor and women's hardships in company towns have resulted, paradoxically, in the notable militancy of miners' wives. By contrast, tobacco factories have tended to employ married women, whose job commitments and associational lives enable them to assume leadership roles in sustained organizing drives. In yet other circumstances, such as the early New England textile mills or the union insurgency of the 1920s and 1930s, single women initiated independent strikes or provided strong support for male-led, mixed-sex campaigns. Where, as in Elizabethton, people were mobilized as family and community members rather than as individual workers, non-wage-earning women could provide essential support. Once in motion, their daughters might outdo men in militancy, perhaps because they had fewer dependents than their male co-workers and could fall back more easily on parental resources, perhaps because the peer culture and increased independence encouraged by factory labor stirred boldness and inspired experimentation.[32]

The fact of women's initiative and participation in collective action is instructive. Even more intriguing is the gender-based symbolism of their protest style. Through dress, language, and gesture, female strikers expressed a complex cultural identity and turned it to their own rebellious purposes.

Consider, for instance, Trixie Perry and a woman who called herself "Texas Bill." Twenty-eight-year-old Trixie Perry was a reeler in the Glanzstoff plant. She had apparently become pregnant ten years before, had married briefly and then divorced, giving her son her maiden name. Her father was a butcher and a farmer, and she lived near her family on the edge of town. Trixie later moved into Elizabethton. She never remarried but went on to have several more children by other men. Texas Bill's background is more elusive. All we know is that she came from out of state, lived in a boardinghouse, and claimed to have been married twice before she arrived in town. These two friends were ringleaders on the picket line. Both were charged with violating the injunction, and both were brought to trial.[33]

Trixie Perry took the stand in a dress sewn from red, white, and blue bunting and a cap made of a small American flag. The prosecuting attorney began his cross-examination:

"You have a United States flag as a cap on your head?"

"Yes."

"Wear it all the time?"

"Whenever I take a notion."

"You are dressed in a United States flag, and the colors?"

"I guess so, I was born under it, guess I have a right to."

The main charge was that Perry and her friend had drawn a line across the road at Gap Creek and dared the soldiers to cross it. Above all they were accused of taunting the National Guard. The defense attorney, a fiery local lawyer playing to a sympathetic crowd, did not deny the charges. Instead, he used the women to mock the government's case. Had Trixie Perry threatened a lieutenant? "He rammed a gun in my face and I told him to take it out or I would knock it out." Had she blocked the road? "A little thing like me block a big road?" What had she said to the threat of a tear gas bomb? "That little old fire cracker of a thing, it won't go off."[34]

Texas Bill was an even bigger hit with the crowd. The defense attorney called her the "Wild Man From Borneo." A guard said she was "the wildest human being I've ever seen." Texas Bill both affirmed and subverted her reputation. Her nickname came from her habit of wearing "cowboy" clothes. But when it was her turn to testify, she "strutted on the stand" in a fashionable black picture hat and a black coat. Besides her other transgressions, she was accused of grabbing a soldier's gun and aiming it at him. What was she doing on the road so early in the morning? "I take a walk every morning before breakfast for my health," Texas replied with what a reporter described as "an assumed ladylike dignity."[35]

Witnesses for the prosecution took pains to contradict Texas Bill's "assumed ladylike dignity." A guardsman complained that she called him a " 'God damned yellow son-of-a-bitch,' and then branched out from that." Texas offered no defense: "When that soldier stuck his gun in my face, that did make me mad and I did cuss a little bit and don't deny it." Far from discrediting the strikers, the soldiers' testimony added to their own embarrassment and the audience's delight. In tune with the crowd, the defense attorney "enjoyed making the guards admit they had been 'assaulted' . . . by 16- and 18-year-old girls."[36]

Mock gentility, transgressive laughter, male egos on the line—the mix made for wonderful theater, and proved effective in court as well. The judge reserved maximum sentences for three especially aggressive men; all the women and most of the men were found not guilty or were lightly fined. In the end even those convictions were overturned by the state court of appeals.[37]

Trixie Perry and Texas Bill certainly donned the role of "disorderly woman." Since, presumably, only extraordinary circumstances call forth feminine aggression, women's assaults against persons and property constitute a powerful witness against injustice. At the same time, since women are considered less rational and taken less seriously than men, they may meet less resistance and be punished less severely for their crimes.[38]

But Trixie Perry and Texas Bill were not just out of line in their public acts; they also led unconventional private lives. It was this erotic subtext that most horrified officialdom and amused the courtroom crowd. The only extended discussion of the strike that appears in the city council minutes resulted in a resolution that read in part:

> WHEREAS, it has come to [our] attention . . . that the moral tone of this community has been lowered by reason of men and women congregating in various houses and meeting-places in Elizabethton and there practicing lewdness all hours of the night, in defiance of morality, law and order. . . .

> NOW, THEREFORE, BE IT RESOLVED, that the police force of the City arrest and place in the City Jail those who are violating the laws by practicing lewdness within the City of Elizabethton. . . .[39]

Union representatives apparently shared, indeed anticipated, the councilmen's concern. Worried by rumors that unemployed women were resorting to prostitution, they had already announced to the press that 25 percent of the strikers had been sent back to their hillside homes, "chiefly young single girls whom we want to keep off the streets." The townsmen and the trade unionists were thus united in drawing a line between good women and bad, with respectability being measured not only by chastity but by nuances of style and language as well.[40] In the heat of the trial, the question of whether or not women—as workers—had violated the injunction took second place to questions about their status *as women*, as members of their sex. Had they cursed? Had they been on the road at odd hours of the day or night? Was Texas Bill a lady or a "wild man from Borneo"? Fearing that "lewd women" might discredit the organizing drive, the organizers tried to send them home. To protect the community's "moral tone," the city council threatened to lock them up.

There is nothing extraordinary about this association between sexual misbehavior and women's labor militancy. Since strikers are often young single women who violate gender conventions by invading public space customarily reserved for men (and sometimes frequented by prostitutes)—and since female aggressiveness stirs up fears of women's sexual power—opponents have often undercut union organizing drives by insinuations of prostitution or promiscuity. Fearing guilt by association, "respectable" women stay away.[41]

What is impressive here is how Trixie Perry and Texas Bill handled the dichotomy between ladyhood and lewdness, good girls and bad. Using words that, for women in particu-

lar, were ordinarily taboo, they refused deference and signaled disrespect. Making no secret of their sexual experience, they combined flirtation with fierceness on the picket line and adopted a provocative courtroom style. And yet, with the language of dress—a cap made of an American flag, an elegant wide-brimmed hat—they claimed their rights as citizens and their place in the female community.

Moreover, that community upheld their claims. The defense attorney chose unruly women as his star witnesses, and the courtroom spectators enthusiastically cheered them on. The prosecuting attorney recommended dismissal of the charges against all the women on trial except Trixie Perry, Texas Bill, and a "hoodlum" named Lucille Ratliffe, on the grounds that the rest came from "good families." Yet in the court transcripts, few differences can be discerned in the behavior of good girls and bad. The other female defendants may have been less flamboyant, but they were no less sharp-tongued. Was Vivian King a member of the UTW? "Yes, and proud of it." Had she been picketing? "Yes, proud of that." What was a young married woman named Dorothy Oxindine doing on Gap Creek at five o'clock in the morning? "Out airing." Did Lena May Jones "holler out 'scab'"? "No, I think the statement made was 'I wouldn't be a scab' and 'Why don't you come and join our organization.'" Did she laugh at a soldier and tell him his gun wouldn't shoot? "I didn't tell him it wouldn't shoot, but I laughed at him . . . and told him he was too much of a man to shoot a lady."[42]

Interviewed over fifty years later, strike participants still refused to make invidious distinctions between themselves and women like Trixie Perry and Texas Bill. Bessie Edens was a settled, self-educated, married woman. But she was also a self-described "daredevil on the picket line," secure in the knowledge that she had a knife hidden in her drawstring underwear. To Edens, who came from a mountain hamlet called Hampton, the chief distinction did not lie between herself and rougher women. It lay between herself and merchants' wives who blamed the trouble on "those hussies from Hampton." When asked what she thought of Trixie Perry and Texas Bill, she answered simply, "There were some girls like that involved. But I didn't care. They did their part."[43]

Nettie Reece, who lived at home with parents who were "pretty particular with [their] daughters," shared Bessie Edens's attitude. After passing along the town gossip about Trixie Perry, she was anxious to make sure her meaning was not misconstrued. "Trixie was not a woman who sold her body," she emphasized. "She just had a big desire for sex. . . . And when she had a cause to fight for, she'd fight." Reece then went on to establish Perry's claim to a certain kind of respectability. After the strike Perry became a hard-working restaurant cook. She was a good neighbor: "If anybody got sick, she was there to wait on them." The children she bore out of wedlock did well in life, and they "never throwed [their mother] aside."[44]

Industrialization, as we know, changed the nature of work, the meaning of time. In Carter County it entailed a shift of economic and political power from the countryside to the town. At issue too were more intimate matters of fantasy, culture, and style.

Implicit in the conflict were two different sexual systems. One, subscribed to by union officials and the local middle class, mandated chastity before marriage, men as breadwinners, and women as housewives in the home. The other, rooted in a rural past and adapted to working-class life, recognized liaisons established without the benefit of clergy or license fees and allowed legitimacy to be broadly construed. It was unfamiliar with—or pragmatic about—prostitution. It circumscribed women's roles without investing in abstract standards of femininity. It was, in short, a society that might produce a Trixie Perry or defend "hussies from Hampton" against the snubs of merchants' wives.

This is not to say that the women of Elizabethton were simply acting on tradition. On the contrary, the strikers dressed the persona of the disorderly woman in unmistakably modern garb. Women's behavior on the witness stand presupposed a certain sophistication: A passing familiarity allowed them to parody ladyhood and to thumb a nose at the genteel standards of the town. Combining garments from the local past with fragments of an expansive consumer culture, the women of Elizabethton assembled their own version of a brash, irreverent Jazz Age style.

By the early 1920s radios and Model Ts had joined railroads and mail-order catalogs as conduits to the larger world. Record companies had discovered hill-country music and East Tennessee's first country-music stars were recording hits that transformed ballad singing, fiddle playing, and banjo picking into one of America's great popular-music sounds. The banjo itself was an Afro-American instrument that had come to the mountains with the railroad gangs. Such cultural interchanges multiplied during the 1920s as rural traditions met the upheavals of industrial life. The result was an explosion of musical creativity—in the hills of Tennessee no less than in New York City and other cosmopolitan centers.[45] Arriving for work in the rayon plants, young people brought with them the useable past of the countryside, but they quickly assimilated the speeded-up rhythms of a changing world.

Work-related peer groups formed a bridge between traditional loyalties and a novel youth culture. Whether married or single, living with parents or on their own, women participated in the strike in same-sex groups. Sisters boarded, worked, and demonstrated together. Girlfriends teamed up in groups or pairs. Trixie Perry and Texas Bill were a case in point. But there were others as well. Nettie Reece joined the union with her parents' approval but also with her whole school girl gang in tow. Ethel and M. C. Ashworth, ages eighteen and seventeen, respectively, came from Virginia to work in the plants. "Hollering and singing [in a] Ford touring car," they were arrested in a demonstration at Watauga Point. Ida and Evelyn Heaton boarded together on Donna Avenue. Evelyn Heaton was hit by a car on the picket line, swore out a warrant, and had the commander of the National Guard placed under arrest. After the strike she was blacklisted, and Ida attended the Southern Summer School.[46]

The sudden gathering of young people in the town nourished new patterns of heterosociability, and the strike's erotic undercurrent surfaced not only in Trixie Perry's "big desire for sex" but also in the behavior of her more conventional peers. The loyalties of the national guardsmen were divided, but their sympathy was obvious, as was their interest in the female strikers. Most of the Elizabethton women were in their teens or early twenties, the usual age of marriage in the region, and the strike provided unaccustomed opportunities for courtship. Rather than choosing a neighbor they had known all their lives, under watchful parental eyes, women flirted on the picket lines or the shop floor. Romance and politics commingled in the excitement of the moment, flowering in a spectrum of behavior—from the outrageousness of Trixie Perry to a spate of marriages among other girls.

What needs emphasis here is the dynamic quality of working-class women's culture—a quality that is sometimes lost in static oppositions between modernism and traditionalism, individualism and family values, consumer and producer mentalities. This is especially important where regional history has been so thoroughly mythologized. Appalachian culture, like all living cultures, embraced continuity and discontinuity, indigenous and borrowed elements.[47] As surely as Anna Weinstock—or Alabama's Zelda Fitzgerald—or any city flapper, the Elizabethton strikers were "new women," making their way in a world their mothers could not have known but carrying with them values handed down through the female line.

Two vignettes may serve to illustrate that process of grounded change.

Flossie Cole's mother, known by everyone on Stoney Creek as "Aunt Tid," was Sheriff Moreland's sister, but that didn't keep her from harboring cardplayers, buckdancers, and whiskey drinkers in her home. Aunt Tid was also a seamstress who "could look at a picture in a catalog and cut a pattern and make a dress just like it." But like most of her friends, Cole jumped at the chance for store-bought clothes: "That first paycheck, that was it ... I think I bought me some new clothes with the first check I got. I bought me a new pair of shoes and a dress and a hat. Can you imagine someone going to a plant with a hat on? I had a blue dress and black shoes—patent leather, honey, with real high heels—and a blue hat." Nevertheless, before Cole left home in the morning for her job in the rayon plant, Aunt Tid made sure that around her neck—beneath the new blue dress—she wore a bag of asafetida, a strong-smelling resin, a folk remedy to protect her from diseases that might be circulating in the town.[48]

Second, there is visual evidence: a set of sixteen-millimeter films made by the company in order to identify—and to blacklist—workers who participated in the union. In those films groups of smiling women traipse along the picket line dressed in up-to-date clothes.[49] Yet federal conciliator Anna Weinstock, speaking

to an interviewer forty years later, pictured them in sunbonnets, and barefooted. "They were," she explained, "what we would normally call hillbillies": women who "never get away from their shacks."[50] This could be seen as the treachery of memory, a problem of retrospection. But it is also an illustration of the power of stereotypes, of how cultural difference is registered as backwardness, of how images of poverty and backwardness hide the realities of working-class women's lives.

The strike, as we know, was defeated. Participants were blacklisted. The Great Depression settled over the mountains, rekindling reliance on older ways of making do. Flossie Cole, for instance, had been new to factory labor, but she was no stranger to women's work. While her brothers had followed their father's lead to the coal mines, she had pursued the two most common occupations of the poorest mountain girls: agricultural labor and domestic service. "We would hire out and stay with people until they got through with us and then go back home. And when we got back home, it was workin' in the corn or wash for people." When Cole lost her job after the strike she went back to domestic service, "back to the drudge house," as she put it.[51]

Young women had poured eagerly into the rayon mills, drawn at least in part by the promise of independence, romance and adventure. As hard times deepened, such motives paled beside stark necessity. Two statistics make the point: The percentage of Carter County women who were gainfully employed held steady through the thirties. But by the end of the period a larger proportion than before worked as servants in other people's homes. When Flossie Cole went "back to the drudge house," she had plenty of company.[52]

Still, despite subsequent hardships, the spirit of the 1920s flickered on. Setting out to explore the strike through oral-history interviews, we expected to find disclaimers or silences. Instead, we heard unfaded memories and no regrets. "I knew I wasn't going to get to go back, and I didn't care," said Bessie Edens. "I wrote them a letter and told them I didn't care whether they took me back or not. I didn't! If I'd starved I wouldn't of cared, because I knew what I was a'doing when I helped to pull it. And I've never regretted it in any way.... And it did help the people, and it's helped the town and the country."[53] For those, like Edens, who went on to the Southern Summer School or remained active in the union, the strike was a pivot around which the political convictions and personal aspirations of a lifetime turned. For them, there were intangible rewards: a subtle deepening of individual power, a belief that they had made history and that later generations benefited from what they had done.

The strike, of course, made a fainter impression on other lives. Women's rebelliousness neither redefined gender roles nor overcame economic dependency. Their desire for the trappings of modernity could blur into a self-limiting consumerism. An ideology of romance could end in sexual danger or a married woman's burdensome double day. Still, the women of Elizabethton left a legacy. A norm of female public work, a new style of sexual expressiveness, the entry of women into public space and political struggles previously monopolized by men—all these pushed against traditional constraints even as they created new vulnerabilities. The farm daughters who left home for the rayon plants pioneered a new pattern of female experience, and they created for their post–World War II daughters an environment far different from the one they, in their youth, had known. It would be up to later generations to wrestle with the costs of commercialization and to elaborate a vision that embraced economic justice and community solidarity as well as women's liberation.

NOTES

This study began as a collaborative endeavor with Sara Evans of the University of Minnesota, who helped to gather many of the interviews on which I have relied. Rosemarie Hester and Jennifer Dowd also joined me on trips to the mountains, and I benefited from their companionship, ideas, and research. I owe a special debt to Christopher Daly, Lu Ann Jones, Robert Korstad, James Leloudis, and Mary Murphy, with whom I have co-written *Like a Family: The Making of a Southern Cotton Mill World* (Chapel Hill, 1987).

1. Dan Crowe, *Old Town and the Covered Bridge* (Johnson City, Tenn., 1977), pp. 32, 71; Florence (Cole) Grindstaff interview by Jacquelyn Hall, July 10, 1981 (in Hall's possession).

2. For this strike wave, see Tom Tippett, *When Southern Labor Stirs* (New York, 1931); James A. Hodges, "Challenge to the New South: The Great Textile Strike in Elizabethton, Tennessee, 1929," *Tennessee Historical Quarterly* 23 (Dec. 1964):343–57; . . .

3. Contemporary observations include, *Knoxville News Sentinel*, May 17, 1929; Florence Kelley,

"Our Newest South," *Survey*, June 15, 1929, pp. 342–44; . . .

4. Anne Firor Scott, "On Seeing and Not Seeing: A Case of Historical Invisibility," *Journal of American History* 71 (June 1984):7–8.

5. Natalie Zemon Davis, *Society and Culture in Early Modern France* (Stanford, 1975), pp. 124–51. . . .

6. Michel Foucault, *Power/Knowledge: Selected Interviews and Other Writings, 1972–1977*, trans. and ed. Colin Gordon (New York, 1980), p. 81.

7. Joseph Leeming, *Rayon: The First Man-Made Fiber* (Brooklyn, 1950), pp. 1–82; Jesse W. Markham, *Competition in the Rayon Industry* (Cambridge, Mass., 1952), pp. 1–38, 97, 186, 193, 209.

8. Bruce Roberts and Nancy Roberts, *Where Time Stood Still: A Portrait of Appalachia* (New York, 1970); William Goodell Frost, "Our Contemporary Ancestors in the Southern Mountains," *Atlantic Monthly* 83 (March 1899):311; Arnold J. Toynbee, *A Study of History*, 2 vols. (New York, 1947), II:312; . . .

9. For this preindustrial economy, and its transformation, see Eller, *Miners, Millhands, and Mountaineers*, pp. 3–38, 86–127. . . .

10. *Mountaineer*, Dec. 28, Dec. 31, 1887.

11. U.S. Department of the Interior, Census Office, *Report on the Productions of Agriculture as Returned at the Tenth Census (June 1, 1880)* (Washington, 1883), pp. 84–85, 132, 169; U.S. Department of Commerce, Bureau of the Census, *Fourteenth Census of the United States Taken in the Year 1920: Agriculture*, vol. VI, pt. 2 (Washington, [D.C.] 1922), pp. 446–47.

12. Holly, "Elizabethton, Tennessee," pp. 123, 133–38, 156, 198; U.S. Congress, Senate, Committee on Manufactures, *Working Conditions of the Textile Industry in North Carolina, South Carolina, and Tennessee*, 71 Cong., 1 sess., May 8, 9, and 20, 1929, p. 95; Henry Schuettler interview by Hall, n.d. [1981] (in Hall's possession).

13. Thirteenth Census of the United States, 1910, Manuscript Population Schedule, Carter County, Tenn., district 7; ibid., district 15; ibid., district 10; ibid., district 12.

14. Grindstaff interview.

15. *Scraps of Work and Play*, Southern Summer School for Women Workers in Industry, Burnsville, N.C., July 11–Aug. 23, 1929, typescript, pp. 21–22, 24, box 111, American Labor Education Service Records (Martin P. Catherwood Library, New York State School of Industrial and Labor Relations, Cornell University, Ithaca, N.Y.); Bessie Edens interview by Mary Frederickson, Aug. 14, 1975, pp. 1–2, 31–32, Southern Oral History Program Collection, Southern Historical Collection (Wilson Library, University of North Carolina at Chapel Hill) [hereafter SOHP].

16. Edens interview, Aug. 14, 1975, p. 32; Grindstaff interview.

17. Nettie Reece [pseud.] interview by Hall, May 18 and 19, 1983 (in Hall's possession).

18. *Knoxville News Sentinel*, May 13, 1929; *American Bemberg Corporation* v. *George Miller, et al.*, East Tennessee District Supreme Court, Jan. 29, 1930, record of evidence, typescript, box 660 (Tennessee State Library and Archives, Nashville) [hereafter Record of Evidence]. . . .

19. *Knoxville News Sentinel*, Mar. 14, 1929; Christine (Hinkle) Galliher and Dave Galliher interview by Hall, Aug. 8, 1979, pp. 8–9, SOHP; Tom Tippett,

"Southern Situation," speech typescript, meeting held at the National Board, May 15, 1929, p. 3, box 25, Young Women's Christian Association Papers, Sophia Smith Collection (Smith College, Northampton, Mass.); Tom Tippett, "Impressions of Situation at Elizabethton, Tenn., May 10, 11, 1929," typescript, p. 1, ibid.

20. *Knoxville News Sentinel*, Mar. 20, Mar. 29, 1929; "Instructions for Adjustment of Wage Scale for Girl Help," Mar. 15, 1929, Records of the Conciliation Service, RG 280 (National Archives); Committee of Striking Workers[,] Members of United Textile Workers of America to the Honorable Herbert Hoover, Apr. 16, 1929, ibid; "Preliminary Report of Commissioner of Conciliation," Apr. 16, 1929, ibid.

21. Dr. J. A. Hardin to Hon. H. H. Horton, May 16, 1929, box 12, Governor Henry H. Horton Papers (Tennessee State Library and Archives); *Knoxville News Sentinel*, May 6, May 10, May 12, May 14, May 19, May 24, 1929.

22. Edens interview, Aug. 14, 1975, pp. 40, 49; Galliher interview, 33; *Knoxville News Sentinel*, Mar. 15, May 16, 1929.

23. *Knoxville News Sentinel*, May 27, 1929; Ina Nell (Hinkle) Harrison interview by Hall, Aug. 8, 1979, p. 2, SOHP; Mary Heaton Vorse, "Rayon Strikers Reluctantly Accept Settlement," press release, May 27, 1929, box 156, Mary Heaton Vorse Papers, Archives of Labor and Urban Affairs (Walter P. Reuther Library, Wayne State University, Detroit, Mich.).

24. "Rays of Sunshine in the Rayon War," *Literary Digest*, June 8, 1929, p. 12; *Charlotte Observer*, June 2, 1929; *Raleigh News and Observer*, May 24, 1929.

25. Edens interview, Aug. 14, 1975, pp. 43–44; Myrtle Simmerly interview by Hall, May 18, 1983 (in Hall's possession); Ollie Hardin interview by Hall and Sara Evans, Aug. 9, 1979 (in Hall's possession); Effie (Hardin) Carson interview by Hall and Evans, Aug. 6, 1979, p. 41, SOHP; Holly, "Elizabethton, Tennessee," 306–7.

26. James Myers, "Field Notes: Textile Strikes in the South," box 374, Archive Union Files (Martin P. Catherwood Library); *Raleigh News and Observer*, Mar. 15, 1929.

27. Hoffmann, "Mountaineer in Industry," 2–5; Robert (Bob) Moreland and Barbara Moreland interview by Hall, July 11, 1981 (in Hall's possession); *Knoxville News Sentinel*, Mar. 15, 1929; Honard Ward interview by Hall, n.d. [1981] (in Hall's possession).

28. *Knoxville News Sentinel*, May 15, 1929; Reece interview; . . .

29. For the argument that precisely because they are "left behind" by the economic developments that pull men into wage labor, woman-centered families may harbor alternative or oppositional visions, see Mina Davis Caulfield, "Imperialism, the Family, and Cultures of Resistance," *Socialist Revolution* 4 (Oct. 1974):67–85; . . .

30. Bessie Edens, "Why a Married Woman Should Work," in *Scraps of Work and Play*, pp. 30–31; Edens interview, Aug. 14. 1975, pp. 14, 21, 34–35; Bessie Edens interview by Hall, Aug. 5, 1979 (in Hall's possession); Millie Sample, "Impressions," Aug. 1931, box 9, American Labor Education Service Records.

31. Mirion Bonner, "Behind the Southern Textile Strikes," *Nation*, Oct. 2 , 1929, pp. 351–52; "Scraps From Our Lives," in *Scraps of Work and Play*, pp. 5–11; . . .

32. Corbin, *Life, Work, and Rebellion*, pp. 92–93; Louise A. Tilly, "Paths of Proletarianization: Organization of Production, Sexual Division of Labor, and Women's Collective Action," *Signs* 7 (Winter 1981):400–17; . . .

33. *Elizabethton Star*, Nov. 14, 1953, Jan. 31, 1986; Reece interview; Carson interview, 25; Nellie Bowers interview by Hall, May 15, 1983 (in Hall's possession); *Knoxville News Sentinel*, May 17, May 18, 1929.

34. Record of Evidence.

35. *Knoxville News Sentinel*, May 17, 1929.

36. Ibid.; Record of Evidence.

37. *American Bemberg Corporation* v. *George Miller, et al.*, minute books "Q" and "R," Chancery Court minutes, Carter County, Tenn., July 22, 1929 (Carter County Courthouse, Elizabethton, Tenn.); *American Bemberg Corporation* v. *George Miller, et al.*, Court of Appeals, #1, Sept. 5, 1930 (Supreme Court and Courts of Appeal, State of Tennessee, Knoxville).

38. Davis, *Society and Culture in Early Modern France*, pp. 124–51; Laurel Thatcher Ulrich, *Good Wives* (New York, 1982), pp. 191–97.

39. Elizabethton City Council, Minutes, May 23, 1929, Minute Book, vol. 5, pp. 356–57 (City Hall, Elizabethton, Tenn.).

40. *Knoxville News Sentinel*, May 5, 1929; Myers, "Field Notes." . . .

41. See, for instance, Alice Kessler-Harris, "The Autobiography of Ann Washington Craton," *Signs* 1 (Summer 1976):1019–37.

42. *Knoxville News Sentinel*, May 18, 1929; Record of Evidence.

43. Edens interview, Aug. 5, 1979.

44. Reece interview, May 19, 1983.

45. Charles K. Wolfe, *Tennessee Strings: The Story of Country Music in Tennessee* (Knoxville, 1977), pp. 22–90; Barry O'Connell, "Dick Boggs, Musician and Coal Miner," *Appalachian Journal* 11 (Autumn–Winter 1983–84):48.

46. *Miller's Elizabethton, Tenn., City Directory*, 1930; Reece interview; Record of Evidence; *Knoxville News Sentinel*, May 16, May 17, 1929; . . .

47. David E. Whisnant, *All That Is Native and Fine: The Politics of Culture in an American Region* (Chapel Hill, 1983), p. 48.

48. Grindstaff interview; Moreland interview.

49. *Knoxville Journal*, Apr. 22, 1929; sixteen-millimeter film (1 reel), ca. 1929, Helen Raulston Collection, Archives of Appalachia (East Tennessee State University, Johnson City); sixteen-millimeter film (20 reels), ca. 1927–1928, Bemberg Industry Records (Tennessee State Library and Archives). . . .

50. Anna Weinstock Schneider interview by Julia Blodgett Curtis, 1969, pp. 161, 166, 172–3, 177, Anna Weinstock Schneider Papers, box 1 (Martin P. Catherwood Library).

51. Grindstaff interview.

52. Bureau of the Census, *Fifteenth Census of the United States: 1930. Population*, vol. III, pt. 2 (Washington, [D.C.], 1932), p. 909; U.S. Department of Commerce, Bureau of the Census, *Sixteenth Census of the United States: 1940. Population*, vol. II, pt. 6 (Washington, [D.C.], 1943), p. 616.

53. Edens interview, Aug. 14, 1975, p. 50. . . .

JACQUELINE JONES
Harder Times: The Great Depression

The chronic scarcity of jobs that characterized the Appalachian South where the Eliza-bethton strike occurred became a national phenomenon in the 1930s. As the Great De-pression tightened its hold on the economy, the plight of America's working people generated protest in the farm belt as well as industrial centers. Government aid even-tually alleviated some of the suffering while New Deal legislation and a revitalized labor movement brought improved working conditions. Nevertheless many workers, agricul-tural as well as industrial, struggled daily to survive. They, especially, remained at the mercy of any employers who would hire them.

African-Americans were especially vulnerable. Jacqueline Jones's study of black women reminds us once again of the extent to which race and class shape women's experience. Consider the difference that race made in both the job opportunities available to women in the 1930s and the debate about whether married women should work. Observe how the experience of black domestics demonstrated the power of race and class to override "the bonds of womanhood." Note, too, how the speed-ups generating such dissatisfaction among the textile workers in the 1920s described by Hall were ex-tended in the 1930s to private household service.

High unemployment rates among their hus-bands and sons forced many white wives to enter the labor market for the first time in the 1930s.[1] But black men experienced even higher rates of joblessness, causing their wives to cling more desperately to the positions they already had, despite declining wages and deteriorating working conditions. During the Great Depres-sion, most black women maintained only a pre-carious hold on gainful employment; their po-sitions as family breadwinners depended upon, in the words of one social worker, "the breath of chance, to say nothing of the winds of economic change."[2] Unemployment statis-tics for the 1930s can be misleading because they do not reveal the impact of a shifting oc-cupational structure on job options for women of the two races. Just as significantly, the rela-tively high rate of black females' participation in the labor force obscures the highly tempo-rary and degrading nature of their work ex-periences. Specifically, most of these women could find only seasonal or part-time employ-ment; racial and sexual discrimination de-prived them of a living wage no matter how hard they labored; and they endured a degree and type of workplace exploitation for which the mere fact of having a job could not com-pensate. During the decade, nine out of ten black women workers toiled as agricultural la-borers or domestic servants. Various pieces of federal legislation designed to protect and raise the purchasing power of workers (most nota-bly the National Industrial Recovery Act [1933], the Social Security Act [1935], and the Fair Labor Standards Act [1938]) exempted these two groups of workers from their provi-sions. In essence, then, no more than 10 percent of gainfully employed black women derived any direct benefit from the new federal policies related to minimum wages, maximum hours, unemployment compensation, and social se-curity.[3]

Despite the rapid decline in a wide variety

of indicators related to production and economic growth in the early 1930s, and despite the sluggishness of the pre-1941 recovery period, the numbers and kinds of job opportunities for white women expanded, as did their need to help supplement household income. The clerical sector grew (as it had in the 1920s) and would continue to do so in the 1940s, and in the process attracted more and more women into the work force and employed a larger proportion of all white women workers. (The percentage of white women who were gainful workers steadily increased throughout the period 1920 to 1940 from 21.3 to 24.1 percent of all adult females.) Recent historians have stressed the "benefits of labor segregation" for women, arguing that, at least during the early part of the depression decade, unemployment in the male-dominated industrial sector was generally greater than in the female-dominated areas of sales, communications, and secretarial work. But this was a race-specific phenomenon. In a job market segmented by both race and sex, black women had no access to white women's work even though (or perhaps because) it was deemed integral to both industrial capitalism and the burgeoning federal bureaucracy. In 1940 one-third of all white, but only 1.3 percent of all black, working women had clerical jobs. On the other hand, 60 percent of all black female workers were domestic servants; the figure for white women was only 10 percent. . . .[4]

KITCHEN SPEED-UPS: DOMESTIC SERVICE

Contemporary literary and photographic images of a stricken nation showed dejected white men waiting in line for food, jobs, and relief. Yet observers sensitive to the racial dimensions of the crisis provided an alternative symbol— that of a middle-aged black woman in a thin, shabby coat and men's shoes, standing on a street corner in the dead of winter and offering her housecleaning services for 10 cents an hour. If the migrant labor camp symbolized the black agricultural worker's descent into economic marginality, then the "slave markets" in northern cities revealed a similar fate for domestic servants.

"The 'mart' is but a miniature mirror of our economic battle front," wrote two investigative reporters in a 1935 issue of the NAACP's monthly journal, *The Crisis*. A creature of the depression, the slave market consisted of groups of black women, aged seventeen to seventy, who waited on sidewalks for white women to drive up and offer them a day's work. The Bronx market, composed of several small ones—it was estimated that New York City had two hundred altogether—received the most attention from writers during the decade, though the general phenomenon recurred throughout other major cities. Before 1929, many New York domestics had worked for wealthy white families on Long Island. Their new employers, some of them working-class women themselves, paid as little as $5.00 weekly for full-time laborers to wash windows and clothes, iron (as many as twenty-one shirts a shift), and wax floors. The black women earned radically depressed wages: lunch and 35 cents for six hours of work, or $1.87 for an eight-hour day. They had to guard against various ruses that would deprive them of even this pittance—for example, a clock turned back an hour, the promised carfare that never materialized at the end of the day. As individuals they felt trapped, literally and figuratively pushed to the limits of their endurance. A thirty-year-old woman told federal interviewer Vivian Morris that she hated the people she worked for: "Dey's mean, 'ceitful, an' 'ain' hones'; but what ah'm gonna do? Ah got to live—got to hab a place to steh," and so she would talk her way into a job by boasting of her muscle power. But some days groups of women would spontaneously organize themselves and "run off the corner" those job seekers "who persist[ed] in working for less than thirty cents an hour."[5]

Unlike their country cousins, domestics contended directly with white competitors pushed out of their factory and waitressing jobs. The agricultural labor system served as a giant sieve; for the most part, displaced farm families went to the city rather than vying for the remaining tenant positions. The urban economy had no comparable avenues of escape; it was a giant pressure cooker, forcing the unemployed to look for positions in occupations less prestigious than the ones they held formerly or, in the event of ultimate failure, to seek some form of charity or public assistance. A 1937 Women's Bureau survey of destitute women in Chicago revealed that, although only 37 percent of native-born white women listed their "usual occupation" as domestic service, a much greater number had tried to take advantage of employers' preferences for white servants before they gave up the quest for jobs altogether and applied for relief. Meanwhile, the 81 percent of black women who had worked in service had nowhere else to go. Under these circumstances, the mere act of hiring a black woman seemed to some to represent a humanitarian gesture. In 1934 an observer of the social-welfare scene noted approvingly, with unintentional irony, that "From Mistress Martha Washington to Mistress Eleanor Roosevelt is not such a long time as time goes. There may be some significance in the fact that the household of the first First Lady was manned by Negro servants and the present First Lady has followed her example."[6]

The history of domestic service in the 1930s provides a fascinating case study of the lengths to which whites would go in exploiting a captive labor force. Those who employed live-in servants in some cases cut their wages, charged extra for room and board, or lengthened on-duty hours. But it was in the area of day work that housewives elevated labor-expanding and money-saving methods to a fine art. General speed-ups were common in private homes throughout the North and South. Among the best bargains were children and teenagers; in Indianola, Mississippi, a sixteen-year-old black girl worked from 6 A.M. to 7 P.M. daily for $1.50 a week. In the same town a maid could be instructed to do her regular chores, plus those of the recently fired cook, for less pay than she had received previously. (A survey of Mississippi's domestics revealed that the average weekly pay was less than $2.00.) Some women received only carfare, clothing, or lunch for a day's work. Northern white women also lowered wages drastically. In 1932 Philadelphia domestics earned $5.00 to $12.00 for a forty-eight- to sixty-seven-hour work week. Three years later they took home the same amount of money for ninety hours' worth of scrubbing, washing, and cooking (an hourly wage of 15 cents).[7]

The deteriorating working conditions of domestic servants reflected the conscious choices of individual whites who took advantage of the abundant labor supply. Social workers recorded conversations with potential employers seeking "bright, lively" domestics (with the very best references) to do all the cooking, cleaning, laundry, and childcare for very little pay, because, in the words of one Pittsburgh woman, "There are so many people

out of work that I am sure I can find a girl for $6.00 a week." Indeed, at times it seemed as if there existed a perversely negative relationship between expectations and compensation. An eighty-three-year-old South Carolina black woman, Jessie Sparrow, resisted working on Sundays because, she told an interviewer in 1937, "when dey pays you dat little bit of money, dey wants every bit your time." A southern white man demonstrated his own brand of logic when he "admitted as a matter of course that his cook was underpaid, but explained that this was necessary, since, if he gave her more money, she might soon have so much that she would no longer be willing to work for him."[8]

The field of domestic service was virtually unaffected by national and state welfare policies. In the 1930s Women's Bureau officials tried to compensate for this inaction with a flurry of correspondence, radio and luncheon-meeting speeches, and voluntary guidelines related to the "servant problem." In her talks on the subject, bureau head Mary Anderson tried to appeal to employers' sense of fairness when she suggested that they draw up job descriptions, guard against accidents in the workplace, and establish reasonable hours and wages. But the few housewives privy to Anderson's exhortations were not inclined to heed them, especially when confronted by a seemingly accommodating "slave" on the street corner. Consequently, black domestic workers in several cities, often under the sponsorship of a local Young Women's Christian Association, Urban League branch, or labor union, made heroic attempts to form employees' organizations that would set uniform standards for service. However, they remained a shifting, amorphous group immune to large-scale organizational efforts. For example, founded in 1934 and affiliated with Building Service Union Local 149 (AFL), the New York Domestic Workers Union had only 1,000 (out of a potential of 100,000) members four years later. It advocated two five-hour shifts six days a week and insisted, "last but not least, no window washing." Baltimore's Domestic Workers Union (in the CIO fold) also welcomed members of both races and remained a relatively insignificant force in the regulation of wages and working conditions. Without adequate financial resources, leaders like New York's Dora Jones labored to organize women who "still believe in widespread propaganda that all unions are rackets." As a result, efforts by domestics to control wage rates informally through peer pressure or failure to report for work as promised represented spontaneous job actions more widespread and successful than official "union" activity.[9]

During the depression, a long life of work was the corollary of a long day of work. Black women between the ages of twenty-five and sixty-five worked at consistently high rates; they simply could not rely on children or grandchildren to support them in their old age. The Federal Writers Project interviews with former slaves recorded in the late 1930s contain hundreds of examples of women in their seventies and eighties still cooking, cleaning, or hoeing for wages on a sporadic basis in order to keep themselves and their dependents alive. An interviewer described the seventy-seven-year-old widow Mandy Leslie of Fairhope, Alabama, as "a pillar of strength and comfort to several white households" because she did their washing and ironing every week. Living alone, her children gone, this elderly woman boiled clothes in an iron pot heated by a fire, and then rubbed them on a washboard and hung them on lines so they could be ironed the following day. Such was the price exacted from black women for the "strength and comfort" they provided whites.[10]

Notes

1. Lois Scharf, *To Work and To Wed: Female Employment, Feminism, and the Great Depression* (Westport, Conn.: Greenwood Press, 1980), pp. 107–8. . . .

2. Marion Cuthbert, "Problems Facing Negro Young Women," *Opportunity* 14 (Feb. 1936):47–49.

3. U.S. Department of Commerce, Bureau of the Census, *The Labor Force*, Pt. 1, U.S. Summary, p. 90; Mary Elizabeth Pidgeon, "Employed Women Under N.R.A. Codes," United States Department of Labor, Women's Bureau, *Bulletin*, no. 130 (1935); "Women at Work: A Century of Industrial Change," United States Department of Labor, Women's Bureau, *Bulletin*, no. 161 (1939). . . .

4. Alice Kessler-Harris, *Out to Work: A History of Wage-Earning Women in the United States* (New York: Oxford University Press, 1982), pp. 250–72; Ruth Milkman, "Women's Work and Economic Crisis: Some Lessons of the Great Depression," *Review of Radical Political Economics* 8 (Spring 1976):73–97; Winifred D. Wandersee, *Women's Work and Family Values, 1920–1940* (Cambridge, Mass.: Harvard University

Press, 1981), pp. 84–102; U.S. Dept. of Commerce, Bureau of the Census, *The Labor Force*, Pt. 1, U.S. Summary, p. 90.

5. Ella Baker and Marvel Cooke, "The Bronx Slave Market," *Crisis* 42 (Nov. 1935):330, 340; Vivian Morris, "Bronx Slave Market," Dec. 6, 1938, Federal Writers Project, Negro Folklore Division (New York), p. 1, Archive of Folk Song, Manuscript Division, Library of Congress, Washington, D.C. . . .

6. Harriet A. Byrne and Cecile Hillyer, "Unattached Women on Relief in Chicago, 1937," United States Department of Labor, Women's Bureau, *Bulletin*, no. 158 (1938); Elmer Anderson Carter, "The Negro Household Employee," *Woman's Press* 28 (July–Aug. 1934):351.

7. John Dollard, *Caste and Class in a Southern Town* (New Haven, Conn.: Yale University Press, 1937), pp. 107–8; Jean Collier Brown, "The Negro Woman Worker," United States Department of Labor, Women's Bureau, *Bulletin*, no. 165 (1938); pp. 3–4, 7; Charles T. Haley, "To Do Good and Do Well: Middle-Class Blacks and the Depression, Philadelphia, 1929–1941" (Ph.D. diss., State University of New York at Binghamton, 1980), p. 59. . . .

8. Harold A. Lett, "Work: Negro Unemployed in Pittsburgh" *Opportunity* 9 (Mar. 1931):79–81; "Women Workers in Indianapolis," *Crisis* 37 (June 1930):189–91; *The American Slave: A Composite Autobiography*, ed. George Rawick, 41 vols., Series 1, Supp. Series 1 and 2 (Westport, Conn.: Greenwood Press, 1972, 1978, 1979), Series 1, *South Carolina Narratives*, pt. IV, vol. 3, p. 146; Hortense Powdermaker, *After Freedom: A Cultural Study in the Deep South* (New York, 1939), pp. 117–18.

9. "The Domestic Worker of Today," Radio Talk by Miss Mary Anderson, Sept. 21, 1932, Station WJAY, sponsored by Cleveland Parent Teachers Association, Speeches No. 112 (Box 71), Women's Bureau Collection, Department of Labor Archives, Record Group 86, National Archives, Washington, D.C.; Dora Jones quoted in "The Domestic Workers' Union," in *Black Women in White America: A Documentary History*, ed. Gerda Lerner, (New York, 1972), pp. 231–34. On the New York union, see Evelyn Seeley, "Our Feudal Housewives," *The Nation* 46 (May 28, 1938):613–15; on Baltimore, see article reprinted from *Baltimore Afro-American*, Oct. 1936, in *The Black Worker: A Documentary History from Colonial Times to the Present*, vol. 6, *The Era of Post-War Prosperity and the Great Depression, 1920–1936*, eds. Philip S. Foner and Ronald L. Lewis (Philadelphia: Temple University Press, 1981), pp. 184–85; Roderick N. Ryon, "An Ambiguous Legacy: Baltimore Blacks and the CIO, 1936–1941," *Journal of Negro History* 65 (Winter 1980):29. For evidence of the Urban League's efforts in this area, see "Program of Mass Meeting of General House Work Employees, Sept. 21, 1933 (St. Louis)" in Correspondence—Household (Domestic) File, General Correspondence Prior to 1934 (Box 926), Women's Bureau Collection, RG 86, National Archives.

10. Rawick, ed., *American Slave, Alabama Narratives*, vol. 6, p. 251.

LINDA GORDON
"The Powers of the Weak": Wife-Beating and Battered Women's Resistance

Heightened awareness of family violence in the present—an estimated 3 to 4 million American women are battered each year by their husbands or partners—has led to questions about battering in the past. Has wife-beating, which currently occurs among all races and socioeconomic groups, been a persistent aspect of family life? Have women always been more vulnerable to assault, injury, rape, and even murder from male partners than from other assailants?* How was family violence viewed in the past? Have views of both problem and solution changed over time?

Until very recently historians had no answers to such questions because family violence had so long been considered a personal rather than a social problem—the action of a particularly violent individual or evidence of a bad marital relationship. Just as the feminist movement of the 1970s took the lead in defining family violence as a social problem, heightening our awareness of its incidence and exposing its social basis, so, too, feminist historians in the 1980s produced the pioneering investigations that made family violence a subject of historical study.

Linda Gordon is one of those pioneers. Exploring case records of welfare workers serving poor immigrant families in Boston from 1880 to 1960, she found that definitions of domestic violence, like gender, have been constructed. She also discovered how those definitions changed as American thoughts on the family changed. Note her point about male dominance as the basis, not the cause, of wife-beating. What does she find to have been the causes of wife-beating in the families she studied? What approaches did these battered women use to enlist the support of social workers? What factors limited the ability of the latter to deal with the problem? How does Gordon explain the tendency of social workers in the 1930s through the 1960s to blame the victim rather than address her real needs?

The basis of wife-beating is male dominance—not superior physical strength or violent temperament (both of which may well have been effects rather than causes of male dominance), but social, economic, political, and psychological power. It is less useful to call male dominance the cause of wife-beating, because we usually mean something more specific when we speak of cause; after all, most men, including many very powerful and sexist men, do not beat women.[1] But it is male dominance that makes wife-beating a social rather than a personal problem. Wife-beating is not comparable to a drunken barroom assault or the hysterical

*Current information about domestic violence is taken from the National Women Abuse Prevention Project's "Domestic Violence Fact Sheets."

attack of a jealous lover, which may be isolated incidents. Wife-beating is the chronic battering of a person of inferior power who for that reason cannot effectively resist.

Defining wife-beating as a social problem, not merely a phenomenon of particular violent individuals or relationships, was one of the great achievements of feminism. Women always resisted battering, but in the last hundred years they began to resist it politically and ideologically, with considerable success. While that success is far from complete, it is important to recognize the gains, and to give credit where it is due. Wife-beating is now not only illegal but also, to a majority of Americans, shameful. . . . Moreover, women have gained substantially, if unevenly, in the economic and psychological strengths needed to escape abusive men.

If the achievements of feminism in countering wife-beating have been inadequately recognized, those of battered women themselves have been practically invisible. It is not a denial of their victimization to notice also their bravery, resilience, and ingenuity, often with very limited resources, in trying to protect and nurture themselves and their children. Elizabeth Janeway has eloquently called such gifts the "powers of the weak."[1a] . . . [I]n the process of protecting themselves, battered women helped to formulate and promulgate the view that women have a right not to be beaten. . . .

Wife-beating usually arises out of specific domestic conflicts, in which women were by no means always passive, angelically patient, and self-sacrificing. To analyze these conflicts, and women's role in them, does not mean blaming the victim, a common distortion in the literature on wife-beating. That women are assertive in domestic power struggles is not a bad thing; women's suppression of their own needs and opinions is by far the greater danger. . . . Examining the construction of specific marital violence in historical context may contribute to understanding how male supremacy worked and is resisted.

CHILD PROTECTORS AND THE PROTECTION OF WOMEN

It seems at first surprising that the United States, with the most powerful women's rights movement in the world, never produced a major campaign specifically directed against cruelty to women. Historian Elizabeth Pleck has unearthed records of a Chicago group for the protection of both women and children, but it was exceptional.[2] Why was there never a [Society for the Prevention of Cruelty to Women?] . . . Since the brutalizer of women and children had the same face—the drunken, brutal, poor immigrant male—women were defended within the defense of children. The issue of wife-beating was influential throughout the nineteenth-century women's-rights movement, but it was addressed primarily indirectly, through temperance, child-welfare, and social purity campaigns, and only marginally through direct lobbying for legislative or judicial reforms regarding wife-beating.

Temperance in the nineteenth century had been in many ways a proto-feminist movement, reflecting the gradual development of a critique of male supremacy. The image of the beaten wife, the indirect victim of drink, was prominent in temperance rhetoric from the 1830s.[3] In the latter half of the century, particularly in the work of the Women's Christian Temperance Union, drinking was a veritable code word for male violence.[4] . . . [T]emperance agitation . . . made drunkenness a gendered vice—male. . . . [A]t the peak of the anti-alcohol agitation, there was no question but that Prohibition was considered a women's victory, and that political "wets" were expected to be hostile to women's rights. . . .

The feminist campaign for divorce also allowed the telling of shocking stories about wife-beating.[5] Some women's rights leaders took on wife-beating as a political struggle directly, primarily by publicizing particular cases involving victimized women of substantial social standing. Feminists sheltered runaway wives, agitated in particular divorce and child-custody cases, held a few public meetings on egregious cases of injustice—and used these cases to argue again for women's right to divorce and to vote.[6]

A small campaign for increased criminal prosecutions and severe sentences, including corporal punishment, for wife-beaters, beginning in the late 1870s, was led almost exclusively by men. Women and feminists were conspicuously absent, probably lacking in enthusiasm for violent remedies to violence. This campaign illustrates another source of the new opposition to wife-beating: a specifically male objection to this form of coercing women, as signifying an unacceptable pattern of masculinity.... Middle-class reformers argued that brutality against the weak was "unmanly," cowardly.... [M]asculinity required self-control, containment, rule through authority—i.e., symbolic force—which required no violence to impose itself. The new fatherhood, moreover, implied a distance from home and children which in turn entailed entrusting substantial autonomy over the household to women.... [These reformers believed that] the ... sexual division of labor characteristic of the urban middle class ... should minimize conflict between husband and wife, and the latter should be in charge of domestic matters....

The condemnation of wife-beating and child-beating ... had made substantial progress by the late nineteenth century.... [W]ife-beating ... was considered a disreputable, seamy practice, and was effectively illegal in most states of the United States by 1870.[7]

Although wife-beating was not widely considered legitimate, neither was public discussion of it.... [I]t is not surprising [, therefore,] that child-protection clients also opted for an indirect approach. In the strategies adopted by these battered women, we can see the outlines of a veritable history of the changing meanings of wife-beating among the immigrant working class. Many of the pre-industrial communities from which these clients, largely immigrants, had come tolerated a male privilege to hit ("punish") wives. However,... [u]nlimited family violence was never tolerated, and there were always standards as to what constituted excessive violence....

... [I]n the nineteenth and early twentieth centuries, many women clients did not seem to believe they had a "right" to freedom from physical violence. When social workers expressed disgust at the way they were treated, the clients sometimes considered that reaction naïve. They spoke of the inevitability of male violence.... [But] these women were [not] passive.... They often resisted assault in many ways: fighting back, running away, attempting to embarrass the men before others, calling the police. And they did express moral outrage if their men crossed some border of tolerability. There is no contradiction here. The language of absolute "rights" is only one legitimate approach to self-defense. In a patriarchal system there were neither institutions nor concepts de-

fending absolute rights, but rather custom and bargaining. Because the client women did not conduct a head-on challenge to their husbands' prerogatives does not mean that they liked being hit or believed that their virtue required accepting it....

What was new in the nineteenth-century middle-class reform sensibility was the notion that wife-beating was entirely intolerable. Family reformers proposed, like abolitionists toward slavery and prohibitionists toward drink, to do away with physical violence in marriage altogether.... By contrast, many poor battered women had a more complex view of the problem than their benefactors: welcoming all the help they could get in their individual struggles against assault, they also needed economic help in order to provide a decent family life for children. Given a choice, they might have preferred economic aid to prosecution of wife-beaters.

Feminist reformers also avoided women's violence toward men, whether offensive or defensive. The Victorian sensibility made them feel they should offer charity only to "true women," peaceful and long-suffering. There were political advantages to their myopia: they kept the focus on battered women and declined to redefine the problem as mutual marital violence; they knew that it was a whole system of male power, not just physical violence, that made women battered.[8] On the other hand, their view of women's proper role ruled out the possibility that women could create independent lives and reject violent husbands. To these nineteenth-century child-savers, women's victimization meant virtue more than weakness; women who submitted to abuse were more praised than those who left their husbands. For example, in the random sample of this study, battered women frequently left or kicked out their husbands, then repeatedly reconciled or reunited with them.[9] In the 1960s such a record would probably have made a social worker question a woman's sincerity and doubt the point of continuing to offer help. In the nineteenth century these women's ambivalence was interpreted as evidence of their commitment to fulfilling wifely duties.

A "RIGHT" NOT TO BE BEATEN

Women's invention of a right not to be beaten came from a dialectic between changing social possibilities and aspirations. When women's best hope was husbands' kindness, because they were economically dependent on marriage, they did not protest violations of their individual rights but rested their case on their importance as mothers. As women's possibilities expanded to include wage-earning, remarriage after divorce, birth limitation, and aid to single mothers, their best hopes escalated to include escape from marital violence altogether.

For example, in the earlier decades of this study, several women clients complained bitterly about their husband's obscene language. A 1916 wife who had left her husband agreed that she would "keep his house if he would treat her respectfully and use decent language before the chn."[10] A 1920 mother thought her husband's "dirty mouth" was "the hardest thing we have to bear in this house, harder even than [his] not working."[11]

By far the most striking and consistent women's complaint, however, through the 1930s, focused on their husbands' non-support rather than abuse. . . . In 1910 a mother who was permanently crippled by her husband's beatings, who had appeared to the police and her priest so badly bruised that they advised her to have him arrested, complained to the [Massachusetts Society for the Prevention of Cruelty to Children] (MSPCC) only about his failure to provide.[12] In 1901 a young mother complained only about non-support; the abuse then uncovered was so severe that an MSPCC agent began making secret plans to sneak the mother and two children out of the house after the father had gone off to work![13]

In approaching child-saving agencies, the mothers had to present evidence of mistreatment of children. . . . They emphasized non-support not because they considered it more unbearable than beating, but because they thought it was a more criminal and therefore actionable grievance to social workers. These women believed that they had a claim on the community, as represented by the social-work agencies, for their support by husbands, but not to protection from physical violence in marriage. Nineteenth-century women also used the courts to bring wife-beating charges, but with little success. . . .

Surprisingly, women's complaints about wife-beating escalated just as feminism was at its nadir. The 1930s were the divide . . . after which the majority of women clients complained directly rather than indirectly about wife-beating. In 1934, for example, a young mother of three, married through a matchmaker at sixteen to an Italian-born man, repeatedly made assault-and-battery complaints against him. He was also a non-supporter, but her logic differed from that of earlier clients, and it was the beating that appeared actionable to her. It should not be surprising that this was an American-born woman much younger than her immigrant husband, a woman who may have had higher or perhaps less conventional aspirations than was the average among family-violence clients. Her husband's probation officer described her as a "high-type Italian," and the caseworker thought she expected "people to do things for her."[14] . . .

In other cases in [1940], women rationalized their battering in new ways: not as an inevitable part of the female condition, as a result of the male nature, but as something they individually deserved. One woman said, "This is my punishment for marrying against my mo.'s wishes."[15] Even in blaming themselves women expressed a new sensibility that wife-beating should not be the general lot of women.

Wife-beating accusations stood out even more [in these later years] because of the virtual disappearance of non-support complaints. . . . [E]conomic dependence [may have] prevented women's formulation of a sense of entitlement to protection against marital violence, but it also gave them a sense of entitlement to support; by contrast, the growth of a wage labor economy, bringing unemployment, transience, and dispersal of kinfolk, lessened women's sense of entitlement to support from their husbands, but allowed them to insist on their physical integrity. It is a reasonable hypothesis that the Depression, by the leveling impact of its widespread unemployment, actually encouraged women regarding the possibilities of independence.

An oblique kind of supporting evidence for this process of consciousness change is provided by wife-beaters' defenses, . . . [which are] important evidence of a consensus among men about the services they expected from wives—or about what complaints might be effective with social workers. Men accused of wife-beating usually countered that their wives were poor housekeepers and neglectful mothers, making themselves the aggrieved parties. The men's counter-accusations were, of course, a means of seeking to reimpose a threatened domination. Yet they simultaneously expressed a sense of an injustice, the violation of a traditional and/or contractual agreement, and their dismay at the historical changes that made women less able or willing to meet these expectations. . . .

Women as well as men professed allegiance to male-supremacist understanding of what relations between the sexes should be like. These shared assumptions, however, by no means prevented conflict. Women's assumptions of male dominance did not mean that they quit trying to improve their situations. . . .

By emphasizing mutual conflict as the origin of wife-beating, I do not mean to suggest an equality in battle. Marital violence almost always resulted in the defeat of women and served to enforce women's subordination. Nor did every act of marital violence emerge from an argument. Contestation could be chronic, structured into the relationship. Male violence often became a pattern, virtually normal, appearing regularly or erratically, without relation to any particular interaction. One man who eventually murdered his wife beat her because their children "had no shoe lacings."[16] Some men simply came home drunk and angry enough to hit anyone in the way. But their drinking, as we shall see below, was often an assertion of privilege, as was their violence an assertion of dominance.

Women's assertiveness against battering was both strengthened and limited by child-raising. Most wife-beating victims are mothers—even more so in the past than today, for women using birth control to defer child-bearing were unusual in this study. They negotiated living with their husbands not as individuals but as mothers responsible for children. We can see the impact of this double position of women—as themselves victims and as guardians of children—in the connections between wife-beating and violence against children. Wife-beating was most highly correlated with incest. . . . It was often correlated with child neglect—28 percent of battered women were also allegedly child neglecters. Only 13 percent of wife-beating victims were child abusers, but 41 percent of wife-beaters were also child abusers.[17]

Let us consider what these abstract correlations meant in real cases. One native-born family, recently moved to Boston from Utica, New York, was reported by neighbors for the father's great brutality. He was fifteen years older than his wife; married in 1903, they had six children at the case opening date in 1917 and were to have three more. Mr. Schmidt, a hard-working boilermaker, claimed that he chose to move his family to Boston because his mother-in-law and neighbors gave him a hard time; whatever his experience with the relatives, the result was that the family was isolated from kin. In 1917 we meet an abusive father, trying to accumulate enough money to buy the house they live in; his ambition escalates his abuse, and he overworks his children and turns over all but two rooms of the house to boarders. The social worker described Mr. Schmidt as energetic, industrious, wanting to get ahead; these qualities are valued and they serve to mitigate the condemnation of his violence. His ability to tyrannize his family members must have been extraordinary, because on one occasion when he claimed to have found his wife and visiting mother-in-law "a little drunk," he called his wife upstairs and she returned with a black eye! By 1922 the MSPCC agent sensed some deep exhaustion in Mrs. Schmidt and recommended that she take a vacation!—hardly a possibility for a woman with, by now, eight children. In 1924 the oldest daughter had married "a shiftless character" and Mr. Schmidt, holding his wife responsible, had beaten her for it; she came to the MSPCC trying to get this marriage annulled. Then in 1926 a male boarder was arrested for the rape of another daughter, sixteen. This girl, in telling her story, claimed that her father had often tried to force sexual relations with his wife in front of the children; the father alleged that his wife and daughter had jointly been having immoral relations with boarders. When asked about these things, Mrs. Schmidt could not speak but only cried. In 1928 the MSPCC filed a neglect complaint: the father and children were living in filthy conditions; Mrs. Schmidt was spending nights at home but leaving early in the morning and staying away from home, no one knew where, all day. When Mr. Schmidt lost his license to keep boarders because of the terrible conditions, she returned to housekeeping. The family reentered the agency records again in 1935, when Mrs. Schmidt was arrested for breaking and entering and was sent to the psychopathic hospital for observation; she was classified as an imbecile; the remaining children were committed to state guardianship.[18]

This case illustrates how a battered woman was transformed into a neglectful mother. Indeed, the process virtually deconstructed the woman's ego: a grown woman, about whom there is no hint of incompetence in 1917, is called an imbecile, with a mental age of 6.6 years, in 1934. She has no way of defending herself except to leave her children and becomes increasingly depressed and slack. . . .

The relationship between wife-beating and child abuse was different. "Triangular" conflicts involving parents and children often escalated marital conflict. Women were beaten for protecting children. Men also beat their wives in anger at their mothering: because the men considered them too lenient, or were jealous of the attention paid to children, for women were often more intimate with their children than with their husbands. One man threw a bread knife at his wife for "indulging" a baby by giving it milk in the middle of the night.[19] The structure of the family and, indeed, the whole sexual division of labor created implicit alliances of women and children against men. Many women got beaten because their husbands perceived their alliance with children as insubordinate; and children were beaten because of their attempts to defend their mothers.

While alliance with children made women vulnerable to male abuse, it also strengthened women, because defense of children against abuse was the factor most likely to increase women's resistance to battering. Women resisted the abuse of their children more than their own abuse, in the past as well as today. . . . They believed that they were obligated to protect their children and that they could expect help from outsiders in doing so, even when they did not seek or expect help for themselves. As mothers they felt entitled; as women, not.

THE CAUSES OF WIFE-BEATING

Today as in the nineteenth century, many people blame wife-beating on drinking.[20] . . . [T]he second wave of anti-wife-beating work was also affected by "temperance": the first U.S. battered women's shelters, opened in 1973 to 1974, were for wives of alcoholics, funded by Al-Anon and state money. . . .

It is only very recently that experts and ac-tivists have challenged this temperance orientation, and it is a radical challenge indeed. Associating wife-beating with drinking placed it in a male culture of recreation—or depravity, depending on the perspective—and kept it defined in trivial and fatalistic terms. It was a male foible, not a crime against women. By the twentieth century a man did not often claim the right to punish a wife; more often, the story was that he had lost control; it was a plea from weakness, not from authority.[21] Liquor provides the evidence of loss of self-control.[22]

But there is anthropological evidence that liquor does not in itself cause aggressive behavior, or even loosen inhibition against it; in different societies the conventional drunken behavior varies widely, suggesting that drunken behavior is itself learned.[23] Interviews with batterers conducted by EMERGE, an organization dedicated to reforming wife-beaters, show that they are enough in "control" to regulate the amount of injury they cause. Arresting and jailing wife-beaters has been shown to create immediate reductions in battering, providing evidence that when there are definite costs to the assailant, he can usually control his aggression.[24] Still, drinking and wife-beating are correlated. For example, in 67 percent of our cases, social workers or victims believed that drinking was a cause of wife-beating incidents. Does drunkenness cause wife-beating or do batterers drink in order to assault?[25] Our case records provide an opportunity to look closely at the relation between drinking and wife-beating.

These cases supplied little evidence that the physiological, chemical effects of alcohol were causes of wife-beating (or other forms of family violence). Rather, the social relations involved in drinking escalated hostilities. For example, liquor "caused" wife-beating because of its cost. Many couples fought about the sums spent, usually by the husband, on drink—i.e., drinking up the pay envelope instead of turning it over to the woman for housekeeping needs.[26] It is not that the women in these cases did not drink, although they appear to have drunk less than men. Rather, the major difference is that the women—mothers, it must be remembered—felt responsible for feeding their families. . . .

A related source of dispute was that men often drank in taverns, while women—again, mothers—were bound at home. Women were doubly enraged when the men not only drank but did so out of reach of remonstrance, enjoying a mobility which women did not have. Moreover, saloon camaraderie tended to escalate men's hostility to women, or at least consolidated and encouraged it. Anthropologist Ann Whitehead has given us an incisive participant-observer's view of that process in a British pub of the 1960s. She described how "firm" treatment of wives was encouraged, and how individual men who gave their wives "privileges," such as the right to go out with women friends, were ridiculed by their bar mates.[27] . . .

Another major source of marital conflict was money. . . . [W]omen's frequent complaints of non-support reflected the area in which they felt entitled; . . . conflicts *about* non-support detonated wife-beating. . . . [M]any wives interpreted their husbands' failure to support as willful. Women had few resources other than their husband in the task of supporting children. They simultaneously resented their dependency and the failure of those on whom they were dependent to make good their side of the presumed wage-labor bargain between the sexes. This is one of the reasons, along with the anger and depression it created in men, that unemployment intensified marital tensions.[28] . . .

Women frequently complained of inconsistency between what their husbands should have earned and what they were given for housekeeping. Even though few women had direct knowledge of the size of their husband's pay packet, most were clever at computing its approximate size. . . . Men not only felt persecuted by these complaints, and perhaps by the reminders of their inadequacy, but often blamed their wives. . . . [H]usbands accused their wives of poor budgeting. . . . One man responded to agency criticism of his violence by demanding that his wife be required to turn in accounts of what she had done with his money.[29] . . .

If liquor and money were two of the major sources of marital conflicts leading to violence, they were closely followed by work and sex. Indeed, all four were connected. Both men's and women's senses of their spouses' inadequacy as workers were of course escalated by poverty, and their sexual antagonisms were in part reflections of hostility provoked by other aspects of their relations.

Men's and women's discontent with each other's work took different forms for the reason that men were primarily engaged in wage labor, and in labor outside the home, while women were usually exclusively responsible for children. Men's adequacy as workers was therefore measured exclusively by their earnings, and women's anger at men's poor support was intensified by their responsibility for children. Women's and children's work was, by contrast, task-defined. Particularly immigrant men, accustomed to a family economy, sometimes claimed patriarchal powers to deploy their family's labor. For example, in 1917 a man forced his older children to work and turn over their wages, the younger children to work in a vegetable patch, and his wife to care for many boarders, beating them all if he was dissatisfied with their performance.[30]

Women's work, moreover, because it consisted primarily of housekeeping and mothering labor, had intense emotional meanings for other family members. Men's dependence on that labor, and its symbolic affirmation of his domination and her submission, made them vulnerable to extreme disappointment and frustration if it was not forthcoming. Women's rage at non-supporting husbands could be substantial, but, on the evidence of these case records, it never approached in intensity, bitterness, and self-pity the rage of men at wives they considered inadequately caring. . . .

Husbands' laments were often very specific. One 1916 father described his wife as putting dirty clothes to soak in the sink and leaving them there for weeks until they "rotted" and she threw them away.[31] Moreover, it is clear that the men were complaining not only on their children's behalf but also on their own. "She cooks only when she is hungry";[32] "She refuses to put up lunches for him in the morning so he is forced to buy his lunch. Sometimes he is forced to buy his breakfast. He comes home nights and she refuses to cook meals."[33] The intensity of these complaints suggests the men's sense of entitlement to wives who took care not only of children but also of husbands.

Despite the common cultural image of the shrewish wife, violent husbands did not cite wives' nagging in their defense until after World War II. The word "nagging" had been in use since the early nineteenth century, and its synonyms for many centuries. But in comparison to the intensity of men's anger at women's failure to fulfill labor, sexual, and reproductive duties, these poor men did not display much demand for harmony in marriage.

In many ways marital battles about sex took a form similar to those about work. Spouses had conflicting—and changing—ideas of their obligations and entitlements. The single most common sexual grievance expressed in the case notes was wives' charges that their husbands made excessive and/or perverse sexual demands. From 1917 to 1934 (the period after detailed record-keeping began, and before modern "sexual-liberation" ideas came to dominate social work interpretation), over one-fifth of wife-beating cases contained such accusations by wives.[34] "Excessive sexual demands" was the usual code in which social workers noted the complaint, but occasionally the women's insistence led to the inclusion of specifics in the notes, usually referring to demands for anal intercourse, fellatio, sex in front of witnesses, and enforced prostitution.[35] In some cases the men's controlling motivations could be distinguished from their sexual ones. For example, a 1934 Italian man told his wife whenever he saw her dressed up, "it's time for you to have another baby."[36] . . .

Fear of pregnancy was only rarely articulated as part of women's resistance to these sexual demands. As one woman in 1931 said, "she does not have anything to do with fa as she has all the chn she can handle now on the amount of money he gives her to run the house on." But her emphasis was on money, and she implied that if he would give her more housekeeping money, she would sleep with him—a fairly direct exchange of money for sex.[37]

Before about 1934 there was also a marked conflict of standards between male clients and social workers. The latter did not accept the assumption that wives owed sexual availability to their husbands, but retained a rather Victorian suspicion of male sexual demands and sympathy for women's right to refuse. Thus husbands were not able to defend their violence on the grounds of sexual frustration or deprivation. This lack of sympathy from social workers may help explain why so many husbands accused of sexual excess responded by accusing their wives of "immorality." Most frequently, these were allegations of unspecified "running around," not accusations of specific liaisons with specific lovers. It appears that they were, however, not only responses to agency workers but also expressive of intense jealousy, as they were often accompanied by wives' complaints of their husbands' attempts to seclude and imprison them. . . .

A remarkable change in the nature of these sexual recriminations was evident after the 1940s. The very complaints that had previously been recorded as allegations of "sexual excess" were now rendered as evidence of female frigidity and sexual withholding. For example, in one 1950 case we meet exactly the same frank articulation that marriage entailed an exchange of sex for money that we met in the 1931 case. The client said that "she used refusal of intercourse as a weapon so that he would turn over his paychecks to her . . . it seemed to be the only way." For this she was condemned and his non-support ignored, as were her allegations that he was a drunkard, an abuser, a non-supporter, intensely jealous and unnaturally suspicious, and had threatened her with a knife.[38] An MSPCC social worker wrote the following analysis of a marital problem in her 1960 case notes:

> [Father began] to act out a good deal, drinking, getting into trouble, killing a pedestrian [sic]. According to mo, fa was quite insistent sexually. (It is my feeling that mo is probably very frigid.) He used to have to beat mo down to have intercourse with her . . .[39]

Denial of work and sex converge when one partner in a relationship threatens to leave. Such threats may have been the most dangerous acts of all for women in battering relationships: much of the marital violence in this study was aimed at forcing a wife to remain.[40] As employment, welfare provisions, and custom made it more possible for women to leave their husbands, the proportion of violence representing attacks on women trying to leave marriages may have increased. In a study of domestic murder in Australia, Judith Allen showed a steady increase in the citing of women's "desertion" as a precipitating factor in homicides by men: 40 percent of 1880s cases, 56 percent of 1900–1909 cases, 77 percent of 1920s cases, 81 percent of 1930s cases.[41]

VICTIMS' RESISTANCE

While the first-wave women's movement had asserted women's right to personal freedom even in marriage, it had not provided any organized, institutional means for poor women to secure and defend that right, a power which was necessary for women really to believe in their own entitlement. Until the revival of feminism and the establishment of battered-women's shelters in the 1970s, wife-beating victims had three resources: their own individual strategies of resistance; the help of relatives, friends, and neighbors; and the intervention of child-welfare agencies. None was adequate to the task. The first two were easily outweighed by the superior power of husbands and the sanctity of marriage itself, and the last did not well represent the interests of the women themselves. Still, on some occasions victims were able to use these inadequate resources to construct definite improvements, if not permanent solutions.

Women in abusive relationships with men still face great difficulties in extricating themselves. These difficulties in turn weaken their ability to insist that the men's behavior change, since the woman's threat to leave is often her most powerful lever and his only incentive to change. Such difficulties were greater fifty or one hundred years ago, and greater for the poor and uneducated women who dominated in these cases. . . . The biggest obstacle for most women facing abusive men was that they did not wish to lose their children; indeed, their motherhood was for most of them (including, it must be emphasized, many who were categorized as abusive or neglectful parents) their greatest source of pleasure, self-esteem, and social status. In escaping they had to find a way simultaneously to earn and raise children in an economy of limited jobs for women, little child care, and little or no reliable aid to single mothers. They had to do this with the often low confidence characteristic of women trying to take unconventional action. Moreover, these women of the past had the added burden of defying a social norm condemning marital separation and encouraging submission as a womanly virtue.

Mrs. O'Brien, for example, changed her mind repeatedly about how she wanted to deal with her problem, and her seeming ambivalence reflects the lack of options she and so many others had. Living with a husband so brutal even the police advised her to have him arrested, she told them, speaking for thousands, "She does not want to lose her chn. however and the little money which she does receive from fa. enables her to keep her home together." Instead, she tried to get the MSPCC agent to "scare" him into treating her and her children "right." This was, arguably, impossible, since previous jail terms had not "reformed" him. She agreed to another prosecu-

tion at one point of rage—"would rather starve than endure the treatment"—then changed her mind and agreed to let him return to live with her if he would give her all his wages. The MSPCC then got her to agree that it would collect $10 per week from him and give it to her. When he agreed to this, she raised her demand to $11 per week, evidently dreading taking him back. But he agreed to this too, and three months later he was sentenced to six months for assaulting her; she was pregnant and soon began campaigning to get him out of jail. This pattern continued for years; in 1914 and again in 1920 she was threatening to murder him, describing herself as in a "desperate state of mind."[42]

Mrs. O'Brien's ambivalence was a rational response to her situation. Her children, numbering six by 1920, literally forced her into submission to her husband. Her problems illustrate the limited usefulness of prosecution as a remedy in the absence of economic provisions for single mothers. (It also suggests why prosecution might have different meanings today, when greater employment opportunities, ADC, and shelters offer women somewhat more chance of survival alone with their children.) But Mrs. O'Brien, like many victims, believed in the potential benefit of prosecution as a deterrent; this was not an option forced on her by social control agents. The resulting contradictory behavior was common. Many women prosecuted and then withdrew their complaints or petitioned for pardons for their husbands. . . . Elizabeth Pleck's tentative conclusion that black and immigrant women were more likely than other women to complain to the police for wife-beating may indicate that prosecution was a weapon of last resort, and that native-born women, with more resources, more likelihood of being adequately supported by husbands, and more respectability to protect, feared the stigma of dealing with police and courts.[43]

Batterers also knew women could not seek prosecution for fear of losing economic support. One husband threatened that "if she ever sues for divorce or separation or if she ever has him brought into court . . . he will throw up his job and then she will be without support . . ."[44] . . .

Mrs. O'Brien's ultimate desire, having rejected prosecution as a solution, was for a "separation and maintenance" agreement, as such provisions were then known: she wanted the state to guarantee her the right to a separate household and require her husband to pay support. Such plans were the most common desire of the beaten wives in this study. As another woman explained to a caseworker, also in 1920, "She did not wish him to be put away as he is a steady worker but wd. like the case arranged so that he wd. live apart and support her and the chn."[45] Mrs. O'Brien managed to get aid from the new Massachusetts mothers' pension program in 1920, but only after she had been struggling against her husband's abuse for at least ten years, he having built up a record of convictions and jail terms for assault and non-support.

Failing to get separation-and-maintenance agreements, and unable to collect support even when it was promised, the remaining option—called desertion—was taken only by the most depressed, disheartened, and desperate women. . . . The low female desertion rate revealed the strength of women's attachment to their children. Moreover, the guilt and stigma attached to such action usually meant that women "deserters" simultaneously cut themselves off from friends and kin. All in all, it was unlikely that ridding themselves of the burdens of children would lead to better futures for wife-beating victims.

Another response to beatings was fighting. For differing reasons, both feminists and sexists have been reluctant to recognize or acknowledge women's physical aggression. Yet fighting was common and accepted among poor women of the past, more so than among "respectable" women and contemporary women.[46] Fourteen percent of the marital violence cases contained some female violence—8 percent mutual violence and 8 percent husband-beating.

Most of the women's violence was responsive or reactive. This distinguished it from men's violence, which grew out of mutual conflict, to be sure, but was more often a regular tactic in an ongoing power struggle. . . . Women's violence toward husbands in these records fell into three typical patterns. The most common was mutual violence. Consider the 1934 case of an Irish Catholic woman married to a Danish fisherman. He was gone at sea all but thirty days a year, and there was violence whenever he returned. One particular target of his rage was Catholicism: he beat his sons, she claimed, to prevent them going to church with

her and loudly cursed the Irish and the Catholics—he was an atheist. The neighbors took her side, and would hide her three sons when their father was in a rage. The downstairs tenants took his side. They reported that she swore, yelled, hit him, and chased him with a butcher knife; that she threw herself down some stairs to make it look as if he had beaten her. Amid these conflicting charges it was certain, however, that she wanted to leave her husband, but he refused to let her have custody of the children; after a year of attempted mediation, the MSPCC ultimately lent its support for a separation.[47] In this case the woman responded with violence to a situation that she was eager to leave, while he used violence to hold her in the marriage. Her violence, as well as her maintenance of neighborhood support, worked relatively effectively to give her some leverage and ultimately to get her out of the situation. An analogous pattern with the sexes reversed could not be found—indeed, probably could not occur. Women's violence in these situations was a matter of holding their own and/or hurting a hated partner whom they were not free to leave. . . .

A second pattern consisted of extremely frightened, usually fatalistic wives who occasionally defended themselves with a weapon. In 1960, for example, the MSPCC took on a case of such a woman, underweight and malnourished, very frightened of her profane, abusive, alcoholic, and possibly insane husband. One day she struck him on the head so hard he had to be hospitalized.[48] This is the pattern that most commonly led, and leads, to murder. Female murderers much more commonly kill husbands or lovers than men do; the overwhelming majority (93 percent) claim to have been victims of abuse.[49]

In a third pattern, the least common, women were the primary aggressors. One 1932 mother, obese, ill, described as slovenly, kicked and slammed her six children around, locked them out of the house, knocked them down the stairs, and scratched them, as well as beating her husband and forcing him and an oldest daughter to do all the housework. His employer described him as "weak and spineless, but very good-hearted." Ultimately this woman was committed to a state mental hospital at her own request on the basis of a diagnosis of an unspecified psychosis.[50]

Of the three patterns of female violence,

the latter two usually involved extremely distressed, depressed, even disoriented women. The fighting women in mutual violence cases were not depressed, and may have been better off than more peaceful ones. Over time there appeared to be a decline in mutual violence and women's aggression.[51] The apparent decline in women's violence was offset by an increase in women's leaving marriages. A likely hypothesis is that there is a trade-off between women's physical violence and their ability to get separations or divorces. . . .

SOCIAL-WORK RESPONSE

Battered women turned to child-protection agencies in part because of the inadequacy of police protection.[52] Women not only expected more sympathy from social workers but also wanted something beyond the powers of the police, particularly separation and maintenance agreements. But such agreements, establishing female-headed households, provoked opposition. . . . Caught in a contradictory set of constraints—attempting to shore up two-parent families, failing to find levers with which to reform violent men—many social workers and their supervisors tried to ignore wife-beating. When it could not be ignored, caseworkers, especially those of a therapeutic orientation, began to define it as a problem for the woman to work on.

For several reasons a woman-blaming response to wife-beating became more pervasive after the 1930s. Changes in social work procedures created a structural imperative to map the problem onto the client who was present and influenceable. In the early years of child protection, caseworkers tried to reform men. The unembarrassed moralism of the earlier period, combined with the wider range of pre-professional techniques, gave agency workers a choice of tactics to influence male behavior: they hectored, threatened, and cajoled; they used short jail sentences, frequent home visits, including surprise visits, visits to employers and relatives; and they dunned non-supporting men for money. As professionalized casework concentrated on office visits, fewer men were seen. Moreover, women were more introspective and self-critical—more productive in casework. Men infrequently originated cases, were rarely willing to meet with caseworkers, and were more defensive about their own behavior.

In search of any ways to influence troubled families, social workers not unnaturally focused on those most open to influence.

More fundamentally, blaming family problems on women was part of a change in family and gender ideology evident by the 1930s. . . . Women were no longer pictured as helpless in the manner of the nineteenth-century victim, and indeed, women were not so helpless, having greater ability to divorce and create separate households or new marriages than they had had earlier. As child neglect became, virtually by definition, a sign of maternal inadequacy, so did marital violence become a sign of wifely dysfunction. "Instead of aligning our agency with the mother," the MSPCC reported in 1959, "we felt it only proper to have the father present his side of the picture. . . . The mother was seen and, instead of encouraging her laments about her husband, efforts were made to help her to understand his needs and the strains he was under."[53]

After World War II a particularly intense anxiety about wifely sexual and gender maladjustment became evident. Nor was there parallelism: if men suffered similar maladjustment, no one noticed. Freudian thought influenced many caseworkers in this direction, with its story that women's maturity required self-sacrifice and renunciation. But the social workers' concern about maladjusted women was also an observation of the stresses of actual social and economic change, the conflicts women were experiencing between earning and housekeeping, raised aspirations and continued constriction of opportunity, public rights and continued subordination. They had to counsel women to perform in contradictory ways. . . .

Caseworkers frequently offered analyses that deepened women's double binds. For example, although accepting the necessity for marital separation at times, both child-protection and psychiatric social workers communicated to women their convictions that being single was always undesirable, not only for children—"no man in the house with whom he can identify"—but also for adult women. . . . A woman who had left her husband was criticized for enjoying her job too much, allegedly putting it ahead of her child.[54] Some caseworkers remained intolerant of divorce in any situation. An MSPCC agent in the 1950s repeatedly urged a battered wife to reconcile with her husband despite her long struggle to leave. The story is consistently written in terms critical of her. For example, "fa had social disease before married of which he informed mo but she willingly accepted him and later she contracted same from fa . . . Mo finds fault w fa bec he is not gay and does not want to go places. . . . refuses to associate w her friends." The wife agreed to reconsider her current plan to separate if the agent would "restrain fa from using his fists. Agt warned mo that she places emphasis on the wrong values and that she should learn to distinguish between undesirable acquaintances and the genuine love of a devoted husband."[55] . . .

Not all social workers were so . . . insensitive. In another MSPCC 1950s case, also originated by a husband's neglect complaint against his wife, the caseworker was originally hostile to the wife because she drank. Within four months this analysis was revised to the diagnosis that wife-beating was the root of the problem, of which her drinking was a symptom.[56] In every period there were caseworkers who listened well and helped clients to value their own resources, both personal and social. But the success stories usually involved exceptionally tenacious, determined clients.

The denial of wife-beating was expressed in the language. By the 1940s gender-neutral euphemisms like marital discord and marital disharmony began to dominate.[57] Where the violence was directly named by the women, social workers sought to probe "deeper." For example, in 1960, a woman told the worker that "fa had thrown her onto the floor. Worker said that she did not believe that mo had to accept this from fa but that if mo removed the cause for fa's doing this, namely mo's excessive drinking, and inability to get along with fa [sic], perhaps this would never have happened."[58] This language not only places onto the woman the responsibility for "getting along" with a violent man but, through use of the passive, makes it appear as if the violence just "happens"; there is no attribution of responsibility. Women's attribution of responsibility to their husbands was an infantile "blaming," a denial of adult responsibility.[59]

These analyses became psychologized. . . . Masochism was a repeated diagnosis.[60] An MSPCC agent wrote in 1956,

> She did say he was very abusive to her when he was drunk and it was difficult to ascertain if

mo derived masochistic pleasure in the abuse or if she is too limited because of physical disabilities and emotional difficulties to do anything about the situation.[61]

These kinds of diagnoses emerged even in cases in which workers were obviously sympathetic to the women. A Polish-American woman from a rigid and religious family was seduced with a promise of marriage by a Protestant man twelve years her senior, who then refused to marry her. She had three out-of-wedlock children with him and was distraught with guilt. His non-support finally sent her to the Catholic Charity organization, which forced him to marry her. He had beaten her severely throughout their relationship and she retaliated by refusing to sleep with him as soon as they were married, using sex as a lever to get money from him: "that was one thing she didn't like to do but it seemed the only way." In 1950, in a drunken rage, he had beaten their son so badly that she overcame her fears and left, returning to her parents. Her caseworker said of her, with sympathy as well as condescension, "I think it becomes quite a problem just how one can make life have more meaning for these women . . . bitter for having to return home with the children and live with their parents with no husband. . . ." (One might suspect, on the contrary, that she would be feeling elated.) Working part-time as a dishwasher, she was diagnosed as a "woman who doesn't like making a home and probably didn't want children." (One might surmise, on the contrary, that her work reflected her concern to support her children decently.) Worried that men made "passes" at her, she expressed her characteristic sexual guilt, wondering "if she looks tough or hard or if she in some way unconsciously encourages without really meaning to." The social worker responded, "I tell her that the latter is possible." The clinicians were concerned about the "feminization" of her seven-year-old son, his "castration fear . . . given frightening reality by the accidental loss of his eye. . . . I wonder if this so-called accident—this loss of the eye—wasn't provoked by him." His mother, of course, is the castrator, because she "banished" the father from the home. (In fact, she had to leave the home, lacking the power to banish him.) The fact that the boy reportedly told his mother, "Mummy I won't chase you with a knife like Daddy did," might suggest an alternative explanation for the boy's castration fears, if they existed, but this alternative was not explored.[62]

WIFE-BEATING, GENDER, AND SOCIETY

Wife-beating arose not just from subordination but also from contesting it. Had women consistently accepted their subordinate status, and had men never felt their superior status challenged, there might have been less marital violence. To focus on women's "provocations," and to examine men's grievances against their wives, is not to blame women but, often, to praise them. It is to uncover the evidence of women's resistance.

To some extent the female gender itself has been influenced by millennia of violence, and a socialization toward passivity. But the relationship between battering and femininity is more complex. Women have been as aggressive, irrational, and self-destructive as men in marital conflict. But by and large, because women had the most to lose in relationships structured by coercion, women developed greater cooperative, socially manipulative skills. Their much-reputed wicked tongues were evident in these case records. Indeed, women's verbal skills were often honed to sharpness precisely to do battle against men's superior power, including violence. Their verbal style was a better tool for creating familial and community cohesion than was violence. This superiority was not, however, a result of moral superiority, as the nineteenth-century reformers believed; rather, it was a collective characteristic developed as a result of the structural position of the gender.

Wife-beaters' behavior was also highly gendered. Accustomed to supremacy, acculturated to expect service and deference from women, and integrating these expectations into the ego itself, men were understandably disoriented to encounter resistance and unskilled at negotiating compromises. Within this context, some men have a smaller range of responses to anger, less constructive responses to stress and frustration than others. Wife-beaters are by no means commonly crazy or even temporarily disoriented, but they may indeed have more self-destructive behaviors than less violent men. We have seen how wife-beating was commonly associated with heavy drinking, desertion, and sexual abuse of children. Men's plea of loss of self-control as an extenuating factor was not convincing, as I have argued above, but it expressed a subjective experience of weak ego.

The batterers I have described were not ideologues defending the dominance of their sex. Neither were they necessarily insecure. They were using violence to increase their control over particular women, defending real, material benefits. Beatings kept women from leaving, kept them providing sexual, housework, and child care services (or were intended to do so).[63] Wife-beating was not usually a mere emotional expression of annoyance, or a symbolic display of power. It did not result from an individual man's "need" to demonstrate masculinity; if masculinity was threatened, that threat arose in a struggle with another person. Some beatings resulted from demands for deference or from conflicts about status, apparently symbolic issues. But in these relationships the symbolism of power functioned to organize and reinforce real power relationships, which in turn provided real benefits and privileges to the "boss." . . .

Batterers were not necessarily conscious of their goals. Often they felt so wounded by women's behavior, and so desperately longed for a wife's services, that they experienced their violence as uncontrollable; they felt they had no recourse. Their sense of entitlement was so strong it was experienced as a need. Their wives did not feel so entitled. And when, stimulated often by responsibility for children, they gave up trying to wheedle and pacify, and tried to escape, they found what they had always suspected: a set of obstacles, any one of which might have been definitive—poverty, motherhood, isolation, and the hostility or indifference of social control agencies. When the context is supplied, many seemingly ineffective responses to wife-beating, including resignation, pandering, and changes of mind, are revealed to be rational, trial-and-error, even experienced and skilled survival and escape tactics. . . .

NOTES

1. No studies to date have identified characteristics which distinguish wife-beaters from other men. The reason may be the either-or approach, some scholars looking for psychological disorders and others for social-stress factors, e.g., Frank A. Elliott, "The Neurology of Explosive Rage: The Dyscontrol Syndrome"; John R. Lion, "Clinical Aspects of Wifebattering," M. Faulk, "Men Who Assault Their Wives,"

and Natalie Shainess, "Psychological Aspects of Wifebattering," all in *Battered Women. A Psychosociological Study of Domestic Violence* ed. Maria Roy, (New York: Van Nostrand, 1977). . . .

1a. Elizabeth Janeway, *The Powers of the Weak* (New York: Alfred A. Knopf, 1980).

2. See her "Feminist Responses to 'Crimes against Women,' 1868–1896," *Signs* 8, no. 3 (Spring 1983):465–69. . . .

3. Jerome Nadelhaft, "Domestic Violence in the Literature of the Temperance Movement," unpub. paper, University of Maine, 1986.

4. Ruth Bordin, *Woman and Temperance. The Quest for Power and Liberty, 1873–1900* (Philadelphia: Temple University Press, 1981), e.g., p. 162; Barbara Leslie Epstein, *The Politics of Domesticity. Women, Evangelism and Temperance in Nineteenth-Century America* (Middletown, Conn.: Wesleyan University Press, 1981), e.g., p. 114.

5. For an early example of this propaganda, see *The Una* I, no. 6 (1855):84. . . .

6. "Address to the Legislature of New York on Women's Rights," 1854, in *Elizabeth Cady Stanton, Susan B. Anthony, Correspondence, Writings, Speeches,* ed. Ellen Carol DuBois (New York: Schocken, 1981), p. 95; Elizabeth Pleck, "Feminist Reponses to 'Crimes Against Women,' 1868–1896," *Signs* 8 no. 3 (Spring 1983):465–69.

7. Elizabeth Pleck, "Wife Beating in Nineteenth-Century America," *Victimology* 4, no. 1 (1979):60–74. . . .

8. The few cases of beaten husbands were not used, as they might have been later, to call attention to women's culpability, but the men were portrayed as "of low type," drunken, immoral. # 2008, 2561. [These numbers are based on the records of The Massachusetts Society for the Prevention of Cruelty to Children (MSPCC), The Boston Children's Service Association (BCSA), and the Judge Baker Guidance Center (JBGC). These numbers are not the actual case numbers assigned by the agencies, but part of a coding system devised by the author. See Gordon, pp. 301–303; 313–14.]

9. For just a few examples, #0315A, 0813A, 2003, 2008, 2054A, 2058A.

10. #3646.

11. #3240.

12. #2027.

13. #3363.

14. #4007A.

15. #4284.

16. #1825A.

17. Altogether 34 percent of all the cases of child mistreatment contained wife-beating. . . .

18. #2523.

19. #3363.

20. Margaret Borkowski, Mervyn Murch, Val Walker, *Marital Violence. The Community Response* (London: Tavistock, 1983), pp. 57–59.

21. The source of these particular records, of course, made that particular justification more popular, as the wife-beaters knew that social workers would be unreceptive to their claims of a right to hit a woman.

22. James Ptacek, "Wifebeaters' Accounts of Their Violence: Loss of Control as Excuse and as Sub-

jective Experience," M.A. thesis, University of New Hampshire, 1985.

23. Craig MacAndrew and Robert B. Edgerton, *Drunken Comportment: A Social Explanation* (Chicago: Aldine, 1969); Richard J. Gelles, *The Violent Home: A Study of Physical Aggression Between Husbands and Wives* (Beverly Hills: Sage, 1974), p. 114.

24. Lawrence W. Sherman and Richard A. Berk, "The Specific Deterrent Effects of Arrest for Domestic Assault," *American Sociological Review* 49, no. 2 (1984):261–72.

25. Murray Straus, Richard Gelles, Suzanne Steinmetz, "Violence in the Family: An Assessment of Knowledge and Research Needs," paper for AAAS, 1976, typescript, p. 32; Gelles, *The Violent Home,* pp. 116–17; Del Martin, *Battered Wives* (New York: Pocket Books, 1976), pp. 56– 58.

26. E.g., #2027, Richard Gelles found the same fighting about drinking in his contemporary study; ibid., e.g., pp. 161–63.

27. Whitehead, "Sexual Antagonism in Herefordshire," in *Dependence and Exploitation in Work and Marriage,* eds. Diana Leonard Barker and Sheila Allen (London: Longman, 1976), pp. 169–203.

28. For recognition of this influence of unemployment by other social observers, see, e.g., Mary C. Blehar, "Family Adjustment to Unemployment," summarizing Louis A. Ferman's research, in *Families Today: A Research Sampler on Families and Children,* ed. Eunice Corfman (Washington, D.C.: NIMH, 1979), pp. 413–39. . . .

29. #2008.

30. #2523.

31. #3101.

32. #3821A.

33. #3560A.

34. Eleven out of fifty-one.

35. #2523, 2548A, 3554A, 3560A, 3585, 3643, 4000, 4004A, 4100, 4141, 4284, 5560, 5601, 5740, 5743A, 6000, 6200, for examples.

36. #4284.

37. #6040.

38. #5740.

39. #6000. . . .

40. Contemporary studies of wife-beaters reveal the same pattern; in fact, separated and divorced women today are more often victimized by their estranged husbands than are women living with their husbands; e.g., Leroy G. Shultz, "The Wife Assaulter," *Journal of Social Therapy* 6, no. 2 (1960):103–12; Patsy A. Klaus and Michael R. Rand, *Family Violence* (Washington, D.C.: U.S. Department of Justice, Bureau of Justice Statistics, 1984).

41. Judith Allen, "The State and Domestic Violence," typescript, n.d.

42. #2027.

43. Pleck, "Wife Beating in Nineteenth-Century America," p. 65.

44. #6040.

45. #3040.

46. These case records contain, for example, instances of fights among women, particularly among neighbors, but also among family members.

47. #4060. See also, e.g., #2008, 2561, 3541, 3546, 5085.

48. #6042. See also, e.g., #3363, 5543.

49. Jane Totman, *The Murderess. A Psychosocial Study of Criminal Homicide* (San Francisco: R. and E. Research Associates, 1978), pp. 3, 48.

50. #3024. . . .

51. Particularly noticeable was the disappearance of women attacking other women. In the first decades of this study the random sample turned up several cases like that of a 1910 Irish-American woman who had "drinking parties" with other women, not infrequently ending in name-calling and fights; she and her daughter fought physically in front of an MSPCC agent; and her daughter was arrested for a fight with another girl. (See #2047.) . . .

52. Martin Rein, unpublished paper, quoted in Judith Areen, "Intervention Between Parent and Child: A Reappraisal of the State's Role in Child Neglect and Abuse Cases," *Georgetown Law Journal* 63, no. 3 (1975):919.

53. AR 1959, p. 9.

54. #5781.

55. #5040.

56. #5560.

57. E.g., #6041.

58. #6041.

59. E.g., #6081.

60. E.g., #6200, 6201.

61. #5585.

62. #5740.

63. Two works that make this argument are Susan Schechter's *Women and Male Violence: The Visions and Struggles of the Battered Women's Movement* (Boston: South End Press, 1982), chap. 9, and Emerson R. and Russell Dobash's *Violence Against Wives: A Case Against the Patriarchy* (New York: The Free Press, 1979).

MARGARET JARMAN HAGOOD

Of the Tenant Child as Mother to the Woman

In the midst of the Great Depression, President Franklin D. Roosevelt identified the South as the nation's number one "problem." Farm tenancy, sharecropping, eroding land, grinding poverty, and persistent illiteracy plagued the region; it also had the lowest rate of urbanization and the highest birth rate in the nation. These problems were human as well as economic, and they attracted the attention of a remarkable nucleus of scholars at the University of North Carolina at Chapel Hill who were interested not only in documentation but also in solutions. One of this small group was Margaret Jarman Hagood, who visited 254 carefully selected tenant houses in Piedmont North Carolina, Georgia, and Alabama to study "mothers of the South," as her book would be entitled when published in 1939. She brought to her task a fine blending of attributes that lent credibility to her work. As a professional sociologist, she used scientific methods of inquiry. As a wife and mother, she used the experience she shared with other women to overcome barriers of class and education so that she might enter the "distinctly feminine culture . . . centered around mating, child care and home-making" that she believed existed among these tenant farm women. (Note the woman's world that Carroll Smith-Rosenberg found among women of a different class and generation.) The portraits resulting from Hagood's study provide a glimpse into the lives of women who bore their poverty and powerlessness with stoic courage and strength. Hagood's study shows how cotton,

Dorothea Lange was working for the Farm Security Administration in the mid-1930s. Along with her colleagues Russell Lee and Roy Stryker, she documented the problems of farm tenancy in images that would become classic. This photograph was taken at a pea-picker's camp in Nipomo, California. Later Lange recalled, "I saw and approached the hungry and desperate mother, as if drawn by a magnet. I do not remember how I explained my presence or my camera to her, but I do remember she asked me no questions. I made five exposures, working closer and closer. . . . I did not ask her name or her history. She told me her age, that she was thirty-two. She said that they had been living on frozen vegetables from the surrounding fields, and birds that the children killed. She had just sold the tires from their car to buy food. There she sat in that lean-to tent with her children huddled around her, and seemed to know that my picture might help her, and so she helped me. There was a sort of equality about it." (Quoted in Milton Meltzer, Dorothea Lange: A Photographer's Life. *[New York: Farrar Straus Giroux, 1978]* Photograph courtesy of the Library of Congress)

tobacco, and children—the economic production of society and the physical *re*production of society—were intertwined in the lives of rural southern women.

The story of the tenant child begins more than a quarter of a century ago. On Monday ten-year-old Mollie woke up when her mother lifted the stove lid and began making the fire. She slipped from underneath the cover easily, so as not to disturb her little brother, and took down her last year's red dress, which had been fleecy and warm, but now was slick and thin. Their bed was in the log kitchen of the Goodwins' two-room cabin, which would be warm enough in a half hour for the sickly knee-baby, who slept with Mollie, to face the December morning. . . .

Mollie's plump arms stretched tight the seams of her outgrown dress, and as she leaned over to pick up fresh wood for the fire, she felt her dress split at the shoulder. She wondered what she would do the washing in if she couldn't get into the old dress next Monday or the one after that. Her father's rule was that her two new dresses of the same cotton fleece lined material, one red and one blue, must never be worn except for school or Sunday School. She had no sisters to hand down clothes to her, for the other four children were boys. Some girls she knew wore overalls for working, but her father would not allow that either. A wicked thought came to her mind—maybe if she had nothing to wear to wash in next Monday, she wouldn't have to wash and instead could go to school with her brothers. She could iron on Tuesday inside the house in her underwear—then a vision of her mother bending over the wash tubs, moaning with the pain in her back, made her put aside the daydream of a washless Monday.

After breakfast Mollie's older brother cut wood and started a fire under the wash pot while she and the brother next younger drew and carried water from the well. Then the boys left for the mile walk to the one-teacher school and Mollie started back for the house to get up the clothes. She lingered on the way, debating whether her father's overalls, stiff with a week's accumulation of winter mud and stable stains, were harder to wash than the baby's soiled diapers. They *were* harder, but the odor from the diapers made you feel you couldn't go on. It was a sensory symbol of babies, of her sick mother, of crying, little brothers, and now was vaguely mixed with her distaste for what two girl friends had told her at recess last week

about how babies come. Mollie tried not to think about this and hoped she never had any babies.

The school bell's ringing interrupted her musing and reminded Mollie of how much she wanted to be there. Her dress was as new as any in school and its color still bright. The teacher had smiled approvingly at Mollie last week when the visiting preacher pinched her dimpled cheek and said, "Miss Grace, you have a fine looking bunch of little girls." Mollie thought now of having, when she was grown, a dress like Miss Grace's Sunday one. The bell stopped ringing and Mollie resolved to stop thinking and to work very hard and fast. Once before she had finished all the washing in time to go back with the boys after dinner. And so she scrubbed with all her force against the washboard and paid no attention to the pain from her knuckles scraped raw.

By dinner time all the clothes were on the line and the first ones out already frozen stiff. Mollie, numbed by cold and fatigue, ate peas, fat pork, and cornbread without joining in the family talk. When she got up from the table, her back ached—she wondered how many years of washing it would take to make it as bent over as her mother's. She changed to her new dress in time to set off for the afternoon session of school. She pulled herself together to respond to the teacher's beaming look of approval for having come to school that afternoon, and then relaxed into a lethargy from weariness and missed words she knew in the Third Reader and was spelled down quickly. . . .

One stormy winter night three months before Mollie was twelve, she was put to bed early. Her father moved the trundle bed from the main room and all the children went to sleep in the kitchen—all but Mollie. She had a terrible feeling of impending disaster to her mother and herself. When she had asked her mother about babies not long before, her mother had told her she was going to have another and that something would happen to Mollie soon, too. From the front room Mollie heard groans and knew her mother was suffering. Her own body began to ache. Her mother's sounds grew louder and each time an anguished scream reached Mollie's ears, a shooting pain went through her. Hardly daring, Mollie reached down under the cover and felt that her legs were wet. All the boys were asleep and so she drew back the cover and in the moonlight saw black stains which had come from her body. Suddenly she thought she was having a baby. She tried to scream like her mother, but the terror of the realization paralyzed her. Fright overwhelmed her until she was no longer conscious of pain. She remained motionless for a long time, knowing and feeling nothing but a horrible fear of disgrace and dread. Then she became aware that the moaning in the next room had stopped and that someone had unlatched the kitchen door. Trembling, she eased out of bed and crept into her mother's room. There was a new baby lying on one side, but she slipped into the other side of the bed and nestled against her mother. The relaxing warmth and comfort of another's body released the inner tensions and Mollie melted into tears and weak, low sobs. Her mother stroked her but said nothing. She lay there for some minutes until the Negro "granny" said she must leave her mother and led her back to bed. Early in the morning she hid the soiled bedclothes in a corner until she could wash them secretly in the creek and found some cloths in her mother's drawer which she asked for without giving any reason. Not for two years, when a girl friend told her, did she have any instruction about how to fix and wear sanitary pads.

The summer Mollie was fourteen her mother persuaded Ben to buy her a silk dress. Mollie had worked so well that year that her father, in an appreciative mood, took her to town and let her select the material, which was a glamorous, changeable, rose and green taffeta. Mrs. Bynum helped her make it, and when her father consented to take the whole family to a Fourth of July celebration ten miles away, Mollie's cup overflowed with joy. She rolled up her hair in rags the night before. She helped bathe and dress the younger children two hours before leaving time so that she might extract the full delight from dressing leisurely in her new clothes for the first time. By eight o'clock in the morning, the family, now nine, piled into the wagon and set off. To keep from going through the county seat, they cut through a shorter, back road, which was rocky and went over steep hills. The boys got out and pushed on the

worst places, but Mollie sat on the bench with her mother and father—accorded special privileges because of her new dress. The jolting and hot sun bearing down were unnoticed for the joy anticipated in being the most beautifully dressed girl at the celebration. Mollie was scarcely aware of her family in the wagon as she rode along with her head in the clouds.

They reached the tabernacle, where there were to be political speeches interspersed with hymn singing contests between churches. Mollie hopped down lightly and was about to run over to join a group of girls she knew when her mother, climbing over the edge of the wagon more slowly, called her back and took her a few steps away from the wagon.

"Your dress is ruined behind," she whispered to Mollie, "you'll have to set still over here by this tree all day." Excitement and the jolting had brought on her menstrual period early and the realization of this brought about a flush of hot shame which obliterated the festive scene of picnic tables and merry people. Mollie's heart seemed to close up and with it her capacity to perceive or respond. Passively she allowed herself to be led to a sheltered spot under an oak with protruding roots which afforded a seat. The loss of her life's triumph and the indescribable embarrassment kept her from comprehending meanings. She felt that she was dead and after a while she leaned against the tree and slept. No one approached, for there seemed to be a tacit understanding of her plight. Late in the afternoon she rode home without speaking to her family. The next day she and her mother were unable to remove the stain from her dress and the beautiful taffeta was never worn. Her father never bought her another silk dress.

Two years later, Mollie finished the seventh grade at sixteen. The other girls were now having boys drop by their houses, but Ben Goodwin was known for his sternness and none came to see Mollie.

That summer one of Mrs. Bynum's many nieces went to a town in another county to work in a tobacco factory and her sister reveled in telling Mollie about the money she made and spent. They planned what sort of things Mollie could buy if she were to go to work in town. After weeks of whispered plans, the sister in town arranged for Mollie to have a job weighing and wrapping cigarettes. Without even telling her mother, Mollie bundled up her clothes and left early one morning, just as the cotton picking season was beginning. A neighbor boy drove her to town and she went to a relative of Ben's to board.

For four months Mollie worked in the tobacco factory and exulted in making $20 a week. This was during the postwar boom period and labor was scarce. As fast as the money came in, she spent $15 for a coat, $11 for high-top shoes, $8 for a hat, and smaller amounts for slippers, dresses, beads, and brooches. There were five other women boarding in the same house and Mollie's greatest delight was in the just-before-bedtime lunches they shared. Each one chipped in a nickel every night for cheese, crackers, and fancy canned things. Mollie had never before eaten "store bought" food and had never had even one cent to spend on self-indulgence. After she had bought an entire outfit of new clothes, she went to a county fair with the women. A boy who worked in the cigarette factory asked her to go with him, but she thought she would have a better time with the other women. This boy always hung around Mollie in the factory and said things she thought were fresh, but the landlady wouldn't allow her to go out with him. Once in December he asked Mollie to marry him but she laughed and said, "Why should I marry and keep house and have babies when I've got such a good job and can buy myself such fine clothes?"

Just before Christmas Ben Goodwin got someone to write a letter to Mollie for him. He told her she had to come back home, but that he would make arrangements for her to live during the week with an aunt in the county seat so that she could go to high school in town. Mollie cried and at first said she wouldn't go, but in the end she knew she had to mind her father. She spent her last week's wages buying presents for all the family and went home on Christmas Eve. The next day her mother took flu and one by one the children came down with it. The weakly brother's flu went into pneumonia and finally into tuberculosis, which required so much waiting on that Mollie didn't get to start to school after all.

The following summer Mollie's mother gave birth to her ninth child. It was in the daytime and the baby came in a hurry. No one was in the house except Mollie and the sick brother in the back room. Ben had gone for a doctor but not soon enough and the doctor did not get there in time. The suffering woman begged for help but Mollie did not know what to do. She even pled with Mollie to kill her and put an end to her tortures. Finally the baby was born, but with the covers pulled up so that Mollie could not see. The mother wrapped the baby up and let it lie there until the doctor came and cut the cord.

With a sick brother, a sickly mother, and a new baby in the house, Mollie had a busy summer. About the only times she had off from household duties were when she spent the night with her cousins or with Mrs. Bynum's nieces. On one such night the young people all went to watch a Negro revival meeting. While they were standing on the outside listening to the shouting through the windows, a man who knew some of the boys came up and joined them. His name was Jim and he was ten years older than Mollie, but he "took a shine" to her from their first meeting. For the rest of the summer he rode his mule for nine miles to come to see her whenever she could spend a night away from home, as Ben was still adamant about no sports coming into his house.

In the fall the brother was better and the original plan for Mollie to go to school in town was feasible. Because Ben had no buggy of his own, and because he wished so much to have his favorite daughter at home on week-ends, he finally consented for Jim to drive her out on Fridays and back to town on Sundays. His mule was the fastest one for miles around, but walked very slowly when Jim was taking Mollie home. This was when they did their courting, for Jim was never permitted to linger after delivering Mollie to her parents. He pressed his suit with urgency, for he was nearly thirty and felt it was time for him to be getting married. Mollie wasn't enjoying going back to school after being out for a year, since she was older than the town girls in her grade and felt awkward with them. She liked Jim although she never felt gay or excited with him the way she did with younger boys. She still did not want to think of marrying and settling down to repeat her mother's life—ruining her health and looks with overwork and childbearing. She made one last appeal to her father to let her go back to work in the cigarette factory, for her onetime job has remained to this day a symbol of money for clothes and luxuries. Ben would not consent, however; he said that factories were no place for his womenfolks and that she could never go back. And so Mollie gave Jim a lukewarm "yes" and they planned to marry on Christmas Day. . . .

Five years later Mollie was pregnant for the third time. She felt very hopeful because this was "the kickingest baby you ever felt." Her first child had been a girl, but a terrible disappointment to Mollie in looks. At four she was big, cumbersome, awkward, and slow moving, resembling her two-hundred-pound father so much that he was frequently told, "You couldn't deny that child if you wanted to!" The second baby was a boy, weakly and always crying just like the little brother Mollie used to sleep with and take care of. The alertness of the child she was now carrying promised better success.

Mollie showed more interest in everything that spring and summer. Jim's family had left them to go live and work in a cotton mill town and for the first time they were "tending" a farm and living in a house alone. Their family of four was the smallest she had ever cooked, cleaned, and washed for, and their tobacco crop looked good in July. She was glad Jim was raising tobacco instead of cotton because it meant more money in the fall. He was still kind about buying her one Sunday dress every year with the first tobacco money he got. Mollie was still pretty at twenty-three and during her nine months of pregnancy she often daydreamed of the child, who was to be a pert, attractive daughter whom she could dress daintily.

In midsummer when her time was nearing, the baby suddenly stopped moving one night, "right short like." Mollie knew that minute the baby was dead and alarmed she woke up Jim and told him about it. He reassured her, but on her insistence the next morning went to town and told the doctor about it. The doctor said there was nothing to do but wait, although it was eleven days before labor set in. The delivery was difficult for the dead fetus had begun disintegrating. The body was too much in pieces to be dressed for burial but they showed Mollie the face of her little girl and she thought it was the prettiest she had ever seen. Blood poison, complications, and a long illness afterwards made Mollie temporarily infertile and she had no more children for ten years.

At thirty-seven Mollie is again pregnant. She is not bitter about it, although she wishes doctors would tell you what to do when they say, "Now you shouldn't have any more children." She was quite surprised when she found she was "that way" four years ago, but she made up her mind she wouldn't hope or imagine anything because, "it's like counting your chickens before they're hatched." Then, too, Mollie has had many lessons in disappointment since her baby died. Several years there was not enough money even to "pay out," much less to buy the annual Sunday dress. Jim can't understand why he hasn't been able to buy a team. Of course, his labor force is small, but Mollie and the oldest daughter do almost full-time work in the summer. He has moved from one place to another in several counties trying to change his luck, but it has done no good. Mollie's greatest disappointment, next to the death of her pretty baby, was the year when they were living in a county where the land is supposed to be the best in the State for tobacco. Jim decided his luck had changed at last, for a week before time to begin priming, his tobacco was looking the finest of any crop he'd ever raised. He was so confident over the proceeds it would bring that he promised to give Mollie not only a finer dress than usual, but a permanent wave as soon as they sold the first load of tobacco. Mollie's straight hair had always been a source of dissatisfaction to her and she felt an almost girlish glow of anticipation over the thought of curls. Then hail came and tore the leaves, battered down the stalks, and ruined their tobacco crop. They had to sell their cow that year to pay up what they owed their landlord for furnishing.

And so Mollie, hoping no longer, was none the less delighted when her fourth child was again a pretty girl—not so pretty as the dead one, and a little plump, but much more nearly a replica of herself. Mollie began selling eggs to bring in a little money all during the year so she could buy cloth to make her daughter pretty clothes. At three now the little girl, always clean and dainty with a hair ribbon, seems incongruous with the meagerly furnished, not too well kept, three-room log cabin in which the family live. Mollie has already laid down the law that this child shall never have to do field work or heavy household tasks. She must go to school regularly and get an education so she can get a job early—"maybe a beauty parlor job"—and get away from farming with its hardships. . . .

Mollie doesn't worry too much about the child yet to be born. She is sorry about the trouble it will be, but she accepts the "Lord's will" here as she does when they have a bad crop year. She no longer expects to realize the goals of life herself, but has transferred her efforts to achieving them for her daughter. Last year she even chose to forgo the Sunday dress in order to buy a fur-trimmed coat for her baby. And yet Mollie is cheerful, except when impatient with her two older children, and works routinely at her farm and housework without complaint.

BETH BAILEY AND DAVID FARBER
Prostitutes on Strike: The Women of Hotel Street During World War II

On a Sunday afternoon the nation listened as radio announcers spoke in shocked tones of the Japanese attack on Pearl Harbor. The date was December 7, 1941. World War II would transform these then remote, ethnically diverse islands no less than the mainland as the military made Hawaii its midpoint stopover in the Pacific. For those returning from combat as well as for those going into it, the place to go in Honolulu was Hotel Street.

The following essay focuses on the women of Hotel Street, more particularly the sex workers who populated its brothels. Note the conditions of work, the complicity and concerns of military authorities, and the conflict between the military and the local police, who acted as agents of the local elite. Note, too, the way the prostitutes maneuvered to improve their lives. What did these women have in common with the battered women described by Linda Gordon? How did the Hotel Street prostitutes inadvertently serve to undermine Hawaii's racial hierarchy? In what other respects did their strategy foreshadow that of postwar civil rights activists?

Hotel Street was the center of Honolulu's eponymous vice district, through which some 30,000 or more soldiers, sailors, and war workers passed on any given day during most of World War II. . . . On Hotel Street, some of the most complex issues in America's history came together. Systems of race and of gender (complicated by both sex and war) structured individual experience and public policy. At the same time, the story of Hawaii's vice district revolves around the changing role of the State, as it asserted its interests in counterpoint to local elites. For most of the war Hawaii was under martial law, ruled by a military governor. Even if not fully by intention, agents of the federal government—ironically in the form of the military and martial law—emerged as limited guarantors of equality and created openings for social struggle. . . . A critical part of this struggle for power centered on prostitution and its control. . . .

Hotel Street was more than just brothels,

Excerpted from "Hotel Street: Prostitution and the Politics of War" by Beth Bailey and David Farber, in *Radical History Review* 52 (Winter 1992):54–77. Copyright © 1992 by MARHO: The Radical Historian's Organization, Inc. Reprinted by permission of the authors and publisher. Notes have been renumbered and edited.

but it was the brothels, for most of the men, that gave the district its identity and its dark magic. During the war years fifteen brothels operated in this section of Chinatown, their presence signaled by neatly lettered, somewhat circumspect signs ("The Bronx Rooms," "The Senator Hotel," "Rex Rooms") and by the lines of men that wound down the streets and alleyways. The brothels were not new; they had developed along with Honolulu's status as a port city, and had, in recent years, served both the growing military population and the plantation workers who came to town on paydays.[1]

Prostitution was illegal in Hawaii. Nonetheless, it existed as a highly and openly regulated system, involving the police department, government officials, and the military. Red-light districts in Honolulu had survived a Progressive Era campaign to close them down, and flourished in the face of the World War II–era May Act until late 1944, when an emerging new political elite succeeded in closing the houses.[2]

Some of the reasons for the brothels' survival are found in Hawaii's multiracial and multicultural society. To many of the people who made up the islands' varied population, prostitution was not a "social evil." And many of the islands' white elite, the "respectable" people who would have provided the necessary pressure to have the brothels closed down, approved of a regulated system of prostitution. The brothels, many believed, kept the predominately lower-class white soldiers and sailors and especially the overwhelmingly male and dark-skinned population of plantation workers [who lived in communities with few women] away from the islands' respectable women, who were, by their definition, white.[3] The head of the Honolulu Police Commission (which was comprised solely of leading white businessmen) said it directly: too many men in and around Honolulu were "just like animals."[4] An editorial in *Hawaii*, a magazine published and supported by the *haole* elite, explained further: "If the sexual desires of men in this predominately masculine community are *going to be satisfied*, certainly not one of us but would rather see them satisfied in regulated brothels than by our young girls and women—whether by rape, seduction or the encouraging of natural tendencies.[5] . . ." The brothels, they thought, helped keep the peace.

The military was pleased with the system, for regulated prostitution kept venereal disease rates relatively low in Hawaii. During World War II, this consideration became especially important. Like any other illness, venereal disease hurt the war effort by cutting into military manpower. At the end of World War I more men left military service with a contagious venereal disease than had been wounded in battle. While the military officials in Hawaii *never* said publicly and directly that they supported regulated vice districts, the military participated fully in the regulation process, putting houses off limits to the men if they broke rules that would compromise venereal disease control, and setting up prophylaxis stations in Honolulu. Each brothel had a sign in its waiting room reminding the men where the "pro" stations were and why it was important for them to make use of the service. The prophylaxis stations were free and open to all—civilian and military—and the Hotel Street stations could handle 1,500 men an hour.[6]

The police department, while to some extent acting on behalf of the *haole* elite, also benefited from the system. Like most police departments, the Honolulu police understood that shutting down the vice district would not end prostitution. Police officials believed that unregulated, dispersed prostitution would more likely be rife with pimps, procurers, and other men who used violence to enforce their criminal order on both the prostitutes and their customers, thus creating much unpleasantness for the police department. In Honolulu, the chief of police personally decided who might open a brothel and who would suffer penalties. The department, according to several sources, received steady payoff money to overlook the varied forms of vice that accompanied the quasi-legal acts of prostitution.[7]

The central charge of the police department was to keep the district orderly and to keep the prostitutes out of sight of respectable Honolulu. The majority of official Honolulu prostitutes were white women recruited through San Francisco. Both police and madams preferred it that way, for women from the mainland had fewer choices but to go along with the system. Each prostitute arriving from the mainland was met at the ship by a member of the vice squad. After she was fingerprinted but before she received her license, she was instructed in the rules that would govern her stay on Hotel Street:

She may not visit Waikiki Beach or any other beach except Kailua Beach (a beach across the mountains from Honolulu).

She may not patronize any bars or better class cafés.

She may not own property or an automobile.

She may not have a steady "boyfriend" or be seen on the streets with any men.

She may not marry service personnel. She may not attend dances or visit golf courses.

She may not ride in the front seat of a taxicab or with a man in the back seat.

She may not wire money to the mainland without permission of the madam.

She may not telephone the mainland without permission of the madam.

She may not change from one house to another. She may not be out of the brothel after 10:30 at night.[8]

... To break these rules was to risk a beating at the hands of the police and possible removal from the islands.

Before the war, few white women served in the houses for more than six months before they returned to the West Coast. The Honolulu service, while lucrative, was not paradise. A few months was often all a woman could take. Some probably earned what money they had hoped for and left the trade. One "sporting girl," writing at the time, said that the police forced prostitutes to leave the islands after about six months "whether the girl's record was up to standard or not . . . [because] she got to know too much in that length of time." Once a prostitute left Hawaii the police prohibited her from returning for a year.[9]

Not all the prostitutes in the Hotel Street district were white. At the Bronx, which was one of the largest houses during the war years, approximately twenty-five prostitutes worked. About half were white women from the mainland and the other half local women. Five of the women were Hawaiian or part Hawaiian. Two were Puerto Rican. The Bronx also had six Japanese prostitutes, which was highly unusual and probably due to Tomi Abe, the Japanese-American woman who ran the Bronx during the war. Most of the madams were white women from the mainland, with names like "Norma Lane," "Peggy Staunton," and

"Molly O'Brian." The owners of the buildings in which the brothels operated were almost all Chinese or Chinese American, but almost none were actively involved in running the brothels.[10]

A less fully regulated set of brothels existed across the river—a very narrow river—from the Hotel Street district. Brothels such as the "Local Rooms" were staffed by local women [of color] only, and charged lower prices. Despite their cheaper rates these brothels were much less popular, for their venereal disease rates were astronomical. Men referred to the prostitutes as "white meat" or "dark meat."

During the war, most of the brothels only served white men. Before the war, the brothels had also maintained a color line, but of a more complicated soft. The major Hotel Street brothels used a two-door system, one for whites (almost all of whom were soldiers and sailors) and the other for local men. This segregated system, in a city where segregation was not commonplace, was aimed at the servicemen. Many were Southern, most had been raised with racist beliefs. Some did not like to think of colored men preceding them in the vagina or mouth of a prostitute. Because the district was rough, and the men likely to be drunk and easily moved to violence, segregation was deemed the safest policy.

With the influx of servicemen and war workers following Pearl Harbor, demand for prostitutes soared. With so many white men lining up outside the brothels, the two-door policy was abandoned for the duration and men of color were simply not served. A couple of brothels in the district did not observe a color line and were open to all who could pay. But almost always the men of color had to pay more.

The color line, as far as the white servicemen and war workers saw it, ran only in one direction. While they did not want to share prostitutes with men of color, some white men preferred the "exotic" women.

While the regulated brothels of Hotel Street had been lucrative, thriving businesses through the 1920s and 1930s, the war changed the scale of success. War conditions presented an amazing economic opportunity to the sex workers of Hotel Street. During the war, approximately 250 prostitutes were registered with the Honolulu Police Department—as "entertainers." They paid $1 a year for their licenses, and could make $30,000–$40,000 a year when the average working woman was considered fortunate to make $2,000. The houses took in over $10 million each during the war years, and the twenty-five to thirty madams who ran and/or owned them each took away between $150,000 and $450,000 every year. As a group, the prostitutes and madams of Hotel Street were incredibly successful economically.

But the conditions of sale, "$3 for 3 minutes," suggests how hard they must have worked. Most houses enforced a quota for each woman of 100 men a day, at least twenty days out of every month. The risks of sexually transmitted diseases were extremely high; in 1943, 120 professional prostitutes were hospitalized 166 times for a contagious venereal disease. A bad dose put the woman into the hospital—she had to go—for at least two weeks.[11]

Some women could accept the physically brutal and health-threatening conditions. They fixed their attention on the payoff. Others found the life, the numbers of men, and the social contempt degrading. Many sought distance from what they did by shooting morphine or by smoking opium. . . . Opiates gave them back some of the feelings of inviolability their roles as prostitutes worked to take from them.

During the war, even more than before, the women of Hotel Street did their best to exercise as much practical control as they could over their punishing livelihood and over the men who paid them for their services. First of all, the brothels were all owned and operated by women. The prostitutes maximized their economic control by allowing no pimps and there were no behind-the-scenes male owners. Even the doorkeepers at the brothels were women, often powerfully built women of Hawaiian descent. While the brothels existed for men, women controlled access.

The men who wanted sex had to wait in line, sometimes for hours, and in full public view. Because the curfew limited brothel hours, all of this took place only during daylight hours. From souvenir shops and beauty parlors and upstairs windows, the older Chinese women of the district watched and laughed at the lines of white men. Lines were generally quiet, but the shoeshine boys kidded the men who seemed visibly nervous, and

quite a few of the men were drunk. But those who fortified themselves with drink faced a further obstacle: the women who kept door at the brothels rejected any man they did not trust to behave properly or to perform quickly. Adeline Naniole, the Hawaiian woman who kept door at the Bronx through part of the war, kept out any man who seemed too drunk. . . . "I don't think you can make business," she would say.[12]

Inside, the system was streamlined for maximum efficiency and control. At the head of the hall that led to the prostitutes' cubicles, a madam stood behind a money booth. Some of the booths were caged; there was no pretense that the houses offered gracious entertainment. The madam collected $3, almost always in singles, and gave the man a token, usually a poker chip. He then waited for an available woman.[13] . . .

Even in the sex act, most men felt little control. That was partly due to the setup: in the interest of time, women rotated from room to room; thus, no time was lost in cleaning up and waiting for the man to dress. When a man's turn came, he went into a cubicle—a regular room divided in half by a flimsy sheet of plywood or wall board that reached only two-thirds of the way to the ceiling. The room was bare except for a single cot, a table with a wash bowl, and a wastebasket. Sometimes, if the maids had been overwhelmed by the pace of business, soiled towels littered the floor. Often the man undressed and waited alone while the prostitute finished up in the cubicle on the other side of the half wall. The man could hear what went on the other side, and he knew that he would be heard in turn.

As time was money, and three minutes was the limit, prostitutes used various strategies to control the sex act itself. After quickly inspecting and washing the man's genitals (as a patron of other brothels described the routine):

She'd lay on her back and get you on top of her so fast, you wouldn't even know you'd come up there on your own power. She'd grind so that you almost felt like you had nothing to do with it. Well, after that, she had you. She could make it go off as quickly as she wanted to. . . .[14]

About a quarter of the men chose fellatio, a fact that worried the senior shore-patrol officer in charge of the district, for he believed that "it is not a far cry from such sex perversions ["buccal coitus," he termed it] to homosexual acts."[15] The women, their minds on the lines outside their doors and always seeking control, seemed to prefer fellatio—it was quicker. For many of the men, sexually inexperienced and fresh from months at sea or long weeks in a battle zone, three minutes was more than enough. As one veteran recalls, "They put it in and they're gone. Sometimes they're gone washing off in the pail. . . ."[16]

Despite the impersonal efficiency of the system, it could break down. One regular customer told his favorite, a half-Chinese, half-Mexican prostitute, at the end of a three-minute session, "Judy, you're the bummest fuck I ever had." As he tells it, she was so angry she spent the rest of the night proving him a liar—for free. It meant a lot; he named his daughter after her.[17] . . .

In the houses, men's money bought women's sexual favors; that was undeniable, and to that extent the men commanded and controlled the women. Women's bodies were commodified. Yet the system was structured to emphasize the women's control over the men. Standing in line, facing the doorkeeper, taking one's place in the day's quota of 100 anonymous acts: none of those experiences served to confirm a sense of male power or control. . . .

While the prostitutes and madams asserted control within the brothels during the war, it is perhaps more significant that they also attempted to challenge the larger system of controls and regulations within which they lived. After the Pearl Harbor attack the Hotel Street district, like much of the city, was shut down for a few weeks. Soon after the houses reopened, with the troops pouring through Honolulu and the men's pay upped from the prewar scale, the women raised their fee to $5 for three minutes. As they saw it, market conditions had changed.

Word of the price hike immediately reached Frank Steer, at that point an army major who had come to the islands in September 1940 to head the military police. Steer . . . served during the war as provost marshall under the state of martial law imposed on Hawaii after the Japanese attack. Under martial law, he had final authority over matters of vice. . . . Steer had no problem with the existence of brothels, but he did have a problem with the price hike. Raising prices on the fighting men

was bad for morale and, as he saw it, unfair. Steer ordered the prices dropped: "The price of meat is still three dollars," he told the madams, and they backed down. They trusted Steer, and they knew he was their ally against the dictates of the police department. But though the prices returned to normal, Hotel Street business would not.

Right after the attack on Pearl Harbor, the women of the houses had rushed to the hospitals and temporary facilities set up for the burned and wounded men. Some of those who came to help were turned away when they admitted their occupations or gave their addresses—the official reason was fear of infection. But more than a few prostitutes nursed the men and did what they could to help. The madams turned over the brothels' living quarters to the overflow of wounded, and for a few days Hotel Street looked like a Red Cross annex.[18]

With their beds filled—and with normal lines of authority disrupted—the women took a chance. They moved out of the district and out of the shadows. They bought and leased houses all around Honolulu—up the rises (mountain slopes), down by the beaches, in fashionable neighborhoods. They told anyone who asked that the district was too risky, that it was a firetrap if the Japanese came back. The explanation was not just a cover; many on the islands believed invasion was imminent. Several prostitutes passed up the promised boom times and joined other women, longtime residents and wives of army and navy officers, who arranged passage on the 20 December special evacuation transport bound for San Francisco.

For several weeks, even as the brothels reopened and long after the wounded had moved out of the prostitutes' living quarters, no one seemed to pay any attention to the women's quiet movement out of the district. The women of Hotel Street, long subject to the dictates of the vice squad, had reason to hope that those days were over.[19]

At first, the women who had moved out of the district attracted little attention; gradually that changed. One businesswoman worked out a lucrative scheme: through an agent, she would buy a house in a fashionable neighborhood and then make clear to her neighbors what her line of work was. The investments paid off handsomely and rapidly, as

the neighbors banded together to buy her out—
at a premium.[20]

Other women, their minds less on business
than on pleasure, simply began to enjoy their
earnings. They flouted the rules—rules that
had not been officially relaxed—appearing in
"respectable" public places, having "wild"
parties, doing as they wished. The military police, under martial law holding more authority
than the civilian police, let such behavior
pass.[21]

The police, especially their chief, William
Gabrielson, were outraged at the new order of
things. Prostitutes had invaded every neighborhood. Hawaii's carefully calibrated social
stratification was being mocked. Mainland
whores—white women—were out in public,
demonstrating how little difference white skin
had to mean in the way of moral superiority or
some sort of "natural" right to rule the majority
of Hawaii's people of darker hues. Already the
hordes of working-class white soldiers, sailors,
and war workers had damaged the equilibrium
that gave stability to the island's ruling white
elite. Now the white prostitutes made a mockery of the whole racist and racialist system.
Their too-public presence signaled to all who
watched that one set of controls was being challenged. The prostitutes' rejection of hierarchy
seemed a foreshadowing of what could happen
on a larger scale politically, economically, and
culturally after the war. Worse yet, supporting
the new laissez-faire approach to the prostitutes was General Emmons, the military governor. . . .

For General Emmons, and for Major Steer,
maintaining orderly troops, low rates of venereal diseases, and a reasonably high morale superseded long-range thinking about racial or
ethnic boundaries and the elite's postwar control of the islands. . . . The men, judging by the
hundreds of thousands of them who went up
and down the Hotel Street brothel stairs in the
months after the Pearl Harbor attack, wanted
prostitutes. The regulated brothels supplied
the prostitutes and ensured that they were relatively disease-free (the Hawaii military district had the lowest venereal disease rates in the
armed forces). The prostitutes had nursed the
wounded and given over their rooms after
Pearl Harbor. They had accepted the command
not to raise their prices. Many high-ranking
military officers believed that "any man who
won't fuck, won't fight"; they saw the women

of Hotel Street as important to morale and to
maintaining a manly spirit among the
"boys."[22] All in all, Emmons, Steer, and others
who played a role in enforcing martial law believed that keeping the prostitutes safe from
needless harassment and hypocritical near-
bondage was a commonsense way of keeping
the more or less disease-free houses operating
smoothly under what were obviously extraordinary conditions.

The matter came to a head quickly. In
April of 1942, chief of police Gabrielson ordered his men to evict four prostitutes living
together in a house in Waikiki, one of the areas
most strictly off-limits to prostitutes in the prewar years. Waikiki before the war was not the
bustling tourist center it would become. It was
an exclusive resort for the well-to-do, and Jews
and people of color knew better than to try to
stay in any of its three luxurious hotels. Although a mixture of Hawaii's ethnic/racial
groups lived in its residential section, Waikiki
was carefully maintained as a respectable area.
The war had changed Waikiki: tourism halted
for the duration, and servicemen had taken
over even one of the exclusive hotels. At least
a few of the Hotel Street prostitutes saw an opportunity in wartime Waikiki—for pleasure, if
not for profit.

When Gabrielson's man told the women to
leave, they complained to Captain Benson of
the military police, who seemed well acquainted with their affairs. He told them that
the police did not run things anymore, and that
his commander did not care where they lived
as long as they did not ply their trade outside
the Hotel Street district. All this was relayed to
Gabrielson, whose angry queries were met
with official but vague statements that the military police would take care of such issues in
the future.[23]

Gabrielson, angry but thinking strategically, issued Administrative Order No. 83, acknowledging the military control of vice in
Honolulu. He then had the memo leaked to the
Honolulu *Star-Bulletin*. He wanted to watch the
military squirm.

To reiterate what must have slipped many
minds in the face of the public and highly regulated system, prostitution was illegal in Honolulu. It was also outlawed through the federal-
level May Act, which . . . stated that the federal
government would, where local officials were
unwilling or unable to do the job themselves,

stamp out prostitution aimed at the servicemen. The May Act was not just window-dressing; it was rigorously enforced throughout the country. Though most of the military administration in Hawaii preferred the regulated brothels to what they saw as the alternative, more dangerous system, no one wanted to take the credit for running the brothels and breaking federal law—least of all General Emmons, the military governor of Hawaii. . . .

In a letter to Police Chief Gabrielson . . . Emmons made his position clear:

> I desire to inform you that your understanding regarding the responsibility for vice conditions in the City and County of Honolulu is in error. . . . No directive had been issued to the Police Department in any way limiting its responsibility for any phase of law enforcement. . . . Cancel Administrative Order No. 83.

Chief Gabrielson, with pleasure, resumed control. But the issue had been settled only on the administrative level. The MPs and the vice squad continued to skirmish, with the vice squad trying to round the women up and return them to their living quarters in the quarter, and the MPs undermining those efforts whenever possible. The MPs told the women they were within their rights.

The women of Hotel Street were caught in the middle. They did not want to go back to the prewar order. It was one thing to choose to service 100 men a day, but it was another to abide by rules that denied them their basic freedoms. They framed the issues that way, and they went on strike.[24]

For close to three weeks in June of 1942 a group of prostitutes walked a picket line outside the police department headquarters, which was just a few blocks from the district. The police headquarters also housed Major Steer and his MPs. The women carried placards protesting their treatment and the rules that restricted their freedoms. This strike was not for better pay but for better treatment, for fuller rights of citizenship.

While no documentation of their *specific* arguments at that time exists, a clear line of reasoning appears in an angry appeal to Honolulu's citizens written by a prostitute in the fall of 1944. In it, she asserted her right to freedom of movement and to adequate police protection, basing her claims on a traditional liberal concept of citizenship. "We pay some of the highest taxes in this town," she wrote. "Where, I ask you, are the beneficial results of our taxes?"

This woman and many of her coworkers believed they were doing vital war work. In addition to the obvious but controversial contributions, the prostitutes had acquitted themselves well after the Pearl Harbor attack and had been willing participants in war-bond drives. One madam had received a special citation from Secretary of the Treasury Henry Morganthau for selling $132,000 in war bonds, most of them, no doubt, to fellow sex workers. The prostitutes believed their good citizenship and patriotism should be recognized as such.[25]

The striking prostitutes gambled that the military police would keep the police department from using force against them and that their military supporters would back them up. What they did took courage, for they had no public allies.

Establishment Hawaii did its best to ignore the strike, and the newspapers carried not a single word about it. General Emmons, however, saw the situation as both embarrassing and serious, and moved quickly to resolve it. . . . Though he had the power under martial law to order the police to do as he wanted, he instead argued his case in what one participant called a "constructive and cooperative" manner. His arguments were simple and straightforward, avoiding the complicated terrains of morality and the political order and focusing instead on the women's working conditions. He said that "the girls are overworked and need periods of rest; that their work is not during daylight hours; that formerly they could go to the Coast for a rest and could be replaced by new girls arriving by steamer; that this is not possible today." Emmons also offered, on behalf of the military, to take over the unpleasant task of ensuring that the women had their regular medical checkups and inspecting the houses for breaches of the sanitary code. The police department, he assured all concerned, would have the right to enforce all other laws and regulations that applied to the women. The police commission and Chief Gabrielson, who really had little choice in the matter, accepted the compromise. The prostitutes ended their strike. Their right to appear in public and to live outside the brothels, while fragile, was won.[26]

Ultimately, the struggle over Hotel Street was not played out in terms of gender, or even with the prostitutes as players. As the prostitutes had seen an opportunity in the context between the military government and the police department, which acted as an agent of the traditional *haole* elite, so too another group saw an opportunity in the divided lines of authority. During the war years a new elite was taking shape, drawn largely from the more liberal range of the *haole* community. By mid-1944, with Hawaii completely out of harm's way and Allied victory seemingly a matter of time, some in Hawaii had begun to look to the future, toward statehood and economic development.

In trying to orchestrate Hawaii's future and maneuver toward statehood, [they] worried about ungovernable prostitutes and regulated brothels. Open prostitution somehow seemed to confirm mainland stereotypes of Hawaii as a primitive, licentious place populated by dark-skinned "natives.". . . One of the [group's] earliest goals was to demolish the unbridled vice district.

The Social Protection Committee of the Honolulu Council of Social Agencies [which] led the way in fighting the regulated brothel system . . . resembled the kind of well-educated, modern reformers who had closed down regulated brothel systems in dozens of American cities during the Progressive Era.[27] On 1 August 1944, the committee issued a bulletin, "Prostitution in Honolulu," that described (in absolutely untitillating prose) the Hotel Street system. The bulletin included a map that showed where every known prostitute in Honolulu lived. The message was clear: the prostitutes live in YOUR neighborhood.[28]. . .

As military control waned, the first phase of the antiprostitution campaign went into effect. All prostitutes were ordered to vacate houses in residential areas and to move back into the district, to the houses in which "they carry on their trade." News of this dictate was carried in the Honolulu newspapers.[29]

One month after the prostitutes had been ordered back into the district, Governor Stainback joined the antiprostitution campaigns, . . . in part, as [a way of] attack[ing] military control [and, in part, as an effort to link] interests with the progressive elite. . . . On 21 September 1944, in one of his first major reversals of military policy, Governor Stainback ordered the regulated brothels shut down. The Social Protection Committee had maneuvered very cleverly, using their greatest weapon: publicity, or

at least the threat of publicity. In letters to Admiral Nimitz, Admiral Furlong, and General Richardson, the committee asked whether each supported the system of regulated brothels. The admirals and the general replied, in writing, that they did not support the system. This was, of course, official policy, even though military practice was quite different. When Stainback closed the brothels, the military offered no resistance. A public debate about the issue, in the face of a determined campaign by an influential group of citizens, was not something anyone in the armed forces could weather. The leaders of the Social Protection Committee knew that.[30]

The actual closing of the brothels went smoothly. On 22 September three uniformed members of the vice squad visited the brothels during working hours, between 11 A.M. and 1:30 P.M. The madams had already heard about the governor's order issued the day before and so had the customers. Business had virtually come to a halt in most houses. The vice-squad officers informed the madams that after 2 P.M. any acts of prostitution committed on their premises would subject them to arrest. The prostitutes were told not to practice their trade, in the houses or elsewhere, and to move out of the district as soon as possible.

According to newspaper reports, many of the prostitutes welcomed the end of an era, and not without humor. One greeted the announcement that she could not longer "practice prostitution" with the old witticism, "I don't practice, I'm an expert." Another woman, wearing "an abbreviated red apron, short-short skirt and a pair of cowboy riding boots," gave a loud "whoopie" at the news. Madams took the news in a variety of ways. . . . But in general the[y] seemed to feel they had little about which to complain. One, and probably not the most successful, had voluntarily paid taxes on an income of $383,000 in 1943. . . . No one had expected the wartime boom to last; most prostitutes and madams had only meant to make the most money they could while it lasted. With the new clampdown in effect, some prostitutes left Honolulu as soon as they could arrange transportation back to the mainland. [Others continued to work outside of brothels.]. . .

The struggle of the Honolulu prostitutes, in retrospect, was charged not only by the usual issues surrounding illicit sex trade and lines of authority, but by concerns specific to prestatehood Hawaii. The women who made such claims on the citizens of Hawaii were white women, and their public presence and vocal demands called into question all the associations of race and gender and the ideology of the purity of white women to be defended against the sexual threat of colored races that were implicit and sometimes explicit in underpinning Hawaii's social structure. In the history of prostitution in America, many have justified the "sacrifice" of lower-class women to "protect" the purity of women of the middle and upper classes. The system in Hawaii was in many ways similar, except that race played a crucial role, and the racial lines were more complex in Hawaii than on the mainland. The public struggles—and yes, excesses—of these "impure" white women called the whole ideological system into question.

At least in small part the system had been dependent on the complicity of the white prostitutes. The prostitutes were seen as a means to keep the low-status white service personnel and the plantation workers sexually satisfied. It was crucial to the system that the prostitutes not claim any public role in Hawaii. In fact, in exchange for a great deal of money, the prostitutes (despite their white skin) were supposed to accept total pariah status. They were not to live or visit outside the vice district; they were supposed to remain silent and hidden. They could amass capital but they could not exercise their economic power in Hawaii. They were required to return to the mainland. But with their strike and with the aid of the military government, the prostitutes had demanded—and in part had gotten—the rights economic power normally guaranteed in the United States. . . .

The prostitutes' strike was only one small and indirect part of a larger movement toward a more pluralistic postwar society in Hawaii. But it is especially significant because it brought together issues of race and gender in such a way that it worked to undermine the ideology of racial superiority. White prostitutes demanded full rights of citizenship, and while the very public fact of their race had, in some small way, helped to undermine Hawaii's racial hierarchy, their race was not sufficient to guarantee their rights. Instead, the public power they were able to display for a short while in wartime Hawaii depended on the utility the federal authorities found in them.

The prostitutes' temporary victory—their ability to emerge from the dangerous shadows and to operate as legitimate, fully protected war workers—could not have happened without the intervention of the State, in the form of the military government. The concern of the federally authorized participants was not with the rights of prostitutes (though several seemed to have some respect or liking for members of the profession), but with winning the war. [What that] intervention . . . signaled [was] the increased and continuing willingness of the federal government to impose its nationally minded agendas upon local entities. . . . The ways in which socially marginal groups like the prostitutes of Hotel Street could succeed in furthering their struggles by publicly aligning themselves with the relatively autonomous federal government's often mercurial concerns would become an ever-more critical characteristic of social change movements in the postwar years.

NOTES

1. Herman Gist, interviewed by David Farber, Germantown, Md., Dec. 1989.

2. Barbara Meils Hobson, *Uneasy Virtue: The Politics of Prostitution and the American Reform Tradition* (New York: Basic Books, 1987).

3. Memo from Commissioner Houston to the Honolulu Police Commission, "Abatement of Houses of Prostitution in the City and County of Honolulu" (n.d. [1 Sept. 1941?]), Lawrence M. Judd Papers ([hereafter cited] LJ), Hawaii State Archives (HA).

4. Quoted by James Cummings in a letter to Dr. Theodore Richards, 11 July 1944, "Prostitution" file, Governor Stainback Papers, HA.

5. "Why Talk about Prostitution," *Hawaii* (31 July 1944):5.

6. Eric A. Funnel, "Venereal Disease Control: A Bedtime Story," *Hawaii Medical Journal* (Nov.–Dec. 1942):67–71; Hobson, *Uneasy Virtue.*

7. Frank Steer interviewed by David Farber, Kailua, Oahu, Hawaii, June 1989; Brian Nicol, "Interview with Col. Frank Steer," *Honolulu* (Nov. 1981):83.

8. Jean O'Hara, "My Life as a Honolulu Prostitute," (n.p. [Nov. 1944?]), Hawaii Collection of the University of Hawaii (HC-UH), pp. 15–16.

9. Ibid., pp. 15–18.

10. Letter to Governor Stainback by Senator Alice Kamokila Campbell, 5 Feb. 1945, "Prostitution" folder, Governor Stainback Papers (GS), HA.

11. Social Protection Committee, *Prostitution in Honolulu, Bulletin* 1 (1 Aug. 1944):2–3.

12. Quote from former brothel employee Adeline Naniole, interviewed by Vivian Lee, 2 March 1979, Women Workers in Pineapple, Ethnic Studies Oral History Project, University of Hawaii, p. 769;

interviews with Colonel Steer, Herman Gist, and Robert Cowan.

13. Dr. G. Gary Schram, "Suppressed Prostitution," *Honolulu Advertiser* (6 Oct. 1944); interviews with "C" (July 1990, by telephone); Herman Gist, Elton Brown (Nov. 1990, by telephone).

14. Ruth Rosen, *The Lost Sisterhood* (Baltimore: Johns Hopkins University Press, 1982), p. 96.

15. Lt. Commander Carl G. Stockholm, "The Effects of Closing Houses of Prostitution on the Navy" (paper given at the Meeting of the Social Protection Committee), 7 Feb. 1945, HC-UH.

16. Elton Brown, telephone interview, Nov. 1990.

17. Ibid.

18. "Hotel Street Harry," *Midpacifican* (15 Aug. 1943):10; Frank Steer interview, June 1989; Peggy Hickok, "In the Midst of War," *Hawaii* (30 June 1942):17.

19. O'Hara, "My Life."

20. "Hotel Street Harry," *Midpacifican* (15 Jan. 1944):10; Naniole, p. 771; and "Police Clamp Lid on Houses," *Honolulu Advertiser* (24 Sept. 1944):1.

21. O'Hara, p. 41.

22. Elizabeth Fee, "Venereal Disease: The Wage of Sin?" in Kathy Peiss and Christina Simmons, *Pas-sion and Power* (Philadelphia: Temple University Press, 1989), p. 189.

23. 014.12 Civil Authorities, Decimal File 1941–45, RG 338, MGH, National Archives.

24. Colonel Steer's assistant in "Memoranda of Conference with Major Slattery. . . ." May 1945, office of Interior Secretary, Research and Historical Sector, RG338, NA.; J. Garner Anthony, *Hawaii Under Army Rule*, p. 440.

25. O'Hara, "My Life," p. 47.

26. 014.12 Civil Authorities, Decimal File 1941–45, RG 338 MGH, NA.

27. "Prostitution" file, Governor Stainback Papers, HA; Lawrence H. Fuchs, *Hawaii Pono: A Special History* (New York: Harcourt Brace, 1961), p. 279, 286–88; Hobson, *Uneasy Virtue*.

28. Social Protection Committee, "Prostitution in Hawaii" (1 Aug. 1944).

29. "Residential Areas Banned Prostitutes," *Honolulu Advertiser* (20 July 1944).

30. Dr. Charles L. Wilbar Jr., "The Effects of Closing Houses of Prostitution on Community Health," (paper given at the Meeting of the Social Protection Committee), 7 Feb. 1945, 2–3, HC-UH; and "Prostitution" file, GS, HA.

VALERIE MATSUMOTO

Japanese-American Women During World War II

On no group of U.S. citizens did the war have greater impact than upon Japanese Americans. Fearful of a Japanese fifth column on American shores, military and civilian leaders urged Franklin Roosevelt to issue an executive order removing Americans of Japanese descent on the West Coast to relocation camps inland. Despite the fact that a vast majority of the nearly 120,000 Japanese Americans in the United States were citizens with the same rights and obligations as any other citizen, the president succumbed to pressure and issued Executive Order 9066 in February 1942, which ultimately resulted in the establishment of ten concentration camps in remote areas of the West. Forced to leave their homes and businesses at great financial cost, both Japanese-born parents, the Issei, and their American-born children, the Nisei, faced the trauma of removal and the shame of implied disloyalty. Not until 1990 would the nation acknowledge the magnitude of its offense and begin providing financial redress for survivors of the camps.

The following essay explores what life in the camps was like for women and the efforts of younger ones to reconstruct a life after internment.

Excerpted from "Japanese-American Women During World War II" by Valerie Matsumoto in *Frontiers* 8 (1984):6, 8–13. Copyright © 1984 by Frontiers Editorial Collective. Reprinted by permission of the author and *Frontiers*. Notes have been renumbered.

The life here cannot be expressed. Sometimes, we are resigned to it, but when we see the barbed wire fences and the sentry tower with floodlights, it gives us a feeling of being prisoners in a "concentration camp." We try to be happy and yet oftentimes a gloominess does creep in. When I see the "I'm an American" editorial and write-ups, the "equality of race etc."—it seems to be mocking us in our faces. I just wonder if all the sacrifices and hard labor on [the] part of our parents has gone up to leave nothing to show for it?

Letter from Shizuko Horiuchi,
Pomona Assembly Center, May 24, 1942

Overlying the mixed feelings of anxiety, anger, shame, and confusion [of the Japanese Americans who were forced to relocate] was resignation. As a relatively small minority caught in a storm of turbulent events that destroyed their individual and community security, there was little the Japanese Americans could do but shrug and say, *"Shikata ga nai,"* or "It can't be helped," the implication being that the situation must be endured. The phrase lingered on many lips when the Issei, Nisei [second generation], and the young Sansei (third generation) children prepared for the move—which was completed by November 1942—to the ten permanent relocation camps organized by the War Relocation Authority: Topaz, Utah; Poston and Gila River, Arizona; Amache, Colorado; Manzanar and Tule Lake, California; Heart Mountain, Wyoming; Minidoka, Idaho; Denson and Rohwer, Arkansas.[1] Denson and Rohwer were located in the swampy lowlands of Arkansas; the other camps were in desolate desert or semi-desert areas subject to dust storms and extreme temperatures reflected in the nicknames given to the three sections of the Poston Camp: Toaston, Roaston, and Duston.

The conditions of camp life profoundly altered family relations and affected women of all ages and backgrounds. Family unity deteriorated in the crude communal facilities and cramped barracks. The unceasing battle with the elements, the poor food, the shortages of toilet tissue and milk, coupled with wartime profiteering and mismanagement, and the sense of injustice and frustration took their toll on a people uprooted, far from home.

The standard housing in the camps was a spartan barracks, about twenty feet by one hundred feet, divided into four to six rooms furnished with steel army cots. Initially each single room or "apartment" housed an average of eight persons; individuals without kin nearby were often moved in with smaller families. Because the partitions between apartments did not reach the ceiling, even the smallest noises traveled freely from one end of the building to the other. There were usually fourteen barracks in each block, and each block had its own mess hall, laundry, latrine, shower facilities, and recreation room.... The even greater lack of privacy in the latrine and shower facilities necessitated adjustments in former notions of modesty. There were no partitions in the shower room, and the latrine consisted of two rows of partitioned toilets "with nothing in front of you, just on the sides".[2]... A married woman with a family wrote from Heart Mountain:

Last weekend, we had an awful cold wave and it was about 20° to 30° below zero. In such a weather, it's terrible to try going even to the bath and latrine house.... It really aggravates me to hear some politicians say we Japanese are being coddled, for *it isn't so!!* We're on ration as much as outsiders are. I'd say welcome to anyone to try living behind barbed wire and be cooped in a 20 ft. by 20 ft. room.... We do our sleeping, dressing, ironing, hanging up our clothes in this one room.[3]

After the first numbness of disorientation, the evacuees set about making their situation bearable, creating as much order in their lives as possible. With blankets they partitioned their apartments into tiny rooms and created benches, tables, and shelves as piles of scrap lumber left over from barracks construction vanished; victory gardens and flower patches appeared....

Despite the best efforts of the evacuees to restore order to their disputed world, camp conditions prevented replication of their prewar lives. Women's work experiences, for example, changed in complex ways during the years of internment. Each camp offered a wide range of jobs, resulting from the organization of the camps as model cities administered through a series of departments headed by Caucasian administrators. The departments handled everything from accounting, agriculture, education, and medical care to mess hall service and the weekly newspaper. The scramble for jobs began early in the assembly centers and camps, and all able-bodied persons were expected to work.

Even before the war many family members had worked, but now children and parents, men and women all received the same low wages. In the relocation camps, doctors, teachers, and other professionals were at the top of the pay scale, earning $19 per month. The majority of workers received $16, and apprentices earned $12. The new equity in pay and the variety of available jobs gave many women unprecedented opportunities for experimentation, as illustrated by one woman's account of her family's work in Poston:

> First I wanted to find art work, but I didn't last too long because it wasn't very interesting . . . so I worked in the mess hall, but that wasn't for me, so I went to the accounting department—timekeeping—and I enjoyed that, so I stayed there. . . . My dad . . . went to a shoe shop . . . and then he was block gardener. . . . He got $16. . . . [My sister] was secretary for the block manager; then she went to the optometry department. She was assistant optometrist; she fixed all the glasses and fitted them. . . . That was $16.[4]

As early as 1942, the War Relocation Authority began to release evacuees temporarily from the centers and camps to do voluntary seasonal farm work in neighboring areas hard hit by the wartime labor shortage. The work was arduous, as one young woman discovered when she left Topaz to take a job plucking turkeys:

> The smell is terrific until you get used to it. . . . We all wore gunny sacks around our waist, had a small knife and plucked off the fine feathers.
>
> This is about the hardest work that many of us have done—but without a murmur of complaint we worked 8 hours through the first day without a pause.
>
> We were all so tired that we didn't even feel like eating. . . . Our fingers and wrists were just aching, and I just dreamt of turkeys and more turkeys.[5]

Work conditions varied from situation to situation, and some exploitative farmers refused to pay the Japanese Americans after they had finished beet topping or fruit picking. One worker noted that the degree of friendliness on the employer's part decreased as the harvest neared completion. Nonetheless, many workers, like the turkey plucker, concluded that "even if the work is hard, it is worth the freedom we are allowed." . . .

Like their noninterned contemporaries, most young Nisei women envisioned a future of marriage and children. They—and their parents—anticipated that they would marry other Japanese Americans, but these young women also expected to choose their own husbands and to marry "for love." This mainstream American ideal of marriage differed greatly from the Issei's view of love as a bond that might evolve over the course of an arranged marriage that was firmly rooted in less romantic notions of compatibility and responsibility. The discrepancy between Issei and Nisei conceptions of love and marriage had sturdy prewar roots; internment fostered further divergence from the old customs of arranged marriage. In the artificial hothouse of camp, Nisei romances often bloomed quickly. As Nisei men left to prove their loyalty to the United States in the 442nd Combat Team and the 100th Battalion, young Japanese Americans strove to grasp what happiness and security they could, given the uncertainties of the future. Lily Shoji, in her "Fem-a-lites" newspaper column, commented upon the "changing world" and advised Nisei women: "This is the day of sudden dates, of blind dates on the up-and-up, so let the flash of a uniform be a signal to you to be ready for any emergency. . . . Romance is blossoming with the emotion and urgency of war."[6]

In keeping with this atmosphere, camp newspaper columns like Shoji's in *The Mercedian*, *The Daily Tulean Dispatch*'s "Strictly Feminine," and the *Poston Chronicle*'s "Fashionotes" gave their Nisei readers countless suggestions on how to impress boys, care for their complexions, and choose the latest fashions. These evacuee-authored columns thus mirrored the mainstream girls' periodicals of the time. Such fashion news may seem incongruous in the context of an internment camp whose inmates had little choice in clothing beyond what they could find in the Montgomery Ward or Sears and Roebuck mail-order catalogues. These columns, however, reflect women's efforts to remain in touch with the world outside the barbed wire fence; they reflect as well women's attempt to maintain morale in a drab, depressing environment. "There's something about color in clothes," speculated Tule Lake columnist "Yuri"; "Singing colors have a heart-building effect. . . . Color is a stimulant we need—both for its effect on ourselves and on others."[7] . . .

RESETTLEMENT: COLLEGE AND WORK

Relocation began slowly in 1942. Among the first to venture out of the camps were college students, assisted by the National Japanese American Student Relocation Council, a non-governmental agency that provided invaluable placement aid to 4,084 Nisei in the years 1942–46.[8] Founded in 1942 by concerned educators, this organization persuaded institutions outside the restricted Western Defense zone to accept Nisei students and facilitated their admissions and leave clearances. A study of the first 400 students to leave camp showed that a third of them were women.[9] Because of the cumbersome screening process, few other evacuees departed on indefinite leave before 1943. In that year, the War Relocation Authority tried to expedite the clearance procedure by broadening an army registration program aimed at Nisei males to include all adults. With this policy change, the migration from the camps steadily increased.[10]

Many Nisei, among them a large number of women, were anxious to leave the limbo of camp and return "to normal life again."[11]... An aspiring teacher wrote: "Mother and father do not want me to go out. However, I want to go so very much that sometimes I feel that I'd go even if they disowned me. What shall I do? I realize the hard living conditions outside but I think I can take it."[12] Women's developing sense of independence in the camp environment and their growing awareness of their abilities as workers contributed to their self-confidence and hence their desire to leave. Significantly, Issei parents, despite initial reluctance, were gradually beginning to sanction their daughters' departures for education and employment in the Midwest and East. One Nisei noted: "[Father] became more broadminded in the relocation center.... At first he didn't want me to relocate, but he gave in.... He didn't say I could go ... but he helped me pack, so I thought, 'Well, he didn't say no.'"[13]

The decision to relocate was a difficult one.... Many internees worried about their acceptance in the outside world. The Nisei considered themselves American citizens, and they had an allegiance to the land of their birth.... But evacuation had taught the Japanese Americans that in the eyes of many of their fellow Americans, theirs was the face of the enemy. Many Nisei were torn by mixed feelings of shame, frustration, and bitterness at the denial of their civil rights.... "A feeling of uncertainty hung over the camp; we were worried about the future. Plans were made and remade, as we tried to decide what to do. Some were ready to risk anything to get away. Others feared to leave the protection of the camp."[14]

Thus, those first college students were the scouts whose letters back to camp marked pathways for others to follow. May Yoshino sent a favorable report to her family in Topaz from the nearby University of Utah, indicating that there were "plenty of schoolgirl jobs for those who want to study at the University."[15] Correspondence from other Nisei students shows that although they succeeded at making the dual transition from high school to college and from camp to the outside world, they were not without anxieties as to whether they could handle the study load and the reactions of the Caucasians around them. One student at Drake University in Iowa wrote to her interned sister about a professor's reaction to her autobiographical essay, "Evacuation": "Today Mr.—, the English teacher that scares me, told me that the theme that I wrote the other day was very interesting.... You could just imagine how wonderful and happy I was to know that he liked it a little bit.... I've been awfully busy trying to catch up on work and the work is so different from high school. I think that little by little I'm beginning to adjust myself to college life."[16]... Lillian ... Ota, a Wellesley student, reassured [her interned friends contemplating college:] "During the first few days you'll be invited by the college to teas and receptions. Before long you'll lose the awkwardness you might feel at such doings after the months of abnormal life at evacuation centers."[17] Although Ota had not noticed "that my being a 'Jap' has made much difference on the campus itself," she offered cautionary and pragmatic advice to the Nisei, suggesting the burden of responsibility these relocated students felt, as well as the problem of communicating their experiences and emotions to Caucasians.

It is scarcely necessary to point out that those who have probably never seen a nisei before will get their impression of the nisei as a whole from the relocated students. It won't do you or your family and friends much good to dwell on what you consider injustices when you are questioned about evacuation. Rather, stress the contributions of [our] people to the nation's war effort.[18]...

Armed with [such] advice and drawn by encouraging reports, increasing numbers of women students left camp.[19] . . . The trickle of migration from the camps grew into a steady stream by 1943, as the War Relocation Authority developed its resettlement program to aid evacuees in finding housing and employment in the East and Midwest. . . . [But] leaving camp meant [more changes.] Even someone as confident as Marii Kyogoku . . . found that re-entry into the Caucasian-dominated world beyond the barbed wire fence was not a simple matter of stepping back into old shoes. Leaving the camps—like entering them—meant major changes in psychological perspective and self-image.

> I had thought that because before evacuation I had adjusted myself rather well in a Caucasian society, I would go right back into my former frame of mind. I have found, however, that though the center became unreal and was as if it had never existed as soon as I got on the train at Delta, I was never so self-conscious in all my life.

Kyogoku was amazed to see so many men and women in uniform and, despite her "proper" dining preparation, felt strange sitting at a table set with clean linen and a full set of silverware.

> I felt a diffidence at facing all these people and things, which was most unusual. Slowly things have come to seem natural, though I am still excited by the sounds of the busy city and thrilled every time I see a street lined with trees, I no longer feel that I am the cynosure of all eyes.[20] . . .

Many relocating Japanese Americans received moral and material assistance from a number of service organizations and religious groups, particularly the Presbyterians, the Methodists, the Society of Friends, and the Young Women's Christian Association. One such Nisei, Dorcas Asano, enthusiastically described to a Quaker sponsor her activities in the big city:

> Since receiving your application for hostel accommodation, I have decided to come to New York and I am really glad for the opportunity to be able to resume the normal civilized life after a year's confinement in camp. New York is really a city of dreams and we are enjoying every minute working in offices, rushing back and forth to work in the ever-speeding subway trains, counting our ration points, buying war bonds, going to church, seeing the latest shows, plays, operas,

making many new friends and living like our neighbors in the war time. I only wish more of my friends who are behind the fence will take advantage of the many helpful hands offered to them.[21]

The Nisei also derived support and strength from networks—formed before and during internment—of friends and relatives. The homes of those who relocated first became way stations for others as they made the transition into new communities and jobs. In 1944, soon after she obtained a place to stay in New York City, Miné Okubo found that "many of the other evacuees relocating in New York came ringing my doorbell. They were sleeping all over the floor!"[22] Single women often accompanied or joined sisters, brothers, and friends as many interconnecting grapevines carried news of likely jobs, housing, and friendly communities. . . .

For Nisei women, like their non-Japanese sisters, the wartime labor shortage opened the door into industrial, clerical, and managerial occupations. Prior to the war, racism had excluded the Japanese Americans from most white-collar clerical and sales positions, and, according to sociologist Evelyn Nakano Glenn, "the most common form of nonagricultural employment for the immigrant women (Issei) and their American-born daughters (Nisei) was domestic service."[23] The highest percentage of job offers for both men and women continued to be requests for domestic workers. In July 1943, the Kansas City branch of the War Relocation Authority noted that 45 percent of requests for workers were for domestics, and the Milwaukee office cited 61 percent.[24] However, Nisei women also found jobs as secretaries, typists, file clerks, beauticians, and factory workers. By 1950, 47 percent of employed Japanese American women were clerical and sales workers and operatives; only 10 percent were in domestic service.[25] The World War II decade, then, marked a turning point for Japanese American women in the labor force. . . .

[Improved opportunities could not compensate for the] uprooting [of] communities and [the] severe psychological and emotional damage [inflicted upon Japanese Americans by internment.] The vast majority returned to the West Coast at the end of the war in 1945—a move that, like the initial evacuation, was a grueling test of flexibility and fortitude. Even with the assistance of old friends and service organizations, the transition was taxing and painful; the end of the war meant not only long-awaited freedom but more battles to be fought in social, academic, and economic arenas. The Japanese Americans faced hostility, crude living conditions, and a struggle for jobs. Few evacuees received any compensation for their financial losses, estimated conservatively at $400 million, because Congress decided to appropriate only $38 million for the settlement of claims.[26] It is even harder to place a figure on the toll taken in emotional shock, self-blame, broken dreams, and insecurity. One Japanese American woman still sees in her nightmares the watchtower searchlights that troubled her sleep forty years ago.

The war altered Japanese American women's lives in complicated ways. In general, evacuation and relocation accelerated earlier trends that differentiated the Nisei from their parents. Although most young women, like their mothers and non-Japanese peers, anticipated a future centered on a husband and children, they had already felt the influence of mainstream middle-class values of love and marriage and quickly moved away from the pattern of arranged marriage in the camps. There, increased peer group activities and the relaxation of parental authority gave them more independence. The Nisei women's expectations of marriage became more akin to the companionate ideals of their peers than to those of the Issei.

As before the war, many Nisei women worked . . . , but the new parity in wages they received altered family dynamics. And though they expected to contribute to the family economy, a large number did so in settings far from the family, availing themselves of opportunities provided by the student and worker relocation programs. In meeting the challenges facing them, Nisei women drew not only upon the disciplined strength inculcated by their Issei parents but also upon firmly rooted support networks and the greater measure of self-reliance and independence that they developed during the crucible of the war years.

NOTES

1. Many of the Japanese community leaders arrested by the FBI before the evacuation were interned in special all-male camps in North Dakota, Louisiana, and New Mexico. Some Japanese Americans living outside the perimeter of the Western defense zone in Arizona, Utah, etc., were not interned.

2. Chieko Kimura, personal interview, Apr. 9, 1978, Glendale, Arizona.

3. Shizuko Horiuchi to Henriette Von Blon, Jan. 24, 1943, Henriette Von Blon Collection, Hoover Institution Archives ([hereafter] HIA).

4. Ayako Kanemura, personal interview, Mar. 10, 1978, Glendale, Arizona.

5. Anonymous, *Topaz Times*, Oct. 24, 1942, p. 3.

6. Lily Shoji, "Fem-a-lites," *The Mercedian*, Aug. 7, 1942, p. 4.

7. "Yuri," "Strictly Feminine," Sept. 29, 1942, p. 2.

8. From 1942 to the end of 1945 the Council allocated about $240,000 in scholarships, most of which were provided through the donations of the church and the World Student Service Fund. The average grant for student for was $156.73, which in that area was a major contribution towards the cost of higher education. Source: National Japanese American Student Relocation Council, Minutes of the Executive Committee Meeting, Philadelphia, Pennsylvania, Dec. 19, 1945.

9. Robert O'Brien, *The College Nisei* (Palo Alto: Pacific Books, 1949), pp. 73–74.

10. The disastrous consequences of the poorly conceived clearance procedure had been examined by Wilson and Hosokawa, pp. 226–27, and Girdner and Loftis, pp. 342–43.

11. May Nakamoto to Mrs. Jack Shoup, Nov. 20, 1943, Mrs. Jack Shoup Collection, HIA.

12. Toshiko Imada to Margaret Cosgrave Sowers, Jan. 16, 1943, Margaret Cosgrave Sowers Collection, HIA.

13. Ayako Kanemura, personal interview, Mar. 24, 1978, Glendale, Arizona.

14. Mine Okubo, *Citizen 13660* (New York: Columbia University Press, 1946), p. 66.

15. *Topaz Times*, Oct. 24, 2942, p. 3.

16. Masako Ono to Atsuko Ono, Sept. 28, 1942, Margaret Cosgrave Sowers Collection, HIA. Prior to the war, few Nisei had college experience: the 1940 census lists 674 second-generation women and 1,507 men who had attended or who were attending college.

17. Lillian Ota, "Campus Report," *Trek* (Feb. 1943), p. 33.

18. Ota, pp. 33–34.

19. O'Brien, p. 84.

20. Marii Kyogoku, *Resettlement Bulletin* (July 1943), p. 5.

21. Dorcas Asano to Josephine Duveneck, Jan. 22, 1944, Conard-Duveneck Collection, HIA.

22. Miné Okubo, *Miné Okubo: An American Experience*, exhibition catalogue (Oakland: Oakland Museum, 1972), p. 84.

23. Evelyn Nakana Glenn, "The Dialectics of Wage Work: Japanese American Women and Domestic Servants, 1905–1940," *Feminist Studies* 6, no. 3 (Fall 1980):412.

24. Advisory Committee of Evacuees, *Resettlement Bulletin* (July 1943), p. 3.

25. 1950 United States Census, Special Report.

26. Susan M. Hartmann, *The Home Front and Beyond, American Women in the 1940s* (Boston: Twayne Publishers, 1982), p. 126. There is some debate regarding the origins of the assessment of evacuee losses at $400 million. However, a recent study by the Commission on Wartime Relocation and Internment of Civilians has estimated that the Japanese Americans lost between $149 million and $370 million in 1945 dollars, and between $810 million and $2 billion in 1983 dollars. See the *San Francisco Chronicle,* June 16, 1983, p. 12.

RUTH MILKMAN

Gender at Work: The Sexual Division of Labor During World War II

As the nation, struggling with economic depression, began to fight its second world war, unemployment lines quickly vanished. Manpower shortages meant that women would once again move into jobs in industry and experience new vocational opportunities; a lessening of discrimination based on marital status, age, and race; and public praise for their wartime contribution as workers. The potential provided by the war for refashioning gender roles was enormous, but the results were disappointing. The expectation was that once the men came home, women would happily exchange industrial tools for the broom and mop or new vacuum cleaner and the baby bottle. Polls showed that up to 85 percent of these women needed to continue working and expected that job seniority would entitle them to return after veterans had been absorbed in the work force.

The redefining of "men's jobs" and "women's jobs" precipitated by wartime mobilization and the rapid return to the prewar sexual division of labor is the subject of Ruth Milkman's study. Focusing especially on the auto and electronics industry, she provides unmistakable evidence of the persistence of occupational segregation at a time when the very survival of democracy was at stake. Note how job segregation demonstrates the double meaning of Milkman's title *Gender at Work.* What was the rationale for segregating jobs by sex? What evidence does Milkman provide to suggest that the designation of jobs as "male" or "female" was often arbitrary? Given management's assessment of women's job performance during the war, how does she explain the reversion to old patterns? What factors were involved? What explanation is offered for the fact that black men were able to hold on to wartime gains in industry whereas white and black women were not?

If it is true that occupational sex typing becomes even more important when women's labor force participation increases, what trends do you foresee for the postwar decades given the changes in the pattern of women's labor force participation noted by Jones for the 1930s and by Milkman for the 1940s? How does job segregation help to explain the fact that for the past thirty years women have earned roughly 55 cents for every $1.00 by men when both are full-time workers?

Conversion to war production involved redefinition of the entire employment structure. Some civilian automobile production jobs were also necessary for the production of tanks, aircraft, engines and ordnance; other war jobs were completely new. The changeover to war production in electrical manufacturing was less dramatic, but also involved shifts in the character and distribution of jobs. Thus, many of the war jobs that had to be filled (in both industries) were not clearly labeled as "women's" or "men's" work, at least at first. . . .

While the government had actively pressured some firms to hire women, it made no effort whatsoever to influence their placement within industry once management complied. The U.S. Employment Service routinely filled employer job openings that called for specific numbers of women and men. Although ceilings were imposed on the number of men who could be allocated to each plant, employers had a free hand in placing women and men in particular jobs within this constraint.[1] Although the unions sometimes contested the sexual division of labor after the fact, the initial job assignments were left entirely to management.

Women were not evenly distributed through the various jobs available in the war plants, but were hired into specific classifications that management deemed "suitable" for women and were excluded from other jobs. Some employers conducted special surveys to determine the sexual division of labor in a plant; probably more often such decisions were made informally by individual supervisors.[2] Although data on the distribution of women through job classifications in the wartime auto and electrical industries are sketchy, there is no mistaking the persistence of segregation by sex. A 1943 survey of the auto industry's Detroit plants, for example, found more than one-half of the women workers clustered in only five of seventy-two job classifications. Only 11 percent of the men were employed in these five occupations.[3]

Jobs were also highly segregated in the electrical industry during the war. A 1942 study of electrical appliance plants (most of which had already been converted to military production when surveyed) found women, who were 30 percent of the workers, in only twenty-one job classifications, whereas men were spread across seventy-two of them. Nearly half of the women (47 percent) were employed in a single job category, and 68 percent were clustered in four occupations. Only 16 percent of the men were in these four job classifications.[4] . . .

Job segregation by sex was explicitly acknowledged in many war plants: jobs were formally labeled "male" and "female." The two largest electrical firms, GE and Westinghouse, continued this practice until the end of the war. And in 45 percent of the auto plants with sexually mixed work forces responding to a survey conducted in mid-1944 by the UAW Women's Bureau, jobs were formally categorized as "male" or "female."[5] Available records suggest that sex segregation also existed elsewhere, even if it was not formally acknowledged. . . .

Segregation appears to be a constant across both industries during the war years. However, in both industries there was considerable plant-to-plant variation in patterns of employment by sex. In the Detroit area, for example, there was a wide range in the proportion of women employed, even among plants manufacturing the same products. In April 1943, women were 29 percent of the workers at the GM Cadillac plant, which was producing engine parts, but women made up 59 percent of the work force at the Excello Corporation's Detroit plant, which made the same product. Similarly, although women were only 2 percent of the workers at Continental Motors, they were 27 percent of those at the Jefferson Avenue plant of the Hudson Motor Car Company. Both plants made aircraft motors.[6] In the electrical industry, too, there was considerable variation of this sort, even among plants owned by the same company and producing similar goods. . . .

Whatever the sexual division of labor happened to be at a given point in time, management always seemed to insist that there was no alternative. When a War Department representative visited an airplane plant where large numbers of women were employed, he was told that the best welder in the plant was a woman. "Their supervisors told me that their work is fine, even better than that of the men who were formerly on those jobs," he reported. "In another plant in the same area, I remarked on the absence of women and was told that women just can't do those jobs—the very same jobs. It is true, they can't do that type of work—as long as the employer refuses to hire and train them."[7]

Although the specifics varied, everywhere management was quick to offer a rationale for the concentration of women in some jobs and their exclusion from others. . . . "Womanpower differs from manpower as oil fuel differs from coal," proclaimed the trade journal *Automotive War Production* in October 1943, "and an understanding of the characteristics of the energy involved was needed for obtaining best results." Although it was now applied to a larger and quite different set of jobs, the basic characterization of women's abilities and limitations was familiar. As *Automotive War Production* put it:

> On certain kinds of operations—the very ones requiring high manipulative skill—women were found to be a whole lot quicker and more efficient than men. Engineering womanpower means realizing fully that women are not only different from men in such things as lifting power and arm reach—but in many other ways that pertain to their physiological and their social functions. To understand these things does not mean to exclude women from *the jobs for which they are peculiarly adapted,* and where they can help to win this war. It merely means using them as women, and not as men.[8]

The idiom of women's war work in the electrical industry closely paralleled that in auto. "Nearly every Westinghouse plant employs women, especially for jobs that require dexterity with tiny parts," reported an article in *Factory Management and Maintenance* in March 1942. "At the East Pittsburgh plant, for instance, women tape coils. The thickness of each coil must be identical to within close limits, so the job requires feminine patience and deft fingers. Another job that calls for unlimited patience is the inspection of moving parts of electric instruments. . . ." Repeatedly stressed, especially in auto, was the lesser physical strength of the average woman worker. "Woman isn't just a 'smaller man,'" *Automo-*

tive War Production pointed out. "Compensations in production processes must be made to allow for the fact that the average woman is only 35 percent muscle in comparison to the average man's 41 percent. Moreover, industrial studies have shown that only 54 percent of woman's weight is strength, as against man's 87 percent, and that the hand squeeze of the average woman exerts only 48 pounds of pressure, against man's 81 pounds."[9]

Accompanying the characterization of women's work as "light" was an emphasis on cleanliness. "Women can satisfactorily fill all or most jobs performed by men, subject only to the limitations of strength and physical requirements," a meeting of the National Association of Manufacturers concluded in March 1942. "However . . . jobs of a particularly 'dirty' character, jobs that subject women to heat process or are of a 'wet' nature should not be filled by women . . . despite the fact that women could, if required, perform them."[10]

The emphasis in the idiom of sex-typing on the physical limitations of women workers had a dual character. It not only justified the sexual division of labor, but it also served as the basis for increased mechanization and work simplification. "To adjust women's jobs to such [physical] differences, automotive plants have added more mechanical aids such as conveyors, chain hoists, and load lifters," reported *Automotive War Production.* A study by Constance Green found job dilution of this sort widespread in electrical firms and other war industries in the Connecticut Valley as well. "Where ten men had done ten complete jobs, now . . . eight women and two, three, or possibly four men together would do the ten split-up jobs," she noted. "Most often men set up machines, ground or adjusted tools, and generally 'serviced' the women who acted exclusively as machine operators."[11]

Although production technology was already quite advanced in both auto and electrical manufacturing, the pace of development accelerated during the war period. Management attributed this to its desire to make jobs easier for women, but the labor shortage and the opportunity to introduce new technology at government expense under war contracts were at least as important. However, the idiom that constructed women as "delicate" and, although poorly suited to "heavy" work, amenable to monotonous jobs, was now marshaled to justify the use of new technology and work "simplification." At Vultee Aircraft, for example, a manager explained:

> It definitely was in Vultee's favor that the hiring of women was started when production jobs were being simplified to meet the needs of fast, quantity production.... Special jigs were added to hold small tools, such as drills, so that women could concentrate on employing more effectively their proven capacity for repetitive operations requiring high digital dexterity.
>
> Unlike the man whom she replaced, she as a woman, had the capacity to withstand the monotony of even more simplified repetitive operations. To have suspended the air wrench from a counterbalanced support for him would have served merely to heighten his boredom with the job. As for the woman who replaced him, she now handles two such counterbalanced, air-driven wrenches, one in each hand.[12] ...

There was a contradiction in the management literature on women's war work. It simultaneously stressed the fact that "women are being trained in skills that were considered exclusively in man's domain" and their special suitability for "delicate war jobs."[13] These two seemingly conflicting kinds of statements were reconciled through analogies between "women's work" at home and in the war plants. "Note the similarity between squeezing orange juice and the operation of a small drill press," the Sperry Gyroscope Company urged in a recruitment pamphlet. "Anyone can peel potatoes," it went on. "Burring and filing are almost as easy." An automotive industry publication praised women workers at the Ford Motor Company's Willow Run bomber plant in similar terms. "The ladies have shown they can operate drill presses as well as egg beaters," it proclaimed. "Why should men, who from childhood on never so much as sewed on buttons," inquired one manager, "be expected to handle delicate instruments better than women who have plied embroidery needles, knitting needles and darning needles all their lives?"[14] The newsreel *Glamour Girls of '43* pursued the same theme: "Instead of cutting the lines of a dress, this woman cuts the pattern of aircraft parts. Instead of baking cake, this woman is cooking gears to reduce the tension in the gears after use...."[15] In this manner, virtually any job could be labeled "women's work."

Glamour was a related theme in the idiom through which women's war work was demarcated as female. As if calculated to assure women—and men—that war work need not involve a loss of femininity, depictions of women's new work roles were overlaid with allusions to their stylish dress and attractive appearance. "A pretty young inspector in blue slacks pushes a gauge—a cylindrical plug with a diamond-pointed push-button on its side—through the shaft's hollow chamber," was a typical rendition.[16] Such statements, like the housework analogies, effectively reconciled woman's position in what were previously "men's jobs" with traditional images of femininity.

Ultimately, what lay behind the mixed message that war jobs were at once "men's" and "women's" jobs was an unambiguous point: Women *could* do "men's work," but they were only expected to do it temporarily. The ideological definition of women's war work explicitly included the provision that they would gracefully withdraw from their "men's jobs" when the war ended and the rightful owners returned. Women, as everyone knew, were in heavy industry "for the duration." This theme would become much more prominent after the war, but it was a constant undercurrent from the outset.

Before the war, too, women had been stereotyped as temporary workers, and occupational sex-typing had helped to ensure that employed women would continue to view themselves as women first, workers second. Now this took on new importance, because the reserves of "womanpower" war industries drew on included married women, even mothers of young children, in unprecedented numbers. A study by the Automotive Council for War Production noted that of twelve thousand women employed during the war by one large automotive firm in Detroit, 68 percent were married, and 40 percent had children. And a 1943 WPB study found that 40 percent of one hundred fifty thousand women war workers employed in Detroit were mothers. "With the existing prejudice against employing women over forty, the overwhelming majority of these women workers are young mothers with children under 16."[17]

This was the group of women least likely to have been employed in the prewar years. "In this time of pressure for added labor supply," the U.S. Women's Bureau reported, "the married women for the first time in this country's history exceeded single women in the employed group."[18] . . .

Some firms made deliberate efforts to recruit the wives and daughters of men whom they had employed before the war. A 1942 study by Princeton University's Industrial Relations Section reported on the reasons given by employers for this policy: "(1) It increases the local labor supply without affecting housing requirements; (2) it brings in new employees who are already acquainted with the company and who are likely to be as satisfactory employees as their male relatives; and (3) it may help to minimize postwar readjustment since wives of employed men are not looking for permanent employment."[19] Similarly, the Detroit Vickers aircraft plant had a policy of hiring "members of men's families who have gone to forces so that when these men come back there will be less of a problem in getting the women out of the jobs to give them back to the men."[20]

The dramatic rise in married women's employment during the war raised the long-standing tension between women's commitment to marriage and family and their status as individual members of the paid work force to a qualitatively different level. Before the war, the bulk of the female labor force was comprised of unmarried women; young wives with no children; and self-supporting widowed, divorced, and separated women. When married women and mothers went to work during the war, the occupational sex-typing that linked women's roles in the family and in paid work, far from disintegrating, was infused with new energy. . . .

DEMOBILIZATION AND THE RECONSTRUCTION OF "WOMAN'S PLACE" IN INDUSTRY

The war's end generated renewed upheaval in the sexual division of labor. As reconversion brought massive layoffs and then new hiring, the issue of women's position in industry came to the fore. . . . Would there be a return to the "traditional," prewar sexual division of labor as the mobilization-era ideology of "woman's place" in the war effort had promised? Or would the successful wartime deployment of women in "men's jobs" lead to a permanent shift in the boundaries between women's and men's jobs? Or—a third alternative—would

completely new, postwar exigencies reshape, or even eliminate, the sexual division of labor?

Reversion to prewar patterns, which ultimately did occur, might appear to have been the only real possibility. Had not the nation been repeatedly assured that women's entrance into industry was a temporary adaptation to the extraordinary needs of war? . . . Such a view is consistent with the prevailing ideology of the demobilization period, but it obscures the significance of the war years themselves. Wartime conditions were indeed transitory, yet the extraordinary period between Pearl Harbor and V-J Day left American society permanently transformed. One legacy of the war years, from which no retreat would be possible, was the increase in female labor force participation. On an individual basis, to be sure, many women faced conflicting pressures after the war—to continue working for pay on the one hand, and to go back to the home on the other. Yet a permanent shift had occurred for women as a social group. Despite the postwar resurgence of the ideology of domesticity, by the early 1950s the number of gainfully employed women exceeded the highest wartime level. And as early as 1948, the labor force participation rate of married women was higher than in 1944, the peak of the war boom. The rise in female employment, especially for married women, would continue throughout the postwar period, and at a far more rapid rate than in the first half of the century. In this respect, far from being a temporary deviation, the war was a watershed period that left women's relationship to work permanently changed.[21]

The crucial issue, then, was not whether women would remain in the work force, but rather which women would do so and on what terms. What would the postwar sexual division of paid labor look like? Would women retain their wartime foothold in basic industries like auto and electrical manufacturing? To what extent would they be able to find work in fields that had been predominantly male before the war? For women who worked for pay, whether by choice or necessity, exclusion from "men's jobs" did not mean the housewifery first celebrated and later decried as the "feminine mystique." Instead, it meant employment in low-wage "female" jobs, especially clerical, sales, and service work—all of which expanded enormously in the postwar decades.

That the war brought a permanent increase in female employment made the demobilization transition particularly consequential. The opportunity was there for incorporating the dramatic wartime changes in women's position in industry into the fabric of a postwar order in which paid work would become increasingly central to women's lives. In the absence of any events affecting the labor market as fundamentally and cataclysmically as the war, there has been no comparable occasion for a wholesale restructuring of the sexual division of labor since the 1940s. The fact that the opportunity the wartime upheaval presented was lost had enormous implications for the entire postwar era.

Why, then, was the potential for an enduring transformation in the sexual division of labor not fulfilled in the 1940s? There are two standard explanations. One focuses on the postwar resurgence of domesticity, both as a practice and as an ideology, and suggests that women war workers themselves relinquished the "men's jobs" they held during the war—either because of the genuine appeal of traditional family commitments or because they were ideologically manipulated. The second explanation, in contrast, suggests that the key problem was the operation of union-instituted seniority systems, and their manipulation by male unionists, to exclude women and to favor returning male veterans in postwar employment.

... [B]oth these accounts of the postwar transition, while partially correct, are inadequate.... A large body of evidence demonstrates that management took the lead both in purging women from "men's jobs" after the war and in refusing to rehire them (except in traditionally "female" jobs) as postwar production resumed. Management chose this course despite the fact that most women war workers wanted to keep doing "men's work," and despite the fact that refusing to rehire women often violated seniority provisions in union contracts....

I will offer a two-part explanation for management's postwar policy. First, in both auto and electrical manufacturing, the "traditional" sexual division of labor had a historical logic embodied in the structure of each industry, which remained compelling in the demobilization period. At one level, indeed, reconstructing the prewar sexual division of labor

was a foregone conclusion from management's perspective. Wartime female substitution was an experiment that employers had undertaken unwillingly and only because there was no alternative. Despite the success with which women were integrated into "men's jobs," the war's end meant an end to the experiment, and management breathed a collective sigh of relief.

But that is only half of the story. The postwar purge of women from men's jobs also reflected management's assessment of labor's position on the issue. For one thing, the CIO's wartime struggles for equal pay for women workers, which narrowed sex differentials in wages considerably, made permanent female substitution less appealing than it might otherwise have been. Moreover, in the reconversion period, male workers displayed a great deal of ambivalence about the postwar employment rights of women war workers, even those with seniority standing. The CIO's official policy was to defend women's job rights in line with the seniority principle, but in practice there was substantial opposition to retaining women in "men's jobs." This, I will suggest, effectively reinforced management's determination to reconstruct the prewar sexual division of labor. . . .

MANAGERIAL POLICY TOWARD WOMEN
WORKERS DURING THE WAR—AND AFTER

... Why was management so determined to oust women from the positions that they had occupied during the war? Women war workers wanted to keep their jobs, and union seniority policies did not stand in the way of hiring women, yet they were purged. The problem is all the more puzzling in light of contemporary evidence that management was highly satisfied with women war workers' abilities and performance. While initially employers had strenuously resisted replacing men with women in war industries, once having reconciled themselves to the inevitable, they seemed very pleased with the results. Moreover, because sex differentials in wages, although smaller than before, persisted during the war, one might expect management to have seriously considered the possibility of permanent female substitution on economic grounds.

There is no doubt that women's wartime performance proved satisfactory to management. Under the impact of the "manpower" crunch in the seven months following Pearl Harbor, the proportion of jobs for which the nation's employers were willing to consider women rose from 29 to 55 percent. And management praised women's industrial performance extravagantly during the mobilization period. "Women keep piling up evidence that they *can do,* and *do well,* a multitude of jobs," proclaimed the American Management Association in a 1943 report. "The distribution of basic aptitudes between the two sexes does not differ to any appreciable extent.... What is needed is *training*—training to develop latent aptitudes, to increase mechanical knowledge and skill, and to overcome any fear of the machine."[22] . . .

. . . In a 1943 National Industrial Conference Board survey of 146 executives, nearly 60 percent stated without qualification that women's production was equal to or greater than that of men on similar work. Similarly, a study by the Bureau of Employment Security of several California war plants found an increase in production per hour of workers of both sexes, and a lowering of costs per hour when women were employed, in every plant studied. The BES study also found that women were easier to supervise, and that labor turnover and accident rates decreased with the introduction of women.[23]

Many traditional management policies toward women workers were revised or eliminated with their successful incorporation into war industry. For example, physical segregation of the sexes was no longer deemed necessary; the belief "that men and women could work satisfactorily side by side" was held by the majority of executives questioned by the magazine *Modern Industry* as early as mid-1942. There were also many efforts to promote women to supervisory posts, especially at the lower levels, although women were almost never given authority over male workers, and there was a lingering conviction that women workers themselves preferred male bosses.[24]

Women workers' wartime performance, then, stood as evidence that they could be successfully incorporated into the industrial labor force. In addition, wage differentials between the sexes persisted during the war years—a consideration that one might expect to have enhanced management's interest in retaining women permanently in the postwar era. The

unions, to be sure, had successfully contested sex discrimination in wages in many "equal pay for equal work" cases before the War Labor Board. But although sex differentials were narrowed as a result of these struggles, they were not eliminated. The Conference Board's composite earnings index for twenty-five manufacturing industries registered only a modest increase in the ratio of female to male average hourly earnings, from 61.5 percent in 1941 to 66.4 percent in 1945.[25] . . .

Still, because men and women rarely did "equal work" even during the war, the outcome of successful WLB equal pay cases was to narrow sex differentials in wages, not to eliminate them. And the Board's equal pay policy was not fully enforced, so that even when jobs were identical, or nearly so, women were often paid less than men. The Conference Board found differentials in starting rates paid to men and to "women hired for men's jobs" in nearly half the one hundred and forty-eight plants that it surveyed in 1943, well after equal pay "for comparable quality and quantity of work" had become official WLB policy. Of the ninety-two plants in the survey that had systems of automatic progression in wage rates, twenty-five had sex differentials built into the progression systems despite the fact that the WLB had declared this practice improper.[26]

Similarly, a study of women's wages by the New York State Department of Labor found that 40 percent of the 143 plants surveyed had different starting rates for men and women on "men's jobs." When the state's investigators asked employers to account for such differences, most simply referred to "tradition," standard practice, prevailing wage rates, and custom. "It's also cheaper," said one manager.[27] . . .

There were some extra costs associated with the employment of women, to be sure, particularly in previously all-male plants. Women's absenteeism was generally higher than men's, especially if they were married and had domestic responsibilities, although employers succeeded in narrowing or even eliminating the gap in some plants.[28] UAW President R. J. Thomas, summarizing the reasons auto industry employers were reluctant to hire women for postwar jobs, noted other costs associated with expanding or introducing female employment in a plant. "First is that as you know on most jobs equal rates are paid for equal jobs today," he pointed out. "Management doesn't want to pay women equal rates with men. Not only that but in many of these plants additional facilities have to be put in, such as toilet facilities to take care of women. More space has to be taken to give an opportunity of changing clothes and more safety measures have to be instituted. I think it is pretty well recognized that it is an additional expense to a management to have women."[29]

This is an accurate rendition of the reasons auto industry managers themselves adduced for their reluctance to employ women. Yet it is an inadequate explanation for managerial hostility toward female employment. The costs of maintaining special "facilities" for women were largely absorbed by the government during the war, and could hardly have been a major financial consideration in any event. Surely the savings associated with sex differentials in pay would outweigh any expense firms would incur in continuing to maintain such facilities. Indeed, if only the direct economic costs and benefits of female employment are taken into account, one would expect management to have consistently discriminated *in favor of* women and against men in postwar layoffs and rehiring. Particularly in view of the vigorous efforts of employers to increase labor productivity in the reconversion period, management should have preferred to retain women permanently in the "men's jobs" they had just demonstrated their ability to perform.[30]

Industrial employers chose the opposite course, however, defying not only the apparent imperatives of economic rationality, but also the stated preference of women war workers to keep their war jobs and the unions' official policy that layoffs and rehiring be done strictly by seniority. Rather than institutionalizing the wartime incorporation of women into male jobs, management returned to its prewar practices. . . .

THE ROOTS OF MANAGEMENT'S POSTWAR POLICY

In retrospect, then, management's determination to restore the *status quo ante* seems altogether irrational. Yet from the perspective of employers themselves at the time, it was a foregone conclusion. Management viewed the successful performance of women war workers as,

at best, the fortunate outcome of an experiment in which it had participated with great trepidation and only because there was no alternative. To be sure, women had proved better workers than anyone had expected during the war. But now men's jobs were men's jobs once more. The ideology of sex-typing emerged triumphant again, defining the postwar order along prewar lines in both auto and electrical manufacturing.

In part, the explanation for management's postwar policy involves the logic of the sexual division of labor as it had first developed within the auto and electrical industries a half-century earlier. Not only did the traditions of sex-typing established then have a continuing influence in the post–World War II period, but the factors that had originally shaped those traditions remained salient. In auto, wage levels were still high relative to other industries and would continue to increase in the postwar decades. As in the prewar years, automotive management's efforts to boost productivity focused on tightening control over labor, not on reducing pay levels.[31] Under these conditions, female substitution had little to recommend it, and employers continued to indulge the conviction . . . that women simply were not suitable for employment in automotive production jobs.

In electrical manufacturing, too, prewar traditions of sex-typing persisted in the postwar [era]. But in this industry, the prewar sexual division of labor was historically rooted in a logic of feminization linked to labor-intensity and piecework systems. So why should the further extension of feminization during the war have been rolled back? Even in the case of the automobile industry, why was there a permanent departure from prewar tradition in regard to black employment while the sexual division of jobs persisted virtually unaltered? The historical, industry-specific logic of sex-typing seems to constitute only a partial explanation for management's postwar determination to reconstruct the prewar order.

It is tempting to look outside of the industrial setting to the arena of family and social reproduction in seeking a better solution to the conundrum of management's postwar policies. The interest of capital in reconstructing a family structure in which women are responsible for the generational and daily reproduction of the working class, one might argue, ruled out the permanent employment of women in the well-paid manufacturing jobs that they had during the war. In this view, if women—and more significantly, married women—were to be employed outside the home in ever-increasing numbers in the postwar era, it was crucial that they be confined to poorly paid, secondary jobs that would not jeopardize their primary allegiance to family.

The difficulty with this line of argument is in specifying how the presumed interest of collective capital in reconstituting traditional family forms was translated into the actual employer policies with respect to women workers that emerged in this period. The historical record offers no evidence that such familial considerations played a role in shaping managerial policy in the postwar transition.[32] Although the idea that "woman's place is in the home" was pervasive in the postwar period, it was seldom invoked by employers as a justification for restoring the prewar sexual division of jobs. Instead, management tended to define the issue in economic terms and, above all, by reference to women's physical characteristics and supposed inability to perform "men's jobs."

Although it would be extremely difficult to demonstrate that management policy was rooted in conscious concern over social reproduction, there is evidence for a different kind of explanation: that the postwar purge of women from "men's jobs" involved employers' assessment of the implications of their policies toward women for labor relations. The wartime struggles over equal pay indicated that the unions were committed to resisting any effort to substitute women for men in order to take advantage of their historically lower wages. If wage savings could not be garnered from substitution, or if they could only be garnered at substantial political cost, then why attempt to preserve the wartime sexual division of jobs after the war? In addition, given the widespread fear of postwar unemployment, management might reasonably have anticipated that unemployed male workers would be a source of potential political instability, given the working-class cultural ideal of the "family wage" and the obvious ambivalence of male unionists about women's postwar employment rights.

In short, management had good reason to

believe that a wholesale postwar reorganization of the sexual division of labor, in defiance of the wartime assurances that women were in "men's jobs" only for the duration, could precipitate widespread resistance from labor. The unions were at the peak of their strength at this time, and at the war's end they were no longer constrained by the no-strike pledge. As one contemporary analyst noted, consideration of labor's reaction figured prominently in employers' postwar policies:

> Employers in plants where women had long been assigned to some jobs were disposed favorably to widening the fields of work open to women, unless the job dilutions had proved complicated and costly. In fact, union men declared that some companies, unless prevented by organized labor, would try to continue to use women on men's work because they could be hired at lower initial base pay, be upgraded more slowly, and would be throughout more docile. With the installation of mechanical aids, which using women had necessitated, already paid for out of war profits, management had frequently no particular reason to oppose keeping women on.... Yet most companies frankly admitted that, given full freedom of choice after the war, if only out of deference to prevailing male opinion in the shops, management would revert to giving men's jobs, so called, only to men. *And employers generally assumed that labor would permit no choice.*[33]

Understanding management's postwar policy in these terms helps explain why, in the auto case, women and blacks were treated differently. Despite their common history of exclusion from most auto jobs in the prewar era, the two groups stood in very different positions at the war's end. Organized feminism was at its nadir in the 1940s, and the labor movement's commitment to sexual equality was limited, so that management had little reason to fear that purging women from the industry would meet with substantial political opposition. In contrast, at least in the North, there was a large and vital black civil rights movement, which enjoyed substantial UAW support and from which management could expect vigorous protests if it pursued racially discriminatory employment policies.[34]

Only a few years earlier, when blacks were first hired in large numbers in Detroit's auto factories during the war mobilization, white workers had been vocal in their opposition, most notably in the numerous hate strikes which erupted in the plants and in the race riot of the summer of 1943.[35] But during the war, Detroit became a stronghold of the civil rights movement. The Motor City had the largest branch of the National Association for the Advancement of Colored People (NAACP) of any city in the nation, with a membership of twenty thousand by 1943, and the UAW had become a strong ally of the NAACP and other civil rights groups. While racial discrimination persisted in the auto industry in regard to promotion to the elite skilled trades, no one contested blacks' claims to semi-skilled jobs in the aftermath of the war.[36]

The sharp regional variation in racial patterns of hiring within the auto industry suggests the critical importance of the political dimension in shaping management's employment policies. Although the proportion of blacks in Detroit's auto plants rose dramatically in the 1940s and 1950s, reaching well over 25 percent of the production work force by 1960, in the nation as a whole the percentage of nonwhite auto workers grew much more modestly, from 4 percent in 1940 to only 9 percent in 1960. The national figures reflect the continuing practice of excluding blacks from employment in southern plants. As a manager at a GM plant in Atlanta told the *Wall Street Journal* in 1957, "When we moved into the South, we agreed to abide by local custom and not hire Negroes for production work. This is no time for social reforming and we're not about to try it."[37]

The situation of women auto workers was entirely different from that of northern blacks. Although the incorporation of women into the industry during the war had not provoked riots or hate strikes, this was primarily because female employment was explicitly understood to be a temporary expedient, "for the duration" only. After the war, women were expected to go "back to the home." There was no parallel expectation regarding black men. And while women war workers wanted to remain in the auto industry, as we have seen, their preferences (unlike blacks') lacked legitimacy. While black workers had the civil rights movement behind them, there was no mass feminist movement or even popular consciousness of women's job rights at this critical juncture, when the sexual division of labor that would

characterize the postwar period was crystallizing. . . .

NOTES

1. U.S. Senate Hearings, *Manpower Problems in Detroit,* 79th Cong. 1st sess., pp. 9–13 (Mar. 1945), pp. 13534, 13638; interview with Edward Cushman.

2. Reference to such a survey made "to determine those operations which were suitable for female operators" is made on pp. 2–3 of the Summary Brief Submitted by Buick Motor Division, Melrose Park, General Motors Corporation, "In the Matter of GMC—Buick, Melrose Park, Ill., and UAW-CIO," 14 June 1943, Walter Reuther Collection, WSU Archives, box 20, folder: "WLB, GM Women's Rates." A survey of this type was also conducted at the Ford Willow Run plant; see the section on "Training of Women" in *Willow Run Bomber Plant, Record of War Effort* (notebook), vol. 2, pt. 2, Jan.–Dec. 1942, p. 30, La Croix Collection, Accession 435, Ford Archives, Dearborn, Michigan, box 15.

3. Computed from data in U.S. Department of Labor, Bureau of Labor Statistics, Division of Wage Analysis, Regional Office no. 8-A, Detroit, Michigan, 3 Dec. 1943, serial no. 8-A–16 (mimeo), "Metalworking Establishments, Detroit, Michigan, Labor Market Area, Straight-Time Average Hourly Earnings, Selected Occupations, July, 1943." UAW Research Department Collection, WSU Archives, box 28, folder: "Wage Rates (Detroit) Bureau of Labor Statistics, 1943–45." . . .

4. Computed from data in "Earnings in Manufacture of Electrical Appliances, 1942," p. 532.

5. Regarding GE and Westinghouse, see U.S. National War Labor Board, *War Labor Reports,* vol. 28, pp. 677–78. . . .

6. See "Summary Employment Status Report for Michigan," 30 Apr. 1943, Records of the U.S. Employment Service, National Archives, Record Group 183, box 181, folder: "Michigan Statewide."

7. Press release of Office of Production Management, Labor Division, 5 Dec. 1941, UAW Research Department Collection, WSU Archives, box 32, folder: "Women Employment 1941."

8. "Engineers of Womanpower," *Automotive War Production* 2 (Oct. 1943):4–5 (emphasis added). . . .

9. "What Women Are Doing in Industry," *Factory Management and Maintenance* 100 (March 1942):63; "Provisions in Plants for Physical Differences Enable Women to Handle Variety of War Jobs," *Automotive War Production* 2 (Sept. 1943):7.

10. "Report of Two Special Meetings on Employing and Training Women for War Jobs," attended by executives from 85 N. A. M. companies from the East and Midwest, 27 and 30 Mar. 1942, in Records of the Automotive Council for War Production, Detroit Public Library, folder: "Manpower: Source Material: New Workers," p. 1.

11. "Provisions in Plants"; Constance Green, "The Role of Women as Production Workers in War

Plants in the Connecticut Valley," *Smith College Studies in History* 28 (1946):32. . . .

12. W. Gerald Tuttle, "Women War Workers at Vultee Aircraft," *Personnel Journal* 21 (Sept. 1942): 8–9.

13. "Women Work for Victory," *Automotive War Production* 1 (Nov. 1942):4; "Engineers of Womanpower," p. 4.

14. "There's a Job for You at Sperry . . . Today" (pamphlet), Records of UE District 4, UE Archives, University of Pittsburgh folder 877; "Hiring and Training Women for War Work," *Factory Management and Maintenance* 100 (Aug. 1942):73; "Engineers of Womanpower," p. 4.

15. The transcript of this newsreel was made available to me by the Rosie the Riveter Film Project, Emeryville, California.

16. "Engineers of Womanpower," p. 4.

17. "New Workers," *Manpower Reports*, 10 (published by the Manpower Division of the Automotive Council for War Production), p. 4; Anne Gould, "Problems of Woman War Workers in Detroit," 20 Aug. 1943, Records of the War Production Board, National Archives, RG 179, box 203, folder: "035.606 Service Trades Divisions, WPB Functions," p. 2.

18. U.S. Department of Labor, Women's Bureau, Special Bulletin no. 20, *Changes in Women's Employment During the War* (1944), p. 18.

19. Helen Baker, *Women in War Industries* (Princeton: Princeton University Press, 1942), p. 15.

20. "Report of Mrs. Betty Sturges Finan on Cleveland Detroit Trip, Feb. 9–17 [1943] inclusive," pp. 3–4, Records of the War Manpower Commission, National Archives, Record Group 211, Series 137, box 977, folder: "Consultants—Betty Sturges Finan." See also "Report of Two Special Meetings," p. 6.

21. See U.S. Bureau of the Census, *Historical Statistics of the U.S.: Colonial Times to 1970* (1975), pp. 131, 133. This claim is considerably more modest than William Chafe's controversial thesis that the wartime changes in female labor force participation make the 1940s a key "turning point in the history of American women." See William H. Chafe, *The American Woman: Her Changing Social, Economic, and Political Role, 1920–1970* (New York: Oxford University Press, 1972), p. 195. . . .

22. Chafe, *The American Woman*, p. 137; American Management Association. Special Research Report no. 2, *Supervision of Women on Production Jobs: A Study of Management's Problems and Practices in Handling Female Personnel* (1943), pp. 8–10 (emphasis in the original).

23. National Industrial Conference Board, "Wartime Pay of Women in Industry," *Studies in Personnel Policy*, no. 58 (1943):27; "Woman's Place," *Business Week* (16 May 1942):20–22. . . .

24. *Modern Industry*, 15 July 1942, summarized in *Management Review* 31 (Sept. 1942):303–4. Regard-

ing the use of women as supervisors, see *Supervision of Women on Production Jobs*, pp. 24–27. . . .

25. Computed from data in *The Management Almanac 1946* (New York: National Industrial Conference Board, 1946), p. 77.

26. "Wartime Pay of Women in Industry," pp. 18–19. . . .

27. New York State Department of Labor, Division of Women in Industry, *Women's Wages on Men's Jobs* (1944), p. 26.

28. See New York State Department of Labor, Division of Women in Industry, *Absenteeism in New York State War Production Plants* (1943); National Industrial Conference Board, "The Problem of Absenteeism," *Studies in Personnel Policy*, no. 53 (1943); "Women Workers on War Production," *UAW Research Report 3* (Mar. 1943):3. . . .

29. *Manpower Problems in Detroit*, pp. 13112–13.

30. See Howell John Harris, *The Right to Manage: Industrial Relations Policies of American Business in the 1940s* (Madison: University of Wisconsin Press, 1982), pp. 66–67, 91–93.

31. Ibid. This is Harris's main thesis.

32. Denise Riley, " 'The Free Mothers': Pronatalism and Working Women in Industry at the End of the Last War in Britain," *History Workshop* II (Spring 1981):59–118, presents the most convincing case for this argument in regard to the postwar transition for the British case, but she relies on evidence about state policy with virtually none directly from employers.

33. Green, "Role of Women as Production Workers," pp. 64–65 (emphasis added).

34. August Meier and Elliot Rudwick, *Black Detroit and the Rise of the U.A.W.* (New York: Oxford University Press, 1979).

35. Ibid.; Robert C. Weaver, *Negro Labor: A National Problem* (New York: Harcourt, Brace, and World, 1946).

36. Meier and Rudwick, *Black Detroit*, p. 113. See also Karen Anderson, "Last Hired, First Fired: Black Women Workers during World War II," *Journal of American History* 69 (June 1982), especially pp. 86–87, where white male workers' attitudes toward women and blacks are compared.

37. Both the employment figures and the quote are cited in Herbert R. Northrup, Richard L. Rowan, et al., *Negro Employment in Basic Industry*, Industrial Research Unit, Wharton School of Finance and Commerce, University of Pennsylvania (1970), pp. 65–75. The national employment figures are from the U.S. Census, and because (unlike the figures for Detroit) they include both production and nonproduction workers, they overstate the difference between Detroit and the nation as a whole, for the vast majority of nonproduction workers were white in this period. The quote is from the *Wall Street Journal*, 24 Oct. 1957.

REGINA G. KUNZEL

Unwed Mothers, Social Workers, and the Postwar Family: White Neurosis, Black Pathology

One of the many concerns of a nation at war was the rise in female promiscuity. It was not just professional prostitutes that aroused alarm, or even the "Victory Girls," those thrill-seeking working-class girls who mingled with soldiers on the streets and in restaurants and dance halls. Rather, it was the young women showing up at maternity homes who were the properly brought up daughters of good families. Hardly "bad girls" in the traditional sense, they nonetheless deviated from the family norm.

In the following essay, Regina Kunzel explores how social workers (who had replaced the missionary women of an earlier generation) dealt with the "new" unwed white mother. However, hers was not the only out-of-wedlock pregnancy that had to be explained. Vying for attention was the unwed black mother. Illegitimacy had long been largely ignored among social workers and policymakers who assumed it to be the natural and unsurprising result of black women's hypersexuality and immorality. In the immediate postwar years, however, it no longer seemed so benign.

Kunzel's account of the cultural meanings attached to out-of-wedlock pregnancy for middle-class white women, working-class white women, and black women provides a compelling example of how class and especially race construct our understanding. Note, too, how these new constructions of illegitimacy, like efforts to return Rosie the Riveter to the home, addressed anxieties about women's sexual and economic behavior unleashed during wartime. In the cold war years containment applied not only to the expansion of communism, but also to the sexual and economic independence of American women, as historian Elaine Tyler May has pointed out.

In September of 1941, Robert South Barrett sent out a warning to . . . workers [who staffed the Florence Crittenton maternity homes]: "I think it necessary that I should raise the storm signal to our Homes in the same way the Weather Bureau raises one at the approach of a hurricane," he wrote. "We are facing a very serious time, and I beg you to make plans now to meet a situation that is fraught with many dangers."[1] These dangers—"the lure of uniforms, the emotional disturbances produced by men being taken away from their usual habitats, the assembling of large numbers of men in military camps"—were those of the home front during wartime. Maternity home workers expected World War II to swell the illegitimacy rate and deluge the homes with applications. . . .

Those concerned with unmarried mothers had reason to sound the alarm. . . . [By] 1944, [when] the first large wartime increase in the number of illegitimate births [occurred], many maternity homes were so overcrowded that they had to turn applicants away.[2] But to those working with unmarried mothers in the 1940s, the changing demographic profile of unmarried mothers seeking aid was as striking as their numerical increase. In contrast to the pre-dominantly working-class clientele that had filled maternity homes in the first half of the twentieth century, maternity home staffs and social workers all over the country reported a rise in the number of white middle-class women seeking the services of homes and so-cial agencies. Social worker Helen Perlman at-tributed this demographic change to marriage postponements during wartime, the rising in-cidence of "illicit coition," and the more fre-quent use of social agencies by unmarried mothers.[3] [Historian Rickie] Solinger has spec-ulated that middle-class girls and women might have turned to maternity homes in greater numbers during and after the war be-cause out-of-wedlock pregnancy threatened the aspirations of middle-class families in a new way. Whereas the illegitimate pregnancy of a middle-class daughter was once a "private sorrow," to be attended with an appropriately private solution, the wartime and postwar fam-ily ideology rendered her a "public humilia-tion" that required a professional curative.[4]

Whatever the cause, the upsurge in the number of white middle-class women seeking aid drew considerable comment, and observa-tions on the class status of unmarried mothers marked every description of the clientele of homes and agencies in the 1940s. Cases cited by social workers in the professional literature, previously populated by the paradigmatic working-class sex delinquent characterized by a fondness for the dance hall, an excessive use of makeup, and an inclination toward using slang, now pondered an altogether different unmarried mother. Social work theorist Leon-tine Young's description of a woman "in her mid twenties, quietly attractive, and well-dressed," who "spoke in a soft voice and with an educated accent," was filled with the signi-fiers of middle-class status.[5] Psychiatrist J. Ka-sanin and social worker Sieglinde Handschin also drew attention to the "new" unmarried mother—"a girl of good family, a good student in high school or perhaps university . . . prop-erly brought up."[6]

Social workers were initially baffled by what to make of unmarried mothers who were "poised, calm and assured, quiet, unruffled, friendly and smiling," and to whom the con-ventional causes of illegitimacy did not seem to apply.[7] "They are no longer limited to the ten-ement dwellers," Sara Edlin noted of the war-

time and postwar residents of Staten Island's Lakeview home, whose history of "overcrowd-ing, large families, and the deprivations and struggles of poverty" had explained their con-dition in the past.[8] Crittenton social worker Rose Bernstein was candid in her confusion when she noted that "the extension of unmar-ried motherhood into our upper and educated classes in sizeable numbers further confounds us by rendering our former stereotypes less tenable. Immigration, low mentality, and hy-persexuality," she wrote, "can no longer be comfortably applied when the phenomenon has invaded our own social class—when the unwed mother must be classified to include the nice girl next door, the physician's or pastor's daughter."[9]

In their departures from the stereotypical unmarried mother, those women seeking the aid of social agencies and maternity homes in the 1940s seemed to defy conventional expla-nations of out-of-wedlock pregnancy. The in-creasing presence of middle-class girls and women in maternity homes and social agencies led social workers to reevaluate the causes be-hind out-of-wedlock pregnancy in an attempt to remove them from the larger category of "sex delinquency." In an effort to comprehend this new group of unmarried mothers, social workers turned from explanations of illegiti-macy grounded in sociology, criminology, and sexology and called instead on psychiatry. Be-ginning in the 1940s, social workers viewed il-legitimacy among white middle-class girls and women as a symptom of unconscious needs and desires. Rather than regarding them as "delinquents, moral defectives, or prostitutes," social workers diagnosed them as neurotic.[10]

Social workers in this decade were not the first of their profession to turn to psychoana-lytic explanations of behavior. The first wave of interest in psychiatry and psychoanalysis rose in the years immediately following World War I and crested in the 1920s, amounting to what historians of social work have since termed the "psychiatric deluge."[11] Especially influential in the mental hygiene movement, the child guidance movement, and the devel-opment of veterans' services, psychiatric social workers proposed an interior approach to the client's problems to replace the more sociolog-ical focus on external circumstances. As social work theory substituted personal maladjust-ment for environmental causes as the root of social problems, social workers proposed adjusting the individual to the environment rather than reforming that environment.[12]. . .

Some social workers, reluctant to dismiss so cavalierly the previous three decades of work on illegitimacy, proposed a bridge between psychiatric and sociological explanations. In 1938, Mandel Sherman argued that "a clear-cut differentiation cannot be made between the psychiatric and the social factors" and posited an "interrelationship" between the two.[13] But the psychological soon overwhelmed the sociological in psychiatrists' and social workers' assessments of unmarried mothers. Beginning in the 1940s, social workers joined psychiatrists and psychologists in viewing out-of-wedlock pregnancy as the unmarried mother's attempt to ease a larger unresolved psychic conflict. . . . Dorothy Hutchinson, professor of casework at the New York School of Social Work, often used psychiatric concepts in her work with unmarried mothers in the 1940s. Judging one unmarried mother "a very neurotic girl," Hutchinson wrote that "unconsciously I feel that Marjorie was working out a love relationship with a man her father's age who represented her father to her but of all this she was totally unaware."[14] Of another client, Hutchinson proposed that "in the pregnancy situation, Jennie seems to be somehow acting out oedipus difficulties and oedipal attachment to father."[15]. . .

Even the Salvation Army's Door of Hope in Jersey City embraced the new understanding of unmarried motherhood. [When] Jane Wrieden, [the] Salvation Army officer and trained social worker . . . principally responsible for bringing psychiatric social work to the Door of Hope, [was] asked to assess the cause of out-of-wedlock pregnancy, Wrieden stated: "I have come to think of these pregnancies as only symptoms of more deep-seated problems.". . . To illustrate, Wrieden told the story of a Door of Hope resident, "Mary Roe," who had had an affair with a man she expected to marry. "But when she found she was pregnant, the man told her that he was not free to marry, and that he did not intend to divorce the wife of whom Mary never before had heard." Although Mary's case contained the essential ingredients of the many tales of seduction and abandonment spun by Door of Hope workers in the past, Wrieden offered a different interpretation of the meaning of Mary's pregnancy.

After receiving a psychological examination at the Door of Hope, "Mary finally gained real insight into her experience, and saw her love affair and her pregnancy as related to her conflict with her own mother."[16]

Although psychiatrists and social workers agreed that illegitimacy was a neurotic symptom, they varied in their specific analyses of the deeper pathology that produced it. Explanations of out-of-wedlock pregnancy ran the gamut of psychoanalytic diagnoses, covering a range of deep-seated problems including self-punishment for forbidden sex fantasies, unresolved oedipal relationships with either or both parents, and fantasies of rape, prostitution, or immaculate conception. Many social workers believed that either a dependency upon or rejection by the mother or a seductive attachment to the father could precipitate illegitimacy.[17] Others described out-of-wedlock pregnancy as a masochistic act. "This passive-masochistic tendency probably characterizes a large proportion of unmarried mothers," psychiatrist Helene Deutsch wrote; "it is a feminine tendency, intensified by guilt feelings, that, once cruelly gratified through illegitimate motherhood, seeks repetition of the same situation." Deutsch transformed the traditional story of seduction and abandonment—"being left 'on the street' with the illegitimate child of a seducer"—into the "masochistic fantasy" of an unmarried mother.[18]

However they diagnosed its underlying cause, psychiatrists and social workers believed out-of-wedlock pregnancy to be a purposeful, albeit unconscious act on the part of a neurotic woman; although she sought pregnancy, she did so for reasons lodged deep in her unconscious. Leontine Young likened the unmarried mother to a "sleepwalker," who "acts out what she must do without awareness or understanding of what it means or of the fact that she plans and initiates the action," and claimed that "there is nothing haphazard or accidental in the causation that brought along this specific situation with these specific girls."[19]

The psychiatric reconceptualization of out-of-wedlock pregnancy was accomplished in less than a decade, so that by the mid-1940s, neurotic unmarried mothers were entirely predictable. Helene Deutsch described Ida, whose pregnancy she diagnosed as the result of "the rebellious struggle against her mother," as "a fundamentally banal story of illegitimacy."[20] In 1944, Viola Bernard remarked on the redundancy of the case of the neurotic unmarried mother: "With repetitious regularity the background histories of all the cases ... show conspicuous maternal and paternal failure to meet the essential lifelong emotional needs of these girls."[21] By the 1940s, social workers were as little surprised to find an unmarried mother with seductive designs on her father as they had been just ten years earlier to find her the promiscuous patron of dance halls or as evangelical women before them had been to find her the victim of an unscrupulous man.

Like these earlier narratives of out-of-wedlock pregnancy, the new psychiatric understanding of the unmarried mother was heavily weighted with meaning for its authors. Despite their many gains, social workers continued to fret over the insecurity of their professional status into the 1940s. To anxious professionals, psychiatry's appeal was inescapable. Because psychiatry was invested with such cultural authority in the postwar period, it boosted social workers' claims to expertise. . . . The psychiatric understanding of unmarried motherhood offered social workers a discourse of illegitimacy cast in an esoteric language appropriate to the professional, filled with medical terms and cloaked in the legitimizing mantle of science. Social workers were afforded unprecedented opportunities to label and categorize and to assign unmarried mothers to "types.". . . [In 1939, social worker] Miriam Powell classified thirty unmarried mothers according to the following categories: "Primary behavior disorder, 17; psychoneurosis, 3; schizophrenia, with excessive sexuality, 2; schizoid personality, with homosexual tendencies, 1; psychopathic personality, 3; neurotic character of the hysterical type, 1; adult maladjustment, 1; childish personality with a nonexistent ego, 1."[22] In an act of surprising humility, Powell listed one unmarried mother as "undiagnosed."

More broadly, the recasting of illegitimacy as a psychological rather than a sociological problem—the causes of which were to be sought not in environmental conditions but in individual psyches—must be understood in the context of the World War II and postwar period, when a family-centered culture and rigidly differentiated and prescriptive gender roles took shape and a therapeutic approach to

social problems gained immense popularity.[23] At a time when "health" was measured in terms of how well an individual adjusted to his or her appropriate place in the nuclear family, it should come as no surprise that out-of-wedlock pregnancy was stigmatized as an "abnormal" departure from "normal" gender roles. Out-of-wedlock pregnancy thus became an index of abnormality that was defined in opposition to normal femininity. According to Marynia Farnham and Ferdinand Lundberg in their 1947 antifeminist classic *Modern Woman: The Lost Sex*, not only was the unmarried mother "a psychological mess"; she was also "a complete failure as a woman."[24] In large part, the core of the unmarried mother's failure lay in her refusal of married heterosexuality—newly sexualized, privileged, and compulsory in wartime and postwar America. "Certainly, the girl's wish to have a baby without a husband is neither an adult nor a normal desire," Young wrote, invoking two damning postwar epithets—immaturity and abnormality—in a single sentence. She continued: "The urge for a child is a fundamental biological force without which the race would not long survive, but normally that urge is an inextricable part of the love of a man and a woman for each other. . . . The serious problem of the unmarried mother is that her urge for a baby has been separated from its normal matrix, love for a mate."[25] . . .

Professional aspirations of social workers and their participation in a culture that stigmatized all departures from conventional gender roles as neurotic go some distance toward explaining the rise of the neurotic unmarried mother. But the fact that not all unmarried mothers were so diagnosed suggests that class and race informed this new conceptualization in powerful ways. In large part, social workers' reframing of illegitimacy as neurotic seems to have been linked to their attempt to explain the changing demographic profile of unmarried mothers seeking aid during the war. Helen Perlman was careful to specify race when she wrote that "prevailing social work theory about the illegitimately pregnant white girl or woman is heavily dependent on psychoanalytic theory." Exploring the reasons behind the new concern for "the psychological well-being of the unmarried mothers" in the 1940s, Perlman argued that "there arose some wish to protect the 'good girl' of 'good family' who was considered to have 'made a mistake.' "[26] Diagnosing the unmarried mother as neurotic rather than as a sex delinquent offered that protection. Psychiatric explanations gave social workers a way to comprehend the illicit sexual behavior of young white women of the middle class as something other than willful promiscuity.

Accordingly, psychiatric explanations desexualized out-of-wedlock pregnancy. Branding unmarried mothers as sexual delinquents had defined them as hypersexual; diagnosing white middle-class unmarried mothers as neurotic recast them as sexually passive, even asexual. In fact, "contrary to the layman's notion," Viola Bernard reported, not one of the ten unmarried mothers in her study experienced "full sexual enjoyment," and for most of them "intercourse proved chiefly unpleasant."[27] . . . Helene Deutsch asserted that "conception takes place under specific conditions that have nothing to do with love or sexual excitement.". . . "The idea that all the girls are boycrazy, oversexed, or downright bad is idiotic," Hildegarde Dolson argued in 1942. To support this claim, Dolson noted that the unmarried mothers she observed at the Youth Consultation Service included "a nurse, a debutante, a waitress, a highschool junior, two college graduates, a young schoolteacher, and the nineteen-year-old daughter of a well-to-do businessman."[28] Dolson's assumption, shared by many of her colleagues, was that class exempted these women from the label of sex delinquency. . . .

One social worker surely spoke for many of her colleagues when she identified the sexual behavior of the unmarried mother as "one of the most difficult problems for the worker."[29] And indeed, it must have been difficult for social workers to transform behavior that had been understood as unambiguously promiscuous into behavior consistent with the sexual passivity that social workers and psychiatrists insisted was characteristic of the white middle-class unmarried mother of the 1940s. They accomplished this feat, in large part, by focusing attention on the pregnancy rather than the precipitating sexual act; the new psychiatric understanding of illegitimacy deemphasized sex and foregrounded maternity. Whereas sex with a casual acquaintance would have once marked a woman as sexually aggressive, it was now understood as a deliberate and neurotic attempt to become pregnant outside of marriage, the man in question being

simply a "tool" by which to achieve the pregnancy and the steps a woman took to accomplish that end only incidentally sexual. "All the evidence points to the fact that most of the girls in this group are truly disinterested in the actual fathers of the babies," Young wrote: "For such a girl, the man is apparently a necessary biological accessory which serves only one purpose—to make her pregnant—and then is of no further interest or concern."[30] By transforming illegitimacy from a discourse of illicit sexuality into a discourse of motherhood, psychoanalytic diagnoses deemphasized the sexuality of overtly sexual women, maternalized women who flouted so many postwar family imperatives, and repositioned unmarried mothers within a structure of family relations rather agnosing the unmarried mother as neurotic rather than as a sex delinquent offered that protection. Psychiatric explanations gave social workers a way to comprehend the illicit sexual behavior of young white women of the middle class as something other than willful promiscuity.

Interestingly, this new focus on unmarried mothers as mothers rather than as sex delinquents did not garner any more respect for their right to make their own decisions regarding the disposition of their children. Social workers had argued that sex delinquents were unfit to be mothers, and neurotic unmarried mothers were considered no more competent to care for their children. "In my experience," Young asserted, "the majority of unmarried mothers are not strong, mature, well adjusted people, and the reality is that only such a person can assume and carry out responsibility for an out-of-wedlock child without serious damage to both herself and the child."[32] In the 1940s, then, social workers took a more active role in encouraging unmarried mothers to put their children up for adoption.[33] . . .

While illegitimacy among white middle-class women appeared less menacing when cast as a problem of individual pathology, illegitimacy among other groups began to take on a more threatening hue. "Bad girls" had not disappeared in the 1940s; on the contrary, they loomed large on the national public landscape. The psychiatric narrative of out-of-wedlock pregnancy that essentially desexualized white middle-class unmarried mothers is all the more striking when viewed in the larger context of the national preoccupation with female promiscuity that accompanied World War II. Observers in the 1940s noted with alarm "the increase in the number of footloose, unprotected girls roaming Main Street, loitering in parks, hanging around juke joints, and often getting themselves into serious trouble."[34] Much of this fear focused on the threat of venereal disease to men in the armed services and precipitated a massive drive against prostitution.[35] Many came to believe, however, that prostitution, traditionally defined as sex for money, was less a problem than "promiscuity," although contemporaries were disconcerted to find the line dividing the two "difficult, if not impossible to draw."[36] Of the girls and women who came to Hartford, Connecticut, to be near soldiers and defense workers, Helen Pigeon wrote, "They do not belong to the rank of professional prostitutes but it is evident from case histories that many are promiscuous."[37] "Sex delinquency" had been a working-class diagnosis since the 1910s, and class assumptions continued to inflect understandings of wartime promiscuity.[38] Mrs. Laura Waggoner of the Community Welfare Council of San Antonio, Texas, identified these girls and women as "almost entirely from farming and working-class homes of low economic level" and characterized them as "casual fun-seeking girls wanting male companionship, immature in judgment, sometimes lonely, unstable, and easily influenced."[39] These women who drew so much attention, condemnation, and fear from public officials and wartime media—those dubbed "Victory Girls," "khaki-wackies," and "patriotic prostitutes" who socialized with soldiers on the streets, in restaurants, and in dance halls—were not given psychiatric examinations; rather, they were rounded up by local law enforcement officials and described in the older terms of sex delinquency.[40] . . . The discourse of sex delinquency retained its explanatory appeal to social workers who attempted to understand the behavior of girls and women whose out-of-wedlock pregnancy still seemed to spring from familiar causes long assumed to have a working-class etiology: broken homes, bad companions, a disdain for authority, and an addiction to urban pleasures. The psychiatric understanding of out-of-wedlock pregnancy simply ensured that white middle-class unmarried mothers would no longer be cast among their ranks.

Even more than working-class white women, black unmarried mothers attracted increasingly intense concern beginning in the late 1930s and accelerating during and after the war. Social workers who went to great lengths to defuse the "problem" of the white unmarried mother drew attention to that posed by her black counterpart. While the psychiatric discourse of illegitimacy attempted to remove white middle-class unmarried mothers from the roster of problems facing postwar America, a reconceptualization of black illegitimacy catapulted African American women to the top of that list.

Observers had commented on a disproportionately high black illegitimacy rate since the early twentieth century, but black unmarried mothers had not attracted a great deal of attention or interest before the late 1930s.[41] Indeed, in the early twentieth century, when illegitimacy among working-class white women came under such intense scrutiny, their African American counterparts seemed hardly worthy of notice. Most of those who did investigate black illegitimacy wrote in the racist tradition that viewed out-of-wedlock pregnancy as the natural and unsurprising result of the constitutional hypersexuality and immorality believed to be characteristic of the race. Beginning in the 1920s and 1930s, however, historians, sociologists, anthropologists, and social workers moved from arguments based on racial degeneracy to new arguments that highlighted the "cultural acceptance" of illegitimacy in some black communities. Rather than providing an index of immorality, illegitimacy, these investigators argued, was better understood as an adaptation to environmental and social conditions. Some, most notably anthropologist Melville Herskovits, argued that African American attitudes toward illegitimacy were rooted in preslavery African traditions.[42] In contrast, E. Franklin Frazier, in his pathbreaking 1939 study *The Negro Family in the United States,* argued that black family patterns were born of the conditions of enslavement in the United States. Social workers were quick to incorporate sociological and anthropological arguments into their own investigations of black illegitimacy. Frazier, in particular, exerted enormous influence among social workers, perhaps because of his background in the profession.[43] . . .

Beginning in the late 1930s, black illegitimacy came under closer scrutiny and began to appear less benign. Frazier was perhaps the first to question the casual acceptance of black out-of-wedlock pregnancy and to complicate its causes. By Frazier's own account, the necessary survival strategies adopted by black families during slavery—including a "matriarchal" family structure, "disorganized" kinship ties, and illegitimacy—took on new meaning in twentieth-century urban life. Before that time, Frazier argued, illegitimacy in rural black communities reflected "the simple and naive behavior of peasant folks"—behavior that was "not licentious and could scarcely be called immoral."[44] The new subjects that captured Frazier's attention, however, were no longer rural blacks, but those who had migrated from the rural South to southern, northern, and western cities. The migration of illegitimacy from rural areas into newly visible urban venues accompanied the geographical migration of blacks that began in the 1910s and accelerated during World War II. . . . Frazier was among the first to assert that the migration of blacks to cities rendered illegitimacy, once harmless, newly problematic: "during the course of their migration to the city, family ties are broken, and the restraints which once held in check immoral sex conduct lose their force."[45] Declaring black illegitimacy in Chicago to be "the result of family and community disorganization," Frazier argued that out-of-wedlock pregnancy was "the result of casual and impersonal contacts through which random and undisciplined impulses found expression." In its new urban incarnation, illegitimacy no longer ensued from an adaptive black family structure but rather from "an awakened imagination fed by the cheap romance of the movies and the popular magazines" that Frazier argued "led some to licentiousness and debauchery in the sex relation."[46]

The wartime migration of African Americans to cities seemed to Frazier to reconfigure rural folkways into urban problems, and disproportionate black illegitimacy rates that had once seemed expressive of naive peasant customs now signaled a dangerously dysfunctional black family. To Frazier, illegitimacy was not only a product of unstable family relations but, more dangerously, the catalyst for "matriarchal" families, which, he claimed, "originate through illegitimacy." Illegitimacy, then, was simultaneously cause and effect of the disorganized black family. In a passage that illumi-

nates the anxiety about black women's autonomy that underlay this characterization of the black family, Frazier wrote that "the man's or father's function generally ceases with impregnation. . . . He has no authority in the household or over his children."[47]

The manifestation of this new matriarchal autonomy most disturbing to Frazier was his belief that black women were more inclined to give up their illegitimate children, to him an important indicator of the new and dangerous character of black illegitimacy. This charge was altogether new and reflected a complete reversal in representations. For decades, social commentators had invested black unmarried mothers with instinctive maternal warmth and praised their tendency to keep their children. But by the 1940s, many observers were noting with great anxiety the desire on the part of some black unmarried mothers in urban areas to give up their children. Frazier found that, "on the whole, the unmarried mothers in the city exhibit less of the elemental maternal sympathy toward their children which one finds in rural communities in the South."[48] Frazier went so far as to accuse black single mothers of infanticide: "In the alleys of southern cities as well as in the tenements in northern cities, the unmarried mother sometimes kills her unwanted child by throwing it in the garbage can."[49]

In attempting to understand the forces generating this reconceptualization of black illegitimacy, one should note that many scholars and social workers, Frazier foremost among them, initially invoked the argument of cultural acceptance to repudiate the racist assumptions of biological theories of black family life and morality that underlay earlier prevailing explanations of black illegitimacy.[50] . . . As eager as many sociologists and social workers were to present black illegitimacy as culturally constructed rather than biologically ordained, they were also concerned that distinctive African-American family patterns presented obstacles to racial integration. Thus, they found some relief in their "discovery" that not all black Americans regarded illegitimacy with the same apparent nonchalance. Studies of urban black communities that proliferated in the 1930s and 1940s sought to show how the family patterns of the most "advanced" black families resembled those of the white middle class, a resemblance that was most often measured according to morality and sexuality. In her 1944 study of illegitimacy in Durham, North Carolina, Hilda Hertz noted that middle- and upper-class blacks "accept the same values in regard to sex behavior and family life accepted in white society."[51] Investigators of black urban communities turned to moral and sexual measures as often as economic indicators to map the geography of class. Believing out-of-wedlock pregnancy to be the most accessible index of moral values and sexual behavior, those investigators used illegitimacy to chart the emergence of a class-stratified black urban community. Hertz, for example, distinguished the "Negro upper and middle class" from the "lower class" by their respective "sex codes," and psychologist Margaret Brenman cited the difference in sexual standards and behavior between middle- and "lower-class" black teenage girls as "probably the most reliable single criterion in establishing class membership."[52] . . .

This sexual cartography of class had two purposes. First, it enabled both investigators of black communities and middle-class residents of those communities to combat the popular notion of a homogeneous and pathological black family and to distinguish a new black bourgeoisie from its "lower-class" neighbors. Representing this new middle class required contrasting its assimilated manners with those of a new black proletariat.[53] Second, and at least as important, this formulation allowed sociologists to posit a hopeful trajectory: if black illegitimacy was most prevalent among recent migrants who had brought their rural ways to the city—if, as St. Clair Drake and Horace Cayton argued, illegitimacy among blacks was a reflection not of immorality but "of the incomplete urbanization of the rural southern migrants"—then perhaps the black family was moving on an evolutionary path toward the standard set by the middle-class white family.[54] The argument that illegitimacy was "culturally accepted" among blacks served the intellectual and political interests of sociologists and social workers of the 1930s and 1940s—some of whom were themselves African American— and the class interests of a new black bourgeoisie, each of whom used this conceptualization of out-of-wedlock pregnancy to plot a liberal path toward racial integration and assimilation.

Frazier's work had a tremendous impact on social workers; it also captured the interest of a new group of "experts" in social policy. In 1935, the Carnegie Corporation commissioned a massive study of American race relations and invited Swedish economist Gunnar Myrdal to synthesize and popularize scholarly work and statistical data on African American life. Published in 1944, *An American Dilemma* was a monument to 1940s racial liberalism. . . . In arguing that "the uniqueness of the Negro family is a product of slavery," Myrdal joined Frazier in characterizing the black family as pathological and in placing ultimate blame for "deviant" black family patterns on white racism.[55]

Postwar social policymakers and politicians were as impressed as Myrdal with Frazier's research on the African American family and as inclined to appropriate his arguments. They were less inclined, however, to focus on the aspects of his analysis that indicted racism and more likely to name the black family itself as the dilemma that demanded national attention. As the specter of black illegitimacy that would dominate public policy debates about the black family in the 1950s and 1960s began to take shape under the weight of wartime and postwar pressures, what was once seen as "cultural acceptance" became "cultural pathology."

The principal architect of this new construction, Daniel Patrick Moynihan, positioned illegitimacy at the heart of the "tangle of pathology" of the black family.[56] Whereas Frazier had blamed white racial oppression for "pathology" and "disorganization," Moynihan suggested that the causes were intrinsic to African American culture. Moynihan's strategy of locating the causes of problems faced by black Americans in the structure of their families served to deflect blame from broader structural problems and institutionalized racism at a time when a militant civil rights movement was directing attention to them. Invoking both Frazier and Myrdal, sometimes virtually verbatim, Moynihan's *The Negro Family: The Case for National Action,* published in 1965, articulated a view of the black family that has proved to have remarkable staying power.[57] Investigations of the "culture of poverty" nurtured by a pathological "underclass" in the 1960s and 1970s further collapsed cultural difference and cultural pathology and moved closer to attributing illegitimacy to innate immorality. In the 1980s and 1990s, the discourse of "family values" even more aggressively racialized the "decent" American family and pathologized black single mothers.

It was in a way ironic that policymakers and politicians would use an argument that sociologists and social workers posed to integrate blacks into the urban social order to further marginalize and pathologize them. As grimly as Frazier depicted black illegitimacy, he went to great lengths to locate its roots in a history of enslavement and oppression. But in many ways, Frazier lent himself to appropriations of his work that would indict the black family and black women in particular. In 1939, Frazier predicted that illegitimacy would result in "disease and in children who are unwanted and uncared for"—a double-edged warning that resonated portentously in wartime and postwar America.[58] The first reference invoked long-held racist associations between African Americans and venereal disease and was particularly threatening in the 1940s, when fears about the health of men in the armed services ran high.[59] The second half of this warning—the specter of unwanted black children—reinforced a growing fear that black illegitimacy would drain welfare coffers. This fear was fueled in the 1940s, when, for the first time, unmarried mothers and their children became eligible for public assistance under the Aid to Dependent Children (ADC) program. Although many more white single mothers than black obtained public assistance, black women bore the brunt of white anger at increasing public welfare costs and became the targets of efforts to deny public assistance to illegitimate children.[60]

As with the psychiatric discourse of white illegitimacy, new fears surrounding black illegitimacy took shape in the larger context of the powerful familial ideology that crystallized during and after the war. It was no accident that the black family should alarm policymakers at a time when family values were being so rigidly prescribed and the normal family was portrayed as white, middle-class, male-headed, and suburban-dwelling. This hegemonic postwar family both implicitly and explicitly excluded black Americans. Mass-mediated celebrations of the American family rendered blacks all but invisible, and suburban developments restricted housing to whites. A crucial site for fighting cold war battles, the family was charged with nothing less than providing refuge from nuclear weapons, halting communist

subversion, ensuring economic progress by operating as a consuming unit, and reviving conventional gender roles from the beating they had taken during the Great Depression and World War II. The stakes invested in the postwar family rendered any deviation from its norms tantamount to treason.

In the first decades of the twentieth century, class had resided at the heart of discourses about illegitimacy. By the 1940s, race had taken center stage. In 1927, social worker Henry Schumacher declared illegitimacy a "socio-psychiatric" problem.[61] During and after the war, the hyphen in that label came to separate rigidly dichotomized constructions of black and white illegitimacy. The wartime and postwar years witnessed the construction of white out-of-wedlock pregnancy as a symptom of individual pathology and the simultaneous reconceptualization of black illegitimacy as a symptom of cultural pathology. While psychiatric explanations for out-of-wedlock pregnancy were almost exclusively applied to white women, black unmarried mothers were burdened with the heavy weight of explanations that were sociological in nature.

Both constructions enlisted new groups of experts in the study of illegitimacy, and the ways in which illegitimacy was cast and recast reveal the extent to which those discourses were shaped by concern for professional legitimacy. But the fracturing of discourses on illegitimacy in the 1940s illuminates a contest over more portentous concerns about sexuality and the family. Illegitimacy had long been a lightning rod that attracted anxieties about gender, race, class, and sexuality. In the wartime and postwar years, out-of-wedlock pregnancy distilled far broader issues of social change and sexual and racial conflict. The psychiatric explanation for white middle-class out-of-wedlock pregnancy promised to forestall the "woman question," which resurfaced in the 1940s when women's sexual and economic autonomy collided with efforts to reinvigorate traditional gender roles. Mounting fears over black illegitimacy expressed larger anxieties about race relations that crystallized and intensified during and after the war. The new militancy and assertiveness on the part of blacks, expressed both in an incipient civil rights movement and in the wartime race riots of the summer of 1943, brought new urgency to the politics of race and posed the "Negro question" in new and unsettling terms that raised doubts as to its resolution. The wartime and postwar discourse on illegitimacy illuminates the way in which anxieties about gender and race were mapped onto sexuality and maternity in the larger culture.

The new constructions of illegitimacy were fraught with meaning for their authors. More difficult to gauge is the meaning of these new discourses to their subjects. On the rare occasions that the voices of unmarried mothers came through in the literature that defined them as "problems," they made clear that they were not passive recipients of others' constructions. One white woman suggested that the "experts' " understanding of illegitimacy as purposeful and neurotic bore little resemblance to her understanding of her own pregnancy: "I've been reading a book on the psychology of the unwed mother," Jean Thompson wrote in 1967. "The book says such a pregnancy is rarely accidental. It says the girl nearly always wants it—as a crutch, an excuse to fail, a way to rebel or demonstrate against her parents. . . . Phew, that sounds like a mouthful, as if the author is really looking for symptoms where there aren't any."[62] One black single mother of five told Chicago investigators that her boyfriend "wants to marry, but I don't want to be bothered. I've been my boss too long now. I go and come and do what I want to do. I can't see where I can have anyone bossing me around now."[63] Although her forthright defense might have reinforced assumptions of black matriarchal power, she made it clear that she understood out-of-wedlock pregnancy as something other than cultural pathology. Perhaps more significantly, she transformed pathology into autonomy, insisting on her own independence in the face of a construction that denied individuality to African American women.

Yet women struggling to construct their own identities as single mothers had to contend with the terms of the dominant postwar discourses that defined them as either mentally ill or culturally deviant. Although out-of-wedlock pregnancy relegated postwar women and girls to outcast status regardless of race, "neurosis" was, in a relative sense, a privileged category. As Solinger argues, since psychiatric diagnoses made illegitimacy "contingent upon the mutable mind, rather than upon fixed, physical entities," they offered the hope of rehabilitation.[64] In short, the (white) girl could

change. At the same time, however, the diagnosis subjected white middle-class girls and women to ever more intrusive scrutiny and aggressive intervention. Although the mostly white, predominantly working-class unmarried mothers who had sought the services of social workers and maternity homes before World War II had been subjected to the intrusions of casework for decades—interrogated by social workers about how many times they had had sex, with whom, and under what circumstances—the new psychiatric diagnoses, which located the cause of out-of-wedlock pregnancy not in the environment but in the mind, legitimized a widening of the scope of intrusion from women's behavior to their psyches. On the other hand, the argument that the pathological black family produced illegitimate children was used to justify public policies directed against African American single mothers and their children, to subject them to harassment by welfare officials, to deny them public funds and services, and in some cases, to license their sterilization.[65]

Racialized discourses of out-of-wedlock pregnancy had material consequences for single mothers. For historians, they underline a phenomenon we have only begun to explore in any detail: the mutual constitution of ideologies of gender and race. Each a reference point for the other, race-specific etiologies of illegitimacy illuminate the ways in which gender and sexuality were enlisted in constructing racial hierarchies in the wartime and postwar period. Recent studies have revealed the ways in which postwar politics were profoundly gendered, but these representations of unmarried mothers suggest that race, as powerfully and pervasively as gender, determined the form and shape of the ideology of the family that stood at the heart of the postwar political agenda.

NOTES

1. "Annual Report of the National Officers," *Florence Crittenton Bulletin* 16 (Sept. 1941):10.

2. Illegitimacy rose from 82,586 in 1943 to 87,001 in 1944. Bureau of the Census, Vital Statistics—Special Report, *Illegitimate Births by Race: United States and Each State, 1944*, vol. 25 [Oct. 31, 1946], p. 255.

3. Helen Harris Perlman, "Unmarried Mothers," in *Social Work and Social Problems*, ed. Nathan E. Cohen (New York: National Association of Social Workers, 1964), p. 301.

4. Rickie Solinger, *Wake Up Little Susie: Single*

Pregnancy and Race before Roe v. Wade (New York: Routledge, 1992), p. 93.

5. Leontine R. Young, *Out of Wedlock* (New York: McGraw-Hill, 1954), p. 1.

6. J. Kasanin and Sieglinde Handschin, "Psychodynamic Factors in Illegitimacy," *American Journal of Orthopsychiatry* 11 (Jan. 1941):68.

7. Kasanin and Handschin, "Psychodynamic Factors":71, 68.

8. Sara B. Edlin, *The Unmarried Mother in Our Society* (New York: Farrar, Straus & Young, 1954), p. 85.

9. Rose Bernstein, "Are We Still Stereotyping the Unmarried Mother?" *Social Work* 5 (1960):24.

10. Young, *Out of Wedlock*, p. 241; Solinger, *Wake Up Little Susie*, chap. 3.

11. Grace Marcus, "The Status of Social Case Work Today," *Compass* 16 (1935):8; Kathleen Woodroofe, *Charity to Social Work in England and the United States* (Toronto: University of Toronto Press, 1962), chap. 6.

12. Clarke A. Chambers, "Creative Effort in an Age of Normalcy, 1918–33," *Social Welfare Forum* (New York: Columbia University Press, 1961), pp. 257–58.

13. Mandel Sherman, "The Unmarried Mother," 1938, box 52, folder 3, United Charities of Chicago Collection, held at the Chicago Historical Society, Chicago, Illinois; Florence Clothier, "Psychological Implications of Unmarried Parenthood," *American Journal of Orthopsychiatry* 13 (July 1943):548.

14. Case of Marjorie, July 26, 1946, p. 6, box 1, folder 3, Dorothy Hutchinson Papers ([hereafter] DH), Columbia University Archives (CUA).

15. Case of Jennie, May 13, 1942, p. 13, box 2, folder 18, DH, CUA.

16. Beulah Amidon, "Front Line Officer," *Survey Graphic* 37 (Oct. 1948):439–40.

17. Babette Block, "The Unmarried Mother: Is She Different?" *NCSW Proceedings* (1945):283; Viola W. Bernard, "Psychodynamics of Unmarried Motherhood in Early Adolescence," *Nervous Child* 4 (Oct. 1944):40.

18. Helene Deutsch, *The Psychology of Women: A Psychiatric Interpretation* (New York: Grune & Stratton, 1945), pp. 345, 369.

19. Young, *Out of Wedlock*, p. 36; Leontine R. Young, "Personality Problems in Unmarried Mothers," *Family* 26 (Dec. 1945):7.

20. Deutsch, *Psychology of Women* 2:349.

21. Bernard, "Psychodynamics," p. 40; Young, *Out of Wedlock*, p. 40.

22. Miriam Powell, "Illegitimate Pregnancy in Emotionally Disturbed Girls," *Smith College Studies in Social Work* 19 (June 1949):173.

23. Elaine Tyler May, *Homeward Bound: American Families in the Cold War Era* (New York: Basic Books, 1988), p. 20.

24. Marynia Farnham and Ferdinand Lundberg, *Modern Woman: The Lost Sex* (New York: Harper & Brothers, 1947), p. 280.

25. Young, *Out of Wedlock*, p. 37.

26. Perlman, "Unmarried Mothers," pp. 288, 301.

27. Bernard, "Psychodynamics," p. 39.

28. Hildegarde Dolson, "My Parents Mustn't Know," *Good Housekeeping* (May 1942):159.

29. Sherman, "The Unmarried Mother," p. 13.

30. Young, *Out of Wedlock*, p. 50.

31. May, *Homeward Bound*, chap. 5.

32. Leontine R. Young, "The Unmarried Mother's Decision about Her Baby," *Journal of Social Casework* (Jan. 28, 1947):33; Ruth F. Brenner, "Case Work Services for Unmarried Mothers," *Family* 22 (Nov. 1941):218.

33. Solinger, *Wake Up Little Susie*, chap. 5.

34. Karen Anderson, *Wartime Women: Sex Role, Family Relations and the Status of Women during World War II* (Westport: Greenwood Press, 1981).

35. Allan M. Brandt, *No Magic Bullet: A Social History of Venereal Disease since 1880* (New York: Oxford University Press, 1985), pp. 165–69.

36. Francis E. Merrill, *Social Problems on the Home Front: A Study of War-Time Influences* (New York: Harper & Brothers, 1948), p. 99.

37. Helen D. Pigeon, *Effect of War Conditions on Children and Adolescents in the City of Hartford, Connecticut* (New Haven: Connecticut Child Welfare Association, 1944), p. 24.

38. James Gilbert, *A Cycle of Outrage: America's Reaction to the Juvenile Delinquent in the 1950s* (New York: Oxford University Press, 1986), p. 18.

39. Venereal Disease Control Conference, pp. 24, 25.

40. Ibid., p. 33; U.S. Children's Bureau, "Services for Unmarried Mothers and Their Children" (Washington, D.C.: Government Printing Office, 1945), p. 1.

41. Ruth Reed, *Social and Health Care of the Illegitimate Family in New York City* (New York: Research Bureau Welfare Council of New York City, 1932), p. 17; Ruth Reed, "Illegitimacy Among Negroes," *Journal of Social Hygiene* 11 (Feb. 1925):73–91.

42. Melville J. Herskovits, *The Myth of the Negro Past* (New York: Harper & Brothers, 1941), p. 167.

43. Anthony M. Platt, *E. Franklin Frazier Reconsidered* (New Brunswick: Rutgers University Press, 1991), chap. 7.

44. E. Franklin Frazier, "Analysis of Statistics on Negro Illegitimacy in the United States," *Social Forces* 11 (Dec. 1932):255.

45. E. Franklin Frazier, *Negro Family in the United States* (New York: Citadel Press, 1948), p. 267.

46. Frazier, "Analysis of Statistics on Negro Illegitimacy":56.

47. Frazier, "Traditions and Patterns of Negro Family Life in the United States," in Edward Byron Reuter, ed., *Race and Culture Contacts* (New York: McGraw-Hill, 1943), pp. 194–95.

48. Frazier, *Negro Family in the United States*, p. 265; Reed, *Social and Health Care*, p. 17.

49. Frazier, *Negro Family in the United States*, p. 265.

50. Platt, *Frazier Reconsidered*.

51. Hilda Hertz and Sue Warren Little, "Negro Illegitimacy in Durham, North Carolina," (M.A. thesis, Duke University, 1944), p. 75; Margaret Brenman, "Urban Lower-Class Negro Girls," *Psychiatry* 6 (Aug. 1943):308.

52. St. Clair Drake and Horace R. Cayton, *Black Metropolis: A Study of Negro Life in a Northern City*

(New York: Harcourt, Brace, 1945), p. 593; Allan Spear, *Black Chicago: The Making of a Negro Ghetto, 1890 to 1920* (Chicago: University of Chicago Press, 1967).

53. Hazel V. Carby, "Policing the Black Woman's Body in an Urban Context," *Critical Inquiry* (Summer 1992):754.

54. Drake and Cayton, *Black Metropolis*, p. 593.

55. Gunnar Myrdal, *All American Dilemma: The Negro Problem and the Modern Democracy* (New York: Harper & Brothers, 1944), pp. 930–31.

56. Daniel P. Moynihan, *The Negro Family: The Case for National Action* (Washington, D.C.: U.S. Department of Labor, 1965).

57. Platt, *Frazier Reconsidered*, pp. 115–20.

58. Frazier, *Negro Family in the United States*, p. 100.

59. Brandt, *No Magic Bullet*, pp. 116, 157–58, 169–70; Elizabeth Fee, "Venereal Disease: The Wages of Sin?" in Kathy Peiss and Christina Simmons, eds., *Passion and Power: Sexuality in History* (Philadelphia: Temple University Press, 1989), pp. 181–83.

60. Solinger, *Wake Up Little Susie*, pp. 29–34, 56–76; Winifred Bell, *Aid to Dependent Children* (New York: Columbia University Press, 1965).

61. Henry C. Schumacher, "The Unmarried Mother: A Socio-Psychiatric Viewpoint," *Journal of Medical Hygiene* 11 (Oct. 1927):775–82.

62. Jean Thompson, *House of Tomorrow* (New York: Harper & Row, 1967), pp. 7–8.

63. Drake and Cayton, *Black Metropolis*, pp. 592–93.

64. Solinger, *Wake Up Little Susie*, p. 16.

65. Ibid., p. 84.

SUSAN K. CAHN

"Mannishness," Lesbianism, and Homophobia in U.S. Women's Sports

In the cold war years Americans sought to assuage concerns about female sexuality and reaffirm traditional family norms in many ways. Defining women attempting to construct their own identities as single mothers as either mentally ill or culturally deviant was only one. Lesbians also presented a challenge. While much of the homophobia of the McCarthy era focused on males who, by virtue of their homosexuality and presumed susceptibility to blackmail, were thought to be tempting targets to Communist agents in search of government secrets, lesbians were also vulnerable. Dismissed from the armed services and civilian agencies as "undesirable," they tried to organize to gain rights, only to discover subsequently that the Daughters of Bilitis had been infiltrated with informants who were supplying names to the FBI and CIA. In an era when sexual conformity was seen as essential to national security, it is hardly surprising that all women engaged in any same-sex activity were suspect.

In the following article, Susan Cahn explores the suspicions and the reality behind those suspicions in women's athletics. Note the persistence of concerns about female sexuality, whether heterosexual or homosexual, throughout the history of women's sports. What measures did colleges and universities take to protect women's sports from charges of lesbianism? What was the price of such actions?

Excerpted from "From the 'Muscle Moll' to the 'Butch' Ballplayer: 'Mannishness,' Lesbianism, and Homophobia in U.S. Women's Sports" by Susan Cahn, in *Feminist Studies* 19 (Summer 1992):343–68. Copyright © 1993 by Feminist Studies, Inc. Reprinted by permission of the author and publisher, Feminist Studies, Inc., c/o Women's Studies Program, University of Maryland, College Park, Maryland 20742. Notes have been renumbered and edited.

In 1934, *Literary Digest* subtitled an article on women's sports, "Will the Playing Fields One Day Be Ruled by Amazons?" The author, Fred Wittner, answered the question affirmatively and concluded that as an "inevitable consequence" of sport's masculinizing effect, "girls trained in physical education to-day may find it more difficult to attract the most worthy fathers for their children."[1] The image of women athletes as mannish, failed heterosexuals represents a thinly veiled reference to lesbianism in sport. At times, the homosexual allusion has been indisputable, as in a journalist's description of the great athlete Babe Didrikson as a "Sapphic, Brobdingnagian woman" or in television comedian Arsenio Hall's more recent witticism, "If we can put a man on the moon, why can't we get one on Martina Navratilova?"[2] More frequently, however, popular commentary on lesbians in sport has taken the form of indirect references, surfacing through denials and refutations rather than open acknowledgment. When in 1955 an *Ebony* magazine article on African American track stars insisted that "off track, girls are entirely feminine. Most of them like boys, dances, club affairs," the reporter answered the implicit but unspoken charge that athletes, especially Black women in a "manly" sport, were masculine manhaters, or lesbians.[3]

The figure of the mannish lesbian athlete has acted as a powerful but unarticulated "bogey woman" of sport, forming a silent foil for more positive, corrective images that attempt to rehabilitate the image of women athletes and resolve the cultural contradiction between athletic prowess and femininity. As a stereotyped figure in U.S. society, the lesbian athlete forms part of everyday cultural knowledge. Yet historians have paid scant attention to the connection between female sexuality and sport.[4] This essay explores the historical relationship between lesbianism and sport by tracing the development of the stereotyped "mannish lesbian athlete" and examining its relation to the lived experience of mid-twentieth-century lesbian athletes.

I argue that fears of mannish female sexuality in sport initially centered on the prospect of unbridled heterosexual desire. By the 1930s, however, female athletic mannishness began to connote heterosexual failure, usually couched in terms of unattractiveness to men, but also suggesting the possible absence of heterosexual

interest. In the years following World War II, the stereotype of the lesbian athlete emerged full blown. The extreme homophobia and the gender conservatism of the postwar era created a context in which longstanding linkages among mannishness, female homosexuality, and athletics cohered around the figure of the mannish lesbian athlete. Paradoxically, the association between masculinity, lesbianism, and sport had a positive outcome for some women. The very cultural matrix that produced the pejorative image also created possibilities for lesbian affirmation. Sport provided social and psychic space for some lesbians to validate themselves and to build a collective culture. Thus, the lesbian athlete was not only a figure of discourse but a living product of women's sexual struggle and cultural innovation.

The athletic woman sparked interest and controversy in the early decades of the twentieth century. In the United States and other Western societies, sport functioned as a male preserve, an all-male domain in which men not only played games together but also demonstrated and affirmed their manhood.[5] The "maleness" of sport derived from a gender ideology which labeled aggression, physicality, competitive spirit, and athletic skill as masculine attributes necessary for achieving true manliness. This notion found unquestioned support in the dualistic, polarized concepts of gender which prevailed in Victorian America. However, by the turn of the century, women had begun to challenge Victorian gender arrangements, breaking down barriers to female participation in previously male arenas of public work, politics, and urban nightlife. Some of these "New Women" sought entry into the world of athletics as well. On college campuses students enjoyed a wide range of intramural sports through newly formed Women's Athletic Associations. Off-campus women took up games like golf, tennis, basketball, swimming, and occasionally even wrestling, car racing, or boxing. As challengers to one of the defining arenas of manhood, skilled female athletes became symbols of the broader march of womanhood out of the Victorian domestic sphere into once prohibited male realms.

The woman athlete represented both the appealing and threatening aspects of modern womanhood. In a positive light, she captured the exuberant spirit, physical vigor, and brazenness of the New Woman. The University of Minnesota student newspaper proclaimed in 1904 that the athletic girl was the "truest type of All-American coed."[6] Several years later, *Harper's Bazaar* labeled the unsportive girl as "not strictly up to date," and *Good Housekeeping* noted that the "tomboy" had come to symbolize "a new type of American girl, new not only physically, but mentally and morally."[7]

Yet, women athletes invoked condemnation as often as praise. Critics ranged from physicians and physical educators to sportswriters, male athletic officials, and casual observers. In their view, strenuous athletic pursuits endangered women and threatened the stability of society. They maintained that women athletes would become manlike, adopting masculine dress, talk, and mannerisms. In addition, they contended, too much exercise would damage female reproductive capacity [interfering with menstruation and causing reproductive organs to harden or atrophy]. And worse yet, the excitement of sport would cause women to lose [sexual] control, . . . unleash[ing] nonprocreative, erotic desires identified with male sexuality and unrespectable women. . . . These fears collapsed into an all-encompassing concept of "mannishness," a term signifying female masculinity . . .

The public debate over the merits of women's athletic participation remained lively throughout the 1910s and 1920s. On all sides of the issue, however, the controversy about sports and female sexuality presumed heterosexuality. Neither critics nor supporters suggested that "masculine" athleticism might indicate or induce same-sex love. And when experts warned of the "amazonian" athlete's possible sexual transgressions, they linked the physical release of sport with a loss of heterosexual *control*, not of *inclination*.

In the 1930s, however, the heterosexual understanding of the mannish "amazon" began to give way to a new interpretation which educators and promoters could not long ignore. To the familiar charge that female athletes resembled men, critics added the newer accusation that sport-induced mannishness disqualified them as candidates for heterosexual romance. In 1930, an *American Mercury* medical reporter decried the decline of romantic love, pinning the blame on women who entered sport, business, and politics. He claimed that such women "act like men, talk like men, and

think like men." The author explained that "women have come closer and closer to men's level," and, consequently, "the purple allure of distance has vamoosed."[8] . . . Although the charges didn't exclusively focus on athletes, they implied that female athleticism was contrary to heterosexual appeal, which appeared to rest on women's difference from and deference to men.

The concern with heterosexual appeal reflected broader sexual transformations in U.S. society. Historians of sexuality have examined the multiple forces which reshaped gender and sexual relations in the first few decades of the twentieth century. Victorian sexual codes crumbled under pressure from an assertive, boldly sexual working-class youth culture, a women's movement which defied prohibitions against public female activism, and the growth of a new pleasure-oriented consumer economy. In the wake of these changes, modern ideals of womanhood embraced an overtly erotic heterosexual sensibility. At the same time, medical fascination with sexual "deviance" created a growing awareness of lesbianism, now understood as a form of congenital or psychological pathology. The medicalization of homosexuality in combination with an antifeminist backlash in the 1920s against female autonomy and power contributed to a more fully articulated taboo against lesbianism. The modern heterosexual woman stood in stark opposition to her threatening sexual counterpart, the "mannish" lesbian.[9]

By the late 1920s and early 1930s, with a modern lesbian taboo and an eroticized definition of heterosexual femininity in place, the assertive, muscular female competitor roused increasing suspicion. It was at this moment that both subtle and direct references to the lesbian athlete emerged in physical education and popular sport. Uncensored discussions of intimate female companionship and harmless athletic "crushes" disappear from the record, pushed underground by the increasingly hostile tone of public discourse about female sexuality and athleticism. Fueled by the gender antagonisms and anxieties of the Depression, the public began scrutinizing women athletes—known for their appropriation of masculine games and styles—for signs of deviance.

Where earlier references to "amazons" had signaled heterosexual ardor, journalists now used the term to mean unattractive, failed heterosexuals. Occasionally, the media made direct mention of athletes' presumed lesbian tendencies. A 1933 *Redbook* article, for example, casually mentioned that track and golf star Babe Didrikson liked men just to horse around with her and not "make love," adding that Babe's fondness for her best girlfriends far surpassed her affection for any man.[10] The direct reference was unusual; the lesbian connotation of mannishness was forged primarily through indirect links of association. . . .

Tentatively voiced in the 1930s, these accusations became harsher and more explicit under the impact of wartime changes in gender and sexuality and the subsequent panic over the "homosexual menace." In a post–World War II climate markedly hostile to nontraditional women and lesbians, women in physical education and in working-class popular sports became convenient targets of homophobic indictment.

World War II opened up significant economic and social possibilities for gay men and women. Embryonic prewar homosexual subcultures blossomed during the war and spread across the midcentury urban landscape. Bars, nightclubs, public cruising spots, and informal social networks facilitated the development of gay and lesbian enclaves. But the permissive atmosphere did not survive the war's end. Waving the banner of Cold War political and social conservatism, government leaders acted at the federal, state, and local levels to purge gays and lesbians from government and military posts, to initiate legal investigations and prosecutions of gay individuals and institutions, and to encourage local police crackdowns on gay bars and street life. The perceived need to safeguard national security and to reestablish social order in the wake of wartime disruption sparked a "homosexual panic" which promoted the fear, loathing, and persecution of homosexuals.[11]

Lesbians suffered condemnation for their violation of gender as well as sexual codes. The tremendous emphasis on family, domesticity, and "traditional" femininity in the late 1940s and 1950s reflected postwar anxieties about the reconsolidation of a gender order shaken by two decades of depression and war. As symbols of women's refusal to conform, lesbians endured intense scrutiny by experts who regularly focused on their subjects' presumed masculinity. Sexologists attributed lesbianism to masculine tendencies and freedoms encouraged by the war, linking it to a general collapsing of gender distinctions which, in their view, destabilized marital and family relations.[12]

Lesbians remained shadowy figures to most Americans, but women athletes—noted for their masculine bodies, interests, and attributes—were visible representatives of the gender inversion often associated with homosexuality. Physical education majors, formerly accused of being unappealing to men, were increasingly charged with being uninterested in them as well. The 1952 University of Minnesota yearbook snidely reported: "Believe it or not, members of the Women's Athletic Association are normal" and found conclusive evidence in the fact that "at least one . . . of WAA's 300 members is engaged."[13]

The lesbian stigma began to plague popular athletics too. . . . The career of Babe Didrikson, which spanned the 1920s to the 1950s, illustrates the shift. In the early 1930s the press had ridiculed the tomboyish track star for her "hatchet face," "door-stop jaw," and "button-breasted" chest. After quitting track, Didrikson dropped out of the national limelight, married professional wrestler George Zaharias in 1938, and then staged a spectacular athletic comeback as a golfer in the late 1940s and 1950s. Fascinated by her personal transformation and then, in the 1950s, moved by her battle with cancer, journalists gave Didrikson's comeback extensive coverage and helped make her a much-loved popular figure. In reflecting on her success, however, sportswriters spent at least as much time on Didrikson's love life as her golf stroke. Headlines blared, "Babe Is a Lady Now: The World's Most Amazing Athlete Has Learned to Wear Nylons and Cook for Her Huge Husband," and reporters gleefully described how "along came a great big he-man wrestler and the Babe forgot all her man-hating chatter."[14]. . . The challenge for women athletes was not to conquer new athletic feats, which would only further reduce their sexual appeal, but to regain their womanhood through sexual surrender to men.

Media coverage in national magazines and metropolitan newspapers typically focused on the sexual accomplishments of white female athletes, but postwar observers and promoters of African American women's sport also confronted the issue of sexual normalcy. In earlier decades, strong local support for women's sport within Black communities and the racist gender ideologies that prevailed outside Black communities may have weakened the association between African American women athletes and "mannish" lesbianism. Historically, European American racial thought characterized African American women as aggressive, coarse, passionate, and physical—the same qualities assigned to manliness and sport.[15] Excluded from dominant ideals of womanhood, Black women's success in sport could therefore be interpreted not as an unnatural sexual deviation but, rather, as the natural result of their reputed closeness to nature, animals, and masculinity.[16] ... Moreover, stereotypes of Black females as highly sexual, promiscuous, and unrestrained in their heterosexual passions further discouraged the linkage between mannishness and lesbianism....

Although Black athletes may initially have encountered few lesbian stereotypes ... circumstances in the broader society eventually pressed African American sport promoters and journalists to address the issue of mannish sexuality. The strong postwar association of sports with lesbianism developed at the same time as Black athletes became a dominant presence in American sport culture.... Therefore, while there was no particular correlation between Black women and lesbianism, the association of each with mannishness and sexual aggression potentially linked the two.... In the late 1950s, Black sport promoters and journalists joined others in taking up the question of sexual "normalcy." One Black newspaper in 1957 described tennis star Althea Gibson as a childhood "tomboy" who "in later life ... finds herself victimized by complexes."[17] The article did not elaborate on the nature of Gibson's "complex," but lesbianism is inferred in the linkage between "tomboys" and psychological illness. This connotation becomes clearer by looking at the defense of Black women's sport. Echoing *Ebony*'s avowal that "entirely feminine" Black female track stars "like boys, dances, club affairs," in 1962 Tennessee State University track coach Ed Temple asserted, "None of my girls have any trouble getting boy friends.... We don't want amazons."[18]

Constant attempts to shore up the heterosexual reputation of athletes can be read as evidence that the longstanding reputation of fe-

male athletes as mannish women had become a covert reference to lesbianism. By midcentury, a fundamental reorientation of sexual meanings fused notions of femininity, female eroticism, and heterosexual attractiveness into a single ideal. Mannishness, once primarily a sign of gender crossing, assumed a specifically lesbian-sexual connotation. In the wake of this change, the strong cultural association between sport and masculinity made women's athletics ripe for emerging lesbian stereotypes. This meaning of athletic mannishness raises further questions. What impact did the stereotype have on women's sport? And was the image merely an erroneous stereotype, or did lesbians in fact form a significant presence in sport? ...

The image of the mannish lesbian athlete had a direct effect on women competitors, on strategies of athletic organizations, and on the overall popularity of women's sport. The lesbian stereotype exerted pressure on athletes to demonstrate their femininity and heterosexuality, viewed as one and the same. Many women adopted an apologetic stance toward their athletic skill. Even as they competed to win, they made sure to display outward signs of femininity in dress and demeanor. They took special care in contact with the media to reveal "feminine" hobbies like cooking and sewing, to mention current boyfriends, and to discuss future marriage plans.[19]

Leaders of women's sport took the same approach at the institutional level. In answer to portrayals of physical education majors and teachers as social rejects and prudes, physical educators revised their philosophy to place heterosexuality at the center of professional objectives.... Curricular changes implemented between the mid-1930s and mid-1950s institutionalized the new philosophy. In a paper on postwar objectives, Mildred A. Schaeffer explained that physical education classes should help women "develop an interest in school dances and mixers and a desire to voluntarily attend them."[20] To this end, administrators revised coursework to emphasize beauty and social charm over rigorous exercise and health. They exchanged old rationales of fitness and fun for promises of trimmer waistlines, slimmer hips, and prettier complexions.... Some departments also added co-educational classes to foster "broader, keener, more sympathetic understanding of the opposite sex."[21] Department heads cracked down on "mannish" students and faculty, issuing warnings against "casual styles" which might "lead us back into some dangerous channels."[22] They implemented dress codes which forbade slacks and men's shirts or socks, adding as well a ban on "boyish hair cuts" and unshaven legs.[23]

Popular sport promoters adopted similar tactics. Martialing sexual data like they were athletic statistics, a 1954 AAU poll sought to sway a skeptical public with numerical proof of heterosexuality—the fact that 91 percent of former female athletes surveyed had married.[24] Publicity for the midwestern All-American Girls Baseball League included statistics on the number of married players. . . . Behind the scenes, teams passed dress and conduct codes. For example, the All-American Girls Baseball League prohibited players from wearing men's clothing or getting "severe" haircuts.[25] That this was an attempt to secure the heterosexual image of athletes was made even clearer when league officials announced that AAGBL policy prohibited the recruitment of "freaks" and "Amazons."[26]

In the end, the strategic emphasis on heterosexuality and the suppression of "mannishness" did little to alter the image of women in sport. The stereotype of the mannish lesbian athlete grew out of the persistent commonsense equation of sport with masculinity. Opponents of women's sport reinforced this belief when they denigrated women's athletic efforts and ridiculed skilled athletes as "grotesque," "mannish," or "unnatural." Leaders of women's sport unwittingly contributed to the same set of ideas when they began to orient their programs around the new feminine heterosexual idea. As physical education policies and media campaigns worked to suppress lesbianism and marginalize athletes who did not conform to dominant standards of femininity, sport officials embedded heterosexism into the institutional and ideological framework of sport. The effect extended beyond sport to the wider culture, where the figure of the mannish lesbian athlete announced that competitiveness, strength, independence, aggression, and physical intimacy among women fell outside the bounds of womanhood. As a symbol of female deviance, she served as a powerful reminder to all women to toe the line of heterosexuality and femininity or risk falling into a despised category of mannish (not-women) women. . . .

[But] was the mannish lesbian athlete merely a figure of homophobic imagination, or was there in fact a strong lesbian presence in sport? When the All-American Girls Baseball League adamantly specified, "*Always appear in feminine attire* . . . MASCULINE HAIR STYLING? SHOES? COATS? SHIRTS? SOCKS, T-SHIRTS ARE BARRED AT ALL TIMES," and when physical education departments threatened to expel students for overly masculine appearance, were administrators merely responding to external pressure?[27] Or were they cracking down on women who may have indeed enjoyed the feel and look of a tough swagger, a short haircut, and men's clothing? And if so, did mannishness among athletes correspond to lesbianism, as the stereotype suggested? In spite of the public stigmatization, [is it probable that] some women may have found the activities, attributes, and emotions of sport conducive to lesbian self-expression and community formation?

As part of a larger investigation of women's athletic experience, I conducted oral histories with women who played competitive amateur, semiprofessional, and professional sports between 1930 and 1970. The interviews included only six openly lesbian narrators and thirty-six other women who either declared their heterosexuality or left their identity unstated.[28] Although the sample is too small to stand as a representative study, the interviews . . . and scattered other sources indicate that sport, particularly softball, provided an important site for the development of lesbian subculture and identity in the United States.[29] Gay and straight informants alike confirmed the lesbian presence in popular sport and physical education. Their testimony suggests that from at least the 1940s on, sport provided space for lesbian activity and social networks and served as a path into lesbian culture for young lesbians coming out and searching for companions and community.

Lesbian athletes explained that sport had been integral to their search for sexual identity and lesbian companionship. Ann Maguire, a softball player, physical education major, and top amateur bowler from New England, recalled that as a teenager in the late 1950s,

> I had been trying to figure out who I was and couldn't put a name to it. I mean it was very—no gay groups, no literature, no characters on "Dynasty"—I mean there was just nothing at that

time. And trying to put a name to it. . . . I went to a bowling tournament, met two women there [and] for some reason something clicked and it clicked in a way that I was not totally aware of.

She introduced herself to the women, who later invited her to a gay bar. Maguire described her experience at age seventeen:

I was being served and I was totally fascinated by the fact that, oh god, here I am being served and I'm not twenty-one. And it didn't occur to me until after a while when I relaxed and started realizing that I was at a gay bar. I just became fascinated. . . . And I was back there the next night. . . . I really felt a sense of knowing who I was and feeling very happy. Very happy that I had been able to through some miracle put this into place.[30] . . .

For women like Maguire, sport provided a point of entry into lesbian culture.

The question arises of whether lesbians simply congregated in athletic settings or whether a sports environment could actually "create" or "produce" lesbians. Some women fit the first scenario, describing how, in their struggle to accept and make sense out of lesbian desire, sport offered a kind of home that put feelings and identities into place. For other women, it appears that the lesbian presence in sport encouraged them to explore or act on feelings that they might not have had or responded to in other settings. Midwestern baseball player Nora Cross remembered that "it was my first exposure to gay people. . . . I was pursued by the one I was rooming with, that's how I found out." She got involved with her roommate and lived "a gay lifestyle" as long as she stayed in sport. Dorothy Ferguson Key also noticed that sport changed some women, recalling that "there were girls that came in the league like this . . . yeah, gay," but that at other times "a girl came in, and I mean they just change. . . . When they've been in a year they're completely changed. . . . They lived together."[31]

The athletic setting provided public space for lesbian sociability without naming it as such or excluding women who were not lesbians. This environment could facilitate the coming-out process, allowing women who were unsure about or just beginning to explore their sexual identity to socialize with gay and straight women without having to make immediate decisions or declarations. Gradually and primarily through unspoken communica-

tion, lesbians in sport recognized each other and created social networks. Gloria Wilson, who played softball in a mid-sized midwestern city, described her entry into lesbian social circles as a gradual process in which older lesbians slowly opened up their world to her and she grew more sure of her own identity and place in the group.

A lot was assumed. And I don't think they felt comfortable with me talking until they knew me better. Then I think more was revealed. And we had little beer gatherings after a game at somebody's house. So then it was even more clear who was doing what when. And then I felt more comfortable too, fitting in, talking about my relationship too—and exploring more of the lesbian lifestyle, I guess.[32]

In an era when women did not dare announce their lesbianism in public, the social world of popular sport allowed women to find each other as teammates, friends, and lovers. But if athletics provided a public arena and social activity in which lesbians could recognize and affirm each other, what exactly was it that they recognized? This is where the issue of mannishness arises. Women athletes consistently explained the lesbian reputation of sport by reference to the mannishness of some athletes. . . . Suspected lesbians were said to "act like a man, you know, the way they walked, the way they talked, the things they did."

Such comments could merely indicate the pervasiveness of the masculine reputation of athletes and lesbians. However, lesbian narrators also suggested connections, although more complicated and nuanced, between athletics, lesbianism, and the "mannish" or "butchy" style which some lesbians manifested. None reported any doubt about their own gender identification as girls and women, but they indicated that they had often felt uncomfortable with the activities and attributes associated with the female gender. They preferred boyish clothes and activities to the conventional styles and manners of femininity.

Several spoke of . . . their relief upon finding athletic comrades who shared this sensibility. Josephine D'Angelo recalled that as a lesbian participating in sport, "you brought your culture with you. You brought your arm swinging . . . , the swagger, the way you tilted or cocked your head or whatever. You brought that with you." She explained that this style was acceptable in sports: "First thing you did was to kind of imitate the boys because you know, you're not supposed to throw like a girl." Although her rejection of femininity made her conspicuous in other settings, D'Angelo found that in sport "it was overlooked, see. You weren't different than the other kids.... Same likeness, people of a kind."[33]

These athletes were clearly women playing women's sports. But in the gender system of U.S. society, the skills, movements, clothing, and competition of sport were laden with impressions of masculinity. Lesbianism too crossed over the bounds of acceptable femininity. Consequently, sport could relocate girls or women with lesbian identities or feelings in an alternative nexus of gender meanings, allowing them to "be themselves"—or to express their gender and sexuality in an unconventional way. This applied to heterosexual women as well, many of whom also described themselves as "tomboys" attracted to boyish games and styles. As an activity that incorporated prescribed "masculine" physical activity into a way of being in the female body, athletics provided a social space and practice for reorganizing conventional meanings of embodied masculinity and femininity. *All* women in sport gained access to activities and expressive styles labeled masculine by the dominant culture. However, because lesbians were excluded from a concept of "real womanhood" defined around heterosexual appeal and desire, sport formed a milieu in which they could redefine womanhood on their own terms....

However, the connections among lesbianism, masculinity, and sport require qualification. Many lesbians in and out of sport did not adopt "masculine" markers. And even among those who did, narrators indicated that butch styles did not occlude more traditionally "feminine" qualities of affection and tenderness valued by women athletes. Sport allowed women to combine activities and attributes perceived as masculine with more conventionally feminine qualities of friendship, cooperation, nurturance, and affection. Lesbians particularly benefited from this gender configuration, finding that in the athletic setting, qualities otherwise viewed as manifestations of homosexual deviance were understood as inherent, positive aspects of sport.[34] Aggressiveness, toughness, passionate intensity, expanded use of motion

and space, strength, and competitiveness contributed to athletic excellence. With such qualities defined as athletic attributes rather than psychological abnormalities, the culture of sport permitted lesbians to express the full range of their gendered sensibilities while sidestepping the stigma of psychological deviance. For these reasons, athletics, in the words of Josephine D'Angelo, formed a "comforting" and "comfortable" place.[35]

Yet lesbians found sport hospitable only under certain conditions. Societal hostility toward homosexuality made lesbianism unspeakable in any realm of culture, but the sexual suspicions that surrounded sport made athletics an especially dangerous place in which to speak out. Physical educators and sport officials vigilantly guarded against signs of "mannishness," and teams occasionally expelled women who wore their hair in a "boyish bob" or engaged in obvious lesbian relationships. Consequently, gay athletes avoided naming or verbally acknowledging their sexuality. Loraine Sumner explained that "you never talked about it.... You never saw anything in public amongst the group of us. But you knew right darn well that this one was going with that one. But yet it just wasn't a topic of conversation. Never."[36] Instead, lesbian athletes signaled their identity through dress, posture, and look, reserving spoken communication for private gatherings among women who were acknowledged and accepted members of concealed communities.

Although in hindsight the underground nature of midcentury lesbian communities may seem extremely repressive, it may also have had a positive side. Unlike the bars where women's very presence declared their status as sexual outlaws, in sport athletes could enjoy the public company of lesbians while retaining their membership in local communities where neighbors, kin, and coworkers respected and sometimes even celebrated their athletic abilities. The unacknowledged, indefinite presence of lesbians in sport may have allowed for a wider range of lesbian experience and identity than is currently acknowledged in most scholarship. For instance, among women who did not identify as lesbian but were sexually drawn to other women, sport provided a venue in which they could express their desires without necessarily having articulated their feelings as a distinct sexual identity. The culture of sport provided space for some women to create clearly delineated lesbian identities and communities, at the same time allowing other women to move along the fringes of this world, operating across sexual and community lines without a firmly differentiated lesbian identity.

Women in sport experienced a contradictory array of heterosexual imperatives and homosexual possibilities. The fact that women athletes disrupted a critical domain of male power and privilege made sport a strategic site for shoring up existing gender and sexual hierarchies. The image of the mannish lesbian confirmed both the masculinity of sport and its association with female deviance. Lesbian athletes could not publicly claim their identity without risking expulsion, ostracism, and loss of athletic activities and social networks that had become crucial to their lives. Effectively silenced, their image was conveyed to the dominant culture primarily as a negative stereotype in which the mannish lesbian athlete represented the unfeminine "other," the line beyond which "normal" women must not cross.

The paradox of women's sport history is that the mannish athlete was not only a figure of homophobic discourse but also a human actor engaged in sexual innovation and struggle. Lesbian athletes used the social and psychic space of sport to create a collective culture and affirmative identity. The pride, pleasure, companionship, and dignity lesbians found in the athletic world helped them survive in a hostile society. The challenge posed by their collective existence and their creative reconstruction of womanhood formed a precondition for more overt, political challenges to lesbian oppression which have occurred largely outside the realm of sport.

NOTES

1. Fred Wittner, "Shall the Ladies Join Us?" *Literary Digest* 117 (19 May 1934):43.

2. Jim Murray, *Austin American Statesman* (n.d.), Zaharias scrapbook, Barker Texas History Center ([hereafter] BTHC), University of Texas, Austin; Arsenio Hall Show, 1988.

3. "Fastest Women in the World," *Ebony* 10 (June 1955):28.

4. Helen Lenskyj, *Out of Bounds: Women, Sport, and Sexuality* (Toronto: Women's Press, 1986); Yvonne Zipter, *Diamonds Are a Dyke's Best Friend: Reflections, Reminiscences, and Reports from the Field on the Lesbian National Pastime* (Ithaca: Firebrand Books, 1988).

5. J. A. Mangan and Roberta J. Park, eds., *"Fair Sex" to Feminism: Sport and the Socialization of Women in the Industrial and Post-Industrial Era* (London: Frank Cays, 1987).

6. 1904–5 Scrapbooks of Anne Maude Butner, Butner Papers, University of Minnesota Archives, Minneapolis (UMA).

7. Violet W. Mange, "Field Hockey for Women," *Harper's Bazaar* 44 (Apr. 1910):246; Anna de Koven, "The Athletic Woman," *Good Housekeeping* 55 (Aug. 1912):150.

8. George Nathan, "Once There Was a Princess," *American Mercury* 19 (Feb. 1930):242.

9. This is an extremely brief and simplified summary of an extensive literature. For a good synthesis, see Estelle Freedman and John D'Emilio, *Intimate Matters: A History of Sexuality in America* (New York: Harper & Row, 1988), chaps. 8–10.

10. William Marston, "How Can a Woman Do It?" *Redbook* (Sept. 1933):60.

11. John D'Emilio, *Sexual Politics, Sexual Communities: The Making of a Homosexual Minority in the United States, 1940–1970* (Chicago: University of Chicago Press, 1983), pp. 9–53; Alan Berube, *Coming Out Under Fire: The History of Gay Men and Women in World War Two* (New York: Free Press, 1990).

12. Donna Penn, "The Meanings of Lesbianism in Post-War America," *Gender and History* 3 (Summer 1991):190–203; Wini Breines, "The 1950s: Gender and Some Social Science," *Sociological Inquiry* 56 (Winter 1986):69–92.

13. *Gopher Yearbook* (1952), p. 257, UMA.

14. Paul Gallico, *Houston Post*, 22 Mar. 1960; Pete Martin, "Babe Didrikson Takes Off Her Mask," *Saturday Evening Post* 20 (Sept. 1947):26–27.

15. Paula Giddings, *When and Where I Enter: The Impact of Black Women on Race and Sex in America* (New York: William & Morrow, 1984), chaps. 1, 2, 4; Patricia Hill Collins, *Black Feminist Thought: Knowledge, Consciousness, and the Politics of Empowerment* (Boston: Unwin Hyman, 1990), chaps. 4, 8.

16. Elizabeth Lunbeck, "'A New Generation of Women': Progressive Psychiatrists and the Hypersexual Female," *Feminist Studies* 13 (Fall 1987):513–43.

17. *Baltimore Afro-American*, 29 June 1957.

18. "Fastest Women in the World," pp. 28, 32; *Detroit News* 31 (July 1962):1.

19. Patricia Del Rey, "The Apologetic and Women in Sport," in Carole Oglesby, ed., *Women and Sport* (Philadelphia: Lea & Febiger, 1978), pp. 107–11.

20. Mildred A. Schaeffer, "Desirable Objectives in Post-war Physical Education," *Journal of Health and Physical Education* 16 (Oct. 1945):44–47.

21. "Coeducational Classes," *Journal of Health, Physical Education, and Recreation* 26 (Feb. 1955):18. For curricular changes, I examined physical education records at the universities of Wisconsin, Texas, and Minnesota, Radcliffe College, Smith College, Tennessee State University, and Hampton University.

22. Dudley Ashton, "Recruiting Future Teachers," *Journal of Health, Physical Education, and Recreation* 28 (Oct. 1957):49.

23. The 1949–50 Physical Training Staff Handbook at the University of Texas stated, "Legs should

be kept shaved" (p. 16). Box 3R213 of Department of Physical Training for Women Records, BTHC.

24. Roxy Andersen, "Statistical Survey of Former Women Athletes," *Amateur Athlete* (Sept. 1954):10–11.

25. All-American Girls Baseball League (AAGBL) 1951 Constitution, AAGBL Records.

26. Morris Markey, "Hey Ma, You're Out!" (n.d.), 1951 Records of the AAGBL; and "Feminine Sluggers," *People and Places* 8 (1952), AAGBL Records.

27. AAGBL 1951 Constitution, AAGBL Records.

28. The sample included forty-two women, ranging in age from their forties to their seventies, who had played a variety of sports in a range of athletic settings in the West, Midwest, Southeast, and Northeast. The majority were white women from urban working-class and rural backgrounds.

29. Zipter, *Diamonds Are a Dyke's Best Friend;* Lillian Faderman, *Odd Girls and Twilight Lovers: A History of Lesbian Life in Twentieth-Century America* (New York: Columbia University Press, 1991), pp. 154, 161–62.

30. Ann Maguire, interview with the author, Boston, 18 Feb. 1988.

31. Nora Cross (pseudonym), interview with the author, 20 May 1988; Dorothy Ferguson Key, interview with the author, Rockford, Ill., 19 Dec. 1988.

32. Gloria Wilson (pseudonym), interview with the author, 11 May 1988.

33. Josephine D'Angelo, interview with the author, Chicago, 21 Dec. 1988.

34. Joseph P. Goodwin, *More Man Than You'll Ever Be! Gay Folklore and Acculturation in Middle America* (Bloomington: Indiana University Press, 1989), p. 62.

35. D'Angelo interview.

36. Loraine Sumner, interview with the author, West Roxbury, Mass., 18 Feb. 1988.

DOCUMENTS: *Making the Personal Political: Fighting Injustice*

Pauli Murray, "I had entered law school preoccupied with the racial struggle . . . but I graduated an unabashed feminist as well. . . ."

Pauli Murray was a remarkable woman. Born into a family that blended slaves, slave-owning whites, Cherokee Indians, freeborn African Americans—a family whose history she would later celebrate in her book *Proud Shoes*—she grew up an orphan in her grand-parents' home in Durham, North Carolina. Bright and energetic but poor, Murray grad-uated from the city's segregated schools in 1926. In a display of characteristic determi-nation, she applied to Hunter College in New York City. Rejected because she was so poorly prepared, she moved in with a cousin, enrolled in high school in New York, and entered Hunter a year later. The struggle to find work and stay in school in the midst of the Great Depression was so intense, however, that Murray, already suffering from mal-nutrition, nearly succumbed to tuberculosis. Shortly after her graduation from Hunter in 1933, she found brief sanctuary in Camp Tera, one of the handful of women's camps established by the New Deal as a counterpart to the men's Civilian Conservation Corps, and then as an employee of remedial reading and workers' education projects funded by the WPA.

"World events were breeding a new militancy in younger Negroes like me," she would write; "One did not need Communist propaganda to expose the inescapable par-allel between Nazi treatment of Jews in Germany and the repression of Negroes in the American South. Daily occurrences pointed up the hypocrisy of a United States policy that condemned Fascism abroad while tolerating an incipient Fascism within its own borders." In 1938, she applied to the law school at the University of North Carolina at Chapel Hill, attracted by the work of its sociologists on race relations and farm tenancy. (Margaret Hagood's study of white tenant farm women, as we have seen, was part of that work.) Many law school students supported her admission, as did Frank Porter Graham, the president of the university, but state law mandated her rejection because of race.

Torn between her writing and law, Murray threw herself into working for social justice. Her involvement in the unsuccessful struggle to obtain clemency for Odell Waller, a black sharecropper whose right to be tried by a representative jury had been denied

Excerpted from "Writing or Law School?," "Jim Crow in the Nation's Capital," "Don't Get Mad, Get Smart," in *Song in a Weary Throat: An American Pilgrimage* by Pauli Murray (New York: HarperCollins, 1987), pp. 183–85, 205–9, 238–45. Copyright © 1987 by The Estate of Pauli Murray. Reprinted by permission of HarperCollins Publishers, Inc.

because Virginia called to jury service only those who had paid a poll tax, brought her to the attention of Leon Ransom of Howard University Law School in Washington, D.C. When Howard University offered her a scholarship in 1941, she entered law school "with the single-minded intention of destroying Jim Crow."

The following account of Murray's years at Howard University focuses on her discovery of sexism amidst her battle with racism. It ends with a reference to her work thirty-five years later as an Episcopal priest. Murray had an extraordinary legal career as a champion of racial and gender justice, serving as a consultant to the President's Committee on the Status of Women in preparing its 1963 report [see pp. 545–46] and on the National Board of the American Civil Liberties Union. In January 1977, she became one of the first women to be ordained an Episcopal priest. Not long after, she was invited to celebrate her first Holy Eucharist in the Chapel of the Cross in Chapel Hill, the same church where the daughter of a prominent slaveholding family had many years before brought for baptism an infant whose father was her own lawyer brother, and whose mother was her own servant, Harriet. The infant was Pauli Murray's grandmother. On that occasion, "all the strands of my life came together," Murray wrote in an autobiography aptly subtitled "Activist, Feminist, Lawyer, Priest, and Poet." For Pauli Murray, the personal was indeed political.

Ironically, if Howard Law School equipped me for effective struggle against Jim Crow, it was also the place where I first became conscious of the twin evil of discriminatory sex bias, which I quickly labeled Jane Crow. In my preoccupation with the brutalities of racism, I had failed until now to recognize the subtler, more ambiguous expressions of sexism. In the all-female setting of Hunter College, women were prominent in professional and leadership positions. My awareness of the additional burden of sex discrimination had been further delayed by my WPA experience. Hilda Smith, national director of the WPA Workers' Education Project, was a woman, my local project director and my immediate supervisor were both women, and it had not occurred to me that women as a group received unequal treatment. Now, however, the racial factor was removed in the intimate environment of a Negro law school dominated by men, and the factor of gender was fully exposed.

During my first year at Howard there were only two women in the law school student body, both of us in the first-year class. When the other woman dropped out before the end of the first term, I was left as the only female for the rest of that year, and I remained the only woman in my class for the entire three-year course. While I was there, not more than two or three women enrolled in the lower classes of the law school. We had no women on the fac-

ulty, and the only woman professional on staff was . . . the registrar, who had graduated from the law school many years earlier.

The men were not openly hostile; in fact, they were friendly. But I soon learned that women were often the objects of ridicule disguised as a joke. I was shocked on the first day of class when one of our professors said in his opening remarks that he really didn't know why women came to law school, but that since we were there the men would have to put up with us. His banter brought forth loud laughter from the male students. I was too humiliated to respond, but though the professor did not know it, he had just guaranteed that I would become the top student in his class. Later I began to notice that no matter how well prepared I was or how often I raised my hand, I seldom got to recite. It was not that professors deliberately ignored me but that their freewheeling classroom style of informal discussion allowed the men's deeper voices to obliterate my lighter voice, and my classmates seemed to take it for granted that I had nothing to contribute. For much of that first year I was condemned to silence unless the male students exhausted their arguments or were completely stumped by a professor's question.

My real awakening came several months after school began, when I saw a notice on the official bulletin board inviting "all male students of the First Year Class" to a smoker at the residence of Professor Leon A. Ransom. The exclusion of women from the invitation was so pointed that I went to Dr. Ransom's office to seek an explanation. He told me blandly that Sigma Delta Tau, a legal fraternity limited to male students and members of the legal profession, had established a chapter at the law school and that the purpose of the smoker was to look over first-year men for likely prospects. Through their association with experienced lawyers these young men would enhance their professional development. I had not yet become aware of the sexist bias of the English language, and recalling that the national professional English "fraternity" to which I had been elected while in college included both sexes, I asked Dr. Ransom, "What about us women?"

To my surprise, Dr. Ransom merely chuckled and said that if we women wanted an organization we could set up a legal sorority. Angrily, I said it was ridiculous to speak of a legal sorority for two women, but he did not seem concerned about our plight. I left Dr. Ransom's office feeling both bewildered and betrayed, especially because he was one of the most liberal professors on the university campus and had always treated me as a person. He had encouraged me to come to law school and used his influence to have me awarded a scholarship. Yet he did not seem to appreciate fully that barring women from an organization purporting to promote professional growth had the same degrading effect upon women as compelling us as Negroes to sit in the back of a bus or refusing to admit black lawyers to white bar associations. The discovery that Ransom and other men I deeply admired because of their dedication to civil rights, men who themselves had suffered racial indignities, could countenance exclusion of women from their professional association aroused an incipient feminism in me long before I knew the meaning of the term "feminism."...

The fact that an accident of gender exempted me from military service and left me free to pursue my career without interruption made me feel an extra responsibility to carry on the integration battle. Many other Howard University women were feeling a similar responsibility, which was heightened by the dramatic leave-taking of sixty-five Howard men, who marched off campus in a body to report for military duty. We women reasoned that it was our job to help make the country for which our black brothers were fighting a freer place in which to live when they returned from wartime service.

From the nightly bull sessions in Truth Hall a plan of action emerged.... It was designed to attract the widest possible support from all segments of the university community, with direct action reserved for the last of a series of steps. My role as student "legal adviser" was to make sure that our proposed actions were within the framework of legality so as not to arouse the official disapproval of the university administration.... Although we were engaged in serious business, our planning sessions were fun and challenged our power of imagination. The fact that we were doing something creative about our racial plight was exhilarating and increased our self-esteem. The Direct Action subcommittee attracted some of the leading students on campus, for it was important that those undertaking unorthodox activities maintain academic excellence. Also, we proceeded cautiously, aware that a misstep would compromise our goal. Instead of rushing precipitously into "hostile" territory, a group of students surveyed public eating places in the neighboring, mostly Negro community on Northwest U Street that still catered to the "White Trade Only." One of the most notorious of these lily-white establishments was the Little Palace Cafeteria, located at the busy intersection of Fourteenth and U streets, N.W., and run by a Mr. Chaconas. Because of its strategic location, the Little Palace had long been a source of mortification for countless unsuspecting Negroes, who entered it assuming that at least they would be served in the heart of the Negro section of the city.

The Little Palace Cafeteria was selected as our first target. For a week prior to our move against the cafeteria we held campus pep rallies and drummed up support for our effort through noon-hour broadcasts from the tower of Founder's Library. We decorated hot-chocolate cups and used them around campus as collection cans to solicit the funds we needed for paper, postage, and picket signs. We held a midweek Town Hall meeting and brought in experienced political leaders ... to lead a forum on civil rights legislation and methods of achieving it. We conducted classes on the legal aspects of picketing and disorderly conduct in the District of Columbia, spent hours in small groups discussing public decorum, anticipating and preparing for the reactions of the black public, the white public, white customers, and white management respectively. We stressed the importance of a dignified appearance, and the subcommittee directed that all participants dress well for the occasion. We also pledged ourselves to exemplary nonviolent conduct, however great the provocation.

Finally, on April 17, a rainy Saturday afternoon, we assembled on campus and began to leave the Howard University grounds in groups of four, about five minutes apart, to make the ten-minute walk to the Little Palace Cafeteria. The demonstration was limited to a carefully selected group of volunteers—less than twenty students—who felt confident they could maintain self-restraint under pressure. As each group arrived, three entered the cafeteria while the fourth remained outside as an "observer." Inside, we took our trays to the steam table and as soon as we were refused service carried our empty trays to a vacant seat at one of the tables, took out magazines, books of poetry or textbooks, notebooks and pencils, and assumed an attitude of concentrated study. Strict silence was maintained. Minutes later the next group arrived and repeated the process. Outside, the observers began to form a picket line with colorful signs reading "Our Boys, our Bonds, our Brothers are Fighting for YOU! Why Can't We Eat Here?"; "We Die Together—Why Can't We Eat Together?"; "There's No Segregation Law in D.C. What's Your Story, Little Palace?" Two pickets carried posters (prepared for the War Manpower Commission by the Office of War Information) depicting two workers—one black and the other white—working together as riveters on a steel plate. The inscription on the poster read "UNITED WE WIN!"

My heart thumped furiously as I sat at a table awaiting developments. The management was stunned at first, then after trying unsuccessfully to persuade us to leave, called the police. Almost immediately a half-dozen uniformed officers appeared. When they approached us we said simply, "We're waiting for service," and since we did not appear to be violating any law, they made no move to arrest us.

After forty-five minutes had passed and twelve Negro students were occupying most of the tables of the small cafeteria, Chaconas gave up and closed his restaurant eight hours earlier than his normal closing time. Those of us who

were inside joined the picket line and kept it going for the rest of the afternoon. Chaconas told reporter Harry McAlpin, who covered the demonstration for the *Chicago Defender:* "I'll lose money, but I'd rather close up than practice democracy this way. The time is not ripe." When Juanita Morrow, a journalism student, interviewed Chaconas several days later, he admitted that he had lost about $180 that Saturday afternoon and evening, a considerable sum for a small business.

Actually, the incident did not arouse the furor we had feared but revealed the possibilities for change. When told why the place was closed and being picketed, a white customer named Raymond Starnes, who came from Charlotte, North Carolina, said, "I eat here regularly, and I don't care who eats here. All I want is to eat. I want the place to stay open. After all, we are all human." Another white bystander, asked what he thought of the students' action, replied, "I think it's reasonable. Negroes are fighting to win this war for democracy just like whites. If it came to a vote, it would get my vote."

When Chaconas opened his place on Monday morning, our picket line was there to greet him, and it continued all day. Within forty-eight hours he capitulated and began to serve Negro customers. We were jubilant. Our conquest of a small "greasy spoon" eating place was a relatively minor skirmish in the long battle to end segregation in the nation's capital—a battle that was ended by a Supreme Court decision ten years later—but it loomed large in our eyes. We had proved that intelligent, imaginative action could bring positive results and, fortunately, we had won our first victory without an embarrassing incident. (One other small restaurant in the area was desegregated that spring before final examinations and summer vacation interrupted our campaign.)

Significantly, the prominent role of women in the leadership and planning of our protest was a by-product of the wartime thinning of the ranks of male students. Twelve of the nineteen Howard University demonstrators at the Little Palace on April 17 were female. . . . Many of those young women who had joined together to defy tradition would continue to make breakthroughs in their respective fields after their college days. . . . The youngest member of that little band of demonstrators, Patricia Roberts, carried the impact of her civil rights experiences from Howard University to the cabinet level of the federal government [Patricia Roberts served as President Carter's Secretary of Housing and Urban Development from 1977 to '79]. . . .

I had entered law school preoccupied with the racial struggle and single-mindedly bent upon becoming a civil rights attorney, but I graduated an unabashed feminist as well. Ironically, my effort to become a more proficient advocate in the first struggle led directly into the second through an unanticipated chain of events which began in the late fall of my senior year.

One day Dean Hastie called me into his office to discuss what I planned to do after graduation. To my utter surprise, he spoke of the possibility of my returning to teach at the law school after a year of graduate study, and with that possibility in mind he recommended that I apply for a Rosenwald fellowship. For a number of reasons, "graduate study" meant to me "graduate study at Harvard University." At least half of the Howard Law School faculty had studied at Harvard, both Hastie and Ransom held doctorates from its law school, and it had become a tradition at Howard to groom an exceptionally promising law graduate for a future faculty position by sending him to Harvard "to put on the gloss" of a prestigous graduate degree in law. My greatest rival in the preceding class, Francisco Carniero, who had graduated with top honors and as Chief Justice of the Court of Peers, was not completing his year of graduate law there. We had run neck and neck in courses we took together, he topping me by a couple of points in one and I topping him in another.

Naively unaware of Harvard's policy toward women, I was stunned when my schoolmates began kidding me. "Murray," someone said, "don't you know they're not going to let you into Harvard?" Harvard, it became clear, did not admit women to its law school.

Then my hopes were raised by a rumor which circulated around campus that Harvard was opening up to women students. Accordingly, when filling out my application to the Rosenwald Fund, I wrote in the space provided for choice of law school: "I should like to obtain my Master's degree at Harvard University, in the event they have removed their bar against women students. If not, then I should like to work at Yale University or at any other University which has advanced study in the field

of labor law." I also wrote to the secretary of Harvard Law School, requesting confirmation or denial of the rumor I had heard. The answer was prompt. On January 5, 1944, the secretary's office wrote back: "Harvard Law School . . . is not open to women for registration."

This verdict was disappointing, of course, but with all the other preoccupations of my senior year, the matter probably would have rested there if I had not won the Rosenwald fellowship or at least if the names of the award winners had not been published nationwide. The announcement, made in late spring, listed me among fifteen white Southerners and twenty-two Negroes (including such notables as E. Franklin Frazier, Adelaide Cromwell Hill, Chester Himes, Rayford W. Logan, Dorothy Porter, and Margaret Walker) who received awards "for creative talent or distinguished scholarship." Mine was the only award in the field of law, and all the news stories reported that I was to do graduate study in labor law at Harvard University.

I was embarrassed to receive congratulatory messages from a number of people who were either unaware of Harvard's restrictive policy or assumed I had broken the barrier. At the same time, some of the men at Howard stepped up their banter, not without a touch of malicious glee. Until then I had been able to lick my wounds in private, but the public disclosure of my dilemma mortified me and presented a challenge I could not pass over lightly. If my schoolmates expected me to dissolve into tears under their stinging gibes, they were disappointed. I simply sat down and wrote a letter of application to Harvard Law School, which was duly processed, and I received a written request for my college transcript and a photograph.

In due course there came from Professor T. R. Powell, who chaired Harvard Law School's Committee on Graduate Studies, a letter that must have been dictated with an impish smirk. As nearly as I can recall, it ran: "Your picture and the salutation on your college transcript indicate that you are not of the sex entitled to be admitted to Harvard Law School." To appreciate the impact of this letter upon me, it is only necessary to remember the similar letter of rejection I had received in 1938 from the dean of the graduate school of the University of North Carolina in Chapel Hill: "Under the laws of North Carolina and under the resolutions of the Board of Trustees of the University of North Carolina, members of your race are not admitted to the University."

The personal hurt I felt now was no different from the personal hurt I had felt then. The niceties of distinction that in one case rejection was based upon custom and involved my sex and in the other was grounded in law and involved my race were wholly irrelevant to me. Both were equally unjust, stigmatizing me for a biological characteristic over which I had no control. But at least in the case of racial rebuffs long experience had taught me some coping mechanisms and I did not feel alone in that struggle. The fact that Harvard's rejection was a source of mild amusement rather than outrage to many of my male colleagues who were ardent civil rights advocates made it all the more bitter to swallow.

The harsh reality was that I was a minority within a minority, with all the built-in disadvantages such status entailed. Because of the considerable snobbery that—even apart from race and sex—existed in the highly competitive field of law, one's initial entry into the profession was profoundly affected by the law school one attended. This was particularly true for anyone who had ambitions to teach law. Since in my case the most common hurdles—lack of funds and a poor scholastic record—did not apply, I felt the injustice of the rejection even more strongly. I knew that however brilliant a record I had made at Howard, among my teaching colleagues I would never be considered on equal academic footing with someone who could boast of Harvard training. I also knew that the school of my second choice, Yale, had suspended its graduate program in law during the wartime emergency. [Professors William H.] Hastie and [Leon] Random, my law school mentors, understood my academic dilemma and were quietly supportive of my decision to pursue the Harvard matter further. Dr. [Caroline] Ware, whose great-great-grandfather Henry Ware had been the first dean of Harvard Divinity School and who grew up surrounded by the Harvard tradition, identified with me wholly in my fight. The only one of five generations of Phi Beta Kappas in her family not to take a Harvard degree, she held a Ph.D. from Radcliffe.

Then began the disheartening effort to budge a sluggishly corpulent bureaucracy on which my protests and appeals made about as much impression as a gnat on an elephant's hide. Harvard, being a private institution, was immune from legal attack and thus I had only the force of reason and logic with which to plead my case. A letter to Professor Powell asking what procedure to follow in appealing the law school's policy brought the information that the law school was bound by the rule of the Harvard Corporation not to admit women, and any appeal from that ruling would have to be submitted to the Corporation through its secretary, A. Calvert Smith.

Since my exclusion from Harvard was based solely on gender, my appeal necessarily was strongly feminist in tone:

> I have met a number of women and have heard of many more who wished to attend Harvard and yet were refused. This fight is not mine, but that of women who feel they should have free access to the very best of legal education. . . .
>
> Women are practicing before the Supreme Court, they have become judges and good lawyers, they are represented on the President's Cabinet and greater demand is being made for women lawyers in administrative positions as the men move into the armed forces. They are proving themselves worthy of the confidence and trust placed in them. . . . They are taking an intelligent view toward the political events at home and abroad, and statistics show they are in the majority of the voting population this year. A spot-check on memory would indicate there are only four important places they are not now holding— (1) As graduates of Harvard University, (2) as President of the United States, (3) as a member of the United States Supreme Court, and (4) as workers in the mines. Although [by admitting women] Harvard might lose in the sense of a loss of tradition, it might gain in the quality of the law school student personnel.

Meanwhile, two influential (if wholly unanticipated) male supporters sympathetic to the rights of women materialized. One was President Franklin D. Roosevelt! I had sent copies of the correspondence with Harvard to Mrs. Roosevelt, suggesting that the President might be amused at this attempt to storm the walls of his alma mater, never dreaming it would evoke more than a chuckle on his part. FDR was not merely amused; he actually wrote a letter on my behalf to President James B. Conant of Harvard University.

It would take more than one of that institution's most illustrious graduates to overturn a three-hundred-year tradition of male exclusiveness, however. President Conant's reply, sent on to me by FDR's secretary, only confused the issue. The letter assured President

Roosevelt that I was free to do graduate work at Radcliffe, and even sent along a Radcliffe catalogue—never mind the obvious fact that Radcliffe did not offer graduate courses in law. I was flattered that the President of the United States had intervened on my behalf, but I was no nearer my goal. Mrs. Roosevelt was unequivocally in my corner, and wrote me a note saying: "I loved your Harvard appeal."

Lloyd K. Garrison, who was to become a lifelong friend and sponsor, was my second unexpected supporter. Mr. Garrison, former dean of the University of Wisconsin School of Law, was then a member of the National War Labor Board, which he later chaired. He was also a member of the Harvard Board of Overseers. I first met him through an ambitious undertaking of our student organization, the First Annual Court of Peers Dinner, jointly sponsored by the faculty and the Student Guild of Howard University School of Law. Mr. Garrison was our guest speaker, and as chief officer of the Student Guild it was my function to preside over the dinner and sit next to him at the speakers' table.

The great-grandson of abolitionist William Lloyd Garrison, Lloyd K. Garrison bore a striking resemblance to his famous ancestor and had inherited his commitment to human freedom. Unlike the fiery nineteenth-century Garrison, however, Lloyd K. Garrison combined a gentleness of disposition with a tough-minded pragmatism. . . . He was intensely interested in my effort to get into Harvard but warned me that I did not have a chance against the archconservative Harvard Corporation. Under the circumstances he encouraged me to follow an alternative plan for graduate study elsewhere, in the meantime pressing my appeal.

A. Calvert Smith informed me that the Harvard Corporation would review my appeal on July 10, by which time I had already applied to Boalt Hall [School] of Law, University of California at Berkeley, one of the few schools in the country whose wartime faculty of distinguished scholars remained relatively intact. On July 12, Mr. Smith wrote me to say that since I was asking, in effect, for a change in the long-established practice of the law school not to admit women, and since the conditions of admission to any department were in general set up by the faculty governing that department, "Whether or not women should be admitted to the Law School is . . . a decision for the Faculty of the Law School." Mr. Smith indicated that

since no recommendation from the faculty of the law school was then before the Corporation, "it does not feel itself in a position to take any action on your application."

By sidestepping my appeal, the Harvard Corporation had rid itself temporarily of an annoying question, but it had also called into play a theory about the significance of individual action I had once announced half-seriously to Dr. Ware: "One person plus one typewriter constitutes a movement." If I could not compel admission to Harvard, at least I could raise the issue in such a way that its law school would be unable to avoid it. I was also learning the process of patiently following whatever administrative procedure was available even when there was every reason to believe the result would be futile.

My next letter was addressed to the Faculty of the Harvard Law School, summarizing the correspondence to date and requesting a meeting of the faculty "to reconsider my application and to decide whether it will recommend a change of the policy now in practice." I included a copy of my appeal to the Harvard Corporation and closed on a humorous note:

> [G]entlemen, I would gladly change my sex to meet your requirements but since the way to such change has not been revealed to me, I have no recourse but to appeal to you to change your minds on this subject. Are you to tell me that one is as difficult as the other?

As I had learned in the case of the University of North Carolina, correspondence could accomplish little more than stir up interest among a few key individuals and keep the issue flickering feebly. At the suggestion of Dr. Ware, I wrote to Judge Sarah T. Hughes of the United States District Court of Texas, who also chaired the Committee on Economic and Legal Status of Women. She replied that this was not a matter her committee had considered, but she said, "I shall be glad to discuss the problem at the next meeting which is in September," and asked that I keep her informed. After I left Washington, Dean Hastie wrote: "My best information on the Harvard situation is that the faculty is sharply divided on the matter of admitting women and will probably take the position that no action should be taken while a majority of the permanent faculty are on leave for war work." Lloyd K. Garrison's analysis prepared me for the inevitable. He wrote:

From what I could pick up in Cambridge, my guesses are:

(1) That the corporation will do nothing unless the Law School takes the initiative in asking that the rules be changed to admit women.

(2) That the Law School will do nothing . . . , certainly not until Dean Landis gets back next fall and probably not then.

(3) That this is due to a combination of long tradition, an excessively high enrollment which has become an increasing headache [and]

(4) A touch of some undefinable male egoism, which is, I think, rather particularly strong in and around Boston as compared let us say with the middle west where we take our co-education for granted.

At my last meeting on the Board of Overseers [at Harvard] there was a great debate as to whether women should be admitted to the Medical School and, so I was told (I had to leave the meeting early), the proposal mustered only two votes out of a dozen. . . .

I was in California when the faculty of the Harvard School of Law met on August 7, 1944, and took action on my petition for review. A few days later, Acting Dean E. M. Morgan informed me of their decision. His letter said in part:

In October, 1942, the Faculty thoroughly considered a proposal to request the University authorities to change the general rule. The first proposition was to admit women only during the emergency. This was almost immediately and unanimously rejected. The second proposal was for a permanent policy admitting women on exactly the same basis as men. This was debated by the Faculty at intervals for about three months, and the views of all members fully considered. There was much difference of opinion, but it was finally unanimously voted that no action looking to a change in the present practice be taken until after the emergency and after the School has returned to normal conditions with its full Faculty in residence. At that time the question will be debated anew. Accordingly it has been necessary to deny all applications for admission by women.

At its meeting on August 7, the Faculty determined to abide by its previous decision.

Having lost my first battle against "Jane Crow," I was somewhat comforted to learn indirectly that the effort was not entirely wasted. That fall when I registered at the University of California's Boalt Hall [School] of Law, I was surprised to discover that news of the Harvard affair had traveled across country, and I was greeted with the remark, "So you're the woman who caused the Harvard Law School faculty to split 7–7 on your application." I also learned later of Harvard's announcement that women would be admitted to its medical school in 1945.

Fortunately, my controversy with Harvard was unresolved when I graduated from Howard in June, and it did not affect the high excitement of the ceremonies. Aunt Pauline came from Durham and Uncle Lewis Murray from Baltimore, each filled with proprietary pride and vying to share the honor of a niece who had "turned out so well." The high point of Aunt Pauline's visit was having tea at the White House with Mrs. Roosevelt. Then on Commencement Day an unexpected recognition electrified the huge outdoor gathering. Harry McAlpin, a reporter for the *Pittsburgh Courier*, captured the mood of the occasion in a story headlined "Flowers from the First Lady." He wrote:

Flowers—a huge bouquet of them—delivered near the close of the Howard University commencement exercises last Friday, overshadowed all the previous proceedings of the impressive occasion. They were from Mrs. Roosevelt, wife of the President of the United States. They were for brilliant, active, strong-willed Pauli Murray, graduate cum laude of the Howard Law School.

According to McAlpin—no stranger to hyperbole—the arrival of the flowers overshadowed the commencement address . . . [and] the conferring of honorary degree[s]. . . .

Actually, the flowers had been delivered to the law school a half hour before the ceremonies began. When I came in to get my cap and gown, I glanced at them admiringly. . . . When someone finally made me realize it was *my* name on the card, I removed it, suggesting the flowers be placed on the platform for all the graduates to share. A few minutes later, the sight of University Secretary . . . parading across campus with the spectacularly beautiful display only moments before the academic procession began created an extra touch of excitement and added a special luster to the pageantry of the event.

On Sunday morning Aunt Pauline and I attended Holy Communion at the Church of the Atonement, where our former vicar at Saint Titus in Durham, the Reverend Eugene L. Henderson, was the celebrant. Mrs. Roosevelt's flowers graced the altar and later were taken to hospitals to cheer the sick. No one could have conceived that morning that thirty-five years later I would be serving in the same church as an Episcopal priest.

Jessie Lopez de la Cruz, "The first woman farmworker organizer out in the fields"

As the twentieth century progressed, Chicana women of the American Southwest were forced to follow their men in search of work, abandoning the communal village life described by Deutsch (see Part IIB). Joined by migrants from Mexico, they found jobs in factories, service work, and in the fields. Although entire families were incorporated into wage labor in the fields of Colorado and California, women, who had fewer job opportunities than men, gradually lost the power base and economic autonomy that had sustained them in their communal villages. They did not lose their resourcefulness or their determination to improve their working conditions, as the following account makes clear.

The movement of Jessie de la Cruz from farmworker to union organizer to community leader and Chicana spokeswoman to membership on the California Commission on the Status of Women is an example of one woman's determination to make the personal political. Contrary to popular stereotypes, Latina women have a tradition of activism. The best-known example is provided by the miners' wives at Silver City whose exploits on the picket line are documented in the classic film *Salt of the Earth*. Historians have recently added other examples: Mexican American women in textile factories and canneries who fought, often unsuccessfully, to gain the benefits for themselves and their families that unions could provide. Their efforts were preceded by those Cuban American women a continent away whose labor militancy and political activism in turn-of-the-century Florida further demonstrates the continuous intertwining of family and work, of home, factory, and field in the lives of many immigrant women as well as their willingness to fight economic and political oppression.

Note the similarities involved in the response to unionization of women workers described by Lopez de la Cruz and by Alice Kessler-Harris (see p. 244) and the critical difference made by the contrasting attitudes of Gompers and Chavez. Note, too, the persistent opposition of employers to unionization, whether in 1990 or 1960.

CHILDHOOD

My grandmother was born in Mexico in Aguas Calientes, near Guadalajara. She was raised by a very strict father and she married at thirteen. That was the custom. The girls, as soon as they were old enough to learn cooking and sewing, would get married. She had my mother and my oldest brother when she and my grandfather came across. My grandfather worked for the railroad laying the ties and tracks. Then he worked for a mining company. And after that we moved to Anaheim. We lived in a big four-bedroom house my grandfather built. With my grandparents and their children, three children of my mother's sister who had died, and the three of us, that made a big crowd.

My grandfather would get up Sunday

mornings and start the fire in a great big wood-burning stove. He would wrap us up in blankets and seat us around that stove on chairs and say, "Now, don't get too close to the stove. Take care of the younger children." Then he would go out to the store and get bananas and oranges and cereal that he'd cook for us to eat, and milk, and he would feed us Sunday mornings. . . .

Then my grandfather had an accident. The middle finger of his right hand was crushed and he couldn't work for about two weeks. When he went back he was told that he'd already been replaced by another worker. So he was out of a job. He decided we'd better go on and pick the crops. We had done that before, during the summer. But this time we went for good.

We came North. The families got together; the women would start cooking at night, boiling eggs and potatoes and making piles of tortillas and tacos, and these lunches would be packed in pails and boxes. There was as much fruit as they could get together, and roasted pumpkin seeds. My uncle had a factory where he made Mexican candy in East Los Angeles. And he used to give us a lot of pumpkin seeds. So my mother dried these, and she roasted and salted them for the trip to keep the drivers awake. We'd start in a car caravan, six or seven families together, one car watching for the other, and when it got a little dark they'd pull onto the roadside and build a fire and start some cooking to feed us. Then they'd spread blankets and quilts on the ground and we would sleep there that night. The next morning the women and older children would get up first and start the breakfast. And we smaller children, it was our job to fold the blankets and put them back in the cars and trucks. Then my brothers and the men would check the cars over again, and after breakfast all the women would wash the dishes and pack them, get 'em in the cars, and we'd start again.

We'd finally get to Delano and would work there a little. If work was scarce we would keep on going till San Jose. I did the same thing my mother and my grandfather and my uncles did, picking prunes on our hands and knees off the ground, and putting them in the buckets. We were paid four dollars a ton and we had to fill forty boxes to make it a ton. They made us sign a contract that we would stay there until all the prunes were picked. When we would finish the prunes, in early Sep-

tember, we would start back. And stop on the way to Mendota to pick cotton.

When I was about 13, I used to lift a 12-foot stack of cotton weighing 104 or 112 pounds. When you're doing this work, you get to be an expert. I could get that sack and put it on my shoulder, and walk with that sack for about a city block or maybe a little less, to where the scale was. I could hook this sack up on the scale, have it weighed, take it off the hook and put it back on my shoulder and walk up a ladder about eight feet high and dump all that cotton in the trailer.

My brothers taught me how to do it. When I first started picking cotton, they had to untie their sack and go on my side of the row and help me put this sack on my shoulder, so they taught me how to do it when it was full. It's stiff. My brother said, "Just walk over it, pick up one end, and sort of pull it up, up, and then bend down, and when the middle of the sack hits your shoulder, you just stand up slowly. Then put your arm on your waist and the sack will sit on your shoulder and you can just walk with it." At 13, 14 I was lifting 104 and 112 pounds. I weighed 97, I guess!

As a child I remember we had tents without any floors. I think it was Giffen's Camp Number Nine. I remember the water coming from under the tent at night to where we were sleeping. My brothers would get up with shovels and put mud around the tent to keep the water out. But our blankets and our clothes were always damp during the winter. . . .

In thirty-three we came up North to follow the crops because my brothers couldn't find any work in Los Angeles during the Depression. I remember going hungry to school. I didn't have a sweater. I had nothing. I'd come to school and they'd want to know, "What did you have for breakfast?" They gave us a paper, to write down what we had! I *invented* things! We had eggs and milk, I'd say, and the same things the other kids would write, I'd write. There weren't many Mexican people at school, mostly whites, and I'd watch to see what they were writing or the pictures that they'd show. You know: glasses of milk, and toast, and oranges and bananas and cereal. I'd never had *anything.* . . .

COURTSHIP AND MARRIAGE

When I was a girl, boys were allowed to go out and have friends and visit there in camp, and even go to town. But the girls—my mother was always watching them. We couldn't talk to nobody. If I had a boyfriend he had to send me letters, drop notes on his way or send them along with somebody. We did no dating. If girls came to visit at my house, my grandmother sat right there to listen to what we were talking about. We weren't allowed to speak English because she couldn't understand. . . . We were allowed nowhere except out to the field, and then we always worked between my two older brothers. The only one they trusted was Arnold. He's the one I married! I was fourteen when I met Arnold, in 1933. We lived next door to his family, which was a big one. . . .

Arnold and I got married in 1938 in Firebaugh, where we'd all moved. We had a big party with an orchestra: some of Arnold's friends played the violin and guitar. But we had no honeymoon. On the second day after our wedding, he went back to his job—irrigating. I'd get up at four o'clock in the morning to fix his breakfast and his lunch. He'd start the fire for me. I did the cooking in his mother's kitchen. In the morning I'd get up and run across and I'd fix his breakfast and his lunch and he'd go off and I'd go back to bed. There was no women's liberation at the time! I felt I was overworked in the house. . . . But I felt, "What can she (her mother-in-law) do without the help I'm giving her?" I felt sorry for her. She'd worked very hard and she had so many children, and had to wash her clothes in a tub with a rock board and do the ironing by heating the irons on top of the stove. All of us had to do this, but not many families had eight or nine little children.

I cooked with her until May. But I kept after Arnold: "I want my own kitchen!" So in May we drove all the way into Fresno. We got a few spoons and plates and pots and skillets and I started my own housekeeping. I still went to his mother's to help her during the day when Arnold was working. But I cooked in my own stove.

After I was married, sometime in May, my husband was chopping cotton and I said, "I want to go with you."

"You can't. You have to stay at home!"

"I just feel like going outside somewhere. I haven't gone anyplace. I want to at least go out to the fields. Take another hoe and I'll help you." I went, but only for one or two days. Then he refused to take me. He said, "You have

to stay home and raise children." I was pregnant with my first one. "I want you to rest," he said. "You're not supposed to work. You worked ever since I can remember. Now that you're married, you are going to rest." So I stayed home but I didn't call it rest doing all the cooking for his mother.

Arnold was raised in the old Mexican custom—men on the one side, women on the other. Women couldn't do anything. Your husband would say, "Go here," you'd do it. You didn't dare go out without your husband saying you could. . . .

After a time I said, "I have really had it. Why do you have to go with your friends all the time when I'm being left alone?"

"Well, what's wrong with that? You can go visit my mother." I said, "Big deal, you want me to visit your mother and help make some tortillas." So he finally started giving me money, five or six dollars. He'd say, "My mother's going to Fresno. If you want to go with them you can go." Or he would say, "Donna Genoveva," a friend of ours, "is going to Fresno and she said you can come along." I'd get my two kids ready early in the morning and we'd go to Fresno or to visit her husband, who was up in the mountains in the hospital for TB. One day I just said, "Why do I have to depend on other people to take me out somewhere? I'm married, I have a husband—who should be taking me out." The next time he was home and said, "Here's the money," I said, "I don't want to go." He let it go at that and I did too, I didn't say another word. The following weekend he said, "Do you want to go to a show? My mother's going. They're going to Fresno." I said, "No." Then about the third time this happened he said, "Why don't you want to go anymore?"

"I do, I do want to go. I want to go somewhere, but not with anyone else. I want to go with you." So then he started staying home and he'd say, "Get ready, we're going into Fresno." And both of us would come in, bring the children, go to a show and eat, or just go to the park.

Arnold would never teach me how to drive. One day I asked him to. We were on a ditch bank about eight feet wide. He says, "Get on the driver's side. Now turn around and go back." I got out. I said, "*You* do it! Just tell me you don't want me to learn if that's what you want." Then in 1947 I asked my sister, Margaret, and she showed me. We practiced in a field. After a few times she said, "Hey! You know how to drive! Let's go into town so you can buy your groceries."

So one day I said to Arnold, "I'm going out to get the groceries."

"Who's going to take you?"

"Me. I'm going to do the buying from now on."

I stopped working toward the last months of my pregnancies, but I would start again after they were born. When I was working and I couldn't find somebody I would take them with me. I started taking Ray with me when he wasn't a year old yet. I'd carry one of those big washtubs and put it under the vine and sit him there. I knew he was safe; he couldn't climb out. Arnold and I would move the tub along with us as we worked. I hated to leave him with somebody that probably wouldn't take care of him the way I could.

In 1944 we moved to a labor camp in Huron and we stayed there 'til 1956. But before that we had a single-room cabin. I used to separate the bed section from the kitchen by nailing blankets or pieces of canvas to divide. We had our bed and another bed for the children. All the boys slept in the bed and the girl slept with us in our bed. During the night Bobby being the youngest of the boys would wake up and be scared and he always ended up in our bed! It was pretty crowded, but what could you do? I was always nailing orange crates on the walls to use as cupboards for dishes. . . .

There was a lot of sickness. I remember when my kids got whooping cough. Arnold was sick, too, he was burning hot. During this time instead of staying in my own cabin at night I'd go to my mother-in-law's. The children would wake up at night coughing and there was blood coming out of their noses. I cried and cried, I was afraid they'd choke. I went to the clinic and they told me the children had whooping cough. That cough lasted six months.

It was like that for all of us. I would see babies who died. It was claimed if you lifted a young baby up fast, the soft spot would cave in and it would get diarrhea and dehydrate and die. After all these years, I know it wasn't that that killed them. It was hunger, malnutrition, no money to pay the doctors. When the union came, this was one of the things we fought against.

FIELD WORK

From 1939 until 1944 we stayed at Giffen's Camp Number Three. We were still following the crops. We would go out to pick cotton or apricots or grapes here near Fresno or we would go father north to Tracey to pick peas. When there was no work chopping or picking cotton we'd go to Patterson or San Jose to pick apricots. Arnold did the picking and I did cutting for the drying-out in the sheds. . . .

We always went where we wanted to make sure the women and men were going to work because if it were just the men working it wasn't worth going out there because we wouldn't earn enough, to support a family. We would start early, around 6:30 A.M., and work for four or five hours, then walk home and eat and rest until about 3:30 in the afternoon when it cooled off. We would go back and work until we couldn't see. Then we'd get home and rest, visit, talk, then I'd clean up the kitchen. I was doing the housework and working out in the fields, and taking care of the kids. I had two children by this time. . . .

The hardest work we did was thinning beets. You were required to use a short-handled hoe. The cutting edge is about seven to eight inches wide and the handle is about a foot long. Then you have to be bent over with the hoe in one hand. You walk down the rows stooped over. You have to work hard, fast, as fast as you can because you were paid by the row, not by the hour. . . .

I used a short-handled hoe in the lettuce fields. The lettuce grows in a bed. You work in little furrows between two rows. First you thin them with the hoe, then you pick off the tops. My brothers-in-law and Arnold and I and some other friends worked there picking the tops off the lettuce. By the time they had taken up one row I had taken up two. The men would go between the two beds and take one row and break the little balls off. But I took two rows at a time, one with each hand. By the time I finished my two rows at the other end, it was close to a mile long, and my brother-in-law had only taken one row part-way. He said, "I'm quitting! If Jessie can beat me at this kind of work, I'm no good at it." So he never came back. About three or four other men wouldn't go back to work because they were beaten by a woman. They said, "I'm ashamed to have a woman even older than I am work faster than

I can. This is women's job." I said, "Hey! What do you mean? You mean the men's job is washing dishes and baking tortillas?" They said working out in the fields was women's work because we were faster at it!

Out in the fields there were never any restrooms. We had to go eight or ten hours without relief. If there wasn't brush or a little ditch we were forced to wait until we got home! Just the women. The men didn't need to pull their clothes down. Later, when I worked for the Farmworkers, in a hearing, I said, "I was working for Russell Giffen, the biggest grower in Huron. These big growers have a lot of money because we earned all that money for them. Because of our sweat and our labor that we put on the land. What they do instead of supplying restrooms and clean water where we can wash our hands, is put posts on the ground with a piece of gunny sack wound around them." That's where we went. And that thing was moved along with us. It was just four stakes stuck in the ground and then there was canvas or a piece of gunny sack around it. You would be working and this restroom would be right there. The canvas didn't come up high enough in front for privacy. We made it a practice to go two at a time. One would stand outdoors and watch outside that nobody came along. And then the other would do the same for the one inside.

LA CAUSA

One night in 1962 there was a knock at the door and there were three men. One of them was Cesar Chavez. And the next thing I knew, they were sitting around our table talking about a union. I made coffee. Arnold had already told me about a union for the farmworkers. He was attending their meetings in Fresno, but I didn't. I'd either stay home or stay outside in the car. But then Cesar said, "The women have to be involved. They're the ones working out in the fields with their husbands. If you can take the women out to the fields, you can certainly take them to meetings." So I sat up straight and said to myself, "*That's* what I want!"

When I became involved with the union, I felt I had to get other women involved. Women have been behind men all the time, always. In my sister-in-law and brother-in-law's families the women do a lot of shouting and cussing and they get slapped around. But that's not

standing up for what you believe in. It's just trying to boss and not knowing how. I'd hear them scolding their kids and fighting their husbands and I'd say, "Gosh! Why don't you go after the people that have you living like this? Why don't you go after the growers that have you tired from working out in the fields at low wages and keep us poor all the time? . . . Then I would say we had to take a part in the things going on around us. "Women can no longer be taken for granted—that we're just going to stay home and do the cooking and cleaning. It's way past the time when our husbands could say, 'You stay home! You have to take care of the children. You have to do as I say.'"

Then some women I spoke to started attending the union meetings, and later they were out on the picket lines.

I was well-known in the small towns around Fresno. Wherever I went to speak to them, they listened. I told them about how we were excluded from the NLRB in 1935, how we had no benefits, no minimum wage, nothing out in the fields—no restrooms, nothing. I'd ask people how they felt about all these many years they had been working out in the fields, how they had been treated. And then we'd all talk about it. They would say, "I was working for so-and-so, and when I complained about something that happened there, I was fired." I said, "Well! Do you think we should be putting up with this in this modern age? You know, we're not back in the 20s. We can stand up! We can talk back! It's not like when I was a little kid and my grandmother used to say, 'You have to especially respect the Anglos, "Yessir," "Yes, Ma'am!"'' That's over. This country is very rich, and we want a share of the money those growers make of our sweat and our work by exploiting us and our children!" I'd have my sign-up book and I'd say, "If anyone wants to become a member of the union, I can make you a member right now." And they'd agree!

So I found out that I could organize them and make members of them. Then I offered to help them, like taking them to the doctor's and translating for them, filling out papers that they needed to fill out, writing their letters for those that couldn't write. A lot of people confided in me. Through the letter-writing, I knew a lot of the problems they were having back home, and they knew they could trust me, that I wouldn't tell anyone else about what I had written or read. So that's why they came to me.

I guess when the union found out how I was able to talk to people, I was called into Delano to one of the meetings, and they gave me my card as an organizer. I am very proud to say I was the first woman organizer out in the fields organizing the people. There have been Dolores Huerta and others, but they were in cities organizing the people, and I was the first woman farmworker organizer out in the fields. . . .

It was very hard being a woman organizer. Many of our people my age and older were raised with old customs in Mexico: where the husband rules, he is the king of his house. The wife obeys, and the children, too. So when we first started it was very, very hard. Men gave us the most trouble—neighbors there in Parlier! They were for the union, but they were not taking orders from women, they said. When they formed the ranch committee at Christian Brothers—that's a big wine company, part of it is in Parlier—the ranch committee was all men. We were working under our first contract in Fresno County. The ranch committee had to enforce the contract. If there are any grievances they meet with us and the supervisors. But there were no women on that first committee.

That year, we'd have a union meeting every week. Men, women, and children would come. Women would ask questions and the men would just stand back. I guess they'd say to themselves, "I'll wait for someone to say something before I do." The women were more aggressive than the men.

When the first contract was up, we talked about there being no women on the ranch committee. I suggested they be on it, and the men went along with this. And so women were elected.

The women took the lead in calling for picketing and we would talk to the people. It got to the point that we would have to find them, because the men just wouldn't go and they wouldn't take their wives. So we would say, "We're having our picket line at the Safeway in Fresno, and those that don't show up are going to have to pay a five dollar fine." We couldn't have four or five come to a picket line and have the rest stay home and watch T.V. In the end, we had everybody out there. . . .

At White River Farms one morning very early, we were out there by the hundreds by the road, and these people got down and started working out there in the grapes. We were asking them not to work, telling them that there was a strike going on. The grower had two guards at the entrance and there was a helicopter above us. At other White River Farm ranches they had the sheriff, the county police, *everybody*. But there were pickets at three different ranches and where we were picketing there wasn't anybody except these two guards. So I said, "Hey! What about the women getting together and let's rush 'em!" And they said, "Do you think we could do that?" And I said, "Of course we can! Let's go in there. Let's get 'em out of there any way we can." So about fifty of us rushed. We went under the vines. We had our banners and you could see them bobbing up and down, up and down, and we'd go under those rows on our knees and roll over. When the scabs saw us coming they took off. All of them went and they got on the bus. The guards had guns that they would shoot, and something black like smoke or teargas would come out. That scared us, but we still kept on. After we saw all those workers get back on the busses, we went back. Instead of running this time, we rolled over and over all the way out. The vines are about four feet tall, and they have wire where you string up the vines. So you can't walk or run across one of these fences. You have to keep going under these wires. When I got out there on the road they were getting these big, hard dirty clods and throwing them at us. And then the pickets started doing the same thing. When the first police car came, somebody broke the windshield. We don't know if it was the scabs or someone on the picket lines, but the picketers were blamed.

When we women ran into the fields we knew we'd be arrested if they caught us. But we went in and we told the scabs, "If you're not coming out we're gonna pull you out!"

In Kern County we were sprayed with pesticides. They would come out there with their sprayers and spray us on the picket lines. They have these big tanks that are pulled by a tractor with hoses attached and they spray the trees with this. They are strong like a water hose, but wider. When we were picketing they came out there to spray the pickets. They had goons with these big police dogs on leashes.

One of the things the growers did to break our strikes was to bring in "illegal aliens." I would get a list of names of the scabs and give them to the border patrol. At that time, you see, we were pitted against each other, us and the people from Mexico, so it was either us or them. When I went to the border patrol office I'd go in and say, "Can I come in?" They'd say, "You can't come in. This is a very small office." They kept telling us they were short of men. But every time I went there, there were all of them with their feet up on the desks in their air-conditioned office. They told me they were under orders not to interfere with labor disputes. So I called Bernie Sisk's office and talked to them about it. Then I came home and called a lot of students who'd been helping us, and other people, and the next morning there we were at the border patrol. I said, "We're paying our tax money, but not for you to sit here while the illegal aliens are being used to break our strike."

While we were in Parlier, I was put in charge of the hiring hall. My house was right next to the office, and I had an extension to the office phone in my house. I could do the housework and take care of the children, but I could take care of the office, too. Before the contract, the hiring hall was just a union office where people came to learn about the union. When they got the first contracts we began dispatching people out to work. The hiring hall was also a place where people could meet and talk. A lot of people were migrants who needed to get to know each other. The people who were there all the time were against the migrants. I said, "We have to get these people together. We can't be divided." I was at the hall all day. People would drop by and I'd introduce them.

The second year we had a contract I started working for Christian Brothers. The men were doing the pruning on the grape vines. After they did the pruning the women's crew would come and tie the vines. (That was something we got changed; we made them give pruning jobs to women.) I was made a steward on the women's crew. . . . the first time we were paid when I started working, during the break the supervisor would come out there with our checks. It was our fifteen minute break, which the contract gave us the right to. We had to walk to the other end of the row; it took us about five minutes to get there, the rest of the fifteen to get our checks, and walk back, and we'd start working. This happened twice. The third time I said, "We're not going to go after our check this time. They always come

during our break and we don't get to rest." So when we saw the pickup coming with the men who had the checks I said, "Nobody move. You just sit here." I walked over to the pickup. I said to the man inside, "Mr. Rager, these women refuse to come out here on their break time. It's their time to rest. So we're asking you, if you must come during our rest period, you take the checks to these ladies." From that day on, every payday he would come to us. That was the sort of thing you had to do to enforce the contract.

I became involved in many of the activities in the community—school board meetings, city council meetings, everything that I could get into. For example I went to fighting for bilingual education at Parlier, went to a lot of meetings about it and spoke about it. Parlier is over 85 percent Chicano, yet during that time there were no Chicanos on the school board, on the police force, nowhere. Now it's changed: we fought to get a Chicano mayor and officials. But then I was asking people, "Why are we always asked to go to the public school for our meetings? Why can't they come over to our side of town in Parlier?" So we began having meetings in *la colonia* at the Headstart Center, and there we pushed for bilingual education.

Fresno County didn't give food stamps to the people—only surplus food. There were no vegetables, no meat, just staples like whole powdered milk, cheese, butter. At the migrant camp in Parlier the people were there a month and a half before work started, and since they'd borrowed money to get to California they didn't have any food. I'd drive them into Fresno to the welfare department and translate for them and they'd get food, but half of it they didn't eat. We heard about other counties where they had food stamps to go to the store and buy meat and milk and fresh vegetables for the children. So we began talking about getting that in Fresno. Finally we had Senate hearings at the Convention Center in Fresno. There were hundreds of people listening. I started in Spanish, and the Senators were looking at each other, you know, saying, "What's going on?" So then I said, "Now, for the benefit of those who can't speak Spanish, I'll translate. If there is money enough to fight a war in Vietnam, and if there is money enough for Governor Reagan's wife to buy a $3000 dress for the Inauguration Ball, there should be money enough to feed these people. The nutrition experts say surplus food is full of vitamins. I've taken a look at that food, this corn meal, and I've seen them come up and down, but you know, we don't call them vitamins, we call them weevils!" Everybody began laughing and whistling and shouting. In the end, we finally got food stamps.

AMY SWERDLOW

Ladies' Day at the Capitol: Women Strike for Peace Versus HUAC

In the years surrounding World War I, women played a significant role in the peace movement. Justifying their involvement in the language of "Reformist Motherhood," Crystal Eastman wrote to Jane Addams in 1915 that, as mothers or potential mothers, women "have a more intimate sense of the value of human life"; therefore, "there can be more meaning and passion in the determination of a woman's organization to end war than in an organization of men and women with the same aim."*

Nearly half a century later, American women would again invoke their role as mothers to urge the end of nuclear testing on behalf of the world's children. The women's peace movement, which Swerdlow explores in the following article, coalesced at a time when the Cuban Missile Crisis had brought the United States and the Soviet Union to the brink of war. It also occurred during a period when virtually any form of political protest was automatically labeled by its critics as "communist inspired." Although the most virulent phase of McCarthyism had subsided by 1962, the machinery of repression was still intact; the women's peace movement was promptly investigated by the House Un-American Activities Committee.

Note how participants in the peace strike countered committee tactics by manipulating traditional gender stereotypes. Who were these women? How can their emergence as political activists be explained?

In mid-December of 1962 in the Old House Office Building of the United States Congress, a confrontation took place between a recently formed women's peace movement called Women Strike for Peace (WSP) and the House Committee on Un-American Activities (HUAC). The confrontation took place at a HUAC hearing to determine the extent of Com-

---

*Crystal Eastman to Jane Addams, January 16, 1915, Woman's Peace Party Papers, Swarthmore College Peace Collection, Swarthmore, Pa.

"Ladies' Day at the Capitol: Women Strike for Peace versus HUAC" by Amy Swerdlow, in *Feminist Studies* 8 (1982):493–520. Copyright © 1982 by Feminist Studies, Inc. Reprinted by permission of the publisher, Feminist Studies, Inc., c/o Women's Studies Program, University of Maryland, College Park, Maryland 20742. Notes have been edited.

munist party infiltration into "the so-called 'peace movement' in a manner and to a degree affecting the national security."[1] This three-day battle of political and sexual adversaries, which resulted in a rhetorical victory for the women of WSP and a deadly blow to the committee, occurred only twenty-five years ago.[2] It is a moment in the history of peace movements in the United States in which women led the way by taking a more courageous and principled stand in opposition to cold war ideology and political repression than that of their male counterparts.[3] However, in keeping with the historical amnesia which besets both the history of women and radical movements in America, the WSP-HUAC struggle is largely forgotten.[4]

This article seeks to reconstruct the WSP-HUAC confrontation and the reasons it took the form it did. By analyzing the ideology, consciousness, political style, and public demeanor of the WSP women as they defended their right as mothers "to influence the course of government," we can learn a great deal about the strengths and weaknesses of women's movements for social change that build on traditional sex role ideology and on female culture.[5]

WSP burst upon the American political scene on November 1st, 1961, when an estimated fifty thousand women in over sixty cities across the United States walked out of their kitchens and off their jobs in a one-day women's strike for peace. As a radioactive cloud from a Russian nuclear test hung over the American landscape, these women strikers staged the largest female peace action in the nation's history.[6] In small towns and large cities from New York to California, the women visited government officials demanding that they take immediate steps to "End the Arms Race—Not the Human Race."[7] Coming on the heels of a decade noted for cold war consensus, political conformity, and the celebration of female domesticity, this spontaneous women's initiative baffled both the press and the politicians. The women seemed to have emerged from nowhere. They belonged to no unifying organizations, and their leaders were totally unknown as public figures.

The women strikers were actually responding to a call from a handful of Washington, D.C., women who had become alarmed by the acceleration of the nuclear arms race. So disheartened were they by the passivity of traditional peace groups, that they had sent a call

to women friends and contacts all over the country urging them to suspend their regular routine of home, family, and job to join with friends and neighbors in a one-day strike to end the nuclear arms race.[8]

The call to strike spread rapidly from Washington through typical female networks: word of mouth and chain letter fashion from woman to woman, from coast to coast, through personal telephone calls, and Christmas card lists. Contacts in Parent Teacher Associations (PTAs), the League of Women Voters, church and temple groups, as well as the established peace organizations such as the Women's International League for Peace and Freedom (WILPF) and the Committee for a Sane Nuclear Policy (SANE), also spread the word.

The nature of the strike in each community depended entirely on what the local women were willing, and able, to do. Some marched, others lobbied local officials, a few groups took ads in local newspapers. Thousands sent telegrams to the White House and to the Soviet embassy, calling upon the two first ladies of the nuclear superpowers, Jacqueline Kennedy and Nina Khrushchev, to urge their husbands on behalf of all the world's children to "stop all nuclear tests—east and west." Amazed by the numbers and composition of the turnout on November 1st, *Newsweek* commented:

> They were perfectly ordinary looking women, with their share of good looks; they looked like the women you would see driving ranch wagons, or shopping at the village market, or attending PTA meetings. It was these women by the thousands, who staged demonstrations in a score of cities across the nation last week, protesting atomic testing. A "strike for peace," they called it and—carrying placards, many wheeling baby buggies or strollers—they marched on city halls and Federal buildings to show their concern about nuclear fallout.[9]

The strikers' concern about the nuclear arms race did not end with the November 1st actions. Within only one year, the one-day strike for peace was transformed by its founders and participants into a national women's movement with local groups in sixty communities and offices in ten cities. With no paid staff and no designated leaders, thousands of women in different parts of the country, most of them previously unknown to each other, managed to establish a loosely structured communications network capable of swift and effective direct action on both a national and international scale.

From its inception, the WSP movement was a non-hierarchical participatory network of activists opposed both to rigid ideologies and formal organizational structure. The WSP women called their format simply "our un-organization." It is interesting to note that the young men of Students for a Democractic Society (SDS), a movement founded in the same year as WSP, more aware of their place in the radical political tradition, more aware of the power of naming, and more confident of their power to do so, named their loose structure "participatory democracy." Eleanor Garst, one of the Washington founders, explained the attractions of the un-organizational format:

> No one must wait for orders from headquarters—there aren't any headquarters. No one's idea must wait for clearance through the national board. No one waits for the president or the director to tell her what to do—and there is no president or director. Any woman who has an idea can propose it through an informal memo system; if enough women think it's good, it's done. Those who don't like a particular action don't have to drop out of the movement; they just sit out that action and wait for one they like. Sound "crazy"?—it is, but it also brings forth and utilizes the creativity of thousands of women who could never be heard from through ordinary channels.[10]

The choice of a loose structure and local autonomy was a reaction to hierarchical and bureaucratic structures of traditional peace groups like WILPF and SANE to which some of the early leaders belonged. These women perceived the WILPF structure, which required that all programmatic and action proposals be cleared with state and national offices, as a roadblock to spontaneous and direct responses to the urgent international crisis.[11] The willingness of the Washington founders to allow each group to act in the way that suited its particular constituency was WSP's greatest strength and the source of the confidence and admiration that women across the country bestowed on the Washington founders. Washington came to be considered the WSP national office not only because it was located in the nation's capital, but also because the Washington group was trusted by all.

There was also another factor militating against a traditional membership organization. Only the year before the WSP strike, Linus Pauling, the Nobel Laureate in physics and opponent of nuclear testing, had been directed by the Senate Internal Security Subcommittee to turn over the names of those who had helped him gather signatures on a scientists' antinuclear petition. The commandeering of membership lists was not an uncommon tactic of political intimidation in the 1950s. Membership lists of radical organizations could therefore be a burden and responsibility. As they served no purpose in the WSP format, it was a sensible strategy to eliminate them. Another benefit was that WSP never had to assess accurately its numerical strength, thus allowing its legend to grow even when its numbers did not.

From its first day onward, WSP tapped a vast reservoir of moral outrage, energy, organizational talent, and sisterhood—female capacities that had been submerged and silenced for more than a decade by McCarthyism and the "feminine mystique." Using standard pressure group tactics, such as lobbying and petitioning, coupled with direct demonstrative action and civil disobedience, executed with imagination and "feminine flair," the WSP women succeeded in putting women's political demands on the front pages of the nation's newspapers, from which they had largely disappeared since the days of the suffrage campaign. WSP also managed to influence public officials and public policy. At a time when peace marchers were ignored, or viewed as "commies" or "kooks," President John F. Kennedy gave public recognition to the women strikers. Commenting on WSP's first antinuclear march at the White House, on January 15, 1962, the president told the nation that he thought the WSP women were "extremely earnest."

> I saw the ladies myself. I recognized why they were here. There were a great number of them, it was in the rain. I understand what they were attempting to say, therefore, I consider their message was received.[12]

In 1970, *Science* reported that "Wiesner (Jerome Wiesner, Pres. Kennedy's Science Advisor) gave the major credit for moving President Kennedy toward the limited Test Ban Treaty of 1963, not to arms controllers inside the government but to the Women Strike for Peace and to SANE and Linus Pauling."[13]

Although WSP, in its first year, was well received by liberal politicians and journalists, the surveillance establishment and the right-wing press were wary. They recognized early what the Rand Corporation described obliquely as the WSP potential "to impact on military policies."[14] Jack Lotto, a Hearst columnist, charged that although the women described themselves as a "group of unsophisticated wives and mothers who are loosely organized in a spontaneous movement for peace, there is nothing spontaneous about the way the pro-Reds have moved in on our mothers and are using them for their own purposes."[15] On the West Coast, the *San Francisco Examiner* claimed to have proof that "scores of well-intentioned, dedicated women . . . were being made dupes of by known Communists . . . operating openly in the much publicized Women Strike for Peace demonstrations."[16]

That WSP was under Federal Bureau of Investigation (FBI) surveillance from its first public planning meeting in Washington in October 1961, is abundantly evidenced in the forty-three volumes of FBI records on WSP which have been made available to the movement's attorneys under the provisions of the Freedom of Information Act. The records show that FBI offices in major cities, North, East, South, and West—and even in such places as Mobile, Alabama; Phoenix, Arizona; and San Antonio, Texas; not known for WSP activities—were sending and receiving reports on the women, often prepared in cooperation with local "red squads."[17]

Having just lived through the Cuban Missile Crisis of October 1962, WSP celebrated its first anniversary in November with a deep sense of urgency and of heightened political efficacy. But, as the women were making plans to escalate their commitment and their protests, they were stopped in their tracks in the first week of December by HUAC subpoenas to thirteen women peace activists from the New York metropolitan area, as well as Dagmar Wilson of Washington, D.C., the WSP national spokesperson.[18]

It is difficult today to comprehend the emotions and fears such a summons could invoke in individuals and organizations. Lillian Hellman's *Scoundrel Time* gives a picture of the tension, isolation, and near hysteria felt by an articulate and prominent public figure, as she prepared her defense against the committee in 1953.[19] By 1962, cold war hysteria had abated somewhat, as the United States and the USSR were engaged in test ban negotiations, but

HUAC represented those forces and those voices in American politics that opposed such negotiations. As a congressional committee, it still possessed the awesome power of an agency of the state to command headlines; cast suspicion; and by labeling individuals as subversives, to destroy careers, lives, and organizations.

The HUAC subpoenas gave no indication of the subject of the hearings, or of their scope. So there was, at first, some confusion about whether it was the WSP connection or other aspects of the subpoenaed women's political lives that were suspect. To add to the confusion, it was soon discovered that three of the women called were not even active in WSP. They were members of the Conference of Greater New York Peace Groups, an organization founded by New Yorkers who had either been expelled from, or who had willingly left, SANE because of its internal red hunt. Of these three women, two had already been named by the committee informers as communists in previous HUAC hearings. One of these women, Elizabeth Moss, had achieved considerable notoriety when she was identified by accused Russian spy William Remington as his mother-in-law and a card-carrying communist. Given these circumstances it was clear that the WSP leadership had some important decisions to make regarding their response to the HUAC hearings. There were two important questions to be faced. First, as WSP had no official membership list, would the movement embrace any woman working for peace even if she were not directly involved in WSP activity? Second, would WSP disavow its members who had past or present communist affiliations, and if WSP did not disavow them, would the movement lose its following and its effectiveness?

The key to WSP unity in the face of the "communist issue" which had divided and disrupted peace, labor, and even civil liberties organizations in the previous decade, was the fact that WSP had previously decided to handle forthrightly and in advance of any attack, the issue of communist inclusion. WSP had, even before the HUAC hearings, decided to reject political screening of its members, deeming it a manifestation of outdated cold war thinking. This decision, the women claimed, was based not on fear or expediency, but on principle. The issue of accepting communists in the movement was brought to the floor of the first national WSP conference in June 1962 by the Los Angeles coordinating council. A prepared statement by the Los Angeles group declared: "Unlike SANE and Turn Toward Peace, WSP must not make the error of initiating its own purges." Treating the issue of communist membership as a question of personal conscience, the Los Angeles group asked, "If there are communists or former communists working in WSP, what difference does that make? We do not question one another about our religious beliefs or other matters of personal conscience. How can we justify political interrogation?" The Los Angeles statement continued, "If fear, mistrust and hatred are ever to be lessened, it will be by courageous individuals who do not hate and fear and can get together to work out tolerable compromises."[20] The argument that "this is a role women would be particularly equipped to play," won over the conference and resulted in the inclusion of a section in the WSP national policy statement which affirmed, "we are women of all races, creeds and political persuasions who are dedicated to the achievement of general and complete disarmament under effective international control."[21]

An emergency meeting of about fifty New York area "key women," along with Dagmar Wilson and other representatives from Washington, was called a few days after the HUAC summonses began to arrive.[22] The first decision made at this meeting was that WSP would live up to the national policy statement that had been arrived at six months earlier and make a reality of the phrase, "We are women of all . . . political persuasions." Following from this decision it was clear that WSP would support and embrace every woman summoned before HUAC, regardless of her past or present affiliations, as long as she supported the movement's campaign against both Russian and American nuclear policies. This meant that in addition to supporting its own women, the three women not active in WSP would also come under the movement's protection if they so desired. They would be given access to the same lawyers as the WSP activists. They would not be isolated or attacked either for their affiliations or for the way they chose to conduct themselves at the hearing. This decision was in sharp contrast to the action taken by SANE in 1960 when it expelled a leading member of its New York chapter after he invoked the Fifth

Amendment at a Senate Internal Security Subcommittee hearing, and then refused to tell Norman Cousins, a cochairman of SANE, whether or not he had ever been a communist.[23]

The decision made by the New York and Washington women not "to cower" before the committee, to conduct no internal purges, to acknowledge each woman's right to act for peace and to conduct herself according to the dictates of her conscience was bold for its day. It was arrived at within the movement, by the women themselves, without consultation with the male leaders of traditional peace and civil liberties groups, many of whom disagreed with this WSP policy.[24] It was based not only on the decision to resist the demonology of the cold war, but also on a sense of sisterhood, on feelings of identification with and empathy for the women singled out for attack. Even the subpoenaed women themselves turned for counsel and support more to each other and the WSP leadership than to their families and lawyers. Working together at a feverish pace, night and day for three weeks, writing, phoning, speaking at rallies, the key women seemed to be acting as if they were a family under attack, for which all personal resources, passions, and energies had to be marshaled. But the family, this time, was "the movement" and it was the sisters, not the fathers, who were in charge.

In response to the subpoenas, a massive campaign was organized for the cancellation of the hearings and for support of WSP from national organizations and public figures. An anti-HUAC statement was composed in New York and Washington which spoke so well to the concerns and the consciousness of "the women" that it succeeded in unifying a movement in shock. The WSP statement on the HUAC inquisition was quoted widely by the press, used by local groups in ads and flyers, in letters to editors, and in speeches. "With the fate of humanity resting on a push button," the statement declared, "the quest for peace has become the highest form of patriotism."[25] In this first sentence, the women set the ground rules for their confrontation with the committee: it was going to be a contest over which group was more patriotic. But the test of "Americanism," according to the WSP rules, was the extent of one's dedication to saving America's children from nuclear extinction. Addressing the issue of communism in the movement, WSP declared: "Differences of politics, economics or social belief disappear when we recognize man's common peril ... we do not ask an oath of loyalty to any set of beliefs. Instead we ask loyalty to the race of man. The time is long past when a small group of censors can silence the voice of peace." These words would be the WSP *leitmotif* in the Washington hearings. The women were saying, once again, as they had throughout their first year, that for them, the arms race, cold war ideology, and cold war politics, were obsolete in the nuclear age, as was the committee itself. This is the spirit Eric Bentley caught and referred to when he wrote: "In the 1960s a new generation came to life. As far as HUAC is concerned it began with Women Strike for Peace."[26]

The WSP strategy against HUAC was innovative. An organizing memorandum from the Washington office declared, "the usual response of protest and public statements is too traditional and ineffectual.... Let's Turn the Tables! Let's meet the HUAC challenge in the Good New WSP way!"[27] The "new way" suggested by women all over the country was to insist that WSP had nothing to hide. Instead of refusing to testify, as radicals and civil libertarians had done in the 1950s, large numbers of WSP participants volunteered to "talk." Approximately one hundred women sent wires to Representative Francis Walter, chairman of HUAC, offering to come to Washington to tell all about their movement. The offers were refused by HUAC. But this new WSP tactic pointed up the fact that the committee was less interested in securing information than in exposing and smearing those it chose to investigate. Some WSP groups objected to the free testimony strategy on the grounds that there was a contradiction between denying the right of the committee to exist, and at the same time offering to cooperate with it. But these groups were in a minority. Carol Urner of Portland, Oregon, spoke for all those who volunteered to testify, making it clear that she would not be a "friendly witness." "I could not, of course, divulge the names of others in the movement," she wrote to Representative Walter. "I suppose such a refusal could lead one to 'contempt' and prison and things like that ... and no mother can accept lightly even the remote possibility of separation from the family which needs her. But mankind needs us too...."[28]

Only three weeks' time elapsed between the arrival of the first subpoenas from HUAC and the date of the Washington hearings. In this short period, the WSP key women managed to develop a legal defense, a national support system for those subpoenaed, and a broad national campaign of public protest against the committee. The women's performance at the hearings was so original, so winning, and so "feminine" in the traditional sense, that it succeeded in capturing the sympathy and the support of large sections of the national media and in strengthening the movement instead of destroying it.

The hearings opened on December 11, 1962, at 10:00 A.M. in the caucus room of the Old House Office Building of the United States Congress in Washington, D.C. Fear, excitement, and exhilaration were in the air as each WSP woman in the audience looked around to see every seat in the room occupied by sisters who had come from eleven states, some from as far as California, in response to a call for their presence from the national leadership. Clyde Doyle, chairman of the subcommittee of HUAC conducting the WSP hearings, opened with a statement of their purpose. Quoting from Lenin, Stalin, Khrushchev, and Gus Hall, he explained:

> Communists believe that there can be no real peace until they have conquered the world.... The initiated Communist, understanding his Marxist-Leninist doctrine, knows that a Moscow call to intensify the "fight for peace" means that he should intensify his fight to destroy capitalism and its major bastion, the United States of America.[29]

The WSP women in the audience rose as one as the committee called its first witness, Blanche Posner, a retired schoolteacher who was the volunteer office manager for New York WSP. The decision to rise with the first witness, to stand *with* her, was spontaneous. It was proposed only a few minutes before Posner was called, as a note from an unknown source was circulated around the room. Posner refused to answer any questions about the structure or personnel of WSP. She resorted to the Fifth Amendment forty-four times, as the press pointed out in dozens of news stories covering the first day of the hearings. They also reported the way in which Posner took matters into her own hands, lecturing the committee members as though they were recalcitrant boys at DeWitt

Clinton High School in the Bronx, where she had taught. Talking right through the interruptions and objections raised by the chairman and by committee counsel, Alfred Nittle, Posner declared:

> I don't know, sir, why I am here, but I do know why you are here, I think . . . because you don't quite understand the nature of this movement. This movement was inspired and motivated by mothers' love for children. . . . When they were putting their breakfast on the table, they saw not only the wheaties and milk, but they also saw strontium 90 and iodine 131. . . . They feared for the health and life of their children. That is the only motivation.[30]

Each time Posner resorted to the Fifth Amendment, she did it with a pointed criticism of the committee or a quip that endeared her to the women in the hearing room who needed to keep their spirits up in the face of charges that Posner had been identified by an FBI informer as a Communist party member while working in New York City as a schoolteacher. One prize exchange between Nittle and Posner led to particularly enthusiastic applause and laughter from WSP women. Nittle asked, "Did you wear a colored paper daisy to identify yourself as a member of the Women Strike for Peace?" Posner answered, "It sounds like such a far cry from communism it is impossible not to be amused. I still invoke the Fifth Amendment."[31]

Most of the witnesses were called because the committee believed it had evidence to link them with the Communist party through identification by FBI informers or the signing of party nominating petitions. But the strategy backfired with Ruth Meyers, of Roslyn, Long Island. She stepped forward, according to Mary McGrory's report in the *Washington* (D.C.) *Evening Star*, "swathed in red and brown jersey, topped by a steeple crowned red velvet hat," and "she was just as much of a headache to the committee as Posner had been."[32] There was much sparring between Meyers and the committee about the nature and structure of WSP. "Are you presently a member of a group known as Women Strike for Peace?" Nittle asked. "No, sir, Women Strike for Peace has no membership," Meyers answered. Nittle then asked, "You are familiar, I understand, with the structural organization of Women Strike for Peace as evidenced by this plan?" Meyers replied, "I am familiar to the extent of the role that I play in it. I must say that I was not par-

ticularly interested in the structure of Women Strike for Peace. I was more involved in my own community activities. . . . I felt that structure, other than the old telephone, has not much of what I was interested in." Nittle then proceeded to deliver what he believed would be the coup de grâce for Meyers. "Mrs. Meyers," he barked, "it appears from the public records that a Ruth Meyers, residing at 1751 East 10th Street, Brooklyn, New York, on July 27, 1948, signed a Communist Party nominating petition. . . . Are you the Ruth Meyers who executed that petition?" Meyers shot back, "No, sir." She then examined the petition carefully, and announced, "I never lived in Brooklyn, and this is not my signature."[33] Although the official transcript does not contain this statement, many, including the author, remember that she added, "My husband could never get me to move there." This female remark brought an explosion of laughter and applause. Meyers also invoked the Fifth Amendment. As she left the witness stand, Meyers received a one-minute ovation for humor, grace, and mistaken identity. In the corridor outside the caucus room in front of the TV cameras, she told reporters that she had never been a Communist. "But I'll never acknowledge the Committee's right to ask me that question."[34]

Another witness, Lyla Hoffman, chose to tell the committee of her past communist affiliation, asserting that she had left the Communist Party, but would not cooperate in naming names or in citing the cause of her resignation. In a statement written after the hearings Hoffman explained, "I felt that it was high time to say, 'What difference does it make what anyone did or believed many years ago? That's not the problem facing humanity today.' But I had to say this in legal terms." She found it very difficult to do so, as the committee was interested only in whether she was a genuine anticommunist or a secret fellow-traveler.[35] Hoffman invoked the Fifth Amendment.

The witnesses that followed Posner, Meyers, and Hoffman, each in her own style, invoked whatever legal and rhetorical strategy her conscience and her situation dictated. They lectured the committee eloquently and courageously on the danger of nuclear holocaust, on women's rights and responsibility to work for peace. In attempting to explain the nonstructured format of WSP, several witnesses suggested that the movement was too fluid and too unpredictable to be comprehended by the masculine mind.

In their most optimistic projections, the WSP women could not have predicted the overwhelmingly favorable press and public response they would receive, and the support and growth for the movement that would result from the HUAC episode. From the outset, the WSP leadership understood that HUAC needed the press to make its tactics of intimidation and punishment work. So, WSP played for the press—as it had done from its founding—and won! The Washington and New York leadership knew that it had two stories; both were developed to the hilt. The first was "motherhood under attack" and the second was the age-old "battle of the sexes." The contest between the sexes, according to the WSP version, involved female common sense, openness, humor, hope and naiveté versus male rigidity, solemnity, suspicion, and dark theories of conspiracy and subversion. The WSP women, in their middle-class, feminine, political style turned the hearings into an episode of the familiar and funny "I Love Lucy," rather than the tragic and scary inquisition of Alger Hiss.

For the first time, HUAC was belittled with humor and treated to a dose of its own moral superiority. Headlines critical of the committee and supportive of WSP were featured on the front pages of prominent newspapers from coast to coast. The *Chicago Daily News* declared: "It's Ladies' Day at Capitol: Hoots, Howls—and Charm; Congressmen Meet Match." Russell Baker's column was headed "Peace March Gals Make Red Hunters Look Silly" and a *Detroit Free Press* story was entitled, "Headhunters Decapitated." A cartoon by Herblock in the *Washington* (D.C.) *Post* of December 13th showed three aging and baffled committee members: One is seated at the hearing table. One is holding a gavel. Another turns to him and says, "I Came in Late, Which Was It That Was Un-American—Women or Peace?"[36] A story in the *Vancouver* (B.C.) *Sun* of December 14 was typical of many other reports:

> The dreaded House Un-American Activities Committee met its Waterloo this week. It tangled with 500 irate women. They laughed at it. Klieg lights glared, television cameras whirred, and 50 reporters scribbled notes while babies cried and cooed during the fantastic inquisition.

Bill Galt, author of the *Vancouver Sun* story, gave a blow-by-blow description of WSP civil disobedience in the Old House Office Building:

> When the first woman headed to the witness table, the crowd rose silently to its feet. The irritated Chairman Clyde Doyle of California outlawed standing. They applauded the next witness and Doyle outlawed clapping. Then they took to running out to kiss the witness.... Finally, each woman as she was called was met and handed a huge bouquet. By then Doyle was a beaten man. By the third day the crowd was giving standing ovations to the heroines with impunity.[37]

The hearings were a perfect foil for the humor of Russell Baker, syndicated columnist of the *New York Times*.

> If the House Un-American Activities Committee knew its Greek as well as it knows its Lenin, it would have left the women peace strikers alone.... Instead with typical male arrogance it has subpoenaed 15 of the ladies, ... spent several days trying to show them that women's place is not on the peace march route, and has come out of it covered with foolishness.

Baker, a liberal columnist, understood the committee's purpose and also the "drama of the absurd" that WSP had staged to defeat that purpose. "The Committee's aim was simple enough," Baker pointed out,

> their sleuths studying an organization known as Women Strike for Peace had learned that some of the strikers seemed to have past associations with the Communist Party or its front groups. Presumably if these were exposed, right thinking housewives would give up peace agitation and go back to the kitchen.

The committee had reckoned without female logic, according to Baker:

> How could WSP be infiltrated, witness after witness demanded, when it was not an organization at all? ... Try as he might, Alfred Nittle, the committee counsel, never managed to break through against this defense.[38]

The *Detroit Free Press* commented: "The House Committee can get away with attacking college students in California, government flunkies who are forced to shrive their souls to save their jobs, and assorted misguided do-gooders. But when it decides to smear an estimated half-million angry women, it's in deep trouble. We wish them nothing but the worst."[39]

Mary McGrory in the *Washington* (D.C.)

Evening Star played up the difference between the male, HUAC perceptions and those of the female, WSP:

> "Why can't a woman be like a man?" sings Henry Higgins in *My Fair Lady.* That is precisely the question the House Committee on Un-American Activities is asking itself today. . . . The committee is trying to find out if the ladies' group is subversive. All it found out was that their conduct in the caucus room certainly was.

"The leader of the group kept protesting that she was not really the leader at all," McGrory observed. Pointing out that few men would deny being leaders, or admit they didn't know what was going on, Mary McGrory reported that:

> Dagmar Wilson of Washington, when asked if she exercised control over the New York chapter merely giggled and said, "Nobody controls anybody in the Women Strike for Peace. We're all leaders."

Characterizing Wilson's appearance as the "coup de grâce in the battle of the sexes," McGrory noted that the ladies had been using the Congress as a babysitter, while their young crawled in the aisles and noisily sucked their bottles during the whole proceedings. With a mixture of awe and wonder McGrory described how the ladies themselves, as wayward as their babies, hissed, gasped, clapped entirely at will. When several of their number took the Fifth Amendment, to McGrory's surprise, the women applauded, and

> when Mrs. Wilson, trim and beguiling in red wool, stepped up to take the stand, a mother with a baby on one hip worked her way through the crowd and handed her a bouquet of purple and white flowers, exactly as if she were the principal speaker at a ladies' luncheon.

McGrory caught the flavor of Wilson's testimony which was directed not only at the committee, but also at her sisters in the audience. She reported that when Mr. Nittle asked whether the New York chapter had played a dominant role in the group, Wilson replied, "Other cities would be mortified if you said that."

> "Was it," Mr. Nittle wanted to know, "Mrs. Wilson's idea to send delegates to a Moscow peace conference?" "No," said Mrs. Wilson regretfully, "I wish I'd thought of that." When Mr. Nittle pursued the question of whose idea it was to send

observers to Moscow, Dagmar Wilson replied, "This is something I find very difficult to explain to the masculine mind."

And, in a sense, it was. "Mr. Nittle pressed forward to the clutch question," one, according to McGrory, "that would bring a man to his knees with patriotic protest: 'I would like to ask you whether you would knowingly permit or encourage a Communist Party member to occupy a leadership position in Women Strike for Peace.'" Wilson replied:

> Well, my dear sir, I have absolutely no way of controlling, do not desire to control, who wishes to join in the demonstrations and the efforts that women strikers have made for peace. In fact, I would also like to go even further. I would like to say that unless everybody in the whole world joins us in this fight, then God help us.

"Would you knowingly permit or welcome Nazis or Fascists?" asked Mr. Nittle. Mrs. Wilson replied, "if we could only get them on our side."[40] Mr. Doyle then thanked Wilson for appearing and being so helpful. "I want to emphasize," he said,

> that the Committee recognizes that there are many, many, many women, in fact a great great majority of women, in this peace movement who are absolutely patriotic and absolutely adverse to everything the Communist Party stands for. We recognize that you are one of them. We compliment you on your leadership and on your helpfulness to us this morning.

Dagmar Wilson tried to get the last word: "I do hope you live to thank us when we have achieved our goal." But Doyle replied, "Well, we will."[41]

The way in which WSP, a movement of middle-class, middle-aged, white women, mobilized to meet the attack by a feared congressional committee was energetic and bold, politically nontraditional, pragmatic rather than ideological, moralistic and maternal. It was entirely consistent with the already established program, tactics, rhetoric, and image of this one-year-old movement, labeled by the University of Wisconsin's student newspaper as "the bourgeois mother's underground."[42]

Were these courageous women who bowed to traditional notions of female behavior merely using the politics of motherhood for political advantage? Or had they internalized the feminine mystique? It is useful to examine the backgrounds of the WSP women in seeking to understand their use of their own female culture to legitimate a radical critique of national, foreign, and military policies. The WSP key women were mostly in their late thirties to mid forties at the inception of the movement in 1961. Most of them, then, had come into adulthood in the late 1930s and early 1940s. They were students or workers in the years of political ferment preceding World War II. Many had married just before, during, or right after the war. The majority of these women participated in the postwar baby boom, the rise of middle-class affluence, and the privatism and consumerism connected with suburban life. It was during the 1950s that they made their adjustment to family, parenting, community, and consensus politics.

As a movement born out of, and responding to, the consciousness of the 1950s, WSP projected a middle-class and politically moderate image. In an article celebrating WSP's first anniversary, Eleanor Garst, one of WSP's early image makers, proclaimed:

> Breaking all the rules and behaving with incredible disorder and naivete, "the women" continue to attract recruits until the movement now numbers hundreds of thousands. . . . Furthermore, many of the women behaving in these unaccustomed ways are no odd-ball types, but pillars of the community long courted by civic organizations. Others—perhaps the most numerous—are apolitical housewives who have never before lifted a finger to work for peace or any other social concern.[43]

Although the movement projected an image of political innocence and inexperience, WSP was actually initiated by five women who were already active members of SANE. The women—Dagmar Wilson, Jeanne Bagby, Folly Fodor, Eleanor Garst, and Margaret Russell—had gravitated toward each other because of their mutual distaste for SANE's internal red hunt, which they felt contributed to an escalation, rather than an end to cold war hysteria. Perhaps, more important, they shared a frustration over the slow pace with which the highly structured SANE reacted to international crises. They also resented the reluctance of SANE's male leadership to deal with "mother's issues" such as the contamination of milk by radioactive fallout from nuclear tests.

Dagmar Wilson was forty-five years old, and a political novice when she was moved to call a few friends to her home in the late summer of 1961 to discuss what could be done about the nuclear crisis. At this meeting WSP was born. Wilson was at that time a successful freelance children's book illustrator, the mother of three daughters and wife of Christopher Wilson, a commercial attaché at the British embassy. Wilson had been born in New York City, had moved to Germany as a very young child, and had spent most of her adult years in England where her father, Cesar Searchinger, was a well-known broadcast correspondent for the Columbia Broadcasting System and the National Broadcasting Company.

Wilson came to the United States prior to World War II, held a variety of professional jobs as an artist and teacher, and finally became a freelance illustrator. She worked in a studio at home, so as to be available to her children and to ensure a smooth-running household. Despite the fact that Wilson was so successful an artist that one of her children's books had become a best-seller, she nevertheless identified herself as a housewife.

> My idea in emphasizing the housewife rather than the professional was that I thought the housewife was a downgraded person, and that we, as housewives, had as much right to an opinion and that we deserved as much consideration as anyone else, and I wanted to emphasize . . . this was an important role and that it was time we were heard.[44]

A gifted artist, an intelligent person of good sense, good grace, and charm, Wilson possessed the charisma of those who accurately represent the feelings and the perceptions of their constituency, but excel them in passion and the capacity for creative articulation. Having been most of her life a "nonjoiner" Wilson was, as the *New York Times Magazine* reported in a feature story in May 1962, a "political neophyte."[45] Because Wilson had not been involved in U.S. radical politics of the 1940s, she was free from the self-conscious timidity that plagued those who had been involved in leftist organizations and who feared either exposure or a repetition of the persecution and the political isolation they had experienced in the 1950s.

Among the women who met at Wilson's house to plan the emergency peace action was Eleanor Garst, whose direct, friendly, practical, yet passionate political prose played a powerful role in energizing and unifying the WSP women in their first year. It was she who drafted the call for November 1st, and later helped create most of the anti-HUAC rhetoric.

Garst came from a conservative Baptist background. She recalls that everything in her upbringing told her that the only thing a woman should do was to marry, have babies, care for her husband and babies, and "never mind your own needs." Despite this, Garst was the only one of the inner circle of Washington founders, who in 1961 was a completely self-supporting professional woman, living on her own. She was the mother of two grown children. At the time of the founding of WSP, Garst was employed as a community organizer for the Adams Morgan Demonstration Project, administered by American University, working to maintain integrated neighborhoods in Washington, D.C. She had become a pacifist in her early childhood after reading about war in novels and poems. Her husband, a merchant seaman, refused to be drafted prior to World War II, a decision that he and Eleanor made together without consulting any other pacifists because they knew none. They spent their honeymoon composing an eighty-page brief against peacetime conscription.

After the war, Garst became a professional political worker, writer, and peace activist on the West Coast before coming to Washington. She had been a founder of the Los Angeles SANE and editor of its newsletter. A forceful and easy writer, Garst had already been published in the *Saturday Evening Post, Reporter, Ladies' Home Journal,* and other national publications when she was asked to draft the letter that initiated the successful November 1st strike.

Folly Fodor, a leading figure in the founding group, had come to Washington in 1960 to follow her husband's job with the U.S. Labor Department. She joined SANE on her arrival in Washington and had been elected to the board. Thirty-seven years old at the time of the founding of WSP, Fodor was the mother of two. Folly Fodor was not new to politics. She was the daughter of parents who had been involved in liberal-to-communist political causes and had herself been a leader in political organizations since her youth. As an undergraduate at Antioch College, in Yellow Springs, Ohio, Folly Fodor had become active in the Young People's Socialist League, eventually becoming "head of it," as she put it. In retrospect she believes she spent too much time fighting the communists on campus, and "never did a goddamn thing."

Fodor had been chairperson of the Young Democrats of California and as a Democrat she had clandestinely supported Henry Wallace in 1948. During the mid-1950s, after the birth of her second child, Fodor organized a mother's group to oppose nuclear testing. So Fodor, like Garst, was not new to radical causes, to peace activity, or to women's groups. She was ready and eager for a separate women's peace action in the fall of 1961.

Two other women who founded WSP, Jeanne Bagby and Margaret Russell, were also already active in the peace cause at the time of the founding of WSP. Bagby was a frequent contributor to *Liberation* magazine. Together the founders possessed research, writing, organizing, and speaking talents that were not unusual for women active in a variety of community, civic, and church groups in the 1950s. All the founders shared a conviction that the men in the peace movement and the government had failed them and that women had to take things into their own hands.

But what of the thousands of women who joined the founders? What was their social and political background and their motivation to take to the streets in peace protest? Elise Boulding, a sociologist and longtime pacifist activist, who became involved in the WSP communications network right after November 1st, decided to try to find out. During the six months in which Boulding edited the *Women's Peace Movement Bulletin,* an information exchange for WSP groups, she kept asking herself whether the WSP women were really political neophytes as they claimed, or "old pros with a well defined idea of some kind of world social order?" Using the resources of the Institute for Conflict Resolution in Ann Arbor, Michigan, where she was working, and with the help of WSP colleagues in Ann Arbor, she composed a questionnaire that was sent to every eighth name on the mailing lists of forty-five local groups. By the fall of 1962, shortly before the summonses from HUAC, 279 questionnaires had been returned from thirty-seven localities in twenty-two states. According to Boulding, the respondents represented a cross-section of the movement—not only leaders.[46]

Boulding found that the overwhelming majority of the WSP women were well-educated mothers, and that 61 percent were not employed outside the home. But she concluded that the women who went out on strike for peace on November 1, 1961, and stayed on in the movement in the following months, appeared to be a more complex and sophisticated group than the "buggy-pushing housewife" image the movement conveyed. She characterized the early WSP participants as "largely intellectual and civic-minded people, mostly of the middle class"—very much like the Washington founders themselves.[47]

Most of the women strikers had been liberals, radicals, or pacifists in the 1940s. Although few had been political leaders of any kind, they shared the 1940s belief that society could be restructured on humanistic lines through the direct political action of ordinary people. Dorothy Dinnerstein described the psychological process of depoliticization and privatization that many politically active people experienced in the 1950s. Many radicals, according to Dinnerstein, spent the 1950s in a state of moral shock, induced by the twin catastrophes of Stalinism and McCarthyism. They lost their capacity for social connectedness and, "in this condition they withdrew from history—more or less totally, more or less gradually, more or less blindly into intensely personalistic, inward-turning, magically thing-and-place-oriented life." According to Dinnerstein they withdrew their passion from the larger human scene and sought to invest in something less nightmarish, more coherent and mentally manageable.[48] What the WSP women withdrew into, with society's blessing and encouragement, was the domestic sphere, the management of family, children, home, and local community. Many, when their school-aged children no longer required fulltime care, were propelled into the PTAs, League of Women Voters, Democratic party politics, church, synagogue, or cultural activities by their earlier social, political, and humanitarian concerns.

It took the acceleration of nuclear testing by both the capitalist United States and the socialist USSR to convince the WSP women of something they already suspected: that there was no political force in the world acting morally and humanely in the interest of the preservation of life. It took a series of international crises, the example of the civil rights sit-ins, and the Aldermarston antibomb marches in Britain to give the WSP women both the sense of urgency, and of possibility, that are the necessary ingredients for a political movement. Once out

in the political arena, the women found that their moral outrage, their real fear for their children's future, and their determination never to be pushed back into the non-political domestic sphere, made them unafraid of a mere congressional committee before which others had quaked.

The women who were drawn to WSP certainly took the job of motherhood seriously. They had willingly chosen to sacrifice careers and personal projects to raise society's children because they had been convinced by the post-Freudians that the making of human beings is a far more important vocation than anything else; and that the making of human beings was a sex-specific vocation requiring the full-time duties of a resident mother.[49] But where the WSP women differed from the majority of their middle-class cohorts was that they saw motherhood not only as a private function, but also as a contribution to society in general and to the future. When they built on their rights and responsibilities to act politically in defense of the world's children, they were invoking not only their maternal consciousness, but their social conscience as well. They were women of heart, emotion, ingenuity, wit, and guile, but they were also serious political thinkers and activists. They chose to rely on their femininity, as most women did in the fifties and early sixties, to create whatever space and power they could carve out for themselves.

The Birmingham (England) Feminist History Group in an article, "Feminism as Femininity in the Nineteen Fifties?" suggests that feminism of the fifties seemed to be more concerned with integrating and foregrounding femininity than in transforming it in a fundamental way.[50] The conduct of WSP before the House Committee on Un-American Activities follows this pattern. The WSP women were not concerned with transforming the ideology of femininity, but rather with using it to enhance women's political power. But in so doing they were transforming that ideology and foreshadowing the feminism that emerged later in the decade.

Very much in the way that the concept of Republican motherhood was used in the late eighteenth century to justify the demand for women's education, and the cult of true womanhood was built upon to project women into the ante-bellum reform movements, WSP used the feminine mystique of the 1950s to legitimize women's right to radical dissent from foreign and military policies. In the repressive political climate of the early 1960s, WSP relied heavily upon sex role stereotypes to legitimize its opposition to cold war policies. But by emphasizing the fact that the men in power could no longer be counted on for protection in the nuclear age, WSP implied that the traditional sex-gender contract no longer worked. And by stressing global issues and international sisterhood, rather than domestic responsibilities, WSP challenged the privatization and isolation of women which was a key element of the feminine mystique. Most important, by performing in relation to HUAC with more courage, candor, and wit than most men had done in a decade of inquisitions, WSP raised women's sense of political power and self-esteem. One of the negative effects for WSP of relying so heavily on the politics of motherhood to project its political message was that it alienated a new generation of younger women who admired the movement's stand for peace, but saw its acquiescence to sex role stereotypes as regressive. In the late 1960s these younger women insisted upon working for peace not as wives, mothers, and sisters, but as autonomous persons.

Sara Evans, in *Personal Politics*, points out that those few young women in the civil rights movement who first raised feminist issues within the movement had to step *outside* the sex role assumptions on which they were raised in order to articulate a radical critique of women's position.[51] For WSP it was obviously different. The founders and leaders of WSP certainly did not step outside the traditional sex role assumptions; rather, they stood squarely upon them, with all their contradictions. By using these contradictions to present a radical critique of man's world, WSP began the transformation of woman's consciousness and woman's role.

NOTES

1. U.S. Congress, House, Committee on Un-American Activities, *Communist Activities in the Peace Movement (Women Strike for Peace and Certain Other Groups), Hearings before the Committee on Un-American Activities on H.R. 9944.* 87th Cong., 2d. sess., 1962, p. 2057.

2. Historians and political opponents of HUAC agree that the WSP hearing marked the beginning of the end of the committee's power. Eric Bentley called the WSP-HUAC confrontation, "the fall of HUAC's Bastille." See Eric Bentley, *Thirty Years of Treason* (New York: Viking Press, 1971), p. 951. . . .

3. In May 1960, Senator Thomas Dodd, vice-chairman of the Senate International Security Subcommittee, threatened SANE with congressional investigation if it did not take steps to rid itself of communist infiltrators. SANE responded by voting to exclude all those with communist sympathies. Whole chapters that did not go along with internal red hunts were expelled, as was Henry Abrams, a leading New York activist who refused to tell the Senate committee whether or not he was a communist. Turn Toward Peace also rejected communists or former communists. See Milton S. Katz, "Peace, Politics, and Protest: SANE and the American Peace Movement, 1957–1972" (Ph.D. diss., St. Louis University, 1973), pp. 109–130. . . .

4. The way in which WSP's militant role in the peace movement has been either ignored or trivialized by journalists, peace movement leaders, and historians is illustrated by the following examples. Mary McGrory in her syndicated column described a WSP visit to the White House in the following manner: "This week's Cinderella story has to do with Women Strike for Peace, which after 15 years of drudgery in the skullery of anti-war activity has been invited to the White House" (*New York Post*, 8 Mar. 1977, p. 27). Dave Dellinger, one of the most prominent of the male leaders of the 1960s peace movement, devoted about 10 lines to WSP in a 317-page book on the history of the civil rights and peace movements from 1965 to 1973. He described WSP as a group fearful of engaging in civil disobedience in the 1967 "Mobilization March on the Pentagon." Nowhere in the book did Dellinger mention that nine months earlier 2,500 WSP women broke through police barricades to bang their shoes on the Pentagon doors which had been shut in their faces. See Dave Dellinger, *More Power Than We Know* (Garden City, N.Y.: Anchor Press, 1975). . . .

5. For a symposium on the relationship of feminism, women's culture, and women's politics, see Ellen DuBois, Mari Jo Buhle, Temma Kaplan, Gerda Lerner, and Carroll Smith-Rosenberg, "Politics and Culture in Women's History: A Symposium," *Feminist Studies* 6 (Spring 1980):26–64. . . .

6. The figure of fifty thousand claimed by the Washington founders after November 1st was accepted in most press accounts and became part of the WSP legend. It was based on reports from women in sixty cities and from newspapers across the country. . . .

7. "End the Arms Race—Not the Human Race" was the central slogan of the November 1st "strike": "Help Wanted" flyer, 25 Oct. 1961, Washington, D.C. See WSP Document Collection in custody of the author. (Mimeographed.)

8. "Dear —, Last night I sat with a few friends in a comfortable living room talking of atomic war." Draft of call to strike by Eleanor Garst, Washington, D.C., 22 Sept. 1961. WSP Document Collection. (Mimeographed.)

9. *Newsweek*, 13 Nov. 1961, p. 21.

10. Eleanor Garst, "Women: Middle-Class Masses," *Fellowship* 28 (1 Nov. 1962):10–12.

11. Minutes of the WILPF National Executive Committee stated: "Each branch taking direct action should clear with the National Action Projects Com-

mittee. The committee should have, and send out to branches, a list of approved action and a list of the organizations with which we formally cooperate." Women's International League for Peace and Freedom, Minutes of the National Executive Committee meeting of 28–29 Sept. 1961. Swarthmore College Peace Collection, DG 43, Series A-2, Box 18, p. 5.

12. "Transcript of the President's News Conference on World and Domestic Affairs," *New York Times*, 16 Jan. 1962, p. 18.

13. *Science* 167 (13 Mar. 1970):1476.

14. A. E. Wessel, *The American Peace Movement: A Study of Its Themes and Political Potential* (Santa Monica: Rand Corporation, 1962), p. 3.

15. *New York Journal American*, 4 Apr. 1962, p. 10.

16. *San Francisco Examiner*, 21 May 1962, p. 10.

17. The FBI files on WSP are located in the offices of the Washington, D.C., law firm of Gaffney, Anspach, Shember, Klimasi, and Marx. These contain hundreds of documents from security officers in major cities to the director of the FBI and from the directors to the security officers. For instance, as early as 23 Oct. 1961, one week before the November 1st strike, the Cleveland office of the FBI already identified one of the WSP planning groups as communist. (FBI Document 100-39566-8)....

18. Those subpoenaed were (in order of appearance) Blanche Posner, Ruth Meyers, Lyla Hoffman, Elsie Neidenberg, Sylvia Contente, Rose Clinton, Iris Freed, Anna Mackenzie, Elizabeth Moss, Ceil Gross, Jean Brancato, Miriam Chesman, Norma Spector, and Dagmar Wilson. Spector never testified; she was excused due to illness. *Hearings before Committee on Un-American Activities*, p. iii.

19. Lillian Hellman, *Scoundrel Time* (Boston: Little, Brown & Co., 1976), p. 99.

20. Los Angeles WISP, Statement I, Ann Arbor Conference, June 9–10, 1962 (WSP Document Collection); ...

21. "WSP National Policy Statement," *Women Strike for Peace Newsletter*, New York, New Jersey, Connecticut, Summer 1962, pp. 1–2.

22. "Key women" was the name used by WSP for those women who were part of the national and local communications network. They were the ones who were called upon to initiate actions or who called upon others to do so.

23. Katz, "Peace, Politics, and Protest," pp. 122–26.

24. Homer Jack, "The Will of the WISP versus the Humiliation of HUAC," transcript of a talk on Radio Station WBAI, New York, 28 Dec. 1962 (WSP Document Collection).

25. The anti-HUAC statement by WSP was composed by the New York and Washington leadership in their usual collaborative fashion, with no pride or claim of authorship, so it is difficult to know which group wrote what part. It was distributed through official WSP channels via the national office in Washington.

26. Bentley, *Thirty Years of Treason*, p. 951.

27. Women Strike for Peace, Washington, D.C. to "Dear WISP's," 6 Dec. 1962 (WSP Document Collection).

28. Carol Urner to Representative Francis Walter reprinted in the *Women's Peace Movement Bulletin* 1 (20 Dec. 1962):5.

29. *Hearings before Committee on Un-American Activities*, pp. 2064–65.

30. Ibid., p. 2074.

31. Ibid., p. 2085.

32. Mary McGrory, "Prober Finds 'Peacemakers' More Than a Match," *Washington* (D.C.) *Evening Star*, 12 Dec. 1962, p. A-1.

33. *Hearings before Committee on Un-American Activities*, pp. 2095, 2101.

34. McGrory, "Prober Finds 'Peacemakers' More Than a Match," p. A-1.

35. Lyla Hoffman, undated typewritten statement (WSP Document Collection).

36. Thirty-seven favorable news stories, columns and editorials were reprinted in a hastily prepared WSP booklet, published less than two weeks after the hearings....

37. *Vancouver* (B.C.) *Sun*, 14 Dec. 1962, p. 2.

38. "The Ladies Turn Peace Quiz into Greek Comedy," *Detroit Free Press*, 16 Dec. 1962, p. 1.

39. *Detroit Free Press*, 13 Dec. 1962, p. A-8.

40. Mary McGrory, "Nobody Controls Anybody," *Washington* (D.C.) *Evening Star*, 14 Dec. 1962, pp. A-1, A-9.

41. *Hearings before Committee on Un-American Activities*, p. 2201.

42. *Madison* (Wis.) *Daily Cardinal*, 14 Dec. 1962, p. 2.

43. Garst, "Women: Middle-Class Masses," pp. 10–11.

44. Interview with Dagmar Wilson, Leesburg, Va., Sept. 1977.

45. *New York Times Magazine*, 6 May 1962, p. 32.

46. On a WSP activity measure, 38 percent rated themselves as "very active," 10 percent as "active," and 42 percent rated themselves as "not active," or only "slightly active." The profile of the majority of the WSP participants that emerged was indeed that of middle-class, well-educated housewives....

Thirty-eight percent of the women who responded claimed to belong to no other organizations, or at least did not record the names of any organizations in response to questions concerning other community activities. Forty percent of the women were active in a combination of civic, race relations, civil liberties, peace, and electoral political activity. Only 11 percent were members of professional organizations....

47. Ibid., p. 15.

48. Dorothy Dinnerstein, *The Mermaid and the Minotaur: Sexual Arrangements and Human Malaise* (New York: Harper Colophon Books, 1976), pp. 259–62.

49. Ashley Montagu, "The Triumph and Tragedy of the American Woman," *Saturday Review*, 27 (Sept. 1958):14; ...

50. "Feminism as Femininity in the Nineteen Fifties?" Birmingham (England) Feminist History Group, *Feminist Review*, no. 3 (1979):48–65.

51. Sara Evans, *Personal Politics: The Roots of Women's Liberation in the Civil Rights Movement and the New Left* (New York: Alfred A. Knopf, 1979), p. 23.

Maxine Hong Kingston, "She said I would grow up a wife and a slave, but she taught me the song of the warrior woman . . ."

Born in 1940, Maxine Hong Kingston grew up in Stockton, California, the eldest of her immigrant parents' six children. As a child working in her parents' laundry and attending public school, she experienced the tensions typical of immigrant children caught between their parents' culture and the dominant culture. Yet the family ideology and gender prescriptions associated with cold war America were, in many respects, a much more benign version of the views her parents had brought with them from China. That Maxine resisted those prescriptions is evident not only in the bitterness with which she would later write about them, but in her decision to enroll in the University of California at Berkeley in 1958 (where she is now a Distinguished Professor) and to become an author.

In what respects did Maxine's mother actually give her quite conflicting messages about the fate of Asian American women? In what respects did Maxine, no less than Murray and Lopez de la Cruz, make the personal political?

"You must not tell anyone," my mother said, "what I am about to tell you. In China your father had a sister who killed herself. She jumped into the family well. We say that your father has all brothers because it is as if she had never been born.

"In 1924 just a few days after our village celebrated seventeen hurry-up weddings—to make sure that every young man who went 'out on the road' would responsibly come home—your father and his brothers and your grandfather and his brothers and your aunt's new husband sailed for America, the Gold Mountain. . . . Those lucky enough to get contracts waved goodbye from the decks. They fed and guarded the stowaways and helped them off in Cuba, New York, Bali, Hawaii. 'We'll meet in California next year,' they said. All of them sent money home. . . .

"Don't let your father know that I told you. He denies her. Now that you have started to menstruate, what happened to her could happen to you. Don't humiliate us. You wouldn't like to be forgotten as if you had never been born. The villagers are watchful."

Whenever she had to warn us about life, my mother told stories that ran like this one, a story to grow up on. She tested our strength to establish realities. Those in the emigrant generations who could not reassert brute survival died young and far from home. Those of us in the first American generations have had to figure out how the invisible world the emigrants built around our childhoods fit in solid America.

The emigrants confused the gods by diverting their curses, misleading them with crooked streets and false names. They must try

Excerpted from "No Name Woman," "White Tigers," and "A Song for a Barbarian Reed Pipe," chaps. 1, 2, and 5 of *The Woman Warrior: Memoirs of a Girlhood Among Ghosts* by Maxine Hong Kingston (New York: Alfred A. Knopf, 1975). Copyright © 1975, 1976 by Maxine Hong Kingston. Reprinted by permission of Alfred A. Knopf, Inc.

to confuse their offspring as well, who, I suppose, threaten them in similar ways—always trying to get things straight, always trying to name the unspeakable. The Chinese I know hide their names; sojourners take new names when their lives change and guard their real names with silence.

Chinese Americans, when you try to understand what things in you are Chinese, how do you separate what is peculiar to childhood, to poverty, insanities, one family, your mother who marked your growing with stories, from what is Chinese? What is Chinese tradition and what is the movies?

If I want to learn what clothes my aunt wore, whether flashy or ordinary, I would have to begin, "Remember Father's drowned-in-the-well sister?" I cannot ask that. My mother has told me once and for all the useful parts. She will add nothing unless powered by Necessity, a riverbank that guides her life. . . .

Adultery is extravagance. Could people who hatch their own chicks and eat the embryos and the heads for delicacies and boil the feet in vinegar for party food, leaving only the gravel, eating even the gizzard lining—could such people engender a prodigal aunt? To be a woman, to have a daughter in starvation time was a waste enough. My aunt could not have been the lone romantic who gave up everything for sex. Women in the old China did not choose. Some man had commanded her to lie with him and be his secret evil. I wonder whether he masked himself when he joined the raid on her family. . . .

She may have gone to the pigsty as a last act of responsibility: she would protect this child as she had protected its father. It would look after her soul, leaving supplies on her grave. But how would this tiny child without family find her grave when there would be no marker for her anywhere, neither in the earth nor the family hall? No one would give her a family hall name. She had taken the child with her into the wastes. At its birth the two of them had felt the same raw pain of separation, a wound that only the family pressing tight could close. A child with no descent line would not soften her life but only trail after her, ghost-like, begging her to give it purpose. At dawn the villagers on their way to the fields would stand around the fence and look.

Full of milk, the little ghost slept. When it awoke, she hardened her breasts against the milk that crying loosens. Toward morning she picked up the baby and walked to the well.

Carrying the baby to the well shows loving. Otherwise abandon it. Turn its face into the mud. Mothers who love their children take them along. It was probably a girl; there is some hope of forgiveness for boys.

"Don't tell anyone you had an aunt. Your father does not want to hear her name. She has never been born." I have believed that sex was unspeakable and words so strong and fathers so frail that "aunt" would do my father mysterious harm. I have thought that my family, having settled among immigrants who had also been their neighbors in the ancestral land, needed to clean their name, and a wrong word would incite the kinspeople even here. But there is more to this silence: they want me to participate in her punishment. And I have.

In the twenty years since I heard this story I have not asked for details nor said my aunt's name; I do not know it. People who can comfort the dead can also chase after them to hurt them further—a reverse ancestor worship. The real punishment was not the raid swiftly inflicted by the villagers, but the family's deliberately forgetting her. Her betrayal so maddened them, they saw to it that she would suffer forever, even after her death. . . .

My aunt haunts me—her ghost drawn to me because now, after fifty years of neglect, I alone devote pages of paper to her, though not origamied into houses and clothes. I do not think she always means me well. I am telling on her, and she was a spite suicide, drowning herself in the drinking water. The Chinese are always very frightened of the drowned one, whose weeping ghost, wet hair hanging and skin bloated, waits silently by the water to pull down a substitute.

When we Chinese girls listened to the adults talking-story, we learned that we failed if we grew up to be but wives or slaves. We could be heroines, swordswomen. Even if she had to rage across all China, a swordswoman got even with anybody who hurt her family. Perhaps women were once so dangerous that they had to have their feet bound. . . .

My mother told other [stories] that followed swordswomen through the woods and palaces for years. Night after night my mother would talk-story until we fell asleep. I couldn't tell where the stories left off and the dreams began, her voice the voice of the heroines in my sleep. And on Sundays, from noon to midnight, we went to the movies at the Confucius Church. We saw swordswomen jump over houses from a standstill; they didn't even need a running start.

At last I saw that I too had been in the presence of great power, my mother talking-story. After I grew up, I heard the chant of Fa Mu Lan, the girl who took her father's place in battle. Instantly I remembered that as a child I had followed my mother about the house, the two of us singing about how Fa Mu Lan fought gloriously and returned alive from war to settle in the village. I had forgotten this chant that was once mine, given me by my mother, who may not have known its power to remind. She said I would grow up a wife and a slave, but she taught me the song of the warrior woman, Fa Mu Lan. I would have to grow up a warrior woman.

My American life has been such a disappointment.

"I got straight A's, Mama."

"Let me tell you a true story about a girl who saved her village."

I could not figure out what was my village. And it was important that I do something big and fine, or else my parents would sell me when we made our way back to China. In China there were solutions for what to do with little girls who ate up food and threw tantrums. You can't eat straight A's.

When one of my parents or the emigrant villagers said, "Feeding girls is feeding cowbirds," I would thrash on the floor and scream so hard I couldn't talk. I couldn't stop.

"What's the matter with her?"

"I don't know. Bad, I guess. You know how girls are. 'There's no profit in raising girls. Better to raise geese than girls.'"

"I would hit her if she were mine. But then there's no use wasting all that discipline on a girl. 'When you raise girls, you're raising children for strangers.'"

"Stop that crying!" my mother would yell. "I'm going to hit you if you don't stop. Bad girl! Stop!" I'm going to remember never to hit or to scold my children for crying, I thought, because then they will only cry more.

"I'm not a bad girl," I would scream. "I'm not a bad girl. I'm not a bad girl." I might as well as have said, "I'm not a girl."

"When you were little, all you had to say was 'I'm not a bad girl,' and you could make yourself cry," my mother says, talking-story about my childhood.

I minded that the emigrant villagers shook their heads at my sister and me. "One girl—and another girl," they said, and made our parents ashamed to take us out together. The good part about my brothers being born was that people stopped saying, "All girls," but I learned new grievances. "Did you roll an egg on *my* face like that when *I* was born?" "Did you have a full-month party for *me?*" "Did you turn on all the lights?" "Did you send *my* picture to Grandmother?" "Why not? Because I'm a girl? Is that why not?" "Why didn't you teach me English?" "You like having me beaten up at school, don't you?"

"She is very mean, isn't she?" the emigrant villagers would say.

I went away to college—Berkeley in the sixties—and I studied, and I marched to change the world, but I did not turn into a boy. I would have liked to bring myself back as a boy for my parents to welcome with chickens and pigs. That was for my brother, who returned alive from Vietnam.

If I went to Vietnam, I would not come back; females desert families. It was said, "There is an outward tendency in females," which meant that I was getting straight A's for the good of my future husband's family, not my own. I did not plan ever to have a husband. I would show my mother and father and the nosey emigrant villagers that girls have no outward tendency. I stopped getting straight A's.

And all the time I was having to turn myself American-feminine, or no dates.

There is a Chinese word for the female I—which is "slave." Break the women with their own tongues!

I refused to cook. When I had to wash dishes, I would crack one or two. "Bad girl," my mother yelled, and sometimes that made me gloat rather than cry. Isn't a bad girl almost a boy? . . .

I live now where there are Chinese and Japanese, but no emigrants from my own village looking at me as if I had failed them. Living among one's own emigrant villagers can give a good Chinese far from China glory and a place. "That old busboy is really a swordsman," we whisper when he goes by. "He's a swordsman who's killed fifty. He has a tong ax in his closet." But I am useless, one more girl who couldn't be sold. When I visit the family now, I wrap my American successes around me like a private shawl; I *am* worthy of eating the food. From afar I can believe my family loves me fundamentally. They only say, "When fishing for treasures in the flood, be careful not to pull in girls," because that is what one says about daughters. But I watched such words come out of my own mother's and father's mouths; I looked at their ink drawing of poor people snapping their neighbors' flotage with long flood hooks and pushing the girl babies on down the river. And I had to get out of hating range. I read in an anthropology book that Chinese say, "Girls are necessary too"; I have never heard the Chinese I know make this concession. Perhaps it was a saying in another village. . . .

I learned that young men were placing ads in the *Gold Mountain News* to find wives when my mother and father started answering them. Suddenly a series of new workers showed up at the laundry; they each worked for a week before they disappeared. They ate with us. They talked Chinese with my parents. They did not talk to us. We were to call them "Elder Brother," although they were not related to us. They were all funny-looking FOB's, Fresh-off-the-Boats, as the Chinese-American kids at school called the young immigrants. . . . My mother took one home from the laundry, and I saw him looking over our photographs. "This one," he said, picking up my sister's picture.

"No. No," said my mother. "This one," my picture. "The oldest first," she said. Good. I was an obstacle. I would protect my sister and myself at the same time. As my parents and the FOB sat talking at the kitchen table, I dropped two dishes. I found my walking stick and limped across the floor. I twisted my mouth and caught my hand in the knots of my hair. I spilled soup on the FOB when I handed him his bowl. "She can sew, though," I heard my mother say, "and sweep." I raised dust swirls sweeping around and under the FOB's chair— very bad luck because spirits live inside the broom. I put on my shoes with the open flaps and flapped about like a Wino Ghost. From then on, I wore those shoes to parties, when-

ever the mothers gathered to talk about marriages. The FOB and my parents paid me no attention, half ghosts half invisible, but when he left, my mother yelled at me about the dried-duck voice, the bad temper, the laziness, the clumsiness, the stupidity that comes from reading too much. The young men stopped visiting; not one came back. "Couldn't you just stop rubbing your nose?" she scolded. "All the village ladies are talking about your nose. They're afraid to eat our pastries because you might have kneaded the dough." But I couldn't stop at will anymore, and a crease developed across the bridge. My parents would not give up, though. "Though you can't see it," my mother said, "a red string around your ankle ties you to the person you'll marry. He's already been born, and he's on the other end of the string." . . .

The hulk, the hunching sitter [a retarded person who pursued Kingston; she feared her parents planned to marry her to him], brought a third box now, to rest his feet on. He patted his boxes. He sat in wait, hunching on his pile of dirt. My throat hurt constantly, vocal cords taut to snapping. One night when the laundry was so busy that the whole family was eating dinner there, crowded around the little round table, my throat burst open. I stood up, talking and burbling. I looked directly at my mother and father and screamed, "I want you to tell that hulk, that gorilla-ape, to go away and never bother us again. I know what you're up to. You're thinking he's rich, and we're poor. You think we're odd and not pretty and we're not bright. You think you can give us away to freaks. You better not do that, Mother. I don't want to see him or his dirty boxes here tomorrow. If I see him here one more time, I'm going away. I'm going away anyway. I am. Do you hear me? I may be ugly and clumsy, but one thing I'm not, I'm not retarded. There's nothing wrong with my brain. Do you know what the Teacher Ghosts say about me? They tell me I'm smart, and I can win scholarships. I can get into colleges. I've already applied. I'm smart. I can do all kinds of things. I know how to get A's, and they say I could be a scientist or a mathematician if I want. I can make a living and take care of myself. So you don't have to find me a keeper who's too dumb to know a bad bargain. I'm so smart, if they say write ten pages, I can write fifteen. I can do ghost things even better than ghosts can. Not everybody thinks I'm nothing. I am not going to be a slave or a wife. Even if I am stupid and talk funny and get sick, I won't let you turn me into a slave or a wife. I'm getting out of here. I can't stand living here anymore. It's your fault I talk weird. The only reason I flunked kindergarten was because you couldn't teach me English, and you gave me a zero IQ. I've brought my IQ up, though. They say I'm smart now. Things follow in lines at school. They take stories and teach us to turn them into essays. I don't need anybody to pronounce English words for me. I can figure them out by myself. I'm going to get scholarships, and I'm going away. And at college I'll have the people I like for friends. I don't care if their great-great-grandfather died of TB. I don't care if they were our enemies in China four thousand years ago. So get that ape out of here. I'm going to college. And I'm not going to Chinese school anymore. I'm going to run for office at American school, and I'm going to join clubs. I'm going to get enough offices and clubs on my record to get into college. And I can't stand Chinese school anyway; the kids are rowdy and mean, fighting all night. And I don't want to listen to any more of your stories; they have no logic. They scramble me up. You lie with stories. You won't tell me a story and then say, 'This is a true story,' or, 'This is just a story.' I can't tell the difference. I don't even know what your real names are. I can't tell what's real and what you make up. Ha! You can't stop me from talking. You tried to cut off my tongue, but it didn't work." So I told the hardest ten or twelve things on my list all in one outburst.

My mother, who is champion talker, was, of course, shouting at the same time. "I cut it to make you talk more, not less, you dummy. You're still stupid. You can't listen right. I didn't say I was going to marry you off. Did I ever say that? Did I ever mention that? Those newspaper people were for your sister, not you. Who would want you? Who said we could sell you? We can't sell people. Can't you take a joke? You can't even tell a joke from real life. You're not so smart. Can't even tell real from false."

"I'm never getting married, never!"

"Who'd want to marry you anyway? Noisy. Talking like a duck. Disobedient. Messy. And I know about college. . . . Everybody else is sending their girls to typing school. 'Learn to type if you want to be an American girl.' Why don't you go to typing school? The cousins and village girls are going to typing school."

"And you leave my sister alone. You try that with the advertising again, and I'll take her with me." . . .

"You're the one to leave your little sisters alone," my mother was saying. "You're always leading them off somewhere. I've had to call the police twice because of you." She herself was shouting out things I had meant to tell her—that I took my brothers and sisters to explore strange people's houses, ghost children's houses, and haunted houses blackened by fire. We explored a Mexican house and a redheaded family's house, but not the gypsies' house; I had only seen the inside of the gypsies' house in mind-movies. We explored the sloughs, where we found hobo nests. My mother must have followed us.

"You turned out so unusual. I fixed your tongue so you could say charming things. You don't even say hello to the villagers."

"They don't say hello to me."

"They don't have to answer children. When you get old, people will say hello to you."

"When I get to college, it won't matter if I'm not charming. And it doesn't matter if a person is ugly; she can still do schoolwork."

"I didn't say you were ugly."

"You say that all the time."

"That's what we're supposed to say. That's what Chinese say. We like to say the opposite."

It seemed to hurt her to tell me that—another guilt for my list to tell my mother, I thought. And suddenly I got very confused and lonely because I was at that moment telling her my list, and in the telling, it grew. No higher listener. No listener but myself.

"Ho Chi Kuei," she shouted. "Ho Chi Kuei. Leave then. Get out, you Ho Chi Kuei. Get out. I knew you were going to turn out bad, Ho Chi Kuei." My brothers and sisters had left the table, and my father would not look at me anymore, ignoring me. . . .

I've been looking up "Ho Chi Kuei," which is what the immigrants call us—Ho Chi Ghosts. "Well, Ho Chi Kuei," they say, "what silliness have you been up to now?" "That's a Ho Chi Kuei for you," they say, no matter what we've done. It was more complicated (and therefore worse) than "dogs," which they say affectionately, mostly to boys. They use "pig" and "stink pig" for girls, and only in an angry voice. . . .

I'll send the relatives money, and they'll write me stories about their hunger. . . . I'd like to go to China and see those people and find out what's a cheat story and what's not. Did my grandmother really live to be ninety-nine? Or did they string us along all those years to get our money? Do the babies wear a Mao button like a drop of blood on their jumpsuits? When we overseas Chinese send money, do the relatives divide it evenly among the commune? Or do they really pay 2 percent tax and keep the rest? It would be good if the Communists were taking care of themselves; then I could buy a color t.v.

Betty Friedan, "The problem that has no name. . . . I understood first as a woman . . ."

If the lives of working-class women were still dominated by the struggle for economic survival, the same cannot be said of middle-class women who enjoyed unprecedented prosperity, especially in the years after World War II. Ensconced in their well-equipped homes in the suburbs, they flourished in an atmosphere of domesticity and affluence that characterized the new consumer culture. Such, at least, was the message of the women's magazines with their advertisements of the latest household appliances and advice columns on marriage and child care. Although there were rumblings of discontent in the 1950s, it was 1963 when Betty Friedan, a suburban housewife herself, exposed the triviality and frustrations of a resurgent domesticity. Friedan's indictment, a brief portion of which appears here, was the subject of much controversy. Women who found the gratification associated with child care and housework vastly overemphasized applauded Friedan's forceful articulation of their own dissatisfactions. Other women objected vehemently, insisting that, as wives and mothers and perhaps community activists, they enjoyed a life style that not only benefited both their families and communities but provided them personally with freedom, pleasure, and a sense of self-worth. How are we to explain such different responses? Is the housewife described by Friedan foreshadowed in Ruth Schwartz Cowan's article on housework? In what sense is the role of housewife a product of the fusing of biology, economics, and ideology?

The problem lay buried, unspoken, for many years in the minds of American women. It was a strange stirring, a sense of dissatisfaction, a yearning that women suffered in the middle of the twentieth century in the United States. Each suburban wife struggled with it alone. As she made the beds, shopped for groceries, matched slipcover material, ate peanut butter sandwiches with her children, chauffeured Cub Scouts and Brownies, lay beside her husband at night—she was afraid to ask even of herself the silent question—"Is this all?"

For over fifteen years there was no word of this yearning in the millions of words writ-

The assumption that women found their true happiness in domesticity could be carried to extremes; here the film star Joan Crawford posed for a publicity photograph that showed her engaged in household tasks. She does not look very happy. (Photograph courtesy of the Museum of Modern Art, Film Stills Archive)

ten about women, for women, in all the columns, books and articles by experts telling women their role was to seek fulfillment as wives and mothers. Over and over women heard in voices of tradition and of Freudian sophistication that they could desire no greater destiny than to glory in their own femininity. Experts told them how to catch a man and keep him, how to breastfeed children and handle their toilet training, how to cope with sibling rivalry and adolescent rebellion; how to buy a dishwasher, bake bread, cook gourmet snails, and build a swimming pool with their own hands; how to dress, look, and act more feminine and make marriage more exciting; how to keep their husbands from dying young and their sons from growing into delinquents. They were taught to pity the neurotic, unfeminine, unhappy women who wanted to be poets or physicists or presidents. They learned that truly feminine women do not want careers, higher education, political rights—the independence and the opportunities that the old-fashioned feminists fought for. Some women, in their forties and fifties, still remembered painfully giving up those dreams, but most of the younger women no longer even thought about them. A thousand expert voices applauded their femininity, their adjustment, their new maturity. All they had to do was devote their lives from earliest girlhood to finding a husband and bearing children.

By the end of the nineteen-fifties, the average marriage age of women in America dropped to 20, and was still dropping, into the teens. Fourteen million girls were engaged by 17. The proportion of women attending college in comparison with men dropped from 47 per cent in 1920 to 35 per cent in 1958. A century earlier, women had fought for higher education; now girls went to college to get a husband. By the mid-fifties, 60 per cent dropped out of college to marry, or because they were afraid too much education would be a marriage bar. Colleges built dormitories for "married students," but the students were almost always the husbands. A new degree was instituted for the wives—"Ph.T." (Putting Husband Through).

Then American girls began getting married in high school. And the women's magazines, deploring the unhappy statistics about these young marriages, urged that courses on marriage, and marriage counselors, be in-

stalled in the high schools. Girls started going steady at twelve and thirteen, in junior high. Manufacturers put out brassieres with false bosoms or foam rubber for little girls of ten. And an advertisement for a child's dress, size 3–6x, in the *New York Times* in the fall of 1960, said: "She Too Can Join the Man-Trap Set."

By the end of the fifties, the United States birthrate was overtaking India's. The birth-control movement, renamed Planned Parenthood, was asked to find a method whereby women who had been advised that a third or fourth baby would be born dead or defective might have it anyhow. Statisticians were especially astounded at the fantastic increase in the number of babies among college women. Where once they had two children, now they had four, five, six. Women who had once wanted careers were now making careers out of having babies. So rejoiced *Life* magazine in a 1956 paean to the movement of American women back to the home.

In a New York hospital, a woman had a nervous breakdown when she found she could not breastfeed her baby. In other hospitals, women dying of cancer refused a drug which research had proved might save their lives: its side effects were said to be unfeminine. "If I have only one life, let me live it as a blonde," a larger-than-life-sized picture of a pretty, vacuous woman proclaimed from newspaper, magazine, and drugstore ads. And across America, three out of every ten women dyed their hair blonde. They ate a chalk called Metrecal, instead of food, to shrink to the size of the thin young models. Department-store buyers reported that American women, since 1939, had become three and four sizes smaller. "Women are out to fit the clothes, instead of vice-versa," one buyer said.

Interior decorators were designing kitchens with mosaic murals and original paintings, for kitchens were once again the center of women's lives. Home sewing became a million-dollar industry. Many women no longer left their homes, except to shop, chauffeur their children, or attend a social engagement with their husbands. Girls were growing up in America without ever having jobs outside the home. In the late fifties, a sociological phenomenon was suddenly remarked: a third of American women now worked, but most were no longer young and very few were pursuing careers. They were married women who held part-time jobs, selling or secretarial, to put their husbands through school, their sons through college, or to help pay the mortgage. Or they were widows supporting families. Fewer and fewer women were entering professional work. The shortages in the nursing, social work, and teaching professions caused crises in almost every American city. Concerned over the Soviet Union's lead in the space race, scientists noted that America's greatest source of unused brainpower was women. But girls would not study physics: it was "unfeminine." A girl refused a science fellowship at Johns Hopkins to take a job in a real-estate office. All she wanted, she said, was what every other American girl wanted—to get married, have four children and live in a nice house in a nice suburb.

The suburban housewife—she was the dream image of the young American women and the envy, it was said, of women all over the world. The American housewife—freed by science and labor-saving appliances from the drudgery, the dangers of childbirth and the illnesses of her grandmother. She was healthy, beautiful, educated, concerned only about her husband, her children, her home. She had found true feminine fulfillment. As a housewife and mother, she was respected as a full and equal partner to man in his world. She was free to choose automobiles, clothes, appliances, supermarkets; she had everything that women ever dreamed of.

In the fifteen years after World War II, this mystique of feminine fulfillment became the cherished and self-perpetuating core of contemporary American culture. Millions of women lived their lives in the image of those pretty pictures of the American suburban housewife, kissing their husbands goodbye in front of the picture window, depositing their station wagons full of children at school, and smiling as they ran the new electric waxer over the spotless kitchen floor. They baked their own bread, sewed their own and their children's clothes, kept their new washing machines and dryers running all day. They changed the sheets on the beds twice a week instead of once, took the rug-hooking class in adult education, and pitied their poor frustrated mothers, who had dreamed of having a career. Their only dream was to be perfect wives and mothers; their highest ambition to have five children and a beautiful house, their only fight to get and keep their husbands. They

had no thought for the unfeminine problems of the world outside the home; they wanted the men to make the major decisions. They gloried in their role as women, and wrote proudly on the census blank: "Occupation: housewife."

For over fifteen years, the words written for women, and the words women used when they talked to each other, while their husbands sat on the other side of the room and talked shop or politics or septic tanks, were about problems with their children, or how to keep their husbands happy, or improve their children's school, or cook chicken or make slipcovers. Nobody argued whether women were inferior or superior to men; they were simply different. Words like "emancipation" and "career" sounded strange and embarrassing; no one had used them for years. When a Frenchwoman named Simone de Beauvoir wrote a book called *The Second Sex*, an American critic commented that she obviously "didn't know what life was all about," and besides, she was talking about French women. The "woman problem" in America no longer existed.

If a woman had a problem in the 1950's and 1960's she knew that something must be wrong with her marriage, or with herself. Other women were satisfied with their lives, she thought. What kind of a woman was she if she did not feel this mysterious fulfillment waxing the kitchen floor? She was so ashamed to admit her dissatisfaction that she never knew how many other women shared it. If she tried to tell her husband, he didn't understand what she was talking about. She did not really understand it herself. For over fifteen years women in America found it harder to talk about this problem than about sex. Even the psychoanalysts had no name for it. When a woman went to a psychiatrist for help, as many women did, she would say, "I'm so ashamed," or "I must be hopelessly neurotic." "I don't know what's wrong with women today," a suburban psychiatrist said uneasily. "I only know something is wrong because most of my patients happen to be women. And their problem isn't sexual." Most women with this problem did not go to see a psychoanalyst, however. "There's nothing wrong really," they kept telling themselves. "There isn't any problem."

But on an April morning in 1959, I heard a mother of four, having coffee with four other mothers in a suburban development fifteen miles from New York, say in a tone of quiet desperation, "the problem." And the others knew, without words, that she was not talking about a problem with her husband, or her children, or her home. Suddenly they realized they all shared the same problem, the problem that has no name. They began, hesitantly, to talk about it. Later, after they had picked up their children at nursery school and taken them home to nap, two of the women cried, in sheer relief, just to know they were not alone.

Gradually I came to realize that the problem that has no name was shared by countless women in America. As a magazine writer I often interviewed women about problems with their children, or their marriages, or their houses, or their communities. But after a while I began to recognize the telltale signs of this other problem. I saw the same signs in suburban ranch houses and split-levels on Long Is-

land and in New Jersey and Westchester County; in colonial houses in a small Massachusetts town; on patios in Memphis; in suburban and city apartments; in living rooms in the Midwest. Sometimes I sensed the problem, not as a reporter, but as a suburban housewife, for during this time I was also bringing up my own three children in Rockland County, New York. I heard echoes of the problem in college dormitories and semi-private maternity wards, at PTA meetings and luncheons of the League of Women Voters, at suburban cocktail parties, in station wagons waiting for trains, and in snatches of conversation overheard at Schrafft's. The groping words I heard from other women, on quiet afternoons when children were at school or on quiet evenings when husbands worked late, I think I understood first as a woman long before I understood their larger social and psychological implications.

Ellen Willis, "I see men who consider themselves dedicated revolutionaries, yet exploit their wives and girl friends shamefully without ever noticing a contradiction. . . ."

In January 1968, Ellen Willis went to Washington to take part in a demonstration against the Vietnam war and for black liberation, which was staged to coincide with Richard Nixon's inaugural as president. At the demonstration, women in the group had asked to make a statement about their subordinate position within the New Left and on behalf of their own liberation. When they tried to make what they described as a "moderate, pro-movement statement," Willis reports, men in the audience "booed, laughed, cat-called and yelled enlightened remarks like 'Take her off the stage and fuck her.'" Instead of reprimanding the hecklers (as was done during an unpopular speech by a black GI), male organizers hurried the women off the stage.

On her return to New York, Willis wrote an article entitled "Women and the Left" (*Notes from the Second Year*, n.v. [1970]:55–56), in which she argued that the New Left was dominated by men and its theory, priorities, and strategy reflected male interests. Radical men would not take women seriously, she insisted, unless "we build an independent movement so strong that no revolution at all is possible without our cooperation."

The article elicited criticism in the form of letters-to-editor, one of which Willis answered. Although the editor chose not to publish her reply, it is a cogent statement of the thinking of young women who would come to be known as radical feminists.

Dear Wanda,

I was disturbed by your comments on my *Guardian* article, not because you disagreed but because you accused me of not thinking seriously. . . .

You say "the basic misperception is that our enemy is man, not capitalism." I say, the basic misperception is the facile identification of "the system" with "capitalism." In reality, the American system consists of two interdependent but distinct parts—the capitalist state, and the patriarchal family. Engels, in *Origin of the Family, Private Property and the State,* explains that the material basis of history is twofold: the means of production of commodities, and the means of production of new human beings. The social organization for the production of commodities is the property system, in this case the capitalist state. The social organization for the production of new human beings is the family system. And within the family system, men function as a ruling class, women as an exploited class. Historically, women and their children have been the property of men (until recently, quite literally, even in "advanced" countries). The mistake many radicals make is to assume that the family is simply part of the cultural superstructure of capitalism, while actually both capitalism and the family system make up the material substructure of society. It is difficult to see this because capitalism is so pervasive and powerful compared to the family, which is small, weak, and has far less influence on the larger economic system than vice versa. But it is important for women to recognize and deal with their exploited position in the family system, for it is primarily in terms of the family system that we are oppressed *as women.* Of course capitalism also exploits us, but the way in which it exploits us is primarily by taking advantage of, turning to its own purposes, our subordinate position in the family system and our historical domination by man, which stems from a time when the family system was all-powerful and the state did not yet exist. If you really *think* about our exploi-

tation under capitalism—as cheap labor and as consumers—you will see that our position in the family system is at the root. This does not mean we shouldn't fight capitalism. Unless the power of the corporate state is broken, there can be no revolution in the family system. Furthermore, to attack male supremacy (i.e., man's class dominance in the family system) consistently inevitably means attacking capitalism in vulnerable areas. But if we simply work to destroy capitalism, without working to destroy male supremacy on all levels, we will find that the resulting revolution is only vicarious. . . .

So much for ideology. Now for some practical politics. Our position here is exactly analogous to the black power position, with male radicals playing the part of white liberals. White liberals (and radicals, too, before they got wise to themselves) made exactly the same argument you're making. "Racism affects us too, we should work together, divisions between us only help the common enemy." (Incidentally, I thought you were being a little disingenuous in saying there are no "women's issues." A women's issue—or a black issue—means, in the accepted usage, a way in which women are oppressed because they are women, or blacks because they are black. This doesn't mean that men, and whites, are not affected by such issues.) Blacks answered, "We can't work together because you don't understand what it is to be black; because you've grown up in a racist society, your behavior toward us is bound to be racist whether you know it or not and whether you mean it or not; your ideas about how to help us are too often self-serving and patronizing; besides, part of our liberation is in thinking for ourselves and working for ourselves, not accepting the domination of the white man in still another area of our lives. If you as whites want to work on eliminating your own racism, if you want to support our battle for liberation, fine. If we decide that we have certain common interests with white activists and can form alliances with white organizations, fine. But we want to make the decisions in our own movement." Substitute man-woman for black-white and that's where I stand. With one important exception: while white liberals and radicals always understood the importance of the black liberation struggle, even if their efforts in the blacks' behalf were often misguided, radical men simply do not understand the importance of our struggle. . . . All around me I see men who consider themselves dedicated revolutionaries, yet exploit their wives and girl friends shamefully without ever noticing a contradiction. Anyone who was at that incredible rally in Washington knows it will be a long time before the majority of men, even those on the Left that should be closest to us, grasp that we have a grievance, and that we are serious. When they do grasp this, then we can talk about working together.

Sincerely,
Ellen Willis

DOCUMENT: *Remembering Vietnam*

"We were the first American women sent to live and work in the midst of guerrilla warfare . . ."

The American ships and planes that went to Vietnam carried women as well as men. There were approximately 10,000 military women and more than 13,000 Red Cross women, as well as smaller numbers of women foreign service officers, staff of the U.S. Agency for International Development, and employees of the USO. In 1980, Congress authorized a memorial to be built "in honor and recognition of the men and women of the Armed Forces of the United States who served in Vietnam." The competition for the design of the memorial was won by 21-year old Maya Lin, an undergraduate architecture student at Yale. The memorial stands today in Washington, visited by millions of people each year. They leave offerings as at a shrine: flowers, photographs, mementos.

The design of the memorial—whose black granite walls bear the names of 58,000 Americans who died, including 8 women—was controversial from the beginning. Many veterans groups insisted on a more traditional, representational design. In 1984 an additional statue that depicted three soldiers was placed in a grove of trees nearby. When the additional statue failed to include the figure of a woman, women veterans began to urge the addition of another statue honoring the women who had served.

In 1988 Congress authorized a statue recognizing women, to be constructed on federal property at the Vietnam Veterans Memorial from funds (like those of the other memorials) raised from private donations. The comments that follow were made at hearings conducted by Senator Dale Bumpers of Arkansas, chair of the Senate Subcommittee on Public Lands, National Parks and Forests.

Each of the veterans had complex memories of their experience in Vietnam, twenty years before. How do the women explain the meaning of their service? How is Robert Doubek's testimony affected by concerns about class, race, and gender?

Both Karen Johnson's testimony and the arguments of the Supreme Court in *Rostker* v. *Goldberg* (pp. 598–600) address the issue of whether men and women have an equal obligation to serve in the military. Do you think men and women have an equal obligation to serve in the military in time of war, as Karen Johnson believes? Does that obligation extend to service in combat? Does the exclusion of women from combat suggest that American society attaches greater value to women's lives than men's? What other factors might also be relevant in explaining the exclusion of women from combat?

Vietnam Women's Memorial. Hearing Before the Subcommittee on Public Lands, National Parks and Forests of the Committee on Energy and Natural Resources, United States Senate 100th Congress, 2nd session. February 23, 1988, pp. 89–90, 99–100, 108–9, 124–25.

STATEMENT OF DONNA-MARIE BOULAY, CHAIRMAN, VIETNAM WOMEN'S MEMORIAL PROJECT

Mr. Chairman, people who serve in wars have unique experiences. War was never meant to be. War makes death. Day after day, even hour after hour, we lived and worked amidst the wounded, the dead, and the dying.

I arrived in Vietnam at the end of February 1967. A few days later I was assigned to triage for the first time. The medevac helicopters brought twelve soldiers into our emergency room. Ten were already dead. Two were bleeding to death.

Mr. Chairman, our daily duty was to care for the badly wounded, the young men whose legs had been blown off, whose arms had been traumatically amputated, whose bodies and faces had been burned beyond recognition.

We eased the agony of a young marine, his legs amputated, his wounds dangerously infected. We worked hard to stop the bleeding of a sailor who had been shot in his liver. He died three days after, in immense pain.

We cared for a young Army lieutenant from New York named Pat who had been admitted with a badly mangled leg and later evacuated to Japan, like many of the other seriously wounded soldiers we treated. I do not know whether Pat's leg was saved. I hope so. Pat was a good soldier.

Mr. Chairman, "Pat" is not short for "Patrick." Pat is a nurse. Patty was a nurse. She was stationed at the 24th Evacuation Hospital in Long Binh.

We were the first American women sent to live and work in the midst of guerrilla warfare. The month-long Tet offensive was especially frightening. The Viet Cong blew up the ammunition dump down the street, causing a wall in our unit to collapse on some patients.

VC snipers shot at us. The North Vietnamese Army artillery roared throughout the nights. Those of us not at work huddled in our bunkers, wondering if we would survive until dawn.

At work, listening to the thundering sounds around us, we tried to keep our hands from shaking, the fear out of our voices and off of our faces, so that the wounded would not see or hear it.

Women served in Vietnam in many capacities. We served as personnel specialists, journalists, clerk-typists, intelligence officers, and nurses. There was no such thing as a generic woman soldier, as there was no such thing as a generic male soldier. Men served as mechanics, engineers, pilots, divers, and infantrymen.

The design of the men's statue at the Veterans Memorial was selected, according to Frederick Hart, the sculptor, because they "depict the bonds of men at war and because the infantry bore the greatest burden."

Mr. Chairman, we are proposing that the design for the women's statue be that of a nurse who served in Vietnam. The statue of a nurse is so compatible with the existing trio of figures because the nurses' experience so closely parallels the experience of the infantrymen—the intensity, the trauma, the carnage of war.

The statue design which we are proposing is an easily recognizable symbol of healing and hope, consistent with the spirit and the experience of the Vietnam Veterans Memorial. . . .

STATEMENT OF KAREN K. JOHNSON, LITTLE ROCK, AR

I was born in Petersburg, Virginia. My father was in the military. He was killed in France on November the 11th, 1944.

I was raised in Oklahoma. I graduated from college in 1964 and explored the military as a career and joined the Army in 1965.

My family was very patriotic because of the trials and tribulations that we had to go through because of being raised without a father. Considering that everyone in my family had experienced all that patriotism, when I said that I was going to join the Army it was not a new thought, even though I was the first woman to have joined.

My family felt that all Americans owed their country any sacrifice needed for the national good, regardless of their race or sex, that patriotism should be a blind emotion, and it should be accepted by our country without any thought or qualm as to who offered such patriotism.

Consequently, after I served in Germany from 1966 to 1968, when my country asked me to go overseas again to Vietnam, I went. I served in Vietnam from July of 1970 to March of 1972, for a total of 20 months in country.

When I tell people these facts, they always ask me, was I a nurse, that I did not see any combat, and that I must have volunteered. When I tell them that I was awarded a Bronze Star, they ask me what for.

For 18 years I have answered these questions with several long-winded explanations which were really an apology for my Vietnam service, because I was not a nurse and I was not a combat soldier, and there were many others who had served who the public much better understood their service in their traditional roles.

I have kept silent on what I did in Vietnam because it was easier than making the apologies or trying to educate my listener. I know now that I have done many Vietnam veterans a great disservice by my silence. Thanks to the support of the Arkansas Vietnam Veterans, my husband and my grandchildren, I have made my last apology, felt my last twinge of embarrassment, and I will not remain silent to the detriment of my comrades in arms.

I am a veterans' veteran and I am proud of it. I was not a nurse. I saw very little full-fledged combat, and when my country called I went willingly. I see no disgrace in answering such a call or in volunteering to serve in the United States Army.

I served as the Command Information Officer of the United States Army, Vietnam Headquarters, located at Long Binh. However, my job entailed finding out what Army troops were doing, photographing those troops, writing news reports, and printing the internal publications to keep the troops informed.

I could not do that from Long Binh. I traveled all over Vietnam. Wherever there were Army troops, I went, too. I have flown in attack helicopters, been shot at in jeeps, and I went over the Hay Van Pass in several convoys.

Whatever it took to get the news out to the troops is what I and my staff did, and we did it very well. "Uptight Magazine," one of our publications, was awarded the Thomas Jefferson Award for the outstanding military publication in its field, an award that was given to me by "Time Magazine."

Our office published a twice-daily news bulletin, a weekly Long Binh paper, the weekly "Army Reporter," "Uptight Magazine Quarterly"; and "Tour 364," the history of the war, was updated every six months so that troops rotating home had a written history of their service. We were also responsible for the free distribution of "Stars and Stripes" to ensure that every U.S. military personnel serving in Vietnam had daily access to a newspaper.

There were a lot of obstacles to resolve to make all of this happen. My staff made it happen every day for 20 months, in 12 hour shifts, seven days a week, including Christmas, when we worked harder because we were responsible for making Operation Jingle Bells work so that the troops could see Bob Hope.

I am here today to tell you that I am very proud of that staff, and especially of Spec. 5 Steven Henry Warner, who gave his life so the American soldier could be the best informed and most motivated soldier in the world. I do not believe they would want me to apologize for our service or the fact that Steve Warner gave his life as a journalist and not as a combat soldier.

If there is any apology owed, it is the one I owe my staff for not standing up for them for the last 18 years because I did not like the questions my admission to being a Vietnam veteran elicited because I was a woman, something not well understood by the American public.

Their service and mine should be given equal recognition with all who served, not diminished because of the non-traditional position I held.

I come before you today to ask you to legislate equal dignity for the women who served their country by answering the call to arms. The Vietnam Women's Memorial would do much to give women veterans a new sense of self-respect and it will make a strong public statement that bias, prejudice, or ignorance of the sacrifices that women veterans have made for their country will no longer be tolerated.

Today the flag that covered my father's casket when he was put to final rest in 1948 lies in front of me, because I have always wanted him to be proud of me, his only child. And I believe he would be proudest of me today when I say, after 18 long years of silence: I was an American soldier; I answered my country's call to arms; and I am an American veteran, a title I should be able to share with equal dignity with all who have served before me and will serve after me. . . .

STATEMENT OF ROBERT W. DOUBEK . . .

Mr. Chairman, my name is Robert W. Doubek of Washington, D.C. I am a Vietnam veteran. I am employed in the private sector. I was a founder of the Vietnam Veterans Memorial Fund. I served as its Executive Director and Project Director. I was responsible for building the memorial. I did the work. In recognition of my achievement, I was nominated for a Congressional Gold Medal which was a bill passed by the Senate on November 14, 1985.

The fact is that women are not represented by the Vietnam Veterans Memorial. The fact is also that the memorial does not represent anyone. It is not a legislative body. It is a symbol of honor, and as such, it is complete as a tribute to all who served their country in the Vietnam War.

It is a basic rule of common sense that mandates that something which is not broken should not be fixed. The genius of the wall is its equalizing and unifying effect. All veterans are honored, regardless of rank, service branch, commission, sex, or any other category. The names of the eight women casualties take their rightful places of honor. To ensure that this fact is never overlooked, the inscription on the first panel of the wall states that the memorial is in honor of the men and women of the Armed Forces. The reason I know this is because I was instrumental in drafting the inscription.

In 1982, politics required that we add a figurative sculpture as a more specific symbol of the Vietnam veteran. Even with the heroic and dangerous service rendered by other combatants such as Air Force and Navy pilots, Navy swiftboat crews, and the life saving efforts of nurses, helicopter pilots and medics, there was only one possible choice of what category would be literally depicted to symbolize the Vietnam veteran, and that could only be the enlisted infantrymen, grunts. They account for the majority of names on the wall; they bore the brunt of the battle. The fact is all grunts were men.

The addition of a statue of a woman or of any other category, for that matter, would reduce the symbolism of the existing sculpture from honoring or symbolizing the Vietnam veterans community as a whole to symbolizing only enlisted infantrymen. This in turn would open a Pandora's box of proliferating statuary toward the goal of trying to depict every possible category. The National Park Service has already received requests for a statue to literally depict Native Americans and even for scout dogs, and in fact, I want to say that the figure for Native American casualties was 225.

The addition of a statue solely on the basis of gender raises troubling questions about proportion. Is gender of such overriding importance among veterans that we should have a specific statue to women who suffered eight ca-

sualties, and none for the Navy which suffered over 2,500, nor for the Air Force which suffered over 2,400? Is gender of such importance to outweigh that some 90 percent of the women who served in Vietnam in the military were officers [nurses were commissioned officers], while over 87 percent of all casualties were enlisted? . . . Approval . . . would set the precedent that strict literal depiction of both genders is an absolute requirement of all military related memorials. What about the new Navy memorial? Will Congress mandate an additional figure at the Iwo Jima Memorial?

STATEMENT OF COL. MARY EVELYN BANE, USMC (RETIRED), ARLINGTON, VA

Mr. Chairman, my name is Mary Evelyn Bane. I live in Arlington, Virginia, and I have lived in the Washington metropolitan area for a total of almost 19 nonconsecutive years. I retired in 1977 from a 26-year career in the United States Marine Corps in the grade of colonel. I never served in Vietnam, only a few women Marines did, and they were in Saigon, but I was in active service during the entire period of the war there. My career was in personnel management and, like most Marine officers, I had a variety of assignments and experiences, including two tours at our famous or infamous Parris Island training recruits, and an assignment with the Joint Staff in France. All of my male Marine colleagues did serve in Vietnam, many of them more than once, and some of their names are on the Vietnam Veterans Memorial.

I am opposed to the installation of a statue of a woman at the site of the VVM for both artistic and philosophical reasons, artistically, because it is at odds with the design as well as the theme of the memorial. . . . [and] philosophically simply because I am a woman. This may seem unfathomable to the statue's proponents, but perhaps I can explain. From the beginning of my chosen career in what most will agree is a macho outfit, I tried hard to be the best Marine I was capable of being. When I was commissioned, fewer than 1 percent of the officers in the Marine Corps were female. Women were assigned to women's billets, and restricted to a handful of occupational specialties considered appropriate for women. Over the years, through the combined efforts of many, many people, of which I am happy to say I am one, the concept of how women could and should serve their country has changed. The huge increase in the military's population required by the Vietnam War hastened the changes.

Nevertheless, in 1973 when I, then a lieutenant colonel, was assigned as the Marine Corps member of a Department of Defense ad hoc group studying the recruitment and processing of non-prior service personnel, the Civil Service GS-15 chair of the group complained to the Commandant of the Marine Corps that he had not appointed a real Marine.

My point here is that sex is an accident of birth. I chose to be a Marine and worked hard at it, and spent a career combatting discrimination based on sex. I feel every service person should be recognized for what he or she accomplished as a soldier, sailor, Marine or airman. The Vietnam Veterans Memorial recognizes American military members for their service in Vietnam, irrespective of sex, rank, service, race, or occupational specialty. To single out one of these criteria for special recognition in the form of a statue on the site of the Vietnam Veterans Memorial would not only violate the integrity of the design, but would be discriminatory.

KRISTIN LUKER
Abortion, Motherhood, and Morality

Abortion, as we have seen, was commonly used in the first half of the nineteenth century by women, married as well as unmarried, middle and upper class as well as working class, when other methods of fertility control were unreliable or unavailable. When in the post–Civil War decades states began to impose restrictions on abortion, they did so primarily at the urging of the newly established American Medical Association. Concerned about the health risks posed for pregnant women, "regular" physicians were also eager to put out of business "irregular" caregivers (abortionists and midwives), thereby securing for themselves a monopoly on medical practice. One hundred years later, the medical profession once again sought changes in abortion policy, this time urging liberalization of state laws in the wake of technological advances that made possible early detection of fetal abnormalities and medically safe abortion procedures. Although nonmedical factors played a role in these policy decisions, especially in the earlier effort to criminalize abortion, physicians, not women, were the chief participants in the abortion debate.

That situation changed dramatically with *Roe* v. *Wade,* the 1973 Supreme Court decision liberalizing abortion restrictions. (See pp. 592–96.) Women mobilized in large numbers both in opposition to and support of the Court's decision as the abortion debate "went public." The growing intensity of that debate suggests that much is at stake for both sides.

Kristin Luker has examined both pro-choice and pro-life activists in California in an

Excerpted from "Motherhood and Morality in America," chap. 8 of *Abortion and the Politics of Motherhood* by Kristin Luker (Berkeley: University of California Press, 1984). Copyright © 1984 by The Regents of the University of California. Reprinted by permission of the author and the publisher. Notes have been renumbered and edited.

effort to discover precisely what is contested. While her California sample may not be representative of activists nationwide, Luker's illuminating study reveals two groups of women coming from very different social worlds. Their contrasting life choices and life experiences, coupled with different ethical and religious beliefs, have given rise to dramatically divergent views about the purpose of women's lives and the meaning of motherhood. In examining the differences, Luker makes clear just why compromise on this issue seems increasingly ellusive.

According to interested observers at the time, abortion in America was as frequent in the last century as it is in our own. And the last century . . . had its own "right-to-life" movement, composed primarily of physicians who pursued the issue in the service of their own professional goals. When abortion reemerged as an issue in the late 1950s, it still remained in large part a restricted debate among interested professionals. But abortion as we now know it has little in common with these earlier rounds of the debate. . . . Instead of the elite male professionals who commanded the issue until recently, ordinary people—and more to the point, ordinary women—have come to predominate in the ranks of those concerned. From a quiet, restricted technical debate among concerned professionals, abortion has become a debate that seems at times capable of tearing the fabric of American life apart. How did this happen? What accounts for the remarkable transformation of the abortion debate?

The history of the debate . . . provides some preliminary answers. Technological advances in obstetrics led to a decline in those abortions undertaken strictly to preserve the life of the woman, using the narrowly biological sense of the word *life*. These technological advances, in turn, permitted (and indeed forced) physicians over time to make more and more nuanced decisions about abortion and eventually brought to the fore the underlying philosophical issue that had been obscured by a century of medical control over abortion: is the embryo a person or only a potential person? . . . [O]nce this question is confronted directly, a unified world view—a set of assumptions about how the world is and ought to be organized—is called into play. . . . [W]orld views are usually the product of values so deeply held and dearly cherished that an assault upon them is a deeply disturbing assault indeed. . . . [T]he abortion debate has been transformed because it has "gone public" and

in so doing has called into question individuals' most sacrosanct beliefs.

But this is only part of the story. . . . By bringing the issue of the moral status of the embryo to the fore, the new round focuses on the relative rights of women and embryos. Consequently, the abortion debate has become a debate about women's contrasting obligations to themselves and others. New technologies and the changing nature of work have opened up possibilities for women outside of the home undreamed of in the nineteenth century; together, these changes give women—for the first time in history—the option of deciding exactly how and when their family roles will fit into the larger context of their lives. In essence, therefore, this round of the abortion debate is so passionate and hard-fought *because it is a referendum on the place and meaning of motherhood.*

Motherhood is at issue because two opposing visions of motherhood are at war. Championed by "feminists" and "housewives," these two different views of motherhood represent in turn two very different kinds of social worlds. The abortion debate has become a debate among women, women with different values in the social world, different experiences of it, and different resources with which to cope with it. How the issue is framed, how people think about it, and, most importantly, where the passions come from are all related to the fact that the battlelines are increasingly drawn (and defended) by women. While on the surface it is the embryo's fate that seems to be at stake, the abortion debate is actually about the meanings of *women's* lives. . . .

. . . [I]n our interviews we routinely asked both male and female activists on both sides of the issue to supply information on several "social background variables," such as where they were born, the extent of their education, their income level, the number of children they had, and their occupations. When male activists on the two sides are compared on these variables, they are virtually indistinguishable from one another. But when female activists are compared, it is dramatically clear that for the women who have come to dominate the ranks of the movement, the abortion debate is a conflict between two different social worlds and the hopes and beliefs those worlds support.

WHO ARE THE ACTIVISTS?

On almost every social background variable we examined, pro-life and pro-choice women differed dramatically.... Keeping in mind that the statistical use of averages has inherent difficulties, we ask, who are the "average" pro-choice and pro-life advocates? When the social background data are looked at carefully, two profiles emerge. The average pro-choice activist is a forty-four-year-old married woman who grew up in a large metropolitan area and whose father was a college graduate. She was married at age twenty-two, has one or two children, and has had some graduate or professional training beyond the B.A. degree. She is married to a professional man, is herself employed in a regular job, and her family income is more than $50,000 a year. She is not religiously active, feels that religion is not important to her, and attends church very rarely if at all.

The average pro-life woman is also a forty-four-year-old married woman who grew up in a large metropolitan area. She married at age seventeen and has three children or more. Her father was a high school graduate, and she has some college education or may have a B.A. degree. She is not employed in the paid labor force and is married to a small businessman or a lower-level white-collar worker; her family income is $30,000 a year. She is Catholic (and may have converted), and her religion is one of the most important aspects of her life: she attends church at least once a week and occasionally more often.

INTERESTS AND PASSIONS

To the social scientist (and perhaps to most of us) these social background characteristics connote lifestyles as well. We intuitively clothe these bare statistics with assumptions about beliefs and values. When we do so, the pro-choice women emerge as educated, affluent, liberal professionals, whose lack of religious affiliation suggests a secular, "modern," or (as pro-life people would have it) "utilitarian" outlook on life. Similarly, the income, education, marital patterns, and religious devotion of pro-life women suggest that they are traditional, hard-working people ("polyester types" to their opponents), who hold conservative views on life. We may be entitled to assume that individuals' social backgrounds act to shape and mold their social attitudes, but it is important to realize that the relationship between social worlds and social values is a very complex one.

Perhaps one example will serve to illustrate the point. A number of pro-life women in this study emphatically rejected an expression that pro-choice women tend to use almost unthinkingly—the expression *unwanted pregnancy*. Pro-life women argued forcefully that a better term would be a *surprise* pregnancy, asserting that although a pregnancy may be momentarily unwanted, the child that results from the pregnancy almost never is. Even such a simple thing—what to call an unanticipated pregnancy—calls into play an individual's values and resources. Keeping in mind our profile of the average pro-life person, it is obvious that a woman who does not work in the paid labor force, who does not have a college degree, whose religion is important to her, and who has already committed herself wholeheartedly to marriage and a large family is well equipped to believe that an unanticipated pregnancy usually becomes a beloved child. Her life is arranged so that for her, this belief is true. This view is consistent not only with her values, which she has held from earliest childhood, but with her social resources as well. It should not be surprising, therefore, that her world view leads her to believe that everyone else can "make room for one more" as easily as she can and that therefore it supports her in her conviction that abortion is cruel, wicked, and self-indulgent.

It is almost certainly the case that an unplanned pregnancy is never an easy thing for anyone. Keeping in mind the profile of the average pro-choice woman, however, it is evident that a woman who is employed full time, who has an affluent lifestyle that depends in part on her contribution to the family income, and who expects to give a child as good a life as she herself has had with respect to educational, social, and economic advantages will draw on a different reality when she finds herself being skeptical about the ability of the average person to transform unwanted pregnancies into well-loved (and well-cared-for) children.

The relationship between passions and interests is thus more dynamic than it might appear at first. It is true that at one level, pro-choice and pro-life attitudes on abortion are self-serving: activists on each side have different views of the morality of abortion because their chosen lifestyles leave them with different needs for abortion; and both sides have values that provide a moral basis for their abortion needs in particular and their lifestyles in general. But this is only half the story. The values that lead pro-life and pro-choice women into different attitudes toward abortion are the same values that led them at an earlier time to adopt different lifestyles that supported a given view of abortion.

For example, pro-life women have *always* valued family roles very highly and have arranged their lives accordingly. They did not acquire high-level educational and occupational skills, for example, because they married, and they married because their values suggested that this would be the most satisfying life open to them. Similarly, pro-choice women postponed (or avoided) marriage and family roles because they chose to acquire the skills they needed to be successful in the larger world, having concluded that the role of wife and mother was too limited for them. Thus, activists on both sides of the issue are women who have a given set of values about what are the most satisfying and appropriate roles for women, and they have made *life commitments that now limit their ability to change their minds.* Women who have many children and little education, for example, are seriously handicapped in attempting to become doctors or lawyers; women who have reached their late forties with few children or none are limited in their ability to build (or rebuild) a family. For most of these activists, therefore, their position on abortion is the "tip of the iceberg," a shorthand way of supporting and proclaiming not only a complex set of values but a given set of social resources as well.

To put the matter differently, we might say that for pro-life women the traditional division of life into separate male roles and female roles

still works, but for pro-choice women it does not. Having made a commitment to the traditional female roles of wife, mother, and homemaker, pro-life women are limited in those kinds of resources—education, class status, recent occupational experiences—they would need to compete in what has traditionally been the male sphere, namely, the paid labor force. The average pro-choice woman, in contrast, is comparatively well endowed with exactly those resources: she is highly educated, she already has a job, and she has recent (and continuous) experience in the job market.

In consequence, anything that supports a traditional division of labor into male and female worlds is, broadly speaking, in the interests of pro-life women because that is where their resources lie. Conversely, such a traditional division of labor, when strictly enforced, is against the interests of pro-choice women because it limits their abilities to use the valuable "male" resources that they have in relative abundance. It is therefore apparent that attitudes toward abortion, even though rooted in childhood experiences, are also intimately related to present-day interests. Women who oppose abortion and seek to make it officially unavailable are declaring, both practically and symbolically, that women's reproductive roles should be given social primacy. Once an embryo is defined as a child and an abortion as the death of a person, almost everything else in a woman's life must "go on hold" during the course of her pregnancy: any attempt to gain "male" resources such as a job, an education, or other skills must be subordinated to her uniquely female responsibility of serving the needs of this newly conceived person. Thus, when personhood is bestowed on the embryo, women's nonreproductive roles are made secondary to their reproductive roles. The act of conception therefore creates a pregnant woman rather than a woman who is pregnant; it creates a woman whose life, in cases where roles or values clash, is defined by the fact that she is—or may become—pregnant.

It is obvious that this view is supportive of women who have already decided that their familial and reproductive roles are the major ones in their lives. By the same token, the costs of defining women's reproductive roles as primary do not seem high to them because they have already chosen to make those roles primary anyway. For example, employers might choose to discriminate against women because they might require maternity leave and thus be unavailable at critical times, but women who have chosen not to work in the paid labor force in the first place can see such discrimination as irrelevant to them.

It is equally obvious that supporting abortion (and believing that the embryo is not a person) is in the vested interests of pro-choice women. Being so well equipped to compete in the male sphere, they perceive any situation that both practically and symbolically affirms the primacy of women's reproductive roles as a real loss to them. Practically, it devalues their social resources. If women are only secondarily in the labor market and must subordinate working to pregnancy, should it occur, then their education, occupation, income, and work become potentially temporary and hence discounted. Working becomes, as it tradiionally was perceived to be, a pastime or hobby pursued for "pin money" rather than a central part of their lives. Similarly, if the embryo is defined as a person and the ability to become pregnant is the central one for women, a woman must be prepared to sacrifice some of her own interests to the interests of this newly conceived person.

In short, in a world where men and women have traditionally had different roles to play and where male roles have traditionally been the more socially prestigious and financially rewarded, abortion has become a symbolic marker between those who wish to maintain this division of labor and those who wish to challenge it. . . . [T]raditional relationships between men and women are still satisfying, rewarding, and meaningful for pro-life women, and they therefore resist the lure of "liberation." For pro-choice women, however, with their access to male resources, a division of labor into the public world of work and the private world of home and hearth seems to promise only restriction to "second-class" citizenship.

Thus, the sides are fundamentally opposed to each other not only on the issue of abortion but also on what abortion *means*. Women who have many "human capital" resources of the traditionally male variety want to see motherhood recognized as a private, discretionary choice. Women who have few of these resources and limited opportunities in the job market want to see motherhood recog-

nized as the most important thing a woman can do. In order for pro-choice women to achieve their goals, therefore, they *must* argue that motherhood is not a primary, inevitable, or "natural" role for all women; for pro-life women to achieve their goals, they *must* argue that it is. In short, the debate rests on the question of whether women's fertility is to be socially recognized as a resource or as a handicap. . . .

Because of their commitment to their own view of motherhood as a primary social role, pro-life women believe that other women are "casual" about abortions and have them "for convenience." There are no reliable data to confirm whether or not women are "casual" about abortions, but many pro-life people believe this to be the case and relate their activism to their perception of other people's casualness.[1] For example:

> Every time I saw some article [on abortion] I read about it, and I had another friend who had her second abortion in 1977 . . . and both of her abortions were a matter of convenience, it was inconvenient for her to be pregnant at that time. When I talked to her I said, "O.K., you're married now, your husband has a good job, you want to have children eventually, but if you became pregnant now, you'd have an abortion. Why?" "Because it's inconvenient, this is not when I want to have my child." And that bothered me a lot because she is also very intelligent, graduated magna cum laude, and knew nothing about fetal development.

The assertion that women are "casual" about abortion, one could argue, expresses in a shorthand way a set of beliefs about women and their roles. First, the more people value the personhood of the embryo, the more important must be the reasons for taking its life. Some pro-life people, for example, would accept an abortion when continuation of the pregnancy would cause the death of the mother; they believe that when two lives are in direct conflict, the embryo's life can be considered the more expendable. But not all pro-life people agree, and many say they would not accept abortion even to save the mother's life. (Still others say they accept the idea in principle but would not make that choice in their own lives if faced with it.) For people who accept the personhood of the embryo, any reason besides trading a "life for a life" (and sometimes even that) seems trivial, merely a matter of "convenience."

Second, people who accept the personhood of the embryo see the reasons that pro-abortion people give for ending a pregnancy as simultaneously downgrading the value of the embryo and upgrading everything else but pregnancy. The argument that women need abortion to "control" their fertility means that they intend to subordinate pregnancy, with its inherent unpredictability, to something else. . . . [T]hat something else is participation in the paid labor force. Abortion permits women to engage in paid work on an equal basis with men. With abortion, they may schedule pregnancy in order to take advantage of the kinds of benefits that come with a paid position in the labor force: a paycheck, a title, and a social identity. The pro-life women in this study were often careful to point out that they did not object to "career women." But what they meant by "career women" were women whose *only* responsibilities were in the labor force. Once a woman became a wife and a mother, in their view her primary responsibility was to her home and family.

Third, the pro-life activists we interviewed, the overwhelming majority of whom are full-time homemakers, also felt that women who worked *and* had families could often do so only because women like themselves picked up the slack. Given their place in the social structure, it is not surprising that many of the pro-life women thought that married women who worked outside the home were "selfish"—that they got all the benefits while the homemakers carried the load for them in Boy and Girl Scouts, PTA, and after school, for which their reward was to be treated by the workers as less competent and less interesting persons.[2]

Abortion therefore strips the veil of sanctity from motherhood. When pregnancy is discretionary—when people are allowed to put anything else they value in front of it—then motherhood has been demoted from a sacred calling to a job. In effect, the legalization of abortion serves to make men and women more "unisex" by deemphasizing what makes them different—the ability of women to visibly and directly carry the next generation. Thus, pro-choice women are emphatic about their right to compete equally with men without the burden of an unplanned pregnancy, and pro-life women are equally emphatic about their belief that men and women have different roles in life and that pregnancy is a gift instead of a burden.

The pro-life activists we interviewed do not want equality with men in the sense of having exactly the same rights and responsibilities as men do, although they do want equality of status. In fact, to the extent that *all* women have been touched by the women's movement and have become aware of the fact that society often treats women as a class as less capable than men, quite a few said they appreciated the Equal Rights Amendment (ERA), except for its implied stand on abortion. The ERA, in their view, reminded them that women are as valuable *in their own sphere* as men are in theirs. However, to the extent that the ERA was seen as downplaying the differences between men and women, to devalue the female sphere of the home in the face of the male sphere of paid work, others saw it as both demeaning and oppressive to women like themselves. As one of the few married employed pro-life women argued:

> I oppose it [the ERA]. Because I've gotten where I am without it. I don't think I need it. I think a woman should be hired on her merits, not on her sex or race. I don't think we should be hiring on sex or on race. I think we should be taking the competent people that are capable of doing the job . . . I don't think women should be taking jobs from the breadwinner, you know. I still think that our society should be male . . . the male should be the primary breadwinner. For example, my own husband cannot hope for promotion because he is white and Anglo, you know, I mean white male. He's not going to get a promotion. If he could get the promotion that others of different minorities have gotten over him, I probably wouldn't have to work at all. So from my own point of view, purely selfishly, I think we've got to consider it. On the other hand, if I'm doing the same job [as a man], I expect to get the same pay. But I've always gotten it. So I really don't think that's an issue. I see the ERA as causing more problems than it's going to [solve]. . . . As I see it, we were on a pedestal, why should we go down to being equal? That's my feeling on the subject.

It is stating the obvious to point out that the more limited the educational credentials a woman has, the more limited the job opportunities are for her, and the more limited the job opportunities, the more attractive motherhood is as a full-time occupation. In motherhood, one can control the content and pace of one's own work, and the job is *intrinsically meaningful.* Compared with a job clerking in a supermarket (a realistic alternative for women with limited educational credentials) where the work is poorly compensated and often demeaning, motherhood can have compensations that far transcend the monetary ones. As one woman described mothering: "You have this little, rough uncut diamond, and you're the artist shaping and cutting that diamond, and bringing out the lights . . . that's a great challenge."

All the circumstances of her existence will therefore encourage a pro-life woman to highlight the kinds of values and experiences that support childbearing and childrearing and to discount the attraction (such as it is) of paid employment. Her circumstances encourage her to resent the pro-choice view that women's most meaningful and prestigious activities are in the "man's world."

Abortion also has a symbolic dimension that separates the needs and interests of homemakers and workers in the paid labor force. Insofar as abortion allows a woman to get a job, to get training for a job, or to advance in a job, it does more than provide social support for working women over homemakers; it also seems to support the value of economic considerations over moral ones. Many pro-life people interviewed said that although their commitment to traditional family roles meant very real material deprivations to themselves and their families, the moral benefits of such a choice more than made up for it. . . .

For pro-life people, a world view that puts the economic before the noneconomic hopelessly confuses two different kinds of worlds. For them, the private world of family as traditionally experienced is the one place in human society where none of us has a price tag. Home, as Robert Frost pointed out, is where they have to take you in, whatever your social worth. Whether one is a surgeon or a rag picker, the family is, at least ideally, the place where love is unconditional.

Pro-life people and pro-life women in particular have very real reasons to fear such a state of affairs. Not only do they see an achievement-based world as harsh, superficial, and ultimately ruthless; they are relatively less well-equipped to operate in that world. A considerable amount of social science research has suggested, at least in the realm of medical treatment, that there is an increasing tendency to judge people by their official (achieved) worth.[3] Pro-life people have relatively fewer official achievements in part because they have been doing what they see as a moral task, namely, raising children and making a home; and they

see themselves as becoming handicapped in a world that discounts not only their social contributions but their personal lives as well.

It is relevant in this context to recall the grounds on which pro-life people argue that the embryo is a baby: that it is genetically human. To insist that the embryo is a baby because it is genetically human is to make a claim that it is both wrong and impossible to make distinctions between humans at all. Protecting the life of the embryo, which is by definition an entity whose social worth is all yet to come, means protecting others who feel that they may be defined as having low social worth; more broadly, it means protecting a legal view of personhood that emphatically rejects social worth criteria.

For the majority of pro-life people we interviewed, the abortions they found most offensive were those of "damaged" embryos. This is because this category so clearly highlights the aforementioned concerns about social worth. To defend a genetically or congenitally damaged embryo from abortion is, in their minds, defending the weakest of the weak, and most pro-life people we interviewed were least prepared to compromise on this category of abortion.

The genetic basis of the embryo's claim to personhood has another, more subtle implication for those on the pro-life side. If genetic humanness equals personhood, then biological facts of life must take precedence over social facts of life. One's destiny is therefore inborn and hence immutable. To give any ground on the embryo's biologically determined babyness, therefore, would by extension call into question the "innate," "natural," and biological basis of women's traditional roles as well.

Pro-choice people, of course, hold a very different view of the matter. For them, social considerations outweigh biological ones: the embryo becomes a baby when it is "viable," that is, capable of achieving a certain degree of social integration with others. This is a world view premised on achievement, but not in the way pro-life people experience the world. Pro-choice people, believing as they do in choice, planning, and human efficacy, believe that biology is simply a minor given to be transcended by human experience. Sex, like race and age, is not an appropriate criterion for sorting people into different rights and responsibilities. Pro-choice people downplay these "natural" ascriptive characteristics, believing that true equality means achievement based on talent, not being restricted to a "women's world," a "black world," or an "old people's world." Such a view, as the profile of pro-choice people has made clear, is entirely consistent with their own lives and achievements.

These differences in social circumstances that separate pro-life from pro-choice women on the core issue of abortion also lead them to have different values on topics that surround abortion, such as sexuality and the use of contraception. With respect to sexuality, for example, the two sides have diametrically opposed values; these values arise from a fundamentally different premise, which is, in turn, tied to the different realities of their social worlds. If pro-choice women have a vested interest in subordinating their reproductive capacities, and pro-life women have a vested interest in highlighting them, we should not be surprised to find that pro-life women believe that the purpose of sex is reproduction whereas pro-choice women believe that its purpose is to promote intimacy and mutual pleasure.

These two views about sex express the same value differences that lead the two sides to have such different views on abortion. If women plan to find their primary role in marriage and the family, then they face a need to create a "moral cartel" when it comes to sex. If sex is freely available outside of marriage, then why should men, as the old saw puts it, buy the cow when the milk is free? If many women are willing to sleep with men outside of marriage, then the regular sexual activity that comes with marriage is much less valuable an incentive to marry. And because pro-life women are traditional women, their primary resource for marriage is the promise of a stable home, with everything it implies: children, regular sex, a "haven in a heartless world."

But pro-life women, like all women, are facing a devaluation of these resources. As American society increasingly becomes a service economy, men can buy the services that a wife traditionally offers. Cooking, cleaning, decorating, and the like can easily be purchased on the open market in a cash transaction. And as sex becomes more open, more casual, and more "amative," it removes one more resource that could previously be obtained only through marriage.

Pro-life women, as we have seen, have both value orientations and social characteristics that make marriage very important. Their alternatives in the public world of work are, on the whole, less attractive. Furthermore, women who stay home full-time and keep house are becoming a financial luxury. Only very wealthy families or *families whose values allow them to place the nontangible benefits of a full-time wife over the tangible benefits of a working wife* can afford to keep one of its earners off the labor market. To pro-life people, the nontangible benefit of having children—and therefore the value of procreative sex—is very important. Thus, a social ethic that promotes more freely available sex undercuts pro-life women two ways: it limits their abilities to get into a marriage in the first place, and it undermines the social value placed on their presence once within a marriage.

For pro-choice women, the situation is reversed. Because they have access to "male" resources such as education and income, they have far less reason to believe that the basic reason for sexuality is to produce children. They plan to have small families anyway, and they and their husbands come from and have married into a social class in which small families are the norm. For a number of overlapping reasons, therefore, pro-choice women believe that the value of sex is not primarily procreative: pro-choice women value the ability of sex to promote human intimacy more (or at least more frequently) than they value the ability of sex to produce babies. But they hold this view because they can afford to. When they bargain for marriage, they use the same resources that they use in the labor market: upper-class status, an education very similar to a man's, side-by-side participation in the man's world, and, not least, a salary that substantially increases a family's standard of living.

It is true, therefore, that pro-life people are "anti-sex." They value sex, of course, but they value it for its traditional benefits (babies) rather than for the benefits that pro-choice people associate with it (intimacy). Pro-life people really do want to see "less" sexuality—or at least less open and socially unregulated sexuality—because they think it is morally wrong, they think it distorts the meaning of sex, and they feel that it *threatens the basis on which their own marital bargains are built.* . . .

Pro-choice women . . . value (and can afford) an approach to sexuality that, by sidelining reproduction, diminishes the differences between men and women; they can do this *because they have other resources on which to build a marriage*. The pro-choice women we met have approximately the same kinds of education as their husbands do, and many of them have the same kinds of jobs—they are lawyers, physicians, college professors, and the like. Even those who do not work in traditionally male occupations have jobs in the paid labor market and thus share common experiences. They and their husbands share many social resources in common: they both have some status outside the home, they both have a paycheck, and they both have a set of peers and friends located in the work world rather than in the family world. In terms of the traditional studies of family power, pro-choice husbands and wives use the same bargaining chips and have roughly equal amounts of them.[4] Since their value is intimacy and since the daily lives of men and women on the pro-choice side are substantially similar, intimacy in the bedroom is merely an extension of the intimacy of their larger world.

Pro-life women and men, by contrast, tend to live in "separate spheres." Because their lives are based on a social and emotional division of labor where each sex has its appropriate work, to accept contraception or abortion would devalue the one secure resource left to these women: the private world of home and hearth. This would be disastrous not only in terms of status but also in terms of meaning: if values about fertility and family are not essential to a marriage, what supports does a traditional marriage have in times of stress? To accept highly effective contraception, which actually and symbolically subordinates the role of children in the family to other needs and goals, would be to cut the ground of meaning out from under at least one (and perhaps both) partners' lives. Therefore, contraception, which sidelines the reproductive capacities of men and women, is both useless and threatening to pro-life people.

THE CORE OF THE DEBATE

In summary, women come to be pro-life and pro-choice activists as the end result of lives that center around different definitions of motherhood. They grow up with a belief about the nature of the embryo, so events in their lives lead them to believe that the embryo is a unique person, or a fetus; that people are intimately tied to by their biological roles, or that these roles are but a minor part of life; that motherhood is the most important and satisfying role open to a woman, or that motherhood is only one of several roles, a burden when defined as the only role. These beliefs and values are rooted in the concrete circumstances of women's lives—their educations, incomes, occupations, and the different marital and family choices they have made along the way—and they work simultaneously to shape those circumstances in turn. Values about the relative place of reason and faith, about the role of actively planning for life versus learning to accept gracefully life's unknowns, of the relative satisfactions inherent in work and family—all of these factors place activists in a specific relationship to the larger world and give them a specific set of resources with which to confront that world.

The simultaneous and ongoing modification of both their lives and their values by each other finds these activists located in a specific place in the social world. They are financially successful, or they are not. They become highly educated, or they do not. They become married and have a large family or they have a small one. And at each step of the way, both their values and their lives have undergone either ratification or revision.

Pro-choice and pro-life activists live in different worlds, and the scope of their lives, as both adults and children, fortifies them in their belief that their own views on abortion are the more correct, more moral, and more reasonable. When added to this is the fact that should "the other side" win, one group of women will see the very real devaluation of their lives and life resources, it is not surprising that the abortion debate has generated so much heat and so little light.

NOTES

1. . . . While I know of no direct data of how women feel who choose abortions, in the course of research for my previous book (*Taking Chances: Abortion and the Decision Not to Contracept* [1975]), I interviewed over 100 women in deep, unstructured verbatim interviews. In subsequent research, I have talked with or interviewed over 500 women who have had abortions. In my own—and possibly biased—experience, few of these women were "casual" about having an abortion. Some were more conflicted about the abortion decision than others,

but for all the women I interviewed, the decision to seek abortion has been serious, thoughtful, and carefully considered.

2. In fact, pro-life women, especially those recruited after 1972, were *less* likely to be engaged in formal activities such as Scouts, church activities, and PTA than their pro-choice peers. Quite possibly they have in mind more informal kinds of activities, premised on the fact that since they do not work, they are home most of the time.

3. See, e.g., Victor Fuchs, *Who Shall Live? Health Economics and Social Choice* (New York: Basic Books, 1974). . . .

4. There is a long sociological research tradition on the relative power status of husbands and wives and what contributes to their relative power; see [for example,] . . . Robert Blood and Robert Hamlin, ''The Effects of the Wife's Employment on the Family Power Structure,'' *Social Forces* 36, no. 4 (1958):347–52. . . .

Phyllis Schlafly, "The thoughts of one who loves life as a woman . . ."

Phyllis Stewart Schlafly had much in common with Betty Goldstein Friedan. Separated in age by only three years, both were the first child born to their respective families, the Stewarts who were Roman Catholic and the Goldsteins who were Jewish. Both grew up during the depression years in Illinois and were valedictorians of their high school class. Both attended women's colleges, Goldstein choosing prestigious Smith College in Massachusetts and Stewart attending College of the Sacred Heart in Maryville, Illinois, before transferring to Washington University in St. Louis. Excelling in college, both entered graduate school, Goldstein studying for an M.A. in psychology at the University of California, Berkeley. Stewart earning an M.A. in political science at Radcliffe College and Harvard University. (She would later return to Washington University for a law degree.)

Both went on to interesting jobs, Stewart as a congressional researcher in Washington, Goldstein as a journalist in New York City. Both subsequently married, Stewart choosing John Fred Schlafly, Jr., a lawyer and fellow conservative, and Goldstein choosing Carl Friedan, a theatrical producer and later an advertising executive. Both women had children, Schlafly six and Friedan three, whom they reared in suburbia along with the millions of other middle-class families caught up in the resurgent domesticity of the postwar years.

Energetic and intelligent, neither found domesticity sufficient. Friedan continued to write, as did Schlafly, who also became a community volunteer, Republican party activist, and, in 1952, a congressional candidate, winning her primary but losing in the general election. In the early 1960s, both published first books that became best-sellers—Friedan, *The Feminine Mystique* (see pp. 512–16), and Schlafly, *A Choice Not an Echo*, a political endorsement of conservative Arizona senator Barry Goldwater, the Republican presidential candidate in 1964.

Yet despite these similarities, the personal became political for these two women in ways that would lead them in sharply divergent directions in the years ahead. Friedan's name would become synonymous with a resurgent feminism, Schlafly's with antifeminism. Friedan, as a founder and the first president of the National Organization for Women (NOW), would champion equal rights for women. Schlafly, creator and author

Excerpted from "Preface" and "Understanding the Difference," pp. 9–28 of *The Power of the Positive Woman* by Phyllis Schlafly (New Rochelle, N.Y.: Arlington House Publishers, 1977). Copyright © 1977 by Phyllis Schlafly. Reprinted by permission of Crown Publishers, Inc.

Phyllis Schlafly demonstrated the domestic ideal by posing cooking her husband's breakfast the morning after her 1952 primary victory. (St. Louis Globe-Democrat *photo. Courtesy of the St. Louis Mercantile Library Association.)*

of the *Phyllis Schlafly Report*, would devote her extraordinary energy as well as formidable organizational and speaking skills to defeat of the Equal Rights Amendment (see p. 589). Equality between the sexes, she would insist, will harm rather than help women.

While Schlafly's antistatism partially explains her opposition to using the federal government on behalf of sexual equality—she was always very conservative politically—more is involved, as is evident in the following document. Why would Schlafly's characterization of the "positive woman" appeal to antiabortion activists described by Luker?

The cry of "women's liberation" leaps out from the "lifestyle" sections of newspapers and the pages of slick magazines, from radio speakers and television screens. Cut loose from past patterns of behavior and expectations, women of all ages are searching for their identity—the college woman who has new alternatives thrust upon her via "women's studies" courses, the young woman whose routine is shattered by a chance encounter with a "consciousness-raising session," the woman in her middle years who suddenly finds herself in the "empty-nest syndrome," the woman of any age whose lover or lifetime partner departs for greener pastures (and a younger crop).

All of these women, thanks to the women's liberation movement, no longer see their predicament in terms of personal problems to be confronted and solved. They see their own difficulties as a little cog in the big machine of establishment restraints and stereotypical injustice in which they have lost their own equilibrium. Who am I? Why am I here? Why am I just another faceless victim of society's oppression, a nameless prisoner behind walls too high for me to climb alone? . . .

For a woman to find her identity in the modern world, the path should be sought from the Positive Women who have found the road and possess the map, rather than from those who have not. In this spirit, I share with you the thoughts of one who loves life as a woman and lives love as a woman, whose credentials are from the school of practical experience, and who has learned that fulfillment as a woman is a journey, not a destination.

Like every human being born into this world, the Positive Woman has her share of sorrows and sufferings, of unfulfilled desires and bitter defeats. But she will never be crushed by life's disappointments, because her positive mental attitude has built her an inner security that the actions of other people can never fracture. To the Positive Woman, her par-

ticular set of problems is not a conspiracy against her, but a challenge to her character and her capabilities.

The first requirement for the acquisition of power by the Positive Woman is to understand the differences between men and women. Your outlook on life, your faith, your behavior, your potential for fulfillment, all are determined by the parameters of your original premise. The Positive Woman starts with the assumption that the world is her oyster. She rejoices in the creative capability within her body and the power potential of her mind and spirit. She understands that men and women are different, and that those very differences provide the key to her success as a person and fulfillment as a woman.

The women's liberationist, on the other hand, is imprisoned by her own negative view of herself and of her place in the world around her. . . . Someone—it is not clear who, perhaps God, perhaps the "Establishment," perhaps a conspiracy of male chauvinist pigs—dealt women a foul blow by making them female. It becomes necessary, therefore, for women to agitate and demonstrate and hurl demands on society in order to wrest from an oppressive male-dominated social structure the status that has been wrongfully denied to women through the centuries. . . . Confrontation replaces cooperation as the watchword of all relationships. Women and men become adversaries instead of partners. . . . Within the confines of the women's liberationist ideology, therefore, the abolition of this overriding inequality of women becomes the primary goal.

This goal must be achieved at any and all costs—to the woman herself, to the baby, to the family, and to society. Women must be made equal to men in their ability *not* to become pregnant and *not* to be expected to care for babies they may bring into the world. This is why women's liberationists are compulsively involved in the drive to make abortion and child-care centers for all women, regardless of religion or income, both socially acceptable and government-financed. . . .

If man is targeted as the enemy, and the ultimate goal of women's liberation is independence from men and the avoidance of pregnancy and its consequences, then lesbianism is logically the highest form in the ritual of women's liberation. . . .

The Positive Woman will never travel that dead-end road. It is self-evident to the Positive Woman that the female body with its baby-producing organs was not designed by a conspiracy of men but by the Divine Architect of the human race. Those who think it is unfair that women have babies, whereas men cannot, will have to take up their complaint with God because no other power is capable of changing that fundamental fact. . . . The Positive Woman looks upon her femaleness and her fertility as part of her purpose, her potential, and her power. She rejoices that she has a capability for creativity that men can never have.

The third basic dogma of the women's liberation movement is that there is no difference between male and female except the sex organs, and that all those physical, cognitive, and emotional differences you *think* are there, are merely the result of centuries of restraints imposed by a male-dominated society and sex-stereotyped schooling. The role imposed on women is, by definition, inferior, according to the women's liberationists. . . .

There are countless physical differences between men and women. The female body is 50 to 60 percent water, the male 60 to 70 percent water, which explains why males can dilute alcohol better than women and delay its effect. The average woman is about 25 percent fatty tissue, while the male is 15 percent, making women more buoyant in water and able to swim with less effort. Males have a tendency to color blindness. Only 5 percent of persons who get gout are female. Boys are born bigger. Women live longer in most countries of the world, not only in the United States where we have a hard-driving competitive pace. Women excel in manual dexterity, verbal skills, and memory recall. . . .

Does the physical advantage of men doom women to a life of servility and subservience? The Positive Woman knows that she has a complementary advantage which is at least as great—and, in the hands of a skillful woman, far greater. The Divine Architect who gave men a superior strength to lift weights also gave women a different kind of superior strength. . . . A Positive Woman cannot defeat a man in a wrestling or boxing match, but she can motivate him, inspire him, encourage him, teach him, restrain him, reward him, and have power over him that he can never achieve over her with all his muscle. How or whether a Positive Woman uses her power is determined solely by the way she alone defines her goals and develops her skills.

The differences between men and women are also emotional and psychological. Without woman's innate maternal instinct, the human race would have died out centuries ago. . . . The overriding psychological need of a woman is to love something alive. A baby fulfills this need in the lives of most women. If a baby is not available to fill that need, women search for a baby-substitute. This is the reason why women have traditionally gone into teaching and nursing careers. They are doing what comes naturally to the female psyche. The schoolchild or the patient of any age provides an outlet for a woman to express her natural maternal need. . . . The Positive Woman finds somebody on whom she can lavish her maternal love so that it doesn't well up inside her and cause psychological frustrations. Surely no woman is so isolated by geography or insulated by spirit that she cannot find someone worthy of her maternal love. . . .

One of the strangest quirks of women's liberationists is their complaint that societal restraints prevent men from crying in public or showing their emotions, but permit women to do so, and that therefore we should "liberate" men to enable them, too, to cry in public. The public display of fear, sorrow, anger, and irritation reveals a lack of self-discipline that should be avoided by the Positive Woman just as much as by the Positive Man. Maternal love, however, is not a weakness but a manifestation of strength and service, and it should be nurtured by the Positive Woman. . . .

Another silliness of the women's liberationists is their frenetic desire to force all women to accept the title *Ms* in place of *Miss* or *Mrs*. If Gloria Steinem and Betty Friedan want to call themselves *Ms* in order to conceal their marital status, their wishes should be respected. But most married women feel they worked hard for the *r* in their names; and they don't care to be gratuitously deprived of it. . . .

Finally, women are different from men in dealing with the fundamentals of life itself. Men are philosophers, women are practical, and 'twas ever thus. Men may philosophize about how life began and where we are heading; women are concerned about feeding the kids today. No woman would ever, as Karl Marx did, spend years reading political philosophy in the British Museum while her child starved to death. Women don't take naturally to a search for the intangible and the abstract. . . . Where man is discursive, logical, abstract, or philosophical, woman tends to be emotional, personal, practical, or mystical. Each set of qualities is vital and complements the other. Among the many differences explained in [Amaury] de Riencourt's book, [*Sex and Power in History*], are the following:

> Women tend more toward conformity than men—which is why they often excel in such disciplines as spelling and punctuation where there is only one correct answer, determined by social authority. Higher intellectual activities, however, require a mental independence and power of abstraction that they usually lack, not to mention a certain form of aggressive boldness of the imagination which can only exist in a sex that is basically aggressive for biological reasons.
>
> To sum up: The masculine proclivity in problem solving is analytical and categorical; the feminine, synthetic and contextual. . . . Deep down, man tends to focus on the object, on external results and achievements; woman focuses on subjective motives and feelings. If life can be compared to a play, man focuses on the theme and structure of the play, woman on the innermost feelings displayed by the actors.

De Riencourt provides impressive refutation of two of the basic errors of the women's liberation movement: (1) that there are no emotional or cognitive differences between the sexes, and (2) that women should strive to be like men. . . . An effort to eliminate the differences by social engineering or legislative or constitutional tinkering cannot succeed, which is fortunate, but social relationships and spiritual values can be ruptured in the attempt. . . .

The Torch Relay, opening the International Women's Year Conference, Houston, Texas, 1977. The torch, brought by runners from Seneca Falls to Houston, symbolized the link between those early feminists who drafted the Declaration of Sentiments and their contemporary counterparts who assembled to present new proposals designed to achieve the still-elusive goal of equality. From left to right: Billie Jean King, Susan B. Anthony II, Bella Abzug, Sylvia Ortiz, Peggy Kokernot, Michele Cearcy, Betty Friedan. (Photograph by Diana Mara Henry)

Conclusion
Jane Sherron De Hart
The New Feminism and the
Dynamics of Social Change

Fifty years after gaining the right to vote, women who had been suffragists and women young enough to be their great-granddaughters embarked on a new feminist movement. Referred to as feminism's second wave to distinguish it from an earlier surge occurring around 1910, this new movement was vigorous, diffuse, and highly controversial. It was, in fact, many movements. Some were predominantly white and acquired the labels liberal, radical, socialist, and cultural feminism. Others consisted largely of women of color who identified themselves variously as Black, Chicana, Asian American, Native American, or U.S. Third World Feminists. One cannot make simplistic assumptions about which variant an individual woman might embrace. (For example, Pauli Murray, an African American lawyer and writer, would have been more likely to describe herself as a liberal feminist rather than a Black feminist.) Nor can one assume that only women embraced this new feminism or that all women did so. "As an *ism* (an ideology), feminism presupposed a set of principles not necessarily belonging to every woman—nor limited to women," wrote historian Nancy Cott of first wave feminism.[1] Her observation also applies to second wave feminism. Some men, but not all women, embraced those principles and joined this renewed struggle to dismantle gender hierarchy. For those who did so, the goal became not mere formal equality, but genuine liberation. Their objective: to change not only laws and institutions, but values, patterns of behavior, personal relationships, and ultimately themselves.

The feminism explored in this essay is sometimes referred to as mainstream feminism. Emerging out of liberal and radical feminism, it has been a predominantly white phenomenon. In order to understand its origins and agendas, its opponents, and most important, its potential for changing society, it is necessary to examine the long-term economic and social changes that created an environment within which this strand of the movement could emerge. It is important also to appreciate the ferment of the 1960s, much of it initiated by African Americans, that provided white mainstream feminism with its ideological core, vitality, and impetus. To explore such origins is also to explore the extent to which these feminists confronted issues that their ideological foremothers had left unresolved.

UNFULFILLED EXPECTATIONS

By winning the vote in 1920, many women believed that the decisive battle in the long struggle for sexual equality had been won. The atmosphere was electric with a sense of achievement and expectation generated by the euphoria of the moment. The fact that enfranchisement had come on the heels of other reforms identified with women seemed evidence of their growing influence. Congress had passed legislation to protect women in industry, outlaw child labor, and enact prohibition—measures important to those who believed that women and children were the primary victims of exploitative employment and alcohol-related abuse. Champions of women's rights also celebrated gains in education and employment. Since 1900 female enrollment had shot up 1,000 percent in public colleges and universities and nearly 500 percent in private ones. As ambitious graduates gained access to advanced training, the proportion of women in the professions climbed by 1920 to an unprecedented 11.9 percent.[2] During World War I women in record numbers had moved into skilled jobs and administrative positions formerly held by men.

These very real achievements had been won by a movement that was successful only so long as large numbers of women remained committed to each other and to common goals. This collective commitment had secured the vote and corrected some of the wrongs associated with women's exclusion from full participation in the public sphere of ballot box and marketplace. Few suffragists and reformers, however, were any more prepared to confront the barriers to equality in the domestic sphere of family than they were to dismantle racial barriers. Most women as well as men still accepted as one of the few unchanging facts of life the conviction that woman's primary duty was to be "helpmate, housewife, and mother." Feminists who hoped to provide additional, complementary, or alternative possibilities gradually found themselves a diminishing minority. Since their understanding of the many kinds of change yet required to ensure full emancipation was shared by so few women, enfranchisement failed to create a bloc of female voters prepared to use the ballot to remove additional barriers to equality. Like their male counterparts, they found issues of class, race, and ethnicity more compelling factors in the voting booth than the need to improve women's status. The collective power of the "woman's vote" through which suffragists had hoped to achieve further gains never fully materialized in the decade ahead.

Part of the reason for this failure lay in the physical and emotional fatigue of the suffragists themselves. The fight for the ballot, compounded by the stress of World War I, had taken its toll. As one suffragist explained: "After we [got] the vote, the crusade was over. It was peacetime and we went back to a hundred different causes and tasks that we'd been putting off all those years. We just demobilized."[3] For those who still had the energy, there were new causes. Pacifism and disarmament acquired an added urgency not only for pre-war pacifists such as Crystal Eastman and Jane Addams but also for more recent enthusiasts such as suffragist leader Carrie Chapman Catt, who established the National Conference on the Cause and Cure of War. Other women, whose feminist sympathies and political activism had been tenuous even in the yeasty reformist milieu of the progressive era, gradually yielded to the political conservatism of the 1920s. They could not be effectively mobilized for protest even when the Supreme Court in 1922 and 1923 invalidated two of the major legislative gains of the pre-war women's movement—minimum wages for women and the abolition of child labor. Younger women who might have become new recruits found old visions of female equality less exciting than the quest for personal fulfillment associated with the relaxed social and sexual mores and affluence of the new consumer culture.

As these and other disappointments mounted, divisions developed within the movement itself. The organizations most responsible for winning the vote, the National American Woman Suffrage Association (NAWSA) and its militant offshoot, the Congressional Union, had regrouped under new names. The Congressional Union, under Alice Paul's leadership, became the National Woman's Party. It enrolled between four and five thousand members, many of them professional women, whose first priority was improvement of women's status. Many NAWSA members moved in a different direction, finding their way into the new League of Women Voters created in 1919 to educate women for citizenship. The League represented the persistence of a broad progressive impulse along with the commitment to the advancement of women. Its bipartisan concern for "good government" and legislation protecting women and children made it the more broadly reformist of the two organizations. Disagreement over tactics during the suffrage campaign continued in the debate over the next tactic in the struggle for equality. The Woman's Party advocated a constitutional amendment to guarantee equality before the law. The League and other organizations—such as the General Federation of Women's Clubs, the Women's Trade Union League, the Young Women's Christian Association, and the American Association of University Women—preferred to deal with the many discriminatory aspects of the law through a state-by-state effort to change specific statutes.

The League's preference derived in part from fears that an equal rights amendment would jeopardize legislation regulating hours, wages, and working conditions for thousands of unskilled, nonunionized female workers. Their health and safety, insisted the League, required the special protection of government. The courts, having denied this legislation to men on the ground that such laws interfered with their "freedom of contract," permitted it to women workers only because of their traditional role as mothers. Women workers, opponents of the amendment argued, could ill afford to surrender concrete gains for the abstract principle of equality.

By the end of the 1920s the League and its allies could point to a few transitory gains in the area of maternal and infant health care and to the easing of legal strictures affecting marriage, divorce, property holding, and contracts. But they failed to shake the unswerving conviction of Woman's Party loyalists that the key to equality lay in amending the Constitution. As a result of these disagreements, intense and acrimonious debate persisted throughout years of fragmentation and frustration. Feminism as an organized mass movement virtually disappeared. To be sure, a loose network of individuals and organizations continued to work to improve the status of women; however, only the Woman's Party, unwavering in its single-minded advocacy of an equal rights amendment, persistently wore the feminist label as a badge of honor. Modest gains in the postsuffrage decades could not obscure the fact that the fundamental circumstances of most women's lives remained little changed.[4]

For working-class women, especially women of color, life was still one of constant toil—on farms, in factories and mills, or in other women's homes. The factory job that had promised escape from poverty or the drudgery of farm work or the servility of domestic service often carried with it new problems. To be sure, increases in productivity during the 1920s allowed a handful of companies to initiate a five-day workweek, the eight-hour day, or a two-week annual vacation with pay. But low wages, long hours, frequent lay-offs, monotony, noise, dirt, and danger still characterized many industrial jobs, especially in the non-unionized South. Moreover, wage work brought no escape from domestic duties.

Middle-class white women fared better than their working-class counterparts. More advantaged economically, they had easier access to birth control devices and to the educational and professional opportunities that would equip them to function in the world outside the home. Yet if progress is measured by achievements in professional, commercial, and political life, middle-class women made few gains in the postsuffrage decades. The proportion of women attending colleges and universities actually declined between 1920 and 1960, as did the proportion of women on college faculties. By 1960 only 4 percent of the lawyers and judges in this nation were women, only 6 percent of the medical doctors, and less than 1 percent of the architects. Percentages, of course, can be misleading in that they indicate a share rather than absolute numbers.[5] In the final analysis, however, there was no escaping the fact that access had not meant parity, even for the most privileged. In certain areas of business, notably real estate, women had increased in both numbers and percentage. But a seat on the Stock Exchange was as difficult to come by as a seat on the president's cabinet. Boards of directors of major corporations were a male preserve. So, too, the higher echelons of government. The number of women elected to Congress throughout this entire forty-year period totaled a mere three in the Senate and forty-four in the House. The number of female cabinet members was a scant two.[6]

UNRESOLVED ISSUES

The discrepancy between early feminists' expectations and the actual accomplishments of women in the postsuffrage decades is a measure of how effectively internal and external barriers interacted to bind white women especially to the traditional pattern of domesticity. That so many rejected the new possibilities of public life for the old expectations of a private one when the former *seemingly* offered more challenging and potentially rewarding options is testimony both to the power of cultural constraints that undermined real freedom of choice and to the reality of external barriers that ensured inequality in the workplace. Although women themselves may have thought they chose "freely," few were actually in a position to do so. Most had grown up in an atmosphere of profound conditioning that from infancy through adulthood assigned individuals of each sex social roles defined essentially by gender.

The cumulative impact of this socialization shaped young women's sense of themselves as females and the options open to them by the time the more fortunate reached college. There, as in high school, the curriculum reinforced established patterns. Students taking home economics courses learned about the tasks that awaited them as consumer, homemaker, and mother. By the 1940s and 1950s many sociology courses portrayed the "normal" family as one based on a sexual division of labor and "sex-determined" behavioral characteristics. If the campus served as an environment within which to pursue a husband rather than an independent intellectual life or preprofessional training, that acknowledged a basic reality. Getting a man, especially one with bright prospects, was itself a vocational objective, one preferable to others.

The reason was that in a labor force segregated by sex as well as race and ethnicity positions filled predominantly by women carried little pay and prestige—to the financial detriment of the few males involved as well as the many females. Fields such as business, engineering, architecture, law, medicine, science, and university teaching were only slightly open to women. Female applicants to professional schools were usually confronted with admission quotas limiting the number of women, often to 5 percent. University faculties frequently assumed that female students would marry, get pregnant, and drop out, or, if they did graduate, never practice the profession for which they had been trained. Those young women who persisted, ultimately receiving the Ph.D. or the M.D., could expect continued discrimination in hiring, pay, or promotion once their active work life began.

They also had to face the problem of combining work and family in a society governed by traditional assumptions relating to both. Many business and professional women in the early years of the twentieth century solved the problem by staying single. Successive generations, less attracted to that option, had to find husbands willing to have a spouse pursue an active work life outside the home in an era in which a working wife was thought to reflect poorly on a man's ability to provide for his family. Those who were able to do so had to contend with still other problems. Nagging fears that successful careers were inconsistent with marital happiness—at least for women— found reinforcement in Hollywood movies, women's magazines, and scholarly studies. The conventional assumption that an achieving woman would lose "her chance for the kind of love she wants" was criticized by the anthropologist Margaret Mead in 1935 to no avail.[7] In a society in which the normative ideology of middle-class Americans reinforced such assumptions, women whose personal and professional lives provided refutation were simply too few to make a difference.

Parenting complicated the situation even further, creating practical problems and compounding internal anxieties. To be a lawyer and a father in America was to be "normal"; to be a lawyer and a mother was to be "deviant" because motherhood was assumed to be a full-time occupation, especially in middle-class circles. How to cope with the physical and psychological demands of family while simultaneously meeting the performance criteria and competitive pressures of work challenged even the most dedicated and resourceful woman. Pregnancy and child care leaves, tax benefits for child care expenses, public day care centers with strong programs to encourage physical and intellectual growth: these measures had become well established in advanced European nations such as Sweden. But they were never fully incorporated into the structure of American society during the first three-quarters of this century.

Families, too, were ill prepared to accommodate the special needs of women who worked outside the home. With kin networks often scattered about in distant cities and towns, it was difficult to find a grandparent or aunt who could take care of children during an emergency. Husbands, even when supportive in principle, often proved reluctant in practice to assume additional responsibilities at home.

The assumption that family responsibilities would not interfere with work efficiency was built into the very structure of their jobs, as was the expectation that the corporate manager, for example, would have at his disposal a wife who could devote significant time and energy to the needs of *his* career.

For the vast majority of middle-class women the problems of combining a professional career and family were simply too great. Moreover, their social position was such that most of the working women they knew—clerks, waitresses, domestics—were lower-middle and working-class people. *Not* working for pay outside the home indicated the high status so important to millions of Americans. As internal constraints and external constraints reinforced each other, most middle-class women concluded that they would have a better chance for security and status as wives and mothers than as workers.

There were, to be sure, achieving women whose lives were not defined only by domesticity—Helen Keller, Amelia Earhart, Mary McLeod Bethune, and Eleanor Roosevelt. But this was a culture that, while celebrating the "exceptional woman" and urging all women to work for community betterment, endlessly extolled the joys of the housewife-mother who lovingly tended her garden and a bumper crop of children. Even the heroines hawked by Hollywood in the 1950s fell into two categories: sex objects and wives. Gone were the brainy, resourceful, independent working women of an earlier era; depicted in their stead were lonely, frustrated neurotics whose unhappiness signaled the futility of sacrificing home and children for career.

THE GROWING GAP BETWEEN IDEOLOGY AND REALITY

The apparent retreat from feminism into domesticity after 1920 hid a more complex reality. Impersonal economic, scientific, and demographic forces were subtly undermining old patterns and assumptions. Although in themselves these new developments did not produce a resurgence of feminism, they did add impetus to the growing gap between conventional attitudes and changing conditions. This in turn lent credibility to a feminist critique of society.

One of the economic realties of modern America has been that many women were never fully in their "place"—the home. They have long been part of a paid labor force (see graph on percentage of men and women in the labor force, 1890–2000, at page 562). Their numbers increased significantly throughout the twentieth century. Even during the Depression the proportion of women in the work force remained constant, hovering around 25 percent. This occurred despite the fact that many employers, including local school boards and the federal civil service, sought to deny employment to married women, assuming, often mistakenly, that their husband's earnings were adequate to support the family and that, as working women, they took jobs away from other men with families to support. But if hard times forced some women back into the home, others were forced out. Many mothers desperately needed even meager wages to keep the family afloat at a time when one out of every five children in this country was not getting enough nourishing food to eat.

As the nation shifted from fighting economic depression to waging global war, women responded by the millions to patriotic appeals to get a war job so as to bring their men home sooner. Between 1940 and 1945 the proportion of women in the work force rose to 37 percent. Money as well as patriotism was involved. The women who flocked to factories were beneficiaries of New Deal legislation governing wages and hours for both sexes. They also benefited from the Congress of Industrial Organizations' (CIO) successful unionization effort during the 1930s and became the first generation of female industrial employees to receive good wages. Not surprisingly many were reluctant to return home when "Rosie the Riveter," that symbol of women war workers, was told to put down her riveting machine at the return of peace. Forced out of well-paying "male" jobs, many women returned to low-paying "female" jobs in restaurants, laundries, shops, and offices. Moreover, their wartime experience seemingly had little impact on public attitudes. When asked whether married women whose husbands made enough to support them should be allowed to hold jobs if they wanted to, the majority of Americans responded with a resounding no.[8] Yet as white-collar and clerical jobs expanded rapidly in the post-war years, so did the number of working women.[9]

By 1960 some 40 percent of American women were employed in full- or part-time jobs. Moreover, those who worked outside the home were no longer predominantly young, single, or poor. Nearly half were mothers of school-age children; many of them were middle class. When asked why they worked most responded that they regarded their jobs as an extension of family responsibilities as well as a matter of economic need. A second salary made possible a family vacation, a large home better suited to the children's needs, savings for college tuition, or simply a color television set for the family room. During the period when all America seemed about to become one great shopping mall, the definition of economic need was clearly changing. But even if one allows for a rising level of expectations consistent with the consumer culture of the 1950s as well as a higher inflation rate, the fact remains that, while rhetoric still conformed to the old domestic ideology, the growing presence of women in the work force did not.

The gap between the old ideology of home and family and the new reality of office and work widened still further as medical advances resulted in improved birth control devices and longer life expectancy. Referring to the extent to which women's lives had been determined by their reproductive role, Sigmund Freud had observed that "anatomy is destiny." But as women gained the ability to control "destiny"—to decide whether to have children, when, and how many—they were no longer victims of biological processes (see graph on American birth rates at page 563). Use of condoms and diaphragms, widespread especially among middle-class couples, made birth control a reality even before the introduction in 1960 of an oral contraceptive—"the pill." As medical science also devised new weapons against disease, the non-childbearing years during which one could expect to function as a healthy, active adult increased accordingly.

The implications were enormous. That they were not immediately grasped is not surprising for a generation seeking in the private world of home and family the security unavailable in a public world wracked successively by economic depression, world war, and the threat of global annihilation. Throughout the 1950s, family experts emphasized the impor-

tance of early marriage and motherhood if the "atomic age" family were to be a bulwark of morality and stability. Specialists in marketing techniques continued to fuse the role of homemaker and mother with that of consumer, stressing that true feminine fulfillment lay in maternity, domesticity, and purchase of the "right" products. Yet by glorifying women as homemakers and mothers at precisely the same time important changes were occurring that served to undermine those roles, advertisers, like the family experts, were unwittingly helping to sharpen the dissonance between the domestic myth and the new reality of many women's lives.

The gap between reality and the dominant ideology, often present for many minority women, now existed for women who were both white and middle class. It was a gap that could be ignored initially because it was a "bad fit"—a size six foot in a five-and-one-half shoe—a small discomfort with which people thought they could live. Yet even as more women felt the pinch, they still had difficulty seeing themselves as permanent members of the work force. Many seemed reluctant to join unions or press for equal treatment in the workplace, perhaps because they saw themselves as supplementary breadwinners or as housewives whom misfortune had trapped in monotonous, low-paying jobs.[10] Or perhaps they knew that most unions tended to marginalize women, denying them equal access to positions of leadership within the union and excluding gender equality as a demand in collective bargaining agendas.[11] That so many women continued to see themselves and their work primarily as serving family needs is hardly surprising in a culture in which their rights to participate in the labor force was contested and homemaking was described as "the most important and difficult profession any woman can have."[12] But the bad fit was there. So, too, was the unfairness of unequal pay for the same or comparable work, the low value placed on jobs women performed, the double burden of housework and wage work. Those women who felt the growing discomfort needed a new way of looking at things that would allow them to examine afresh the condition of their lives, moving from endurance of painful inequities to confrontation and change. They needed, in short, a feminist consciousness.

THE CREATION OF A FEMINIST CONSCIOUSNESS

Revolutions are seldom started by the powerless. The revolution of mainstream feminists was no exception. It was begun largely by educated, middle-class women whose diverse experiences had sharpened their sensitivity to the fundamental inequality between the sexes at a time when America had been thrust into the throes of self-examination by a movement for racial equality. Some were young veterans of the civil rights movement and the New Left, steeped in a commitment to equality and the techniques of protest. Others were young professionals increasingly aware of their secondary status. Still others were older women who in their long careers as professionals or as activists had used organizations such as the American Civil Liberties Union (ACLU), the Young Women's Christian Association (YWCA) and the United Auto Workers (UAW) to fight sex-based discrimination. Included, too, were those whose outwardly conformist lives belied an intense awareness of the malaise of domesticity and the untenably narrow boundaries of their prescribed roles. To explore how they came self-consciously to appraise women's condition as one demanding collective action is to explore the process of radicalization that helped to create a new feminist movement.

In its early state, a major component of that movement consisted of two different groups—women's rights advocates and women's liberationists. Although the differences between the two groups began to blur as the movement matured, initial distinctions were sharp. Women's rights advocates were likely to have been older, to have had professional training or work experience, to have been more inclined to form or join organized feminist groups. Reform oriented, these organizations used traditional pressure group tactics to achieve changes in laws and public policy that would guarantee women equal rights. Emphasis on ''rights'' meant extending to women in life outside the home the same ''rights'' men had, granting them the same options, privileges, and responsibilities that men enjoyed. There was little suggestion initially of personal or cultural transformation.

Women's liberationists were younger women, less highly educated, whose ideology and political style, shaped in the dissent and violence of the 1960s, led them to look at women's predicament differently. Instead of relying upon traditional organizational structure and lobbying techniques, they developed a new style of politics. Instead of limiting their goals to changes in public policy, they embraced a transformation in private, domestic life as well. They sought liberation from ways of thinking and behaving that they believed stunted or distorted women's growth and kept them subordinate to men. Through the extension of their own personal liberation they hoped to remake the male world, changing it as they had changed themselves. For women's liberationists as for women's rights advocates, however, the first step toward becoming feminists demanded a clear statement of women's position in society, one that called attention to the gap between the egalitarian ideal and the actual position of women in American culture. There also had to be a call to action from women themselves, *for* women, *with* women, *through* women. Redefining themselves, they had to make being a woman a political fact; and, as they did so, they had to live with the radical implications of what could only be called a rebirth.

The Making of Liberal Feminists: Women's Rights Advocates

For some women, the process of radicalization began with the appointment of a Presidential Commission on the Status of Women in 1961. Presidents, Democrat and Republican, customarily discharged their political debt to female members of the electorate, especially to those who had loyally served the party, by appointing a few token women, usually party stalwarts, to highly visible posts. John Kennedy was no exception. He was, however, convinced by Esther Peterson, the highest-ranking woman in his administration, that the vast majority of women would be better served if he also appointed a commission charged with investigating obstacles to the full participation of women in society. Peterson, who was assistant secretary of labor and head of the Women's Bureau, believed that the report of such a commission could sensitize the public to barriers to equality just as her own experience as a labor organizer had sensitized her to the particular problems confronting women workers. Citizens thus informed could then be mobilized on behalf of governmental efforts at reform.[13] Accordingly, the commission was appointed with Eleanor Roosevelt serving as chair until her death a year later. Its report, *American Women* (1963), was conservative in tone, acknowledging the importance of women's traditional roles within the home and the progress they had made in a "free democratic society." Acknowledging also that women were an underutilized resource that the nation could ill afford to ignore, the report provided extensive documentation of discriminatory practices in government, education, and employment, along with substantial recommendations for change.[14] Governors, replicating Kennedy's move, appointed state commissions on the status of women. In these commissions hundreds of men and women encountered further evidence of the economic, social, and legal disabilities that encumbered the nation's "second sex." For some, the statistics were old news; for others, they were a revelation.

Although there were variations from state to state, the pattern documented by the North Carolina Commission soon became increasingly familiar to a small but growing number of women throughout the nation. According to that commission's report, women workers, who made up over one-third of the state's labor force, suffered economically from job segregation and pay inequities. Of the 600,000 women employed outside the home in 1960, most (68 percent) were concentrated in blue-collar jobs or in traditionally low-paying "female" professions such as teaching and nursing. Whatever their occupational level, women earned significantly less than their male counterparts with comparable skills, experience, and responsibilities. They also had fewer opportunities for advancement. (Female mill operatives, for example, earned nearly 30 percent less than male operatives.)

Educational experience, seemingly more equitable, actually foreshadowed economic inequities. At the graduate level, women constituted only a tiny fraction of those enrolled in schools training future members of high-paying professions such as medicine. At the undergraduate level, female students clustered in the humanities, avoiding the math and science courses necessary for providing greater career choice. Whatever their educational level, most women lacked access to diversified vocational training, enlightened career guidance, and the

kind of role models provided by women, especially minority women, holding important nontraditional jobs. Worse still, they lacked expert, readily available child care. (Licensed day care facilities had only one space available for every seventeen preschool children of working mothers.)

Legally, women in North Carolina, as elsewhere, were handicapped not only by hundreds of discriminatory federal statutes but also by state laws denying them equal treatment under the law. For example, married women still lacked complete control over their own property; state law required the written assent of the husband before a wife could convey her real property to someone else. Nor did women function as political equals. In North Carolina, as in other states, women were less likely to vote than men and far less likely to hold elective office or significant policy-making jobs. Especially disturbing to the commission was the failure of most women to understand "the direct connection between their own active and informed participation in politics . . . and the solution to many of their most pressing problems."[15]

Some women, however, could make that connection. Aroused by growing evidence of "the enormity of our problem," members of state commissions gathered in Washington in 1966 for the Third National Conference of the Commissions on the Status of Women. Individuals who were coming to know and rely on one another as they pooled their growing knowledge of widespread inequities, they were a network in the making. They were also women who wanted something done. This time they encountered a situation that transformed at least some of those present into activists in a new movement for women's equality. The catalyst proved to be a struggle involving Representative Martha Griffiths and the Equal Employment Opportunity Commission (EEOC), the federal agency in charge of implementing the Civil Rights Act of 1964.

Despite the fact that the law proscribed discrimination on the basis of sex as well as race, the commission refused to take seriously the problem of sexual discrimination. The first executive director of EEOC, believing that "sex" had been injected into the bill by opponents seeking to block its passage, regarded the sex provision as a "fluke" best ignored. Representative Griffiths from Michigan thought otherwise. While the bill was still in Congress she encouraged a small group of women in the House to become part of an unlikely alliance with legislative opponents of a federal civil rights act in order to keep the sex provision in the bill. Liberals objected, fearing that so encumbering a bill would prevent passage of much-needed legislation on behalf of racial equality. But despite such objections—and the ridicule of many of her male colleagues—Griffiths persisted. She urged her fellow representatives not to give black women and men advantages which white women were denied. A racist appeal, it revealed the exclusivity of Griffiths's vision of sisterhood. Her commitment to the sex provision, however, was unqualified. Once the bill passed she was determined to see the new law enforced in its entirety. When EEOC failed to do so, she lambasted the agency for its inaction in a biting speech delivered on the House floor only days before the Conference of the Commissions on the Status of Women met.

Griffiths's concern was shared by a group of women working within EEOC. Echoing an argument made the year before by a black trade unionist in the Women's Bureau,[16] they insisted that the agency could be made to take gender-related discrimination more seriously if women had a civil rights organization as adept at applying pressure on their behalf as was the National Association for the Advancement of Colored People (NAACP) on behalf of blacks. Initially the idea was rejected. Conference participants most upset by EEOC's inaction decided instead to propose a resolution urging the agency to treat sexual discrimination with the same seriousness it applied to racial discrimination. When the resolution was ruled inappropriate by conference leaders, they were forced to reconsider. After a whispered conversation over lunch they concluded the time for discussion of the status of women was over. It was time for action. Before the day was out twenty-eight women had paid five dollars each to join the National Organization for Women (NOW), including author Betty Friedan, who happened to be in Washington at the time of the conference.[17]

Friedan's presence in Washington was auspicious; her involvement in NOW, virtually inevitable. The author of a brilliant polemic published in 1963, she not only labeled the resurgent domestic ideology of recent decades but exposed the groups perpetuating it. Editors of women's magazines, advertising experts, Freudian psychologists, social scientists, and educators—all, according to Friedan, contributed to a romanticization of domesticity she termed "the feminine mystique." The result, she charged, was the infantilization of intelligent women and the transformation of the suburban home into a "comfortable concentration camp."[18] Harsh words, they rang true to those who found the creativity of homemaking and the joys of motherhood vastly exaggerated. Sales of the book ultimately zoomed past the million mark.

By articulating heretofore inarticulated grievances, *The Feminine Mystique* had advanced a process initiated by more dispassionate investigations of women's status and the discriminatory practices which made that status inferior. That process was the collective expression of discontent. It is not surprising that the voices initially heard were those of women who were overwhelmingly white, educated, and middle or upper middle class. College women who regarded themselves the equals of male classmates by virtue of intellect and training were, as Jo Freeman points out, more likely to develop expectations they saw realized by their male peers but not, in most cases, by themselves. The frustrations were even greater for women with professional training. The very fact that many had sought advanced training in fields not traditionally "female" meant that they were less likely to find in traditional gender roles the identity and self-esteem such roles provided other women. Moreover, when measuring themselves against fellow professionals who happened to be men, the greater rewards enjoyed by their white male counterparts seemed especially galling. Privileged though they were, such women *felt* more deprived in many cases than did those women who were in reality less privileged. By 1966 this sense of deprivation had been sufficiently articulated and shared and the networks of like-minded women sufficiently developed so that collective discontent could be translated into collective action. The formation of NOW signaled a feminist resurgence.[19]

The three hundred men and women who gathered in October for the organizational meeting of NOW included mainly professionals, some of them veterans of commissions on the status of women as well as a few feminist union activists, notably Dorothy Haener. Adopting bylaws and a statement of purpose, they elected officers, naming Friedan president. Her conviction that intelligent women needed purposeful, generative work of their own was reflected in NOW's statement of purpose, which attacked "the traditional assumption that a woman has to choose between marriage and motherhood on the one hand and serious participation in industry or the professions on the other." Determined that women should be allowed to develop their full potential as human beings, the organization's goal was to bring them into "full participation in the mainstream of American society NOW, exercising all the privileges and responsibilities thereof in truly equal partnership with men." To that end NOW developed a Bill of Rights, adopted at its 1967 meeting, that exhorted Congress to pass an equal rights amendment to the Constitution, called on EEOC to enforce antidiscrimination legislation, and urged federal and state legislators to guarantee equal and unsegregated education. To ensure women control over their reproductive lives, these new feminists called for removal of penal codes denying women contraceptive information and devices as well as safe, legal abortions. To ease the double burden of working mothers, they urged legislation that would ensure maternity leaves without jeopardizing job security or seniority, permit tax deductions for child care expenses, and create public, inexpensive day care centers. To improve the lot of poor women, they urged reform of the welfare system and equality with respect to benefits, including job-training programs.[20]

Not content simply to call for change, NOW leaders, following the lead of equality advocates within the labor movement, worked to make it happen. Using persuasion, pressure, and even litigation, they, with other newly formed women's rights groups such as the Women's Equity Action League (WEAL), launched a massive attack on sex discrimination. By the end of the 1960s NOW members had filed legal suits against newspapers listing jobs under the headings "Help Wanted: Male" and "Help Wanted: Female," successfully arguing that such headings discouraged women from applying for jobs they were perfectly capable of doing. Building on efforts begun in the Kennedy administration such as the passage of the Equal Pay Act, they pressured the federal

government to intensify its commitment to equal opportunity. They urged congressmen and labor leaders to persuade the Department of Labor to include women in its guidelines designed to encourage the hiring and promotion of blacks in firms holding contracts with the federal government. They persuaded the Federal Communications Commission to open up new opportunities for women in broadcasting. Tackling the campus as well as the marketplace, WEAL filed suit against more than three hundred colleges and universities, ultimately securing millions of dollars in salary raises for women faculty members who had been victims of discrimination. To ensure that women receive the same pay men received for doing the same work, these new feminists lobbied for passage of a new Equal Employment Opportunity Act that would enable EEOC to fight discrimination more effectively.

NOW also scrutinized the discriminatory practices of financial institutions, persuading them to issue credit to single women and to married women in their own—not their husband's—name. WEAL, in turn, filed charges against banks and other lending institutions that refused to grant mortgages to single women, or in the case of married couples, refused to take into account the wife's earnings in evaluating the couple's eligibility for a mortgage. Colleges and universities that discriminated against female students in their sports programs came under fire, as did fellowship programs that failed to give adequate consideration to female applicants.

While NOW and WEAL attacked barriers in industry and education, the National Women's Political Caucus (NWPC) focused on government and politics. Formed in 1971, the caucus was initiated by Friedan, New York congresswomen Bella Abzug and Shirley Chisholm—both outspoken champions of women's rights—and Gloria Steinem, soon to become founding editor of the new mass-circulation feminist magazine *Ms*. Abzug, a lawyer and veteran activist for peace and civil rights, and Chisholm, the first black woman elected to Congress, were especially concerned about the small numbers of women in government. Accordingly the caucus concentrated on getting women elected and appointed to public office while also rallying support for issues such as the Equal Rights Amendment (see p. 589). Meanwhile women in the professions, aware of their small numbers and inferior status, began to organize as well. Physicians, lawyers, and university professors fought for equal opportunity in the meetings of such overwhelmingly male groups as the American Medical Association, the American Association of University Professors, and the American Historical Association.[21] Union women also mobilized. In 1974, three thousand women from fifty-eight unions attended the founding convention of the Coalition of Labor Union Women (CLUW), resolving to fight for equality in the workplace and within organized labor.

Collectively such protests served notice that more women were becoming radicalized. The particular combination of events that transformed these women into feminists varied with the individual. A southern legislator, describing the process that brought home the reality of her own second-class citizenship, wrote:

> As a State Senator, I succeeded in getting Mississippi women the right to sit on juries (1968); the opposition's arguments were appalling. When women began hiring me in order to get credit, I became upset at the discrimination I saw. After I was divorced in 1970, I was initially denied a home loan. The effect was one of the worst traumas I've suffered. Denial of a home loan to one who was both a professional and a member of the legislature brought things to a head.[22]

Although the number of women who understood what it meant to be the "second sex" were still only a tiny minority, they were nonetheless a minority whose energy, talents, and experience enabled them to work for changes necessary to ensure equal rights.

THE MAKING OF RADICAL FEMINISTS: WOMEN'S LIBERATIONISTS

The process of radicalization that transformed some individuals into liberal feminists occurred simultaneously—but in different fashion and with somewhat different results— among a younger generation of women who were also predominantly white and middle class. Many of them veterans of either the civil rights movement or of the New Left, these were the activists who would initially become identified as women's liberationists. Differing in perspective as well as style, they would ultimately push many of their older counterparts beyond the demand for equal rights to recog-

nition that true emancipation would require a far-reaching transformation of society and culture.

The experiences awakening in this 1960s generation a feminist consciousness have been superbly described by Sara Evans in her book, *Personal Politics*.[23] "Freedom, equality, love and hope," the possibility of new human relationships, the importance of participatory democracy—letting the people decide—were, as Evans points out, part of an egalitarian ideology shared by both the southern-based Student Nonviolent Coordinating Committee (SNCC) in its struggle for racial equality and the Students for Democratic Society (SDS) in its efforts to mobilize an interracial organization of the urban poor in northern ghettos. Membership in both organizations—"the movement"—thus reinforced commitment to these ideals among the women who joined. In order to translate ideals into reality, however, young, college-age women who had left the shelter of middle-class families for the hard and dangerous work of transforming society found themselves doing things that they would never have thought possible. Amidst the racial strife of the South, they joined picket lines, created freedom schools, and canvassed for voter registration among blacks, often enduring arrest and jailing. SDS women from affluent suburbs entered decaying tenements and were surrounded by the grim realities of the ghetto. They trudged door-to-door in an effort to reach women whose struggle to survive made many understandably suspicious of intruding strangers. In the process, not only did these young activists achieve a heightened sense of self-worth and autonomy, they also learned the skills of movement building and the nuts and bolts of organizing.

Particularly important was the problem of getting people, long passive, to act on their own behalf. SDS women began by encouraging ghetto women to come together to talk about their problems. This sharing of experiences, they believed, would lead these women to recognize not only that their problems were common but that solutions required changes in the system. In the process of organizing, the organizers also learned. They began to understand the meaning of oppression and the valor required of those who fought it. They found new role models, Evans suggests, in extraordinary southern black women whose courage seemed never to waiver in the face of violence and in those welfare mothers of the North who confronted welfare bureaucrat and slum lord after years of passivity.

But if being in the movement brought a new understanding of equality, it also brought new problems. Men who were committed to equality for one group were not necessarily committed to equality for another group. Women in SNCC, as in SDS, found themselves frequently relegated to domestic chores and treated as sex objects, denied most leadership positions, and refused a key voice in the formulation of policy. Moreover, the sexual freedom that had been theirs as part of the cultural revolution taking place in the 1960s soon began to feel more like sexual exploitation as they saw their role in the movement spelled out in the draft resister's slogan: "Girls Say Yes to Guys Who Say No." Efforts to change the situation were firmly rebuffed. When SNCC leader Stokely Carmichael joked that the only "position for women in SNCC is prone," he encapsulated views which, while not his own, reflected all too accurately the feelings of males in the New Left as well as many in SNCC.[24]

By 1967 the tensions had become so intense that white women left the movement to organize on behalf of their own "liberation." Black women stayed, resolving to work for change from within and give voice to their own priorities.

The women who left did not leave empty-handed. As radicals, they were impatient with liberalism, critical of capitalism, and profoundly suspicious of authority. Accustomed to challenging prevailing ideas and practices, they had acquired a language of protest, an organizing tactic, and a deep-seated conviction that the personal was political. How that legacy would shape this burgeoning new feminist movement became evident as small women's liberation groups began springing up spontaneously in major cities and university communities across the nation.

STRUCTURE, LEADERSHIP, AND CONSCIOUSNESS-RAISING

Initially, at least, the two branches of mainstream feminism seemed almost to be two different movements, so unlike were they in structure and style. Linked only by newsletters, notices in underground newspapers, and networks of friends, women's liberation groups rejected both traditional organizational structure and leadership. Unlike NOW and the other women's rights groups associated with liberal feminism, they had no central headquarters, no elected officers, no bylaws. There was no legislative agenda and little of the activism that transformed the more politically astute women's rights leaders into skilled lobbyists and tacticians. Instead this younger generation of feminists, organizing new groups wherever they found themselves, concentrated on a kind of personal politics rooted in movement days. Looking back on male-dominated meetings in which, however informal the gathering, a few highly verbal, aggressive men invariably controlled debate and dictated strategy and left less articulate and assertive women effectively excluded, they recalled the technique they had used in organizing the poor. They remembered how they had encouraged those women to talk among themselves until the personal became political, that is, until problems which, at first glance, seemed to be personal were finally understood to be social in cause—rooted in society rather than in the individual—and political in solution. Applying this same process in their own informal "rap groups," women's liberationists developed the technique of "consciousness-raising." Adopted by women's rights groups such as local chapters of NOW, consciousness-raising sessions became one of the most important innovations of mainstream feminism.[25]

The immediate task of the consciousness-raising session was to bring together in a caring, supportive, noncompetitive setting women accustomed to relating most intimately not with other women but with men—husbands, lovers, "friends." As these women talked among themselves, exchanging confidences, reassessing old options, and mentally exploring new ones, a sense of shared problems began to emerge. The women themselves gradually gained greater understanding of how profoundly their lives had been shaped by the constraints of culture. Personal experience with those constraints merged with intellectual awareness of women's inferior status and the factors that made it so. By the same token, new understanding of problems generated new determination to resolve them. Anger, aggression, and frustration formerly turned inward in unconscious self-hatred began to be directed outward, becoming transformed into new energy directed toward constructive goals. If society and culture had defined who women were through their unconscious internalization of tradition, they could reverse the process, and, by redefining themselves, redefine society and culture. Or, to put it another way, if woman was a *social construct*—the product not so much of biology, but of what people in a particular society and culture believed to be the implications of biology—then women themselves would re-create the construct. At work was a process of discovery so radicalizing that the individuals undergoing it ultimately emerged in a very real sense as different people. Now feminists, these were women with a different understanding of reality—a new "consciousness," a new sense of "sisterhood," and a new commitment to change.

Consciousness-raising was an invigorating and sometimes frightening experience. As one young woman wrote, "This whole movement is the most exhilarating thing of my life. The last eight months have been a personal revolution. Nonetheless, I recognize there is dynamite in this and I'm scared shitless."[26] "Scared" or not, such women could no longer be contained. Veterans of one rap group fanned out, creating others, often with arresting names such as Cell 16, the Furies, Redstockings, or simply Radical Women. For the feminist movement, this mushrooming of groups meant increased numbers and added momentum. For some of the women involved, it meant confronting and articulating theoretically as well as personally what "oppression," "sexism," and "liberation" really meant: in short, developing a feminist ideology.

TOWARD A FEMINIST IDEOLOGY: OPPRESSION, SEXISM, AND CHANGE

To explain the significance of the discovery that woman is a *social construct* and that subordination was built into that construct was no simple process. The concept itself was complex. Moreover, women's rights advocates who were essentially pragmatic were more interested in practical results than in theoretical explanations. Even among women's liberationists who were far more theoretically oriented and ideologically fractious, intellectual perspectives reflected differences in experience, temperament, style, and politics. Manifestos, po-

sition papers, and books began to pile up as liberationists searched for the historical origins of female oppression. Those whose primary loyalty was still to the New Left—soon dubbed "politicos"—attributed women's oppression to capitalism. Others, who would come to be known as socialist-feminists, insisted that both male supremacy and capitalism were responsible for women's subordination and that feminists must be allied with, but apart from, the left. Still other liberationists argued that male supremacy, not class or race, was the more fundamental and universal form of oppression and that women as a group constituted an oppressed class. Known as radical feminists, their emphasis on the primacy of gender would prevail, although it would be ultimately challenged by feminists of color. In the meantime, however, radical feminists' identification of the family as the basic unit in the system of oppression led to new debates among radical feminists themselves. If marriage as an intersexual alliance divided women, leading them to identify with the oppressor from whom they derived economic advantages rather than each other, ought marriage to be abolished? If so, what new structure should take its place? Pushing the logic of this position, lesbian feminists argued that the ultimate rejection of male domination required not just the rejection of marriage, but the rejection of sexual intimacy with men. Other radical feminists, seeking to desexualize lesbianism, argued that sexual behavior—who one slept with—was less important than being "woman identified." Still others insisted that heterosexual relationships were essential: men should be reformed, not abandoned. Feminists familiar with role theory pointed to sex-based role differentiation as a source of oppression, arguing that work and family roles should be restructured in ways that would encourage greater mutuality and fulfillment for both sexes. Other feminists argued that personality—men and women's psychic identity—were also overly differentiated by sex. Only by merging role and personality characteristics of both sexes within each individual could androgynous men and women be developed and real liberation achieved.[27]

Given the great variety of perspectives and positions even among women's liberationists alone, it is impossible to talk about *a* feminist ideology to which all those who identified with the women's movement subscribed. The ascendancy of radical feminism among women's liberationists in the early 1970s and the eventual embrace of many of their insights by liberal feminists, however, does make it possible to talk about a common conceptual framework shared by mainstream feminists. Most believed that *gender hierarchy* is a primary factor essential to any understanding of why women *as a group* suffer from an unequal distribution of power and resources in a society. They agreed that men have been the dominant sex and that women as a group are subordinate. While not all mainstream feminists were comfortable talking about a *system* of oppression or even using the word "oppression," they were quick to list the many areas where inequities were—and still are—evident.

At the top of the list was the economy. Men, they agreed, are more likely to be economically independent than women because the latter work within the home where their labor has no monetary value and/or outside the home in sex-segregated jobs for wages too meager to ensure economic self-sufficiency. Society and culture also provided numerous examples of the higher status, greater options, and greater power conferred upon men by virtue of their sex. Just as traditional male roles provide access to power and independence, whereas female roles do not, so, feminists pointed out, masculine values define what attributes are admired and rewarded. The very fact that strength, competence, independence, and rationality are considered masculine values, that they are more highly regarded by both sexes, *and* that they constitute the standard by which mental health is judged these new feminists found revealing indeed. The problem, they insisted, is not simply that the qualities themselves, intrinsically neither "male" or "female," are the product of gender socialization. It is the preference, conscious and unconscious, for whatever society regards as "masculine" that is so persistent and so objectionable—a preference feminists termed *sexism*.

Sexism, they believed, is persistent, pervasive, and powerful. It is internalized by women as well as men. It is most dramatically evident in the programmed-to-please women who search for happiness through submissiveness to men and in the men who use their power to limit women's options and keep them dependent. It is also evident in a more subtle fashion among women who emulate male models and values, refusing to see those aspects of women's lives that are positive and life-affirming, and among men who are unaware of the unconscious sexism permeating their attitudes and actions. Internalized in individuals, sexism is also embedded in institutions—the family, the education system, the media, the economy, politics, law, organized religion, language, and sexual morality.

Given the pervasiveness of sexism, many feminists saw no possibility for real equality short of transformation not only of individuals but also of social institutions and cultural values. Even what was once seen as the relatively simple demand of women's rights advocates for equal pay for equal work no longer looked so simple. What seemed to be a matter of obtaining equal rights *within* the existing system in reality demanded changes that *transform* the system. Involved was:

> a reevaluation of women as workers, of women as mothers, of mothers as workers, of work as suitable for one gender and not for the other. The demand implies equal opportunity and thus equal responsibilities. It implies a childhood in which girls are rewarded for competence, risk taking, achievement, competitiveness and independence—just like boys. Equal pay for equal work means a revision in our expectations about women as equal workers and it involves the institutional arrangements to make them so.

"There is nothing small here," a feminist scholar observed.[28] And indeed there was not.

FEMINISM IN ACTION

While mainstream feminism contains under its broad umbrella women who differ significantly in the degree of their radicalism, the changes implied in achieving sexual equality are of such scope as to make radical by definition those who genuinely understand what is involved in equality and, beyond that, emancipation.[29] To change self and society so that all women can achieve legal, economic, and social parity requires courage, energy, and commitment—commitment that has to be sustained over time and through defeat. To fundamentally restructure private and public life so as to benefit both sexes constitutes an even greater challenge. Yet despite the obstacles, millions of women during the past decades have participated in the process.

For some the changes have consisted largely of private actions—relationships renegotiated, careers resumed. Others, preferring to make public statements of new commitments, used flamboyant methods to dramatize the subtle ways in which society so defined woman's place as to deny not only her full participation but also her full humanity. As part of the confrontational politics of the 1960s, radical feminists picketed the 1968 Miss America contest, protesting the commercialization of beauty and our national preoccupation with bust size and "congeniality" rather than brain power and character. (In the process they were dubbed "bra burners," despite the fact that no bras were burned.) Activists pushed their way into all-male bars and restaurants as a way of forcing recognition of how these bastions of male exclusivity were themselves statements about "man's world/woman's place." They sat in at the offices of *Ladies' Home Journal* and *Newsweek* protesting the ways in which the media's depiction of women perpetuated old stereotypes at the expense of new realities. They demonstrated on behalf of legalized abortion, arguing that the right to terminate unwanted pregnancy is essential if women are to control the direction of their lives.

Still other feminists chose to work for social change in a different fashion. They created nonsexist day care centers, wrote and published nonsexist children's books, monitored sex stereotyping in textbooks, lobbied for women's studies programs in high schools and colleges, and founded women's health clinics. They formed rape crisis centers so that rape victims could be treated by caring females; they agitated for more informed, sympathetic treatment on the part of hospital staffs, the police, and the courts. They created shelters for battered women, insisting that physical abuse was not a private family matter but a social problem requiring a public response. Feminists also lobbied for programs to retrain displaced homemakers so that such women could move from economic dependency to self-support. Feminist scholars used their talents to recover and interpret women's experience, opening new areas for research and in the process furthering change. Feminist legislators, especially black Congresswoman Shirley Chisholm, sponsored legislation to extended minimum wage coverage to domestic workers. Other lawmakers sponsored bills, not always successful, to help

housewives to secure some form of economic recognition for work performed, to enable women workers to obtain insurance that would give them the same degree of economic security afforded male coworkers, and to secure for battered women protection from the physical violence that is the most blatant form of male oppression. Black feminists, speaking out on the "double jeopardy" of being black and female—"the most pressed down of us all"—lent their support to feminist measures of especial importance to minority women.[30] Trade union feminists, concerned about their dual oppression as wage workers and as women, struggled to keep the needs of working women in the forefront. Actions, like voices, differed. Such diversity, however, was basic to the movement.

FEMINISM: THE PUBLIC IMPACT

In a society in which the media create instant awareness of social change, feminism burst upon the public consciousness with all the understated visibility of a fireworks display on the Fourth of July. The more radical elements of the movement, with their talk of test tube conception, the slavery of marriage, and the downfall of capitalism, might be dismissed out of hand. But it was hard to ignore 50,000 women parading down New York's Fifth Avenue, the presence of *Ms.* magazine on newsstands, feminist books on the best-seller lists, women in hard hats on construction jobs, or the government-mandated affirmative action programs that put them there. It was harder still to ignore the publicity that accompanied the appointment of women to the Carter cabinet, the enrollment of coeds in the nation's military academies, and the ordination of women to the ministry. A Harris poll of December 1975 reported that 63 percent of the women interviewed favored most changes designed to improve the status of women, although some were quick to insist that they were not "women's libbers."[31]

Evidence of changing views was everywhere. The list of organizations lined up in support of ratification of the Equal Rights Amendment included not only such avowedly feminist groups as NOW, WEAL, and NWPC as well as longtime supporters such as the National Woman's Party and the National Federation of Business and Professional Women's Clubs, but also well-established women's organizations such as the General Federation of Women's Clubs, the American Association of University Women, the League of Women Voters, the National Council of Jewish Women, the National Council of Negro Women, and the YWCA.

Even more potent evidence that feminism had "arrived" was the 1977 International Women's Year Conference in Houston. Before more than two thousand delegates from every state and territory in the United States and twenty thousand guests, three First Ladies—Lady Bird Johnson, Betty Ford, and Rosalynn Carter—endorsed the Equal Rights Amendment and the goals of the Houston Conference, their hands holding a lighted torch carried by women runners from Seneca Falls where, in 1848, the famous Declaration of Sentiments had been adopted. Confessing that she once thought the women's movement belonged more to her daughters than to herself, Lady Bird Johnson added, "I have come to know that it belongs to women of all ages." Such an admission, like the presence of these three women on the platform, proclaimed a message about feminists that was boldly printed on balloons throughout the convention hall: "We Are Everywhere!"[32]

OPPOSITION TO FEMINISM

For some women the slogan was not a sign of achievement but of threat. Gathered at a counter-convention in Houston were women who shared neither the critique nor the goals of the movement. They were an impressive reminder that social change generates opposition and that opposition to feminism had crystallized in the struggle for ratification of the Equal Rights Amendment. ERA—as the amendment is called—simply stated: "Equality of rights under the law shall not be denied or abridged by the United States or by any State on account of sex." First suggested in 1923 as the logical extension of suffrage, the amendment had long been opposed by those who feared it would be used to strike down laws intended to protect women in the workplace. By the 1960s, those concerns no longer applied. Prodded by NOW, Congress once again turned its attention to a constitutional amendment removing sexual bias from common, statutory, and constitutional law. After a massive lobbying effort by women's rights advocates and their allies, the Senate finally joined the House and sent ERA

to the states for ratification by a lopsided vote of eighty-four to eight in 1972. Almost immediately twenty-one states rushed to ratify. Within a year, however, opponents of ratification had begun a counterattack that ultimately stalled the number of ratified states at thirty-five, three short of the needed three-fourths majority when the deadline for ratification expired on June 30, 1982. Opponents even induced some ratifying states to rescind their approval. Early successes indicated a majority of Americans favored ERA—but not a large enough majority.

Opposition to ERA is starkly paradoxical. A constitutional amendment proposed especially to benefit women was opposed by women. The paradox is resolved in part by remembering that many Americans who claim to believe in equality become profoundly apprehensive when the principle is identified with specific governmental policies they consider to be intrusive and unreasonable. When supporters of ERA said that implementation of a constitutional ban on sex discrimination would be left to the Supreme Court, conservatives of both sexes were reminded that this was the same Supreme Court that had not only mandated racial integration, but prohibited prayer in the public schools and struck down bans on birth control, abortion, and pornography. Court-enforced sexual equality, like racial equality, many people believed, would further diminish the power of state and local governments and the right of individuals to live as they choose. As one woman wrote her U.S. senator: "*Forced* busing, *forced* mixing, *forced* housing. Now *forced* women! No thank you!"[33]

Such logic also illuminates antiratificationist charges, mystifying to ratificationists, that ERA would destroy the family. Although ERA supporters correctly pointed out that the amendment had nothing to do with private relationships, social conservatives were not convinced; they had seen what a federal agenda in feminist hands looked like at the International Women's Year Conference in Houston. A meeting subsidized by the U.S. government had endorsed not only women's rights and ERA, but government-sponsored child care, federal funding of abortions for poor women, contraception for minors without parental consent, and gay rights. If Big Brother or, more appropriately, Big Sister, had her way in Washington, women might well be forced to live in the kind of post-ERA world invoked by anti-ERA spokeswoman Phyllis Schlafly—a world in which mothers, no longer financially able to remain at home, would be forced to surrender their children to government-sponsored day-care centers. There child-care personnel would supplant parental authority and family identification with loyalty to the state.

The danger, as anti-ERA women saw it, was not just to family, but to women themselves. Feminists believed that theirs was a struggle for justice and liberation—liberation from economic inequities, social roles, and cultural values that denied rights and limited autonomy. To require *all* women to endure constraints dictated not by biology (sex) but by culture (gender) was, from the standpoint of feminists, to deny freedom and self-determination to half the population simply because they were born female. To women who did not believe they were oppressed, feminists' efforts at liberation, especially the rhetoric of radical feminists, appeared *not* as an attack on traditional gender categories, but rather an assault on familar patterns that provided security, identity, and meaning. Fusing feminism and ERA, an antiratificationist begged her senator not to vote for the amendment, insisting that she did not want to be liberated. "My husband," she wrote, "works for me and takes care of me and our three children, doesn't make me do things that are hard for me (drive in town), loves me and doesn't smoke, drink, gamble, run around or do anything that would upset me. I do what he tells me to do. I like this arrangement. *It's the only way I know how to live.*" Insisted another: "I am a widow, have three children, and work to make ends meet. I am still against ERA. I am a woman—and want to be treated as a woman."[34]

When ERA supporters responded that treating women as individuals legally rather than classifying them by sex had nothing to do with the division of labor between husbands and wives, social etiquette, or the masculinization of women, their reassurances fell on deaf ears. The free-floating anxiety aroused by the enormity of the social change inherent in feminism had acquired concrete focus in ERA. Opponents' predictions of the terrible consequences that would result from ratification of the amendment were not so important as the function such statements served—an indictment of what Schlafly called the "unisex" so-

ciety and an affirmation of traditional gender categories. For women living in a world in which personal identity, social legitimacy, economic viability, and moral order were rooted in traditional gender categories, calling those categories into question in the name of gender-neutral law meant that feminists must want men and women to be "the same." Finding it difficult to separate gender from sex—to see gender as a social construction—ERA opponents could only conclude that this latest drive for equality was not only absurd ("you can't fool Mother Nature") but dangerous. By rallying women to this danger, Schlafly revealed that the issue was not whether women should stay at home minding the children and cooking the food—Schlafly herself did not do that. The issue was the *meaning* of sexual differences between men and women.

In the early years of the movement, both radical and liberal feminists minimized those differences, believing reproductive control and work in the public sector have made women's lives more like men's. Antifeminists inflated those differences. Their response is a measure both of their belief that women are "eternal in their attributes and unchanged by events" and their anger and distress at changes that had already occurred.[35] It is a reminder, too, of how far the feminist movement has still to go to achieve the reforms sought by women's rights advocates, much less its more far-reaching goals.

NEW PROGRESS AND OLD PROBLEMS

There were gains to be sure. New reproductive freedom came in 1973 with the Supreme Court's liberalization of abortion laws that removed the danger of the illegal, back-alley abortions so long the recourse of desperate women. Sexual preference and practice became less an occasion for denial of civil rights and more a matter of individual choice. Evidence of expanding educational and employment opportunities seemed to be everywhere. Women assumed high-level posts in government, the judiciary, the military, business, and labor. In a new batch of female "firsts," Sandra Day O'Connor assumed a seat on the Supreme Court, NASA's Sally Ride zoomed into space, and Geraldine Ferraro won the vice-presidential slot on the 1984 Democratic ticket. From an expanding population of female college graduates, younger women moved in record numbers into professional schools, dramatically changing enrollment patterns in such fields as law, medicine, and business. Their blue-collar counterparts, completing job training programs, trickled into the construction industry and other trades, finding in those jobs the decent wage that had eluded them as waitresses, hairdressers, salesclerks, or domestics. Political participation also increased. Women emerged from years of lobbying for ERA with a new understanding of the political process. (So, too, did their opponents.) More female candidates filed for office and more female politicians worked themselves into positions of power. Revision of discriminatory statutes, while by no means completed, brought a greater measure of legal equality. A heightened public consciousness of sexism ushered in other changes. School officials began admitting boys to home economics classes, girls to shop. Some employers transformed maternity leaves into child-care leaves, making them available to fathers as well as mothers. Liberal religious leaders talked of removing gender-related references from prayer books.

Such gains, while in some cases smacking of tokenism, are not to be minimized. Most required persistent pressure from feminists, from government officials, and often from both. They were by no means comprehensive, however. As in the case of the civil rights movement, the initial beneficiaries of the feminist movement were predominantly middle-class, often highly educated, and relatively young. The increase in the number of single women, the older age at which women married for the first time, the declining birth rate—changes characteristic of the entire female population during the 1970s—were especially characteristic of a younger generation of career-oriented women.[36] But even for these women and their partners, financial as well as personal costs were sometimes high: couples living apart for some portion of the week or year in order to take advantage of career opportunities; married women devoting virtually all of their salaries to domestic and child-care costs, especially during their children's preschool years. Perhaps the personal recognition, independence, and sense of fulfillment associated with career success made the costs "affordable"— especially given the alternatives.

The women who stood to gain most from the implementation of feminists' efforts to change the nation's economic and social structure were not those who were young, talented, and educated but those who were less advantaged. Yet by the 1990s the latter could with good reason argue that two decades of feminist activity had left their lives little changed in ways that really count. While the number of women in the work force continued to rise from less than 20 percent in 1920 to 59 percent by June 1991, with a projected 87 percent by 2000, working women in the 1970s and 1980s saw the gap between male and female income remain virtually unchanged. By 1990 female workers earned 70 cents for every dollar earned by males. College graduates were no exception. Their earnings averaged $21,362 compared to $19,241 earned by men *without* even a high school diploma, although the gap has substantially narrowed among younger women. Part of the explanation for this persistent gap lies in pay inequities.[37] More fundamental, however, is the continuation of occupational segregation and the undervaluation of work done by women. Around 80 percent of all working women still cluster in gender-segregated occupations in which wages are artificially low. That women made up two-thirds of all minimum-wage workers in the United States is, therefore, hardly surprising.[38]

With the dramatic rise in the number of female-headed households—33 percent of all working mothers are their family's breadwinners—the continuation of this occupational ghetto has disturbing implications not only for women workers but also for their children. Female heads of households, often lacking both child-care facilities and skills that would equip them for better-paying jobs if such jobs were available, earn enough to enable less than two-thirds to stay above the poverty level. Their struggle for economic survival is shared by other women, especially older women—widows or divorcées whose years of housework have left them without employment skills. Indeed divorce often contributes to the problem, for with the breaking up of a marriage, the standard of living for most women falls dramatically. The fact that child support, if awarded, is frequently inadequate, unpaid, and uncollectible further exacerbates the economic plight of those women who have custody of their children. Thus, ironic as it may seem, the decade that witnessed the revival of the feminist movement also saw the feminization of poverty. By the end of the 1970s, two out of every three poor persons in the United States were female. If this trend continues at the present rate, it is estimated that by the year 2000 the poverty population will be composed entirely of women and their children.[39]

Ironic, too, given the feminist insistence that child-care and household responsibilities should be shared by working spouses, is the persistence of the double burden borne by women working outside the home. Working women continue to do 80 to 90 percent of the chores related to running a household, with husbands and children "helping out."[40] For all the talk about the changing structure of family roles, major shifts have occurred slowly, even in households in which women were informed and engaged enough to be familiar with current feminist views.[41] Although some fathers, especially among the middle class, have become more involved in parenting, the primary responsibility for children still remains the mother's. And working mothers still receive little institutional help despite the fact that by 1990 over half of all mothers with children under six worked outside the home.[42] Without a fundamental rethinking of both work and family, women will continue to participate in the labor force in increasing numbers. Many, however, will remain in its lower echelons as marginal members.

In sum, economic and demographic change has been the basis of important changes in attitudes and behavior. As a result, life is more challenging for many women, but the feminization of poverty reminds the nation of its failures. We have yet to see the new social policies necessary to create the egalitarian and humane society envisioned by feminists.

Indeed, in the climate of political conservatism of the 1980s feminists had to fight hard to maintain gains already won. The reproductive freedom of poor women had already been eroded by limitations on federal funding of abortions, and the reproductive freedom of all women had been threatened by congressional advocates of the Human Life Bill. Although that bill never received the votes necessary to become law, an increasingly conservative Supreme Court dealt reproductive rights a further blow. The 1989 *Webster* and the 1992 *Planned Parenthood* decisions, while not overturning the right to an abortion, upheld the right of states to limit access. With reproductive rights now a contested issue in state legislatures, the struggle to keep abortion legal and unrestricted has escalated dramatically.[43]

During the 1980s legislation mandating equal opportunity in education and employment was also weakened by the courts and assaulted by the Reagan and Bush administrations, whose budget cuts further hampered EEOC's antidiscrimination efforts. There were also cuts in funds for Title IX, which seeks to ensure sex equality on campus; cuts in grants for traditionally female programs such as nursing; cuts in Small Business Administration funding for programs benefiting women. Also under attack was comparable worth, a policy designed to reduce pay inequities by evaluating skills, effort, and responsibilities associated with jobs traditionally held by men and those traditionally held by women so that pay can be equalized for jobs that are indeed comparable.

Setbacks occurred in other areas as well. Day care centers, battered women's shelters, and legal aid centers have had their work curtailed by budget cuts. Legal equality has also suffered. Without an equal rights amendment requiring legislators to revise the discriminatory statutes that remain, the impetus will have to come not from the governments—state and local—but from individual women and men genuinely committed to equality before the law. Although the election of 1992 brought a pro-choice president to the White House and new feminist legislators to Capital Hill, the need for collective action on the part of feminists is as great in the 1990s as it was in the 1970s and 1980s.

Social change is complex and results from the interplay of many factors. Nowhere is this truer than in the women's movement. The swiftness with which a resurgent feminism captured the imagination of millions of American women dramatized the need for change. The inability of feminists to win ratification of ERA dramatized the limits of change. The irony of the polarization, however, was that the failure of ERA did not and could not stop feminism in its tracks and that antifeminist women, in mobilizing to fight the amendment, were themselves assuming a new role whether they acknowledged that fact or not. They organized lobbies, political action committees, and conventions; they also ran for and won public office. Where feminists have led, antifeminists would not be too far behind, defining themselves within the context of change they could not stop. But the rhetoric of liberation that had been so important to the awakening and maturation of women in the 1970s seemed by the 1980s to be less appealing. Women could happily benefit from the achievements of feminism without understanding or embracing its critique of style. Transformational politics seemed to have given way to a bevy of career women armed with a copy of *Savvy* or *Working Woman*, "dressed for success," and busily playing "games their mothers never taught them" with scant realization, as one observer noted, that "only a decade ago they would never have been allowed to play."[44] Commentators, speculating that feminism had become careerism, pronounced the movement dead.

Although press speculation was off the mark, feminism had changed. By the mid-seventies, radical feminism had given way to cultural feminism. The appeal that alternative institution-building held for cultural feminists in the conservative eighties was understandable. But the kind of valorization of the female reflected in the search for lost matriarchies and goddess worship seemed to radical and liberal feminists to represent not only female separatism but a retreat from political struggle. Both seemed alien to women whose aim had been to transcend gender, not reaffirm it. Valorization of female difference was also at the heart of still newer varieties of feminism such as eco-feminism: women as natural nurturers were presumed to be uniquely concerned with ecological ruin. If eco-feminism focused on issues that radical and liberal feminists of the 1960s would have regarded as broad human issues rather than distinctively feminist ones, the groups themselves functioned as a sharp reminder that second wave feminism had always been an ideologically pluralistic, decentralized, and structurally amorphous movement. Indeed diversity is a source of strength—a point made with renewed intensity in the 1980s by women of color. Their insistence that racism, classism, and sexism are multiple and interlocking forms of oppression has served to remind mainstream feminists that women speak in different voices from multiple historical, cultural, racial, economic, and sexual locations. The need to move beyond totalizing notions of "sisterhood," recognizing the extent to which women have themselves been oppressors of other women, requires of mainstream femi-

nism further transformation. There can be no mistaking black poet and feminist Audre Lorde's meaning when she asked, "What woman here is so enamored of her own oppression that she cannot see her heelprint upon another woman's face?"[45] If feminism is to become genuinely egalitarian and multicultural, mainstream feminists who bear the greater responsibility for that transformation will have much to do.

Meanwhile the movement continues to expand even in the midst of antifeminist backlash as women continue to make the connection between the personal and political as they confront in their own lives or the lives of others the trauma of sexual harassment, job discrimination, inequitable divorce settlements, as well as rape and other forms of sexual violence. Moreover, the challenge of the New Right has made abundantly clear that old patterns of gender-based discrimination have not lost their force. Those patterns had hindered efforts of women to establish a public role in the nineteenth century; they had restricted that public role once it was won. The same patterns, so indelible even under attack, continue to obstruct contemporary efforts to dismantle gender hierarchy in the drive for equality. The tension between past position and future possibility, however, demands of all women—not merely feminists—a definition of self that extends beyond the definitions of the past.

NOTES

1. Nancy F. Cott, *The Grounding of Modern Feminism* (New Haven, Conn., 1987), p. 3.

2. William H. Chafe, *The Paradox of Change: American Women in the 20th Century* (New York, 1991), pp. 99–100.

3. Marion K. Sanders, *The Lady and the Vote* (Boston, 1956), p. 142.

4. For new studies of feminism in the postsuffrage decades, see Nancy F. Cott, *The Grounding of Modern Feminism* (New Haven, 1987), and Leila J. Rupp and Verta Taylor, *Survival in the Doldrums: The American Women's Rights Movement, 1945 to the 1960s* (New York, 1987).

5. For a discussion of statistics relating to women in professional as well as attitudes of college-educated women to careers, see Frank Stricker, "Cookbooks and Law Books: The Hidden History of Career Women in Twentieth Century America," *Journal of Social History* 10 (1976):1–19.

6. Excluded are women who were appointed to congressional office simply to finish out the term of a deceased husband. Among these forty-seven in Congress, however, are women who were initially

appointed or elected in a special election to fill the seat of a deceased incumbent, often a husband, and who went on to win election to a subsequent term—or terms—on their own. Figures were compiled from Rudolf Engelbart, *Women in the United States Congress, 1917–1972* (Littleton, Colo., 1974).

7. Margaret Mead, "Sex and Achievement," *Forum* 94 (1935):303.

8. According to a Gallup Poll, 86 percent of American people objected to married women working; according to a *Fortune* poll, 67 percent. See Hadley Cantril, *Public Opinion, 1935–1946* (Princeton, 1951), p. 1047, and "The Fortune Survey: Women in America," *Fortune* 34 (1946):8. For the impact of the cold war on the resurgent domesticity of women, see Elaine Tyler May, *Homeward Bound: American Families in the Cold War Era* (New York, 1988).

9. For a much more detailed analysis, see Valerie Kincade Oppenheimer, *The Female Labor Force in the United States: Demographic and Economic Factors Governing Its Growth and Changing Composition* (Berkeley, 1970).

10. For a perceptive discussion of this issue, see Leslie Woodstock Tentler, *Wage-Earning Women: Industrial Work and Family Life in the United States, 1900–1930* (New York, 1979), pp. 180–85.

11. Nancy F. Gabin, *Feminism in the Labor Movement: Women and the United Auto Workers, 1935–1975* (Ithaca, N.Y., 1990), p. 4.

12. Quoted in Marguerite Wykoff Zapoleon, *The College Girl Looks Ahead to Her Career Opportunities* (New York, 1956), p. 9. See also Ashley Montagu, "The Triumph and Tragedy of the American Woman," *Saturday Review* 41 (1958):14.

13. Cynthia E. Harrison, "A 'New Frontier' for Women: The Public Policy of the Kennedy Administration," *Journal of American History* 67 (1980):630–46.

14. U.S. President's Commission on the Status of Women, *American Women* (Washington, D.C., 1963).

15. N. C. Governor's Commission on the Status of Women, *The Many Lives of North Carolina Women* (n.p., 1964). The report benefited from the fact that the study was funded—some state commissions were not—and from the expertise of some of its members, among whom were the then U.S. commissioner of welfare, Ellen Winston, and economist and later secretary of commerce, Juanita Kreps. The phrase quoted is that of Anne Firor Scott, who chaired the commission. Although none of these three found their involvement with the commission a "consciousness-raising" experience in that the data were already familiar, the findings were new to other members. Scott speculates that the many regional and national meetings attended by chairs of state commissions were important both for growing concern with women's issues and for network building. Interviews with Ellen Winston and Anne Firor Scott, Dec. 7 and 8, 1980.

16. Gabin, *Feminism in the Labor Movement*, p. 188.

17. For events leading to the founding of NOW, see Jo Freeman, *The Politics of Women's Liberation: A Case Study of an Emerging Social Movement and Its Relation to the Social Policy Process* (New York, 1975), pp.

53–55; and Cynthia Harrison, *On Account of Sex: The Politics of Women's Issues, 1945–1968* (Berkeley, 1988), pp. 192–209.

18. Betty Friedan, *The Feminine Mystique* (New York, 1963).

19. Freeman, *Politics of Women's Liberation*, pp. 35–37.

20. National Organization of Women, Statement of Purpose, 1966, reprinted in *Up from the Pedestal*, ed. Aileen S. Kraditor (Chicago, 1968), pp. 363–64; National Organization of Women, Bill of Rights, 1967, reprinted in *Sisterhood is Powerful: An Anthology of Writings on the Women's Liberation Movement*, ed. Robin Morgan (New York, 1970), pp. 512–14.

21. Freeman, *Politics of Women's Liberation*, chap. 3; Maren Lockwood Carden, *The New Feminist Movement* (New York, 1974), chaps. 8–10; also Gayle Graham Yates, *What Women Want: The Ideas of the Movement* (Cambridge, Mass., 1975), chap. 2; Gabin, *Feminism in the Labor Movement*, p. 226.

22. Quoted in Carolyn Hadley, "Feminist Women in the Southeast," *Bulletin of the Center of the Study of Southern Culture and Religion* 3 (1979):10.

23. Sara Evans, *Personal Politics: The Roots of Women's Liberation in the Civil Rights Movement and the New Left* (New York, 1979); see also Evans, "Tomorrow's Yesterday: Feminist Consciousness and the Future of Women," in *Women of America: A History*, ed. Carol Ruth Berkin and Mary Beth Norton (Boston, 1979), pp. 390–415. The following paragraphs rely heavily on this essay and on Evans's *Personal Politics*.

24. Mary King, one of the authors of the manifesto protesting the treatment of women in SNCC, insists that Carmichael was personally responsive to their concerns if others were not. See Mary King, *Freedom Song* (New York, 1987), pp. 450–52.

25. Carden, *New Feminist Movement*, chaps. 5–7, and Yates, *What Women Want*, chap. 3.

26. Quoted in Evans, "Tomorrow's Yesterday," p. 407.

27. The literature is extensive, beginning with Simone de Beauvoir, *The Second Sex*, trans. and ed. by H. M. Parshley (New York, 1961). Kate Millett, *Sexual Politics* (Garden City, N.Y., 1970); Shulamith Firestone, *The Dialectic of Sex: The Case for a Feminist Revolution* (New York, 1970); Germaine Greer, *The Female Eunuch* (New York, 1970); Juliet Mitchell, *Women's Estate* (New York, 1971); Evelyn Reed, *Problems of Women's Liberation: A Marxist Approach* (New York, 1971); Mary Daly, *Beyond God the Father: Toward a Philosophy of Women's Liberation* (New York, 1968); Carolyn Heilbrum, *Toward a Recognition of Androgyny* (New York, 1973). Anthologies include *Sisterhood is Powerful*, ed. Robin Morgan; *The Black Woman: An Anthology*, ed. Toni Cade; (New York, 1970); *Liberation Now: Writings from the Women's Liberation Movement*, eds. Deborah Babcox and Madeline Belkin (New York, 1971). The best historical treatment of radical feminism is Alice Echols, *Daring to Be Bad: Radical Feminism in America, 1967–1975* (Minneapolis, 1989).

28. Judith M. Bardwick, *In Transition: How Feminism, Sexual Liberation and the Search for Self-Fulfillment Have Altered America* (New York, 1979), p. 26.

29. For a fuller discussion of what is meant by the term *emancipation*, see Gerda Lerner's statement

in "Politics and Culture in Women's History," *Feminist Studies* 6 (1980):50.

30. The phrases are those of Frances Beale in "Double Jeopardy: To Be Black and Female," in *The Black Woman,* ed. Toni Cade, pp. 90–100, and of Patricia Haden, Donna Middleton, and Patricia Robinson in "A Historical and Critical Essay for Black Women," in *Voices from Women's Liberation,* ed. Leslie B. Tanner (New York, 1971), pp. 316–24. According to the 1972 Louis Harris Virginia Slims poll, a higher percentage of black women than white supported efforts to improve women's condition. Black feminists such as Pauli Murray, Elizabeth Koontz, Shirley Chisholm, and Florynce Kennedy have been important to the movement, and black feminist groups have developed; the initial response of many black women, however, was to regard the women's movement as a white woman's movement.

31. Louis Harris, "Changing Views on the Role of Women," *The Harris Survey,* Dec. 11, 1975.

32. Caroline Bird and the Members and Staff of the National Commission on the Observance of International Woman's Year, *What Women Want: From the Official Report to the President, the Congress, and the People of the United States* (New York, 1979), p. 68 for Johnson's statement.

33. Violet S. Devieux to Senator Sam J. Ervin, Jr., Mar. 23, 1972, Samuel J. Ervin Papers, #3847 Southern Historical Collection, Library of the University of North Carolina at Chapel Hill. For a fuller analysis of the significance of the struggle over ERA and the debate over feminism, see Donald G. Mathews and Jane S. De Hart, *Sex, Gender, and the ERA: A State and the Nation* (New York, 1990).

34. See also De Hart, "Gender on the Right: Meanings Behind the Existential Scream," *Gender and History* 3 (1991):246–67.

35. This apt characterization is William Chafe's; see *The Paradox of Change,* p. 209.

36. The percentage of single women over age eighteen has risen substantially—from 11.9 percent in 1960 to 19.3 percent in 1991—while the birth rate has dropped from an average of over three children per family in 1960 to less than one in 1991. See U.S. Bureau of the Census, *Statistical Abstract of the United States: 1992,* p. 43; U.S. Bureau of the Census, *Current Population Reports, Household and Family Characteristics: March 1989* (Washington, D.C., 1989), p. 54.

37. Despite the dramatic narrowing of the gap between the numbers of men and women in the labor force that had occurred by June 1991 (59.3 percent of all women age sixteen and over compared to 77.5

percent of all men) and the minimal differences in educational level (25 percent of females had four or more years of college compared with 28.2 percent of all males), the median earnings for workers fourteen years old and over, working fifty-two weeks per year, indicate a sex-based earnings gap that has changed relatively little. A Rand Corporation study estimates that in 1930 the average earnings of women were 43 percent of those of men; in 1950, 48 percent; in 1980, 53 percent; and in 1987, 62 percent, with sufficient increases coming in the 1980s. The study projects women's earnings in the year 2000 to be about 74 percent. See U.S. Bureau of the Census, *Statistical Abstracts of the United States: 1992,* pp. 14–15, 382, 385; and James P. Smith, *The Wage Gap and Comparable Worth,* Rand Paper Series (Santa Monica, 1985), pp. 4–5.

38. For a fuller discussion, see *Women's Work, Men's Work: Sex Segregation on the Job,* eds. Barbara F. Reskin and Heidi I. Hartmann (Washington, D.C., 1986).

39. Diane Pearce, "The Feminization of Poverty: Women, Work, and Welfare," *Urban and Social Change Review* 11 (1978):28–36; Barbara Ehrenreich and Francis Fox Piven, "The Feminization of Poverty: When the 'Family Wage System' Breaks Down," *Dissent* 31 (1984):162–70; Leonore J. Weitzman, *The Divorce Revolution and the Unanticipated Consequences for Women and Children in America* (New York, 1985).

40. *The American Woman, Status Report 1988–1989,* ed. Sara E. Rix (New York, 1988), p. 151.

41. Arlie Hochshild, *Second Shift: Working Parents and the Revolution at Home* (New York, 1989).

42. *The American Woman, 1990–1991: A Status Report,* ed. Sara E. Rix (New York, 1990), p. 380.

43. For a fuller account of court decisions affecting women during the 1980s, see Jane Sherron De Hart, "Equality Challenged: Equal Rights and Sexual Difference," *Journal of Policy History* 6 (1994):40–72.

44. Quoted in Verta Taylor, "The Future of Feminism in the 1980s: A Social Movement Analysis," in *Feminist Frontiers,* eds. Laurel Richardson and Verta Taylor (Reading, Mass., 1983), p. 442.

45. The quote is from Audre Lorde, *Sister Outsider* (Trumansburg, N.Y., 1984), p. 60. See also Angela Y. Davis, *Women, Race, and Class* (New York, 1981). For a more theoretical discussion, see Patricia Hill Collins, *Black Feminist Thought: Knowledge, Consciousness, and the Politics of Empowerment* (New York, 1990); and Nancie Caraway, *Segregated Sisterhood: Racism and the Politics of American Feminism* (Knoxville, Tenn., 1991).

Statistics, Statutes, Judicial Decisions

Census data have been collected on all Americans, but some particularly pertain to women. The law of the United States affects all inhabitants, but some statutes have had a special significance for women. This section includes two statistical charts and the following selection of statutes, constitutional amendments, court decisions, and other documents that have had important impact on the status of women in America:

Percentage of Men and Women in the Labor Force, 1890–2000

American Birth Rates, 1820–1990

The Law of Domestic Relations: Examples from Colonial Connecticut, 1640, 1672, 1702

Declaration of Sentiments, 1848

Married Women's Property Acts, New York State, 1848, 1860

Reconstruction Amendments, 1868, 1870

Bradwell v. *Illinois*, 1873

Comstock Law, 1873

Minor v. *Happersett*, 1875

Muller v. *Oregon*, 1908

MacKenzie v. *Hare*, 1915

Equal Suffrage (Nineteenth) Amendment, 1920

Adkins v. *Children's Hospital*, 1923

Hoyt v. *Florida*, 1961; *Taylor* v. *Louisiana*, 1975

Civil Rights Act, Title VII, 1964

Equal Rights Amendment, 1972

Frontiero v. *Richardson*, 1973

Roe v. *Wade*, 1973; *Planned Parenthood* v. *Casey*, 1992

Rostker v. *Goldberg*, 1981

Meritor Savings Bank v. *Mechelle Vinson et al.*, 1986

EDITORS' NOTE: Commentary on the legal documents in this section is written by Linda K. Kerber.

Percentage of Men and Women in the Labor Force, 1890–2000 ("Labor Force Participation Rate—Annual" [%])

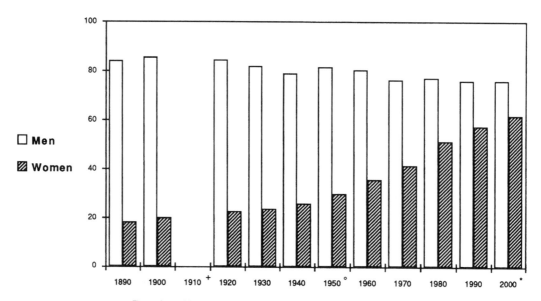

Figures from 1890 - 1970: *Historical Statistics of the United States, Colonial Times to 1970,* Part 1
U.S. Department of Commerce, Bureau of the Census (Washington, D.C., 1975), pp. 131-32.
Figures from 1980 - 2000: *Statistical Abstract of the United States, 1993,* U.S. Department of Commerce,
Bureau of the Census (Washington, D.C., 1993), p. 393.

*   **Figures for 2000 are projections**
+   **Figures for 1910 not available**
°   **Prior to 1950, ages 14 and over; 1950 and after, 16 years old and over.**

Sources: *1890–1930: Historical Statistics of the United States, Colonial Times to 1970,* Part 1, U.S. Department of Commerce, Bureau of the Census (Washington, D.C., 1975), pp. 131–32. *1980–2000: Statistical Abstract of the United States, 1993,* U.S. Department of Commerce, Bureau of the Census (Washington, D.C., 1993), p. 393.

American Birth Rates, 1820–1990

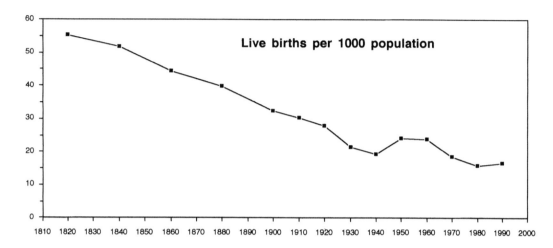

Live births per 1000 population

Sources: *1820–1970: Historical Statistics of the United States, Colonial Times to 1970,* Part 1, U.S. Department of Commerce, Bureau of the Census, (Washington, D.C., 1975), p. 49. *1980–1990: Statistical Abstract of the United States, 1993,* U.S. Department of Commerce, Bureau of the Census (Washington, D.C., 1993), p. 74.

ESSENTIAL DOCUMENTS

The Law of Domestic Relations: Examples from Colonial Connecticut, 1640–1702

Each American colony developed its own code of laws. There were major variations from colony to colony, but the thirteen Atlantic seaboard colonies that would eventually rebel against England were governed by English law and the modifications their legislatures made in it. Marriage is the result of private choice, but it is also a public act and has important legal implications for women. In seventeenth- and eighteenth-century English law and practice, the great legal theorist William Blackstone wrote, "husband and wife are one person in law, that is, the very being or legal existence of the woman is suspended during the marriage, or at least is incorporated and consolidated into that of the husband; under whose wing, protection, and *cover*, she performs every thing; and is therefore called . . . a *feme covert*." This doctrine of "unity of person" underlay a complex system of law of domestic relations; when an English woman married, her husband became the owner of all the movable things she possessed and of all the property or wages she might earn during their marriage. He also received the right to manage and collect the rents and profits on any real estate she owned; if they had a child, the child could not inherit the dead mother's lands until after the death of the father.

French law and Spanish law both derived from Roman law, a considerably different legal tradition than the Anglo-Saxon tradition from which the English common law had developed. Roman law recognized the husband and wife to be separate persons, who could each continue to own separately the property they brought to the marriage, who were co-owners of the property they acquired during their marriage, and who passed the property down evenly to their heirs. The husband, however, was "the head and master" of the household, with broad powers over wife and children and over the use of the property during the duration of the marriage. In practice, women living under community property rules were only slightly better situated than those who lived under English legal systems. The concept of "community property" was unknown in the English colonies and the states that succeeded them, but when as a result of the Louisiana Purchase in 1803 the United States absorbed thousands of people who were already engaged in complex property and commercial relationships, it seemed wisest to maintain established property law. Community property continued to be the norm not only in Louisiana but in other states that developed from French or Spanish settlement—California, New Mexico, Arizona, Texas. (See essay by Sarah Deutsch, pp. 276–85).

All colonies placed in their statutes a law regulating marriage. This step reflected a

The Public Statute Laws of the State of Connecticut (Hartford, 1808) I:236, 239–40, 477–81.

concern that marriage be celebrated publicly in order to guard against bigamy. Connecticut did not forbid interracial marriage, but many other colonies did (see Virginia law, p. 66). Laws also defined incest; note the large number of relatives prohibited from marrying in the statute from colonial Connecticut that follows. In the course of the next century the list of prohibited relatives was gradually reduced. Note that the Connecticut marriage law included a provision against cross-dressing.

AN ACT FOR REGULATING AND ORDERLY CELEBRATING OF MARRIAGES . . . . 1640, WITH REVISIONS 1672, 1702

Forasmuch as the ordinance of marriage is honourable amongst all; so it is meet it should be orderly and decently solemnized:

Be it therefore enacted . . . That no persons shall be joined in marriage, before the purpose or intention of the parties proceeding therein, hath been sufficiently published in some public meeting or congregation on the Lord's day, or on some public fast, thanksgiving, or lecture-day, in the town, parish, or society where the parties, or either of them do ordinarily reside; or such purpose or intention be set up in fair writing, upon some post or door of their meeting-house, or near the same, in public view, there to stand so as it may be read, eight days before such marriage.

. . . And in order to prevent incestuous and unlawful marriages, be it further enacted, That no man shall marry . . . his grand-father's wife, wife's grandmother, father's sister, mother's sister, father's brother's wife, mother's brother's wife, wife's father's sister, wife's mother's

sister, father's wife, wife's mother, daughter, wife's daughter, son's wife, sister, brother's wife, son's daughter, daughter's daughter, son's son's wife, daughter's son's wife, wife's son's daughter, wife's daughter's daughter, brother's daughter, sister's daughter, brother's son's wife, sister's son's wife.

And if any man shall hereafter marry, or have carnal copulation with any woman who is within the degrees before recited in this act, every such marriage shall be . . . null and void; And all children that shall hereafter be born of such incestuous marriage or copulation, shall be forever disabled to inherit by descent, or by being generally named in any deed or will, by father or mother. . . .

And that if any man shall wear women's apparel, or if any woman shall wear men's apparel, and be thereof duly convicted; such offenders shall be corporally punished or fined at the discretion of the county court, not exceeding *seventeen* dollars. . .

Early America was a divorceless society. South Carolina boasted that it granted no divorce until 1868. Most colonies followed the British practice of treating marriage as a moral obligation for life. Occasional special dissolutions of a marriage were granted by legislatures in response to individual petitions or by courts of equity, but these were separations from bed and board, which normally did not carry with them freedom to marry again.

Colonial Connecticut was unusual in treating marriage as a civil contract, which might be broken if its terms were not carried out. Connecticut enacted the earliest divorce law in the colonies. It made divorce available after a simple petition to the superior court under certain circumstances. People who did not fit these circumstances were able to present special petitions to the legislature. Normally a divorce in Connecticut implied that the innocent party had the right to marry again.

Most petitioners for divorce in early America were women. On what grounds might Connecticut women petition for divorce?

AN ACT RELATING TO BILLS OF DIVORCE, 1667

Be it enacted . . . that no bill of divorce shall be granted to any man or woman, lawfully mar-

ried, but in case of adultery, or fraudulent contract, or wilful desertion for three years with total neglect of duty; or in case of seven years absence of one party not heard of: after due enquiry is made, and the matter certified to the superior court, in which case the other party may be deemed and accounted single and un-married. And in that case, and in all other cases afore-mentioned, a bill of divorce may be granted by the superior court to the aggrieved party; who may then lawfully marry or be married again.

Perhaps no statutes were more important to women in the first 250 years after settlement of the English colonies than the laws protecting their claims to dower. The "widow's dower" should be distinguished from the dowry a bride might bring with her into marriage. "The widow's dower" or the "widow's third" was the right of a widow to use one-third of the real estate that her husband held at the time of his death. It was an old English tradition that he might leave her more in his will, but he could not leave her less. If a man died without a will, the courts would ensure that his widow received her "third."

It is important to note that she only had the right to use the land and buildings. She might live on this property, rent it out, farm the land, and sell the produce. But she could not sell or bequeath it. After her death the property reverted to her husband's heirs, who normally would be their children, but in the case of a childless marriage it might go to others whom he identified.

In Lousiana law, community property was acquired during the marriage; the wife had her own separate claim to the property she brought to the marriage. "Dotal" property, or dowry, was intended to help with the expenses of the marriage; the husband could manage this property and spend its income, but at the end of the marriage it was restored to the wife or her heirs, thus keeping it in her own family line of succession. She also kept her own "paraphernalia"—personal clothing and other items—which she could trade as a merchant without her husband's consent or dispose of in her own will.

In the Connecticut statute, printed below, note the provisions protecting the widow's interests. Normally colonial courts were scrupulous about assigning the widow's portion. Observe, however, that widows could not claim dower in "movable" property, which might represent a larger share of their husband's wealth than real estate. As time passed and the American economy became more complex, it became increasingly likely that a man's property would not be held in the form of land. If the land were heavily mort-gaged, the widow's prior right to her "third" became a barrier to creditors seeking to collect their portion of a husband's debts. By the early nineteenth century courts were losing their enthusiasm for protecting widows' thirds.

By the middle of the century the married women's property acts began to refor-mulate a definition of the terms by which married women could claim their share of the property of wife and husband. But between 1790 and 1840, when the right to dower was more and more laxly enforced and the new married women's property acts had not yet been devised, married women were in a particularly vulnerable position. See Keziah Kendall, pp. 201–203.

AN ACT CONCERNING THE DOWRY OF WIDOWS, 1672

That there may be suitable provision made for the maintenance and comfortable support of widows, after the decease of their husbands, Be it enacted . . . that every married woman, living with her husband in this state, or absent elsewhere from him with his consent, or through his mere default, or by inevitable providence; or in case of divorce where she is the innocent party, that shall not before marriage be estated by way of jointure in some houses, lands, tenements or hereditaments for term of life . . . shall immediately upon, and after the death of her husband, have right, title and interest by way of dower, in and unto one third part of the real estate of her said deceased husband, in houses and lands which he stood possessed of in his own right, at the time of his decease, to be to her during her natural life: the remainder of the estate shall be disposed of according to the will of the deceased. . . .

And for the more easy, and speedy ascertaining such rights of dower, It is further enacted, That upon the death of any man possessed of any real estate . . . which his widow . . . hath a right of dower in, if the person, or persons that by law have a right to inherit said

estate, do not within sixty days next after the death of such husband, by three sufficient freeholders of the same county; to be appointed by the judge of probate . . . and sworn for that purpose, set out, and ascertain such right of dower, that then such widow may make her complaint to the judge of probate . . . which judge shall decree, and order that such woman's dowry shall be set out, and ascertained by three sufficient freeholders of the county . . . and upon approbation thereof by said judge, such dower shall remain fixed and certain. . . .

And every widow so endowed . . . shall maintain all such houses, buildings, fences, and inclosures as shall be assigned, and set out to her for her dowry; and shall leave the same in good and sufficient repair.

Declaration of Sentiments, 1848

The "Convention to discuss the social, civil, and religious condition and rights of women" that was announced by Elizabeth Cady Stanton, Lucretia Mott, and two of their friends in 1848 was simply an open meeting to which the public was invited. It provided an occasion for debating and publicizing a set of reform proposals. The meeting in Seneca Falls, New York, was followed by a series of other public meetings—in Rochester, New York; Akron, Ohio; and Worcester, Massachusetts. But the manifesto of the Seneca Falls Convention, written by Elizabeth Cady Stanton, remained the basic statement of reformers' goals throughout the nineteenth century.

The rhetoric of the Declaration of Sentiments was borrowed from the Declaration of Independence. Through its lines flowed the conviction that the Revolution had made implicit promises to women which had not been kept.

Seneca Falls, New York,
July 19–20, 1848
When, in the course of human events, it becomes necessary for one portion of the family of man to assume among the people of the earth a position different from that which they have hitherto occupied, but one to which the

laws of nature and of nature's God entitle them, a decent respect to the opinions of mankind requires that they should declare the causes that impel them to such a course.

We hold these truths to be self-evident: that all men and women are created equal; that they are endowed by their Creator with certain

Declaration of Sentiments, in *History of Woman Suffrage,* edited by Elizabeth Cady Stanton, Susan B. Anthony, and Matilda Joslyn Gage, vol. 1 (New York: Fowler & Wells, 1881), pp. 70–71.

inalienable rights; that among these are life, liberty, and the pursuit of happiness; that to secure these rights governments are instituted, deriving their just powers from the consent of the governed. Whenever any form of government becomes destructive of these ends, it is the right of those who suffer from it to refuse allegiance to it, and to insist upon the institution of a new government, laying its foundation on such principles, and organizing its powers in such form, as to them shall seem most likely to effect their safety and happiness. Prudence, indeed, will dictate that governments long established should not be changed for light and transient causes; and accordingly all experience hath shown that mankind are more disposed to suffer, while evils are sufferable, than to right themselves by abolishing the forms to which they were accustomed. But when a long train of abuses and usurpations, pursuing invariably the same object evinces a design to reduce them under absolute despotism, it is their duty to throw off such government, and to provide new guards for their future security. Such has been the patient sufferance of the women under this government, and such is now the necessity which constrains them to demand the equal station to which they are entitled.

The history of mankind is a history of repeated injuries and usurpations on the part of man toward woman, having in direct object the establishment of an absolute tyranny over her. To prove this, let facts be submitted to a candid world.

He has never permitted her to exercise her inalienable right to the elective franchise.

He has compelled her to submit to laws, in the formation of which she had no voice.

He has withheld from her rights which are given to the most ignorant and degraded men—both native and foreigners.

Having deprived her of this first right of a citizen, the elective franchise, thereby leaving her without representation in the halls of legislation, he has oppressed her on all sides.

He has made her, if married, in the eye of the law, civilly dead.

He has taken from her all right in property, even to the wages she earns.

He has made her, morally, an irresponsible being, as she can commit many crimes with impunity, provided they be done in the presence of her husband. In the covenant of marriage, she is compelled to promise obedience to her husband, he becoming, to all intents and purposes, her master—the law giving him power to deprive her of her liberty, and to administer chastisement.

He has so framed the laws of divorce, as to what shall be the proper causes, and in case of separation, to whom the guardianship of the children shall be given, as to be wholly regardless of the happiness of women—the law, in all cases, going upon a false supposition of the supremacy of man, and giving all power into his hands.

After depriving her of all rights as a married woman, if single, and the owner of property, he has taxed her to support a government which recognizes her only when her property can be made profitable to it.

He has monopolized nearly all the profitable employments, and from those she is permitted to follow, she receives but a scanty remuneration. He closes against her all the avenues to wealth and distinction which he considers most honorable to himself. As a teacher of theology, medicine, or law, she is not known.

He has denied her the facilities for obtaining a thorough education, all colleges being closed against her.

He allows her in Church, as well as State, but a subordinate position, claiming Apostolic authority for her exclusion from the ministry, and, with some exceptions, from any public participation in the affairs of the Church.

He has created a false public sentiment by giving to the world a different code of morals for men and women, by which moral delinquencies which exclude women from society, are not only tolerated, but deemed of little account in man.

He has usurped the prerogative of Jehovah himself, claiming it as his right to assign for her a sphere of action, when that belongs to her conscience and to her God.

He has endeavored, in every way that he could, to destroy her confidence in her own powers, to lessen her self-respect, and to make her willing to lead a dependent and abject life.

Now, in view of this entire disfranchisement of one-half the people of this country, their social and religious degradation—in view of the unjust laws above mentioned, and because women do feel themselves aggrieved, oppressed, and fraudulently deprived of their most sacred rights, we insist that they have immediate admission to all the rights and privileges which belong to them as citizens of the United States.

In entering upon the great work before us, we anticipate no small amount of misconception, misrepresentation, and ridicule; but we shall use every instrumentality within our power to effect our object. We shall employ agents, circulate tracts, petition the State and National legislatures, and endeavor to enlist the pulpit and the press in our behalf. We hope this Convention will be followed by a series of Conventions embracing every part of the country.

The following resolutions were discussed by Lucretia Mott, Thomas and Mary Ann McClintock, Amy Post, Catharine A. F. Stebbins, and others, and were adopted:

WHEREAS, The great precept of nature is conceded to be, that "man shall pursue his own true and substantial happiness." Blackstone in his Commentaries remarks, that this law of Nature being coeval with mankind, and dictated by God himself, is of course superior in obligation to any other. It is binding over all the globe, in all countries, and at all times; no human laws are of any validity if contrary to this, and such of them as are valid, derive all their force, and all their validity, and all their authority, mediately and immediately, from this original; therefore;

Resolved, That such laws as conflict, in any way, with the true and substantial happiness of woman, are contrary to the great precept of nature and of no validity, for this is "superior in obligation to any other."

Resolved, That all laws which prevent woman from occupying such a station in society as her conscience shall dictate, or which place her in a position inferior to that of man, are contrary to the great precept of nature, and therefore of no force or authority.

Resolved, That woman is man's equal—was intended to be so by the Creator, and the highest good of the race demands that she should be recognized as such.

Resolved, That the women of this country ought to be enlightened in regard to the laws under which they live, that they may no longer

publish their degradation by declaring themselves satisfied with their present position, nor their ignorance by asserting that they have all the rights they want.

Resolved, That inasmuch as man, while claiming for himself intellectual superiority, does accord to woman moral superiority, it is preeminently his duty to encourage her to speak and teach, as she has an opportunity, in all religious assemblies.

Resolved, That the same amount of virtue, delicacy, and refinement of behavior that is required of woman in the social state, should also be required of man, and the same transgressions should be visited with equal severity on both man and woman.

Resolved, That the objection of indelicacy and impropriety, which is so often brought against woman when she addresses a public audience, comes with a very ill-grace from those who encourage, by their attendance, her appearance on the stage, in the concert, or in feats of the circus.

Resolved, That woman has too long rested satisfied in the circumscribed limits which corrupt customs and a perverted application of the Scriptures have marked out for her, and that it is time she should move in the enlarged sphere which her great Creator has assigned her.

Resolved, That it is the duty of the women of this country to secure to themselves their sacred right to the elective franchise.

Resolved, That the equality of human rights results necessarily from the fact of the identity of the race in capabilities and responsibilities.

Resolved, therefore, That, being invested by the Creator with the same capabilities, and the same consciousness of responsibility for their exercise, it is demonstrably the right and duty of woman, equally with man, to promote every righteous cause by every righteous means; and especially in regard to the great subjects of morals and religion, it is self-evidently her right to participate with her brother in teaching them, both in private and in public, by writing and by speaking, by any instrumentalities proper to be used, and in any assemblies proper to be held; and this being a self-evident truth growing out of the divinely implanted principles of human nature, any custom or authority adverse to it, whether modern or wearing the hoary sanction of antiquity, is to be regarded as a self-evident falsehood, and at war with mankind.

At the last session Lucretia Mott offered and spoke to the following resolution:

Resolved, That the speedy success of our cause depends upon the zealous and untiring efforts of both men and women, for the overthrow of the monopoly of the pulpit, and for the securing to woman an equal participation with men in the various trades, professions, and commerce.

Married Women's Property Acts, New York State, 1848, 1860

Americans inherited the ancient English custom of *coverture,* by which the married woman's civil identity was covered by or absorbed into her husband's. By common law tradition a husband might spend his wife's property, punish her physically, and provide her with only minimal food, clothing, and shelter. The rigor of the common law was in fact substantially eased both in England and the colonies by courts of equity, which permitted more judicial discretion. The common law rights of the husband might, for example, be circumvented by premarital contracts or trusteeships.

But these options were most realistic for women who could obtain the benefit of sophisticated legal advice and who had substantial property to protect. They were not readily available to poorer women who needed them most. The Declaration of Sentiments sharply attacked contemporary practice as "civil death" for women. Reformers gave high priority to legislation that would confirm the right of married women to the property they had brought into their marriages and to wages and income they earned after marriage.

Ironically, the first married women's property acts, passed in Mississippi in 1839 and in New York in 1848, were supported by many male legislators out of a desire to preserve the estates of married daughters against spendthrift sons-in-law. Four out of the five sections of the Mississippi act broadened the rights of married women over their own slaves.

Note the limits of the 1848 New York law and the ways in which women's rights were extended by the 1860 revision. In 1860 married women were also confirmed in their guardianship of their children.

1848

The real and personal property of any female [now married and] who may hereafter marry, and which she shall own at the time of marriage, and the rents issues and profits thereof shall not be subject to the disposal of her husband, nor be liable for his debts, and shall continue her sole and separate property, as if she were a single female. . . .

Laws of the State of New-York, Passed at the Seventy-First Session of the Legislature . . . (Albany, 1848), pp. 307–8; *Laws of the State of New York, Passed at the Eighty-Third Session of the Legislature . . .* (Albany, 1860), pp. 157–59.

It shall be lawful for any married female to receive, by gift, grant, devise or bequest, from any person other than her husband and hold to her sole and separate use, as if she were a single female, real and personal property, and the rents, issues and profits thereof, and the same shall not be subject to the disposal of her husband, nor be liable for his debts. . . .

1860

[The provisions of the law of 1848 were retained, and others were added:]

A married woman may bargain, sell, assign, and transfer her separate personal property, and carry on any trade or business, and perform any labor or services on her sole and separate account, and the earnings of any married woman from her trade . . . shall be her sole and separate property, and may be used or invested by her in her own name. . . .

Any married woman may, while married, sue and be sued in all matters having relation to her . . . sole and separate property . . . in the same manner as if she were sole. And any married woman may bring and maintain an action in her own name, for damages, against any person or body corporate, for any injury to her person or character, the same as if she were sole; and the money received upon the settlement . . . shall be her sole and separate property.

No bargain or contract made by any married woman, in respect to her sole and separate property . . . shall be binding upon her husband, or render him or his property in any way liable therefor.

Every married woman is hereby constituted and declared to be the joint guardian of her children, with her husband, with equal powers, rights, and duties in regard to them, with the husband. . . .

Reconstruction Amendments, 1868, 1870

Until 1868, the United States Constitution made no explicit distinctions on the basis of gender. Of qualifications for voters, it said only that "the electors in each State shall have the qualifications requisite for electors of the most numerous branch of the State legislature" (Article I, section 2). Reformers merely needed to persuade each state legislature to change its own rules in order to enfranchise women in national elections.

The word *male* was introduced into the Constitution in section 2 of the Fourteenth Amendment, as part of a complex provision—never enforced—intended to constrain former Confederates from interfering with the civil rights of newly freed slaves. Suffragists were bitterly disappointed at the failure to include sex as a category in the Fifteenth Amendment. But until the test case of *Minor* v. *Happersett* (pp. 575–76), they clung to the hope that the first article of the Fourteenth Amendment would be interpreted broadly enough to admit women to the polls.

FOURTEENTH AMENDMENT, 1868

1. All persons born or naturalized in the United States, and subject to the jurisdiction thereof, are citizens of the United States and of the State wherein they reside. No State shall make or enforce any law which shall abridge the privileges or immunities of citizens of the United States; nor shall any State deprive any person of life, liberty, or property, without due process of law; nor deny to any person within its jurisdiction the equal protection of the laws.

2. Representatives shall be apportioned among the several States according to their respective numbers, counting the whole number of persons in each State, excluding Indians not

taxed. But when the right to vote at any election for the choice of electors for President and Vice-President of the United States, Representatives in Congress, the executive and judicial officers of a State, or the members of the legislature thereof, is denied to any of the male inhabitants of such State, being twenty-one years of age and citizens of the United States, or in any way abridged, except for participation in rebellion, or other crime, the basis of representation therein shall be reduced in the proportion which the number of such male citizens shall bear to the whole number of male citizens twenty-one years of age in such State. . . .

FIFTEENTH AMENDMENT, 1870

The right of citizens of the United States to vote shall not be denied or abridged by the United States or by any State on account of race, color, or previous condition of servitude. . . .

Bradwell v. *Illinois,* 1873

Although she could not practice in the courts until the end of her career, Myra Bradwell was perhaps the most notable female lawyer of the nineteenth century. She read law in the office of her husband, a prominent Chicago attorney and county judge. In 1868 she began to publish the *Chicago Legal News,* a weekly newspaper covering developments in courts and legislatures throughout the country. Because she had received a special charter from the state legislature under which she was permitted to act without the usual legal disabilities of a married woman, she ran the *News* as her own business. She wrote vigorous editorials, evaluating legal opinions and new laws, assessing proposed state legislation, and supporting progressive developments like prison reform, the establishment of law schools, and women's rights. She drafted bills improving married women's rights to child custody and to property, including the Illinois Married Woman's Property Act of 1869. Thanks in part to her own lobbying efforts, Illinois permitted women to own property and to control their own earnings.

It was only logical that Myra Bradwell should seek admission to the bar. Although she passed the entrance tests in 1869, although the Illinois Married Woman's Property Act permitted her to own property, and although the law that gave the state supreme court the power to license attorneys did not explicitly exclude women, her application was rejected by the Illinois Supreme Court on the grounds that she was a married woman, and therefore not a truly free agent. Appealing to the United States Supreme Court, her attorney argued that among the "privileges and immunities" guaranteed to each citizen by the Fourteenth Amendment was the right to pursue any honorable profession. "Intelligence, integrity and honor are the only qualifications that can be prescribed . . . the broad shield of the Constitution is over all, and protects each in that measure of success which his or her individual merits may secure."

The Court's decision came in two parts. Speaking for the majority and citing the most recent decision of the Supreme Court in the slaughterhouse cases, Justice Samuel

83 U.S. 130.

F. Miller held that the right to practice law in the courts of any particular state was a right that had to be granted by the individual state; it was not one of the "privileges and immunities" of national citizenship. This judgment was supplemented by a concurring opinion, in which Justice Joseph P. Bradley offered an ideological justification for the Court's decision that was based on inherent differences between men and women and that was to be widely used thereafter to defend the exclusion of women from professional careers.

While her case was pending before the U.S. Supreme Court, Bradwell and Alta M. Hulett, another woman who had been refused admission to the bar even though she was otherwise qualified, successfully lobbied for a law that granted freedom of occupational choice to all Illinois citizens, both male and female. The bill was passed in 1872; a year later Alta Hulett was sworn in before the Illinois Bar. Bradwell did not think she should have to beg for admission, and she never formally applied for a license to practice law under the new statute. In the *Chicago Legal News* she observed that "having once complied with the rules and regulations of the court . . . [I] declined to . . . again ask for admission." In 1890, twenty years after her initial application, the Illinois Supreme Court admitted Bradwell to the bar. Two years before her death in 1894 she was admitted to practice before the U.S. Supreme Court, but she never did argue a case there.*

MR. JUSTICE JOSEPH P. BRADLEY:

The claim of the plaintiff, who is a married woman, to be admitted to practice as an attorney and counselor at law, is based upon the supposed right of every person, man or woman, to engage in any lawful employment for a livelihood. The supreme court of Illinois denied the application on the ground that, by the common law, which is the basis of the laws of Illinois, only men were admitted to the bar, and the legislature had not made any change in this respect. . . .

The claim that, under the 14th Amendment of the Constitution, which declares that no state shall make or enforce any law which shall abridge the privileges and immunities of citizens of the United States, and the statute law of Illinois, or the common law prevailing in that state, can no longer be set up as a barrier against the right of females to pursue any lawful employment . . . assumes that it is one of the privileges and immunities of women as citizens to engage in any and every profession, occupation or employment in civil life.

It certainly cannot be affirmed, as a historical fact, that this has ever been established as one of the fundamental privileges and immunities of the sex. On the contrary, the civil law,

as well as nature herself, has always recognized a wide difference in the respective spheres and destinies of man and woman. Man is, or should be, woman's protector and defender. The natural and proper timidity and delicacy which belongs to the female sex evidently unfits it for many of the occupations of civil life. The constitution of the family organization, which is founded in the divine ordinance, as well as in the nature of things, indicates the domestic sphere as that which properly belongs to the domain and functions of womanhood. The harmony, not to say identity, of interests and views which belong or should belong to the family institution, is repugnant to the idea of a woman adopting a distinct and independent career from that of her husband. So firmly fixed was this sentiment in the founders of the common law that it became a maxim of that system of jurisprudence that a woman had no legal existence separate from her husband, who was regarded as her head and representative in the social state; and, notwithstanding some recent modifications of this civil status, many of the special rules of law flowing from and dependent upon this cardinal principle still exist in full force in most

---

*See also Frances Olsen, "From False Paternalism to False Equality: Judicial Assaults on Feminist Community, Illinois 1869–1895," *Michigan Law Review* 84 (1986):1518–43.

states. One of these is, that a married woman is incapable, without her husband's consent, of making contracts which shall be binding on her or him. This very incapacity was one circumstance which the supreme court of Illinois deemed important in rendering a married woman incompetent fully to perform the duties and trusts that belong to the office of an attorney and counselor.

It is true that many women are unmarried and not affected by any of the duties, complications, and incapacities arising out of the married state, but these are exceptions to the general rule. The paramount destiny and mission of woman are to fulfill the noble and benign offices of wife and mother. This is the law of the Creator. And the rules of civil society must be adapted to the general constitution of things, and cannot be based upon exceptional cases. . . .

Comstock Law, 1873

This "Act for the Suppression of Trade in, and Circulation of Obscene Literature and Articles of Immoral Use" was passed at the urging of Anthony Comstock, the head of the New York Society for the Suppression of Vice. The first section prohibited the sale of the described materials in the District of Columbia and the territories; subsequent sections prohibited the sending of these materials through the mails or their importation into the United States. In the 1870s many states passed their own versions of the federal law.

The law reflected a widespread belief that both contraception and abortion were acts of interference with the natural order and with God's intentions. No distinction was made between drugs used for abortion and materials used for contraception; all were treated in the same terms as pornographic materials. Note the heavy penalties provided.

A century after the Comstock Law, its limitations on birth control information and on pornography had eroded. By 1973 the Supreme Court finally agreed on the definition of obscene material, that is, material unprotected as an exercise of free speech under the First Amendment: "the average person, applying contemporary community standards, would find that the work, taken as a whole, appeals to the prurient interest . . . [describes sexual conduct] in a patently offensive way . . . and . . . lacks serious literary, artistic, political, or scientific value" (*Miller* v. *California*, 413 U.S. 15 [1973]). In the 1980s some feminists began to argue that pornography ought to be defined not merely as obscenity but as "sexually explicit subordination of women"; that is, that pornography was not simply an expression of free speech, protected under the First Amendment, but an actual injury, to be protected against as a civil liberty. "Depictions of subordination tend to perpetuate subordination. The subordinate status of women in turn leads to affront and lower pay at work, insult and injury at home, battery and rape on the streets," observed a federal court in the course of evaluating an Indianapolis ordinance outlawing pornog-

Public Laws of the United States of America, Passed at the Third Session of the Forty-Second Congress (Boston, 1873), p. 598.

raphy in 1985 (*American Booksellers Association* v. *Hudnut*, 771 F.2d 323 [1985]). Although the Court refused to uphold the ordinance, the issue continues to be debated.

Be it enacted . . . That whoever, within the District of Columbia or any of the Territories of the United States . . . shall sell . . . or shall offer to sell, or to lend, or to give away, or in any manner to exhibit, or shall otherwise publish or offer to publish in any manner, or shall have in his possession, for any such purpose or purposes, any obscene book, pamphlet, paper, writing, advertisement, circular, print, picture, drawing or other representation, figure, or image on or of paper or other material, or any cast, instrument, or other article of an immoral nature, or any drug or medicine, or any article whatever, for the prevention of conception, or for causing unlawful abortion, or shall adver-

tize the same for sale, or shall write or print, or cause to be written or printed, any card, circular, book, pamphlet, advertisement, or notice of any kind, stating when, where, how, or of whom, or by what means, any of the articles in this section . . . can be purchased or obtained, or shall manufacture, draw, or print, or in any wise make any of such articles, shall be deemed guilty of a misdemeanor, and on conviction thereof in any court of the United States . . . he shall be imprisoned at hard labor in the penitentiary for not less than six months nor more than five years for each offense, or fined not less than one hundred dollars nor more than two thousand dollars, with costs of court. . . .

Minor v. *Happersett,* 1875

In 1872 suffragists in a number of places attempted to test the possibilities of the first section of the Fourteenth Amendment. "The power to regulate is one thing, the power to prevent is an entirely different thing," observed Virginia Minor, president of the Woman Suffrage Association of Missouri, and she presented herself at the polls in St. Louis in 1872. When the registrar refused to permit her to register to vote, she and her husband sued him for denying her one of the "privileges and immunities of citizenship"; when they lost the case they appealed to the Supreme Court.

In a unanimous opinion the justices held that if the authors of the Constitution had intended that women should vote, they would have said so explicitly. The decision of the Court meant that woman suffrage could not be developed by way of a quiet reinterpretation of the Constitution but would require an explicit amendment to the Constitution or a series of revisions in the laws of the states.

MR. CHIEF JUSTICE MORRISON R. WAITE DELIVERED THE OPINION OF THE COURT:
The question is presented in this case, whether, since the adoption of the fourteenth amendment, a woman, who is a citizen of the United States and of the State of Missouri, is a voter in that State, notwithstanding the provision of the constitution and laws of the State, which confine the right of suffrage to men alone. . . . The

argument is, that as a woman, born or naturalized in the United States and subject to the jurisdiction thereof, is a citizen of the United States and of the State in which she resides, she has the right of suffrage as one of the privileges and immunities of her citizenship, which the State cannot by its laws or constitution abridge.

88 U.S. 162.

There is no doubt that women may be citizens. They are persons, and by the fourteenth amendment "all persons born or naturalized in the United States and subject to the jurisdiction thereof" are expressly declared to be "citizens of the United States and of the State wherein they reside." But, in our opinion, it did not need this amendment to give them that position . . . sex has never been made one of the elements of citizenship in the United States. In this respect men have never had an advantage over women. The same laws precisely apply to both. The fourteenth amendment did not affect the citizenship of women any more than it did of men. . . . Mrs. Minor . . . has always been a citizen from her birth, and entitled to all the privileges and immunities of citizenship.

If the right of suffrage is one of the necessary privileges of a citizen of the United States, then the constitution and laws of Missouri confining it to men are in violation of the Constitution of the United States, as amended, and consequently void. The direct question is, therefore, presented whether all citizens are necessarily voters.

The Constitution does not define the privileges and immunities of citizens. For that definition we must look elsewhere. In this case we need not determine what they are, but only whether suffrage is necessarily one of them.

It certainly is nowhere made so in express terms. The United States has no voters in the States of its own creation. The elective officers of the United States are all elected directly or indirectly by state voters. . . . it cannot for a moment be doubted that if it had been intended to make all citizens of the United States voters,

the framers of the Constitution would not have left it to implication. . . .

It is true that the United States guarantees to every State a republican form of government. . . . No particular government is designated as republican, neither is the exact form to be guaranteed, in any manner especially designated. . . . When the Constitution was adopted . . . all the citizens of the States were not invested with the right of suffrage. In all, save perhaps New Jersey, this right was only bestowed upon men and not upon all of them. . . . Under these circumstances it is certainly now too late to contend that a government is not republican, within the meaning of this guaranty in the Constitution, because women are not made voters. . . . If suffrage was intended to be included within its obligations, language better adapted to express that intent would most certainly have been employed. . . .

. . . For nearly ninety years the people have acted upon the idea that the Constitution, when it conferred citizenship, did not necessarily confer the right of suffrage. If uniform practice long continued can settle the construction of so important an instrument as the Constitution of the United States confessedly is, most certainly it has been done here. Our province is to decide what the law is, not to declare what it should be.

We have given this case the careful consideration its importance demands. If the law is wrong, it ought to be changed; but the power for that is not with us. . . . No argument as to woman's need of suffrage can be considered. We can only act upon her rights as they exist. . . .

Muller v. *Oregon*, 1908

The farmer's workday was sunrise to sunset. When the first factories were established in the early nineteenth century, they were operated for equally long hours. It was a particular interest of laborers and of progressive reformers to support enactment of limits

208 U.S. 412.

on the workday. The ten-hour day was on the agenda of early labor unions, and the federal civil service adopted it shortly after the Civil War.

But in 1905 the United States Supreme Court refused to uphold a state law limiting the hours of bakers to ten hours a day. Ruling in *Lochner* v. *New York* (198 U.S. 45 [1905]), the Court held that such a law was not "a legitimate exercise of the police power of the State, but an unreasonable, unnecessary, and arbitrary interference with the right and liberty of the individual to contract in relation to his labor. . . ."

After the *Lochner* decision progressives were forced to conclude that it was impractical to support limitations on hours that applied to *all* workers. But it occurred to some that a special case might be made in defense of a limit on working hours for women.

When the constitutionality of the Oregon ten-hour law for women was challenged, the National Consumers' League undertook the defense of the statute and hired attorney Louis D. Brandeis to present the case before the Supreme Court. The brief he presented to the court in *Muller* v. *Oregon* was startling and unprecedented. It consisted of only two pages of legal argument and over one hundred pages describing the "world's experience regarding women's hours of labor." Although the document became known as the Brandeis Brief, it was prepared largely by his sister-in-law Josephine Goldmark, a social worker and a staff member of the Consumers' League. Goldmark wrote a closely reasoned monograph, drawing on reports of factory inspectors, bureaus of labor statistics, commissioners of hygiene, and observations of physicians, and demonstrating that everywhere in the civilized world long hours had been shown to be detrimental to the health, safety, and morals of employed women. The style of argument, drawing as it did on social evidence as much as upon abstract legal reasoning, came to be known as "sociological jurisprudence." The style was widely employed; the government's case in 1954 in *Brown* v. *Board of Education,* on the desegregation of schools, had much in common with the Brandeis Brief.

In 1908 the Supreme Court upheld the constitutionality of the Oregon law, though making it clear that it was swayed primarily by the case made for women's physical vulnerability and couching the decision in terms of traditional sex roles. Fifteen years later, only five states lacked maximum hour legislation of some sort, although provisions varied widely.

Protective legislation for women had complex consequences. Obviously an eight-hour workday was vastly preferable to a longer one. But in the absence of a minimum wage, women living at the margin of subsistence found that limitations on the hours they could work cut their income or speeded up their piecework; some would not have chosen to trade time for money. Maximum hour legislation was often supplemented by restrictions against night work and "heavy" work (the latter often conveniently defined to include well-paying skilled work like iron molding), which further segregated women in the workplace and gave men an advantage in the competition for jobs. There is substantial evidence that male unions understood this when they supported protective legislation.*

Compare the reasoning in *Muller* to that offered in the *Bradwell* case (pp. 572–74) more than thirty-five years before. What were the advantages of pressing the argument of female weakness? What were the disadvantages?

---

*See Alice Kessler-Harris, *Out to Work: A History of Wage-Earning Women in the United States* (New York, 1982), pp. 201–5.

Mr. Justice David J. Brewer:

... It may not be amiss, in the present case, before examining the constitutional question, to notice the course of legislation, as well as expressions of opinion from other than judicial sources. In the brief filed by Mr. Louis D. Brandeis for the defendant . . . is a very copious collection of all these matters. . . .

The legislation and opinions referred to . . . may not be, technically speaking, authorities, and in them is little or no discussion of the constitutional question presented to us for determination, yet, they are significant of a widespread belief that woman's physical structure, and the functions she performs in consequence thereof, justify special legislation restricting or qualifying the conditions under which she should be permitted to toil. . . .

That woman's physical structure and the performance of maternal functions place her at a disadvantage in the struggle for subsistence is obvious. This is especially true when the burdens of motherhood are upon her. Even when they are not, by abundant testimony of the medical fraternity continuance for a long time on her feet at work, repeating this from day to day, tends to injurious effects upon the body, and, as healthy mothers are essential to vigorous offspring, the physical well-being of woman becomes an object of public interest and care in order to preserve the strength and vigor of the race.

... Differentiated by these matters from the other sex, she is properly placed in a class by herself, and legislation designed for her protection may be sustained, even when like legislation is not necessary for men, and could not be sustained. It is impossible to close one's eyes to the fact that she still looks to her brother and depends upon him. . . . her physical structure and a proper discharge of her maternal functions—having in view not merely her own health, but the well-being of the race—justify legislation to protect her from the greed as well as the passion of man. The limitations which this statute places upon her contractual powers, upon her right to agree with her employer as to the time she shall labor, are not imposed solely for her benefit, but also largely for the benefit of all. Many words cannot make this plainer. The two sexes differ in structure of body, in the functions to be performed by each, in the amount of physical strength, in the capacity for long continued labor, particularly when done standing, the influence of vigorous health upon the future well-being of the race, the self-reliance which enables one to assert full rights, and in the capacity to maintain the struggle for subsistence. This difference justifies a difference in legislation, and upholds that which is designed to compensate for some of the burdens which rest upon her.

We have not referred in this discussion to the denial of the elective franchise in the State of Oregon, for while it may disclose a lack of political equality in all things with her brother, that is not of itself decisive. The reason runs deeper, and rests in the inherent difference between the two sexes.

For these reasons, and without questioning in any respect the decision in *Lochner v. New York*, we are of the opinion that it cannot be adjudged that the act in question is in conflict with the Federal Constitution, so far as it respects the work of a female in a laundry, and the judgment of the Supreme Court of Oregon is Affirmed.

MacKenzie v. *Hare*, 1915

The persistent expansion of Married Women's Property Laws and the development of support for suffrage makes it tempting to conclude that the practice of coverture—women's civic subordination to men—steadily dissolved over the course of the nineteenth

239 U.S. 299.

and early twentieth centuries. But while it is true that some aspects of coverture eroded, others were sustained and even strengthened.

Although Chief Justice Morrison R. Waite had been right when he observed in *Minor v. Happersett* (1875) [pp. 575–76] "[t]here is no doubt that women may be citizens," he was wrong when he went on to claim that "sex has never been made one of the elements of citizenship. . . . [M]en have never had an advantage over women." According to the common law and early American practice, women, like men, became citizens either by birth or by their own choice to be naturalized. But in 1855, following practices established in France by the conservative Code Napoleon (1804) and in Britain in 1844, the U.S. Congress extended the principle of marital unity to provide that "any woman who might lawfully be naturalized under the existing laws, married, or shall be married to a citizen of the United States shall be deemed and taken to be a citizen." That is, foreign women who married male citizens did not need to go through a naturalization process or even take an oath of allegiance. The law made no comment about foreign-born men who might marry American women; for the next fifty years, there was little consistency in how courts dealt with the cases that came before them. But when the principle of "marital unity" prevailed, women who were American citizens actually lost their citizenship, and in 1907, Congress passed a statute that explicitly provided that women take the nationality of their husbands.

Expatriation—the loss of citizenship—traditionally has been a very severe punishment, usually reserved for cases of treason. If a married woman had to assume the nationality of her husband, she might become the subject of a king or tsar in a political system that offered her even less protection than did the United States. She might even become stateless. If Americans claimed to base their political system on the "consent of the governed," could women's "consent" be arbitrarily denied? In time of war, the American woman who married, say, a German national, could overnight change her status from a citizen to an alien enemy.

Ethel MacKenzie, who had been born in California, married Gordon Mackenzie, a British subject, in 1909—two years after the passage of the Citizenship Act of 1907. She was active in the woman suffrage movement in California, and when it was successful in 1911 she worked in the San Francisco voter registration drive. It is not surprising that she herself should try to register to vote. When the Board of Election Commissioners denied her application, holding that upon her marriage to a British subject she had "ceased to be a citizen of the United States," she refused to let her husband apply for citizenship and instead challenged the law, claiming that Congress had exceeded its authority. She could not believe that Congress had actually *intended* to deprive her of the citizenship she understood to be her birthright. Why did the Supreme Court deny her claim? What "ancient principle of jurisprudence" did they rely on? Why did the Court think that the marriage of an American woman to a foreign man should be treated differently than the marriage of an American man to a foreign woman?

MR. JUSTICE MCKENNA:

. . . The question . . . is, Did [Ethel MacKenzie] cease to be a citizen by her marriage? . . . [MacKenzie contends] that it was not the intention [of Congress] to deprive an American-born woman, remaining within the jurisdiction of the United States, of her citizenship by reason of her marriage to a resident foreigner. . . . [She is trying to persuade the Court that the citizenship statute was] beyond the authority of Congress. . . . [She offered the] earnest argument . . . that . . . under the Constitution and laws of the United States, [citizenship] became a right, privilege and immunity which could not be taken away from her except as a punishment for crime or by her voluntary expatriation. . . .

[But the Court concludes:] . . . The identity of husband and wife is an ancient principle of our jurisprudence. It was neither accidental nor arbitrary and worked in many instances for her protection. There has been, it is true, much relaxation of it but in its retention as in its origin it is determined by their intimate relation and unity of interests, and this relation and unity may make it of public concern in many instances to merge their identity, and give dominance to the husband. It has purpose, if not necessity, in purely domestic policy; it has greater purpose and, it may be, necessity, in international policy. . . . Having this purpose, has it not the sanction of power?

. . . The law in controversy deals with a condition voluntarily entered into. . . . The marriage of an American woman with a foreigner has consequences . . . [similar to] her physical expatriation. . . . Therefore, as long as the relation lasts it is made tantamount to expatriation. This is no arbitrary exercise of government. . . . It is the conception of the legislation under review that such an act [marriage to a foreign man] may bring the Government into embarrassments and, it may be, into controversies. . . . [Marriage to a foreign man] is as voluntary and distinctive as expatriation and its consequence must be considered as elected.

The decision in *MacKenzie* angered suffragists and energized them; American women needed suffrage to protect themselves against involuntary expatriation and statelessness. The repeal of the Citizenship Act of 1907 was high on the suffragists' agenda, and they turned to it as soon as suffrage was accomplished (see Equal Suffrage [Nineteenth] Amendment). The Cable Act of 1922 provided that "the right of a person to become a naturalized citizen shall not be denied to a person on account of sex or because she is a married woman," but it permitted American women who married foreigners to retain their citizenship only if they married men from countries whose subjects were eligible for U.S. citizenship—that is, not from China or Japan. American-born women who married aliens from China or Japan still lost their citizenship. American-born women who married aliens not from China or Japan were treated as naturalized citizens who would lose their citizenship should they reside abroad for two years. The Cable Act was extended by amendments well into the 1930s, but loopholes remained, and not all of it was made retroactive. As late as the 1950s, some American-born women were denied passports because they had married aliens before 1922.*

*This information relies heavily on Virginia Sapiro, "Women, Citizenship, and Nationality: Immigration and Naturalization Policies in the United States," *Politics and Society* XIII (1984):1–26; and Candice Dawn Bredbenner, "Toward Independent Citizenship: Married Women's Nationality Rights in the United States, 1855–1937," Ph.D. diss., University of Virginia, 1990.

Equal Suffrage (Nineteenth) Amendment, 1920

When the Fourteenth and Fifteenth Amendments (pp. 571–72) failed to provide for universal suffrage, a federal amendment was introduced into the Senate by S. C. Pomeroy of Kansas in 1868 and into the House by George W. Julian of Indiana in March 1869.

Historian Ellen DuBois has observed, "Previously the case for suffrage had consistently been put in terms of the individual rights of all persons, regardless of their sex and race. Angered by their exclusion from the Fifteenth Amendment, women's rights advocates began to develop fundamentally different arguments for their cause. They claimed their right to the ballot not as individuals but as a sex. . . . The reason women should vote was not that they were the same as men but that they were different. That made for a rather thorough reversal of classic women's rights premises."*

Arguing for the vote on the basis of women's *difference* from men could be effective in strengthening women's sense of group consciousness, but it also was compatible with racist and nativist arguments that white women needed the vote to counteract the suffrage of black and immigrant men. The old alliance of woman suffrage and abolitionist activism eroded, even though voting rights for black men were increasingly threatened after Reconstruction. The suffrage efforts of 1870 to 1920 continued to display arguments from equality, but younger generations of activists were increasingly likely to emphasize difference—what one activist called "the mother instinct for government."

Woman suffrage was not accomplished easily. One scholar has counted 480 suffrage campaigns between 1870 and 1910, but only seventeen referenda were held, with only two successes. Stanton died in 1902; Anthony in 1906. But a new, younger generation adopted new strategies; Americans were inspired by the militancy of the British suffrage movement; in 1902 Carrie Chapman Catt was simultaneously president of the International Woman Suffrage Alliance and the National American Woman Suffrage Association. By 1910 it was clear that a reinvigorated movement was underway, using door-to-door campaigns, street-corner speakers, poll watchers on election day. For the first time, cross-class suffrage organizations, like New York's Equality League of Independent Women, were mobilizing support for suffrage. Suffragists staged public parades that attracted tens of thousands of supporters.

Although many suffragists had claimed that when women got the vote there would be no more war, Catt swung NAWSA behind Woodrow Wilson and American support for the Allies and eventually support for American entry into World War I. In 1918, the House of Representatives passed the suffrage amendment, barely achieving the required two-thirds majority, but despite a personal appearance of President Wilson, it failed by only two votes to carry the Senate. As state after state fell into line, the number of congressmen dependent on women's votes increased; when a federal amendment was proposed in Congress, these men were likely to feel they had no choice but to support it. NAWSA targeted four senators in the fall elections; two of them failed to be re-elected. Energetic campaigns in the states to elect prosuffrage people to Congress worked. When the amendment came up in the new Congress, Anne F. Scott and Andrew Scott report, "224 of those voting yes came from suffrage states, and eighty from nonsuffrage states." It squeaked by in the Senate. It was ratified by thirty-five states by August 1920; after a bitter fight in Tennessee, it was ratified by a single vote, just in time to permit women to vote in the elections of 1920.

When Puerto Rican women attempted to register to vote in 1920, however, the U.S. Bureau of Insular Affairs decided that the Nineteenth Amendment did not automatically

*Ellen Carol DuBois, "Outgrowing the Compact of the Fathers: Equal Rights, Woman Suffrage, and the United States Constitution 1820–1878," *Journal of American History* 74 (1987):848.

apply to U.S. territories. Suffragist groups mobilized in Puerto Rico, lobbying throughout the next decade both on the island and in Washington, D.C., with support from the National Women's Party. In 1929 the territorial legislature granted suffrage to women restricted by a literacy requirement; not until Puerto Rico became a commonwealth, in 1952, was universal suffrage established.

Many southern states had excluded African-American men from voting by using literacy tests, poll taxes, and intimidation; in those states black women could vote no more easily than black men, and suffrage was an empty victory. The state of Georgia effectively discouraged white women from voting as well by providing that any woman who did not choose to register to vote did not have to pay the poll tax. This law, which encouraged women—and their husbands—to see voting as an expensive extravagance, was upheld by the U.S. Supreme Court in 1937. [*Breedlove* v. *Suttles,* 302 U.S. 277]

Section 1. The right of the citizens of the United States to vote shall not be denied or abridged by the United States or by any State on account of sex.

Section 2. Congress shall have power to enforce this article by appropriate legislation.

Adkins v. *Children's Hospital,* 1923

Minimum wage legislation was the counterpart to maximum hour laws. In 1918 Congress authorized the Wage Board of the District of Columbia to fix minimum wages for women and children in order to protect them "from conditions detrimental to their health and morals, resulting from wages which are inadequate to maintain decent standards of living."

This act was attacked, much as maximum hour legislation had been, as an interference with the right of the employer and employee to contract freely. Suit was brought against it by a hospital that employed many women at lower than minimum wages. Arguing for the Wage Board and on behalf of the Consumers' League was Felix Frankfurter, who used a Brandeis Brief researched by Molly Dewson that was a thousand pages long. He convinced Justices William Howard Taft and Oliver Wendell Holmes, Jr., that low wages and long hours were linked. In their dissenting opinion they stated that if Congress could regulate one it could regulate the other. Holmes also observed that the phrase "liberty of contract" did not appear in the Constitution.

The majority of the Court was not persuaded, however. The members of the majority distinguished between maximum hours legislation, which they saw as directly allied to health concerns, and minimum wage legislation, which they thought "simply and exclusively a price-fixing law." The majority also observed that the Nineteenth Amendment obviated the need for protective legislation for women. In taking that position, the

261 U.S. 525.

Justices were endorsing the arguments of Alice Paul and the National Women's Party, who had no faith in protective labor legislation and who were lobbying for an Equal Rights Amendment.

The *Adkins* decision blocked progress in minimum wage legislation for fifteen years, until there was a new president (Franklin D. Roosevelt) and a new approach in Congress. In 1938 the Fair Labor Standards Act established a federal minimum wage for *both* men and women. However, women continued often to be paid less than men for the same jobs. In 1963 the Equal Pay Act prohibited different pay for men and women when their jobs require "equal skill, effort and responsibility and are performed under similar working conditions." The Court has ruled that jobs meriting equal pay must be substantially equal but not necessarily identical: "Dusting is dusting is dusting" said one court in ruling that the pay of maids and janitors must be equal. More recently, the definition of what constitutes "equal skill, effort and responsibility" has been broadened to a public debate over what constitutes "comparable worth."

MR. JUSTICE GEORGE SUTHERLAND DELIVERED THE OPINION OF THE COURT:

... the ancient inequality of the sexes, otherwise than physical, as suggested in the *Muller Case* has continued "with diminishing intensity." In view of the great—not to say revolutionary—changes which have taken place since that utterance, in the contractual, political and civil status of women, culminating in the Nineteenth Amendment, it is not unreasonable to say that these differences have now come almost, if not quite, to the vanishing point. ... we cannot accept the doctrine that women of mature age, ... require or may be subjected to restrictions upon their liberty of contract which could not lawfully be imposed in the case of men under similar circumstances. To do so would be to ignore all the implications to be drawn from the present day trend of legislation, as well as that of common thought and usage, by which woman is accorded emancipation from the old doctrine that she must be given special protection or be subjected to special restraint in her contractual and civil relationships. ...

... What is sufficient to supply the necessary cost of living for a woman worker and maintain her in good health and protect her morals is obviously not a precise or unvarying sum. ... The amount will depend upon a variety of circumstances: the individual temperament, habits of thrift, care, ability to buy necessaries intelligently, and whether the woman live alone or with her family. ... It cannot be shown that well paid women safeguard their morals more carefully than those who are poorly paid. Morality rests upon other considerations than wages. ...

Hoyt v. Florida, 1961; Taylor v. Louisiana, 1975

Some members of the founding generation thought that service on juries was a more significant aspect of citizenship than voting; voting, after all, is complete in a moment, while service on juries requires extended periods of time, debate, and deliberation among the jurors, and ultimately the exercise of judgment, which can result in important consequences—including the death sentence—for an accused fellow citizen. The Constitu-

368 U.S. 57.

tion promises an "impartial" jury drawn from "the district wherein the crime shall have been committed." The conditions of impartiality are not spelled out; the Constitution promises neither "a jury of one's peers," nor one drawn from a "cross-section" of the community. It is tradition that has linked the concept of the jury with "peers," neighbors, and the community in which the crime is committed and from which the jury is chosen.

When women achieved the vote in Wyoming in 1869, it seemed to follow that they could hold office and serve on juries, but after only a few years the objection of male voters and officeholders was so severe that the law was changed to exclude them.

In some states, the achievement of jury service followed painlessly on the heels of suffrage. In Iowa, Michigan, Nevada, and Pennsylvania, where statutes defined as competent jurors "all qualified electors . . . of good moral character, sound judgment, and in full possession of the senses of hearing and seeing, and who can speak, write and read the English language," the admission of women to the electorate automatically defined them as competent jurors. When these interpretations were tested in state courts, judges usually upheld them. Not all state courts, however, thought it was obvious that "electors" could be properly construed to mean women as well as men. In 1925 the Illinois Supreme Court ruled that because only men had been voters in 1874 when the jury statute had been passed, the terms "legal voters" and "electors" referred only to male persons. Not until 1939 did the Illinois state legislature permit women to serve on juries.

In most states, new statutes were required. By 1923, eighteen states and the territory of Alaska had arranged for women to serve on juries. But then the momentum ran out; subsequently the issue had to be debated afresh in each state. A few states continued to exclude women completely, but most developed some form of "voluntary" jury service, in which women could be called to serve but could easily decline. In Florida, no women at all served on juries until 1949, when the legislature passed a law providing that women who wished to be eligible could go to their county courthouses and register their willingness to have their names placed in the jury pool.

When Gwendolyn Hoyt came to trial in Tampa in 1957, charged with manslaughter for killing her husband, only 218 women of the more than 46,000 women voters in Hillsborough County had registered to serve; the jury commissioner placed only 10 of those women's names in a pool of 10,000 names. It was no surprise that she was tried—and found guilty—by an all-male jury. It took the six-man jury only twenty-five minutes to convict Gwendolyn Hoyt of second-degree murder; on January 20, 1958, she was sentenced to imprisonment at hard labor for thirty years.

Hoyt appealed, first to the Florida Supreme Court, and then to the U.S. Supreme Court, which heard the case in 1961. Hoyt claimed temporary insanity, brought on by her suspicions of her husband's infidelity, his rejection of her offer of reconciliation, and her own vulnerability to epilepsy. She believed that women would understand her distress better than would men. Her lawyers did not claim that a fair jury was required to have women as members; rather, they claimed that a fair jury would have been drawn at random from a list of names from which women had not been excluded. Hoyt claimed that in order to have enjoyed the right to a trial by a jury of her peers, other women would have to be obligated to serve on juries. To grant other women the privilege of easy avoidance of jury duty, she and her lawyers thought, was to diminish Hoyt's right to a fair trial. The prosecution argued, instead, that if men and women were truly equal, Hoyt should have no objection to being judged by men.

MR. JUSTICE JOHN MARSHALL HARLAN:

At the core of appellant's argument is the claim that the nature of the crime of which she was convicted peculiarly demanded the inclusion of persons of her own sex on the jury. She was charged with killing her husband ... in the context of a marital upheaval involving, among other things, the suspected infidelity of appellant's husband, and culminating in the husband's final rejection of his wife's efforts at reconciliation. It is claimed, in substance, that women jurors would have been more understanding or compassionate than men in assessing the quality of appellant's act and her defense of "temporary insanity." No claim is made that the jury as constituted was otherwise afflicted by any elements of supposed unfairness.

... [T]he right to an impartially selected jury assured by the Fourteenth Amendment ... does not entitle one accused of crime to a jury tailored to the circumstances of the particular case, whether relating to the sex or other condition of the defendant, or to the nature of the charges to be tried. It requires only that the jury be indiscriminately drawn from among those eligible in the community for jury service, un-

trammelled by any arbitrary and systematic exclusions.... The result of this appeal must therefore depend on whether such an exclusion of women from jury service has been shown.

... Florida's [law] does not purport to exclude women from state jury service. Rather, the statute "gives to women the privilege to serve but does not impose service as a duty." It accords women an absolute exemption from jury service unless they expressly waive that privilege.... [W]e [cannot] ... conclude that Florida's statute is ... infected with unconstitutionality. Despite the enlightened emancipation of women from the restrictions and protections of bygone years, and their entry into many parts of community life formerly considered to be reserved to men, woman is still regarded as the center of home and family life. We cannot say that it is constitutionally impermissible for a State, acting in pursuit of the general welfare, to conclude that a woman should be relieved from the civil duty of jury service unless she herself determines that such service is consistent with her own special responsibilities.

II

... Finding no substantial evidence whatever in this record that Florida has arbitrarily undertaken to exclude women from jury service

... we must sustain the judgment of the Supreme Court of Florida.

JUSTICES WARREN, BLACK, AND DOUGLAS:

We cannot say from this record that Florida is not making a good faith effort to have women perform jury duty without discrimination on

the ground of sex. Hence we concur in the result, for reasons set forth in Part II of the Court's opinion.

Why do you think Warren, Black, and Douglas wrote a separate concurring opinion? To what extent was the Court's opinion based on arguments from equality? on arguments from difference?

When Ruth Bader Ginsburg began to work on the ACLU's Women's Rights Project (see *Frontiero* v. *Richardson*, pp. 590–92), she was committed to persuading the Supreme Court to reverse its decisions on several major cases that had sustained sex discrimination; one of those cases was *Hoyt*. Not until 1975, in a case arising in Louisiana, a state in which women were still required to file a written declaration of their desire to be subject to jury service, was *Hoyt* reversed by the Supreme Court. Billy Taylor, convicted of rape and kidnapping, successfully appealed his conviction on the grounds that women had been systematically excluded from the jury pool. His lawyers drew an analogy between his experience and the Court's decision three years before that a white man was entitled to have a jury from which blacks had not been systematically barred. The majority opinion upheld Taylor's claim. It made extensive use of an opinion written by Justice William O. Douglas in 1946. What did Douglas mean when he said, "the two sexes are not fungible"? Do you agree?

MR. JUSTICE BYRON R. WHITE DELIVERED THE OPINION OF THE COURT:*

The Louisiana jury-selection system does not disqualify women from jury service, but in operation its conceded systematic impact is that only a few women, grossly disproportionate to the number of eligible women in the community, are called for jury service. In this case, no women were on the venire from which the petit jury was drawn. . . .

The State first insists that Taylor, a male, has no standing to object to the exclusion of women from his jury. . . . Taylor was not a member of the excluded class; but there is no rule that claims such as Taylor presents may be made only by those defendants who are members of the group excluded from jury service. In [1972] . . . a white man [successfully] challenged his conviction on the ground that Negroes had been systematically excluded from jury service. . . .

We are . . . persuaded that the fair-cross-section requirement is violated by the systematic exclusion of women, who in the judicial district involved here amounted to 53 percent of the citizens eligible for jury service. . . . This very matter was debated in *Ballard* v. *U.S.* [1946]. . . . The . . . view that an all-male panel drawn from various groups in the community would be as truly representative as if women were included, was firmly rejected:

> . . . who would claim that a jury was truly representative of the community if all men were intentionally and systematically excluded from the panel? The truth is that the two sexes are not fungible; a community made up exclusively of one is different from a community composed of both; the subtle interplay of influence one on the other is among the imponderables. . . . The exclusion of one may indeed make the jury less representative of the community than would be true if an economic or racial group were excluded. [Justice William O. Douglas, 1946]

. . . It is untenable to suggest these days that it would be a special hardship for each and every woman to perform jury service . . . it may be burdensome to sort out those who should be exempted from those who should serve. But that task is performed in the case of men, and the administrative convenience in dealing with women as a class is insufficient justification for diluting the quality of community judgment represented by the jury in criminal trials.

The decision in *Taylor* addressed only the problem of who is included in the panels from whom jurors are chosen. Not until 1994 did the Supreme Court rule that the Fourteenth Amendment's Equal Protection Clause prohibits the use of peremptory jury challenges on the basis of gender. Overturning a paternity suit in which a woman challenged virtually all the men in the jury pool, leaving an all-female jury to decide on her claims for child support, the majority held "that gender, like race, is an unconstitutional proxy for juror competence and impartiality."†

Taylor v. *Louisiana*, 419 U.S. 522 (1975).

†*J.E.B.* v. *Alabama ex rel. T.B.*, No. 92-1239 (April 19, 1994).

Civil Rights Act, Title VII, 1964

The Civil Rights Act of 1964 was a comprehensive law of enormous significance. It was a complex statute, twenty-eight printed pages long and divided into eleven major sections, or *Titles*. Title I dealt with voting rights; Title III with the desegregation of public facilities; Title V established a Commission on Civil Rights. Title VII defined a long list of practices that would be forbidden to employers and labor unions, obliged the federal government to undertake an "affirmative" program of equal employment opportunity for all employees and job applicants, and created an Equal Employment Opportunity Commission (EEOC) to monitor compliance with the law.

Title VII was notable in that it outlawed discrimination on the basis of gender as well as of race. Sex was added to the categories "race, color, religion and national origin" by Congressman Howard Smith of Virginia, who hoped to defeat the legislation; he joked that an amendment adding the category "sex" would guarantee the "right" of every woman to a husband. Representative Martha Griffiths of Michigan and other congresswomen supported the bill, ironically receiving support from conservative colleagues who spoke on behalf of the amendment in the hope that the prospect of sexual equality might cause the entire bill to fail.

The Equal Employment Opportunity Commission, which began to operate in the summer of 1965, anticipated that virtually all its complaints would come from blacks. They were surprised to discover that 25 percent of the complaints received during the first year were from women. In the course of responding to these complaints, both the commission and the courts were driven to a more subtle analysis of female job categories and work patterns. Section 703(e)1 required that employers wishing to define a job category by sex had to show that sex was a "bona fide occupational qualification"; it was not enough to say that men or women had traditionally filled any given job.

The act was amended in 1972 and again in 1978; on both occasions the EEOC was given substantial additional powers and responsibilities. The three major areas of EEOC activity are: (1) furnishing assistance to comparable state agencies, (2) furnishing advice to employers and labor unions about compliance, and (3) enforcing compliance by conciliation and by legal action. In 1978 Congress passed the Pregnancy Discrimination Act, which amplified the definition of *sex* to include pregnancy, childbirth, or related medical conditions. EEOC has been willing to view sexual harassment as a form of sex discrimination but has not endorsed the concept of comparable worth.

Sec. 703. (a) It shall be an unlawful employment practice for an employer—

(1) to fail or refuse to hire or to discharge any individual, or otherwise to discriminate against any individual with respect to his compensation, terms, conditions, or privileges of employment, because of such individual's race, color, religion, sex, or national origin; or

(2) to limit, segregate, or classify his employees in any way which would deprive or tend to deprive any individual of employment oppor-

U.S. Statutes at Large, 78:253–66. For a full discussion of Title VII, see Donald Allen Robinson, "Two Movements in Pursuit of Equal Employment Opportunity," *Signs: Journal of Women in Culture and Society* 4 (1979):413–33.

tunities or otherwise adversely affect his status as an employee, because of such individual's race, color, religion, sex, or national origin.

(b) It shall be an unlawful employment practice for an employment agency to fail or refuse to refer for employment, or otherwise to discriminate against, any individual because of his race, color, religion, sex, or national origin, or to classify or refer for employment any individual on the basis of his race, color, religion, sex, or national origin.

(c) It shall be an unlawful employment practice for a labor organization—

(1) to exclude or to expel from its membership, or otherwise to discriminate against, any individual because of his race, color, religion, sex, or national origin;

(2) to limit, segregate, or classify its membership, or to classify or fail or refuse to refer for employment any individual, in any way which would deprive or tend to deprive any individual of employment opportunities, or would limit such employment opportunities or otherwise adversely affect his status as an employee or as an applicant for employment, because of such individual's race, color, religion, sex, or national origin; or

(3) to cause or attempt to cause an employer to discriminate against an individual in violation of this section. . . .

(e) Notwithstanding any other provision of this title, (1) it shall not be an unlawful employment practice for an employer to hire and employ employees, for an employment agency to classify, or refer for employment any individual, for a labor organization to classify its membership or to classify or refer for employment any individual, or for an employer, labor organization, or joint labor-management committee controlling apprenticeship or other training or retraining programs to admit or employ any individual in any such program, on the basis of his religion, sex, or national origin in those certain instances where religion, sex, or national origin is a bona fide occupational qualification reasonably necessary to normal operation of that particular business or enterprise. . . .

Sec. 705. (a) There is hereby created a Commission to be known as the Equal Employment Opportunity Commission, which shall be composed of five members, not more than three of whom shall be members of the same political party, who shall be appointed by the President by and with the advice and consent of the Senate. . . .

(g) The Commission shall have power—

(1) to cooperate with and, with their consent, utilize regional, State, local, and other agencies, both public and private, and individuals; . . .

(3) to furnish to persons subject to this title such technical assistance as they may request to further their compliance with this title or an order issued thereunder;

(4) upon the request of (i) any employer, whose employees or some of them, or (ii) any labor organization, whose members or some of them, refuse or threaten to refuse to cooperate in effectuating the provisions of this title, to assist in such effectuation by conciliation or such other remedial action as is provided by this title;

(5) to make such technical studies as are appropriate to effectuate the purposes and policies of this title and to make the results of such studies available to the public;

(6) to refer matters to the Attorney General with recommendations for intervention in a civil action brought by an aggrieved party under section 706, or for the institution of a civil action by the Attorney General under section 707, and to advise, consult, and assist the Attorney General on such matters. . . .

Equal Rights Amendment, 1972

An equal rights amendment, with wording slightly different from that passed by Congress in 1972, was sponsored in 1923 by the National Woman's Party. It seemed to party members the logical corollary to suffrage. But that amendment was vigorously opposed by the League of Women Voters and other progressive reformers, lest it undermine the protective legislation for which they had fought so hard.

An equal rights amendment was introduced regularly in Congress virtually every year thereafter, but it received little attention until after World War II. In 1950 and 1953 it was passed by the Senate but ignored by the House.

By 1970 much protective legislation had been applied to both men and women. It was possible to support an equal rights amendment without risking the undoing of labor law reforms. The hope that the Supreme Court would apply the Fourteenth Amendment's "equal protection of the laws" clause to cases involving discrimination on the basis of sex as firmly as it applied the clause to cases involving racial discrimination had not been fulfilled. When the current Equal Rights Amendment was introduced in 1970, it was endorsed by a wide range of organizations, some of which had once opposed it; these organizations included groups as disparate as the United Automobile Workers and the Woman's Christian Temperance Union. Its main sponsor in the House was Martha Griffiths of Michigan; in the Senate, Birch Bayh of Indiana.

The ERA was passed by Congress on March 22, 1972, and sent to the states for ratification. There was much initial enthusiasm; within two days six states had ratified. But the pace of ratification slowed after 1975, and only thirty-five of the needed thirty-eight states had ratified it by 1978. (Four state legislatures voted to rescind ratification, although the legality of that move was open to question.) In October 1978 Congress extended the deadline for ratification to June 30, 1982; the extension expired with no additional ratifications. The amendment was reintroduced in Congress in 1983 but has not been passed.

Section 1. Equality of rights under the law shall not be denied or abridged by the United States or by any State on account of sex.

Section 2. The Congress shall have the power to enforce, by appropriate legislation, the provisions of this article.

Section 3. The amendment shall take effect two years after the date of ratification.

Frontiero v. *Richardson,* 1973

Sharron A. Frontiero was an Air Force officer who was dismayed to discover that she could not claim dependent's benefits for her husband on the same terms that her male colleagues could for their wives. She and her husband brought suit, claiming that statutes requiring spouses of female members of the uniformed services to receive more than half of their support from their wives to be considered dependents, while all spouses of male members were treated as dependents, violated the due process clause of the Fifth Amendment and the equal protection clause of the Fourteenth Amendment.

Until 1971, the Supreme Court had never ruled that discrimination on the basis of sex was a violation of the equal protection clause of the Fourteenth Amendment. So long as a legislature had a "reasonable" basis for making distinctions between men and women, discriminatory laws were upheld. Between 1971 and 1975, in a stunning series of decisions, the Supreme Court placed the burden of proof that discrimination on the basis of sex was reasonable on those who tried to discriminate. Ruth Bader Ginsburg was a 38-year-old lawyer working for the American Civil Liberties Union in 1971 when the Court accepted her argument that an Idaho law requiring that fathers, rather than mothers, always be preferred as executors of their children's estates was unconstitutional. (*Reed* v. *Reed* 404 U.S. 71 [1971].)

The ACLU set up a Women's Rights Project with Ginsburg at its head to follow up on the implications of the *Reed* decision. Ginsburg wrote the brief and managed the argument in *Frontiero;* it was one of a brilliant series of cases that she argued in the early 1970s. With her colleagues, she helped persuade the Court that a wide range of discriminatory practices were illegal. Her career as a litigator would lead to her appointment as a judge on the U.S. Court of Appeals in 1980 and, in 1993, to her appointment to the U.S. Supreme Court.

The Supreme Court ruled in favor of the Frontieros in a complex decision that used statistical information about woman's place in the work force in a manner reminiscent of the Brandeis Brief. Speaking for three of his colleagues Justice William J. Brennan, Jr., prepared a historically based argument, explaining the distance American public opinion had traveled since the *Bradwell* case (see *Bradwell* v. *Illinois,* pp. 572–74). He drew analogies between discrimination on the basis of race, which the court subjected to strict scrutiny, and discrimination on the basis of sex.

In concurring with Brennan's opinion, three justices observed that although they agreed with the Frontieros in this particular case, they were not yet persuaded that sex ought to be regularly treated as a "suspect category." Only when—or if—the Equal Rights Amendment were passed could the Court be sure that the public agreed that discrimination on the basis of sex ought to be evaluated as critically as discrimination

411 U.S. 677. See also *Craig* v. *Boren* 429 U.S. 190 (1976).

on the basis of race. Note that the facts in *Frontiero* relate to discrimination against the husband of the wage earner, not directly against a woman. It is the family of the wage earner that is discriminated against. A similar case, also argued by Ginsburg, is *Weinberger v. Weisenfeld* (420 U.S. 636 [1975]), in which the husband of a dead woman successfully demanded survivor's benefits equal to those available to widows. Ginsburg and her colleagues stressed that both men and women benefited from gender-blind equal treatment under the law.

MR. JUSTICE WILLIAM J. BRENNAN, JR. DELIVERED THE OPINION OF THE COURT:

The question before us concerns the right of a female member of the uniformed services to claim her spouse as a "dependent." . . .

At the outset, appellants contend that classifications based upon sex, like classifications based upon race, alienage, and national origin, are inherently suspect and must therefore be subjected to close judicial scrutiny. We agree. . . .

There can be no doubt that our Nation has had a long and unfortunate history of sex discrimination. Traditionally, such discrimination was rationalized by an attitude of "romantic paternalism" which, in practical effect, put women, not on a pedestal, but in a cage. Indeed, this paternalistic attitude became so firmly rooted in our national consciousness that, 100 years ago, a distinguished Member of this Court was able to proclaim. . . . "The natural and proper timidity and delicacy which belongs to the female sex evidently unfits it for many of the occupations of civil life." . . .

It is true, of course, that the position of women in America has improved markedly in recent decades. Nevertheless, it can hardly be doubted that, in part because of the high visibility of the sex characteristic, women still face pervasive, although at times more subtle, discrimination in our educational institutions, in the job market, and perhaps most conspicuously, in the political arena. . . .

Moreover, since sex, like race and national origin, is an immutable characteristic determined solely by the accident of birth, the imposition of special disabilities upon the member of a particular sex because of their sex would seem to violate "the basic concept of our system that legal burdens should bear some relationship to individual responsibility. . . ." And what differentiates sex from such non-suspect statuses as intelligence or physical disability, and aligns it with the recognized suspect criteria, is that the sex characteristic frequently bears no relation to ability to perform or contribute to society. . . .

. . . over the past decade, Congress has itself manifested an increasing sensitivity to sex-based classifications. In Tit[le] VII of the Civil Rights Act of 1964, for example, Congress expressly declared that no employer, labor union, or other organization subject to the provisions of the Act shall discriminate against any individual on the basis of "race, color, religion, *sex*, or national origin." Similarly, the Equal Pay Act of 1963 provides that no employer covered by the Act "shall discriminate . . . between employees on the basis of sex." . . .

With these considerations in mind, we can only conclude that classifications based upon sex, like classifications based upon race, alienage, or national origin, are inherently suspect, and must therefore be subjected to strict judicial scrutiny. Applying the analysis mandated by that stricter standard of review, it is clear that the statutory scheme now before us is constitutionally invalid. . . .

MR. JUSTICE LEWIS F. POWELL, JR., WITH WHOM THE CHIEF JUSTICE AND MR. JUSTICE HARRY A. BLACKMUN JOIN, CONCURRING IN THE OPINION:

I agree that the challenged statutes constitute an unconstitutional discrimination against servicewomen . . . but I cannot join the opinion of Mr. Justice Brennan, which would hold that all classifications based upon sex . . . are "inherently suspect and must therefore be subjected to close judicial scrutiny." . . . The Equal Rights Amendment, which if adopted will resolve the substance of this precise question, has been approved by the Congress and submitted for ratification by the States. If this Amendment is duly adopted, it will represent the will of the people accomplished in the manner prescribed by the constitution. . . . It seems to me that this reaching out to pre-empt by judicial action a major political decision which is currently in process of resolution does not reflect appropriate respect for duly prescribed legislative processes.

Roe v. *Wade*, 1973; *Planned Parenthood of Southeastern Pennsylvania* v. *Casey*, 1992

The Comstock Law had been echoed by a series of anticontraception and antiabortion laws throughout the country. James Mohr observes, "Every state in the Union had [by 1900] an antiabortion law of some kind on its books . . . except Kentucky, where the state courts outlawed the practice anyway."* In 1962 the ethics of abortion became a pressing problem when it was revealed that thalidomide, a drug extensively used in Europe and occasionally in the United States, resulted in the birth of thousands of babies with phocomelia (deformed or missing arms and legs). Sherry Finkbine, an Arizona woman who had taken the drug, demanded a legal abortion. Although her doctors supported her, the county medical society refused to approve the procedure, and, lacking confidence that she and her doctors would be spared immunity from prosecution, she fled to Sweden, where abortion was legal.

Her plight, and her challenge to hospital practice, helped to shift public opinion, both within the medical profession, which would subsequently be instrumental in advocating liberalization of abortion legislation, and among women's groups, who began to articulate dismay that women were generally denied access to safe abortion services. Estimates of the number of illegal abortions performed each year before 1973 range from 200,000 to 1,200,000; it is estimated that 200 women died each year as a result. Abortion was virtually the only medical procedure to which middle-class women did not have access. The issue was less intense for black women's groups; working-class minority women lacked a wide range of medical services, and abortion was only one among many which they needed. Thus at the beginning of the reinvigorated women's movement of the late 1960s, black and white women were divided about the place that access to legal abortion should hold in their list of priorities for legal change.

In 1970, Alaska, Hawaii, New York, and Washington legalized abortion. Texas law, like the law of most states, continued to prohibit abortion except for the purpose of saving

---

*James C. Mohr, *Abortion in America: The Origins and Evolution of National Policy, 1800–1900* (New York, 1978), pp. 229–30.

410 U.S. 113; 112 S. Ct. 2791.

the mother's life. In 1970, Norma McCorvey, a single pregnant woman, known as Jane Roe to protect her privacy, brought a class action suit challenging the constitutionality of that law as a violation of her right to liberty as guaranteed by the due process clause of the Fourteenth Amendment.

The Supreme Court's decision in *Roe* v. *Wade* marked a sharp change from long-established practice. As the opening lines of the majority decision make clear, the justices were aware they were making a sensitive and important decision.

MR. JUSTICE HARRY A. BLACKMUN DELIVERED THE OPINION OF THE COURT:

We forthwith acknowledge our awareness of the sensitive and emotional nature of the abortion controversy, of the vigorous opposing views, even among physicians, and of the deep and seemingly absolute convictions that the subject inspires. One's philosophy, one's experiences, one's exposure to the raw edges of human existence, one's religious training, one's attitudes toward life and family and their values, and the moral standards one establishes and seeks to observe, are all likely to influence and to color one's thinking and conclusions about abortion.

In addition, population growth, pollution, poverty, and racial overtones tend to complicate and not to simplify the problem.

Our task, of course, is to resolve the issue by constitutional measurement, free of emotion and of predilection. We seek earnestly to do this. . . .

The principal thrust of the appellant's attack on the Texas statutes is that they improperly invade a right, said to be possessed by the pregnant woman, to choose to terminate her pregnancy. Appellant would discover this right in the concept of personal "liberty" embodied in the Fourteenth Amendment's Due Process Clause; or in personal, marital, familial and sexual privacy said to be protected by the Bill of Rights . . . or among those rights reserved to the people by the Ninth Amendment. . . .

It perhaps is not generally appreciated that the restrictive criminal abortion laws in effect in a majority of States today are of relatively recent vintage. Those laws, generally proscribing abortion or its attempt at any time during pregnancy except when necessary to preserve the pregnant woman's life, are not of ancient or even of common-law origin. Instead, they derive from statutory changes effected, for the most part, in the latter half of the nineteenth century. . . . At common law, at the time of the adoption of our Constitution, and throughout the major portion of the nineteenth century . . . a woman enjoyed a substantially broader right to terminate a pregnancy than she does in most states today. . . .

When most criminal abortion laws were first enacted, the procedure was a hazardous one for the woman. This was particularly true prior to the development of antisepsis. . . . Abortion mortality was high. . . . Modern medical techniques have altered this situation. Appellants . . . refer to medical data indicating that abortion in early pregnancy, that is, prior to the end of the first trimester, although not without its risk, is now relatively safe. Mortality rates for women undergoing early abortions, where the procedure is legal, appear to be as low as or lower than the rates for normal childbirth. Consequently, any interest of the State in protecting the woman from an inherently hazardous procedure . . . has largely disappeared. . . . The State has a legitimate interest in seeing to it that abortion, like any other medical procedure, is performed under circumstances that insure maximum safety for the patient. . . .

The Constitution does not explicitly mention any right of privacy. In a line of decisions, however . . . the Court has recognized that a right of personal privacy, or a guarantee of certain areas or zones of privacy, does exist under the Constitution. . . . This right . . . whether it be founded in the Fourteenth Amendment's concept of personal liberty . . . or . . . in the Ninth Amendment's reservation of rights to the people, is broad enough to encompass a woman's decision whether or not to terminate her pregnancy. . . . We . . . conclude that the right of personal privacy includes the abortion decision, but that this right is not unqualified and must be considered against important state interests in regulation. . . .

. . . the State does have an important and legitimate interest in preserving and protecting the health of the pregnant woman ... and ... it has still *another* important and legitimate interest in protecting the potentiality of human life. These interests are separate and distinct. Each grows in substantiality as the woman approaches term, and, at a point during pregnancy, each becomes "compelling."

With respect to the State's important and legitimate interest in the health of the mother, the "compelling" point, in the light of present medical knowledge, is at approximately the end of the first trimester. This is so because of the now-established medical fact ... that until the end of the first trimester mortality in abortion may be less than mortality in normal childbirth. It follows that ... for the period of pregnancy prior to this "compelling" point, the attending physician, in consultation with his patient, is free to determine, without regulation by the State, that in his medical judgment, the patient's pregnancy should be terminated.

... For the state subsequent to approximately the end of the first trimester, the State, in promoting its interest in the health of the mother, may, if it chooses, regulate the abortion procedure in ways that are reasonably related to maternal health.

For the state subsequent to viability, the State in promoting its interest in the potentiality of human life may, if it chooses, regulate, and even proscribe, abortion except where it is necessary, in appropriate medical judgment, for the preservation of the life or health of the mother.

Our conclusion ... is ... that the Texas abortion statutes, as a unit, must fall. ...

In the years before 1973, when abortion was generally illegal, commonly performed in the private offices of doctors and unlicensed practitioners without emergency medical support, and generally without anesthesia, death from abortion was substantial. It is estimated that at least 200 deaths a year occurred when abortion was illegal. In 1985, it was estimated that only two deaths occurred from illegal abortion and only six deaths resulted from legal abortion.

The issues that were raised by *Roe* v. *Wade* have not been fully settled and are not likely to be easily resolved, touching as they do on basic religious and ethical beliefs. Because only women become pregnant, and because there is no obvious parallel to pregnancy in male experience, arguments about abortion are less easily made on the equal treatment grounds that served women's rights activists well in *Frontiero* (see *Frontiero* v. *Richardson*, pp. 590–92). and other similar cases. Advocates must ask what equal treatment would mean for men and women, who are differently situated in relation to abortion.

In the 1980s, a number of states tested what boundaries would be considered reasonable limits on the abortion rights sustained in Roe. In 1980, the Supreme Court upheld the "Hyde Amendment" by which Congress refused to fund even medically necessary abortions for indigent women (*Harris* v. *McRae*, 448 U.S. 297). This decision was not the focus of massive public protest, and it was replicated in the laws of many states. An effort to defeat the Hyde Amendment failed in Congress in 1993, but some states did revise their practice, covering some abortions for indigent women, usually in the case of rape or incest.

Missouri legislators developed further the position that the state could deny any form of public support or facilities for the performance of abortions. A 1986 law prohibited the use of public employees and facilities to perform or assist abortions not necessary to save the life of the mother and also prohibited the use of public funds for counseling a woman in abortion decisions not necessary to save her life. It included a preamble that claimed that the life of each human being begins at conception and a provision that required that medical tests of fetal viability—tests whose efficacy was disputed—be performed before any abortion on a fetus estimated to be twenty weeks or more in gestation.

Since 97 percent of all late abortions (done at an estimated sixteen-week gestational age) were performed at a single hospital in Kansas City that, although private, received public aid and was located on public property, the practical impact of the law was great.

In deciding *Webster* v. *Reproductive Health Services* in July 1989, by a 5–3 vote, the Supreme Court majority claimed that the conclusions of *Roe* had not been changed.* Missouri law left a pregnant woman free to terminate her pregnancy so long as neither public funds nor facilities were used for it; this was, the Court majority said, a "value judgment" favoring childbirth over abortion. But the majority raised a general question about *Roe*. "[T]he rigid Roe framework," wrote Chief Justice Rehnquist in the majority opinion, "is hardly consistent with the notion of a Constitution cast in general terms, as ours is, and usually speaking in general principles, as ours does. The key elements of the *Roe* framework—trimesters and viability—are not found in the text of the Constitution or in any place else one would expect to find a constitutional principle . . . the result has been a web of legal rules that . . . [resemble] a code of regulations rather than a body of constitutional doctrine." Justice Anthony Scalia concurred, adding that in his view, *Roe* should have been overturned; abortion is, he thought, a field in which the Court "has little proper business since the answers to most of the cruel questions posed are political and not juridical." He was appalled at efforts to bring the pressure of public opinion to bear on the decisions of the Court, notably the March on Washington of some 200,000 people that had been sponsored by pro-choice groups shortly before the *Webster* case was argued in April 1989.

Justice Harry A. Blackmun, who had written the Court's opinion in *Roe*, now wrote a bitter dissent for the minority. He denied that Rehnquist's opinion left *Roe* "undisturbed." Rather it challenged a large body of legal precedent that had established a "private sphere of individual liberty," which although not explicitly specified in the Constitution had long been taken to have been implied by the Fourth Amendment guarantee against unreasonable searches. The right to privacy had been invoked in the 1960s when the Court protected the sale and use of birth control devices; the *Webster* decision, Blackmun feared, bypassed "the true jurisprudential debate underlying this case: . . . whether and to what extent . . . a right to privacy extends to matters of childbearing and family life, including abortion." Justice John Paul Stevens argued that the preamble's claim that life begins at conception was a religious view, and to write it into law was to ignore First Amendment requirements for the separation of church and state. Finally, Blackmun argued that the state had a distinct interest in maintaining public health, and that as safe and legal abortions became more difficult to get, an increase in deaths from illegal abortions could be predicted. "For today," he concluded, "the women of this Nation still retain the liberty to control their destinies. But the signs are evident and very ominous, and a chill wind blows."

The Court's decision in *Webster* left many questions open. If states could deny public funds for abortions, what other limitations was it reasonable for state legislatures to impose? Was it reasonable to require a waiting period? Was it reasonable to require minors to get the consent of one parent? of both parents? The Court had ruled in 1976 that a state could not require a married woman to get her husband's consent before

---

*William L. Webster, Attorney General of Missouri v. Reproductive Health Services, 109 Sup. Ct. 3040 (1989).

having an abortion (*Planned Parenthood* v. *Danforth*, 428 U.S. 52 [1976]); could a state require a married woman to *notify* her husband?

In 1988 and 1989 Pennsylvania amended its Abortion Control Act of 1982 extensively, requiring a twenty-four-hour waiting period and the provision of "certain information" twenty-four hours before the abortion is performed. Minors were required to have the consent of one parent, and married women to have notified their husbands, although it was possible for a court to waive that requirement and all requirements could be waived in the event of a "medical emergency." Because most of the Justices had made public substantial reservations about the decision in *Roe*, it seemed to many observers not unreasonable to predict that the Court would uphold the entire Pennsylvania statute and, possibly, overturn *Roe* v. *Wade*. Instead, a majority organized by Justices Sandra Day O'Connor, Anthony Kennedy, and David Souter, joined by Harry Blackmun and John Paul Stevens, wrote a complex opinion, which began with a ringing affirmation of *Roe*. But O'Connor, Kennedy, and Souter also made it clear that they shared Rehnquist's skepticism of the trimester framework of *Roe*. How does the majority think the principle of equal protection of the laws should be applied in abortion decisions?

Note the comments on coverture at the end of the majority opinion; this statement marks the first explicit recognition by the Court of the end of coverture.

Why do the dissenting Justices think *Roe* should be overturned?

PLANNED PARENTHOOD OF SOUTHEASTERN PENNSYLVANIA V. *CASEY*

JUSTICES O'CONNOR, KENNEDY, SOUTER:
Liberty finds no refuge in a jurisprudence of doubt. Yet 19 years after our holding that the Constitution protects a woman's right to terminate her pregnancy in its early stages . . . that definition of liberty is still questioned. . . . After considering the fundamental constitutional questions resolved by *Roe*, principles of institutional integrity, and the rule of *stare decisis* [the principle that decisions of previous courts should be let stand unless there is overwhelming reason to change them], we are led to conclude this: the essential holding of *Roe* v. *Wade* should be retained and once again reaffirmed. . . . Constitutional protection of the woman's decision to terminate her pregnancy derives from the Due Process Clause of the Fourteenth Amendment. It declares that no State shall "deprive any person of life, liberty, or property, without due process of law." . . . It is a premise of the Constitution that there is a realm of personal liberty which the government may not enter. We have vindicated this principle before. Marriage is mentioned nowhere in the Bill of Rights and interracial marriage was illegal in most States in the 19th cen-

tury, but the Court was no doubt correct in finding it to be an aspect of liberty protected against state interference by the substantive component of the Due Process Clause in *Loving* v. *Virginia* 388 U.S. 1 (1967). . . .

Men and women of good conscience can disagree, and we suppose some always shall disagree, about the profound moral and spiritual implications of terminating a pregnancy, even in its earliest stage. Some of us as individuals find abortion offensive to our most basic principles of morality, but that cannot control our decision. Our obligation is to define the liberty of all, not to mandate our own moral code. . . .

Our law affords constitutional protection to personal decisions relating to marriage, procreation, contraception, family relationships, child rearing, and education. . . . These matters, involving the most intimate and personal choices a person may make in a lifetime, choices central to personal dignity and autonomy, are central to the liberty protected by the Fourteenth Amendment. At the heart of liberty is the right to define one's own concept of existence, of meaning, of the universe, and of the mystery of human life. Beliefs about these mat-

112 S. Ct. 2791 (1992).

ters could not define the attributes of personhood were they formed under compulsion of the State. The woman's right to terminate her pregnancy before viability is the most central principle of *Roe* v. *Wade*. It is a rule of law and a component of liberty we cannot renounce.

On the other side of the equation is the interest of the State in the protection of potential life. The *Roe* Court recognized the State's "important and legitimate interest in protecting the potentiality of human life." . . . That portion of the decision in *Roe* has been given too little acknowledgment and implementation by the Court in its subsequent cases. . . . Though the woman has a right to choose to terminate or continue her pregnancy before viability, it does not at all follow that the State is prohibited from taking steps to ensure that this choice is thoughtful and informed. Even in the earliest stages of pregnancy, the State may enact rules and regulations designed to encourage her to know that there are philosophic and social arguments of great weight that can be brought to bear in favor of continuing the pregnancy to full term. . . . We reject the trimester framework, which we do not consider to be part of the essential holding of *Roe*. . . . Measures aimed at ensuring that a woman's choice contemplates the consequences for the fetus do not necessarily interfere with the right recognized in *Roe* . . . not every law which makes a right more difficult to exercise is, ipso facto, an infringement of that right. . . .

. . . We . . . see no reason why the State may not require doctors to inform a woman seeking an abortion of the availability of materials relating to the consequences to the fetus. . . . Whether the mandatory 24-hour waiting period is . . . invalid because in practice it is a substantial obstacle to a woman's choice to terminate her pregnancy is a closer question. [We do not agree with the District Court] that the waiting period constitutes an undue burden. . . . [From Part D: We have already established the precedent, and] we reaffirm today, that a State may require a minor seeking an abortion to obtain the consent of a parent or guardian, provided that there is an adequate judicial bypass procedure. . . .

. . . Pennsylvania's abortion law provides, except in cases of medical emergency, that no physician shall perform an abortion on a married woman without receiving a signed statement from the woman that she has notified her spouse that she is about to undergo an abor-

tion. The woman has the option of providing an alternative signed statement certifying that her husband is not the man who impregnated her; that her husband could not be located; that the pregnancy is the result of spousal sexual assault which she had reported [or that she fears bodily harm from him.] A physician who performs an abortion on a married woman without receiving the appropriate signed statement will have his or her license revoked, and is liable to the husband for damages.

. . . In well-functioning marriages, spouses discuss important intimate decisions such as whether to bear a child. But there are millions of women in this country who are the victims of regular physical and psychological abuse at the hands of their husbands. . . . Many may have a reasonable fear that notifying their husbands will provoke further instances of child abuse [or psychological abuse]. . . .

. . . [A]s a general matter . . . the father's interest in the welfare of the child and the mother's interest are equal. Before birth, however, the issue takes on a very different cast. It is an inescapable biological fact that state regulation with respect to the child a woman is carrying will have a far greater impact on the mother's liberty than on the father's. [That is why the Court has already ruled that when the wife and husband disagree on the abortion decision, the decision of the wife should prevail.]

. . . There was a time, no so long ago, when a different understanding of the family and of the Constitution prevailed. In *Bradwell* v. *Illinois* [see pp. 572–74], three Members of this Court reaffirmed the common-law principle that "a woman had no legal existence separate from her husband." . . . Only one generation has passed since this Court observed that "woman is still regarded as the center of home and family life," with attendant "special responsibilities" that precluded full and independent legal status under the Constitution (*Hoyt* v. *Florida* [pp. 583–85]). These views, of course, are no longer consistent with our understanding of the family, the individual, or the Constitution. . . . [The Pennsylvania abortion law] embodies a view of marriage consonant with the common-law status of married women but repugnant to our present understanding of marriage and of the nature of the rights secured by the Constitution. Women do not lose their constitutionally protected liberty when they marry.

CHIEF JUSTICE REHNQUIST, WITH WHOM JUSTICE WHITE, JUSTICE SCALIA, AND JUSTICE CLARENCE
THOMAS JOIN:

The joint opinion . . . retains the outer shell of *Roe* v. *Wade* . . . but beats a wholesale retreat from the substance of that case. We believe that *Roe* was wrongly decided, and that it can and should be overruled consistently with our traditional approach to *stare decisis* in constitutional cases. We would . . . uphold the challenged provisions of the Pennsylvania statute in their entirety. . . . [B]y foreclosing all democratic outlet for the deep passions this issue arouses, by banishing the issue from the political forum that gives all participants, even the losers, the satisfaction of a fair hearing and an honest fight, by continuing the imposition of a rigid national rule instead of allowing for regional differences, the Court merely prolongs and intensifies the anguish.

We should get out of this area, where we have no right to be, and where we do neither ourselves nor the country any good by remaining.

Abortion is an issue of concern to men as well as to women. It is an issue on which women and men hold a wide variety of views. Among the questions raised are:

1. What are the limits of a woman's right to make her own reproductive decisions?
2. Should the unborn be afforded legal rights?
3. What rights does the father have? In 1976 the Supreme Court held that a state could not require a married woman to get her husband's consent before having an abortion (*Planned Parenthood* v. *Danforth*, 428 U.S. 52 [1976]). Is the husband's claim of a role in an abortion decision a reinstatement of the old law of coverture?
4. What rights does the community have to set general policy? What are the appropriate limits of government intervention? The state may not require a woman to conceive a child; can the state require a woman to bear a child?
5. Will any of these rights change as improvements are made in the technology for the discovery of birth defects and genetic abnormalities, for the implantation of embryos, and for caring for premature infants at earlier ages?

Rostker v. *Goldberg*, 1981

Classical republican tradition linked political identity with property holding and military obligation. In the United States, the obligations of male citizens include military service; the obligations of female citizens do not. Although women had been employed by the army and navy as nurses, not until World War II were they involved in military service in substantial numbers. Women's sections of the Army, Navy, and Air Force accepted volunteers under strict regulations which excluded them from combat duty, limited the

101 Sup. Ct. 2646. For extended comment, see Linda K. Kerber, "'A Constitutional Right to be Treated like . . . Ladies': Women, Civic Obligation and Military Service," *University of Chicago Law School Roundtable* 1 (1993):93–128.

numbers who could be accepted and the rank to which they could rise (until 1967 no woman could serve in a command position), and offered fewer fringe benefits than were received by servicemen of the same rank (see *Frontiero* v. *Richardson*, pp. 590–92). Partly in response to the Vietnam War, many of these restrictions were eased; in 1976 women were admitted to West Point, Annapolis, and the Air Force Academy.

When President Jimmy Carter recommended the resumption of peacetime selective service registration in 1980, he proposed registering women as well as men. The president and his supporters on the Armed Services Committees of the Senate and the House sought to separate the issue of registration, the actual draft, and the use of women in combat. They argued that decisions on whether women would actually be drafted (and, if so, whether mothers would be exempted) and whether women would be placed in combat positions could be left for future debate. They also argued that registration did not necessarily mean that one would be drafted, for men who planned to request exemption as conscientious objectors were still required to register.

Opponents insisted that the issues were linked: if the sexes were treated equally in registration, it would be impossible to reject equity in future treatment. Since the primary goal of Selective Service was to identify combat-ready men, opponents also argued that if women were not used in combat there was no need to register them. In the course of debate contrasting ideas of the role of women in American society were expressed.* This debate overlapped with the debate on the Equal Rights Amendment, taking place at the same time; probably the single most effective argument used by opponents of the ERA was that it would involve women in the draft. In the end, Congress approved registration for men but not for women.

The Military Selective Service Act of 1980 was challenged by a group of men who argued that they had been denied the equal protection of the laws guaranteed by the Fifth Amendment. The Carter administration was now placed in the odd position of having to defend the statute it had opposed.

Note the reasoning of the Supreme Court and its emphasis on the exclusion of women from combat positions. By 1990, women made up 11 percent of the armed forces and were placed in positions on patrol ships and stationed on the fringes of the defense perimeter. They have also been placed in "combat support" units; in the Panama invasion of 1989 Army Captain Linda Bray led a military police unit in an exchange of fire while conducting what had been expected to be a police mission. Five women were killed in the Gulf War of 1991 and two were taken prisoner. What implications do these developments have for the reasoning of the Court in *Rostker*?

Although the argument was not offered in *Rostker*, some men have argued that if women are drafted but not placed in combat positions, the likelihood that any specific man would be assigned to a noncombat job diminishes and men are therefore placed at greater risk for combat assignments. Moreover, some men in similar situations, such as police or prison guards, have demanded the exclusion of women on the grounds that women can not back men up effectively in physical confrontation; thus giving women equal opportunity to become prison guards actually increases the risks to men. Yet an-

*See the *Congressional Record*, June 10, 1980.

other perspective is offered by the legal historian Leo Kanowitz, who argues that "the equanimity with which men's exclusive liability for military service is regarded by the general population, even during times of violent combat . . . [suggests] the philosophy that a man's life is less precious than that of a woman." Do you agree?

MR. JUSTICE WILLIAM H. REHNQUIST DELIVERED THE OPINION OF THE COURT:

The question presented is whether the Military Selective Service Act . . . violates the Fifth Amendment to the United States Constitution in authorizing the President to require the registration of males and not females. Whenever called upon to judge the constitutionality of an Act of Congress—"the gravest and most delicate duty that this Court is called upon to perform," . . . the Court accords "great weight to the decisions of Congress."

. . . This case is quite different from several of the gender-based discrimination cases we have considered in that . . . Congress did not act "unthinkingly" or "reflexively and not for any considered reason." . . . The question of registering women for the draft not only received considerable national attention and was the subject of wide-ranging public debate, but also was extensively considered by Congress in hearings, floor debate, and in committee. Hearings held by both Houses of Congress in response to the President's request for authorization to register women adduced extensive testimony and evidence concerning the issue. . . . the decision to exempt women from registration was not the "accidental byproduct of a traditional way of thinking about women. . . ."

Women as a group, however, unlike men as a group, are not eligible for combat. The restrictions on the participation of women in combat in the Navy and Air Force are statutory. . . . The Army and Marine Corps preclude the use of women in combat as a matter of established policy.* . . . The existence of the combat restrictions clearly indicates the basis for Congress' decision to exempt women from registration. The purpose of registration was to prepare for a draft of combat troops. Since women are excluded from combat, Congress concluded that they would not be needed in the event of a draft, and therefore decided not to register them. . . . This is not a case of Congress arbitrarily choosing to burden one of two similarly situated groups, such as would be the case with an all-black or all-white, or an all-Catholic or all-Lutheran, or an all-Republican or all-Democratic registration. Men and women, because of the combat restrictions on women, are simply not similarly situated for purposes of a draft or registration for a draft. . . . The Constitution requires that Congress treat similarly situated persons similarly, not that it engage in gestures of superficial equality.

*No major country has women in combat jobs in its standing army.

MR. JUSTICE BYRON WHITE, DISSENTING:

I assume . . . that excluding women from combat positions does not offend the Constitution . . . [but] I perceive little, if any, indication that Congress itself concluded that every position in the military, no matter how far removed from combat, must be filled with combat-ready men.

MR. JUSTICE THURGOOD MARSHALL, DISSENTING:

The Court today places its imprimatur on one of the most potent remaining public expressions of "ancient canards about the proper role of women." It upholds a statute that requires males but not females to register for the draft, and which thereby categorically excludes women from a fundamental civic obligation.

Meritor Savings Bank v. *Mechelle Vinson et al.*, 1986

The term "sexual harassment" was unknown before the mid-1970s. One legal scholar has written, "the term was invented by feminist activists, given legal content by feminist litigators and scholars, and sustained by a wide-ranging body of scholarship generated largely by feminist academics." Another legal scholar observes "[f]or the first time in history, women have defined women's injuries in a law."*

Consider Part 1 of Section 703 of Title VII of the Civil Rights Act of 1964 (pp. 587–88). The authors of the statute were defining economic injuries, and for more than a decade the Equal Employment Opportunities Commission supported only economic claims of sex discrimination. But working women had long put up with behavior that, beginning in the 1970s, they began to say was also sex discrimination: supervisors who referred to all women as "whores," whether or not in joking tones; workplaces that had cheesecake or frankly pornographic calenders on the walls; and, worst of all, covert or explicit pressure to have sex with supervisors or employers for fear of losing their jobs if they refused.

Legal scholar Catharine MacKinnon gave names to two forms of sexual harassment: (1) "quid pro quo": when sexual submission to a supervisor becomes, either implicitly or explicitly, a condition of employment; and (2) "offensive working environment": when the conduct of a supervisor, co-employee, or client unreasonably interferes with an individual's work or creates an intimidating and hostile workplace. By the late 1970s, many behaviors that men had described as flirting, and that women had "put up with" because they saw no alternative, could be named and challenged. In 1980, the EEOC published an official set of guidelines describing behavior it would challenge as sexual harassment, even if the actors claimed they were merely flirting or "joking around."

In 1986, a unanimous Supreme Court for the first time formally recognized sexual harassment as a violation of Title VII. Catharine MacKinnon was one of the attorneys for Mechelle Vinson, who complained that she had been hired in 1974 as a teller-trainee by a vice president of Meritor Savings Bank and was steadily promoted for four years until she became assistant branch manager. During those four years, however, she had a sexual relationship with the man (Mr. Taylor) who had hired her; when she tried to decline his attentions, he exposed himself to her, and even forcibly raped her.

Vinson claimed that she had been the victim of both "quid pro quo" and offensive environment forms of sexual harassment. Vinson told the court "that because she was

---

*Martha Chamallas, "Writing About Sexual Harassment: A Guide to the Literature," UCLA *Women's Law Journal* IV (1993):37–38; Catharine MacKinnon, *Feminism Unmodified: Discourses on Life and Law* (Cambridge, Mass.: Harvard University Press, 1987) p. 105.

477 U.S. 57 (1986).

afraid of Taylor she never reported his harassment to any of his supervisors and never attempted to use the bank's complaint procedure." But when she was fired for what the bank claimed was excessive use of sick leave, she sued the bank, claiming sexual harassment and asking for punitive damages. The bank claimed that "any sexual harassment by Taylor was unknown to the bank and engaged in without its consent or approval."

A unanimous Court agreed with Vinson. What analogies do they see with race discrimination? Why do they hold Meritor Bank guilty as well as Mr. Taylor? Taylor argued that Vinson wore sexually provocative clothing. How much responsibility do you think the victim of sexual harassment should be expected to take for avoiding the harassment?

A third wave of attention to sexual harassment in the workplace took place after the fall of 1991, when hearings on the nomination of Clarence Thomas to the Supreme Court were interrupted by the charges of Anita Hill that he had sexually harassed her a decade earlier. Ironically, their encounter had taken place within the EEOC itself, where Thomas had been director and Hill had been a lawyer on his staff. In response, Thomas charged that he was himself victimized by the media attention. Adrienne Davis and Stephanie Wildman observe, "in a stunning sleight of hand, [Thomas] managed to convince all involved, including the Senate, that white racism, rather than a Black woman, had accused him of harassment."* Thomas's nomination to the Supreme Court was confirmed by the Senate.

As of 1994, courts have not held that harassment based on an employee's homosexuality constitutes sex discrimination, but a number of lawsuits have raised the matter and discussion continues.

JUSTICE WILLIAM REHNQUIST:

This case presents important questions concerning claims of workplace "sexual harassment" brought under Title VII of the Civil Rights Act of 1964 . . . [Vinson] argues . . . that unwelcome sexual advances that create an offensive or hostile working environment violate Title VII. Without question, when a supervisor sexually harasses a subordinate because of the subordinate's sex, that supervisor "discriminate[s]" on the basis of sex. [Meritor Bank] does not challenge this proposition. It contends instead that in prohibiting discrimination with respect to "compensation, terms, conditions, or privileges" of employment, Congress was concerned with what petitioner describes as "tangible loss" of "an economic character," not "purely psychological aspects of the workplace environment."

We reject petitioner's view. First, the language of Title VII is not limited to "economic" or "tangible" discrimination. The phrase "terms, conditions, or privileges of employment" evinces a congressional intent "to strike at the entire spectrum of disparate treatment of men and women" in employment. . . . As the Court of Appeals for the Eleventh Circuit wrote . . . in 1982: "Sexual harassment which creates a hostile or offensive environment for members of one sex is every bit the arbitrary barrier to sexual equality at the workplace that racial harassment is to racial equality. Surely a requirement that a man or woman run a gauntlet of sexual abuse in return for the privilege of being allowed to work and make a living can be as demeaning and disconcerting as the harshest of racial epithets."

---

*Adrienne D. Davis and Stephanie M. Wildman, "The Legacy of Doubt: Treatment of Sex and Race in the Hill-Thomas Hearings," *Southern California Law Review* 65 (1992):1367.

. . . [W]e reject the . . . view that the mere existence of a grievance procedure and a policy against discrimination, coupled with respondent's failure to invoke that procedure, must insulate petitioner from liability. . . . the bank's grievance procedure apparently required an employee to complain first to her supervisor, in this case Taylor. Since Taylor was the alleged perpetrator, it is not altogether surprising that respondent failed to invoke the procedure and report her grievance to him. . . . [W]e hold that a claim of "hostile environment" sex discrimination is actionable under Title VII. . . .

Further Resources

Full citations of works preceded by an asterisk may be found in the credit lines for the appropriate selections in this volume or in the initial citation listed below.

Part I: Traditional America, 1600–1820

BIOLOGY

James Axtell, ed., *The Indian Peoples of Eastern America: A Documentary History of the Sexes* (New York, 1981), is organized in terms of life cycle and includes sections on birth, puberty, marriage, and death. Carolyn Merchant, *Ecological Revolutions: Nature, Gender, and Science in New England* (Chapel Hill, 1989), contrasts the ways in which incompatible conceptualizations of gender permeated the world views of Indians and Europeans. *The Diary of Elizabeth Drinker*, ed. Elaine Foreman Crane, 3 vols. (Boston, 1991), includes extensive comments on Drinker's experience of childbearing and motherhood. The intersection of biology and economics is revealed in Laurel Thatcher Ulrich's insightful study of a woman who delivered hundreds of infants safely in a record comparable to that achieved in modern medical practice: *A Midwife's Tale: The Life of Martha Ballard Based on Her Diary 1785–1812* (New York, 1990). See also Daniel Scott Smith and Michael S. Hindus, "Premarital Pregnancy in America, 1640–1971: An Overview and Interpretation," *Journal of Interdisciplinary History* 5 (1975):537–70; Nancy Schrom Dye and Daniel Blake Smith, "Mother Love and Infant Death, 1750–1920," *Journal of American History* 73 (1986):329–53; and *Cornelia Hughes Dayton, "Taking the Trade." An energetic debate has developed on the timing of the "demographic transition" to smaller families; see Daniel Scott Smith, " 'Early' Fertility Decline in America: A Problem in Family History," in *Family History at the Crossroads: A Journal of Family History Reader*, ed. Tamara Hareven and Andrejs Plankans (Princeton, 1987), pp. 73–84.

ECONOMICS

Julia Cherry Spruill, *Women's Life and Work in the Southern Colonies* (Chapel Hill, 1938), is rich in descriptive detail and still repays reading. For thoughtful introductions to work that occupied most women much of the time, see Susan Burrows Swan, *Plain and Fancy: American Women and Their Needlework 1750–1850* (New York, 1977), and Betty Ring, *Let Virtue Be a Guide to Thee: Needlework in the Education of Rhode Island Women, 1730–1830* (Providence, 1983).

Lyle Koehler, *A Search for Power: The "Weaker Sex" in Seventeenth-Century New England* (Urbana, 1980), examines the work options open to women in a single region. A special issue of the *Pennsylvania Magazine of History and Biography* 107 (January 1983) has useful essays on the economic aspects of colonial women's lives; see especially Jean R. Soderland, "Black Women in Colonial Pennsylvania," pp. 49–68, and Sharon V. Salinger, " 'Send No More Women': Female Servants in Eighteenth-Century Philadelphia," pp. 29–48. For women's lives in the Chesapeake, see Lois Green Carr and Lorena Walsh, "The Planter's Wife: The Experience of White Women in Seventeenth-Century Maryland," *William and Mary Quarterly*, 3d ser., 34 (1977):542–71. Richard S. Dunn, "A Tale of Two Plantations: Slave Life at Mesopotamia in Jamaica and Mount Airy in Virginia, 1799–1828," *William and Mary Quarterly*, 3d ser., 34 (1977):32–65, is a comparative study that provides a detailed reconstruction of the work lives of slave women and emphasizes the pressures under which they lived. Carole Shammas, "The Domestic Environment in Early Modern England and America," *Journal of Social History* 31 (1980):3–24, sets American domestic work in transatlantic context; see also Shammas, "Black Women's Work and the Evolution of Plantation Society in Virginia," *Labor History* 26 (1985):5–28. On the law, see Elizabeth Bowles Warbasse's classic *The Changing Legal Rights of Married Women 1800–1861* (New York, 1987, 1960) and Marylynn Salmon, *Women and the Law of Property in Early America* (Chapel Hill, 1986).

POLITICS

For an astute examination of the ways in which social order is maintained through gossip, see Mary Beth Norton, "Gender and Defamation in Seventeenth-Century Maryland," *William and Mary Quarterly*, 3d ser., XLIV (1987):3–39. The witchcraft trials of seventeenth-century New England were occasions on which religious and political concerns mingled. The fact that the targets of the trials were, with few exceptions, female, makes them an important episode in women's history. In addition to *Carol Karlsen's *Devil in the Shape of a Woman*, several other studies are pertinent: Chadwick Hansen, *Witchcraft at Salem* (New York, 1969), and Richard Weisman, *Witchcraft, Magic and Religion in 17th Century Massachusetts* (Amherst, Mass., 1984), treat the theme in the context of religious and folk belief; Paul Boyer and Stephen Nissenbaum, *Salem Possessed: The Social Origins of Witchcraft* (Cambridge, Mass., 1974), examine the trials as an expression of social and economic tension in the community. John Demos, *Entertaining Satan: Witchcraft and the Culture of Early New England* (New York, 1982), is a wide-ranging study that addresses the subject from the perspectives of psychology, history, biography, and political relationships. For the narrative of a captive white woman who chose to stay with the Seneca Indians, see James E. Seaver, ed. *A Narrative of the Life of Mrs. Mary Jemison*, (Syracuse, 1990; originally published 1823).

IDEOLOGY

For diaries rich in insight into the rhythms of daily life, see *The Journal of Esther Edwards Burr, 1754–1757,* ed. Carol F. Karlsen and Laurie Crumpacker (New Haven, 1984), and

Religion and Domestic Violence in Early New England: The Memoirs of Abigail Abbot Bailey,
ed. Ann Taves (Bloomington, 1989). For striking examples of the ways in which some
representative colonial women interpreted their own lives, see Anne Firor Scott, "Self
Portraits: Three Women," in *Uprooted Americans: Essays to Honor Oscar Handlin,* ed. Richard Bushman et al. (Boston, 1979). For the sources on which these portraits are based,
see *The Letters of Benjamin Franklin and Jane Mecom,* ed. Carl Van Doren (Princeton, 1950),
and *The Letterbook of Eliza Lucas Pinckney,* ed. Elise Pinckney (Chapel Hill, 1972). For the
very high rates of literacy among New England women, see William J. Gilmore, *Reading
Becomes a Necessity of Life: Material and Cultural Life in Rural New England, 1780–1835*
(Knoxville, 1989). A thorough review essay is Sally Schwager, "Educating Women in
America," *Signs* 12 (1987):333–72. For the ways in which religious practices affected wom-
en's status, see essays in Janet Wilson James, ed., *Women in American Religion* (Philadel-
phia, 1980), especially Mary Maples Dunn, "Saints and Sisters: Congregational and
Quaker Women in the Early Colonial Period." For the interaction of biology, economics,
politics, and ideology in the Revolutionary era, see Linda K. Kerber, *Women of the Republic:
Intellect and Ideology in Revolutionary America* (Chapel Hill, 1980), and Mary Beth Norton,
Liberty's Daughters: The Revolutionary Experience of American Women, 1750–1800 (Boston,
1980). Essays on law, inheritance, work, and ideology are included in *Women in the Age
of the American Revolution,* ed. Ronald Hoffman and Peter J. Albert (Charlottesville, 1989).
For debate over the relationship of women to the state, see Linda K. Kerber, "The Paradox
of Women's Citizenship in the Early Republic: The Case of *Martin vs. Massachusetts,*
1805," *American Historical Review* 97 (1992):349–78, and Carroll Smith-Rosenberg, "Dis-
Covering the Subject of the 'Great Constitutional Discussion' 1786–1789," *Journal of American History* 79 (1992):841–73.

Part IIA: Industrializing America, 1820–1880

BIOLOGY

For an important overview, see John D'Emilio and Estelle B. Freedman, *Intimate Matters:
A History of Sexuality in America* (New York, 1988), esp. Parts I and II; see also Carl N.
Degler, *At Odds: Women and the Family in America from the Revolution to the Present* (New
York, 1980), especially chaps. 2–9, as well as *James Mohr, *Abortion in America.* For the
relationship of women to the health reform movement, see Jane D. Donegan, *Hydropathic
Highway to Health: Women and Water-Cure in Antebellum America* (New York, 1986), and
Susan E. Cayleff, *Wash and Be Healed: The Water Cure Movement and Women's Health* (Phil-
adelphia, 1987). For problems characteristic of one region, see Sally G. McMillen, *Motherhood in the Old South: Pregnancy, Childbirth and Infant Rearing* (Baton Rouge, 1990).

ECONOMICS

In addition to *Deborah White's *Ar'n't I a Woman?,* see Jacqueline Jones, *Labor of Love,
Labor of Sorrow* (New York, 1985); chaps. 1 and 2 are devoted to the period before 1880.
Dorothy Sterling, ed., *We Are Your Sisters: Black Women in the Nineteenth Century* (New
York, 1984), includes many well-selected documents of the working lives of black
women, slave and free (it also includes documents that have much bearing on politics
and ideology), as does Gerda Lerner, ed., *Black Women in White America* (New York, 1972).
Willie Lee Rose, ed., *A Documentary History of Slavery in North America* (New York, 1976),

and John Balssingame, ed., *Slave Testimony: Two Centuries of Letters, Speeches, Interviews and Autobiographies* (Baton Rouge, 1977), should also be consulted. The most authoritative of the many editions of Harriet A. Jacobs, *Incidents in the Life of a Slave Girl* [Linda Brent] *Written by Herself*, ed. Lydia Maria Child (1860), is the one prepared with a new introduction by Jean Fagen Yellin (Cambridge, Mass., 1987). Elizabeth Keckley, *Behind the Scenes, or Thirty Years a Slave, and Four Years in the White House* (reprinted New York, 1988), includes her experiences during the Civil War and her friendship with Mary Todd Lincoln.

Many elderly women who had been slaves when young were interviewed by the Federal Writers' Project in the 1930s. Selected interviews appear in B. A. Botkin, ed., *Lay My Burden Down: A Folk History of Slavery* (Chicago, 1945), and Norman R. Yetman, ed., *Voices from Slavery* (New York, 1970). Much remains to be done on the experiences of black women sharecroppers, but see Susan A. Mann, "Slavery, Sharecropping, and Sexual Inequality," *Signs* XIV (1989):774–98.

For women's work in the domestic economy, see Nancy F. Cott, *The Bonds of Womanhood: "Woman's Sphere" in New England 1780–1835* (New Haven, 1977), chap. 1. Widowhood was an economic category as well as a demographic one; see Lisa Wilson, *Life After Death: Widows in Pennsylvania 1750–1850* (Philadelphia, 1992). For analyses of the interrelationship between biology, economics, politics, and gender, see Joan Jensen, *Loosening the Bonds: Mid-Atlantic Farm Women, 1750–1850* (New Haven, 1986), and Jeanne Boydston, *Home and Work*. For domestic work and the maintenance of gendered roles in a frontier context there is now a large and growing literature; see Lillian Schlissel, *Women's Diaries of the Westward Journey* (New York, 1982); John Mack Faragher, *Sugar Creek: Life on the Illinois Prairie* (New Haven, 1988); Sandra L. Myres, *Westering Women and the Frontier Experience 1800–1915* (Albuquerque, 1982); and Paula Petrik, *No Step Backward: Women and Family on the Rocky Mountain Mining Frontier, Helena Montana 1865–1900* (Helena, 1987). For an excellent bibliographic essay, see Elizabeth Jameson, "Toward a Multicultural History of Women in the Western United States," *Signs* XIII (1988):761–91.

For the impact of industrialization on working women, see Thomas Dublin, *Women at Work: The Transformation of Work and Community in Lowell, Massachusetts, 1826–1860* (New York, 1979), and Dublin, *Farm to Factory: The Mill Experience and Women's Lives in New England, 1830–1860* (New York, 1981); Judith A. McGaw, *Most Wonderful Machine: Mechanization and Social Change in Berkshire Papermaking, 1801–1885* (Princeton, 1987); and Mary H. Blewett, *Men, Women, and Work: Class, Gender and Protest in the New England Shoe Industry, 1780–1910* (Urbana, 1988). A classic memoir is Lucy Larcom, *A New England Girlhood* (1889; reprint, New York, 1961); for a classic text, see Helen Sumner, *History of Women in Industry in the United States* (Washington, D.C., 1910).

For the feminization of schooling, see Richard M. Bernard and Maris A. Vinovskis, "The Female School Teacher in Ante-Bellum Massachusetts," *Journal of Social History* 10 (1977):332–45, and the important essays on teaching in Anne Firor Scott, *Making the Invisible Woman Visible* (Urbana, 1984). For gender and power in the schools, see Myra H. Strober and David Tyack, "Why Do Women Teach and Men Manage? A Report on Research on Schools," *Signs* V (1980):494–503.

For the origins of the first work force in which women and men worked side by side, see Cindy Sondik Aron, *Ladies and Gentlemen of the Civil Service: Middle-Class Workers in Victorian America* (New York, 1987). For entry into the professions, see Mary Roth

Walsh, *"Doctors Wanted, No Women Need Apply": Sexual Barriers in the Medical Profession 1835–1975* (New Haven, 1977); Regina Morantz-Sanchez, *Sympathy and Science: Women Physicians in America* (New York, 1985); Susan Reverby, *Ordered to Care: The Dilemma of American Nursing, 1850–1945* (Cambridge, Mass., 1987); and Margaret Rossiter, *Women Scientists in America: Struggles and Strategies to 1940* (Baltimore, 1982).

POLITICS

Estelle Freedman, *Their Sisters' Keepers: Women and Prison Reform in Nineteenth-Century America* (Ann Arbor, 1981), introduces an important reform movement. Gerda Lerner, *The Grimké Sisters from South Carolina: Rebels against Slavery* (Boston, 1967), is a readable biography that suggests the way in which abolitionism could lead to a concern for women's rights, a theme more recently pursued in Jean Fagen Yellin, *Women and Sisters: Antislavery Feminists in American Culture* (New Haven, 1990) and Dorothy Sterling, *Ahead of Her Time: Abby Kelley and the Politics of Antislavery* (New York, 1991). Ellen Carol DuBois, *Feminism and Suffrage: The Emergence of an Independent Women's Movement in America, 1848–1869* (Ithaca, 1978), is an important interpretation that stresses the radicalism of the demand for suffrage. Nancy Hewitt, *Women's Activism and Social Change: Rochester, New York, 1822–1872* (Ithaca, 1984), follows the history of women and reform in a single city. Lori Ginzberg, *Women and the Work of Benevolence: Morality and Politics in the 19th Century United States* (New Haven, 1990), incisively examines reformers' tactics and underlying ideologies. For an overview of women's organizations at the local and national levels, see Anne Firor Scott, *Natural Allies: Women's Associations in American History* (Urbana, 1991). For women's participation in a variety of public sectors, see Mary Ryan, *Women in Public: Between Banners and Bullets, 1825–1880* (Baltimore, 1990). Gerda Lerner examines the process of women's politicization in *The Creation of Feminist Consciousness: From the Middle Ages to Eighteen-Seventy* (New York, 1993). Readable biographies of political women are Celia Morris Eckhardt, *Fanny Wright: Rebel in America* (Cambridge, Mass., 1984), and Elisabeth Griffith, *In Her Own Right: The Life of Elizabeth Cady Stanton* (New York, 1984). Six massive volumes of the basic sources on the suffrage movement have been conveniently abridged in *A Concise History of Woman Suffrage: Selections from the Classic Work of Stanton, Anthony, Gage and Harper*, ed. Mari Jo Buhle and Paul Buhle (Urbana, 1978); a selection of the correspondence between Stanton and Anthony and some of their more notable testimony and speeches is conveniently available in Ellen Carol DuBois, ed., *Elizabeth Cady Stanton, Susan B. Anthony Correspondence, Writing and Speeches* (New York, 1981). Sojourner Truth's *Narrative* of her life, prepared by Olive Gilbert, has been thoughtfully edited by Margaret Washington (New York, 1993). Carlton Mabee shows how biography can be detective work in *Sojourner Truth: Slave, Prophet, Legend* (New York, 1993).

There are many memoirs of women's participation in the Civil War; among them are Susie King Taylor, *A Black Woman's Civil War Memoirs*, ed. Patricia W. Romero and Willie Lee Rose (New York, 1988); Sarah Emma Edmonds, *Nurse and Spy in the Union Army* (Hartford, 1865); Louisa May Alcott, *Hospital Sketches* (New York, 1863); Mary A. Livermore, *My Story of the War* (Hartford, 1865); *Civil War Nurse: The Diary and Letters of Hannah Ropes*, ed. John R. Brumgardt (Knoxville, 1980). For the perspective of a Southern woman on the home front, see C. Vann Woodward, ed., *Mary Chestnut's Civil War*, (New Haven, 1981). Mary Elizabeth Massey's *Bonnet Brigades* (New York, 1966) is rapidly being joined by new interpretations; see George C. Rable, *Civil Wars: Women and the Crisis of Southern Nationalism* (Urbana, 1989); Drew Gilpin Faust, "Altars of Sacrifice: Confederate Women and the Narratives of War," *Journal of American History* 76 (1990):1200–1228; and Catherine Clinton and Nina Silber, eds., *Divided Houses: Gender and the Civil War* (New York, 1992). For compelling interpretations of the Reconstruction Era, see Nina Silber, *The Romance of Reunion: Northerners and the South 1865–1900* (Chapel Hill, 1993), and Martha Hodes, "The Sexualization of Reconstruction Politics: White Women and Black Men in the South After the Civil War," *Journal of the History of Sexuality* 3 (1993):402–17.

Ideology

"The Cult of True Womanhood" was given its name in an essay with the same title by Barbara Welter, *American Quarterly* 18 (1966):151–74. A different interpretation of some of the same sources is offered by Gerda Lerner, *The Majority Finds Its Past: Placing Women in History* (New York, 1979), chap. 2. An overview of the literature of separate spheres is provided in Linda K. Kerber, "Separate Spheres, Female Worlds, Woman's Place: The Rhetoric of Women's History," *Journal of American History* 75 (1988):9–39.

The relationship of women's roles to a developing economy is brilliantly dissected in Mary P. Ryan, *Cradle of the Middle Class: The Family in Oneida County, New York, 1790–1865* (Cambridge, Mass., 1981). The social construction of gender is insightfully explored in Carroll Smith-Rosenberg, *Disorderly Conduct: Visions of Gender in Victorian America* (New York, 1985), and Lee Chambers-Schiller, *Liberty, A Better Husband: Single Women in America: The Generations of 1780–1840* (New Haven, 1984). For the intersections of gender, class, and sexuality in a major city, see Christine Stansell, *City of Women: Sex and Class in New York* (New York, 1986); Patricia Cline Cohen, "Unregulated Youth: Masculinity and Murder in the 1830s City," *Radical History Review* 52 (1992):33–52; and Timothy Gilfoyle, *City of Eros: New York City, Prostitution and the Commercialization of Sex, 1790–1920* (New York, 1992). For changes in the legal construction of gender, see Norma Basch, *In the Eyes of the Law: Women, Marriage and Property in Nineteenth-Century New York* (Ithaca, 1982); Ellen Carol DuBois, "Outgrowing the Compact of the Fathers: Equal Rights, Woman Suffrage, and the United States Constitution, 1820–1878," *Journal of American History* 74 (1987):836–862; and Amy Dru Stanley, "Conjugal Bonds and Wage Labor: Rights of Contract in the Age of Emancipation," *Journal of American History* 75 (1988):471–500.

For radical experiments in changing gender roles, see Maren Lockwood Carden, *Oneida: Utopian Community to Modern Corporation* (Baltimore, 1969), and Carol A. Kolmerten, *Women in Utopia: The Ideology of Gender in the American Owenite Communities* (Bloomington, 1990).

For efforts to control domestic violence, see Elizabeth H. Pleck, *Domestic Tyranny: The Making of American Social Policy Against Family Violence from Colonial Times to the Present* (New York, 1987). Fictional visions of women's lives are analyzed in Mary Kelley, *Private Woman, Public Stage: Literary Domesticity in Nineteenth-Century America* (New York, 1984), and Annette Kolodny, *The Land Before Her: Fantasy and Experience of the American Frontiers, 1630–1860* (Chapel Hill, 1984). The making of marriages is evaluated in Ellen K. Rothman, *Hands and Hearts: A History of Courtship in America* (New York, 1984). For the way in which religious beliefs affected women's roles and behavior, see Joan Jacobs Brumberg, *Mission for Life* (New York, 1980), and Donald G. Mathews, *Religion in the Old South* (Chicago, 1978), chap. 2.

The roles of Southern elite white women are discussed in Catherine Clinton, *The Plantation Mistress: Woman's World in the Old South* (New York, 1983); see also Nell Irvin Painter, ed., *The Secret Eye: The Journal of Ella Clanton Thomas, 1848–1889* (Chapel Hill, 1990). The relationship of poor Southern white women to state power is analyzed in Victoria Bynum, *Unruly Women: The Politics of Social and Sexual Control in the Old South, 1840–1865* (Chapel Hill, 1992). Elizabeth Fox-Genovese, *Within the Plantation Household: Black and White Women of the Old South* (Chapel Hill, 1988), is an effort to treat mistresses and enslaved women as part of the same social order. In *The Free Women of Petersburg: Status and Culture in a Southern Town* (New York: 1984), Suzanne Lebsock examines the interconnection of biology, economics, politics, and ideology in a single city. Adele Logan Alexander, *Ambiguous Lives: Free Women of Color in Rural Georgia, 1789–1879* (Fayetteville, 1991), uses autobiography to explore these interconnections.

Part IIB: Industrializing America, 1880–1920

BIOLOGY

Biology and ideology interacted in the medical treatment of women, a subject much discussed in scholarly articles. See, for example, Carroll Smith-Rosenberg and Charles Rosenberg, "The Female Animal: Medical and Biological Views of Woman and Her Role in Nineteenth-Century America," *Journal of American History* 60 (1973):332–56. For differing interpretations of Sanger and the birth control movement, see Linda Gordon, *Woman's Body, Woman's Right: Birth Control in America* (New York, 1977); James Reed, *From Private Vice to Public Virtue: The Birth Control Movement and American Society since 1830* (New York, 1978); David M. Kennedy, *Birth Control in America: The Career of Margaret Sanger* (New Haven, 1970); and Ellen Chesler, *Woman of Valor: Margaret Sanger and the Birth Control Movement in America* (New York, 1992). For an overview of women's sexuality during this period, see *Carl N. Degler, *At Odds*, chaps. 11–12, and *John D'Emilio and Estelle B. Freedman, *Intimate Matters*, chaps. 8–10. See also Anne Snitow, Christine Stansell, and Sharon Thompson, eds., *Powers of Desire: The Politics of Sexuality*, (New York, 1983), and *Passion and Power: Sexuality in History*, ed. Kathy Peiss and Christina Simmons (Philadelphia, 1989). For developments in childbirth, see *Judith Walzer Leavitt, *Brought to Bed*, chaps. 3–6. Another issue that is biologically related and also intersects with ideology and the state is the physical abuse of women's bodies in situations of domestic violence. See *Linda Gordon, *Heroes of Their Own Lives*, chap. 8, and *Elizabeth Pleck, *Domestic Tyranny*, chap. 6.

ECONOMICS

Housework engaged all women, except for the most privileged. See Ruth Schwartz Cowan, *More Work for Mother: The Ironies of Household Technology from the Open Hearth to the Microwave* (New York, 1983), chaps. 4–6, and Susan Strasser, *Never Done: A History of American Housework* (New York, 1982), chaps. 1–12. Farm women had additional burdens as described in Deborah Fink, *Agrarian Women: Wives and Mothers in Rural Nebraska, 1880–1940* (Chapel Hill, 1992), and Nancy Grey Osterud, *Bonds of Community: The Lives of Farm Women in Nineteenth Century New York* (Ithaca, 1991).

Whether women worked outside the home and at what jobs depended on economic need and work options as well as family expectations. How family expectations and work options interacted with different ethnic groups is explored in a variety of studies; see, for example, not only *Jacqueline Jones, *Labor of Love, Labor of Sorrow,* chaps. 4–5, but also Virginia Yans-McLaughlin, *Family and Community: Italian Immigrants in Buffalo, 1880– 1930* (Ithaca, 1977); Louise Lamphere, *From Working Daughters to Working Mothers: Immigrant Women in a New England Industrial Community* (Ithaca, 1989); *Sarah Deutsch, *No Separate Refuge;* Janet A. Nolan, *Ourselves Alone: Women Immigrants from Ireland* (Lexington, 1989); and Susan A. Glenn, *Daughters of the Shtetl: Life and Labor in the Immigrant Generation* (Ithaca, 1990).

For a general study of working-class women who found work options in industry, see Leslie Woodcock Tentler's *Wage-Earning Women: Industrial Work and Family Life in the United States, 1900–1930* (New York, 1979). For those finding new opportunities in others areas, see Patricia A. Cooper, *Once A Cigar Maker: Men, Women, and Work Culture in American Cigar Factories, 1900–1919* (Urbana, 1987); Ileen A. DeVault, *Sons and Daughters of Labor: Class and Clerical Work in Turn-of-the-Century Pittsburgh* (Ithaca, 1990); Miriam Cohen, *Workshop to Office: Two Generations of Italian Women in New York City, 1900–1950* (Ithaca, 1993); and Susan Porter Benson, *Counter Cultures: Saleswomen, Managers, and Customers in American Department Stores: 1890–1940* (Urbana, 1986). Shoplifters rather than shopworkers are the focus of Elaine Abelson's *When Ladies Go A-Thieving: Middle-Class Shoplifters in the Victorian Department Store* (New York, 1989). Prostitution also provided jobs whether women entered such work voluntarily or, as many did, involuntarily as demonstrated in Ruth Rosen's *Lost Sisterhood: Prostitution in America, 1900–1918* (Baltimore, 1982).

How working-class women used their leisure and whether leisure activities contributed to individual and/or collective self-improvement are issues explored by not only *Kathy Peiss, *Cheap Amusements,* but also Elizabeth Ewen, *Immigrant Women in the Land of Dollars: Life and Culture on the Lower East Side, 1890–1925* (New York, 1985). For efforts to improve the economic well-being of working-class women through unionization, see Susan Levine, *Labor's True Woman: Carpet Weavers, Industrialization, and Labor Reform in the Gilded Age* (Philadelphia, 1984); Nancy Schrom Dye, *As Equals and as Sisters: Feminism, the Labor Movement and the Women's Trade Union League of New York* (Columbia, 1980); Elizabeth A. Payne, *Reform, Labor, and Feminism: Margaret Dreier Robins and the Women's Trade Union League* (Urbana, 1988); Stephen H. Norwood, *Labor's Flaming Youth: Telephone Operators and Worker Militancy, 1878–1923* (Urbana, 1990); as well as selected essays in *Women, Work, and Protest: A Century of U.S. Women's Labor History,* ed. Ruth Milkman (Boston, 1985). On the larger issue of working-class consciousness, see Sarah Eisenstein, *Give Us Bread But Give Us Roses: Working Women's Consciousness in the United States, 1890 to the First World War* (London, 1983).

Better-educated, middle-class women also discovered new opportunities for employment in a variety of new professions. See, for example, Barbara Melosh, *The Physician's Hand: Work, Culture, and Conflict in American Nursing* (Philadelphia, 1982); *Susan M. Reverby, *Ordered to Care;* Darlene Clark Hine, *Black Women in White: Racial Conflict and Cooperation in the Nursing Profession, 1890–1950* (Bloomington, 1989); *Regina Morantz-Sanchez, *Sympathy and Science;* Gloria Moldow, *Women Doctors in Gilded Age Washington: Gender, Race, and Professionalization* (Urbana, 1987); *Margaret W. Rossiter, *Women Scientists in America;* Barbara Miller Solomon, *In the Company of Educated Women: A History of Women and Higher Education in America* (New Haven, 1985); Dee Garrison, *Apostles of*

Culture: The Public Librarian and American Society, 1876–1920 (New York, 1979); Margery W. Davies, *Woman's Place Is at the Typewriter: Office Work and Office Workers: 1879–1930* (Philadelphia, 1982); Lisa M. Fine, *The Souls of Skyscrapers: Female Clerical Workers in Chicago, 1890–1930* (Philadelphia, 1990); and *Cindy Sondik Aron, *Ladies and Gentlemen of the Civil Service.* On the first generation of working women to live alone, see Joanne J. Meyerowitz, *Women Adrift: Independent Wage Earners in Chicago, 1880–1930* (Chicago, 1988).

For an important overview of this changing work force, see Alice Kessler-Harris, *Out to Work: A History of Wage-Earning Women in the United States* (New York, 1982), secs. 2–3; Lynn Y. Weiner, *From Working Girl to Working Mother: The Female Labor Force in the United States, 1820–1920* (Chapel Hill, 1985), chap. 3; and Claudia Goldin, *Understanding the Gender Gap: An Economic History of American Women* (New York, 1989). On the application of gender analysis to labor history, see Ava Baron, "Gender and Labor History: Learning from the Past, Looking at the Future," in *Work Engendered: Toward a New History of American Labor* (Ithaca, 1991), pp. 1–46.

POLITICS

There is increasing literature on female political activism. Paula Baker examines the intimate relationship between gender and politics in *The Moral Frameworks of Public Life: Gender, Politics, and the State in Rural New York, 1870–1930* (New York, 1991). On pre- and postsuffrage activism, see *Nancy Hewitt and Suzanne Lebsock, eds., *Visible Women.* Studies of the temperance movement include Ruth Bordin, *Woman and Temperance: The Quest for Power and Liberty, 1873–1900* (Philadelphia, 1980); Barbara Epstein, *The Politics of Domesticity: Women, Evangelism, and Temperance in Nineteenth-Century America* (Middletown, Conn. 1981); Ian Tyrrell, *Woman's World, Woman's Empire: The Woman's Christian Temperance Union in International Perspective, 1880–1930* (Chapel Hill, 1991). On women's clubs see, Karen Blair, *The Clubwoman as Feminist: True Womanhood Redefined, 1868–1914* (New York, 1980), and Theodora Penny Martin, *The Sound of Our Own Voices: Women's Study Clubs, 1860–1910* (Boston, 1987). Women's voluntary associations and philanthropy are examined in Anne Firor Scott, *Natural Allies,* and Kathleen D. McCarthy, *Lady Bountiful Revisited: Women, Philanthropy, and Power* (New Brunswick, 1990). McCarthy also explores women's participation in the business of art in *Women's Culture: American Philanthropy and Art, 1830–1930* (Urbana, 1991). Women missionaries are the subject of Jane Hunter's *The Gospel of Gentility: American Women Missionaries in Turn-of-the-Century China* (New Haven, 1989), and of *Peggy Pascoe's *Relations of Rescue.* For black women's activism, see Paula Giddings, *When and Where I Enter: The Impact of Black Women on Race and Sex in America* (New York, 1984); and Evelyn Brooks Higginbotham, *Righteous Discontent: The Women's Movement in the Black Baptist Church, 1880–1920* (Cambridge, 1993).

The most famous group of reformers were the settlement house women, whose political activism is skillfully probed in Kathryn Kish Sklar's "Hull House in the 1890s: A Community of Women Reformers," *Signs* 10 (1985):658–77. On Jane Addams, see Allen Davis, *American Heroine: The Life and Legend of Jane Addams* (New York, 1973), and Christopher Lasch, ed., *The Social Thought of Jane Addams* (New York, 1965).

On the relationships between social service and the new profession of social work, see Clarke A. Chambers, *Seedtime of Reform: Social Service and Social Action, 1918–1933* (Ann Arbor, 1967); and Robyn Muncy, *Creating a Female Dominion in American Reform,*

1890–1935 (New York, 1991). For a firsthand account of many facets of female activism by a pioneer in industrial medicine, see *Alice Hamilton: A Life in Letters,* ed. Barbara Sicherman (Cambridge, Mass., 1984). Female activists and social scientists had an impact on social policy, as is demonstrated in Ellen Fitzpatrick, *Endless Crusade: Women Social Scientists and Progressive Reform* (New York, 1990); Theda Skocpol, *The Political Origins of Social Policy in the United States* (Cambridge, Mass., 1992); *Regina G. Kunzel, *Fallen Women, Problem Girls,* chaps. 1–4; and Barbara Meil Hobson, *Uneasy Virtue: The Politics of Prostitution and the American Reform Tradition* (Urbana, 1990), chaps. 4–8.

The peace movement and the socialist movement also attracted dedicated activists. On peace movement participation, see Barbara J. Steinson's " 'The Mother Half of Humanity': American Women in the Peace and Preparedness Movements in World War I'' in *Women, War and Revolution,* ed. Carol Berkin and Clara Lovett (New York, 1980). See also Catherine Foster, *Women for All Seasons: The Story of the Women's International League for Peace and Freedom* (Athens, Ga., 1989). Participation in the socialist movement and its politics was also an important part of the process of political socialization for women, as is ably documented by Mari Jo Buhle in *Women and American Socialism, 1870–1920* (Urbana, 1983). New biographies of radicals include Candace Falk, *Love, Anarchy and Emma Goldman: A Biography* (New York, 1989); Dee Garrison, *Mary Heaton Vorse: The Life of an American Insurgent* (Philadelphia, 1989); and Janice R. MacKinnon and Stephen R. MacKinnon, *Agnes Smedley: The Life and Times of an American Radical* (Berkeley, 1987).

The standard history of suffrage is still Eleanor Flexner's *Century of Struggle: The Woman's Rights Movement in the United States* (Cambridge, Mass., 1958). For an illuminating new regional study, see Marjorie Spruill Wheeler's *New Women of the New South: The Leaders of the Woman Suffrage Movement in the Southern States* (New York, 1993). State studies include Sharon Hartman Strom, "Leadership and Tactics in the American Woman Suffrage Movement: A New Perspective from Massachusetts," *Journal of American History* 62 (1975):262–82; Carole Nichols, "Votes and More for Women: Suffrage and After in Connecticut," *Women and History* 5 (1983):1–87; Steven Buechler, *The Transformation of the Woman Suffrage Movement: The Case of Illinois, 1850–1920* (New Brunswick, 1986). On the Women's Party, see Christina A. Leonardi, *From Equal Suffrage to Equal Rights: Alice Paul and the National Woman's Party, 1910–1928* (New York, 1986).

Ideology

*Carroll Smith-Rosenberg, *Disorderly Conduct,* extends its sophisticated and nuanced treatment of gender ideology and social change into the early twentieth century. On ideology and education, see *Barbara Miller Solomon, *In the Company of Educated Women;* Helen L. Horowitz, *Alma Mater: Design and Experience in the Women's Colleges from Their Nineteenth Century Beginning to the 1930's* (New York, 1984); Lynn D. Gordon, *Gender and Higher Education in the Progressive Era* (New Haven, 1990); and Dorothy C. Holland and Margaret A. Eisenhart, *Educated in Romance: Women, Achievement, and Culture* (Chicago, 1990). The way ideology affected both attitudes toward divorce and the debate on changing divorce laws is evident in Glenda Riley, *Divorce: An American Tradition* (New York, 1991). The effect of ideology on changing standards of beauty is explored in Lois Banner, *American Beauty* (New York, 1983). The intersection of ideology and technology is explored in Virginia Scharff, *Taking the Wheel: Women and the Coming of the Motor Age* (New York, 1991). For insight into contemporary feminist thought, see Ann J. Lane, *To "Her-*

land" and Beyond: The Life and Work of Charlotte Perkins Gilman (New York, 1990), and Nancy F. Cott, *A Woman Making History: Mary Ritter Beard through Her Letters* (New Haven, 1991).

Part III: Modern America, 1920–1990

For overviews of the period, see William H. Chafe, *The Paradox of Change: American Women in the 20th Century* (New York, 1991), and Rosalind Rosenberg, *Divided Lives: American Women in the Twentieth Century* (New York, 1992).

BIOLOGY

On sexuality, see *John D'Emilio and Estelle B. Freedman, *Intimate Matters*, chaps. 11–15. On the development of homosexual subcultures, see Elizabeth Laporsky and Madeline Davis, *Boots of Leather, Slippers of Gold: The History of a Lesbian Community* (New York, 1993); see also Allan Berube, *Coming Out Under Fire: Gay Men and Women in World War II* (New York, 1990). For recent scholarship on gay and lesbian studies, see Eric Marcus, *Making History: The Struggle for Gay and Lesbian Equal Rights, 1945–1990: An Oral History* (New York, 1992); and Lillian Faderman, *Odd Girls and Twilight Lovers: A History of Lesbian Life in Twentieth-Century America* (New York, 1991). On birth control and the black community, see Jessie M. Rodrique, "The Black Community and the Birth Control Movement," in *Kathy Peiss and Christina Simmons, eds., *Passion and Power*. For childbirth, see *Judith Walzer Leavitt, *Brought to Bed*, chaps. 7–8. On single pregnancy, see Rickie Solinger, *Wake Up Little Susie: Single Pregnancy and Race before Roe v. Wade* (New York, 1992). The role of the state in relation to both reproductive freedom and domestic violence cuts across biology, ideology, and politics. On abortion, see Rosalind Pollack Petchesky, *Abortion and Woman's Choice: The State, Sexuality and Reproductive Freedom* (New York, 1984); on battering, see *Elizabeth Pleck, *Domestic Tyranny*, chaps. 7–10. Eating disorders and aging also involve the intersection of biology and ideology, as is demonstrated in *Joan Jacob Brumberg's *Fasting Girls*, and *Lois Banner's *In Full Flower*, chaps. 7–9.

ECONOMICS

For an overview, see *Alice Kessler-Harris, *Out to Work*, and *Lynn Y. Weiner, *From Working Girl to Working Mother*, chaps. 4–6. For the 1930s, see Lois Scharf, *To Work and to Wed: Female Employment, Feminism and the Great Depression* (Westport, Conn., 1980); and Winifred Wandersee, *Women's Work and Family Values, 1920–1940* (Cambridge, Mass., 1981). Women who engaged in paid labor in the home are the focus of *Homework: Historical and Contemporary Perspectives on Paid Labor at Home*, ed. Eileen Boris and Cynthia R. Daniels (Urbana, 1989); and Eileen Boris, *Home to Work: Motherhood and the Politics of Industrial Homework in the United States* (Cambridge, 1994). The impact of technology on farm women's work is described in Katherine Jellison, *Entitled to Power: Farm Women and Technology, 1913–1963* (Chapel Hill, 1993). Southern textile workers are the focus of Jacquelyn Dowd Hall et al., *Like a Family: The Making of a Southern Cotton Mill World* (Chapel Hill, 1987).

On women and labor unions, see Dana Frank, *Purchasing Power, Consumer Organizing, Gender and the Seattle Labor Movement, 1919–1929* (Cambridge, 1994); Dorothy Sue Cobble, *Dishing Out: Waitresses and Their Unions in the Twentieth Century* (Urbana, 1991); Nancy F. Gabin, *Feminism in the Labor Movement: Women and the United Auto Workers,*

1935–1975 (Ithaca, 1990); and Elizabeth Faue, *Community of Suffering and Struggle: Women, Men, and the Labor Movement in Minneapolis, 1915–1945* (Chapel Hill, 1991). On Hispanic women and unionization, see Vicki L. Ruiz, *Cannery Women, Cannery Lives: Mexican Women, Unionization, and the California Food Processing Industry, 1930–1950* (Albuquerque, 1987). For the particular problems facing black women, see *Jacqueline Jones, *Labor of Love, Labor of Sorrow*, chaps. 6–7; Dolores Janiewski, *Sisterhood Denied: Race, Class, and Gender in a New South Community* (Philadelphia, 1985); Elizabeth Clark-Lewis, *"This Work Hada' End": The Transition from Live-in to Day Work* (Memphis, 1985); and Phyllis Palmer, *Domesticity and Dirt: Housewives and Domestic Servants in the United States, 1920–1945* (Philadelphia, 1990).

Karen Anderson explores women's work as part of a larger study of women's status during World War II in *Wartime Women: Sex Roles, Family Relations and the Status of Women During World War II* (Westport, Conn., 1981), as does Susan M. Hartmann in *The Home Front and Beyond: American Women in the 1940s* (Boston, 1982). Job segregation in two key industries is the focus of *Ruth Milkman's *Gender at Work*. Discrimination in the professions is examined in such studies as Mary Roth Walsh's *Doctors Wanted, No Women Need Apply: Sexual Barriers in the Medical Profession, 1835–1975* (New Haven, 1977). For women working outside the home, the challenge of combining marriage, family, and career is perhaps best explored in biographies such as Joyce Antler's *Lucy Sprague Mitchell: The Making of a Modern Woman* (New Haven, 1987). On wage equity, see Sara M. Evans and Barbara J. Nelson, *Wage Justice: Comparable Worth and the Paradox of Technocratic Reform* (Chicago, 1989).

POLITICS

The activities of politically active women in the aftermath of suffrage were first probed in J. Stanley Lemons, *The Woman Citizen: Social Feminism in the 1920's* (Urbana, 1975). Recent works include Felice Gordon's *After Winning: The Legacy of New Jersey Suffragists 1920–1946* (New Brunswick, 1986); Nancy F. Cott's rich and persuasive *The Grounding of Modern Feminism* (New Haven, 1987); and for black women, *Paula Giddings's *When and Where I Enter*, and Jacqueline Anne Rouse, *Lugenia Burns Hope: Black Southern Reformers* (Athens, Ga., 1989). Conservative women also became politically active as outlined in Kathleen M. Blee, *Women of the Klan: Racism and Gender in the 1920s* (Berkeley, 1991), and Betty A. DeBerg, *Ungodly Women: Gender and the First Wave of American Fundamentalism* (Minneapolis, 1990). Important biographies of other activists and/or politicians include Jacquelyn Dowd Hall's *Revolt Against Chivalry: Jessie Daniel Ames and the Women's Campaign Against Lynching* (New York, 1974); Christie Miller, *Ruth Hanna McCormick: A Life in Politics, 1880–1944* (Albuquerque, 1992); Susan Ware, *Partner and I: Mollie Dewson, Feminism, and New Deal Politics* (New Haven, 1987); *Blanche Weisen Cook, *Eleanor Roosevelt*; and Ingrid Scobie, *Center Stage: Helen Gahagen Douglas, A Life* (New York, 1992).

Although the 1950s have traditionally been considered a period in which female activism was dormant, new studies suggest there were important exceptions. See, for example, Susan Lynn, *Progressive Women in Conservative Times: Racial Justice, Peace, and Feminism, 1945 to the 1960s* (New Brunswick, 1992); and especially Joanne Meyerowitz, ed., *Not June Cleaver: Women and Gender in Postwar America, 1945–1960* (Philadelphia, 1994). For black women's involvement in the civil rights movement, see Vicki L. Crawford, Jacqueline Anne Rouse, and Barbara Woods, eds., *Women and the Civil Rights Move-*

ment: Trailblazers and Torchbearers, 1941–65 (Brooklyn, 1990); David Garrow, ed., *The Montgomery Bus Boycott and the Women Who Started It: The Memoir of Jo Ann Gibson Robinson* (Knoxville, 1987); and *Jacqueline Jones, *Labor of Love, Labor of Sorrow,* chaps. 7–8. On the peace movement, see Harriet Hyman Alonso, *The Women's Peace Movement and the Outlawry of War, 1921–1942* (Knoxville, 1990), and Amy Swerdlow, *Women Strike for Peace: Traditional Motherhood and Radical Politics in the 1960s* (Urbana, 1993). On women's influence on diplomatic policy, see Edward P. Crapol, *Women and American Foreign Policy: Lobbyists, Critics, and Insiders* (Wilmington, 1992).

For the roots of feminist resurgence, see Leila Rupp and Verta Taylor, *Survival in the Doldrums: The American Women's Rights Movement, 1945 to the 1960s* (New York, 1987); Cynthia Harrison, *On Account of Sex: The Politics of Women's Issues, 1945–1968* (Berkeley, 1988); *Nancy F. Gabin, *Feminism in the Labor Movement;* and Sara Evans, *Personal Politics: The Roots of Women's Liberation in the Civil Rights Movement and the New Left* (New York, 1979). On the rise and demise of radical feminism, see Alice Echols, *Daring to Be Bad: Radical Feminism in America, 1965–1975* (Minneapolis, 1989). For overviews of the impact of the feminist movement, see Winifred D. Wandersee, *On the Move: American Women in the 1970s* (Boston, 1988); and *Susan M. Hartmann, *From Margin to Mainstream: American Women and Politics Since 1960* (New York, 1989). For studies of two highly contested issues that mobilized women politically, see *Kristin Luker, *Abortion and the Politics of Motherhood,* and Donald G. Mathews and Jane Sherron De Hart, *Sex, Gender, and the ERA: A State and the Nation* (New York, 1990). Another policy issue of importance is explored in Mary Frances Berry, *The Politics of Parenthood: Child Care, Women's Rights and the Myth of the Good Mother* (New York, 1993).

IDEOLOGY

Gender representation during the Depression is the focus of Barbara Melosh's *Engendering Culture: Manhood and Womanhood in the New Deal Public Art and Theater* (Washington, D.C. 1991). On the roots of feminist ideology, see Rosalind Rosenberg, *Beyond Separate Spheres: Intellectual Roots of Modern Feminism* (New Haven, 1984). On its development in this century, see *Nancy F. Cott, *The Grounding of Modern Feminism.* For its impact on design, see Delores Hayden, *The Grand Domestic Revolution: A History of Feminist Designs for American Homes, Neighborhoods, and Cities* (Cambridge, Mass., 1982). For antifeminist ideology and its impact during the post–World War II years, see Elaine Tyler May's rich and persuasive. *Homeward Bound: American Families in the Cold War Era* (New York, 1988); for more recent decades, see Rebecca Klatch, *Women of the New Right* (Philadelphia, 1988).

REFERENCES

Important references containing excellent short biographies and a brief bibliography on many of the women appearing in this book are *Notable American Women, 1607–1950: A Biographical Dictionary,* ed. Edward T. James, Janet Wilson James, and Paul Boyer, 3 vols. (Cambridge, Mass., 1971); *Notable American Women: The Modern Period,* eds. Barbara Sicherman and Carol Hurd Green (Cambridge, Mass., 1980); and *Black Women in America: An Historical Encyclopedia,* ed. Darlene Clark Hine, 2 vols. (Brooklyn, 1993). An annually updated reference, first published in 1987, which surveys all aspects of the status of American women, is the series sponsored by the Women's Research and Education Institute in Washington, D.C., entitled *The American Woman, A Status Report.* The most recent edition is 1993–94, edited by Sara Rix (New York, 1993).

Documentary Films

A number of recent films both complement and supplement material in *Women's America.* This list is by no means comprehensive.

Hearts and Hands: A Social History of Nineteenth Century Women and Quilts (1987, 63 min., color) is a beautifully crafted and absorbing documentary, which uses quilts to explore the lives of anonymous and notable women as they intersected with the major movements and events of the nineteenth century. Ideal as an overview for a course in women's history, it also provides an opportunity to explore material culture, especially when used with its companion book, *Hearts and Hands: The Influence of Women and Quilts on American Society* by Pat Ferrero, Elaine Hedges, and Julie Silber, published by the Quilt Digest Press of San Francisco in 1987 (Hearts and Hands Media Arts, 372 Frederick St., San Francisco, Calif. 94117; 415-664-9623).

The Women of Hull-House (1992, 18 min., b/w, color) tells the story of a thirteen-building complex that served as a focal point for education, urban research, and social reform in Chicago during the early twentieth century. Highlighted are the contributions of Hull-House women such as Florence Kelly, Julia Lathrop, Mary Kenney, and Grace and Edith Abbot, as well as founders Jane Addams and Ellen Gates Starr (Jane Addams' Hull-House Museum, The University of Illinois at Chicago, 800 South Halsted Street, Chicago, Ill. 60607-7017).

A scholarly and lively presentation of turn-of-the-century immigrant working women in New York City, *Heaven Will Protect the Working Girl* (1992, 30 min., b/w) captures the drama of the Shirtwaist Strike of 1909 and the challenges of factory work and coming of age in a new land (American Social History Library, 22B Hollywood Avenue, Hohokus, N.J. 07423).

Ida B. Wells: A Passion for Justice (1990, 53 min., color) examines the personal and intense career of slave-born African American journalist and activist Ida B. Wells from her militant opposition to lynchings and discrimination to determined support for the NAACP and the women's suffrage movement. This excellent film is particularly effective at showing how her activism was shaped by both her sex and race (William Greaves Productions, 230 55th St., 26th Floor, New York, N.Y. 10019).

From the perspective of the National Women's Party, *How We Got the Vote* (1975, 52 min., b/w, color) traces the national suffrage movement from its nineteenth-century origins with the Susan B. Anthony Amendment to the passage of the Nineteenth Amendment in 1920. The film contrasts the political styles of the National American Women's Suffrage Association in the years prior to 1917 to those of the more militant National Women's Party, detailing at length the strategy of civil disobedience that Alice Paul and her followers adopted during and after World War I (Republic Pictures Home Video, P.O. Box 66030, Los Angeles, Calif. 90066-0930).

Chronicling her life as a prominent speaker, lobbyist, and grass-roots suffrage organizer, *Jeannette Rankin: The Woman Who Voted No* (1984, 30 min., color) tells the story of the first woman elected to the U.S. Congress, in 1916, who held true to her conscience and cast No votes against America's entry into both World War I and World War II (PBS Video, 1320 Braddock Place, Alexandria, Va. 22314-1698).

The Flapper Story (1985, 29 min., color) examines the flapper ideal, explores the way in which the flapper defied conventional social mores, and also appraises the contradictions and limitations that underlay the "independence" of the "New Woman" of the 1920s (The Cinema Guild, 1697 Broadway, New York, N.Y. 10019).

Wild Women Don't Have the Blues (1989, 58 min., b/w, color) explores how pioneering black female singers transformed the blues in the first half of the twentieth century and reveals how little protection their celebrity status offered them in the face of racial prejudice and exploitation by the music industry (Resolution Inc.—California Newsreel, 149 Ninth Street, #420, San Francisco, Calif. 94103).

A portrayal of the Bryn Mawr Summer School, which flourished between 1921 and 1938, *The Women of Summer* (1975, 55 min., color) documents the effort to expose blue-collar women to humanistic study in such a way as to empower them to go back to their own communities as leaders. Duplicated in the South, these summer schools for women workers were part of the workers' education movement. Their impact on some of the alumnae is conveyed in archival footage, oral histories, and clips of many of the women leaders who served to link Progressivism and the New Deal (FilmMakers Library, Inc., 133 E. 58th Street, New York, N.Y. 10022; 212-355-6545).

Beginning in 1911, *You May Call Her Madam Secretary* (1986, 58 min., b/w, color) follows New Dealer Francis Perkins from teaching to settlement house work to FDR's cabinet as Secretary of Labor, documenting effectively the continuity between Progressivism and the New Deal (Vineyard Video Productions, Elias Lane, West Tisbury, Mass. 02575).

Based on Alice Lynch's account of the labor movement in the 1930s, *Union Maids* (1976, 50 min., b/w) depicts the personal experiences of three women who were labor organizers in Chicago during this period (New Day Films, 22 Riverside Drive, Wayne, N.J. 07470; 201-663-0212).

The story of the Women's Emergency Brigade, *With Babies and Banners* (1979, 45 min., color) is an account of women's critical role in the General Motors sit-down strike in Flint, Michigan, in 1937, which was the key to the success of the Congress of Industrial Organizations' drive for industrial unionism (New Day Films, as above).

The Life and Times of Rosie the Riveter (1980, 65 min., color) presents the powerful and moving reminiscences of five women who welcomed the challenges and higher pay provided by new jobs in industry during World War II and details their loss of wartime opportunities at the war's end when women were told to return home (Clarity Educational Productions, Box 315, Franklin Lakes, N.J. 07414).

Never Turn Back: The Life of Fannie Lou Hamer (1983, 58 min., color) is an informative documentary that follows the career of black activist Fannie Lou Hamer from her early life as a sharecropper in Sunflower County, Mississippi, to national prominence as a civil rights leader and founding member of the Mississippi Freedom Democratic party in the 1960s (Rediscovery Production, 2 Half Mill Common, Westport, Conn. 06880; 203-226-4489).

Focusing solely on Mexican-American/Chicana women, *Adelante, Mujeres* (1992, 30 min., b/w, color) provides a brief history from colonial Mexico to the present. Women are presented in their work and family roles and as community and union activists. (National Women's History Project, 7738 Bell Road, Windsor, Calif. 95492).

Index